MEDIA-RICH LEARNING SPELLS SUCCESS!

Study for results with this book
and its Interactive Student CD-ROM!

You're about to experience effective new ways to study, understand, and retain the key concepts of criminal justice. This current book and its enclosed CD-ROM work as a team—helping you take full advantage of multimedia technology and the vast resources available on the Internet.

VIEW late-breaking CNN® video of criminal justice cases and events

Every chapter in this book opens with an intriguing real-life story—a newsworthy case or event that shows how chapter topics relate to actual experiences in the criminal justice field. Easy-to-spot prompts near these chapter-openers guide you to the CD-ROM for actual CNN video footage relating to the case, as well as to critical thinking questions that help you relate the case to criminal justice concepts you are studying. Most of the chapter-opening stories and their accompanying CNN video segments are new to this edition—the Laci Peterson murder case, the capture of notorious fugitive Eric Rudolph (wanted in connection with the Olympic and abortion center bombings), Mark Hurlbert (a local prosecutor thrust into the limelight when called upon to investigate the Kobe Bryant case), and many more.

View the CNN video clip of this story on your Introduction to Criminal Justice 10e CD.

QUIZ yourself at key points with interactive self-tests

At key junctures in the narrative of this book, you'll find these reminders in the margins that ask you to visit the CD-ROM—your gateway to interactive, online quizzes. By testing yourself on material right after you've read it, you'll retain more and find that studying for final exams is a whole lot easier.

To quiz yourself on this material, go to questions 1.1–1.3 on the Introduction to Criminal Justice 10e CD.

REINFORCE your understanding at the Book Companion Web Site
http://cj.wadsworth.com/siegel_intro10e

This exceptional site features:

- **Concept Builders**—three step modules that 1) briefly review a key chapter concept, 2) apply the concept to a real-world scenario, and 3) challenge you to apply the concept with a related essay question
- **Chapter Summaries and Outlines** that overview the entire chapter
- **Chapter Tutorial Quizzes**—25 multiple-choice, true/false, and essay questions with immediate rejoinders for each answer choice
- **A Final Exam**—includes a random selection of tutorial questions
- **Internet Activities**—as well as InfoTrac® College Edition activities
- **Links to Criminal Justice sites**—organized by chapter

Introduction to Criminal Justice

Tenth Edition

Larry J. Siegel
University of Massachusetts, Lowell

Joseph J. Senna
Northeastern University

THOMSON

WADSWORTH

Australia • Canada • Mexico • Singapore • Spain • United Kingdom • United States

THOMSON

WADSWORTH

Senior Executive Editor, Criminal Justice: Sabra Horne
Development Editor: Shelley Murphy
Editorial Assistant: Elise Smith
Technology Project Manager: Susan DeVanna
Marketing Manager: Dory Schaeffer
Marketing Assistant: Andrew Keay
Advertising Project Manager: Stacey Purviance
Project Manager, Editorial Production: Jennie Redwitz
Art Directors: Vernon Boes/Carolyn Deacy
Print/Media Buyer: Becky Cross
Permissions Editor: Kiely Sexton

Production Service: Robin Lockwood Productions
Text Designer: Jeanne Calabrese
Photo Editor: Linda L Rill
Copy Editor: Colleen McGuiness
Illustrators: Thompson Type, Bob Voigts, and John and Judy Waller
Cover Designer: Yvo
Cover Image: "Lock," © Robert Rauschenberg/licensed by VAGA, New York, NY. Reproduction © Christie's Images/Corbis.
Compositor: Thompson Type
Text and Cover Printer: Transcontinental Printing/Interglobe

Printed in Canada
1 2 3 4 5 6 7 08 07 06 05 04

For more information about our products, contact us at:
Thomson Learning Academic Resource Center
1-800-423-0563

For permission to use material from this text or product, submit a request online at **http://www.thomsonrights.com**. Any additional questions about permissions can be submitted by email to **thomsonrights@thomson.com**.

Library of Congress Control Number: 2003115078

Student Edition: ISBN 0-534-62946-6
Instructor's Edition: ISBN 0-534-62947-4

Thomson Wadsworth
10 Davis Drive
Belmont, CA 94002-3098
USA

Asia
Thomson Learning
5 Shenton Way #01-01
UIC Building
Singapore 068808

Australia/New Zealand
Thomson Learning
102 Dodds Street
Southbank, Victoria 3006
Australia

Canada
Nelson
1120 Birchmount Road
Toronto, Ontario M1K 5G4
Canada

Europe/Middle East/Africa
Thomson Learning
High Holborn House
50/51 Bedford Row
London WC1R 4LR
United Kingdom

About the Authors

Larry J. Siegel was born in the Bronx in 1947. While attending City College of New York in the 1960s he was introduced to the study of crime and justice in courses taught by sociologist Charles Winick. After graduation he attended the newly opened program in criminal justice at the State University of New York at Albany, where he earned both his M.A. and Ph.D. After completing his graduate work, Dr. Siegel began his teaching career at Northeastern University, where he worked closely with colleague Joseph Senna on a number of texts and research projects. After leaving Northeastern, he held teaching positions at the University of Nebraska, Omaha and Saint Anselm College in New Hampshire. He is currently a professor at the University of Massachusetts, Lowell.

Dr. Siegel has written extensively in the area of crime and justice, including books on juvenile law, delinquency, criminology, and criminal procedure. He is a court certified expert on police conduct and has testified in numerous legal cases. He resides in Bedford, New Hampshire, with his wife Therese J. Libby, Esq. and their children.

Joseph J. Senna was born in Brooklyn, New York. He graduated from Brooklyn College, Fordham University Graduate School Service, and Suffolk University Law School. Mr. Senna has spent over fourteen years teaching law and justice courses at Northeastern University. In addition, he has served as an Assistant District Attorney, Director of Harvard Law School Prosecutorial Program, and consultant to numerous criminal justice organizations. His academic specialties include the areas of Criminal Law, Constitutional Due Process, Criminal Justice, and Juvenile Law.

Mr. Senna lives with his wife and sons outside of Boston. He is currently working on a criminal law textbook.

Brief Contents

Contents

v

Chapter 12
The Criminal Trial 357

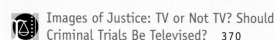

Images of Justice: TV or Not TV? Should Criminal Trials Be Televised? 370

Law in Review:
Batson v. *Kentucky* (1986) 373

Race, Gender, and Ethnicity in Criminal Justice: Jury Selection and Peremptory Challenges 376

Chapter 13
Punishment and Sentencing 389

Analyzing Criminal Justice Issues: Getting Tough: Three Strikes Laws 406

Race, Gender, and Ethnicity in Criminal Justice: Race and Sentencing 412

International Justice:
The Death Penalty Abroad 414

Preface

For the past few years people in Connecticut have been alternately fascinated and revolted by the ongoing saga of Waterbury mayor Philip Giordano, a married father of three who was accused of engaging in sexual relations with minors. Giordano, a highly respected officeholder who had been the Republican candidate for the U.S. Senate in 2000, was snared in a Federal Bureau of Investigation (FBI) probe of municipal corruption. During the investigation, a 17-year-old girl came forward and charged that Giordano had paid her to have sex with him in his private law office. She claimed that Giordano had also engaged in sex acts with her aunt and her two nieces, ages 8 and 10. On March 25, 2003, a federal jury convicted Giordano of violating the civil rights of the two young girls. Giordano received a 37-year prison sentence, which means that, with good behavior, he could be released in 30 years.

This shocking case illustrates the wide range of human behavior that falls within the jurisdiction of criminal justice system agencies. Some involve the wealthy and powerful. Criminal suspects such as Philip Giordano receive the full protection of the legal system. They are able to hire the best attorneys and expert witnesses to help them prepare their defense. But the Giordano case is an unusual high-profile event that captured media attention. Each year the criminal justice system routinely processes millions of cases involving theft, violence, drug trafficking, and other crimes that are rarely reviewed on TV or in the newspapers. It has become an enterprise costing more than $100 billion each year and employs millions of people in law enforcement, courts, and correctional agencies. Justice agencies are engaged in a continuing effort to improve their efficiency and effectiveness. We have written *Introduction to Criminal Justice* to help students interested in justice to better understand this enormous and complex system and to aid their journey in introductory-level criminal justice courses.

Because the study of criminal justice is a dynamic, ever-changing field of scientific inquiry and the concepts and processes of justice are constantly evolving, we have updated *Introduction to Criminal Justice* to reflect the most recent structural and procedural changes, critical legal cases, research studies, and policy initiatives. The text analyzes and describes the agencies of justice and the procedures they use to identify and treat criminal offenders. It covers what most experts believe are the critical issues in criminal justice and analyzes their impact on the justice system. This edition focuses on emerging policy issues in the criminal justice system, inmate reentry, technocorrections, and personal privacy in the age of terrorism.

Our primary goals in writing this tenth edition remain as they have been for the previous nine:

1. To provide students with a thorough knowledge of the criminal justice system.
2. To be as thorough and up-to-date as possible.
3. To be objective and unbiased.
4. To describe current methods of social control and analyze their strengths and weaknesses.

Every attempt has been made to present the material in an interesting, balanced, and objective manner. No single political or theoretical position dominates the text. Instead, the many diverse views that are contained within criminal justice and characterize its interdisciplinary nature are presented. In fact, the diversity of opinion about what justice is and what it should be provides the central focus of the text. We have tried to provide a text that is both scholarly and informative, comprehensive yet interesting, well organized and objective yet provocative and thought-provoking.

Organization of the Text

The tenth edition has been thoroughly revised. We have made a concerted effort to make the text more concise, student-friendly, and accessible.

Part One offers a basic introduction to crime, law, and justice. The first chapter covers the problem of crime in America, agencies of justice, and the formal justice process, and it introduces students to the concept of the informal justice system, which involves discretion, deal making, and plea bargains. Chapter 1 also discusses the major perspectives on justice and uses the "war on drugs" as an example of how different perspectives on justice influence social policy. Chapter 2 discusses the nature and extent of crime and victimization: How is crime measured? Where and when does it occur? Who commits crime? Who are its victims? What social factors influence the crime rate? Chapter 3 covers crime patterns and addresses the critical question: Why do people commit crime and why do some people become the victims of criminal acts? Chapter 4 provides a discussion of the criminal law and its relationship to criminal justice. It focuses on critical issues in both substantive and procedural law.

Part Two provides an overview of the law enforcement field. Four chapters cover the history and development of law enforcement; the role, organization, and function of police in modern society; issues in policing; and police and the rule of law.

Part Three is devoted to the adjudication process, from pretrial indictment to the sentencing of criminal offenders. Chapters focus on organization of the court system, an analysis of the prosecution and defense function, pretrial procedures, the criminal trial, and sentencing. Topics included here range from court structure to sentencing policies such as three strikes laws and capital punishment. There are also sections on the processing of felony cases, indigent defense systems, attorney competence, legal ethics, pretrial services, and bail reform.

Part Four focuses on the correctional system, including probation, intermediate sanctions, and restorative justice. The traditional correctional system of jails, prisons, community-based corrections, and parole are also discussed at length. Issues such as technocorrections and the problem of prisoner reentry are presented in detail.

Part Five explores the juvenile justice system. Information is provided on preventive detention of youth, waiving youth to the adult court, and the death penalty for children.

Great care has been taken to organize the text to reflect the structure and process of justice. Each chapter attempts to be comprehensive, self-contained, and orderly.

What's New in This Edition

• **Chapter 1, "Crime and Criminal Justice,"** has a new opening vignette on the Lovers Lane Bandit, a killer caught 45 years after his murderous spree, and a new Images of Justice feature that analyzes the film *Gangs of New York*. Updates are provided on the number of people in correctional institutions and new data are presented on justice system expenditures. *Board of Education of Independent School District No. 92 of Pottawatomie County et al.* v. *Earls et al.* is also discussed.

- **Chapter 2, "The Nature and Extent of Crime,"** begins by recounting the activities of Eric Rudolph, an abortion clinic bomber. It updates two boxes, "Explaining Crime Trends" and "Should Guns Be Controlled?" We also provide the latest self-report, victim, and Uniform Crime Reports data. A new International Justice box covers the reasons that crime is booming around the world.

- In **Chapter 3, "Understanding Crime and Victimization,"** we open with a new vignette on the Chante Mallard murder case. A new Analyzing Criminal Justice Issues feature discusses the Emerge program. We updated data on poverty and its relation to crime, and also included new data from the most recent youth gang survey, the most recent child maltreatment data, and data from the most recent Arrestee Drug Abuse Monitoring program. Chapter 3 now also covers the results of recent research on psychological deficits and crime. And a new exhibit reviews contemporary forms of terrorism.

- **Chapter 4, "Criminal Law: Substance and Procedure,"** opens with a review of the Laci Peterson murder case. It has new boxes on ex post facto laws, *Chicago v. Morales*, the insanity defense, and criminal law and terrorism. We also include a new section on reforming the criminal law, including discussion of penumbral crimes, criminal acts defined by a high level of noncompliance and nonenforcement.

- **Chapter 5, "Police in Society: History and Organization,"** begins with the story of Gary Ridgway, a serial killer who stalked and killed women over a 20-year period. He was known as the "Green River Killer." A new box describes Operation X-Out, a venture designed to stop the use of ecstasy. New data are included on police salaries. Two new boxes discussing crime mapping and the Information Collecting for Automated Mapping program and biometric technology have been added. We have also included new data on the most recent use of technology in the nation's police departments.

- **Chapter 6, "The Police: Organization, Role, Function,"** begins with the story of Montgomery County, Maryland, police chief Charles Moose, who led the investigation to identify the D.C. snipers. It has new boxes on a variety of topics: the Amber Alert; the Boston Gun Project; Operation Ceasefire; and Community Mapping, Planning, and Analysis for Safety Strategies: COMPASS. It also has an Images of Justice box on the television show *CSI: Crime Scene Investigation.* We have included a new exhibit on the elements of community and a discussion of the Coplink technology program. We also go into the benefits of a "bait car" program in which cars parked in high-theft areas are equipped with technology that alerts law enforcement personnel when they have been stolen.

- **Chapter 7, "Issues in Policing,"** opens with the Donovan Jackson case, an incident in which a 16-year-old African American youth was slammed onto the trunk of a patrol car and punched by a white police officer while being arrested at a service station. It has new boxes on less than lethal weapons, racial profiling, and working with problem cops. It covers a recent settlement in which a police department was forced to pay millions for arresting a suspect based on his race.

- **Chapter 8, "Police and the Rule of Law,"** has two new boxes, one on the future of the exclusionary rule and the other on an important federal case, *United States v. Bin Laden.* We cover *Chavez v. Martinez,* in which the U.S. Supreme Court ruled that a *Miranda* warning applies only to criminal matters, and *United States v. Arvizu,* in which the Supreme Court defined when a police officer can search a suspicious vehicle. The chapter reviews *Kirk v. Louisiana,* in which the Supreme Court ruled on what police officers need to make a lawful entry into a home. New data also are included from a survey on what police chiefs think about the *Miranda* warning.

- **Chapter 9, "The Courts and the Judiciary,"** has a new box on specialized courts that deal exclusively with drug and mental health cases. The chapter covers the crisis in court system funding. It has data from a new survey on judicial pay. New material is presented on the role technology plays in the courtroom, including Internet access to information about criminal cases. New coverage of research on how the fear of reversal influences judicial decision making also is provided.

• **Chapter 10, "The Prosecution and the Defense,"** now begins with a vignette on Mark Hurlbert, a typical hardworking local prosecutor who was thrust into the limelight when called upon to prosecute the Kobe Bryant case. It has two new boxes, one on attorney honesty and the other on attorney competence. It contains new data on state court prosecutors' offices, reviews research on prosecutorial justifications for sexual assault case rejection, and discusses what happens when an increase is seen in the proportion of domestic violence arrests that are prosecuted. The chapter now covers prosecuting the crime of identity theft and has new material on prosecutorial discretion.

• **Chapter 11, "Pretrial Procedures,"** has a new box on pretrial service programs. It covers the New York appellate case of *People* v. *Hicks,* in which a person violated his promise to be truthful during a plea bargain agreement. We include new research on the grand jury, the danger of convicting the innocent in a plea negotiation, and how prosecutors depart from sentencing guidelines.

• **Chapter 12, "The Criminal Trial,"** begins with the story of Sara Jane Olson, who was sentenced to 20 years to life in prison for her role in a failed radical bomb plot to kill Los Angeles police officers in 1975. It covers the 2003 case *Sell* v. *United States,* in which the U.S. Supreme Court set out rules that guide the use of forced medication of inmates. It covers the case of James C. Kopp (the accused killer of Dr. Barnett A. Slepian, a Buffalo-area abortion provider), who waived his right to a jury trial and requested a bench trial. It reviews *Alabama* v. *Shelton* (2002), in which the Court ruled that a defendant must be represented by counsel if he or she receives a probation sentence in which a prison or jail sentence is possible. We include a new feature discussing the issue of televising criminal trials.

• **Chapter 13, "Punishment and Sentencing,"** now begins with the case of Samantha Runnion, age 5, who was kidnapped while playing in front of her California home and was later found dead. We include new boxes on the Capital Jury Project and the Death Penalty Abroad. We cover a 2003 case, *Miller-El* v. *Cockrell,* in which the Supreme Court ruled against selecting biased juries; *Atkins* v. *Virginia,* in which the Court ruled that executions of mentally retarded criminals are "cruel and unusual punishments"; and *Ring* v. *Arizona,* in which the Court held that juries, not judges, must make decisions in death penalty cases. The chapter also contains new summaries of research on regional variation in federal drug offense sentencing, the effect of gender on incarceration, and whether the United States sentencing guidelines can be considered successful.

• **Chapter 14, "Community Sentences: Probation, Intermediate Sanctions, and Restorative Justice,"** begins with an analysis of the Winona Ryder case. It has new boxes on drug treatment alternatives to prison, reintegrative shaming, restorative justice in the community, and alternatives to incarceration abroad. It covers the case of Albert Lee, who had been given probation for transporting child pornography via computer and enticing a minor by computer to engage in sex. The chapter now has more extensive coverage of restorative justice programs as well.

• **Chapter 15, "Corrections: History, Institutions, and Populations,"** now begins with a discussion of the murder of ex-priest John Geoghan, a convicted pedophile, who was strangled while doing time in a Massachusetts prison. It has new boxes on the penal harm movement, ultramaximum-security prisons, the development of parole, and how prisons supervise inmate mail. The latest data on private prisons, jails, and correctional populations are included.

• **Chapter 16, "Prison Life: Living in and Leaving Prison,"** begins with the story of Kathy Boudin, who was released from prison after serving 20 years for an armed robbery during which police officers were killed. It has new boxes on Girl Scouts Behind Bars, the problem of reentry, residential substance abuse

treatment, *Newjack,* technocorrections, and the case of *Hope* v. *Pelzer.* The chapter updates the issue of parole and the difficulty inmates have reentering society.
- **Chapter 17, "The Juvenile Justice System,"** begins with the case of Lee Boyd Malvo, the 17-year-old boy who was identified as one of the two D.C. snipers. It also has boxes on teen courts, the Juvenile Mentoring Program, and whether the juvenile court should be abolished. We also update data on juvenile court processing, detention, and sentencing.

Special Features

To keep up with the changes in the criminal justice system, the tenth edition of *Introduction to Criminal Justice* has been thoroughly revised and renewed. The evolution of crime control policy has been followed by updating the discussion of the criminal justice system with recent court decisions, legislative changes, and theoretical concepts that reflect the changing orientation of the field.

Boxed Features

The text contains six kinds of boxed inserts, which help students analyze material in greater depth.

1. **Analyzing Criminal Justice Issues** This feature helps students to learn and think critically about current justice issues and practices. For example, an Analyzing Criminal Justice Issues box in Chapter 6, "Amber Alert," discusses the initiative to link law enforcement agencies so that they can respond quickly to locate missing children.
2. **Images of Justice** These boxes show how the criminal justice system is portrayed in films and TV shows and also how the media influences crime and justice. For example, in Chapter 12, an Images of Justice box entitled "TV or Not TV? Should Criminal Trials Be Televised?" looks at the advantages (and disadvantages) of broadcasting trials.
3. **Law in Review** This feature gives the facts, decisions, and significance of critical legal cases. In Chapter 4, a new Law in Review box entitled "Ex Post Facto Laws" considers three recent cases in which the Supreme Court reviewed laws that retroactively punish people.
4. **Race, Gender, and Ethnicity in Criminal Justice** These boxes are aimed at helping students better understand the problems of women and minorities in the justice system. For example, in Chapter 7, a Race, Gender, and Ethnicity in Criminal Justice feature on "Racial Profiling: Does Race Influence the Police Use of Discretion?" tackles the controversial issue of the police use of racial profiles to target suspects.
5. **Criminal Justice and Technology** This feature focuses on some of the latest efforts to modernize the system using contemporary technological methods. For example, "Crime Mapping and the ICAM Program" in Chapter 5 discusses the way police departments are using crime maps to investigate and predict future criminal activities.
6. **International Justice** This feature focuses on crime trends and issues around the world. For example, a Chapter 13 box is about "The Death Penalty Abroad."

Other Chapter Features

- **Perspectives on Justice** Throughout the book Perspectives on Justice boxes link the material to the competing viewpoints on what criminal justice is all about and how it should be directed. For example, some people believe that the primary mission of the justice system is punishing criminals, while others focus more on treatment and rehabilitation. The Perspectives on Justice boxes show how each of these competing views has influenced the way the system of justice operates and identifies programs and policies to which they are linked.

• **Web Links and InfoTrac® College Edition Links** These are designed to guide students to Web sites that will provide them with additional information if they want to conduct further research on the topics covered in the text.

• **Chapter Objectives (New in the Tenth Edition)** Each chapter now begins with a list of objectives designed to guide the student through the chapter content. The Chapter Objectives help students to focus on the most critical material found within the chapter.

• **Concept Summaries (New in the Tenth Edition)** Concept summaries distill the content of important concepts so students can compare and contrast ideas, views, cases, and findings. For example, in Chapter 11 a Concept Summary reviews the major Supreme Court decisions regulating plea-bargaining practices.

• **Doing Research on the Web** At the end of each chapter this section sets out a research question and then guides students to Web sites to help them find answers to the proposed topic.

• **Key Terms and Discussion Questions** At the end of each chapter is a list of key terms (with page numbers referencing the page where the term is defined) and a series of discussion questions that are designed to facilitate classroom debate and deliberation.

The book also contains many new figures and tables, which make the presentation easier to understand and conceptualize.

Ancillary Materials

A number of pedagogic supplements are provided by Thomson Wadsworth to help instructors use *Introduction to Criminal Justice,* Tenth Edition, in their courses and to aid students in preparing for exams. These are available to qualified adopters. Please consult your local sales representative for details.

For the Instructor

• **Resource Integration Guide** Located at the Book Companion Web site (http://cj.wadsworth.com/siegel_intro10e) and in the *Instructor's Resource Manual,* a fully annotated Resource Integration Guide will assist instructors in organizing their classroom presentations and reinforcing the themes of the course. Each chapter of the guide ties all of the supplements directly to the topics in the text.

• **Instructor's Resource Manual** The *Instructor's Resource Manual* includes resources lists, lecture outlines, and testing suggestions that will help time-pressed teachers more effectively communicate with their students and also strengthen coverage of course material. Each chapter has multiple choice, true/false, and fill-in-the-blanks test items, as well as review and discussion questions. The *Instructor's Resource Manual* is backed up by Exam View, a computerized test bank available in Windows and Macintosh formats.

• **ExamView®** This computerized testing software helps instructors create and customize exams in minutes. Instructors can easily edit and import their own questions and graphics, change test layouts, and reorganize questions. This software also offers the ability to test and grade online. It is available for both Windows and Macintosh.

- **WebTutor™ Advantage on Blackboard and WebCT**
  http://webtutor.thomsonlearning.com

WebTutor Advantage allows instructors to provide virtual office hours, post syllabi, set up threaded discussions, and track student progress with the quizzing material. WebTutor's communication tools include a course calendar, asynchronous discussion, real-time chat, a whiteboard, and an integrated e-mail system. WebTutor Advantage offers access to a full array of study tools organized by text chapter, including glossary flashcards, practice quizzes, online tutorials, and Web links. "Out of the box" or customizable, this versatile online tool is filled with preloaded, text-specific content, including diagrams and illustrations, and Microsoft® PowerPoint® files organized by text chapter. Teachers can customize the content in any way they choose, from uploading images and other resources to adding Web links, to creating their own practice materials. WebTutor Advantage is designed flexibly for use in a variety of ways, from an electronic study guide to a tool for teaching courses online.

- **Multimedia Manager for Criminal Justice: A Microsoft® Powerpoint® Link Tool** This valuable resource contains all of the art from the book as well as interactive learning tools that will enhance classroom lectures. In addition, instructors can choose from ready-made dynamic slides or customize their own with the art files provided from the text.

- **Introduction to Criminal Justice Transparencies** To help bring key concepts of the text to the classroom, 50 full-color transparency masters for overhead projection are available in the *Criminal Justice 2004* transparencies package. These transparencies help instructors fully discuss concepts and research findings with students.

- **CNN® Today: Introduction to Criminal Justice, Volume VI** Now instructors can integrate the up-to-the-minute programs of CNN and its affiliate networks right into their courses. This video features short, high-interest clips perfect for launching lectures. A current new volume is available to adopters each year. Ask your Thomson Wadsworth representative about the video policy by adoption size. (Volumes I–V are also available.)

- **Wadsworth Criminal Justice Video Library** The Wadsworth Criminal Justice Video Library offers an exciting collection of videos to enrich lectures. Qualified adopters may select from a variety of professionally prepared videos covering various aspects of policing, corrections, and other areas of the criminal justice system. The selections include videos from *Films for the Humanities and Sciences, Court TV* videos that feature provocative one-hour programs to illustrate seminal and high-profile cases in depth, *A&E American Justice Series* videos, *National Institute of Justice: Crime File* videos, *ABC News* videos, and *MPI Home* videos.

- **Opposing Viewpoints Resource Center** This online center allows instructors to expose their students to all sides of today's most compelling issues, including genetic engineering, environmental policy, prejudice, abortion, health care reform, media violence, and dozens more. The Opposing Viewpoints Resource Center (OVRC) draws on Greenhaven Press's acclaimed social issues series, as well as core reference content from other Gale and Macmillan Reference USA sources. The result is a dynamic online library of current event topics—the facts as well as the arguments of each topic's proponents and detractors. Special sections focus on critical thinking (and walk students through critically evaluating point-counterpoint arguments) and researching and writing papers. To take a quick tour of the OVRC, visit http://www.gale.com/OpposingViewpoints/index.htm.

For the Student

- **Introduction to Criminal Justice 10e CD-ROM** Included on the CD are chapter-based self-tests; a Concept Builder that includes review, application, and exercise questions on chapter-based key concepts; and CNN video clips with critical thinking questions relating to key points from the text. Student responses can be saved and e-mailed to instructors.

- **Study Guide** The extensive *Study Guide* has been revised by Charles Crawford. Because students learn in different ways, a variety of pedagogical aids are included in the guide to help them. Each chapter is outlined, major terms are defined, and summaries and sample tests are provided.

- **Companion Web Site** The companion Web site provides Chapter Outlines and Summaries, Tutorial Quizzing, a Final Exam, textbook Glossary, FlashCards, Crossword puzzle, Concentration game, InfoTrac College Edition Exercises, Web Links, Internet Activities, and the multi-step Concept Builder that includes review, application, and exercise questions on chapter-based key concepts.

- **InfoTrac® College Edition** Students automatically receive four months of real-time access to InfoTrac College Edition's online database of continuously updated, full-length articles from hundreds of journals and periodicals. By doing a simple key word search, students can quickly generate a list of related articles, then select relevant articles to explore and print out for reference or further study.

- **Terrorism: An Interdisciplinary Perspective** This 80-page booklet (with companion Web site) discusses terrorism in general and the issues surrounding the events of September 11, 2001. It examines the origins of terrorism in the Middle East, focusing on Osama bin Laden in particular, as well as issues involving bioterrorism, the role played by religion in Middle Eastern terrorism, globalization as it relates to terrorism, and the reactions and repercussions of terrorist attacks.

- **State Supplements for California, Florida, Illinois, New York, and Texas** These concise booklets include state-specific topics, laws, and other criminal justice–related information as they pertain to each state. State crime enforcement, court procedures, correctional systems, and juvenile justice programs are just a few of the issues covered.

- **Crime Scenes: An Interactive Criminal Justice CD-ROM** Recipient of several *New Media Magazine Invision Awards,* this interactive CD-ROM allows students to take on the roles of investigating officer, lawyer, parole officer, and judge in excitingly realistic scenarios.

- **Mind of a Killer CD-ROM (Bundle Version)** Voted one of the top 100 CD-ROMs by an annual *PC Magazine* survey, *Mind of a Killer* gives students a chilling glimpse into the realm of serial killers, with more than 80 minutes of video and 3D simulations, an extensive mapping system, a library, and more.

- **Careers in Criminal Justice Interactive CD-ROM, Version 3.0** This engaging self-exploration CD-ROM provides an interactive discovery of the wide range of careers in criminal justice. The self-assessment helps steer students to suitable careers based on their personal profile. Students can gather information on various careers from the job descriptions, salaries, employment requirements, sample tests, and video profiles of criminal justice professionals presented on this valuable tool.

- **Internet Guide for Criminal Justice, Second Edition** Internet beginners will appreciate this helpful booklet. With explanations and the vocabulary necessary for navigating the Web, it features customized information on criminal justice Web sites and presents Internet project ideas.

- **Internet Activities for Criminal Justice, Second Edition** This completely revised 96-page booklet shows the best ways to use the Internet for research through searches and activities.

- **Criminal Justice Internet Investigator III** This brochure lists the most popular Internet addresses for criminal justice Web sites. It includes URLs for corrections, victimization, crime prevention, high-tech crime, policing, courts, investigations, juvenile justice, research, and fun sites.

- **Seeking Employment in Criminal Justice and Related Fields** Written by J. Scott Harr and Karen Hess, this practical book, now in its fourth edition, helps students develop a search strategy to find employment in criminal justice and related fields. Each chapter includes "insiders' views," written by individuals in the field and addressing promotions and career planning.
- **Guide to Careers in Criminal Justice** This concise 60-page booklet provides a brief introduction to the exciting and diverse field of criminal justice. Students can learn about opportunities in law enforcement, courts, and corrections and how they can go about getting these jobs.

Acknowledgments

Many people helped make this book possible. Those who reviewed the ninth edition and made suggestions that we attempted to follow as best we could include Thomas R. Arnold, The College of Lake County; Michael P. Brown, Ball State University; Steven A. Egger, University of Houston Clear Lake; Michael T. Eskey, Troy State University; Patrick McConnell, Temple University; Karen Terry, John Jay College; and Robert C. Wadman, Weber State University. Those who reviewed the previous edition include Allen Anderson, Indiana University, Kokomo; Kelly Asmussen, Peru State College; Roger Barnes, University of the Incarnate Word; Joe Becraft, Portland Community College; Eugene Bouley Jr., Georgia College and State University; Linda O'Daniel, Mountain View College; Edward Qualey, Hilbert College; and Robert C. Wadman, Weber State University.

The form and content of this new edition were directed by our terrific executive editor, Sabra Horne, who is almost a co-author. Much credit for getting this book out must go to our patient, kind, and competent development editor, Shelley Murphy. Special thanks must also go to production manager Jennie Redwitz, production editor Robin Lockwood, our special friend and photo editor Linda Rill, and the wonderful marketing manager Dory Schaeffer. We enjoyed working with copyeditor Colleen McGuiness and appreciate her thoroughness and dedication.

Larry J. Siegel
Joseph J. Senna

Part One The Nature of Crime, Law, and Criminal Justice

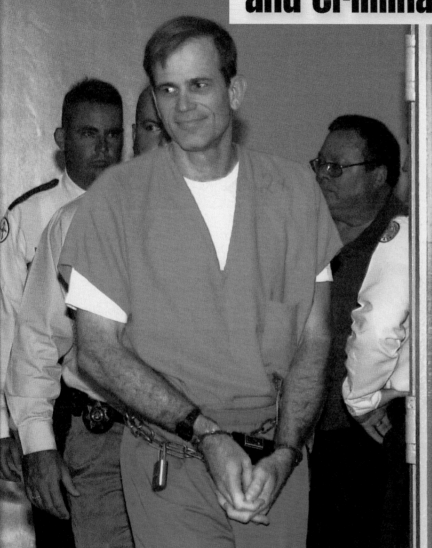

© 2003 AP/Wide World Photos

On September 3, 2003, Paul Hill was executed in Florida for the murders of Dr. John Bayard Britton and his bodyguard, retired Air Force lieutenant colonel James Herman Barrett. The killings had taken place in Pensacola, outside the Ladies Center, an abortion clinic. Though members of the antiabortion movement dismissed Hill as a fringe character, soon after his execution Florida abortion clinics and police were put on alert for reprisals. Several officials connected to the case received threatening letters, accompanied by rifle bullets.

Why do people kill or commit violent acts instead of finding peaceful solutions to their problems? And what should be done to those who commit criminal acts? A great deal of irony can be found in the Hill case: Society chose to kill someone who chose to kill someone because he considered that person a killer. What is the process of justice and how are people such as Hill tried, convicted, and sentenced to death? Are such murders common and is the United States an especially violent society? These questions are addressed in Part One of this text. Chapter 1 covers the justice process and the organizations that are entrusted with conducting its operations: the police, courts, and corrections. Chapter 2 looks at the nature and extent of crime, and Chapter 3 tries to answer the question, why do people commit crime? Finally, Chapter 4 covers the criminal law, analyzing both its substantive and procedural components.

Chapter Outline

Chapter Objectives

After reading this chapter, you should be able to:

1. Describe the development of crime in the United States.
2. Tell how the criminal justice system was created.
3. Describe the origins of federal involvement in criminal justice.
4. List three main types of criminal justice agencies.
5. Know the 15 critical decision points in the criminal justice process.
6. Identify the interrelationship between criminal justice process and agencies.
7. Analyze the importance of the informal justice system.
8. List the four basic stages of the criminal justice "wedding cake."
9. Describe the six most important perspectives on contemporary criminal justice.
10. Analyze how each perspective influences criminal justice policy in the war on drugs.

Viewpoints

 Images of Justice: *Gangs of New York* 6

 Law in Review: *Board of Education of Independent School District No. 92 of Pottawatomie County et al.* v. *Earls et al.* 26

 Analyzing Criminal Justice Issues: Should Drugs Be Legalized? 34

Web Links

London Metropolitan Police
http://www.met.police.uk/police/mps/history/index.htm 7

American Bar Foundation
http://www.abf-sociolegal.org/ 8

National Institute of Justice
http://www.ojp.usdoj.gov/nij/welcome.html 8

National Center for State Courts
http://www.ncsc.dni.us 10

**Brennan Judicial Center at
New York University**
http://brennancenter.org/ 27

InfoTrac College Edition Links

Article: "The Role of Mass Media Campaigns in Reducing High-Risk Drinking among College Students" 4

Article: "Who Was Wyatt Earp?" 4

Article: "The Whole Shootin' Match" 5

Article: "Crime and Punishment" 7

Key Term: "Criminal Justice, Administration of" 10

Key Term: "criminal investigation" 13

Key Term: "models of justice" 22

Article: "Politics: Washington Fumes as Canada Moves to Decriminalize Pot" 28

Key Term: "war on drugs" 30

On January 29, 2003, police arrested 69-year-old Gerald F. Mason for the murder of two El Segundo, California, patrolmen. The murders occurred in 1957, more than 45 years earlier. When the attacks had occurred, the culprit was known as the Lovers Lane Bandit because he ambushed four teenagers in an area known to be a teen hangout, raped a girl, and then gunned down two young police officers when they stopped him for running a stop sign.[1]

How did the police track down Mason? After receiving an anonymous tip, they used fingerprints from a stolen 1949 Ford that the police believed the killer was driving and ran them on the Federal Bureau of Investigation (FBI) national fingerprint database, a technology not available when the crime was committed. The prints from the car matched a set of Mason's on file in South Carolina from when he served time in prison for burglary in 1956. On March 24, 2003, in Los Angeles, Mason pleaded guilty to the murders and was sentenced to two terms of life in prison.

Solving the Lovers Lane murder 45 years after it occurred is unusual but certainly not unique. As crime rates have dropped nationwide over the past decade, police departments have been able to devote more resources to older, tougher cases. Many have formed cold case squads that focus on unsolved crimes. For example, in 2000 the Los Angeles Sheriff's Department, which polices the large area surrounding the city of Los Angeles, launched a review of the county's 3,000 unsolved murder cases dating back to 1980. The depart-

OFFICER MILTON CURTIS   OFFICER RICHARD PHILLIPS

ment hired six former homicide detectives and asked them to go over every open case file and determine which ones might be solved using modern technology. So far, 29 cases have been solved, and more than 80 others are undergoing more testing, including DNA analysis.

The Lovers Lane case is informative for a number of reasons. It illustrates how technology is influencing the day-to-day operations of the justice system. From criminal investigation to correctional security, the system is making use of technology to improve its effectiveness and efficiency. Can the system be going too far? Is technology a threat to personal freedom? Should a citizen's fingerprints be kept in a national database? What about his DNA? Or his medical history? Considering the threat of terrorism, from both domestic sources such as the Washington, D.C., snipers John Allen

Mohammed and Lee Boyd Malvo and foreign sources such as Osama Bin Laden and al Qaeda, should the government be allowed to expand its surveillance of American citizens and increase the amount of information in its computer banks?

The case also illustrates the dilemma of determining what is fair and consistent justice. Should someone be punished 45 years after he committed a crime? What purpose would it serve to incarcerate someone if he turned his life around, raised a family, was gainfully employed, and was not the person he was when he committed the crime? But is it fair and just to absolve someone of responsibility for a crime he committed simply because he was able to avoid detection by the police? Would such a reward for bad behavior encourage other criminals to evade detection, skip out on bail, or try to escape from jail?

And what is a proper punishment for the Lovers Lane killer? Should he be put to death? He did kill two police officers. Why should his punishment be any less than that given to John Mohammed, who was sentenced to death following his conviction?[2] Is it fair to put one murderer behind bars while another is executed? How can the criminal justice system distinguish between two people who commit horrendous crimes?

Though cases such as the arrest of the Lovers Lane Bandit are relatively rare, crime has been an ever-present fixture of American culture.

CNN® *View the CNN video clip of this story on your Introduction to Criminal Justice 10e CD.*

To read more about special investigation units that go after cold cases, go to InfoTrac College Edition and read Brian Parry, "Special Service Unit: Dedicated to Investigating and Apprehending Violent Offenders," *Corrections Today* 63 (2001): 120–23.

Though media exposure may be harmful to some, the media could play a beneficial role in reducing crime. Go to InfoTrac College Edition and access William De-Jong, "The Role of Mass Media Campaigns in Reducing High-Risk Drinking among College Students," *Journal of Studies on Alcohol* 63, no. 2 (March 2002): 182.

criminal justice system
The various sequential stages through which offenders pass, from initial contact with the law to final disposition, and the agencies charged with enforcing the law at each of these stages.

The public relies on the agencies of the **criminal justice system** to provide solutions to the crime problem and to shape the direction of crime policy. This loosely organized collection of agencies is charged with, among other matters, protecting the public, maintaining order, enforcing the law, identifying transgressors, bringing the guilty to justice, and treating criminal behavior. The public depends on this vast system, employing more than 2 million people and costing taxpayers about $150 billion a year, to protect them from evildoers and to bring justice to their lives.

This text serves as an introduction to the study of criminal justice. This chapter covers some basic issues and concepts, beginning with a discussion of the concept and the study of criminal justice. The major processes of the criminal justice system are then examined so that you can develop an overview of how the system functions. Because no single view exists of the underlying goals that help shape criminal justice, the varying perspectives on what criminal justice really is or should be are set out in some detail.

Is Crime a Recent Development?

Older people often say, "Crime is getting worse every day" and "I can remember when it was safe to walk the streets at night," but their memories may be colored by wishful thinking. Crime and violence have existed in the United States for more than two hundred years. In fact, the crime rate may have been much higher in the nineteenth and early twentieth centuries than it is today.

Crime and violence have been common since the nation was first formed.[3] Guerilla activity was frequent before, during, and after the Revolutionary War. Bands supporting the British (Tories) and the American revolutionaries engaged in savage attacks on each other, using hit-and-run tactics, burning, and looting.

The struggle over slavery during the mid-nineteenth century generated decades of conflict, crimes, and violence, including a civil war. After the war, night riders and Ku Klux Klan members were active in the South, using vigilante methods to maintain the status quo and terrorize former slaves. The violence also spilled over into bloody local feuds in the hill country of southern Appalachia. Factional hatreds, magnified by the lack of formal law enforcement and grinding poverty, gave rise to violent attacks and family feuding. Some former Union and Confederate soldiers, heading west with the dream of finding gold or starting a cattle ranch, resorted to theft and robbery.

Crime in the Old West

Some western lawmen developed reputations that have persisted for over a century. Of these, none is more famous than Wyatt Earp. In 1876 he became chief deputy marshal of Dodge City, Kansas, a lawless frontier town, and later moved

To read more about the fascinating life of Wyatt Earp, go to InfoTrac College Edition and read Allen Barra, "Who Was Wyatt Earp?" *American Heritage,* December 1998, p. 76.

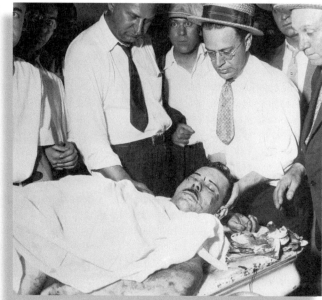

© Bettmann/Corbis

on to Deadwood in the Dakota Territory. In 1879 Earp and his brothers Morgan and Virgil journeyed to Tombstone, Arizona, where he eventually was appointed deputy U.S. marshal for the Arizona Territory. The Earps, along with their gun-slinging dentist friend, Doc Holliday, participated in the famous OK Corral gun-fight in 1881, during which they killed several members of a rustler gang known as the Cowboys led by Curly Bill Brocius and Johnny Ringo. The Cowboys were not the only gang that plied their trade in the old west. Train robbery was popularized by the Reno brothers of Indiana and bank robbery by the James–Younger gang of Missouri.

Crime in the Cities

The old west was not the only area where gang activity flourished. In New York City, bearing colorful monikers such as the Hudson Dusters and Shirttails, gangs played a major role in the city's political power struggles. Their activities were the focus of *Gangs of New York,* a film by director Martin Scorsese, which is reviewed in the Images of Justice feature.

The Civil War also produced widespread business crime. The great robber barons bribed government officials and intrigued to corner markets and obtain concessions for railroads, favorable land deals, and mining and mineral rights on government land. The administration of President Ulysses S. Grant was tainted by numerous corruption scandals.

From 1900 to 1935, the nation experienced a sustained increase in criminal activity. This period was dominated by Depression-era outlaws who later became mythic figures. Charles "Pretty Boy" Floyd was a folk hero among the sharecroppers of eastern Oklahoma, while the nation eagerly followed the exploits of its premier bank robber, John Dillinger, until he was killed in front of a Chicago movie house. The infamous "Ma" Barker and her sons Lloyd, Herman, Fred, and Arthur are credited with killing more than 10 people, while Bonnie Parker and Clyde Barrow killed more than 13 before they were slain in a shootout with federal agents.

The crime problem, then, is not a recent phenomenon; it has been evolving along with the nation itself. Crime has provided a mechanism for the frustrated to vent their anger, for business leaders to maintain their position of wealth and

At the turn of the last century, rural outlaws became mythic figures. At left are photos of the FBI's six most wanted men in 1934. Charles "Pretty Boy" Floyd (left photos, top right) was a folk hero among the sharecroppers of eastern Oklahoma. Floyd robbed as many as thirty banks, filing a notch in his pocket watch for each of the ten men he killed. Floyd was shot dead by police on October 19, 1934. John Dillinger (left photos, top left and right photo) became the nation's premier bank robber until he was killed in front of a Chicago movie house on July 22, 1934. After his death, his body was put on view at the morgue. Hordes of people came to view America's most notorious criminal.

Bonnie and Clyde remain subjects of fascination almost 70 years after their deaths. Read more about them in this article on InfoTrac College Edition: Gary Cartwright, "The Whole Shootin' Match," *Texas Monthly* 29 (February 2001), p. 74.

Gangs of New York

images of justice

The colorful and entertaining 2002 film *Gangs of New York*, directed by Martin Scorsese, was loosely based on Herbert Asbury's book of the same name. Set in New York City, 1840–63, the film tells the story of a young man named Amsterdam (played by Leonardo DiCaprio) who seeks vengeance against Bill "The Butcher" Poole (Daniel Day-Lewis), who killed his father, Priest Vallon (Liam Neeson), during a gang war between Poole's Protestant, American-born Nativist gang and Vallon's Irish-Catholic Dead Rabbits gang that was mostly made up of newly arrived immigrants. The Nativists prevail in the fight and become the cohorts of the Democratic Party political machine known as Tammany Hall, led by the notorious William "Boss" Tweed. Poole serves as Tweed's enforcer in the crime-plagued Five Points section of lower Manhattan (now near the Chinatown area). Here the poor live and work in a labyrinth of underground caves, which in the film are made to look like a scene from Dante's *Inferno*. The Nativists and Dead Rabbits are two among many gangs in the area, including the Plug Uglies, the Swamp Angels, the Daybreak Boys, the Shirttails, and the Bowery Boys. The gang battles are extremely brutal, and men are killed with knives, hatchets, cleavers, and anything else that can puncture or slice flesh.

Returning to the Five Points after spending years in an orphanage, Amsterdam seeks to extract revenge against the man who killed his father. He is aided by a young pickpocket and thief named Jenny Everdeane (Cameron Diaz). Amsterdam joins Poole's gang and at first seems enamored by Poole's worldly ways and personal power. When Poole discovers Amsterdam's true identity, he realizes that one of them must die and sets out to kill Amsterdam.

The film's climactic scene is played out against the Draft Riots of 1863, a four-day rampage that left more than 100 people dead. One of the bloodiest incidents in the city's history, the riot was sparked by the forced conscription of Irish immigrants into the Union Army. While the rich could buy their way out of service for $300, thousands of immigrants were forced to join up. In one telling scene, long lines of young men are taken right off the boat and sent to a table where they are told to sign their citizenship papers and their draft papers at the same time. During the rioting, Amsterdam and Poole begin their final battle. Meanwhile, Union gunboats bomb the area in which the fight is ongoing. Poole is hit by shellfire and says his dying words, "Good-bye, boys: I die a true American!" thus ending the conflict.

How accurate is the film? Bill the Butcher was based on a real character. William Poole, born in 1821, followed in his father's footsteps and opened a New York City butcher shop. In the 1850s his local street gang became the enforcers for the anti-immigrant Know-Nothing or Native American Party. In 1854 he severely beat John Morrissey, an Irish gang leader. Morrissey and his boys swore vengeance and fatally shot him on February 25, 1855, at Stanwix Hall in New York. This was before the Draft Riots and the Civil War. However, legend has it his dying words were "Good-bye, boys: I die a true American!"

The script departs from the historical facts in many other instances. The character of Monk Eastman (played by Brendan Gleeson) is a popular Dead Rabbit who is killed in the film by Bill the Butcher. The real Monk was born in 1873, well after the demise of the Dead Rabbits, the Native Americans, and Bill the Butcher. Monk was gang leader in the Five Points area at the turn of the century, not in the 1860s. He served with distinction in World War I.

The film depicts large numbers of Chinese immigrants, but in reality there were very few in New York City in the 1850s and 1860s and there were almost no Chinese female immigrants. The depiction of the Five Points area as a crime hellhole is also overblown. By the time of the Civil War, crime had begun to decrease there and the Irish were moving up the economic ladder and out of the neighborhood. Union gunboats never shelled the city and Bill the Butcher died in bed after he was shot, not on the streets of the Five Points.

These historical inaccuracies aside, *Gangs of New York* does illustrate a place and time in history that was heretofore unknown to most Americans. It shows the close association between crime and politics and the corruption that led to twentieth-century reform movements in the police and other city agencies. It also graphically depicts the significant amount of crime that took place in the nineteenth century. It shows that crime and violence are not new and existed in an era before rap music, drugs, or any other element of twentieth-century culture, which is a suspected cause of criminality.

Critical Thinking

Gangs of New York portrayed a world in which political figures and crime leaders worked hand in hand. Are there any parallels in contemporary society? Has there been a link, for example, between politics and white-collar criminals?

InfoTrac College Edition Research

To find out all about the making of the film *Gangs of New York*, use it as a subject guide on InfoTrac College Edition.

Source: Tyler Anbinder, *Five Points: The Nineteenth-Century New York City Neighborhood That Invented Tap Dance, Stole Elections, and Became the World's Most Notorious Slum* (New York: Penguin, 2002); Herbert Asbury, *The Gangs of New York: An Informal History of the Underworld* (reprint, New York: Thunder's Mouth Press, 2001).

power, and for those outside the economic mainstream to take a shortcut to the American dream. To protect itself from this ongoing assault, the public has supported the development of a great array of government agencies whose stated purpose is to control and prevent crime; identify, apprehend, and bring to trial those who choose to violate the law; and devise effective methods of criminal correction. These agencies make up what is commonly referred to today as the criminal justice system.

Creating Criminal Justice

The debate over the proper course for effective crime control can be traced back to the publication in 1764 of Cesare Beccaria's famous treatise, *On Crime and Punishment*. Beccaria, an Italian social philosopher, made a persuasive argument against the use of torture and capital punishment, common practices in the eighteenth century. He argued that only the minimum amount of punishment was needed to control crime if criminals could be convinced that their law violations were certain to be discovered and punished.[4] Beccaria's work provides a blueprint for criminal justice: Potential law violators would most certainly be deterred if agencies of government were created that could swiftly detect, try, and punish anyone foolish enough to violate the criminal law.

However, the first police agency, the London Metropolitan Police, was not developed until 1829, to keep the peace and identify criminal suspects. Police agencies began to appear in the United States during the mid-nineteenth century. The penitentiary, or prison, was created to provide nonphysical correctional treatment for convicted offenders. These were considered liberal innovations that replaced corporal punishment or capital punishment or both.

Although significant and far-reaching, these changes were isolated developments. As criminal justice developed over the next century, these fledgling agencies of justice rarely worked together in a systematic fashion. It was not until 1919—when the Chicago Crime Commission, a professional association funded by private contributions, was created—that the work of the criminal justice system began to be recognized.[5] The Chicago Crime Commission acted as a citizens advocate group and kept track of the activities of local justice agencies. The commission still carries out its work today.

In 1931 President Herbert Hoover appointed the National Commission of Law Observance and Enforcement, which is commonly known as the Wickersham Commission. This national study group made a detailed analysis of the U.S. justice system and helped usher in the era of treatment and rehabilitation. Its final report found that thousands of rules and regulations govern the system and made it difficult for justice personnel to keep track of the system's legal and administrative complexity.[6]

The Modern Era of Justice

The modern era of criminal justice can be traced to a series of research projects, first begun in the 1950s, under the sponsorship of the American Bar Foundation (ABF).[7] Originally designed to provide in-depth analysis of the organization, administration, and operation of criminal justice agencies, the ABF project discovered that the justice system contained many procedures that heretofore had been kept hidden from the public view. The research focus then shifted to an examination of these previously obscure processes and their interrelationship—investigation, arrest, prosecution, and plea negotiations. Justice professionals used a great deal of personal choice in decision making, and how this discretion was used became a prime focus of the research effort. For the first time, the term

Wish to read more about Cesare Beccaria's views? Go to InfoTrac College Edition and access Richard Bellamy's article, "Crime and Punishment," *History Review* 28 (September 1997): 24.

To learn more about the history of the London Metropolitan Police, go to the Web page at http://www.met.police.uk/police/mps/history/index.htm.

The American Bar Foundation is a non-profit, independent national research institute committed to basic empirical research on law and legal institutions. For more than 40 years, the foundation's research products have served to expand knowledge of the theory and functioning of law, legal institutions, and the legal profession. Visit its Web site at http://www.abf-sociolegal.org/.

Law Enforcement Assistance Administration (LEAA)
Agency funded by the federal Safe Streets and Criminal Control Act of 1968 that provided technical assistance and hundreds of millions of dollars in aid to local and state justice agencies between 1969 and 1982.

To quiz yourself on this material, go to questions 1.1–1.3 on the Introduction to Criminal Justice 10e CD.

 The National Institute of Justice is the research and development agency of the U.S. Department of Justice and is the only federal agency solely dedicated to researching crime control and justice issues. You can visit its Web site and access online publications at http://www.ojp.usdoj.gov/nij/welcome.html.

criminal justice system began to be used, reflecting a view that justice agencies could be connected in an intricate yet often unobserved network of decision-making processes.

Federal Involvement in Criminal Justice

In 1967 the President's Commission on Law Enforcement and Administration of Justice (Crime Commission), which had been appointed by President Lyndon B. Johnson, published its final report, *The Challenge of Crime in a Free Society*.[8] This group of practitioners, educators, and attorneys was charged with creating a comprehensive view of the criminal justice process and recommending reforms. Concomitantly, Congress passed the Safe Streets and Crime Control Act of 1968, providing for the expenditure of federal funds for state and local crime control efforts.[9] This act helped launch a massive campaign to restructure the justice system. It funded the National Institute of Law Enforcement and Criminal Justice, which encouraged research and development in criminal justice. Renamed the National Institute of Justice in 1979, it has continued its mission as a major source of funding for the implementation and evaluation of innovative experimental and demonstration projects in the criminal justice system.[10]

The Safe Streets Act provided funding for the **Law Enforcement Assistance Administration (LEAA),** which granted hundreds of millions of dollars in aid to local and state justice agencies. Throughout its 14-year history, the LEAA provided the majority of federal funds to states for criminal justice activities. On April 15, 1982, the program came to an end when Congress ceased funding it. Although the LEAA suffered its share of criticism, it supported many worthwhile programs, including the development of a vast number of criminal justice departments in colleges and universities and the use of technology in the criminal justice system.

The federal government continues to fund the National Institute of Justice, the Office of Juvenile Justice and Delinquency Prevention, and the Bureau of Justice Statistics. These agencies carry out a more limited role in supporting criminal justice research and development and in publishing valuable data and research findings. (See Figure 1.1 for the criminal justice system time line.)

The Criminal Justice System Today

The contemporary criminal justice system is society's instrument of **social control.** Some behaviors are considered so dangerous that they must be either strictly controlled or outlawed outright; some people are so destructive that they must

Figure 1.1
Criminal Justice Time Line

Exhibit 1.1 Components of the Criminal Justice System

Police	Courts	Corrections

Police departments are those public agencies created to maintain order, enforce the criminal law, provide emergency services, keep traffic on streets and highways moving freely, and develop a sense of community safety. Police officers work actively with the community to prevent criminal behavior; they help divert members of special needs populations, such as juveniles, alcoholics, and drug addicts, from the criminal justice system; they participate in specialized units such as a drug prevention task force or anti-rape unit; they cooperate with public prosecutors to initiate investigations into organized crime and drug trafficking; they resolve neighborhood and family conflicts; and they provide emergency services, such as preserving civil order during strikes and political demonstrations.

The criminal courthouse is the scene of the trial process. Here the criminal responsibility of defendants accused of violating the law is determined. Ideally, the court is expected to convict and sentence those found guilty of crimes while ensuring that the innocent are freed without any consequence or burden. The court system is formally required to seek the truth, to obtain justice for the individual brought before its tribunals, and to maintain the integrity of the government's rule of law. The main actors in the court process are the judge, whose responsibilities include overseeing the legality of the trial process, and the prosecutor and the defense attorney, who are the opponents in what is known as the adversary system. These two parties oppose each other in a hotly disputed contest—the criminal trial—in accordance with rules of law and procedure.

In the broadest sense, correctional agencies include community supervision or probation, various types of incarceration (including jails, houses of correction, and state prisons), and parole programs for both juvenile and adult offenders. These programs range from the lowest security, such as probation in the community with minimum supervision, to the highest security, such as 24-hour lockdown in an ultra-maximum security prison. Corrections ordinarily represent the postadjudicatory care given to offenders when a sentence is imposed by the court and the offender is placed in the hands of the correctional agency.

be monitored or even confined. The agencies of justice seek to prevent or deter outlawed behavior by apprehending, adjudicating, and sanctioning lawbreakers. Society maintains other forms of informal social control, such as parental and school discipline, but these are designed to deal with moral and not legal misbehavior. Only the criminal justice system maintains the power to control crime and punish outlawed behavior through the arm of the criminal law.

Today the system can be divided into three main components (Exhibit 1.1): law enforcement agencies, which investigate crimes and apprehend suspects; the court system, where a determination is made whether a criminal suspect is guilty as charged; and the correctional system, which treats and rehabilitates offenders as well as incapacitates them so that they may not repeat their crimes.

Contemporary criminal justice agencies are political entities whose structure and function are lodged within the legislative, judicial, and executive branches of the government (Figure 1.2). The **legislature** defines the law by determining what conduct is prohibited and establishes criminal penalties for those who violate the law. The legislative branch of government helps shape justice policy by creating appropriations for criminal justice agencies and acting as a forum for the public expression of views on criminal justice issues.

The judiciary interprets the existing law and determines whether it meets constitutional requirements. It also oversees criminal justice practices and has the power to determine whether existing operations fall within the ambit of the state and ultimately the U.S. Constitution. The courts have the right to overturn or ban policies that are in conflict with constitutional rights.

social control
The ability of society and its institutions to control, manage, restrain, or direct human behavior.

legislature
The branch of government in a state invested with power to make and repeal laws.

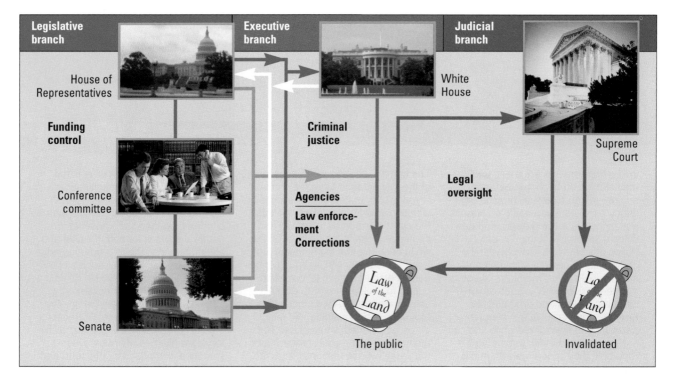

Figure 1.2
The Interrelationship among the
Three Branches of Government

Source: *The United States Government*
Manual 1981/82 (Washington, D.C.:
Government Printing Office, 1981); *The*
United States Government Manual 1982/83
(Washington, D.C.: Government Printing
Office, 1982).

The National Center for
State Courts (NCSC) is
an independent, nonprofit organization dedicated to the improvement
of justice. NCSC activities include
developing policies to enhance state
courts, advancing state courts' interests within the federal government,
fostering state court adaptation to
future changes, securing sufficient
resources for state courts, strengthening state court leadership, facilitating state court collaboration, and
providing a model for organizational
administration. To access its Web
site, go to http://www.ncsc.dni.us.

Use the term "Criminal Justice, Administration of" as
a subject guide on InfoTrac
College Edition to find out more
about this engrossing subject.

Because most justice agencies are within the executive branch of government, elected leaders have a mandate to plan programs, appoint personnel, and
exercise administrative responsibility for criminal justice agencies. Executive
leaders—for example, the president, governor, and mayor—maintain the power
of appointment within key justice agencies, including the right to appoint judges
and heads of administrative agencies, such as police chiefs and commissioners of
corrections. Conversely, they can remove officials who are either inefficient or ineffective.

Scope of the System

The contemporary criminal justice system in the United States is monumental in
size. It consists of more than 55,000 public agencies and costs federal, state, and
local governments about $150 billion per year for civil and criminal justice, which
is an increase of more than 300 percent since 1982 (see Exhibit 1.2).

One reason the justice system is so expensive to run is because it employs
more than 2 million people, including 565,915 full-time law enforcement employees, of which about 441,000 are sworn personnel.[11] It consists of 17,000 police agencies, nearly 17,000 courts, more than 8,000 prosecutorial agencies, about
6,000 correctional institutions, and more than 3,500 probation and parole departments. There are also capital costs. State jurisdictions are now conducting a
massive correctional building campaign, adding tens of thousands of prison cells.
It costs about $70,000 to build a prison cell, and about $22,000 per year is needed
to keep an inmate in prison. Juvenile institutions cost about $30,000 per year per
resident.

The system is so big because it must process, treat, and care for millions of
people each year. Although the crime rate has declined substantially, about
14 million people are still being arrested each year, including more than 2 million
for serious felony offenses.[12] In addition, about 1.5 million juveniles are handled

Exhibit 1.2 Justice System Expenditures

Direct expenditure by criminal justice function, 1982–99

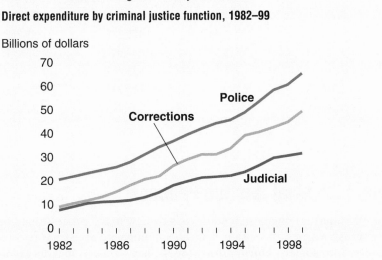

- The percent change from 1982 to 1999 in direct expenditure by police was 244 percent; corrections, 442 percent; and judicial, 314 percent.

- Federal, state, and local governments in the United States spent $147 billion in fiscal year 1999 for criminal and civil justice.

- In 1999 the federal government alone spent $27 billion dollars on the justice system. Between 1982 and 1999, expenditure by the federal government grew 514 percent.

- State governments spent $57 billion on criminal and civil justice in 1999. Sixty percent of state spending was for corrections, at nearly $35 billion. State justice expenditure has grown approximately 9 percent each year since 1982.

- Local governments in 1999 contributed the most (51 percent) to the criminal and civil justice system—almost $75 billion. By far the largest component of local expenditure was police protection, at nearly $46 billion.

- Federal, state, and local governments had 2.2 million justice-related employees in 1999.

- Local governments employed the most people for justice functions, about 1.3 million.

- The total number of justice employees grew 72 percent between 1982 and 1999. The largest growth was in state governments (107 percent).

- From 1977 to 1999 total state and local expenditures for all functions increased 401 percent. Police protection rose 411 percent; corrections rose 946 percent; and judicial and legal rose 1,518 percent. Among some other government functions during the same period, education increased 370 percent; hospitals and health care increased 418 percent; interest on debt increased 490 percent; and public welfare increased 510 percent.

- The three levels of government together spend about $440 for each resident in the United States.

Source: Sidra Lea Gifford, *Justice Expenditure and Employment in the United States, 1999* (Washington, D.C.: Bureau of Justice Statistics, 2002).

by the juvenile courts. Today state and federal courts convict a combined total of more than 1 million adults on felony charges.[13]

Considering the enormous number of people processed each year, the correctional system population is at an all-time high. As Table 1.1 shows, about 6.5 million people are under the control of the correctional system, including about 2 million behind bars and another 4 million on some form of community supervision. The prison population has almost doubled since 1990 despite a decade-long drop in the crime rate.

 To quiz yourself on this material, go to questions 1.4–1.8 on the Introduction to Criminal Justice 10e CD.

Table 1.1 Number of People under Correctional Supervision, 1990–2002

Year	Probation	Parole	Jail	Prison
1990	2,670,234	531,407	405,320	743,382
1995	3,077,861	679,421	507,044	1,078,542
2000	3,826,209	723,898	621,149	1,316,333
2001	3,931,731	732,333	631,240	1,330,007
2002	3,995,165	753,141	665,475	1,367,856

Source: Bureau of Justice Statistics.

The Formal Criminal Justice Process

Another way of understanding criminal justice is to view it as a process that takes an offender through a series of decision points beginning with arrest and concluding with reentry into society. During this process, key decision makers resolve whether to maintain the offender in the system or to discharge the suspect without further action. This decision making is often a matter of individual discretion, based upon a variety of factors and perceptions. Legal factors, including the seriousness of the charges, available evidence, and the suspect's prior record, are usually considered legitimate influences on decision making. Troubling is the fact that such extralegal factors as the suspect's race, gender, class, and age may influence decision outcomes. A significant debate is ongoing over the impact of extralegal factors in the decision to arrest, convict, and sentence a suspect. Critics believe a suspect's race, class, and gender can often determine the direction a case will take, whereas supporters argue that the system is relatively fair and unbiased.[14]

In reality, few cases are processed through the entire formal justice system. Most are handled informally and with dispatch. The system of justice has been roundly criticized for its backroom deals and bargain justice. Although informality and deal making are the rule, the concept of the formal justice process is important because it implies every criminal defendant charged with a serious crime is entitled to a full range of rights under law. Central to the American concept of liberty is that every individual is entitled to his day in court, to be represented by competent counsel in a fair trial before an impartial jury, with trial procedures subject to review by a higher authority. Secret kangaroo courts and summary punishment are elements of political systems that most Americans fear and despise. The fact that most criminal suspects are treated informally may be less important than the fact that all criminal defendants are entitled to a full range of legal rights and constitutional protections.

A comprehensive view of the formal criminal process would normally include the following:

1. *Initial contact.* In most instances, the initial contact with the criminal justice system takes place as a result of a police action. For example, patrol officers observe a person acting suspiciously, conclude the suspect is under the influence of drugs, and take her into custody. In another instance, police officers are contacted by a victim who reports a robbery; they respond by going to the scene of the crime and apprehend a suspect. In a third case, an informer tells police about some ongoing criminal activity to receive favorable treatment. Initial contact may also be launched by the police department's responding to the request of the mayor or other political figures to control a persistent social problem. The police chief may then initiate an undercover investigation into such corrupt practices as gambling, prostitution, or drug trafficking.

Grand jury decision making is a key element in the criminal justice process. Though some critics accuse grand juries of being a "rubber stamp" for the prosecution, they sometimes return a *no bill* of indictment. In this photo, Tim Duncan, left, and other civil rights protesters demonstrate in Louisville, KY, as they wait for a grand jury's report on its investigation of the fatal shooting of James Taylor by Louisville police detective Michael O'Neil on December 5, 2002. Taylor, who was handcuffed, died in his downtown apartment after being shot 11 times. O'Neil was cleared by the grand jury investigating the case.

2. *Investigation.* The purpose of the investigatory stage of justice is to gather sufficient evidence to identify a suspect and support a legal arrest. An investigation can take but a few minutes, as when a police officer sees a crime in progress and can apprehend the suspect at the scene. Or it can take many months and involve hundreds of law enforcement agents, such as the Federal Bureau of Investigation's pursuit of the so-called Unabomber, which led to the arrest of Ted Kaczynski. Investigations may be conducted at the local, state, or federal level and involve coordinated teams of law enforcement agents, prosecutors, and other justice officials.

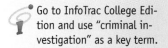 Go to InfoTrac College Edition and use "criminal investigation" as a key term.

3. *Arrest.* The **arrest** power of the police involves taking a person into custody in accordance with lawful authority and holding that person to answer for a violation of the criminal law. A legal arrest occurs when the following conditions exist:

a. The police officer believes that sufficient evidence of a crime exists to restrain the suspect. The officer has *probable cause* to believe a crime has occurred and the person he seeks to arrest is the culprit.
b. The officer deprives the individual of her freedom.
c. The suspect believes that she is in the custody of the officer and cannot voluntarily leave. She has lost her *liberty.*

arrest
Taking a person into legal custody for the purpose of restraining the accused until he or she can be held accountable for the offense at court proceedings.

The police officer is not required to exclaim "You're under arrest!" as usually presented in TV dramas, and the officer does not first have to haul the suspect to the station house. Basically, a person who has been deprived of liberty is under arrest.

An arrest can be made if a police officer personally witnesses the guilty act, if he has probable cause based on a witness or victim statement, or if an **arrest warrant** has been issued by a court. The arrest warrant is a court order that empowers any police officer to arrest the suspect and bring the named person before the court. An arrest warrant must be based on probable cause that the person to be arrested has committed or is attempting to commit a crime. The police will ordinarily go before a judge and obtain a warrant when no danger exists that the suspect will leave the area, when a long-term investigation of a crime is under way, or when they can produce probable cause to arrest the suspect even though they

arrest warrant
Written court order authorizing and directing that an individual be taken into custody to answer criminal charges.

did not directly witness the crime, that is, they have some physical evidence such as fingerprints or a DNA sample.

Most arrests are made without a warrant. The decision to arrest often comes from the police officer during contact with the suspect. In the case of a felony, most jurisdictions provide that police officers may arrest a suspect without a warrant when probable cause exists, even if the officers did not see the crime being committed. In the case of a misdemeanor, officers need to observe the crime firsthand, known as the **in presence requirement,** but many states have eliminated this requirement. This is important for such crimes as domestic violence, shoplifting, or cases in which the suspect will escape if not arrested immediately. As a general rule, if the police make an arrest without a warrant, the arrestee must be brought promptly before a magistrate (within 48 hours) for a **probable cause hearing.**[15]

4. *Custody.* The moment after an arrest is made, the detained suspect is considered in police custody. The police may wish to search the suspect for weapons or contraband, interrogate her to gain more information, find out if the person had any accomplices, or even encourage the suspect to confess to the crime. The police may wish to enter the suspect's home, car, or office to look for further evidence. Similarly, the police may want to bring witnesses to view the suspect in a lineup or in a one-to-one confrontation. Personal information will also be taken from the suspect, including name, address, fingerprints, and photo. Because these procedures are so crucial and can have a great impact at trial, the U.S. Supreme Court has granted suspects in police custody protection from the unconstitutional abuse of police power, such as illegal searches and intimidating interrogations.

5. *Charging.* If the arresting officers or their superiors believe that sufficient evidence exists to charge a person with a crime, the case will be turned over to the prosecutor's office. Minor crimes—that is, misdemeanors—are generally handled with a complaint being filed before the court that will try the case. For serious crimes—that is, felonies—the prosecutor must decide to either bring the case before a grand jury or conduct a preliminary hearing (depending on the procedures used in the jurisdiction; see item 6). In either event, the decision to charge the suspect with a specific criminal act involves many factors, including evidence sufficiency, crime seriousness, case pressure, and political issues, as well as personal factors such as a prosecutor's own specific interests and biases. For example, in some jurisdictions obscenity charges may be vigorously pursued, while in another they are all but ignored. After conducting a preliminary investigation of the legal merits of a case, prosecutors may decide to take no further action, referred to as a **nolle prosequi.**

6. *Preliminary hearing/grand jury.* Because a criminal suspect faces great financial and personal costs when forced to stand trial for a felony, the U.S. Constitution mandates that before a trial can take place, the government must first prove probable cause that the accused committed the crime with which he is being charged. In about half the states and the federal system, this decision is rendered by a group of citizens brought together to form a grand jury, which considers the merits of the case presented only by the prosecutor in a closed hearing. If the evidence is sufficient, the grand jury will issue a bill of indictment, which specifies the charges on which the accused must stand trial. In the remaining states, the grand jury has been replaced with a preliminary hearing. In these jurisdictions, a charging document called an *information* is filed before a lower trial court, which then conducts an open hearing on the merits of the case. During this procedure, sometimes referred to as a *probable cause hearing,* the defendant and her attorney may appear and dispute the prosecutor's charges. The suspect will be called to stand trial if the presiding magistrate or judge accepts the prosecutor's evidence as factual and sufficient. In some states such as California the prosecutor can choose either a preliminary hearing or grand jury.

in presence requirement
A police officer cannot arrest someone for a misdemeanor unless the officer sees the crime occur. To make an arrest for a crime he did not witness, the officer must obtain a warrant.

probable cause hearing
If a person is taken into custody for a misdemeanor, a hearing is held to determine if probable cause exists that he committed the crime.

nolle prosequi
Decision by a prosecutor to drop a case after a complaint has been made because of, for example, insufficient evidence, witness reluctance to testify, police error, or office policy.

7. *Arraignment.* Before the trial begins, the defendant will be arraigned, or brought before the court that will hear the case. Formal charges are read, the defendant informed of his constitutional rights (for example, the right to be represented by legal counsel), an initial plea entered in the case (not guilty or guilty), a trial date set, and bail issues considered.

8. *Bail/detention.* Bail is a money bond levied to ensure the return of a criminal defendant for trial, while allowing the person pretrial freedom to prepare her defense. Defendants who do not show up for trial forfeit their bail. Those people who cannot afford to put up bail or who cannot borrow sufficient funds for it will remain in state custody prior to trial. In most instances, this means an extended stay in a county jail or house of correction. Most jurisdictions allow defendants awaiting trial to be released on their own recognizance (promise to the court), without bail, if they are stable members of the community and have been charged with committing nonviolent crimes.

9. *Plea bargaining.* Soon after an arraignment, if not before, defense counsel will meet with the prosecution to see if the case can be brought to a conclusion without a trial. In some instances, this can involve filing the case while the defendant participates in a community-based treatment program for substance abuse or receives psychiatric care. Most commonly, the defense and prosecution will discuss a possible guilty plea in exchange for reducing or dropping some of the charges or agreeing to a request for a more lenient sentence. Almost 90 percent of all cases end in a plea bargain, instead of a criminal trial.

10. *Trial/adjudication.* If an agreement cannot be reached or if the prosecution does not wish to arrange a negotiated settlement of the case, a criminal trial will be held before a judge or jury, whose duty is to decide whether the prosecution's evidence against the defendant is sufficient beyond a reasonable doubt to prove guilt. If a jury cannot reach a decision—that is, it is deadlocked—the case is left unresolved. The prosecution then decides whether it should be retried at a later date.

11. *Sentencing/disposition.* If after a criminal trial the accused has been found guilty as charged, he will be returned to court for sentencing. Possible dispositions include a fine, probation, a period of incarceration in a penal institution, or some combination of these. In cases involving first-degree murder, more than 35 states and the federal government allow the death penalty. Sentencing is a key decision point in the criminal justice system because, in many jurisdictions, judicial discretion can result in people receiving vastly different sentences even though they have committed the same crime. Some may be released on community supervision, whereas others committing the same crime can receive long prison sentences.

12. *Appeal/postconviction remedies.* After conviction, the defense can ask the trial judge to set aside the jury's verdict because she believes there has been a mistake of law. For example, in 1997 Louise Woodward, a young British nanny, was convicted on the charge of second-degree murder when a Massachusetts jury found her responsible for the death of Matthew Eappen, an infant boy placed in her care. Woodward allegedly shook Eappen, causing his death. The verdict was soon set aside by the trial judge, Hiller Zobel, because he believed that the facts of the case did not substantiate the charge of second-degree murder. He instead reduced the charge to manslaughter and sentenced Woodward to time already served while she was awaiting trial.[16]

An appeal may be filed if after conviction the defendant believes that he has not received fair treatment or that his constitutional rights were violated. Appellate courts review such issues as whether evidence was used properly, a judge conducted the trial in an approved fashion, jury selection was properly done, and the attorneys in the case acted appropriately. If the court rules that the appeal has merit, it can hold that the defendant be given a new trial or, in some instances, be set free. Outright release can be ordered, for example, when the state prosecutes the case in violation of the double jeopardy clause (Fifth Amendment) or when it violates the defendant's right to a speedy trial (Sixth Amendment).

Exhibit 1.3 The Problems of Reentry

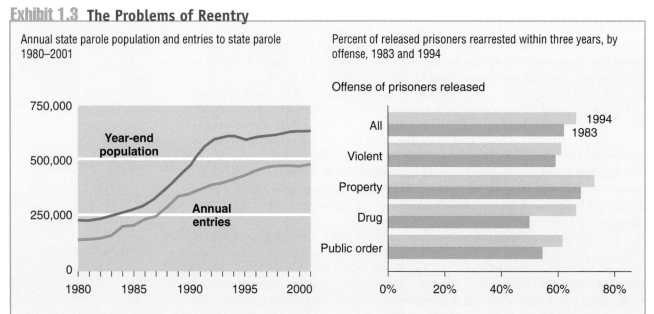

Annual state parole population and entries to state parole 1980–2001

Percent of released prisoners rearrested within three years, by offense, 1983 and 1994

- At least 95 percent of all state prisoners will be released from prison at some point; nearly 80 percent will be released to parole supervision.
- At year-end 2001, 1,406,031 prisoners were under the jurisdiction of state or federal correctional authorities.
- In 2000 about 571,000 state prison inmates were released to the community after serving time in prison.

Source: Bureau of Justice Statistics.

13. *Correctional treatment.* After sentencing, the offender is placed within the jurisdiction of state or federal correctional authorities. She may serve a probationary term, be placed in a community correctional facility, serve a term in a county jail, or be housed in a prison. During this stage of the criminal justice process, the offender may be asked to participate in rehabilitation programs designed to help her make a successful readjustment to society.

14. *Release.* Upon completion of his sentence and period of correction, the offender will be free to return to society. Most inmates do not serve the full term of their sentence but are freed via an early-release mechanism, such as parole or pardon or by earning time off for good behavior. Offenders sentenced to community supervision simply finish their term and resume their lives in the community.

15. *Postrelease.* After termination of their correctional treatment, offenders may be asked to spend some time in a community correctional center, which acts as a bridge between a secure treatment facility and absolute freedom. Offenders may find that their conviction has cost them some personal privileges, such as the right to hold certain kinds of employment. These may be returned by court order once the offenders have proven their trustworthiness and willingness to adjust to society's rules. Reentry is often a difficult process and poses significant risk for the offender, his family, and the community in which he resides (Exhibit 1.3). As millions of former offenders filter back into their community, they create a destabilizing force that unsettles neighbors and increases crime rates. The topic of reentry will be discussed further in Chapter 16.

The Criminal Justice Assembly Line

The image that comes to mind when considering the criminal justice system is an assembly-line conveyor belt that moves an endless stream of cases, never stopping, carrying them to workers who stand at fixed stations and who perform on each case as it comes by the same small but essential operation that brings it one

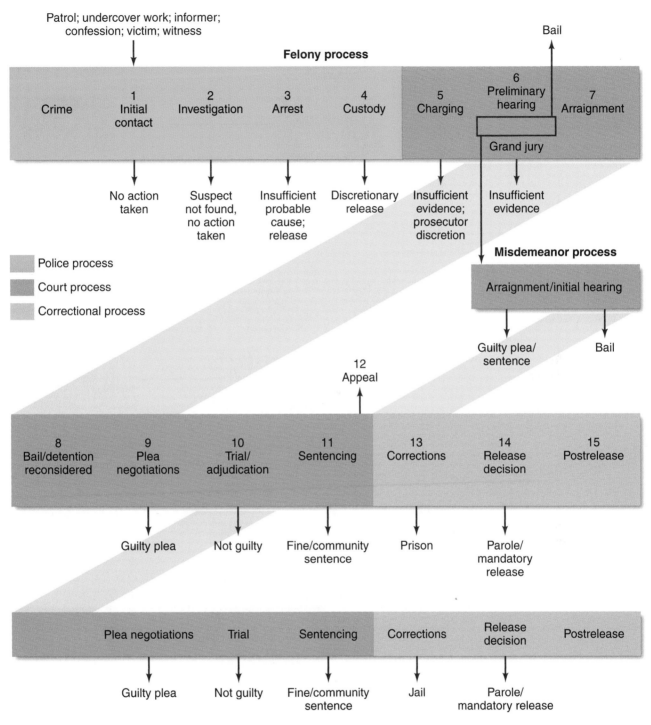

Figure 1.3
The Critical Stages in the Justice Process

step closer to being a finished product, or to exchange the metaphor for the reality, a closed file. The criminal process is seen as a screening process in which each successive stage—pre-arrest investigation, arrest, postarrest investigation, preparation for trial or entry of plea, conviction, disposition—involves a series of routinized operations whose success is gauged primarily by their ability to pass the case along to a successful conclusion.[17]

According to this view, each of the 15 stages is a decision point through which cases flow (Figure 1.3). For example, at the investigatory stage, police must decide whether to pursue the case or terminate involvement because insufficient evidence exists to identify a suspect, the case is considered trivial, the victim decides not to

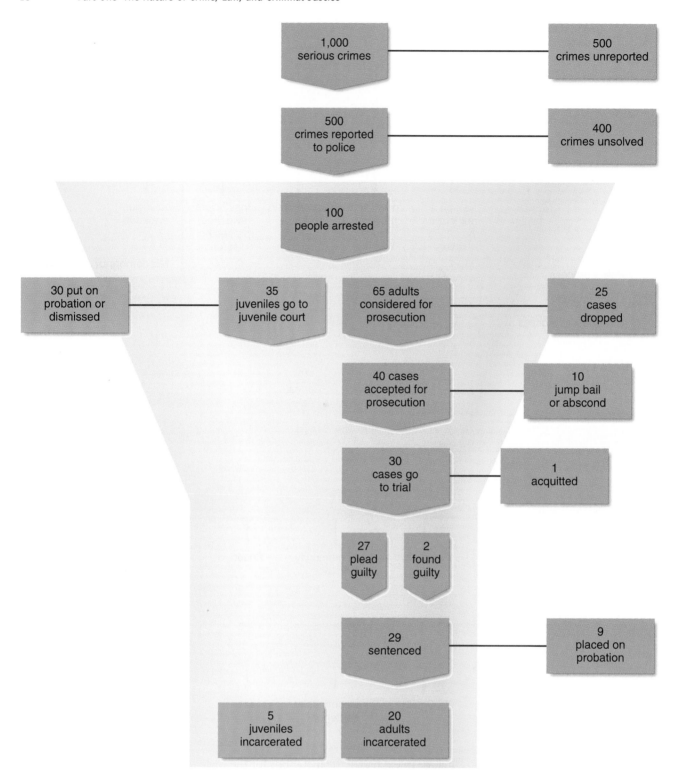

Figure 1.4
The Criminal Justice Funnel

Source: Brian Reeves, *Felony Defendants in Large Urban Counties, 1998* (Washington, D.C.: Bureau of Justice Statistics, 2001).

press charges, and so on. At the bail stage, a decision must be made whether to set so high a bail that the defendant remains in custody, set a reasonable bail, or release the defendant on her own recognizance. Each of these decisions can have a critical effect on the defendant, the justice system, and society. If an error is made, an innocent person may suffer or a dangerous individual may be released to continue to prey upon the community.

Figure 1.4 illustrates the approximate number of offenders removed from the criminal justice system at each stage of the process. Most people who commit

Exhibit 1.4 **The Interrelationship of the Criminal Justice System and the Criminal Justice Process**

The System: Agencies of crime control	The Process
1. Police	1. Contact
	2. Investigation
	3. Arrest
	4. Custody
2. Prosecution and defense	5. Complaint/charging
	6. Grand jury/preliminary hearing
	7. Arraignment
	8. Bail/detention
	9. Plea negotiations
3. Court	10. Adjudication
	11. Disposition
	12. Appeal/postconviction remedies
4. Corrections	13. Correction
	14. Release
	15. Postrelease

crime escape detection, and of those who do not, relatively few are bound over for trial, convicted, and eventually sentenced to prison. About 70 percent of people arrested on felony charges are eventually convicted in criminal court. However, about 25 percent of convictees are released back into the community without having to do time in prison.[18]

In practice, many suspects are released before trial because of a procedural error, evidence problems, or other reasons that result in a case dismissal by the prosecutor (nolle prosequi). Though most cases that go to trial wind up in a conviction, others are dismissed by the presiding judge because of a witness or complainant's failure to appear or procedural irregularities. So, the justice process can be viewed as a funnel that holds many cases at its mouth and relatively few at its end.

Theoretically, nearly every part of the process requires that individual cases be disposed of as quickly as possible. However, the criminal justice process is slower and more tedious than desired because of congestion, inadequate facilities, limited resources, inefficiency, and the nature of governmental bureaucracy. When defendants are not processed smoothly, often because of the large caseloads and inadequate facilities that exist in many urban jurisdictions, the procedure breaks down, the process within the system fails, and the ultimate goal of a fair and efficient justice system cannot be achieved. Exhibit 1.4 shows the interrelationship of the component agencies of the criminal justice system and the criminal justice process.

 To quiz yourself on this material, go to questions 1.9–1.11 on the Introduction to Criminal Justice 10e CD.

The Informal Criminal Justice System

The traditional model of the criminal justice system depicts the legal process as a series of decision points through which cases flow. Each stage of the system, beginning with investigation and arrest and ending after a sentence has been served, is defined by time-honored administrative procedures and controlled by the rule of law. The public's perception of the system, fueled by the media, is that it is composed of daredevil, crime-fighting police officers who never ask for overtime or sick leave, crusading district attorneys who stop at nothing to send the mob boss up the river, wily defense attorneys who neither ask clients for up-front cash nor cut short office visits to play golf, no-nonsense judges who are never inept political appointees, and tough wardens who rule the yard with an iron hand. It would be overly simplistic to assume that the system works this way for every case. Although a few cases receive a full measure of rights and procedures, many are settled in an informal pattern of cooperation between the major actors in the justice process. For example, police may be willing to make a deal with a suspect to gain his cooperation, and the prosecutor may bargain with the defense attorney to get a plea of guilty as charged in return for a promise of leniency. Law enforcement agents and court officers are allowed tremendous discretion in their decision to make an arrest, bring formal charges, handle a case informally, substitute charges, and so on. Crowded courts operate in a spirit of getting the matter settled quickly and cleanly, instead of engaging in long, drawn-out criminal proceedings with an uncertain outcome.

Whereas the traditional model regards the justice process as an adversary proceeding in which the prosecution and defense are combatants, the majority of criminal cases are cooperative ventures in which all parties get together to work out a deal. This is often referred to as the **courtroom work group**.[19] This group, made up of the prosecutor, defense attorney, judge, and other court personnel, functions to streamline the process of justice through the extensive use of plea bargaining and other alternatives. Instead of looking to provide a spirited defense or prosecution, these legal agents, who have often attended the same schools, know each other, and have worked together for many years, try to work out a case to their own professional advantage. In most criminal cases, cooperation, not conflict, between prosecution and defense appears to be the norm. The adversarial process is called into play in only a few widely publicized criminal cases involving rape or murder. Consequently, upward of 80 percent of all felony cases and over 90 percent of misdemeanors are settled without trial.

What has developed is a system in which criminal court experiences can be viewed as a training ground for young defense attorneys looking for seasoning and practice. It provides a means for newly established lawyers to receive government compensation for cases taken to get their practice going or an arena in which established firms can place their new associates for experience before they are assigned to paying clients. Similarly, successful prosecutors can look forward to a political career or a highly paid partnership in a private firm. To further their career aspirations, prosecutors must develop and maintain a winning track record in criminal cases. Although the courtroom work group limits the constitutional rights of defendants, it may be essential for keeping the overburdened justice system afloat. Moreover, though informal justice exists, it is not absolutely certain that it is inherently unfair to both the victim and the offender. Evidence shows that the defendants who benefit the most from informal court procedures commit the least serious crimes, whereas the more chronic offender gains relatively little.[20]

The "Wedding Cake" Model of Justice

Samuel Walker, a justice historian and scholar, has come up with a dramatic way of describing this informal justice process. He compares it with a four-layer cake, as depicted in Figure 1.5.[21]

Level I The first layer of Walker's model is made up of the celebrated cases involving the wealthy and famous, such as O. J. Simpson or Wall Street financier Michael Milken, or the not so powerful who victimize a famous person—for ex-

courtroom work group
All parties in the adversary process working together in a cooperative effort to settle cases with the least amount of effort and conflict.

There are many different "models of justice." To find out more, use it as a key term on InfoTrac College Edition.

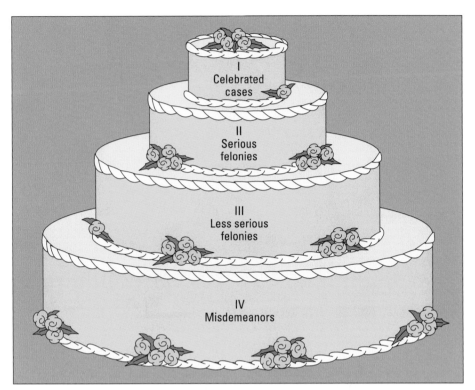

**Figure 1.5
The Criminal Justice
"Wedding Cake"**

Source: Based on Samuel Walker,
Sense and Nonsense about Crime
(Monterey, Calif.: Brooks/Cole, 1985).

ample, John Hinckley Jr., who shot President Ronald Reagan. Other cases fall into the first layer because they are widely reported in the media and become the subject of a TV investigation. The media usually focus on hideous or unusual cases, such as the murder of JonBenet Ramsey or the kidnapping of Utah teen Elizabeth Smart.

Cases in the first layer of the criminal justice "wedding cake" usually receive the full array of criminal justice procedures, including competent defense attorneys, expert witnesses, jury trials, and elaborate appeals. The media typically focus on Level I cases, and the movie-going public are given the impression that most criminals are sober, intelligent people and most victims are members of the upper classes, a patently false impression.

Level II In the second layer are the serious felonies—rapes, robberies, and burglaries—which have become all too routine in U.S. society. They are in the second layer because they are serious crimes committed by experienced offenders. Burglaries are included if the amount stolen is high and the techniques used indicate the suspect is a pro. Violent crimes, such as rape and assault, are vicious incidents against an innocent victim and may involve a weapon and extreme violence. Robberies involve large amounts of money and suspects who brandish handguns or other weapons and are considered career criminals. Police, prosecutors, and judges all agree that these are serious cases, worthy of the full attention of the justice system. Offenders in such Level II cases receive a full jury trial and, if convicted, can look forward to a prison sentence.

Level III Though they can also be felonies, crimes that fall in the third layer of the wedding cake are less serious offenses committed by young or first-time offenders or involving people who knew each other or were otherwise related: An inebriated teenager committed a burglary and netted $50; the rape victim had

The top layer of the criminal justice wedding cake is reserved for the most famous and notorious cases. Here basketball star Kobe Bryant appears at an August 6, 2003 hearing in the courtroom of Judge Fred Gannett in Eagle County, Colorado. Bryant was the target of sexual assault charges in a highly publicized case.

© Barry Gutierrez-Pool/Getty Images

gone on a few dates with her assailant before he attacked her; the robbery involved members of rival gangs and no weapons; the assault was the result of a personal dispute and some question arises as to who hit whom first. Agents of the criminal justice system relegate these cases to the third level because they see them as less important and less deserving of attention. Level III crimes may be dealt with by an outright dismissal, a plea bargain, reduction in charges, and, most typically, a probationary sentence or intermediate sanction, such as victim restitution.

Level IV The fourth layer of the cake is made up of the millions of misdemeanors, such as disorderly conduct, shoplifting, public drunkenness, and minor assault. The lower criminal courts handle these cases in assembly-line fashion. Few defendants insist on exercising their constitutional rights because the delay would cost them valuable time and money. Because the typical penalty is a small fine, everyone wants to get the case over with.[22]

The wedding cake model of informal justice is an intriguing alternative to the traditional criminal justice flowchart. Criminal justice officials handle individual cases differently, yet a high degree of consistency is found with which particular types or classes of cases are dealt in every legal jurisdiction. For example, police and prosecutors in Los Angeles and Boston will each handle the murder of a prominent citizen in similar fashion. They will also deal with the death of an unemployed street person killed in a brawl in a similar manner. Yet, in each jurisdiction, the two cases will be handled very differently. The bigwig's killer will receive a full-blown jury trial (with details on the 6 o'clock news); the drifter's killer will get a quick plea bargain. The model is useful because it shows that all too often public opinion about criminal justice is formed on the basis of what happened in an atypical case.

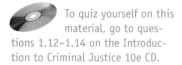

To quiz yourself on this material, go to questions 1.12–1.14 on the Introduction to Criminal Justice 10e CD.

Perspectives on Justice

Though more than 25 years have passed since the field of criminal justice began to be the subject of both serious academic study and attempts at unified policy formation, significant debate continues over the meaning of the term *criminal*

According to the crime control model, the focus of justice should be on the victim, not the criminal. Here, family and friends of Michael Costin listen as a verdict of guilty of involuntary manslaughter is read at Thomas Junta's trial in Cambridge, Massachusetts, January 11, 2002. Junta was sentenced for the beating death of Costin following their sons' hockey practice in July 2000.

© 2002 AP/ Wide World Photos

justice and how the problem of crime control should be approached. After decades of research and policy analysis, criminal justice clearly is far from a unified field. Practitioners, academics, and commentators alike have expressed irreconcilable differences concerning its goals, purpose, and direction. Some conservatives believe the solution to the crime problem is to increase the number of police, apprehend more criminals, and give them long sentences to maximum-security prisons. In contrast, liberals call for increased spending on social services and community organization. Others worry about giving the government too much power to regulate and control behavior and to interfere with individual liberty and freedom.

Given the multitude of problems facing the justice system, this lack of consensus is particularly vexing. The agencies of justice must attempt to eradicate such seemingly diverse social problems as substance abuse, gang violence, pornography, price fixing, and environmental contamination while respecting individual liberties and civil rights. The agencies of the justice system also presumably have adequate resources and knowledge to carry out their complex tasks in an efficient and effective manner, something that so far seems to be wishful thinking. Experts are still searching for the right combination of policies and actions that will significantly reduce crime and increase public safety while maintaining individual freedom and social justice.

Considering the complexity of criminal justice, that no single view, perspective, or philosophy dominates the field is not surprising. What are the dominant views of the criminal justice system today? What is the role of the justice system, and how should it approach its tasks?

Crime Control Perspective

More than 20 years ago political scientist James Q. Wilson made the persuasive argument that most criminals are not poor unfortunates who commit crime to survive but are greedy people who choose theft or drug dealing for quick and easy profits.[23] Criminals, he argued, lack inhibition against misconduct, value

Rehabilitation advocates believe that at-risk youngsters will forgo criminal behavior if they are provided with adequate alternatives to crime. Here, a police officer works with schoolchildren at a community-run, summer gang-resistance program in Boston.

crime control perspective
A model of criminal justice that emphasizes the control of dangerous offenders and the protection of society through harsh punishment as a deterrent to crime.

profile (profiling)
The practice of police targeting members of particular racial or ethnic groups for traffic and other stops because they believe that members of that group are more likely to be engaged in criminal activity even though the individual being stopped has not engaged in any improper behavior.

the excitement and thrills of breaking the law, have a low stake in conformity, and are willing to take greater chances than the average person. If they could be convinced that their actions will bring severe punishment, only the irrational would be willing to engage in crime. Restraining offenders and preventing their future misdeeds, he argued, is a much more practical goal of the criminal justice system than trying to eradicate the root causes of crime: poverty, poor schools, racism, and family breakup. He made this famous observation:

Wicked people exist. Nothing avails except to set them apart from innocent people. And many people, neither wicked nor innocent, but watchful, dissembling, and calculating of their chances, ponder our reaction to wickedness as a clue to what they might profitably do.[24]

Wilson's views helped define the **crime control perspective** of criminal justice. According to this view, the proper role of the justice system is to prevent crime through the judicious use of criminal sanctions. Because the public is outraged by such crimes as mass school shootings (for example, at Columbine High School in Colorado), it demands an efficient justice system that hands out tough sanctions to those who choose to violate the law.[25] If the justice system operated in an effective manner, potential criminals would be deterred from committing law violations, while those who did commit crime would be apprehended, tried, and punished so that they would never dare risk committing crime again. Crime rates trend upward, the argument goes, when criminals do not sufficiently fear apprehension and punishment. If the efficiency of the system could be increased and the criminal law could be toughened, crime rates would decline. Effective law enforcement, strict mandatory punishment, and expanding use of prison are the keys to reduce crime rates. Though crime control may be expensive, reducing the pains of criminal activity is well worth the price.

Focus on the Victim According to the crime control perspective, the focus of justice should be on the victim of crime, not the criminal, so that innocent people can be protected from the ravages of crime. This objective can be achieved through more effective police protection, tough sentences (including liberal use of the death penalty), and the construction of prisons designed to safely incapacitate hardened criminals. If punishment were both certain and severe, then few would be tempted to break the law.

Crime control advocates do not want legal technicalities to help the guilty go free and tie the hands of justice. They lobby for the abolition of legal restrictions that control a police officer's ability to search for evidence and interrogate suspects. For example, they want law enforcement officers to be able to **profile** people at an airport to identify terrorists even if it means singling out people because of their gender, race, or ethnic origin. Isn't this a violation of the Constitution? critics might ask. A crime control advocate might reply that we are in the midst of a national emergency and the ends justify the means. We are not worried about middle-aged, Norwegian woman so why bother to search them? they might retort. They are angry at judges who let obviously guilty people go free because a law enforcement officer made an unintentional procedural error.

Crime control advocates also question the criminal justice system's ability to rehabilitate offenders. Most treatment programs are ineffective because the justice system is simply not equipped to treat people who have a long history of antisocial behavior. Even when agents of the system attempt to prevent crime by working with young people, the results are unsatisfactory. For example, evaluations of the highly touted Drug Abuse Resistance Education (DARE) antidrug program indicate that it has had little impact on students.[26] From both a moral and a practical standpoint, the role of criminal justice should be the control of antisocial people. If not to the justice system, then to whom can the average citizen turn for protection from society's criminal elements?

Rehabilitation Perspective

If the crime control perspective views the justice system in terms of protecting the public and controlling criminal elements, then advocates of the **rehabilitation perspective** may be said to see the justice system as a means of caring for and treating people who cannot manage themselves. They view crime as an expression of frustration and anger created by social inequality. Crime can be controlled by giving people the means to improve their lifestyle through conventional endeavors.

The rehabilitation concept assumes that people are at the mercy of social, economic, and interpersonal conditions and interactions. Criminals themselves are the victims of racism, poverty, strain, blocked opportunities, alienation, family disruption, and other social problems. They live in socially disorganized neighborhoods that are incapable of providing proper education, health care, or civil services. Society must help them to compensate for their social problems.

rehabilitation perspective
A model of criminal justice that sees crime as an expression of frustration and anger created by social inequality that can be controlled by giving people the means to improve their lifestyle though conventional endeavors.

Alternatives to Crime Rehabilitation advocates believe that government programs can help reduce crime on both a societal (macro) and individual (micro) level. For example, on the macro-, or societal, level, research shows that as the number of legitimate opportunities to succeed declines, people are more likely to turn to criminal behaviors, such as drug dealing, to survive. Increasing economic opportunities through job training, family counseling, educational services, and crisis intervention are more effective crime reducers than prisons and jails. As legitimate opportunities increase, violence rates decline.[27]

On a micro-level, rehabilitation programs can help at-risk kids avoid entry into criminal careers by providing them with legitimate alternatives to crime. Even those who find themselves in trouble with the law can avoid recidivism if they are placed in effective, well-designed treatment facilities that can reduce repeat offending. For example, counseling programs, which help offenders develop interpersonal skills, induce a prosocial change in attitudes and improve cognitive thinking patterns, both of which have been shown to significantly reduce recidivism rates.[28]

Punishing offenders and placing them in prison does not seem to deter future criminality. Society has a choice: Pay now, by funding treatment and educational programs, or pay later, when troubled youths enter costly correctional facilities over and over again. This view is certainly not lost on the public. Although the public may want to get tough on crime, many are willing to make exceptions, for example, by advocating leniency for younger offenders.[29]

Due Process Perspective

Advocates of the **due process perspective** argue that the greatest concern of the justice system should be providing fair and equitable treatment to those accused of crime.[30] This means providing impartial hearings, competent legal counsel,

due process perspective
A model of criminal justice that emphasizes individual rights and constitutional safeguards against arbitrary or unfair judicial or administrative proceedings.

Board of Education of Independent School District No. 92 of Pottawatomie County et al. v. Earls et al.

law in review

Facts

The Tecumseh, Oklahoma, school district adopted a student activities drug testing policy that requires all middle and high school students to consent to urinalysis testing for drugs to participate in any extracurricular activity. The policy was a response to increased perceptions of student drug use by faculty and administrators. Teachers saw students who appeared to be under the influence of drugs and heard students speaking openly about using drugs. A drug dog found marijuana near the school parking lot. Police found drugs or drug paraphernalia in a car driven by an extracurricular club member. And the school board president reported that people in the community were calling the board to discuss the "drug situation."

In practice, the policy was applied only to competitive extracurricular activities sanctioned by the Oklahoma Secondary Schools Activities Association (OSSAA). A group of students and their parents filed suit against the policy, arguing that it infringed on a student's right to personal privacy. The Tenth Circuit Court of Appeals

agreed and held that before imposing a suspicionless drug testing program a school must demonstrate some identifiable drug abuse problem among a sufficient number of students such that testing that group will redress its drug problem. The federal court held that the school district had failed to demonstrate such a problem among Tecumseh students participating in competitive extracurricular activities. However, the Supreme Court reversed its decision and ruled that the policy is a reasonable means of furthering the school district's important interest in preventing and deterring drug use among its schoolchildren and does not violate the students' rights to privacy or their due process rights.

Decision

The Court ruled that, so as not to violate due process, drug testing policies had to be "reasonable." However, in contrast to searches for criminal evidence, students could be searched by school authorities (to determine whether they used drugs) without probable cause because the need

for that level of evidence interferes with maintaining swift and informal disciplinary procedures that are needed to maintain order in a public school. Because the schools' responsibility for children cannot be disregarded, it would not be unreasonable to search students for drug usage even if no single student was suspected of abusing drugs.

The Court also ruled that within this context, students have a limited expectation of privacy. In their complaint, the students argued that children participating in nonathletic extracurricular activities have a stronger expectation of privacy than athletes who regularly undergo physicals as part of their participation in sports. However, the Court disagreed, maintaining that students who participate in competitive extracurricular activities voluntarily subject themselves to many of the same intrusions on their privacy as do athletes. Some of these clubs and activities require off-campus travel and communal undress, and all of them have their own rules and requirements that do not apply to the student body as a whole. Each of them must

equitable treatment, and reasonable sanctions. The use of discretion within the justice system should be strictly monitored to ensure that no one suffers from racial, religious, or ethnic discrimination. The system must be attuned to the civil rights afforded every citizen by the U.S. Constitution. It is therefore vexing to due process advocates when the Supreme Court extends the scope of law enforcement's reach, enabling police agencies to monitor and control citizens at the expense of their right to privacy. The Law in Review feature above focuses on one area of justice, student drug testing, and illustrates the eternal struggle between the needs of crime control and the concerns of due process.

Though many views exist of what the true goals of justice should be, the system undoubtedly must operate in a fair and unbiased manner.

Those who advocate the due process orientation point out that the justice system remains an adversary process that pits the forces of an all-powerful state against those of a solitary individual accused of a crime. If concern for justice and fairness did not exist, the defendant who lacked resources could easily be overwhelmed. Miscarriages of justice are common. Numerous criminal convictions had been overturned because newly developed DNA evidence later showed that the accused could not have committed the crimes. Many of the falsely convicted spend years in prison before their release.[31] Evidence also abide by OSSAA rules, and a faculty sponsor monitors students for compliance with the various rules dictated by the clubs and activities. Such regulation diminishes the student's expectation of privacy.

Finally, the Court concluded that the means used to enforce the Drug Policy was not overly invasive or an intrusion on the students' privacy. Under the Policy, a faculty monitor would wait outside a closed restroom stall for the student to produce a sample and must listen for the normal sounds of urination to guard against tampered specimens and ensure an accurate chain of custody. This procedure is virtually identical to the "negligible" intrusion concept which was approved in an earlier case, *Vernonia* v. *Acton,* which applied to student athletes. The Policy requires that test results be kept in confidential files separate from a student's other records and released to school personnel only on a "need to know" basis. Moreover, the test results are not turned over to any law enforcement authority. Nor do the test results lead to the imposition of discipline or

have any academic consequences. Rather, the only consequence of a failed drug test is to limit the student's privilege of participating in extracurricular activities.

Significance

In *Pottawatomie County,* the Court concluded that a drug testing policy effectively serves a school district's interest in protecting its students' safety and health. It reasoned that preventing drug use by schoolchildren is an important governmental concern. School districts need not show that kids participating in a particular activity have a drug problem in order to test them for usage. The need to prevent and deter the substantial harm of childhood drug use itself provides the necessary immediacy for a school testing policy. Given what it considers a "nationwide epidemic of drug use" it was entirely reasonable for the school district to enact a drug testing policy.

Critical Thinking

Pottawatomie County extends the drug testing allowed in the *Vernonia* case from

athletes to all students who participate in any form of school activity. Do you believe this is a reasonable exercise of state authority or a violation of due process? After all, the students being tested have not shown any evidence of drug abuse. Furthermore, nonathletic school activities do not provide the same degree of danger as an athletic activity during the course of which an impaired participant may suffer serious injury.

InfoTrac College Edition Research

 To read what former drug czar and values guru William Bennett has to say about the case, go to InfoTrac College Edition and read "Statement of Empower America Co-Director William J. Bennett on the Supreme Court's Decision in *Pottawatomie County* v. *Earls,*" *US Newswire,* June 27, 2002.

Source: *Board of Education of Independent School District No. 92 of Pottawatomie County et al.* v. *Earls et al.,* 01.332 (2002).

shows that many innocent people have been executed for crimes they did not commit. For example, from 1976 to 1999, 566 people were executed. During that same period of time, 82 convicts awaiting execution were exonerated—a ratio of one freed for every seven put to death.[32] Because such mistakes can happen, even the most apparently guilty offender deserves all the protection the justice system can offer.

Those who question the due process perspective claim that the legal privileges afforded criminal suspects have gone too far and that the effort to protect individual rights now interferes with public safety. Is it fair, they argue, for evidence to be suppressed if it is obtained in violation of the constitutional right to be free from an illegal search and seizure, even if it means that a dangerous person goes free? Is it better to free a guilty person than trample on the civil rights of citizens, even those who commit criminal acts? But what about the rights of actual or potential victims of crime? Should the needs of the victim take precedence over those of criminal offenders? Those who advocate for the due process perspective believe firmly that legal principles of fairness and due process must be upheld even if it means that on occasion a patently guilty person is freed. Preserving the democratic ideals of American society takes precedent over the need to punish the guilty.

WWW To read about such critical due process issues as defending judicial independence, controversial judicial opinions, federal judicial selection, state judicial elections, judicial appointments in the states, impeachment and disciplining of judges, judicial reform, and other similar issues, go to the home page of the Brennan Judicial Center at New York University: http://brennancenter.org/.

Nonintervention Perspective

nonintervention perspective
A model of criminal justice that favors the least intrusive treatment possible: decarceration, diversion, and decriminalization.

Read about the movement to decriminalize marijuana in Canada in "Politics: Washington Fumes as Canada Moves to Decriminalize Pot," *Inter Press Service,* July 27, 2002.

decriminalization
Reducing the penalty for a criminal act without legalizing it.

victimless crime
A crime typically involving behavior considered immoral or in violation of public decency that has no specific victim, such as public drunkenness, vagrancy, or public nudity.

deinstitutionalization
The movement to remove as many offenders as possible from secure confinement and treat them in the community.

pretrial diversion
Informal, community-based treatment programs that are used in lieu of the formal criminal process.

widening the net
To enmesh more offenders for longer periods in the criminal justice system—a criticism of pretrial diversion programs.

Supporters of the **nonintervention perspective** believe that justice agencies should limit their involvement with criminal defendants. Regardless of whether intervention is designed to punish or treat people, the ultimate effect of any involvement is harmful. Whatever their goals or design, programs that involve people with a social control agency—such as the police, a mental health department, the correctional system, or a criminal court—will have long-term negative effects. Once involved with such an agency, criminal defendants may be watched, people might consider them dangerous and untrustworthy, and they can develop a lasting record that has negative connotations. Bearing an official label disrupts their personal and family life and harms parent–child relationships. Eventually, they may even come to believe what their official record suggests; they may view themselves as bad, evil, outcasts, troublemakers, or crazy. Thus, official labels promote rather then reduce the continuity in antisocial activities.[33]

Noninterventionists are concerned about the effect of the stigma that criminal suspects bear when they are given negative labels such as "rapist" or "child abuser." These labels will stick with them forever. Once labeled, people may find it difficult to be accepted back into society, even after they have completed their sentence. It is not surprising, considering these effects of stigma and labeling, that recidivism rates are so high. When fewer people are given less stigmatized forms of punishment such as probation, they are less likely to become repeat offenders.[34]

Fearing the harmful effects of stigma and labels, noninterventionists have tried to place limitations on the government's ability to control people's lives. They have called for the **decriminalization** (reduction of penalties) and legalization of nonserious **victimless crimes,** such as the possession of small amounts of marijuana, public drunkenness, and vagrancy. They demand the removal of nonviolent offenders from the nation's correctional system, a policy referred to as **deinstitutionalization.** First offenders who commit minor crimes should instead be placed in informal, community-based treatment programs, a process referred to as **pretrial diversion.**

Sometimes the passage of new criminal laws help stigmatize offenders beyond the scope of their offense, referred to as **widening the net** of justice. For example, a person who purchases pornography on the Internet is labeled a dangerous sex offender, or someone caught for a second time with marijuana is considered a habitual drug abuser. Noninterventionists have fought implementation of community notification–type laws that require convicted sex offenders to register with state law enforcement officials and allow officials to publicly disclose when a registrant moves into a community. Their efforts have resulted in rulings stating that these laws can be damaging to the reputation and future of offenders who have not been given an opportunity to defend themselves from the charge that they are chronic criminal sex offenders.[35] As a group, noninterventionist initiatives have been implemented to help people avoid the stigma associated with contact with the criminal justice system.

Justice Perspective

The core of the justice perspective is that all people should receive the same treatment under the law. Any effort to distinguish between criminal offenders will create a sense of unfairness that can interfere with readjustment to society. Frustration arises when two people commit the same crime but receive different sentences or punishments. The resulting anger and a sense of unfairness will increase the likelihood of recidivism.

To remedy this situation, the criminal justice system must reduce discretion and unequal treatment. Law violators should be evaluated on the basis of their current behavior, not on what they have done in the past (they have already paid for their behavior) or on what they may do in the future (because future behavior cannot be accurately predicted). The treatment of criminal offenders must be based solely on present behavior: Punishment must be equitably administered and based on just deserts.

The justice perspective has had considerable influence in molding the nation's sentencing policy. An ongoing effort has been made to reduce discretion and guarantee that every offender convicted of a particular crime receives equal punishment. This change has been particularly welcome given the charges of racial discrimination that have beset the sentencing process. A number of initiatives have been designed to achieve this result, including mandatory sentences requiring that all people convicted of a crime receive the same prison sentence. *Truth-in-sentencing laws* require offenders to serve a substantial portion of their prison sentence behind bars, thus limiting their eligibility for early release on parole.[36]

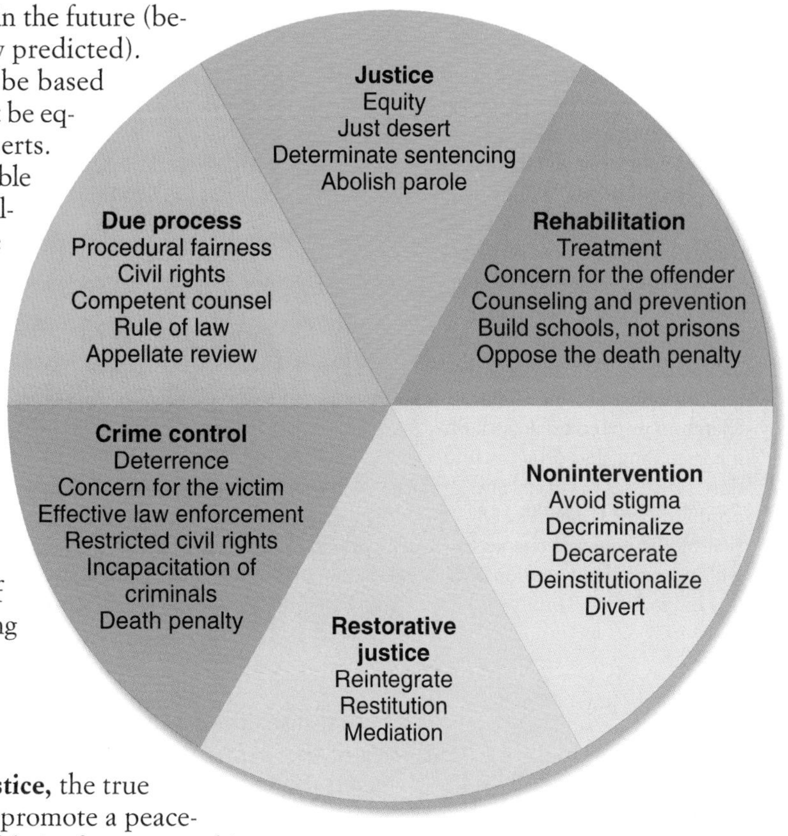

Restorative Justice Perspective

According to the concept of **restorative justice,** the true purpose of the criminal justice system is to promote a peaceful and just society; the justice system should aim for peacemaking, not punishment.[37]

The restorative justice perspective draws its inspiration from religious and philosophical teachings ranging from Quakerism to Zen. Advocates of restorative justice view the efforts of the state to punish and control as crime encouraging rather than crime discouraging. The violent punishing acts of the state, they claim, are not dissimilar from the violent acts of individuals.[38] Therefore, mutual aid, not coercive punishment, is the key to a harmonious society. Without the capacity to restore damaged social relations, society's response to crime has been almost exclusively punitive.

According to restorative justice, resolution of the conflict between criminal and victim should take place in the community in which it originated and not in some far-off prison. The victim should be given a chance to voice his story, and the offender can directly communicate her need for social reintegration and treatment. The goal is to enable the offender to appreciate the damage she has caused, to make amends, and to be reintegrated back into society.

Restorative justice programs are now being geared to these principles. Police officers, as elements of community policing programs, are beginning to use mediation techniques to settle disputes instead of resorting to formal arrest.[39] Mediation and conflict resolution programs are common features in many communities. Financial and community service restitution programs as an alternative to imprisonment have been in operation for more than two decades. The perspectives are summarized in Figure 1.6.

Figure 1.6
Perspectives on Justice: Key Concerns and Concepts

restorative justice
A perspective on justice that views the main goal of the criminal justice system to be a systematic response to wrongdoing that emphasizes healing the wounds of victims, offenders, and communities caused or revealed by crime. It stresses noncoercive and healing approaches whenever possible.

To quiz yourself on this material, go to questions 1.15–1.21 on the Introduction to Criminal Justice 10e CD.

Perspectives in Action: Controlling the Drug Trade

The fact that multiple perspectives of justice exist can no where better be seen than in the "war on drugs." Reducing drug abuse is a top priority, considering its social costs.

One popular crime control strategy is a police crackdown during which law enforcement agencies aggressively focus on a particular crime pattern in an effort to achieve control or elimination of it. Here, Ludwig "Ninny" Bruschi stands in Superior Court during his arraignment on organized crime charges June 10, 2003 in Freehold, New Jersey. Bruschi, a reputed capo with the Genovese crime family, and sixteen others were indicted on charges they operated loansharking, gambling, and drug distribution businesses in central and northern New Jersey. The 68-year-old Bruschi was charged with running the operation out of a bar in Union County.

© Don Murray-Pool/Getty Images

Is the United States fighting a war on drugs? Is it winning? Use "war on drugs" as a key term on InfoTrac College Edition.

source control
Attempting to cut off the supply of illegal drugs by destroying crops and arresting members of drug cartels in drug-producing countries.

Because of the importance and costs associated with the war on drugs, agencies of the criminal justice system have used a number of strategies to reduce drug trafficking and the use of drugs. Some have relied on a strict crime control orientation, whereas others feature nonintervention, justice, and rehabilitation strategies.

Crime Control Strategies

A number of efforts have been made to control the drug trade through strict crime control. These include the following:

Source Control To cut off supplies of drugs, crops are being destroyed and members of drug cartels in drug-producing countries are being arrested; this approach is known as **source control.** The federal government's Drug Enforcement Administration has been in the vanguard of encouraging exporting nations to step up efforts to destroy drug crops and prosecute dealers. Translating words into deeds is a formidable task. Drug lords are willing and able to fight back through intimidation, violence, and corruption. For example, enforcement efforts in Peru and Bolivia have been so successful that drug crops have been significantly reduced. Instead of inhibiting drug shipments, Colombia and Mexico have become the premier coca-cultivating nations. When the Colombian government mounted an effective eradication campaign in the traditional growing areas, the drug cartel linked up with rebel groups in remote parts of the country for its drug supply.[40] In addition to cocaine production, Colombia and Mexico have become the dominant suppliers of heroin to the United States, replacing Asia, and producing upward of 80 percent of the heroin that reaches American streets.[41]

Border Control Another crime control approach to the drug problem has been to interdict drug supplies as they enter the country. Border patrols and military personnel using sophisticated hardware have been involved in massive interdiction efforts. Many impressive multimillion-dollar seizures have been made. Yet U.S. borders are so vast and unprotected that meaningful interdiction is difficult.

To aid law enforcement agencies, the U.S. military has become involved in stemming the flow of drugs across the border. The cost of staffing listening posts and patrolling borders is growing rapidly. Today interdiction and eradication strategies cost billions of dollars, yet they do little to reduce drug supplies.

Police Crackdowns Local, state, and federal law enforcement agents have also been actively fighting drug dealers. One approach is to focus on large-scale drug rings. However, the effect has merely been to decentralize drug dealing. Law enforcement efforts have significantly reduced the strength of traditional organized syndicates. Instead of reducing the inflow of drugs, their place has been taken by Asian, Latino, and Jamaican groups; motorcycle clubs; and local gangs. Colombian syndicates have established cocaine distribution centers on every continent, and Mexican organizations are responsible for large methamphetamine shipments to the United States. Russian, Turkish, Italian, Nigerian, Chinese, Lebanese, and Pakistani heroin-trafficking syndicates are now competing for dominance.

In terms of weight and availability, no commodity is more lucrative than illegal drugs. They cost relatively little to produce and provide large profit margins to dealers and traffickers. At an average street price of $100 per gram in the United States, a metric ton of pure cocaine is worth $100 million. Cutting it and reducing purity can double or triple the value. It is difficult for law enforcement agencies to counteract the inducement of drug profits. When large-scale drug busts are made, supplies become scarce and market values increase, encouraging more people to enter the drug trade.

Aiming efforts at low-level dealers is also problematic. Some street-level enforcement efforts have been successful, but others are considered failures. Drug sweeps have clogged courts and correctional facilities with petty offenders while proving a costly drain on police resources. A displacement effect is also suspected: Stepped-up efforts to curb drug dealing in one area or city simply encourage dealers to seek out friendlier territory.

Justice Model Strategies

According to the justice model, if drug violations were to be punished with criminal sentences commensurate with their harm, then the rational drug trafficker would look for a new line of employment. The cornerstone of this antidrug model is the adoption of mandatory minimum sentences for drug crimes, which ensure that all offenders receive similar punishments for their acts. The justice model advocates lobby for sentencing policies that will standardize punishments. The Federal Anti-Drug Abuse Act of 1988 provides minimum mandatory prison sentences for serious drug crimes, with especially punitive sentences for anyone caught distributing drugs within 1,000 feet of a school playground, youth center, or other areas where minors congregate.[42] Once convicted, drug dealers are subject to very long sentences and the seizure of their homes, automobiles, boats, and other assets bought with drug-trafficking profits.

Rehabilitation Strategies

Advocates of the rehabilitation model criticize punitive efforts to control the drug trade. They suggest that law enforcement efforts such as source and border control are doomed to failure because even if they were effective they would drive up the price of illegal drugs and encourage more people to enter the drug trade. Moreover, severely punishing users with long prison sentences may have little deterrent effect. They point to research such as that conducted by Cassia

Spohn and David Holleran that shows drug-involved offenders are the ones most likely to recidivate after serving a prison sentence.[43] Instead, rehabilitation advocates suggest that the only effective way to reduce drug use is to create strategies aimed at lessening the desire to use drugs and increasing incentives for users to eliminate substance abuse. What strategies have been tried?

Drug Prevention One approach relies on drug prevention—convincing nonusers to not start using drugs. This effort relies heavily on educational programs that teach children to "say no" to drugs. The most well-known program is Drug Abuse Resistance Education, or **DARE,** an elementary school course designed to give students the skills for resisting peer pressure to experiment with tobacco, drugs, and alcohol. Evaluations of the program have been disappointing, indicating that it does increase knowledge about dangerous substances but has been insignificant in shaping attitudes toward drug abuse and law enforcement, increasing self-esteem, or reducing student drug use.[44]

DARE
Drug Abuse Resistance Education, a school-based program designed to give students the skills to resist peer pressure to experiment with tobacco, alcohol, and illegal drugs.

Offender Treatment The rehabilitation model suggests that it is possible to treat known users, get them clean of drugs and alcohol, and help them reenter conventional society.

An active effort has been made to identify drug abusers to get them into treatment. Drug testing of arrestees is common. Public and private institutions now regularly test employees and clients to determine if they are drug abusers.

Once users have been identified, a number of treatment strategies have been implemented. One approach rests on the assumption that users have low self-esteem and holds that treatment efforts must focus on building a sense of self. In this approach, users participate in outdoor activities and wilderness training to create self-reliance and a sense of accomplishment.[45]

More intensive efforts use group therapy approaches relying on group leaders who once were substance abusers. Group sessions try to give users the skills and support that can help them reject the social pressure to use drugs. These programs are based on the Alcoholics Anonymous approach: Users must find within themselves the strength to stay clean, and peer support from those who understand the users' experiences can help them achieve a drug-free life.

Residential programs have been established for the more heavily involved users, and a large network of drug treatment centers has been developed. Some are detoxification units that use medical procedures to wean patients from the more addicting drugs to others, such as **methadone,** the use of which can be more easily regulated. Methadone, a drug similar to heroin, is given under controlled conditions to addicts at clinics. Methadone programs have been undermined because some users sell their methadone on the black market, while others supplement their dosages with illegally obtained heroin.

methadone
A synthetic narcotic used as a substitute for heroin in drug-control efforts.

Despite the good intentions of these treatment programs, little evidence exists that they can efficiently end substance abuse. A stay can help stigmatize residents as addicts, even though they never used hard drugs. While in treatment, they may be introduced to hard-core users with whom they may associate upon release. Users often do not enter these programs voluntarily and have little motivation to change.[46] Even for those who could be helped, there are simply more users who need treatment than there are beds in treatment facilities. Many programs are restricted to users whose health insurance will pay for short-term residential care. When the insurance coverage ends, the patients are often released before their treatment program is completed. Simply put, if treatment strategies are to be successful, far more programs and funding are needed.

Restorative Justice Strategies

Numerous restorative justice–based programs are now in operation. Mediation and conflict resolution programs are common. Financial and community service restitution programs as an alternative to imprisonment have been in operation for more than two decades. These serve as an alternative to traditional criminal justice prosecution for drug-related offenses and work to tailor nonpunitive, effective, and appropriate responses to drug offenders. One restorative effort involves the use of specialized drug courts. Defendants eligible for the drug court program are identified as soon as possible and, if accepted into the program, are referred immediately to multiphased outpatient treatment. Treatment entails multiple weekly (often daily) contacts with the treatment provider for counseling, therapy, and education as well as a rehabilitation program that includes vocational, educational, family, medical, and other support services.[47] The drug court movement will be revisited in Chapter 10.

Nonintervention Strategies

Despite the massive effort to control drug usage through both crime control and rehabilitation strategies, the fight has not been successful. Getting people out of the drug trade is difficult because drug trafficking involves enormous profits and dealers and users both lack meaningful economic alternatives. Controlling drugs by convincing known users to quit is equally hard; few treatment efforts have proven successful.

Considering these problems, some commentators, relying on a noninterventionist strategy, have called for the **legalization** of drugs. If drugs were legalized, the argument goes, distribution could be controlled by the government. Price and the distribution method could be regulated, reducing the addict's cash requirements. Crime rates would be cut because drug users would no longer need the same cash flow to support their habit. Drug-related deaths would decrease because government control would reduce the sharing of needles and thus the spread of HIV/AIDS (human immunodeficiency virus/acquired immune deficiency syndrome). Legalization would also destroy the drug-importing cartels and gangs. Given that drugs would be bought and sold openly, the government would reap a windfall from both taxes on the sale of drugs and on the income of drug dealers, which now is untaxed as part of the hidden economy. Drug distribution would be regulated, keeping narcotics out of the hands of adolescents. Those who favor legalization point to the Netherlands as a country that has legalized drugs and remains relatively crime-free.[48] The issue of legalization is analyzed further in the Analyzing Criminal Justice Issues feature on page 34.

legalization
The removal of all criminal penalties from a previously outlawed act.

Due Process Strategies

Those who advocate due process are concerned that fighting the war on drugs may compromise civil rights and cast suspicion on innocent people. All too often, due process advocates charge, the rights of minorities are breached by overzealous law enforcement agents. For example, in July 1999, 10 percent of the African American population in Tulia, Texas, a small town of 5,000 in the Texas panhandle, was arrested on drug charges. In 2003 a Dallas judge threw out the drug convictions of 38 of those defendants, finding that they were based on questionable testimony from a single undercover agent who may have been motivated by racial prejudice. In another case, 15 percent of young African American men in Hearne, a small community in eastern Texas, were arrested under similar circumstances.[49]

Due process advocates are also concerned about the abuse of forced drug testing, which they charge interferes with the due process rights of non-drug

Should Drugs Be Legalized?

analyzing criminal justice issues

Advocates of drug legalization suggest that, like it or not, drug use is here to stay because using mood-altering substances is customary in almost all human societies. No matter what, people will find ways of obtaining psychoactive drugs. Banning drugs serves to create networks of manufacturers and distributors, many of whom use violence as part of their standard operating procedures. Though some may charge that drug use is immoral, is it any worse than the unrestricted use of alcohol and cigarettes, both of which are addicting and unhealthy? Far more people die each year because they abuse these legal substances than the numbers who are killed in drug wars or from illegal substances (an estimated 100,000 people die each year from alcohol-related causes and another 320,000 from tobacco).

Reformer Ethan Nadelman of the Drug Policy Alliance is an outspoken critic of the ongoing war against drugs. Nadelman argues persuasively that everyone has a stake in ending the war on drugs, whether they be a parent concerned about protecting children from drug-related harm, a social justice advocate worried about racially disproportionate incarceration rates, an environmentalist seeking to protect the Amazon rainforest, or a fiscally conservative taxpayer seeking to save

money. U.S. federal, state, and local governments have spent hundreds of billions of dollars trying to make America drug-free. Yet heroin, cocaine, methamphetamine, and other illicit drugs are cheaper, purer, and easier to get than ever before. Nearly half a million people in the United States are behind bars on drug charges—more than all of western Europe (with a bigger population) incarcerates for all offenses. Moreover, Nadelman suggests that many of the problems the drug war claims to resolve are in fact caused by the drug war itself. For example, public health problems such as HIV and hepatitis C are all increased by laws that restrict access to clean needles. The drug war is not the promoter of family values that some would have us believe, he argues. Children of inmates are at risk of educational failure, joblessness, addiction, and delinquency. In a 2003 publication, Nadelman castigates the federal government's strict law enforcement approach to drug control. By and large, he says, the more punitive the approach, the greater the harms that result. The United States represents 5 percent of the world's population and 25 percent of the world's prison population. The stand against the use of marijuana for medical purposes shows the futility of the get-tough approach. Almost 80 percent of Americans believe marijuana should be

legally available as a medicine, when recommended by a doctor. Every state ballot initiative on the issue has won. Now even state legislatures are approving medical marijuana. The U.S. Institute of Medicine says marijuana has medicinal value. Yet the federal government continues to forbid marijuana use.

Liberals are not the only critics of current drug control policy. Judge James P. Gray, a political conservative, is also an outspoken critic of America's antidrug policies. In his book *Why Our Drug Laws Have Failed and What We Can Do about It* (2001), he decries the program of massive imprisonment and demonization of drug users that has flowed from making drugs illegal. Illegality is futile because it amounts to an attempt to repeal the law of supply and demand, which is an impossible task. Criminalizing drugs raises the price of the goods, which encourages growers and dealers to risk their lives to sell drugs for huge profits. Gray also argues that antidrug efforts have eroded civil liberties and due process, giving police too much power to seize assets and confiscate property or money from criminals to obstruct further criminal activity. Few of those whose assets have been seized are later charged with a crime. Some form of legalization would help reduce these problems. However, instead of condoning drug use he calls for a

users. In addition to violating rights, little evidence exists that testing can reduce drug abuse. For example, a recent study of student substance abuse found no statistical difference in rates of drug use between schools that implemented drug testing policies and those that did not. Drug testing was not a significant predictor of marijuana or other illicit drug use by students, including athletes.[50]

Due process advocates are also concerned about racial disparity in sentencing between black and white drug users. One particular concern is the disparity produced by federal laws that distinguish between powdered cocaine and cocaine base or crack. In 1988 Congress increased the penalties for the sale of crack cocaine so that a dealer with five grams of crack received the same punishment as a dealer who had 500 grams of powder cocaine, a disparity of 100-to-1. Minority group members are more likely to use crack and are therefore subject to significantly more stringent punishments.[51]

program of drug maintenance (allowing addicts a monitored drug intake) and controlled distribution (in which government-regulated drugs are sold in a controlled fashion). Gray goes as far to suggest that generically packaged drugs such as marijuana could be sold by pharmacists, with a steep tax that would fund rehabilitation programs and drug education.

Against Legalization

At a 2003 hearing on legalization of marijuana for medical purposes in Maryland, John P. Walters, director of National Drug Control Policy, stated:

> We owe people with debilitating medical conditions the best that science has to offer—not the results of interest group lobbying and political compromise. Research has not demonstrated that smoked marijuana is safe and effective medicine. Legalizing smoked marijuana under the guise of medicine is scientifically irresponsible and contradictory to our high standards for approval of medications. The legislation being considered in Maryland for so-called medical marijuana would also mean more availability of a dangerous drug in our neighborhoods. The citizens of Maryland deserve better.

Walters, along with other legalization opponents, believes that legalization may harm the well-being of the community by creating health and social damage. Individuals do not have the right to harm society even if it means curbing their freedom and personal choices—that is, the right to use drugs. If injured by their drug use, individuals would have to be cared for by the community at a substantial cost to nondrug users. Legalization would result in an increase in the nation's rate of drug usage, creating an even larger group of nonproductive, drug-dependent people, who must be cared for by the rest of society. If drugs were legalized and freely available, users might significantly increase their daily intake. In countries such as Iran and Thailand, where drugs are cheap and readily available, narcotic-use rates are high.

The problems of alcoholism should serve as a warning of what can happen when controlled substances are made readily available. If legalized, the number of drug-dependent babies could begin to match or exceed the number who are delivered with fetal alcohol syndrome. Drunk-driving fatalities, which today number about 25,000 per year, could be matched by deaths caused by driving under the influence of pot or crack. And though distribution would be regulated, adolescents likely would have the same opportunity to obtain potent drugs as they now have with beer and other forms of alcohol.

Critical Thinking

In the final analysis, and after considering all the issues in this ongoing debate, should drugs be legalized? What is the logic of banning marijuana while dangerous substances such as scotch and bourbon are readily available in stores?

InfoTrac College Edition Research

To conduct further research on this topic, use "drug legislation" as a subject guide on InfoTrac College Edition.

Source: "White House Drug Czar, Chair of Congressional Black Caucus Rep. Elijah Cummings, and Maryland Community Leaders Discuss Harms of 'Medical Marijuana' and Warn of Dangers of Marijuana Legalization," press release, March 24, 2003, http://www.whitehousedrugpolicy.gov/news/press03/032403.html; Ethan Nadelman, "The U.S. Is Addicted to War on Drugs," Globe and Mail, May 20, 2003, p. 1; James P. Gray, Why Our Drug Laws Have Failed and What We Can Do about It: A Judicial Indictment of the War on Drugs by Judge (Philadelphia: Temple University Press, 2001); Erich Goode, Between Politics and Reason: The Drug Legalization Debate (New York: St. Martin's Press, 1997); David Courtwright, "Should We Legalize Drugs? History Answers No," American Heritage, February/March 1993, pp. 43–56; Ethan Nadelman, "America's Drug Problem," Bulletin of the American Academy of Arts and Sciences 65 (1991): 24–40; Ethan Nadelman, "Should We Legalize Drugs? History Answers Yes," American Heritage, February/March 1993, pp. 41–56.

Perspectives in Perspective

The variety of tactics being used in the war on drugs aptly illustrates the impact of the various perspectives on justice on the operations of the criminal justice system (Figure 1.7). Advocates of each view have attempted to promote their vision of what justice is all about and how it should be applied. During the past decade, the crime control and justice models have dominated. Laws have been toughened and the rights of the accused curtailed, the prison population has grown, and the death penalty has been employed against convicted murderers. Because the crime rate has been dropping, these policies seem to be effective. They may be questioned if crime rates once again begin to rise. At the same time, efforts to rehabilitate offenders, to provide them with elements of due process, and to give them the least intrusive treatment have not been abandoned. Police, courts, and correctional agencies supply a wide range of treatment and rehabilitation programs to offenders in all stages

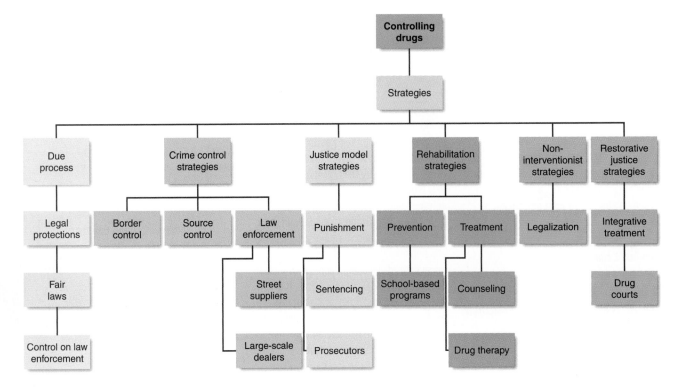

Figure 1.7
Strategies for Controlling Drugs

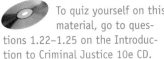

To quiz yourself on this material, go to questions 1.22–1.25 on the Introduction to Criminal Justice 10e CD.

of the criminal justice system. Whenever possible, those accused of a crime are treated informally in nonrestrictive, community-based programs, and the effects of stigma are guarded against. Although the legal rights of offenders are being closely scrutinized by the courts, the basic constitutional rights of the accused remain inviolate. Guardians of the process have made sure that defendants are allowed the maximum protection possible under the law. For example, criminal defendants have been awarded the right to competent legal counsel at trial; merely having a lawyer to defend them is not considered sufficient legal protection. In sum, understanding the justice system today requires analyzing a variety of occupational roles, institutional processes, legal rules, and administrative doctrines. Each predominant view of criminal justice provides a vantage point for understanding and interpreting these complex issues. No single view is the right or correct one. Each individual must choose the perspective that best fits his own ideas and judgment—or they can all be discarded and the individual's own view substituted.

Perspectives on Justice

Throughout the remainder of the book we will link the various perspectives on justice to the practices of the contemporary justice system. This will allow you to assess the impact of the various schools of thought on justice policy and their impact in guiding the system's efforts to reduce the frequency of criminal behaviors.

Summary

- America has experienced crime throughout its history.
- In the old west, justice was administered by legendary lawmen such as Wyatt Earp. There was little in the way of a formal criminal justice system.

- The term *criminal justice* became prominent around 1967, when the President's Commission on Law Enforcement and the Administration of Justice began a study of the nation's crime problem. Since then, a field of study has emerged that uses knowledge from various disciplines in an attempt to understand what causes people to commit crimes and how to deal with the crime problem. Criminal justice, then, consists of the study of crime and of the agencies concerned with its prevention and control.

- The contemporary criminal justice system functions as a cooperative effort among the primary agencies—police, courts, and corrections.
- The criminal justice process consists of the steps the offender takes from the initial investigation through trial, sentencing, and appeal.
- In many instances, the criminal justice system works informally to expedite the disposal of cases. Criminal acts that are very serious or notorious may receive the full complement of criminal justice processes, from arrest to trial. However, less serious cases are often settled when a bargain is reached between the prosecution and the defense. The process has been described by Samuel Walker as the "wedding cake" model of justice.
- There are a number of different perspectives on criminal justice today.
- The crime control perspective is oriented toward deterring criminal behavior and incapacitating serious criminal offenders.
- The rehabilitation model views the justice system as a treatment agency focused on helping offenders. Counseling programs are stressed over punishment and deterrence strategies.
- The due process perspective sees the justice system as a legal process. The concern here is that every defendant receive the full share of legal rights granted under law.
- The justice model is concerned with making the system equitable. The arrest, sentencing, and correctional process should be structured so that every person is treated equally.
- The nonintervention model is concerned about stigma and helping defendants avoid the net of justice. Advocates call for the least intrusive methods possible.
- The restorative justice model focuses on finding peaceful and humanitarian solutions to crime.
- The various perspectives on justice are visible in the way the nation has sought to control substance abuse. Some programs rely on a strict crime control policy featuring the detection and arrest of drug traffickers, whereas others seek the rehabilitation of known offenders. The justice model has influenced development of sentencing policies that emphasize mandatory punishments. Another approach is to legalize drugs, thereby reducing abusers' incentive to commit crimes, a policy that reflects the nonintervention perspective.

Key Terms

criminal justice system 4
Law Enforcement Assistance
    Administration (LEAA) 8
social control 8
legislature 9
arrest 13
arrest warrant 13
in presence requirement 14
probable cause hearing 14

nolle prosequi 14
courtroom work group 20
crime control perspective 23
profile 24
rehabilitation perspective 25
due process perspective 25
nonintervention perspective 28
decriminalization 28
victimless crime 28

deinstitutionalization 28
pretrial diversion 28
widening the net 28
restorative justice 29
source control 30
DARE 32
methadone 32
legalization 33

Doing Research on the Web

**For an up-to-date list of Web links, go to
http://cj.wadsworth.com/siegel_intro10e.**

The issue of drug legalization has been the subject of endless debate. To get more information using Info-Trac College Edition, do a power search using the following terms: "drug legalization" and "decriminalization."

For a good overview of all sides of the issue, read Erich Goode, "Strange Bedfellows: Ideology, Politics, and Drug Legalization," *Society* 35, no. 1 (1998): 18.

For arguments against drug legalization, go to Charles B. Rangel, "Why Drug Legalization Should Be Opposed," *Criminal Justice Ethics* 17, no. 2 (1998): 2.

To read about some of the possible benefits, go to Jeffrey A. Miron, "The Economics of Drug Prohibition and Drug Legalization," *Social Research* 68, no. 3 (2001): 835.

To read more about the drug legalization issue, go to the home of the Drug Policy Alliance: http://www.dpf.org/homepage.cfm.

Pro/Con discussions and Viewpoint Essays on some of the topics in this chapter may be found at the Opposing Viewpoints Resource Center: http://www.gale.com/OpposingViewpoints.

Discussion Questions

1. Which criminal behavior patterns pose the greatest threat to the public? Should the justice system devote greater resources to combating these crimes? If so, which crime patterns should be deemphasized?

2. Describe the differences between the formal and informal justice systems. Is it fair to treat some offenders informally?

3. What are the layers of the criminal justice "wedding cake"? Give an example of a crime for each layer.

4. What are the basic elements of each model or perspective on justice? Which best represents your own point of view?

5. How would each perspective on criminal justice consider the use of the death penalty as a sanction for first-degree murder?

Notes

1 Christina S. N. Lewis, "Reviewing 3,000 Cold Cases, One by One,' Court TV online, May 9, 2003, http://www.courttv.com/news/feature/coldcasereview_ctv.html, accessed on December 8, 2003.

2 James Dao, "Death Sentence for Muhammad; Sniper Jury Cites Lack of Sorrow," *New York Times,* November 25, 2003, p. A1.

3 This section leans heavily on Ted Robert Gurr, "Historical Trends in Violent Crime: A Critical Review of the Evidence," in *Crime and Justice: An Annual Review of Research,* vol. 3, ed. Michael Tonry and Norval Morris (Chicago: University of Chicago Press, 1981); Richard Maxwell Brown, "Historical Patterns of American Violence," in *Violence in America: Historical and Comparative Perspectives,* ed. Hugh Davis Graham and Ted Robert Gurr (Beverly Hills, Calif.: Sage, 1979).

4 Cesare Beccaria, *On Crimes and Punishments* (1764; reprint, Indianapolis: Bobbs-Merrill, 1963).

5 Samuel Walker, *Popular Justice* (New York: Oxford University Press, 1980).

6 Ibid.

7 For an insightful analysis of this effort, see Samuel Walker, "Origins of the Contemporary Criminal Justice Paradigm: The American Bar Foundation Survey, 1953–1969," *Justice Quarterly* 9 (1992): 47–76.

8 President's Commission on Law Enforcement and the Administration of Justice, *The Challenge of Crime in a Free Society* (Washington, D.C.: Government Printing Office, 1967).

9 See Public Law 90-351, Title I—Omnibus Crime Control Safe Streets Act of 1968, 90th Congress, June 19, 1968.

10 For a review, see Kevin Wright, "Twenty-two Years of Federal Investment in Criminal Justice Research: The National Institute of Justice, 1968–1989," *Journal of Criminal Justice* 22 (1994): 27–40.

11 Matthew J. Hickman and Brian A. Reaves, *Local Police Departments 2000* (Washington, D.C.: Bureau of Justice Statistics, 2003).

12 Federal Bureau of Investigation, *Crime in the United States, 2000* (Washington, D.C.: Government Printing Office, 2001), p. 208.

13 Brian Reaves, *Felony Sentences in Large Urban Counties, 1998* (Washington, D.C.: Bureau of Justice Statistics, 2001).

14 For an analysis of this issue, see William Wilbanks, *The Myth of a Racist Criminal Justice System* (Monterey, Calif.: Brooks/Cole, 1987); Stephen Klein, Joan Petersilia, and Susan Turner, "Race and Imprisonment Decisions in California," *Science* 247 (1990): 812–16; Alfred Blumstein, "On the Racial Disproportionality of the United States Prison Population," *Journal of Criminal Law and Criminology* 73 (1982): 1259–81; Darnell Hawkins, "Race, Crime Type, and Imprisonment," *Justice Quarterly* 3 (1986): 251–69.

15 *Riverside County v. McLaughlin,* 500 U.S. 44, 111 S.Ct. 1661, 114 L.Ed.2d 49 (1991).

16 Middlesex SS Superior Court Criminal No. 97-0433, Commonwealth Memorandum, and *Order v. Louise Woodward,* 1997.

17 Herbert L. Packer, *The Limits of the Criminal Sanction* (Stanford, Calif.: Stanford University Press, 1975), p. 21.

18 Jacob Perez, *Tracking Offenders, 1990* (Washington, D.C.: Bureau of Justice Statistics, 1994), p. 2.

19 James Eisenstein and Herbert Jacob, *Felony Justice* (Boston: Little, Brown, 1977); Peter Nardulli, *The Courtroom Elite* (Cambridge, Mass.: Ballinger, 1978); Paul Wice, *Chaos in the Courthouse* (New York: Praeger, 1985); Marcia Lipetz, *Routine Justice: Processing Cases in Women's Court* (New Brunswick, N.J.: Transaction Books, 1983).

20 Douglas Smith, "The Plea Bargaining Controversy," *Journal of Criminal Law and Criminology* 77 (1986): 949–67.

21 Samuel Walker, *Sense and Nonsense about Crime* (Belmont, Calif.: Wadsworth, 1985).

22 Malcolm Feeley, *The Process Is the Punishment* (New York: Russell Sage, 1979).

23 James Q. Wilson, *Thinking about Crime* (New York: Vintage Books, 1983).

24 Ibid., p. 128.

25 John DiIulio, *No Escape: The Future of American Corrections* (New York: Basic Books, 1991).

26 Dennis Rosenbaum and Gordon Hanson, "Assessing the Effects of School-Based Drug Education: A Six-Year Multilevel Analysis of Project DARE," *Journal of Research in Crime and Delinquency* 35 (1998): 381–412.

27 Karen Parker and Patricia McCall, "Structural Conditions and Racial Homicide Patterns: A Look at the Multiple Disadvantages in Urban Areas," *Criminology* 37 (1999): 447–48.

28 Francis Cullen, John Paul Wright, and Mitchell Chamlin, "Social Support and Social Reform: A Progressive Crime Control Agenda," *Crime and Delinquency* 45 (1999): 188–207.

29 Jane Sprott, "Are Members of the Public Tough on Crime? The Dimensions of Public 'Punitiveness,'" *Journal of Criminal Justice* 27 (1999): 467–74.

30 Herbert Packer, *The Limits of the Criminal Sanction* (Stanford, Calif.: Stanford University Press, 1968), p. 175.

31 "DNA Testing Has Exonerated 28 Prison Inmates, Study Finds," *Criminal Justice Newsletter,* June 17, 1996, p. 2.

32 Caitlin Lovinger, "Death Row's Living Alumni," *New York Times,* August 22, 1999, p. 1.

33 Eric Stewart, Ronald Simons, Rand Conger, and Laura Scaramella, "Beyond the Interactional Relationship between Delinquency and Parenting Practices: The Contribution of Legal Sanctions," *Journal of Research in Crime and Delinquency* 39 (2002): 36–60.

34 Cassia Spohn and David Holleran, "The Effect of Imprisonment on Recidivism Rates of Felony Offenders: A Focus on Drug Offenders," *Criminology* 40 (2002): 329-59.

35 *Doe v. Pryor M.D. Ala,* Civ. No. 99-T-730-N, J. Thompson, August 16, 1999.

36 This section is based on Paula M. Ditton and Doris James Wilson, *Truth in Sentencing in State Prisons* (Washington, D.C.: Bureau of Justice Statistics, 1999).

37 Herbert Bianchi, *Justice as Sanctuary* (Bloomington: Indiana University Press, 1994); Nils Christie, "Conflicts as Property," *British Journal of Criminology* 17 (1977): 1–15; L. Hulsman, "Critical Criminology and the Concept of Crime," *Contemporary Crises* 10 (1986): 63–80.

38 Larry Tifft, "Foreword," in Dennis Sullivan, *The Mask of Love* (Port Washington, N.Y.: Kennikat Press, 1980), p. 6.

39 Christopher Cooper, "Patrol Police Officer Conflict Resolution Processes," *Journal of Criminal Justice* 25 (1997): 87–101.

40 U.S. Department of State, *1998 International Narcotics Control Strategy Report* (Washington, D.C.: February 1999).

41 Juan Forero with Tim Weiner, "Latin American Poppy Fields Undermine U.S.

Drug Battle," *New York Times,* June 8, 2003, p. 1.

42 Anti-Drug Abuse Act of 1988, Public Law 100-690, 21 U.S. Ct. 1501; Subtitle A—Death Penalty, Sec. 001, Amending the Controlled Substances Abuse Act, 21 USC 848.

43 Spohn and Holleran, "The Effect of Imprisonment on Recidivism Rates of Felony Offenders," 329-59.

44 Dennis Rosenbaum, Robert Flewelling, Susan Bailey, Chris Ringwalt, and Deanna Wilkinson, "Cops in the Classroom: A Longitudinal Evaluation," *Journal of Research in Crime and Delinquency* 31 (1994): 3–31.

45 See, generally, Peter Greenwood and Franklin Zimring, *One More Chance* (Santa Monica, Calif.: RAND, 1985).

46 Eli Ginzberg, Howard Berliner, and Miriam Ostrow, *Young People at Risk: Is Prevention Possible?* (Boulder, Colo.: Westview Press, 1988), 99.

47 Drug Court Clearinghouse and Technical Assistance Project, *Looking at a Decade of Drug Courts* (Washington, D.C.: Government Printing Office, 1999).

48 See, generally, Ralph Weisheit, *Drugs, Crime, and the Criminal Justice System* (Cincinnati, Ohio: Anderson, 1990).

49 This information is from the American Civil Liberties Union Web site, http://www.aclu.org/DrugPolicy/DrugPolicyMain.cfm, accessed on July 1, 2003.

50 Ryoko Yamaguchi, Lloyd D. Johnston, and Patrick M. O'Malley, "Relationship between Student Illicit Drug Use and School Drug-Testing Policies," *Journal of School Health* 73, no. 4 (April 2003): 163.

51 The report, *ACLU Urges End to Discriminatory Crack vs. Powder Cocaine Sentencing Disparity: Restore Rationality to Sentencing Policy,* May 22, 2002, can be accessed at the American Civil Liberties Union Web site, http://www.aclu.org/DrugPolicy/DrugPolicy.cfm?ID=10367&c=229.

Chapter Outline

Chapter Objectives

After reading this chapter, you should be able to:

1. Name the three major sources of crime data.
2. Know the similarities and differences between the Uniform Crime Reports, National Crime Victimization Survey, and self-report data.
3. Recognize the problems associated with each data form.
4. Describe the factors that explain the rise and fall of crime rates in the United States.
5. Discuss crime trends around the world.
6. Recognize that there are stable patterns in the crime rate.
7. Describe the ecological patterns in crime.
8. Discuss the social, gender, age, and racial differences in the crime rate.
9. Argue the pro and con positions on gun control.
10. Identify the factors that produce chronic offenders.
11. Explain how chronic offending has influenced crime policy.

Viewpoints

 Analyzing Criminal Justice Issues: Explaining Crime Trends 50

 International Justice: Why Is Crime Booming around the World? 56

 Analyzing Criminal Justice Issues: Should Guns Be Controlled? 58

InfoTrac College Edition Links

Key Term: "social class" 61

Key Terms: "gender" and "crime" 63

Key Term: "liberal feminism" 65

Web Links

Uniform Crime Reports
http://www.fbi.gov/ 42

National Incident-Based Reporting System
http://www.ojp.usdoj.gov/bjs/nibrs.htm 45

National Crime Victimization Survey
http://www.ojp.usdoj.gov/bjs/pub/pdf/cv00.pdf 45

Small Arms Survey
http://www.smallarmssurvey.org/ 60

Chapter 2 | The Nature and Extent of Crime

On May 31, 2003, Eric Rudolph was arrested behind a grocery store in rural western North Carolina after five years on the run. He was accused of detonating a bomb outside a Birmingham, Alabama, abortion clinic on January 29, 1998, killing a police officer and critically injuring a nurse. He was also charged with setting off a bomb that killed one person and injured 150 others in a park in downtown Atlanta, Georgia, during the 1996 Olympics. There is also evidence that Rudolph was involved in the 1997 bombings of a gay nightclub and a building that housed an abortion clinic.

Rudolph came under suspicion when someone saw a man believed to be Rudolph leaving the scene of the Birmingham bombing. A truck registered to Rudolph was spotted moments later. In the days following the bombing, law enforcement agents searched a storage locker rented by Rudolph and found nails like those in the devises used to bomb the clinic and an Atlanta building that housed an abortion clinic. Similarities also linked them to the bomb set off during the Olympics.

Rudolph's crime spree is believed to have been motivated by his extreme political beliefs. He was reputedly a member of a white supremacist group called the Army of God. His relatives told authorities that Rudolph was an ardent anti-Semite who claimed that the Holocaust never happened and that the Jews control the media and the government. Ironically, soon after he was arrested, the court appointed attorney Richard S. Jaffe, a practicing Jew, to lead Rudolph's defense team.[1]

The Rudolph case made national headlines in 2003. It illustrates the undercurrent of violence that is still all too common on the American landscape. Yet, while the Rudolph case is a shocking reminder of the damage that a single person can inflict on the public, the overall crime rate seems to be in decline. And while the United States has the reputation of being an extremely violent nation, violence rates here are dropping while increasing abroad. How can this phenomenon be explained? What causes the rise and fall in crime rates and trends?

View the CNN video clip of this story on your Introduction to Criminal Justice 10e CD.

Measuring Crime

Today three significant methods are used to measure the nature and extent of crime: official data, victim data, and self-report data.

Official Data: Uniform Crime Reports

Official data on crime refers to those crimes known to and recorded by the nation's police departments. The **Uniform Crime Reports (UCRs),** issued by the Federal Bureau of Investigation (FBI), are the best known and most widely cited source of official criminal statistics.[2] The FBI receives and compiles records from more than 17,000 police departments serving a majority of the U.S. population. Its major unit of analysis involves **index crimes,** or **Part I crimes:** murder and non-negligent manslaughter, forcible rape, robbery, aggravated assault, burglary, larceny, arson, and motor vehicle theft. Exhibit 2.1 defines these crimes.

The FBI tallies and annually publishes the number of reported offenses by city, county, standard metropolitan statistical area, and geographical divisions of the United States. In addition to these statistics, the UCR shows the number and characteristics (age, race, and gender) of individuals who have been arrested for these and all other crimes, except traffic violations (**Part II crimes**).

Collecting Data for the Uniform Crime Reports The methods used to compile the UCR are complex. Each month law enforcement agencies report the number of index crimes known to them. These data are collected from records of all crime

Uniform Crime Reports (UCRs)
The official crime data collected by the FBI from local police departments.

index crimes
The eight serious crimes—murder, rape, assault, robbery, burglary, arson, larceny, and motor vehicle theft—whose incidence is reported in the annual Uniform Crime Report (UCR).

 You can access the Uniform Crime Reports at the FBI Web site at http://www.fbi.gov/.

Exhibit 2.1 FBI Index Crimes

Criminal Homicide

Murder and non-negligent manslaughter. The willful (non-negligent) killing of one human being by another. Deaths caused by negligence, attempts to kill, assaults to kill, suicides, accidental deaths, and justifiable homicides are excluded. Justifiable homicides are limited to the killing of a felon by a law enforcement officer in the line of duty and the killing of a felon by a private citizen.

Manslaughter by negligence. The killing of another person through gross negligence. Traffic fatalities are excluded. While manslaughter by negligence is a Part I crime, it is not included in the crime index.

Forcible Rape

The carnal knowledge of a female forcibly and against her will. Included are rapes by force and attempts or assaults to rape. Statutory offenses (no force used—victim under age of consent) are excluded.

Robbery

The taking or attempting to take anything of value from the care, custody, or control of a person or persons by force or threat of force or violence or by putting the victim in fear.

Aggravated Assault

An unlawful attack by one person on another for the purpose of inflicting severe or aggravated bodily injury. This type of assault is usually accompanied by the use of a weapon or by means likely to produce death or great bodily harm. Simple assaults are excluded.

Burglary

Breaking or entering. The unlawful entry of a structure to commit a felony or a theft. Attempted forcible entry is included.

Larceny/Theft

The unlawful taking, carrying, leading, or riding away of property from the possession or constructive possession of another. Examples are thefts of bicycles or automobile accessories, shoplifting, pocket picking, or the stealing of any property or article that is not taken by force and violence or by fraud. Attempted larcenies are included. Embezzlement, con games, forgery, worthless checks, and so on are excluded.

Motor Vehicle Theft

The theft or attempted theft of a motor vehicle. A motor vehicle is self-propelled and runs on the surface and not on rails. Specifically excluded from this category are motorboats, construction equipment, airplanes, and farming equipment.

Arson

Any willful or malicious burning or attempt to burn, with or without intent to defraud, a dwelling, house, public building, motor vehicle or aircraft, personal property of another, and so on.

Source: Federal Bureau of Investigation, *Crime in the United States, 2002* (Washington, D.C.: Government Printing Office, 2003).

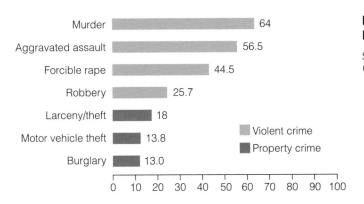

Figure 2.1
Percent of Crimes Cleared by Arrest, 2002

Source: Federal Bureau of Investigation, *Crime in the United States, 2002.*
(Washington, D.C.: Government Printing Office, p. 22).

complaints that victims, officers who discovered the infractions, or other sources reported to these agencies.

Whenever criminal complaints are found through investigation to be unfounded or false, they are eliminated from the count. However, the number of offenses known is reported to the FBI whether or not anyone is arrested for the crime, the stolen property is recovered, or prosecution ensues.

In addition, each month law enforcement agencies report how many crimes were **cleared.** Crimes are cleared in two ways: (1) when at least one person is arrested, charged, and turned over to the court for prosecution; or (2) by exceptional means, when some element beyond police control precludes the physical arrest of an offender (for example, he leaves the country). Data on the number of clearances involving the arrest of only juvenile offenders, data on the value of property stolen and recovered in connection with Part I offenses, and detailed information pertaining to criminal homicide are also reported. Traditionally, slightly more than 20 percent of all reported index crimes are cleared by arrest each year (see Figure 2.1).

Violent crimes are more likely to be solved than property crimes because police devote more resources to these more serious acts. For these types of crime, witnesses (including the victim) are frequently available to identify offenders, and in many instances the victim and offender were previously acquainted.

The UCR uses three methods to express crime data. First, the number of crimes reported to the police and arrests made are expressed as raw figures (for example, 15,980 murders occurred in 2002). Second, crime rates per 100,000 people are computed. That is, when the UCR indicates that the murder rate was 5.6 in 2001, it means that almost 6 people in every 100,000 were murdered between January 1 and December 31 of 2002. This is the equation used:

$$\frac{\text{Number of reported crimes}}{\text{Total U.S. population}} \times 100,000 = \text{Rate per 100,000}$$

Third, the FBI computes changes in the number and rate of crime over time. For example, murder rates climbed 1 percent between 2001 and 2002.

How Accurate Are the Uniform Crime Reports? Despite crime experts' continued reliance on the UCR, its accuracy has been suspect. The three main areas of concern are reporting practices, law enforcement practices, and methodological problems.

Reporting practices. Some crime experts claim that victims of many serious crimes do not report these incidents to police; therefore, these crimes do not become part of the UCR. The reasons for not reporting vary. Some victims do not trust the police or do not have confidence in their ability to solve crimes. Others do not have property insurance and therefore believe it is useless to report theft. In other cases, victims fear reprisals from an offender's friends or family or, in the case of family violence, from their spouse, boyfriend, or girlfriend.[3]

Part I crimes
Those crimes in the FBI's Crime Index, which is composed of offenses used to gauge fluctuations in the overall volume and rate of crime. The offenses included are the violent crimes of murder and non-negligent manslaughter, forcible rape, robbery, and aggravated assault and the property crimes of burglary, larceny-theft, motor vehicle theft, and arson.

Part II crimes
All other crimes reported to the FBI not included in the Crime Index. These are less serious crimes and misdemeanors, excluding traffic violations.

cleared
An offense is cleared by arrest or solved when at least one person is arrested or charged with the commission of the offense and is turned over to the court for prosecution. If the following questions can all be answered "yes," the offense can then be cleared "exceptionally": (1) Has the investigation definitely established the identity of the offender? (2) Is there enough information to support an arrest, charge, and turning over to the court for prosecution? (3) Is the exact location of the offender known so that the subject could be taken into custody now? (4) Is there some reason outside law enforcement control that precludes arresting, charging, and prosecuting the offender?

Exhibit 2.2 Problems Collecting Uniform Crime Reports Data

1. No federal crimes are reported.

2. Reports are voluntary and vary in accuracy and completeness.

3. Not all police departments submit reports.

4. The FBI uses estimates in its total crime projections.

5. If an offender commits multiple crimes, only the most serious is recorded. Thus, if a narcotics addict rapes, robs, and murders a victim, only the murder is recorded. Consequently, many lesser crimes go unreported.

6. Each act is listed as a single offense for some crimes but not for others. If a man robbed six people in a bar, the offense is listed as one robbery; but if he assaulted or murdered them, it would be listed as six assaults or six murders.

7. Incomplete acts are lumped together with completed ones.

8. Important differences exist between the FBI's definition of certain crimes and those used in a number of states.

According to surveys of crime victims, less than 40 percent of all criminal incidents are reported to the police. Some of these victims justify nonreporting by stating that the incident was "a private matter," that "nothing could be done," or that the victimization was "not important enough."[4] These findings indicate that the UCR data may significantly underrepresent the total number of annual criminal events.

Law enforcement practices. The way police departments record and report criminal and delinquent activity also affects the validity of UCR statistics. How law enforcement agencies interpret the definitions of index crimes may also affect reporting practices. Some departments define crimes loosely—for example, reporting a trespass as a burglary or an assault on a woman as an attempted rape—whereas others pay strict attention to FBI guidelines.[5] For example, arson may be seriously underreported because many fire departments do not report to the FBI, and those that do define as "accidental" or "spontaneous" many fires that may have been set by arsonists.[6]

Ironically, boosting police efficiency and professionalism may help increase crime rates. As people develop confidence in the police, they may be more motivated to report crime. Higher crime rates may occur as departments adopt more sophisticated computer technology and hire better-educated, better-trained employees. Crime rates also may be altered based on the way law enforcement agencies process UCR data. As the number of employees assigned to dispatching, record keeping, and criminal incident reporting increases, so, too, will national crime rates. What appears to be a rising crime rate may be simply an artifact of improved police record-keeping ability.[7]

Methodological issues also contribute to questions pertaining to the UCR's validity. The most frequent issues are listed in Exhibit 2.2. The complex scoring procedure means that many serious crimes are not counted. For example, during an armed bank robbery, the offender strikes a teller with the butt of a handgun. The robber runs from the bank and steals an automobile at the curb. Although the offender has technically committed robbery, aggravated assault, and motor vehicle theft, which are three Part I offenses, because robbery is the most serious, it would be the only one recorded in the UCR.[8]

The future of the Uniform Crime Reports. Clearly there must be a more reliable source for crime statistics than the UCR as it stands today. For the past 15 years, the FBI has been implementing some important changes in the Uniform Crime Reports. An attempt is being made to provide more detailed information on individual criminal incidents by using a uniform, comprehensive program called the **National Incident-Based Reporting System (NIBRS).** Instead of submitting statements of the kinds of crime that individual citizens report to the police and summary statements of resulting arrests, the new program requires local police agencies to provide at least a brief account of each incident and arrest within 22 crime patterns, including the incident, victim, and offender information. These expanded crime categories include numerous additional crimes, such as blackmail, embezzlement, drug offenses, and bribery, which would allow a national database on the nature of crime, victims, and criminals to be developed.[9] Other information to be collected includes statistics gathered by federal law enforcement agencies and data on hate or bias crimes. When this new UCR program is fully implemented across the nation, it should bring about greater uniformity in cross-jurisdictional reporting and improve the accuracy of official crime data.

Victim Surveys: National Crime Victimization Survey

The second source of crime data is surveys that ask crime victims about their encounters with criminals. Because many victims do not report their experiences to the police, victim surveys are considered a method of getting at the unknown figures of crime. The most important and widely used victim survey—the **National Crime Victimization Survey (NCVS)**—is sponsored by the Bureau of Justice Statistics of the U.S. Department of Justice. In these national surveys, housing units are selected using a complex, multistage sampling technique. Each year data are obtained from a large nationally representative sample; in 2002, 42,340 households and 76,050 people age 12 or older were interviewed.[10] They are asked to report on the frequency, characteristics, and consequences of criminal victimization for such crimes as rape, sexual assault, robbery, assault, theft, household burglary, and motor vehicle theft. The total sample is interviewed twice a year about victimizations suffered in the preceding six months. Households remain in the sample for about three years, and new homes rotate into the sample continually. The NCVS reports that the interview completion rate in the national sample is usually more than 90 percent in any given period. NCVS data are considered to be a relatively unbiased, valid estimate of all victimizations for the target crimes included in the survey because of the care with which the samples are drawn and the high completion rate.

The NCVS finds that many crimes go unreported to police. For example, the UCR shows that about 418,000 robberies or attempted robberies occurred in 2002, but the NCVS estimates that about 512,000 actually occurred. The reason for such discrepancies is that less than half of all violent crimes, one-third of personal theft crimes (such as pocket picking), and only half of household thefts are reported to police. The reasons most often given by victims for not reporting crime include believing that "the police can do nothing about it," that it was a "private matter," or that they did not want to "get involved." Victims seem to report to the police only crimes that involve considerable loss or injury.

Like the UCR, the NCVS may also suffer from some problems.[11] These are listed in Exhibit 2.3.

Self-Report Surveys

The problems associated with official statistics have led many crime experts to seek alternative sources of information in assessing the true extent of crime patterns. The data provided by the NCVS are important, but they cannot reveal much about the personality, attitudes, and behavior of individual offenders. Neither the NCVS nor UCR is of much value in charting the extent of one of the nation's most important social problems—substance abuse in the teenage population. To address these issues, crime experts have developed the **self-report survey.**

National Incident-Based Reporting System (NIBRS)
A new form of crime data collection created by the FBI requiring local police agencies to provide at least a brief account of each incident and arrest within 22 crime patterns, including the incident, victim, and offender information.

 To read more about the National Incident-Based Reporting System, go to http://www.ojp.usdoj.gov/bjs/nibrs.htm.

National Crime Victimization Survey (NCVS)
The NCVS is the nation's primary source of information on criminal victimization. Each year, data are obtained from a national sample that measure the frequency, characteristics, and consequences of criminal victimization by such crimes as rape, sexual assault, robbery, assault, theft, household burglary, and motor vehicle theft.

 To access the most recent National Crime Victimization Survey data, go to http://www.ojp.usdoj.gov/bjs/pub/pdf/cv00.pdf.

self-report survey
A research approach that questions large groups of subjects, typically high school students, about their own participation in delinquent or criminal acts.

Exhibit 2.3 Problems with the National Crime Victimization Survey

- Overreporting because of victims' misinterpretation of events. For example, a lost wallet may be reported as stolen, or an open door may be viewed as a burglary attempt.
- Underreporting stemming from the embarrassment of reporting crime to interviewers, fear of getting in trouble, or simply forgetting an incident.
- Inability to record the personal criminal activity of those interviewed, such as drug use or gambling; murder is also not included for obvious reasons.
- Sampling errors, which produce a group of respondents who do not represent the nation as a whole.
- Inadequate question format that invalidates responses. Some groups, such as adolescents, may be particularly susceptible to error because of the question format.

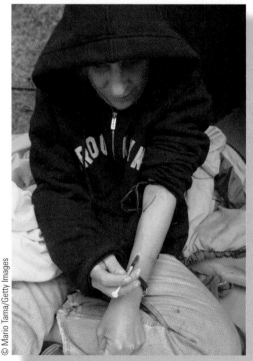

© Mario Tama/Getty Images

A homeless woman, Joan Kimball, 37, injects herself with heroin while sitting beneath the Manhattan Bridge. Self-report surveys are used to gauge the nature and extent of drug use because most episodes go undetected by police. While drug use is still prevalent, surveys indicate that there is less usage today than 30 years ago.

Most often, self-report surveys are administered to groups of subjects through a mass distribution of questionnaires. Although some surveys are able to identify the subjects, most are given anonymously so that respondents feel freer to tell the truth about their behaviors. The basic assumption of self-report studies is that because anonymity and confidentiality are assured, people will be encouraged to accurately describe their illegal activities. Exhibit 2.4 illustrates some typical self-report items.

Because most self-report instruments contain items measuring subjects' attitudes, values, personal characteristics, and behaviors, the data obtained from them can be used for various purposes. These include testing theories, measuring attitudes toward crime, and computing the association between crime and important social variables, such as family relations, educational attainment, and income. They also enable crime experts to evaluate the distribution of criminal behavior across racial, class, and gender lines. It is then possible to determine whether official arrest data truly represent the offender population or if they reflect bias, discrimination, and selective enforcement. For example, if black and white respondents report equal amounts of crime, but official data indicate that minorities are arrested more often than whites, the results would indicate the presence of racial bias in the arrest rate. In sum, self-reports provide an appreciable amount of information about offenders that official statistics and victimization surveys fail to provide.

Are Self-Reports Accurate? Although self-report data have profoundly affected criminological inquiry, some important methodological issues have been raised about their accuracy. Critics of self-report studies frequently suggest that it is unreasonable to expect people to candidly admit illegal acts. They have nothing to gain, and the ones taking the greatest risk are the ones with official records who may be engaging in the most criminality. In addition, some people may exaggerate their criminal acts, forget some of them, or be confused about what is being asked. Some surveys contain an overabundance of trivial offenses, such as shoplifting small amounts of items or using false identification (ID), which are often lumped together with serious crimes to form a total crime index. Consequently, comparisons between groups can be highly misleading.

Various techniques have been used to verify self-report data.[12] The known-group method compares youths who are known to be offenders with those who have not to see whether the former report more delinquency. Research shows

Exhibit 2.4 Self-Report Survey Questions

Please indicate how often in the past 12 months you did each act. (Check the best answer.)	Never did act	One time	2–5 times	6–9 times	10+ times
Stole something worth less than $50	___	___	___	___	___
Stole something worth more than $50	___	___	___	___	___
Used cocaine	___	___	___	___	___
Was in a fistfight	___	___	___	___	___
Carried a weapon such as a gun or knife	___	___	___	___	___
Fought someone using a weapon	___	___	___	___	___
Stole a car	___	___	___	___	___
Used force to steal	___	___	___	___	___
(For boys) Forced a girl to have sexual relations against her will	___	___	___	___	___

that when kids are asked if they have ever been arrested or sent to court their responses accurately reflect their true-life experiences.[13]

Another approach is to use peer informants who can verify the honesty of a subject's answers. Subjects can be tested twice to see if their answers remain stable. Sometimes questions are designed to reveal respondents who are lying on the survey; for example, an item might say, "I have never done anything wrong in my life." Polygraphs, commonly known as lie detectors, have also been used to verify the responses given on self-report surveys. The results often validate the accuracy of self-report survey data.[14] Research studies also indicate a substantial association between official processing and self-reported crime.[15]

Questioning Self-Report Accuracy Although these findings are encouraging, nagging questions still remain about the validity of self-reports. Even if 90 percent of a school population voluntarily participates in a self-report study, researchers can never be sure whether the few who refuse to participate or are absent that day comprise a significant portion of the school's population of persistent high-rate offenders. Research indicates that offenders with the most extensive prior criminality are also the most likely to be "poor historians of their own crime commission rates."[16] It is also unlikely that the most serious chronic offenders in the teenage population are the ones most willing to cooperate with university-based crime experts administering self-report tests.[17] Institutionalized youths, who are not generally represented in the self-report surveys, are not only more delinquent than the general youth population but also are considerably more misbehaving than the most delinquent youths identified in the typical self-report survey.[18] Consequently, self-reports may measure only nonserious, occasional delinquents while ignoring hard-core chronic offenders who may be institutionalized and unavailable for self-reports.

Compatibility of Crime Statistics Sources

Are the various sources of crime statistics compatible? Each has strengths and weaknesses. The FBI survey is carefully tallied and contains data on the number of murders and people arrested, information that the other data sources lack. However, this survey omits the many crimes that victims choose not to report to police, and it is subject to the reporting caprices of individual police departments.

Concept Summary 2.1 Comparing the Three Measures of Crime Data

	Uniform Crime Reports	National Crime Victimization Survey	Self-Report Survey
Source	Police records	Victim surveys	Student survey
Frequency	Annual	Annual	Periodic
Number reporting	17,000 police departments	40,000 households	students
Strengths	Consistent measure Records homicides Includes arrest data	Consistent measure Records unreported crimes Includes victim and offender information	Includes adolescents Includes drug use Includes attitudes and beliefs
Weaknesses	Only measures crimes reported to police Police department recording errors	Relies on victims' memories Does not include substance abuse or homicide	Relies on memory of adolescent drug abusers Omits kids who are out of school

The NCVS contains unreported crime and important information on the personal characteristics of victims, but the data consist of estimates made from relatively limited samples of the total U.S. population. Because of this, even narrow fluctuations in the rates of some crimes can have a major impact on findings. It also relies on personal recollections that may be inaccurate. The NCVS does not include data on important crime patterns, including murder and drug abuse.

Self-report surveys can provide information on the personal characteristics of offenders, such as their attitudes, values, beliefs, and psychological profiles, which is unavailable from any other source. Yet at their core, self-reports rely on the honesty of criminal offenders and drug abusers, a population not generally known for accuracy and integrity.

Despite these differences, a number of prominent crime experts have concluded that the data sources are more compatible than was first believed. Although their tallies of crimes are certainly not in sync, the crime patterns and trends they record are often similar.[19] For example, all three sources generally agree about the personal characteristics of serious criminals (such as age and gender) and where and when crime occurs (such as urban areas, nighttime, and summer months).

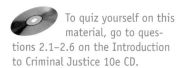

To quiz yourself on this material, go to questions 2.1–2.6 on the Introduction to Criminal Justice 10e CD.

Official Crime Trends

Crime is not a new phenomenon.[20] Studies have indicated that a gradual increase in the crime rate, especially in violent crime, occurred from 1830 to 1860. Following the Civil War, this rate increased significantly for about 15 years. Then, from 1880 up to the time of the First World War, with the possible exception of the years immediately preceding and following the war, the number of reported crimes decreased. After a period of readjustment, the crime rate steadily declined until the onset of the Great Depression (about 1930), when another crime wave was recorded. Crime rates increased gradually following the 1930s until the 1960s, when the growth rate became much greater. The homicide rate, which had declined from the 1930s to the 1960s, also began a sharp increase that continued through the 1970s and most of the 1980s, having reached a total of about 14.6 million crimes. Since then the number and rate of crimes have been in decline. In 2002, about 11.8 million crimes were reported to the police, which is about 25 percent less than it was a decade ago, as measured by the UCR. The number of reported crimes has declined more than 3 million from the 1991 peak. Even the teen murder rate, which had remained stubbornly high, has undergone decline during the past few years.[21] The factors that help explain the upward and downward movements in crime rates are discussed in the Analyzing Criminal Justice Issues feature on page 50.

Trends in Violent Crime

According to the FBI, overall violent crime decreased 1.4 percent between 2001 and 2002. Among individual violent crimes, murder and forcible rape both showed increases, 0.8 percent and 4.0 percent, respectively. The number of robberies in 2002 decreased 1.2 percent from the 2001 total, and the number of aggravated assaults declined 2.0 percent.[22] As Figure 2.2 shows, during the past decade the number of violent crime victimizations reported to the police declined by more than 25 percent.

Murder statistics are generally regarded as the most accurate aspect of the UCR. While the murder rate increased slightly between 2001 and 2002, there has been a decade-long decrease in the number and rate of murders. Figure 2.3 illustrates homicide rate trends since 1900. The rate peaked around 1930, then fell, rose dramatically around 1960, and peaked once again in 1991, when the number of murders topped 24,000 for the first time in the nation's history. An estimated 16,000 murders were committed in 2002, 12 percent less than in 1997 and 33 percent less than in 1992. Some major cities, such as New York, report significant declines of more than 50 percent in their murder rates through the 1990s. It remains to be seen whether the uptick in murders experienced in 2002 portends a long-term trend or is a one-year blip.

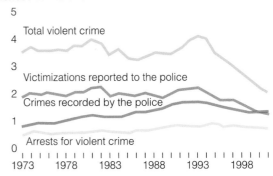

Offenses in millions

Figure 2.2
Four Measures of Serious Violent Crime

Note: The serious violent crimes included are rape, robbery, aggravated assault, and homicide.

Source: Bureau of Justice Statistics.

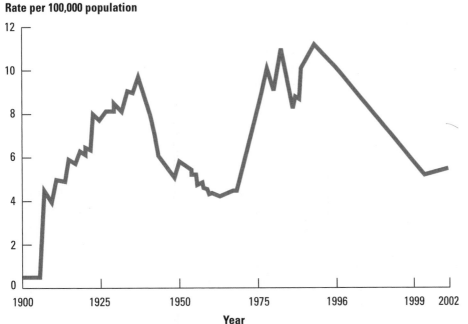

Rate per 100,000 population

Year

Figure 2.3
Homicide Rate Trends, 1900–2002

Source: Federal Bureau of Investigation, *Crime in the United States, 1995* (Washington, D.C.: Government Printing Office, 1996); Federal Bureau of Investigation, *Crime in the United States, 2002* (Washington, D.C.: Government Printing Office, 2003).

Explaining Crime Trends

analyzing criminal justice issues

Crime experts have identified a variety of social, economic, personal, and demographic factors that influence crime rate trends. Although crime experts are still uncertain about how these factors impact crime rate trends, change in their direction seems to be associated with changes in crime rates.

Age

Because teenagers have extremely high crime rates, crime experts view change in the age distribution of the population as having the greatest influence on crime trends. As a general rule, the crime rate follows the proportion of young males in the population. With the graying of society in the 1980s and a decline in the birth rate, it is not surprising that the overall crime rate declined between 1991 and 2002. The number of juveniles should be increasing over the next decade, and some crime experts fear that this will signal a return to escalating crime rates. However, the number of senior citizens is also expanding, and their presence in the population may have a moderating effect on crime rates (seniors do not commit much crime), offsetting the effect of teens.

Economy

A debate is ongoing over the effect the economy has on crime rates. It seems logical that when the economy turns downward people, especially those who are unemployed, will become more motivated to commit theft crimes. However, some crime experts believe a poor economy helps lower crime rates because unemployed parents are at home to supervise children and guard their possessions. Because there is less to spend, a poor economy reduces the number of valuables worth stealing. Also, it seems unlikely that law-abiding, middle-aged workers will suddenly turn to a life of crime if they are laid off during an economic downturn. Not surprisingly, most research efforts fail to find a definitive relationship between unemployment and crime. For example, a 2002 study on the relationship between

unemployment and crime conducted by Gary Kleck and Ted Chiricos reinforces the weak association between the two factors. Kleck and Chiricos discovered that no relationship exists between unemployment rates and the rate of most crimes including those that desperate unemployed people might choose such as the robbery of gas stations, banks, and drug stores. Nor did unemployment influence the rate of nonviolent property crimes including shoplifting, residential burglary, theft of motor vehicle parts, and theft of automobiles, trucks, and motorcycles.

Over the long haul, a strong economy could help lower crime rates, while long periods of sustained economic weakness and unemployment could lead to increased rates. Crime rates fell when the economy surged for almost a decade during the 1990s. A long-term economic recession may produce increases in the crime rate.

Social Malaise

As the level of social problems increases—such as single-parent families, dropout rates, racial conflict, and teen pregnancies—so do crime rates. For example, crime rates are correlated with the number of unwed mothers in the population. Children of unwed mothers could need more social services than children in two-parent families. As the number of kids born to single mothers increases, the child welfare system will be taxed and services depleted. The teenage birth rate began to increase in the late 1980s and so, too, have crime rates.

Racial conflict may also increase crime rates. Areas undergoing racial change, especially those experiencing an in-migration of minorities into predominantly white neighborhoods, seem prone to significant increases in their crime rate. Whites in these areas may be using violence to protect what they view as their home turf. Racially motivated crimes diminish as neighborhoods become more integrated and power struggles are resolved.

Abortion

In a controversial work, John J. Donohue III and Steven D. Levitt found empirical evidence that the recent drop in the crime rate can be attributed to the availability of legalized abortion. In 1973, *Roe* v. *Wade* legalized abortion nationwide. Within a few years of *Roe* v. *Wade,* more than 1 million abortions were being performed annually, or roughly one abortion for every three live births. Donohue and Levitt suggest that the crime rate drop, which began approximately 18 years later, in 1991, can be tied to the fact that at that point the first groups of potential offenders affected by the abortion decision began reaching the peak age of criminal activity. They find that states that legalized abortion before the rest of the nation were the first to experience decreasing crime rates and that states with high abortion rates have seen a greater fall in crime since 1985.

The abortion-related reduction in crime rates is predominantly attributable to a decrease in crime among the young. The link between crime rates and abortion could be the result of two mechanisms: (1) selective abortion on the part of women most at risk to have children who would engage in criminal activity, and (2) improved child-rearing or environmental circumstances caused by better maternal, familial, or fetal circumstances because women are having fewer children. If abortion were illegal, they find, crime rates might be 10 to 20 percent higher than they currently are. If these estimates are correct, legalized abortion can explain about half of the recent fall in crime. All else equal, they predict that crime rates will continue to fall slowly for an additional 15 to 20 years as the full effects of legalized abortion are gradually felt.

Guns

The availability of firearms may influence the crime rate, especially the proliferation of weapons in the hands of teens. Evidence shows that more guns than ever before are finding their way into the hands of young people. Surveys of high school students indicate that between 6 and 10 percent carry guns at least some of the time. Guns also cause escalation in the seriousness of crime. As the number of gun-toting students increases, so will the seriousness of violent crime as, for example, a schoolyard fight turns into murder.

Gangs

Another factor that affects crime rates is the explosive growth in teenage gangs. Surveys indicate that there are more than 750,000 gang members in the United States. Boys who are members of gangs are far more likely to possess guns than non-gang members. Criminal activity increases when kids join gangs. According to Alfred Blumstein, gangs involved in the urban drug trade recruit juveniles because they work cheaply, are immune from heavy criminal penalties, and are "daring and willing to take risks." Arming themselves for protection, these drug-dealing children present a menace to their community, which persuades non-gang-affiliated neighborhood adolescents to arm themselves for protection. The result is an arms race that produces an increasing spiral of violence.

The recent decline in the crime rate may be tied to changing gang values. Some streetwise kids have told researchers that they now avoid gangs because of the "younger brother syndrome"—they have watched their older siblings or parents caught in gangs or drugs and want to avoid the same fate.

Drug Use

Some experts tie increases in the violent crime rate between 1980 and 1990 to the crack cocaine epidemic, which swept the nation's largest cities, and drug-trafficking gangs that fought over drug turf. These well-armed gangs did not hesitate to use violence to control territory, intimidate rivals, and increase market share. As the crack epidemic has subsided, so has the violence in New York City and other metropolitan areas where the crack epidemic was rampant.

Media

Some experts argue that the availability and use of violent media can influence the direction of crime rates. As the availability of media with a violent theme skyrocketed with the introduction of home video players, DVDs, cable TV, computer and video games, and so on, so did teen violence rates. According to a recent analysis of all available scientific data conducted by Brad Bushman and Craig Anderson, watching violence on TV is correlated to aggressive behaviors especially for people with a preexisting tendency toward crime and violence. This conclusion is bolstered by research showing that the more kids watch TV the more often they get into violent encounters. For example, Jeffrey Johnson and his associates at Columbia University found that 14-year-old boys who watched less than one hour of TV per day later got into an average of nine fights resulting in injury. In contrast, adolescent males watching one to three hours of TV per day got into an average of 28 fights; those watching more than three hours of TV got into an average of 42 fights. Of those watching one to three hours per day, 22.5 percent later engaged in violence, such as assaults or robbery, in their adulthood; 28.8 percent of kids who regularly watched more than three hours of TV in a 24-hour period engaged in violent acts as adults.

Medical Technology

Some crime experts believe that the presence and quality of health care can have a significant impact on murder rates. According to research conducted by Anthony Harris and his associates, murder rates would be up to five times higher than they are today if not for medical breakthroughs developed over the past 40 years. They estimate that the United States would suffer between 50,000 and 115,000 homicides per year as opposed to the current number, which has fluctuated around 15,000. Looking back more than 40 years, they found that the aggravated assault rate has increased at a far higher pace than the murder rate, a fact they attribute to the decrease in mortality of violence victims in hospital emergency rooms. The big breakthrough occurred in the 1970s, when technology developed to treat injured soldiers in Vietnam was applied to trauma care in the nation's hospitals. Since then, murder rates can be linked to the level and availability of emergency medical services.

Justice Policy

Some law enforcement experts have suggested that a reduction in crime rates may be attributed to aggressive police practices that target "quality of life" crimes such as panhandling, graffiti, petty drug dealing, and loitering. By showing that even the smallest infractions will be dealt with seriously, aggressive police departments may be able to discourage potential criminals from committing more serious crimes. Also, as the number of police officers on parole increases, crime rates trend downward.

Tough laws targeting drug dealing and repeat offenders with lengthy prison terms also can affect crime rates. The fear of punishment may inhibit some would-be criminals. Lengthy sentences also help boost the nation's prison population. Placing a significant number of potentially high-rate offenders behind bars may help lower crime rates. Some ex-criminals have told researchers that they stopped committing crime because they perceive higher levels of street enforcement and incarceration rates.

Crime Opportunities

Crime rates may drop when market conditions change or when an alternative criminal opportunity develops. For example, the decline in the burglary rate over the past decade may be explained in part by the abundance and subsequent decline in price of commonly stolen merchandise such as VCRs, TVs, and cameras. Improving home and commercial security

(continued)

analyzing criminal justice issues (continued)

devices may also turn off would-be burglars, convincing them to turn to other forms of theft such as stealing from motor vehicles. These are non-index crimes and do not contribute to the national crime rate.

Critical Thinking

While crime rates have been declining in the United States, they have been increasing in Europe. Could factors that correlate with crime rate changes in the United States have little utility in predicting changes in other cultures? What other factors may increase or reduce crime rates?

InfoTrac College Edition Research

Gang activity may have a big impact on crime rates. To read about the effect, see John M. Hagedorn, Jose Torres, and Greg Giglio, "Cocaine, Kicks, and Strain: Patterns of Substance Use in Milwaukee Gangs," *Contemporary Drug Problems* 25, no. 1 (Spring 1998): 113–45; Mary E. Pattillo, "Sweet Mothers and Gangbangers:

Managing Crime in a Black Middle-Class Neighborhood," *Social Forces* 76, no. 3 (March 1998): 747–74.

Sources: Jeffrey Johnson, Patricia Cohen, Elizabeth Smailes, Stephanie Kasen, and Judith Brook, "Television Viewing and Aggressive Behavior during Adolescence and Adulthood," *Science* 295 (2002): 2468–71; Brad Bushman and Craig Anderson, "Media Violence and the American Public," *American Psychologist* 56 (2001): 477–89; Gary Kleck and Ted Chiricos, "Unemployment and Property Crime: A Target-Specific Assessment of Opportunity and Motivation as Mediating Factors," *Criminology* 40 (2002): 649–80; Anthony Harris, Stephen Thomas, Gene Fisher, and David Hirsch, "Murder and Medicine: The Lethality of Criminal Assault 1960–1999," *Homicide Studies* 6 (2002): 128–67; Steven Messner, Lawrence Raffalovich, and Richard McMillan, "Economic Deprivation and Changes in Homicide Arrest Rates for White and Black Youths, 1967–1998: A National Time-Series Analysis," *Criminology* 39 (2001): 591–614; John Laub, "Review of the Crime Drop in America," *American Journal of Sociology* 106 (2001): 1820–22; John J. Donohue III and Steven D. Levitt, "Legalized Abortion and Crime" (Chicago: University of Chicago, June 24, 1999); Donald Green, Dara Strolovitch, and Janelle Wong, "Defended Neighborhoods, Integration, and Racially Motivated Crime," *American Journal of Sociology* 104 (1998):

372–403; Robert O'Brien, Jean Stockard, and Lynne Isaacson, "The Enduring Effects of Cohort Characteristics on Age-Specific Homicide Rates, 1960–1995," *American Journal of Sociology* 104 (1999): 1061–95; Darrell Steffensmeier and Miles Harer, "Making Sense of Recent U.S. Crime Trends, 1980 to 1996/1998: Age Composition Effects and Other Explanations," *Journal of Research in Crime and Delinquency* 36 (1999): 235–74; Desmond Ellis and Lori Wright, "Estrangement, Interventions, and Male Violence toward Female Partners," *Violence and Victims* 12 (1997): 51–68; Richard Rosenfeld, "Changing Relationships between Men and Women: A Note on the Decline in Intimate Partner Homicide," *Homicide Studies* 1 (1997): 72–83; Bruce Johnson, Andrew Golub, and Jeffrey Fagan, "Careers in Crack, Drug Use, Drug Distribution, and Non-Drug Criminality," *Crime and Delinquency* 41 (1995): 275–95; Alfred Blumstein, "Violence by Young People: Why the Deadly Nexus," *National Institute of Justice Journal* 229 (1995): 2–9; Joseph Sheley and James Wright, *In the Line of Fire: Youth, Guns, and Violence in Urban America* (New York: Aldine de Gruyter, 1995); Alan Lizotte, Gregory Howard, Marvin Krohn, and Terence Thornberry, "Patterns of Illegal Gun Carrying among Young Urban Males," *Valparaiso University Law Review* 31 (1997): 376–94; Rosemary Gartner, "Family Structure, Welfare Spending, and Child Homicide in Developed Democracies," *Journal of Marriage and the Family* 53 (1991): 231–40.

Perspectives on Justice

The fact that the violent crime rate has declined at a time when the prison population has increased significantly is used by those who support the crime control model as an indication that get-tough measures can work to reduce crime.

Trends in Property Crime

The property crimes reported in the UCR include larceny, motor vehicle theft, and arson. Property crime rates have declined in recent years, though the drop has not been as dramatic as that experienced by the violent crime rate. The overall property crime total remained the same in 2002 when compared with the 2001 total. Larceny-theft was the lone property crime showing a decrease, 0.7 percent, when compared with the previous year's total. Burglary increased 1.5 percent, and motor vehicle theft went up 1.2 percent. Arson offenses decreased 3.7 percent.

Victimization Trends

According to the National Crime Victimization Survey, U.S. residents age 12 or older in 2002 experienced about 23.0 million violent and property victimizations. This represented a significant downward trend in reported victimization, which began in 1994 and has resulted in the lowest number of criminal victimization recorded since 1973, when an estimated 44 million victimizations were recorded. Between 1993 and 2002 the violent crime rate has decreased 54 percent (from 50 to 23 victimizations per 1,000 persons age 12 or older) and the property crime rate declined 50 percent (from 319 to 159 crimes per 1,000 households). For example, in 2002 the rate for rape was 0.4 per 1,000 persons age 12 or older, 60 percent of the 1993 rate; the rate for robbery was down 63 percent.

© 2003 AP/Wide World Photos

Figure 2.4 shows the recent trends in violent and property victimizations. So while the official crime statistics indicate that the crime rate drop may be stabilizing, the victim data indicate that the crime drop still continues unabated.

Arson is the most recent crime added to the Uniform Crime Reports. While some arsons are for profit, others may be the result of pranks, mental disturbance, revenge, or even terrorism. Here, firemen walk past damaged vehicles at a car dealership in West Covina, California, August 22, 2003. Apparent arson fires destroyed or damaged dozens of Hummers and other SUVs early Friday at the West Covina dealership vandalized by anti-pollution graffiti, and similar slogans were found spray-painted on SUVs at three other dealerships in neighboring cities.

Self-Report Findings

In general, self-reports suggest that the number of people who break the law is far greater than the number projected by official statistics. Almost everyone questioned is found to have violated some law.[23] Furthermore, self-reports dispute the notion that criminals and delinquents specialize in one type of crime or another. Offenders seem to engage in a mixed bag of crime and deviance.[24]

Self-report studies indicate that the most common offenses are truancy, alcohol abuse, use of a false ID, shoplifting or larceny under $50, fighting, marijuana use, and damage to the property of others. It is not unusual for self-reports to find combined substance abuse, theft, violence, and damage rates of more than 50 percent among suburban, rural, and urban high school youths. What is surprising is the consistency of these findings in samples taken around the United States.

Table 2.1 contains data from a self-report study called *Monitoring the Future,* which researchers at the University of Michigan Institute for Social Research (ISR) conduct annually. This national survey of more than 2,500 high school seniors, one of the most important sources of self-report data, shows a widespread yet stable pattern of youth crime since 1978.[25] Young people self-report a great deal of crime: About 30 percent of high school seniors report stealing in the last 12 months; 20 percent said they were involved in a gang fight and more than 10 percent injured someone so badly that the victim had to see a doctor; almost 25 percent engaged in breaking and entering. The fact that so many—at least 33 percent—of all U.S. high school students engaged in theft and about 20 percent committed a serious violent act during the past year shows that criminal activity is widespread and is not restricted to a few bad apples. However, the ISR survey does not report any major upswing in teen crime and, if anything, there has been a slight decline in self-reported behavior in recent years.

To quiz yourself on this material, go to questions 2.7–2.14 on the Introduction to Criminal Justice 10e CD.

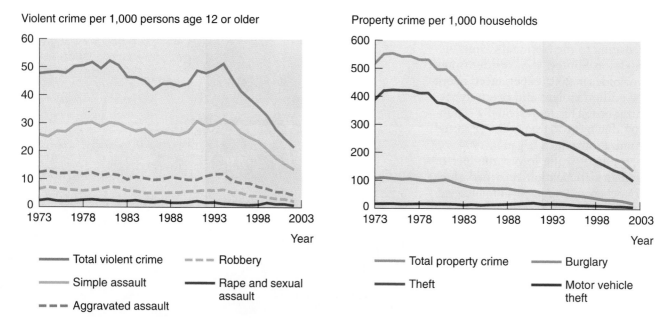

Figure 2.4
Victimization Rate per 1,000 Persons Age 12 or Older, 1973–2002

Source: Callie Marie Rennison and Michael Rand, *Criminal Victimization, 2002* (Washington, D.C.: Bureau of Justice Statistics, 2003).

What the Future Holds

It is risky to speculate about the future of crime trends because current conditions can change rapidly, but some crime experts have tried to predict future patterns. For example, criminologist James A. Fox predicts a significant increase in teen violence if current trends persist. The United States has approximately 50 million school-age children in the United States, and many are under age 10. This is more than there have been for decades. Many lack stable families and adequate supervision. These children will soon enter their prime crime years. As a result, there may be an increase in youth violence.[26]

Fox's predictions are persuasive, but not all crime experts believe an age-driven crime wave is forthcoming. Some, such as Steven Levitt, dispute the fact that the population's age makeup contributes as much to the crime rate as suggested by Fox and others.[27] Even if teens commit more crime in the future, Levitt finds that their contribution may be offset by the aging of the population, which will produce a large number of senior citizens and elderly, a group with a relatively low crime rate.

Such prognostication is reassuring, but there is no telling what changes are in store that may influence crime rates either up or down. Technological developments such as the rapid expansion of e-commerce on the Internet have created new classes of crime. Although crime rates have trended downward, it is too early to predict that this trend will continue into the foreseeable future.

While crime has declined and stabilized for the moment in the United States, it seems to be increasing around the world. The recent boom in crime rates overseas is the subject of the International Justice feature on page 56.

Crime Patterns

Crime experts look for stable crime rate patterns to gain insight into the nature of crime. If crime rates are consistently higher at certain times, in certain areas, and among certain groups, this knowledge might help explain the onset

Table 2.1 Percent of Self-Reported Delinquent Activity during the Past 12 Months among High School Seniors, 2002

Type of Crime	Percent Committing Crime	Once	More than Once
Set fire on purpose	3	1	2
Damaged school property	11	5	6
Damaged work property	7	3	4
Auto theft	5	2	3
Auto part theft	5	2	3
Breaking and entering	23	10	13
Theft worth less than $50	24	12	17
Theft worth more than $50	10	5	5
Shoplifting	28	11	17
Gang fight	17	9	8
Hurt someone bad	12	6	6
Used force to steal	3	1	2
Hit teacher or supervisor	3	1	2
Serious fight	12	6	6

Source: Lloyd Johnston, Patrick O'Malley, and Jerald Bachman, *Monitoring the Future, 2002* (Ann Arbor, Mich.: Institute for Social Research, 2003).

or cause of crime. For example, if criminal statistics show that crime rates are consistently higher in poor neighborhoods in large urban areas, then crime may be a function of poverty and neighborhood decline. If, in contrast, crime rates are spread evenly across society, this would provide little evidence that crime has an economic basis. Instead, crime might be linked to socialization, personality, intelligence, or some other trait unrelated to class position or income.

The Ecology of Crime

Crime is not spread equally across society, and specific patterns in the crime rate seem to be linked to temporal and ecological factors. These factors are stable and unchanging.

Day, Season, and Climate Most reported crimes occur during the warm summer months of July and August. During the summer, teenagers, who usually have the highest crime levels, are out of school and have greater opportunity to commit crime. People spend more time outdoors during warm weather, making themselves easier targets. Similarly, homes are left vacant more often during the summer, making them more vulnerable to property crimes. Two exceptions to this trend are murders and robberies, which occur frequently in December and January (although rates are also high during the summer).

Crime rates also may be higher on the first day of the month than at any other time. Government welfare and Social Security checks arrive at this time and with them come increases in such activities as breaking into mailboxes and accosting recipients on the streets. Also, people may have more disposable income at this time, and the availability of extra money may relate to behaviors associated with crime such as drinking, partying, gambling, and so on.[28]

Why Is Crime Booming around the World?

international justice

While crime rates are trending downward in the United States, they seem to be increasing abroad. Though it is often difficult to compare crime data, international crime expert Gene Stephens notes the following trends.

- The United States in 1980 clearly led the Western world in overall crime, but a decade later statistics show a marked decline in U.S. property crime. Overall crime rates for the United States dropped below those of England and Wales, Denmark, and Finland.
- Homicide rates are still higher in nations undergoing political and social turmoil. Colombia, for instance, had 63 homicides per 100,000 people and South Africa, 51, compared with less than 6 in the United States.
- Until 1990 U.S. rape rates were higher than those of any Western nation, but by 2000 Canada took the lead. The lowest reported rape rates were in Asia and the Middle East.
- As of 2000, countries with more reported robberies than the United States included England and Wales, Portugal, and Spain. Countries with fewer reported robberies include Germany, Italy, and France, as well as Middle Eastern and Asian nations.
- As of 2000 the United States had lower burglary rates than Australia, Denmark, Finland, England and Wales, and Canada. It had higher reported burglary rates than Spain, Korea, and Saudi Arabia.
- Australia, England and Wales, Denmark, Norway, Canada, France, and Italy now have higher rates of vehicle theft than the United States.
- Contrary to the common assumption that Europeans are virtually unarmed, the 15 countries of the European Union have an estimated 84 million firearms. Of that, 67 million (80 percent) are in civilian hands. With a total population of 375 million people, this amounts to 17.4 guns for every 100 people.

Reasons for the Rising Crime Rates

There are two views of the recent crime boom abroad. According to the modernization view, crime rates spiral upward when a nation undergoes rapid change in its social and economic makeup. Modernization causes the family, religion, and education to undergo rapid change, and the resulting social pressures result in escalating crime rates. According to this view, crime booms are most likely to occur in societies that are experiencing rapid industrialization as traditional patterns of behavior are disrupted by rapid social change, urbanization, and the shift from agricultural to industrial and service economies. According to the globalization view, crime rates vary uniformly around the globe. During periods of increase, major cities in Europe, Asia, Africa, and the Americas will experience a boom in their crime rates. Similarly, during periods of decline, crime rates trend downward around the globe.

When Gary LaFree and Kriss Drass tested this view using cross-national homicide data collected by the World Health Organization, they did find substantial support for the modernization hypothesis. Nations undergoing rapid industrial change were the ones most likely to experience twentieth-century crime waves. They found that 12 of the 34 nations they studied had experienced crime waves. They also discovered that the percentage of industrializing countries with crime booms was more than three times greater than was the percentage of industrialized nations with crime booms.

Not all countries fit the pattern. Some industrializing nations (Chile, Hungary, Mexico) did not experience crime booms while some already industrialized nations (Canada, Greece, Italy, Spain, and the United States) did. LaFree and Drass found that several of the industrialized nations with crime booms also had periods of substantial social uproar at about the same time that their homicide rates increased. For example, in the United States and Canada homicides spiked during the politically turbulent years stretching from the mid-1960s to the early 1970s. In Greece, the growth of homicide rates in the 1970s coincided with the establishment of a new civilian government and a constitution, while in Spain homicide rates jumped immediately after the death of dictator Francisco Franco (1975) and the social changes ushered in by the transition to democracy.

These results suggest that, while modernization may help predict crime waves, other social forces must also be considered. However, clear-cut evidence seems to exist that social forces may be responsible for the rise and fall of crime rates. As the countries in Eastern and Central Europe modernize and undergo rapid social change, they are expected to undergo crime booms. And as Asia and the Middle East experience political turmoil, countries in those regions may also see a surge in their crime rates.

Critical Thinking

1. The United States is notorious for employing much tougher penal measures than Europe. Do you believe its tougher measures explain why crime is declining in the United States while increasing abroad?
2. Thinking about current social and economic conditions in the United States, what is your prediction about future crime trends? Should a crime boom be expected in the near future?

InfoTrac College Edition Research

What is being done in Europe to combat the latest crime boom? To find out, read J. F. O. Mcallister, "Shock to the System: The Public Is Scared and Angry about Crime, So Politicians Are Cracking Down with Tough New Laws That Take a Bite Out of Precious Civil Liberties," *Time International,* December 2, 2002, p. 68.

Source: Gene Stephens, "Global Trends in Crime: Crime Varies Greatly around the World, Statistics Show, But New Tactics Have Proved Effective in the United States; To Keep Crime in Check in the Twenty-first Century, We'll All Need to Get Smarter, Not Just Tougher," *Futurist* 37 (2003): 40–47; Gary Lafree and Kriss Drass, "Counting Crime Booms among Nations: Evidence for Homicide Victimization Rates, 1956–1998," *Criminology* 40 (2002): 769–801; Small Arms Survey, 2003, http://www.smallarmssurvey.org/, accessed on July 10, 2003.

Population Density Large urban areas have by far the highest violence rates. Areas with low per capita crime rates tend to be rural. These findings are also supported by victim data. Exceptions to this trend are low population resort areas with large transient or seasonal populations—such as Atlantic City, New Jersey, and Nantucket, Massachusetts.

Crime rates vary by region. For many years, southern states have had consistently higher crime rates in almost all crime categories than those found in other regions of the country. These data convinced some crime experts that there was a "southern subculture of violence." Though the lead has flip-flopped in recent years between the South and the West, the latest UCR data, illustrated in Figure 2.5, indicate that southern crime rates once again are the highest in the nation.

Firearms and Crime

Firearms play a dominant role in criminal activity. According to the NCVS, firearms are typically involved in about 20 percent of robberies, 10 percent of assaults, and 6 percent of rapes. According to the UCR, about two-thirds of all murders involved firearms; most of these weapons were handguns.

According to international crime experts Franklin Zimring and Gordon Hawkins, the proliferation of handguns and the high rate of lethal violence they cause is the single most significant factor separating the crime problem in the United States from the rest of the developed world.[29] Differences between the United States and Europe in non-lethal crimes are only modest at best.[30] Zimring and Gordon's research is reinforced by data showing that in areas where household firearm ownership rates were higher, a disproportionately large number of people die from homicide.[31] Because of this association some experts believe that guns must be carefully controlled. This topic is discussed in the Analyzing Criminal Justice Issues feature on page 58.

Social Class and Crime

A still-unresolved issue in criminological literature is the relationship between social class and crime. Traditionally crime has been thought of as a lower-class phenomenon. After all, people at the lowest rungs of the social structure have the greatest incentive to commit crimes. Those unable to obtain desired goods and services through conventional means may consequently resort to theft and other illegal activities—such as selling narcotics—to obtain

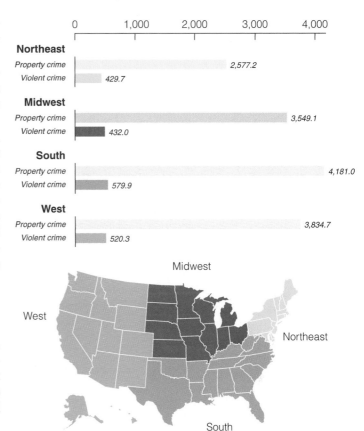

Northeast
Property crime 2,577.2
Violent crime 429.7

Midwest
Property crime 3,549.1
Violent crime 432.0

South
Property crime 4,181.0
Violent crime 579.9

West
Property crime 3,834.7
Violent crime 520.3

Midwest
West
Northeast
South

**Figure 2.5
Regional Crime Rates, 2001**

Ernestine Hill walks past a poster of City Councilman James Davis in Davis' district, where someone has attached a sign reading "Rest in Peace" in Brooklyn, New York, July 23, 2003. Davis was shot by a political opponent, Othniel Askew, who was running for Davis' council seat. Davis was not required to go through metal detectors as he entered City Hall, and as Askew had accompanied him, he bypassed metal detectors as well.

Should Guns Be Controlled?

analyzing criminal justice issues

The 2002 sniper killings in the Washington, D.C., area focused a spotlight on a long-running policy debate in the United States: Should guns be controlled? According to the 2003 Small Arms Survey, the United States has by far the largest number of publicly owned firearms in the world and is approaching the point where there is one gun for every American. An estimated 50 million of these guns are illegal. Handguns are linked to many violent crimes, including 20 percent of all injury deaths (second to autos) and 60 percent of all homicides and suicides. They are also responsible for the deaths of about two-thirds of all police officers killed in the line of duty. Cross-national research conducted by Anthony Hoskin found that countries, including the United States, that have high levels of privately owned firearms also have the highest levels of homicide. To some critics the deadly sniper attacks that paralyzed the Virginia–Maryland area were a sad result of the widespread availability of deadly rifles and handguns.

The association between guns and crime has spurred many Americans to advocate controlling the sale of handguns and banning the cheap mass-produced handguns known as Saturday night specials. In contrast, gun advocates view control as a threat to personal liberty and call for severe punishment of criminals, not control of handguns. They argue that the Second Amendment of the U.S. Constitution protects the right to bear arms. A 2001 survey by J. Robert Jiobu and Timothy Curry found that the typical gun owner has a deep mistrust of the federal government. To such a person, a gun is an "icon for democracy and personal empowerment."

Gun Control Efforts

Efforts to control handguns have come from many different sources. The states and many local jurisdictions have laws banning or restricting sales or possession of guns; some regulate dealers who sell guns. The Federal Gun Control Act of 1968, which is still in effect, requires that all dealers be licensed, fill out forms detailing each trade, and avoid selling to people prohibited from owning guns such as minors, ex-felons, and drug users. Dealers must record the source and properties of all guns they sell and carefully account for their purchase. Gun buyers must provide identification and sign waivers attesting to their ability to possess guns. Unfortunately, the resources available to enforce this law are meager.

On November 30, 1993, the Brady Handgun Violence Prevention Act was enacted, amending the Federal Gun Control Act of 1968. The bill was named after former press secretary James Brady, who was severely wounded in the attempted assassination of President Ronald Reagan by John Hinckley Jr. in 1981. The Brady law imposes a waiting period of five days before a licensed importer, manufacturer, or dealer may sell, deliver, or transfer a handgun to an unlicensed individual. The waiting period applies only in states without an acceptable alternate system of conducting background checks on handgun purchasers. The Brady law provided for an instant check on whether a prospective buyer is prohibited from purchasing a weapon. Federal law bans gun purchases by people convicted of or under indictment for felony charges, fugitives, the mentally ill, those with dishonorable military discharges, those who have renounced U.S. citizenship, illegal aliens, illegal drug users, and those convicted of domestic violence misdemeanors or who are under domestic violence restraining orders (individual state laws may create other restrictions). The Brady law requires background approval not just for handgun buyers but also for those who buy long guns and shotguns.

Although gun control advocates see this legislation as a good first step, some question whether such measures will ultimately curb gun violence. For example, when Jens Ludwig and Philip Cook compared two sets of states, 32 that installed the Brady law in 1994 and 18 states plus the District of Columbia that already had similar types of laws prior to 1994, they found no evidence that implementing the measure contributed to a reduction in homicide.

Another approach is to severely punish people caught with unregistered handguns. The most famous attempt to regulate handguns using this method is the Massachusetts Bartley-Fox law, which provides a mandatory one-year prison term for possessing a handgun (outside the home) without a permit. A detailed analysis of violent crime in Boston after the law's passage found that the use of handguns in robberies and murders did decline substantially (in robberies by 35 percent and in murders by 55 percent in a two-year period). However, these optimistic results must be tempered by two facts: rates for similar crimes dropped significantly in comparable cities that did not have gun control laws, and the use of other weapons, such as knives, increased in Boston.

Some jurisdictions have tried to reduce gun violence by adding extra punishment, such as a mandatory prison sentence for any crime involving a handgun. California's "10-20-life" law requires an additional 10 years in prison for carrying a gun while committing a violent felony and 20 years if the gun is fired. If someone is injured, the penalty increases to 25 years to life in prison. Aiding this effort is a U.S. Supreme Court decision, *U.S.* v. *Rodriguez-Moreno* (1998), holding that a person can be prosecuted for using an illegal handgun to commit a crime even if the person did not use the gun in the prosecuting jurisdiction. *Rodriguez-Moreno* means, for example, that a person who uses a gun in Kansas to steal drugs and then sells them in California can be prosecuted for gun possession in California because both the theft and sale of the drugs are considered part of the same crime.

Can Guns Be Outlawed?

Even if gun ownership is outlawed or severely restricted, the government's ability to control guns is problematic. Even if legitimate gun stores were strictly regulated, private citizens could still sell, barter, or trade handguns. Unregulated gun fairs and auctions are common throughout the United States. Many gun deals are made at gun shows with few questions asked. When Anthony A. Braga and David M. Kennedy reviewed illegal firearms trafficking involving youth and juveniles, they found that most kids obtained firearms illegally through a multitude of unauthorized sources including unlicensed dealers, corrupt licensed dealers, and straw purchasers.

If handguns were banned or outlawed, they would become more valuable. Illegal importation of guns might increase as it has for another controlled substance, narcotics. Increasing penalties for gun-related crimes has also met with limited success because judges may be reluctant to alter their sentencing policies to accommodate legislators. Regulating dealers is difficult, and tighter controls on them would only encourage private sales and bartering. Relatively few guns are stolen in burglaries, but many are sold to licensed gun dealers who circumvent the law by ignoring state registration requirements or making unrecorded or mis-recorded sales to individuals and unlicensed dealers. Even a few corrupt dealers can supply tens of thousands of illegal handguns.

A 2003 report by the Task Force on Community Preventive Services, an independent nonfederal task force, illustrates the problem of employing gun control legislation to control gun violence. After reviewing the effect of laws that banned a variety of gun-related activities including controlling specific firearms and ammunition, placing restrictions on firearm acquisition, creating waiting periods for firearm acquisition, controlling firearm registration and licensing of firearm owners, mandating "shall issue" concealed weapon carry laws, child access prevention laws, zero-tolerance laws for firearms in schools, and combinations of firearms laws, the task force found insufficient evidence to determine the effectiveness of any of the firearms laws or combinations of laws reviewed on violent outcomes.

Is There a Benefit to Having Guns?

Not all experts are convinced that strict gun control is a good thing. Gary Kleck, a leading advocate of gun ownership, argues that guns may inhibit violence. In many assaults, he reasons, the aggressor does not wish to kill but only scare the victim. Possessing a gun gives aggressors so much killing power that they may be inhibited from attacking. For example, research by Kleck and Karen McElrath found that perpetrators of a robbery can control the situation without the need for illegal force. Guns may also enable victims to escape serious injury. They may be inhibited from fighting back without losing face. It is socially acceptable to back down from a challenge if the opponent is armed with a gun. Guns then can de-escalate a potentially violent situation. Kleck, along with Michael Hogan, finds that people who own guns are only slightly more likely to commit homicide than nonowners. The benefits of gun ownership, he concludes, outweigh the costs.

Kleck's findings have been supported by research conducted by John Lott Jr. and David Mustard. Using cross-sectional data for the United States, they found that jurisdictions that allow citizens to carry concealed weapons also have lower violent crime rates. If all states allowed citizens to carry concealed weapons, their analysis indicates that 1,500 murders, 4,000 rapes, 11,000 robberies, and 60,000 aggravated assaults would be avoided yearly. The annual social benefit from each additional concealed handgun permit is as high as $5,000, saving society more than $6 billion per year.

Does Defensive Gun Use Work?

While Kleck and his associates support the use of guns for defensive purposes, other research efforts show that defensive gun use may be more limited than believed. For example, Stephen Schnebly found that possessing a gun may help some but has little utility for women and residents in lower-class neighborhoods. Guns are also of little defensive help outside of urban areas.

The recent spate of gun violence, including the D.C. area sniper, makes a powerful statement against gun ownership. Research shows that people who want to buy guns legally or purchase licenses to carry concealed weapons often have prior criminal records and engage in patterns of heavy drinking. Facilitating their access to weapons may increase instead of reduce violent crime levels. And, in an important analysis, William Wells and Julie Horney found that having a gun in a violent situation was more likely to produce a negative outcome than any other kind of weapon, for example, knives or clubs. Even people with a history of violence or who exhibit abnormal psychological traits are less likely to kill when they used a knife or other weapon in an attack than when they employ a gun. The Wells and Horney research sheds important light on the age-old question, Do guns kill people or do people kill people? According to Wells and Horney, even the most dangerous people are less likely to resort to lethal violence if the gun is taken out of their hands.

Critical Thinking

1. Should the sale and possession of handguns be banned?
2. Which of the gun control methods discussed do you feel would be most effective in deterring crime?

(continued)

analyzing criminal justice issues (continued)

InfoTrac College Edition Research

One method of reducing gun violence may be to make guns safer. Read more about this plan in Krista D. Robinson, Stephen P. Teret, Susan DeFrancesco, and Stephen W. Hargarten, "Making Guns Safer," *Issues in Science and Technology* 14, no. 4 (Summer 1998): 37–41.

Sources: Small Arms Survey, 2003, http://www.smallarmssurvey.org/ accessed on July 10, 2003; Robert A. Hahn, Oleg O. Bilukha, Alex Crosby, Mindy Thompson Fullilove, Akiva Liberman, Eve K. Moscicki, Susan Snyder, Farris Tuma, and Peter Briss, *Evaluating the Effectiveness of Strategies for Preventing Violence: Firearms Laws* (Atlanta, Ga.: Task Force on Community Preventive Services Centers for Disease Control and Prevention, 2003); Stephen Schnebly, "An Examination of the Impact of Victim, Offender, and Situational Attributes on the Deterrent Effect of Gun Use: A Research

Note," *Justice Quarterly* 19 (2002): 377–99; William Wells and Julie Horney, "Weapon Effects and Individual Intent to Do Harm: Influences on the Escalation of Violence," *Criminology* 40 (2002): 265–96; Gary Kleck and Karen McElrath, "The Effects of Weaponry on Human Violence," *Social Forces* 67, no. 3 (March 1991): 669–92; John Lott Jr., *More Guns, Less Crime: Understanding Crime and Gun Control Laws* (Chicago: University of Chicago Press, 2001); John Lott Jr. and David Mustard, "Crime, Deterrence, and Right-to-Carry Concealed Handguns," *Journal of Legal Studies* 26 (1997): 1–68; Anthony A. Braga and David M. Kennedy, "The Illicit Acquisition of Firearms by Youth and Juveniles," *Journal of Criminal Justice* 29 (2001): 379–88; Anthony Hoskin, "Armed Americans: The Impact of Firearm Availability on National Homicide Rates," *Justice Quarterly* 18 (2001): 569–92; J. Robert Jiobu and Timothy Curry, "Lack of Confidence in the Federal Government and the Ownership of Firearms," *Social Science Quarterly* 82 (2001): 77–87, quoted matter on p. 87; Jens Ludwig and Philip Cook, "Homicide and Suicide Rates Associated with the Implemen-

tation of the Brady Violence Prevention Act," *Journal of the American Medical Association* 284 (2000): 585–91; Julius Wachtel, "Sources of Crime Guns in Los Angeles, California," *Policing* 21 (1998): 220–39; Gary Kleck and Michael Hogan, "National Case-Control Study of Homicide Offending and Gun Ownership," *Social Problems* 46 (1999): 275–93; Garen Wintemute, Mora Wright, Carrie Parham, Christina Drake, and James Beaumont, "Denial of Handgun Purchase: A Description of the Affected Population and a Controlled Study of Their Handgun Preferences," *Journal of Criminal Justice* 27 (1999): 21–31; Shawn Schwaner, L. Allen Furr, Cynthia Negrey, and Rachelle Seger, "Who Wants a Gun License?" *Journal of Criminal Justice* 27 (1999): 1–10; Gary Kleck and Marc Gertz, "Armed Resistance to Crime: The Prevalence and Nature of Self-Defense with a Gun," *Journal of Criminal Law and Criminology* 86 (1995): 150–87; Colin Loftin, David McDowall, Brian Wiersma, and Talbert Cottey, "Effects of Restrictive Licensing of Handguns on Homicide and Suicide in the District of Columbia," *New England Journal of Medicine* 325 (1991): 1615–20.

The Small Arms Survey is an independent research project located at the Graduate Institute of International Studies, Geneva, Switzerland. It serves as the principle international source of public information on all aspects of small arms and as a resource center for governments, policy makers, researchers, and activists. Go to its Web site at http://www.smallarmssurvey.org/.

instrumental crimes
Criminal acts intended to improve the financial or social position of the criminal.

expressive crimes
Criminal acts that serve to vent rage, anger, or frustration.

them. These activities are referred to as **instrumental crimes.** Those living in poverty are also believed to engage in disproportionate amounts of **expressive crimes,** such as rape and assault, as a means of venting their rage, frustration, and anger against society. Alcohol and drug abuse, common in impoverished areas, help fuel violent episodes.[32]

When measured with UCR data, official statistics indicate that crime rates in inner-city, high-poverty areas are generally higher than those in suburban or wealthier areas.[33] Surveys of prison inmates consistently show that prisoners were members of the lower class and unemployed or underemployed in the years before their incarceration.

An alternative explanation for these findings is that the relationship between official crime and social class is a function of law enforcement practices, not criminal behavior patterns. Police may devote more resources to poor areas, and consequently apprehension rates may be higher there. Similarly, police may be more likely to formally arrest and prosecute lower-class citizens than those in the middle and upper classes, which may account for the lower class's overrepresentation in official statistics and the prison population.

Class and Self-Reports Self-report data have been used extensively to test the class–crime relationship. If people in all social classes self-report similar crime patterns, but only those in the lower class are formally arrested, that would explain higher crime rates in lower-class neighborhoods. However, if lower-class people report greater criminal activity than their middle- and upper-class peers, it would indicate that official statistics accurately represent the crime problem. Surprisingly, early self-report studies conducted in the 1950s, specifically those by James Short and F. Ivan Nye, did not find a direct relationship between social

Frank Quattrone, center, accompanied by his attorney John Keker, arrives in Manhattan federal court for the first day of his trial. An influential investment banker at Credit Suisse First Boston during the 1990s, Quattrone was accused of encouraging CSFB employees to get rid of documents that were being sought by a grand jury and regulators looking into how CSFB doled out shares of initial public offerings. While crime may be concentrated in lower-class neighborhoods, the affluent are not immune from allegations that they violated the criminal law. On October 24, 2003, the trial judge declared a mistrial after jurors failed to decide whether the former star banker obstructed justice during federal investigations into hot stock offerings.

class and youth crime.[34] They found that socioeconomic class was related to official processing by police, courts, and correctional agencies but not to the commission of crimes. In other words, although lower- and middle-class youth self-reported equal amounts of crime, the lower-class youths had a greater chance of being arrested, convicted, and incarcerated and becoming official delinquents. In addition, factors generally associated with lower-class membership, such as broken homes, were found to be related to institutionalization but not to admissions of delinquency. Other studies of this period reached similar conclusions.[35]

For more than 20 years after the use of self-reports became widespread, a majority of self-report studies concluded that a class–crime relationship did not exist. If the poor possessed more extensive criminal records than the wealthy, this difference was attributed to differential law enforcement and not to class-based behavior differences. That is, police may be more likely to arrest lower-class offenders and treat the affluent more leniently.

More than 20 years ago, Charles Tittle, Wayne Villemez, and Douglas Smith wrote what is still considered the definitive review of the relationship between class and crime.[36] They concluded that little if any support exists for the contention that crime is primarily a lower-class phenomenon. Consequently, Tittle and his associates argued that official statistics probably reflect class bias in processing lower-class offenders. In a subsequent article written with Robert Meier, Tittle once again reviewed existing data on the class–crime relationship and found little evidence of a consistent association between class and crime.[37] More recent self-report studies generally support Tittle's conclusions: No direct relationship exists between social class and crime.[38]

Tittle's findings have sparked significant debate in the criminological community. Many self-report instruments include trivial offenses such as using a false ID or drinking alcohol, which may invalidate findings. Affluent youths could frequently engage in trivial offenses such as petty larceny, using drugs, and simple assault but rarely escalate their criminal involvement. Those who support a class–crime relationship suggest that if only serious felony offenses are considered can a significant association be observed.[39] Some studies find that when only serious crimes, such as burglary and assault, are considered, lower-class youths are significantly more delinquent.[40]

Why does social class have such a great impact on individual behavior? To find out, go to InfoTrac College Edition and use "social class" as a subject guide.

The Class–Crime Controversy The relationship between class and crime is an important one for criminological theory. If crime is related to social class, then it follows that economic and social factors, such as poverty and neighborhood disorganization, cause criminal behavior.

One reason that a true measure of the class–crime relationship has so far eluded crime experts is that the methods employed to determine social class vary widely. For example, father's occupation and education are only weakly related to self-reported crime, but unemployment or receiving welfare are more significant predictors of criminality.[41]

The association between class and crime also could be more complex than a simple linear relationship (that is, the poorer you are, the more crime you commit).[42] Class may affect some subgroups in the population (for example, women, African Americans) more than it does others (for example, males, whites).[43] Sally Simpson and Lori Elis found that white females are more likely to be influenced by social class than are minority females. They speculate that white females have had their financial expectations significantly raised because of the women's movement, which had less effect on minority women. Therefore, white females are more likely to turn to crime when their expectations of wealth are not achieved.[44] In light of these findings, it is not surprising that the true relationship between class and crime is difficult to determine. The effect may be obscured because its impact varies within and between groups.

Like so many other criminological controversies, the debate over the true relationship between class and crime will most likely persist. The weight of recent evidence seems to suggest that serious, official crime is more prevalent among the lower classes, whereas less serious and self-reported crime is spread more evenly throughout the social structure.[45] Income inequality, poverty, and resource deprivation are all associated with the most serious violent crimes, including homicide and assault.[46] Members of the lower class are more likely to suffer psychological abnormality including high rates of anxiety and conduct disorders, conditions that may promote criminality.[47]

Perspectives on Justice

Rehabilitation advocates believe that social class is correlated with crime and that the key to reducing crime rates are programs that emphasize jobs, counseling, and opportunity instead of punishment.

Age and Crime

General agreement exists that age is inversely related to criminality.[48] Regardless of economic status, marital status, race, sex, and so on, younger people commit crime more often than their older peers. Research indicates this relationship has been stable across time periods ranging from 1935 to the present.[49] Official statistics reveal that young people are arrested at a disproportionate rate to their numbers in the population. Victim surveys generate similar findings for crimes in which assailant age can be determined. Whereas youths ages 13 to 17 collectively make up about 6 percent of the total U.S. population, they account for about 25 percent of index crime arrests and 17 percent of arrests for all crimes. As a general rule, the peak age for property crime is believed to be 16, and for violence, 18 (see Figure 2.6). In contrast, adults 45 and over, who make up 32 percent of the population, account for only 7 percent of index crime arrests. The elderly are particularly resistant to the temptations of crime. They make up more than 12 percent of the population and less than 1 percent of arrests. Elderly males 65 and over are predominantly arrested for alcohol-related matters (public drunkenness

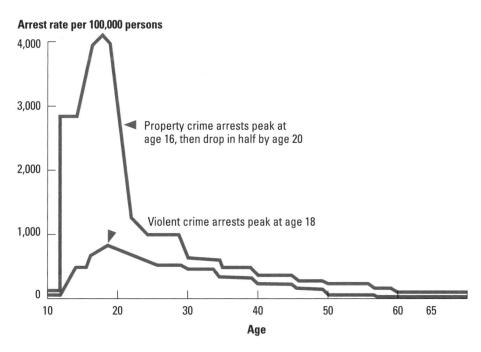

Arrest rate per 100,000 persons

Property crime arrests peak at
age 16, then drop in half by age 20

Violent crime arrests peak at age 18

Age

Figure 2.6
**The Relationship between Age
and Serious Crime Arrests**

Source: Federal Bureau of Investigation,
Crime in the United States, 2002 (Washington, D.C.: Government Printing Office,
2003).

and drunk driving) and elderly females for larceny (shoplifting). The elderly
crime rate has remained stable for the past 20 years.[50]

Gender and Crime

The three data-gathering criminal statistics tools support the theory that male
crime rates are much higher than those of females. Victims report that their assailant was male in more than 80 percent of all violent personal crimes. According to the Uniform Crime Reports arrest statistics, the overall male–female arrest
ratio is about 3.5 male offenders to 1 female offender; for serious violent crimes,
the ratio is closer to 5 males to 1 female; murder arrests are 8:1 male. Recent self-
report data collected by the Institute for Social Research at the University of
Michigan also show that males commit more serious crimes, such as robbery, assault, and burglary, than females. However, although the patterns in self-reports
parallel official data, the ratios are smaller. In other words, males self-report more
criminal behavior than females—but not to the degree suggested by official data.

Traits and Temperment Early crime experts pointed to emotional, physical, and
psychological differences between males and females to explain the differences
in crime rates. Cesare Lombroso's 1895 book, *The Female Offender,* argued that
a small group of female criminals lacked "typical" female traits of "piety, maternity, undeveloped intelligence, and weakness."[51] In physical appearance as well
as in their emotional makeup, delinquent females appeared closer to men than to
other women. Lombroso's theory became known as the **masculinity hypothesis;**
in essence, a few "masculine" females were responsible for the handful of crimes
women commit.

   Another early view of female crime focused on the supposed dynamics of sexual relationships. Female criminals were viewed as either sexually controlling or
sexually naive, either manipulating men for profit or being manipulated by them.
The female's criminality was often masked because criminal justice authorities
were reluctant to take action against a woman.[52] This perspective is known as the
chivalry hypothesis, which holds that much female criminality is hidden because
of American culture's generally protective and benevolent attitude toward

Many explanations can be
cited for the gender differences in the crime rate.
To research this topic on Info-
Trac College Edition, use "gender" and "crime" as key words.

masculinity hypothesis
The view that women who commit
crimes have biological and psychological traits similar to those of men.

chivalry hypothesis
The idea that female defendants
are treated more leniently in sentencing (and are less likely to be
arrested and prosecuted in the first
place) because the criminal justice
system is dominated by men who
have a paternalistic or protective
attitude toward women.

Female criminality is becoming more common and widespread and receiving a great deal of media attention. In this photo, the "Mercedes-Benz Murderer," Clara Harris, center, is flanked by her attorneys Emily Munoz and George Parnham as she receives a 20-year sentence from the jury, February 14, 2003, in Houston. Harris was found guilty of murder for running down her husband with her Mercedes-Benz after catching him with another woman.

© 2003 AP/Wide World Photos

women.[53] In other words, police are less likely to arrest, juries are less likely to convict, and judges are less likely to incarcerate female offenders.

Although these early writings are no longer taken seriously, some crime experts still consider trait differences a key determinant of crime rate differences. For example, some crime experts link antisocial behavior to hormonal influences by arguing that male sex hormones (androgens) account for more aggressive male behavior and that gender-related hormonal differences can also explain the gender gap in the crime rate.[54]

Socialization and Development Another view is that, unlike boys, a majority of young girls are socialized to avoid being violent and aggressive and are supervised more closely by parents. It comes as no surprise when research shows that most girls develop moral values that strongly discourage antisocial behavior.[55] The few female criminals are troubled individuals, alienated at home, who pursue crime as a means of compensating for their disrupted personal lives.[56] The streets are a second home to girls whose physical and emotional adjustment was hampered by a strained home life marked by such conditions as absent fathers, overly competitive mothers, and so on.

For example, a 2002 study conducted by Emily Gaarder and Joanne Belknap of delinquent girls sent to adult prisons found that many of these young women had troubled lives that set them on a criminal career path.[57] One girl told them how her father had attacked her yet her mother shortly let him return home.

I told her I'd leave if he came back, but she let him anyway. I was thinking, you know, she should be worrying about me. I left and went to my cousin's house. Nobody even called me. Mom didn't talk to me for two weeks, and Dad said to me "Don't call." It was like they didn't care. I started smoking weed a lot then, drinking, skipping school, and shoplifting . . . I had no [delinquency] record before this happened.

Some experts explain these differences in socialization by pointing to gender-based differences in human development that help shape behavior choices. Girls are believed to have cognitive traits that shield them from criminal behaviors.

Feminist Views In the 1970s, **liberal feminist theory** focused attention on the social and economic role of women in society and its relationship to female crime rates.[58] This view suggested that the traditionally lower crime rate for women could be explained by their second-class economic and social position. As women's social roles changed and their lifestyles became more like those of males, it was believed that their crime rates would converge.

Crime experts, responding to this research, began to refer to the "new female criminal." The rapid increase in the female crime rate during the 1960s and 1970s, especially in what had traditionally been male-oriented crimes (such as burglary and larceny), supported the liberal feminist view. In addition, self-report studies seem to indicate that the pattern of female criminality, if not its frequency, is similar to that of male criminality and that the factors predisposing male criminals to crime have an equal impact on female criminals.[59] Crime experts began to assess the association between economic issues, gender roles, and criminality.

liberal feminist theory
An ideology holding that women suffer oppression, discrimination, and disadvantage as a result of their sex. Calls for gender equality in pay, opportunity, child care, and education.

To read about the history and nature of the women's movement in the United States, go to InfoTrac College Edition and use "liberal feminism" as a subject guide.

Is Convergence Likely? Will the gender differences in the crime rate eventually dissolve? Some crime experts find that gender-based crime rate differences remain significant and argue that the emancipation of women has had relatively little influence on female crime rates.[60] They dispute that increases in the female arrest rate reflect economic or social change brought about by the women's movement. For one thing, many female criminals come from the socioeconomic class least affected by the women's movement. Their crimes seem more a function of economic inequality than women's rights. For another, the offense patterns of women are still quite different from those of men, who commit a disproportionate share of serious crimes such as robbery, burglary, murder, and assault.[61] This view is supported by recent research showing that women who are living in poverty (for example, on welfare and unemployed) are much more likely than their more affluent sisters to get involved in assaults and engage in petty property crime such as fraudulently claiming welfare benefits, credit card fraud, and public order crimes such as prostitution.[62]

Although male arrest rates are still considerably higher than female rates, female arrest rates seem to be increasing at a faster pace. For example, between 1991 and 2001 the male arrest rate declined by 3.8 percent while the female rate increased by 18 percent. Male arrests for violent crimes dropped by 17.1 percent while the female rate rose 32.7 percent. One reason for this convergence is the increasing female participation in crimes that traditionally have been a male enterprise. For example, females are now joining teen gangs, which at one time was a rare occurrence, in record numbers. Recent national surveys indicate that about 8 percent of females report gang membership (as compared with 14 percent of males); the male–female gang membership ratio is now less than 2:1.[63]

Race and Crime

Official crime data indicate that minority group members are involved in a disproportionate share of criminal activity. According to UCR reports, African Americans make up about 12 percent of the general population, yet they account for about 40 percent of Part I violent crime arrests and 34 percent of property crime arrests. They also are responsible for a disproportionate number of Part II arrests (except for alcohol-related arrests, which detain primarily white offenders).

These data could reflect racial differences in the crime rate, but they also could reflect police bias in the arrest process. This issue can be evaluated by comparing racial differences in self-report data with those found in official delinquency records. Charges of racial discrimination in the arrest process would be substantiated if whites and blacks self-reported equal numbers of crimes but minorities were arrested far more often.

Early efforts found virtually no relationship between race and self-reported delinquency.[64] These research efforts supported a case for police bias in the arrest decision. Other, more recent self-report studies that use large national samples of youths have also found little evidence of racial disparity in crimes committed. For example, the Monitoring the Future self-report survey found that, if anything, black youths self-report less delinquent behavior and substance abuse than whites.[65] These and other self-report studies seem to indicate that the delinquent behavior rates of black and white teenagers are generally similar and that differences in arrest statistics may indicate a differential selection policy by police.[66]

Racial differences in the crime rate remain an extremely sensitive issue. Although official arrest records indicate that African Americans are arrested at a higher rate than members of other racial groups, some question whether this is a function of crime rate differences, racism by police, or faulty data collection.[67] Research shows that suspects who are poor, minority, and male are more likely to be formally arrested than suspects who are white, affluent, and female.[68] Some critics charge that police officers routinely use racial profiling to stop African Americans and search their cars without probable cause or reasonable suspicion. Some cynics have gone so far as to suggest that police officers have created a new from of traffic offense called DWB, "driving while black."[69]

Perspectives on Justice

Advocates of the due process perspective are especially sensitive to charges of race bias and have drawn attention to the practice of racial profiling.

Although the UCR may reflect discriminatory police practices, African Americans are arrested for a disproportionate amount of violent crime, such as robbery and murder, and police discretion alone is unlikely to account for these proportions. It is doubtful that police routinely ignore white killers, robbers, and rapists while arresting violent black offenders. Recent research by Stewart J. D'Alessio and and Lisa Stolzenberg using data from the National Incident-Based Reporting System found that the odds of arrest for white offenders is approximately 22 percent higher for robbery, 13 percent higher for aggravated assault, and 9 percent higher for simple assault than they are for black offenders; race is not related to rape arrests. Their findings suggest that the fact that African Americans account for a disproportionately high percentage of serious crime arrests is most likely attributable to differential involvement in reported crime, not to racially biased law enforcement practices. If these findings are accurate, how can the racial differences in the crime rate be explained?[70]

Racism and Discrimination Most crime experts focus on the impact of economic deprivation and the legacy of racism and discrimination on personality and behavior.[71] The fact that U.S. culture influences African American crime rates is underscored by the fact that black violence rates are much lower in other nations—both those that are predominantly white, such as Canada, and those that are predominantly black, such as Nigeria.[72]

Some crime experts view black crime as a function of socialization in a society where the black family was torn apart and black culture destroyed in such a way that recovery has proven impossible. Early experiences, beginning with slavery, have left a wound that has been deepened by racism and lack of opportunity.[73] Children of the slave society were thrust into a system of forced dependency and ambivalence and antagonism toward one's self and group.

Institutional Racism Racism is still an element of daily life in the African American community, a factor that undermines faith in social and political institutions and weakens confidence in the justice system. Such fears are supported by em-

© 2003 AP/Wide World Photos

Racial differences in the crime rate may be a function of institutional racism. African-Americans may be the subject of "racial profiling" and accused of crimes they did not commit. Here, Dennis Allen, center, hugs and kisses his daughters Rosie, 12 (right), and Christina after his release from the Swisher County courthouse in Tulia, Texas, June 16, 2003. A dozen blacks jailed in a series of small-town drug busts that were based on the now-discredited testimony of a single undercover agent were freed on bail pending appeals. A special prosecutor has said he will dismiss the cases if an appeals court orders new trials.

pirical evidence that, at least in some jurisdictions, young African American males are treated more harshly by the criminal and juvenile justice systems than are members of any other group.[74] Because they are more likely to become the focus of unwarranted police attention, African Americans are more likely to obtain a prior criminal record and, consequently, be eligible for more severe punishments than Caucasian youths if they are re-arrested.[75] Evidence shows that African Americans, especially those who are indigent or unemployed, receive longer prison sentences than whites with the same employment status. Judges could be imposing harsher punishments on unemployed African Americans because they view them as "social dynamite," considering them more dangerous and more likely to recidivate than white offenders.[76] Yet when African Americans are victims of crime, their predicament receives less public concern and media attention than that afforded white victims.[77] For example, research shows that as the percentage of violent felony offenses that involve a black perpetrator and a white victim rises, the likelihood that a black individual will be arrested for a felony crime also increases. Black crime increases the racial fears of whites, which results in increased sanctions against all African Americans. Black-on-black crime does not create the same effect.[78]

Differential enforcement practices take their toll on the black community. For example, a national survey found that more than 13 percent of all African American males have lost the right to vote; that in seven states 25 percent have been disenfranchised; and that in two states, Florida and Alabama, 33 percent of black males have lost their voting privileges.[79] It is not surprising then that African Americans of all social classes hold negative attitudes toward the justice system and view it as an arbitrary and unfair institution.[80]

Economic and Social Disparity Racial differentials in crime rates may also be tied to economic disparity. Blacks and whites face different economic and social realities. African Americans typically have higher unemployment rates and lower incomes than whites. They face a greater degree of social isolation and economic deprivation, a condition that has been linked by empirical research to high murder rates.[81] Not helping the situation is that during tough economic times blacks and whites may find themselves competing for shrinking job opportunities. As economic competition between the races grows, interracial homicides do likewise. Economic and political rivalries lead to greater levels of interracial violence.[82]

Even during times of economic growth, lower-class African Americans are left out of the economic mainstream, a fact that meets with a growing sense of frustration and failure.[83] As a result of being shut out of educational and economic opportunities enjoyed by the rest of society, this population may be prone, some believe, to the lure of illegitimate gain and criminality. Young African American males in the inner city often are resigned to a lifetime of little if any social and economic opportunity. Even when economic data say they are doing better, news accounts of "protests, riots, and acts of civil disobedience" tell them otherwise.[84] African Americans living in lower-class slums may be disproportionately violent because they are exposed to more violence in their daily lives than other racial and economic groups. This exposure is a significant risk factor for violent behavior.[85] Sociologist Julie Philips found that if whites were subjected to the same economic and social disabilities as minorities, interracial homicide rate differences would be dramatically reduced. Based on 1990 data for 129 U.S. metropolitan areas, she found that all of the white–Latino homicide differential and about half of the white–black homicide gap would evaporate if the social and economic characteristics of minorities were improved to levels currently enjoyed by whites.[86]

Family Dissolution Family dissolution in the minority community is tied to low employment rates among African American males, which places a strain on marriages. The relatively large number of single, female-headed households in these communities may be tied to the high mortality rate among African American males due in part to their increased risk of early death by disease and violence.[87] When families are weakened or disrupted, their social control is compromised. It is not surprising, then, that divorce and separation rates are significantly associated with homicide rates in the African American community.[88] However, even among at-risk African American kids growing up in communities categorized by poverty, high unemployment levels, and single-parent households, those who manage to live in stable families with sufficient income and educational achievement are much less likely to engage in violent behaviors than those lacking family support. [89]

Is Convergence Possible? Considering these overwhelming social problems, is it possible that racial crime rates will soon converge? One argument is that if economic conditions improve in the minority community, then differences in crime rates will eventually disappear.[90] A trend toward residential integration, under way since 1980, may also help reduce crime rate differentials.[91] Despite economic disparity, few racial differences are evident in attitudes toward crime and justice today. Convergence in crime rates will occur if economic and social obstacles can be removed.

In sum, the weight of the evidence shows that although little difference exists in the self-reported crime rates of racial groups, African Americans are more likely to be arrested for serious violent crimes. The causes of minority crime have been linked to poverty, racism, hopelessness, lack of opportunity, and urban problems experienced by all too many African American citizens.

Careers and Crime

Crime data show that most offenders commit a single criminal act and upon arrest discontinue their antisocial activity. Others commit a few less serious crimes. A small group of criminal offenders, however, account for a majority of all criminal offenses. These persistent offenders are referred to as **career criminals** or **chronic offenders.**

career criminals
Persistent repeat offenders who organize their lifestyle around criminality.

chronic offenders
As defined by Marvin Wolfgang, Robert Figlio, and Thorsten Sellin, delinquents arrested five or more times before the age of 18 who commit a disproportionate amount of all criminal offenses.

The concept of the chronic or career offender is most closely associated with the research efforts of Marvin Wolfgang, Robert Figlio, and Thorsten Sellin.[92] In their landmark 1972 study, *Delinquency in a Birth Cohort,* they used official records to follow the criminal careers of a cohort of 9,945 boys from the time of their birth in Philadelphia in 1945 until they reached 18 years of age in 1963. Official police records were used to identify delinquents. About one-third of the boys (3,475) had some police contact. The remaining two-thirds (6,470) had none. Each delinquent was given a seriousness weight score for every delinquent act.[93] The weighting of delinquent acts allowed the researchers to differentiate, for example, between a simple assault requiring no medical attention for the victim and serious battery in which the victim needed hospitalization. The best known discovery of Wolfgang and his associates was that of the so-called chronic offender. The cohort data indicated that 54 percent (1,862) of the sample's delinquent youths were repeat offenders, whereas the remaining 46 percent (1,613) were one-time offenders. The repeaters could be further categorized as nonchronic recidivists and chronic recidivists. The former consisted of 1,235 youths who had been arrested more than once but fewer than five times and who made up 35.6 percent of all delinquents. The latter were a group of 627 boys arrested five times or more, who accounted for 18 percent of the delinquents and 6 percent of the total sample of 9,945.

The chronic career criminals (known today as "the chronic 6 percent") were involved in the most dramatic amounts of delinquent behavior. They were responsible for 5,305 offenses, or 51.9 percent of all the offenses committed by the cohort. Even more striking was the involvement of chronic offenders in serious criminal acts. Of the entire sample, they committed 71 percent of the homicides, 73 percent of the rapes, 82 percent of the robberies, and 69 percent of the aggravated assaults.

Wolfgang and his associates found that arrests and court experience did little to deter the chronic offender. In fact, punishment was inversely related to chronic offending: The more stringent the sanction chronic offenders received, the more likely they would be to engage in repeated criminal behavior.

In a second cohort study, Wolfgang and his associates selected a new, larger birth cohort, born in Philadelphia in 1958, which contained both male and female subjects.[94] Although the proportion of delinquent youths was about the same as that in the 1945 cohort, they found a similar pattern of chronic offending. Chronic female delinquency was relatively rare—only 1 percent of the females in the survey were chronic offenders. Wolfgang's pioneering effort to identify the chronic career offender has been replicated by a number of other researchers in a variety of locations in the United States.[95] The chronic offender has also been found abroad.[96]

Who Are Career Criminals? Who is at risk of becoming a career criminal? As might be expected, kids who have been exposed to a variety of personal and social problems at an early age are the most at risk to repeat offending. Other research studies have found that involvement in criminal activity (for example, getting arrested before age 15), relatively low intellectual development, and parental drug involvement were key predictive factors for chronicity.[97] Children who are found to be disruptive and antisocial as early as age 5 or 6 are the most likely to exhibit stable, long-term patterns of disruptive behavior throughout adolescence.[98] They have measurable behavior problems in areas such as learning and motor skills, cognitive abilities, family relations, and other areas of social, psychological, and physical functioning.[99] Youthful offenders who persist are more likely to abuse alcohol, become economically dependent, have lower aspirations, and have a weak employment record.[100] They do not specialize in one type of crime; instead, they engage in a variety of criminal acts, including theft, drugs, and violent offenses.

three strikes laws
Sentencing codes that require that an offender receive a life sentence after conviction for a third felony. Some states allow parole after a lengthy prison stay, for example, 25 years.

Implications of the Career Criminal Concept Concern about repeat offenders has been translated into programs at various stages of the justice process. For example, police departments and district attorneys' offices around the nation have set up programs to focus resources on capturing and prosecuting dangerous or repeat offenders.[101] Legal jurisdictions are developing sentencing policies designed to incapacitate chronic offenders for long periods of time without hope of probation or parole. Among the policies spurred by the chronic offender concept are mandatory sentences for violent or drug-related crimes and **three strikes laws,** which require people convicted of a third felony offense to serve a mandatory life sentence. Whether such policies can reduce crime rates or are merely get-tough measures designed to placate conservative voters remains to be seen.

Perspectives on Justice

The discovery of the chronic offender was a key element in the development of sentences that provide extended terms for repeat offenders. It stands to reason that if only a few hard-core offenders commit most crimes, locking them up for life can have a dramatic effect on the crime rate. This is a cornerstone of the crime control model.

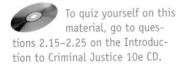 To quiz yourself on this material, go to questions 2.15–2.25 on the Introduction to Criminal Justice 10e CD.

Summary

- The three primary sources of crime statistics are the Uniform Crime Reports based on police data accumulated by the FBI, self-reports from criminal behavior surveys, and victim surveys.
- These sources reveal significant levels of crime in the United States, although the amount of violent crime is decreasing.
- Each data source has its strengths and weaknesses, and although different from one another, they agree on the nature of criminal behavior.
- The data sources show stable patterns in the crime rate. Ecological patterns show that some areas of the country are more crime-prone than others, that there are seasons and times for crime, and that these patterns are stable.
- Evidence also exists of gender and age gaps in the crime rate: Men commit more crime than women,

  and young people commit more crime than the elderly.
- Crime data show that people commit less crime as they age, but the significance and cause of this pattern is still not completely understood.
- Racial and class patterns appear in the crime rate. However, whether these are true differences or a function of discriminatory law enforcement remains unclear.
- One of the most important findings in the crime statistics is the existence of the chronic offender, a repeat career criminal responsible for a significant amount of all law violations. Career criminals begin their careers early in life and, instead of aging out of crime, persist into adulthood.

Key Terms

Doing Research on the Web

For an up-to-date list of Web links, go to http://cj.wadsworth.com/siegel_intro10e.

Eric Rudolph's criminal acts might be classified as hate crimes. Each state defines this type of crime differently. Here is a section of California's hate crime statute.

California PENAL CODE

SECTION 422.6

422.6. (a) No person, whether or not acting under color of law, shall by force or threat of force, willfully injure, intimidate, interfere with, oppress, or threaten any other person in the free exercise or enjoyment of any right or privilege secured to him or her by the Constitution or laws of this state or by the Constitution or laws of the United States because of the other person's race, color, religion, ancestry, national origin, disability, gender, or sexual orientation, or because he or she perceives that the other person has one or more of those characteristics.

Search the Web for sites that discuss hate crimes. This one contains the laws of most states and other information: http://www.religiousfreedomwatch.org/.

This site provides general information and many links: http://www.hatecrime.net/.

You might also use "hate crime" as a subject guide on InfoTrac College Edition.

Pro/Con discussions and Viewpoint Essays on some of the topics in this chapter may be found at the Opposing Viewpoints Resource Center: http://www.gale.com/OpposingViewpoints.

Discussion Questions

1. Would you answer honestly if a national crime survey asked you about your criminal behavior, including drinking and drug use? If not, why not? If you said "no," do you question the accuracy of self-report surveys?
2. How would you explain gender differences in the crime rate? Why do you think males are more violent than females?
3. Assuming that males are more violent than females, does that mean crime has a biological as opposed to a social basis (because males and females share a similar environment)?
4. The UCR states that crime rates are higher in large cities than in small towns. What does that say about the effects of TV, films, and music on teenage behavior?
5. What social and environmental factors do you believe influence the crime rate? For example, do you think a national emergency such as the September 11, 2001, terrorist attacks will increase or decrease crime rates?
6. If the characteristics of chronic offenders could be determined, should people with those traits be monitored from birth?

Notes

1 Information on the Rudolph case can be obtained at http://www.cnn.com/2003/US/05/31/rudolph.arrest/http://www.belleville.com/mld/newsdemocrat/6027216.htm.
2 Federal Bureau of Investigation, *Crime in the United States, 2001* (Washington, D.C.: Government Printing Office, 2002). Updated with preliminary 2002 data.
3 Richard Felson, Steven Messner, Anthony Hoskin, and Glenn Deane, "Reasons for Reporting and Not Reporting Domestic Violence to the Police," *Criminology* 40 (2002): 617–48.
4 Callie Marie Rennison and Michael Rand, *Criminal Victimization 2002* (Washington, D.C.: Bureau of Justice Statistics, 2003).
5 Duncan Chappell, Gilbert Geis, Stephen Schafer, and Larry Siegel, "Forcible Rape: A Comparative Study of Offenses Known to the Police in Boston and Los Angeles," in *Studies in the Sociology of Sex,* ed. James Henslin (New York: Appleton Century Crofts, 1971), pp. 169–93.

6 Patrick Jackson, "Assessing the Validity of Official Data on Arson," *Criminology* 26 (1988): 181–95.
7 Robert O'Brien, "Police Productivity and Crime Rates: 1973–1992," *Criminology* 34 (1996): 183–207.
8 FBI, *UCR Handbook* (Washington, D.C.: Government Printing Office, 1998), p. 33.
9 Roger Hood and Richard Sparks, *Key Issues in Criminology* (New York: McGraw-Hill, 1970), p. 72.
10 Data in this section come from Rennison and Rand, *Criminal Victimization 2002.*
11 L. Edward Wells and Joseph Rankin, "Juvenile Victimization: Convergent Validation of Alternative Measurements," *Journal of Research in Crime and Delinquency* 32 (1995): 287–307.
12 See, for example, Spencer Rathus and Larry Siegel, "Crime and Personality Revisited: Effects of MMPI Sets on Self-Report Studies," *Criminology* 18 (1980): 245–51; John Clark and Larry Tifft, "Polygraph and Interview Validation of Self-

Reported Deviant Behavior," *American Sociological Review* 31 (1966): 516–23.
13 Mallie Paschall, Miriam Ornstein, and Robert Flewelling, "African American Male Adolescents' Involvement in the Criminal Justice System: The Criterion Validity of Self-Report Measures in Prospective Study," *Journal of Research in Crime and Delinquency* 38 (2001): 174–87.
14 Clark and Tifft, "Polygraph and Interview Validation of Self-Reported Deviant Behavior."
15 David Farrington, Rolf Loeber, Magda Stouthamer-Loeber, Welmoet Van Kammen, and Laura Schmidt, "Self-Reported Delinquency and a Combined Delinquency Seriousness Scale Based on Boys, Mothers, and Teachers: Concurrent and Predictive Validity for African Americans and Caucasians," *Criminology* 34 (1996): 501–25.
16 Leonore Simon, "Validity and Reliability of Violent Juveniles: A Comparison of Juvenile Self-Reports with Adult Self-Reports Incarcerated in Adult Prisons," paper presented at the annual meeting of the American

Society of Criminology, Boston, Massachusetts, November 1995, p. 26.

17 Stephen Cernkovich, Peggy Giordano, and Meredith Pugh, "Chronic Offenders: The Missing Cases in Self-Report Delinquency Research," *Journal of Criminal Law and Criminology* 76 (1985): 705–32.

18 Terence Thornberry, Beth Bjerregaard, and William Miles, "The Consequences of Respondent Attrition in Panel Studies: A Simulation Based on the Rochester Youth Development Study," *Journal of Quantitative Criminology* 9 (1993): 127–58.

19 Alfred Blumstein, Jacqueline Cohen, and Richard Rosenfeld, "Trend and Deviation in Crime Rates: A Comparison of UCR and NCVS Data for Burglary and Robbery," *Criminology* 29 (1991): 237–48. See also Michael Hindelang, Travis Hirschi, and Joseph Weis, *Measuring Delinquency* (Beverly Hills, Calif.: Sage, 1981).

20 Clarence Schrag, *Crime and Justice: American Style* (Washington, D.C.: Government Printing Office, 1971), p. 17.

21 Thomas Bernard, "Juvenile Crime and the Transformation of Juvenile Justice: Is There a Juvenile Crime Wave?" *Justice Quarterly* 16 (1999): 336–56.

22 Federal Bureau of Investigation, *Crime in the United States, 2002* (Washington, D.C.: Government Printing Office, 2003).

23 For example, the following studies have noted the great discrepancy between official statistics and self-report studies: Martin Gold, "Undetected Delinquent Behavior," *Journal of Research in Crime and Delinquency* 3 (1966): 27–46; James Short and F. Ivan Nye, "Extent of Undetected Delinquency, Tentative Conclusions," *Journal of Criminal Law, Criminology, and Police Science* 49 (1958): 296–302; Michael Hindelang, "Causes of Delinquency: A Partial Replication and Extension," *Social Problems* 20 (1973): 471–87.

24 D. Wayne Osgood, Lloyd Johnston, Patrick O'Malley, and Jerald Bachman, "The Generality of Deviance in Late Adolescence and Early Adulthood," *American Sociological Review* 53 (1988): 81–93.

25 Lloyd Johnston, Patrick O'Malley, and Jerald Bachman, *Monitoring the Future, 1990* (Ann Arbor, Mich.: Institute for Social Research, 1991); Timothy Flanagan and Kathleen Maguire, *Sourcebook of Criminal Justice Statistics, 1989* (Washington, D.C.: Government Printing Office, 1990), pp. 290–91.

26 James A. Fox, *Trends in Juvenile Violence: A Report to the United States Attorney General on Current and Future Rates of Juvenile Offending* (Boston, Mass.: Northeastern University, 1996).

27 Steven Levitt, "The Limited Role of Changing Age Structure in Explaining Aggregate Crime Rates," *Criminology* 37 (1999): 581–99.

28 Ellen Cohn, "The Effect of Weather and Temporal Variations on Calls for Police Service," *American Journal of Police* 15 (1996): 23–43.

29 See, generally, Franklin Zimring and Gordon Hawkins, *Crime Is Not the Problem: Lethal Violence in America* (New York: Oxford University Press, 1997).

30 Ibid., p. 36.

31 Matthew Miller, Deborah Azrael, and David Hemenway, "Rates of Household Firearm Ownership and Homicide across U.S. Regions and States, 1988–1997," *American Journal of Public Health* 92 (2002): 1988–94.

32 Robert Nash Parker, "Bringing 'Booze' Back In: The Relationship between Alcohol and Homicide," *Journal of Research in Crime and Delinquency* 32 (1995): 3–38.

33 Victoria Brewer and M. Dwayne Smith, "Gender Inequality and Rates of Female Homicide Victimization across U.S. Cities," *Journal of Research in Crime and Delinquency* 32 (1995): 175–90.

34 Short and Nye, "Extent of Undetected Delinquency."

35 Ivan Nye, James Short, and Virgil Olsen, "Socioeconomic Status and Delinquent Behavior," *American Journal of Sociology* 63 (1958): 381–89; Robert Dentler and Lawrence Monroe, "Social Correlates of Early Adolescent Theft," *American Sociological Review* 63 (1961): 733–43. See also Terence Thornberry and Margaret Farnworth, "Social Correlates of Criminal Involvement: Further Evidence of the Relationship between Social Status and Criminal Behavior," *American Sociological Review* 47 (1982): 505–18.

36 Charles Tittle, Wayne Villemez, and Douglas Smith, "The Myth of Social Class and Criminality: An Empirical Assessment of the Empirical Evidence," *American Sociological Review* 43 (1978): 643–56.

37 Charles Tittle and Robert Meier, "Specifying the SES/Delinquency Relationship," *Criminology* 28 (1990): 271–301.

38 R. Gregory Dunaway, Francis Cullen, Velmer Burton, and T. David Evans, "The Myth of Social Class and Crime Revisited: An Examination of Class and Adult Criminality," *Criminology* 38 (2000): 589–632.

39 Delbert Elliott and Suzanne Ageton, "Reconciling Race and Class Differences in Self-Reported and Official Estimates of Delinquency," *American Sociological Review* 45 (1980): 95–110.

40 See also Delbert Elliott and David Huizinga, "Social Class and Delinquent Behavior in a National Youth Panel: 1976–1980," *Criminology* 21 (1983): 149–77. For a similar view, see John Braithwaite, "The Myth of Social Class and Criminality Reconsidered," *American Sociological Review* 46 (1981): 35–58; Hindelang, Hirschi, and Weis, *Measuring Delinquency*, p. 196.

41 David Brownfield, "Social Class and Violent Behavior," *Criminology* 24 (1986): 421–39.

42 Douglas Smith and Laura Davidson, "Interfacing Indicators and Constructs in Criminological Research: A Note on the Comparability of Self-Report Violence Data for Race and Sex Groups," *Criminology* 24 (1986): 473–88.

43 Dunaway, Cullen, Burton, and Evans, "The Myth of Social Class and Crime Revisited."

44 Sally Simpson and Lori Elis, "Doing Gender: Sorting Out the Case and Crime Conundrum," *Criminology* 33 (1995): 47–81.

45 Judith Blau and Peter Blau, "The Cost of Inequality: Metropolitan Structure and Violent Crime," *American Sociological Review* 147 (1982): 114–29; Richard Block, "Community Environment and Violent Crime," *Criminology* 17 (1979): 46–57; Robert Sampson, "Structural Sources of Variation in Race-Age-Specific Rates of Offending across Major U.S. Cities," *Criminology* 23 (1985): 647–73.

46 Chin-Chi Hsieh and M. D. Pugh, "Poverty, Income Inequality, and Violent Crime: A Meta-Analysis of Recent Aggregate Data Studies," *Criminal Justice Review* 18 (1993): 182–99.

47 Richard Miech, Avshalom Caspi, Terrie Moffitt, Bradley Entner Wright, and Phil Silva, "Low Socioeconomic Status and Mental Disorders: A Longitudinal Study of Selection and Causation during Young Adulthood," *American Journal of Sociology* 104 (1999): 1096–1131; Marvin Krohn, Alan Lizotte, and Cynthia Perez, "The Interrelationship between Substance Use and Precocious Transitions to Adult Sexuality," *Journal of Health and Social Behavior* 38 (1997): 87–103, at 88; Richard Jessor, "Risk Behavior in Adolescence: A Psychosocial Framework for Understanding and Action," in *Adolescents at Risk: Medical and Social Perspectives,* ed. D. E. Rogers and E. Ginzburg (Boulder, Colo.: Westview, 1992).

48 Travis Hirschi and Michael Gottfredson, "Age and the Explanation of Crime," *American Journal of Sociology* 89 (1983): 552–84, at 581.

49 Darrell Steffensmeier and Cathy Streifel, "Age, Gender, and Crime across Three Historical Periods: 1935, 1960, and 1985," *Social Forces* 69 (1991): 869–94.

50 For a comprehensive review of crime and the elderly, see Kyle Kercher, "Causes and Correlates of Crime Committed by the Elderly," in *Critical Issues in Aging Policy,* ed. E. Borgatta and R. Montgomery (Beverly Hills, Calif.: Sage, 1987), pp. 254–306; Darrell Steffensmeier, "The Invention of the 'New' Senior Citizen Criminal," *Research on Aging* 9 (1987): 281–311.

51 Cesare Lombroso, *The Female Offender* (New York: Appleton, 1920), p. 122.

52 Otto Pollack, *The Criminality of Women* (Philadelphia: University of Pennsylvania, 1950).

53 For a review of this issue, see Darrell Steffensmeier, "Assessing the Impact of the Women's Movement on Sex-Based Differences in the Handling of Adult Criminal Defendants," *Crime and Delinquency* 26 (1980): 344–57.

54 Alan Booth and D. Wayne Osgood, "The Influence of Testosterone on Deviance in Adulthood: Assessing and Explaining the Relationship," *Criminology* 31 (1993): 93–118.

55 Daniel Mears, Matthew Ploeger, and Mark Warr, "Explaining the Gender Gap in Delinquency: Peer Influence and Moral Evaluations of Behavior," *Journal of Research in Crime and Delinquency* 35 (1998): 251–66.

56 Gisela Konopka, *The Adolescent Girl in Conflict* (Englewood Cliffs, N.J.: Prentice-Hall, 1966); Clyde Vedder and Dora Somerville, *The Delinquent Girl* (Springfield, Ill.: Charles C. Thomas, 1970).

57 Emily Gaarder and Joanne Belknap, "Tenuous Borders: Girls Transferred to Adult Court," *Criminology* 40 (2002): 481–517.

58 Freda Adler, *Sisters in Crime* (New York: McGraw-Hill, 1975); Rita James Simon, *The Contemporary Woman and Crime* (Washington, D.C.: Government Printing Office, 1975).

59 David Rowe, Alexander Vazsonyi, and Daniel Flannery, "Sex Differences in Crime: Do Mean and Within-Sex Variation Have Similar Causes?" *Journal of Research in Crime and Delinquency* 32 (1995): 84–100;

Michael Hindelang, "Age, Sex, and the Versatility of Delinquency Involvements," *Social Forces* 14 (1971): 525–34; Martin Gold, *Delinquent Behavior in an American City* (Belmont, Calif.: Brooks/Cole, 1970); Gary Jensen and Raymond Eve, "Sex Differences in Delinquency: An Examination of Popular Sociological Explanations," *Criminology* 13 (1976): 427–48.

60 Darrell Steffensmeier and Renee Hoffman Steffensmeier, "Trends in Female Delinquency," *Criminology* 18 (1980): 62–85. See also Darrell Steffensmeier and Renee Hoffman Steffensmeier, "Crime and the Contemporary Woman: An Analysis of Changing Levels of Female Property Crime, 1960–1975," *Social Forces* 57 (1978): 566–84; Joseph Weis, "Liberation and Crime: The Invention of the New Female Criminal," *Crime and Social Justice* 1 (1976): 17–27; Carol Smart, "The New Female Offender: Reality or Myth," *British Journal of Criminology* 19 (1979): 50–59; Steven Box and Chris Hale, "Liberation/Emancipation, Economic Marginalization or Less Chivalry," *Criminology* 22 (1984): 473–78.

61 Meda Chesney-Lind, "Female Offenders: Paternalism Reexamined," in *Women, the Courts and Equality,* ed. Laura Crites and Winifred Hepperle (Newbury Park, Calif.: Sage, 1987), pp. 114–39, at 115.

62 Anne Campbell, Steven Muncer, and Daniel Bibel, "Female–Female Criminal Assault: An Evolutionary Perspective," *Journal of Research in Crime and Delinquency* 35 (1998): 413–28.

63 Finn-Aage Esbensen and Elizabeth Piper Deschenes, "A Multisite Examination of Youth Gang Membership: Does Gender Matter?" *Criminology* 36 (1998): 799–828.

64 Leroy Gould, "Who Defines Delinquency: A Comparison of Self-Report and Officially Reported Indices of Delinquency for Three Racial Groups," *Social Problems* 16 (1969): 325–36; Harwin Voss, "Ethnic Differentials in Delinquency in Honolulu," *Journal of Criminal Law, Criminology, and Police Science* 54 (1963): 322–27; Ronald Akers, Marvin Krohn, Marcia Radosevich, and Lonn Lanza-Kaduce, "Social Characteristics and Self-Reported Delinquency," in *Sociology of Delinquency,* ed. Gary Jensen (Beverly Hills, Calif.: Sage, 1981), pp. 48–62.

65 Institute for Social Research, *Monitoring the Future* (Ann Arbor, Mich.:2000).

66 Paul Tracy, "Race and Class Differences in Official and Self-Reported Delinquency," in *From Boy to Man, from Delinquency to Crime,* ed. Marvin Wolfgang, Terence Thornberry, and Robert Figlio (Chicago: University of Chicago Press, 1987), p. 120.

67 Phillipe Rushton, "Race and Crime: An International Dilemma," *Society* 32 (1995): 37–42; for a rebuttal, see Jerome Neapolitan, "Cross-National Variation in Homicides: Is Race a Factor?" *Criminology* 36 (1998): 139–56.

68 Miriam Sealock and Sally Simpson, "Unraveling Bias in Arrest Decisions: The Role of Juvenile Offender Type-Scripts," *Justice Quarterly* 15 (1998): 427–57.

69 "Law Enforcement Seeks Answers to 'Racial Profiling' Complaints," *Criminal Justice Newsletter* 29 (1998): 5.

70 Stewart J. D'Alessio and Lisa Stolzenberg, "Race and the Probability of Arrest," *Social Forces* 81 (2003): 1381–97.

71 Barry Sample and Michael Philip, "Perspectives on Race and Crime in Research and Planning," in *The Criminal Justice System and Blacks,* ed. D. Georges-Abeyie (New York: Clark Boardman, 1984), pp. 21–36.

72 Candace Kruttschnitt, "Violence by and against Women: A Comparative and Cross-National Analysis," *Violence and Victims* 8 (1994): 4.

73 James Comer, "Black Violence and Public Policy," in *American Violence and Public Policy,* ed. Lynn Curtis (New Haven: Yale University Press, 1985), pp. 63–86.

74 Michael Leiber and Jayne Stairs, "Race, Contexts, and the Use of Intake Diversion," *Journal of Research in Crime and Delinquency* 36 (1999): 56–86; Darrell Steffensmeier, Jeffery Ulmer, and John Kramer, "The Interaction of Race, Gender, and Age in Criminal Sentencing: The Punishment Cost of Being Young, Black, and Male," *Criminology* 36 (1998): 763–98.

75 Rodney Engen, Sara Steen, and George Bridges, "Racial Disparities in the Punishment of Youth: A Theoretical and Empirical Assessment of the Literature," *Social Problems* 49 (2002): 194-221.

76 Tracy Nobiling, Cassia Spohn, and Miriam DeLone, "A Tale of Two Counties: Unemployment and Sentence Severity," *Justice Quarterly* 15 (1998): 459–86.

77 Alexander Weiss and Steven Chermak, "The News Value of African American Victims: An Examination of the Media's Presentation of Homicide," *Journal of Crime and Justice* 21 (1998): 71–84.

78 David Eitle, Stewart J. D'Alessio, and Lisa Stolzenberg, "Racial Threat and Social Control: A Test of the Political, Economic, and Threat of Black Crime Hypotheses," *Social Forces* 81 (2002): 557–77.

79 *The Sentencing Project, Losing the Vote: The Impact of Felony Disenfranchisement Laws in the United States* (Washington, D.C.: Sentencing Project, 1998).

80. Ronald Weitzer and Steven Tuch, "Race, Class, and Perceptions of Discrimination by the Police," *Crime and Delinquency* 45 (1999): 494–507.

81 Karen Parker and Patricia McCall, "Structural Conditions and Racial Homicide Patterns: A Look at the Multiple Disadvantages in Urban Areas," *Criminology* 37 (1999): 447–69.

82 David Jacobs and Katherine Woods, "Interracial Conflict and Interracial Homicide: Do Political and Economic Rivalries Explain White Killings of Blacks or Black Killings of Whites?" *American Journal of Sociology* 105 (1999): 157–90.

83 Melvin Thomas, "Race, Class, and Personal Income: An Empirical Test of the Declining Significance of Race Thesis, 1968–1988," *Social Problems* 40 (1993): 328–39.

84 Gary LaFree, Kriss Drass, and Patrick O'Day, "Race and Crime in Postwar America: Determinants of African American and White Rates, 1957–1988," *Criminology* 30 (1992): 157–88.

85 Mallie Paschall, Robert Flewelling, and Susan Ennett, "Racial Differences in Violent Behavior among Young Adults: Moderating and Confounding Effects," *Journal of Research in Crime and Delinquency* 35 (1998): 148–65.

86 Julie Phillips, "White, Black, and Latino Homicide Rates: Why the Difference?" *Social Problems* 49 (2002): 349–74.

87 R. Kelly Raley, "A Shortage of Marriageable Men? A Note on the Role of Cohabitation in Black-White Differences in Marriage Rates," *American Sociological Review* 61 (1996): 973–83.

88 Julie Phillips, "Variation in African American Homicide Rates: An Assessment of Potential Explanations," *Criminology* 35 (1997): 527–59.

89 Thomas Mcnulty and Paul Bellair, "Explaining Racial and Ethnic Differences in Adolescent Violence: Structural Disadvantage, Family Well-Being, and Social Capital," *Justice Quarterly* 20 (2003): 1–32.

90 Roy Austin, "Progress toward Racial Equality and Reduction of Black Criminal Violence," *Journal of Criminal Justice* 15 (1987): 437–59.

91 Reynolds Farley and William Frey, "Changes in the Segregation of Whites from Blacks during the 1980s: Small Steps toward a More Integrated Society," *American Sociological Review* 59 (1994): 23–45.

92 Marvin Wolfgang, Robert Figlio, and Thorsten Sellin, *Delinquency in a Birth Cohort* (Chicago: University of Chicago Press, 1972).

93 See Thorsten Sellin and Marvin Wolfgang, *The Measurement of Delinquency* (New York: Wiley, 1964), p. 120.

94 The following sections rely heavily on Paul Tracy and Robert Figlio, "Chronic Recidivism in the 1958 Birth Cohort," paper presented at the annual meeting of the American Society of Criminology, Toronto, Canada, October 1982; Marvin Wolfgang, "Delinquency in Two Birth Cohorts," in *Perspective Studies of Crime and Delinquency,* ed. Katherine Teilmann Van Dusen and Sarnoff Mednick (Boston: Kluwer-Nijhoff, 1983), pp. 7–17.

95 Lyle Shannon, *Criminal Career Opportunity* (New York: Human Sciences Press, 1988).

96 D. J. West and David P. Farrington, *The Delinquent Way of Life* (London: Hienemann, 1977).

97 Peter Jones, Philip Harris, James Fader, and Lori Grubstein, "Identifying Chronic Juvenile Offenders," *Justice Quarterly* 18 (2001): 478–507.

98 R. Tremblay, R. Loeber, C. Gagnon, P. Charlebois, S. Larivee, and M. LeBlanc, "Disruptive Boys with Stable and Unstable High Fighting Behavior Patterns during Junior Elementary School," *Journal of Abnormal Child Psychology* 19 (1991): 285–300.

99 Jennifer White, Terrie Moffitt, Felton Earls, Lee Robins, and Phil Silva, "How Early Can We Tell? Predictors of Childhood Conduct Disorder and Adolescent Delinquency," *Criminology* 28 (1990): 507–35.

100 Kimberly Kempf-Leonard, Paul Tracy, and James Howell, "Serious, Violent, and Chronic Juvenile Offenders: The Relationship of Delinquency Career Types to Adult Criminality," *Justice Quarterly* 18 (2001): 449–78.

101 Susan Martin, "Policing Career Criminals: An Examination of an Innovative Crime Control Program," *Journal of Criminal Law and Criminology* 77 (1986): 1159–82.

Chapter Outline

Chapter Objectives

After reading this chapter, you should be able to:

1. Describe the problems of violent and economic crimes and substance abuse.
2. Know the reasons that crime seems rational.
3. Recognize the differences between general and specific deterrence.
4. Understand the concept of situational crime prevention.
5. Discuss the biological factors linked to crime.
6. Recognize that psychological factors are related to crime.
7. Describe the relationship between media and violence.
8. Discuss why social and economic factors influence the crime rate.
9. Recognize the sociocultural factors associated with crime.
10. Identify the socialization factors related to crime.
11. Explain how social conflict leads to crime.
12. Understand the concept of human development and crime.
13. Discuss the behavior patterns that increase the chances of becoming a crime victim.

Viewpoints

 Images of Justice: The Media and Violence   90

 Analyzing Criminal Justice Issues: Emerge   92

 Race, Gender, and Ethnicity in Criminal Justice: Building a Bridge over the Racial Divide   98

Web Links

InfoTrac College Edition Links

Chapter 3 | Understanding Crime and Victimization

On July 1, 2003, Chante Mallard, 27, received 50 years for the murder of Gregory Biggs and 10 years for tampering with evidence; she will be eligible for parole in 2028. On October 27, 2001, after a night of clubbing and drug use, Mallard headed home in her 1997 Chevrolet Cavalier with Ecstasy still in her system. As she was rounding a curve, she struck Biggs with her car and drove home with him stuck in her windshield. Because she was too "scared," "ashamed," and "out of control" on Ecstasy to seek help, she did not call the police or emergency services. When Mallard did phone for help, it was to her friend Titilisee Fry. Fry cautioned Mallard against contacting the police, warning that she could be implicated on charges of illegal drug use. Without help or care, Biggs bled to death in Mallard's garage. After

her trial, Mallard said: "I have ruined lives of other people, I have ruined my family's lives, and I have put people through pain, and I am truly sorry."[1]

View the CNN video clip of this story on your Introduction to Criminal Justice 10e CD.

Crime in the United States

Crimes such as the one committed by Chante Mallard have become an all-too-familiar and disturbing aspect of life in the United States. Both the poor and the affluent engage in criminal activity. Crime cuts across racial, class, and gender lines. It involves some acts that shock the conscience such as the Mallard case and others that may seem to be relatively harmless human foibles.

Criminal acts may be the work of strangers, so-called predatory criminals who care little for the lives of their victims. In contrast, many crimes—including date rape and spouse, child, elderly, and sexual abuse—involve family members, friends, or trusted associates. Such acts are referred to as intimate violence.

Surveys indicate that people fear crime and are suspicious of the criminal justice system's ability to reduce its incidence. What are the major forms of crime that concern most Americans?

Violent Crime

Americans are bombarded with television news stories and newspaper articles featuring grisly accounts of violent gangs, terrorism, serial murder, child abuse, and rape. Although rates of violent crime have declined significantly, violence rates in the United States still exceed those of most other industrialized nations. What are the forms of violence that most people fear?

Gang Violence   After remaining dormant for many years, organized youth gangs today terrorize neighborhoods in urban communities around the United States. From Boston to Los Angeles, gangs have become actively involved in drug distribution, extortion, and violence.

Whereas youth gangs once relied on group loyalty and emotional involvement with neighborhood turf to encourage membership, modern gangs seem more motivated by the quest for drug profits and street power. It is common for drug cliques to form within gangs or for established drug dealers to make use of gang bangers for protection and distribution services. As a consequence, gang-related killings have become so commonplace that the term *gang homicide* is now recognized as a separate and unique category of criminal behavior.[2]

At one time, gang activity was restricted to the nation's largest cities, especially Philadelphia, New York, Detroit, Los Angeles, and Chicago. These cities still have large gang populations, but today smaller and medium-size cities—such as Cleveland and Columbus, Ohio, and Milwaukee, Wisconsin—also have been the locus of gang activity. One reason that gang populations are swelling is that established urban gang members migrate to other locales to set up local branches.

The most recent surveys indicate that active in the United States are more than 24,000 gangs, with more than 750,000 gang members. Larger cities with a population of more than 250,000 were the most likely to report persistent gang activity, while smaller cities with populations of between 25,000 and 50,000 experienced some decline in gang numbers.[3] While the number of gang members in smaller cities seems to be on the decline, membership is still rising in larger communities where the bulk of gang members reside.[4]

Serial and Mass Murder   On April 20th, 1999, the nation's most deadly school shooting occurred at Columbine High School in Littleton, Colorado. Two heavily armed students, Eric Harris, 18, and Dylan Klebold, 17, members of a secretive student group called the "Trenchcoat Mafia," went on a shooting spree that claimed the lives of 12 students and one teacher and wounded 24 others, many seriously. As police SWAT (Special Weapons and Tactics) teams closed in, the two boys committed suicide in the school library, leaving authorities to puzzle

Want to know more about gangs? To find out, go to the Office of Juvenile Justice Web site at http://ojjdp.ncjrs.org/pubs/gang.html.

Intimate violence is a sad but common occurrence in American society. Each of the three men shown here, Christian Longo, Robert Bryant, and Edward Morris, killed family members.

over the cause of their deadly act. Later their friends described Harris and Klebold as outsiders whose behavior may have been triggered by their perceived victimization at the hands of school athletes.[5]

Mass murderers, such as Klebold and Harris, and serial killers, such as Jeffrey Dahmer of Milwaukee, have become familiar to the American public.[6] The threat of the unknown, random, and deranged assailant has become a part of modern reality. One type of serial killer roams the country killing a particular type of victim, for example, girls with long brown hair; others, such as Richard Ramirez, the Satan-worshiping Los Angeles "Night Stalker," terrorize a city. A third type of serial murderer—such as hospital orderly Donald Harvey, who murdered 54 patients—kills so cunningly that many victims are dispatched before the authorities even realize that the deaths can be attributed to a single perpetrator. Mass murderers kill many victims in a single violent outburst; **spree killers** spread their murderous outburst over a few days or weeks.

There is no single explanation for serial or mass murder. Such widely disparate factors as mental illness, sexual frustration, neurological damage, child abuse and neglect, smothering maternal relationships, and childhood anxiety have been suggested as possible causes. However, most experts view serial killers as sociopaths who from early childhood demonstrated bizarre behavior (such as torturing animals), enjoy killing, are immune to their victims' suffering, and bask in the media limelight when caught.[7]

spree killer
A killer of multiple victims whose murders take place over a relatively short period of time.

Terrorism The bombing in Oklahoma City on April 19, 1995, made the country aware of the threat that domestic political terrorism presents to the public. The September 11, 2001, attacks thrust the nation into an international war against terrorist activities. Today terrorism comes in many forms, as described in Exhibit 3.1.

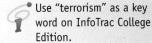
Use "terrorism" as a key word on InfoTrac College Edition.

Intimate Violence Although violent attacks by strangers produce the most fear and create the most graphic headlines, Americans face greater physical danger from people with whom they are in close and intimate contact: spouses, other relatives, and dating partners.

One area of intimate violence that has received a great deal of media attention is child abuse, which is any physical or emotional trauma to a child for which no reasonable explanation, such as an accident or ordinary disciplinary practices, can be found. Child abuse can result from physical beatings administered by hands, feet, weapons, belts, or sticks, or from burning.

An estimated 3 million cases of child abuse are reported to authorities each year. After investigation, less than half of reported cases are considered valid. The most recent national survey conducted by the U.S. Department of Health

© 2003 AP/Wide World Photos

Exhibit 3.1 Contemporary Forms of Terrorism

Revolutionary Terrorism

Revolutionary terrorists aim to replace the existing government with a regime that holds acceptable political or religious views. For example, fundamentalist Muslim groups in Egypt such as Jamaat al-Islamiyya Jihad, which is also known as Al-Gama'a al-Islamiyya (The Islamic Group), and Egyptian Islamic Jihad have attacked foreigners in an effort to sabotage the tourist industry, topple the secular government, and turn Egypt into an Islamic state. On November 17, 1997, more than 60 foreign tourists were killed in an attack by fundamentalist Muslim terrorists near the ruins of Luxor in Southern Egypt.

Political Terrorism

Political terrorists engage in a campaign of violence designed to suppress or destroy those people or groups who oppose the terrorists' political ideology or whom the terrorists define as a threat to their social and religious views and political leanings within their own homeland. In the United States, political terrorists tend to be heavily armed groups organized around such themes as white supremacy, militant tax resistance, and religious revisionism such as the Aryan Republican Army, Fourth Reich, Aryan Revolutionary Front, and Aryan Nation, whose aim is to topple the government that they view as protecting the rights of people and groups they oppose, for example, racial minorities and immigrants.

Nationalist Terrorism

Nationalist terrorists promote the interests of a minority ethnic or religious group that believes it has been persecuted under majority rule and wishes to carve out its own independent homeland. In the Middle East, terrorist activities have been linked to the Palestinians' desire to wrest their former homeland from Israel. In India, Sikh radicals have used violence to recover what they believe to be lost homelands in Kashmir. The Tamil Tigers are fighting for a separate homeland for minority Tamils in the north and east of Sri Lanka. Basque rebels have conducted terror attacks against the Spanish government.

Cause-Based Terrorism

Some terrorist organizations direct their activities against individuals and governments to whom they object to on economic, social, or religious grounds. They do not wish to carve out a homeland or replace the existing government of their own nation but simply destroy all those who oppose their view anywhere in the world. For example, Osama Bin Laden claims that he is conducting a jihad or holy war against the United States because American forces are operating in Saudi Arabia and elsewhere in the Middle East. His cause was based on Islamic tradition holding that it is not permissible for non-Muslims to serve as protectors in Saudi Arabia.

Environmental Terrorism

Environmental terrorists carry out raids against those who they consider to be a threat to the ecosystem. One prominent group, the Earth Liberation Front (ELF), seeks to inflict economic damage on those profiting from the destruction and exploitation of the natural environment; to reveal and educate the public on the atrocities committed against the earth and all species that populate it; and to take all necessary precautions against harming any animal, human and nonhuman. ELF has been active for several years in the United States and abroad and has conducted arson attacks on property ranging from a sport utility vehicles sales lot in Eugene, Oregon; a Nike shop in a shopping mall north of Minneapolis, Minnesota; and new homes on Long Island, New York.

State-Sponsored Terrorism

State-sponsored terrorism occurs when a repressive governmental regime forces its citizens into obedience, oppresses minorities, and stifles political dissent. Death squads and the use of government troops to destroy political opposition parties are often associated with Latin American political terrorism. When Tupac Amaru rebels seized and held hostages at the Japanese ambassadors' villa in Peru on December 17, 1996, the action came in response to a decade-long campaign of human rights violations by national security forces and extensive abuses against opposition groups. Between January 1983 and December 1992, more than 4,000 people disappeared in Peru following detention by the security forces.

Criminal Terrorism

Sometimes terrorist groups become involved in common law crimes such as drug dealing and kidnapping to fund their activities. These illegal activities may on occasion become so profitable that they replace the group's original focus. In some instances the line between being a terrorist organization with political support and vast resources and an organized criminal group engaging in illicit activities for profit becomes blurred. The greatest threat from criminal terrorism is the theft of nuclear material and its subsequent sale to other terrorist groups that will not hesitate to build and use weapons of mass destruction.

---

www→ You can read more about child abuse at the U.S. Department of Health and Human Services Web site: http://www.hhs.gov/children/index.shtml#family.

and Human Services found that approximately 903,000 children were victims of abuse and neglect in a single year (2001). While the rate of abuse has stabilized in recent years, about 12.4 children for every 1,000 children in the population were victims of some form of abuse or neglect.[8]

Regardless of how it is defined, the effects of abuse can be devastating. Children who have experienced some form of maltreatment have a devalued sense of self, a mistrust of others, a tendency toward attributing hostility toward others in situations where the intentions of others are ambiguous, a tendency to generate antagonistic solutions to social problems, and a suspicion of close relationships.[9]

Substance Abuse

The United States has been waging a "war on drugs" for some time. The most commonly abused substance, alcohol, is legal, easily obtained, and suspected of being involved in half of all U.S. murders, suicides, and accidental deaths. Alcohol-related deaths number 100,000 a year, far more than deaths by all illegal drugs combined. Strong links are found between alcohol abuse and violent crime and other antisocial behaviors. For example, drinking among college students is closely associated with episodes of assaultive behavior and vandalism.[10] Strong links also exist between alcohol consumption and certain types of homicide, especially those that occur during robberies and other criminal offenses.[11]

Although drug use has stabilized in the general population, it is still prevalent in the offender population—evidence of the association between drug use and crime. The federally sponsored Arrestee Drug Abuse Monitoring (ADAM) program, which drug-tests people who have been arrested, is active in 35 cities.[12] In its most recent report (2003), the ADAM survey showed that 64 percent or more of adult male arrestees had used at least one of five drugs: cocaine (crack or powder), marijuana, opiates, methamphetamine, or PCP (phencyclidine). Between about one-fourth and one-half of all adult male arrestees in the ADAM sites were found to have been at risk for dependence on drugs, but few had received treatment. Urinalysis also shows that a large percentage of women arrestees had used drugs, with cocaine and marijuana being the top choices.

Economic Crimes

Millions of property- and theft-related crimes occur each year. Most are the work of amateur or occasional criminals whose decision to steal is spontaneous and whose acts are unskilled, unplanned, and haphazard. Many thefts, ranging in seriousness from shoplifting to burglary, are committed by school-age youths who are unlikely to enter into a criminal career.

Added to the pool of amateur thieves are the millions of adults whose behavior may occasionally violate the criminal law—shoplifters, pilferers, tax cheats—but whose main source of income comes from conventional means and whose self-identity is noncriminal. Most of these property crimes occur when an immediate opportunity, or *situational inducement,* arises to commit crime.[13]

Professional thieves, in contrast, derive a significant portion of their income from crime. Professionals do not delude themselves that their acts are impulsive, one-time efforts. They also do not employ elaborate rationalizations to excuse the harmfulness of their action ("Shoplifting doesn't really hurt anyone"). Professionals pursue their craft with vigor, attempting to learn from older, experienced criminals the techniques that will earn them the most money with the least risk. Their numbers are relatively few, but professionals engage in crimes that produce greater losses to society and perhaps cause more significant social harm. Typical forms include pickpocketing, burglary, shoplifting, forgery and counterfeiting, extortion, and swindling.[14]

White-Collar Crime White-collar crime involves the criminal activities of people and institutions whose acknowledged purpose is profit through illegal business transactions. Included within white-collar crime are such acts as income tax evasion, credit card fraud, and bank fraud. White-collar criminals also use their positions of trust in business or government to commit crimes. Their activities might include soliciting bribes or kickbacks as well as embezzlement. Some white-collar

WWW The principal purpose of the Office of National Drug Control Policy is to establish policies, priorities, and objectives for the nation's drug control program, the goals of which are to reduce illicit drug use, manufacturing, and trafficking; drug-related crime and violence; and drug-related health consequences. To read more about its efforts, go to http://www.whitehousedrugpolicy.gov.

white-collar crime
White-collar crimes involve the violation of rules that control business enterprise. They can range from employee pilferage, bribery, commodities law violations, mail fraud, computer fraud, environmental law violations, embezzlement, Internet scams, extortion, forgery, insurance fraud, price fixing, and environmental pollution.

criminals set up businesses for the sole purpose of victimizing the general public. They engage in land swindles, securities theft, medical fraud, and so on. And, in addition to acting as individuals, some white-collar criminals become involved in criminal conspiracies designed to improve the market share or profitability of their corporations. This type of white-collar crime, which includes antitrust violations, price-fixing, and false advertising, is known as corporate crime.

It is difficult to estimate the extent and influence of white-collar crime on victims because victimologists often ignore those who suffer the consequences of such crime. Some experts place its total monetary value in the hundreds of billions of dollars. Beyond their monetary cost, white-collar crimes often damage property and kill people. Violations of safety standards, pollution of the environment, and industrial accidents due to negligence can be classified as corporate violence. White-collar crime also destroys confidence, saps the integrity of commercial life, and has the potential for devastating destruction.

An independent branch of white-collar crime involves the use of ultramodern technology to engage in fraudulent endeavors. In some instances, high-tech crimes involve the use of technology to commit common law crimes, for example, Internet fraud and identity theft. In other instances, the technology itself is the target, for example, illegal copying and sale of computer software. High-tech crimes cost consumers billions of dollars each year and will most likely increase dramatically in the years to come. For example, with the continuing growth of e-commerce, Internet credit card fraud alone will increase worldwide from $1.6 billion in 2000 to an estimated $15.5 billion by 2005.[15]

Organized Crime Organized crime involves the criminal activity of people and organizations whose acknowledged purpose is economic gain through illegal enterprise.[16] These criminal cartels provide those outlawed goods and services demanded by the general public: prostitution, narcotics, gambling, loan sharking, pornography, and untaxed liquor and cigarettes. In addition, organized criminals infiltrate legitimate organizations, such as unions, to drain off their funds and profits for illegal purposes.

Federal and state agencies have been dedicated to wiping out organized crime, and some well-publicized arrests have resulted in the imprisonment of important leaders. The membership of the traditional Italian and Irish crime families has dropped an estimated 50 percent over a 20-year period. New groups—including Russian and Eastern European, Hispanic, and African American gangs—have filled the vacuum created by federal prosecutors. For example, more than 2,000 Russian immigrants are believed to be involved in criminal activity, primarily in Russian enclaves in New York City. Beyond extortion from fellow Eastern European immigrants, Russian organized crime groups have engaged in narcotics trafficking, fencing stolen property, money laundering, and other traditional organized crime schemes.[17]

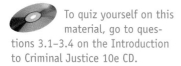
To quiz yourself on this material, go to questions 3.1–3.4 on the Introduction to Criminal Justice 10e CD.

The Cause of Crime

criminology
The scientific study of the nature, extent, cause, and control of criminal behavior.

Despite years of study and research, criminologists are still uncertain about why people commit crime or why some people become crime victims. One of the enduring goals of **criminology** is to develop an understanding of the nature and cause of crime and victimization. Without knowing why crime occurs, it would be difficult to create effective crime reduction programs. No one could be sure if efforts were being aimed at the proper audience or, if they were, whether the prevention efforts were the ones most likely to cause positive change. For example, a crime prevention program based on providing jobs for unemployed teenagers would be effective only if in fact crime is linked to unemployment.

Similarly, a plan to reduce prison riots by eliminating the sugar intake of inmates is feasible only if research shows a link between diet and violence.

Because They Want To: Choice Theory

One prominent view of criminality is that people choose to commit crime after weighing the potential benefits and consequences of their criminal act. They will commit a crime if they believe it will provide immediate benefits without the threat of long-term risks. For example, before concluding a drug sale, experienced traffickers will mentally balance the chances of making a large profit against the probability of being apprehended and punished for drug dealing. They know that most drug deals are not detected and that the potential for enormous, untaxed profits is great. They evaluate their lifestyle and determine how much cash they need to maintain their standard of living, which is usually extravagant. They may have borrowed to finance the drug deal, and their creditors are not usually reasonable if loans cannot be repaid promptly. They also realize that they could be the target of a sting operation by undercover agents and, if caught, will get a long mandatory sentence in a forbidding federal penitentiary. If the greedy culprits conclude that the potential for profits is great enough, their need for cash urgent, and the chances of apprehension minimal, they will carry out the deal. If, however, they believe that the transaction will bring them only a small profit and a large risk of apprehension and punishment, they may forgo the deal, believing it too risky. Crime, then, is a matter of rational decision making in which a motivated offender weighs the potential costs and benefits of crime before deciding to take action.

According to choice theory, to deter crime, punishment must be sufficiently strict, sure, and swift to outweigh any benefits of law violation. For example, a 30-year prison sentence should deter potential bank robbers, regardless of the amount of money in the bank's vault. However, no matter how severely the law punishes a criminal act, it will have little **deterrent** effect if potential law violators believe they have little chance of being caught or that the wheels of justice are slow and inefficient.

Rational Criminals

The decision to commit a specific crime, then, is a matter of personal decision making based on the evaluation of available information. For example, offenders are likely to desist from crime if they believe that their future criminal earnings will be relatively low and that attractive and legal opportunities to generate income are available.[18] In contrast, criminals may be motivated when they know people who have made big scores and are successful at crime. Although the prevailing wisdom is that "crime does not pay," a small but significant subset of criminals earn close to $50,000 a year from crime, and their success may help motivate other would-be offenders.[19] In this sense, rational choice is a function of a person's perception of conventional alternatives and opportunities.

The rational criminal may also decide to forgo or desist from illegal behaviors. Such criminals may fear apprehension and punishment—a target appears too well protected; the police in the area are very active; local judges have vowed to crack down on crime; they simply cannot find a safe site to break the law.[20]

Rational Crimes

That crime is rational can be observed in a wide variety of criminal events. White-collar and organized crime figures engage in elaborate and well-planned conspiracies, ranging from international drug deals to the looting of savings and loan

Organized criminals are getting into new forms of crime, including the smuggling of illegal aliens. Read about their activities at Tim Padgett, Hilary Hylton, and Dolly Mascarenas, "People Smugglers Inc.: Organized Coyote Mafias Want to Dominate the Transport of Illegal Immigrants to the U.S.," *Time International*, July 21, 2003.

deterrent
Preventing crime before it occurs by means of the threat of criminal sanctions.

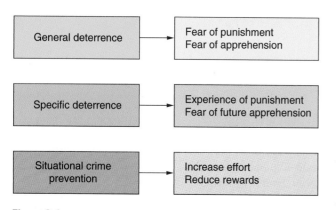

Figure 3.1
Preventing Crime

institutions. But even predatory street criminals exhibit stealth and planning in their criminal acts. Burglars may try to determine which homes are easy targets by reading newspaper stories about weddings or social events that mean the attendees' homes will be unguarded. They choose houses that are easily accessible and screened from public view and offer good escape routes—for example, at the end of a cul-de-sac abutting a wooded area. They target high-value homes that do not have burglar alarms or other security devices.[21] Burglars seem to prefer working between 9 a.m. and 11 a.m. and in midafternoon, when parents are either working or dropping off or picking up children at school. Burglars appear to monitor car and pedestrian traffic and avoid selecting targets on heavily traveled streets.[22]

Even violent criminals exhibit elements of rationality. For example, armed robbers choose targets close to their homes or in areas that they routinely travel. Familiarity with the area gives them knowledge of escape routes; this is referred to as their awareness space.[23] Robbers also report being wary of people who are watching the community for signs of trouble. Robbery levels are relatively low in neighborhoods where residents keep a watchful eye on their neighbors' property.[24] Robbers avoid freestanding buildings because they can more easily be surrounded by police. Others select targets that are known to do a primarily cash business, such as bars, supermarkets, and restaurants.[25]

If crime is a rational choice, how can it be prevented or controlled? See Figure 3.1.

Make 'Em Afraid I: The Concept of General Deterrence

If crime is a matter of choice, it follows that it can be controlled by convincing criminals that breaking the law is a bad or dangerous choice to make. If people believe that they are certain to be apprehended by the police, quickly tried, and severely penalized, they will most likely forgo any thought of breaking the law.[26] In other words, people will not choose crime if they fear legal punishment. This principle is referred to as **general deterrence.**

If the justice system could be made more effective, those who care little for the rights of others would be deterred by fear of the law's sanctioning power.[27] Only by reducing the benefits of crime through sure, swift, and certain punishment can society be sure that a group of new criminals will not emerge to replace the ones who have already been dealt with.[28]

Research shows that some people who report that they fear punishment will be deterred from committing certain crimes.[29] The prevailing wisdom is that the certainty of being punished is a greater deterrent to crime than the severity of punishment. In other words, people will more likely be deterred from crime if they believe that they will get caught. What happens to them after apprehension seems to have a lesser impact.[30]

While certain, not severe, punishment has some influence on crime, little hard evidence is yet available that fear of the law alone can be a general deterrent to crime.[31] Even the harshest punishment, the death penalty, appears to have little effect on the murder rate.[32] What factors inhibit the sanctioning power of the criminal law? One is the lack of efficiency of the justice system. About 20 percent of serious reported crimes result in an arrest. Relatively few criminals are eventually tried, convicted, and sentenced to prison. Chronic offenders and career criminals may believe that the risk of apprehension and imprisonment is limited and conclude that the certainty of punishment, a key element in deterrence, is minimal. Even if they do fear punishment, their anxiety may be neutralized by the be-

general deterrence
A crime control policy that depends on the fear of criminal penalties.

lief that a crime gives them a significant chance for large profit. When criminologists Alex Piquero and George Rengert interviewed active burglars, they were told that fear of capture and punishment was usually neutralized by the hope of making a big score. Greed overcomes fear.[33]

The concept of general deterrence assumes a rational criminal; that is, an offender who carefully weighs and balances the pains and benefits of the criminal act. However, a majority of arrested criminals are under the influence of drugs or alcohol at the time of their arrest. Many offenders, therefore, may be incapable of having the rational thought patterns upon which the concept of general deterrence rests. Relatively high rates of substance abuse, including alcohol and illegal drugs, may render even the harshest criminal penalties for violent crimes ineffective deterrents.[34]

In sum, the theory of rational choice predicts that criminals are calculating individuals who can be deterred by the threat of punishment. Research has so far failed to turn up clear and convincing evidence that the threat of punishment or its implementation can deter would-be criminals.

Perspectives on Justice

Rational choice theory is the philosophical cornerstone of the crime control perspective of justice. It has been used to justify the get-tough law-and-order approach that is predominant today. If criminals choose crime, then it follows that increasing the level of criminal punishment should deter and lower crime. Law enforcement agencies now establish task forces to locate and apprehend chronic offenders, prosecutors target career criminals, and state legislatures enact laws providing lengthy prison sentences for recidivists. Long prison sentences are believed to be the best way to keep repeaters out of circulation, to convince prospective offenders that crime does not pay, and to teach those who decide to commit crimes a lesson not soon forgotten.

Make 'Em Afraid II: Specific Deterrence

Even if the threat of punishment cannot deter would-be criminals, actual punishment at the hands of the justice system should be sufficient to convince arrested offenders never to repeat their criminal acts. If punishment were severe enough, a convicted criminal would never dare repeat his or her offense. What rational person would? This view is referred to as **specific deterrence.** Prior to the twentieth century, specific deterrence was a motive for the extreme tortures and physical punishments commonly used on convicted criminals. By breaking the convicts physically, legal authorities hoped to control their spirit and behavior.[35]

Although the more enlightened society in America today no longer uses such cruel and unusual punishments, long prison sentences, in dangerous and forbidding prisons, are imposed. Yet such measures do not seem to deliver the promise of crime control inherent in the specific deterrence concept. A majority of inmates repeat their criminal acts soon after returning to society, and most inmates have served time previously.[36]

Why have these punishments failed as a specific deterrent? Specific deterrence also assumes a rational criminal, someone who learns from experience. Many offenders could have impulsive personalities that interfere with their ability to learn from experience. And if they do learn, it may be from more experienced offenders who encourage them to commit crime once they are released. A majority of criminal offenders have lifestyles marked by heavy substance abuse, lack of formal education, and disturbed home lives, which inhibit conventional behavior. The pains of imprisonment and the stigma of a prison record do little

specific deterrence
Punishment severe enough to convince convicted offenders never to repeat their criminal activity.

According to the deterrence approach, if people fear the consequences of crime they will be deterred from criminal involvement. Here, Sam Waksal leaves a Federal court after being sentenced on June 10, 2003 to more than seven years in prison and a 4 million dollar fine for his involvement in insider trading on his company stock. Do you think that such a harsh sentence for a business-related crime will deter other businesspeople from violating securities laws?

© 2003 AP/Wide World Photos

to help an already troubled person readjust to society. Rather than deter crime, a prison sentence may encourage future law violations.

Make It Difficult: Situational Crime Prevention

Some advocates of rational choice theory argue that crime prevention can be achieved by reducing the opportunities people have to commit particular crimes, a technique known as *situational crime prevention.*

Situational crime prevention was first popularized in the United States in the early 1970s by Oscar Newman, who coined the term *defensible space.* The idea is that crime can be prevented or displaced through the use of residential architectural designs that reduce criminal opportunity, such as well-lit housing projects that maximize surveillance.[37]

Contemporary choice theorists maintain that situational crime prevention can be achieved by creating a strategy or overall plan to reduce specific crimes and then developing specific tactics to achieve those goals. Ronald Clarke sets out the four main types of crime prevention tactics in use today.[38]

1. Increase the effort needed to commit the crime. Increasing the effort needed to commit crimes involves using target-hardening techniques and access control: placing steering locks on cars; putting unbreakable glass on storefronts; locking gates and fencing yards; having owners' photos on credit cards; controlling the sale of spray paint (to reduce graffiti); installing caller ID (a device that displays the telephone number of the party placing the call, which can reduce the number of obscene or crank calls).
2. Increase the risks of committing the crime. It is also possible to increase the risks of committing a crime by improving surveillance lighting, creating neighborhood watch programs, controlling building entrances and exits, putting in burglar alarms and security systems, and increasing the number and effectiveness of private security officers and police patrols. For example, research shows that crime rates are reduced when police officers use aggressive crime reduction techniques and promote community safety by increasing lighting and cleaning up vacant lots.[39] For instance, a recent initiative by the Dallas Police Department to aggressively pursue truancy and enforce curfew laws has resulted in lower rates of gang violence.[40]

3. Reduce the rewards for committing the crime. Reward reduction strategies include making car radios removable so they can be taken into the home at night, marking property so that it is more difficult to sell when stolen, and having gender-neutral phone lists to discourage obscene phone calls.

4. Induce shame or guilt. Inducing guilt or shame might include such techniques as embarrassing offenders (for example, publishing "John lists" in the newspaper to punish those arrested for soliciting prostitutes) or facilitating compliance by providing trash bins whose easy access might shame chronic litterers into using them. When caller ID was installed in New Jersey, the number of obscene phone calls reported to police declined significantly because of the threat of exposure.[41]

At their core, situational crime prevention efforts seek clearly defined solutions to specific crime problems. Instead of changing criminals, they seek to change the environment so that criminality becomes more difficult and consequently less profitable.

To quiz yourself on this material, go to questions 3.5–3.7 on the Introduction to Criminal Justice 10e CD.

Because They Are Different: Biological Theories

As the nineteenth century came to a close, some criminologists began to suggest that crime was caused not so much by human choice but by inherited and uncontrollable biological and psychological traits: intelligence, body build, personality, biomedical makeup. The newly developed scientific method was applied to the study of social relations, including criminal behavior.

The origin of scientific criminology is usually traced to the research of Cesare Lombroso (1836–1909). Lombroso, an Italian army physician fascinated by human anatomy, became interested in finding out what motivated criminals to commit crimes. He physically examined hundreds of prison inmates and other criminals to discover any similarities among them. On the basis of his research, Lombroso proposed that criminals manifest *atavistic anomalies:* primitive, animal-like physical qualities such as an asymmetric face or excessive jaw, eye defects, large eyes, a receding forehead, prominent cheekbones, long arms, a twisted nose, and swollen lips.[42]

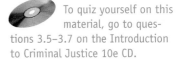 To read a brief biography of Cesare Lombroso go to http://www.epub.org.br/cm/n01/frenolog/lombroso.htm.

Lombroso's views were discredited in the twentieth century, and biological explanations of crime were abandoned. Today, the biology of crime has gained a resurgence of interest, and a number of criminologists are looking once again at the biological underpinnings of crime. At their core, biological theories assume that variation in human physical traits can explain behavior. Instead of being born equal and influenced by social and environmental conditions, each person possesses a unique biochemical, neurological, and genetic makeup. People may develop physical or mental traits at birth, or soon after, that affect their social functioning over the life course and influence their behavior choices. For example, low-birth-weight babies have been found to suffer poor educational achievement later in life; academic deficiency has been linked to delinquency and drug abuse.[43]

Biocriminologists are attempting to link physical traits with tendencies toward violence, aggression, and other antisocial behavior. Their work, which is still in the early stages of development, can be divided into three broad areas of focus: biochemical factors, neurological problems, and genetic influence.

In the Blood: Biochemical Factors

Some biocriminologists focus on the influence of biochemical factors on criminal behavior. Some research efforts have linked vitamin and mineral deficiencies, food additives, improper diet, environmental contaminants, and allergies to antisocial behavior. For example, exposure to environmental contaminants such as

© Christopher Morris/Black Star (iStockphoto.com)

Some children become involved in violent crimes at a very early age. Does this suggest that violence is the result of a biological trait, present at birth, that determines future behavior patterns throughout the life span?

Is there a neurological basis to juvenile violence and what should be done with kids who are extremely violent? To find out, read Mirah A. Horowitz, "Kids Who Kill: A Critique of How the American Legal System Deals with Juveniles Who Commit Homicide," *Law and Contemporary Problems* 63, no. 3 (Summer 2000): 133–77.

neurotransmitters
Chemical substances that carry impulses from one nerve cell to another. Neurotransmitters are found in the space (synapse) that separates the transmitting neuron's terminal (axon) from the receiving neuron's terminal (dendrite).

the now-banned PCB (polychlorinated biphenyls), a chemical that was once used in insulation materials, has been shown to influence brain functioning and intelligence levels.[44] Ingestion of common food additives such as calcium propionate, used to preserve bread, has been linked to problem behaviors.[45] Another suspected biochemical hazard are high levels of lead ingestion, which has been linked to antisocial behaviors.[46] In some cases, the association between chemical and mineral imbalance and crime is indirect. For example, research shows that high levels of mercury may lead to cognitive and learning dysfunctions, factors associated with antisocial behaviors.[47]

Another area of biological research focuses on hypoglycemia, a condition that occurs when blood glucose (sugar) falls below levels necessary for normal and efficient brain functioning. Symptoms of hypoglycemia include irritability, anxiety, depression, crying spells, headaches, and confusion. Research shows that persistent abnormality in the way the brain metabolizes glucose is linked to substance abuse.[48]

Hormonal imbalance has been linked to aggressive behavior. Research shows that children who have low levels of the stress hormone cortisol tend to be more violent and antisocial than those with normal levels.[49] A growing body of evidence suggests that hormonal changes are also related to mood and behavior and that adolescents experience more intense mood swings, anxiety, and restlessness than their elders, explaining in part the high violence rates found among teenage males.[50]

In sum, biochemical studies suggest that criminal offenders have abnormal levels of organic or inorganic substances that influence their behavior and in some way make them prone to antisocial behavior.

The Abnormal Brain: Neurological Problems

Another area of interest to biocriminologists is the relationship of brain activity to behavior. Electroencephalograms (EEGs) have been used to record the electrical impulses given off by the brain. Psychologist Dorothy Otnow Lewis and her associates found that murderous youths suffer signs of major neurological impairment (such as abnormal EEGs, multiple psychomotor impairment, and severe seizures).[51] In her book *Guilty by Reason of Insanity,* Lewis reports that death row inmates have a history of mental impairment and intellectual dysfunction.[52] Other research efforts show that spouse abusers exhibit a variety of neuropsychological disorders and cognitive deficits; many suffered brain injuries in youth.[53]

Another cause of abnormal neurological function is impairment in **neurotransmitters,** which are chemical compounds that influence or activate brain functions. Those studied in relation to aggression include dopamine, serotonin, monoamine oxidase, and Gamma-Aminobutryic Acid. Evidence exists that abnormal levels of these chemicals are associated with aggression.[54] Studies of habitually violent criminals show that low serotonin levels are linked with poor impulse control and hyperactivity, increased irritability, and sensation seeking.[55]

People with an abnormal cerebral structure referred to as minimal brain dysfunction may experience periods of explosive rage. Brain dysfunction is sometimes manifested as an attention-deficit hyperactivity disorder (ADHD), another suspected cause of antisocial behavior. Several studies have shown that children with attention problems experience increased levels of antisocial behavior and aggression during childhood, adolescence, and adulthood.[56] Both boys and girls who suffer from ADHD are impaired both academically and socially, factors that are related to long-term antisocial behaviors.[57]

The condition may cause poor school performance, bullying, stubbornness, and a lack of response to discipline. Although the origin of ADHD is still unknown, suspected causes include neurological damage, prenatal stress, and even food additives and chemical allergies. Research shows that youths with ADHD who grow up in a dysfunctional family are the most vulnerable to chronic delinquency that continues into their adulthood.[58]

The National Attention Deficit Disorder Association disseminates information and policy updates at its Web site: http://www.add.org/.

The Bad Seed: Genetic Factors

Although the earliest biological studies of crime tried and failed to discover a genetic basis for criminality, modern biocriminologists are still concerned with the role of heredity in producing crime-prone people.

If inherited traits are related to criminality, twins should be more similar in their antisocial activities than other sibling pairs. Because most twins are brought up together, however, determining whether behavioral similarities are a function of environmental influences or genetics is difficult. To overcome this problem, biocriminologists usually compare identical, or monozygotic (MZ), twins with fraternal, or dizygotic (DZ), twins of the same sex. MZ twins are genetically identical, so their behavior would be expected to be more similar than that of DZ twins. Preliminary studies have shown that this is true.[59] Some evidence exists that genetic makeup is a better predictor of criminality than either social or environmental variables.[60]

Another approach has been to evaluate the behavior of adopted children. If an adopted child's behavior patterns run parallel to those of his or her biological parents, it would be strong evidence to support a genetic basis for crime. Preliminary studies conducted in Europe have indicated that the criminality of the biological father is a strong predictor of a child's antisocial behavior.[61] The probability that a youth will engage in crime is significantly enhanced when both biological and adoptive parents exhibit criminal tendencies.

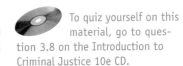 To quiz yourself on this material, go to question 3.8 on the Introduction to Criminal Justice 10e CD.

In Their Heads: Psychological Theories

The view that criminals may be suffering from psychological abnormality or stress has also had a long history.

The Disturbed Mind: Psychodynamic Theory

Psychodynamic theory, the creation of Viennese physician Sigmund Freud (1856–1939), still holds a prominent position in psychological thought.[62] According to the psychodynamic view, some people encounter problems during their early development that cause an imbalance in their personality. Some have mood disorders and are extremely anxious, fearful, and impulsive. *Psychotics* are people whose primitive impulses have broken through and actually control their personality; they may hear voices telling them what to do or see visions. One type of psychosis is *schizophrenia,* a condition marked by incoherent thought processes, a lack of insight, hallucinations, and feelings of persecution.

Psychodynamic theorists believe that law violators may have suffered damage to their egos or superegos early in their development that renders them powerless to control their impulses. They may suffer delusions and feel persecuted, worthless, and alienated.[63] Psychosis is often associated with violent episodes, but even nonviolent criminals may be motivated by a lack of insight and control caused by personality disorders.[64] As a result, they seek immediate gratification of their needs without considering right and wrong or the needs of others.

Mental Illness and Crime Although a link between mental instability and criminality seems logical (and a popular topic in horror movies), the evidence associating the two conditions is still inconclusive.

Those who believe in an association between mental illness and crime suggest that certain symptoms of mental illness are connected to violence—for example, the feeling that others wish the person harm, that the person's mind is dominated by forces beyond his or her control, or that thoughts are being put into the person's head by others.[65] Research also demonstrates a linkage between mental instability and criminal behavior patterns.[66] Studies of adolescent males accused of murder have found that 75 percent could be classified as having some mental illness, including schizophrenia.[67] Abusive mothers have been found to have mood and personality disorders and a history of psychiatric diagnoses.[68] The diagnosed mentally ill appear more often in arrest and court statistics at a rate disproportionate to their presence in the population.[69] In some bizarre cases, people who commit murder hope to be executed for their crimes, a form of suicide-murder.[70]

Nor is the association between mental illness and crime restricted to the United States. Forensic criminologist Henrik Belfrage studied mental patients in Sweden and found that 28 percent of those who were still alive 10 years after being discharged from mental hospitals were found to be registered for a criminal offense. Among those who were 40 years old or younger at the time of discharge, nearly 40 percent had a criminal record as compared with less than 10 percent of the general public.[71] Another study conducted with samples of Australian men with schizophrenia have shown them to be four times more likely than the general population to be convicted for serious violence.[72] And a recent Danish study evaluated all arrests for violence and all hospitalizations for mental illness that occurred in an extremely large sample of 350,000 people and found a significant positive relationship between mental disorder and criminal violence. Persons hospitalized for a major mental disorder were responsible for a disproportionate percentage of violence. Both men and women with schizophrenia were significantly more likely to be arrested for criminal violence than were those who had never been hospitalized.[73]

Despite this evidence, some doubt remains as to whether the mentally ill commit more crime than the mentally sound. Studies focusing on the criminal activity of the mentally ill have failed to establish a clear link between crime and psychiatrically diagnosed problems.[74] The mentally ill may be more likely to withdraw or harm themselves than to act aggressively toward others.[75] Research shows that, after release, prisoners with prior histories of hospitalization for mental disorders are less likely to be rearrested than those who have never been hospitalized.[76] And even if the mentally ill have a higher arrest and conviction rate than the mentally sound, in any given year only 0.2 percent of patients with schizophrenia were convicted of crimes. So while a link between mental illness and crime seems plausible, the association has been the subject of much debate.

Learning to Commit Crime: Behavioral Theory

A second branch of psychological theory views behavior as learned through interactions with others. Behavior that is rewarded becomes habitual; behavior that is punished becomes extinguished. One branch of behavioral theory of particular relevance to criminology is **social learning theory.** According to social learning theorists, people act aggressively because, as children, they modeled their behavior after the violent acts of adults.[77] Later in life, antisocial behavioral patterns are reinforced by peers and other acquaintances.[78]

Social learning theorists conclude that the antisocial behavior of potentially violent people can be triggered by a number of different influences: verbal taunts and threats; the experience of direct pain; and perceptions of relative social disability, such as poverty and racial discrimination. Those who have learned violence and have seen it rewarded are more likely to react violently under these stimuli than those who have not.

One area of particular interest to social learning theorists is whether the entertainment media can influence violence. This topic is discussed in the Images of Justice feature on page 90.

Developing Criminal Ideas: Cognitive Theory

Cognitive psychologists are concerned with the way people perceive and mentally represent the world in which they live. Some focus on how people process and store information, viewing the operation of human intellect as similar to the way computers analyze available information; the emphasis is on *information processing.* Aggressive people may base their behavior on faulty information. They perceive other people to be more aggressive than they are. Consequently, they are more likely to be vigilant, on edge, or suspicious. When they attack victims, they may believe they are defending themselves, when they are simply misreading the situation.[79] The college student who rapes his date may have a cognitive problem, rendering him incapable of distinguishing behavioral cues. He misidentifies rejection as a come-on or playing hard to get.

Another area of cognitive psychology is *moral development theory.* According to this theory, people go through a series of stages beginning early in childhood and continuing through their adult years.[80] Each stage is marked by a different view of right and wrong. For example, a child may do what is right simply to avoid punishment and censure. Later in life, the same person will develop a sensitivity to others' needs and do what is right to avoid hurting others. On reaching a higher level of maturity, the same person may behave in accordance with his or her perception of universal principles of justice, equality, and fairness.

According to developmental psychologists, criminals may lack the ability to make moral judgments. Criminals report that their outlooks are characterized by self-interest and impaired moral development. They are unlikely to consider the rights of others, and they are not concerned with maintaining the rules of society.[81] Some treatment programs help clients improve their cognitive skills. One such program is described in the Analyzing Criminal Justice Issues feature on page 92.

Personality and Crime: The Psychopath

Some psychologists view criminal behavior as a function of a disturbed personality structure. Personality can be defined as the reasonably stable patterns of

social learning theory
The view that human behavior is learned through observation of human social interactions, either directly from those in close proximity or indirectly from the media.

Serial killer suspect Orville Lynn Majors, in handcuffs, smiles as he is led by police. Majors is suspected of killing more than 100 patients while working as a nurse. Is it possible that serial killers like Majors are mentally healthy? Could someone kill 100 people and not be suffering some psychological impairment?

© Jim Avelis/Tribune Star/Sipa Press

The Media and Violence
images of justice

Does the media influence behavior? Does broadcast violence cause aggressive behavior in viewers? This has become a hot topic because of the persistent theme of violence on television and in films. Critics have called for drastic measures ranging from the banning of TV violence to putting warning labels on heavy metal albums because of a fear that listening to hard-rock lyrics produces delinquency.

If a TV-violence link exists, the problem is indeed alarming. Systematic viewing of TV begins at 2½ years of age and continues at a high level during the preschool and early school years. It has been estimated that children age 2 to 5 watch TV for 27.8 hours each week; children age 6 to 11, 24.3 hours per week; and teens, 23 hours per week. Marketing research indicates that adolescents age 11 to 14 rent violent horror movies at a higher rate than any other age group. Children this age use older peers and siblings and apathetic parents to gain access to R-rated films. More than 40 percent of U.S. households now have cable TV, which features violent films and shows. Even children's programming is saturated with violence.

Numerous anecdotal cases of violence linked to TV and films can be cited. For example, in a famous incident, John Hinckley Jr. shot President Ronald Reagan because of his obsession with actress Jodie Foster, which developed after he watched her play a prostitute in the film *Taxi Driver*. Hinckley viewed the film at least 15 times.

A national survey found that almost 80 percent of the general public believe that violence on TV can cause violence "in real life." Psychologists, however, believe that media violence does not in itself cause violent behavior because, if it did, there would be millions of daily incidents in which viewers imitated the aggression they watched on TV or in movies. But most psychologists agree that media violence contributes to aggression. There are several explanations for the effects of television and film violence on behavior.

- Media violence can provide aggressive scripts that children store in memory. Repeated exposure to these scripts can increase their retention and lead to changes in attitudes.
- Children learn from what they observe. In the same way they learn cognitive and social skills from their parents and friends, children learn to be violent from television.
- Television violence increases the arousal levels of viewers and makes them more prone to act aggressively. Studies measuring the galvanic skin response of subjects—a physical indication of arousal based on the amount of electricity conducted across the palm of the hand—show that viewing violent television shows led to increased arousal levels in young children.
- Watching television violence promotes such negative attitudes as suspicious-

ness and the expectation that the viewer will become involved in violence. Those who watch television frequently come to view aggression and violence as common and socially acceptable behavior.
- Television violence allows aggressive youths to justify their behavior. Instead of causing violence, television could help violent youths rationalize their behavior as a socially acceptable and common activity.
- Television violence may disinhibit aggressive behavior, which is normally controlled by other learning processes. **Disinhibition** takes place when adults are viewed as being rewarded for violence and when violence is seen as socially acceptable. This contradicts previous learning experiences in which violent behavior was viewed as wrong.

Such distinguished bodies as the American Psychological Association, the National Institute of Mental Health, and the National Research Council support the TV-violence link. They base their conclusion on research efforts that indicate that watching violence on TV leads to increased levels of violence in the laboratory settings as well as in natural settings.

A number of experimental approaches have been used, including:

- Having groups of subjects exposed to violent TV shows in a laboratory setting, then monitoring their behavior afterward and comparing it with the

---

disinhibition
Unrestricted behavior resulting from a loss of inhibition produced by an external influence, such as drugs or alcohol, or from a brain injury.

psychopath
A person whose personality is characterized by a lack of warmth and feeling, inappropriate behavioral responses, and an inability to learn from experience; also called sociopath or antisocial personality.

behavior, including thoughts and emotions, that distinguish one person from another.[82] An individual's personality reflects characteristic ways of adapting to life's demands and problems. The way you behave is a function of how your personality enables you to interpret life events and make appropriate behavioral choices.

Psychologists have explored the link between personality and crime. Evidence suggests that aggressive youths have unstable personality structures, often marked by hyperactivity, impulsiveness, and instability. Suspected traits include impulsivity, hostility, and aggressiveness.[83] There is also a demonstrated linkage between depression and delinquent behavior patterns.[84]

One area of particular interest to criminology is the identification of the *psychopathic* (also called *antisocial* or *sociopathic*) personality. **Psychopaths** are be-

behavior of control groups who viewed nonviolent programming;

- Observing subjects on playgrounds, athletic fields, and residences after they have been exposed to violent television programs;
- Requiring subjects to answer attitude surveys after watching violent TV shows; and
- Using aggregate measures of TV viewing, for example, tracking the number of violent TV shows on the air during a given time period and comparing it with crime rates during the same period.

According to a recent analysis of available scientific data since 1975, Brad Bushman and Craig Anderson found that the weight of the evidence is that watching violence on TV is correlated to aggressive behaviors and that the newest and most methodologically sophisticated works show the greatest amount of association.

In one of the most important recent studies, L. Rowell Huesmann and his associates at the University of Michigan contacted 329 adults 15 years after they had participated as 6- to 9-year-olds in a study indicating that kids who watched more violent television shows also displayed more aggressive behavior than their peers. As adults, those same children who had viewed violent shows in their adolescence continued to behave in a violent and aggressive manner. Boys who liked violent television grew into men who were signifi-

cantly more likely to have pushed, grabbed, or shoved their wives and attacked others whom they found insulting. They were also much more likely to be convicted of a crime. Ironically, women who watched violent shows as children reported being punched, beaten, or choked as adults at a rate over four times the rate of nonviolence-watching women.

While this research is persuasive, not all criminologists accept that watching TV or movies and listening to heavy metal music eventually leads to violent and antisocial behavior. For example, little evidence is available that residential areas that experience the highest levels of violent TV viewing also have rates of violent crime that are above the norm. If violent TV shows did cause interpersonal violence, then there should be few ecological and regional patterns in the crime rate, of which there are many. Put another way, how can regional differences in the violence rate be explained considering the fact that people all across the nation watch the same TV shows and films? Finally, millions of children watch violence every night, but they do not become violent criminals. Despite the increased availability of violent TV shows, DVDs, films, and video games, the violence rate among teens has been in a significant decline.

Critical Thinking

1. Should the government control the content of TV shows and limit the

amount of weekly violence? How could the national news be shown if violence were omitted? What about boxing matches or hockey games?
2. How do you explain the fact that millions of kids watch violent TV shows and remain nonviolent? If there is a TV-violence link, how do you explain the fact that violence rates may have been higher in the old west than they are today? Do you think violent gang kids stay home and watch TV shows?

InfoTrac College Edition Research

Is the presence of violence on TV increasing or in decline? To find out, check Nancy Signorielli, "Prime-time Violence 1993–2001: Has the Picture Really Changed?" *Journal of Broadcasting and Electronic Media* 47 (March 2003): 36.

Source: L.Rowell Heusmann, Jessica Moise-Titus, Cheryl-Lynn Podolski, and Leonard Eron, "Longitudinal Relations between Children's Exposure to TV Violence and Their Aggressive and Violent Behavior in Young Adulthood: 1977–1992," *Developmental Psychology* 39 (2003): 201–21; Brad Bushman and Craig Anderson, "Media Violence and the American Public," *American Psychologist* 56 (2001): 477–89; Garland White, Janet Katz, and Kathryn Scarborough, "The Impact of Professional Football Games upon Violent Assaults on Women," *Violence and Victims* 7 (1992): 157–71; Albert Reiss and Jeffrey Roth, eds., *Understanding and Preventing Violence* (Washington, D.C.: National Academy Press, 1993).

lieved to be dangerous, aggressive, antisocial individuals who act in a callous manner. They neither learn from their mistakes nor are deterred by punishments.[85] Although they may appear charming and have at least average intelligence, psychopaths lack emotional depth, are incapable of caring for others, and maintain an abnormally low level of anxiety. They are likely to be persistent alcohol and drug abusers.[86] Violent offenders often display psychopathic tendencies such as impulsivity, aggression, dishonesty, pathological lying, and lack of remorse.[87] Psychopathy has also been linked to chronic recidivism and serial murder.[88]A high proportion of serial rapists and repeat sexual offenders exhibit psychopathic personality structures.[89]

A number of factors are believed to contribute to the development of a psychopathic personality.[90] Some factors are related to improper socialization and

Emerge

analyzing criminal justice issues

Established in 1977, Emerge is the first program developed in the United States to address domestic abusers. The major premise of the program is that abusive behavior is learned behavior that can be transformed with the proper help and support. In addition, the program helps men to understand that they should be accountable for their behavior in abusive situations.

The program is available to men who are at least 18 years of age and admit to being abusive either physically, sexually, emotionally, or verbally. Upon entering the program, participants must share their abusive experiences during twice weekly sessions in which they meet with other group members and program facilitators. During these meetings, clients must update their current abusive behavior and share with group members any incidents in which they lost control. Feedback is encouraged. Each meeting contains approximately 12 group members and two program facilitators.

The Emerge program is delivered in two stages. The first stage, with eight lessons, provides information to clients on the following topics:

- What counts as violence
- Negative versus positive self-talk
- Effects of violence
- Quick fixes versus long-term solutions
- Psychological, economical, and sexual abuse
- Effects of domestic violence on children

The second stage of the program requires participants to utilize the information they learned and apply it to their lives. This stage consists of 32 lessons that consist of the following activities:

- Developing goals to change behavior
- Recognizing behavior that results in abusive conduct
- Sharing experiences with others to gain feedback from fellow members
- Practicing the use of positive conflict resolution techniques
- Learning nonabusive ways to resolve problems

Emerge believes that various lessons and activities can help abusers become more aware of the harm they cause and recognize the need for change. The program aims to have abusers reduce intimidating behavior, increase the level of their respect for others, and become account-able for their own actions without blaming family members when things go wrong.

Located in five different sites in the state of Massachusetts, Emerge counsels more than 300 abusers per week. It is the only program that offers help to abusive lesbian and gay partners and is the only program that provides the program in Vietnamese and Khmer, along with English and Spanish. Emerge also provides support groups for male teenagers who are abusive to their partners, siblings, or parents

Critical Thinking

Do you believe that domestic violence should be treated or punished? That is, instead of sending offenders to programs such as Emerge, should they be given strict incarceration sentences?

InfoTrac College Edition Research

To learn more about the nature and extent of domestic violence, use it as a subject guide on InfoTrac College Edition.

Source: Emerge, *Counseling and Education to Stop Domestic Violence* (Cambridge, Mass.: 2003), pp. 1–7. The Emerge Web site can be accessed at www.emergedv.com.

---

include having a psychopathic parent, parental rejection and lack of love during childhood, and inconsistent discipline.

Others suspect that psychopaths suffer from a low level of arousal as measured by the activity of their autonomic nervous system.[91] Therefore, psychopaths could be thrill seekers who engage in high-risk antisocial activities to raise their general neurological arousal level.

Some psychologists believe that antisocial personality traits can be linked to brain dysfunction or damage.[92] In one recent study, Kent Kiehl and his associates performed functional magnetic resonance imaging—that is, scans—on eight psychopathic criminals, eight nonpsychopathic criminals, and eight noncriminal controls. He discovered that psychopathic criminals exhibited less emotion-related activity in several areas of the limbic system in response to negative stimuli than members of the comparison groups. These areas of the brain are associated with attention, emotion, and memory. In addition, the psychopaths exhibited overactivation in the bilateral frontal-temporal cortex, a region of the brain associated with decision-making processes. These findings suggest that psychopaths may have brain-related physical anomalies that cause them to process emotional input differently than nonpsychopaths.[93]

Perspectives on Justice

Biological and psychological explanations of crimes seem to mesh with the crime control perspective. If criminals are damaged goods—genetically damaged or psychologically bent—then it stands to reason that they should be incarcerated for long periods of time if the public is to be protected. However, a supporter of rehabilitation might argue that trait theory suggests that criminals are not responsible for their actions and can be helped by psychological counseling or other efforts to change their behavior.

IQ and Crime

One of the most enduring controversies in the psychology of crime is the relationship between intelligence as measured by standardized intelligence quotient (IQ) tests and violent or criminal behavior. Numerous studies link low IQ to violent and aggressive behavior and crime.[94] Some research examines samples of people to determine whether those with low IQ are also more aggressive in social settings. Evidence shows that people who act aggressively in social settings also have lower IQ scores than their peers.[95] Some studies have found a direct IQ-delinquency link among samples of adolescent boys.[96] When Alex Piquero examined violent behavior among groups of children in Philadelphia, he found that scores on intelligence tests were the best predictor of violent behavior and could be used to distinguish between groups of violent and nonviolent offenders.[97] The IQ-crime relationship has also been found in cross-national studies. A significant relationship between low IQ and delinquency has been found among samples of youth in Denmark, where researchers discovered that children with a low IQ tended to engage in delinquent behaviors because their poor verbal ability was a handicap in the school environment.[98] An IQ-crime link was also found in a longitudinal study of Swedish youth; low IQ measures taken at age 3 were significant predictors of later criminality over the life course.[99]

While this evidence is persuasive, many experts dispute that an IQ-crime relationship exists. It has been suggested that any association is a function of bias in the testing procedures. Furthermore, a number of studies find that IQ level has negligible influence on criminal behavior.[100] Also, a recent evaluation of existing knowledge on intelligence conducted by the American Psychological Association concluded that the strength of an IQ-crime link was "very low."[101]

It is unlikely that the IQ-criminality debate will be settled in the near future. Measurement is beset by many methodological problems. The well-documented criticisms suggesting that IQ tests are class-biased would certainly influence the testing of the criminal population who are besieged with a multitude of social and economic problems. Even if it can be shown that known offenders have lower IQs than the general population, it is difficult to explain many patterns in the crime rate: Why are males three times as likely to get arrested than females (Are females three time smarter than males)? Why do crime rates vary by region, time of year, and even weather patterns? Why does aging out occur? IQs do not increase with age, so why should crime rates fall?

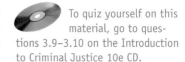 To quiz yourself on this material, go to questions 3.9–3.10 on the Introduction to Criminal Justice 10e CD.

Blame Society: Sociological Theories

Official, self-report, and victim data all indicate social patterns in the crime rate.[102] Some regions are more crime-prone than others. Distinct differences are found in crime rates across states, cities, and neighborhoods. If crime rates are higher in California than Vermont, it is probably not because Californians are more likely to suffer personality defects or eat more sugar than Vermonters. Crime rates are higher in large urban areas that house concentrations of the poor than they are in sparsely populated rural areas in which residents are relatively affluent. Prisons are filled with the poor and the hopeless, not the rich and the famous. Because crime patterns have a decidedly social orientation, sociological explanations of crime have predominated in criminology.

Sociological criminology is usually traced to the pioneering work of sociologist Émile Durkheim (1858–1917), who viewed crime as a social phenomenon.[103] In formulating his theory of **anomie,** Durkheim held that crime is an essential part of society and a function of its internal conflict. As he used the term, *anomie* means the absence or weakness of rules and social norms in any person or group; without these rules or norms, an individual may lose the ability to distinguish between right and wrong.

As the field of sociological criminology emerged in the twentieth century, greater emphasis was placed on environmental conditions, while the relationship between crime and physical or mental traits (or both) was neglected. Equating the cause of criminal behavior with social factors, such as poverty and unemployment, was instrumental in the development of treatment-oriented crime prevention techniques. If criminals are made and not born—if they are forged in the crucible of societal action—then it logically follows that crime can be eradicated by the elimination of the social elements responsible for crime. The focus of crime prevention shifted from punishing criminals to treatment and rehabilitation.

Because They Are Poor: Social Structure Theory

According to **social structure** theory, the United States is a stratified society. Social strata are created by the unequal distribution of wealth, power, and prestige. Social classes are segments of the population whose members have relatively similar attitudes, values, and norms and have an identifiable lifestyle. In U.S. society, people can be identified as belonging to the upper, middle, or lower class, with a broad range of economic variation in each group.

The contrast between the lifestyles of the wealthiest members of the upper class and the poorest segment of the lower class is striking. Though their number has gotten smaller recently, about 3 million households still have "investable assets" including stocks, bonds, and cash in excess of $1 million. If other assets are added, such as vacation homes, 401(K) or 403(b) plans, stock options, investment real estate, annuities, or closely held business partnerships about 8 million American households have assest in excess of $1 million. In contrast, the poverty rate was 12.1 percent in 2002, up from 11.7 percent in 2001 (see Figure 3.2). More than 34 million people now live in poverty, which the federal government defines as earning about $18,500 per year for a family of four. Children are especially hard hit: More than 12 million kids live in poverty, a rate of about 17 percent.[104]

Racial differences are also evident in the poverty rate. About 23 percent of Hispanics and African Americans live in poverty, as compared with about 8 percent of European Americans.[105] Though minority poverty rates have declined significantly during the past 40 years, they are still unacceptably high (see Figure 3.3).

About 20 million high school dropouts face dead-end jobs, unemployment, and social failure. Because of their meager economic resources, lower-class citizens are often forced to live in slum areas marked by substandard housing, inadequate health care, poor educational opportunities, underemployment, and despair. They live in areas with deteriorated housing and abandoned buildings, which research shows are magnets for crime, drug dealing, and prostitution.[106]

The problems of lower-class culture are particularly acute for racial and ethnic minorities. Research indicates that their disproportionate representation in the poverty class may be a result of negative racial stereotyping among potential

anomie
The absence or weakness of rules, norms, or guidelines as to what is socially or morally acceptable.

social structure
The stratifications, classes, institutions, and groups that characterize a society.

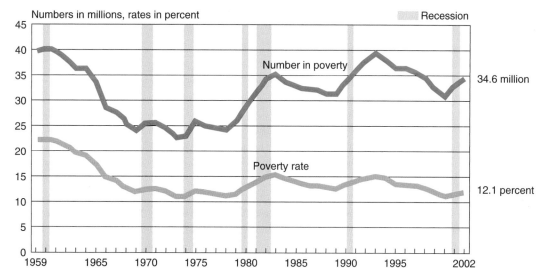

Figure 3.2
Number of Poor and Poverty Rate, 1959–2002

Source: U.S. Census Bureau Current Population Survey 1960–2002

employers, which leads to both lower employment opportunities and greater income inequality.[107]

The crushing burden of urban poverty brings on the development of a **culture of poverty**.[108] This subculture is marked by apathy, cynicism, helplessness, and distrust. The culture is passed from one generation to the next, creating a permanent underclass, referred to as the "truly disadvantaged."[109]

Considering the social disability suffered by the lower class, some people not surprisingly turn to crime as a means of support and survival. According to the social structure approach, a significant majority of people who commit violent crimes and serious theft offenses live in the lower-class culture, and a majority of all serious crimes occur in inner-city areas. The social forces operating in lower-class, inner-city areas produce high-crime rates. What are these forces, and how do they produce crime?

The Disorganized Neighborhood

Some crime experts believe that crime is a product of neighborhoods that are characterized by physical deterioration and by conflicting values and social systems. Disorganized neighborhoods are undergoing the disintegration of their existing culture and services, the diffusion of cultural standards, and successive changes from purely residential to a mixture of commercial, industrial, transient, and residential populations. In these areas, the major sources of informal social control—family, school, neighborhood, civil service—are broken and ineffective.

Urban areas are believed to be crime-prone because their most important social institutions cannot function properly. These neighborhoods are unable to realize the common values of their residents or to solve commonly experienced problems.[110] Disorganized neighborhoods have high population density, large numbers of single-parent households, unrelated people living together, and a lack of employment opportunities.[111] Their residents perceive significant levels of fear, alienation, and social dissatisfaction. These high-crime areas typically have rapid population turnover and lack the ability to socially integrate their residents.[112] Constant population turnover makes it difficult for these communities to understand or assimilate their newest members. Hence, they acquire the reputation of being a changing neighborhood.

culture of poverty
The view that people in the lower class of society form a separate culture with its own values and norms that are in conflict with those of conventional society.

To read more about poverty in the United States, go to Howard Glennerste, "United States Poverty Studies and Poverty Measurement: The Past Twenty-five Years," *Social Service Review* 76, no. 1 (March 2002): 83–108.

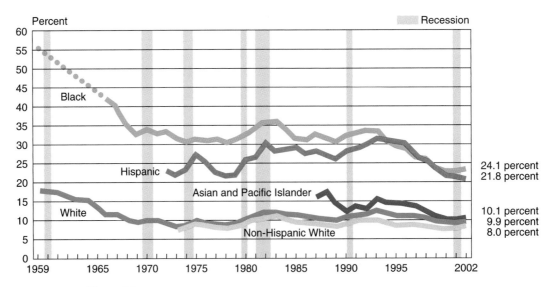

Figure 3.3
Poverty Rates by Race and Hispanic Origin, 1959–2002

Source: U.S. Census Bureau, *Current Population Survey* 1960–2002

The social, economic, and physical conditions that develop in disorganized neighborhoods have been associated with escalating crime rates. Areas that experience a high rate of housing abandonment, neighborhood decline, increased population density, and urban growth have also been found to have increasing crime rates.[113] Even in rural areas, which normally have low crime rates, signs of social disorganization such as residential instability (a large number of people moving in and out), family disruption, and changing ethnic composition are linked to high crime rates.[114] The crime-producing influence of these economic disadvantages are felt by all residents, both male and female.[115] However, minority group members living in these areas suffer the added disadvantages of race-based income inequality and institutional racism.[116] The fact that significant numbers of African Americans are forced to live under these conditions can help explain the distinct racial patterns in the official crime statistics. The powerful effect of living in racially segregated poverty areas is discussed in the Race, Gender, and Ethnicity in Criminal Justice feature on page 98.

Unfortunately, the problems found in disorganized areas are stubborn and difficult to overcome. Even when an attempt is made to revitalize a neighborhood—for example, by creating institutional support programs such as community centers and better schools—the effort may be countered by the enduring lack of economic and social resources.[117]

Perspectives on Justice

Social structure theory is linked to the rehabilitation perspective of justice. If poverty and strain cause crime, then efforts to improve economic opportunity can help reduce crime rates. Job and social welfare programs are part of the government's effort to give members of the lower class opportunities to succeed legitimately. Efforts to reduce crime rates by revitalizing a community's social and economic health are extremely difficult to achieve because the problems of decayed, transitional neighborhoods are overwhelming. Rehabilitation efforts are dwarfed by the social problems ingrained in these areas.

Exhibit 3.2 Miller's Lower-Class Focal Concerns

Trouble

In lower-class communities, people are evaluated by their actual or potential involvement in making trouble. Getting into trouble includes such behavior as fighting, drinking, and sexual misconduct. Dealing with trouble can confer prestige—for example, when a man establishes a reputation for being able to handle himself well in a fight. Not being able to handle trouble, and having to pay the consequences, can make a person look foolish and incompetent.

Toughness

Lower-class males want local recognition of their physical and spiritual toughness. They refuse to be sentimental or soft and instead value physical strength, fighting ability, and athletic skill. Those who cannot meet these standards risk getting a reputation for being weak, inept, and effeminate.

Smartness

Members of the lower-class culture want to maintain an image of being streetwise and savvy and having the ability to outfox and out-con the opponent. Although formal education is not admired, knowing essential survival techniques, such as gambling, conning, and outsmarting the law, is a requirement.

Excitement

Members of the lower class search for fun and excitement to enliven an otherwise drab existence. The search for excitement may lead to gambling, fighting, getting drunk, and sexual adventures. In between, the lower-class citizen may simply "hang out" and "be cool."

Fate

Lower-class citizens believe that their lives are in the hands of strong spiritual forces that guide their destinies. Getting lucky, finding good fortune, and hitting the jackpot are all slum dwellers' daily dreams.

Autonomy

Being independent of authority figures, such as the police, teachers, and parents, is required. Losing control is an unacceptable weakness, incompatible with toughness.

Source: Walter Miller, "Lower-Class Culture as a Generating Milieu of Gang Delinquency," *Journal of Social Issues* 14 (1958): 5–19.

Deviant Values and Cultures Living in deteriorated inner-city neighborhoods, forced to endure substandard housing and schools, and cut off from conventional society, lower-class slum dwellers are faced with a constant assault on their self-image and sense of worth. While the media bombard them with images glorifying a materialistic lifestyle, they cannot purchase fine clothes, a luxury automobile, or their own home. Residents may become resentful and angry when they realize that they are falling further and further behind the social mainstream.[118] Residents who live in these high-crime areas, where drug abuse is common, also suffer. Because they believe that their neighbors lack ties to conventional cultural values, their own ability to maintain social ties in the neighborhood become weak and attenuated. This may further reduce already weakened levels of informal social control.[119]

How is it possible for them to adjust and satisfy their needs? One method of adjusting is to create an independent value system. Whereas middle-class values favor education, hard work, sexual abstinence, honesty, and sobriety, lower-class values in slum areas applaud goals that are realistically obtainable in a disorganized society: being cool, promiscuous, intemperate, and fearless. Thus lower-class **focal concerns** include scorning authority, living for today, seeking excitement, and scoffing at formal education (see Exhibit 3.2).[120]

Some people living in disorganized areas band together to form an independent lower-class subculture—small reference groups that provide members with a unique set of values, beliefs, and traditions distinct from those of conventional society. Within this subculture, lower-class youths can achieve success unobtainable within the larger culture, while gaining a sense of identity and achievement. Members of the criminal subculture adopt a set of norms and principles in direct opposition to middle-class society. They engage in short-run hedonism, living for today by taking drugs, drinking, and engaging in unsafe sex. They resist efforts by family members and other authority figures to control their behavior and

focal concerns
Central values and goals that, according to Walter Miller, differ by social class.

Building a Bridge over the Racial Divide
race, gender, and ethnicity in criminal justice

In his famous 1987 book, *The Truly Disadvantaged,* William Julius Wilson provided a description of the plight of the lowest levels of the underclass. Wilson portrayed members of this group as socially isolated people who dwell in urban inner cities, occupy the bottom rung of the social ladder, and are the victims of discrimination. They live in areas in which the basic institutions of society—family, school, housing—have long since declined. Their decline triggers similar breakdowns in the strengths of inner-city areas, including a loss of community cohesion and the ability of people living in the area to control the flow of drugs and criminal activity. For example, in a more affluent area, neighbors might complain to parents that their children were acting out. In distressed areas, this element of informal social control may be lacking because parents are under stress or, all too often, absent. These effects magnify the isolation of the underclass from mainstream society and promote a ghetto culture and behavior.

Because the truly disadvantaged rarely come into contact with the source of their oppression, they direct their anger and aggression at those with whom they are in close and intimate contact, such as neighbors, businesspeople, and landlords. Members of this group, plagued by underemployment or unemployment, begin to lose self-confidence, a feeling supported by the plight of kin and friendship groups who also experience extreme economic marginality. Self-doubt is a neighborhood norm, overwhelming those forced to live in areas of concentrated poverty.

In his 1996 publication, *When Work Disappears,* Wilson assessed the effect of joblessness and underemployment on residents of poor neighborhoods on Chicago's South Side. He noted that, for the first time in the twentieth century, most adults in inner-city ghetto neighborhoods were not working during a typical week. He found that inner-city life was only marginally affected by the surge in the nation's economy, brought about by new industrial growth connected with technological development. Poverty in these inner-city areas is eternal and unchanging and, if anything, worsening as residents are further shut out of the economic mainstream.

Wilson suggests that as difficult as life was for African Americans in the 1940s and 1950s, they at least had a reasonable hope of steady work. Now, because of the globalization of the economy, those opportunities have evaporated. Although in the past racial segregation had limited opportunity, growth in the manufacturing sector fueled upward mobility and provided the foundation of today's African American middle class. Those opportunities no longer exist because manufacturing plants have moved to nonaccessible rural and overseas locations where the cost of doing business is lower. With manufacturing opportunities all but obsolete in the United States, service and retail establishments that depended on blue-collar spending have similarly disappeared, leaving behind an economy based on welfare and government support. In less than 20 years, formerly active African American communities have become crime-infested slums.

When work becomes scarce, the discipline and structure it provides are absent. Community-wide underemployment destroys social cohesion, increasing the presence of neighborhood social problems ranging from drug use to educational failure. Schools in these areas cannot teach basic skills, and because desirable employment is lacking, few adults can serve as role models. In contrast to more affluent suburban households, where daily life is organized around

instead join autonomous peer groups and gangs.[121] Members may be prone to violence, for example, because the routine activities of their subculture require them to frequent locations, such as bars and dance clubs, where aggressive behavior is the norm and where they are exposed to other violence-prone people.[122] Cultural values might include excluding police officers from social conflicts and handling problems personally. When Charis Kubrin and Ronald Weitzer examined the ecological and socioeconomic correlates of homicide in St. Louis, Missouri, they found that a certain type of homicide (what they call "cultural retaliatory homicide") is more common in some neighborhoods than in others.[123] Residents in these communities often solve problems informally, without calling the police, even if it means having to kill someone in retaliation for a perceived or actual slight or provocation. The neighborhood culture codes support this type of problem solving, even if it leads to violence and death. In sum, in lower-class areas, social, cultural, and economic forces interact to produce a violent environment.

job and career demands, children in inner-city areas are not socialized in the workings of the mainstream economy.

In his newest book, *The Bridge over the Racial Divide: Rising Inequality and Coalition Politics* (1999), Wilson argues that, despite economic gains, inequality is growing in American society and ordinary families of all races and ethnic origins are suffering. Whites, Latinos, African Americans, Asians, and Native Americans must therefore begin to put aside their differences and concentrate more on what they have in common—their aspirations, problems, and hopes. There needs to be mutual cooperation across racial lines.

One reason for this set of mutual problems is that the government tends to aggravate rather than ease the financial stress being placed on ordinary families. Monetary policy, trade policy, and tax policy are harmful to working-class families. A multiracial citizens coalition could pressure national public officials to focus on the interests of ordinary people. As long as middle- and working-class groups are fragmented along racial lines, such pressure is impossible.

Wilson finds that racism is becoming more subtle and harder to detect. Whites believe that African Americans are responsible for their inferior economic status be-

cause of their cultural traits. Because even affluent whites fear corporate downsizing, they are unwilling to vote for government assistance to the poor. Whites live mainly in the suburbs, further isolating poor minorities in central cities and making their problems seem distant and unimportant. The changing marketplace, with its reliance on sophisticated computer technologies, is continually decreasing demand for low-skilled workers, which affects African Americans more negatively than other, better-educated groups.

Wilson argues for a cross-race, class-based alliance of working- and middle-class Americans to pursue policies that will benefit them instead of the affluent. These include full employment, programs to help families and workers in their private lives, and a reconstructed "affirmative opportunity" program that benefits African Americans without antagonizing whites.

With these three volumes, Wilson provides probably the best description of the plight of the poor within an affluent American society and what must be done to bring them within the mainstream.

Critical Thinking

1. Is it unrealistic to assume that a government-sponsored public works

program can provide needed jobs in this era of budget cutbacks?
2. What are some of the hidden costs of unemployment in a community setting?
3. Racism has stained this nation for hundreds of years. Is it realistic to believe that some form of governmental programming can lighten the burden it places on the American people?

InfoTrac College Edition Research

 For more on William Julius Wilson's view of poverty, unemployment, and crime, check out Gunnar Almgren, Avery Guest, George Immerwahr, and Michael Spittel, "Joblessness, Family Disruption, and Violent Death in Chicago, 1970–90," *Social Forces* 76, no. 4 (June 1998): 1465; William Julius Wilson, "Inner-City Dislocations," *Society* 35, no. 2 (January–February 1998): 270.

Source: William Julius Wilson, *The Truly Disadvantaged* (Chicago: University of Chicago Press, 1987); William Julius Wilson, *When Work Disappears: The World of the Urban Poor* (New York: Knopf, 1996); William Julius Wilson, *The Bridge over the Racial Divide: Rising Inequality and Coalition Politics* (Berkeley: University of California Press, 1999).

Strain In lower-class neighborhoods, **strain,** or status frustration, occurs because legitimate avenues for success are all but closed. Frustrated and angry, with no acceptable means of achieving success, people may use deviant methods, such as theft or violence, to achieve their goals.

The concept of strain can be traced to the pioneering work of famed sociologist Robert Merton, who recognized that members of the lower-class experience anomie, or normlessness, when the means they have for achieving culturally defined goals, mainly wealth and financial success, are insufficient.[124] As a result, people will begin to seek alternative solutions to meet their need for success: They will steal, sell drugs, or extort money. Merton referred to this method of adaptation as *innovation*—the use of innovative but illegal means to achieve success in the absence of legitimate means. Other youths, faced with the same dilemma, might reject conventional goals and choose to live as drug users, alcoholics, and wanderers; Merton referred to this as *retreatism*. Still others might join revolutionary political groups and work to change the system to one of their

strain
The emotional turmoil and conflict caused when people believe they cannot achieve their desires and goals through legitimate means.

According to strain theory, people who want to experience the American Dream of wealth, success, and happiness will be frustrated and angry if they lack the means of achieving their goals.

© Lara Jo Regan/Getty Images

liking; Merton refers to this as *rebellion*. Criminologist Robert Agnew has expanded anomie theory by recognizing other sources of strain in addition to failure to meet goals. These include both negative experiences, such as child abuse, and the loss of positive supports, such as the end of a stable romantic relationship (see Figure 3.4).[125]

Research has linked these sources of strain to criminal and delinquent behaviors.[126] People who report feelings of stress- and strain-related anger are more likely to interact with deviant peers and engage in criminal behaviors.[127] Evidence also suggests that people who fail to meet success goals are more likely to engage in criminal activities.[128]

Socialized to Crime: Social Process Theories

Not all criminologists agree that the root cause of crime can be found solely within the culture of poverty.[129] After all, self-report studies indicate that many middle- and upper-class youths take drugs and commit serious criminal acts. As adults, they commit white-collar and corporate crimes. Conversely, the majority of people living in the poorest areas hold conventional values and forgo criminal activity. Simply living in a violent neighborhood does not produce violent people. Research shows that family, peer, and individual characteristics play a large role in predicting violence.[130] These patterns indicate that forces must be operating in all strata of society that influence individual involvement in criminal activity.

If crime is spread throughout the social structure, then it follows that the factors that cause crime should be found within all social and economic groups. People commit crimes as a result of the experiences they have while they are being socialized by the various organizations, institutions, and processes of society. People are most strongly influenced toward criminal behavior by poor family relationships, destructive peer-group relations, educational failure, and labeling by agents of the justice system. Although lower-class citizens have the added burdens of poverty, strain, and blocked opportunities, middle- or upper-class citizens also may turn to crime if their socialization is poor or destructive.

Social process theorists point to research efforts linking family problems to crime as evidence that socialization, not social structure, is the key to understanding the onset of criminality. The quality of family life is considered a significant

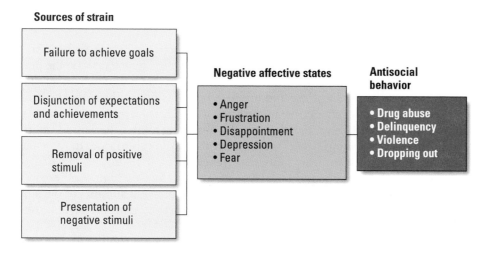

Figure 3.4
Agnew's Sources of Strain and Their Consequences

determining factor in adolescent development.[131] Among the most important research efforts are those showing that inconsistent discipline, poor supervision and discipline, and a lack of warm parent–child relationships are closely related to a child's deviant behavior.[132] Children who grow up in homes where parents use severe discipline and also lack warmth and involvement are prone to engage in antisocial behavior.[133] In contrast, positive parental relationships can insulate children from criminogenic influences in the environment.[134] Child abuse also could be related both to delinquency and to the perpetuation of abusive behavior. Abused children grow up to become child abusers themselves.[135]

Educational experience has also been found to have a significant impact on behavioral choices. Schools contribute to fostering criminality when they set problem youths apart by creating a track system that labels some as college-bound and others as academic underachievers. Studies show that chronic delinquents do poorly in school, lack educational motivation, and are frequently held back.[136] Research indicates that high school dropouts are more likely to become involved in crime than those who complete their education.[137]

Associating with deviant peers also exerts tremendous influence on behavior, attitudes, and beliefs.[138] Deviant peers provide friendship networks and support behaviors such as riding around, staying out late, and partying. They provide the opportunity to commit deviant acts.[139] Because delinquent friends tend to be, as criminologist Mark Warr puts it, "sticky" (once acquired, they are not easily lost), peer influence may continue through the life span.[140] The more antisocial the peer group, the more likely its members will be to engage in delinquency. Nondelinquent friends help moderate delinquency.[141] People who maintain close relations with antisocial peers will sustain their own criminal behavior into adulthood. If peer influence dimishes, so, too, does criminal activity.[142]

In sum, significant evidence exists that the direction and quality of interpersonal interactions and relationships influence behavior throughout the life span. However, disagreement arises over the direction this influence takes. Some crime experts maintain that all people are born innocent, but some are exposed to and learn criminal techniques and attitudes from peers and family members. Another view is that all people have the potential to engage in antisocial behavior, but most are controlled by the bonds they form with society. Still another view is that crime is a by-product of social stigma and the formation of a deviant identity.

Students of Crime: Learning Theories Those who advocate learning theories hold that people enter into a life of crime when, as adolescents, they are taught the attitudes, values, and behaviors that support a criminal career. They may learn the techniques of crime from a variety of intimates, including parents and family members.[143]

The best-known example of the learning perspective is Edwin Sutherland's **differential association theory.**[144] Sutherland, considered by many to be the pre-eminent American criminologist, believed that the attitudes and behaviors that cause crime are learned in close and intimate relationships with significant others. People learn to commit crime in the same way they learn any other behavior. For example, children learn to ride a bike by observing more experienced riders, practicing riding techniques, and hearing how much fun it is to ride. In the same fashion, adolescents learn from more experienced drug users how to buy drugs, how to use them properly, and how to behave when they are high. Adolescents who are exposed to an excess of attitudes ("definitions") in support of deviant behavior will eventually view those behaviors as attractive, appropriate, and suitable and engage in a life of crime.

Testing the principles of differential association theory is difficult, but several notable research efforts have supported its core assumptions. Differential association measures have been correlated with the onset of substance abuse and a career in the drug trade. Adolescent drug users are likely to have intimate relationships with a peer friendship network that supports their substance abuse and teaches them how to deal with the drug world.[145] Differential association has also been found to be a significant predictor of criminal behavior in adult felons.[146]

Out of Control: Control Theories When they were in high school, most students knew a few people who seemed detached and alienated from almost everything and everyone. They did not care about school, they had poor relationships at home, and, although they may have belonged to a tough crowd, their relationships with their peers were superficial and often violent. Very often these same people got into trouble at school, had run-ins with the police, and were involved in drugs and antisocial behaviors.

These observations form the nucleus of **social control theory.** This approach to understanding crime holds that all people may have the inclination to violate the law but most are held in check by their relationships to conventional institutions and individuals, such as family, school, and peer group. For some people, when these relationships are strained or broken, they become free to engage in deviant acts that otherwise would be avoided. Crime occurs when the influence of official and informal sources of social control is weakened or absent.

The most influential advocate of control theory is sociologist Travis Hirschi, who suggests that people's social bonds are formed from a number of different elements (see Figure 3.5). According to Hirschi, people whose bond to society is secure are unlikely to engage in criminal misconduct because they have a strong stake in society. Those who find their social bond weakened are much more likely to succumb to the temptations of criminal activity. After all, crime does have rewards, such as excitement, action, material goods, and pleasures. Hirschi does not give a definitive reason for what causes a person's social bond to weaken, but the process has two likely main sources: disrupted home life and poor school ability (leading to subsequent school failure and dislike of school).

Ongoing research efforts have attempted to test Hirschi's theory about social control and crime. Although results vary, a number of studies have supplied data that support Hirschi's view.[147] For example, youths who maintain positive attachments with others also report low rates of delinquency.[148]

differential association theory
The view that criminal acts are related to a person's exposure to antisocial attitudes and values.

social control theory
The view that most people do not violate the law because of their social bonds to family, peer group, school, and other institutions. If these bonds are weakened or absent, they become free to commit crime.

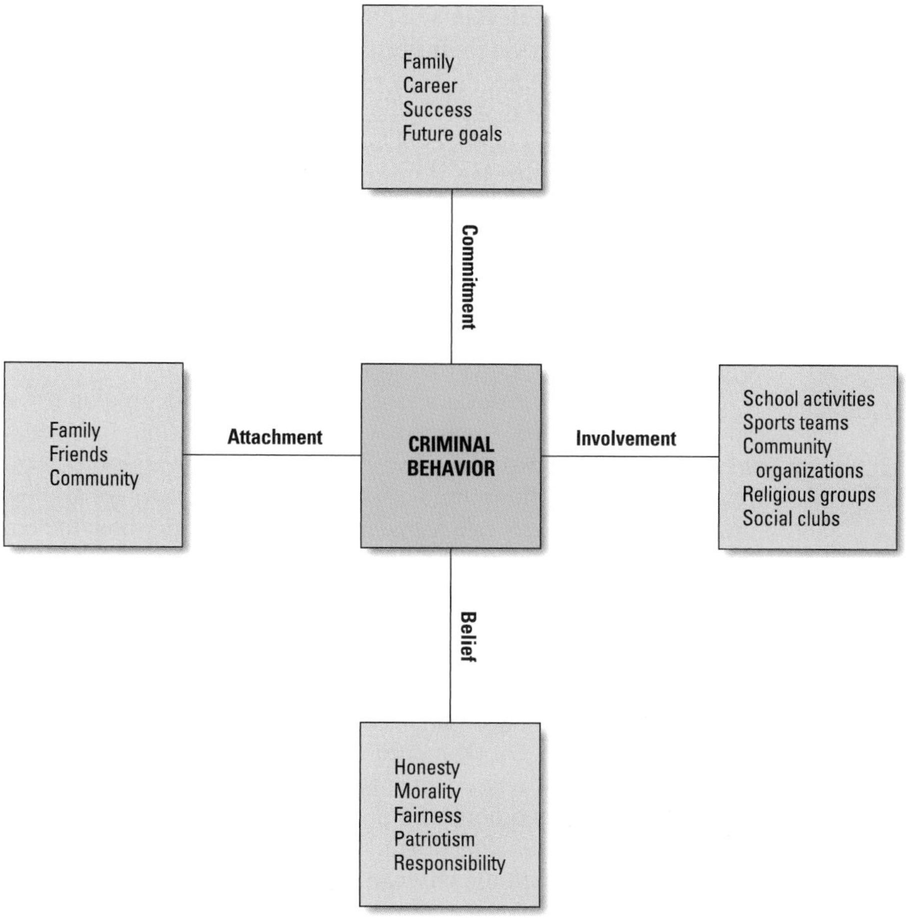

Figure 3.5
Elements of the Social Bond

Those adolescents who are committed to school are less likely to engage in delinquent acts than youths who fail at school and are detached from the educational experience.[149]

Perspectives on Justice

Control theory has been linked to the rehabilitation perspective. Programs have been designed to present alternative values and lifestyles to youths who have bought into a delinquent way of life. These programs often use group process and counseling to attack the criminal behavior orientations of their clients and help them learn conventional values and beliefs. Rehabilitation advocates suggest that community-based programs designed to strengthen young people's bonds to society will insulate them from crime. Family development, counseling programs, and school-based prevention programs are often utilized. In addition, various state youth and adult correctional authorities maintain inmate treatment programs that stress career development, work and educational furloughs, and self-help groups, all designed to help reestablish social bonds.

The Outsider: Labeling Theory   According to **labeling theory,** officially designating people as "troublemakers," stigmatizing them with a permanent deviant label, leads many to become criminals. People who commit undetected

labeling theory
The view that society produces criminals by stigmatizing certain individuals as deviants, a label that they come to accept as a personal identity.

Does self-labeling promote crime? To find out, read Mike S. Adams, Craig T. Robertson, Phyllis Gray-Ray, and Melvin C. Ray, "Labeling and Delinquency," *Adolescence* 38, no. 49 (Spring 2003): 171–86.

Initial criminal act
People commit crimes for a number of reasons.

↓

Detection by the justice system
Arrest is influenced by racial, economic, and power relations.

↓

Decision to label
Some are labeled official criminals by police and court authorities.

↓

Creation of a new identity
Those labeled are known as troublemakers, criminals, and so on, and they are shunned by conventional society.

↓

Acceptance of labels
Labeled people begin to see themselves as outsiders. Secondary deviance. Self-labeling.

↓

Deviance amplificaton
Stigmatized offenders are now locked into criminal careers.

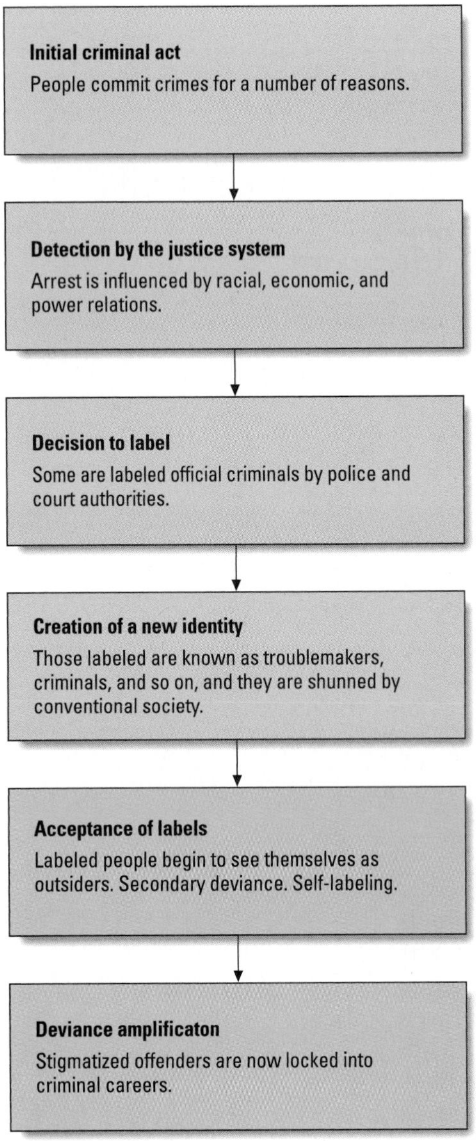

Figure 3.6
The Labeling Process

To quiz yourself on this material, go to questions 3.11–3.16 on the Introduction to Criminal Justice 10e CD.

antisocial acts are called "secret deviants" or "primary deviants." Their illegal act has little influence or impact on their lifestyle or behavior. However, if another person commits the same act and his or her behavior is discovered by social control agents, the labeling process may be initiated. That person may be given a deviant label, such as "mentally ill" or "criminal." The deviant label transforms him or her into an outsider, shunned by the rest of society. In time, the stigmatized person may believe that the deviant label is valid and assume it as a personal identity. For example, the student placed in special education classes begins to view himself as "stupid" or "backward," the mental patient accepts society's view of her as "crazy," and the convicted criminal considers himself "dangerous" or "wicked."

Accompanying the deviant label are a variety of degrading social and physical restraints—handcuffs, trials, incarceration, bars, cells, and a criminal record—which leave an everlasting impression on the accused. These sanctions are designed to humiliate and are applied in what labeling experts call *degradation ceremonies,* in which the target is made to feel unworthy and despised.

Labels and sanctions work to define the whole person, meaning that a label evokes stereotypes that are used to forecast other aspects of the labeled person's character. A person labeled "mentally ill" is assumed to be dangerous, evil, cruel, or untrustworthy, even though he or she has exhibited none of these characteristics.

Faced with such condemnation, negatively labeled people may begin to adopt their new, degraded identity. They may find no alternative but to seek others who are similarly stigmatized and form a deviant subculture. Supported by a deviant peer group that sports similar labels, they enter into a deviant or criminal career. Instead of deterring crime, labeling begins a deviance amplification process. If apprehended and subjected to even more severe negative labels, the offender may be transformed into a real deviant—one whose view of self is in direct opposition to conventional society. The deviant label may become a more comfortable and personally acceptable social status than any other. The individual whose original crime may have been relatively harmless is transformed by social action into a career deviant, a process referred to as *secondary deviance.* The entire labeling process is illustrated in Figure 3.6.

Labeling theorists also believe that there is racial, gender, and economic discrimination in the labeling process. For example, judges may sympathize with white defendants and help them avoid criminal labels, especially if they seem to come from "good families," whereas minority youths are not afforded that luxury.[150] This may help explain racial and economic differences in the crime rate.

Perspectives on Justice

Labeling theory principles support the noninterventionist view that an offender's interface with the criminal justice system should be limited. Among the most prominent policy initiatives based on labeling theory are efforts to divert first offenders from the normal justice process and to shepherd them into treatment programs, to order offenders to pay victim restitution instead of entering them into the justice process, and to deinstitutionalize nonviolent offenders (that is, remove them from the prison system).

It's All about the Benjamins: Conflict Theory

Conflict theory views the economic and political forces operating in society as the fundamental cause of criminality. The criminal law and criminal justice system are seen as vehicles for controlling the poor. The criminal justice system helps the powerful and rich impose their own morality and standards of good behavior on the entire society, while protecting their property and physical safety from the have-nots, even though the cost may be the legal rights of the lower class. Those in power control the content and direction of the law and the legal system. Crimes are defined in a way that meets the needs of the ruling classes. Thus the theft of property worth five dollars by a poor person can be punished much more severely than the misappropriation of millions by a large corporation. Those in the middle class are drawn into this pattern of control because they are led to believe that they, too, have a stake in maintaining the status quo and should support the views of the upper-class owners of production.[151]

Conflict theory has a number of subdivisions. One approach—known as *conflict criminology*—views crime as a product of the class conflict that can exist in any society.[152] A second subbranch—called *critical, radical,* or *Marxist criminology*—focuses on the crime-producing forces contained within the capitalist system. Both branches agree that the law and justice systems are mechanisms through which those in power control the have-not members of society.

Conflict theorists devote their research efforts to exposing discrimination and class bias in the application of laws and justice. They trace the history of criminal sanctions to show how those sanctions have corresponded to the needs of the wealthy. They attempt to show how police, courts, and correctional agencies have served as tools of the powerful members of society. Conflict theorists maintain that, because of social and economic inequality, members of the lower class are forced to commit larceny and burglary, take part in robberies, and sell drugs as a means of social and economic survival. In some instances, the disenfranchised will engage in rape, assault, and senseless homicides as a means of expressing their rage, frustration, and anger.

A considerable body of research supports the conflict view. Criminologists routinely have found evidence that measures of social inequality, such as income level, deteriorated living conditions, and relative economic deprivation are highly associated with crime rates, especially felony murders that typically accompany robberies and burglaries.[153] The conclusion is that as people become economically marginalized they will turn to violent crime for survival, producing an inevitable upswing in the number of street crimes and a corresponding spike in the murder rate.

Critical criminology has evolved over the past two decades and a number of new subbranches have been developed. **Left realism** attempts to reconcile critical views with the social realities of crime and its impact on the lower class. Left realists recognize that predatory crimes are not revolutionary acts and that crime is an overwhelming problem for the poor. Regardless of its origins, according to left realists, crime must be dealt with by the police and courts.[154] **Radical feminism** has tried to explain how capitalism places particular stress on women and to explicate the role of male dominance in female criminality.[155] **Peacemaking criminology** views crime as just one form of violence among others, such as war and genocide. Peacemakers call for universal social justice as a means of eliminating antisocial acts.[156] They argue that the old methods of punishment are a failure and that new less punitive methods must be discovered. When conservatives scoff at their ideas and claim that the crime rate dropped in the 1990s because the number of people in prison was at an all-time high, peacemakers counter by citing studies showing that imprisonment rates are not related to crime rates, that no consistent finding has been reached that locking people up

conflict theory
The view that crime results from the imposition by the rich and powerful of their own moral standards and economic interests on the rest of society.

left realism
A branch of conflict theory that accepts the reality of crime as a social problem and stresses its impact on the poor.

radical feminism
A branch of conflict theory that focuses on the role of capitalist male dominance in female criminality and victimization.

peacemaking criminology
A branch of conflict theory that stresses humanism, mediation, and conflict resolution as means to end crime.

To quiz yourself on this material, go to questions 3.17–3.18 on the Introduction to Criminal Justice 10e CD.

helps reduce crimes, and that upward of two-thirds of all prison inmates recidivate soon after their release.[157]

Perspectives on Justice

Peacemaking criminology serves as the basis of the restorative justice perspective. Rather than being adversarial and punitive, the justice system should strive to restore damaged social relations. Harsh punishments have become the norm. An alternative would be mediation, arbitration, restitution, and forgiveness. This call for social justice has helped focus attention on the plight of the poor, women, and minority groups when they confront the agencies of the justice system. Programs that have been developed as a result include free legal services for indigent offenders, civilian review boards to oversee police, laws protecting battered women, and shelters for victims of domestic abuse.

The Path to Crime: Developmental Theories

developmental theories
A view of crime holding that as people travel through the life course their experiences along the way influence behavior patterns. Behavior changes at each stage of the human experience.

Developmental theories seek to identify, describe, and understand the developmental factors that explain the onset and continuation of a criminal career. As a group, they do not ask the relatively simple question: Why do people commit crime? Instead, they focus on more complex issues: Why do some offenders persist in criminal careers while others desist from or alter their criminal activity as they mature? Why do some people continually escalate their criminal involvement while others slow down and turn their lives around? Are all criminals similar in their offending patterns or are there different types of offenders and paths to offending? Developmental theories not only want to know why people enter a criminal way of life but also why, once they do, are they able to alter the trajectory of their criminal involvement.

Developmental theories seem to fall into two distinct groups: latent trait and life course theories.

Latent Trait Theory

latent trait theories
A view that human behavior is controlled by a master trait, present at birth or soon after, which influences and directs their behavior.

Latent trait theories hold that human development is controlled by a master trait, present at birth or soon after. Some criminologists believe that this master trait remains stable and unchanging throughout a person's lifetime while others suggest that it can be later altered or influenced or changed by experience. In either event, as people travel through their life course this trait is always there, influencing decisions and directing their behavior. Because this master trait is enduring, the ebb and flow of criminal behavior is directed by the impact of external forces such as criminal opportunity and the reaction of others.[158] Suspected latent traits include defective intelligence, impulsive personality, and genetic makeup—characteristics that may be present at birth or established early in life and remain stable over time.[159] People who are antisocial during adolescence are the ones most likely to remain criminals throughout their life span because the latent trait controlling their behavior in youth also does so in adulthood.

The best-known latent trait theory is Michael Gottfredson and Travis Hirschi's general theory of crime (see Figure 3.7).[160] In the general theory, Gottfredson and Hirschi argue that individual differences in the tendency to commit criminal acts can be found in a person's level of self-control. People with limited self-control tend to be impulsive, insensitive, physical (rather than mental), risk-taking, shortsighted, and nonverbal. They have a here-and-now orientation and refuse to work for distant goals. They lack diligence, tenacity, and persistence in a course of action. People lacking self-control tend to be adventuresome, active, physical, and self-centered. As they mature, they have unstable marriages, jobs, and friendships.

Criminal acts are attractive to such individuals because they provide easy and immediate gratification—or, as Gottfredson and Hirschi put it, "money without work, sex without courtship, revenge without court delays." Given the opportunity to commit crime, they will readily violate the law. Under the same set of circumstances, nonimpulsive people will refrain from antisocial behavior.

Criminal activity diminishes when the opportunity to commit crime is limited. People age out of crime because the opportunity to commit crimes diminishes with age. Teenagers simply have more opportunity to commit crimes than the elderly, regardless of their intelligence. Here the general theory integrates the concepts of latent traits and criminal opportunity: Possessing a particular trait + having the opportunity to commit crime = the choice to commit crime.

Life Course Theory

In contrast to this view, the **life course** branch views criminality as a dynamic process, influenced by a multitude of individual characteristics, traits, and social experiences. As people travel through the life course, they are constantly bombarded by changing perceptions and experiences. As a result, their behavior will change directions, sometimes for the better and sometimes for the worse (see Figure 3.8).

According to the life course view, a criminal career is an evolutionary process, and the role of criminal is always changing. Criminals start their journey at different times. Some are precocious, beginning their criminal careers early and persisting into adulthood.[161] Others stay out of trouble in their early adolescence and do not violate the law until late in their teenage years. Some offenders may peak at an early age, whereas others persist into adulthood. Some youth maximize their offending rates at a relatively early age and then reduce their criminal activity. Others persist into their twenties. Some are high-rate offenders, whereas others offend at relatively low rates.[162]

Some criminals may desist from crime, only to resume their activities at a later date. Some commit offenses at a steady pace, whereas others escalate the rate of their criminal involvement. Offenders can begin to specialize in one type of crime or become generalists who commit a variety of illegal acts. The reasons people commit crimes and the frequency of their criminal activity change over the course of their lives. Criminals may be influenced by family matters, financial needs, and changing lifestyle and interests.

Life course theorists dispute the existence of an unchanging master trait that controls human development. Instead, they suggest that as people mature, the factors that influence their behavior also undergo change. At first, family relations may be most influential; in later adolescence, school and peer relations predominate; in adulthood, marital relations may be the most critical influence. Some antisocial youths who are in trouble throughout their adolescence may be able to find stable work and maintain intact marriages as adults. These life events help them desist from crime. In contrast, those who develop arrest records, get involved with the wrong crowd, and can find only menial jobs are at risk for criminal careers. Social forces that are critical at one stage of life may have little meaning or influence at another.

Life course theorists believe that crime is one among a group of antisocial behaviors that cluster together and typically involve family dysfunction, sexual and physical abuse, substance abuse, smoking, precocious sexuality and early pregnancy, educational underachievement, suicide attempts, sensation seeking, and unemployment.[163] People who suffer from one of these conditions typically exhibit many symptoms of the rest.[164] They find themselves with a range of personal

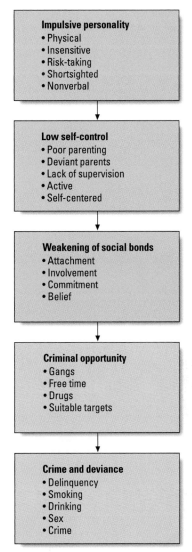

Figure 3.7
General Theory of Crime

life course
The course of social and developmental changes through which an individual passes as he or she travels from birth through childhood, adolescence, adulthood, and finally old age.

Figure 3.8
Life Course Theories

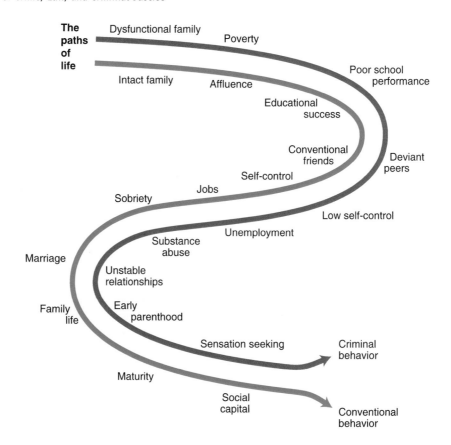

The paths of life

Dysfunctional family

Poverty

Poor school performance

Intact family   Affluence

Educational success

Deviant peers

Conventional friends

Self-control

Jobs

Sobriety

Low self-control

Substance abuse

Unemployment

Marriage

Unstable relationships

Family life

Early parenthood

Sensation seeking

Criminal behavior

Maturity

Social capital

Conventional behavior

dilemmas, from drug abuse to being accident prone, to requiring more health care and hospitalization, to becoming teenage parents to having mental health problems.[165]

Age-Graded Theory   Two of the leading life course theorists, criminologists Robert Sampson and John Laub, have formulated what they call age-graded theory.[166] According to Sampson and Laub, "turning points" in a criminal career are life events that enable people to "knife off" from a criminal career path into one of conventional and legitimate activities. As they mature, people who have had significant problems with the law are able to desist from crime if they can become attached to a spouse who supports and sustains them. They may encounter employers who are willing to give them a chance despite their record. People who cannot sustain secure marital relations or are failures in the labor market are less likely to desist from crime. Getting arrested can help sustain a criminal career because it reduces the chances of marriage, employment, and job stability, factors that are directly related to crime.

social capital
Positive relations with individuals and institutions that foster self-worth and inhibit crime.

According to Sampson and Laub, these life events help people build **social capital**—positive relations with individuals and institutions that are life-sustaining. Building social capital, which includes acquiring personal connections and relationships, is critical if a person hopes to obtain his or her life's objectives.[167] For example, a successful marriage creates social capital when it improves a person's stature, creates feelings of self-worth, and encourages people to give them a chance.[168] Getting a good job inhibits crime by creating a stake in conformity—why commit crimes when you are doing well at your job? The relationship is reciprocal: Persons chosen as employees return the favor by doing the best job possible; those chosen as spouses blossom into devoted partners. Building social capital and strong social bonds reduces the likelihood of long-term deviance. According to research by Alex Piquero and his associates, even people who have long histories of criminal activity and have been convicted of serious offenses reduce the frequency of their offending if they get married and fall into a domestic lifestyle.[169] People who are married often have schedules where they work 9-to-5 jobs, come home for dinner, take care of children if they have them, watch television, go to bed, and repeat the cycle over and over again. People who are not married have free rein to do what they want, especially if they are not employed. Crossing the line of getting married helps these men stay away from crime. If they do not cross that line, they can continue their lifestyles, which are erratic.[170]

 To quiz yourself on this material, go to questions 3.19–3.22 on the Introduction to Criminal Justice 10e CD.

It's How You Live: Theories of Victimization

victim precipitation
The role of the victim in provoking or encouraging criminal behavior.

For many years, criminological theory focused on the actions of the criminal offender. The role of the victim was virtually ignored. Then a number of scholars found that the victim is not a passive target in crime but someone whose behavior can influence his or her own fate. Hans Von Hentig portrayed the crime victim as someone who "shapes and molds the criminal."[171] The criminal may be a predator, but the victim may help the criminal by becoming a willing prey. Stephen Schafer extended this approach by focusing on the victim's responsibility in the "genesis of crime."[172] Schafer accused some victims of provoking or encouraging criminal behavior, a concept now referred to as **victim precipitation.** These early works helped focus attention on the role of the victim in the crime problem and led to further research efforts that have sharpened the image of the crime victim.

Victim Precipitation

The concept of victim precipitation was popularized by Marvin Wolfgang's 1958 study of criminal homicide. Wolfgang found that crime victims were often intimately involved in their demise, and as many as 25 percent of all homicides could be classified as victim-precipitated.[173]

There are two types of victim precipitation. *Active precipitation* occurs when victims act provocatively, use threats or fighting words, or even attack first.[174] For example, some experts have suggested that female rape victims contribute to their attacks by their manner of dress or by pursuing a relationship with the rapist.[175] Although this finding has been disputed, courts have continued to return not guilty verdicts in rape cases if a victim's actions can in any way be construed as consenting to sexual intimacy.[176]

Passive precipitation occurs when the victim exhibits some personal characteristic that unintentionally either threatens or encourages the attacker. The crime may occur because of personal conflict. For example, a woman may become the target of intimate violence when she increases her job status and her success results in a backlash from a jealous spouse or partner.[177] Passive precipitation may also occur when the victim belongs to a group whose mere presence threatens the attacker's reputation, status, or economic well-being. For example, hate crime violence may be precipitated by immigrants arriving in the community and competing for jobs and housing.[178]

© 2003 AP/Wide World Photos

High-risk lifestyles can increase the likelihood of victimization and the Internet has become a risky place. Here, Shelly Riling holds a picture of her niece, Christina Long, 13, outside of Danbury Superior Court in Danbury, Connecticut, May 6, 2003, where Saul Dos Reis, 25, was sentenced to 30 years in prison after he was convicted of one count of manslaughter and three counts of sexual assault. He had met the girl through the Internet.

Lifestyle Theory

Some criminologists believe that people may become crime victims because their lifestyle increases their exposure to criminal offenders. Victimization risk is increased by such behaviors as associating with violent young men, going out in public places late at night, and living in an urban area. Those who have histories of engaging in serious delinquency, getting involved in gangs, carrying guns, and selling drugs have an increased chance of being shot and killed themselves.[179]

Figure 3.9
Routine Activities Theory

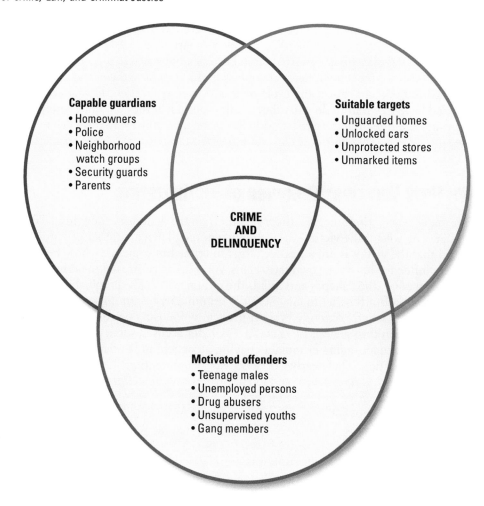

Capable guardians
• Homeowners
• Police
• Neighborhood
  watch groups
• Security guards
• Parents

Suitable targets
• Unguarded homes
• Unlocked cars
• Unprotected stores
• Unmarked items

**CRIME
AND
DELINQUENCY**

Motivated offenders
• Teenage males
• Unemployed persons
• Drug abusers
• Unsupervised youths
• Gang members

Lifestyle risks continue into young adulthood. College students who spend several nights each week partying and who take recreational drugs are much more likely to suffer violent crime than those who avoid such risky behavior.[180]

Lifestyle theory suggests that a person can reduce the chances of victimization by reducing risk-taking behavior: staying home at night, moving to a rural area, staying out of public places, earning more money, and getting married. The basis of this theory is that crime is not a random occurrence but a function of the victim's lifestyle.

Routine Activities Theory

routine activities theory
The view that crime is a product of three everyday factors: motivated offenders, suitable targets, and a lack of capable guardians.

To find out more about "routine activities theory," use the term as a subject guide on InfoTrac College Edition.

Routine activities theory, a variation on the lifestyle model, holds that the incidence of criminal activity and victimization is related to the nature of normal, everyday patterns of human behavior. According to this view, predatory crime rates can be explained by three factors (see Figure 3.9): the supply of *motivated offenders* (such as large numbers of unemployed teenagers), *suitable targets* (goods that have value and can be easily transported, such as VCRs), and the absence of *effective guardians* (protections such as police and security forces or home security devices).[181]

The routine activities view of victimization suggests that people's daily activities may put them at risk. If people leave unguarded valuables in their home, they increase the likelihood of becoming burglary victims. If they walk at night in public places, they increase the risk of becoming targets of violence.[182]

According to this approach, the likelihood of victimization is a function of both criminal motivation and the behavior of potential victims. For example, if average family income increases because of an increase in the number of working mothers, and consequently the average family is able to afford more luxury goods such as portable computers and digital cameras, a comparable increase in the crime rate might be expected because the number of suitable targets has expanded while the number of capable guardians left to protect the home has been reduced.[183] In contrast, crime rates may go down during times of high unemployment, because there is less to steal and more people are at home to guard their possessions. The routine activities approach seems a promising way of understanding crime and victimization patterns and predicting victim risk.

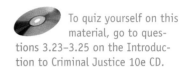

To quiz yourself on this material, go to questions 3.23–3.25 on the Introduction to Criminal Justice 10e CD.

Summary

- Crime in America comes in a number of diverse forms.
- Violent crimes range from gang warfare to serial killing to family violence.
- Substance abuse continues to be a significant social problem.
- Property crimes now include high-tech crimes, which involve the use of computers and the Internet.
- More than one approach can be taken to understanding the cause of crime and its consequences (see Concept Summary 3.1).
- Debate continues over whether crime is a social, economic, psychological, biological, or personal problem; whether it is a matter of free choice or the product of uncontrollable social and personal forces; and whether it can be controlled by the fear of punishment or the application of rehabilitative treatment. Consequently, there are a number of different and diverse schools of criminological theory—some focusing on the individual and others viewing social factors as the most important element in producing crime.
- Choice theories assume that criminals carefully choose whether to commit criminal acts. Evidence shows that crime is a rational event and criminals are rational decision makers.
- According to the general deterrence concept, people are influenced by their fear of the criminal penalties associated with being caught and convicted for law violations. The more severe, certain, and swift the punishment, the more likely it is to control crime. Deterrence theory holds that if criminals are rational, then an inverse relationship should exist between punishment and crime.
- Specific deterrence theory holds that the crime rate can be reduced if known offenders are punished so severely that they never commit crimes again.

- According to the situational crime prevention approach, because criminals are rational, taking steps to reduce their opportunity to commit crimes will result in lower crime rates.
- Biological theories hold that human traits and conditions such as biochemical makeup, neurological deficits, and genetic abnormalities control crime.
- Psychological theories suggest that crime may be a function of mental abnormality, learned behavior, or deficient cognitive ability.
- Sociologists believe that crime is a product of environmental influences.
- Some argue that people living in disorganized inner-city neighborhoods are at risk to commit crime because their environment gives them little hope of achieving success through conventional means. They may become angry and frustrated.
- Another view is that people become socialized to crime because of their upbringing and social learning. Some learn to commit crime. Others may commit crime because their socialization has weakened their bond to society.
- Still another view is that the conflict inherent in a capitalist society is a direct cause of antisocial behavior.
- Some theorists believe that crime is a function of human development. Within this group are those who believe that an underlying master trait directs human behavior. Others believe that criminal careers are part of a developmental process and that the conditions that cause criminal behavior at one point in the life cycle change radically as people mature.
- There are also a number of theories of victimization (see Concept Summary 3.2). One view, called victim precipitation, is that victims provoke criminals and are at least partially responsible for their victimization.

Concept Summary 3.1 Concepts and Theories of Criminology: A Review

Theory	Major premise
Choice Theory	People commit crime when they perceive that the benefits of law violation outweigh the threat and pain of punishment.
Biosocial theory	
Biochemical	Crime, especially violence, is a function of diet, vitamin intake, hormonal imbalance, or food allergies.
Neurological	Criminals and delinquents often suffer brain impairment. Attention deficit disorder and minimum brain dysfunction are related to antisocial behavior.
Genetic	Delinquent traits and predispositions are inherited. The criminality of parents can predict the delinquency of children.
Psychological theory	
Psychoanalytic	The development of personality early in childhood influences behavior for the rest of a person's life. Criminals have weak egos and damaged personalities.
Social learning	People commit crime when they model their behavior after others whom they see being rewarded for the same acts. Behavior is enforced by rewards and extinguished by punishment.
Social structure theory	
Social disorganization	The conflicts and problems of urban social life and communities control the crime rate. Crime is a product of transitional neighborhoods that manifest social disorganization and value conflict.
Strain	People who adopt the goals of society but lack the means to attain them seek alternatives, such as crime.
Social process theory	
Learning theory	People learn to commit crime from exposure to antisocial behaviors. Criminal behavior depends on the person's experiences with rewards for conventional behaviors and punishments for deviant ones. Being rewarded for deviance leads to crime.
Social control theory	A person's bond to society prevents him or her from violating social rules. If the bond weakens, the person is free to commit crime.
Self-control theory	Crime and criminality are separate concepts. People choose to commit crime when they lack self-control. People lacking self-control will seize criminal opportunities.
Conflict theory	
Conflict	People commit crimes when the law, controlled by the rich and powerful, defines their behavior as illegal. The immoral actions of the powerful go unpunished.
Left realism	Crime is a function of relative deprivation. Criminals prey on the poor.
Radical feminism	The capital system creates patriarchy, which oppresses women. Male dominance explains gender bias, violence against women, and repression.
Peacemaking	Peace and humanism can reduce crime. Conflict resolution strategies can work.
Developmental theory	Early in life people begin relationships that determine their behavior through their life course. Life transitions control the probability of offending.

Concept Summary 3.2 Victimization Theories

Victim precipitation	Victims trigger criminal acts by their provocative behavior. Active precipitation involves fighting words or gestures. Passive precipitation occurs when victims unknowingly threaten their attackers.
Lifestyle	Victimization risk is increased when people have a high-risk lifestyle. Placing oneself at risk by going to dangerous places results in increased victimization.
Routine activities	Crime rates can be explained by the availability of suitable targets, the absence of capable guardians, and the presence of motivated offenders.

- Lifestyle theories suggest that victims put themselves in danger by engaging in high-risk activities, such as going out late at night, living in a high-crime area, and associating with high-risk peers.

- The routine activities theory maintains that a pool of motivated offenders exists and that these offenders will take advantage of suitable, unguarded targets.

Key Terms

spree killer 77
white-collar crime 79
criminology 80
deterrent 81
general deterrence 82
specific deterrence 83
neurotransmitters 86
social learning theory 89
disinhibition 90
psychopath 90

anomie 94
social structure 94
culture of poverty 95
focal concerns 97
strain 99
differential association theory 102
social control theory 102
labeling theory 103
conflict theory 105
left realism 105

radical feminism 105
peacemaking criminology 105
developmental theories 106
latent trait theories 106
life course 107
social capital 108
victim precipitation 109
routine activities theory 110

Doing Research on the Web

**For an up-to-date list of Web links, go to
http://cj.wadsworth.com/siegel_intro10e.**

The Web can be used to conduct more in-depth research on the various theories of crime and victimization. For example, to get more information using InfoTrac College Edition, do a power search using the term "general strain theory" to learn more about Robert Agnew's vision of strain. You may want to read Robert Agnew and Timothy Brezina, "Relational Problems with Peers, Gender, and Delinquency," *Youth and Society* 29, no. 1 (September 1997): 84; Lisa Broidy and Robert Agnew, "Gender and Crime: A General

Strain Theory Perspective," *Journal of Research in Crime and Delinquency* 34, no. 2 (August 1997): 275.

To get some more background on other forms of strain theory as well as the general theory, go to the following Web sites: http://home.comcast.net/~ddemelo/crime/gen_strain.html and http://faculty.ncwc.edu/TOConnor/301/301lect09.htm.

Pro/Con discussions and Viewpoint Essays on some of the topics in this chapter may be found at the Opposing Viewpoints Resource Center: http://www.gale.com/OpposingViewpoints.

Discussion Questions

1. What factors are present in a disorganized urban area that produce high crime rates?
2. If research could show that the tendency to commit crime is inherited, what should be done with the young children of violence-prone criminals?
3. It seems logical that biological and psychological factors might explain why some people commit crime. Why would these factors fail to explain crime patterns and trends?
4. Are criminals impulsive? How could impulsivity be used to explain white-collar and organized crime?
5. If crime is a routine activity, what steps should you take to avoid becoming a crime victim?

Notes

1 To read more about the Mallard case, go to the Court TV Web site at http://www.courttv.com/trials/mallard/062703_ctv.html.
2 Gary Bailey and N. Prabha Unnithan, "Gang Homicides in California: A Discriminant Analysis," *Journal of Criminal Justice* 22 (1994): 267–75.
3 Arlen Egley Jr., National Youth Gang Survey Trends from 1996 to 2000 (Washington, D.C.: Office of Juvenile Justice and Delinquency Prevention, 2002); for more, see Walter Miller, *The Growth of the Youth Gang Problem in the United States, 1970–1998* (Washington, D.C.: Office of Juvenile Justice and Delinquency Prevention, 2001).
4 Arlen Egley Jr. and Mehala Arjunan, *Highlights of the 2000 National Youth Gang Survey* (Washington, D.C.: Office of Juvenile Justice and Delinquency Prevention, 2002).

5 "Special Report: The Columbine Tapes," *Time,* December 20, 1999, p. 23.

6 James Alan Fox and Jack Levin, "Multiple Homicide: Patterns of Serial and Mass Murder," in *Crime and Justice: An Annual Edition,* vol. 23, ed. Michael Tonry (Chicago: University of Chicago Press, 1998), pp. 407–55.

7 Ibid.

8 U.S. Department of Health and Human Services, Administration on Children, Youth, and Families, *Child Maltreatment 2001* (Washington, D.C.: Government Printing Office, 2003).

9 Joseph Price and Kathy Glad, "Hostile Attributional Tendencies in Maltreated Children," *Journal of Abnormal Child Psychology* 31 (2003): 329–44.

10 Ruth Engs and David Hanson, "Boozing and Brawling on Campus: A National Study of Violent Problems Associated with Drinking over the Past Decade," *Journal of Criminal Justice* 22 (1994): 171–80.

11 Robert Nash Parker, "Bringing 'Booze' Back In: The Relationship between Alcohol and Homicide," *Journal of Research in Crime and Delinquency* 32 (1993): 3–38.

12 Arrestee Drug Abuse Monitoring Program, 2000 *Annual Report on Drug Use among Adult and Juvenile Arrestees* (Washington, D.C.: National Institute of Justice, 2003).

13 John Hepburn, "Occasional Criminals," in *Major Forms of Crime,* ed. Robert Meier (Beverly Hills, Calif.: Sage, 1984), pp. 73–94.

14 James Inciardi, "Professional Crime," in *Major Forms of Crime,* ed. Robert Meier (Beverly Hills, Calif.: Sage, 1984), p. 223.

15 Jeanne Capachin and Dave Potterton, "Online Card Payments, Fraud Solutions Bid to Win," *Meridien Research Report,* January 18, 2001.

16 See, generally, Jay Albanese, *Organized Crime in America,* 2d ed. (Cincinnati, Ohio: Anderson, 1989), p. 68.

17 James O. Finckenauer and Yuri A. Voronin, *The Threat of Russian Organized Crime* (Washington, D.C.: National Institute of Justice, 2001).

18 Liliana Pezzin, "Earnings Prospects, Matching Effects, and the Decision to Terminate a Criminal Career," *Journal of Quantitative Criminology* 11 (1995): 29–50.

19 Pierre Tremblay and Carlo Morselli, "Patterns in Criminal Achievement: Wilson and Abrahamse Revisited," *Criminology* 38 (2000): 633–60.

20 Gordon Knowles, "Deception, Detection, and Evasion: A Trade Craft Analysis of Honolulu, Hawaii's Street Crack Cocaine Traffickers," *Journal of Criminal Justice* 27 (1999): 443–55.

21 Andrew Buck, Simon Hakim, and George Rengert, "Burglar Alarms and the Choice Behavior of Burglars: A Suburban Phenomenon," *Journal of Criminal Justice* 21 (1993): 497–507; Julia MacDonald and Robert Gifford, "Territorial Cues and Defensible Space Theory: The Burglar's Point of View," *Journal of Environmental Psychology* 9 (1989): 193–205; Paul Cromwell, James Olson, and D'Aunn Wester Avary, *Breaking and Entering: An Ethnographic Analysis of Burglary* (Newbury Park, Calif.: Sage, 1991), pp. 48–51.

22 Matthew Robinson, "Lifestyles, Routine Activities, and Residential Burglary Victimization," *Journal of Criminal Justice* 22 (1999): 27–52.

23 William Smith, Sharon Glave Frazee, and Elizabeth Davison, "Furthering the Integration of Routine Activity and Social Disorganization Theories: Small Units of Analysis and the Study of Street Robbery as a Diffusion Process," *Criminology* 38 (2000): 489–521.

24 Paul Bellair, "Informal Surveillance and Street Crime: A Complex Relationship," *Criminology* 38 (2000): 137–67.

25 John Gibbs and Peggy Shelly, "Life in the Fast Lane: A Retrospective View by Commercial Thieves," *Journal of Research in Crime and Delinquency* 19 (1982): 229–30.

26 James Q. Wilson, *Thinking about Crime* (New York: Basic Books, 1975); Ernest Van den Haag, *Punishing Criminals* (New York: Basic Books, 1975).

27 Herbert Packer, *The Limits of the Criminal Sanction* (Stanford, Calif.: Stanford University Press, 1968).

28 Ernest Van den Haag, "Could Successful Rehabilitation Reduce the Crime Rate?" *Journal of Criminal Law and Criminology* 73 (1985): 1022–35.

29 Steven Klepper and Daniel Nagin, "Tax Compliance and Perceptions of the Risks of Detection and Criminal Prosecution," *Law and Society Review* 23 (1989): 209–40.

30 Daniel Nagin and Greg Pogarsky, "An Experimental Investigation of Deterrence: Cheating, Self-Serving Bias, and Impulsivity," *Criminology* 41 (2003): 167–95.

31 Raymond Paternoster, "Decisions to Participate in and Desist from Four Types of Common Delinquency: Deterrence and the Rational Choice Perspective," *Law and Society Review* 23 (1989): 7–29.

32 Jon Sorenson, Robert Wrinkle, Victoria Brewer, and James Marquart, "Capital Punishment and Deterrence: Examining the Effect of Executions on Murder in Texas," *Crime and Delinquency* 45 (1999): 481–93.

33 Alex Piquero and George Rengert, "Studying Deterrence with Active Residential Burglars," *Justice Quarterly* 16 (1999): 451–62.

34 Parker, "Bringing 'Booze' Back In."

35 Michel Foucault, *Discipline and Punishment* (New York: Random House, 1978).

36 David J. Levin, Patrick A. Langan, and Jodi M. Brown, *State Court Sentencing of Convicted Felons, 1996* (Washington, D.C.: Bureau of Justice Statistics, 2000); Allen Beck and Bernard Shipley, *Recidivism of Young Parolees* (Washington, D.C.: Bureau of Justice Statistics, 1987).

37 Oscar Newman, *Defensible Space: Crime Prevention through Urban Design* (New York: Macmillan, 1972).

38 Ronald Clarke, *Situational Crime Prevention* (Albany, N.Y.: Harrow and Heston, 1992).

39 Anthony Braga, David Weisburd, Elin Waring, Lorraine Green Mazerolle, William Spelman, and Francis Gajewski, "Problem-Oriented Policing in Violent Crime Places: A Randomized Controlled Experiment," *Criminology* 37 (1999): 541–80.

40 Eric Fritsch, Tory Caeti, and Robert Taylor, "Gang Suppression through Saturation Patrol, Aggressive Curfew, and Truancy Enforcement: A Quasi-Experimental Test of the Dallas Anti-Gang Initiative," *Crime and Delinquency* 45 (1999): 122–39.

41 Ronald Clarke, "Deterring Obscene Phone Callers: The New Jersey Experience," *Situational Crime Prevention,* ed. Ronald Clarke (Albany, N.Y.: Harrow and Heston, 1992), pp. 124–32.

42 See, generally, Cesare Lombroso, *Crime: Its Causes and Remedies* (Montclair, N.J.: Patterson Smith, 1968).

43 Dalton Conley and Neil Bennett, "Is Biology Destiny? Birth Weight and Life Chances," *American Sociological Review* 654 (2000): 458–67.

44 Jens Walkowiak, Jörg-A Wiener, Annemarie Fastabend, Birger Heinzow, Ursula Krämer, Eberhard Schmidt, Hans-J Steingürber, Sabine Wundram, and Gerhard Winneke, "Environmental Exposure to Polychlorinated Biphenyls and Quality of the Home Environment: Effects on Psychodevelopment in Early Childhood," *Lancet* 358 (2001): 92–93..

45 S. Dengate and A. Ruben, "Controlled Trial of Cumulative Behavioural Effects of a Common Bread Preservative," *Journal of Pediatrics and Child Health* 38 (2002): 373–76.

46 Herbert Needleman, Christine McFarland, Roberta Ness, Stephen Fienberg, and Michael Tobin, "Bone Lead Levels in Adjudicated Delinquents: A Case Control Study," *Neurotoxicology and Teratology* 24 (2002): 711–17.

47 G. B. Ramirez, O. Pagulayan, H. Akagi, A. Francisco Rivera, L. V. Lee, A. Berroya, M. C. Vince Cruz, and D. Casintahan, "Tagum Study II: Follow-up Study at Two Years of Age after Prenatal Exposure to Mercury," *Pediatrics* 111 (2003): 289–95.

48 Diana Fishbein, "Neuropsychological Function, Drug Abuse, and Violence: A Conceptual Framework," *Criminal Justice and Behavior* 27 (2000): 139–59.

49 Keith McBurnett and others, "Aggressive Symptoms and Salivary Cortisol in Clinic-Referred Boys with Conduct Disorder," *Annals of the New York Academy of Sciences* 794 (1996): 169–77.

50 Christy Miller Buchanan, Jacquelynne Eccles, and Jill Becker, "Are Adolescents the Victims of Raging Hormones? Evidence for Activational Effects of Hormones on Moods and Behavior at Adolescence," *Psychological Bulletin* 111 (1992): 62–107.

51 Dorothy Otnow Lewis, Ernest Moy, Lori Jackson, Robert Aaronson, Nicholas Restifo, Susan Serra, and Alexander Simos, "Biopsychosocial Characteristics of Children Who Later Murder," *American Journal of Psychiatry* 142 (1985): 1161–67.

52 Dorothy Otnow Lewis, *Guilty by Reason of Insanity* (New York: Fawcett Columbine, 1998).

53 Ronald Cohen, Alan Rosenbaum, Robert Kane, William Warneken, and Sheldon

Benjamin, "Neuropsychological Correlates of Domestic Violence," *Violence and Victims* 15 (2000): 397–410.

54 Susan Young, Andrew Smolen, Robin Corley, Kenneth Krauter, John DeFries, Thomas Crowley, and John Hewitt, "Dopamine Transporter Polymorphism Associated with Externalizing Behavior Problems in Children," *American Journal of Medical Genetics* 114 (2002): 144–49.

55 Matti Virkkunen, David Goldman, and Markku Linnoila, "Serotonin in Alcoholic Violent Offenders," *The Ciba Foundation Symposium: Genetics of Criminal and Antisocial Behavior* (Chichester, England: Wiley, 1995).

56 Rolf Loeber and Dale Hay, "Key Issues in the Development of Aggression and Violence from Childhood to Early Adulthood," *Annual Review of Psychology* 48 (1997): 371–410.

57 D. R. Blachman and S. P. Hinshaw, "Patterns of Friendship among Girls with and without Attention-Deficit/Hyperactivity Disorder," *Journal of Abnormal Child Psychology* 30 (2002): 625–40.

58 Terrie Moffitt and Phil Silva, "Self-Reported Delinquency, Neuropsychological Deficit, and History of Attention Deficit Disorder," *Journal of Abnormal Child Psychology* 16 (1988): 553–69.

59 See S. A. Mednick and Karl O. Christiansen, eds., *Biosocial Bases of Criminal Behavior* (New York: Gardner Press, 1977).

60 David Rowe and D. Wayne Osgood, "Heredity and Sociological Theories of Delinquency: A Reconsideration," *American Sociological Review* 49 (1984): 526–40.

61 B. Hutchings and S. A. Mednick, "Criminality in Adoptees and Their Adoptive and Biological Parents: A Pilot Study," in *Biosocial Bases of Criminal Behavior,* ed. S. A. Mednick and Karl O. Christiansen (New York: Gardner Press, 1977), pp. 83–105.

62 For an analysis of Sigmund Freud, see Spencer Rathus, *Psychology* (New York: Holt, Rinehart, and Winston, 1990), pp. 412–20.

63 August Aichorn, *Wayward Youth* (New York: Viking, 1965).

64 Seymour Halleck, *Psychiatry and the Dilemmas of Crime* (New York: Harper and Row, 1967), pp. 99–115.

65 John Monahan, *Mental Illness and Violent Crime* (Washington, D.C.: National Institute of Justice, 1996).

66 Jennifer Beyers and Rolf Loeber, "Untangling Developmental Relations between Depressed Mood and Delinquency in Male Adolescents," *Journal of Abnormal Child Psychology* 31 (2003): 247–67.

67 Richard Rosner, "Adolescents Accused of Murder and Manslaughter: A Five-Year Descriptive Study," *Bulletin of the American Academy of Psychiatry and the Law* 7 (1979): 342–51.

68 Richard Famularo, Robert Kinscherff, and Terence Fenton, "Psychiatric Diagnoses of Abusive Mothers: A Preliminary Report," *Journal of Nervous and Mental Disease* 180 (1992): 658–60.

69 Bruce Link, Howard Andrews, and Francis Cullen, "The Violent and Illegal Behavior of Mental Patients Reconsidered,"

American Sociological Review 57 (1992): 275–92; Ellen Hochstedler Steury, "Criminal Defendants with Psychiatric Impairment: Prevalence, Probabilities and Rates," *Journal of Criminal Law and Criminology* 84 (1993): 354–74.

70 Katherine Van Wormer and Chuk Odiah, "The Psychology of Suicide-Murder and the Death Penalty," *Journal of Criminal Justice* 27 (1999): 361–70.

71 Henrik Belfrage "A Ten-Year Follow-up of Criminality in Stockholm Mental Patients: New Evidence for a Relation between Mental Disorder and Crime," *British Journal of Criminology* 38 (1998): 145–55.

72 C. Wallace, P. Mullen , P. Burgess, S. Palmer, D. Ruschena, and C. Browne, "Serious Criminal Offending and Mental Disorder: Case Linkage Study," *British Journal of Psychiatry* 174 (1998): 477–84.

73 Patricia Brennan, Sarnoff Mednick, and Sheilagh Hodgins, "Major Mental Disorders and Criminal Violence in a Danish Birth Cohort," *Archives of General Psychiatry* 57 (2000): 494–500.

74 John Monahan and Henry Steadman, *Crime and Mental Disorder* (Washington, D.C.: National Institute of Justice, September 1984); David Tennenbaum, "Research Studies of Personality and Criminality," *Journal of Criminal Justice* 5 (1977): 1–19.

75 Marc Hillbrand, John Krystal, Kimberly Sharpe, and Hilliard Foster, "Clinical Predictors of Self-Mutilation in Hospitalized Patients," *Journal of Nervous and Mental Disease* 182 (1994): 9–13.

76 Carmen Cirincione, Henry Steadman, Pamela Clark Robbins, and John Monahan, *Mental Illness as a Factor in Criminality: A Study of Prisoners and Mental Patients* (Delmar, N.Y.: Policy Research Associates, 1991); see also Carmen Cirincione, Henry Steadman, Pamela Clark Robbins, and John Monahan, *Schizophrenia as a Contingent Risk Factor for Criminal Violence* (Delmar, N.Y.: Policy Research Associates, 1991).

77 This discussion is based on three works by Albert Bandura: *Aggression: A Social Learning Analysis* (Englewood Cliffs, N.J.: Prentice-Hall, 1973); *Social Learning Theory* (Englewood Cliffs, N.J.: Prentice-Hall, 1977); "The Social Learning Perspective: Mechanisms of Aggression," in *The Psychology of Crime and Criminal Justice,* ed. H. Toch (New York: Holt, Rinehart, and Winston, 1979), pp. 198–226.

78 Mark Warr and Mark Stafford, "The Influence of Delinquent Peers: What They Think or What They Do?" *Criminology* 29 (1991): 851–66.

79 J. E. Lockman, "Self and Peer Perception and Attributional Biases of Aggressive and Nonaggressive Boys in Dyadic Interactions," *Journal of Consulting and Clinical Psychology* 55 (1987): 404–10.

80 See, generally, Jean Piaget, *The Moral Judgement of the Child* (London: Kegan Paul, 1932).

81 Lawrence Kohlberg and others, *The Just Community Approach in Corrections: A Manual* (Niantic, Conn.: Connecticut Department of Corrections, 1973).

82 Walter Mischel, *Introduction to Personality,* 4th ed. (New York: Holt, Rinehart, and Winston, 1986), p. 1.

83 Edelyn Verona and Joyce Carbonell, "Female Violence and Personality," *Criminal Justice and Behavior* 27 (2000): 176–95.

84 Jennifer Beyers and Rolf Loeber, "Untangling Developmental Relations between Depressed Mood and Delinquency in Male Adolescents," *Journal of Abnormal Child Psychology* 31 (2003): 247–67.

85 See, generally, Albert Rabin, "The Antisocial Personality: Psychopathy and Sociopathy," in *The Psychology of Crime and Criminal Justice,* ed. H. Toch (New York: Holt, Rinehart, and Winston, 1979), pp. 236–51.

86 Steven Smith and Joseph Newman, "Alcohol and Drug Abuse: Dependence Disorders in Psychopathic and Nonpsychopathic Criminal Offenders," *Journal of Abnormal Psychology* 99 (1990): 430–39.

87 Richard Rogers, Randall Salekin, Kenneth Sewell, and Keith Cruise, "Prototypical Analysis of Antisocial Personality Disorder," *Criminal Justice and Behavior* 27 (2000): 234–55.

88 Jack Levin and James Alan Fox, *Mass Murder* (New York: Plenum, 1985).

89 Stephen Porter, David Fairweather, Jeff Drugge, Huues Herve, Angela Birt, and Douglas Boer, "Profiles of Psychopathy in Incarcerated Sexual Offenders," *Criminal Justice and Behavior* 27 (2000): 216–33.

90 David Lykken, "Psychopathy, Sociopathy, and Crime," *Society* 34 (1996): 30–38.

91 Christopher J. Patrick "Emotion and Psychopathy: Startling New Insights," *Psychophysiology* 31 (1994): 319–30.

92 Adrian Raine, Todd Lencz, Susan Bihrle, Lori LaCasse, and Patrick Colletti, "Reduced Prefrontal Gray Matter Volume and Reduced Autonomic Activity in Antisocial Personality Disorder," *Archives of General Psychiatry* 57 (2000): 119–27.

93 Kent Kiehl, Andra Smith, Robert Hare, Adrianna Mendrek, Bruce Forster, Johann Brink, and Peter F. Liddle, "Limbic Abnormalities in Affective Processing by Criminal Psychopaths as Revealed by Functional Magnetic Resonance Imaging," *Biological Psychiatry* 5 (2001): 677–84.

94 Deborah Denno, "Sociological and Human Developmental Explanations of Crime: Conflict or Consensus," *Criminology* 23 (1985): 711–41; Christine Ward and Richard McFall, "Further Validation of the Problem Inventory for Adolescent Girls: Comparing Caucasian and Black Delinquents and Nondelinquents," *Journal of Consulting and Clinical Psychology* 54 (1986): 732–33; L. Hubble and M. Groff, "Magnitude and Direction of WISC-R Verbal Performance IQ Discrepancies among Adjudicated Male Delinquents," *Journal of Youth and Adolescence* 10 (1981): 179–83.

95 Peter R. Giancola and Amos Zeichner, "Intellectual Ability and Aggressive Behavior in Nonclinical-Nonforensic Males," *Journal of Psychopathology and Behavioral Assessment* 16 (1994): 20–32.

96 Donald Lynam, Terrie Moffitt, and Magda Stouthamer-Loeber, "Explaining the Relation between IQ and Delinquency: Class,

Race, Test Motivation, School Failure, or Self-Control," *Journal of Abnormal Psychology* 102 (1993): 187–96.

97 Alex Piquero, "Frequency, Specialization, and Violence in Offending Careers," *Journal of Research in Crime and Delinquency* 37 (2000): 392–418.

98 Terrie Moffitt, William Gabrielli, Sarnoff Mednick, and Fini Schulsinger, "Socioeconomic Status, IQ, and Delinquency," *Journal of Abnormal Psychology* 90 (1981): 152–56.

99 Hakan Stattin and Ingrid Klackenberg-Larsson, "Early Language and Intelligence Development and Their Relationship to Future Criminal Behavior," *Journal of Abnormal Psychology* 102 (1993): 369–78.

100 H. D. Day, J. M. Franklin, and D. D. Marshall, "Predictors of Aggression in Hospitalized Adolescents," *Journal of Psychology* 132 (1998): 427–35; Scott Menard and Barbara Morse, "A Structuralist Critique of the IQ-Delinquency Hypothesis: Theory and Evidence," *American Journal of Sociology* 89 (1984): 1347–78; Denno, "Sociological and Human Developmental Explanations of Crime."

101 Ulric Neisser and others, "Intelligence: Knowns and Unknowns," *American Psychologist* 51 (1996): 77–101, at 83.

102 See, generally, Terance Miethe and Robert Meier, *Crime and Its Social Context: Toward an Integrated Theory of Offenders, Victims, and Situations* (Albany, N.Y.: State University of New York Press, 1994).

103 Émile Durkheim, *The Division of Labor in Society* (New York: Free Press, 1964); Émile Durkheim, *Rules of the Sociological Method,* trans. S. A. Solvay and J. H. Mueller, ed. G. Catlin (New York: Free Press, 1966).

104 *Poverty in the United States: 2002* (U.S. Department of the Census, 2003).

105 Ibid.

106 William Spelman, "Abandoned Buildings: Magnets for Crime," *Journal of Criminal Justice* 21 (1993): 481–95.

107 William Julius Wilson, "Poverty, Joblessness, and Family Structure in the Inner City: A Comparative Perspective," paper presented at the annual meeting of the American Society of Criminology, San Francisco, California, November 1991.

108 Oscar Lewis, "The Culture of Poverty," *Scientific American* 215 (1966): 19–25.

109 William Julius Wilson, *The Truly Disadvantaged* (Chicago: University of Chicago Press, 1987).

110 Robert Bursik, "Social Disorganization and Theories of Crime and Delinquency: Problems and Prospects," *Criminology* 26 (1988): 519–551, at 521.

111 Robert Sampson, "Structural Sources of Variation in Race-Age-Specific Rates of Offending across Major U.S. Cities," *Criminology* 23 (1985): 647–73; Janet Heitgerd and Robert Bursik Jr., "Extracommunity Dynamics and the Ecology of Delinquency," *American Journal of Sociology* 92 (1987): 775–87; Ora Simcha-Fagan and Joseph Schwartz, "Neighborhood and Delinquency: An Assessment of Contex-

tual Effects," *Criminology* 24 (1986): 667–703.

112 E. Britt Patterson, "Poverty, Income Inequality, and Community Crime Rates," *Criminology* 29 (1991): 755–76.

113 Leon Pettiway, "Urban Spatial Structure and Incidence of Arson: Differences between Ghetto and Nonghetto Environments," *Justice Quarterly* 5 (1988): 113–29.

114 D. Wayne Osgood and Jeff Chambers, "Social Disorganization Outside the Metropolis: An Analysis of Rural Youth Violence," *Criminology* 38 (2000): 81–117.

115 Darrell Steffensmeier and Dana Haynie, "Gender, Structural Disadvantage, and Urban Crime: Do Macrosocial Variables Also Explain Female Offending Rates?" *Criminology* 38 (2000): 403–38.

116 Karen Parker and Matthew Pruitt, "Poverty, Poverty Concentration, and Homicide," *Social Science Quarterly* 81 (2000): 555–82.

117 Ruth Peterson, Lauren Krivo, and Mark Harris, "Disadvantage and Neighborhood Violent Crime: Do Local Institutions Matter?" *Journal of Research in Crime and Delinquency* 37 (2000): 31–63.

118 Beverly Stiles, Xiaoru Liu, and Howard Kaplan, "Relative Deprivation and Deviant Adaptations: The Mediating Effects of Negative Self-Feelings," *Journal of Research in Crime and Delinquency* 37 (2000): 64–90.

119 Barbara Warner, "The Role of Attenuated Culture in Social Disorganization Theory," *Criminology* 41 (2003): 73–97.

120 Walter Miller, "Lower Class Culture as a Generating Milieu of Gang Delinquency," *Journal of Social Issues* 14 (1958): 5–19; see also Thorsten Sellin, *Culture Conflict and Crime,* bulletin no. 41 (New York: Social Science Research Council, 1938).

121 Richard Cloward and Lloyd Ohlin, *Delinquency and Opportunity* (Glencoe, Ill.: Free Press, 1960).

122 Leslie Kennedy and Stephen Baron, "Routine Activities and a Subculture of Violence: A Study of Violence on the Street," *Journal of Research in Crime and Delinquency* 30 (1993): 88–112.

123 Charis Kubrin and Ronald Weitzer, "Retaliatory Homicide: Concentrated Disadvantage and Neighborhood Culture," *Social Problems* 50 (2003): 157–81.

124 Robert Merton, "Social Structure and Anomie," *American Sociological Review* 3 (1938): 672–82.

125 Robert Agnew, "Foundation for a General Strain Theory of Crime and Delinquency," *Criminology* 30 (1992): 47–87; Robert Agnew, "Stability and Change in Crime over the Life Course: A Strain Theory Explanation," in *Advances in Criminological Theory,* vol. 7, *Developmental Theories of Crime and Delinquency,* ed. Terence Thornberry (New Brunswick, N.J.: Transaction Books, 1994).

126 Raymond Paternoster and Paul Mazerolle, "General Strain Theory and Delinquency: A Replication and Extension," *Journal of Research in Crime and Delinquency* 31 (1994): 235–63.

127 Paul Mazerolle, Velmer Burton, Francis Cullen, T. David Evans, and Gary Payne,

"Strain, Anger, and Delinquent Adaptations: Specifying General Strain Theory," *Journal of Criminal Justice* 28 (2000): 89–101.

128 Stephen Cernkovich, Peggy Giordano, and Jennifer Rudolph, "Race, Crime and the American Dream," *Journal of Research in Crime and Delinquency* 37 (2000): 131–70.

129 Charles Tittle, Wayne Villemez, and Douglas Smith, "The Myth of Social Class and Criminality: An Empirical Assessment of the Evidence," *American Sociological Review* 43 (1978): 643–56.

130 Eric Stewart, Ronald Simons, and Rand Conger, "Assessing Neighborhood and Social Psychological Influences on Childhood Violence in an African American Sample," *Criminology* 40 (2002): 801–30.

131 Rolf Loeber and Magda Stouthamer-Loeber, "Family Factors as Correlates and Predictors of Juvenile Conduct Problems and Delinquency," in *Crime and Justice,* vol. 7, ed. Michael Tonry and Norval Morris (Chicago: University of Chicago Press, 1986), pp. 29–151.

132 John Laub and Robert Sampson, "Unraveling Families and Delinquency: A Reanalysis of the Gluecks' Data," *Criminology* 26 (1988): 355–80.

133 Ronald Simons, Chyi-In Wu, Kuei-Hsiu Lin, Leslie Gordon, and Rand Conger, "A Cross-Cultural Examination of the Link between Corporal Punishment and Adolescent Antisocial Behavior," *Criminology* 38 (2000): 47–79.

134 Joan McCord, "Family Relationships, Juvenile Delinquency, and Adult Criminality," *Criminology* 29 (1991): 397–419.

135 Lawrence Rosen, "Family and Delinquency: Structure or Function?" *Criminology* 23 (1985): 553–73.

136 Lyle Shannon, *Assessing the Relationship of Adult Criminal Careers to Juvenile Careers: A Summary* (Washington, D.C.: Government Printing Office, 1982); Donald J. West and David P. Farrington, *The Delinquent Way of Life* (London: Heineman, 1977); Marvin Wolfgang, Robert Figlio, and Thorsten Sellin, *Delinquency in a Birth Cohort* (Chicago: University of Chicago Press, 1972).

137 Terence Thornberry, Melanie Moore, and R. L. Christenson, "The Effect of Dropping Out of High School on Subsequent Criminal Behavior," *Criminology* 23 (1985): 3–18.

138 Scott Menard, "Demographic and Theoretical Variables in the Age-Period-Cohort Analysis of Illegal Behavior," *Journal of Research in Crime and Delinquency* 29 (1992): 178–99.

139 D. Wayne Osgood, Janet Wilson, Patrick O'Malley, Jerald Bachman, and Lloyd Johnston, "Routine Activities and Individual Deviant Behavior," *American Sociological Review* 61 (1996): 635–55.

140 Mark Warr, "Age, Peers, and Delinquency," *Criminology* 31 (1993): 17–40.

141 Sara Battin, Karl Hill, Robert Abbott, Richard Catalano, and J. David Hawkins, "The Contribution of Gang Membership to Delinquency Beyond Delinquent Friends," *Criminology* 36 (1998): 93–116.

142 David Fergusson, L. John Horwood, and Daniel Nagin, "Offending Trajectories in a New Zealand Birth Cohort," *Criminology* 38 (2000): 525–51.

143 Denise Kandel and Mark Davies, "Friendship Networks, Intimacy, and Illicit Drug Use in Young Adulthood: A Comparison of Two Competing Theories," *Criminology* 29 (1991): 441–67.

144 Edwin Sutherland and Donald Cressey, *Criminology* (Philadelphia: J. B. Lippincott, 1970), pp. 71–91.

145 Denise Kandel and Mark Davies, "Friendship Networks, Intimacy, and Illicit Drug Use in Young Adulthood: A Comparison of Two Competing Theories," *Criminology* 29 (1991): 441–67.

146 Leanne Fiftal Alarid, Velmer Burton, and Francis Cullen, "Gender and Crime among Felony Offenders: Assessing the Generality of Social Control and Differential Association Theory," *Journal of Research in Crime and Delinquency* 37 (2000) 171–99.

147 See, for example, Randy La Grange and Helen Raskin White, "Age Differences in Delinquency: A Test of Theory," *Criminology* 23 (1985): 19–45; Marvin Krohn and James Massey, "Social Control and Delinquent Behavior: An Examination of the Elements of the Social Bond," *Sociological Quarterly* 21 (1980): 529–44.

148 Bobbi Jo Anderson, Malcolm Holmes, and Erik Ostresh, "Male and Female Delinquents' Attachments and Effects of Attachments on Severity of Self-Reported Delinquency," *Criminal Justice and Behavior* 26 (1999): 435–52.

149 Patricia Jenkins, "School Delinquency and the School Social Bond," *Journal of Research in Crime and Delinquency* 34 (1997): 337–67.

150 Christina DeJong and Kenneth Jackson, "Putting Race into Context: Race, Juvenile Justice Processing, and Urbanization," *Justice Quarterly* 15 (1998): 487–504.

151 W. Byron Groves and Robert Sampson, "Critical Theory and Criminology," *Social Problems* 33 (1986): 58–80.

152 Gresham Sykes, "The Rise of Critical Criminology," *Journal of Criminal Law and Criminology* 65 (June 1974): 206; see also Ian Taylor and others, *The New Criminology: For a Social Theory of Deviance* (New York: Harper and Row, 1973).

153 Travis Pratt and Christopher Lowenkamp, "Conflict Theory, Economic Conditions, and Homicide: A Time-Series Analysis," *Homicide Studies* 6 (2002): 61–84.

154 See, generally, Jock Young, *Realist Criminology* (London: Sage, 1989).

155 Kathleen Daly and Meda Chesney-Lind, "Feminism and Criminology," *Justice Quarterly* 5 (1988): 438–97.

156 Kevin Anderson, "Richard Quinney's Journey: The Marxist Dimension," *Crime and Delinquency* 48 (2002): 232–43; Harold Pepinsky, "Violence as Unresponsiveness: Toward a New Conception of Crime," *Justice Quarterly* 5 (1988): 539–87.

157 Robert DeFina and Thomas Arvanites, "The Weak Effect of Imprisonment on Crime: 1971–1998," *Social Science Quarterly* 83 (2002): 635–54.

158 David Rowe, D. Wayne Osgood, and W. Alan Nicewander, "A Latent Trait Approach to Unifying Criminal Careers," *Criminology* 28 (1990): 237–70.

159 David Rowe and Daniel Flannery, "An Examination of Environmental and Trait Influences on Adolescent Delinquency," *Journal of Research in Crime and Delinquency* 31 (1994): 374–89.

160 Michael Gottfredson and Travis Hirschi, *A General Theory of Crime* (Stanford, Calif.: Stanford University Press, 1990).

161 Ick-Joong Chung, Karl G Hill, J. David Hawkins, Lewayne Gilchrist, and Daniel Nagin, "Childhood Predictors of Offense Trajectories," *Journal of Research in Crime and Delinquency* 39 (2002): 60–91.

162 Amy D'Unger, Kenneth Land, Patricia McCall, and Daniel Nagin, "How Many Latent Classes of Delinquent/Criminal Careers? Results from Mixed Poisson Regression Analyses," *American Journal of Sociology* 103 (1998): 1593–1630.

163 Helene Raskin White, Peter Tice, Rolf Loeber, and Magda Stouthamer-Loeber, "Illegal Acts Committed by Adolescents under the Influence of Alcohol and Drugs," *Journal of Research in Crime & Delinquency* 39 (2002): 131–53; Xavier Coll, Fergus Law, Aurelio Tobias, Keith Hawton, and Josep Tomas, "Abuse and Deliberate Self-Poisoning in Women: A Matched Case-Control Study," *Child Abuse and Neglect* 25 (2001): 1291–93.

164 Richard Miech, Avshalom Caspi, Terrie Moffitt, Bradley Entner Wright, and Phil Silva, "Low Socioeconomic Status and Mental Disorders: A Longitudinal Study of Selection and Causation during Young Adulthood," *American Journal of Sociology* 104 (1999): 1096–1131; Marvin Krohn, Alan Lizotte, and Cynthia Perez, "The Interrelationship between Substance Use and Precocious Transitions to Adult Sexuality," *Journal of Health and Social Behavior* 38 (1997): 87–103.

165 Rolf Loeber, David Farrington, Magda Stouthamer-Loeber, Terrie Moffitt, Avshalom Caspi, and Don Lynam, "Male Mental Health Problems, Psychopathy, and Personality Traits: Key Findings from the First 14 Years of the Pittsburgh Youth Study," *Clinical Child and Family Psychology Review* 4 (2002): 273–97.

166 Robert Sampson and John Laub, *Crime in the Making: Pathways and Turning Points through Life* (Cambridge, Mass.: Harvard University Press, 1993).

167 Nan Lin, *Social Capital: A Theory of Social Structure and Action* (Cambridge, England: Cambridge University Press, 2002).

168 Doris Layton MacKenzie and Spencer De Li, "The Impact of Formal and Informal Social Controls on the Criminal Activities of Probationers," *Journal of Research in Crime and Delinquency* 39 (2002): 243–78.

169 Alex Piquero, John MacDonald, and Karen Parker. "Race, Local Life Circumstances, and Criminal Activity over the Life Course," *Social Science Quarterly* 83 (2002): 654–71.

170 Personal communication with Alex Piquero, September 24, 2002.

171 Hans Von Hentig, *The Criminal and His Victim: Studies in the Sociobiology of Crime* (New Haven, Conn.: Yale University Press, 1948), p. 384.

172 Stephen Schafer, *The Victim and His Criminal* (New York: Random House, 1968), p. 152.

173 Marvin Wolfgang, *Patterns of Criminal Homicide* (Philadelphia: University of Pennsylvania Press, 1958).

174 Ibid.

175 Menachem Amir, *Patterns in Forcible Rape* (Chicago: University of Chicago Press, 1971).

176 Susan Estrich, *Real Rape* (Cambridge, Mass.: Harvard University Press, 1987).

177 Edem Avakame, "Females' Labor Force Participation and Intimate Femicide: An Empirical Assessment of the Backlash Hypothesis," *Violence and Victims* 14 (1999): 277–83.

178 Rosemary Gartner and Bill McCarthy, "The Social Distribution of Femicide in Urban Canada, 1921–1988," *Law and Society Review* 25 (1991): 287–311.

179 Rolf Loeber, Mary DeLamatre, George Tita, Jacqueline Cohen, Magda Stouthamer-Loeber, and David Farrington, "Gun Injury and Mortality: The Delinquent Backgrounds of Juvenile Offenders," *Violence and Victims* 14 (1999): 339–51.

180 Bonnie Fisher, John Sloan, Francis Cullen, and Chunmeng Lu, "Crime in the Ivory Tower: The Level and Sources of Student Victimization," *Criminology* 36 (1998): 671–710.

181 Lawrence Cohen and Marcus Felson, "Social Change and Crime Rate Trends: A Routine Activities Approach," *American Sociological Review* 44 (1979): 588–608; Lawrence Cohen, Marcus Felson, and Kenneth Land, "Property Crime Rates in the United States: A Macrodynamic Analysis, 1947–1977, with Ex-Ante Forecasts for the Mid-1980s," *American Journal of Sociology* 86 (1980): 90–118; for a review, see James LeBeau and Thomas Castellano, "The Routine Activities Approach: An Inventory and Critique," Center for the Studies of Crime, Delinquency, and Corrections, Southern Illinois University, Carbondale, Illinois, 1987.

182 Steven Messner and Kenneth Tardiff, "The Social Ecology of Urban Homicide: An Application of the 'Routine Activities' Approach," *Criminology* 23 (1985): 241–67; Philip Cook, "The Demand and Supply of Criminal Opportunities," in *Crime and Justice,* vol. 7, ed. Michael Tonry and Norval Morris (Chicago: University of Chicago Press, 1986), pp. 1–28; Ronald Clarke and Derek Cornish, "Modeling Offenders' Decisions: A Framework for Research and Policy," in *Crime and Justice,* vol. 6, ed. Michael Tonry and Norval Morris (Chicago: University of Chicago Press, 1985), pp. 147–187.

183 Cohen, Felson, and Land, "Property Crime Rates in the United States."

Chapter Outline

Chapter Objectives

After reading this chapter, you should be able to:

1. Understand the concept of substantive criminal law and its history.
2. Know the similarities and differences between criminal law and civil law.
3. Recognize the differences between felonies and misdemeanors.
4. Name the various elements of a crime.
5. Discuss the concept of criminal intent.
6. Recognize the recent changes in the criminal law.
7. Describe the role of the Bill of Rights.
8. Know which constitutional amendments are the most important to the justice system.
9. List the elements of due process of law.
10. Show how interpretations of due process affect civil rights.

Viewpoints

 Law in Review:
Ex Post Facto Laws   126

 Law in Review: *Chicago* v. *Morales*
(1999)   128

 Analyzing Criminal Justice
Issues: The Insanity Defense   135

 Analyzing Criminal Justice
Issues: The Criminal Law and
Terrorism   140

Web Links

Roman Twelve Tables
http://members.aol.com/pilgrimjon/private/LEX/
12tables.html   121

Justinian code
http://www.fordham.edu/halsall/basis/
535institutes.html   121

Online legal dictionary
http://dictionary.law.com/   121

Historical legal documents and codes
http://www.wagonerlaw.com/
DKmilestones.html   121

Negligence interpreted
http://www.duhaime.org/tort/ca-negl.htm   123

O. J. Simpson case
http://www.cnn.com/US/OJ/   124

New York public safety statutes
http://assembly.state.ny.us/leg/
?cl=82&a=69   132

American Psychiatric Association
http://www.psych.org/public_info/
insanity.cfm   134

InfoTrac College Edition Links

Chapter 4 | Criminal Law: Substance and Procedure

On April 18, 2003, California law enforcement officials announced that the two unidentified bodies found in San Francisco Bay earlier that week were Laci Peterson and her unborn baby boy, Connor. Laci had been the subject of intense national attention. Soon after the bodies were discovered, Scott Peterson, Laci's husband, was taken into police custody and charged with two counts of murder. The media alleged that Scott, who was having an affair, had killed his wife. Peterson had told police he last saw 27-year-old Laci on Christmas Eve 2002, when he left to go fishing at a Berkeley, California, marina, located only three miles from where the bodies were found. Scott maintained his innocence and his legal defense team soon claimed that Laci may have been murdered by the same people who had killed a young mother, Evelyn Hernandez, whose body had been found under similar circumstances. When Scott Peterson's attorneys asked to have access to the police file on the Hernandez case so that they could find the "real killers," their request was refused by a Superior Court judge who claimed that opening the file on the murder of the 24-year-old Hernandez might hinder police efforts to solve that case. The

judge ordered that both the prosecution and the defense be given copies of Hernandez's autopsy report as well as 30 autopsy photographs.

The Peterson case illustrates a number of important issues affecting the legal system today. Can Scott Peterson hope to get a fair trial in the wash of all the media publicity given to his wife's disappearance? Can the suspect in a celebrated case benefit from the same level of procedural fairness, such as an unbiased jury, enjoyed by a more anonymous criminal suspect? Or could Scott's notoriety

be beneficial if it turns him into a sympathetic character? The Peterson case also illustrates how the rule of law, as applied by the court system, controls the outcome. Here, in the early part of the proceedings, a judge's ruling on the availability of evidence, for example, the Hernandez police file, may shape the final disposition of the case.

View the CNN video clip of this story on your Introduction to Criminal Justice 10e CD.

civil law

All law that is not criminal, including tort, contract, personal property, maritime, and commercial law.

criminal law

The body of rules that define crimes, set out their punishments, and mandate the procedures for carrying out the criminal justice process.

The present English system of law came into existence during the reign of Henry II (1154–1189) when royal judges began to publish their decisions in local cases. This allowed judicial precedents to be established, and a national law established. In this early image, a petitioner goes before the Royal judges.

The Substantive Criminal Law

The substantive criminal law defines crime and punishment in U.S. society. Each state government and the federal government has its own criminal code, developed over many generations and incorporating moral beliefs, social values, and political, economic, and other societal concerns. The criminal law is a living document, constantly evolving to keep pace with society and its needs. The rules designed to implement the substantive law are known as procedural law. It is concerned with the criminal process—the legal steps through which an offender passes—commencing with the initial criminal investigation and concluding with release of the offender. Some elements of the law of criminal procedure are the rules of evidence, the law of arrest, the law of search and seizure, questions of appeal, and the right to counsel. Many of the rights that have been extended to offenders over the past two decades lie within procedural law.

In modern American society, the rule of law governs almost all phases of human enterprise, including commerce, family life, property transfer, and the regulation of interpersonal conflict. It contains elements that control personal relationships between individuals and public relationships between individuals and the government. The former is known as **civil law,** and the latter is called **criminal law.** Because the law defines crime, punishment, and procedure, which are the basic concerns of the criminal justice system, it is essential for students to know something of the nature, purpose, and content of the substantive and procedural criminal law.

The Historical Development of Criminal Law

The roots of the criminal codes used in the United States can be traced back to such early legal charters as the Babylonian Code of Hammurabi (2000 B.C.), the Mosaic Code of the Israelites (1200 B.C.), and the Roman Twelve Tables (451 B.C.), which were formulated by a special commission of ten noble Roman men in response to pressure from the lower classes, who complained that the existing, unwritten legal code gave arbitrary and unlimited power to the wealthy classes. The original code was written on bronze plaques, which have been lost, but records of sections, which were memorized by every Roman male, survive. The remaining laws deal with debt, family relations, property, and other daily matters.

During the sixth century, under the leadership of Byzantine emperor Justinian, the first great codification of law in the Western world was prepared. Justinian's Corpus Juris Civilis, or body of civil law, summarized the system of Roman law that had developed over a thousand years. Rules and regulations to ensure the safety of the state and the individual served as the basis for future civil and criminal legal classifications. Centuries later, French emperor Napoleon I created the French civil code, using Justinian's code as a model.[1]

Though the early formal legal codes were lost during the Dark Ages, early German and Anglo-Saxon societies developed legal systems featuring monetary compensation, called wergild (*wer* means worth and refers to what the person, and therefore the crime, was worth), for criminal violations. Guilt was determined by two methods: compurgation, which involved having the accused person swear an oath of innocence while being backed up by a group of 12 to 25 oath helpers, who would attest to his or her character; and claims of innocence and ordeal, which were based on the principle that divine forces would not allow an innocent person to be harmed.

Perspectives on Justice

Wergild was the forerunner of the modern fine. Efforts are being made to gear fines to a person's income, a procedure that is in sync with the justice perspective.

Determining guilt by ordeal involved such measures as having the accused place his or her hand in boiling water or hold a hot iron. If the wound healed, the person was found innocent; if the wound did not heal, the accused was deemed guilty. Trial by combat allowed the accused to challenge his accuser to a duel, with the outcome determining the legitimacy of the accusation. Punishments included public flogging, branding, beheading, and burning.

Development of Common Law

After the Norman Conquest of England in 1066, royal judges began to travel throughout the land, holding court in each county several times a year. When court was in session, the royal administrator, or judge, would summon a number of citizens who would, on their oath, tell of the crimes and serious breaches of the peace that had occurred since the judge's last visit. The royal judge then would decide what to do in each case, using local custom and rules of conduct as his guide—a system known as **stare decisis** (Latin for "to stand by decided cases").

Courts were bound to follow the law established in previous cases unless a higher authority, such as the king or the pope, overruled the law.

The present English system of law came into existence during the reign of Henry II (1154–1189) when royal judges began to publish their decisions in local cases. Judges began to use these written decisions as a basis for their decision making and eventually a fixed body of legal rules and principles was produced. If the new rules were successfully applied in a number of different cases, they would become precedents, which would then be commonly applied in all similar cases—hence the term *common law.* Crimes such as murder, burglary, arson, and rape are common law crimes whose elements were initially defined by judges. They are referred to as **mala in se,** inherently evil and depraved. When the situation required it, the English Parliament enacted legislation to supplement the judge-made common law. These were referred to as statutory or mala prohibitum crimes, which reflected existing social conditions.

English common law evolved constantly to fit specific incidents that the judges encountered. In fact, legal scholars have identified specific cases in which judges created new crimes, some of which exist today. For example, in the *Carriers* case (1473), an English court ruled that a merchant who had been hired to transport merchandise was guilty of larceny (theft) if he kept the goods for his own purposes.[2] Before the *Carriers* case, the common law had not recognized a crime when people kept something that was voluntarily placed in their possession, even if the rightful owner had given them only temporary custody of the merchandise. Breaking with legal tradition, the court recognized that the commercial system could not be maintained unless the laws of theft were changed. Thus, larcenies defined by separate and unique criminal laws—such as embezzlement, extortion, and false pretenses—came into existence.

 To read some of the original elements of the Roman Twelve Tables, go to http://members.aol.com/pilgrimjon/private/LEX/12tables.html.

To read some of the statutes in the Justinian code, go to http://www.fordham.edu/halsall/basis/535institutes.html.

To read more about life in the barbarian tribes, use "Germanic tribes" as a subject guide on InfoTrac College Edition.

stare decisis
To stand by decided cases; the legal principle by which the decision or holding in an earlier case becomes the standard by which subsequent similar cases are judged.

Need to look up legal terms such as *stare decisis*? Here is a link to a good online legal dictionary: http://dictionary.law.com/.

Use "stare decisis" as a key work on InfoTrac College Edition to learn more about this common law concept.

mala in se
In common law, offenses that are from their own nature evil, immoral, and wrong. Mala in se offenses include murder, theft, and arson.

 For a site with numerous links to important historical legal documents and codes, go to http://www.wagonerlaw.com/DKmilestones.html.

Exhibit 4.1 Common Law Crimes

	Crime	Definition	Example
Crimes against the person	First-degree murder	Unlawful killing of another human being with malice aforethought and with premeditation and deliberation.	A woman buys some poison and pours it into a cup of coffee her husband is drinking, intending to kill him. Her motive is to get the insurance benefits of the victim.
	Voluntary manslaughter	Intentional killing committed under extenuating circumstances that mitigate the killing, such as killing in the heat of passion after being provoked.	A husband coming home early from work finds his wife in bed with another man. The husband goes into a rage and shoots and kills both lovers with a gun he keeps by his bedside.
	Battery	Unlawful touching of another with intent to cause injury.	A man seeing a stranger sitting in his favorite seat in the cafeteria goes up to that person and pushes him out of the seat.
	Assault	Intentional placing of another in fear of receiving an immediate battery.	A student aims an unloaded gun at her professor who believes the gun is loaded. The student says she is going to shoot.
	Rape	Unlawful sexual intercourse with a female without her consent.	After a party, a man offers to drive a young female acquaintance home. He takes her to a wooded area and, despite her protests, forces her to have sexual relations with him.
	Robbery	Wrongful taking and carrying away of personal property from a person by violence or intimidation.	A man armed with a loaded gun approaches another man on a deserted street and demands his wallet.
Inchoate (incomplete) offenses	Attempt	An intentional act for the purpose of committing a crime that is more than mere preparation or planning of the crime. The crime is not completed, however.	A person intending to kill another places a bomb in the second person's car, so that it will detonate when the ignition key is used. The bomb is discovered before the car is started. Attempted murder has been committed.
	Conspiracy	Voluntary agreement between two or more persons to achieve an unlawful object or to achieve a lawful object using means forbidden by law.	A drug company sells larger-than-normal quantities of drugs to a doctor, knowing that the doctor is distributing the drugs illegally. The drug company is guilty of conspiracy.
Crimes against property	Burglary	Breaking and entering of a dwelling house of another with the intent to commit a felony.	Intending to steal some jewelry and silver, a young man breaks a window and enters another's house.
	Arson	Intentional burning of a dwelling house of another.	A secretary, angry that her boss did not give her a raise, goes to her boss's house and sets fire to it.
	Larceny	Taking and carrying away the personal property of another with the intent to steal the property.	While a woman is shopping, she sees a diamond ring displayed at the jewelry counter. When no one is looking, the woman takes the ring and walks out of the store.

Before the American Revolution, the colonies, then under British rule, were subject to the common law. After the colonies won their independence, state legislatures standardized common law crimes such as murder, burglary, arson, and rape by putting them into statutory form in criminal codes. As in England, whenever common law proved inadequate to deal with changing social and moral issues, the states and Congress supplemented it with legislative statutes. Similarly, statutes prohibiting such offenses as the sale and possession of narcotics or the pirating of videotapes have been passed to control human behavior unknown at the time the common law was formulated. Today, criminal behavior is defined primarily by statute. With few exceptions, crimes are removed, added, or modified by the legislature of a particular jurisdiction. See Exhibit 4.1 for definitions and examples of common law crimes.

Exhibit 4.2 A Comparison of Criminal and Tort Law

Similarities

- Goal of controlling behavior
- Imposition of sanctions
- Some common areas of legal action—for example, personal assault and control of white-collar offenses such as environmental pollution

Differences

Criminal law	Tort law
Crime is a public offense.	Tort is a civil or private wrong.
The sanction associated with criminal law is incarceration or death.	The sanction associated with tort law is monetary damages.
The right of enforcement belongs to the state.	The individual brings the action.
The government ordinarily does not appeal.	Both parties can appeal.
Fines go to the state.	The individual receives the damages as compensation for harm done.

Criminal Law and Civil Law

Over time, law came to be divided into two broad categories: criminal law and civil law. Criminal law is the law of crimes and their punishments. Civil law includes tort law (personal wrongs and damages), property law (the law governing the transfer and ownership of property), and contract law (the law of personal agreements). The differences between criminal law and civil law are significant because, in the U.S. legal system, criminal proceedings are completely separate from civil actions.

The major objective of the criminal law is to protect the public against harm by preventing criminal offenses. The primary concern of the civil law is the control and regulation of human interaction. It regulates agreements and contracts, ownership of property, inheritance, and personal relationships such as marriage and child custody. However, it is in the area of private wrongs, or torts, in which the criminal and civil law are most similar. A tort typically involves some harm such as an injury that occurs because of the negligence of a motor vehicle operator. It can also involve injury caused by malicious intent, such as when a person strikes another and causes injury. A tort action is a lawsuit aimed at collecting damages for harm done. While similar to a crime because a victim has been injured, the two actions are somewhat different. When a crime is committed, the state initiates the legal process and imposes a punishment in the form of a criminal sanction. Furthermore, in criminal law, the emphasis is on the intent of the individual committing the crime. A civil proceeding gives primary attention to affixing the blame each party deserves for producing the damage or conflict.

Despite these major differences, criminal and civil law share certain features. Both seek to control people's behavior by preventing them from acting in an undesirable manner, and both impose sanctions on those who commit violations of the law. The payment of damages to the victim in a tort case, for example, serves some of the same purposes as the payment of a fine in a criminal case. In addition, many actions, such as assault and battery, various forms of larceny, and negligence, are the basis for criminal as well as civil actions. Exhibit 4.2 summarizes the major similarities and differences between criminal law and tort law.

How is the concept of negligence interpreted? To find out, go to http://www.duhaime.org/Tort/ca-negl.htm.

www   Want to read more about the O. J. Simpson case? Numerous Web sites are devoted to it, including one maintained by CNN: http://www.cnn.com/US/OJ/.

To quiz yourself on this material, go to questions 4.1–4.4 on the Introduction to Criminal Justice 10e CD.

The Simpson Case The widely publicized case of O. J. Simpson provides a good example of the similarities and differences between tort and criminal law. In the so-called Trial of the Century—Part I, the famous athlete was tried by the state of California and acquitted of the murder of his ex-wife, Nicole, and her friend, Ron Goldman, in a criminal prosecution. As a defendant, Simpson was required to be in court but did not have to testify during the trial. The standard of proof "beyond a reasonable doubt" was used to assess the evidence, and the verdict had to be unanimous. A conviction would have brought a sentence of life in prison.

In the Trial of the Century—Part II, the Estate of Nicole Brown Simpson and the family of Ron Goldman sued O. J. Simpson for the wrongful deaths of his ex-wife and her friend in a civil trial. This was a lawsuit brought by the family of the deceased against the person believed to have caused the death. Simpson was not required to be in court, but when called by either side he had to provide testimony. No television cameras were allowed in the courtroom, whereas the criminal trial was televised. The burden of proof in the civil case was "preponderance of the evidence," or which side had the most convincing case before the jury. In addition, only nine of the twelve jurors had to agree on a general verdict, and any judgment involved money and not imprisonment. While found not guilty at his criminal trial, Simpson was required to pay significant damages at his civil case.

Sources of the Criminal Law

The three major sources of the criminal law are (1) common law, statutes, and case decisions; (2) administrative rules and regulations; and (3) constitutional laws.[3]

Common Law, Statutes, and Case Decisions

The common law crimes adopted into state codes form one major source of the substantive criminal law today. As common law, crimes had a general meaning, and everyone basically understood the definition of such actions as murder, larceny, and rape. Today, statutes enacted by state and federal legislative bodies have built on these common law meanings and often contain more detailed and specific definitions of the crimes. Statutes are thus a way in which the criminal law is created, modified, or expunged. They reflect existing social conditions and deal with issues of morality, such as gambling and sexual activity, as well as traditional common law crimes, such as murder, burglary, and arson.

Case law and judicial decision making also change and influence laws. For example, a statute may define murder as the "unlawful killing of one human being by another with malice." Court decisions might help explain the meaning of the term *malice* or clarify whether "human being" includes a fetus. A judge may rule that a statute is vague, deals with an act no longer of interest to the public, or is an unfair exercise of state control over an individual. Conversely, some judges may interpret the law so that behaviors previously acceptable become outlawed. For example, judges in a particular jurisdiction might find all people who sell magazines depicting nude men and women guilty of the crime of selling obscene material, whereas in the past obscenity was interpreted much more narrowly. Or some courts might consider drunken driving a petty crime, whereas others might interpret the statute on driving under the influence more severely.

Administrative Rule Making

Administrative agencies with rule-making authority also develop measures to control conduct in society.[4] Some agencies regulate taxation, health, environment, and other public functions; others control drugs, illegal gambling, or porno-

State and federal agencies, such as the Environmental Protection Agency, have administrative rules that are designed to protect citizens. The EPA, for example, has rules that prohibit indiscriminate hazardous waste dumping that might result in serious injuries and death.

graphic material. For example, the major enforcement arm against environmental crimes is the Environmental Protection Agency (EPA), which was given full law enforcement authority in 1988. The EPA has successfully prosecuted significant violations across all major environmental statutes, including data fraud cases (for example, private laboratories submitting false environmental data to state and federal environmental agencies); indiscriminate hazardous waste dumping that resulted in serious injuries and death; industry-wide ocean dumping by cruise ships; oil spills that caused significant damage to waterways, wetlands, and beaches; international smuggling of CFC (chlorofluorocarbon) refrigerants that damage the ozone layer and increase skin cancer risk; and illegal handling of hazardous substances such as pesticides and asbestos that exposed children, the poor, and other especially vulnerable groups to potentially serious illness.[5]

Perspectives on Justice

Efforts to control the crimes of big business through administrative rule making reflect the concerns of the conflict perspective.

Administrative laws also control the operations of the justice system. Parole boards are administrative agencies that implement the thousands of regulations governing the conduct of criminal offenders after their release from prison. Such rules are called administrative rules with criminal sanctions, and agency decisions about these rules have the force and authority of law.

Constitutional Law and Its Limits

Regardless of its source, all criminal law in the United States must conform to the rules and dictates of the U.S. Constitution.[6] In other words, any criminal law that conflicts with the various provisions and articles of the Constitution will eventually be challenged in the appellate courts and stricken from the legal code by judicial order (or modified to adhere to constitutional principles). As Chief Justice John Marshall's opinion in *Marbury* v. *Madison* indicated, "If the courts are to regard the Constitution and the Constitution is superior to any ordinary

Ex Post Facto Laws

law in review

The Constitution forbids laws that retroactively punish people. That is, a person cannot be punished for an act that was legal at the time of its occurrence. However, can a person be treated or helped for a prior act? Can a state pass laws that apply retroactively if their intention is nonpunitive? The U.S. Supreme Court addressed this issue in three recent cases involving sex offenders: *Kansas* v. *Hendricks* (1997), *Smith* v. *Doe* (2003), and *Stogner* v. *California* (2003).

Kansas *v.* Hendricks

The Kansas Sexually Violent Predator Act allows for indefinite civil confinement for sexual predators after their criminal term has concluded. Leroy Hendricks, a habitual offender, was serving a prison term for sexual misconduct when the law was implemented. He appealed on the grounds that his ex post facto rights were violated because he now could be confined under a law that did not exist when he was first convicted.

The Supreme Court upheld his confinement, concluding that the act was nonpunitive in nature and designed to treat, not harm, offenders. Therefore, it did not violate ex post facto laws against retroactive punishment.

Smith et al. *v.* Doe et al.

Under the Alaska Sex Offender Registration Act, an incarcerated sex offender or child kidnapper must register with the Department of Corrections within 30 days before his release. Even if convicted of a single, nonaggravated sex crime, the offender must register with authorities and provide information to authorities for 15 years. The offender's information is forwarded to the Department of Public Safety, which maintains a central registry of sex offenders. Some of the data is kept confidential, while other information such as the offender's name, aliases, address, photograph, and physical description are published on the Internet. Both the act's registration and notification requirements were made retroactive to previously convicted offenders.

The petitioners were convicted of aggravated sex offenses and released from prison after completing rehabilitative programs for sex offenders. Although convicted before the act's passage, respondents were covered by its provisions and were required to register with authorities and make quarterly contacts. They brought suit to void the restrictions under the ex post facto clause of the Constitution.

On review the Supreme Court upheld the Alaska Sex Offender Registration Act's requirement that offenders who had been incarcerated prior to its passage be made to conform to its provisions because it is nonpunitive. It ruled that the Alaska legislature's intent was to create a civil, nonpunitive requirement for release that is designed to protect the public from sex offenders as the law's primary interest. The Court found that nothing in the statute's language suggests that the Alaska legislature sought to create anything other than a civil scheme designed to protect the public from harm. The act does not impose physical restraint and so does not resemble imprisonment, and no evidence exists that the act has led to substantial occupational or housing disadvantages for former sex offenders that would not have otherwise occurred. Therefore,

---

act of the legislature, the Constitution and not such ordinary act must govern the case to which they apply."[7] This landmark case of 1803 established the concept of judicial review. All laws, including criminal statutes, must therefore meet constitutional standards or be declared invalid.

Among the general limitations set by the Constitution are those that forbid the government to pass **ex post facto laws,** which make an action a crime that was not a crime at the time it was committed. They create laws or penalties or both that are enforced. However, as the Law in Review feature (above) shows, every legal rule has numerous interpretations.

The Constitution also forbids bills of attainder; that is, legislative acts that inflict punishment without a judicial trial. In addition, criminal laws have been interpreted as violating constitutional principles if they are too vague or overbroad to give clear meaning of their intent. For example, a law forbidding adults to engage in "immoral behavior" could not be enforced because it does not use clear and precise language or give adequate notice as to which conduct is forbidden. The Law in Review feature on page 128 concerns an important case dealing with the concept of vagueness.[8]

The Constitution also forbids laws that make a person's status a crime. For example, addiction to narcotics cannot be made a crime, though laws can forbid the sale, possession, and manufacture of dangerous drugs.

In general, the Constitution has been interpreted to forbid any criminal law that violates a person's right to be treated fairly and equally. This principle is referred to

ex post facto law
A law that makes an act criminal after it was committed or retroactively increases the penalty for a crime.

requiring offenders convicted and or incarcerated prior to the law's passage to register and report is not illegal.

Stogner *v.* California

In 1993 California enacted a new criminal statute of limitations permitting prosecution for sex-related child abuse within one year of a victim's report of the abuse to the police even if the statute of limitations had already run out. In 1998 Mario Stogner was indicted for sex-related child abuse committed between 1955 and 1973. At the time those crimes were allegedly committed, the limitations period was three years. Stogner argued that his indictment was illegal on the ground that the ex post facto clause forbids revival of a previously time-barred prosecution.

The Court ruled that a law enacted to allow criminal prosecutions after expiration of a previously applicable statute of limitations period violates the ex post facto clause. California's law extends the time in which prosecution is allowed and authorized prosecutions that the passage of time had previously barred. Such laws

are forbidden by the Constitution because they inflict punishments when the party was not, by law, liable to any punishment.

Significance of the Cases

All three cases show that the Supreme Court can use its discretion to interpret law in unusual ways. In *Smith* v. *Doe,* the Alaska law in question applied only to sex offenders and not other types of criminals. Isn't that a special form of punishment? The law applied to every sex offender without allowing discretion and imposed severe restrictions, yet the Court ruled that the burdens were nonpunitive. As a group, the cases show that the Court draws a clear distinction between a person being "treated" and a person who is being "punished," even though to an outsider the distinction between them may become muddled. In *Hendricks,* continued treatment was allowed even if it meant a longer period of confinement. In contrast, *Stogner* shows that when an ex post facto law is clearly punitive, that is, allows criminal prosecution, it will not be upheld by the Court.

Critical Thinking

In his dissent in *Smith* v. *Doe,* Justice John Paul Stevens wrote: "In my opinion, a sanction that (1) is imposed on everyone who commits a criminal offense, (2) is not imposed on anyone else, and (3) severely impairs a person's liberty is punishment. It is therefore clear to me that the Constitution prohibits the addition of these sanctions to the punishment of persons who were tried and convicted before the legislation was enacted." Do you agree with Stevens?

InfoTrac College Edition Research

To read more about the *Hendricks* case and the ex post facto clause, go to Wayne A. Logan, "The Ex Post Facto Clause and the Jurisprudence of Punishment," *American Criminal Law Review* 35, no. 4 (Summer 1998): 1261.

Source: *Kansas v. Hendricks,* 117 S. Ct. 2072, 2078 (1997); *Smith et al.* v. *Doe et al.,* No. 01–729, decided March 5, 2003; *Stogner* v. *California,* No. 01–1757, decided June 26, 2003.

as substantive due process. Usually, this means that, before a new law can be created, the state must show a compelling need to protect public safety or morals.[9]

Perspectives on Justice

Constitutional controls over the substantive criminal law is a cornerstone of the due process model. Laws that may erode such personal rights as notice of charges or the right to a hearing raise red flags. Efforts to control terrorism through legislation may create a conflict between constitutional rights and national security issues.

To quiz yourself on this material, go to questions 4.5–4.7 on the Introduction to Criminal Justice 10e CD.

Classifying Crimes

The decision of how a crime should be classified rests with the individual jurisdiction. Each state has developed its own body of criminal law and consequently determines its own penalties for the various crimes. Thus, the criminal law of a given state defines and grades offenses, sets levels of punishment, and classifies crimes into categories. Over the years, crimes have been generally grouped into (1) felonies, misdemeanors, and violations and (2) other statutory classifications, such as juvenile delinquency, sex offender categories, and multiple- or first-offender

Chicago v. *Morales* (1999)

law in review

Facts

Because of an epidemic of gang violence, Chicago passed the Gang Congregation Ordinance in 1997, which prohibited "criminal street gang members" from loitering in public places. Under the ordinance, if a police officer observed a person whom she believes to be a gang member loitering in a public place with one or more persons, she can order them to disperse. Failure to disperse was a violation of the ordinance and grounds for arrest. The police department's General Order 92–4 attempted to limit the officers' enforcement discretion by confining arrest authority to designated officers, establishing detailed criteria for defining street gangs and membership, and providing for designated, but publicly undisclosed, enforcement areas.

In 1998, after a number of arrests of gang members by the police, the Illinois Supreme Court found that the statute violated due process of law because it was vague and an arbitrary restriction on personal liberty. An appeal was filed before the U.S. Supreme Court.

Decision

In a 6–3 decision, the U.S. Supreme Court affirmed the Illinois court and ruled that the ordinance's broad sweep violates the requirement that the legislature establish minimal guidelines to govern law enforcement activities. The Court said the ordinance criminalized too much behavior that would otherwise be considered harmless and normative. Persons in the company of a gang member could be ordered to disperse even if their purpose is not apparent to an officer and even though they were committing no offensive or illegal act. More important, the state courts had interpreted the statutory language of loitering as being "to remain in any one place with no apparent purpose." This vague language gave police officers enormous discretion to determine what activities constitute loitering. They ruled the three features of the ordinance that limit the officer's discretion (it does not permit issuance of a dispersal order to anyone who is moving along or who has an apparent purpose; it does not permit an arrest if individuals obey a dispersal order; and no order can be issued unless the officer reasonably believes that one of the loiterers is a gang member) were insufficient. Ironically, the Court noted that the ordinance was also "under-inclusive"; it did not cover loitering with an apparent purpose even if the purpose was to conceal drug trafficking or claim territory for a gang.

Significance of the Case

This case reinforces the constitutional principle that criminal laws with unlimited discretion and vagueness will be struck down. The problem with the statute was that it covered a broad range of innocent conduct and delegated too much discretion to the police. The Court also said that the statute could be "made constitutional by requiring that loiterers have some harmful purpose before being arrested, or making it clear that only gang members could be arrested rather than people standing nearby." This language has been taken by legal scholars as a cue that a properly drafted ordinance could be constitutional.

Critical Thinking

Considering the threat of terrorism, should greater powers be given to law enforcement agencies to stop, question, detain, and arrest suspicious people under statutes that are loosely worded and vague? For example, should the police be allowed to question people if they "seem suspicious" or make arrests for "suspicious behavior"?

InfoTrac College Edition Research

 For a more detailed analysis of this case, go to Kim Strosnider, "Anti-Gang Ordinances after *City of Chicago* v. *Morales:* The Intersection of Race, Vagueness Doctrine, and Equal Protection in the Criminal Law," *American Criminal Law Review* 39, no 1 (Winter 2002): 101.

Source: *City of Chicago* v. *Jesus Morales et al.,* 527 U.S. 41 (1999).

---

classifications. In general terms, felonies are considered serious crimes, misdemeanors are seen as less serious crimes, and violations may be noncriminal offenses such as traffic offenses and public drunkenness. Some states consider violations civil matters, whereas others classify them as crimes.

Felonies and Misdemeanors

The most common classification in the United States is the division between felonies and misdemeanors.[10] This distinction is based primarily on the degree of seriousness of the crime. Distinguishing between a felony and a misdemeanor is sometimes difficult.

Black's Law Dictionary defines the two terms as follows:

A felony is a crime of a graver or more atrocious nature than those designated as misdemeanors. Generally it is an offense punishable by death or imprisonment in a penitentiary. A misdemeanor is lower than a felony and is generally punishable by fine or imprisonment otherwise than in a penitentiary.[11]

Each jurisdiction in the United States determines by statute what types of conduct constitute felonies or misdemeanors. The most common definition of a felony is a crime punishable in the statute by death or by imprisonment in a state or federal prison. Another way of determining what category an offense falls into is by providing in the statute that a felony is any crime punishable by imprisonment for more than one year. In the former method, the place of imprisonment is critical; in the latter, the length of the prison sentence distinguishes a felony from a misdemeanor.

In the United States today, felonies include serious crimes against the person, such as criminal homicide, robbery, and rape, as well as such crimes against property as burglary and larceny. Misdemeanors include petit (or petty) larceny, assault and battery, and the unlawful possession of marijuana. The least serious, or petty, offenses, which often involve criminal traffic violations, are called infractions or violations.

The felony–misdemeanor classification has a direct effect on the offender charged with the crime. A person convicted of a felony may be barred from certain fields of employment or some professions, such as law and medicine. A felony offender's status as an alien in the United States might also be affected, or the offender might be denied the right to hold public office, vote, or serve on a jury.[12] These and other civil liabilities exist when a person is convicted only of a felony offense, not a misdemeanor.

Whether the offender is charged with a felony or a misdemeanor also makes a difference at the time of arrest. Normally, the law of arrest requires that if the crime is a misdemeanor and has not been committed in the presence of a police officer, the officer cannot make an arrest. This is known as the *in presence requirement*. However, the police officer does have the legal authority to arrest a suspect for a misdemeanor at a subsequent time by the use of a validly obtained arrest warrant. In contrast, an arrest for a felony may be made regardless of whether the crime was committed in the officer's presence, as long as the officer has reasonable grounds to believe that the person has committed the felony.

The Legal Definition of a Crime

Occasionally people admit at trial that they committed the act of which they are accused, yet they are not found guilty of the crime. For example, there was little question that John Hinckley Jr. attempted to assassinate President Ronald Reagan in 1981; the shooting and Hinckley's capture were shown on national TV. Yet Hinckley was not found guilty of a crime because he lacked one of the legal requirements needed to prove his guilt—mental competency. The jury concluded he was not mentally competent at the time of the crime. In most instances, this occurs because state or federal prosecutors have not proven that the defendants' behavior falls within the legal definition of a crime. To fulfill the legal definition, all elements of the crime must be proven. For example, the common law crime of armed burglary in the first degree (Massachusetts) is set out in Exhibit 4.3.

Armed burglary has the following elements:

- It happens at night.
- It involves breaking or entering or both.
- It happens at a dwelling house.
- The accused is armed or arms himself or herself after entering the house or commits an assault on a person who is lawfully in the house.

Exhibit 4.3 Armed Burglary in Massachusetts

CHAPTER 266. CRIMES AGAINST PROPERTY.

Chapter 266: Section 14. Burglary; armed; assault on occupants; weapons; punishment.

Section 14. Whoever breaks and enters a dwelling house in the night time, with intent to commit a felony, or whoever, after having entered with such intent, breaks into such dwelling house in the night time, any person being then lawfully therein, and the offender being armed with a dangerous weapon at the time of such breaking or entry, or so arming himself in such house, or making an actual assault on a person lawfully therein, shall be punished by imprisonment in the state prison for life or for any term of not less than ten years.

Whoever commits any offense described in this section while armed with a firearm, rifle, shotgun, machine gun or assault weapon shall be punished by imprisonment in the state prison for life or for any term of years, but not less than 15 years. Whoever commits a subsequent such offense shall be punished by imprisonment in the state prison for life or for any term of years, but not less than 20 years. The sentence imposed upon a person who, after being convicted of any offence mentioned in this section, commits the like offence, or any other of the offences therein mentioned, shall not be suspended, nor shall he be placed on probation.

Source: State of Massachusetts Web site, http://www.state.ma.us/legis/laws/mgl/266-14.htm.

- The accused intends to commit a felony.
- If the accused brought a firearm with him or her, the punishment is increased.

For the state to prove a crime occurred, and that the defendant committed it, the prosecutor must show that the accused engaged in the guilty act (**actus reus**) and had the intent to commit the act (**mens rea**). Under common law, both the actus reus and the mens rea must be present for the act to be considered a crime. Thoughts of committing an act do not alone constitute a crime.

actus reus
An illegal act, or failure to act when legally required.

mens rea
A guilty mind; the intent to commit a criminal act.

Actus Reas The actus reus is an aggressive act, such as taking someone's money, burning a building, or shooting someone. The action must be voluntary for an act to be considered illegal. An accident or involuntary act would not be considered criminal. For example, if while walking down the street, a person has a seizure and as a result strikes another person in the face, he cannot be held criminally liable for assault. But if he had known beforehand that he could have a seizure and

The actus reas is the illegal act: stealing money, shooting a gun, selling drugs, even robbing banks. This bank video surveillance camera image, released by the FBI March 18, 1999, shows a young woman believed to be responsible for six Boston-area bank robberies. The woman, described as blond, in her 30s and about 5-foot-2, is under suspicion for a robbery in Wilmington, Massachusetts, where she allegedly drew a gun and escaped with thousands of dollars in cash.

© 2003 AP/Wide World Photos

unreasonably put himself in a position where he was likely to harm others—for instance, by driving a car—he would be criminally liable for his behavior.

In addition, the failure or omission to act can be considered a crime on some occasions:

Failure to perform a legally required duty that is based on relationship or status. These relationships include parent and child and husband and wife. If a husband finds his wife unconscious because she took an overdose of sleeping pills, he is obligated to seek medical aid. If he fails to do so and she dies, he can be held responsible for her death. Parents are required to look after the welfare of their children; failure to provide adequate care can be a criminal offense.

Imposition by statute. Some states have passed laws that require a person who observes an automobile accident to stop and help the other parties involved.

A contractual relationship. These relationships include lifeguard and swimmer, doctor and patient, and baby-sitter or au pair and child. Because lifeguards have been hired to ensure the safety of swimmers, they have a legal duty to come to the aid of drowning persons. If a lifeguard knows a swimmer is in danger and does nothing about it and the swimmer drowns, the lifeguard is legally responsible for the swimmer's death.

The duty to act is a legal and not a moral duty. The obligation arises from the relationship between the parties or from explicit legal requirements. For example, a private citizen who sees a person drowning is under no legal obligation to save that person. Although it may be considered morally reprehensible, the private citizen could walk away and let the swimmer drown without facing legal sanctions.

Mens Rea Under common law, for an act to constitute a crime, the actor must have criminal intent or mens rea. For example, a person enters a store with a gun and shouts at the clerk to "open the cash register." His actions signal his intent to commit a robbery. Mens rea is also present when a person's reckless or negligent act produces social harm. For example, a drunk driver may not have intended to kill his victim, yet his negligent and reckless behavior, that is, driving while drunk, creates a condition in which a reasonable person can assume will lead to injury.

Criminal intent is implied if the results of an action, though originally unintended, are certain to occur. For example, when Mohammed Atta and his terrorist band crashed aircraft into the World Trade Center on September 11, 2001, they did not intend to kill any particular person in the building. Yet, the law would hold that anybody would be substantially certain that people in the building would be killed in the blast and the terrorists therefore had the criminal intent to commit the crime of first-degree murder.

The Relationship of Mens Rea and Actus Reus The third element needed to prove a crime was committed is the immediate relationship of the act to the criminal intent or result. The law requires that the offender's conduct be the approximate cause of any injury resulting from the criminal act. If, for example, a man chases a victim into the street intending to assault him and the victim is struck and killed by a car, the accused could be convicted of murder if the court felt that his actions made him responsible for the victim's death. In other words, the victim would not have run into the street on his own accord and therefore would not have been killed. If, however, a victim dies from a completely unrelated illness after being assaulted, the court must determine

While the concept of mens rea implies that to be guilty of crime a defendant must have intended to commit a criminal act, it is also possible to infer intent if a person's negligent behavior resulted in an injury or even death to another. U.S. Rep. Bill Janklow was charged with manslaughter in the second degree, a class-four felony in South Dakota, when he was accused of causing the death of a motorcyclist on August 16, 2003. Janklow was accused of failing to stop at a stop sign, one count of driving "at least" 71 mph in a 55 mph zone and one count of reckless driving, crimes which could bring him 10 years in the state penitentiary and a $10,000 fine.

© 2003 AP/Wide World Photos

To read more about the concept of mens rea, go to Claire Finkelstein, "The Inefficiency of Mens Rea (The Morality of Criminal Law: A Symposium in Honor of Professor Sanford Kadish)," *California Law Review* 88, no. 3 (May 2000): 89.

Exhibit 4.4 New York State Law: S 270.10 Creating a Hazard

A person is guilty of creating a hazard when:

1. Having discarded in any place where it might attract children, a container which has a compartment of more than one and one-half cubic feet capacity and a door or lid which locks or fastens automatically when closed and which cannot easily be opened from the inside, he fails to remove the door, lid, locking or fastening device; or

2. Being the owner or otherwise having possession of property upon which an abandoned well or cesspool is located, he fails to cover the same with suitable protective construction.

Creating a hazard is a class B misdemeanor.

Source: New York State Consolidated Laws, Article 270 Other Offenses Relating to Public Safety, Section 270.10 Creating a Hazard (2002).

whether the death was a probable consequence of the defendant's illegal conduct or whether it would have resulted even if the assault had not occurred.

public safety or strict liability crime
A criminal violation—usually one that endangers the public welfare—that is defined by the act itself, irrespective of intent.

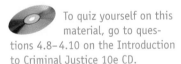

To access the public safety statutes in New York, go to http://assembly.state.ny.us/leg/?cl=82&a=69.

To quiz yourself on this material, go to questions 4.8–4.10 on the Introduction to Criminal Justice 10e CD.

Strict Liability   Certain statutory offenses exist in which mens rea is not essential. These offenses fall within a category known as a **public safety** or **strict liability crime.** A person can be held responsible for such a violation independent of the existence of intent to commit the offense. Strict liability criminal statutes generally include narcotics control laws, traffic laws, health and safety regulations, sanitation laws, and other regulatory statutes. For example, a driver could not defend herself against a speeding ticket by claiming that she was unaware of how fast she was going and did not intend to speed, and a bartender could not claim that a juvenile to whom he sold liquor looked older. No state of mind is generally required where a strict liability statute is violated.[13] For example, consider the New York State law § 270.10, about creating a hazard, which is set out in Exhibit 4.4.[14]

Intent to commit is not required to be found guilty on charges of creating a hazardous condition.

Criminal Defenses

When people defend themselves against criminal charges, they must refute one or more of the elements of the crime of which they have been accused. Defendants may deny the actus reus by arguing that they were falsely accused and the real culprit has yet to be identified. Defendants may also claim that, while they did engage in the criminal act they are accused of, they lacked the mens rea, or mental intent needed to be found guilty of the crime. If a person whose mental state is impaired commits a criminal act, the person could be excused of his or her criminal actions by claiming he or she lacked the capacity to form sufficient intent to be held criminally responsible. Insanity, intoxication, and ignorance are also among the types of excuse defenses.

justification
A defense for a criminal act claiming that the criminal act was reasonable or necessary under the circumstances.

Another type of defense is **justification.** Here, the individual usually admits committing the criminal act but maintains that the act was justified and that he or she, therefore, should not be held criminally liable. Among the justification defenses are necessity, duress, self-defense, and entrapment. Persons standing trial for criminal offenses may defend themselves by claiming either that their actions were justified under the circumstances or that their behavior can be excused by their lack of mens rea. If either the physical or mental elements of a crime cannot be proven, then the defendant cannot be convicted.

Ignorance or Mistake

Ignorance or mistake can be an excuse if it negates an element of a crime. As a general rule, however, ignorance of the law is no excuse. Some courts have had to accept this excuse in cases in which the government failed to make enactment of a new law public. It is also a viable justification when the offender relies on an official statement of the law that is later deemed incorrect. Barring that, even immigrants and other new arrivals to the United States are required to be aware of the content of the law. For example, on October 7, 1998, Chris Ahamefule Iheduru, a Nigerian immigrant, was convicted of sexual assault on the grounds that he had intimate relations with his 14-year-old stepdaughter after signing a contract with the girl to bear him a son (she gave birth to a daughter in September 1998).[15] At trial, Iheduru testified that it is not illegal in his native country to have sex with a juvenile and that he did not know it was against the law in the United States. His ignorance of American law did not shield him from conviction.

Insanity

Insanity is a defense to criminal prosecution in which the defendant's state of mind negates his or her criminal responsibility. A successful insanity defense results in a verdict of "not guilty by reason of insanity." Insanity, in this case, is a legal category. As used in U.S. courts, it does not necessarily mean that everyone who suffers from a form of mental illness can be excused from legal responsibility. Many people who are depressed, suffer mood disorders, or have a psychopathic personality can be found legally sane. Instead, insanity means that the defendant's state of mind at the time the crime was committed made it impossible for him to have the necessary mens rea to satisfy the legal definition of a crime. Thus, a person can be undergoing treatment for a psychological disorder but still be judged legally sane if it can be proven that at the time he committed the crime he had the capacity to understand the wrongfulness of his actions.

If a defendant uses the insanity plea, it is usually left to psychiatric testimony to prove that a person understood the wrongfulness of his actions and was therefore legally sane or, conversely, was mentally incapable of forming intent. The

Use "the insanity defense" as a subject guide on InfoTrac College Edition to learn more about this controversial criminal defense.

The American Psychiatric Association is a medical specialty society dedicated to the humane care and effective treatment for all persons with a mental disorder, including mental retardation and substance-related disorders. To read its take on the insanity plea, go to http://www.psych.org/public_info/insanity.cfm.

Concept Summary 4.1 Various Insanity Defense Standards

Test	Legal standard of mental illness	Final burden of proof	Who bears burden of proof
M'Naghten	"Didn't know what he was doing or didn't know it was wrong"	Balance of probabilities	Defense
Irresistible impulse	"Could not control his conduct"	Beyond reasonable doubt	Prosecutor
Durham	"The criminal act was caused by his mental illness"	Beyond reasonable doubt	Prosecutor
Substantial capacity	"Lacks substantial capacity to appreciate the wrongfulness of his conduct or to control it"	Beyond reasonable doubt	Prosecutor
Present federal law	"Lacks capacity to appreciate the wrongfulness of his conduct"	Clear and convincing evidence	Defense

Source: Norval Morris, *Crime Study Guide: Insanity Defense* (Washington, D.C.: U.S. Department of Justice, 1986), p. 3.

KAYLA ROLLAND
AGE 6
5/12/93 - 2/29/00
BUELL SCHOOL
Beecher Community School District

Age may be a defense for crime and it is rare that a child under seven be prosecuted. On February 29, 2000, Kayla Rolland, a first grader, was killed by a six-year-old classmate who had taken a gun from his home. Though the boy could not be prosecuted, a grand jury indicted one man for stealing and two others for buying the gun that he used to shoot the girl in her classroom. This, a tribute to Kayla, now hangs in her elementary school.

jury then must weigh the evidence in light of the test for sanity currently used in the jurisdiction. These tests vary throughout the United States. The commonly used ones are listed in Concept Summary 4.1.

See the Analyzing Criminal Justice Issues feature on page 135 for more about the insanity defense.

Intoxication

As a general rule, intoxication, which may include drunkenness or being under the influence of drugs, is not considered a defense. However, a defendant who becomes involuntarily intoxicated under duress or by mistake may be excused for crimes committed. Involuntary intoxication may also lessen the degree of the crime. For example, a judgment may be decreased from first- to second-degree murder because the defendant uses intoxication to prove the lack of the critical element of mens rea, or mental intent. Thus, the effect of intoxication on criminal liability depends on whether the defendant uses alcohol or drugs voluntarily. For example, a defendant who enters a bar for a few drinks, becomes intoxicated, and strikes someone can be convicted of assault and battery. If, however, the defendant ordered a nonalcoholic drink that subsequently was spiked by someone else, the defendant may have a legitimate legal defense.

Because of the frequency of crime-related offenses involving drugs and alcohol, the impact of intoxication on criminal liability is a persistent issue in the criminal justice system. The connection between drug use, alcoholism, and violent street crime has been well documented. Although those in law enforcement and the judiciary tend to emphasize the use of the penal process in dealing with problems of chronic alcoholism and drug use, others in corrections and crime prevention favor approaches that depend more on behavioral theories and the social sciences. For example, in the case of *Robinson* v. *California,* the U.S. Supreme Court struck down a California statute making addiction to narcotics a crime, on the ground that it violated the defendant's rights under the Eighth and Fourteenth Amendments to the Constitution.[16] However, the landmark decision in *Powell* v. *Texas* placed severe limitations on the behavioral science approach in *Robinson* when it rejected the defense of chronic alcoholism of a defendant charged with the crime of public drunkenness.[17]

Age

The law holds that a child is not criminally responsible for actions committed at an age that precludes a full realization of the gravity of certain types of behavior. Under common law, there is generally a conclusive presumption of incapacity for a child under age 7, a reliable presumption for a child between the ages of 7 and 14, and no presumption for a child over the age of 14. This generally means that a child under age 7 who commits a crime will not be held criminally responsible for these actions and that a child between ages 7 and 14 may be held responsible. These common law rules have been changed by statute in most jurisdictions. Today, the maximum age of criminal responsibility for children ranges from ages 14 to 17 or 18, while the minimum age may be set by statute at age 7 or under age 14.[18] In addition, every ju-

The Insanity Defense

analyzing criminal justice issues

The insanity defense has been the source of debate and controversy. Many critics of the defense maintain that inquiry into a defendant's psychological makeup is inappropriate at the trial stage. They would prefer that the issue be raised at the sentencing stage, after guilt has been determined. Opponents also charge that criminal responsibility is separate from mental illness and that the two should not be equated. It is a serious mistake, they argue, to consider criminal responsibility as a trait or quality that can be detected by a psychiatric evaluation. Moreover, some criminals avoid punishment because they are erroneously judged by psychiatrists to be mentally ill. Meanwhile, some people who are found not guilty by reason of insanity because they suffer from a mild personality disturbance are then incarcerated in mental health facilities far longer than they would have been imprisoned if they had been convicted of a criminal offense.

Advocates of the insanity defense say that it serves a unique purpose. Most successful insanity verdicts result in the defendant's being committed to a mental institution until he or she has recovered. The general assumption is that the insanity defense makes it possible to single out for special treatment certain persons who would otherwise be subjected to further penal sanctions following conviction.

The insanity plea was thrust into the spotlight in the case against John Hinckley Jr., who attempted to assassinate President Ronald Reagan in 1981. Hinckley was found not guilty by reason of insanity. Public outcry against this seeming miscarriage of justice prompted some states to revise their insanity statutes. Alaska, Delaware, Georgia, Illinois, Indiana, Michigan, and New Mexico, among

other states, have created the plea of guilty but insane, in which the defendant is required to serve the first part of his or her sentence in a hospital and, once cured, to be then sent to prison.

In 1984 the federal government revised its criminal code to restrict insanity as a defense solely to individuals who are unable to understand the nature and wrongfulness of their acts. The burden of proof has made an important shift from the prosecutor's need to prove sanity to the defendant's need to prove insanity. About 11 states have followed the federal government's lead and made significant changes in their insanity defenses, such as shifting the burden of proof from prosecution to defense. Three states (Idaho, Montana, and Utah) no longer use evidence of mental illness as a defense in court, though psychological factors can influence sentencing. On March 28, 1994, the U.S. Supreme Court failed to overturn the Montana law (*Cowan* v. *Montana*), thereby giving the states the right to abolish the insanity defense if they so choose.

Although such backlash against the insanity plea is intended to close supposed legal loopholes allowing dangerous criminals to go free, the public's fear may be misplaced. It is estimated that the insanity plea is used in less than 1 percent of all cases. Moreover, evidence shows that relatively few insanity defense pleas are successful.

Even if the insanity defense is successful, the offender must be placed in a secure psychiatric hospital or the psychiatric ward of a state prison. Because many defendants who successfully plead insanity are nonviolent offenders, their hospital stay certainly could be longer than the prison term they would have received if

they had been convicted of the crimes of which they were originally accused.

Despite efforts to ban its use, the insanity plea is probably here to stay. Most crimes require mens rea, and unless that standard of law is lifted those people whose mental state makes it impossible for them to rationally control their behavior will be found not guilty.

Critical Thinking

1. Is it fair to excuse the criminal responsibility of someone who acted under an irresistible impulse?
2. Aren't all criminals impulsive people who lack the capacity to control their behavior?
3. If not, why would they commit crimes in the first place? Is it possible that child molesters, for example, are rational creatures who do not have irresistible impulses?

InfoTrac College Edition Research

To research the impact of the insanity plea on criminal defenses, check out Richard J. Bonnie, Norman G. Poythress, Steven K. Hoge, John Monahan, and Marlene Eisenberg, "Decision Making in Criminal Defense: An Empirical Study of Insanity Pleas and the Impact of Doubted Client Competence," *Journal of Criminal Law and Criminology* 87, no. 1 (Fall 1996): 48–62.

Source: Richard Moran, *Knowing Right from Wrong: The Insanity Defense of Daniel McNaughtan* (New York: Free Press, 2000); Daniel N. Robinson, *Wild Beasts and Idle Humours: The Insanity Defense from Antiquity to the Present* (Cambridge, Mass.: Harvard University Press, 1998); Ralph Slovenko, *Psychiatry and Criminal Culpability* (New York: John Wiley and Sons, 1995).

risdiction has established a juvenile court system to deal with juvenile offenders and children in need of court and societal supervision. Thus, the mandate of the juvenile justice system is to provide for the care and protection of children under a given age, established by state statute. In certain situations, a juvenile court may transfer a more serious chronic youthful offender to the adult criminal court.

Justification and Excuse

In 1884 two British sailors, desperate after being shipwrecked for days, made the decision to kill and eat a suffering cabin boy. Four days later, they were rescued by a passing ship and returned to England. English authorities, wanting to end the practice of shipwreck cannibalism, tried and convicted the two men for murder. Clemency was considered and a reluctant Queen Victoria commuted the death sentences to six months.[19] Were the seamen justified in killing a shipmate to save their lives? If they had not done so, they likely all would have died. Can there ever be a good reason to take a life? Can the killing of another ever be justified? Before you answer, remember that people can kill in self-defense, to prevent lethal crimes, or in times of war. The passengers aboard United Airlines Flight 93 are considered heroes for attacking the hijackers on September 11. Certainly no rational person would condemn their acts even though they may have resulted in the death of others. Oftentimes, the quality of the act is not most important; the way society defines and reacts to it determines whether a crime has been committed.

Criminal defenses may be based on the concepts of justification or excuse. In these instances, defendants normally acknowledge that they committed the act but claim that they cannot be prosecuted because they were justified in doing so. Major types of criminal defenses involving justification or excuse are consent; self-defense; and entrapment, duress, and necessity.

Consent As a general rule, the victim's consent to a crime does not justify or excuse the defendant who commits the action. The type of crime involved generally determines the validity of consent as an appropriate legal defense. Such crimes as common law rape and larceny require lack of consent on the part of the victim. In other words, a rape does not occur if the victim consents to sexual relations. In the same way, a larceny cannot occur if the owner voluntarily consents to the taking of property. Consequently, in such crimes, consent is an essential element of the crime, and it is a valid defense where it can be proven or shown that it existed at the time the crime was committed. But in other crimes, such as sexual relations with a minor child, consent cannot be a defense because the state presumes that young people are not capable of providing adequate or mature consent. Similarly, it is still against the law to help someone commit suicide even if the person consented to the procedure. Dr. Jack Kevorkian was convicted in 1999 on charges of second-degree murder growing out of the death of Thomas Youk, a man he helped commit suicide. As of fall 2003, Oregon was the only state that allowed assisted suicide but narrowly controlled when it could be used, such as with a terminally ill patient.

Self-Defense In certain instances, a criminal defendant can claim to be not guilty because he acted in self-defense. To establish self-defense, the defendant must prove he acted with a reasonable belief that he was in danger of death or great harm and had no reasonable means of escape from the assailant.

As a general legal rule, a person defending herself may use only such force as is reasonably necessary to prevent personal harm. A person who is assaulted by another with no weapon is ordinarily not justified in hitting the assailant with a baseball bat. A person verbally threatened by another is not justified in striking the other party with his fists. If a woman hits a larger man, generally speaking the man would not be justified in striking the woman and causing her physical harm. In other words, to exercise the self-defense privilege, the danger to the defendant must be immediate. And, depending on the legal jurisdiction and facts of the case, the defendant may be obligated to prove that he sought

Should people be allowed to carry handguns for self-defense? See Linda Gorman and David Kopel, "Self-Defense: The Equalizer," *Forum for Applied Research and Public Policy* 15, no. 4 (Winter 2000): 92.

alternative means of avoiding the danger, such as escape, retreat, or assistance from others.

Entrapment, Duress, and Necessity Under the rule of law, a defendant may be excused from criminal liability if he can convince the jury that law enforcement agents used traps, decoys, and deception to induce criminal action. Law enforcement officers can legitimately set traps for criminals by getting information about crimes from informers, undercover agents, and codefendants. Police officers are allowed to use ordinary opportunities for defendants to commit crime and to create these opportunities without excessive inducement. However, when the police instigate the crime, implant criminal ideas, and coerce individuals into bringing about crime, defendants can claim to have been entrapped.

Entrapment then must be viewed within the context of the defendant's predisposition to commit a crime. A defendant with a criminal record would have a tougher time using this defense successfully than one who had never been in trouble. However, in one of the most important entrapment cases, *Jacobson* v. *United States* (1992), the Supreme Court ruled that a defendant with a past history of child pornography had been entrapped by the government into purchasing more. Keith Jacobson had ordered *Bare Boys* magazines depicting nude children. When his name came up in their *Bare Boys* files, government agents sent him mailings for more than two-and-a-half years in an effort to get him to purchase more kiddie porn. Such purchases are a violation of the Child Protection Act of 1984. Jacobson was arrested after he gave in to the inducements and ordered a magazine showing young boys engaged in sexual activities. A search of his house revealed no materials other than those sent by the government (and the original *Bare Boys* magazines). On appeal, the Court held that Jacobson was entrapped because the state could not prove a predisposition to break the law and the purchase of the sexually charged magazines was the result of government coaxing.[20]

A duress (also called compulsion or coercion) defense may be used when the defendant claims he had been forced to commit a crime as the only means of preventing death or serious harm to himself or others. For example, a bank employee might be excused from taking bank funds if she can prove that her family was being threatened and that consequently she was acting under duress. But widespread general agreement exists that duress is no defense for an intentional killing.

The defense of necessity is used when a crime was committed under extreme circumstances and could not be avoided. For example, a husband steals a car to bring his pregnant wife to the hospital for an emergency delivery, or a hunter shoots an animal of an endangered species that was about to attack her child. Unlike the duress defense, which involves threats made by another person, people act out of necessity according to their own judgment.

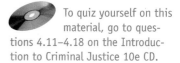 To quiz yourself on this material, go to questions 4.11–4.18 on the Introduction to Criminal Justice 10e CD.

Reforming the Criminal Law

In recent years, many states and the federal government have been examining their substantive criminal law. Because the law, in part, reflects public opinion and morality regarding various forms of behavior, what was considered criminal 40 years ago may not be considered so today. In some cases, states have reassessed their law and reduced the penalties on some common practices such as public intoxication; this is referred to as decriminalization. Such crimes, which in the past might have resulted in a prison sentence, may now be punished with a fine. In other instances, what was considered a criminal act may be declared noncriminal or legalized. For example, sexual relations between consenting same-sex adults was punished as a serious felony under sodomy statutes in a number of states until the Supreme Court ruled such statutes illegal in 2003.

On occasion the criminal law can be amended or changed in response to emerging social issues. Though Dr. Jack Kevorkian (above) attempted to change the law and legalize physician-assisted suicides, he was convicted in 1999 on charges of second-degree murder based on the death of Thomas Youk, a man he helped commit suicide.

penumbral crimes
Criminal acts defined by a high level of noncompliance with the stated legal standard, an absence of stigma associated with violation of the stated standard, and a low level of law enforcement or public sanction.

obitiatry
Helping people take their own lives; assisted suicide.

States may take action to decriminalize or legalize some crimes because the general public simply ignores the laws and law enforcement agents are reluctant to press charges even when they apprehend violators. Legal scholar Margaret Raymond calls these **penumbral crimes**—criminal acts defined by a high level of noncompliance with the stated legal standard, an absence of stigma associated with violation of the stated standard, and a low level of law enforcement or public sanction.[21] Because otherwise law-abiding people routinely violate these laws, they may be targets for penalty reduction and eventual legalization. For example, given that the 55 mile per hour speed limit has been so widely ignored, states have increased limits to 65 and even 70 miles per hour.

Creating New Penalties

In some instances, new criminal laws have been created to conform to emerging social issues. For example, physician-assisted suicide became the subject of a national debate when Dr. Jack Kevorkian began practicing what he calls **obitiatry,** helping people take their lives.[22] In an attempt to stop Kevorkian, Michigan passed a statutory ban on assisted suicide, reflecting what lawmakers believed to be prevailing public opinion.[23]

Assisted suicide is but one of many emerging social issues that has prompted change in the criminal law. More than 25 states have enacted **stalking** statutes, which prohibit and punish acts described typically as "the willful, malicious and repeated following and harassing of another person."[24] Stalking laws were originally formulated to protect women terrorized by former husbands and boyfriends, although celebrities often are plagued by stalkers as well. In celebrity cases, these laws often apply to stalkers who are strangers or casual acquaintances of their victims.

Community notification laws are a response to concern about sexual predators moving into neighborhoods. One of the most well known is Megan's Law, named after 7-year-old Megan Kanka of Hamilton Township, N.J., who was killed in 1994. Charged with the crime was a convicted sex offender who unknown to the Kankas lived across the street. On May 17, 1996, President Bill Clinton signed Megan's Law, which contained two components:

Sex Offender Registration—A revision of the 1994 Jacob Wetterling Act, which had required the states to register individuals convicted of sex crimes against children, to also establish a community notification system.
Community Notification—Compels the states to make private and personal information on registered sex offenders available to the public.

Changing technology and the ever-increasing role of technology in people's daily lives will require modification in the criminal law. For example, such technologies as automatic teller machines and cellular phones have already spawned a new generation of criminal acts involving theft of access numbers and software piracy. The criminal law has also undergone extensive change in both substance and procedure in the aftermath of the September 11 terrorist attacks. This change is addressed in the Analyzing Criminal Justice Issues feature on page 140.

While criminal law reform may be guided by good intentions, it is sometimes difficult to put the changes into operation. Law reform may require new enforcement agencies to be created, a process that is both lengthy and often hampered by budget considerations. A case in point occurred in Massachusetts. A recently passed community notification law created a sex offender registry designed to warn neighbors and police about past offenders living in their midst. After a particularly brutal murder was committed in 2002 by a known sex offender, the state revealed that only 1,000 out of 18,000 past offenders had been registered because there was only a staff of 11 hearing examiners to process cases.[25]

Constitutional Criminal Procedure

Whereas substantive criminal law primarily defines crimes, the law of criminal procedure consists of the rules and procedures that govern the pretrial processing of criminal suspects and the conduct of criminal trials. The main source of the procedural law is the ten amendments added to the U.S. Constitution on December 15, 1791, collectively known as the Bill of Rights. The purpose of these amendments was to prevent the government from usurping the personal freedoms of citizens. The U.S. Supreme Court's interpretation of these amendments has served as the basis for the creation of legal rights of the accused. Of primary concern are the Fourth, Fifth, Sixth, and Eighth Amendments, which limit and control the manner in which the federal government operates the justice system. In addition, the due process clause of the Fourteenth Amendment has been interpreted to apply limits on governmental action on the state and local level.

- The Fourth Amendment bars illegal "searches and seizures," a right especially important for the criminal justice system because it means that police officers cannot indiscriminately use their authority to investigate a possible crime or arrest a suspect. Stopping, questioning, or searching an individual without legal justification represents a serious violation of the Fourth Amendment right to personal privacy.
- The Fifth Amendment limits the admissibility of confessions that have been obtained unfairly. In 1966 in the landmark case of *Miranda* v. *Arizona,* the Supreme Court held that a person accused of a crime has the right to refuse to answer questions when placed in police custody.[26] The Fifth Amendment also guarantees defendants the right to a grand jury and not to be tried twice for the same crime, that is, they are protected from double jeopardy. Its due process clause guarantees defendants the right to fundamental fairness and the expectation of fair trials, fair hearings, and similar procedural safeguards.
- The Sixth Amendment guarantees the defendant the right to a speedy and public trial by an impartial jury, the right to be informed of the nature of the charges, and the right to confront any prosecution witnesses. It also contains the right of a defendant to be represented by an attorney, a privilege that has been extended to numerous stages of the criminal justice process, including pretrial custody, identification and lineup procedures, preliminary hearing, submission of a guilty plea, trial, sentencing, and postconviction appeal.
- According to the Eighth Amendment, "Excessive bail shall not be required, nor excessive fines imposed, nor cruel and unusual punishments inflicted." Bail is a money bond put up by the accused to attain freedom between arrest and trial. Bail is meant to ensure a trial appearance, because the bail money is forfeited if the defendant misses the trial date. The Eighth Amendment does not

stalking
The willful, malicious, and repeated following, harassing, or contacting of another person. It becomes a criminal act when it causes the victim to feel fear for his or safety or the safety of others.

Can community notification laws stand the test of legal scrutiny by the Supreme Court or do they unfairly single out sex offenders and deprive them of due process? To find out, read Wayne A. Logan, "Liberty Interests in the Preventive State: Procedural Due Process and Sex Offender Community Notification Laws," *Journal of Criminal Law and Criminology* 89, no. 4 (Summer 1999): 1167.

 To quiz yourself on this material, go to questions 4.19–4.20 on the Introduction to Criminal Justice 10e CD.

The Criminal Law and Terrorism

analyzing criminal justice issues

Soon after the September 11, 2001, terrorist attacks, the federal government enacted several laws focused on preventing further acts of violence against the United States. President George W. Bush signed the USA Patriot Act (USAPA) into law on October 26, 2001. The bill was more than 342 pages long, created new laws, and made changes to more than 15 different existing statutes. Its aim was to give sweeping new powers to domestic law enforcement and international intelligence agencies in an effort to fight terrorism, to expand the definition of terrorist activities, and to alter sanctions for violent terrorism.

Among its provisions, USAPA expands all four traditional tools of surveillance—wiretaps, search warrants, pen/trap orders (installing devices that record phone calls), and subpoenas. The Foreign Intelligence Surveillance Act, which allows domestic operations by intelligence agencies, also was expanded. USAPA gave greater power to the FBI to check and monitor phone, Internet, and computer records without first needing to demonstrate that the devices were being used by a suspect or target of a court order.

The government may now serve a single wiretap or pen/trap order on any person regardless of whether that person or entity is named in a court order. Prior to the act, telephone companies could be ordered to install pen/trap devices on their networks, which would monitor calls coming to a surveillance target and to whom the surveillance target made calls. The USAPA extends this monitoring to the Internet. Law enforcement agencies may now obtain the e-mail addresses and Web sites visited by a target as well as e-mails of those people with whom they communicate. An Internet service provider could

be required to install a device that records e-mail and other electronic communications on its servers, looking for communications initiated or received by the target of an investigation. Under USAPA, the government does not need to show a court that the information or communication is relevant to a criminal investigation, and it does not have to report where it served the order or what information it received.

The act also allows enforcement agencies to monitor cable operators and obtain access to cable operators' records and systems. Before the act, the cable company had to give prior notice to the customer, even if that person was a target of an investigation. Information can be obtained about people with whom the cable subscriber communicates, the content of their communications, and their subscription records. Prior notice is still required if law enforcement agencies want to learn what television programming a subscriber purchases.

The act also expands the definition of terrorism and enables the government to monitor more closely those people suspected of "harboring" and giving "material support" to terrorists. It further increases the authority of the attorney general to detain and deport noncitizens with little or no judicial review. The attorney general may certify that he has "reasonable grounds to believe" that a noncitizen endangers national security and therefore is eligible for deportation. The attorney general and secretary of state are also given the authority to designate domestic groups as terrorist organizations and deport any noncitizen who is a member.

While law enforcement agencies may applaud these new laws, civil libertarians are troubled because they view the act as eroding civil rights. Political commentator

Morton Halperin complains that provisions in the law permit the government to share information from grand jury proceedings and from criminal wiretaps with intelligence agencies. He also argues that First Amendment activities of American citizens, for example, watching TV, may be violated. He is concerned that this new and sweeping authority is not limited to true terrorism investigations but covers a much broader range of activity involving reasonable political protest. The USAPA will also be used against common law criminals such as drug traffickers and members of organized crime.

Critical Thinking

1. Are you concerned that the government's efforts to control terrorism have produced a reduction in civil liberties? Does the danger presented by future September 11–type attacks justify erosion of the law of personal privacy?
2. Should noncitizens residing in the United States enjoy the same rights, liberties, and protections as citizens?

InfoTrac College Edition Research

Use "USA Patriot Act" as a key term to find out more about its scope and provisions. See also Douglas A. Kash, "Hunting Terrorists Using Confidential Informant Reward Programs," *FBI Law Enforcement Bulletin* 71(2002): 26–28; Sara Sun Beale and James Felman, "The Consequences of Enlisting Federal Grand Juries in the War on Terrorism: Assessing the USA Patriot Act's Changes to Grand Jury Secrecy," *Harvard Journal of Law and Public Policy* 25 (2002): 699–721; Morton Halperin, "Less Secure, Less Free: Striking Terror at Civil Liberty," *American Prospect* 12 (November 19, 2001): 10–13.

guarantee a constitutional right to bail but instead prohibits the use of excessive bail, which is typically defined as an amount far greater than that imposed on similar defendants who are accused of committing similar crimes.

The Eighth Amendment also forbids the use of cruel and unusual punishment. This prohibition protects both the accused and convicted offenders from actions regarded as unacceptable by a civilized society, including corporal punishment and torture.

- The Fourteenth Amendment is the vehicle used to apply the protection of the Bill of Rights to the states. It affirms that no state shall "deprive any person of life, liberty, or property, without due process of law." In essence, the same general constitutional restrictions previously applicable to the federal government can be imposed on the states.

To read more about these issues, use "constitutional law" as a subject guide on InfoTrac College Edition

Due Process of Law

The concept of due process, found both in the Fifth and Fourteenth Amendments, has been used to evaluate the constitutionality of legal statutes and to set standards and guidelines for fair procedures in the criminal justice system.

In seeking to define the meaning of the term, most legal experts believe that it refers to the essential elements of fairness under law.[27] This definition basically refers to the legal system's need for rules and regulations that protect individual rights.

Due process can be divided into two distinct categories: substantive and procedural. Substantive due process refers to the citizen's right to be protected from criminal laws that may be biased, discriminatory, and otherwise unfair. These laws may be vague or apply unfairly to one group over another. For example, in an important 2003 case, *Lawrence et al.* v. *Texas,* the Supreme Court declared that laws banning sodomy were unconstitutional because they violated the due process rights of citizens because of their sexual orientation. A neighbor in 1998 had reported a "weapons disturbance" at the home of John G. Lawrence, and when police arrived they found Lawrence and another man, Tyron Garner, having sex. The two were held overnight in jail and later fined $200 each for violating the state's homosexual conduct law. In its decision, the Court said:

> *Although the laws involved . . . here . . . do not do more than prohibit a particular sexual act, their penalties and purposes have more far-reaching consequences, touching upon the most private human conduct, sexual behavior, and in the most private of places, the home. They seek to control a personal relationship that, whether or not entitled to formal recognition in the law, is within the liberty of persons to choose without being punished as criminals. The liberty protected by the Constitution allows homosexual persons the right to choose to enter upon relationships in the confines of their homes and their own private lives and still retain their dignity as free persons.*

As a result of the decision, all sodomy laws in the United States are now unconstitutional and unenforceable.[28]

Perspectives on Justice

The *Lawrence* v. *Texas* case is a milestone in the ongoing effort to grant due process rights to all Americans. No one, according to the due process perspective, should be denied the protection of the law simply because of their personal status—race, religion, ethnicity, or sexual orientation.

In contrast, procedural due process seeks to ensure that no person will be deprived of life, liberty, or property without proper and legal criminal process. Basically, procedural due process is intended to guarantee that fundamental fairness exists in each individual case. Specific due process procedures include:

- Prompt notice of charges,
- A formal hearing,
- The right to counsel or some other representation,
- The opportunity to respond to charges,
- The opportunity to confront and cross-examine witnesses and accusers,

- The privilege to be free from self-incrimination,
- The opportunity to present one's own witnesses,
- A decision made on the basis of substantial evidence and facts produced at the hearing,
- A written statement of the reasons for the decision, and
- An appellate review procedure.

The Meaning of Due Process

Exactly what constitutes due process in a specific case depends on the facts of the case, the federal and state constitutional and statutory provisions, previous court decisions, and the ideas and principles that society considers important at a given time and in a given place.[29] Justice Felix Frankfurter emphasized this point in *Rochin* v. *California* (1952):

> Due process of law requires an evaluation based on a disinterested inquiry pursued in the spirit of science on a balanced order of facts, exactly and clearly stated, on the detached consideration of conflicting claims[,] . . . on a judgment not ad hoc and episodic but duly mindful of reconciling the needs both of continuity and of change in a progressive society.[30]

The interpretations of due process of law are not fixed but reflect what society deems fair and just at a particular time and place. The degree of loss suffered by the individual (victim or offender) balanced against the state's interests also determines which and how many due process requirements are ordinarily applied. When the Supreme Court justices are conservative, as they are now, they are less likely to create new rights and privileges under the guise of due process. For example, the Court's decision in the case of *Sattazahn* v. *Pennsylvania* (2003) helped define the concept of double jeopardy. David Sattazahn had been sentenced to death under a Pennsylvania law requiring that the sentencing jury unanimously find that the case warranted capital punishment. If the jury cannot unanimously agree on the sentence, the court must then enter a life sentence. After Sattazahn was convicted of murder, his jury became deadlocked on the sentence. The trial judge discharged the jury members and entered a life sentence against the defendant. Sattazahn subsequently appealed the conviction and received a new trial. At the second trial, the prosecutor again sought the death penalty and Sattazahn was again convicted, but this time the jury imposed a death sentence. Sattazahn appealed on the grounds that the imposition of the death sentence after he was originally awarded a life sentence was a violation of double jeopardy. However, the Supreme Court disagreed, finding that jeopardy was not compromised in this case. When a defendant is convicted of murder and sentenced to life imprisonment and succeeds in having the conviction set aside on appeal, jeopardy has not terminated, so that a life sentence imposed in connection with the initial conviction raises no double jeopardy bar to a death sentence on retrial. The Court also concluded that double jeopardy protections were not triggered in this case because the jury deadlocked at the first sentencing and made no findings with respect to the alleged aggravating circumstance. The result could not be called an acquittal within the context of double jeopardy. The Court could have ruled that the second capital sentence was a violation of the defendant's constitutional rights but chose not to, instead finding:

> Nothing in §1 of the Fourteenth Amendment indicates that any "life" or "liberty" interest that Pennsylvania law may have given petitioner in the first proceeding's life sentence was somehow immutable, and he was "deprived" of any such interest only by operation of the "process" he invoked to invalidate the underlying first-degree murder conviction. This Court declines to hold that the Due Process Clause provides greater double-jeopardy protection than does the Double Jeopardy Clause.[31]

This complicated case aptly illustrates how judicial interpretation controls the meaning of due process.

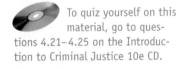
To quiz yourself on this material, go to questions 4.21–4.25 on the Introduction to Criminal Justice 10e CD.

Summary

- The criminal justice system is basically a legal system. Its foundation is the criminal law, which is concerned with people's conduct.
- The purpose of criminal law is to regulate behavior and maintain order in society. What constitutes a crime is defined primarily by the state and federal legislatures and reviewed by the courts. What is considered criminal conduct changes from one period to another. Social norms, values, and community beliefs play major roles in determining what conduct is antisocial.
- Crimes are generally classified as felonies or misdemeanors, depending on their seriousness.
- There are different elements, both mental and physical, in a crime.
- Crimes have a mental element known as mens rea or intent.
- The actus reas is the physical element of the crime. Thought alone is not enough; a crime must involve action.
- The law does not hold an individual blameworthy unless that person is capable of intending to com-

mit the crime of which he is accused and that intent causes him to commit an illegal action.
- A person can defend himself against crime by denying he committed the act.
- Defendants can also deny their intent to commit crime. They may claim that they were intoxicated, acted under duress or out of necessity, or in self-defense. They can argue that the police entrapped them into committing crime. Such factors as insanity, a mental defect, or age mitigate a person's criminal responsibility.
- States periodically revise and update the substantive criminal law. The definition of crime and criminal defense change to reflect existing social and cultural change. For example, recent changes in the law to control terrorism reflect the public condemnation of the September 11 terrorist attacks.
- Procedural laws set out the rules for processing the offender from arrest through trial, sentencing, and release. An accused must be provided with the guarantees of due process under the Fifth and Fourteenth Amendments to the U.S. Constitution.

Key Terms

civil law   120
criminal law   120
stare decisis   121
mala in se   121
ex post facto law   126

actus reus   130
mens rea   130
public safety or strict
    liability crime   132
justification   132

penumbral crimes   138
obitiatry   138
stalking   138

Doing Research on the Web

For an up-to-date list of Web links, go to http://cj.wadsworth.com/siegel_intro10e.

The jury in the 1997 Massachusetts trial of British au pair Louise Woodward, who was accused of killing the baby she was caring for, had four possible outcomes. It could (1) convict Woodward of first-degree murder (intent to kill, cause harm or injury or atrocity, and inflict extreme cruelty); (2) convict her of second-degree murder (acted with malice); (3) acquit her (not guilty because the prosecution failed to prove guilt beyond a reasonable doubt); or (4)result in a hung jury (jury is divided and cannot reach a verdict).

After the jury found her guilty of second-degree murder, the judge reduced Woodward's sentence to manslaughter because the intent to do bodily harm or act with malice was not present. Involuntary manslaughter is a killing with no intention to cause

serious bodily harm, such as acting without proper caution.

Suppose you work in the prosecutor's office and you have been assigned the task of coming up with information on criminal homicide to assist the government in its appeal. Search for articles using InfoTrac College Edition regarding the distinction between murder and manslaughter. Use key words such as "malice," "intent to kill," and "provocation."

To read a critique of the decision from a conservative perspective, look up William F. Buckley Jr., "Scrambled Justice," *National Review,* December 8, 1997, p. 62.

> Pro/Con discussions and Viewpoint Essays on some of the topics in this chapter may be found at the Opposing Viewpoints Resource Center: http://www.gale.com/OpposingViewpoints.

Discussion Questions

1. What are the specific aims and purposes of the criminal law? To what extent does the criminal law control behavior?
2. What kinds of activities should be labeled criminal in contemporary society? Why?
3. What is a criminal act? What is a criminal state of mind? When are individuals liable for their actions?
4. Discuss the various kinds of crime classifications. To what extent or degree are they distinguishable?
5. Numerous states are revising their penal codes. Which major categories of substantive crimes do you think should be revised?
6. Entrapment is a defense used when the defendant was lured into committing the crime. To what extent should law enforcement personnel induce the commission of an offense?
7. What legal principles can be used to justify self-defense? As the law seeks to prevent, not promote, crime, are such principles sound?
8. What are the minimum standards of criminal procedure required in the criminal justice system?

Notes

1 Some of the historical criminal law concepts discussed here are a synthesis of those contained in Peter Stein, *Roman Law in European History* (London, England: Cambridge University Press, 1999); Norman Cantor, *Imagining the Law: Common Law and the Foundations of the American Legal System* (New York: Harper Collins, 1999); Jerome Hall, *General Principles of Criminal Law* (Charlottesville, Va.: Michie, 1961).
2 *Carriers Case Yearbook,* 13 Edward IV 9.pL.5 (1473).
3 See, generally, Wayne R. LaFave and Austin W. Scott, *Criminal Law* (St. Paul, Minn.: West Publishing Horn Book Series, 1986).
4 E. Gellhorn, *Administrative Law and Process* (St. Paul, Minn.: West Publishing Nutshell Series, 1981).
5 Environmental Protection Agency, Criminal Enforcement Division, http://www.epa.gov/compliance/criminal/index.html.
6 See John Weaver, *Warren—The Man, the Court, the Era* (Boston: Little, Brown, 1967).
7 *Marbury* v. *Madison,* 5 U.S. (1 Cranch) 137, 2 L.Ed. 60 (1803).
8 *City of Chicago* v. *Jesus Morales et al.,* 527 US 41 (1999).
9 *Kansas* v. *Hendricks,* 117 S.Ct. 2072 (1997); *City of Chicago* v. *Jesus Morales et al.,* 119 S.Ct. 246 (1999).
10 See American Law Institute, Model Penal Code, Sec. 104.
11 Henry Black, *Black's Law Dictionary,* rev. 5th ed. (St. Paul, Minn.: West, 1979), pp. 744, 1150.
12 Sheldon Krantz, *Law of Corrections and Prisoners' Rights, Cases, and Materials,* 3d ed. (St. Paul, Minn.: West, 1986), p. 702; Barbara Knight and Stephen Early Jr., *Prisoners' Rights in America* (Chicago: Nelson-Hall, 1986), chap. 1; see also Fred Cohen, "The Law of Prisoners' Rights—An Overview," *Criminal Law Bulletin* 24 (1988): 321–49.
13 See *United States* v. *Balint,* 258 U.S. 250, 42 S.Ct. 301, 66 L.Ed. 604 (1922); see also *Morissette* v. *United States,* 342 U.S. 246, 72 S.Ct. 240, 96 L.Ed. 288 (1952).
14 New York State Consolidated Laws, Article 270 Other Offenses Relating to Public Safety, Section 270.10 Creating a Hazard (2002).
15 Associated Press, "Nigerian Used Stepdaughter, 14, for a Son, Jury Finds," *Boston Globe,* October 8, 1998, p. 9.
16 370 U.S. 660, 82 S.Ct. 1417, 8 L.Ed.2d 758 (1962).
17 392 U.S. 514, 88 S.Ct. 2145, 20 L.Ed.2d 1254 (1968).
18 Samuel M. Davis, *Rights of Juveniles: The Juvenile Justice System* (New York: Boardman, 1974; update 1993), chap. 2; Larry Siegel and Joseph Senna, *Juvenile Delinquency: Theory, Practice, and Law* (St. Paul, Minn.: West, 1996).
19 *Regina* v. *Dudley and Stephens,* 14 Q.B.D. 273 (1884).
20 503 U.S. 540, 112 S.Ct. 1535, 118 L.Ed.2d 174 (1992).
21 Margaret Raymond, "Penumbral Crimes," *American Criminal Law Review* 39 (2002): 1395–1440.
22 Marvin Zalman, John Strate, Denis Hunter, and James Sellars, "Michigan Assisted Suicide Three Ring Circus: The Intersection of Law and Politics," *Ohio Northern Law Review* 23 (1997): 863–903.
23 1992 P.A. 270 as amended by 1993 P.A.3, M.C.L. ss. 752.1021 to 752. 1027.
24 National Institute of Justice, *Project to Develop a Model Anti-Stalking Statute* (Washington, D.C.: National Institute of Justice, 1994).
25 Michele Kurtz, "Predator Laws Hit by Rulings, Backlogs," *Boston Globe,* July 20, 2002, p. 1.
26 384 U.S. 436, 86 S.Ct. 1602, 16 L.Ed.2d 694 (1966).
27 James MacGregor Burns and Steward Burns, *The Pursuit of Rights in America* (New York: Knopf, 1991).
28 *Lawrence et al.* v. *Texas,* No. 02–102, June 26, 2003.
29 342 U.S. 165, 72 S.Ct. 205, 95 L.Ed. 183 (1952).
30 Ibid., at 172, 72 S.Ct. at 209.
31 *Sattazahn* v. *Pennsylvania,* No. 01–7574, decided January 14, 2003.

Part Two   The Police and Law Enforcement

© 2003 AP/Wide World Photos

On September 5, 2003, 242 U.S. and international law enforcement officers graduated from the 214th class of the Federal Bureau of Investigation National Academy. They came from 49 states and 25 countries, including Egypt, Gambia, Jordan, Korea, Kyrgyzstan, Rwanda, Turkey, and Venezuela. Each was a member of a sheriff's department, police department, military police unit, or federal agency. They went through 11 weeks of academic classes and physical training designed to give them a fuller understanding of current issues, law enforcement trends, the need for global partnerships against crime, and the best methods to combat terrorism. Opened in 1935, the FBI academy has trained more than 36,000 law enforcement managers, nearly 2,500 of them from international agencies.

The academy is one component of the nation's largest federal law enforcement agency. The next four chapters cover the most important law enforcement agencies, including the FBI, and discuss their role, organization, tasks, and objectives as well as the problems they face on a daily basis. Chapter 5 discusses the history of law enforcement and the various contemporary agencies, Chapter 6 covers the role and function of police agencies, Chapter 7 analyzes the most pressing issues facing police agencies, and Chapter 8 is devoted to police and the rule of law.

Chapter Outline

Chapter Objectives

After reading this chapter, you should be able to:

1. Recount the early development of the police in England.
2. Know the reasons that police departments were created in the United States.
3. Recognize the problems of the early police agencies.
4. Identify the various levels of law enforcement.
5. Discuss the differences between local, state, county, and federal law enforcement agencies.
6. Describe how local police agencies evolved over time.
7. Discuss what social and economic factors influence policing.
8. Know what is meant by the term *biometric technology*.
9. Identify the different types of DNA testing and tell how they are used.
10. Explain how some critics fear the spread of police technology.

Viewpoints

 Analyzing Criminal Justice Issues: Operation X-Out   161

 Criminal Justice and Technology: Crime Mapping and the ICAM Program   166

 Criminal Justice and Technology: Added Security: Biometric Technology   169

Web Links

Sir Robert Peel
http://www.spartacus.schoolnet.co.uk/
PRpeel.htm   149

Boston police strike
http://www.geocities.com/fcpa.geo/
no1union.htm   152

Drug Enforcement Administration
http://www.usdoj.gov/dea/   160

Police Officer Internet Dictionary
http://www.officer.com/   164

Western Identification Network
http://www.winid.org/history.htm   168

Automated Fingerprint Identification System
http://www.ci.mesa.az.us/police/identification/
fptech_job.htm   168

Science of DNA testing
http://arbl.cvmbs.colostate.edu/hbooks/
genetics/medgen/dnatesting/   170

InfoTrac College Edition Links

Article: "The Old English Constabulary"   149

Article: "The Origins of the Modern Police"   150

Key term: "vigilante"   150

Article: "A Police Force Stands Ready"   151

Key term: "police unions"   154

Key term: "Rodney King case"   154

Key term: "FBI and terrorism"   158

Chapter 5 | Police in Society: History and Organization

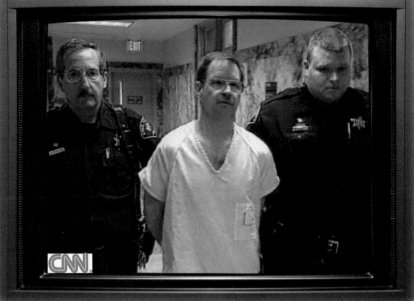

In the 1980s the Seattle, Washington, area was terrorized by a serial killer who stalked and killed prostitutes and runaways. He was given the name "Green River Killer" after the area where the first victims' bodies were found. In 1984, police attention began to focus on a local man, Gary Ridgway, when the boyfriend of one victim told police that he last saw her getting into a pickup truck owned by Ridgway. Ridgway claimed he had never met the girl, and a police investigator from a nearby town cleared him as a suspect. Ridgway also passed a polygraph test. Because detectives continued to suspect him, they searched his house and took a saliva sample.

Area detectives were so desperate to identify the killer that, in an effort mimicking events in the films *Silence of the Lambs* and *Red Dragon,* some even traveled to Florida to interview the notorious serial killer Ted Bundy to examine the mind of a remorseless murderer. Thirteen years after the Seattle killing spree began, DNA technology had developed sufficiently so that the evidence taken from the bodies of three victims could be matched to Ridgway. On November 6, 2003, to escape the death penalty, Ridgway plead guilty to killing 48 women. He is the most prolific convicted serial killer in the nation's history.

The Green River case is a triumph of police persistence. Local

detectives did everything in their power to catch a notorious and brutal killer. Some of the officers on the case followed leads for more than 20 years. The case also shows how sophisticated investigation techniques such as the use of DNA are shaping police work.

The Green River case is but one of many high-profile law enforcement investigations undertaken by local, county, state, and Federal agencies. It aptly illustrates how law enforcement is of critical importance for the criminal justice system. The police are the gatekeepers of the justice process. They initiate contact with alleged law violators and decide whether to for-

mally arrest them and start their journey through the criminal justice system, to settle the issue in an informal way (such as by issuing a warning), or to simply take no action at all. The strategic position of law enforcement officers, their visibility and contact with the public, and their use of weapons and arrest power have kept them in the forefront of public thought in criminal justice matters.

CNN *View the CNN video clip of this story on your Introduction to Criminal Justice 10e CD.*

The public may applaud police efforts that have brought the crime rate down, but they are also concerned by media reports of police officers who abuse their power by either using unnecessary force and brutality or routinely violating the civil rights of suspects. Even when community members believe police officers are competent and dependable, many question their priorities and often consider them disrespectful.[1] For example, some critics charge that police officers routinely induce or force

confessions from criminal suspects. Later at trial, these false confessions may influence jurors even if they seem inconsistent with the facts of the case.[2] Another concern is that police are racially and ethnically biased and use racial profiling to routinely stop African Americans and search their cars. Some have suggested that police have created a new form of crime: DWB, "driving while black."[3] In the post–September 11 age, police are focusing their attention on suspected terrorists of Middle East descent.

Despite these concerns, the majority of citizens give their police force high marks. Though African Americans were believed to hold less positive attitudes toward police, recent research finds that racial differences are slight.[4] Citizens are especially likely to value local police if they view their neighborhood as safe and believe that the efficiency of the local police is a key to its protection.[5] Metropolitan police departments are attracting applicants who value an exciting, well-paid job that also holds the opportunity to provide valuable community service. Salaries in municipal police agencies are becoming more competitive (see Table 5.1).

The History of Police

The origin of U.S. police agencies, like that of criminal law, can be traced to early English society.[6] England had no regular police force before the Norman Conquest. Every person living in the villages scattered throughout the countryside was responsible for aiding neighbors and protecting the settlement from thieves and marauders. This was known as the pledge system. People were grouped in collectives of 10 families, called **tithings,** and were entrusted with policing their own minor problems. When trouble occurred, a citizen was expected to make a **hue and cry.** Ten tithings were grouped into a **hundred,** whose affairs were supervised by a constable appointed by the local nobleman. The **constable,** who might be considered the first real police officer, dealt with more serious breaches of the law.[7]

Empirical evidence shows that, in at least some jurisdictions, young African American males are treated more harshly by the criminal and juvenile justice system than are members of any other group. Elements of institutional racism have become so endemic that terms such as "DWB" (Driving While Black) are now part of the vernacular, used to signify the fact that young African American motorists are routinely stopped by police.

tithings
During the Middle Ages, groups of about 10 families responsible for maintaining order among themselves and dealing with disturbances, fire, wild animals, or other threats.

hue and cry
In medieval England, a call for mutual aid against trouble or danger.

Caption for photo: © 2001 AP/Wide World Photos

Table 5.1 Police Salaries, 2003

Position	Minimum Base	Maximum Salary
Police chief	$62,640	$78,580
Deputy chief	53,740	67,370
Police captain	51,680	64,230
Police lieutenant	47,750	57,740
Police sergeant	42,570	50,670
Police corporal	35,370	43,830
Police officer	31,410	43,450

Source: Bureau of Labor Statistics, *Occupational Outlook Handbook, 2002–03 Edition* (Washington, D.C.: 2003), http://www.bls.gov/oco/ocos160.htm, accessed on July 9, 2003.

Shires, which resembled the counties of today, were controlled by the shire reeve appointed by the Crown or local landowner to supervise the territory and ensure that order would be kept. The **shire reeve,** a forerunner of today's sheriff, soon began to pursue and apprehend law violators as part of his duties.

In the thirteenth century, the **watch system** was created to help protect property in England's larger cities and towns. Watchmen patrolled at night and helped protect against robberies, fires, and disturbances. They reported to the area constable, who became the primary metropolitan law enforcement agent. In larger cities, such as London, the watchmen were organized within church parishes and were usually members of the parish they protected.

In 1326 the office of **justice of the peace** was created to assist the shire reeve in controlling the county. Eventually, these justices took on judicial functions in addition to their primary role as peacekeeper. The local constable became the operational assistant to the justice of the peace, supervising the night watchmen, investigating offenses, serving summonses, executing warrants, and securing prisoners. This system helped delineate the relationship between police and the judiciary, which has continued for more than 670 years.

Eighteenth-Century Developments

As the eighteenth century began, rising crime rates encouraged a new form of private monied police who were able to profit both legally and criminally from the lack of formal police departments. These private police agents, referred to as thief takers, were universally corrupt, taking profits not only from catching and informing on criminals but also from receiving stolen property, theft, intimidation, perjury, and blackmail. They often relieved their prisoners of money and stolen goods and made more income by accepting hush money, giving perjured evidence, swearing false oaths, and operating extortion rackets. Petty debtors were especially easy targets for those who combined thief taking with the keeping of alehouses and taverns. While incarcerated, the health and safety of prisoners were entirely at the whim of the keepers or thief takers who were virtually free to charge what they wanted for board and other necessities. Court bailiffs who also acted as thief takers were the most passionately detested legal profiteers. They seized debtors and held them in small lockups where they forced their victims to pay exorbitant prices for food and lodging. The thief takers' use of violence was notorious. They went armed and were prepared to maim or kill to gain their objectives.

Henry Fielding, the famed author of *Tom Jones,* along with Saunders Welch and Sir John Fielding, sought to clean up the thief-taking system. Appointed a city magistrate in 1748, Henry Fielding operated his own group of monied police out of Bow Street in London, directing and deploying them throughout the city and its environs, deciding which cases to investigate and what streets to protect. His agents were carefully instructed on their legitimate powers and duties. Fielding's Bow Street Runners were a marked improvement over the earlier monied police because they had an administrative structure that improved record-keeping and investigative procedures. Although an improvement, Fielding's forces were not adequate, and by the nineteenth century, state police officers were needed.

In 1829 Sir Robert Peel, England's home secretary, guided through Parliament an "Act for Improving the Police in and near the Metropolis." The **Metropolitan Police Act** established the first organized police force in London. Composed of more than 1,000 men, the London police force was structured along military lines. Its members would be known from then on as bobbies, after their creator. They wore a distinctive uniform and were led by two magistrates, who were later given the title of commissioner. However, the ultimate responsibility for the police fell to the home secretary and consequently the Parliament.

hundred
In medieval England, a group of 100 families responsible for maintaining order and trying minor offenses.

constable
In early English towns, an appointed peacekeeper who organized citizens for protection and supervised the night watch.

What was the life of an English constable like? Read on InfoTrac College Edition, Robert D. Storch, "The Old English Constabulary," *History Today* 49, no. 11 (November 1999): 43.

shire reeve
In early England, the chief law enforcement official in a county, forerunner of today's sheriff.

watch system
In medieval England, men organized in church parishes to guard at night against disturbances and breaches of the peace under the direction of the local constable.

justice of the peace
Official appointed to act as the judicial officer in a county.

Metropolitan Police Act
In 1829, when Sir Robert Peel was home secretary, the first Metropolitan Police Act was passed and the Metropolitan Police Force was established to replace the local watch and constable system in the London area.

To read about Sir Robert Peel's life and political career, go to http://www.spartacus.schoolnet.co.uk/PRpeel.htm.

The early bobbies suffered many problems. Many were corrupt, they were unsuccessful at stopping crime, and they were influenced by the wealthy. Owners of houses of ill repute who in the past had guaranteed their undisturbed operations by bribing watchmen now turned their attention to the bobbies. Metropolitan police administrators fought constantly to terminate cowardly, corrupt, and alcoholic officers, dismissing in the beginning about one-third of the bobbies each year.

Despite its recognized shortcomings, the London experiment proved a vast improvement over what had come before. It was considered so successful that the metropolitan police soon began providing law enforcement assistance to outlying areas that requested it. Another act of Parliament allowed justices of the peace to establish local police forces, and by 1856 every borough and county in England was required to form its own police force.

Law Enforcement in Colonial America

Law enforcement in colonial America paralleled the British model. In the colonies, the county **sheriff** became the most important law enforcement agent. In addition to keeping the peace and fighting crime, sheriffs collected taxes, supervised elections, and handled a great deal of other legal business.

The colonial sheriff did not patrol or seek out crime. Instead, he reacted to citizens' complaints and investigated crimes that had occurred. His salary, related to his effectiveness, was paid on a fee system. Sheriffs received a fixed amount for every arrest made. Unfortunately, their tax-collecting chores were more lucrative than fighting crime, so law enforcement was not one of their primary concerns.

In the cities, law enforcement was the province of the town marshal, who was aided, often unwillingly, by a variety of constables, night watchmen, police justices, and city council members. However, local governments had little power of administration, and enforcement of the criminal law was largely an individual or community responsibility. After the American Revolution, larger cities relied on elected or appointed officials to serve warrants and recover stolen property, sometimes in co-operation with the thieves themselves. Nightwatchmen, referred to as leatherheads because of the leather helmets they wore, patrolled the streets calling the hour while equipped with a rattle to summon help and a nightstick to ward off lawbreakers. Watchmen were not widely respected. Rowdy young men enjoyed tipping over watch houses with a leatherhead inside, and a favorite saying in New York was: "While the city sleeps the watchmen do too."[8]

In rural areas in the South, "slave patrols" charged with recapturing escaped slaves were an early, if loathsome, form of law enforcement.[9] In the western territories, individual initiative was encouraged by the practice of offering rewards for the capture of felons. If trouble arose, the town vigilance committee might form a posse to chase offenders. These **vigilantes** were called on to eradicate such social problems as theft of livestock, through force or intimidation. The San Francisco Vigilance Committee actively pursued criminals in the mid-nineteenth century.

As cities grew, it became exceedingly difficult for local leaders to organize ad hoc citizen vigilante groups. Moreover, the early nineteenth century was an era of widespread urban unrest and mob violence. Local leaders began to realize that a more structured police function was needed to control demonstrators and keep the peace.

Early Police Agencies

The modern police department was born out of urban mob violence that wracked the nation's cities in the nineteenth century. Boston created the first formal U.S. police department in 1838. New York formed its police department in

---

To read a detailed account of the creation of the first police forces, go to Clive Emsley, "The Origins of the Modern Police," *History Today* 49, no. 4 (April 1999): 8.

sheriff
The chief law enforcement officer in a county.

vigilantes
In the old west, members of a vigilance committee or posse called upon to capture cattle thieves or other felons.

Vigilantes still operate today. To read about the modern versions, use "vigilante" as a key word on InfoTrac College Edition.

1844; Philadelphia, in 1854. The new police departments replaced the night-watch system and relegated constables and sheriffs to serving court orders and running jails.

At first, the urban police departments inherited the functions of the institutions they replaced. For example, Boston police were charged with maintaining public health until 1853, and in New York, the police were responsible for street sweeping until 1881. Politics dominated the departments and determined the recruitment of new officers and promotion of supervisors. An individual with the right connections could be hired despite a lack of qualifications. Early police agencies were corrupt, brutal, and inefficient.[10]

In the late nineteenth century, police work was highly desirable because it paid more than most other blue-collar jobs. By 1880 the average factory worker earned $450 a year, while a metropolitan police officer made $900 annually. For immigrant groups, having enough political clout to be appointed to the police department was an important step up the social ladder.[11] However, job security was uncertain because it depended on the local political machine's staying in power.

Police work itself was primitive. Few of even the simplest technological innovations common today, such as call boxes or centralized record keeping, were in place. Most officers patrolled on foot, without backup or the ability to call for help. Officers were commonly taunted by local toughs and responded with force and brutality. The long-standing conflict between police and the public was born in the difficulty that untrained, unprofessional officers had in patrolling the streets of nineteenth-century U.S. cities and in breaking up and controlling labor disputes. Police were not crime fighters as they are known today. Their major role was maintaining order, and their power was almost unchecked. The average officer had little training, no education in the law, and a minimum of supervision, yet the police became virtual judges of law and fact with the ability to exercise unlimited discretion.[12]

At mid-nineteenth century, the detective bureau was set up as part of the Boston police. Until then, thief taking had been the province of amateur bounty hunters, who hired themselves out to victims for a price. When professional police departments replaced bounty hunters, the close working relationships that developed between police detectives and their underworld informants produced many scandals and, consequently, high personnel turnover.

Police during the nineteenth century were regarded as incompetent and corrupt and were disliked by the people they served. The police role was only minimally directed at law enforcement. Its primary function was serving as the enforcement arm of the reigning political power, protecting private property, and keeping control of the ever-rising numbers of foreign immigrants.

Police agencies evolved slowly through the second half of the nineteenth century. Uniforms were introduced in 1853 in New York. The first technological breakthroughs in police operations came in the area of communications. The linking of precincts to central headquarters by telegraph began in the 1850s. In 1867 the first telegraph police boxes were installed. An officer could turn a key in a box, and his location and number would automatically register at headquarters. Additional technological advances were made in transportation. The Detroit Police Department outfitted some of its patrol officers with bicycles in 1897. By 1913 the motorcycle was being used by departments in the eastern part of the nation. The first police car was used in Akron, Ohio, in 1910, and the police wagon became popular in Cincinnati in 1912.[13] Nonpolice functions, such as care of the streets, began to be abandoned after the Civil War.

Big-city police were still disrespected by the public, unsuccessful in their role as crime stoppers, and uninvolved in progressive activities. The control of police departments by local politicians impeded effective law enforcement and fostered an atmosphere of graft and corruption.

To read about the operations of an early police department, go to L. Wayne Hicks, "A Police Force Stands Ready," *Denver Business Journal* 51, no. 12 (November 12, 1999): 24.

Perspectives on Justice

The fact that police agencies grew out of the desire of the upper classes to suppress the social behavior and economic aspirations of the lower classes agrees with the restorative justice perspectives vision that American justice is traditionally coercive and must be changed to become humanistic.

Twentieth-Century Reform

In an effort to reduce police corruption, civic leaders in a number of jurisdictions created police administrative boards to lessen local officials' control over the police. These tribunals were responsible for appointing police administrators and controlling police affairs. In many instances, these measures failed because the private citizens appointed to the review boards lacked expertise in the intricacies of police work.

Another reform movement was the takeover of some big-city police agencies by state legislators. Although police budgets were financed through local taxes, control of police was usurped by rural politicians in the state capitals. New York City temporarily lost authority over its police force in 1857. It was not until the first decades of the twentieth century that cities regained control of their police forces.

One of the few policemen who stayed at work during the Boston police strike of 1919. Police earned about twenty-five cents an hour and were expected to work up to ninety-eight hours a week!

The Boston police strike of 1919 heightened interest in police reform. The strike came about basically because police officers were dissatisfied with their status in society. Other professions were unionizing and increasing their standards of living, but police salaries lagged behind. The Boston police officers organization, the Boston Social Club, voted to become a union affiliated with the American Federation of Labor. The officers struck on September 9, 1919. Rioting and looting broke out, resulting in Governor Calvin Coolidge's mobilization of the state militia to take over the city. Public support turned against the police, and the strike was broken. Eventually, all the striking officers were fired and replaced by new recruits. The Boston police strike ended police unionism for decades and solidified power in the hands of reactionary, autocratic police administrators. In the aftermath of the strike, various local, state, and federal crime commissions began to investigate the extent of crime and the ability of the justice system to deal with it and made recommendations to improve police effectiveness.[14] However, with the onset of the Great Depression, justice reform became a less important issue than economic revival and, for many years, little changed in the nature of policing.

www What effect did the Boston police strike have on police labor unions? To find out, go to http://www.geocities.com/fcpa.geo/no1union.htm.

The Emergence of Professionalism

Around the turn of the century, a number of nationally recognized leaders called for measures to help improve and professionalize the police. In 1893 the International Association of Chiefs of Police (IACP), a professional society, was formed. Under the direction of its first president (District of Columbia chief of police

Richard Sylvester), the IACP became the leading voice for police reform during the first two decades of the twentieth century. The IACP called for creating a civil service police force and for removing political influence and control. It also advocated centralized organizational structure and record keeping to curb the power of politically aligned precinct captains. Still another professional reform the IACP fostered was the creation of specialized units, such as delinquency control squads.

The most famous police reformer of the time was August Vollmer. While serving as police chief of Berkeley, California, Vollmer instituted university training for young officers. He also helped develop the School of Criminology at the University of California at Berkeley, which became the model for justice-related programs around the United States. Vollmer's disciples included O. W. Wilson, who pioneered the use of advanced training for officers when he took over and reformed the Wichita (Kansas) Police Department in 1928. Wilson was also instrumental in applying modern management and administrative techniques to policing. His text, *Police Administration,* became the single most influential work on the subject.

During this period, police professionalism was equated with an incorruptible, tough, highly trained, rule-oriented department organized along militaristic lines. The most respected department was that in Los Angeles, which emphasized police as incorruptible crime fighters who would not question the authority of the central command.

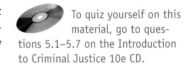

To quiz yourself on this material, go to questions 5.1–5.7 on the Introduction to Criminal Justice 10e CD.

The Modern Era of Policing: 1960 to the Present Day

The modern era of policing can be traced from 1960 to the present day. What are the major events that occurred during this period?

Policing in the 1960s

Turmoil and crisis were the hallmarks of policing during the 1960s. Throughout this decade, the U.S. Supreme Court handed down a number of decisions designed to control police operations and procedures. Police officers were now required to obey strict legal guidelines when questioning suspects, conducting searches and wiretapping, and so on. As the civil rights of suspects were significantly expanded, police complained they were being "handcuffed by the courts."

Also during this time, civil unrest produced a growing tension between police and the public. African Americans, who were battling for increased rights and freedoms in the civil rights movement, found themselves confronting police lines. When riots broke out in New York, Detroit, Los Angeles, and other cities between 1964 and 1968, the spark that ignited conflict often involved the police. When students across the nation began marching in anti–Vietnam War demonstrations, local police departments were called on to keep order. Police forces were ill equipped and poorly trained to deal with these social problems. Not surprisingly, the 1960s were marked by a number of bloody confrontations between the police and the public.

Confounding these problems was a rapidly growing crime rate. The number of violent and property crimes increased dramatically. Drug addiction and abuse grew to be national concerns, common in all social classes. Urban police departments could not control the crime rate, and police officers resented the demands placed on them by dissatisfied citizens.

Policing in the 1970s

The 1970s witnessed many structural changes in police agencies themselves. The end of the Vietnam War significantly reduced tensions between students and police. However, the relationship between police and minorities was still rocky.

Local fears and distrust, combined with conservative federal policies, encouraged police departments to control what was perceived as an emerging minority group "threat."[15]

Increased federal government support for criminal justice greatly influenced police operations. During the decade, the Law Enforcement Assistance Administration (LEAA) devoted a significant portion of its funds to police agencies. Although a number of police departments used this money to purchase little-used hardware, such as antiriot gear, most of it went to supporting innovative research on police work and advanced training of police officers. Perhaps most significant, LEAA's Law Enforcement Education Program helped thousands of officers further their college education. Hundreds of criminal justice programs were developed on college campuses around the country, providing a pool of highly educated police recruits. LEAA funds were also used to import or transfer technology originally developed in other fields into law enforcement. Technological innovations involving computers transformed the way police kept records, investigated crimes, and communicated with one another. State training academies improved the way police learn to deal with such issues as job stress, community conflict, and interpersonal relations.

More women and minorities were recruited to police work. Affirmative action programs helped, albeit slowly, alter the ethnic, racial, and gender composition of U.S. policing.

Policing in the 1980s

As the 1980s began, the police role seemed to be changing significantly. A number of experts acknowledged that the police were not simply crime fighters and called for police to develop a greater awareness of community issues, which resulted in the emergence of the community policing concept.[16]

Police unions, which began to grow in the late 1960s, continued to have a great impact on departmental administration in the 1980s. Unions fought for and won increased salaries and benefits for their members. In many instances, unions eroded the power of the police chief to make unquestioned policy and personnel decisions. During the decade, chiefs of police commonly consulted with union leaders before making major decisions concerning departmental operations.

While police operations improved markedly during this time, police departments were also beset by problems that impeded their effectiveness. State and local budgets were cut back during the Reagan administration, while federal support for innovative police programs was severely curtailed with the demise of the LEAA.

Police–community relations continued to be a major problem. Riots and incidents of urban conflict occurred in some of the nation's largest cities.[17] They triggered continual concern about what the police role should be, especially in inner-city neighborhoods.

Policing in the 1990s

The 1990s began on a sour note and ended with an air of optimism. The incident that helped change the face of American policing occurred on March 3, 1991, when two African American men, Rodney King and Bryant Allen, were driving in Los Angeles, California. They refused to stop when signaled by a police car, instead increasing their speed. King, who was driving, was apparently drunk or on drugs. When police finally stopped the car, they delivered 56 baton blows and six kicks to King, in a period of two minutes, producing 11 skull fractures, brain damage, and kidney damage. They did not realize that their actions were being videotaped by an observer who later gave the tape to the media. The officers involved were tried and acquitted in a suburban court by an all-white jury. The acquittal set off six days of rioting in South Central Los Angeles, which was brought under

Use the term "police unions" as a subject guide on InfoTrac College Edition to learn more about them in the United States and around the world.

To read more about the infamous L.A. incident, use "Rodney King case" as a subject guide on InfoTrac College Edition.

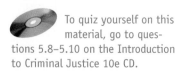
To quiz yourself on this material, go to questions 5.8–5.10 on the Introduction to Criminal Justice 10e CD.

control by the California National Guard. In total, 54 people were killed, 2,383 were known to have been injured, and 13,212 people were arrested.[18] The police officers involved in the beatings were later tried and convicted in federal court.

The King case prompted an era of reform. Several police experts decreed that the nation's police forces should be evaluated not on their crime-fighting ability but on their courteousness, deportment, and helpfulness. Interest renewed in reviving an earlier style of police work featuring foot patrols and increased citizen contact. Police departments began to embrace new forms of policing that stressed cooperation with the community and problem solving; this is referred to as the **community policing** model. Ironically, urban police departments began to shift their focus to becoming community organizers at a time when technological improvements increased the ability to identify suspects. An ongoing effort was made to bring diversity to police departments, and African Americans began to be hired as chiefs of police, particularly in Los Angeles. Exhibit 5.1 lists some of the most notable achievements of the decade.

Policing and Law Enforcement Today

Policing and Law enforcement today is divided into four broad categories: federal, state, county, and local policing agencies (and many subcategories within).

© 2000 AP/Wide World Photos

Although police agencies are learning from the mistakes of the past, racial and ethnic conflict and charges of police brutality are still quite common. Here, police speak to protestors rallying against racial profiling and police brutality in front of the Ramparts police station in downtown Los Angeles. Some of the protestors, who urged police to arrest them, were later arrested peacefully.

Exhibit 5.1 **The Most Notable Achievements of Contemporary American Police**

- The intellectual caliber of the police has risen dramatically. American police today at all ranks are smarter, better informed, and more sophisticated than police in the 1960s.

- Senior police managers are more ambitious for their organizations than they used to be. Chiefs and their deputies want to leave their own distinctive stamp on their organizations. Many recognize that management is a specialized skill that must be developed.

- An explicit scientific mind-set has taken hold in American policing that involves an appreciation of the importance of evaluation and the timely availability of information.

- The standards of police conduct have risen. Despite recent well-publicized incidents of brutality and corruption, American police today treat the public more fairly, more equitably, and less venally than police did 30 years ago.

- Police are remarkably more diverse in terms of race and gender than a generation ago. This amounts to a revolution in American policing, changing both its appearance and, more slowly, its behavior.

- The work of the police has become intellectually more demanding, requiring an array of new specialized knowledge about technology, forensic analysis, and crime. This has had profound effects on recruitment — notably, civilianization — organizational structure, career patterns, and operational coordination.

- Civilian review of police discipline has gradually become accepted by police. Although the struggle is not yet over, expansion is inevitable as more and more senior police executives see that civilian review reassures the public and validates their own favorable opinion of the overall quality of police performance.

community policing
A law enforcement program that seeks to integrate officers into the local community to reduce crime and gain good community relations. It typically involves personalized service and decentralized policing, citizen empowerment, and an effort to reduce community fear of crime, disorder, and decay.

Source: David H. Bayley, "Policing in America," *Society* 36 (December 1998): 16–20.

There is no real hierarchy, and each branch has its own sphere of operations, though overlap may exist.

Federal Law Enforcement Agencies

The federal government has a number of law enforcement agencies designed to protect the rights and privileges of U.S. citizens. No single agency has unlimited jurisdiction, and each has been created to enforce specific laws and cope with particular situations. Federal police agencies have no particular rank order or hierarchy of command or responsibility, and each reports to a specific department or bureau.

The Justice Department, Federal Bureau of Investigation The U.S. Department of Justice is the legal arm of the federal government. Headed by the attorney general, it is empowered to enforce all federal laws, represent the United States when it is party to court action, and conduct independent investigations through its law enforcement services.

The Department of Justice maintains several separate divisions that are responsible for enforcing federal laws and protecting U.S. citizens. The Civil Rights Division proceeds legally against violations of federal civil rights laws that protect citizens from discrimination on the basis of their race, creed, ethnic background, age, or sex. Areas of greatest concern include discrimination in education, housing, and employment, including affirmative action cases. The Tax Division brings legal actions against tax violators. The Criminal Division prosecutes violations of the Federal Criminal Code. Its responsibility includes enforcing statutes relating to bank robbery (because bank deposits are federally insured), kidnapping, mail fraud, interstate transportation of stolen vehicles, and narcotics and drug trafficking.

The Justice Department first became involved in law enforcement when the attorney general hired investigators to enforce the Mann Act (forbidding the transportation of women between states for immoral purposes). These investigators were formalized in 1908 into a distinct branch of the government, the Bureau of Investigation. The agency was later reorganized into the **Federal Bureau of Investigation (FBI),** under the direction of J. Edgar Hoover (1924–72).

Today's FBI is not a police agency but an investigative agency with jurisdiction over all law enforcement matters in which the United States is or may be an interested party. Its jurisdiction, however, is limited to federal laws, including all federal statutes not specifically assigned to other agencies. Areas covered by these laws include espionage, sabotage, treason, civil rights violations, murder and assault of federal officers, mail fraud, robbery and burglary of federally insured banks, kidnapping, and interstate transportation of stolen vehicles and property. The FBI headquarters in Washington, D.C., oversees 56 field offices, approximately 400 satellite offices known as resident agencies, four specialized field installations, and more than 40 foreign liaison posts. The foreign liaison offices, each of which is headed by a legal attaché or legal liaison officer, work abroad with American and local authorities on criminal matters within FBI jurisdiction. In all, the FBI has approximately 11,400 special agents and more than 16,400 other employees who perform professional, administrative, technical, clerical, craft, trade, or maintenance operations. About 9,800 employees are assigned to Washington headquarters; nearly 18,000 are assigned to field installations.

The FBI offers a number of important services to local law enforcement agencies. Its identification division, established in 1924, collects and maintains a vast fingerprint file that can be used by local police agencies. Its sophisticated crime laboratory, established in 1932, aids local police in testing and identifying such evidence as hairs, fibers, blood, tire tracks, and drugs. The Uniform Crime Reports (UCR) is another service of the FBI. The UCR is an annual compilation of crimes reported to local police agencies, arrests, police killed or wounded in

Federal Bureau of Investigation (FBI)
The arm of the Justice Department that investigates violations of federal law, gathers crime statistics, runs a comprehensive crime laboratory, and helps train local law enforcement officers.

Exhibit 5.2 Special Programs and Divisions of the Federal Bureau of Investigation

The **Criminal Justice Information Services (CJIS) Division**, located in Clarksburg, West Virginia, centralizes criminal justice information. It serves as the national repository for fingerprint information and criminal record data and also manages Law Enforcement On-Line, a law enforcement "intranet," which provides secure communications, distance learning, and information services to the law enforcement community. CJIS operates the National Instant Check System, mandated by the Brady bill to check on the backgrounds of people desiring to purchase firearms. It is currently developing the Integrated Automated Fingerprint Identification System.

The **Crime Laboratory,** one of the largest and most comprehensive forensic laboratories in the world, examines evidence free of charge for federal, state, and local law enforcement agencies. Among its activities are:

- Scientific analysis of physical evidence submitted for examination, followed by expert testimony in court;
- Operational and technical support to investigations;
- Research and development of forensic techniques and procedures;
- Development and deployment of new forensic technologies; and
- Training programs and symposia for U.S. and international crime laboratory practitioners and law enforcement personnel.

The **Child Abduction and Serial Killer Unit,** created in 1994, responds upon request from local law enforcement agencies to kidnappings and to serial killer cases.

Combined DNA Index System (CODIS) is a national database of DNA profiles from convicted offenders, unsolved crime scenes, and missing persons. CODIS allows state and local law enforcement crime labs to exchange and compare DNA profiles electronically.

The **Critical Incident Response Group** is ready to assist law enforcement agencies in hostage-taking and barricade situations, terrorist activities, and other critical incidents.

The **Uniform Crime Report (UCR)** is another service of the FBI. The UCR is an annual compilation of crimes reported to local police agencies, arrests, police killed or wounded in action, and other information.

The **National Crime Information Center (NCIC)** is a computerized network linked to local police departments that provides ready information on stolen vehicles, wanted persons, stolen guns, and other crime-related materials.

Source: Federal Bureau of Investigation, *FBI Facts and Figures* (Washington, D.C.: 2002).

action, and other information. Finally, the FBI's National Crime Information Center is a computerized network linked to local police departments that provides ready information on stolen vehicles, wanted persons, stolen guns, and so on. The major activities of the FBI are described in Exhibit 5.2.

The FBI mission has been evolving to keep pace with world events. With the end of the cold war and the reduction of East–West tension, the FBI's counterintelligence mission has diminished. In some offices, agents have been reassigned to antigang and drug control efforts.[19]

Since the September 11, 2001, terrorist attacks, the FBI has dedicated itself to combating terrorism. The FBI has announced a reformulation of its priorities (see Exhibit 5.3), which makes protecting the United States from terrorist attack its number 1 commitment.

To carry out its newly formulated mission, the FBI is expanding its force, hiring approximately 1,000 more agents. In addition to helping in counterterrorism activities, these agents will staff the new Cyber Division, which was created in 2001, to coordinate, oversee, and facilitate FBI investigations when the Internet, online services, and computer systems and networks are the principal instruments

Exhibit 5.3 Reformulated FBI Priorities

1. Protect the United States from terrorist attack.
2. Protect the United States against foreign intelligence operations and espionage.
3. Protect the United States against cyber-based attacks and high-technology crimes.
4. Combat public corruption at all levels.
5. Protect civil rights.
6. Combat transnational and national criminal organizations and enterprises.
7. Combat major white-collar crime.
8. Combat significant violent crime.
9. Support federal, state, local, and international partners.
10. Upgrade technology to successfully perform the FBI's mission.

Source: Federal Bureau of Investigation, http://www.fbi.gov/priorities/priorities.htm.

Use "FBI and terrorism" as key words on InfoTrac College Edition to find out what the bureau is doing to counter terrorist acts.

Department of Homeland Security (DHS)

A federal agency created to coordinate national efforts to prevent terrorist attacks from occurring within the United States, to respond if an attack takes place, and to reduce or minimize the damage from attacks that do happen.

or targets of terrorists. Exhibit 5.4 describes some of the other actions the FBI has undertaken to combat terrorist activities.

Department of Homeland Security (DHS) Following the September 11 attacks, a new cabinet-level agency called the **Department of Homeland Security** received congressional approval and was assigned the mission of preventing terrorist attacks within the United States; reducing America's vulnerability to terrorism; and minimizing the damage and recovering from attacks that do occur. The DHS has five independent branches.

1. *Border and Transportation Security.* BTS is responsible for maintaining the security of the nation's borders and transportation systems. It is home to agencies such as the Transportation Security Administration, U.S. Customs Service, the border security functions of the Immigration and Naturalization Service, the

Exhibit 5.4 Key Near-Term Actions to Combat Terrorism

1. Restructure the Counterterrorism Division at FBI headquarters.
    *   Redefine relationship between headquarters and field offices.
    *   Shift from reactive to proactive orientation.
2. Establish "flying squads" to coordinate national and international investigations.
3. Establish national Joint Terrorism Task Force.
4. Substantially enhance analytical capabilities with personnel and technology.
    *   Expand use of data mining, financial record analysis, and communications analysis to combat terrorism.
    *   Establish the Office of Intelligence.
5. Build a national terrorism response capability that is more mobile, agile, and flexible, for example, use of flying squads and regional assets.
6. Permanently shift additional resources to the Counterterrorism Division.
7. Augment overseas capabilities and partnerships.
8. Target recruitment to acquire agents, analysts, translators, and others with specialized skills and backgrounds.
9. Enhance counterterrorism training for FBI and law enforcement partners.

The Department of Homeland Security is a new federal agency charged with protecting the United States from terrorism. Here at one of their command bases, images from 400 remote cameras are monitored to ensure the security of ports of entry around the United States.

Animal and Plant Health Inspection Service, and the Federal Law Enforcement Training Center.

2. *Emergency Preparedness and Response.* This branch ensures that the nation is prepared for, and able to recover from, terrorist attacks and natural disasters.

3. *Science and Technology.* Coordinates the department's efforts in research and development, including preparing for and responding to the full range of terrorist threats involving weapons of mass destruction.

4. *Information Analysis and Infrastructure Protection (IAIP).* IAIP merges the capability to identify and assess intelligence information concerning threats to the homeland under one roof, issue timely warnings, and take appropriate preventive and protective action.

5. *Management.* Responsible for budget, management, and personnel issues in DHS.

Besides the five DHS directorates, several other critical agencies are being folded into the new department or being newly created.

• The United States Coast Guard maintains an independent status, but its commandant reports directly to the secretary of homeland security. Upon declaration of war or when the president so directs, the Coast Guard would operate as an element of the Department of Defense, consistent with existing law.

• The United States Secret Service serves to protect the president and other government leaders, as well as to provide security for designated national events. The Secret Service is also the primary agency responsible for protecting U.S. currency from counterfeiters and safeguarding Americans from credit card fraud.

• The Bureau of Citizenship and Immigration Services dedicates its full energies to providing efficient immigration services and easing the transition to American citizenship. The director of citizenship and immigration services reports directly to the deputy secretary of homeland security.

• The Office of State and Local Government Coordination ensures that close coordination takes place with state and local first responders, emergency services, and governments.

• The Office of Private Sector Liaison provides America's business community a direct line of communication to the Department of Homeland Security.

• The Office of Inspector General serves as an independent and objective inspection, audit, and investigative body to promote effectiveness, efficiency, and economy in the Department of Homeland Security's programs and operations and to prevent and detect fraud, abuse, mismanagement, and waste in such programs and operations

While not a law enforcement agency per se, the DHS combines elements of law enforcement with national security.

Drug Enforcement Administration Government interest in drug trafficking can be traced back to 1914, when the Harrison Act established federal jurisdiction over the supply and use of narcotics. A number of drug enforcement units, including the Bureau of Narcotics and Dangerous Drugs, were charged with enforcing drug laws. In 1973 these agencies were combined to form the Drug Enforcement Administration.

DEA agents assist local and state authorities in investigating illegal drug use and carrying out independent surveillance and enforcement activities to control the importation of narcotics. For example, DEA agents work with foreign governments in cooperative efforts aimed at destroying opium and marijuana crops at their source, hard-to-find fields tucked away in the interiors of Latin America, Asia, Europe, and Africa. Undercover DEA agents infiltrate drug rings and simulate buying narcotics to arrest drug dealers.

DEA is also asked to respond to the challenges presented by the ever-changing cornucopia of illicit drugs used by the American public. The Analyzing Criminal Justice Issues feature on page 161 describes a recent initiative designed to disrupt the proliferation of club drugs.

WWW The Drug Enforcement Administration's home page is located at http://www.usdoj.gov/dea/.

Treasury Department The U.S. Treasury Department maintains three enforcement branches.

The Bureau of Alcohol, Tobacco, and Firearms helps control sales of untaxed liquor and cigarettes and, through the Gun Control Act of 1968 and the Organized Crime Control Act of 1970, has jurisdiction over the illegal sales, importation, and criminal misuse of firearms and explosives.

The Internal Revenue Service (IRS), established in 1862, enforces violations of income, excise, stamp, and other tax laws. Its Intelligence Division actively pursues gamblers, narcotics dealers, and other violators who do not report their illegal financial gains as taxable income. For example, the career of Al Capone, the famous 1920s gangster, was brought to an end by the efforts of IRS agents.

The Customs Service guards points of entry into the United States and prevents smuggling of contraband into (or out of) the country. It ensures that taxes and tariffs are paid on imported goods and helps control the flow of narcotics into the country.

State Law Enforcement Agencies

Unlike municipal police departments, state police were legislatively created to deal with the growing incidence of crime in nonurban areas, a consequence of the increase in population mobility and the advent of personalized mass transportation in the form of the automobile. County sheriffs — elected officials with occasionally corrupt or questionable motives — had proven to be ineffective in dealing with the wide-ranging criminal activities that developed during the latter half of the nineteenth century. In addition, most local police agencies were unable to effectively protect against highly mobile lawbreakers who randomly struck at cities and towns throughout a state. In response to citizens' demands for effective and efficient law enforcement, state governors began to develop plans for police agencies that would be responsible to the state, instead of being tied to local politics and possible corruption.

The Texas Rangers, created in 1835, was one of the first state police agencies formed. Essentially a military outfit that patrolled the Mexican border, it was fol-

Operation X-Out

analyzing criminal justice issues

Operation X-Out was created in 2002 and aimed at detecting and dismantling organizations that are manufacturing and trafficking party and predatory drugs such as Ecstasy, Rohypnol, GHB (Gamma Hydroxy Butyrate), Ketamine, and other lesser known drugs and selling them to individuals who often do not understand their potentially devastating effects. For example, evidence shows that taking just one or two Ecstasy pills can cause long-lasting brain damage leading to depression. Individuals who tried Ecstasy on only a few occasions have depression levels four times higher than those who took a range of other drugs but not Ecstasy.

The goals of the initiative include

- Drastically increasing the amount of investigations occurring at suspect clubs that allow drug use and trafficking within their business,
- Improving current task forces and also developing new task forces to monitor packages entering the country through the airports,
- Developing new task forces in major cities where Ecstasy enters, and
- Deterring drug trafficking occurring over the Internet and collaborating with other countries to curtail international drug trafficking.

To reach these objectives, the DEA planned to

- Double the number of club and predatory drug investigations across the country,
- Enhance airport interdiction task forces at specific airports,
- Create three task forces in South Florida,
- Utilize the 21 Mobile Enforcement Teams,
- Increase DEA resources in the Netherlands, and
- Form an Internet task force to coordinate investigations targeting E-drug traffickers.

With 70 percent of all Ecstasy coming from the Netherlands and Belgium, the DEA had to work with European authorities to effectively reduce the amount of drugs entering the United States from Holland. Agents assigned to Operation X-Out also collaborated with organizations, such as the Partnership for a Drug Free America, the Rape, Abuse, and Incest National Network, and the National Foundation of Women Legislators to educate the public about the dangers of these predatory and party drugs.

Can such an international effort work? On November 5, 2002, the Drug Enforcement Administration's New York Division announced the arrest of 20 defendants, 11 in New York and 9 in the Netherlands, involved in an international Ecstasy trafficking organization. The defendants were charged with conspiring to smuggle approximately 30 kilograms of Ecstasy hav-

ing a street value of over $2 million dollars into the United States. Among the methods used to smuggle the Ecstasy were concealing it in a print of a Rembrandt painting, "The Nightwatch."

Critical Thinking

As long as young people want to take drugs such as Ecstasy, dealers and traffickers will find a way to get it into their hands. Do you believe that law enforcement efforts, no matter how complex and well planned, are eventually doomed to fail in the war against drugs?

InfoTrac College Edition Research

 Is Ecstasy use related to crime? Read the following article on InfoTrac College Edition: "Ecstasy Use among Juvenile Offenders Higher Than for Students in General Population," *Brown University Digest of Addiction Theory and Application* 21, no. 12 (December 2002): 2.

Source: Drug Enforcement Administration, *Ecstasy and Predatory Drugs* (February 2003), www.usdoj.gov/dea/pubs/ecstasy/predatory_drugs-4.pdf, pp. 1–28; Drug Enforcement Administration, "DEA to Launch 'Operation X-Out': New Club and Predatory Drug Initiative," press release, November 21, 2002, pp. 1–2, www.dea.gov/pubs/states/newsrel/mia112102.html.

lowed by the Massachusetts state constables in 1865 and the Arizona Rangers in 1901. Pennsylvania formed the first truly modern state police in 1905.[20]

Today about 23 state police agencies have the same general police powers as municipal police and are territorially limited in their exercise of law enforcement regulations only by the state's boundaries. The remaining state police agencies are primarily responsible for highway patrol and traffic law enforcement. Some state police, such as those in California, direct most of their attention to the enforcement of traffic laws. Most state police organizations are restricted by legislation from becoming involved in the enforcement of certain areas of the law. For example, in some jurisdictions, state police are prohibited from becoming involved in strikes or other labor disputes, unless violence erupts.

The nation's 80,000 state police employees (55,000 officers and 25,000 civilians) not only are involved in law enforcement and highway safety but also carry out a variety of functions, including maintaining a training academy and providing emergency medical services. State police crime laboratories aid local departments in

© 2000 AP/Wide World Photos

In some jurisdictions, the county sheriff's department has primary law enforcement duties. Here, Trumbull County (Ohio) sheriff's deputies, along with police from Brookfield, Howland, and Johnston, search a 140-car train that passed by the Corrections Corporation of America prison in Youngstown shortly after six inmates escaped.

investigating crime scenes and analyzing evidence. State police also provide special services and technical expertise in such areas as bomb-site analysis and homicide investigation. Other state police departments, such as California's, are involved in highly sophisticated traffic and highway safety programs, including the use of helicopters for patrol and rescue, the testing of safety devices for cars, and the conducting of postmortem examinations to determine the causes of fatal accidents.

County Law Enforcement Agencies

The county sheriff's role has evolved from that of the early English shire reeve, whose primary duty was to assist the royal judges in trying prisoners and enforcing sentences. From the time of the westward expansion in the United States until municipal departments were developed, the sheriff was often the sole legal authority over vast territories.

Today, nearly 3,100 sheriff's offices operate nationwide, employing more than 290,000 full-time staffers, including about 165,000 sworn personnel. Employment was up an average of about 4 percent per year since 1990.[21] Nearly all sheriff's offices provided basic law enforcement services such as routine patrol (97 percent), responding to citizen calls for service (95 percent), and investigating crimes (92 percent).[22]

The duties of a county sheriff's department vary according to the size and degree of development of the county. The standard tasks of a typical sheriff's department are serving civil process (summons and court orders), providing court security, operating the county jail, and investigating crimes. Less commonly, sheriff's departments may serve as coroners, tax collectors, overseers of highways and bridges, custodians of the county treasury, and providers of fire, animal control, and emergency medical services. In years past, sheriff's offices also conducted executions. Typically, a sheriff department's law enforcement functions are restricted to unincorporated areas within a county, unless a city or town police department requests its help.

Some sheriff's departments are exclusively law enforcement–oriented; some carry out only court-related duties; some are involved solely in correctional and judicial matters and not in law enforcement. However, a majority are full-service programs that carry out judicial, correctional, and law enforcement activities. As a rule, agencies serving large population areas (more than 1 million people) are devoted to maintaining county correctional facilities, while those in smaller population areas are focused on law enforcement.

In the past, sheriffs' salaries were almost always based on the fees they received for the performance of official acts. They received fees for every summons, warrant, subpoena, writ, or other process they served. They were also compensated for summoning juries or locking prisoners in cells. Today, sheriffs are salaried to avoid conflict of interest.

Metropolitan Law Enforcement Agencies

Local police make up the majority of the nation's authorized law enforcement personnel. Metropolitan police departments range in size from the New York City Police Department with almost 40,000 full-time officers and 10,000 civilian employees, to rural police departments, which may have a single officer. Local police departments employ about 441,000 sworn personnel, an increase of about 2 percent per year since 1990.[23] In addition to sworn personnel, many police agencies hire civilian employees who bring special skills to the department. For example, in this computer age, departments often employ information resource managers who are charged with improving data processing; integrating the department's computer information database with others in the state; operating computer-based fingerprint identification systems and other high-tech investigation devices; and linking with national computer systems such as the FBI's national crime information system, which holds the records of millions of criminal offenders. To carry out these tasks, local departments employ an additional 120,000 civilians.

Most TV police shows feature the trials of big-city police officers, but the overwhelming number of departments have fewer than 50 officers and serve a population of less than 25,000. About 70 law enforcement agencies employed 1,000 or more full-time sworn personnel, including 47 local police departments with 1,000 or more officers. These agencies accounted for about a third of all local police officers. In contrast, nearly 800 departments employed just one officer.

Regardless of their size, most individual metropolitan police departments perform a standard set of functions and tasks and provide similar services to the community. These include the following:

traffic enforcement	narcotics and vice control
accident investigation	radio communications
patrol and peacekeeping	crime prevention
property and violent crime investigation	fingerprint processing
death investigation	search and rescue

The police role is expanding, so procedures must be developed to aid special-needs populations, including AIDS-infected suspects, the homeless, and victims of domestic and child abuse.

These are only a few examples of the multiplicity of roles and duties assumed today in some of the larger urban police agencies around the nation. Smaller agencies can have trouble effectively carrying out these tasks. The hundreds of small police agencies in each state often provide duplicative services. Whether unifying smaller police agencies into superagencies would improve services is often debated among police experts. Smaller municipal agencies can provide important specialized services that might have to be relinquished if they were combined and incorporated into larger departments. Another approach has been to maintain smaller departments but to link them via computerized information-sharing and resource management networks.[24]

To quiz yourself on this material, go to questions 5.11–5.17 on the Introduction to Criminal Justice 10e CD.

Perspectives on Justice

Police departments are evolving because leaders recognize that traditional crime control–oriented models have not been effective. In the future, the police role may shift to a more restorative justice emphasis, moving away from a legalistic style that isolates officers from the public to a service orientation that holds officers accountable to the community and encourages them to learn from the people they serve. This means that the police must actively create a sense of community where none has existed and recruit neighborhood cooperation for crime prevention activities.

Technology and Law Enforcement

Policing is relying more and more on modern technology to increase effectiveness. And the influence of technology on policing will continue to grow. Police officers now trained to prevent burglaries may someday have to learn to create high-tech forensic labs that can identify suspects who are involved in theft of genetically engineered cultures from biomedical labs.[25]

Criminal investigation will be enhanced by the application of sophisticated electronic gadgetry: computers, cellular phones, and digital communication devices. A majority of predatory crimes are concentrated in geographic hot spots.

Using Computer Software

Police are becoming more sophisticated in their use of computer software to identify and convict criminals. For example, some have begun to use computer software to conduct analysis of behavior patterns, a process called *data mining*, in an effort to identify crime patterns and link them to suspects.[26] By discovering patterns in burglaries, especially those involving multiple offenders, computer programs can be programmed to recognize a particular way of working at crime and thereby identify suspects most likely to fit the working profile. Advanced computer software has helped in the investigations of Internet crime. For example, in a recent case in England, police used forensic software to show in court that a defendant had used a particular Internet search engine to find Web pages that contained information about child pornography and then followed links to sites that he used to obtain and view kiddie porn. The Internet evidence was used to obtain his conviction.[27]

Computer mapping programs that can translate addresses into map coordinates allow departments to identify problem areas for particular crimes, such as drug dealing. Computer maps allow police to identify location, time of day, and linkage among criminal events and to concentrate their forces accordingly. Crime mapping is discussed in the Criminal Justice and Technology feature on page 166.

Information Technology

Crime mapping is not the only way technology will be used to improve the effectiveness of police resources. Budget realities demand that police leaders make the most effective use of their forces, and technology seems to be an important method of increasing productivity at a relatively low cost. The introduction of technology has already been explosive. In 1964, for example, only one city, St. Louis, had a police computer system; by 1968, 10 states and 50 cities had state-level criminal justice information systems; today, almost every city of more than 50,000 people has some sort of computer-support services.[28] The most recent federally sponsored survey of the nation's police forces found that most have embraced technology. Some of the advances are described in Exhibit 5.5.

One of the most important computer-aided tasks is the identification of criminal

For news about police technology and other related issues, go to the Police Officer Internet Directory at http://www.officer.com/.

New breakthroughs in fingerprint identification have revolutionized suspect identification. Here, Jeffrey Graham reviews an enlargement of the latent fingerprint taken from the motor home of David Westerfield, during Westerfield's murder trial, June 19, 2002, in San Diego. Graham is employed by the San Diego Police Department as a latent print examiner. His fingerprint analysis helped prosecutors convict Westerfield of the death of seven-year-old Danielle van Dam.

Exhibit 5.5 The Use of Technology in the Nation's Police Departments

- From 1990 to 2000, the percentage of local police departments using in-field computers increased from 5 to 40. Departments using in-field computers employed 75 percent of all officers in 2000, up from 30 percent in 1990.

- The percentage of local police departments using computers for Internet access rose from 24 in 1997 to 56 in 2000. During 2000, about 9 in 10 departments serving 50,000 or more residents had this capability.

- From 1997 to 2000, the percentage of officers employed by a department with in-field computer access to vehicle records increased from 56 to 69, driving records from 51 to 58, calls for service histories from 23 to 37, and criminal histories from 25 to 29.

- In 2000, 75 percent of departments used paper reports as the primary means to transmit criminal incident field data to a central information system, down from 86 percent in 1997. During the same time period, use of computer and data devices increased from 9 percent to 19 percent.

Source: Matthew Hickman and Brian Reaves, *Local Police Departments 2000* (Washington, D.C.: Bureau of Justice Statistics, 2003).

suspects. Computers link neighboring agencies so that they can share information on cases, suspects, and warrants. On a broader jurisdictional level, the FBI in 1967 implemented the National Crime Information Center, which provides rapid collection and retrieval of data about persons wanted for crimes anywhere in the 50 states.

Some police departments are using computerized imaging systems to replace mug books. Photos or sketches are stored in computer memory and easily retrieved for viewing. Several software companies have developed identification programs that help witnesses create a composite picture of the perpetrator. A vast library of photographed or drawn facial features can be stored in computer files and accessed on a terminal screen. Witnesses can scan through thousands of noses, eyes, and lips until they find those that match the suspect's. Eyeglasses, mustaches, and beards can be added; skin tones can be altered. When the composite is created, an attached camera makes a hard copy for distribution.

Criminal Identification

Computer systems used in the booking process can also help in the suspect identification process. During booking, a visual image of the suspect is stored in a computer's memory, along with other relevant information. By calling up color photos on the computer monitor, police can then easily create a photo lineup of all suspects having a particular characteristic described by a witness.

New techniques are constantly being developed. Soon, through the use of genetic algorithms (mathematical models), a computerized composite image of a suspect's face will be constructed from relatively little information. Digitization of photographs will enable the reconstruction of blurred images. Videotapes of bank robbers or blurred photos of license plates, even bite marks, can be digitized using highly advanced mathematical models.

Computer software is being created that allows two-dimensional mug shots to be re-created on a three-dimensional basis. This technology has the human face divided into 64 features, such as noses, mouths, and chins. There are 256 different types of each feature to choose from within the program. The result is that virtually anyone's face can be re-created according to a witness or victim's description. The image then can be compared with more than 1 million mug

Crime Mapping and the ICAM program

criminal justice and technology

Crime maps offer police administrators graphic representations of where crimes are occurring in their jurisdiction. Computerized crime mapping gives the police the power to analyze and correlate a wide array of data to create immediate, detailed visuals of crime patterns. The most simple maps (such as that depicted in Figure A, which shows the occurrence of part I crimes in Tempe, Arizona, during the month of August 1999) display crime locations or concentrations and can be used to help direct patrols to places they are most needed. More complex maps can be used to chart trends in criminal activity and have even proven valuable in solving individual criminal cases. For example, a serial rapist may be caught by observing and understanding the patterns of his crime so that detectives may predict where he will strike next and stake out the area with police decoys.

Crime mapping makes use of the new computer technology to replace the old-fashioned system of locating crimes on maps with pins. Computerized crime mappings let the police detect patterns of crimes and pathologies of related problems. It enables them to work with multiple layers of information and scenarios, thus far more successfully to identify emerging hot spots of criminal activity and target resources accordingly.

Figure A
Crime Map of Tempe, Arizona,
August 1999

Source: Courtesy of Tempe (Arizona) Police Department.

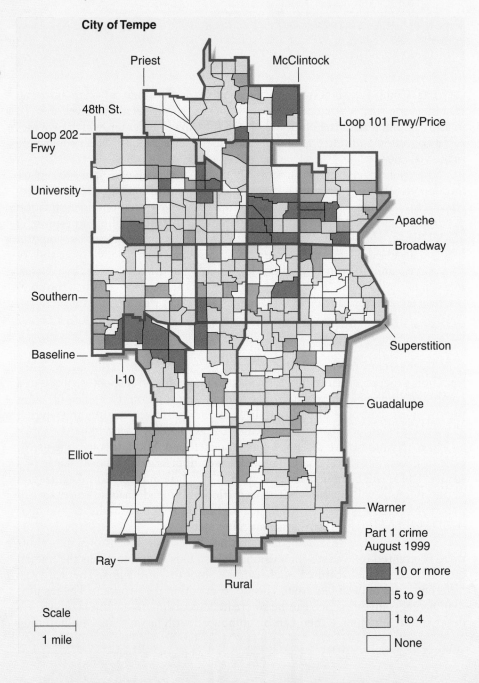

A survey conducted by the National Institute of Justice found that 36 percent of agencies with 100 or more sworn officers are now using some form of computerized crime mapping. A number of the nation's largest departments are now using mapping techniques. The New York City Police Department's CompStat process relies on computerized crime mapping to identify crime hot spots and hold officers accountable for crime reduction along the department's chain of command. The department credits CompStat for dramatic and continuing reductions in crime in New York City.

Chicago ICAM

Information technology, such as crime mapping, has gained enormous popularity among police departments in the past decade. One city that has been a leader in implementing mapping systems into its police departments is Chicago, which has focused its attention on a collaborative approach among law enforcement agencies and the city's community. In the mid-1990s the Chicago Police Department implemented the Citizen and Law Enforcement Analysis and Reporting (CLEAR) program. The program's objective is to use information technology to improve data sharing between law enforcement and residents of the community. CLEAR seeks to identify community problems with help from people within the neighborhoods and, together with law enforcement, target the problems to reduce the amount of crime occurring. Together citizens and police identify hot spots, then citizens and police officers meet and share knowledge about community problems and discuss ways to intervene to stop the occurrence of these problems. One effective component of the CLEAR program has been the Citizen Information Collecting for Automated Mapping (ICAM). Citizen ICAM is an Internet program that contains current crime data that are inputted by the police daily and are accessible to the public.

Citizen ICAM allows the community to track the number of crimes being committed within their neighborhoods. More specifically, the program includes reported crimes and arrests for a 90-day period. Residents have access to information gathered in the last 90 days, with the most recent data being from seven days prior to the current day. This delay in time allows police officers to properly input the information and classify each incident. ICAM allows citizens to search crime incidents by address and intersections or by police beats and type of crime. The information provides specifics of the incident: time, day, and type of crime. However, because of the need for privacy, exact addresses are not given and the victim's identity remains confidential. These data are located within a secure program to which only police officers have access. In addition, residents can view maps displaying the crime within the city. Therefore, they can learn which areas are crime-ridden and which are crime-free.

By allowing access to crime information over an Internet site, residents of the community can be more aware of the illegal activities occurring in their neighborhood without having to continuously attend neighborhood meetings. However, Chicago has found that when citizens are more informed of community problems, they are more likely to get involved to combat the crimes that plague their neighborhoods. Some residents do not mind attending meetings, and together with the direction of the police they organize neighborhood watches and other helpful tactics. In addition, the program has a "Top 10 feature," which supplies officers with the 10 most common crimes occurring on their beats over a specific duration: days, weeks, or months. This feature is helpful in designating where police officers and citizens should focus their attention.

Chicago is not the only city using technology to collaborate its efforts with the community. A few jurisdictions in California have also implemented similar mapping systems. The hope is that the system will allow a collaborative approach between law enforcement and citizens to successfully deter crime in their communities. As more people are willing to get involved, the more productive they become in deterring crime from occurring on their streets.

Some mapping efforts cross jurisdictional boundaries. Examples of this approach include the Regional Crime Analysis System in the greater Baltimore–Washington, D.C., area and the Charlotte-Mecklenburg Police Department (North Carolina), which uses data collected by other city and county agencies in its crime mapping efforts. By coordinating the tax assessor's, public works, planning, and sanitation departments, the Charlotte-Mecklenburg Police Department's analysts have made links between disorder and crime that have been instrumental in supporting the department's community policing philosophy.

Critical Thinking

1. Crime mapping represents one of the latest technological advances in the allocation of police resources to fight crime effectively. Is it possible that recent downturns in the crime rate reflect this emphasis on technology?

2. Does a growing police technology capability present a danger to personal privacy? How far should the police go to keep tabs on potentially dangerous people? For example, should DNA samples be taken at birth from all people and kept on file to match with genetic materials collected at crime scenes?

InfoTrac College Edition Research

 To read more about developments in police technology, read Christina Couret, "Police and Technology: The Silent Partnership," *American City and County* 114, no. 9 (August 1999): 31.

Sources: City of Chicago, *Information Collection for Automated Mapping* (Chicago Police Department, 2002), pp. 1–2; Kent Reichert, *Use of Information Technology by Law Enforcement* (University of Pennsylvania, Jerry Lee Center of Criminology Forum on Crime and Justice, December 2001), pp. 1–4; William W Bratton and Peter Knobler, *Turnaround: How America's Top Cop Reversed the Crime Epidemic* (New York: Random House, 1998), p. 289; Jeremy Travis, "Computerized Crime Mapping," *NIJ News* (January 1999).

shots in less than a second to search for a match. Instead of relying on an artist's sketch based on a victim's description of a suspect, investigators can work with a victim on a computer to come up with a matching description. Once detectives have mug shots, they can take the three-dimensional facial images contained in the software and create a match with the mug shot. Once this is done for all 64 features, a two-dimensional mug shot can be enhanced to make a three-dimensional head. Effects on the three-dimensional image such as lighting and angles can also be changed to make a better re-creation of an environment in which a crime has taken place.[29]

Perspectives on Justice

In the future, police departments will be relying more heavily on new technologies for investigation efficiency. The use of improved computer-based record keeping and long-range electronic surveillance devices create the fear that police will have carte blanche to intrude into the private lives of citizens. How much information will go on police databases? Some question the wisdom of emphasizing the technological aspects of police productivity at the expense of public service. As technology improves, the threat to privacy and security will increase, pitting crime control advocates against due process–oriented civil libertarians.

Some of the most recent advances in identification have come through the use of biometric technology, which is the topic of the Criminal Justice and Technology feature on page 169.

Automated Fingerprint Identification Systems

The use of computerized automated fingerprint identification systems (AFIS) is growing in the United States. Using mathematical models, AFIS can classify fingerprints and identify up to 250 characteristics (minutiae) of the print. These automated systems use high-speed silicon chips to plot each point of minutiae and count the number of ridge lines between that point and its four nearest neighbors. They are a substantial improvement over earlier systems in their speed and accuracy. Some police departments report that computerized fingerprint systems are allowing them to make more than 100 identifications a month from fingerprints taken at a crime scene. AFIS files have been regionalized. For example, the Western Identification Network consists of eight central site members (Alaska, Idaho, Montana, Nevada, Oregon, Utah, Wyoming, and the Portland, Oregon, Police Bureau), two interface members (California and Washington), multiple local members, and six federal members (Drug Enforcement Administration, Federal Bureau of Investigation, Immigration and Naturalization Service, Internal Revenue Service, Postal Inspection Service, and Secret Service).[30] When it first began, the system had a centralized automated database of 900,000 fingerprint records; today, with the addition of new jurisdictions (Alaska, California, and Washington), the number of searchable fingerprint records increased to more than 14 million.

If these computerized fingerprint files become standardized and a national database is formed, records in all 50 states will be able to be checked to determine whether a suspect's fingerprints match those taken at the crime scene of previously unsolved cases. A national fingerprint identification system should become an even more effective tool because laser technology should vastly improve fingerprint analysis. Investigators will soon be able to recover prints that in the past were too damaged to be used as evidence. New breeds of fingerprint analysis will soon be available. The FBI plans to create an integrated AFIS that will

The Western Identification Network Web site is at http://www.winid.org/history.htm.

Want to work with automated fingerprint identification system files? Go to this Web site for a job description: http://www.ci.mesa.az.us/police/identification/fptech_job.htm.

Added Security: Biometric Technology

criminal justice and technology

Since the terrorist attacks on September 11, 2001, added security measurements have been installed to help protect the country's citizens. Biometrics, the science of using digital technology to identify individuals, has been implemented in many facets of the country's security system. Although biometrics is not a new technique, additional ways of administering the science have been adopted. Biometrics allows an individual to be identified through physical and biological qualities. More specifically, through the use of fingerprints, handprints, face recognition, iris scans, voice samples, and handwriting, people can no longer fake their identities. The system has two modes in which it functions: an identification mode and a verification mode. The identification mode identifies an individual from the entire population enrolled in the system by searching the system for a match. The verification mode allows a person to claim his or her identity from a previous registered pattern. Biometric technology has been installed in both airports and prisons to ensure that people are not using other identities to partake in illegal behavior.

Airports

Airports have started to implement the use of biometrics into their systems to prevent nonemployees from entering secured locations. Biometrics also allows for control of passengers onto airplanes. For example, the most popular type of biometrics being used within airports is iris scanning. While looking into a cam-

era, a computer scans your eye, records information regarding your iris, and stores the information into a database. Once your eye has been scanned, you are then permitted to board the plane. To depart from the plane at your destination your iris scan must match the one in the database to ensure that you are the person who is supposed to be departing the plane. For those who travel frequently, this procedure has proved effective, not requiring the individual to continuously stop at checkpoints and have identification checked. The person simply looks into a camera and within seconds is permitted to pass through all the checkpoints.

In addition, an airport in Charlotte, North Carolina, has used the system to keep unwanted individuals from entering secure facilities. With the use of swipe cards or codes, people were allowed to walk in behind personnel to gain entry into an area. However, this is no longer a problem with biometrics. Employees of the Charlotte airport have their irises scanned and the information gained remains in a database. To access the secured areas, personnel must look into a tube and have their match confirmed to be allowed entrance. Although fingerprints have also been used for this purpose, an iris scan can match more than 400 different points of identification compared with that of only 60–70 points of a fingerprint.

Other airports have incorporated another type of biometric technology within their security system: facial recognition. Facial recognition systems measure facial features

of people, noting the distance of one feature from another, along with sizes of features and so on. An airport in Florida uses a facial recognition system that contains the images of the FBI's top 10 most wanted, along with other sought-after individuals. Passengers are required to look into cameras to verify that they do not match any of the images in the system. If no matches are found, passengers are permitted to board the airplane. With the continued success of this system, facial recognition systems may be able to help locate fugitives, terrorists, and abducted children who are passing through transportation terminals.

Critical Thinking

Are you afraid that futuristic security methods such as biometric technology will lead to the loss of personal privacy and the erosion of civil liberties? Would you want your personal medical information to be posted on a computer Web site, where it can be potentially accessed by future employers and others?

InfoTrac College Edition Research

 To learn more about the subject, use "biometric technology" as a key word on InfoTrac College Edition.

Source: National Law Enforcement and Corrections Technology Center, "Counting with Fingers," *TechBeat* (Spring 2003); National Law Enforcement and Corrections Technology Center, "Counting on Biometrics," *TechBeat* (Winter 2003): 1–2.

allow local departments to scan fingerprints, send them electronically to a national depository, and receive the identification and criminal history of a suspect.

DNA Testing

Advanced technology is also spurring new forensic methods of identification and analysis.[31] The most prominent technique is **DNA profiling,** a procedure that has gained national attention because of the O. J. Simpson case. This technique allows suspects to be identified on the basis of the genetic material found in hair, blood, and other bodily tissues and fluids. When DNA is used as evidence in a

DNA profiling
The identification (or elimination) of criminal suspects by comparing DNA samples (genetic material) taken from them with specimens found at crime scenes.

rape trial, DNA segments are taken from the victim and suspect and from the blood and semen found on the victim. A DNA match indicates a 4 billion-to-1 chance that the suspect is the offender.

Two methods of DNA matching are used. The most popular technique, known as RFLP (restriction fragment length polymorphism), uses radioactive material to produce a DNA image on an X-ray film. The second method, PCR (polymerase chain reaction), amplifies DNA samples through molecular photocopying.[32]

The use of DNA evidence in criminal trials received a boost in 1997 when the FBI announced that the evidence has become so precise that experts no longer have to supply a statistical estimate of accuracy while testifying at trial (for example, "The odds are one in a billion that this is the culprit"). They can now state in court that "a reasonable degree of scientific certainty" exists that evidence came from a single suspect.[33]

Leading the way in the development of the most advanced forensic techniques is the Forensic Science Research and Training Center operated by the FBI in Washington, D.C., and Quantico, Virginia. The lab provides information and services to hundreds of crime labs throughout the United States. The National Institute of Justice is also sponsoring research to identify a wider variety of DNA segments for testing and is involved in developing a PCR-based DNA-profiling examination, using fluorescent detection, that will reduce the time required for DNA profiling. The FBI operates the DNA Index System, a computerized database that will allow DNA taken at a crime scene to be searched electronically to find matches against samples taken from convicted offenders and other crime scenes. The first database will allow suspects to be identified, and the second will allow investigators to establish links between crimes, such as those involving serial killers or rapists. In 1999 the FBI announced the system made its first cold hit by linking evidence taken from crime scenes in Jacksonville, Florida, to ones in Washington, D.C., thereby tying nine crimes to a single offender.[34] When Timothy Spence was executed in Virginia on April 27, 1994, he was the first person convicted and executed almost entirely on the basis of DNA evidence.[35]

While DNA is a very useful tool, some ethical and practical questions have arisen concerning its use. Critics such as Paul Tracy and Vincent Morgan find that the cost of maintaining a national DNA database is significant, upward into the hundreds of millions of dollars, while the number of criminals identified using DNA is relatively small.[36] They argue that DNA databases cannot be used to solve the vast majority of serious crimes and few, if any, nonserious ones. Even if crime scenes contain DNA evidence, local law enforcement agencies do not have the necessary resources to collect evidence and identify criminals. Tracy and Morgan also warn that having DNA evidence on file poses a serious threat to civil liberties. Should a person who is arrested for placing a bet on a football game have his DNA kept on files with convicted rapists and child molesters?

WWW If you want to read more about the science of DNA testing, go to http://arbl. cvmbs.colostate.edu/hbooks/ genetics/medgen/dnatesting/.

Communications

Computer technology will enhance communications and information dissemination. Many larger departments have equipped officers with portable computers, which significantly cuts down on the time needed to write and duplicate reports. Police can use terminals to draw accident diagrams, communicate with city traffic engineers, and merge their incident reports into other databases. Pen computing, in which officers write directly on a computer screen, eliminates paperwork and increases the accuracy of reports.[37] To make this material more accessible to the officer on patrol, head-up display units project information onto screens located on patrol car windshields. Police officers can access computer readouts without taking their eyes off the road.[38]

Future police technology will involve more efficient communications systems. Officers are using cellular phones in their cars to facilitate communications with victims and witnesses.[39] Departments that cover wide geographical areas and maintain independent precincts and substations are experimenting with tele-conferencing systems that provide both audio and video linkages. Police agencies may use advanced communications gear to track stolen vehicles. Some departments are linking advanced communications systems with computers, making use of electronic bulletin boards that link officers in an active online system, enabling them to communicate faster and more easily.

Combating Terrorism with Communications Communication technology has become even more important now that police agencies are involved in a war on terrorism. Keeping surveillance on suspected terrorist groups is not an easy task. However, the 1994 Communications Assistance for Law Enforcement Act (CALEA) aided law enforcement's ability to monitor suspects. The act required that communication equipment manufacturers and carriers design equipment, facilities, and services that are compatible with electronic surveillance needs.[40] Under the law, telecommunications carriers must ensure that equipment has the capability to facilitate the isolation and interception of communications content and call-identifying information and make it easy to deliver this data to law enforcement agencies.[41] CALEA allows that, upon issue of a court order or other lawful authorization, communication carriers must be able to expeditiously isolate all wire and electronic communications of a target transmitted by the carrier within its service area; expeditiously isolate call-identifying information of a target; provide intercepted communications and call-identifying information to law enforcement; and carry out intercepts unobtrusively, so targets are not made aware of the electronic surveillance, and in a manner that does not compromise the privacy and security of other communications. Under CALEA the government reimburses telecommunications carriers for the costs of developing software to intercept communications.

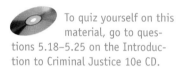 To quiz yourself on this material, go to questions 5.18–5.25 on the Introduction to Criminal Justice 10e CD.

Summary

- Early in British history, law enforcement was a personal matter.
- Tithings and hundreds (10 tithings) were early forms of law enforcement.
- In the Middle Ages, constables were appointed to keep peace among groups of 100 families. This rudimentary beginning was the seed of today's police departments.
- In 1838 the first true U.S. police department was born in Boston.
- The first U.S. police departments were created because of the need to control mob violence, which was common during the nineteenth century.
- The early police were viewed as being dominated by political bosses who controlled their hiring practices and policies.
- Reform movements begun during the 1920s culminated in the concept of professionalism in the 1950s and 1960s. Police professionalism was interpreted to mean tough, rule-oriented police work

featuring advanced technology and hardware. However, the view that these measures would quickly reduce crime proved incorrect.
- Between 1960 and the 1990s police were beset by many problems including their treatment of minorities and their lack of effectiveness. This paved the way for a radical change in policing and the development of community policing.
- There are several major law enforcement agencies. On the federal level, the FBI is the premier law enforcement organization. Other agencies include the Drug Enforcement Administration, the U.S. marshals, and the Secret Service. After September 11, 2001, Congress approved formation of the Department of Homeland Security.
- County-level law enforcement is provided by sheriff's departments, and most states, except Hawaii, maintain state police agencies. Some of these agencies specialize in traffic control, while other are full-fledged law enforcement departments.

- Most law enforcement is conducted by local police agencies, which carry out patrol, investigative, and traffic functions, as well as many support activities.
- Today, most police departments rely on advanced computer-based technology to identify suspects and collate evidence.
- Automated fingerprint systems and computerized identification systems have become widespread. Some believe technology may make police overly intrusive and interfere with civil liberties.

Key Terms

tithings   148
hue and cry   148
hundred   148
constable   148
shire reeve   149
watch system   149

justice of the peace   149
Metropolitan Police Act   149
sheriff   150
vigilantes   150
community policing   155

Federal Bureau of
   Investigation (FBI)   156
Department of Homeland
   Security (DHS)   158
DNA profiling   159

Doing Research on the Web

**For an up-to-date list of Web links, go to
http://cj.wadsworth.com/siegel_intro10e.**

Supplementing local police forces has been a burgeoning private security industry. Private security service has become a multibillion-dollar industry with 10,000 firms and 1.5 million employees. Even federal police services have been privatized to cut expenses, a move that was opposed by the American Federation of Government Employees. To learn more about this growth, see http://www.bls.gov/oco/ocos159.htm.

You can also learn more about private security by going to the Web site of state agencies that monitor the industry. For example, the site for California's Bureau of Security and Investigative Services is http://www.dca.ca.gov/bsis/ppo.htm.

InfoTrac College Edition also provides some important research on the private security industry. Do a search using the key words "private security" and "private police." See Gayle M. B. Hanson, "Private Protection Is Secure Industry," *Insight on the News* 13 (1997): 19.

There will be more legal scrutiny as the private security business blossoms. For example, are security guards subject to the same search and seizure standards as police officers? The U.S. Supreme Court has repeatedly stated that purely private search activities do not violate the Fourth Amendment's prohibitions. Might security guards be subject to Fourth Amendment requirements if they are performing services that are traditionally reserved for the police, such as guarding communities? To find out, read John B. Owens, "Westec Story: Gated Communities and the Fourth Amendment," *American Criminal Law Review* 34 (1997): 127–60.

Pro/Con discussions and Viewpoint Essays on some of the topics in this chapter may be found at the Opposing Viewpoints Resource Center: http://www.gale.com/OpposingViewpoints.

Discussion Questions

1. List the problems faced by today's police departments that were also present during the early days of policing.
2. Distinguish between the duties of the state police, sheriff's departments, and local police departments.
3. What is the Department of Homeland Security? What are its component agencies?
4. What are some of the technological advances that should help the police solve more crimes? What are the dangers of these advances?
5. Discuss the trends that may influence policing during the coming decade. What other social factors may affect police?

Notes

1 Sara Stoutland, "The Multiple Dimensions of Trust in Resident/Police Relations in Boston," *Journal of Research in Crime and Delinquency* 38 (2001): 226–56.

2 Richard A. Leo and Richard J. Ofshe, "The Consequences of False Confessions: Deprivations of Liberty and Miscarriages of Justice in the Age of Psychological Interrogation," *Journal of Criminal Law and Criminology* 88 (1998): 429–96.

3 "Law Enforcement Seeks Answers to 'Racial Profiling' Complaints," *Criminal Justice Newsletter* 29 (1998): 5.

4 Liqun Cao, James Frank, and Francis Cullen, "Race, Community Context, and Confidence in the Police," *American Journal of Police* 15 (1996): 3–15.

5 Thomas Priest and Deborah Brown Carter, "Evaluations of Police Performance in an African American Sample," *Journal of Criminal Justice* 27 (1999): 457–65.

6 This section relies heavily on such sources as Malcolm Sparrow, Mark Moore, and David Kennedy, *Beyond 911: A New Era for Policing* (New York: Basic Books, 1990); Daniel Devlin, *Police Procedure, Administration, and Organization* (London: Butterworth, 1966); Robert Fogelson, *Big-City Police* (Cambridge, Mass.: Harvard University Press, 1977); Roger Lane, *Policing the City, Boston 1822–1885* (Cambridge, Mass.: Harvard University Press, 1967); J. J. Tobias, *Crime and Industrial Society in the Nineteenth Century* (New York: Schocken Books, 1967); Samuel Walker, *A Critical History of Police Reform: The Emergence of Professionalism* (Lexington, Mass.: Lexington Books, 1977); Samuel Walker, *Popular Justice* (New York: Oxford University Press, 1980); John McMullan, "The New Improved Monied Police: Reform Crime Control and Commodification of Policing in London," *British Journal of Criminology* 36 (1996): 85–108.

7 Devlin, *Police Procedure,* p. 3.

8 Wilbur Miller, "The Good, the Bad, and the Ugly: Policing America," *History Today* 50 (2000): 29–32.

9 Phillip Reichel, "Southern Slave Patrols as a Transitional Type," *American Journal of Police* 7 (1988): 51–78.

10 Walker, *Popular Justice,* p. 61.

11 Ibid., p. 8.

12 Dennis Rousey, "Cops and Guns: Police Use of Deadly Force in Nineteenth-Century New Orleans," *American Journal of Legal History* 28 (1984): 41–66.

13 Law Enforcement Assistance Administration, *Two Hundred Years of American Criminal Justice* (Washington, D.C.: Government Printing Office, 1976).

14 National Commission on Law Observance and Enforcement, *Report on the Police* (Washington, D.C.: Government Printing Office, 1931), pp. 5–7.

15 Pamela Irving Jackson, *Minority Group Threat, Crime, and Policing* (New York: Praeger, 1989).

16 James Q. Wilson and George Kelling, "Broken Windows," *Atlantic Monthly* March 1982, pp. 29–38.

17 Frank Tippett, "It Looks Just Like a War Zone," *Time,* May 27, 1985, pp. 16–22; "San Francisco, New York Police Troubled by Series of Scandals," *Criminal Justice Newsletter* 16 (1985): 2–4; Karen Polk, "New York Police: Caught in the Middle and Losing Faith," *Boston Globe,* December 28, 1988, p. 3.

18 The Staff of the Los Angeles Times, *Understanding the Riots: Los Angeles before and after the Rodney King Case* (Los Angeles, Calif.: Los Angeles Times, 1992).

19 Kathleen Grubb, "Cold War to Gang War," *Boston Globe,* January 22, 1992, p. 1.

20 Bruce Smith, *Police Systems in the United States* (New York: Harper and Row, 1960).

21 Matthew Hickman and Brian Reaves, *Sheriffs' Office 2000* (Washington, D.C.: Bureau of Justice Statistics, 2003).

22 Matthew Hickman and Brian Reaves, *Local Police Departments 2000* (Washington, D.C.: Bureau of Justice Statistics, 2003).

23 Hickman and Reaves, *Local Police Departments 2000.*

24 See, for example, Robert Keppel and Joseph Weis, *Improving the Investigation of Violent Crime: The Homicide Investigation and Tracking System* (Washington, D.C.: National Institute of Justice, 1993).

25 Larry Coutorie, "The Future of High-Technology Crime: A Parallel Delphi Study," *Journal of Criminal Justice* 23 (1995): 13–27.

26 Bill Goodwin, "Burglars Captured by Police Data Mining Kit," *Computer Weekly,* August 8, 2002, p. 3.

27 "Forensic Computing Expert Warns Interpol about Computer Crime," *Information Systems Auditor* (August 2002): 2.

28 Lois Pliant, "Information Management," *Police Chief* 61 (1994): 31–35.

29 "Spotlight on Computer Imaging," Police Chief 66 (1999): 6–8.

30 Laura Moriarty and David Carter, *Criminal Justice Technology in the Twenty-first Century* (Springfield, Ill.: Charles C. Thomas Publishers, 1998).

31 See, generally, Ryan McDonald, "Juries and Crime Labs: Correcting the Weak Links in the DNA Chain," *American Journal of Law and Medicine* 24 (1998): 345–63; "DNA Profiling Advancement," *FBI Law Enforcement Bulletin* 67 (1998): 24.

32 Ronald Reinstein, *Postconviction DNA Testing: Recommendations for Handling Requests* (Philadelphia, Pa.: DIANE Publishing. 1999).

33 "Under New Policy, FBI Examiners Testify to Absolute DNA Matches," *Criminal Justice Newsletter* 28 (1997): 1–2.

34 "FBI's DNA Profile Clearinghouse Announce First 'Cold Hit,' " *Criminal Justice Newsletter* (March 16 1999): 5.

35 "South Side Strangler's Execution Cited as DNA Evidence Landmark," *Criminal Justice Newsletter* (May 2, 1994): 3.

36 Paul Tracy and Vincent Morgan, "Big Brother and His Science Kit: DNA Databases for Twenty-first Century Crime Control?" *Journal of Criminal Law and Criminology* 90 (2000): 635–90.

37 "Pen Computing: The Natural 'Next Step' for Field Personnel," *Law and Order* 43 (1995): 37.

38 Miller McMillan, "High Tech Enters the Field of View," *Police Chief* 62 (1994): 29.

39 Ibid., p. 24.

40 Communications Assistance for Law Enforcement Act of 1994, Pub. L. No. 103-414, 108 Stat. 4279.

41 Michael P. Clifford, "Communications Assistance for Law Enforcement Act (CALEA)," *FBI Law Enforcement Bulletin* 71 (2002): 11–14.

Chapter Outline

Chapter Objectives

After reading this chapter, you should be able to:

1. Understand the organization of police departments.
2. Know the similarities and differences between patrol and detective operations.
3. Recognize the problems associated with the time-in-rank system.
4. Describe the efforts being made to improve patrol effectiveness.
5. Discuss the organization of police detectives.
6. Understand the concept of community policing.
7. Describe various community policing strategies.
8. Discuss the concept of problem-oriented policing.
9. Explain the various police subsystems.
10. Identify the factors that may be used to improve police productivity.

Viewpoints

Analyzing Criminal Justice Issues:
Amber Alert   183

Images of Justice: *CSI: Crime Scene Investigation*   187

Analyzing Criminal Justice Issues:
Boston Gun Project: Operation
Ceasefire   194

Analyzing Criminal Justice Issues:
Police Oversight: Civilian Review
Boards   198

Analyzing Criminal Justice Issues:
Community Mapping, Planning,
and Analysis for Safety Strategies
(COMPASS)   202

InfoTrac College Edition Links

Key Term: "police patrol"   180

Key Term: "undercover operations"   186

Key Term: "broken windows"   190

Article: "Equity and Community
Policing: A New View of
Community Partnerships"   191

Key Term: "police training"   199

Web Links

New York City Police Department
http://www.nyc.gov/html/nypd/home.html   176

Copsonline
http://www.copsonline.com/   177

**Michigan State University,
School of Criminal Justice**
http://www.ssc.msu.edu/~cj/cp/cptoc.html   190

**COPY Kids and community policing initiative
in Spokane, Washington**
http://www.ncjrs.org/nij/cops_casestudy/
spokane.html   191

Community Policing Consortium
http://www.communitypolicing.org/   192

Community policing
http://www.policing.com   196

Chapter 6 | The Police: Organization, Role, Function

Millions of people got to know Montgomery County, Maryland, police chief Charles Moose when he became the point man in the investigation of the Washington-area sniper attacks in October 2002. His coordination of the investigation turned Moose into one of the most recognized law enforcement agents in the nation.

Moose, who had grown up in Lexington, North Carolina, is a multitalented man. He is highly educated, earning a bachelor's degree in U.S. history from the University of North Carolina at Chapel Hill and a master's degree in public administration and a doctorate in urban studies from Portland State University. He began his career as a patrol officer in Portland, Oregon, in 1975, eventually serving as chief of police from 1993 to 1999. He then moved to Montgomery County, where the police department had more than 1,000 sworn officers serving an area with some 850,000 residents. Chief Moose also served as a major in the District of Columbia Air National Guard and is an adjunct faculty member at Montgomery (Maryland) College. He graduated from the FBI National Academy's 154th Session and the FBI National Executive Institute's 17th Session in 1988 and 1994, respectively.[1]

Moose resigned his position as Montgomery County police chief after a county ethics commission re-

fused him permission to write a book on the investigation into the D.C. sniper case, presumably fearing that he would release confidential information. Moose was eventually able to reach a settlement with the commission, and he was allowed to write the book and pursue a movie project.

Charles Moose's career can serve as a model of the successful law enforcement agent. Yet, there is no question that the job can be challenging. Police officers are told to be enforcers of the law in some of the

toughest areas in urban America, while they are criticized or even jailed when their tactics become too aggressive. Some are considered heroes when they risk their lives to protect citizens from dangers ranging from drunk drivers to international terrorists, while others are vilified for practicing racial profiling. Is it unrealistic to expect police officers to fulfill society's demand for order while maintaining a tight grip on their behavior and emotions?

To read the latest on Charles Moose, go to http://charlesmoose.newstrove.com/.

CNN. *View the CNN video clip of this story on your Introduction to Criminal Justice 10e CD.*

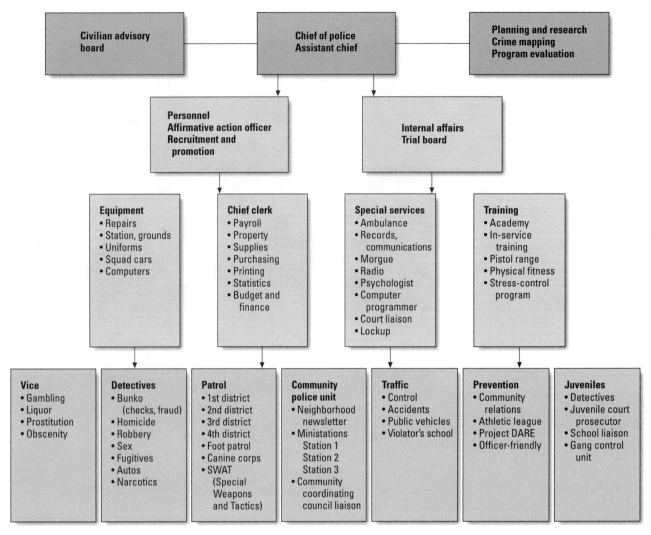

Figure 6.1
Organization of a Traditional
Metropolitan Police Department

The Police Organization

Most municipal police departments in the United States are independent agencies within the executive branch of government and operating without specific administrative control from any higher governmental authority. On occasion, police agencies will cooperate and participate in mutually beneficial enterprises, such as sharing information on known criminals, or they may help federal agencies investigate interstate criminal cases. Aside from such cooperative efforts, police departments tend to be functionally independent organizations with unique sets of rules, policies, procedures, norms, budgets, and so on. The structure of police agencies greatly influences their function and effectiveness.

Although many police agencies are in the process of rethinking their organization and goals, the majority are still organized in a militaristic, hierarchical manner, as illustrated in Figure 6.1. Within this organizational model, each element of the department normally has its own chain of command. For example, in a large municipal department, the detective bureau might have a captain who serves as the director of a particular division (such as homicide), a lieutenant who oversees individual cases and acts as liaison with other police agencies, and sergeants and inspectors who carry out field work. Smaller departments may have a captain or lieutenant as head of all detectives, while he or she supervises individual subsystems (such as robbery or homicide). At the head of the organization is the police chief, who sets policy and has general administrative control over all the department's various operating branches.

The typical police department's organizational structure has several problems. First, citizens often have difficulty in determining who is responsible for the department's policies and operations. Second, the large number of operating divisions and the lack of any clear relationship among them almost guarantee that the decision-making practices of one branch will be unknown to another. Two divisions may unknowingly compete with each other over jurisdiction on a particular case.

Most departments also follow a military-like system in promoting personnel called the **time-in-rank system.** At an appropriate time, a promotion test may be given and, based on his scores and recommendations, an officer may be advanced in rank. This organizational style frustrates some police officers from furthering their education, because a college or advanced degree may have little direct impact on their promotion potential or responsibilities. Furthermore, some otherwise competent police officers cannot increase their rank because of their inability to take tests well.

Most police departments employ a time-in-rank system for determining promotion eligibility. This means that before moving up the administrative ladder, an officer must spend a certain amount of time in the next lowest rank. For example, a sergeant cannot become a captain without serving an appropriate amount of time as a lieutenant. Although this system is designed to promote fairness and limit favoritism, it also restricts administrative flexibility. Unlike the private sector, where talented people can be pushed ahead in the best interests of the company, the time-in-rank system prohibits rapid advancement. A police agency would probably not be able to hire a computer systems expert with a Ph.D. and give her a command position in charge of its data analysis section. The department would be forced to hire the expert as a civilian employee under the command of a ranking senior officer who may not be as technically proficient.

Under this rank system, a title can rarely be taken away or changed once it is earned. Police administrators become frustrated when qualified junior officers cannot be promoted or reassigned to appropriate positions because they lack time in rank or because less qualified officers have more seniority. Inability to advance through the ranks convinces numerous educated and ambitious officers to seek private employment. The rank system also means that talented police officers cannot transfer to other departments or sell their services to the highest bidder. Time in rank ensures the stability — for better or worse — of police agencies.

Copsonline is a police Internet resource. It provides information on how to become a police officer, information on the latest books, training, and jobs. The Web address is http://www.copsonline.com/.

time-in-rank system
The promotion system in which a police officer can advance in rank only after spending a prescribed amount of time in the preceding rank.

To quiz yourself on this material, go to questions 6.1–6.3 on the Introduction to Criminal Justice 10e CD.

The Police Role

In countless books, movies, and TV shows, the public has been presented with a view of policing that romanticizes police officers as fearless crime fighters who think little of their own safety as they engage in daily shoot-outs with Uzi-toting drug runners, psychopathic serial killers, and organized crime hit men. Occasionally, but not often, fictional patrol officers and detectives seem aware of departmental rules, legal decisions, citizens groups, civil suits, or physical danger. They are rarely faced with the economic necessity of moonlighting as security guards, taking on

Police patrol means more than fighting crime. Here, Indiana State Police officer J. D. Maxwell checks Terry Martin of Ellettsville, fifty miles south of Indianapolis, on September 20, 2002, after Martin survived a tornado that ripped the roof off his home. He said he got through the ordeal by lying in the fetal position next to his entertainment center after he failed to reach a closet in his bedroom in time. Some twelve houses were destroyed and an apartment complex was damaged.

© 2002 AP/Wide World Photos

Figure 6.2
Police Encounters with Citizens

Source: Patrick A. Langan, Lawrence A. Greenfield, Steven K. Smith, Matthew R. Durose, and David J. Levin, *Contacts between Police and the Public: Findings from the 1999 National Survey* (Washington, D.C.: Bureau of Justice Statistics, 2001).

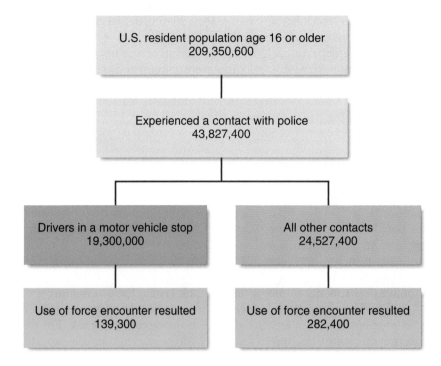

extra details, caring about an annual pay raise, or griping when someone less deserving gets promoted ahead of them for political reasons.

How close is this portrayal of a selfless crime fighter to real life? Not very, according to most research efforts. Police officers are asked to deal with hundreds of incidents each year. Most research shows that a police officer's crime-fighting efforts are only a small part of his overall activities. Studies of police work indicate that a significant portion of an officer's time is spent handling minor disturbances, service calls, and administrative duties. Police work, then, involves much more than catching criminals. Figure 6.2 shows the results of a national survey of police behavior. About 44 million Americans have contacts with the police each year.[2] About half of these involve some form of motor vehicle or traffic-related issues. About 5 million annual contacts involve citizens asking for assistance, for example, responding to a neighbor's complaint about music being too loud during a party or warning kids not to shoot fireworks. This survey indicates that the police role is both varied and complex.[3]

These results are not surprising when Uniform Crime Reports arrest data are considered. Each year, about 700,000 local, county, and state police officers make about 14 million arrests, or about 20 each. Of these, about 2.2 million are for serious index crimes (Part I), or about three per officer. Given an even distribution of arrests, the average police officer makes less than two arrests per month and less than one felony arrest every four months.

Perspectives on Justice

Rehabilitation advocates would suggest that the police role should be reconsidered because a majority of police activities involve community activities instead of crime control. Police might better serve by preventing crime than catching criminals after a crime occurs.

These figures should be interpreted with caution because not all police officers are engaged in activities that allow them to make arrests, such as patrol or detective work. About one-third of all sworn officers in the nation's largest police departments are in such units as communications, antiterrorism, administration, and personnel and are therefore unlikely to make arrests. Even if the number of arrests per officer were adjusted by one-third, it would still amount to only nine or 10 serious crime arrests per officer per year. So, though police handle thousands of calls each year, relatively few result in an arrest for a serious crime, such as a robbery and burglary. In suburban and rural areas, years may go by before a police officer arrests someone for a serious felony offense.

The evidence, then, shows that the police role involves many non-crime-related activities. While TV and movies show police officers busting criminals and engaging in high-speed chases, the true police role is much more complex. Police officers function in a variety of roles ranging from dispensers of emergency medical care to the keepers of the peace on school grounds. Although officers in large urban departments may be called on to handle more felony cases than those in small towns, they, too, will probably find that the bulk of their daily activities are not crime-related.

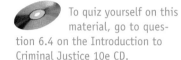 To quiz yourself on this material, go to question 6.4 on the Introduction to Criminal Justice 10e CD.

The Patrol Function

Regardless of style of policing, uniformed patrol officers are the backbone of the police department, usually accounting for about two-thirds of a department's personnel.[4] Patrol officers are the most highly visible components of the entire criminal justice system. They are charged with supervising specific areas of their jurisdiction, called **beats,** whether on foot, in a patrol car, or by motorcycle, horse, helicopter, or even boat. Each beat, or patrol area, is covered 24 hours a day by different shifts. The major purpose of patrol is to

beats
Designated police patrol areas.

- Deter crime by maintaining a visible police presence,
- Maintain public order (peacekeeping) within the patrol area,
- Enable the police department to respond quickly to law violations or other emergencies,
- Identify and apprehend law violators,
- Aid individuals and care for those who cannot help themselves,
- Facilitate the movement of traffic and people, and
- Create a feeling of security in the community.[5]

Patrol officers' responsibilities are immense. They may suddenly be faced with an angry mob, an armed felon, or a suicidal teenager and be forced to make split-second decisions on what action to take. At the same time, they must be sensitive to the needs of citizens who are often of diverse racial and ethnic backgrounds. When police are present and visible, a sense of security is created in a neighborhood and residents' opinions of the police improve.[6]

Patrol Activities

Most experts agree that the great bulk of patrol effort is devoted to what has been described as **order maintenance,** or **peacekeeping:** maintaining order and civility within their assigned jurisdiction.[7] Order-maintenance functions fall on the border between criminal and noncriminal behavior. The patrol officer's discretion often determines whether a noisy neighborhood dispute involves the crime of disturbing the peace or whether it can be controlled with street-corner diplomacy and the combatants sent on their way. Similarly, teenagers milling around in the shopping center parking lot can be brought in and turned over to the juvenile authorities or handled in a less formal and often more efficient manner.

order maintenance (peacekeeping)
Maintaining order and authority without the need for formal arrest; "handling the situation"; keeping things under control by means of threats, persuasion, and understanding.

The major role of police seems to be handling the situation. Police encounter many troubling incidents that need some sort of fixing up.[8] Enforcing the law might be one tool a patrol officer uses; threat, coercion, sympathy, understanding, and apathy might be others. Most important is keeping things under control so that no complaints arise that the officer is doing nothing or doing too much. The real police role, then, may be as a community problem solver.

Police officers practice a policy of selective enforcement, concentrating on some crimes but handling the majority in an informal manner. A police officer is supposed to know when to take action and when not to, whom to arrest and whom to deal with by issuing a warning or some other informal action. If a mistake is made, the officer can come under fire from his peers and superiors, as well as the general public. Consequently, the patrol officer's job is extremely demanding and often unrewarding and unappreciated. The attitudes of police officers toward the public, not surprisingly, are sometimes characterized as being ambivalent and cynical.[9]

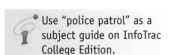
Use "police patrol" as a subject guide on InfoTrac College Edition.

Does Patrol Deter Crime?

For many years, preventive police patrol has been considered one of the greatest deterrents to criminal behavior. The visible presence of patrol cars on the street and the rapid deployment of police officers to the scene of the crime were viewed as particularly effective law enforcement techniques.

However, research efforts have questioned the basic assumptions of patrol. The most widely heralded attempt at measuring patrol effectiveness was undertaken during the early 1970s in Kansas City, Missouri, under sponsorship of the Police Foundation, a private institute that studies police behavior.[10]

To evaluate the effectiveness of patrol, the researchers divided 15 police districts into three groups: One group retained normal patrol; the second (proactive) set of districts were supplied with two to three times the normal amount of patrol forces; the third (reactive) group had its preventive patrol eliminated, and police officers responded only when summoned by citizens to the scene of a particular crime.

Data from the Kansas City study indicated that these variations in patrol techniques had little effect on the crime patterns in the 15 districts. The presence or absence of patrol did not seem to affect residential or business burglaries, motor vehicle thefts, larcenies involving auto accessories, robberies, vandalism, or other criminal behavior.[11] Moreover, variations in patrol techniques appeared to have little influence on citizens' attitudes toward the police, their satisfaction with police, or their fear of future criminal behavior.[12]

Although the Kansas City study found little evidence that police patrol could deter crime, police in a number of jurisdictions have attempted to test the effectiveness of patrol by targeting areas for increased police presence. For example, a police task force might target street-level narcotics dealers by using undercover agents and surveillance cameras in known drug-dealing locales. Or they may actively enforce public nuisance laws in an effort to demonstrate the department's crime-fighting resolve. These efforts have not proven to be successful mechanisms for lowering crime rates.[13] In addition, there is the problem of **displacement:** Criminals move from an area targeted for increased police presence to another that is less well protected. When the police leave, they return to business as usual.

displacement
An effect that occurs when criminals move from an area targeted for increased police presence to another that is less well protected.

Improving Patrol

Police departments have initiated a number of programs and policies to try to improve patrol effectiveness.

Proactive Patrol The Kansas City study, although subject to criticism because of its research design, greatly influenced the way police experts viewed the effectiveness of patrol. Its lukewarm findings set the stage for community and problem-oriented policing models, which stress social service over crime deterrence. However, it may be too soon to dismiss police patrol as a crime-fighting technique. Although the mere presence of police may not be sufficient to deter crime, the manner in which they approach their task may make a difference. Evidence shows that cities with larger police departments, which have more officers per capita than the norm, also experience lower levels of violent crimes.[14] Police departments that use a proactive, aggressive law enforcement style may help reduce crime rates. Jurisdictions that encourage patrol officers to stop motor vehicles to issue citations and to aggressively arrest and detain suspicious persons also experience lower crime rates than jurisdictions that do not follow such proactive policies.[15] Departments that more actively enforce minor regulations, such as disorderly conduct and traffic laws, are also more likely to experience lower felony rates.[16]

Pinpointing why proactive policing works so effectively is difficult. It may have a deterrent effect: Aggressive policing increases the community perception that police arrest many criminals and that most violators get caught. Criminals, therefore, are scared to commit crimes in a town that has such an active police force. **Proactive policing** may also help control crime because it results in conviction of more criminals. Because aggressive police arrest more suspects, fewer criminals are left on the street to commit crime, and fewer criminals produce lower crime rates.

Aggressive police patrol efforts have been a critical success. The downturn in the New York City violent crime rate during the 1990s has been attributed to aggressive police work aimed at lifestyle crimes: vandalism, panhandling, and graffiti.[17]

proactive policing
An aggressive law enforcement style in which patrol offices take the initiative against crime instead of waiting for criminal acts to occur. For example, they stop motor vehicles to issue citations and aggressively arrest and detain suspicious persons.

Does the Amber Alert program actually work? Here, Patricia Bradbury sits at a news conference held in Austin, Texas on July 17, 2002, with her daughter Rae-Leigh. When Rae-Leigh's babysitter did not bring her home, the Bradbury's called local police, who instituted the Amber Alert. Swift action resulted in Rae-Leigh's safe return.

Perspectives on Justice

These results are encouraging to crime control enthusiasts, but the downside of aggressive tactics must be considered before a general policy of vigorous police work can be adopted. Proactive police strategies may cause resentment in minority areas where citizens believe they are being unfairly targeted by police. Aggressive police tactics such as stopping, frisking, and rousting teenagers who congregate on street corners may be the seeds from which racial conflict grows. Overly aggressive police may also be the ones who are continually involved in incidents of unnecessary brutality. Due process advocates are troubled by these side effects and demand review boards to oversee police activities. Despite such reservations, many large police jurisdictions have adopted a crime control philosophy by having patrol officers become more aggressive and concentrate on investigating and deterring crimes.

Targeting Crimes Evidence also shows that targeting specific crimes can be successful. One aggressive patrol program, known as the Kansas City Gun Experiment, was directed at restricting the carrying of guns in high-risk places at high-risk times. Working with academics from the University of Maryland, the Kansas City Police Department focused extra patrol attention on a hot-spot high-crime area identified by computer analysis of all gun crimes. Over a 29-week period, the gun patrol officers made thousands of car and pedestrian checks and traffic stops, and they made more than 600 arrests. Using frisks and searches, they found 29 guns, and an additional 47 weapons were seized by other officers in the experimental area. There were 169 gun crimes in the target beat in the 29 weeks prior to the gun patrol but only 86 while the experiment was under way, a decrease of 49 percent. Drive-by shootings dropped significantly, as did homicides, without any displacement to other areas in the city. The weapons

seized could have been taken from high-rate offenders who were among the most likely perpetrators of gun-related crimes. Their lost opportunity to commit violent crimes may have resulted in an overall rate decrease. The gun sweeps also could have caused some of the most violent criminals to be taken off the streets. And as word of the patrol got out, there may have been a general deterrent effect: People contemplating violent crime may have been convinced that apprehension risks were unacceptably high.[18]

One of the most frightening of all crimes — child abduction — has been targeted through the Amber Alert protocol, which is the subject of the Analyzing Criminal Justice Issues feature on page 183.

To quiz yourself on this material, go to questions 6.5–6.8 on the Introduction to Criminal Justice 10e CD.

Making Arrests   Can more formal police action, such as an arrest, reduce crime? Research studies show that contact with the police may cause some offenders to forgo repeat criminal behavior and deter future criminality.[19] For example, an arrest for drunk driving has been shown to reduce the likelihood of further driving while intoxicated because arrestees are afraid that they will be rearrested if they drink and drive.[20] The effect of arrest may be immediate: As the number of arrests increase, reported crimes decrease substantially the following day.[21] News of increased and aggressive police activity could be rapidly diffused through the population and have an immediate impact that translates into lower crime rates. Some cities have adopted a zero-tolerance approach making arrests for even nuisance crimes, for example, panhandling, to deter repeat offenders and give citizens the impression that crime will not be tolerated.

Adding Patrol Officers   One reason patrol activity may be less effective than desired is the lack of adequate resources. Does adding more police help bring down the crime rate? The evidence is mixed. Some reviews find that the number of law enforcement officers in a jurisdiction seems to have little effect on area crimes.[22] Comparisons of police expenditures in U.S. cities indicate that cities with the highest crime rates also spend the most on police services.[23]

Can adding patrol officers bring the crime rate down? The most recent research suggests that as the number of officers on the street increases, crime rates decline.

While these results are disappointing, a number of recent studies, using different methodologies, have found that police presence may reduce crime levels and that adding police may bring crime levels down.[24] In addition, increasing the size of the local police force may have other benefits for the overall effectiveness of the justice system. For example, adding police and bolstering resources can increase the prosecution and conviction rates.[25] Inadequate resources make it difficult to gather sufficient evidence to ensure a conviction, and prosecutors are likely to drop these cases. Adding police resources helps increase prosecutorial effectiveness. See Concept Summary 6.1.

The Investigation Function

Since the first independent detective bureau was established by the London Metropolitan Police in 1841, criminal investigators have been romantic figures vividly portrayed in novels, such as Detective Alex Cross in James Patterson's widely read books (such as *Kiss the Girls* and *Along Came a Spider*), in movies such as Eddie Murphy's portrayal of Axel Foley in *Beverly Hills Cop* and Clint Eastwood's role as Dirty Harry, and in television shows such as *CSI: Crime Scene Investigation, NYPD Blue,* and *Law & Order.*[26] The fictional police detective is usually depicted as a loner who is

Amber Alert
analyzing criminal justice issues

An abducted child is a parent's worst nightmare. Even more horrifying is the fact that approximately 74 percent of children who are abducted and murdered are found to have been killed within three hours of being snatched. For these reasons alone, abducted children must be found immediately. To help ensure the recovery of abducted children, an emergency alert system has been instituted to help notify the public of missing children.

America's Missing Broadcast Emergency Response, also known as the Amber Alert, was developed after Amber Hagerman, a 9-year-old girl, was abducted while riding her bike near her home in Texas when she was kidnapped and brutally killed by her abductor. As a result of that tragic incident, Texas in 1996 developed the Amber Alert, which combines the efforts of law enforcement, media, and the public to broadcast the most recent abduction information. The Amber Alert protocol quickly alerts and interrupts local television and radio programs with information regarding the abduction and with photographs of the missing child. The program operates under some stipulations, including the following.

- Only law enforcement personnel can activate the program.
- The program is used only for children 17 years of age or younger.

- The alert is used solely for serious abductions in which law enforcement fear that the child is in imminent danger of his or her life.
- The program is not generally used when the abductor is a parent of the child, unless extenuating circumstances indicate that the child is in serious danger of being harmed.

California instituted the Amber Alert as a regional program in 1999 and incorporated it as a statewide program in 2002. The program went nationwide in April 2003, when President George W. Bush signed the Child Protection Act of 2003. So far the program has been successful in helping rescue 64 children from their abductors.

The TRAK Program

Working in conjunction with the Amber Alert is the TRAK (technology to recover abducted kids) system, which aids law enforcement in creating high-quality photos and fliers of the missing child along with photos of the abductor. Instead of taking many hours for these photos and fliers to be made, the system has the power to create them within minutes, which is essential to getting information out quickly to the public. In addition, these photos can be sent electronically through TRAK electronics or by fax machine.

SocialTech, in San Francisco, California, developed the TRAK system. The company works closely with law enforcement to help in child abduction cases. The system is growing in popularity and is used within at least eight states.

Critical Thinking

Would other types of criminal investigations benefit from an Amber Alert–type system, or is it unique to child abductions? What about a Terror Alert system?

InfoTrac College Edition Research

 Use "Amber Alert" in a key word search on InfoTrac College Edition to find out more about how the system is being used.

Source: Joann Donnellan and Nicole Hayes, *President to Sign Amber into Law* (Arlington, Va.: National Center for Missing and Exploited Children, April 30, 2003), pp. 1–2, www.missingkids.com/missingkids; Richard Kirkland, *TRAK-Technology to Recover Abducted Kids* (Nevada Department of Public Safety, June 4, 2002), p. 1, http://nvrepository.state.nv.us/TRAK.htm; C. O. Bradford, "TRAKing Abducted Kids," *Community Police Exchange* (July/August 1998): 1–2, www.communitypolicing.org/publications/exchange; "What Is California AMBER Alert?" *California Amber Alert Manual* (State of California, 2003), p. 1; *California Highway Patrol* (State of California, 2003), pp. 1–2, www.chp.ca.gov/html/amber-en.html.

Concept Summary 6.1 Improving Patrol

Strategy	Tactic	Goal
Aggressive patrol	Enforce law vigorously	Give message that crime will not be tolerated
Target specific crimes	Crack down on persistent problems such as gun possession	Stopping one type of crime may have spillover effect
Make arrests	Arrest even minor offenders; zero-tolerance approach	Convince people that crime does not pay
Add police	Increase number of officers on the street	Improve system efficiency

Criminal investigation is a key element of police work. Here, police officers scour a crime scene for evidence during the Washington, D.C., sniper investigation, October 19, 2002.

© 2000 AP/Wide World Photos

willing to break departmental rules, perhaps even violate the law, to capture the suspect. The average fictional detective views departmental policies and U.S. Supreme Court decisions as unfortunate roadblocks to police efficiency. Civil rights are either ignored or actively scorned.[27]

Although every police department probably has a few aggressive detectives who may take matters into their own hands at the expense of citizens' rights, the modern criminal investigator is most likely an experienced civil servant, trained in investigatory techniques, knowledgeable about legal rules of evidence and procedure, and at least somewhat cautious about the legal and administrative consequences of her actions.[28] *CSI*'s Gil Grissom, head of the Crime Scene Investigation team in Las Vegas, may be a more realistic portrayal of the modern investigator than Dirty Harry or Axel Foley. Although detectives are often handicapped by limited time, money, and resources, they are certainly aware of how their actions will one day be interpreted in a court of law.

Detectives may enter a case after patrol officers have made the initial contact, such as when a patrol car interrupts a crime in progress and the offenders flee before they can be apprehended. They can investigate a case entirely on their own, sometimes by following up on leads provided by informants. Typically, the more serious the case, with murder being the extreme example, the longer detectives will devote to a single crime and the more likely they will eventually be able to identify and arrest the culprit.[29]

Detective divisions are typically organized into sections or bureaus, such as homicide, robbery, or rape (see Exhibit 6.1).

vice squads
Police officers assigned to enforce morality-based laws, such as those on prostitution, gambling, and pornography.

Some jurisdictions maintain **vice squads,** which are usually staffed by plainclothes officers or detectives specializing in victimless crimes, such as prostitution or gambling. Vice squad officers may set themselves up as customers for illicit activities to make arrests. For example, male undercover detectives may frequent public men's rooms and make advances toward other men. Those who respond are arrested for homosexual soliciting. In other instances, female police officers may pose as prostitutes. These covert police activities have often been

Exhibit 6.1 Detective Division Organization in Baton Rouge

Division I. Crimes against Persons

The **Homicide** division is responsible for investigating all criminal calls when a death or life-threatening injury has occurred, any officer-involved shooting, or the attempted murder of a police officer.

The **Armed Robbery** division is responsible for investigating all criminal calls involving all degrees of robbery.

The **Juvenile/Sex Crimes** division is responsible for maintaining juvenile investigation records, cases of child abuse, and all types of sex crimes.

The **Major Assaults/Missing Persons** division is responsible for investigating a wide range of non-life-threatening felony personal crimes and missing person cases.

The **Computer Crimes** division investigates crimes committed against persons or computer systems using the Internet, e-mail, or other electronic means.

Division II. Property Crimes

The **Burglary** division is responsible for coordinating all follow-up investigations of burglaries, as well as the recovery of stolen property from local pawnshops.

The **Auto Theft/Impound** division is responsible for conducting follow-up investigations of auto thefts and unauthorized use of movables. The unit also coordinates all records and information relating to vehicles stored and impounded by the department and monitoring local towing services to ensure compliance with applicable standards and ordinances.

The **Forgery** division is responsible for investigating all crimes involving thefts by fraudulent use of access cards as well as forgeries of negotiable documents.

The **Felony Theft** unit is responsible for all felony theft investigations that do not fall under the Auto Theft, Burglary, or Forgery divisions. The office is also responsible for felony damage to property cases. Priority is placed on business embezzlement incidents.

Division III. Investigative Support

The **Evidence** division is responsible for the collection, storage, cataloguing, and disposition of all evidence and property seized by, or turned in to, the department.

The **Crime Scene** division is responsible for assisting in investigations by taking photographs, sketching major crime scenes, collecting and tagging evidence, and performing various scientific tests on suspects and evidence as needed.

The **Polygraph** division conducts all polygraph, or lie detector, tests given to recruits, employees, or criminal suspects.

The **Crime Stoppers** office coordinates all facets of the Crime Stoppers program with local news media, businesses, and the public.

Division IV. Special Operations

The **Narcotics Division** is responsible for investigating crimes involving illegal drugs as well as related vice crimes.

The **School Drug Task Force** investigates crimes involving narcotics, explosives and weapons in schools, and school buses and at school-sponsored events within the parish.

The **Liaison Detectives** assigned to outside state and federal agencies work jointly with these agencies to participate in multijurisdictional investigations

Source: Baton Rouge Louisiana Police Department, http://brgov.com/dept/brpd/criminal.htm.

criticized as violating the personal rights of citizens, and their appropriateness and fairness have been questioned.

Sting Operations

Another approach to detective work, commonly referred to as a **sting operation,** involves organized groups of detectives who deceive criminals into openly committing illegal acts or conspiring to engage in criminal activity. Numerous sting operations have been aimed at capturing professional thieves and seizing stolen merchandise. Undercover detectives pose as fences, set up ongoing fencing operations, and encourage thieves interested in selling stolen merchandise. Transactions are videotaped to provide prosecutors with strong cases. Sting operations have netted millions of dollars in recovered property and resulted in the arrests of many criminals. These results seem impressive, but sting operations have drawbacks.[30] By its very nature, a sting involves deceit by police agents that often comes close to entrapment. Sting operations may encourage criminals to commit new crimes because they have a new source for fencing stolen goods. Innocent people may hurt their reputations by buying merchandise from a sting operation when they had no idea the items had been stolen. By putting the government in the fencing business, such operations blur the line between law enforcement and criminal activity.

sting operation
Organized groups of detectives who deceive criminals into openly committing illegal acts or conspiring to engage in criminal activity.

Undercover Work

Sometimes detectives go undercover to investigate crime.[31] Undercover work can take a number of forms. A lone agent can infiltrate a criminal group or organization to gather information on future criminal activity. For example, a Drug Enforcement Administration agent may go undercover to gather intelligence on drug smugglers. Undercover officers can also pose as victims to capture predatory criminals who have been conducting street robberies and muggings.

Undercover work is considered a necessary element of police work, although it can prove dangerous for the agent. Police officers may be forced to engage in illegal or immoral behavior to maintain their cover. They also face significant physical danger in playing the role of a criminal and dealing with mobsters, terrorists, and drug dealers. In far too many cases, undercover officers are mistaken for real criminals and are injured by other law enforcement officers or private citizens trying to stop a crime. Arrest situations involving undercover officers may also provoke violence when suspects do not realize they are in the presence of police and therefore violently resist arrest.

Undercover officers may also experience psychological problems. Being away from home, keeping late hours, and always worrying that their identity will be uncovered all create enormous stress. Officers have experienced post-undercover strain, resulting in trouble at work and, in many instances, ruined marriages and botched prosecutions. Hanging around with criminals for a long period of time, making friends with them, and earning their trust can also have a damaging psychological impact.

Use the term "undercover operations" as a subject guide on InfoTrac College Edition to learn more about this form of investigation.

Evaluating Investigations

Serious criticism has been leveled at the nation's detective forces for being bogged down in paperwork and relatively inefficient in clearing cases. One famous study of 153 detective bureaus found that a great deal of a detective's time was spent in nonproductive work and that investigative expertise did little to solve cases. Half of all detectives could be replaced without negatively influencing crime clearance rates.[32]

Although some question remains about the effectiveness of investigations, police detectives do make a valuable contribution to police work because their skilled interrogation and case-processing techniques are essential to eventual criminal conviction.[33] Nonetheless, a majority of cases that are solved are done so when the perpetrator is identified at the scene of the crime by patrol officers. Research by the Police Executive Research Forum shows that, if a crime is reported while in progress, the police have about a 33 percent chance of making an arrest; the arrest probability declines to about 10 percent if the crime is reported one minute later; and to 5 percent if more than 15 minutes has elapsed. As the time between the crime and the arrest grows, the chances of a conviction are also reduced, probably because the ability to recover evidence is lost. Put another way, once a crime has been completed and the investigation is put in the hands of detectives, the chances of identifying and arresting the perpetrator diminish rapidly.[34]

Improving Investigations

A number of efforts have been made to revamp and improve investigation procedures. One practice has been to give patrol officers greater responsibility for conducting preliminary investigations at the scene of the crime. In addition, specialized units, such as homicide or burglary squads, now operate over larger areas and can bring specific expertise to bear. Technological advances in DNA and fingerprint identification have also aided investigation effectiveness. The Images of Justice feature on page 187 highlights how advances are being portrayed on one popular TV series.

CSI: Crime Scene Investigation

images of justice

CSI: Crime Scene Investigation is a surprise television hit. Instead of relying on shoot-outs and car chases, it pits criminals against a dedicated team of forensic scientists who work for the Las Vegas, Nevada, Police Department. Instead of using their brawn, the CSI investigators rely on their wits and scientific training.

The team is led by Gil Grissom, played by William Peterson. The character is a trained scientist whose specialty is forensic entomology, which is the study of insects found on or near a crime scene. He searches for clues within victims' bodies, outside of their bodies, or in any other way that can provide evidence to identify the suspect or solve the crime. For example, he can test the waste products from an insect found in the body of the deceased to determine the time of death, whether the body has been moved, and so on. The opposite of a hard-drinking, two-fisted crime fighter, Grissom is a shy, quiet guy who, when not working, can be found doing crossword puzzles.

While not all CSI members were trained as scientists, most have the skills and education that make them formidable forensic specialists. For example, Sara Sidle, played by Jorja Fox, holds a B.S. degree in physics from Harvard University. Brought in specifically by Grissom, she is dedicated to her work and seems to spend her free time studying forensics.

Each show revolves around a seemingly unsolvable crime. In some instances, a leading suspect is exonerated when the team uses its skills to show that, despite appearances, he or she could not have committed the crime. For example, in "Sex, Lies, and Larvae," which first aired on December 22, 2000, the team investigates the shooting death of a young woman whose bloodied and bug-infested body is found on a nearby mountain. At first glance, it seems that the woman's abusive husband is the killer. But Grissom's analysis of the bugs found on the woman's body indicates that the victim was killed three days earlier, when her husband was out of town. The *CSI* series has proven so popular that a second version set in Miami, Florida, premiered in 2002.

The *CSI* series draws attention to the developing field of forensics in police work. Forensic means "pertaining to the law," and forensic scientists perform comprehensive chemical and physical analyses on evidence submitted by law enforcement agencies. Although most forensic scientists focus on criminal cases (they are sometimes referred to as criminalists), others work in the civil justice system — for example, performing handwriting comparisons to determine the validity of a signature on a will. Nevertheless, their analyses involve a variety of sciences, mathematical principles, and problem-solving methods, including use of complex instruments and chemical, physical, and microscopic examining techniques. In addition to analyzing crime scene investigations, forensic scientists provide testimony in a court of law when the case is brought to trial. While some forensic scientists are generalists, other such as Gil Grissom, specialize is a particular scientific area, including the following:

Controlled substances and toxicology. Crime lab professionals specializing in this area examine blood and other body fluids and tissues for the presence of alcohol, drugs, and poisons.

Biology. Crime lab professionals compare body fluids and hair for typing factors, including DNA analysis. Analysis of a hair found at a crime scene can determine factors such as whether the hair belongs to a human or animal, the body area a hair came from, diseases the person or animal has, and, sometimes, race.

Chemistry. Forensic scientists analyze trace physical evidence such as blood spatters, paint, soil, and glass. For example, blood spatters help reconstruct a crime scene. The patterns of spatters and the shapes of blood droplets tell how the crime was committed.

Document examination. Document examination includes many areas of expertise, including forgery, document dating, and analysis of handwriting, typewriting, computer printing, and photocopying.

Firearms and toolmark identification. Firearms examination involves matching identifying characteristics between a firearm and projectile and between a projectile and target. Typically, this includes matching bullets to the gun that fired them. Toolmark identification involves matching some identifying characteristics of a tool, such as a pry bar, to the object on which it was used, such as a door frame. It also includes explosives and imprint evidence.

Critical Thinking

They say that life imitates art. As the popularity of the *CSI* series grows, more students likely will be drawn into forensics and more police and law enforcement agencies probably will utilize forensic specialists in their daily operations. Do you think that crime would be better solved in the lab or on the beat?

InfoTrac College Edition Research

How accurate is *CSI*? To find out, read Michael Lipton and Lorenzo Benet, "Getting Dead Right: Forensics Expert Elizabeth Devine Makes Sure *CSI*'s Corpses Are Ready for Their Close-Ups," *People Weekly,* April 22, 2002, p. 77. Use "*Crime Scene Investigation*" as a subject guide on InfoTrac College Edition to learn more about the show.

Source: Hall Dillon, "Forensic Scientists: A Career in the Crime Lab," *Occupational Outlook Quarterly* 43 (1999): 2–5.

One reason for investigation ineffectiveness is that detectives often lack sufficient resources to carry out a lengthy ongoing probe of any but the most serious cases. Research shows the following.[35]

Unsolved cases. Almost 50 percent of burglary cases are screened out by supervisors before assignment to a detective for a follow-up investigation. Of those assigned, 75 percent are dropped after the first day of the follow-up investigation. Although robbery cases are more likely to be assigned to detectives, 75 percent of them are also dropped after one day of investigation.

Length of investigation. The vast majority of cases are investigated for no more than four hours stretching over three days. An average of 11 days elapses between the initial report of a crime and the suspension of the investigation.

Sources of information. Early in an investigation, the focus is on the victim; as the investigation is pursued, emphasis shifts to the suspect. The most critical information for determining case outcome is the name and description of the suspect and related crime information. Victims are most often the source of information. Unfortunately, witnesses, informants, and members of the police department are consulted far less often. However, when these sources are tapped, they are likely to produce useful information.

Effectiveness. Preliminary investigations by patrol officers are critical. In situations in which the suspect's identity is not known immediately after the crime is committed, detectives make an arrest in less than 10 percent of all cases.

Considering these findings, detective work may be improved if greater emphasis is placed on collecting physical evidence at the scene of the crime, identifying witnesses, checking departmental records, and using informants. The probability of successfully settling a case is improved if patrol officers gather evidence at the scene of a crime and effectively communicate it to detectives working the case. Police managers should pay more attention to screening cases, monitoring case flow and activity, and creating productivity measures to make sure that individual detectives and detective units are meeting their goals. Also recommended is the use of targeted investigations that direct attention at a few individuals, such as career criminals, who are known to have engaged in the behavior under investigation.

Using Technology

Police departments are now employing advanced technology in all facets of their operations, from assigning patrol routes to gathering evidence. Investigators are starting to use advanced technology to streamline and enhance the investigation process. For example, gathering evidence at a crime scene and linking those clues to a list of suspects can be a tedious job for many investigators. Yet linkage is critical if suspects are to be quickly apprehended before they are able to leave the jurisdiction, intimidate witnesses, or cover up any clues they may have left behind.

One innovative use of technology allows investigators to compare evidence found at the crime scene with material collected from similar crimes by other police agencies. Police agencies are using a program called Coplink to facilitate this time-consuming task. Coplink integrates information from different jurisdictions into a single database that detectives can access when working investigations.[36] The Coplink program allows investigators to search the entire database of past criminal records and compute a list of possible suspects even if only partial data, such as first or last name, partial license plate numbers, vehicle type, vehicle color, location of crime, or weapon used, are available. The Coplink program allows police to access data from other police agencies in minutes, a process that normally could take days or weeks. The Coplink system allows for easy information sharing between law enforcement agencies, a task that has been problematic in the past and is one of the new breed of computer-aided investigation techniques that are beginning to have a significant impact on capture ratios in the nation's police departments.

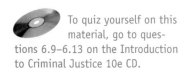
To quiz yourself on this material, go to questions 6.9–6.13 on the Introduction to Criminal Justice 10e CD.

Community policing has paid dividends for local police departments. A group of Hispanic students listens to Community Policing Officer, Corporal H. Borges, left, and Senior Police Attorney Arnetta Herring, right, June 2, 2003, at the Durham Police Department, in Durham, North Carolina, during the Latino Citizen Police Academy. The city's first Spanish Police Academy has helped bridge language and culture barriers between police and the Hispanic community in Durham.

Community Policing

For more than 30 years, police agencies have been trying to gain the cooperation and respect of the communities they serve. At first, efforts at improving the relationships between police departments and the public involved programs with the general title of police–community relations (PCR). Developed at the station house and departmental levels, these initial PCR programs were designed to make citizens more aware of police activities, alert them to methods of self-protection, and improve general attitudes toward policing.

Though PCR efforts showed a willingness for police agencies to cooperate with the public, some experts believed that law enforcement agencies must undergo a significant transformation to create meaningful partnerships with the public. These views were articulated in a critical 1982 paper by two justice policy experts, George Kelling and James Q. Wilson, who espoused a new approach to improving police relations in the community, which has come to be known as the **broken windows model**.[37] Kelling and Wilson made three points.

1. Neighborhood disorder creates fear. Urban areas filled with street people, youth gangs, prostitutes, and the mentally disturbed are the ones most likely to maintain a high degree of crime.
2. Neighborhoods give out crime-promoting signals. A neighborhood filled with deteriorated housing, unrepaired broken windows, and untended disorderly behavior gives out crime-promoting signals. Honest citizens live in fear in these areas, and predatory criminals are attracted to them.
3. Police need citizen cooperation. If police are to reduce fear and successfully combat crime in these urban areas, they must have the cooperation, support, and assistance of the citizens.[38]

According to the broken windows approach, community relations and crime control effectiveness cannot be the province of a few specialized units housed within a traditional police department. Instead, the core police role must be altered if community involvement is to be won and maintained. To accomplish this goal, urban police departments should return to the earlier style of policing in which officers on the

broken windows model
Role of the police as maintainers of community order and safety.

Use "broken windows" as a subject guide on InfoTrac College Edition to learn more about this concept.

wwww The School of Criminal Justice at Michigan State University maintains a comprehensive Web site devoted to community policing. It contains an extensive collection of full text papers on all aspects of community policing. Access it at http://www.ssc.msu.edu/~cj/cp/cptoc.html.

beat had intimate contact with the people they served. Modern police departments generally rely on motorized patrol to cover wide areas, to maintain a visible police presence, and to ensure rapid response time. Although effective and economical, the patrol car removes officers from the mainstream of the community, alienating people who might otherwise be potential sources of information and help to the police.

Perspectives on Justice

According to the broken windows model, police administrators would be served by deploying their forces where they can encourage public confidence, strengthen feelings of safety, and elicit cooperation from citizens. Community preservation, public safety, and order maintenance — not crime fighting — should become the primary focus of patrol. Just as physicians and dentists practice preventive medicine and dentistry, police should help maintain an intact community structure, not simply fight crime. Broken windows policing has shifted police from a purely crime control model to one that embraces elements of rehabilitation and restorative justice.

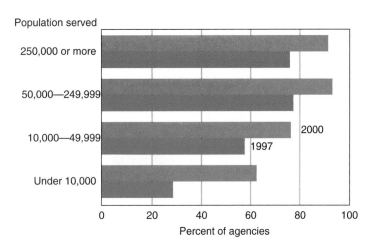

Figure 6.3
Departments with Community Policing

Percent of local police departments using full-time community policing officers, 1997 and 2000

Source: Matthew Hickman and Brian Reeves, *Local Police Department, 2000* (Washington, D.C.: Bureau of Justice Statistics, 2003), p. 15.

foot patrol
Police patrol that takes officers out of cars and puts them on a walking beat to strengthen ties with the community.

community-oriented policing (COP)
Programs designed to bring police and the public closer together and create a more cooperative working environment between them.

Implementing Community Policing

The community policing concept was originally implemented through a number of innovative demonstration projects.[39] Among the most publicized were experiments in foot patrol, which took officers out of cars and set them to walking beats in the neighborhood. Foot patrol efforts were aimed at forming a bond with community residents by acquainting them with the individual officers who patrolled their neighborhood, letting them know that police were caring and available. The first **foot patrol** experiments were conducted in cities in Michigan and New Jersey. An evaluation of foot patrol indicated that, although it did not bring down the crime rate, residents in areas where foot patrol was added perceived greater safety and were less afraid of crime.[40]

Since the advent of these programs, the federal government has encouraged the growth of community policing by providing millions of dollars to hire and train officers.[41] Hundreds of communities have adopted innovative forms of decentralized, neighborhood-based community policing models. Recent surveys indicate that a significant increase is evident in community policing activities in recent years and that certain core programs such as crime prevention activities have become embedded in the police role (see Figure 6.3).[42]

Community-oriented policing (COP) programs have been implemented in large cities, suburban areas, and rural communities.[43] The most successful programs give officers the time to meet with local residents to talk about crime in the neighborhood and to use personal initiative to solve problems (see Exhibit 6.2).

While not all programs work (police–community newsletters and cleanup campaigns do not seem to do much good), the overall impression has been that patrol officers can reduce the level of fear in the community. Some COP programs assign officers to neighborhoods, organize training programs for community leaders, and feature a bottom-up approach to deal with community problems; that is, decision making involves the officer on the scene, not a directive from central headquarters. Programs also have been created for juveniles who might ordinarily have little to do but get involved in gangs but are now directed at such

Exhibit 6.2 The Elements of Community Policing

Community policing focuses on crime and social disorder through the delivery of police services that includes aspects of traditional law enforcement, as well as prevention, problem solving, community engagement, and partnerships. The community policing model balances reactive responses to calls for service with proactive problem solving centered on the causes of crime and disorder. Community policing requires police and citizens to join together as partners in the course of both identifying and effectively addressing these issues.

The core elements of community policing are described below.

Organizational elements	*Tactical elements*	*External elements*
Philosophy adopted organization-wide	Enforcement of laws	Public involvement in community partnerships
Decentralized decision making and accountability	Proactive, crime prevention–oriented	Government and other agency partnerships
Fixed geographic accountability and generalist responsibilities	Problem solving	
Utilization of volunteer resources		
Enhancers		

Source: COPS Office Web site, http://www.cops.usdoj.gov/default.asp?Item=36, accessed on July 18, 2003.

activities as neighborhood cleanup efforts.[44] In Spokane, Washington, for example, the community–police effort created a program called COPY Kids, a summer outreach program for disadvantaged youths, which promotes a positive work ethic, emphasizes the values of community involvement, and helps create a positive image of the police department.[45]

Neighborhood Policing

Community policing means more than implementing direct-action programs. It also refers to a philosophy of policing that requires departments to reconsider their recruitment, organization, and operating procedures. What are some of the most important community policing concepts? First, community policing emphasizes results, not bureaucratic process. Instead of reacting to problems in the community, police departments take the initiative in identifying issues and actively treating their cause. Problem-solving and analysis techniques replace emphasis on bureaucratic detail. There is less concern with playing by the book and more with getting the job done.

To achieve the goals of COP, some agencies have tried to decentralize, an approach sometimes referred to as innovative **neighborhood-oriented policing (NOP)**.[46] Problem solving is best done at the neighborhood level where issues originate, not at a far-off central headquarters. Because each neighborhood has its own particular needs, police decision making must be flexible and adaptive. For example, neighborhoods undergoing change in racial composition all experience high levels of racially motivated violence.[47] Police must be able to distinguish these neighborhood characteristics and allocate resources to meet their needs.

Changing the Police Role

Community policing also stresses sharing power with local groups and individuals. A key element of the community policing philosophy is that citizens must actively participate with police to fight crime.[48] This participation might involve

To read more about COPY Kids and the community policing initiative in Spokane, go to Peter M. Sheingold, "National COPS Evaluation Organizational Change Case Study: Spokane, Washington," http://www.ncjrs.org/nij/cops_casestudy/spokane.html.

neighborhood-oriented policing (NOP)
A philosophy of police suggesting that problem solving is best done at the neighborhood level, where issues originate, not at a far-off central headquarters.

What needs to be done to involve the community in community policing? Read David Thacher, "Equity and Community Policing: A New View of Community Partnerships." *Criminal Justice Ethics* 20, no. 1 (Winter-Spring 2001): p. 3.

The Community Policing Consortium was created and funded in 1993 by the Bureau of Justice Assistance of the U.S. Department of Justice to deliver community policing training and technical assistance to police departments and sheriff's offices that receive federal grant money. Its site is at http://www.communitypolicing.org/.

To quiz yourself on this material, go to question 6.14 on the Introduction to Criminal Justice 10e CD.

problem-oriented policing
A style of police management that stresses proactive problem solving instead of reactive crime fighting.

hot spots of crime
The view that a significant portion of all police calls in metropolitan areas typically radiate from a relatively few locations: bars, malls, the bus depot, hotels, and certain apartment buildings.

providing information in area-wide crime investigations or helping police reach out to troubled youths.

Community policing also means the eventual redesign of police departments. Management's role must be reordered to focus on the problems of the community, not the needs of the police department. The traditional vertical police organizational chart must be altered so that top-down management gives way to bottom-up decision making. The patrol officer becomes the manager of his beat and a key decision maker.

Community policing requires that police departments alter their recruitment and training requirements. Future officers must develop community-organizing and problem-solving skills, along with traditional police skills. Their training must prepare them to succeed less on their ability to make arrests or issue citations and more on their ability to solve problems effectively.

Problem-Oriented Policing

Closely associated with, yet independent from, the community policing concept are **problem-oriented policing** strategies. Traditional police models focus on responding to calls for help in the fastest possible time, dealing with the situation, and then getting on the street again as soon as possible.[49] In contrast, the core of problem-oriented policing is a proactive orientation.

Problem-oriented policing strategies require police agencies to identify particular long-term community problems — street-level drug dealers, prostitution rings, gang hangouts — and to develop strategies to eliminate them.[50] As with community policing, being problem solvers requires that police departments rely on local residents and private resources. This means that police managers must learn how to develop community resources, design cost-efficient and effective solutions to problems, and become advocates as well as agents of reform.[51]

A significant portion of police departments is using special units to confront specific social problems. For example, a significant number of departments employ special units devoted to youth issues ranging from child abuse to gangs.

Problem-oriented policing models are supported by the fact that a great deal of urban crime is concentrated in a few hot spots.[52] A large number of all police calls in metropolitan areas typically radiate from a relatively few locations: bars, malls, the bus depot, hotels, and certain apartment buildings.[53] By implication, concentrating police resources on these **hot spots of crime** could appreciably reduce crime.[54]

Criminal Acts, Criminal Places

Problem-oriented strategies are being developed that focus on specific criminal problem areas or specific criminal acts or both.

Combating Auto Theft   Because of problem-oriented approaches (combined with advanced technology), car thieves in many jurisdictions are no longer able to steal cars with as much ease as before. To reduce the high number of car thefts occurring each year, some police departments have invested in bait cars, which are parked in high-theft areas and are equipped with technology that alarms law enforcement personnel when someone has stolen a vehicle. A signal goes off when either a door is opened or the engine begins. Then, equipped with Global Positioning Satellite technology, police officers are able to watch the movement of the car. Some cars are also equipped with microscopic videos and audio recorders, which allow officers to see and hear the suspect(s) within the car, and remote engine and door locks, which can trap the thief inside. The technology has been used in conjunction with an advertising campaign to warn potential car thieves about the program. The system has been instituted in Vancouver, Canada, and Minneapolis, Minnesota, with impressive results. Motor vehicle theft dropped over 40 percent in Minneapolis over a three-year period in which bait cars were used and 30 percent in Vancouver within six months of being instituted. In addition to cutting down on auto theft, the system, which costs roughly $3,500 per car, seems to decrease the chance of danger of high-speed pursuits because police officers can put obstacles on the road to stop the car.[55]

Reducing Violence A number of efforts have been made to reduce violence using problem-oriented community policing techniques. Police in Richmond, California, successfully applied such techniques, including citizen involvement, to help reduce murder rates.[56] Problem-oriented techniques have also been directed at combating gang-related violence. For example, the Tucson, Arizona, Police Department has created a **Gang Tactical Detail** unit, which is aimed at proactively attacking neighborhood gang problems by targeting known offenders who have shown a propensity toward gang violence or criminal activity. Members of the tactical unit work directly with neighborhood community groups to identify specific gang problems within individual neighborhoods. Once the problem is identified, the unit helps devise a working solution combining community involvement, intergovernmental assistance, and law enforcement intervention. The officers of the Gang Tactical Detail attend meetings with community groups to identify gang-related problems. They assist with gang awareness presentations for schools and civic groups.[57]

Another well-known program, Operation Ceasefire, is a problem-oriented policing intervention aimed at reducing youth homicide and youth firearms violence in Boston, Massachusetts. Evaluations of the program found that Ceasefire produced significant reductions in youth homicide victimization and gun assault incidents in Boston that were not experienced in other communities in New England or elsewhere in the nation.[58] A more detailed description of the program is contained in the Analyzing Criminal Justice Issues feature on page 194.

The Jersey City, New Jersey, police recently applied a variety of aggressive crime-reducing techniques in some of the city's gang-ridden areas. Evaluations of the program show that crime rates were reduced when police officers used aggressive problem solving (for example, drug enforcement) and community improvement (for example, increased lighting and cleaned vacant lots) techniques in high-crime areas.[59] Another recent initiative by the Dallas Police Department assigned officers to aggressively pursue truancy and curfew enforcement, a tactic that resulted in lower rates of gang violence.[60]

While programs such as these seem successful, the effectiveness of any street-level problem-solving efforts must be interpreted with caution.[61] Criminals could be displaced to other, safer areas of the city and could return shortly after the program is called a success and the additional police forces have been pulled from the area.[62] Nonetheless, evidence shows that merely saturating an area with police may not deter crime, but focusing efforts at a particular problem may have a crime-reducing effect.

Gang Tactical Detail
A police unit created to combat neighborhood gang problems by targeting known offenders who have shown a propensity toward gang violence or criminal activity.

The Challenges of Community Policing

The core concepts of police work are changing as administrators recognize the limitations and realities of police work in modern society. If they are to be successful, community policing strategies must be able to react effectively to some significant administrative problems.

Defining community. Police administrators must be able to define the concept of community in terms of an ecological area defined by common norms, shared

Boston Gun Project: Operation Ceasefire

analyzing criminal justice issues

The Boston Gun Project, which later became known as Operation Ceasefire, was a problem-oriented policing initiative designed to reduce the number of youth gang homicides. The program was a response to an upsurge in youth homicides, which began in the early 1990s and resulted in approximately 44 youthful homicides each year between 1991 and 1995.

Operation Ceasefire was implemented in 1996. The program was two-pronged. First, the program sought to crack down on firearm traffickers who supplied guns to children. Law enforcement officers assigned to the project began targeting illicit firearm dealers. In addition, research was conducted to learn which guns were most popular among the gangs, and investigations were aimed at gun dealers who specialized in selling those particular guns. Second, violent gangs and their leaders were targeted. Gangs were given ample warning that the police were taking gangs seriously. Messages were continuously spread throughout the city informing gang members that violence would no longer be tolerated and that those who ignored this warning and continued their violent ways would suffer severe consequences.

Those involved with Operation Ceasefire immediately began using every possible legal method to stop violence. Groups of probation officers, parole officers, and church representatives communicated

with gang members to express the importance of the new program. They helped send the message that gangs would be smart to end their violence and also offered assistance including health services, food, shelter, substance abuse programs, educational courses, and opportunities to partake in legitimate recreational activities.

The police and other criminal justice personnel took a proactive stand against gang activity. They increased monitoring of probationers and made sure outstanding arrest warrants were served. If violence was detected in gang areas, law enforcement officers responded immediately, arresting and quickly prosecuting suspects. Federal agents were involved in the crackdown, and federal prosecutions were sought where applicable.

Informing gang members that violence would no longer be tolerated and then immediately enforcing consequences if warnings were ignored proved to be highly effective. Many gang boys were intimidated by the threat of prosecution and dropped out. The rate of homicides and other gun-related crimes dropped significantly. An evaluation of the program recorded monthly declines in youth homicides (63 percent), shot-fired calls for service (32 percent), gun assaults (25 percent), and youth assaults (44 percent). The average number of youths killed in gang actions dropped from 44 per year

from 1991 to 1995 to 26 in 1996 and 15 in 1999. Because of this astounding success, the program was copied in Washington, D.C., and Richmond, Virginia (where it was called Operation Exile).

Critical Thinking

1. What other problem areas do you think deserve special police operations such as Ceasefire?

2. How would you go about controlling a specific problem in your town or city, for example, reducing underage drinking?

InfoTrac College Edition Research

To read more about Ceasefire, go to "Swift and Certain Punishment: How to Keep Young Toughs from Committing Violent Acts," *U.S. News and World Report,* December 29, 1997, p. 67.

Sources: David Kennedy, Anthony Braga, Ann Piehl, and Elin Waring, *Reducing Gun Violence: The Boston Gun Project's Operation Ceasefire* (Washington, D.C.: National Institute of Justice, 2001); Winifred Reed and Scott Decker, *Responding to Gangs: Evaluation and Research* (Washington, D.C.: National Institute of Justice, 2003); U.S. Bureau of Alcohol, Tobacco, and Firearms, "Operation Ceasefire" (2003), www.atf.gov/pub/fire-explo_pub/ceasefire/index.htm; Office of Juvenile Justice and Delinquency Prevention, "Project Exile, U.S. Attorney's Office — Eastern District of Virginia" (2003), http://ojjpd.ncjrs.org/pubs/gun_violence/profile38.html.

values, and interpersonal bonds.[63] After all, the main focus of community policing is to activate the community norms that make neighborhoods more crime-resistant. To do so requires identification of distinct ecological areas. If, in contrast, community policing projects cross the boundaries of many different neighborhoods, any hope of learning and accessing community norms, strengths, and standards will be lost.[64] And even if natural community structures can be identified, policing agencies will have to continually monitor the changing norms, values, and attitudes of the community they serve, a process that has the positive side effect of creating positive interactions between the community and the police.[65]

Defining roles. Police administrators must also establish the exact role of community police agents. How should they integrate their activities with those of regular patrol forces? For example, should foot patrols have primary responsibility for policing in an area, or should they coordinate their activities with officers assigned to patrol cars? Should community police officers be solely problem

© 2003 AP/Wide World Photos

Community policing can help re-orient the police role to re- duce community tensions. Here, Alicia Robinson, 8, holds a bear given to her by Michigan state troopers after falling from her bicycle, as police patrol the streets of Benton Harbor, Michigan, June 19, 2003. Police are patrolling the streets after a fatal chase by suburban police ignited two nights of rioting in this city that for years has strug- gled with poverty, high unem- ployment, and racial tensions.

identifiers and neighborhood organizers, or should they also be expected to be law enforcement agents who get to the crime scene rapidly and later do inves- tigative work? Can community police teams and regular patrols work together, or must a department abandon traditional police roles and become purely com- munity policing-oriented?

Emphasizing supervision style. The way patrol officers are supervised may en- hance or detract from their dedication to community policing. For example, Robin Shepard Engel studied supervisory styles and found that active supervi- sors who she found to embrace a philosophy of leading by example had the great- est impact on their subordinates. These active supervisors become heavily involved in the field. They performed the dual function of being street officer and supervisor. Officers with active supervisors were more likely than those with other types of supervisors to use force and spent more time on self-initiated ac- tivities including community policing and problem solving.[66] In contrast, some supervisors are wary of community policing because it supports a decentralized command structure. This would mean fewer supervisors and, consequently, less chance for promotion and a potential loss of authority.[67]

Reorienting police values. Research shows that police officers who have a tra- ditional crime control orientation are less satisfied with community policing ef- forts than those who are public service–oriented.[68] Officers who embrace the community policing model are the ones who are most willing to engage in com- munity policing–type behaviors. Even loyal police officers who are committed to the police organization as a whole are unlikely to be successful in community policing activities unless they form a commitment to community policing itself.[69] While this finding comes as no surprise, it is indicative of the difficulty police managers will face in convincing experienced officers, many of whom hold tradi- tional law and order values, to embrace community policing models.

Revise training. Because the community policing model calls for a revision of the police role from law enforcer to community organizer, police training must be revised to reflect this new mandate. If community policing is to be adopted on a wide scale, a whole new type of police officer must be recruited and trained in a new way. Retraining and reorienting police from their traditional roles into a

www   To find a Web site dedicated to providing the latest information, training, advice, and discussion on community policing, go to http://www.policing.com. Its view is that community policing is a philosophy based on the recognition that nothing can outperform dedicated people working together to make their communities better and safer places in which to live and work and raise children.

more social service orientation may also be difficult. Most police officers do not have the social service skills required of effective community agents. Community policing requires that police departments alter their recruitment and training requirements. Future officers must develop community-organizing and problem-solving skills, along with traditional police skills. Their training must prepare them to succeed less on their ability to make arrests or issue citations and more on their ability to solve problems, prevent crime effectively, and deal with neighborhood diversity and cultural values.[70]

Reorient recruitment. To make community policing successful, midlevel managers must be recruited and trained who are receptive to and can implement community-change strategies.[71] The selection of new recruits must be guided by a desire to find individuals with the skills and attitudes that support community policing. They must be open to the fact that community policing will help them gain knowledge of the community, give them opportunities to gain skill and experience, and help them engage in proactive problem solving.[72] Selecting people who find these values attractive and then providing training that accentuates the community vision of policing is essential to the success of the COP model.

Overcoming Obstacles

Although these are formidable obstacles to overcome, growing evidence shows that community and problem-oriented policing can work and fit well with traditional forms of policing.[73] Many police experts and administrators have embraced the community and problem-oriented policing concepts as revolutionary revisions of the basic police role. Community policing efforts have been credited with helping reduce crime rates in large cities such as New York and Boston. The most professional and highly motivated officers are the ones most likely to support community policing efforts.[74]

These results are encouraging, but clear-cut evidence does not exist that community policing is highly successful at either reducing crime or changing the traditional values and attitudes of police officers involved in the programs.[75] Crime rate reductions in cities that have used COP may be the result of an overall downturn in the nation's crime rate or some other factor such as an improved economy.

National surveys find that police administrators still consider law enforcement their top priority; providing community and social services is not considered a significant police role.[76] Instead of reflecting community policing needs, most police agencies still mostly value crime control and improving professional standards.[77]

Despite these professional obstacles, community policing has become a stable part of municipal police departments. Even critics, such as Ralph Taylor, recognize the usefulness of community policing. In his book *Breaking Away from Broken Windows,* Taylor argues that the policing policies based on the broken windows model are not a sole panacea for crime control. While efforts by policing programs to improve levels of physical decay and disorder are helpful, in the long term neighborhood economic decline is a more important crime-producing factor. He concludes that community policing programs can provide some relief, but that for crime rates to remain low, politicians, businesses, and community leaders must work together to improve the economic climate in high-crime areas.[78]

Support Functions

As the model of a typical police department indicates (Figure 6.1), not all members of a department engage in what the general public regards as real police work — patrol, detection, and traffic control. Even in departments that are embracing community and problem-oriented policing, a great deal of police resources is devoted to support and administrative functions.

Many police departments maintain their own personnel service, which carries out such functions as recruiting new police officers, creating exams to determine the most qualified applicants, and handling promotions and transfers. Innovative selection techniques are constantly being developed and tested. For example, the Behavioral-Personnel Assessment Device (B-PAD) requires police applicants to view videotaped scenarios and respond as if they were officers handling the situation. Reviews indicate that this procedure may be a reliable and unbiased method of choosing new recruits.[79]

Larger police departments often maintain an internal affairs branch, which is charged with policing the police. The **internal affairs** division processes citizen complaints of police corruption, investigates what may be the unnecessary use of force by police officers, and even probes police participation in criminal activity, such as burglaries or narcotics violations. In addition, the internal affairs division may assist police managers when disciplinary action is brought against individual officers. Internal affairs is a controversial function given that investigators are feared and distrusted by fellow police officers. Nonetheless, rigorous self-scrutiny is the only way police departments can earn the respect of citizens. Because of these concerns, it has become commonplace for police departments to institute citizen oversight of police practices and insitute civilian review boards that have the power to listen to complaints and conduct investigations. Citizen oversight is the subject of the Analyzing Criminal Justice Issues feature on page 198.

Most police departments are responsible for the administration and control of their own budgets. This task includes administering payroll, purchasing equipment and services, planning budgets for future expenditures, and auditing departmental financial records.

Police departments maintain separate units that are charged with maintaining and disseminating information on wanted offenders, stolen merchandise, traffic violators, and so on. Modern data management systems enable police to use their records in a highly sophisticated fashion. For example, officers in a patrol car who spot a suspicious-looking vehicle can instantly receive a computerized rundown on whether it has been stolen. Or, if property is recovered during an arrest, police using this sort of system can determine who reported the loss of the merchandise and arrange for its return.

Another important function of police communication is the effective and efficient dispatching of patrol cars. Again, modern computer technologies have been used to make the most of available resources.[80]

In many departments, training is continuous throughout an officer's career. Training usually begins at a police academy, which may be run exclusively for larger departments or be part of a regional training center servicing smaller and varied governmental units. More than 90 percent of all police departments require preservice training, including almost all departments in larger cities

© 2002 AP/Wide World Photos

A Kansas City, Missouri, police officer directs rush hour traffic at a darkened intersection. Freezing rain had left a heavy coat of ice on trees and power lines, resulting in a loss of power to large parts of the metropolitan area. Traffic control remains a significant part of the police role.

internal affairs
Unit that investigates allegations of police misconduct.

Citizen Oversight of Police: Civilian Review Boards
analyzing criminal justice issues

Two Rochester, New York, police officers approach two young males walking down the street for allegedly dealing drugs. During an ensuing melee, one of the youths reportedly is pushed through a plate glass window. The mother of one of the boys claims that these innocent young men were the victims of police brutality.

At a hearing, the city's citizen review finds out that the arrestees had drugs in their possession, that the officers had remained polite and professional during the encounter, and that one of the boys had pushed an officer into the store window, not the other way around. The officers were exonerated by the review board.

Citizen oversight of police conduct can be a critical method of improving community relations, but it is also one that has caused conflict with police officers. Nonetheless, citizen oversight of police has been on the rise in the United States.

Typically, there are four models of oversight systems.

1. Citizens investigate allegations of police misconduct and recommend a finding to the head of the agency.
2. Officers investigate allegations and develop findings. Then, citizens review and recommend that the head of the agency approve or reject the findings.
3. Complainants may appeal findings established by the agency to citizens who review them and make recommendations to the head of the agency.
4. An auditor investigates the process the agency uses to accept and investigate complaints and reports to the agency and the community the thoroughness and fairness of the process.

Many variations exist on these basic models. For example, the Minneapolis, Minnesota, civilian police review operates in two stages. First, paid, professional investigators and a director examine citizen complaints to determine if there is reasonable evidence that police misconduct occurred. Then, volunteer board members conduct closed-door hearings

to decide whether they should support the allegations that came from the initial screening process. In Orange County, Florida, a nine-volunteer citizen review board holds hearings, open to the public and the media, on all cases involving the alleged use of excessive force and abuse of power after the sheriffs department has conducted an investigation.

While police agencies in some communities have embraced citizen review, others find them troublesome. Departmental opposition is most likely when oversight procedures represent outside interference, oversight staff lack experience with and understanding of police work, and oversight processes are unfair. Most police administrators believe that their agencies should have the final say in matters of discipline, policies and procedures, and training, and some bridle at the hint of outside interference by nonprofessionals. In some communities, local governments have established oversight bodies that act only in an advisory capacity and make nonbinding recommendations to law enforcement agencies.

Another familiar complaint is that civilians are unable to understand the complexities of police work. To compensate, candidates for the review board in Rochester, New York, attend a condensed version of a police academy run by the police department. The 48-hour course involves three hours per evening for two weeks and two all-day Saturday sessions. The members use a shoot–don't shoot simulator, practice handcuffing, and learn about department policies and procedures, including the use-of-force continuum.

In addition to these issues, many officers believe that review members hold them accountable for minor infractions, such as placing the wrong offense code on a citation or failing to record the end mileage on a vehicle transport. Some also believe that the review process is often lengthy and that delays both harm the credibility of the oversight process and cause officers considerable stress as they

wait for their cases to be decided. To overcome these problems, some police administrators have taken the initiative by helping set up a citizen oversight system before being required to do so and then becoming involved in the planning process.

Despite serious reservations about citizen oversight, many law enforcement administrators have identified positive outcomes from having a review board in place. These include improving community relations, enhancing an agency's ability to police itself, and, most important, improving an agency's policies and procedures. Citizen oversight bodies can recommend changes in the way the department conducts its internal investigation into alleged misconduct and also improve department policies governing officer behavior.

Critical Thinking

1. The research conducted by Liqun Cao and Bu Huang shows that having a civilian review board is not a panacea that will eliminate or significantly reduce citizen complaints. One reason is police resistance to civilian oversight. If you were the chief of police, would you want civilians to oversee how you ran your department or handled citizen complaints?
2. If you were the head of a civilian review board, how would you get the local police to accept your authority?

InfoTrac College Edition Research

 Should there be civilian oversight over police? For one viewpoint, read Sidney L. Harring, "The Diallo Verdict: Another 'Tragic Accident' in New York's War on Street Crime?" *Social Justice* 27 (2000): 9–18.

Sources: Liqun Cao and Bu Huang, "Determinants of Citizen Complaints against Police Abuse of Power," *Journal of Criminal Justice* 28 (2000): 203–13; Peter Finn, "Getting Along with Citizen Oversight," *FBI Law Enforcement Bulletin* 69 (2000): 22–27.

Table 6.1 Training Requirements for New Officer Recruits in Local Police Departments, by Size of Population Served, 2000

Population Served	Average Number of Hours Required					
	Academy			Field		
	Total	State-mandated	Other Required	Total	State-mandated	Other Required
All sizes	637	514	123	417	228	189
1,000,000 or more	1,051	564	487	534	189	345
500,000–999,999	950	586	364	784	425	359
250,000–499,999	991	577	414	659	336	323
100,000–249,999	853	601	252	757	425	322
50,000–99,999	790	604	186	689	414	275
25,000–49,999	763	586	177	680	334	346
10,000–24,999	751	574	177	537	297	240
2,500–9,999	611	514	97	389	235	154
Under 2,500	532	469	63	244	153	91

Note: Average number of training hours excludes departments not requiring training.

Source: Matthew Hickman and Brian Reaves, *Local Police Departments, 2000* (Washington, D.C.: Bureau of Justice Statistics, 2003), p. 6.

(population over 100,000). The average officer receives more than 600 hours of preservice training, including 400 hours in the classroom and the rest in field training (see Table 6.1). Police in large cities receive more than 1,000 hours of instruction divided almost evenly between classroom and field instruction.[81] Among the topics usually covered are law and civil rights, firearms handling, emergency medical care, and restraint techniques.[82]

After assuming their police duties, new recruits are assigned to field-training officers who break them in on the job. However, training does not stop here. On-the-job training is a continuous process in the modern police department and covers such areas as weapons skills, first aid, crowd control, and community relations. Some departments use roll-call training, in which superior officers or outside experts address police officers at the beginning of the workday. Other departments allow police officers time off to attend annual training sessions to sharpen their skills and learn new policing techniques.

Police departments provide emergency aid to the ill, counsel youngsters, speak to school and community agencies on safety and drug abuse, and provide countless other services designed to improve citizen–police interactions.

Larger police departments maintain specialized units that help citizens protect themselves from criminal activity. For example, they advise citizens on effective home security techniques or conduct Project ID campaigns — engraving valuables with an identifying number so that they can be returned if recovered after a burglary. Police also work in schools teaching kids how to avoid drug use.[83]

Police agencies maintain (or have access to) forensic laboratories that enable them to identify substances to be used as evidence and to classify fingerprints.

Planning and research functions include designing programs to increase police efficiency and strategies to test program effectiveness. Police planners monitor recent technological developments and institute programs to adapt them to police services.

Use "police training" as a subject guide on InfoTrac College Edition to learn more about the topic.

Police training helps officers be prepared for the sometimes dangerous encounters they will face while on patrol. Officer Jim Franklin, left, a twelve-year veteran with the Hannibal, Missouri Police Department, fires a simulation round at Sergeant Jim Hark, who was playing an armed, mentally unstable attacker during police training scenarios held May 16, 2003, at the HPD Firearm Range. Each scenario placed officers in encounters with armed "suspects" and was videotaped to evaluate performance.

© 2003 AP/Wide World Photos

Improving Police Productivity

Police administrators have sought to increase the productivity of their line, support, and administrative staff. As used today, the term *police productivity* refers to the amount of order, maintenance, crime control, and other law enforcement activities provided by individual police officers and concomitantly by police departments as a whole. By improving police productivity, a department can keep the peace, deter crime, apprehend criminals, and provide useful public services without necessarily increasing its costs. This goal is accomplished by having each police officer operate with greater efficiency, thus using fewer resources to achieve greater effectiveness.

Despite the emphasis on increasing police effectiveness, serious questions have been raised about how the police accomplish their assigned tasks.[84] One basic complaint has been that the average patrol officer spends relatively little time on what is considered real police work. More often than not, highly skilled police officers can be found writing reports, waiting in court corridors, getting involved in domestic disputes, and handling what are generally characterized as miscellaneous noncriminal matters. Police departments are now experimenting with cost-saving reforms that maximize effectiveness while saving taxpayer dollars. For example, J. David Hirschel and Charles Dean describe how a program to summon offenders to court via a field citation is considerably cheaper than a formal arrest. Factoring in the cost of rearresting offenders who fail to appear in court, a citation program would save about $72 per case. Considering the millions of arrests made each year, the adoption of a citation policy could produce considerable savings, not to mention the positive effects on the overcrowded jail system.[85] Other cost-saving productivity measures include consolidation, informal arrangements, sharing, pooling, contracting, police service districts, use of civilian employees, multiple tasking, special assignment programs, budget supplementation, and differential police responses.[86]

Consolidation One way to increase police efficiency is to consolidate police services. This means combining small departments (usually with under 10 employees) in adjoining areas into a superagency that services the previously fragmented jurisdictions. Consolidation has the benefit of creating departments large enough to use expanded services, such as crime labs, training centers, communications centers, and emergency units, that are not cost-effective in smaller departments. This procedure is controversial, because it demands that existing lines of political and administrative authority be drastically changed.

Informal Arrangements Unwritten cooperative agreements may be made between localities to perform a task collectively that would be mutually beneficial (such as monitoring neighboring radio frequencies so that needed backup can be provided).

Sharing Sharing is the provision or reception of services that aid in the execution of a law enforcement function (such as the sharing of a communications system by several local agencies). Some agencies form mutual aid pacts so that they can share infrequently used emergency services such as SWAT (Special Weapons and Tactics) and Emergency Response Teams.[87] Some states have gone as far as setting up centralized data services that connect most local police agencies into a statewide information net.[88]

Pooling Some police agencies combine resources by two or more agencies to perform a specified function under a predetermined, often formalized arrangement with direct involvement by all parties. An example is the use of a city–county law enforcement building or training academy or the establishment of a crime task force. An example of a pooling arrangement is discussed in the Analyzing Criminal Justice Issues feature on page 202.

Contracting Another productivity measure is a limited and voluntary approach in which one government enters into a formal binding agreement to provide all or certain specified law enforcement services (such as communications or patrol service) to another government for an established fee. Many communities that contract for full law enforcement service do so at the time they incorporate to avoid the costs of establishing their own police capability. For example, five small towns in Florida (Pembroke Park, Lauderdale Lakes, Tamarac, Dania, and Deerfield Beach) contract with the Broward County Sheriff's Department to provide law enforcement for their communities. Contracting saves each town millions of dollars.[89]

Service Districts Some jurisdictions have set aside areas, usually within an individual county, where a special level of service is provided and financed through a special tax or assessment. In California, residents of an unincorporated portion of a county may petition to form such a district to provide more intensive patrol coverage than is available through existing systems. Such service may be provided by a sheriff, another police department, or a private person or agency. This system is used in Contra Costa and San Mateo counties in California and Suffolk and Nassau counties in New York.

Civilian Employees One common cost-saving method is to use civilians in administrative support or even in some line activities. Civilians' duties have included operating communications gear; performing clerical work, planning, and doing research; and staffing traffic control (meter monitors). Using civilian employees can be a considerable savings to taxpayers, because their salaries are considerably lower than those of regular police officers. In addition, trained, experienced officers are then allowed to spend more time on direct crime control and enforcement activities.

Multiple Tasking Some police officers are trained to carry out other functions of municipal government. For example, in a number of smaller departments, the roles of firefighters and police officers have been merged into a job called a public safety officer. The idea is to increase the number of people trained in both areas to have the potential for putting more police at the scene of a crime or more firefighters at

Community Mapping, Planning, and Analysis for Safety Strategies (COMPASS)
analyzing criminal justice issues

Community Mapping, Planning, and Analysis for Safety Strategies (COMPASS) is an initiative that was created to pool resources from different agencies within the community to target public safety issues by implementing tactical interventions using technology. Instead of requiring departments to develop their own mapping and communication program, COMPASS would allow smaller departments to pool their resources to access advanced technology such as using Internet resources and multiagency information resources. For example, COMPASS creates data sharing and also a common site for data analysis.

The program has four main components.

1. A collaborative approach by police agencies as well as the community to develop community safety strategies and to work on necessary initiatives.
2. An all-inclusive data set containing information from various sources such as crime incidents, public safety, school records, social data, and demographic environmental information.
3. Spatial and temporal analysis of the data to observe specific problems and develop programs to target the problems.
4. A partnership with a research firm to analyze data and help in the incorporation of interventions and to study the impact of the interventions.

The program has adopted strategies from previous successful programs including New York's Compstat program and the Boston Gun Project. By referring to earlier intervention strategies, the COMPASS program uses successful tactics in reducing crime through partnerships among agencies along with the community and also by implementing different computer technologies that have been beneficial in other programs.

An important feature of COMPASS it to get the community involved along with police agencies. Together they focus on specific problems that are occurring in the communities and, through sharing data, develop good problem-solving strategies to target the problems. By pooling information, critical data from multiple sites can be kept in a single database, which can be easily accessed by the law enforcement community.

To gain community involvement, crime-mapping data are made available via the Internet. This feature allows community residents to observe the trends and services occurring in their neighborhoods. Crime maps allow residents to visually observe where problems are occurring within their community while the Internet allows for communication to occur more easily between citizens and government agencies. To date three different COMPASS sites have been developed, in Seattle, Washington; Milwaukee, Wisconsin; and East Valley California. These sites were chosen as part of a demonstration project because they vary in their level of experience in incorporating computer technology, collaborating in community partnerships, and establishing a data set from multiple outlets.

Critical Thinking

Are programs such as COMPASS a fad or can they help reduce crime rates? Could the current decline in crime be a result of the use of sophisticated police technology? How could you test the effect of technology?

InfoTrac College Edition Research

Can crime-mapping programs help capture serial killers? To find out, read Spencer Chainey, "Mapping Evil: Spencer Chainey Assesses the Impact of Crime Mapping in the Case of Dr. Harold Shipman," *GEO: Connexion* 1, no. 10 (November 2002): 52–55.

Source: Erin Dalton, "Overview: Community Mapping, Planning, and Analysis for Safety Strategies," *Crime Mapping News* 4 (2002): 1–12; Bill Huxhold and Jochen Albrecht, "Compass Background," University of Maryland, Department of Geography, 2002, pp. 1–3, www.gepg.umd.edu/research/projects/UMD_COMPASS.html.

---

a blaze than was possible when the two tasks were separated. The system provides greater coverage at far less cost.

Special Assignments Some departments train officers for special assignments that are required only occasionally, such as radar operation, as crowd control and security.

Differential Police Response These strategies maximize resources by differentiating among police requests for services in terms of the form the police response takes. Some calls will result in the dispatch of a sworn officer, others in the dispatching of a less highly trained civilian. Calls considered low priority are handled by asking citizens to walk in or to mail in their requests.[90]

In sum, police departments are now implementing a variety of administrative models designed to stretch resources while still providing effective police services.

Summary

- Today's police departments operate in a military-like fashion. Policy generally emanates from the top of the hierarchy.
- Most police officers therefore use a great deal of discretion when making on-the-job decisions.
- The most common law enforcement agencies are local police departments, which carry out patrol and investigative functions, as well as many support activities.
- Many questions have been raised about the effectiveness of police work, and while some research efforts seem to indicate that police are not effective crime fighters, evidence shows that aggressive police work, the threat of formal action, and cooperation between departments can have a measurable impact on crime.
- Recent research indicates that adding police can help reduce crime rates.

- For some crimes, making arrests can help reduce criminal activity.
- To improve effectiveness, police departments have developed new methods of policing that stress community involvement and problem solving.
- Community policing typically involves programs with law enforcement and community involvement.
- Police agencies face many challenges in transforming themselves into community-based problem solvers.
- Police departments contain many subareas including training, communications, personnel, and other administrative systems.
- Police agencies are constantly trying to improve their productivity because of budget demands. They have learned how to share tasks, perform multitasks, and pool resources with other agencies.

Key Terms

time-in-rank system 177
beats 179
order maintenance (peacekeeping) 179
displacement 180
proactive policing 181

vice squads 184
sting operation 185
broken windows model 189
foot patrol 190
community-oriented policing (COP) 190

neighborhood-oriented policing (NOP) 191
problem-oriented policing 192
hot spots of crime 192
Gang Tactical Detail 193
internal affairs 197

Doing Research on the Web

For an up-to-date list of Web links, go to http://cj.wadsworth.com/siegel_intro10e.

Community policing has been one of the most significant innovations in law enforcement in the past few decades. Numerous sources are available on InfoTrac College Edition to research the topic of community-oriented policing. First, do a search on the concept of "problem-oriented policing." Then, to find out what COP means to various police departments in terms of strategies, philosophy, and officer skills, check out Michael G. Breci and Timothy E. Erickson, "Community Policing: The Process of Transitional Change," *FBI Law Enforcement Bulletin* 67 (1998): 16.

To check out the effectiveness of citizen participation in community policing, read Eli Lehrer, "Communities and Cops Join Forces," *Insight on the News* 15 (1999): 16. This paper finds that communities in which the residents watch out for one another and take active steps in crime prevention have a crime rate that is 40 percent lower than equivalent communities that do not take such measures.

Finally, to see how community policing strategies can be applied in other milieus, read Stephen Dohery, "How Can Workplace Violence Be Deterred? The Community Policing Model Has Been Successfully Applied to the Problem of Domestic Violence: The Same Model Can Be Used to Address Workplace Violence," *Security Management* 46, no. 4 (April 2002): 134.

The Community Policing Consortium is a partnership of five of the leading police organizations in the United States: International Association of Chiefs of Police, National Organization of Black Law Enforcement Executives, National Sheriffs' Association, Police Executive Research Forum, and Police Foundation. To read about their activities, go to http://www.communitypolicing.org/.

Pro/Con discussions and Viewpoint Essays on some of the topics in this chapter may be found at the Opposing Viewpoints Resource Center: http://www.gale.com/OpposingViewpoints.

Discussion Questions

1. Should the primary police role be law enforcement or community service? Explain.
2. Should a police chief be permitted to promote an officer with special skills to a supervisory position, or should all officers be forced to spend time in rank? Why or why not?
3. Do the advantages of proactive policing outweigh the disadvantages? Explain.
4. Should all police recruits take the same physical tests, or are different requirements permissible for male and female applicants? Explain.
5. Can the police and the community ever form a partnership to fight crime? Why or why not? Does the community policing model remind you of early forms of policing? Explain.

Notes

1 For more on Charles Moose's background, go to the National Law Enforcement Officers Memorial Fund Web site at http://www.nleomf.com/WhatsNew/OfficerofMonth/moose.html. See also Charles Moose and Charles Fleming, *Three Weeks in October: The Manhunt for the Serial Sniper* (New York: E. P. Dutton, 2003).

2 Patrick A. Langan, Lawrence A. Greenfeld, Steven K. Smith, Matthew R. Durose, and David J. Levin, *Contacts between Police and the Public: Findings from the 1999 National Survey* (Washington, D.C.: Bureau of Justice Statistics, 2001).

3 Lawrence A. Greenfeld, Patrick A. Langan, and Steven K. Smith, *Police Use of Force: Collection of National Data* (Washington, D.C.: Bureau of Justice Statistics, 1997).

4 Brian Reaves and Pheny Smith, *Law Enforcement Management and Administrative Statistics, 1993: Data for Individual State and Local Agencies with 100 or More Officers* (Washington, D.C.: Bureau of Justice Statistics, 1995).

5 American Bar Association, *Standards Relating to Urban Police Function* (New York: Institute of Judicial Administration, 1974), Standard 2.2.

6 James Hawdon and John Ryan, "Police–Resident Interactions and Satisfaction with Police: An Empirical Test of Community Policing Assertions," *Criminal Justice Policy Review* 14 (2003): 55–74

7 Albert J. Reiss, *The Police and the Public* (New Haven, Conn.: Yale University Press, 1971), p. 19.

8 James Q. Wilson, V*arieties of Police Behavior: The Management of Law and Order in Eight Communities* (Cambridge, Mass.: Harvard University Press, 1968).

9 See Harlan Hahn, "A Profile of Urban Police," in *The Ambivalent Force*, ed. A. Niederhoffer and A. Blumberg (Hinsdale, Ill.: Dryden Press, 1976), p. 59.

10 George Kelling, Tony Pate, Duane Dieckman, and Charles Brown, *The Kansas City Preventive Patrol Experiment: A Summary Report* (Washington, D.C.: Police Foundation, 1974).

11 Ibid., pp. 3–4.

12 Ibid.

13 Kenneth Novak, Jennifer Hartman, Alexander Holsinger, and Michael Turner, "The Effects of Aggressive Policing of Disorder on Serious Crime," *Policing* 22 (1999): 171–90.

14 David Jacobs and Katherine Woods, "Interracial Conflict and Interracial Homicide: Do Political and Economic Rivalries Explain White Killings of Blacks or Black Killings of Whites?" *American Journal of Sociology* 105 (1999): 157–90.

15 James Q. Wilson and Barbara Boland, "The Effect of Police on Crime," *Law and Society Review* 12 (1978): 367–84.

16 Robert Sampson, "Deterrent Effects of the Police on Crime: A Replication and Theoretical Extension," *Law and Society Review* 22 (1988): 163–91.

17 For a thorough review of this issue, see Andrew Karmen, *Why Is New York City's Murder Rate Dropping So Sharply?* (New York: John Jay College, 1996).

18 Lawrence Sherman, James Shaw, and Dennis Rogan, *The Kansas City Gun Experiment* (Washington, D.C.: National Institute of Justice, 1994).

19 Mitchell Chamlin, "Crime and Arrests: An Autoregressive Integrated Moving Average (ARIMA) Approach," *Journal of Quantitative Criminology* 4 (1988): 247–55.

20 Perry Shapiro and Harold Votey, "Deterrence and Subjective Probabilities of Arrest: Modeling Individual Decisions to Drink and Drive in Sweden," *Law and Society Review* 18 (1984): 111–49.

21 Stewart D'Alessio and Lisa Stolzenberg, "Crime, Arrests, and Pretrial Jail Incarceration: An Examination of the Deterrence Thesis," *Criminology* 36 (1998): 735–61.

22 Thomas Marvell and Carlysle Moody, "Specification Problems, Police Levels, and Crime Rates," *Criminology* 34 (1996): 609–46; Colin Loftin and David McDowall, "The Police, Crime, and Economic Theory: An Assessment," *American Sociological Review* 47 (1982): 393–401.

23 Craig Uchida and Robert Goldberg, *Police Employment and Expenditure Trends* (Washington, D.C.: Bureau of Justice Statistics, 1986).

24 Tomislav V. Kovandzic and John J. Sloan, "Police Levels and Crime Rates Revisited: A County-Level Analysis from Florida (1980–1998)," *Journal of Criminal Justice* 30 (2002): 65–75; Tomislav V. Kovandzic and John J. Sloan, "Police Levels and Crime Rates Revisited: A County-Level Analysis from Florida (1980–1998)," *Journal of Criminal Justice* 30 (2002): 65–76; Steven Levitt, "Using Electoral Cycles in Police Hiring to Estimate the Effect of Police on Crime," *American Economic Review* 87 (1997): 270–91.

25 Joan Petersilia, Allan Abrahamse, and James Q. Wilson, "A Summary of RAND's Research on Police Performance, Community Characteristics, and Case Attrition," *Journal of Police Science and Administration* 17 (1990): 219–29.

26 See Belton Cobb, *The First Detectives* (London: Faber and Faber, 1957).

27 See, for example, James Q. Wilson, "Movie Cops — Romantic vs. Real," *New York Magazine,* August 19, 1968, pp. 38–41.

28 For a view of the modern detective, see William Sanders, *Detective Work: A Study of Criminal Investigations* (New York: Free Press, 1977).

29 Janice Puckett and Richard Lundman, "Factors Affecting Homicide Clearances: Multivariate Analysis of a More Complete Conceptual Framework," *Journal of Research in Crime and Delinquency* 40 (2003): 171–94.

30 Robert Langworthy, "Do Stings Control Crime? An Evaluation of a Police Fencing Operation," *Justice Quarterly* 6 (1989): 27–45.

31 Mark Porgebin and Eric Poole, "Vice Isn't Nice: A Look at the Effects of Working Undercover," *Journal of Criminal Justice* 21 (1993): 385–96; Gary Marx, *Undercover: Police Surveillance in America* (Berkeley: University of California Press, 1988).

32 Peter Greenwood and Joan Petersilia, *The Criminal Investigation Process: Summary and Policy Implications,* ed. Peter Greenwood and others (Santa Monica, Calif.: RAND Corporation, 1975).

33 Mark Willman and John Snortum, "Detective Work: The Criminal Investigation Process in a Medium-Size Police Department," *Criminal Justice Review* 9 (1984): 33–39.

34 Police Executive Research Forum, *Calling the Police: Citizen Reporting of Serious Crime* (Washington, D.C.: Police Executive Research Forum, 1981).

35 John Eck, *Solving Crimes: The Investigation of Burglary and Robbery* (Washington, D.C.: Police Executive Research Forum, 1984).

36 A. Fischer, "Coplink Nabs Criminals Faster," *Arizona Daily Star,* January 7, 2001, p. 1; Alexandra Robbins, "A. I. Cop on the Beat," *PC Magazine,* 22 (2002); M. Sink, "An Electronic Cop That Plays Hunches," *New York Times,* November 2, 2002, p. B1.

37 George Kelling and James Q. Wilson, "Broken Windows: The Police and Neighborhood Safety," *Atlantic Monthly* 249 (March 1982): 29–38.

38 Ibid.

39 For a general review, see Robert Trojanowicz and Bonnie Bucqueroux, *Community Policing: A Contemporary Perspective* (Cincinnati, Ohio: Anderson, 1990).

40 Police Foundation, *The Newark Foot Patrol Experiment* (Washington, D.C.: Police Foundation, 1981).

41 John Worrall and Jihong Zhao, "The Role of the COPS Office in Community Policing," *Policing: An International Journal of Police Strategies and Management* 26 (2003): 64–87.

42 Jihong Zhao, Nicholas Lovrich, and Quint Thurman, "The Status of Community Policing American Cities," *Policing* 22 (1999): 74–92.

43 Albert Cardarelli, Jack McDevitt, and Katrina Baum, "The Rhetoric and Reality of Community Policing in Small and Medium-Sized Cities and Towns," *Policing* 21 (1998): 397–415.

44 Quint Thurman, Andrew Giacomazzi, and Phil Bogen, "Research Note: Cops, Kids, and Community Policing — An Assessment of a Community Policing Demonstration Project," *Crime and Delinquency* 39 (1993): 554–64.

45 Quint Thurman and Phil Bogen, "Research Note: Spokane Community Policing Officers Revisited," *American Journal of Police* 15 (1996): 97–114.

46 Susan Sadd and Randolph Grinc, *Implementation Challenges in Community Policing* (Washington, D.C.: National Institute of Justice, 1996).

47 Donald Green, Dara Strolovitch, and Janelle Wong, "Defended Neighborhoods, Integration, and Racially Motivated Crime," *American Journal of Sociology* 104 (1998): 372–403.

48 Walter Baranyk, "Making a Difference in a Public Housing Project," *Police Chief* 61 (1994): 31–35.

49 Ibid., p. 17.

50 Herman Goldstein, "Improving Policing: A Problem-Oriented Approach," *Crime and Delinquency* 25 (1979): 236–58.

51 Jerome Skolnick and David Bayley, *Community Policing: Issues and Practices around the World* (Washington, D.C.: National Institute of Justice, 1988), p. 12.

52 Lawrence Sherman, Patrick Gartin, and Michael Buerger, "Hot Spots of Predatory Crime: Routine Activities and the Criminology of Place," *Criminology* 27 (1989): 27–55.

53 Ibid., p. 45.

54 Dennis Roncek and Pamela Maier, "Bars, Blocks, and Crimes Revisited: Linking the Theory of Routine Activities to the Empiricism of 'Hot Spots,'" *Criminology* 29 (1991): 725–53.

55 C. Jewett, "Police Use Bait Cars to Reduce Theft," *Knight Ridder/Tribune Buisness News,* March 3, 2003, p. 1.

56 Michael White, James Fyfe, Suzanne Campbell, and John Goldkamp, "The Police Role in Preventing Homicide: Considering the Impact of Problem-Oriented Policing on the Prevalence of Murder," *Journal of Research in Crime and Delinquency* 40 (2003): 194–226.

57 Tucson Police Department, Gang Tactical Detail, http://www.ci.tucson.az.us/police/Organization/Investigative_Services_/Violent_Crimes_Section/Gang_Tactical_Detail/gang_tactical_detail.html, accessed on July 18, 2003.

58 Anthony Braga, David Kennedy; Elin Waring, and Anne Morrison Piehl, "Problem-Oriented Policing, Deterrence, and Youth Violence: An Evaluation of Boston's Operation Ceasefire," *Journal of Research in Crime and Delinquency* 38 (2001): 195–225.

59 Anthony Braga, David Weisburd, Elin Waring, Lorraine Green Mazerolle, William Spelman, and Francis Gajewski, "Problem-Oriented Policing in Violent Crime Places: A Randomized Controlled Experiment," *Criminology* 37 (1999): 541–80.

60 Eric Fritsch, Tory Caeti, and Robert Taylor, "Gang Suppression through Saturation Patrol, Aggressive Curfew, and Truancy Enforcement: A Quasi-Experimental Test of the Dallas Anti-Gang Initiative," *Crime and Delinquency* 45 (1999): 122–39.

61 Bureau of Justice Assistance, *Problem-Oriented Drug Enforcement: A Community-Based Approach for Effective Policing* (Washington, D.C.: National Institute of Justice, 1993).

62 Ibid., pp. 64–65.

63 Jack R. Greene, "The Effects of Community Policing on American Law Enforcement: A Look at the Evidence," paper presented at the International Congress on Criminology, Hamburg, Germany, September 1988, p. 19.

64 Roger Dunham and Geoffrey Alpert, "Neighborhood Differences in Attitudes toward Policing: Evidence for a Mixed-Strategy Model of Policing in a Multi-Ethnic Setting," *Journal of Criminal Law and Criminology* 79 (1988): 504–522.

65 Mark E. Correia, "The Conceptual Ambiguity of Community in Community Policing — Filtering the Muddy Waters," *Policing: An International Journal of Police Strategies and Management* 23 (2000): 218–233.

66 Robin Shepard Engel, *How Police Supervisory Styles Influence Patrol Officer Behavior* (Washington, D.C.: National Institute of Justice, 2003).

67 Scott Lewis, Helen Rosenberg, and Robert Sigler, "Acceptance of Community Policing among Police Officers and Police Administrators," *Policing: An International Journal of Police Strategies and Management* 22 (1999): 567–88.

68 Amy Halsted, Max Bromley, and John Cochran, "The Effects of Work Orientations on Job Satisfaction among Sheriffs' Deputies Practicing Community-Oriented Policing," *Policing: An International Journal of Police Strategies and Management* 23 (2000): 82–104.

69 Kevin Ford, Daniel Weissbein, and Kevin Plamondon, "Distinguishing Organizational from Strategy Commitment: Linking Officers' Commitment to Community Policing to Job Behaviors and Satisfaction," *Justice Quarterly* 20 (2003): 159–86.

70 Michael Palmiotto, Michael Birzer, and N. Prabha Unnithan, "Training in Community Policing: A Suggested Curriculum," *Policing: An International Journal of Police Strategies and Management* 23 (2000): 8–21.

71 Lisa Riechers and Roy Roberg, "Community Policing: A Critical Review of Underlying Assumptions," *Journal of Police Science and Administration* 17 (1990): 105–14.

72 John Riley, "Community Policing: Utilizing the Knowledge of Organizational Personnel," *Policing: An International Journal of Police Strategies and Management* 22 (1999): 618–33.

73 David Kessler, "Integrating Calls for Service with Community- and Problem-Oriented Policing: A Case Study," *Crime and Delinquency* 39 (1993): 485–508.

74 L. Thomas Winfree, Gregory Bartku, and George Seibel, "Support for Community Policing versus Traditional Policing among Nonmetropolitan Police Officers: A Survey of Four New Mexico Police Departments," *American Journal of Police* 15 (1996): 23–47.

75 Jihong Zhao, Ni He, and Nicholas Lovrich, "Value Change among Police Officers at a Time of Organizational Reform: A Follow-up Study of Rokeach Values," *Policing* 22 (1999): 152–70.

76 Jihong Zhao and Quint Thurman, "Community Policing: Where Are We Now?" *Crime and Delinquency* 43 (1997): 345–57.

77 Jihong Zhao, Nicholas Lovrich, and T. Hank Robinson, "Community Policing: Is It Changing the Basic Functions of Policing? Findings from a Longitudinal Study of 200+ Municipal Police Agencies," *Journal of Criminal Justice* 29 (2001): 365–77

78 Ralph B. Taylor, *Breaking Away from Broken Windows: Baltimore Neighborhoods and the Nationwide Fight against Crime, Grime, Fear, and Decline* (Boulder, Colo.: Westview Press, 2000).

79 William Doerner and Terry Nowell, "The Reliability of the Behavioral-Personnel Assessment Device (B-PAD) in Selecting Police Recruits," *Policing* 22 (1999): 343–52.

80 See, for example, Richard Larson, *Urban Police Patrol Analysis* (Cambridge, Mass.: MIT Press, 1972).

81 Brian Reaves, *State and Local Police Departments, 1990* (Washington, D.C.: Bureau of Justice Statistics, 1992), p. 6.

82 Philip Ash, Karen Slora, and Cynthia Britton, "Police Agency Officer Selection Practices," *Journal of Police Science and Administration* 17 (1990): 258–69.

83 Dennis Rosenbaum, Robert Flewelling, Susan Bailey, Chris Ringwalt, and Deanna Wilkinson, "Cops in the Classroom: A Longitudinal Evaluation of Drug Abuse Resistance Education (DARE)," *Journal of Research in Crime and Delinquency* 31 (1994): 3–31.

84 Peter Greenwood, Jan Chaiken, Joan Petersilia, and others, *The Criminal Investigation Process: Observations and Analysis,* ed. Peter Greenwood and others (Santa Monica, Calif.: RANDCorporation, 1975).

85 J. David Hirschel and Charles Dean, "The Relative Cost-Effectiveness of Citation and Arrest," *Journal of Criminal Justice* 23 (1995): 1–12.

86 Adapted from Terry Koepsell and Charles Gerard, *Small Police Agency Consolidation: Suggested Approaches* (Washington, D.C.: Government Printing Office, 1979).

87 Mike D'Alessandro and Charles Hoffman, "Mutual Aid Pacts," *Law and Order* 43 (1995): 90–93.

88 Leonard Sipes Jr., "Maryland's High-Tech Approach to Crime Fighting," *Police Chief* 61 (1994): 18–20.

89 Nick Navarro, "Six Broward County Cities Turn to the Green and Gold," *Police Chief* 59 (1992): 60.

90 Robert Worden, "Toward Equity and Efficiency in Law Enforcement: Differential Police Response," *American Journal of Police* 12 (1993): 1–24.

Chapter Objectives

After reading this chapter, you should be able to:

1. Explain the concept of a police culture.
2. Know the reasons that experts believe police have a unique personality.
3. Recognize the different types of police officer style.
4. Understand how police use discretion.
5. Discuss the issue of racial profiling.
6. Describe how the role of women in local police agencies has evolved over time.
7. Discuss some of the problems of minority police officers.
8. Know what is meant by police stress.
9. Identify the different methods used to control the police use of force.
10. Explain the concept of police corruption.

Viewpoints

Race, Gender, and Ethnicity in Criminal Justice: Racial Profiling: Does Race Influence the Police Use of Discretion? 216

Analyzing Criminal Justice Issues: Working with Problem Cops: Early Intervention Programs 227

Criminal Justice and Technology: Less Than Lethal Weapons 233

Web Links

Police Foundation
http://www.policefoundation.org/ 208

Police discretion and controlling behavior that violates community standards
http://www.ncjrs.org/pdffiles1/nij/178259.pdf 212

Police attitudes toward abuse of authority
http://www.ncjrs.org/pdffiles1/nij/181312.pdf 236

InfoTrac College Edition Links

Article: "Behind the Window Dressing: Ethnic Minority Police Perspectives on Cultural Diversity" 208

Article: "Changing Police Culture" 209

Article: "Education and Training Requirements for Big-City Police Officers Increases, Starting Salaries Remain Flat" 218

Article: "Police Officers' Judgments of Blame in Family Violence: The Impact of Gender and Alcohol" 222

Key Term: "police shootings" 230

Chapter 7 | Issues in Policing

On July 6, 2002, Donovan Jackson, a 16-year-old African American youth, was slammed onto the trunk of a patrol car and punched by Jeremy Morse, an Inglewood, California, patrol officer, while being arrested at a service station. The incident was caught on videotape. Morse subsequently was charged with five counts of assault and his partner, Bijan Darvish, with filing a false police report. The report failed to mention Jackson being slammed into the car and instead said he was being "assisted to his feet" during the arrest.

Though race was never mentioned during the trial, the image of a white officer beating a black youth made national headlines and sparked angry charges of racism in Inglewood. After a lengthy trial, Darvish was acquitted, and the jury was deadlocked 7–5 in favor of convicting Morse. Though many people feared that civil unrest would follow an acquittal, as it did in Los Angeles after the first Rodney King trial, the city remained calm after the verdict was announced on July 29, 2003.[1] The Inglewood case was another in a series of incidents involving videotaped police violence of which the King case is the one best remembered.

CNN. *View the CNN video clip of this story on your Introduction to Criminal Justice 10e CD.*

Incidents such as the Jackson case highlight the critical and controversial role police play in the justice system and the need for developing a professional, competent police force. The police are the gatekeepers of the criminal justice process. They initiate contact with law violators and decide whether to formally arrest them and start their journey through the criminal justice system, settle the issue in an informal way (such as by issuing a warning), or simply take no action at all. The strategic position of law enforcement officers, their visibility and contact with the public, and their use of weapons and arrest power have kept them in the forefront of public thought about law enforcement.

For the past three decades, much public interest has focused on the function of the police. The U.S. public seems genuinely concerned today about the quality and effectiveness of local police. Most citizens seem to approve of their local law enforcement agents. About 60 percent say they have a "great deal of confidence" in the police.[2] While this is encouraging, approval is often skewed along racial lines.[3] It may not be surprising that minority citizens report having less confidence in the police compared with Caucasians and are less likely to report crime to police agencies.[4] To combat these perceptions, police departments have gone to great lengths to improve relationships with the minority community, and efforts may have begun to pay off. Surveys show improvement in the African American community's view of the local police. Some evidence suggests that minority groups value police services, welcome the presence of both white and African American police officers, and are generally supportive of the local police.[5]

The general public is not the only group concerned about police attitudes and behavior. Police administrators and other law enforcement experts have focused their attention on issues that may influence the effectiveness and efficiency of police performance in the field. Some of their concerns are outgrowths of the development of policing as a profession: Does an independent police culture exist, and what are its characteristics? Do police officers develop a unique working personality, and if so, does it influence their job performance? Are there police officer styles that make some police officers too aggressive and others inert and passive? Is policing too stressful an occupation?

Another area of concern is the social composition of police departments: Who should be recruited as police officers? Are minorities and women being attracted to police work, and what have their experiences been on the force? Should police officers have a college education?

Important questions are also being raised about the problems police departments face interacting with the society they are entrusted with supervising: Are police officers too forceful and brutal, and do they discriminate in their use of deadly force? Are police officers corrupt, and how can police deviance be controlled?

The Police Profession

All professions have unique characteristics that distinguish them from other occupations and institutions. Policing is no exception. Police experts have long sought to understand the unique nature of the police experience and to determine how the challenges of police work shape the field and its employees.

Police Culture

Police experts have found that the experience of becoming a police officer and the nature of the job itself cause most officers to band together in a police subculture, characterized by cynicism, clannishness, secrecy, and insulation from others in society — the so-called **blue curtain.** Police officers tend to socialize together and believe that their occupation cuts them off from relationships with civilians. Police officers perceive their working environment to be laden with

---

How does the general public view the police in England? Are perceptions different from those in the United States and are they influenced by race? Read the findings from a study on InfoTrac College Edition to find out: Ellis Cashmore, "Behind the Window Dressing: Ethnic Minority Police Perspectives on Cultural Diversity," Journal of Ethnic and Migration Studies 28, no. 2 (April 2002): 327.

The Police Foundation is a nonprofit organization dedicated to conducting research on law enforcement. To check out its activities and publications, go to the Web site at http://www.policefoundation.org/.

blue curtain
The secretive, insulated police culture that isolates officers from the rest of society.

Some experts believe there is a police subculture, referred to as the *blue curtain,* characterized by cynicism, clannishness, secrecy, and insulation from others in society. Members of the police subculture stick up for fellow officers against outsiders and distrust outsiders' motives and behavior.

danger or the risk of danger, and they become preoccupied with the danger and violence that surrounds them, always anticipating both.[6] Perceptions of danger have a unifying effect on officers and work to separate them from the chief source of danger — the public — and help create the boundaries of a police subculture. Joining the police subculture means always having to stick up for fellow officers against outsiders, maintaining a tough, macho exterior personality, and distrusting the motives and behavior of outsiders.[7] Six core beliefs are viewed as being the heart of the police culture.

1. Police are the only real crime fighters. The public wants the police officer to fight crime; other agencies, both public and private, only play at crime fighting.
2. No one else understands the real nature of police work. Lawyers, academics, politicians, and the public in general have little concept of what it means to be a police officer.
3. Loyalty to colleagues counts above everything else. Police officers have to stick together because everyone is out to get the police and make the job more difficult.
4. The war against crime cannot be won without bending the rules. Courts have awarded criminal defendants too many civil rights.
5. Members of the public are basically unsupportive and unreasonably demanding. People are quick to criticize police unless they need police help themselves.
6. Patrol work is the pits. Detective work is glamorous and exciting.[8]

The forces that support a police culture generally are believed to develop out of on-the-job experiences. Most officers originally join the police force because they want to help people, fight crime, and have an interesting, exciting, prestigious career with a high degree of job security.[9] Recruits often find that the social reality of police work does not mesh with their original career goals. They are unprepared for the emotional turmoil and conflict that accompany police work today.

Membership in the police culture helps recruits adjust to the rigors of police work and provides the emotional support needed for survival.[10] The culture encourages decisiveness in the face of uncertainty and the ability to make split-second judgments that may later be subject to extreme criticism. Officers who view themselves as crime fighters are the ones most likely to value solidarity and depend on the support and camaraderie of their fellow officers.[11] The police subculture

Is there a police culture in other nations? To find out, read Janet Chan, "Changing Police Culture," *British Journal of Criminology* 36, no. 1 (Winter 1996): 109–34, on InfoTrac College Edition.

encourages its members to draw a sharp distinction between good and evil. Officers, more than mere enforcers of the law, are warriors in the age-old battle between right and wrong.[12] In contrast, criminals are referred to as "terrorists" and "predators," terms that convey the fact that they are evil individuals ready to prey upon the poor and vulnerable. Because the predators represent a real danger, the police culture demands that its members be both competent and concerned with the safety of their peers and partners. Competence is often translated into respect and authority, and citizens must obey lest they face payback.[13]

In sum, the police culture has developed in response to the insulated, dangerous lifestyle of police officers. Policing is a dangerous occupation, and the availability of unquestioned support and loyalty of their peers is not something officers could readily do without.[14]

Police Personality

cynicism
The belief that most people's actions are motivated solely by personal needs and selfishness.

Along with an independent police culture, some experts believe that police officers develop a unique set of personality traits that distinguish them from the average citizen.[15] To some commentators, the typical police personality can be described as dogmatic, authoritarian, and suspicious.[16] **Cynicism** has been found on all levels of policing, including chiefs of police, and throughout all stages of a police career.[17] Maintenance of these negative values and attitudes is believed to cause police officers to be secretive and isolated from the rest of society, producing the blue curtain.[18]

The police officer's working personality is shaped by constant exposure to danger and the need to use force and authority to reduce and control threatening situations.[19] Police feel suspicious of the public they serve and defensive about the actions of their fellow officers. There are two opposing viewpoints on the cause of this phenomenon. One position holds that police departments attract recruits who are by nature cynical, authoritarian, secretive, and so on.[20] Other experts maintain that socialization and experience on the police force itself cause these character traits to develop in police officers.

Since the first research measuring police personality was published, numerous efforts have been made to determine whether the typical police recruit possesses a unique personality that sets her apart from the average citizen. The results have been mixed.[21] While some research concludes that police values are different from those of the general adult population, other efforts reach an opposing conclusion. Some have found that police officers are more psychologically healthy than the general population, less depressed and anxious, and more social and assertive.[22] Still other research on police personality found that police officers highly value such personality traits as warmth, flexibility, and emotion. These traits are far removed from rigidity and cynicism.[23] Given that research has found evidence supportive of both viewpoints, no one position dominates on the issue of how the police personality develops, or even if one exists.

In his classic study of police personality, *Behind the Shield* (1967), Arthur Niederhoffer examined the assumption that most police officers develop into cynics as a function of their daily duties.[24] Among his most important findings were that police cynicism increased with length of service and that military-like police academy training caused new recruits to quickly become cynical about themselves.[25]

Police Style

Policing encompasses a multitude of diverse tasks, including peacekeeping, criminal investigation, traffic control, and providing emergency medical service. Part of the socialization as a police officer is developing a working attitude, or style, through which he approaches policing. For example, some police officers may view their job as a well-paid civil service position that stresses careful compliance with written departmental rules and procedures. Other officers may see them-

Exhibit 7.1 The Four Basic Styles of Policing

The Crime Fighter. To crime fighters, the most important aspect of police work is investigating serious crimes and apprehending criminals. Their focus is on the victim, and they view effective police work as the only force that can keep society's "dangerous classes" in check. They are the "thin blue line" protecting society from murderers and rapists. They consider property crimes to be less significant, while such matters as misdemeanors, traffic control, and social service functions would be better handled by other agencies of government. The ability to investigate criminal behavior that poses a serious threat to life and safety, combined with the power to arrest criminals, separates a police department from other municipal agencies. They see diluting these functions with minor social service and nonenforcement duties as harmful to police efforts to create a secure society.

The Social Agent. Social agents believe that police should be involved in a wide range of activities without regard for their connection to law enforcement. Instead of viewing themselves as criminal catchers, the social agents consider themselves community problem solvers. They are troubleshooters who patch the holes that appear where the social fabric wears thin. They are happy to work with special-needs populations, such as the homeless, school kids, and those who require emergency services. Social agents fit well within a community policing unit.

The Law Enforcer. According to this view, duty is clearly set out in law, and law enforcers stress playing it "by the book." Because the police are specifically charged with apprehending all types of lawbreakers, they see themselves as generalized law enforcement agents. Although law enforcers may prefer working on serious crimes — which are more intriguing and rewarding in terms of achievement, prestige, and status — they see the police role as one of enforcing all statutes and ordinances. They perceive themselves as neither community social workers nor vengeance-seeking vigilantes. Simply put, they are professional law enforcement officers who perform the functions of detecting violations, identifying culprits, and taking the lawbreakers before a court. Law enforcers are devoted to the profession of police work and are the officers most likely to aspire to command rank.

The Watchman. The watchman style is characterized by an emphasis on the maintenance of public order as the police goal, not on law enforcement or general service. Watchmen choose to ignore many infractions and requests for service unless they believe that the social or political order is jeopardized. Juveniles are expected to misbehave and are best ignored or treated informally. Motorists will often be left alone if their driving does not endanger or annoy others. Vice and gambling are problems only when the currently accepted standards of public order are violated. Like the watchmen of old, these officers only take action when and if a problem arises. Watchmen are the most passive officers, more concerned with retirement benefits than crime rates.

Source: William Muir, *Police: Streetcorner Politicians* (Chicago: University of Chicago Press, 1977); James Q. Wilson, *Varieties of Police Behavior* (Cambridge, Mass.: Harvard University Press, 1968).

selves as part of the "thin blue line" that protects the public from wrongdoers. They will use any means to get the culprit, even if it involves such cheating as planting evidence on an obviously guilty person who so far has escaped arrest. Should the police bend the rules to protect the public? This has been referred to as the "Dirty Harry problem," after the popular Clint Eastwood movie character who routinely (and successfully) violated all known standards of police work.[26]

Several studies have attempted to define and classify **police styles** into behavioral clusters. These classifications, called typologies, attempt to categorize law enforcement agents by groups, each of which has a unique approach to police work. The purpose of such classifications is to demonstrate that the police are not a cohesive, homogeneous group, as many believe, but individuals with differing approaches to their work.[27] The way police take on their task and their attitude toward the police role, as well as their peers and superior officers, have been shown to affect police work.[28]

An examination of the literature suggests that four styles of police work seem to fit the current behavior patterns of most police agents: the crime fighter, the social agent, the law enforcer, and the watchman, which are described in Exhibit 7.1.

police styles
The working personalities adopted by police officers that can range from being a social worker in blue to a hard-charging crime fighter.

Police Personality, Culture, Styles While some police experts have found that a unique police personality and culture do exist, others have challenged that assumption. No clearcut agreement has been reached on the matter. In either event, changes in contemporary police agencies likely will have a significant impact on police culture and personality, if they have not done so already. Police departments have become diverse, attracting women and minorities in growing numbers. Police are becoming more educated and technologically sophisticated. The

To quiz yourself on this material, go to questions 7.1–7.3 on the Introduction to Criminal Justice 10e CD.

vision of a monolithic department whose employees share similar and uniform values, culture, and personality traits seems somewhat naïve in the presence of such diversity.

Furthermore, today's police officer is unlikely to be able to choose to embrace a particular style of policing while excluding others. While some police officers may emphasize one area of law enforcement over another, their daily activities most likely require them to engage in a wide variety of duties. A contemporary police officer probably cannot choose to concentrate on crime fighting and ignore her other duties. Police departments are today seeking public support through community police models and are reorienting the police role toward community outreach.[29]

Police Discretion

discretion
The use of personal decision making and choice in carrying out operations in the criminal justice system.

A critical aspect of a police officer's professional responsibility is the personal discretion each officer has in carrying out his daily activities. **Discretion** can involve the selective enforcement of the law, as when a vice-squad plainclothes officer decides not to take action against a tavern that is serving drinks after hours. Patrol officers use discretion when they decide to arrest one suspect for disorderly conduct but escort another home. Because police have the ability to deprive people of their liberty, arrest them and take them away in handcuffs, and even use deadly force to subdue them, their use of discretion is a vital concern.

low-visibility decision making
Decision making by police officers that is not subject to administrative review; for example, when a decision is made not to arrest someone or not to stop a speeding vehicle.

The majority of police officers use a high degree of personal discretion in carrying out daily tasks, sometimes referred to as **low-visibility decision making** in criminal justice.[30] This terminology suggests that, unlike members of almost every other criminal justice agency, police are neither regulated in their daily procedures by administrative scrutiny nor subject to judicial review (except when their behavior clearly violates an offender's constitutional rights). As a result, the exercise of discretion by police may sometimes deteriorate into discrimination, violence, and other abusive practices. A number of factors influence police discretion.

WWW How do police use their discretion and what can be done to control behaviors that violate community standards? The answer to this question may be found in a 1999 publication of the National Institute of Justice entitled *"Broken Windows" and Police Discretion* by criminologist George Kelling. Check http://www.ncjrs.org/pdffiles1/nij/178259.pdf.

Legal Factors

Police discretion is inversely related to the severity of the offense. Far less personal discretion is available when police confront a suspect in a case involving murder or rape than a simple assault or trespass. The likelihood of a police officer taking legal action then may depend on how the individual officer views offense severity. For example, some police officers may treat all drug-related crimes as serious and deserving of formal action, while other officers, less concerned about the drug problem, may confiscate illegal substances and let the perpetrator off with a warning.

Victim Factors

The relationship between the parties involved influences decision making and discretion. An altercation between two friends or relatives may be handled differently than an assault on a stranger. A case in point is policing domestic violence cases. Research indicates that police are reluctant to even respond to these kinds of cases because they are a constant source of frustration and futility.[31] Evidence shows that police intentionally delay responding to domestic disputes, hoping that by the time they get there the problem will be settled.[32] Victims, they believe, often fail to get help or change their abusive situation.[33] Even when they are summoned, police are likely to treat domestic violence cases more casually than other assault cases. If, however, domestic abuse involves extreme violence, especially if a weapon is brandished or used, police are much more likely to respond with a formal arrest.[34] Police, therefore, use their discretion to separate what they consider nuisance cases from those serious enough to demand police action.

Environmental Factors

The degree of discretion an officer will exercise is at least partially defined by the living and working environment.[35] Police officers may work or dwell within a community culture that either tolerates eccentricities and personal freedoms or expects extremely conservative, professional, no-nonsense behavior on the part of its civil servants. Communities that are proactive and contain progressive governmental institutions also may influence the direction of a police officer's discretion. For example, police in communities that provide training in domestic violence prevention and maintain local shelters are more likely to take action in cases involving spousal abuse.[36]

An officer who lives in the community she serves is probably strongly influenced by and shares a large part of the community's beliefs and values and is likely to be sensitive to and respect the wishes of neighbors, friends, and relatives. Conflict may arise, however, when the police officer commutes to an assigned area of jurisdiction, as is often the case in inner-city precincts. The officer who holds personal values in opposition to those of the community can exercise discretion in ways that conflict with the community's values and result in ineffective law enforcement.[37]

A police officer's perception of community alternatives to police intervention may also influence discretion. A police officer may exercise discretion to arrest an individual in a particular circumstance if it seems that nothing else can be done, even if the officer does not believe that an arrest is the best possible example of good police work. In an environment that has a proliferation of social agencies — detoxification units, drug control centers, and child care services, for example — a police officer will have more alternatives to choose from in deciding whether to make an arrest. Referring cases to these alternative agencies saves the officer both time and effort, as records do not have to be made out and court appearances can be avoided. Thus, social agencies provide greater latitude in police decision making.

Departmental Factors

The policies, practices, and customs of the local police department are another influence on discretion. These conditions vary from department to department and strongly depend on the judgment of the chief and others in the organizational hierarchy. For example, departments can issue directives aimed at influencing police conduct. Patrol officers may be asked to issue more traffic tickets and make more arrests, refrain from arresting under certain circumstances, or limit their hot pursuits to avoid accidents. Occasionally, a directive will instruct officers to be particularly alert for certain types of violations or to make some sort of interagency referral when specific events occur. For example, the department may order patrol officers to crack down on street panhandlers or to take formal action in domestic violence cases.[38] Most experts believe that written rules, either directing or prohibiting action, can be highly effective at controlling police discretion and a valuable administrative tool.[39] Many departments now rely on written rules to control discretion in violent confrontations. More than 90 percent have strict rules governing such activities as controlling domestic abuse and when to use lethal force.

Supervisory Factors

Along with departmental policy, a patrol officers supervisor can influence discretion. The ratio of supervisory personnel to subordinates may also influence discretion. Departments with a high ratio of sergeants to patrol officers may experience fewer officer-initiated actions than one in which fewer eyes are observing the action in the streets. Supervisory style also may have an influence on how police use discretion. For example, Robin Shepard Engel found that patrol officers supervised by sergeants who are take-charge types and like to participate in high levels of activity in the field themselves spend significantly more time per shift engaging in self-initiated and community policing or problem-solving activities than they do in administrative activities. In contrast, officers with supervisors whose style involves spending time mentoring and coaching subordinates are more likely to devote significantly more attention to engaging in administrative tasks.[40] The size of the department may also determine the level of officer discretion. In larger departments, looser control by supervisors seems to encourage a level of discretion unknown in smaller, more tightly run police agencies.

Peer Factors

Police discretion is also subject to peer pressure.[41] Police officers suffer a degree of social isolation because the job involves strange working conditions and hours, including being on 24-hour call, and their authority and responsibility to enforce the law may cause embarrassment during social encounters. At the same time, officers must handle irregular and emotionally demanding encounters involving the most personal and private aspects of people's lives. As a result, police officers turn to their peers for both on-the-job advice and off-the-job companionship, essentially forming a subculture to provide a source of status, prestige, and reward.

The peer group affects how police officers exercise discretion on two distinct levels. First, in an obvious, direct manner, other police officers dictate acceptable responses to street-level problems by displaying or withholding approval in office discussions. Second, the officer who takes the job seriously and desires the respect and friendship of others will take their advice, abide by their norms, and seek out the most experienced and most influential patrol officers on the force and follow their behavior models.

Situational Factors

The situational factors attached to a particular crime provide another extremely important influence on police actions and behavior. Regardless of departmental or community influences, the officer's immediate interaction with a criminal act, offender, citizen, or victim will weigh heavily on the use of discretionary powers. Some early research efforts found that a police officer relies heavily on **demeanor** (the attitude and appearance of the offender) in making decisions. If an offender is surly, talks back, or otherwise challenges the officer's authority, formal action is more likely to be taken.[42] According to this view, a negative demeanor will result in formal police action.[43]

In a series of research studies, David Klinger challenged the long-held belief that bad demeanor has a significant influence on police decision making. Klinger, a police officer turned criminologist, suggests that it is criminal behavior and actions (touching, hitting, or grappling with an officer) that occur during police detention and not negative attitudes that influence the police decision to take formal action. Police officers are unimpressed by a bad attitude; they have seen it all before.[44] Research in support of Klinger's views indicate that suspects who offer physical resistance were much more likely to receive some form of physical coercion in return, but those who offer verbal disrespect are not likely to be physically coerced.[45] Po-

demeanor
The way in which a person outwardly manifests his or her personality.

lice officers' response to a suspect's challenge to their authority is dependent then on the way the challenge is delivered. Verbal challenges are met with verbal responses; physical with physical.[46]

Another set of situational influences on police discretion concerns the manner in which a crime or situation is encountered. If, for example, a police officer stumbles on an altercation or break-in, the discretionary response may be different from a situation in which the officer is summoned by police radio. If an act has received official police recognition, such as the dispatch of a patrol car, police action must be taken, or an explanation made as to why it was not. Or if a matter is brought to an officer's attention by a citizen observer, the officer can ignore the request and risk a complaint or take discretionary action. When an officer chooses to become involved in a situation, without benefit of a summons or complaint, maximum discretion can be used. Even in this circumstance, however, the presence of a crowd or of witnesses may influence the officer's decision making.

And, the officer who acts alone is also affected by personal matters — physical condition, mental state, police style, and whether she has other duties to perform. Other factors that might influence police are the use of a weapon, seriousness of injury, and the presence of alcohol or drugs.

© 2003 AP/Wide World Photos

Donovan Jackson sits at the witness stand in a Los Angeles courtroom as the videotape of his arrest and beating plays on a laptop computer. Incidents such as the Jackson case give the impression that race plays a significant role in shaping police discretion.

Extralegal Factors

On October 4, 2000, federal investigators looking into the activities of the Street Crime Unit of the New York Police Department (NYPD) issued a report claiming that its officers, as they conducted an aggressive campaign of street searches, had been singling out African American and Hispanic citizens, a practice known as *racial profiling*.[47] The elite undercover unit had come under official scrutiny in the aftermath of the highly publicized 1999 shooting death of Amadou Diallo, an unarmed black man. Not taking the accusations lightly, Mayor Rudolph Giuliani charged that if police were forced to stop and search people based on their representation in the city's population, then about 17 percent of those detained must be senior citizens. He argued that, although the federal report said that about 85 percent of the people searched by police were African American or Hispanic, in truth about 89 percent of the criminal suspects in New York City were identified by victims as being African American or Hispanic.[48] Were members of the Street Crime Unit behaving in a racist fashion, or did their behavior merely reflect the sad realities of urban life in which the poor and minority group members are disproportionately involved in criminal behavior?

One often-debated issue is whether police take race, class, and gender into account when making arrest decisions. For example, research shows that police are less likely to make arrests in cases of elder mistreatment than in other assaults; the age of the victim influences their decision making.[49] The question then is whether police discretion is shaped by such extralegal factors as age, gender, income, and race. Because this issue is so important, it is the topic of the Race, Gender, and Ethnicity in Criminal Justice feature on page 216.

Police discretion is one of the most often debated issues in criminal justice (see Concept Summary 7.1 on page 218). On its face, the unequal enforcement of the law

Racial Profiling: Does Race Influence the Police Use of Discretion?

race, gender, and ethnicity in criminal justice

Should and do police use race as a factor when making decisions such as stopping and questioning a suspect or deciding to make an arrest, a practice referred to as racial profiling? The issue is complex. While some commentators believe that considering race in police decision making is racial discrimination per se, others demur, finding that consideration of a suspect's race or ethnic group may be appropriate if members of that group are known to have a much higher crime rate than members of other racial or ethnic groups. Police may stop minority motorists more than white drivers, the argument goes, but rather than being a function of racism, it may be that the police are responding to the fact that Latinos and African Americans are more likely to live in high crime rate areas.

Profiling Remains a Problem

Profiling may be a function of institutional policies and not individual racism. For example, Robert Kane's research shows that as the minority population increases in a neighborhood the number of police officers assigned to that area also increases. These new officers may view their role to be one of aggressive police work. Police who patrol these higher crime rate areas may be more vigilant and suspicious than those assigned to lower crime rate areas and more likely to stop and question minority group members. What appears to be racially motivated stops may be a function of departmental policies and concerns.

Regardless of its cause, members of the minority community believe they are unfairly targeted by the police use of profiling and discrimination. When Ronald Weitzer and Steven Tuch used data from a national survey of 2,000 people, they found that about 40 percent of African American respondents claimed they were stopped by police because of their race as compared with just 5 percent of Caucasians. Almost three quarters of young African American men, age 18–34, said they were the victim of profiling. African Americans who were better educated and wealthier were more likely to indicate being the victim of profiling than their lower-class, less educated peers.

Weitzer and Tuch speculate that more affluent minority group members have greater mobility and therefore are more likely to encounter police suspicious of them because they are "out of place" as they travel to different neighborhoods (p. 451). Recent research (2002) by Albert Meehan and Michael Ponder confirm this hypothesis. They found that police are more likely to use racial profiling to stop black motorists as they travel further into the boundaries of predominantly white neighborhoods.

Is the Tide Turning?

Efforts to control racial profiling and discrimination are now ongoing in most major police departments, and some evidence suggests that these programs and policies are paying off. For example, a

recent national study of police contact by Patrick Langin and his associates found that most drivers, regardless of race, who experienced a traffic stop said that they felt the officer had a legitimate reason for making the stop. Nearly 9 out of 10 white drivers and 3 out of 4 African American drivers described the officer as having had a legitimate reason for the stop. Both African American and Caucasian drivers maintained these perceptions regardless of the race of the officer making the stop. Even though relatively more African Americans than Caucasians felt the police were motivated by race, the survey found that a clear majority of members of both racial groups believe the police acted in a forthright fashion, that they were not the victim of profiling, and the race of the police officer had no influence on their performance.

According to legal experts Dan Kahan and Tracey Meares, racial discrimination may be on the decline because minorities now possess sufficient political status to protect them from abuses within the justice system. And in the event that political influence is insufficient to control profiling, members of the minority community have used the court system to seek legal redress. For example, in a 2003 decision, Cincinnati, Ohio, was forced to establish a $4.5 million settlement fund to compensate 16 people for instances of racial profiling. One plaintiff was held at gunpoint after being stopped for a traffic infraction, and another had been shot in the back while running away, unarmed.

To quiz yourself on this material, go to questions 7.4–7.8 on the Introduction to Criminal Justice 10e CD.

smacks of unfairness and violates the Constitution's doctrines of due process and equal protection. Yet if some discretion were not exercised, police would be forced to function as robots merely following the book. Administrators have sought to control discretion so that its exercise may be both beneficial to citizens and nondiscriminatory.[50]

Who Are the Police?

The composition of the nation's police forces is changing. Traditionally, police agencies were composed of white males with a high school education who viewed policing as a secure position that brought them the respect of family and friends and a step up the social ladder. It was not uncommon to see police families in which one member of

Community policing efforts may also be helping to reduce profiling because community-oriented police are trained to be sensitive to community issues such as profiling. As part of their community policing efforts, some departments have made race relations a top priority.

The aggressive tactics of external groups such as the American Civil Liberties Union acting as racial auditors who amass data on police stop-and-arrest patterns have also helped bring attention to and deter racial profiling. A number of states are conducting widespread data collections on police stopping practices, which should help police officials determine whether there are problem departments and problem officers.

To end racial profiling, according to some experts such as Bela August Walker, police departments should not even use racial identifiers as a crucial part of suspect descriptions. She finds that the use of race as a physical descriptor in suspect identification is both discriminatory and inefficient because more and more Americans are of mixed race heritage. She argues that employing race as an identifying characteristic allows law enforcement officers broad discretionary powers that can be used in a discriminatory manner, while ultimately proving counterproductive to the aims of effective law enforcement. She argues for an alternative solution: a universal complexion chart to replace "black" or "Hispanic" as descriptors.

Critical Thinking

1. What, if anything, can be done to reduce racial bias on the part of police? Would adding minority officers help? Would it be a form of racism to assign minority officers to minority neighborhoods?

2. Would research showing that police are more likely to make arrests in interracial incidents than intraracial incidents constitute evidence of racism?

InfoTrac College Edition Research

Use "racial profiling" as a key word to review articles on the use of race as a determining factor in the police use of discretion.

Sources: Andrew E. Taslit, "Racial Auditors and the Fourth Amendment: Data with the Power to Inspire Political Action," *Law and Contemporary Problems* 66 (2003): 221–99; *In re Cincinnati Policing*, No. C-1-99-3170 (S.D. Ohio, 2003); Bela August Walker, "Color of Crime: The Case," *Columbia Law Review* 103 (2003): 662–69; Robert Kane, "Social Control in the Metropolis: A Community-Level Examination of the Minority Group-Threat Hypothesis," *Justice Quarterly* 20 (2003): 265–96; Matthew Petrocelli, Alex R. Piquero, and Michael R. Smith, "Conflict Theory and Racial Profiling: An Empirical Analysis of Police Traffic Stop Data," *Journal of Criminal Justice* 31 (2003): 1–11; Robin Shepard Engel, Jennifer Calnon, and Thomas Bernard, "Theory and Racial Profiling: Shortcomings and Future Directions in Research," *Justice Quarterly* 19 (2002): 19–45; Albert Meehan and Michael Ponder, "Race and Place: The Ecology of Racial Profiling African American Motorists," *Justice Quarterly* 29 (2002): 399–431; Stephen Mastrofski, Michael Reisig, and John McCluskey, "Police Disrespect toward the Public: An Encounter-Based Analysis,"*Criminology* 40 (2002): 519–32; Ronald Weitzer and Steven Tuch, "Perceptions of Racial Profiling: Race, Class, and Personal Experience," *Criminology* 40 (2002): 435–56; Patrick A. Langan, Lawrence A. Greenfeld, Steven K. Smith, Matthew R. Durose, and David J. Levin, *Contacts between Police and the Public: Findings from the 1999 National Survey* (Washington, D.C.: Bureau of Justice Statistics, 2001); Richard Felson and Jeff Ackerman, "Arrest for Domestic and Other Assaults," *Criminology* 39 (2001): 655–76; Sidney L. Harring, "The Diallo Verdict: Another 'Tragic Accident' in New York's War on Street Crime?" *Social Justice* 27 (2000): 9–14; Robert Worden and Robin Shepard, "Demeanor, Crime, and Police Behavior: A Reexamination of the Police Services Study Data," *Criminology* 34 (1996): 83–105; Stephen Mastrofski, Robert Worden, and Jeffrey Snipes, "Law Enforcement in a Time of Community Policing," *Criminology* 33 (1995): 39–563; Matt De Lisi and Bob Regoli, "Race, Conventional Crime, and Criminal Justice: The Declining Importance of Skin Color," *Journal of Criminal Justice* 27 (1999): 549–57; David Cole, *No Equal Justice: Race and Class in the American Criminal Justice System* (New York: New Press, 2000); Randall Kennedy, *Race, Crime, and the Law* (New York: Vintage Books, 1998); Dan M. Kahan and Tracey L. Meares, "The Coming Crisis of Criminal Procedure," *Georgetown Law Journal* 86 (1998): 1153–84. Ronald Weitzer, "Racial Discrimination in the Criminal Justice System: Findings and Problems in the Literature," *Journal of Criminal Justice* 24 (1996): 309–22; Samuel Walker, Cassia Spohn, and Miriam DeLone, *The Color of Justice, Race, Ethnicity, and Crime in America* (Belmont, Calif.: Wadworth, 1996), p. 115; Sandra Lee Browning, Francis Cullen, Liqun Cao, Renee Kopache, and Thomas Stevenson, "Race and Getting Hassled by the Police: A Research Note," *Police Studies* 17 (1994): 1–10.

each new generation would enter the force. This picture has been changing and will continue to change. As criminal justice programs turn out thousands of graduates every year, an increasing number of police officers have at least some college education. In addition, affirmative action programs have helped slowly change the racial and gender composition of police departments to reflect community makeup.

Police Education

In recent years, many police experts have argued that police recruits should have a college education. This development is not unexpected, considering that higher education for police officers has been recommended by national commissions since 1931.[51]

Concept Summary 7.1 Police Discretion

Factors influencing discretion	Individual influences
Legal factors	Crime seriousness; prior record
Victim factors	Victim–criminal relationship
Environmental factors	Community culture and values
Departmental factors	Policies and orders
Supervision factors	Supervisors style and control
Peer factors	Peer influence and culture
Situational factors	Suspect demeanor
Extralegal factors	Race, gender, age

You can access some data from the national survey of larger police departments on InfoTrac College Edition at *M2 Presswire*. See "Education and Training Requirements for Big-City Police Officers Increase, Starting Salaries Remain Flat," *M2 Presswire*, May 13, 2002.

Figure 7.1
Local Police Officers in Departments with a College Education Requirement for New Recruits, 1990 and 2000

aNondegree requirements only.

Source: Matthew Hickman and Brian Reeves, *Local Police Departments 2000* (Washington, D.C.: Bureau of Justice Statistics, 2003), p. 6.

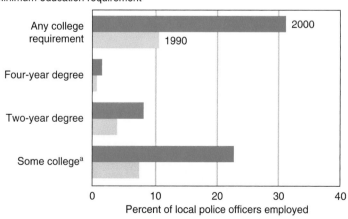

Though most law enforcement agencies still do not require recruits to have an advanced degree, the number requiring advanced education in the hiring and promotion process is growing. A recent national survey of larger police departments (serving populations of 500,000–1 million) found that during the past decade the percentage of departments requiring new officers to have at least some college rose from 19 to 37 and the percentage requiring a two-year or four-year degree grew from 6 to 14.[52] About half of the surveyed departments expressed a preference for criminal justice majors, most often because of their enhanced knowledge of the entire criminal justice system and issues in policing. Another promising trend is that, although not requiring college credits for promotion, 82 percent of the departments recognized that college education is an important element in promotion decisions. (See Figure 7.1.)

What are the benefits of higher education for police officers? Better communication with the public, especially minority and ethnic groups, is believed to be one. Educated officers write better and more clearly and are more likely to be promoted. Police administrators believe that education enables officers to perform more effectively, generate fewer citizen complaints, show more initiative in performing police tasks, and generally act more professionally.[53] In addition, educated officers are less likely to have disciplinary problems and are viewed as better decision makers.[54] Studies have shown that college-educated police officers generate fewer citizen complaints and have better behavioral and performance characteristics than their less educated peers. Research indicates that educated officers are more likely to rate themselves higher on most performance indicators, indicating that, if nothing else, higher education is associated with greater self-confidence and assurance.[55]

Though education has its benefits, little conclusive evidence has been found that educated officers are more effective crime fighters.[56] The diversity of the police role, the need for split-second decision making, and the often boring and mundane tasks police are required to do are all considered reasons that formal education may not improve performance on the street.[57] Nonetheless, because police administrators value educated officers and citizens find them to be exceptional in the use of good judgment and problem solving, the trend toward having a more educated police force likely will continue.[58]

The number of women and minorities in police agencies is increasing. Here, acting Assisting Chief Heather Fong of the San Francisco police department faces the media on March 4, 2003.

© 2003 AP/Wide World Photos

Minorities in Policing

For the past two decades, U.S. police departments have made a concerted effort to attract minority police officers, and there have been some impressive gains. As might be expected, cities with large minority populations are the ones having a higher proportion of minority officers in their police departments.[59]

The reasons for this effort are varied. Viewed in its most positive light, police departments recruit minority citizens to field a more balanced force that truly represents the communities they serve. African Americans generally have less confidence in the police than whites and are skeptical of their ability to protect them from harm.[60] African Americans also seem to be more adversely affected than whites when well-publicized incidents of police misconduct occur.[61] It comes as no surprise then that public opinion polls and research surveys show that African American citizens report having less confidence in the police when compared with both Hispanics and Caucasians.[62] African American juveniles seem particularly suspicious of police even when they deny having a negative encounter with a police officer.[63] A heterogeneous police force can be instrumental in gaining the confidence of the minority community by helping dispel the view that police departments are generally bigoted or biased organizations. Furthermore, minority police officers possess special qualities that can serve to improve police performance. For example, Spanish-speaking officers can help with investigations in Hispanic neighborhoods, while Asian officers are essential for undercover or surveillance work with Asian gangs and drug importers. Figure 7.2 shows the racial and gender breakdown of the nation's largest police departments.

Minority Police Officers

The earliest known date of when an African American was hired as a police officer was 1861 in Washington, D.C.; Chicago hired its first African American officer in 1872.[64] By 1890 an estimated 2,000 minority police officers were employed in the United States. At first, African American officers suffered a great deal of discrimination. Their work assignments were restricted, as were their chances for promotion. Minority officers were often assigned solely to the patrol of African American neighborhoods, and in some cities they were required to call a white

Figure 7.2
Female and Minority Local Police Officers, 1990 and 2000

^aIncludes Asians, Pacific Islanders, American Indians, and Alaska Natives.

Source: Matthew Hickman and Brian Reeves, *Local Police Departments 2000* (Washington, D.C.: Bureau of Justice Statistics, 2003), p. iii.

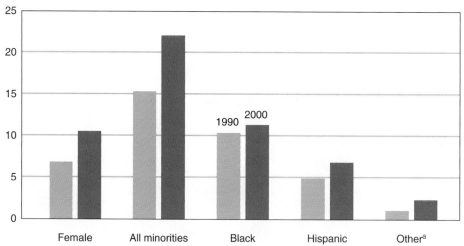

double marginality
According to Nicholas Alex, the social burden African American police officers carry by being both minority group members and law enforcement officers.

officer to make an arrest. White officers held highly prejudicial attitudes, and as late as the 1950s some refused to ride with African Americans in patrol cars.[65]

The experience of African American police officers has not been an easy one. In his classic 1969 book, *Black in Blue,* Nicholas Alex pointed out that African American officers of the time suffered from what he called **double marginality.**[66] On the one hand, African American officers had to deal with the expectation that they would give members of their own race a break. On the other hand, they often experienced overt racism from their police colleagues. Alex found that African American officers' adaptation to these pressures ranged from denying that African American suspects should be treated differently from whites to treating African American offenders more harshly than white offenders, to prove their lack of bias. Alex offered several reasons for some African American officers being tougher on African American offenders: They desired acceptance from their white colleagues; they were particularly sensitive to any disrespect given them by African American teenagers; and they viewed themselves as protectors of the African American community. Ironically, minority citizens may be more likely to accuse a minority officer of misconduct than they are white officers, a circumstance that underscores the difficult position of the minority officer in contemporary society.[67]

These conflicts have become more muted as the number of minority officers has increased. For example, in larger cities (over 250,000), Hispanics' representation among officers increased from 9 percent to 14 percent, and African Americans' from 18 percent to 20 percent, between 1990 and 2000.[68]

Minority police officers now seem more aggressive and self-assured, less willing to accept any discriminatory practices by the police department.[69] They appear to be experiencing some of the same problems and issues encountered by white officers.[70] For example, minority officers report feeling similar if somewhat higher rates of job-related stress and strain than white officers.[71] However, they may deal with stress in a somewhat different fashion. Minority officers are more likely to seek aid from fellow minority officers, whereas white officers are more likely to try to express their feelings to others, form social bonds, and try to get others to like them more.[72]

African American and white police officers share similar attitudes toward community policing (although minority officers report being even more favorable toward it than white officers).[73] African American officers may today be far less detached and alienated from the local community than white or Hispanic officers.[74] Also helping is the fact that the number of African American officers in some of the nation's largest cities is now proportionate to minority representation in the population. So, although minority officers report feeling somewhat more job-related stress and strain than white officers do, they appear to be on the path to overcoming the problems of double marginality.[75]

When affirmative action was first instituted, white police officers viewed it as a threat to their job security.[76] As more minorities join U.S. police forces, their situation seems to be changing. Caucasian officers are more likely to appreciate the contribution of minority officers. For example, when Charles Katz examined the formation of a police gang unit in a Midwestern city, he found that commanders chose minority officers so that the unit could be representative of the community they served.[77] One Hispanic officer told Katz, "When you talk to Hispanics, you have to know and be familiar with their culture. . . . [Y]ou always talk to the man of the house, never presenting your position to the kid or to the mother."[78] These benefits are not lost on citizens either, and research shows that the general public cares little about the racial or ethnic makeup of the police officers in their neighborhood and more about their effectiveness.[79]

Women in Policing

In 1910 Alice Stebbins Wells became the first woman to hold the title of police officer (in Los Angeles) and to have arrest powers.[80] For more than half a century, female officers endured separate criteria for selection, were given menial tasks, and were denied the opportunity for advancement.[81] Some relief was gained with the passage of the 1964 Civil Rights Act and its subsequent amendments. Courts have consistently supported the addition of women to police forces by striking down entrance requirements that eliminated almost all female candidates but could not be proven to predict job performance (such as height and upper-body strength).[82] Women do not do as well as men on strength tests and are much more likely to fail the entrance physical than male recruits. Critics contend that many of these tests do not reflect the actual tasks police do on the job.[83] Nonetheless, the role of women in police work is still restricted by social and administrative barriers that have been difficult to remove. Today, about 16 percent of all sworn officers in larger cities (over 250,000) are women; in all about 11 percent of sworn officers are female.[84]

Studies of policewomen indicate that they are still struggling for acceptance, believe that they do not receive equal credit for their job performance, and report that it is common for them to be sexually harassed by their coworkers.[85] One reason may be that many male police officers tend to view policing as an overtly masculine profession not appropriate for women. For example, officers in the Los Angeles Police Department make an important distinction between two models of officers — "hard chargers" and "station queens." The former display such characteristics as courage and aggressiveness; they are willing to place themselves in danger and handle the most hazardous calls.[86] The latter like to work in the station house doing paperwork or other administrative tasks. The term *queen* is designed as a pejorative to indicate that these officers are effeminate.[87]

Female police officers may also be targeted for more disciplinary actions by administrators and, if cited, are more likely to receive harsher punishments than male officers. That is, a larger percentage receives punishment greater than a reprimand.[88] Considering the sometimes hostile reception they receive from male colleagues and supervisors, female officers not surprisingly report significantly higher levels of job-related stress than male officers.[89]

Job Performance Gender bias is certainly not supported by existing research indicating that female officers are highly successful police officers.[90] In an important study of recruits in the Metropolitan Police Department of Washington, D.C., policewomen were found to display extremely satisfactory work performances.[91] Compared with male officers, women were found to respond to similar types of

Do male and female police officers differ in their reaction to domestic violence situations? To find out, read Anna Stewart and Kelly Maddren, "Police Officers' Judgements of Blame in Family Violence: The Impact of Gender and Alcohol," *Sex Roles: A Journal of Research* 37, no. 11-12 (December 1997): 921.

calls, and the arrests they made were as likely to result in conviction. Women were more likely then their male colleagues to receive support from the community and were less likely to be charged with improper conduct.

Research also shows that female officers are less likely to use force than male officers.[92] Because female officers seem to have the ability to avoid violent encounters with citizens and to de-escalate potentially violent arrest situations, they are typically the target of fewer citizen complaints.[93]

Gender Conflicts Despite the overwhelming evidence supporting their performance, policewomen have not always been fully accepted by their male peers or the general public.[94] Surveys of male officers show that only one-third accept a woman on patrol and that more than half do not think that women can handle the physical requirements of the job as well as men.[95] This form of bias is not unique to the United States. Research shows that policewomen working in northern England report being excluded from full membership in the force, based on gender inequality. Though policewomen in England are enthusiastic for crime-related work, their aspirations are frequently frustrated in favor of male officers.[96]

Women working in this male-dominated culture can experience stress and anxiety.[97] Not surprisingly, then, significantly more female than male officers report being the victim of discrimination on the job. And the male officers who claim to have experienced gender-based discrimination suggest that it comes at the hands of policewomen who use their sexuality for job-related benefits.[98]

Female officers are frequently caught in the classic catch-22 dilemma: If they are physically weak, male partners view them as a risk in street confrontations; if they are more powerful and aggressive than their male partners, they are regarded as an affront to a male officer's manhood. Ironically, to adapt to this paternalistic culture they may develop values and attitudes that support traditional concepts of police work instead of the new community policing models, which are viewed as taking a more humanistic, people-oriented approach.[99]

Minority Female Officers African American women, who account for less than 5 percent of police officers, occupy a unique status. In a study of African American policewomen serving in five large municipal departments, Susan Martin found that they perceive significantly more racial discrimination than both other female officers and African American male officers.[100] However, white policewomen were significantly more likely to perceive sexual discrimination than African American policewomen were.

Martin found that African American policewomen often incur the hostility of both white women and African American men who feel threatened that they will take their place. On patrol, African American policewomen are treated differently than white policewomen by male officers. Neither group of women is viewed as equals. White policewomen are protected and coddled, whereas African American policewomen are viewed as passive, lazy, and unequal. In the station house, male officers show little respect for African American women, who face "widespread racial stereotypes as well as outright racial harassment."[101] African American women also report having difficult relationships with African American male officers. Their relationships are strained by tensions and dilemmas "associated with sexuality and competition for desirable assignments and promotions."[102] Surprisingly, little unity is found among the female officers. Martin concludes: "Despite changes in the past two decades, the idealized image of the representative of the forces of 'law and order' and protector who maintains 'the thin blue line' between 'them' and 'us' remains white and male."[103]

Despite these problems, the future of women in policing grows continually brighter.[104] Female officers want to remain in policing because it pays a good salary, offers job security, and is a challenging and exciting occupation.[105] These factors should continue to bring women to policing for years to come.

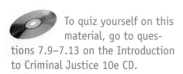
To quiz yourself on this material, go to questions 7.9–7.13 on the Introduction to Criminal Justice 10e CD.

Table 7.1 Circumstances of Accidental Police Deaths, 1996–2000

Circumstances	Total	1996	1997	1998	1999	2000
Total	344	51	63	81	65	84
Automobile accidents	197	33	33	48	41	42
Motorcycle accidents	23	4	4	3	6	6
Aircraft accidents	19	0	4	4	4	7
Struck by vehicles	59	7	15	14	9	14
Traffic stops or roadblocks	22	4	4	4	3	7
Directing traffic or assisting motorists	37	3	11	10	6	7
Accidental shootings	12	2	1	3	3	3
Other (for example, drownings and falls)	34	5	6	9	2	12

Source: U.S. Department of Justice, Federal Bureau of Investigation, *Law Enforcement Officers Killed and Assaulted 2000* (Washington, D.C.: 2001), p. 64.

Problems of Policing

Law enforcement is not an easy job. The role ambiguity, social isolation, and threat of danger present in working the street are the police officer's constant companions. What effects do these strains have on police? Three of the most significant problems are job stress, violence, and corruption.

Job Stress

The complexity of their role, the need to exercise prudent discretion, the threat of using violence and having violence used against them, and isolation from the rest of society all take a toll on law enforcement officers. Police officer stress leads to negative attitudes, burnout, loss of enthusiasm and commitment (cynicism), increased apathy, substance abuse problems, divorce, health problems, and many other social, personal, and job-related problematic behaviors.[106] Evidence suggests that police officers are often involved in marital disputes and even incidents of domestic violence, which may be linked to stress.[107] Stress may not be constant, but at some time during their career (usually the middle years), most officers will feel its effects.[108]

Causes of Stress A number of factors have been associated with job stress.[109] Some are related to the difficulties police officers have in maintaining social and family relationships, considering their schedule and workload.[110] Police suffer stress in their personal lives when they bring the job home or when their work hours are shifted, causing family disruptions.[111]

Some stressors are job-related. The pressure of being on duty 24 hours a day leads to stress and emotional detachment from both work and public needs. Policing is a dangerous profession and officers are at risk to many forms of job-related accidental deaths (see Table 7.1).

Stress has been related to internal conflict with administrative policies that deny officers support and a meaningful role in decision making.[112] For example, stress may result when officers are forced to adapt to a department's new methods of policing, such as community-oriented policing, and they are skeptical about the change in policy.[113] Other stressors include poor training, substandard equipment, inadequate pay, lack of opportunity, job dissatisfaction, role conflict, exposure to brutality, and fears about competence, success, and safety.[114] Some officers may feel stress because they believe that the court system favors the rights of the criminal and handcuffs the police; others might be sensitive to a perceived lack of support from governmental officials and the general public.[115] Some officers believe that their superiors care little about their welfare.[116]

Police psychologists have divided these stressors into four distinct categories.

1. External stressors, such as verbal abuse from the public, justice system inefficiency, and liberal court decisions that favor the criminal. What are perceived to be antipolice judicial decisions may alienate police and reduce their perceptions of their own competence.[117]
2. Organizational stressors, such as low pay, excessive paperwork, arbitrary rules, and limited opportunity for advancement.
3. Duty stressors, such as rotating shifts, work overload, boredom, fear, and danger.
4. Individual stressors, such as discrimination, marital difficulties, and personality problems.[118]

The effects of stress can be shocking. Police work has been related to both physical and psychological ailments. Police have a significantly high rate of premature death caused by such conditions as heart disease and diabetes. They also experience a disproportionate number of divorces and other marital problems. Research indicates that police officers in some departments, but not all, have higher suicide rates than the general public. (Recent research shows that New York City police have equal or lower suicide rates that the general public and that some researchers have found a lower than average police suicide rate in other areas of the country.)[119] Police who feel stress may not be open to adopting new ideas and programs such as community policing.[120]

Combating Stress Research efforts have shown that the more support police officers get in the workplace, the lower their feelings of stress and anxiety.[121] Consequently, departments have attempted to fight job-related stress by training officers to cope with its effects. Today, stress training includes diet information, biofeedback, relaxation and meditation, and exercise. Many departments include stress management as part of an overall wellness program, also designed to promote physical and mental health, fitness, and good nutrition.[122] Some programs have included family members: They may be better able to help the officer cope if they have more knowledge about the difficulties of police work. Still other efforts promote total wellness programming, which enhances the physical and emotional well-being of officers by emphasizing preventive physical and psychological measures.[123] Research also shows that because police perceive many benefits of their job and enjoy the quality of life it provides, stress reduction programs might help officers focus on the positive aspects of police work.[124]

© 2002 AP/Wide World Photos

Because police are called on to handle difficult interactions and situations, stress is a routine aspect of their work. Here, Tory Kennedy, ten, is comforted by Little Rock, Arkansas, police officers after being held hostage in a Little Rock neighborhood, March 12, 2002. The child, one of four, escaped through a window before the three others were released by a man police identified as Allen Lewis.

Stress is a critically important aspect of police work. Further research is needed to create valid methods of identifying police officers under considerable stress and to devise effective stress reduction programs.[125]

Violence

In the late summer of 1997 New Yorkers were shocked as an astounding case of **police brutality** case began to unfold in the daily newspapers. Abner Louima, 33, a Haitian immigrant, had been arrested outside Club Rendezvous, a Brooklyn nightclub, after a fight had broken out. Louima later claimed that the arresting officers had become furious when he protested his arrest, twice stopping the patrol car to beat him with their fists.[126] When they arrived at the station house, two officers, apparently angry because some of the club-goers had fought with the police, led Louima to the men's room. They removed his trousers and attacked him with the handle of a toilet plunger, first shoving it into his rectum and then into his mouth, breaking teeth. Louima screamed: "Why are you doing this to me? Why? Why?" The officers also shouted racial slurs at Louima during the attack. Louima, who witnesses said had no bruises or injuries when officers took him into custody, arrived at the hospital three hours later bleeding profusely. He underwent emergency surgery to repair a puncture in his small intestine and injuries to his bladder.

In the aftermath of the case, NYPD investigators granted departmental immunity to nearly 100 officers to gain information. In the aftermath of the blue curtain of silence being cracked, a number of police officers were given long prison sentences on charges of sexual abuse and first-degree assault.

The Louima case and other incidents involving the police illustrate the persistent problems police departments have in regulating violent contacts with citizens. Police officers are empowered to use force and violence in pursuit of their daily tasks. Some scholars argue that the use of violent measures is the core of the police roles.[127]

Since their creation, U.S. police departments have wrestled with the charge that they are brutal, physically violent organizations. Early police officers resorted to violence and intimidation to gain the respect that was not freely given by citizens. In the 1920s, the Wickersham Commission detailed numerous instances of police brutality, including the use of the third degree to extract confessions.

Today, police brutality continues to be a concern, especially when police use excessive violence against members of the minority community. The nation looked on in disgust when a videotape was aired on network newscasts showing members of the Los Angeles Police Department beating, kicking, and using electric stun guns on Rodney King. Earlier, Los Angeles police stopped using a restraining choke hold, which cuts off blood circulation to the brain, after minority citizens complained that it caused permanent damage and may have killed as many as 17 people. Three quarters of all complaints filed against the police for misconduct tend to be by nonwhite males under the age of 30.[128]

How Common Is the Use of Force Today? How much force is being used by the police today?[129] Despite some highly publicized incidence, the research data show that the use of force is not a common event. A national survey on police contacts with civilians found that in a single year (1999), of an estimated 43 million police–citizen interactions, approximately 1 percent, or 422,000, involved the use or threatened use of force. Of these, an estimated 2 in 10 involved the threat of force only. When force was used, it typically involved the citizen being pushed or grabbed. Less than 20 percent of those experiencing force reported an injury.[130] The least intrusive types of force, such as handcuffing, are used much more often than the most intrusive, such as lethal violence. The use of weapons is

police brutality
Actions such as using abusive language, making threats, using force or coercion unnecessarily, prodding with nightsticks, and stopping and searching people to harass them.

rare. For every 1,000 police officers there are about four incidents in which an officer shoots at a civilian.[131]

While this data indicate that the police use of force may not be as common as previously believed, it still remains a central part of the police role. Although getting an accurate figure is difficult, at least 6,600 civilians have been killed by the police since 1976 and the true number is probably much higher.[132] Considering these numbers, police use of force is an important topic for study.

Race and Force The routine use of force may be diminishing, but debate is ongoing over whether police are more likely to get rough with minority suspects. Some studies find that police are more likely to use force against minorities, while others reach an opposing conclusion. A national survey of police contacts found that African Americans (2 percent) and Hispanics (2 percent) were more likely than whites (just under 1 percent) to experience police threat or use of force as a consequence of police contact.[133] This finding was substantiated by research conducted by William Terrill and Stephen Mastrofski of police in St. Petersburg, Florida, and Indianapolis, Indiana.[134]

While these findings are troubling, research also finds no racial differences in the use of force. For example, Joel Garner's recent study of police encounters with citizens using a wide variety of samples taken in different locales found that race played an insignificant role in the decision to use force. The Garner research indicates that a suspect's behavior is a much more powerful determinant of police response than age or race. People who resisted police orders or grappled with officers were much more likely to be the target of force than those who were respectful, passive, and noncombative.[135]

These different findings provide inconclusive evidence that police officers routinely use more force against minority citizens. Nonetheless, minority citizens are much more likely to perceive that police are more likely to hassle them; that is, stop them or watch them closely when they have done nothing wrong. They are also more likely to know someone who has been hassled by police. Perceptions of hassling may erode an individual's future relations with police and affect police–community relations as a whole.[136]

Who Are the Problem Cops? Evidence shows that only a small proportion of officers is continually involved in use-of-force incidents.[137] What kind of police officer gets involved in problem behavior? Are some officers chronic offenders? Research conducted in a southeastern city by Kim Michelle Lersch and Tom Mieczkowski found that a few officers (7 percent) were chronic offenders who accounted for a significant portion of all citizen complaints (33 percent). Those officers receiving the bulk of the complaints tended to be younger and less experienced and had been accused of harassment or violence after a proactive encounter that they had initiated. Although repeat offenders were more likely to be accused of misconduct by minority citizens, little evidence existed that attacks were racially motivated.[138] Efforts to deal with these problem cops are now being undertaken in police departments around the nation. The Analyzing Criminal Justice Issues feature on page 227 describes these efforts in some detail.

Curbing the Use of Force Because incidents of brutality undermine efforts to build a bridge between police and the public, police departments around the United States have instituted specialized training programs to help police officers to conduct their duties without resorting to force. For example, recent research finds that police are most likely to use force when responding to calls in which they do not expect a violent confrontation, such as a property offense call, when compared with violent service calls, such as a domestic disturbance. When caught unprepared, police officers may respond with unnecessary violence. Proper training can

Working with Problem Cops: Early Intervention Programs

analyzing criminal justice issues

Research indicates about 10 percent of all officers account for 90 percent of the problems experienced by police departments. In some departments as few as 2 percent of all officers are responsible for 50 percent of all citizen complaints. In 1981, the U.S. Commission on Civil Rights recommended that all police departments create an early warning system to identify problem officers, those who are frequently the subject of complaints or who demonstrate identifiable patterns of inappropriate behavior. During the past two decades, a number of police departments have set up such systems, to identify officers whose behavior is problematic and provide a form of intervention, such as counseling or training, to correct that performance before disciplinary action is required.

A 2001 survey by police experts Samuel Walker, Geoffrey P. Alpert, and Dennis J. Kenney found that, as of 1999, 39 percent of all municipal and county law enforcement agencies that served populations greater than 50,000 either had an early warning system in place or were planning to implement one. While these systems are becoming prevalent, Walker and his associates found that questions still arose about their effectiveness and about the various program elements that are associated with effectiveness. Walker and his colleagues found that early warning systems have three basic phases: selection, intervention, and postintervention monitoring.

Selecting Officers for the Program. No standards have been established for identifying officers for early warning programs, but general agreement has been reached about the criteria that should influence their selection. Performance indicators that can help identify officers with problematic behavior include citizen complaints, firearm-discharge and use-of-force reports, civil litigation, resisting-arrest incidents, and high-speed pursuits and vehicular damage. Most departments use a combination of these indicators to select officers for help. Of those that rely

solely on citizen complaints, most (67 percent) require three complaints in a given time frame (76 percent specify a 12-month period) to identify an officer.

Intervening with the Officer. The primary goal of early warning systems is to change the behavior of individual officers who have been identified as having performance problems. The basic intervention strategy involves a combination of deterrence and education. According to the deterrence strategy, officers who are subject to intervention presumably will change their behavior in response to a perceived threat of punishment. Early warning systems operate on the assumption that training, as part of the intervention, can help officers improve their performance.

In most systems, the initial intervention generally consists of a review by the officer's immediate supervisor. Almost half of the responding agencies involve other command officers in counseling the officer. Also, these systems frequently include a training class for groups of officers identified by the system.

Monitoring the Officer's Subsequent Performance. Nearly all the agencies that have an early warning system in place report that they monitor an officer's performance after the initial intervention. Such monitoring is generally informal and conducted by the officer's immediate supervisor, but some departments have developed a formal process of observation, evaluation, and reporting. Almost half of the agencies monitor the officer's performance for 36 months after the initial intervention. Half of the agencies indicate that the follow-up period is not specified and that officers are monitored either continuously or on a case-by-case basis.

Do the Early Warning Systems Work?

Walker and his associates made detailed evaluations of the early warning systems in three cities — Minneapolis, Minnesota; Miami, Florida; and New Orleans, Louisiana — to assess the impact of the systems on

officers' performance. They found that early warning systems appear to have a dramatic effect on reducing citizen complaints and other indicators of problematic police performance among those officers subject to intervention. In Minneapolis, the average number of citizen complaints received by officers subject to early intervention dropped by 67 percent one year after the intervention; in New Orleans, by 62 percent. In Miami-Dade, 96 percent of the officers sent to early intervention had experienced complaints about excessive use of force. Following the intervention, that number dropped to 50 percent.

Critical Thinking

While early intervention systems alone may not be a panacea that can neutralize the inappropriate behavior of problem officers, it is emerging as an important tool that can be used along with other techniques to reduce unacceptable behaviors. Could it be used as an intervention to combat racial profiling? For example, would it be appropriate to identify officers who make a disproportionate number of traffic stops of racial or ethnic minorities (relative to other officers with the same assignment) and place them in an early intervention program? Is this a violation of their civil rights, for example, labeling them without a hearing or trial?

InfoTrac College Edition Research

To read an article on psychologists who work with problem cops, go to Alan W. Benner, "COP DOCS," *Psychology Today,* November 2000, p. 36, on InfoTrac College Edition.

Source: Samuel Walker, Geoffrey P. Alpert, and Dennis J. Kenney, *Early Warning Systems: Responding to the Problem Police Officer, Research in Brief* (Washington, D.C.: National Institute of Justice, 2001).

help reduce these incidents. Even if a police officer is mentally prepared to handle a property offense call, a lack of proper training in the physical aspects of policing may result in undesirable consequences.[139]

Research into police violence and its relation to calls for service usually focuses on so-called dangerous encounters. The dangerous encounters, based on rankings on assaults and injuries to police officers, are almost exclusively considered to be traffic stops, domestic disturbances, or violent crime calls.

Urban police departments are implementing or considering implementing neighborhood and community policing models to improve relations with the public. In addition, detailed rules of engagement that limit the use of force are common in major cities. However, the creation of departmental rules limiting behavior is often haphazard and is usually a reaction to a crisis situation (for example, a citizen is seriously injured) instead of part of a systematic effort to improve police–citizen interactions.[140] Some departments have developed administrative policies that stress limiting the use of **deadly force** and containing armed offenders until specially trained backup teams are sent to take charge of the situation. Administrative policies have been found to be an effective control on deadly force, and their influence can be enhanced if given the proper support by the chief of police.[141]

Some cities are taking an aggressive proactive stance to curb violent cops. Since 1977 the New York City Police Department has been operating a Force-Related Integrity Testing program in which undercover officers pose as angry citizens in elaborate sting operations intended to weed out officers with a propensity for violence. In a typical encounter, officers responding to a radio call on a domestic dispute confront an aggressive husband who spews hatred at everyone around, including the police. The husband is actually an undercover officer from the Internal Affairs Bureau, who is testing whether the officers, one of whom has had a history of civilian complaints, will respond to verbal abuse with threats or violence. The NYPD conducts about 600 sting operations each year to test the integrity of its officers, including several dozen devoted to evaluating the conduct of officers with a history of abuse complaints.[142]

What may be the greatest single factor that can control the use of police brutality is the threat of civil judgments against individual officers who use excessive force, police chiefs who ignore or condone violent behavior, and the cities and towns in which they are employed. Civilians routinely file civil actions against police departments when they believe that officers have violated their civil rights. Police may be sued when a victim believes that excessive force was used during his or her arrest or custody. Civilians may collect damages if they can show that the force used was unreasonable, considering all the circumstances known to the officer at the time he or she acted. Excessive force suits commonly occur when police use a weapon, such as a gun or baton, to subdue an unarmed person who is protesting his or her treatment. The U.S. Supreme Court in 1978 (*Monell* v. *Department of Social Services*) ruled that local agencies could be held liable under the federal Civil Rights Act (42 U.S.C. 1983) for actions of their employees if it was part of an official custom or practice.[143]

Deadly Force

As commonly used, the term *deadly force* refers to the actions of a police officer who shoots and kills a suspect who is fleeing from arrest, assaulting a victim, or attacking an officer.[144] The justification for the use of deadly force can be traced to English common law, in which almost every criminal offense was a felony and bore the death penalty. The use of deadly force in the course of arresting a felon was considered expedient, saving the state the burden of trial (the "fleeing felon" rule).[145]

Although the media depict hero cops in a constant stream of deadly shootouts in which scores of bad guys are killed, the number of people killed by the police each year is most likely between 250 and 300.[146] Although these data are

deadly force
Police killing of a suspect who resists arrest or presents a danger to an officer or the community.

encouraging, some researchers believe that the actual number of police shootings is far greater and may be hidden or masked by a number of factors. For example, coroners may be intentionally or accidentally underreporting police homicides by almost half.[147]

Factors Related to Police Shootings

Is police use of deadly force a random occurrence, or are there social, legal, and environmental factors associated with its use? The following seven patterns have been related to police shootings.

1. **Violence Levels.** The higher the levels of violence in a community, the more likely police in the area will use deadly force.[148] A number of studies have found that fatal police shootings were closely related to reported violent crime rates and criminal homicide rates. Police officers kill civilians at a higher rate in years when the general level of violence in the nation is higher. The perception of danger may contribute to the use of violent means for self-protection.[149]

2. **Exposure to Violence.** Police officers may become exposed to violence when they are forced to confront the emotionally disturbed. Some distraught people attack police as a form of suicide.[150] This tragic event has become so common that the term *suicide by cop* has been coined to denote victim-precipitated killings by police. For example, during a 10-year period (1988–98) more than 10 percent of the shootings by police officers in Los Angeles involved suicidal people intentionally provoking police.[151]

3. **Workload.** A relationship exists among police violence and the number of police on the street, the number of calls for service, the number and nature of police dispatches, the number of arrests made in a given jurisdiction, and police exposure to stressful situations.

4. **Firearms Availability.** Cities that experience a large number of crimes committed with firearms are also likely to have high police violence rates. A strong association has been found between police use of force and gun density (the proportion of suicides and murders committed with a gun).[152]

5. **Social Conflict.** The greatest number of police shootings occurs in areas that have significant disparities in economic opportunity and high levels of income inequality.[153] One conflict-reduction approach is to add minority police officers. However, recent research by Brad Smith shows that the mere addition of minority officers to a department is not a sufficient means to reduce levels of police violence.[154] David Jacobs and Jason Carmichael, however, found that the presence of an African American mayor significantly reduces the likelihood of police–citizen violence.[155] They conclude that economic disadvantage within the minority community coupled with political alienation leads to climate in which police–citizen conflict is sharpened. Politically excluded groups may turn to violence to gain ends that those not excluded can acquire with conventional tactics. The presence of an African American mayor may reduce feelings of powerlessness in the minority community, which in turn reduces anger against the state of which the police are the most visible officials.

6. **Administrative Policies.** The philosophy, policies, and practices of individual police chiefs and departments significantly influence the police use of deadly force.[156] Departments that stress restrictive policies on the use of force generally have lower shooting rates than those that favor tough law enforcement and encourage officers to shoot when necessary. Poorly written or ambivalent policies encourage shootings because they allow the officer at the scene to decide when deadly force is warranted, often under conditions of high stress and tension.

7. **Race.** No other issue is as important to the study of the police use of deadly force as that of racial discrimination. A number of critics have claimed that police are more likely to shoot and kill minority offenders than they are whites.

Police can control deadly force in a number of different ways. Murder suspect Dennis Czajkowski is escorted by Pennsylvania State Police Officers after being taken into custody for shooting two nurses he held captive at Norristown State Hospital on June 19, 1999. The police officer in charge of the investigation had given an order not to use deadly force.

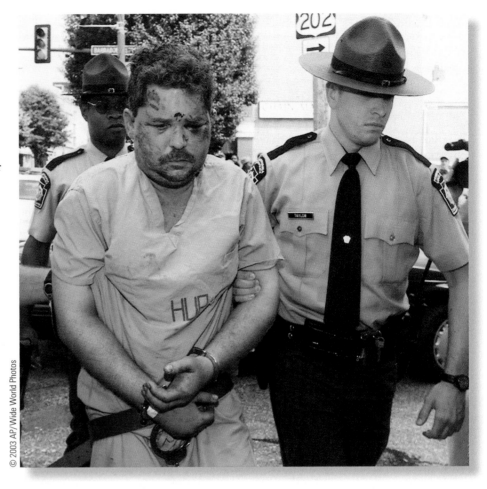

© 2003 AP/Wide World Photos

In a famous statement, sociologist Paul Takagi charged that police have "one trigger finger for whites and another for African-Americans."[157] Takagi's complaint was supported by a number of research studies that showed that a disproportionate number of police killings involved minority citizens — almost 80 percent in some of the cities surveyed.[158]

Do these findings alone indicate that police discriminate in the use of deadly force? Some pioneering research by James Fyfe helps provide an answer to this question. In his study of New York City shootings over a five-year period, Fyfe found that police officers were most likely to shoot suspects who were armed and with whom they became involved in violent confrontations. Once such factors as being armed with a weapon, being involved in a violent crime, and attacking an officer were considered, the racial differences in the police use of force ceased to be significant. Fyfe found that African American officers were almost twice as likely as white officers to have shot citizens. Fyfe attributes this finding to the fact that African American officers work and live in high-crime, high-violence areas where shootings are more common and that African American officers hold proportionately more line positions and fewer administrative posts than white officers, which would place them more often on the street and less often behind a desk.[159]

InfoTrac College Edition has numerous articles on the police use of force. Use "Police Shootings" as a subject guide to locate the most recent ones.

Controlling Deadly Force Given that the police use of deadly force is such a serious problem, ongoing efforts have been made to control it.

One of the most difficult problems that influenced its control was the continued use of the fleeing felon rule in a number of states. However, in 1985 the

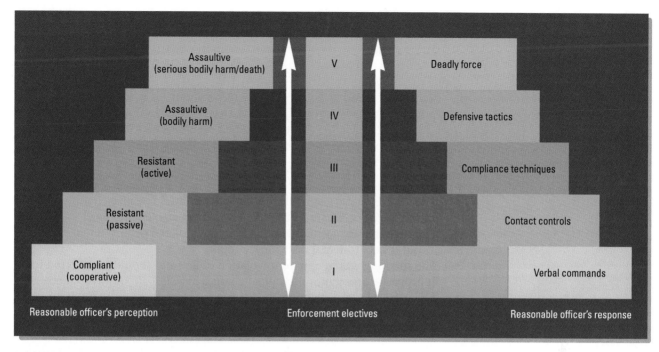

Figure 7.3
The Federal Law Enforcement Training Center's Use-of-Force Model

Source: Franklin Graves and Gregory Connor, Federal Law Enforcement Training Center, Glynco, Georgia.

U.S. Supreme Court outlawed the indiscriminate use of deadly force with its decision in the case of *Tennessee* v. *Garner.* In this case, the Court ruled that the use of deadly force against apparently unarmed and nondangerous fleeing felons is an illegal seizure of their person under the Fourth Amendment. Deadly force may not be used unless it is necessary to prevent escape and the officer has probable cause to believe that the suspect poses a significant threat of death or serious injury to the officer or others. The majority opinion stated that, when the suspect poses no immediate threat to the officer and no threat to others, the harm resulting from failing to apprehend the suspect does not justify the use of deadly force to do so: "A police officer may not seize an unarmed, nondangerous suspect by shooting him dead."[160]

With *Garner,* the Supreme Court effectively put an end to any local police policy that allowed officers to shoot unarmed or otherwise nondangerous offenders if they resisted arrest or attempted to flee from police custody. However, the Court did not ban the use of deadly force or otherwise control police shooting policy. Consequently, in *Graham* v. *Connor,* the Court created a reasonableness standard for the use of force: Force is excessive when, considering all the circumstances known to the officer at the time he acted, the force used was unreasonable.[161] For example, an officer is approached in a threatening manner by someone wielding a knife. The assailant fails to stop when warned and is killed by the officer. The officer would not be held liable if it turns out that the shooting victim was deaf and could not hear the officer's command and if the officer at the time of the incident had no way of knowing the person's disability.

Individual state jurisdictions still control police shooting policy. Some states have adopted statutory policies that restrict the police use of violence. Others have upgraded training in the use of force. The Federal Law Enforcement Training Center (FLETC) has developed the FLETC use-of-force model, illustrated in Figure 7.3, to teach officers the proper method to escalate force in response to the threat they face. As the figure shows, resistance ranges from compliant and cooperative to assaultive with the threat of serious bodily harm or death. Officers are taught via lecture, demonstration, computer-based instruction, and training scenarios to assess the suspect's behavior and apply an appropriate and corresponding amount of force.[162]

Another method of controlling police shootings is through internal review and policy making by police administrative review boards. For example, New York's Firearm Discharge Review Board was established to investigate and adjudicate all police firearm discharges. Among the dispositions available to the board are the following.

- The discharge was in accordance with law and departmental policy.
- The discharge was justifiable, but the officer should be given additional training in the use of firearms or in the law and departmental policy.
- The shooting was justifiable under law but violated departmental policy and warrants departmental disciplinary action.
- The shooting was in apparent violation of law and should be referred to the appropriate prosecutor if criminal charges have not already been filed.
- The officer involved should be transferred (or offered the opportunity to transfer) to a less sensitive assignment.
- The officer involved should receive testing or alcoholism counseling.[163]

The review board approach is controversial because it can mean that the department recommends that one of its own officers be turned over for criminal prosecution.[164]

Non-Lethal Weapons In the last few years, about 1,000 local police forces have started using some sort of less than lethal weapon designed to subdue suspects. The most widely used non-lethal weapons are wood, rubber, or polyurethane bullets shot out of modified 37-mm pistols or 12-gauge shotguns. At short distances, officers use pepper spray and tasers, which deliver electric shocks with long wire tentacles, producing intense muscle spasms. Other technologies still in development include guns that shoot giant nets, guns that squirt sticky glue, and lights that can temporarily blind a suspect filled with lead pellets, which have a range of 100 feet and pack the wallop of a pro boxer's punch.[165]

Recent research efforts indicate that non-lethal weapons may help reduce police use of force.[166] Greater effort must be made to regulate these non-lethal weapons and create effective policies for their use.[167] See the Criminal Justice and Technology feature on page 233.

Police as Victims Police use of force continues to be an important issue, but control measures seem to be working. Fewer people are being killed by police, and fewer officers are being killed in the line of duty than ever before — about 50 each year. The number rose dramatically in 2001 because 23 officers were killed in the

A New York City police officer is assisted by colleagues after being injured while trying to control a union protest march. Policing is a dangerous profession, and death and injury are part of the job.

© 2003 AP/Wide World Photos

Less than Lethal Weapons

criminal justice and technology

After the U.S. Supreme Court ruling in *Tennessee* v. *Garner,* law enforcement officers were prohibited from using deadly force to capture a fleeing, nonviolent, unarmed suspect. Because an alternative to deadly force was needed, police departments around the country turned to non-lethal weapons for use in many incidents.

Pepper Spray

One of the most popular less than lethal weapons being used by law enforcement personnel is oleoresin capsicum, also known as pepper spray. The product, which is made from peppers, is so strong that when suspects are sprayed their eyes will automatically shut and they will experience shortness of breath. Pepper spray is used in a variety of scenarios, ranging from the subduing of an agitated individual to subjugating groups that are uncooperative and causing problems.

Some law enforcement agencies have adopted more high-powered pepper spray models including the the PepperBall System, which is a semiautomatic high-pressure launcher that fires projectiles containing the strongest form of oleoresin capsicum that are built to burst on impact. The launcher is accurate up to 30 feet and can saturate an area up to 100 feet, which allows police officers to safely stand back while incapacitating suspects. Now used by 1,200 different agencies including law enforcement, corrections, security, and other government agencies, the Pepper-Ball System projectiles impact with 8–10 foot-pounds of force to stop suspects without causing permanent injury. The PepperBall System is used for handling violent suspects who may have barricaded themselves in a hard to get at area as well as for riot control and hostage rescue.

Though billed as a non-lethal weapon, some critics fear that pepper spray is dangerous. After 63 people had died after being exposed to pepper spray in three North Carolina counties, the federal government sponsored research to determine whether this non-lethal weapon was more

lethal then previously believed. The research cleared use of the spray, finding that only two of the 63 deaths could be blamed on being pepper sprayed; the other fatalities were attributed to drug use, illness, or a combination of the two. As a result, police are continuing to use incapacitating sprays, and new ones are being developed.

Bean Bag Gun

Some law enforcement agencies are using the bean bag gun, which delivers a projectile the size of a tea bag filled with lead birdshot. Once an assailant is hit by the projectile, he or she will experience a muscle spasm that will either drop the person in his or her tracks or at least slow the person down so he or she can easily be subdued by law enforcement agents.

While effective, bean bag guns have also caused injuries and deaths. Approximately 12 people have been killed in the United States and Canada after being struck by the bean bags. While the projectiles are supposed to unfold once they are released from the gun, when they malfunction, they can rip through the skin, resulting in devastating effects, especially when discharged too close to the target. Because of these concerns, bean bag guns are being used less frequently while new versions, lacking the sharp edges of previous projectiles, are being developed.

Tasers

Tasers fire electrified darts at fleeing individuals who when hit can experience up to 50,000 volts of electricity. The darts can travel approximately 20 feet and can pierce through two inches of clothing, attack the individual's central nervous system, and cause muscle contractions and temporary paralysis. Currently, 2,400 law enforcement agencies in the country are using Tasers, and little evidence exists that they cause permanent injury or death. The biggest complaint is that they have little effect on extremely large or overweight people whose muscles are not located as

close to the skin surface as the average person.

Other weapons such as net launchers and sticky foams, two products that would also help capture fleeing offenders, are still being developed. So far safety issues regarding these products have deterred them from being used frequently among agencies.

Critical Thinking

1. Would the easy availability of non-lethal weapons encourage their use by police officers, thus increasing the risk of civilian injuries?
2. Would you prohibit most police officers from carrying firearms and rely more on non-lethal weapons? Should police in non-death penalty states be allowed to shoot and kill criminal suspects even though they would not face death if they were caught, tried, and convicted?

InfoTrac College Edition Research

To read about the Pepperball System in more detail, go to "Law Enforcement across the Nation Uses PepperBall to Save Lives: Non-Lethal Weapon Helps Police and Civilians Avoid Death, Serious Injury," *PR Newswire,* June 9, 2003.

Sources: National Institute of Justice, *The Effectiveness and Safety of Pepper Spray* (Washington, D.C.: Department of Justice, 2003); Patricia Biggs. "Officers Take to Shock, Awe of Taser Guns," *Arizona Republic,* May 13, 2003, pp. 1–2; Tamara Lush, "Deputies to Test 50,000-Volt Weapon," *St. Petersburg Times,* March 17, 2003, pp. 1–2; Jennifer LeClaire, "Police Now Carry Guns, Badges . . . Beanbags, *Christian Science Monitor,* December 18, 2001, pp. 1–3; Jack Leonard, "Police Dropping 'Non-Lethal' Bean Bags as Too Dangerous," *Nation,* June 3, 2002, pp. 1–5; Terry Flynn, "Ft. Thomas Police Get Non-Lethal Weapons," *Cincinnati Enquirer,* June 15, 2001, pp. 1–2.

September 11 terrorist attacks, along with 343 firefighters. Before the 2001 spike, the number of officers slain in the line of duty had been trending downward for the past decade.[168] About half of the officers were killed while making arrests or conducting a traffic stop.

One long-cherished myth is that police officers who answer domestic violence calls are at risk for violent victimization. The scenario goes that, when confronted, one of the two battling parties turns on the outsider who dares interfere in a private matter. Research conducted in Charlotte, North Carolina, however, indicates that domestic violence calls may be no more dangerous than many other routine police interactions.[169] So while police officers should be on their guard when investigating a call for assistance from an abused spouse, the risk of violence against them may be no greater than when they answer a call for a burglary or car theft.

Corruption

In July 1996 the elite antigang unit from the Los Angeles Police Department's Rampart Division raided gang-infested apartments at Shatto Place. Their target was the notorious 18th Street Gang, one of Los Angeles's most violent gangs. During the raid, police officers killed one gang member and wounded another. A departmental investigation found nothing wrong and exonerated the police involved. Then, in 1999, Rafael A. Perez, an officer who took part in the raid, was caught stealing eight pounds of cocaine from police evidence lockers. After pleading guilty in September 1999, he bargained for a lighter sentence by telling departmental investigators about police brutality, perjury, planted evidence, drug corruption, and attempted murder within the Rampart Division and its antigang unit, known as CRASH (Community Resources Against Street Hoodlums). Perez told authorities that, during the Shatto raid, the victims may have been unarmed so that the raiding officers resorted to a "throwdown" — slang for a weapon being planted to make a shooting legally justifiable. Perez's testimony resulted in at least 12 Rampart cops being fired or relieved from duty. But Perez was not done. He also said he and his partner, Nino Durden, shot an unarmed 18th Street Gang member named Javier Ovando, then planted a semiautomatic rifle on the unconscious suspect and claimed that Ovando had tried to shoot them during a stakeout. Their testimony helped get Ovando, confined to a wheelchair for life because of the shooting, a 23-year sentence for assault. Ovando has since been freed from prison and is suing the city for more than $20 million.[170]

From their creation, U.S. police departments have wrestled with the problem of controlling illegal and unprofessional behavior by their officers. Corruption pervaded the American police when the early departments were first formed. In the nineteenth century, police officers systematically ignored violations of laws related to drinking, gambling, and prostitution in return for regular payoffs. Some entered into relationships with professional criminals, especially pickpockets. Illegal behavior was tolerated in return for goods or information. Police officers helped politicians gain office by allowing electoral fraud to flourish. Some senior officers sold promotions to higher rank within the department.[171]

Since the early nineteenth century, scandals involving police abuse of power have occurred in many urban cities, and elaborate methods had been devised to control or eliminate the problem. Although most police officers are not corrupt, the few who are dishonest bring discredit to the entire profession.

Varieties of Corruption Police deviance can include a number of activities. In a general sense, it involves misuse of authority by police officers in a manner designed to produce personal gain for themselves or others.[172] However, debate continues over whether a desire for personal gain is an essential part of corruption. Some experts argue that police misconduct also involves such issues as the unnecessary use of force, unreasonable searches, or an immoral personal life and that these should be considered as serious as corruption devoted to economic gain.

Scholars have attempted to create typologies categorizing the forms that the abuse of police powers can take. For example, the **Knapp Commission,** a public body set up to investigate the New York City police in the 1970s, classified abusers into two categories: **meat eaters** and **grass eaters.**[173] Meat eaters aggressively misuse police power for personal gain by demanding bribes, threatening legal action, or cooperating with criminals. Across the country, police officers have been accused, indicted, and convicted of shaking down club owners and other business-people.[174] In contrast, grass eaters accept payoffs when their everyday duties place them in a position to be solicited by the public. For example, police officers have been investigated for taking bribes to look the other way while neighborhood bookmakers ply their trade.[175] The Knapp Commission concluded that the vast majority of police officers on the take are grass eaters, although the few meat eaters who are caught capture all the headlines. In 1993 another police scandal prompted formation of the **Mollen Commission,** which found that some New York cops were actively involved in violence and drug dealing.

Other police experts have attempted to create models to better understand police corruption. Police corruption can be divided into four major categories.[176]

1. **Internal Corruption.** This corruption takes place among police officers themselves, involving both the bending of departmental rules and the outright performance of illegal acts. For example, Chicago police officers conspired to sell relatively new police cars to other officers at cut-rate prices, forcing the department to purchase new cars unnecessarily. A major scandal hit the Boston Police Department when a captain was indicted in an exam-tampering-and-selling scheme. Numerous officers bought promotion exams from the captain, while others had him lower the scores of rivals who were competing for the same job.[177]

2. **Selective Enforcement or Nonenforcement.** This form occurs when police abuse or exploit their discretion. If an officer frees a drug dealer in return for valuable information, that is considered a legitimate use of discretion; if the officer does so for money, that is an abuse of police power.

3. **Active Criminality.** This is participation by police in serious criminal behavior. Police may use their positions of trust and power to commit the very crimes they are entrusted with controlling. For example, a police burglary ring in Denver was so large that it prompted one commentator to coin the phrase "burglars in blue." During the past 20 years, police burglary rings have been uncovered in Chicago, Illinois; Reno, Nevada; Nashville, Tennessee; Cleveland, Ohio; and Burlington, Vermont, among other cities.[178] Another disturbing trend has been police use of drugs and alcohol. Police departments have been active in referring officers to treatment programs when substance abuse problems are detected.[179]

4. **Bribery and Extortion.** This includes practices in which law enforcement roles are exploited specifically to raise money. Bribery is initiated by the citizen; extortion is initiated by the officer. Bribery or extortion can be a one-shot transaction, as when a traffic violator offers a police officer $100 to forget about issuing a summons. Or the relationship can be an ongoing one, in which the officer solicits (or is offered) regular payoffs to ignore criminal activities, such as gambling or narcotics dealing. This is known as "being on the pad."

Sometimes police officers accept routine bribes and engage in petty extortion without considering themselves corrupt. They consider these payments as some of the unwritten benefits of police work. For example, mooching involves receiving free gifts of coffee, cigarettes, meals, and so on in exchange for possible future acts of favoritism. Chiseling occurs when officers demand admission to entertainment events or price discounts. And shopping involves taking small items, such as cigarettes, from a store whose door was accidentally left unlocked after business hours.[180]

Knapp Commission
A public body that conducted an investigation into police corruption in New York City in the early 1970s and uncovered a widespread network of payoffs and bribes.

meat eater
A term used to describe a police officer who actively solicits bribes and vigorously engages in corrupt practices.

grass eater
A term used for a police officer who accepts payoffs when everyday duties place him or her in a position to be solicited by the public.

Mollen Commission
An investigative unit set up to inquire into police corruption in New York City in the 1990s.

How do police feel about the abuse of power themselves? To find out, you can read the findings of a national survey on police attitudes toward abuse of authority at http://www.ncjrs.org/pdffiles1/nij/181312.pdf.

The Causes of Corruption No single explanation satisfactorily accounts for the various forms the abuse of power takes.

Police personality. One view puts the blame on the type of person who becomes a police officer. This position holds that policing tends to attract lower-class individuals who do not have the financial means to maintain a coveted middle-class lifestyle. As they develop the cynical, authoritarian police personality, accepting graft seems an all-too-easy method of achieving financial security.

Institutions and practices. A second view is that the wide discretion police enjoy, coupled with low visibility they maintain with the public and their own supervisors, makes them likely candidates for corruption. In addition, the code of secrecy maintained by the police subculture helps insulate corrupt officers from the law. Similarly, police managers, most of whom have risen through the ranks, are reluctant to investigate corruption or punish wrongdoers. Thus, corruption may also be viewed as a function of police institutions and practices.[181]

Moral ambivalence. A third position holds that corruption is a function of society's ambivalence toward many forms of vice-related criminal behavior that police officers are sworn to control. Unenforceable laws governing moral standards promote corruption because they create large groups with an interest in undermining law enforcement. These include consumers — people who gamble, wish to drink after the legal closing hour, or patronize a prostitute — who do not want to be deprived of their chosen form of recreation. Even though the consumers may not actively corrupt police officers, their existence creates a climate that tolerates active corruption by others.[182] Because vice cannot be controlled and the public apparently wants it to continue, the officer may have little resistance to inducements for monetary gain offered by law violators.

Environmental conditions. A fourth position is that corruption may be linked to specific environmental and social conditions that enhance the likelihood police officers may become involved in misconduct. For example, in some areas a rapid increase in the minority residential populations may be viewed as a threat to dominant group interests. Police in these areas may become overly aggressive and routinely use coercive strategies. The conflict produced by these outcomes may lead to antagonism between the police and the minority public and eventual police misconduct of all types. One recent study, in which social ecological conditions in New York City police precincts and divisions were associated with patterns of police misconduct from 1975 to 1996, found that misconduct cases involving bribery, extortion, excessive force, and other abuses of police authority were linked to trends in neighborhood structural disadvantage, increasing population mobility, and increases in the Latino population. It is possible that neighborhood disorganization reduced informal social control mechanisms, population mobility disrupted neighborhood bonds and networks, and the rapidly increasing Latino population was regarded as a threat to the existing social order. These factors provided a source of conflict necessary to encourage police misconduct. Ironically, the communities most in need of protection by the police because of environmental conditions were also the ones in need of the greatest protection from the police because of conditions favoring deviance.[183]

Corrupt departments. It has also been suggested that police corruption is generated at the departmental level and that conditions within the department produce and nurture deviance.[184] In some departments corrupt officers band together and form what is called a "rotten pocket."[185] Rotten pockets help institutionalize corruption because their members expect newcomers to conform to their illegal practices and to a code of secrecy.

Controlling Corruption How can police misconduct be controlled? One approach is to strengthen the internal administrative review process within police departments. A strong and well-supported internal affairs division has been linked to lowered corruption rates.[186] However, asking police to police themselves is not a simple task. Officers are often reluctant to discipline their peers.

Police misbehavior often provokes public outcries. These people are demonstrating in Portland, Oregon, on November 26, 2002, after police shot to death a Mexican national and the police department awarded them medals for their bravery.

For example, a 1999 review of disciplinary files found that hundreds of New York City police officers escaped punishment when their cases were summarily dismissed by the police department without ever interviewing victims or witnesses or making any other efforts to examine the strength of the evidence.[187]

Another approach, instituted by then New York commissioner Patrick Murphy in the wake of the Knapp Commission, is the accountability system. This holds that supervisors at each level are directly accountable for the illegal behaviors of the officers under them. Consequently, a commander can be demoted or forced to resign if one of her command is found guilty of corruption.[188] Close scrutiny by a department, however, can lower officer morale and create the suspicion that the officers' own supervisors distrust them.

Some departments have set up guidelines to help reduce corruption. In 1996 the city of Philadelphia agreed to implement a set of reforms to combat corruption to settle a lawsuit brought by civil rights organizations. The following were among the measures taken to reduce corruption.

• A policy mandating that all citizens' complaints be forwarded for investigation by the internal affairs division.
• Development of computer files that contain all types of complaints and suits against individual officers that could be easily accessed during investigations.
• A policy requiring that internal affairs give a high priority to any officer's claim that another officer was corrupt or used excessive force.
• Mandatory reporting and recording of all incidents in which an officer used more than incidental force.
• Training of officers to treat citizens without racial bias; assigning a deputy commissioner to monitor charges of race discrimination.
• Reviewing all policies and practices to ensure they do not involve or have the potential for race bias.[189]

Another approach is to create outside review boards or special prosecutors, such as the Mollen Commission in New York and the Christopher Commission in Los Angeles, to investigate reported incidents of corruption. However, outside investigators and special prosecutors are often limited by their lack of intimate knowledge of day-to-day operations. As a result, they depend on the testimony of a few officers who are willing to cooperate, either to save themselves from prosecution or because they have a compelling moral commitment. Outside evaluators also face the problem of the blue curtain, which is quickly closed when police officers feel their department is under scrutiny.

A more realistic solution to corruption, albeit a difficult one, might be to change the social context of policing. Police operations must be made more visible, and the public must be given freer access to controlling police operations. All too often, the public finds out about police problems only when a scandal hits the newspaper. Some of the vice-related crimes the police now deal with might be decriminalized or referred to other agencies. Although decriminalization of vice cannot in itself end the problem, it could lower the pressure placed on individual police officers and help eliminate their moral dilemmas.

To quiz yourself on this material, go to questions 7.14–7.25 on the Introduction to Criminal Justice 10e CD.

Summary

- Police departments today are faced with many critical problems in their development and relationship with the public.
- One area of concern is the existence of an independent and unique police culture, which insulates police officers from the rest of society. This culture has distinct rules and loyalties.
- Some experts hold that police officers have distinct personality characteristics marked by authoritarianism and cynicism.
- Police officers may develop a unique working style. Four distinct police styles have been identified, and each influences police decision making.
- Today, many police officers are seeking higher education. The jury is still out on whether educated officers are more effective.
- Women and minorities are being recruited into the police in increasing numbers. Research indicates that, with few exceptions, they perform as well or even better than white or male officers.
- In some larger departments, the percentage of minorities on police forces now reflects their representation in the general population.

- The number of female officers still lags behind the number of male officers.
- Women and minorities still lag white males in supervisory positions.
- The complexity and danger of the police role produce an enormous amount of stress that harms police effectiveness. Police departments have tried a variety of techniques designed to limit police stress.
- Police have been charged with being brutal and have worked hard to reduce their use of force through training and rule making. Surveys indicate that today the police use of force seems limited, indicating that these techniques may be working.
- One critical concern is the police use of deadly force. Research indicates that anti-shooting policies can limit deaths resulting from police action. The U.S. Supreme Court has ruled that police cannot shoot unarmed fleeing felons.
- Another effort has been to identify and eliminate police corruption, which still mars the reputation of police forces.

Key Terms

blue curtain 208
cynicism 210
police styles 211
discretion 212
low-visibility decision making 212

demeanor 214
double marginality 220
police brutality 225
deadly force 228
Knapp Commission 235

meat eater 235
grass eater 235
Mollen Commission 235

Doing Research on the Web

For an up-to-date list of Web links, go to http://cj.wadsworth.com/siegel_intro10e.

To control police use of force, a number of force continuums such as the FLETC model have been created. However, some question has arisen as to whether this a wise move. Should law enforcement abide by force continuums and should police continue to require their officers to start at the lowest level of force and escalate to higher levels without considering the effectiveness such action has in serving the law enforcement mission?

The Federal Law Enforcement Training Center, which developed the FLETC model, is the government's provider of law enforcement training. Its goal is to prepare law enforcement professionals to fulfill their re-

sponsibilities in a safe manner and at the highest level of proficiency. You can reach its Web site at http://www.fletc.gov/.

To read more about this important topic, go to InfoTrac College Edition and read George T. Williams, "Force Continuums: A Liability to Law Enforcement?" *FBI Law Enforcement Bulletin* 71, no. 6 (June 2002):14.

You can also use "police violence" as a subject guide on InfoTrac College Edition.

> Pro/Con discussions and Viewpoint Essays on some of the topics in this chapter may be found at the Opposing Viewpoints Resource Center: http://www.gale.com/OpposingViewpoints.

Discussion Questions

1. Should male and female officers have exactly the same duties in a police department? If not, why not?
2. Do you think that an officer's working the street will eventually produce a cynical personality and distrust for civilians? Explain.
3. How can education help police officers?
4. Should a police officer who accepts a free meal from a restaurant owner be dismissed from the force? Why or why not?
5. A police officer orders an unarmed person running away from a burglary to stop; the suspect keeps running and is shot and killed by the officer. Has the officer committed a crime? Explain.
6. Would you like to live in a society that abolished police discretion and used a full enforcement policy? Why or why not?

Notes

1 Nick Madigan, "Brutality Trial for Officer Concludes in Hung Jury," *New York Times,* July 29, 2003, p. 1

2 Kathleen Maguire and Ann Pastore, eds., *Sourcebook of Criminal Justice Statistics,* online version, //www.albany.edu/sourcebook/1995/pdf/t216.pdf, accessed on October 25, 2003.

3 Steven Tuch and Ronald Weitzer, "The Polls: Trends, Racial Differences in Attitudes toward the Police," *Public Opinion Quarterly* 61 (1997): 642–63.

4 Robert Sigler and Ida Johnson, "Reporting Violent Acts to the Police: A Difference by Race," *Policing: An International Journal of Police Strategies and Management* 25 (2002): 274–93.

5 Thomas Priest and Deborah Brown Carter, "Evaluations of Police Performance in an African American Sample," *Journal of Criminal Justice* 27 (1999): 457–65; Ronald Weitzer "White, Black, or Blue Cops? Race and Citizen Assessments of Police Officers," *Journal of Criminal Justice* 28 (2000): 313–24.

6 Eugene Paoline, "Taking Stock: Toward a Richer Understanding of Police Culture,"

Journal of Criminal Justice 31 (2003): 199–214.

7 See, for example, Richard Harris, *The Police Academy: An Inside View* (New York: Wiley, 1973); John Van Maanen, "Observations on the Making of a Policeman," in *Order Under Law,* ed. R. Culbertson and M. Tezak (Prospect Heights, Ill.: Waveland Press, 1981), pp. 111–26; Jonathan Rubenstein, *City Police* (New York: Ballantine Books, 1973); John Broderick, *Police in a Time of Change* (Morristown, N.J.: General Learning Press, 1977).

8 Malcolm Sparrow, Mark Moore, and David Kennedy, *Beyond 911: A New Era for Policing* (New York: Basic Books, 1990), p. 51.

9 M. Steven Meagher and Nancy Yentes, "Choosing a Career in Policing: A Comparison of Male and Female Perceptions," *Journal of Police Science and Administration* 16 (1986): 320–27.

10 Michael K. Brown, *Working the Street* (New York: Russell Sage, 1981), p. 82.

11 Stan Shernock, "An Empirical Examination of the Relationship between Police Solidarity and Community Orientation,"

Journal of Police Science and Administration 18 (1988): 182–98.

12 Ibid., p. 360.

13 Ibid., p. 359.

14 Egon Bittner, *The Functions of Police in Modern Society* (Cambridge, Mass.: Oelgeschlager, Gunn, and Hain, 1980), p. 63.

15 Wallace Graves, "Police Cynicism: Causes and Cures," *FBI Law Enforcement Bulletin* 65 (1996): 16–21.

16 Richard Lundman, *Police and Policing* (New York: Holt, Rinehart, and Winston, 1980). See also Jerome Skolnick, *Justice without Trial* (New York: Wiley, 1966).

17 Robert Regoli, Robert Culbertson, John Crank, and James Powell, "Career Stage and Cynicism among Police Chiefs," *Justice Quarterly* 7 (1990): 592–614.

18 William Westly, *Violence and the Police: A Sociological Study of Law, Custom, and Morality* (Cambridge, Mass.: MIT Press, 1970).

19 Skolnick, *Justice without Trial,* pp. 42–68.

20 Milton Rokeach, Martin Miller, and John Snyder, "The Value Gap between Police and Policed," *Journal of Social Issues* 27 (1971): 155–71.

21 Bruce Carpenter and Susan Raza, "Personality Characteristics of Police Applicants: Comparisons across Subgroups and with Other Populations," *Journal of Police Science and Administration* 15 (1987): 10–17.

22 Larry Tifft, "The 'Cop Personality' Reconsidered," *Journal of Police Science and Administration* 2 (1974): 268; David Bayley and Harold Mendelsohn, *Minorities and the Police* (New York: Free Press, 1969); Robert Balch, "The Police Personality: Fact or Fiction?" *Journal of Criminal Law, Criminology, and Police Science* 63 (1972): 117.

23 Lowell Storms, Nolan Penn, and James Tenzell, "Policemen's Perception of Real and Ideal Policemen," *Journal of Police Science and Administration* 17 (1990): 40–43.

24 Arthur Niederhoffer, *Behind the Shield: The Police in Urban Society* (Garden City, N.Y.: Doubleday, 1967).

25 Ibid., pp. 216–20.

26 Carl Klockars, "The Dirty Harry Problem," *Annals* 452 (1980): 33–47.

27 Jack Kuykendall and Roy Roberg, "Police Manager's Perceptions of Employee Types: A Conceptual Model," *Journal of Criminal Justice* 16 (1988): 131–35.

28 Stephen Matrofski, R. Richard Ritti, and Jeffrey Snipes, "Expectancy Theory and Police Productivity in DUI Enforcement," *Law and Society Review* 28 (1994): 113–38.

29 Paoline, "Taking Stock."

30 Skolnick, *Justice without Trial.*

31 Helen Eigenberg, Kathryn Scarborough, and Victor Kappeler, "Contributory Factors Affecting Arrest in Domestic and Nondomestic Assaults," *American Journal of Police* 15 (1996): 27–51.

32 Leonore Simon, "A Therapeutic Jurisprudence Approach to the Legal Processing of Domestic Violence Cases," *Psychology, Public Policy, and Law* 1 (1995): 43–79.

33 Peter Sinden and B. Joyce Stephens, "Police Perceptions of Domestic Violence: The Nexus of Victim, Perpetrator, Event, Self and Law," *Policing* 22 (1999): 313–26.

34 Robert Kane, "Patterns of Arrest in Domestic Violence Encounters: Identifying a Police Decision-Making Model," *Journal of Criminal Justice* 27 (1999): 65–79.

35 Gregory Howard Williams, *The Law and Politics of Police Discretion* (Westport, Conn.: Greenwood Press, 1984).

36 Dana Jones and Joanne Belknap, "Police Responses to Battering in a Progressive Pro-Arrest Jurisdiction," *Justice Quarterly* 16 (1999): 249–73.

37 Douglas Smith and Jody Klein, "Police Control of Interpersonal Disputes," *Social Problems* 31 (1984): 468–81.

38 Jones and Belknap, "Police Responses to Battering," pp. 249–73.

39 Wendy L. Hicks, "Police Vehicular Pursuits: An Overview of Research and Legal Conceptualizations for Police Administrators," *Criminal Justice Policy Review* 14 (2003): 75-95.

40 Robin Shepard Engel, "Patrol Officer Supervision in the Community Policing Era," *Journal of Criminal Justice* 30 (2002): 51–64.

41 Westly, *Violence and the Police.*

42 Nathan Goldman, *The Differential Selection of Juvenile Offenders for Court Appearance* (New York: National Council on Crime and Delinquency, 1963).

43 Richard Lundman, "Demeanor or Crime? The Midwest City Police–Citizen Encounters Study," *Criminology* 32 (1994): 631–53; Robert Worden and Robin Shepard, "On the Meaning, Measurement, and Estimated Effects of Suspects' Demeanor toward the Police," paper presented at the annual meeting of the American Society of Criminology, Miami, Florida, November 1994.

44 David Klinger, "Bringing Crime Back In: Toward a Better Understanding of Police Arrest Decisions," *Journal of Research in Crime and Delinquency* 33 (1996): 333–36; David Klinger, "More on Demeanor and Arrest in Dade County," *Criminology* 34 (1996): 61–79; David Klinger, "Demeanor or Crime? Why 'Hostile' Citizens Are More Likely to Be Arrested," *Criminology* 32 (1994): 475–93.

45 William Terrill and Stephen Mastrofski, "Situational And Officer-Based Determinants of Police Coercion," *Justice Quarterly* 19 (2002): 215–48.

46 William Terrill, *Police Coercion: Application of the Force Continuum* (New York: LFB Scholarly Publishing LLC, 2001).

47 Benjamin Weiser, "Federal Inquiry Finds Racial Profiling in Street Searches," *New York Times,* October 5, 2000, p. 1.

48 Thomas J. Lueck, "Mayor Disputes Finding of Profiling by Police," *New York Times,* October 6, 2000, p. B2.

49 R. Steven Daniels, Lorin Baumhover, William Formby, and Carolyn Clark-Daniels, "Police Discretion and Elder Mistreatment: A Nested Model of Observation, Reporting, and Satisfaction," *Journal of Criminal Justice* 27 (1999): 209–25.

50 Brown, *Working the Street,* 290.

51 See Larry Hoover, *Police Educational Characteristics and Curricula* (Washington, D.C.: Government Printing Office, 1975).

52 Brian Reaves and Matthew J. Hickman, *Police Departments in Large Cities, 1990–2000* (Washington, D.C.: Bureau of Justice Statistics, 2002).

53 Bruce Berg, "Who Should Teach Police: A Typology and Assessment of Police Academy Instructors," *American Journal of Police* 9 (1990): 79–100.

54 David Carter and Allen Sapp, *The State of Police Education: Critical Findings* (Washington, D.C.: Police Executive Research Forum, 1988), p. 6.

55 John Krimmel, "The Performance of College-Educated Police: A Study of Self-Rated Police Performance Measures," *American Journal of Police* 15 (1996): 85–95.

56 Robert Worden, "A Badge and a Baccalaureate: Policies, Hypotheses, and

Further Evidence," *Justice Quarterly* 7 (1990): 565–92.

57 See Lawrence Sherman and Warren Bennis, "Higher Education for Police Officers: The Central Issues," *Police Chief* 44 (1977): 32.

58 Worden, "A Badge and a Baccalaureate," 587–89.

59 Jihong Zhao and Nicholas Lovrich, "Determinants of Minority Employment in American Municipal Police Agencies: The Representation of African American Officers," *Journal of Criminal Justice* 26 (1998): 267–78.

60 David Murphy and John Worrall, "Residency Requirements and Public Perceptions of the Police in Large Municipalities," *Policing* 22 (1999): 327–42.

61 Tuch and Weitzer, "The Polls."

62 Sutham Cheurprakobkit, "Police–Citizen Contact and Police Performance: Attitudinal Differences between Hispanics and Non-Hispanics," *Journal of Criminal Justice* 28 (2000) 325–36; Kathleen Maguire and Ann L. Pastore, eds., *Sourcebook of Criminal Justice Statistics* (2001), online version, http://www.albany.edu/sourcebook, accessed on October 25, 2003.

63 Yolander G. Hurst, James Frank, and Sandra Lee Browning, "The Attitudes of Juveniles toward the Police: A Comparison of African-American and White Youth," *Policing: An International Journal of Police Strategies, and Management* 23 (2000): 37–53.

64 Jack Kuykendall and David Burns, "The African-American Police Officer: An Historical Perspective," *Journal of Contemporary Criminal Justice* 1 (1980): 4–13.

65 Ibid.

66 Nicholas Alex, *Black in Blue: A Study of the Negro Policeman* (New York: Appleton-Century-Crofts, 1969).

67 Kim Michelle Lersch, "Predicting Citizen's Race in Allegations of Misconduct against the Police," *Journal of Criminal Justice* 26 (1998): 87–99.

68 Reaves and Hickman, *Police Departments in Large Cities.*

69 Nicholas Alex, *New York Cops Talk Back* (New York: Wiley, 1976).

70 Stephen Leinen, *African-American Police, White Society* (New York: New York University Press, 1984).

71 Donald Yates and Vijayan Pillai, "Frustration and Strain among Fort Worth Police Officers," *Sociology and Social Research* 76 (1992): 145–49.

72 Robin Haarr and Merry Morash, "Gender, Race, and Strategies of Coping with Occupational Stress in Policing," *Justice Quarterly* 16 (1999): 303–36.

73 Kenneth Novak, Leanne Fiftal Alarid, and Wayne Lucas, "Exploring Officers' Acceptance of Community Policing: Implications for Policy Implementation," *Journal of Criminal Justice* 31 (2003): 57–71; Donald Yates and Vijayan Pillai, "Race and Police Commitment to Community Policing," *Journal of Intergroup Relations* 19 (1993): 14–23.

74 Bruce Berg, Edmond True, and Marc Gertz, "Police, Riots, and Alienation," *Journal of Police Science and Administration* 12 (1984): 186–90.

75 Yates and Pillai, "Frustration and Strain among Fort Worth Police Officers."

76 James Jacobs and Jay Cohen, "The Impact of Racial Integration on the Police," *Journal of Police Science and Administration* 6 (1978): 182.

77 Charles Katz, "The Establishment of a Police Gang Unit: An Examination of organizational and Environmental Factors," *Criminology* 39 (2001): 37–73.

78 Ibid., p. 61.

79 Weitzer, "White, Black, or Blue Cops?"

80 For a review of the history of women in policing, see Dorothy Moses Schulz, "From Policewoman to Police Officer: An Unfinished Revolution," *Police Studies* 16 (1993): 90–99; Cathryn House, "The Changing Role of Women in Law Enforcement," *Police Chief* 60 (1993): 139–44.

81 Susan Martin, "Female Officers on the Move? A Status Report on Women in Policing," in *Critical Issues in Policing*, ed. Roger Dunham and Geoffery Alpert (Grove Park, Ill.: Waveland Press, 1988), 312–31.

82 Le Bouef v. Ramsey, 26 FEP Cases 884 (September 16, 1980).

83 Michael Birzer and Delores Craig, "Gender Differences in Police Physical Ability Test Performance," *American Journal of Police* 15 (1996): 93–106.

84 Reaves and Hickman, *Police Departments in Large Cities.*

85 James Daum and Cindy Johns, "Police Work from a Woman's Perspective," *Police Chief* 61 (1994): 46–49.

86 Steve Herbert, " 'Hard Charger' or 'Station Queen'? Policing and the Masculinist State," *Gender Place and Culture: A Journal of Feminist Geography* 8 (2001): 55–72.

87 Ibid., p. 58.

88 Matthew Hickman, Alex Piquero, and Jack Greene, "Discretion and Gender Disproportionality in Police Disciplinary Systems," *Policing: An International Journal of Police Strategies and Management* 23 (2000): 105–16.

89 Robin Haarr and Merry Morash, "Gender, Race, and Strategies of Coping with Occupational Stress in Policing," *Justice Quarterly* 16 (1999): 303–36.

90 Merry Morash and Jack Greene, "Evaluating Women on Patrol: A Critique of Contemporary Wisdom," *Evaluation Review* 10 (1986): 230–55.

91 Peter Bloch and Deborah Anderson, *Policewomen on Patrol: Final Report* (Washington, D.C.: Police Foundation, 1974).

92 Joel Garner, Christopher Maxwell, and Cederick Heraux, "Characteristics Associated with the Prevalence and Severity of Force Used by the Police," *Justice Quarterly* 19 (2002): 705–47.

93 Steven Brandl, Meghan Stroshine, and James Frank, "Who Are the Complaint-Prone Officers? An Examination of the Relationship between Police Officers' Attributes, Arrest Activity, Assignment, and Citizens' Complaints about Excessive Force," *Journal of Criminal Justice* 29 (2001): 521–29.

94 Daum and Johns, "Police Work from a Woman's Perspective."

95 Mary Brown, "The Plight of Female Police: A Survey of NW Patrolmen," *Police Chief* 61 (1994): 50–53.

96 Simon Holdaway and Sharon K. Parker, "Policing Women Police: Uniform Patrol, Promotion, and Representation in the CID," *British Journal of Criminology* 38 (1998): 40–48.

97 Curt Bartol, George Bergen, Julie Seager Volckens, and Kathleen Knoras, "Women in Small-Town Policing, Job Performance, and Stress," *Criminal Justice and Behavior* 19 (1992): 245–59.

98 Susan Martin, "Outsider within the Station House: The Impact of Race and Gender on African-American Women Police," *Social Problems* 41 (1994): 383–400.

99 Michael Birzer and Robert Nolan, "Learning Strategies of Selected Urban Police Related to Community Policing," *Policing: An International Journal of Police Strategies and Management* 25 (2002): 242–55.

100 Martin, "Outsider within the Station House," p. 387.

101 Ibid., p. 392.

102 Ibid., p. 394.

103 Ibid., p. 397.

104 Ibid.

105 Eric Poole and Mark Pogrebin, "Factors Affecting the Decision to Remain in Policing: A Study of Women Officers," *Journal of Police Science and Administration* 16 (1988): 49–55.

106 Richard Lumb and Rondald Breazeale, "Police Officer Attitudes and Community Policing Implementation: Developing Strategies for Durable Organizational Change," *Policing and Society* 13 (2003): 91–107.

107 Karen Kruger and Nicholas Valltos, "Dealing with Domestic Violence in Law Enforcement Relationships," *FBI Law Enforcement Bulletin* 71 (2002): 1–7.

108 Yates and Pillai, "Frustration and Strain among Fort Worth Police Officers."

109 Richard Farmer, "Clinical and Managerial Implication of Stress Research on the Police," *Journal of Police Science and Administration* 17 (1990): 205–17.

110 Ni He, Jihong Zhao, and Carol Archbold, "Gender and Police Stress: The Convergent and Divergent Impact of Work Environment, Work–Family Conflict, and Stress Coping Mechanisms of Female and Male Police Officers," *Policing* 25 (2002): 687–709.

111 Francis Cullen, Terrence Lemming, Bruce Link, and John Wozniak, "The Impact of Social Supports on Police Stress," *Criminology* 23 (1985): 503–22.

112 Jihong Zhao, Ni He, and Nicholas Lovrich, "Predicting Five Dimensions of Police Officer Stress: Looking More Deeply into Organizational Settings for Sources of Police Stress," *Police Quarterly* 5 (2002): 43–63.

113 Lawrence Travis III and Craig Winston, "Dissension in the Ranks: Officer Resistance to Community Policing and Support for the Organization," *Journal of Crime and Justice* 21 (1998): 139–55.

114 Farmer, "Clinical and Managerial Implications of Stress Research on the Police"; Nancy Norvell, Dale Belles, and Holly Hills, "Perceived Stress Levels and Physical Symptoms in Supervisory Law Enforcement Personnel," *Journal of Police Science and Administration* 16 (1988): 75–79.

115 Donald Yates and Vijayan Pillai, "Attitudes toward Community Policing: A Causal Analysis," *Social Science Journal* 33 (1996): 193–209.

116 Harvey McMurray, "Attitudes of Assaulted Police Officers and Their Policy Implications," *Journal of Police Science and Administration* 17 (1990): 44–48.

117 Robert Ankony and Thomas Kelly, "The Impact of Perceived Alienation of Police Officers' Sense of Mastery and Subsequent Motivation for Proactive Enforcement," *Policing* 22 (1999): 120–32.

118 John Blackmore, "Police Stress," in *Policing Society*, ed. Clinton Terry (New York: Wiley, 1985), 395.

119 Stephen Curran, "Separating Fact from Fiction about Police Stress," *Behavioral Health Management* 23 (2003): 38–40; Peter Marzuk, Matthew Nock, Andrew Leon, Laura Portera, and Kenneth Tardiff, "Suicide among New York City Police Officers, 1977–1996," *American Journal of Psychiatry* 159 (2002): 2069–72; Rose Lee Josephson and Martin Reiser, "Officer Suicide in the Los Angeles Police Department: A Twelve-Year Follow-up," *Journal of Police Science and Administration* 17 (1990): 227–30.

120 Yates and Pillai, "Attitudes toward Community Policing," 205–06.

121 Ibid.

122 Rosanna Church and Naomi Robertson, "How State Police Agencies Are Addressing the Issue of Wellness," *Policing* 22 (1999): 304–12.

123 Farmer, "Clinical and Managerial Implications of Stress Research on the Police," 215.

124 Peter Hart, Alexander Wearing, and Bruce Headey, "Assessing Police Work Experiences: Development of the Police Daily Hassles and Uplifts Scales," *Journal of Criminal Justice* 21 (1993): 553–73.

125 Vivian Lord, Denis Gray, and Samuel Pond, "The Police Stress Inventory: Does It Measure Stress?" *Journal of Criminal Justice* 19 (1991): 139–49.

126 David Kocieniewski, "Man Says Officers Tortured Him after Arrest," *New York Times,* August 13, 1997, p.1.

127 Bittner, *The Functions of Police in Modern Society,* p. 46.

128 Richard R. Johnson, "Citizen Complaints: What the Police Should Know," *FBI Law Enforcement Bulletin* 67 (1998): 1–6.

129 For a general review, see Tom McEwen, *National Data Collection on Police Use of Force* (Washington, D.C.: National Institute of Justice, 1996).

130 Patrick A. Langan, Lawrence A. Greenfeld, Steven K. Smith, Matthew R. Durose, and David J. Levin, *Contacts between Police and the Public: Findings from the 1999 National Survey* (Washington, D.C.: Bureau of Justice Statistics, 2001).

131 Antony Pate and Lorie Fridell, *Police Use of Force: Official Reports, Citizen Complaints, and Legal Consequences* (Washington, D.C.: Police Foundation, 1993).

132 Colin Loftin, David McDowall, Brian Wiersema, and Adam Dobrin, "Underreporting of Justifiable Homicides Committed by Police Officers in the United States, 1976–1998," *American Journal of Public Health* 93 (2003): 1117–21.

133 Langan,. Greenfeld,. Smith,. Durose, and. Levin, *Contacts between Police and the Public.*

134 William Terrill and Stephen Mastrofski, "Situational and Officer-Based Determinants of Police Coercion," *Justice Quarterly* 19 (2002): 215–48.

135 Joel Garner, Christopher Maxwell, and Cederick Heraux, "Characteristics Associated with the Prevalence and Severity of Force Used by the Police," *Justice Quarterly* 19 (2002): 705–47.

136 Sandra Lee Browning, Francis Cullen, Liqun Cao, Renee Kopache, and Thomas Stevenson, "Race and Getting Hassled by the Police: A Research Note," *Police Studies* 17 (1994): 1–11.

137 Ibid.

138 Kim Michelle Lersch and Tom Mieczkowski, "Who Are the Problem-Prone Officers? An Analysis of Citizen Complaints," *American Journal of Police* 15 (1996): 23–42.

139 John MacDonald, Patrick Manz, Geoffrey Alpert, and Roger Dunham, "Police Use of Force: Examining the Relationship between Calls for Service and the Balance of Police Force and Suspect Resistance," *Journal of Criminal Justice* 31 (2003): 119–27.

140 Samuel Walker, "The Rule Revolution: Reflections on the Transformation of American Criminal Justice, 1950–1988," Working Papers, Series 3 (Madison: University of Wisconsin Law School, Institute for Legal Studies, December 1988).

141 Michael D. White, "Controlling Police Decisions to Use Deadly Force: Reexamining the Importance of Administrative Policy," *Crime and Delinquency* 47 (2001): 131.

142 Kevin Flynn, "New York Police Sting Tries to Weed Out Brutal Officers," *New York Times,* September 24, 1999, p. 2.

143 Victor Kappeler, Stephen Kappeler, and Rolando Del Carmen, "A Content Analysis of Police Civil Liability Cases: Decisions of the Federal District Courts, 1978–1990," *Journal of Criminal Justice* 21 (1993): 325–37.

144 Lawrence Sherman and Robert Langworthy, "Measuring Homicide by Police Officers," *Journal of Criminal Law and Criminology* 4 (1979): 546–60.

145 Ibid.

146 James Fyfe, "Police Use of Deadly Force: Research and Reform," *Justice Quarterly* 5 (1988): 165–205.

147 Sherman and Langworthy, "Measuring Homicide by Police Officers."

148 Brad Smith, "The Impact of Police Officer Diversity on Police-Caused Violence," *Policy Studies Journal* 31 (2003): 147–63.

149 John MacDonald, Geoffrey Alpert, and Abraham Tennenbaum, "Justifiable Homicide by Police and Criminal Homicide: A Research Note," *Journal of Crime and Justice* 22 (1999): 153–64.

150 Richard Parent and Simon Verdun-Jones, "Victim-Precipitated Homicide: Police Use of Deadly Force in British Columbia," *Policing* 21 (1998): 432–49.

151 "10% of Police Shootings Found to Be 'Suicide by Cop,'" *Criminal Justice Newsletter* 29 (1998): 1.

152 Sherman and Langworthy, "Measuring Homicide by Police Officers."

153 Jonathan Sorenson, James Marquart, and Deon Brock, "Factors Related to Killings of Felons by Police Officers: A Test of the Community Violence and Conflict Hypotheses," *Justice Quarterly* 10 (1993): 417–40; David Jacobs and David Britt, "Inequality and Police Use of Deadly Force: An Empirical Assessment of a Conflict Hypotheses," *Social Problems* 26 (1979): 403–12.

154 Smith, "The Impact of Police Officer Diversity on Police-Caused Violence."

155 David Jacobs and Jason Carmichael, "Subordination and Violence against State Control Agents: Testing Political Explanations for Lethal Assaults against the Police," *Social Forces* 80 (2002): 1223–52.

156 Fyfe, "Police Use of Deadly Force," p. 181.

157 Paul Takagi, "A Garrison State in a 'Democratic' Society," *Crime and Social Justice* 5 (1974): 34–43.

158 Mark Blumberg, "Race and Police Shootings: An Analysis in Two Cities," in *Contemporary Issues in Law Enforcement,* ed. James Fyfe (Beverly Hills, Calif.: Sage, 1981), 152–66.

159 James Fyfe, "Shots Fired," Ph.D. dissertation, State University of New York, Albany, 1978.

160 *Tennessee* v. *Garner,* 471 U.S. 1, 105 S.Ct. 1694, 85 L.Ed.2d 889 (1985).

161 *Graham* v. *Connor,* 490 U.S. 386, 109 S.Ct. 1865, 104 L.Ed.2d 443 (1989).

162 Franklin Graves and Gregory Connor, "The FLETC Use-of-Force Model," *Police Chief* 59 (1992): 56–58.

163 See James Fyfe, "Administrative Interventions on Police Shooting Discretion: An Empirical Examination," *Journal of Criminal Justice* 7 (1979): 313–25.

164 Frank Zarb, "Police Liability for Creating the Need to Use Deadly Force in Self-Defense," *Michigan Law Review* 86 (1988): 1982–2009.

165 Warren Cohen, "When Lethal Force Won't Do," *U.S. News and World Report,* June 23, 1997, p. 12.

166 Richard Lumb and Paul Friday, "Impact of Pepper Spray Availability on Police Officer Use-of-Force Decisions," *Policing* 20 (1997): 136–49.

167 Tom McEwen, "Policies on Less-Than-Lethal Force in Law Enforcement Agencies," *Policing* 20 (1997): 39–60.

168 Federal Bureau of Investigation, "Law Enforcement Officers Killed and Assaulted, 2000," press release, November 26, 2001.

169 J. David Hirschel, Charles Dean, and Richard Lumb, "The Relative Contribution of Domestic Violence to Assault and Injury of Police Officers," *Justice Quarterly* 11 (1994): 99–118.

170 John Cloud, "L.A. Confidential, for Real: Street Cops Accused of Frame-ups in Widening Scandal," *Time,* September 27, 1999, p. 44; "L.A.'s Dirty War on Gangs: A Trail of Corruption Leads to Some of the City's Toughest Cops," *Newsweek,* October 11, 1999, p. 72.

171 Samuel Walker, *Popular Justice* (New York: Oxford University Press, 1980), p. 64.

172 Herman Goldstein, *Police Corruption* (Washington, D.C.: Police Foundation, 1975), p. 3.

173 Knapp Commission, Report on Police Corruption (New York: Braziller, 1973), pp. 1–34.

174 Elizabeth Neuffer, "Seven Additional Detectives Linked to Extortion Scheme," *Boston Globe,* October 25, 1988, p. 60.

175 Kevin Cullen, "U.S. Probe Eyes Bookie Protection," *Boston Globe,* 25 October 25, 1988, p. 1.

176 Michael Johnston, *Political Corruption and Public Policy in America* (Monterey, Calif.: Books/Cole, 1982), p. 75.

177 William Doherty, "Ex-Sergeant Says He Aided Bid to Sell Exam," *Boston Globe,* February 26, 1987, p. 61.

178 Anthony Simpson, *The Literature of Police Corruption,* vol. 1 (New York: John Jay Press, 1977), 53.

179 Peter Kraska and Victor Kappeler, "Police On-Duty Drug Use: A Theoretical and Descriptive Examination," *American Journal of Police* 7 (1988): 1–28.

180 Ellwyn Stoddard, "Blue Coat Crime," in *Thinking about Police,* ed. Carl Klockars (New York: McGraw-Hill, 1983), 338–49.

181 Lawrence Sherman, *Police Corruption: A Sociological Perspective* (Garden City, N.Y.: Doubleday, 1974), pp. 40–41.

182 Samuel Walker, *Police in Society* (New York: McGraw-Hill, 1983), p. 181.

183 Robert Kane, "The Social Ecology of Police Misconduct," *Criminology* 40 (2002): 867–97 .

184 Sherman, *Police Corruption.*
185 Robert Daley, *Prince of the City* (New York: Houghton Mifflin, 1978).
186 Sherman, *Police Corruption,* p. 194.
187 Kevin Flynn, "Police Dept. Routinely Drops Cases of Officer Misconduct, Report Says," *New York Times,* September 15, 1999, p. 1.
188 Barbara Gelb, *Tarnished Brass: The Decade after Serpico* (New York: Putnam, 1983); Candace McCoy, "Lawsuits against Police: What Impact Do They Have?" *Criminal Law Bulletin* 20 (1984): 49–56.
189 "Philadelphia Police Corruption Brings Major Reform Initiative," *Criminal Justice Newsletter* 27 (1996): 4–5.

Chapter Outline

Chapter Objectives

After reading this chapter, you should be able to:

1. Understand the concept of legal control over police activity.
2. Know what is meant by the term *search and seizure*.
3. Recognize the controls the courts have placed on the use of informers to get warrants.
4. Explain the term *totality of the circumstances*.
5. Recognize that searches can occur without a warrant.
6. Know the term *stop and frisk*.
7. Describe the postarrest warrantless search.
8. Discuss the instances that police can search a car without a warrant.
9. Explain the *Miranda* v. *Arizona* decision.
10. Identify the ways incriminating statements can be used in the absence of a *Miranda* warning.
11. Understand the concept of the lineup.

Viewpoints

 Law in Review: *United States* v. *Bin Laden* 264

 Analyzing Criminal Justice Issues: The Future of the Exclusionary Rule 267

InfoTrac College Edition Links

Articles: "*Miranda* Revisited" and "Is *Miranda* Case Law Inconsistent? A Fifth Amendment Synthesis" 262

Web Links

U.S. Supreme Court decisions on criminal procedure
http://www.law.cornell.edu 246

Search and seizure
http://www.lawinfo.com/legalfaqs/search_seizure.html 249

***Miranda* v. *Arizona* opinion**
http://laws.findlaw.com/us/384/436.html 260

Chief Justice Earl Warren's notes on *Miranda*
http://www.loc.gov/exhibits/treasures/trr038.html 262

***Mapp* v. *Ohio* decision**
http://laws.findlaw.com/us/367/643.html 265

Exclusionary rule
http://caselaw.lp.findlaw.com/data/constitution/amendment04/06.html 268

Chapter 8 | Police and the Rule of Law

As the Kobe Bryant rape case unfolded in 2003, it became quickly evident that the State's case against the famed athlete would hang on the quality of evidence the police gathered soon after being called to the crime scene. Bryant readily admitted having a sexual encounter with his accuser but also claimed it was consensual. Nonetheless, police investigators in a sexual assault case such as Bryant's routinely gather evidence such as blood samples, saliva, fingernail scrapings, and hair samples from the victim and suspect in order to prove that a sex act had actually occurred. As experienced investigators, they know that non-laboratory evidence such as witness accounts, photos showing physical abuse, and so on are actually more crucial in a case where the fact that the suspect and victim engaged in sex is not in doubt. The investigators would scour the scene for torn clothing or curtains, broken objects and furniture, and blood on bed sheets and rugs. The objective is to gather sufficient evidence to corroborate the victim's story or support the suspect's denial of a crime.

The police are charged with preventing crime before it occurs and identifying and arresting criminals who have already broken the law.

To carry out these tasks, police officers want a free hand to search for evidence, to seize contraband such as guns and drugs, to interrogate suspects, and to have witnesses and victims identify suspects. They know their investigation must be thorough. At trial, they will need to provide the prosecutor with sufficient evidence to prove guilt "beyond a reasonable doubt." Therefore, soon after the crime is committed, they must make every effort to gather physical evidence, obtain confessions, and take witness statements that will be

adequate to prove the case in court. Police officers also realize that evidence the prosecutor is counting on to prove the case, such as the testimony of a witness or co-conspirator, may evaporate before the trial begins. Then the case outcome may depend on some piece of physical evidence or a suspect's statement taken early in the investigation.

View the CNN video clip of this story on your Introduction to Criminal Justice 10e CD.

245

The need for police officers to gather conclusive evidence can conflict with the constitutional rights of citizens. For example, although police want a free hand to search homes and cars for evidence, the Fourth Amendment restricts police activities by requiring that they obtain a warrant before conducting a search. When police want to vigorously interrogate a suspect, they must honor the Fifth Amendment's prohibition against forcing people to incriminate themselves.

Police and the Courts

Once a crime has been committed and the purpose of the investigation has been determined, the police may use various means to collect the evidence needed for criminal prosecution. With each crime, police must decide how best to conduct an investigation. Should surveillance techniques be employed to secure information? Is there reasonable suspicion to justify stopping and frisking a suspect? Has the investigation shifted from a general inquiry and begun to focus on a particular suspect so that police can start a legally appropriate interrogation?

The U.S. Supreme Court has taken an active role in considering the legality of police operations in the areas of investigation. Of primary concern has been to balance the law enforcement agent's need for a free hand to investigate crimes with the citizen's consitutional right to be free from illegal searches and interrogations. In some instances, the Supreme Court has expanded police power — for example, by increasing the occasions when police can search without a warrant. In other cases, the Supreme Court has restricted police operations — for example, by ruling that every criminal suspect has a right to an attorney when being interrogated by police. Changes in the law often reflect such factors as the justices' legal philosophy and concern for the ability of police to control crime, their views on the need to maintain public safety versus their commitment to the civil liberties of criminal defendants, and current events such as the September 11, 2001, terrorist attacks.

Search and Seizure

One of the key elements of police investigation is the search for incriminating evidence, the seizure of that evidence, and its use during a criminal trial. The Fourth Amendment protects criminal suspects against unreasonable searches and seizures by requiring that evidence cannot be siezed without a lawful **search warrant** issued only after police agents can show in court that they had probable cause to believe that an offense has been or is being committed.

A search warrant is an order from a court authorizing and directing the police to search a designated place for property stated in the order and to bring that property to court. To obtain a warrant, a police officer must offer sworn testimony that the facts on which the request for the search warrant is made are trustworthy and true. If the judge issues the warrant, it will authorize police officers to search for particular objects, at a specific location, at a certain time. For example, a warrant may authorize the search of "the premises at 221 Third Avenue, Apt. 6B between the hours of 8 a.m. to 6 p.m." and direct the police to search for and seize "subtances, contraband, paraphernalia, scales, and other items used in connection with the sale of illegal substances."

Generally, warrants allow the seizure of a variety of types of evidence described in Exhibit 8.1.

Search Warrant Requirements

The Fourth Amendment contains two elements that protect the public against intrusions of their privacy and shape the issuance of warrants.

search warrant
An order, issued by a judge, directing officers to conduct a search of specified premises for specified objects or persons and to bring them before the court.

A great site for U.S. Supreme Court decisions on criminal procedure is http://www.law.cornell.edu.

Exhibit 8.1 Categories of Evidence

Warrants are typically issued to search for and seize a variety of evidence.

- Property that represents evidence of the commission of a criminal offense; for example, a bloody glove or shirt.

- Contraband, the fruits of crime, smuggled goods, illegal material, or anything else that is of a criminal nature.

- Property intended for use or which has been used as the means of committing a criminal offense; for example, burglary tools, safecracking equipment, and drug paraphernalia.

- People may be seized when there is probable cause for their arrest.

- Conversation involving criminal conspiracy and other illegalities can be seized via tape recordings and wiretaps.

1. It protects individuals against unreasonable searches and seizures by the government. This protective envelope extends to any area in which an individual has a reasonable expectation of privacy including their homes, possessions, and persons.
2. It provides that under normal circumstances a search cannot be conducted unless a warrant is issued by a magistrate based upon probable cause, supported by oath or affirmation, and describing in particular detail the place to be searched.

Reasonableness The reasonableness clause means that a search is invalid when an officer exceeds the scope of police authority. Searches are considered unreasonable if the police did not have sufficient information to justify the search and not because they used unreasonable force or coercion to gain evidence. However, a search conducted through stealth, deception, or disguise to gain admittance to a home or business would be considered unreasonable. So, for example, it would be considered an unreasonable search if police officers dressed up as building inspectors to gain entry into a home and then once inside searched for drugs.

A search would also be considered unreasonable if it were conducted simply because of an offender's prior behavior or status. For example, it would also be unreasonable to stop and search a vehicle driven by a known drug dealer unless some other factors supported the search. Unless there was something discernible to a police officer that indicates a crime was then being committed, the mere act of a known drug dealer driving an automobile on a public highway would not justify an officer forcing him to stop to be searched or arrested for a suspected violation. Nor would it be considered reasonable if police decided to search someone simply because he was seen engaging in a pattern of behavior that seemed similar or comparable to the activity of known criminals. For example, a person could not be searched because he was seen driving a flashy new car and making routine stops at the same places each day merely because that is a pattern of behavior common to drug dealing. However, in the 2002 case *United States* v. *Arvizu,* the Supreme Court allowed a police officer to search a suspicious vehicle based on a vehicle registration check showing that the van was registered to an address in an area notorious for alien and narcotics smuggling, patrol experience informing the officer that the suspect had set out on a route used by drug smugglers, and the driver's intention to pass through the area during a border patrol shift change. While each fact alone was insufficient to form reasonable suspicion, taken together they sufficed to allow him to stop the vehicle.[1]

Probable Cause The Fourth Amendment requires that before a search warrant is issued by a court, the police need to have at least **probable cause** to believe that the item being searched for was involved in criminal activity and will be

probable cause
The evidentiary criterion necessary to sustain an arrest or the issuance of an arrest or search warrant; a set of facts, information, circumstances, or conditions that would lead a reasonable person to believe that an offense was committed and that the accused committed that offense.

© 2003 AP/Wide World Photos

In order for police to search a home for evidence they must have a warrant based on probable cause. Here, an officer removes evidence from the home of Scott Peterson, accused of killing his wife, Laci, in 2003.

particularity
The requirement that a search warrant state precisely where the search is to take place and what items are to be seized.

located at the site to be searched. Under normal circumstances a search warrant cannot be obtained unless the request for it is supported by facts, supplied under oath by a law enforcement officer, that are sufficient to convince the court that a crime has been or is being committed.

To show probable cause, the police usually provide the judge or magistrate with information in the form of written affidavits, which report either their own observations or those of private citizens or police undercover informants. If the magistrate believes that the information is sufficient to establish probable cause to conduct a search, he or she will issue a warrant. Though the suspect is not present when the warrant is issued and therefore cannot contest its issuance, he can later challenge the validity of the warrant before trial.

The Fourth Amendment does not explicitly define probable cause and its precise meaning still remains unclear. However, the police officers have to provide factual evidence to define and identify suspicious activities, not simply offer the officer's beliefs or suspicions. In addition, the officer must show how he obtained the information and provide evidence of its reliability. Some common sources are listed in Exhibit 8.2.

Particularity The Fourth Amendment requires that the police limit their search to only those places and property described in the warrant; this is referred to as **particularity.** The police cannot search the basement of a house if the warrant specifies the attic; they cannot look in a desk drawer if the warrant specifies a search for a missing piano. However, this does not mean that police officers can seize only those items listed in the warrant. If, during the course of their search, police officers come across contraband or evidence of a crime that is not listed in the warrant, they can lawfully seize the unlisted items. But they cannot look in places that are off-limits within the scope of the warrant. For more on search warrants, see Concept Summary 8.1.

Obtaining a Warrant

Police can obtain a warrant if their investigation turns up sufficient evidence to convince a judge that a crime likely has been committed and the person or place the police wish to search probably is materially involved in that crime. This might mean presenting photos and other physical evidence before a judge. This can be an extremely time-consuming process. Consequently, in many instances, the evidence used by the police in requesting a search warrant originates not with the police themselves but with an informer who may be trying to avoid criminal

Exhibit 8.2 Sources for a Warrant

- A police informant whose reliability has been established because he has provided information in the past.
- Someone who has firsthand knowledge of illegal activities.
- A co-conspirator who implicates herself as well as the suspect.
- An informant whose information can be partially verified by the police.
- A victim of a crime who offers information.
- A witness to the crime related to the search.
- A fellow law enforcement officer.

Concept Summary 8.1 The Elements of a Search Warrant

Reasonableness	The warrant must not violate what society considers a reasonable intrusion of privacy under the circumstances. Operating on someone to seize cocaine they swallowed would not be a reasonable search. Searching the glove compartment of a car for a missing rifle would be unreasonable.
Probable cause	Probable cause is determined by whether a police officer, based on fact, has objective, reasonable, and reliable information that the person under investigation has committed or was committing an offense.
Particularity	The warrant must set forth and precisely specify the places to be searched and items to be seized so that it can provide reasonable guidance to the police officers and prevent them from having unregulated and unrestricted discretion to search for evidence.

charges. Because informers are often acting out of self-interest instead of civic duty, the reliability of the evidence they provide may be questionable. Moreover, their statements reflect only what they say and heard, and are not substantiated by hard evidence, and thus are defined as **hearsay evidence.**

The U.S. Supreme Court has been concerned about the reliabilty of evidence obtained from informers. The Court has determined that hearsay evidence must be corroborated to serve as a basis for probable cause and thereby justify the issuance of a warrant. In the case of *Aguilar* v. *Texas* (1964), the Court articulated a two-part test for issuing a warrant on the word of an informant. The police had to show (1) why they believed the informant and (2) how the informant acquired personal knowledge of the crime.[2] This ruling restricted informant testimony to people who were in direct contact with police and whose information could be verified.

hearsay evidence
Testimony that is not firsthand but relates information told by a second party.

For answers to frequently asked questions about search and seizure, go to http://www.lawinfo.com/legalfaqs/search_seizure.html.

Anonymous Tips

Because the *Aguilar* case required that an informer be known and their information be proven knowledgeable, it all but ruled out using anonymous tips to secure a search warrant. This was changed in a critical 1983 ruling, *Illinois* v. *Gates,* in which the Court eased the process of obtaining search warrants by developing a *totality of the circumstances* test to determine probable cause for issuing a search warrant. In *Gates,* the police received a knowledgeable and detailed anonymous letter describing the drug-dealing activities of Lance and Sue Gates. Based on that tip, the police began a surveillance and eventually obtained a warrant to search their home. The search was later challenged on the grounds that it would be impossible to determine the accuracy of information provided by an anonymous letter, a condition required by the *Aguilar* case. However, the Court ruled that, to obtain a warrant, the police must prove to a judge that, considering the totality of the circumstances, an informant has relevant and factual knowledge that a fair probability exists that evidence of a crime will be found in a certain place.[3] The anonymous letter, rich in details, satisfied that demand.

Can the police conduct a search based on an anonymous tip that is verbal, for example, one that is given via telephone? In *Alabama* v. *White,* the police received an anonymous tip that a woman was carrying cocaine.[4] Only after police observation showed that the tip had accurately predicted the woman's movements did it become reasonable to believe the tipster had inside knowledge about the suspect and was truthful in his assertion about the cocaine. The Supreme Court ruled that the search based on the tip was legal because it was corroborated by independent police work. In its ruling, the Court stated:

Police can use anonymous tips to gather evidence and regain stolen property. Here, Larae Pickett and her daughter, Vana Rae, are shown in Billings, Montana on Monday, June 2, 2003 with the reclaimed cradleboard that Pickett hand-beaded for her daughter. Perseverance, an anonymous tip, and a lot of detective work helped Pickett recover the stolen cradleboard.

© 2003 AP/Wide World Photos

Standing alone, the tip here is completely lacking in the necessary indicia of reliability, since it provides virtually nothing from which one might conclude that the caller is honest or his information reliable and gives no indication of the basis for his predictions regarding [Vannesa] White's criminal activities. However, although it is a close question, the totality of the circumstances demonstrates that significant aspects of the informant's story were sufficiently corroborated by the police to furnish reasonable suspicion. . . . Thus, there was reason to believe that the caller was honest and well informed, and to impart some degree of reliability to his allegation that White was engaged in criminal activity.[5]

The *White* case seemed to give police powers to search someone after corroborating an anonymous tip. However, in the more recent (2000) case, *Florida* v. *J. L.,* the Court narrowed that right. In *J. L.,* an anonymous caller reported to the Miami-Dade police that a young, black male standing at a particular bus stop, wearing a plaid shirt, was carrying a gun.[6] The tip was not recorded and no information was known about the caller. Two officers went to the bus stop and saw three black males there. One of them, the 15-year-old J. L., was wearing a plaid shirt. Apart from the anonymous tip, the officers had no reason to suspect that any of the males were involved in any criminal activity. The officers did not see a firearm, and J. L. made no threatening or unusual movements. One officer approached J. L., frisked him, and seized a gun from his pocket. The Court disallowed the search, ruling that a police officer must have reasonable suspicion that criminal activity is being conducted prior to stopping a person. Because anonymous tips are generally considered less reliable than tips from known informants, they can be used to search only if they include specific information that shows they are reliable. Unlike the *White* case, the police in *J. L.* failed to provide independent corroboration of the tipster's information.

Warrantless Searches

Under normal circumstances, the police must obtain a warrant to conduct a search. However, the Supreme Court has over the years carved out some significant exceptions to the search warrant requirement of the Fourth Amendment.

To quiz yourself on this material, go to questions 8.1–8.4 on the Introduction to Criminal Justice 10e CD.

Most of these deal with **exigent** or emergency situations in which police are allowed to search without a warrant being issued to protect their lives or to ensure that evidence is not moved or destroyed. For example, police become involved in a shoot-out with three suspects who run into a home. After arresting the suspects the police would be allowed to search the area the suspects were in without a warrant to find weapons or contraband.

The definition of exigency is not written in stone, and situations that a police officer considers exigent may be disputed by the courts. For example, in *Kirk* v. *Louisiana* (2002), police officers observed a suspect engaging in what they considered to be drug deals. Without a warrant, they entered his home, arrested him, frisked him, found a drug vial in his underwear, and seized contraband that was in plain view in the apartment. Only after these actions did the officers obtain a warrant. The Supreme Court ruled that police officers need either a warrant or probable cause plus exigent circumstances to make a lawful entry into a home. While the Court left unclear the factors that define "exigent circumstances," the facts of the *Kirk* case indicate that merely observing a suspect committing what appears to be a nonviolent crime is not enough to justify a warrantless entry of a person's home.[7]

The Supreme Court has identified a number of exigent circumstances in which a search warrant might have normally been required but because of some immediate emergency police officers can search suspects and places without benefit of a warrant. These include stop-and-frisk search, search incident to a lawful arrest, automobile searches, and consent searches.

Field Interrogation: Stop and Frisk

One important exception to the rule requiring a search warrant is the **threshold inquiry,** or the **stop-and-frisk** procedure. This type of search typically occurs when a police officer encounters a suspicious person on the street and frisks or pats down his outer garments to determine if he is in possession of a concealed weapon. The police officer need not have probable cause to arrest the suspect but is reasonably suspicious based on the circumstances of the case, that is, time and place, and his experience as a police officer. The stop-and-frisk search consists of two distinct components.

(1) The Stop: In which a police officer wishes to briefly detain a suspicious person in an effort to effect crime prevention and detection.
(2) The Frisk: In which an officer pats down or frisks a person who is stopped, for the protection of the officer making the stop.

The stop and the frisk therefore are separate stages in the process, and each requires its own factual basis. Stopping a suspect allows for brief questioning of the person, while frisking him for weapons affords the officer an opportunity to avoid the possibility of attack. For instance, a police officer patrolling a high-crime area observes two young men loitering outside a liquor store after dark. The two men confer several times and stop to talk to a third person who pulls up alongside the curb in an automobile. From this observation, the officer may conclude that the men are casing the store for a possible burglary. He can then stop the suspects and ask them for some identification and an explanation of their conduct. However, the facts that support a stop do not automatically allow a frisk. The officer must have reason to believe that the suspect is armed or dangerous. In this instance, confronting a suspected armed robber is enough in and of itself to frisk the subject.

The landmark case of *Terry* v. *Ohio* (1968) shaped the contours of the stop and frisk.[8] In *Terry* a police officer found a gun in the coat pocket of one of three men he frisked when their suspicious behavior convinced him that they were planning a robbery. At trial the defendants futilely moved to suppress the gun on

exigent
Emergency or immediate circumstance.

threshold inquiry
A term used to describe a stop and frisk.

stop and frisk
The situation in which police officers who are suspicious of an individual run their hands lightly over the suspect's outer garments to determine if the person is carrying a concealed weapon; also called a threshold inquiry or pat-down.

the grounds that it was the product of an illegal search. On appeal, the Supreme Court ruled that if a reasonably prudent police officer believes that her safety or that of others is endangered, she may make a reasonable search for weapons of the person regardless of whether she has probable cause to arrest that individual for crime or the absolute certainty that the individual is armed. The *Terry* case illustrated the principle that although the police officer, whenever possible, must secure a warrant to make a search and seizure, when swift action, based upon on-the-spot observations, is called for the need for the warrant is removed.

What kind of behavior can trigger a *Terry* search? How suspicious does a person have to look before the police can legally stop him and pat him down? In *Illinois* v. *Wardlow,* the defendant was walking on the street in an area known for narcotics trafficking. When he made eye contact with a police officer riding in a marked police car, he ran away. The officer caught up with the defendant on the street, stopped him, and conducted a protective pat-down search for weapons. A handgun was discovered in the frisk, and the defendant was convicted of unlawful use of a weapon by a felon. The Illinois Supreme Court ruled that the frisk violated *Terry* v. *Ohio* because flight may simply be an exercise of the right to "go on one's way" and does not constitute reasonable suspicion. However, on appeal, the U.S. Supreme Court, reversed the state court ruling that a person's presence in a "high crime area," standing alone, is not enough to support a reasonable, particularized suspicion of criminal activity.[9] It held that a location's characteristics are sufficiently suspicious to warrant further investigation, and, in this case, the additional factor of the defendant's unprovoked flight added up to reasonable suspicion. The officers found that the defendant possessed a handgun and, as a result of the pat-down and search, had probable cause to arrest him for violation of a state law. The frisk and arrest were thus proper under *Terry* v. *Ohio.*

Search Incident to a Lawful Arrest

search incident to a lawful arrest
An exception to the search warrant rule; limited to the immediate surrounding area.

Traditionally, a search without a warrant is permissible if it is made incident to a lawful arrest. For example, if shortly after the armed robbery of a grocery store, officers arrest a suspect with a briefcase hiding in the basement, a search of the suspect's person and of the briefcase would be a proper **search incident to a lawful arrest** without a warrant. The legality of this type of search depends almost entirely on the lawfulness of the arrest. The arrest will be upheld if the police officer observed the crime being committed or had probable cause to believe that the suspect committed the offense. If the arrest is found to have been invalid, then any warrantless search made incident to the arrest would be considered illegal, and the evidence obtained from the search would be excluded from trial.

The police officer who searches a suspect incident to a lawful arrest must generally observe two rules. (1) The search must be conducted at the time of or immediately following the arrest. (2) The police may search only the suspect and the area within the suspect's immediate control. The search may not legally go beyond the area where the person can reach for a weapon or destroy any evidence.

The U.S. Supreme Court defined the permissible scope of a search incident to a lawful arrest in *Chimel* v. *California.*[10] According to the *Chimel* doctrine, the police can search a suspect without a warrant after a lawful arrest to protect themselves from danger and to secure evidence. But a search of his home is illegal even if the police find contraband or evidence during the course of that search and the police would be forced to obtain a warrant to search the premises.

Automobile Searches

The U.S. Supreme Court has also established that certain situations justify the warrantless search of an automobile on a public street or highway. For example, evidence can be seized from an automobile when a suspect is taken into custody in a lawful arrest. In *Carroll* v. *United States,* which was decided in 1925, the Supreme Court ruled that distinctions should be made between searches of automobiles, persons, and homes. The Court also concluded that a warrantless search of an automobile is valid if the police have probable cause to believe that the car contains evidence they are seeking.[11]

The legality of searching automobiles without a warrant has always been a trouble spot for police and the courts. Should the search be limited to the interior of the car, or can the police search the trunk? What about a suitcase in the trunk? What about the glove compartment? Does a traffic citation give the police the right to search an automobile? These questions have produced significant litigation over the years. To clear up the matter, the Supreme Court decided the landmark case of *United States* v. *Ross* in 1982.[12] The Court held that, if probable cause exists to believe that an automobile contains criminal evidence, a warrantless search by the police is permissible, including a search of closed containers in the vehicle.

In sum, the most important requirement for a warrantless search of an automobile is that it must be based on the legal standard of probable cause that a crime related to the vehicle has been or is being committed. Under such conditions, the car may be stopped and searched, the contraband seized, and the occupant arrested.

Roadblock Searches Police departments often wish to set up roadblocks to check drivers' licenses or the condition of drivers. Is such a stop an illegal search and seizure? In *Delaware* v. *Prouse* (1979), the Supreme Court forbade the practice of random stops in the absence of any reasonable suspicion that some traffic or motor vehicle law has been violated.[13] Unless there is at least reasonable belief that a motorist is unlicensed, that an automobile is not registered, or that the occupant is subject to seizure for violation of the law, stopping and detaining a driver to check his or her license violates the Fourth Amendment. In *City of Indianapolis* v. *Edmund,* the Court ruled that the police may not routinely stop

© 2003 AP/Wide World Photos

all motorists in the hope of finding a few drug criminals.[14] The general rule is that any seizure must be accompanied by individualized suspicion; the random stopping of cars to search for drugs is illegal.

While random stops are forbidden, a police department could set up a roadblock to stop cars in some systematic fashion to ensure public safety. As long as the police can demonstrate that the checkpoints are conducted in a uniform manner and that the operating procedures have been determined by someone other than the officer at the scene, roadblocks can be used to uncover violators of even minor traffic regulations. In *Michigan Dept. of State Police* v. *Sitz,* the Court held that brief, suspicionless seizures at highway checkpoints for the purposes of combating drunk driving were constitutional.[15]

Roadblocks have recently become popular for combating drunk driving. Courts have ruled that police can stop a predetermined number of cars at a checkpoint and can request each motorist to produce his or her license, registration, and insurance card. While doing so, they can check for outward signs of intoxication.

Police use roadblocks in order to stop cars and search them if the driver is suspected of criminal activity. Sometimes things don't work as planned. Here, Fleming County Sheriff Jerry Wagner holds a shotgun on two bank robbery suspects as Maysville, Kentucky Police Chief Van Ingram reaches for one of the suspects after they crashed through a roadblock and hit a coal truck. One of the two suspects in the car was dead at the scene. Three suspects had robbed the Security Bank and Trust in Maysville about an hour earlier. No police officers were injured.

Searching Drivers and Passengers Can police officers search drivers and passengers during routine traffic stops? In 1977 the Supreme Court ruled in *Pennsylvania* v. *Mimms* that officers could order drivers out of their cars and frisk them during routine traffic stops. Officers' safety outweighed the intrusion on individual rights.[16] In 1997 the Court held in *Maryland* v. *Wilson* that the police had the same authority with respect to passengers.[17] In the *Wilson* case, a state patrol officer lawfully stopped a vehicle for speeding. While the driver was producing his license, the front-seat passenger, Jerry Lee Wilson, was ordered out of the vehicle. As he exited, crack cocaine dropped to the ground. Wilson was arrested and convicted of drug possession. His attorney moved to suppress the evidence, but the U.S. Supreme Court disagreed and extended the *Mimms* rule to passengers. The Court noted that lawful traffic stops had become progressively more dangerous to police officers. From 1994 to 1996, 5,700 officers had been assaulted and 11 killed during such stops. The decision means that passengers must comply when ordered out of a lawfully stopped vehicle.

Generally police can search a suspect after he has exited a vehicle to determine if he had a weapon. They can also search the area in the car, for example, the driver's seat, where the suspect was sitting or that was under his control. However, lower courts have limited this right to search if the passenger or driver was in the vehicle before police arrived. For example, in *U.S.* v. *Green,* police searched a suspect's auto and found a weapon after he was tackled and cuffed 6–10 feet outside the vehicle. The Fifth Circuit concluded that the warrantless search of the vehicle was improper, noting that law enforcement agents first approached the suspect when he was about 25 feet away from his auto and arrested him before he entered his car.[18]

"Free to Go" Must police officers inform detained drivers that they are "free to go" before asking consent to search the vehicle? In *Ohio* v. *Robinette* (1996), the Court concluded that no such warning is needed to make consent to a search reasonable. Robert D. Robinette was stopped for speeding. After checking his license, the officer asked if Robinette was carrying any illegal contraband in the car. When the defendant answered in the negative, the officer asked for and received permission to search the car. The search turned up illegal drugs. The Supreme Court ruled that a police officer does not have to inform a driver that they are "free to go" before asking if they can search the car. According to the Court, the touchstone of the Fourth Amendment is reasonableness, which is assessed by examining the totality of the circumstances.[19] In this case the search was ruled a reasonable exercise of discretion.

Pretext Stops A pretext stop is one in which police officers stop a car because they suspect the driver is involved in a crime such as drug trafficking, but, lacking probable cause, they use a pretext such as a minor traffic violation to stop the car and search its interior. The legality of pretext stops was challenged in *Whren* v. *United States* (1996).[20] Two black defendants claimed that plainclothes police officers used traffic violations as an excuse to stop their vehicle because the officers lacked objective evidence that they were drug couriers. The Court ruled, however, that if probable cause exists to stop a person for a traffic violation, the actual motivation of the officers is irrelevant and therefore the search was legal. This point was reiterated in *Arkansas* v. *Sullivan,* in which the Court ruled that if an officer has a legal basis for making a custodial arrest for a particular crime, it does not matter if he has suspicions that the suspect is involved in any other criminal activity.[21] Thus, as long as there is a legal basis for making an arrest, officers may do so, even in cases in which they are motivated by a desire to gather evidence of other suspected crimes.

Consent Searches

Police officers may also undertake warrantless searches when the person in control of the area or object voluntarily consents to the search. Those who consent to a search essentially waive their constitutional rights under the Fourth Amendment. Ordinarily, courts are reluctant to accept such waivers and require the state to prove that the consent was voluntarily given. In addition, the consent must be given intelligently, and in some jurisdictions, consent searches are valid only after the suspect is informed of the option to refuse consent.

The major legal issue in most consent searches is whether the police can prove that consent was given voluntarily. For example, in the case of *Bumper* v. *North Carolina* (1968), police officers searched the home of an elderly woman after informing her that they possessed a search warrant.[22] At the trial, the prosecutor informed the court that the search was valid because the woman had given her consent. When the government was unable to produce the warrant, the court decided that the search was invalid because the woman's consent was not given voluntarily. On appeal, the U.S. Supreme Court upheld the lower court's finding that the consent had been illegally obtained by the false claim that the police had a search warrant.

In most consent searches, however, voluntariness is a question of fact to be determined from all the circumstances of the case. In *Schneckloth* v. *Bustamonte* (1973), for example, where the defendant helped the police by opening the trunk and glove compartment of the car, the Court said this demonstrated that the consent was voluntarily given.[23] Furthermore, the police are usually under no obligation to inform a suspect of the right to refuse consent. Failure to tell a suspect of this right does not make the search illegal, but it may be a factor used by the courts to decide if the suspect gave consent voluntarily.

The Bus Sweep Today, consent searches have additional significance because of their use in drug control programs. On June 20, 1991, the U.S. Supreme Court, in *Florida* v. *Bostick,* upheld the drug interdiction technique known as the **bus sweep,** in which police board buses and, without suspicion of illegal activity, question passengers, ask for identification, and request permission to search luggage.[24] Police in the *Bostick* case boarded a bus bound from Miami to Atlanta during a stopover in Fort Lauderdale. Without suspicion, the officers picked out the defendant and asked to inspect his ticket and identification. After identifying themselves as narcotics officers looking for illegal drugs, they asked to inspect the defendant's luggage. Although there was some uncertainty about whether the defendant consented to the search in which contraband was found and whether he was informed of his right to refuse consent, the defendant was convicted.

The Supreme Court was faced with deciding whether consent was freely given or whether the nature of the bus sweep negated the defendant's consent. The Court concluded that drug enforcement officers, after obtaining consent, may search luggage on a crowded bus without meeting the Fourth Amendment requirements for a search warrant or probable cause.

This case raises fundamental questions about the legality of techniques used to discourage drug trafficking. Are they inherently coercive? In *Bostick,* when the officers entered the bus, the driver exited and closed the door, leaving the defendant and passengers alone with two officers. Furthermore, Terrance Bostick was seated in the rear of the bus, and officers blocked him from exiting the bus. Finally, one of the officers was clearly holding his handgun in full view. In light of these circumstances, was this a consensual or coercive search? The Supreme Court ruled that it was in fact appropriate.

bus sweep
Police investigation technique in which officers board a bus or train without suspicion of illegal activity and question passengers, asking for identification and seeking permission to search their baggage.

Plain View

The Courts have also ruled that police can search for and seize evidence without benefit of a warrant is if it is in plain view. For example, if a police officer is conducting an investigation and notices while questioning some individuals that one has drugs in her pocket, the officer can seize the evidence and arrest the suspect. Or if the police are conducting a search under a warrant authorizing them to

plain view doctrine
Evidence that is in plain view of
police officers may be seized without a search warrant.

look for narcotics in a person's home and they come upon a gun, the police can seize the gun, even though it is not mentioned in the warrant. The 1986 case of *New York* v. *Class* illustrates the **plain view doctrine.**[25] A police officer stopped a car for a traffic violation. Wishing to check the vehicle identification number (VIN) on the dashboard, he reached into the car to clear away material that was obstructing his view. While clearing the dash, he noticed a gun under the seat — in plain view. The U.S. Supreme Court upheld the seizure of the gun as evidence because the police officer had the right to check the VIN; therefore, the sighting of the gun was legal.

The doctrine of plain view was applied and further developed in *Arizona* v. *Hicks* in 1987.[26] Here, the Court held that moving a stereo component in plain view a few inches to record the serial number constituted a search under the Fourth Amendment. When a check with police headquarters revealed that the item had been stolen, the equipment was seized and offered for evidence at James Hicks's trial. The Court held that a plain-view search and seizure could be justified only by probable cause, not reasonable suspicion, and suppressed the evidence against the defendant. In this case, the Court decided to take a firm stance on protecting Fourth Amendment rights. The *Hicks* decision is uncharacteristic in an era when most decisions have tended to expand the exceptions to the search warrant requirement.

curtilage
Grounds or fields attached to a
house.

Curtilage An issue long associated with plain view is whether police can search open fields that are fenced in but otherwise open to view. In *Oliver* v. *United States* (1984), the U.S. Supreme Court distinguished between the privacy granted persons in their own home or its adjacent grounds (**curtilage**) and a field. The Court ruled that police can use airplane surveillance to spot marijuana fields and then send in squads to seize the crops, or they can peer into fields from cars for the same purpose.[27]

In *California* v. *Ciraola* (1986), the Court expanded the police ability to spy on criminal offenders. In this case, the police received a tip that marijuana was growing in the defendant's backyard.[28] The yard was surrounded by fences, one of which was 10 feet high. The officers flew over the yard in a private plane at an altitude of 1,000 feet to ascertain whether it contained marijuana plants. On the basis of this information, a search warrant was obtained and executed, and with the evidence against him, the defendant was convicted on drug charges. On appeal, the Supreme Court found that his privacy had not been violated.

This holding was expanded in 1989 in *Florida* v. *Riley,* when the Court ruled that police do not need a search warrant to conduct even low-altitude helicopter searches of private property.[29] The Court allowed Florida prosecutors to use evidence obtained by a police helicopter that flew 400 feet over a greenhouse in which defendants were growing marijuana plants. The Court said the search was constitutionally permissible because the flight was within airspace legally available to helicopters under federal regulations.

These cases illustrate how the concepts of curtilage and open fields have added significance in defining the scope of the Fourth Amendment in terms of the doctrine of plain view.

Plain Touch If the police touch contraband, can they sieze it legally? Is "plain touch" like "plain view"? In the 1993 case of *Minnesota* v. *Dickerson,* two Minneapolis police officers noticed the defendant acting suspiciously after leaving an apartment building they believed to be a crack house. The officers briefly stopped Timothy Dickerson to question him and conducted a pat-down search for weapons. The search revealed no weapons, but one officer felt a small lump in the pocket of Dickerson's nylon jacket. The lump turned out to be one-fifth of a gram of crack cocaine, and Dickerson was arrested and charged with drug possession. In its decision, the

D.M. AND R.L. SEEN TOGETHER AT WAREHOUSE ON 2/28/03

© 2003 AP/Wide World Photos

The use of surveillance cameras and videos is growing. Some civil libertarians see them as a threat to personal privacy, but police view them as important law enforcement tools. Here, a surveillance video, released during a Phoenix press conference on Tuesday, June 24, 2003, of Arizona Cardinals' Dennis McKinley, left, and Robert Lee puts them at the scene of a south Phoenix warehouse that was the site of a drug bust. McKinley and three other men were arrested as suspects in an investigation of a drug ring based in Phoenix.

Court added to its "plain view" doctrine a "plain touch" or "plain feel" corollary. The pat-down, however, must be limited to a search for weapons, and the officer may not extend the "feel" beyond that necessary to determine if it is a weapon.[30]

While *Dickerson* created the plain-feel doctrine, the Supreme Court limited its scope in *Bond* v. *United States.*[31] Here a federal border patrol agent boarded a bus near the Texas–Mexico border to check the immigration status of the passengers. As he was leaving the bus, he squeezed the soft luggage that passengers had placed in the overhead storage space. When he squeezed a canvas bag belonging to the defendant, he noticed that it contained a "brick-like" object. The defendant consented to a search of the bag, the agent discovered a "brick" of methamphetamine, and the defendant was charged with and convicted of possession. The court of appeals ruled that the agent's manipulation of the bag was not a search under the Fourth Amendment. On appeal, however, the Supreme Court held that the agent's manipulation of the bag violated the Fourth Amendment's rule against unreasonable searches. Personal luggage, according to the Court, is protected under the Fourth Amendment. The defendant had a privacy interest in his bag, and his right to privacy was violated by the police search.

Electronic Surveillance

The use of wiretapping to intercept conversations between parties has significantly affected police investigative procedures. Electronic devices allow people to listen to and record the private conversations of other people over telephones, through walls and windows, and even over long-distance phone lines. Using these devices, police are able to intercept communications secretly and obtain information related to criminal activity.

The earliest and most widely used form of electronic surveillance is wiretapping. With approval from the court and a search warrant, law enforcement officers place listening devices on telephones to overhear oral communications of suspects.

Such devices are also often placed in homes and automobiles. The evidence collected is admissible and used in the defendant's trial.

Many citizens believe that electronic eavesdropping through hidden microphones, radio transmitters, telephone taps, and bugs represents a grave threat to personal privacy.[32] Although the use of such devices is controversial, the police are generally convinced of their value in investigating criminal activity. Opponents, however, believe that these techniques are often used beyond their lawful intent to monitor political figures, harass suspects, or investigate cases involving questionable issues of national security.

In response to concerns about invasions of privacy, the U.S. Supreme Court has increasingly limited the use of electronic eavesdropping in the criminal justice system. In *Katz* v. *United States* (1967), the Court ruled that when federal agents eavesdropped on a phone conversation using a listening device that could penetrate the walls of a phone booth they had conducted an illegal search and seizure.[33] The *Katz* doctrine is usually interpreted to mean that the government must obtain a court order if it wishes to listen in on conversations in which the parties have a reasonable expectation of privacy, such as in their own homes or on the telephone. Public utterances or actions, meanwhile, are fair game. *Katz* concluded that electronic eavesdropping is a search, even though there is no actual trespass. Therefore, it is unreasonable and a warrant is needed.

More sophisticated devices have come into use in recent years. A pen register, for instance, is a mechanical device that records the numbers dialed on a telephone. Trap and tracer devices ascertain the number from which calls are placed to a particular telephone. Law enforcement agencies also obtain criminal evidence through electronic communication devices, such as electronic mail, video surveillance, and computer data transmissions, and even through thermal imaging devices that can do infrared searches of dwellings. The Court has examined the impact of these devices on privacy and in some instances has limited the ability of law enforcement agencies to use them for investigatory purposes. In its decision in *Kyllo* v. *U.S.,* the Court reigned in the use of thermal imaging devices. Suspicious that marijuana was being grown in Danny Kyllo's home, agents used a thermal imaging device to determine if the amount of heat emanating from it was consistent with the high-intensity lamps typically used for indoor marijuana growth.[34] The scan showed that Kyllo's garage roof and a side wall were relatively hot compared with the rest of his home and substantially warmer than the neighboring units. Based in part on the thermal imaging, a federal magistrate judge issued a warrant to search Kyllo's home, where the agents found marijuana growing. On appeal, the Court ruled that when government agents use a device that is not in general public use, to explore details of a private home that would previously have been unknowable without physical intrusion, it is considered a search and must be accompanied by a warrant. For more about warrantless searches, see Concept Summary 8.2.

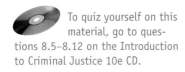 To quiz yourself on this material, go to questions 8.5–8.12 on the Introduction to Criminal Justice 10e CD.

Concept Summary 8.2 Warrantless Searches

Action	Scope of search
Stop and frisk	Pat-down of a suspect's outer garments.
Search incident to arrest	Full body search after a legal arrest.
Automobile search	If probable cause exists, full search of car including driver, passengers, and closed containers found in trunk. Search must be reasonable.
Consent search	Warrantless search of person or place is justified if the suspect knowingly and voluntarily consents to a search.
Plain view	Suspicious objects seen in plain view can be seized without a warrant.
Electronic surveillance	Material can be seized electronically without a warrant if the suspect has no expectation of privacy.

Arrest

The arrest power of the police involves taking a person into custody in accordance with lawful authority and holding that person to answer for a violation of the criminal law. Police officers have complete law enforcement responsibility and unrestricted powers of arrest in their jurisdictions. Private citizens also have the right to make an arrest, generally when a crime is committed in their presence.

An arrest occurs when a police officer takes a person into custody or deprives a person of freedom for having allegedly committed a criminal offense. The police stop unlimited numbers of people each day for a variety of reasons, so the time when an arrest occurs may be hard to pinpoint. Some persons are stopped for short periods of questioning; others are informally detained and released; and still others are formally placed under arrest. However, a legal arrest occurs when the following conditions exist.

- The police officer believes that sufficient legal evidence, that is, probable cause, exists that a crime is being or has been committed and intends to restrain the suspect.
- The police officer deprives the individual of freedom.
- The suspect believes that he is in the custody of the police officer and cannot voluntarily leave. He has lost his liberty.

Arrests can be initiated when an officer observes a crime or otherwise develops sufficient probable cause to take a suspect into custody or when an arrest warrant, a writ that directs the police to bring the named person before the court, has been issued. In either case, an arrest must be based on probable cause that the person has committed or is attempting to commit a crime.

The decision to arrest is often made by the police officer during contact with the suspect and does not rely on a warrant being used. In the case of a felony, most jurisdictions provide that a police officer may arrest a suspect without a warrant where probable cause exists, even though the officer was not present when the offense was committed. The arrest can be based on statements made by victims and witnesses. In the case of a misdemeanor, probable cause and the officer's presence at the time of the offense are required; this is referred to as the in presence requirement. For example, if someone informs the police that he had been slapped during an altercation, the assailant could not be arrested. He would be asked to appear before a court via summons.

As a general rule, if the police make an arrest without a warrant, the arrestee must be brought before a magistrate promptly for a probable cause hearing. The U.S. Supreme Court dealt with the meaning of "promptly" in the 1991 case of *Riverside County* v. *McLaughlin*.[35] The Court said that the police may detain an individual arrested without a warrant for up to 48 hours without a court hearing to determine whether arrest was justified.

Arrest in Noncriminal Acts

Can police arrest someone for a noncriminal act such as a traffic violation? This issue was decided in the case of *Atwater et al.* v. *City of Lago Vista et al.*[36] Gail Atwater was stopped for failing to wear a seat belt as she drove her two children home from soccer practice in Lago Vista, near Austin. She unbuckled for just a moment, she said, to look for a toy that had fallen from the pickup truck onto the street. The Lago Vista patrolman pulled her over, berated her, and arrested her. Under Texas law, she had committed a misdemeanor. Atwater subsequently was found to be driving without a license and to lack proof of insurance.

The standard for determining whether a police action was reasonable under the circumstances in this case is difficult. Some might argue that Atwater's traffic violation was not a breach of the peace, while others might suggest that Atwater's

To quiz yourself on this material, go to question 8.13 on the Introduction to Criminal Justice 10e CD.

arrest was legal because she had violated a state statute. Whatever your opinion is, in April 2001 the Supreme Court upheld the right to arrest a suspect for a traffic violation.

Custodial Interrogation

A suspect taken into police custody — on the street, in a police car, or at the police station — must be warned at the time of arrest of the right under the Fifth Amendment to be free from self-incrimination before police conduct any questioning.

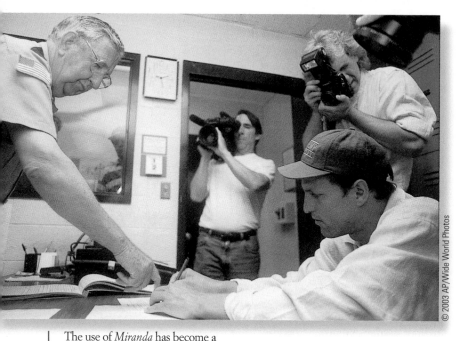

© 2003 AP/Wide World Photos

The *Miranda* Warning

In the landmark case of *Miranda* v. *Arizona* (1966), the Supreme Court held that the police must give the *Miranda* warning to a person in custody before questioning begins.[37] Suspects in custody must be told that they have the following rights.

- They have the right to remain silent.
- If they decide to make a statement, the statement can and will be used against them in a court of law.
- They have the right to have an attorney present at the time of the interrogation, or they will have an opportunity to consult with an attorney.
- If they cannot afford an attorney, one will be appointed for them by the state.

The use of *Miranda* has become a fixture of American life. Here, actor Woody Harrelson signs a form saying that he was read his *Miranda* rights at the Lee County Courthouse in Beattyville, Kentucky, June 1, 1996. Harrelson was arrested by Lee County Sheriff William Kilburn, left, for misdemeanor cultivation of marijuana for planting four industrial hemp seeds on an acre of land four miles south of Beattyville that Harrelson owns. Harrelson staged the event causing the arrest as part of an effort to promote legalization of industrial hemp.

Read the full text of the *Miranda* v. Arizona opinion at http://laws.findlaw.com/us/384/436.html.

Some suspects choose to remain silent, and because oral as well as written statements are admissible in court, police officers often do not elicit any statements without making certain a defense attorney is present. If an accused decides to answer any questions, he or she may also stop at any time and refuse to answer further questions.

A suspect's constitutional rights under *Miranda* can be given up (waived). A suspect can choose to talk to the police or sign a confession. However, for the waiver to be effective, the state must first show that it was voluntary and that the defendant was aware of all of his *Miranda* rights. People who cannot understand the *Miranda* warning because of their age, mental handicaps, or language problems cannot be legally questioned absent an attorney. If they can understand their rights, they may be questioned.[38]

Once the suspect asks for an attorney, all questioning must stop unless the attorney is present. And if the criminal suspect has invoked his or her *Miranda* rights, police officials cannot reinitiate interrogation in the absence of counsel even if the accused has consulted with an attorney in the meantime.[39] However, even if the suspect has invoked his *Miranda* rights and demanded an attorney, the police can question the offender about another separate crime (as long as they give the *Miranda* warning for the second crime also). For example, a person is arrested on burglary charges and requests an attorney. The next day, police question him about a murder after reading the suspect his *Miranda* rights. He decides to waive his rights and confesses to the murder without a lawyer being present. The murder confession would be legal even though the suspect had requested an attorney in the burglary case because they are two separate legal matters.[40]

The *Miranda* Rule Today

The Supreme Court has used case law to define the boundaries of the *Miranda* warning since its inception. While statements made by a suspect who was not given the *Miranda* warning or received it improperly cannot be used against him in a court of law, it is possible to use illegally gained statements and the evidence they produce in some well-defined instances.

- If a defendant perjures himself, evidence obtained in violation of the *Miranda* warning can be used by the government to impeach his testimony during trial.[41]
- At trial, the testimony of a witness is permissible even though his or her identity was revealed by the defendant in violation of the *Miranda* rule.[42]
- Information provided by a suspect who has not been given the *Miranda* warning that leads to the seizure of incriminating evidence is permissible if the evidence would have been obtained anyway by other means or sources; this is now referred to as the **inevitable discovery rule.**[43]
- Initial errors by police in getting statements do not make subsequent statements inadmissible. A subsequent *Miranda* warning that is properly given can cure the condition that made the initial statements inadmissible.[44]
- The admissions of mentally impaired defendants can be admitted in evidence as long as the police acted properly and there is a preponderance of the evidence that they understood the meaning of *Miranda.*[45]
- The erroneous admission of a coerced confession at trial can be ruled a harmless error that would not automatically result in overturning a conviction.[46]

The Supreme Court has also ruled that in some instances the *Miranda* warning may not have to be given before a suspect is questioned and has also narrowed the scope of *Miranda,* for example by restricting with whom a suspect may ask to consult.

- The *Miranda* warning applies only to the right to have an attorney present. The suspect cannot demand to speak to a priest, probation officer, or any other official.[47]
- A suspect can be questioned in the field without a *Miranda* warning if the information the police seek is needed to protect public safety. For example, in an emergency, suspects can be asked where they hid their weapons.[48] This is known as the **public safety doctrine.**
- Suspects need not be aware of all the possible outcomes of waiving their rights for the *Miranda* warning to be considered properly given.[49]
- An attorney's request to see the defendant does not affect the validity of the defendant's waiver of the right to counsel. Police misinformation to an attorney does not affect waiver of *Miranda* rights.[50] For example, a suspect's statements may be used if they are given voluntarily even though his family has hired an attorney and the statements were made before the attorney arrived. Only the suspect can request an attorney, not his friends or family.
- A suspect who makes an ambiguous reference to an attorney during questioning, such as "Maybe I should talk to an attorney," is not protected under *Miranda.* The police may continue their questioning.[51]
- Failure to give a suspect a *Miranda* warning is not illegal unless the case becomes a criminal matter. In *Chavez* v. *Martinez,* the Supreme Court ruled that a *Miranda* warning applies only to criminal matters.[52] While Oliverio Martinez was being treated for gunshot wounds received during a fight with police, he was interrogated without a *Miranda* warning being administered by a patrol supervisor and admitted to having engaged in criminal acts. He was never charged with a crime, and his answers were never used against him in any criminal proceeding.

inevitable discovery rule
Evidence can be used in court even though the information that led to its discovery was obtained in violation of the *Miranda* rule if a judge finds it would have been discovered anyway by other means or sources.

public safety doctrine
A suspect can be questioned in the field without a *Miranda* warning if the information the police seek is needed to protect public safety.

Many experts consider the *Miranda v. Arizona* case the hallmark decision of the Warren Court. To learn more about this landmark case, go to InfoTrac College Edition and read Richard Leo, "Miranda Revisited," *Journal of Criminal Law and Criminology* 86 (1996): 621; Donald Dripps, "Is *Miranda* Case Law Inconsistent? A Fifth Amendment Synthesis," *Constitutional Community* 17 (2000): 19.

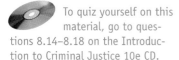

The Library of Congress contains more than 121 million items. Some of these are designated "treasures." One of them is Chief Justice Earl Warren's handwritten notes on the *Miranda* case. You can view them at http://www.loc.gov/exhibits/treasures/trr038.html.

To quiz yourself on this material, go to questions 8.14–8.18 on the Introduction to Criminal Justice 10e CD.

booking
The administrative record of an arrest listing the offender's name, address, physical description, date of birth, employer, time of arrest, offense, and name of arresting officer; also includes photographing and fingerprinting of the offender.

lineup
Placing a suspect in a group for the purpose of being viewed and identified by a witness.

Later Martinez filed a civil rights suit charging that his Fifth Amendment and Fourteenth Amendment rights had been violated by the coercive questioning. The Court ruled that Martinez could not sue because a police officer is entitled to immunity from lawsuits if his alleged misconduct did not violate a constitutional right and the interrogation did not violate a constitutional right because the confession was never used in a criminal case. The court ruled that a criminal case at the very least requires the initiation of legal proceedings, and police questioning by itself does not constitute such a case. Statements compelled by police interrogation may not be used against a defendant in a criminal case, but it is not until such use that the self-incrimination clause is violated.

The Impact of *Miranda*

After *Miranda* was decided, law enforcement officials became concerned that the Supreme Court had gone too far in providing procedural protections to the defendant. However, subsequent research indicates that the decision has had little effect on the number of confessions obtained by the police and that it has not affected the rate of convictions.[53] It now seems apparent that the police formerly relied too heavily on confessions to prove a defendant's guilt. Other forms of evidence, such as witness statements, physical evidence, and expert testimony, have proved adequate to win the prosecution's case. Blaming *Miranda* for increased crime rates in the 1970s and 1980s now seems problematic given that rates are down and *Miranda* is still the law.[54]

Though recent case law has narrowed the scope of *Miranda* and given police greater leeway in their actions, the Supreme Court is unlikely to ever reverse course. In the critical case *Dickerson* v. *United States,* the Court made it clear that the *Miranda* ruling is here to stay and has become enmeshed in the prevailing legal system.[55] Not surprisingly, police administrators who in the past might have have been wary of the restrictions forced by *Miranda* now favor its use.[56] One recent survey (2002) found that nearly 60 percent of police chiefs believe that the *Miranda* warning should be retained and the same number report that abolishing *Miranda* would change the way the police function.[57]

With the ongoing war on terrorism, law enforcement officers may find themselves in unique situations involving national security and forced to make an immediate decision as to whether the *Miranda* rule applies. For example, the Law in Review feature on page 264 considers whether *Miranda* applies to noncitizens arrested outside the United States.

Pretrial Identification

After the accused is arrested, he or she is ordinarily brought to the police station, where the police list the possible criminal charges. At the same time, they obtain other information, such as a description of the offender and the circumstances of the offense, for booking purposes. The **booking** process is a police administrative procedure in which generally the date and time of the arrest are recorded; arrangements are made for bail, detention, or removal to court; and any other information needed for identification is obtained. The defendant may be fingerprinted, photographed, and required to participate in a lineup.

In a **lineup,** a suspect is placed in a group for the purpose of being viewed and identified by a witness. Lineups are one of the primary means the police have of identifying suspects. Others are show-ups, which occur at the crime scene, and photo displays or mug shots of possible suspects. In accordance with the U.S. Supreme Court decisions in *United States* v. *Wade* (1967) and *Kirby* v. *Illinois* (1972), the accused has the right to have counsel present at this postindictment lineup or identification procedure.[58]

© 2003 AP/Wide World Photos

The pretrial identification process enables police officers to gather eyewitness evidence to be used at trial, and allows victims of unsolved crimes to view potential suspects. Here, Mark Martin Bennett is shown in his police booking photo on February 20, 2003. Bennett, a Dallas man who may have assaulted young girls in Texas and Minnesota, was arrested by the Pasadena, Texas Police Department and charged with three counts of sexually assaulting a 15-year-old girl at a hotel room after picking her up at Deer Park High School. Bennett, 26, was jailed without bond as police asked teenaged girls who may have met him in Internet chat rooms and were later assaulted by him to come forward.

In the *Wade* case, the Supreme Court held that a defendant has a right to counsel if the lineup takes place after the suspect has been formally charged with a crime. This decision was based on the Court's belief that the postindictment lineup procedure is a critical stage of the criminal justice process. In contrast, the suspect does not have a comparable right to counsel at a pretrial lineup when a complaint or indictment has not been issued. Right to counsel does not apply until judicial proceedings have begun and the defendant is formally charged with a crime. When the right to counsel is violated, the evidence of any pretrial identification must be excluded from the trial.

One of the most difficult legal issues in this area is determining if the identification procedure is suggestive and consequently in violation of the due process clause of the Fifth and Fourteenth Amendments.[59] In *Simmons* v. *United States* (1968), the Supreme Court said, "The primary evil to be avoided is a very substantial likelihood of irreparable misidentification."[60] In its decision in *Neil* v. *Biggers* (1972), the Court established the following general criteria to judge the suggestiveness of a pretrial identification procedure.

- The opportunity of the witness to view the criminal at the time of the crime.
- The degree of attention by the witness and the accuracy of the prior description by the witness.
- The level of certainty demonstrated by the witness.
- The length of time between the crime and the confrontation.[61]

Weighing all these factors, the Court determines the substantial likelihood of misidentification.

To quiz yourself on this material, go to questions 8.19–8.21 on the Introduction to Criminal Justice 10e CD.

United States v. Bin Laden

law in review

The war against terrorism presents many challenges for law enforcement agencies, especially when they are working under extreme circumstances abroad. The case of *United States* v. *Bin Laden,* decided in a federal appeals court, is an example of this problem.

Bin Laden involved the prosecution of several members of the al Qaeda network who were thought to be responsible for the terrorist attacks on American embassies in Kenya and Tanzania on August 7, 1998. Following the bombing, a team of FBI agents and other American law enforcement officers were assigned to Nairobi, Kenya, to investigate. On August 12, 1998, FBI agents received a tip that led them to Mohamed Rashed Daoud Al'Owhali. The Kenyan National Police, who had accompanied the FBI agents, arrested Al'Owhali without a warrant because of his lack of identification papers. Under Kenyan law, the absence of identification papers was a valid basis for arrest.

Al'Owhali was administered the following *Miranda* warning by FBI agents, which had been modified from the standard *Miranda* warnings because the interrogation was taking place in Kenya and in accordance with Kenyan law.

> We are representatives of the United States government. Under our laws, you have certain rights. Before we ask

you any questions, we want to be sure that you understand those rights.

> You do not have to speak to us or answer any questions. Even if you have already spoken to the Kenyan authorities, you do not have to speak to us now.

> If you do speak with us, anything that you say may be used against you in a court in the United States or elsewhere.

> In the United States, you would have the right to talk to a lawyer to get advice before we ask you any questions and you could have a lawyer with you during questioning. In the United States, if you could not afford a lawyer, one would be appointed for you, if you wish, before any questioning.

> Because we are not in the United States, we cannot ensure that you will have a lawyer appointed for you before any questioning.

> If you decide to speak with us now, without a lawyer present, you will still have the right to stop answering questions at any time.

> You should also understand that if you decide not to speak with us, that fact cannot be used as evidence against you in a court in the United States.

Al'Owhali then acknowledged:

> I have read this statement of my rights and I understand what my rights are. I am willing to make a statement and answer questions. I do not want a lawyer at this time. I understand and know

what I am doing. No promises or threats have been made to me and no pressure or coercion of any kind has been used against me.

After indicating that he understood his rights, Al'Owhali agreed to speak to the investigators. He continually denied his involvement in the bombing. On August 21, however, FBI agents confronted Al'Owhali with all the evidence they had collected linking him to the Kenyan bombing. "[A]cknowledging that the agents 'knew everything,'" Al'Owhali stated that he would tell the truth about his role in the bombing if he could be tried in the United States instead of Kenya. At that moment, an assistant United States attorney, who was assisting the FBI in its questioning of Al'Owhali, administered from memory the standard domestic *Miranda* warnings — without making reference to the modified Kenyan version of the warnings that had been administered to him previously. Al'Owhali proceeded to implicate himself in the Kenyan bombing in detail.

After being brought to the United States for trial, Al'Owhali moved to suppress all the statements he had made to the American investigators in Kenya on the ground that the modified *Miranda* warnings that had been administered to him when he was first taken into Kenyan custody were deficient under American

The Exclusionary Rule

exclusionary rule
The principle that prohibits using illegally obtained evidence in a trial.

No review of the legal aspects of policing would be complete without a discussion of the **exclusionary rule,** the principal means used to restrain police conduct. The Fourth Amendment guarantees individuals the right to be secure in their persons, homes, papers, and effects against unreasonable searches and seizures. The exclusionary rule provides that all evidence obtained by illegal searches and seizures is inadmissible in criminal trials. Similarly, it excludes the use of illegal confessions under Fifth Amendment prohibitions.

For many years, evidence obtained by unreasonable searches and seizures that consequently should have been considered illegal was admitted by state and federal governments in criminal trials. The only criteria for admissibility were whether the evidence was incriminating and whether it would assist the judge or jury in ascertaining the innocence or guilt of the defendant. How the evidence

law. He argued that the modified warnings advised him of the limited right to counsel in light of the uncertainties of Kenyan law, not the explicit American right to counsel as required by the *Miranda* decision. The government responded that, as a non-American whose only connection to America was hostile, Al'Owhali was not protected by the Fifth Amendment's privilege against self-incrimination, and thus, he was not entitled to *Miranda* warnings in the first place. As a result, the government contended that the failure to give correct *Miranda* warnings could not be a basis for suppression. The government argued alternatively that even if the court were to rule that the Fifth Amendment attached to Al'Owhali, the modified warnings that he received were sufficient to satisfy *Miranda* under the circumstances.

The *Bin Laden* court disagreed with the government on both points. First, the court held that the Fifth Amendment's privilege against self-incrimination did in fact apply to Al'Owhali. Second, the court held that *Miranda*'s requirements must be satisfied in overseas interrogations just as they must be satisfied in domestic interrogations. According to the decision, a suspect must be told that he has the right to remain silent and anything that he does say may be used against him in a court of law. If he were in the United States, he would have an absolute right to counsel before and

during any questioning. Because he is not in the United States, his right to an attorney depends on foreign law, but the United States government will do its best to help him obtain retained or appointed counsel, if the suspect desires, by making that request of the host country. If the foreign authorities will not provide him with a lawyer, he does not have to speak with United States authorities, and if he does choose to speak, he may stop at any time. The *Bin Laden* court also required FBI agents abroad to make "a detailed inquiry into a specific nation's law" regarding what *Miranda*-type rights are available to the suspect and speak to local authorities to determine whether they will allow the suspect to consult with an attorney. Because the modified *Miranda* warnings did not accomplish all of these things, the court suppressed the statements made by Al'Owhali following these warnings. The court further ruled that the statements made by Al'Owhali after the assistant United States attorney recited the full domestic warnings to him could be admitted into evidence, as these warnings cured the deficiencies in the previously administered modified version of the *Miranda* warnings.

According to legal scholar Mark A. Godsey, the *Bin Laden* court was correct in holding that the privilege against self-incrimination protects non-Americans interrogated abroad but tried in the United

States. The court's analysis of the warnings required pursuant to *Miranda* was flawed, however. In creating the way the warnings were required in the international context, the court did not analyze the competing interests and established a rule that is unworkable within an international context. It remains to be seen whether the *Bin Laden* decision will be considered by the U.S. Supreme Court. But as it stands, it shows how the rule of law enjoyed by American citizens is also available to noncitizens, even those bent on terrorism and destruction.

Critical Thinking

Do you believe that suspected terrorists, apprehended abroad, should receive the same civil rights as American citizens involved in the legal process at home? Does it matter that they will be tried in American courts?

InfoTrac College Edition Research

 Use the term "Miranda warning" as a key term on InfoTrac College Edition.

Source: *United States* v. *Bin Laden,* 132 F. Supp. 2d 168, 181 (S.D.N.Y. 2001); Mark A. Godsey, "Miranda's Final Frontier, the International Arena: A Critical Analysis of *United States* v. *Bin Laden,* and a Proposal for a New *Miranda* Exception Abroad," *Duke Law Journal* 51 (2002): 1703–82.

---

was obtained was unimportant; its admissibility was determined by its relevance to the criminal case.

In 1914, however, the rules on the admissibility of evidence underwent a change of direction when the Supreme Court decided the case of *Weeks* v. *United States.*[62] The defendant, Freemont Weeks, was accused by federal law enforcement authorities of using the mail for illegal purposes. After his arrest, the home in which Weeks was staying was searched without a valid search warrant. Evidence in the form of letters and other materials was found in his room and admitted at the trial. Weeks was then convicted of the federal offense based on the incriminating evidence. On appeal, the Supreme Court held that evidence obtained by unreasonable search and seizure must be excluded in a federal criminal trial.

Thus, for the first time, the Court held that the Fourth Amendment barred the use of evidence obtained through illegal search and seizure in a federal prosecution. With this ruling, the Court established the exclusionary rule. The rule

Read the full text of the *Mapp* v. *Ohio* decision at http://laws.findlaw.com/us/367/643.html.

was based not on legislation but on judicial decision making. Can the criminal go free because the constable blunders? That became the question.

In 1961, the Supreme Court made the exclusionary rule applicable to the state courts in the landmark decision of *Mapp* v. *Ohio.* In *Mapp,* police officers forcibly searched a home while using a fake warrant. The Court held that although the search had turned up contraband it violated the Fourth Amendment's prohibition against unreasonable searches and seizures and the illegally seized evidence could not be used in court. Justice Tom Clark, delivering the majority opinion of the Court, made clear the importance of this constitutional right in the administration of criminal justice.

> *There are those who say, as did Justice [then Judge Benjamin] Cardozo, that under our constitutional exclusionary doctrine "[t]he criminal is to go free because the constable has blundered." In some cases this will undoubtedly be the result. But . . . there is another consideration — the imperative of judicial integrity. . . . The criminal goes free, if he must, but it is the law that sets him free. Nothing can destroy a government more quickly than its failure to observe its own laws, or worse its disregard of the charter of its own existence.[63]*

Current Status

good faith exception
The principle that evidence may be used in a criminal trial even though the search warrant used to obtain it was technically faulty, so long as the police acted in good faith when they sought the warrant from a judge.

In the 1980s, a more conservative U.S. Supreme Court gradually began to limit the scope of the exclusionary rule. In *Illinois* v. *Gates* (1983), the Court made it easier for police to search a suspect's home, by allowing an anonymous letter to be used as evidence in support of a warrant.[64] In another critical case, *United States* v. *Leon* (1984), the Court ruled that evidence seized by police relying on a warrant issued by a detached and neutral magistrate can be used in a court proceeding, even if the judge who issued the warrant may have relied on less than sufficient evidence.[65] In this case, the Court articulated a **good faith exception** to the exclusionary rule: Evidence obtained with a less than adequate search warrant may be admissible in court if the police officers acted in good faith on obtaining court approval for their search. However, deliberately misleading a judge or using a warrant that the police know is unreasonably deficient would be grounds to invoke the exclusionary rule. Although prosecutors initially applauded the *Leon* decision and defense lawyers feared that police would be inclined to secure warrants from sympathetic judges, both groups agree that *Leon* has had little practical effect on the processing of criminal cases. Further, most experts believe that no important data exist to prove that the exclusionary rule has had a direct impact on police behavior.

In 1995, in one of the most important exclusionary rule cases since *Leon, Arizona* v. *Evans* presented a compelling argument for further applying the good faith exception.[66] The facts in *Evans* are relatively simple. Phoenix police officers stopped the defendant for a vehicular violation and ran a computer check, which showed an outstanding arrest warrant. As Isaac Evans was being arrested, he dropped a marijuana cigarette. More of the drug was seized after being found in the car.

There was one problem with the seizure. Seventeen days earlier, the Phoenix justice court had quashed the arrest warrant. It was unclear why the arrest warrant had not been removed from the police computer. The trial judge refused to admit the evidence gathered during the traffic stop on grounds that the computer error was caused by negligence of the law enforcement authorities. The Arizona Supreme Court affirmed the trial court, stating that it is repugnant to the principles of a free society that a person should ever be taken into custody because of a careless computer error.

In a close vote, the U.S. Supreme Court ruled that the evidence did not have to be suppressed under the exclusionary rule. The exclusionary rule was designed as a means of deterring police misconduct, not mistakes by employees, and it does not apply when police have acted in objectively reasonable reliance on an apparently valid warrant.

In these and other cases, the Court has made it easier for the police to conduct searches of criminal suspects and their possessions and then use the seized

The Future of the Exclusionary Rule

analyzing criminal justice issues

The exclusionary rule has long been a controversial subject in the administration of criminal justice. It was originally conceived to control illegitimate police practices, and that remains its primary purpose. It is justified on the basis that it deters illegal searches and seizures. Yet most experts believe that no impartial data exist to prove that the rule has a direct impact on police behavior. This is by far the most significant criticism of the rule. By excluding evidence, the rule has a more direct effect on the criminal trial than on the police officer on the street. Furthermore, the rule is powerless when the police have no interest in prosecuting the accused or in obtaining a conviction. In addition, it does not control the wholesale harassment of individuals by law enforcement officials bent on disregarding constitutional rights.

The most popular criticism of the exclusionary rule, however, is that it allows guilty defendants to go free. Because courts frequently decide in many types of cases (particularly those involving victimless offenses, such as gambling and drug use) that certain evidence should be excluded, the rule is believed to result in excessive court delays and to negatively affect plea-bargaining negotiations. However, the rule appears to result in relatively few case dismissals.

Though it is assumed that political conservatives oppose the exclusionary rule because it allows the guilty to go free, Timothy Lynch, a director of the Cato Institute, argues that the rule is fundamentally sound and can be justified on the basis of such legal principles as checks and balances and separation of power. Lynch argues that, when agents of the executive branch (the police) disregard or side-step the terms of court-issued search warrants, the judicial branch can respond by overruling the misbehavior. Judges thus can act when executive branch prosecutors attempt to introduce illegally seized evidence in court. Because the exclusionary rule helps the judiciary to uphold the integrity of its warrant-issuing process, it is a powerful weapon against executive branch transgressions and helps ensure the checks and balances between the judicial and executive branch. The exclusionary rule is especially relevant for warrantless searches, considering the fact that the judge is not on the scene when a search takes place and only becomes aware of the circumstances surrounding the search when prosecutors are in court seeking to present the evidence the police acquired. The rule gives the judge the opportunity to correct executive branch excesses before they can influence the outcome of the proceedings.

Suggested approaches to dealing with violations of the exclusionary rule include criminal prosecution of police officers who violate constitutional rights, internal police control, civil lawsuits against state or municipal police officers, and federal lawsuits against the government under the Federal Tort Claims Act.

Law professor Donald Dripps has derived a novel approach for modifying the exclusionary rule. The contingent exclusionary rule would apply when a judge who finds police testimony questionable concludes that the release of the guilty would be unpleasant and unwarranted. Instead of excluding the evidence, she could request that the prosecution or police pay a fee, similar in form to a fine, to use the evidence in court. Exclusion of the evidence would be contingent on the failure of the police department to pay the damages set by the court. The judge thereby could uphold the Constitution without freeing the guilty. The contingent exclusionary rule would force the prosecution to decide whether justice was worth the damages.

The United States is the only nation that applies an exclusionary rule to protect individuals from illegal searches and seizures. Whether the U.S. Supreme Court or legislative bodies adopt any more significant changes to the rule remains to be seen. However, like the *Miranda* warning, the exclusionary rule has been incorporated in modern police procedure and seems to be a permanent fixture.

Critical Thinking

1. Instead of abolishing the exclusionary rule, what do you think of the idea of allowing illegally seized evidence to be used at trial while allowing criminal defendants to sue the police officers who violated their constitutional rights when they made the seizure?
2. As it stands, doesn't the exclusionary rule punish the crime victim and not the offending police officer?

InfoTrac College Edition Research

 Use "Exclusionary rule" as a key term on InfoTrac College Edition.

Sources: Timothy Lynch, *In Defense of the Exclusionary Rule* (Washington, D.C.: Cato Institute, Center for Constitutional Studies, 1998); Donald Dripps, "The Case for the Contingent Exclusionary Rule," *American Criminal Law Review* 38 (2001): 1–47; Harold Rothwax, *The Collapse of Criminal Justice* (New York: Random House, 1996); Tom Smith, "Legislative and Legal Developments," *American Bar Association Journal of Criminal Justice* 11 (1996): 46–47.

evidence in court proceedings. The Court has indicated that, as a general rule, the protection afforded the individual by the Fourth Amendment may take a back seat to concerns about public safety if criminal actions pose a clear threat to society. What is the future of the exclusionary rule? That is the topic of the Analyzing Criminal Justice Issues feature above.

 To quiz yourself on this material, go to questions 8.22–8.25 on the Introduction to Criminal Justice 10e CD.

To learn more about the exclusionary rule, go to http://caselaw.lp.findlaw.com/data/constitution/amendment04/06.html.

Perspectives on Justice

Throughout the past decade, the U.S. Congress has tried to loosen the admissibility of evidence from illegal searches and seizures through legislation. Curtailing the use of the exclusionary rule would widen the scope of justice and favor the crime control perspective.

Summary

- Law enforcement officers use many different investigatory techniques to detect and apprehend criminal offenders, including searches, electronic eavesdropping, interrogation, informants, surveillance, and witness identification procedures.
- Over the past three decades, the U.S. Supreme Court has placed constitutional limitations on the police ability to conduct investigations.
- Under interpretations of the Fourth Amendment, police are required to use warrants to conduct searches except in some clearly defined situations.
- Police are required to have probable cause to obtain a warrant.
- Many warrants are obtained with the help of informants. The Court has ruled that the informant's information must, considering the totality of the circumstances, be valid and factual.
- The exceptions to the search warrant rule include searches of automobiles used in a crime, stop and frisk, searches incident to an arrest, consent searches, and searches of material in plain view.
- If police violate the legal rule controlling search and seizure, then the evidence they collected cannot be used in court.
- Through the *Miranda* rule, the Supreme Court established a procedure required for all custodial

interrogations that focuses on the need to warn criminal suspects of their right to remain silent and be advised by an attorney.

- Many issues concerning *Miranda* continue to be litigated. The Supreme Court has shaped *Miranda* protections, increasing them in some instances and reducing them in others.
- Statements made without a *Miranda* warning being given can now be used in court under some circumstances such as an emergency situation or to impeach a witness who is committing perjury.
- Lineups and other suspect identification practices have been subject to court review. Police cannot manipulate lineups. Defendants are entitled to counsel being present in postindictment lineups.
- The exclusionary rule continues to be one of the most controversial issues in the criminal justice system. Even though the courts have curtailed its application in recent years, it still generally prohibits the admission of evidence obtained in violation of the defendant's constitutional rights.
- Some critics have called for the abolition of the exclusionary rule, while others believe it can be successfully modified.

Key Terms

search warrant 246
probable cause 247
particularity 248
hearsay evidence 249
exigent 251
threshold inquiry 251

stop and frisk 251
search incident to a
    lawful arrest 252
bus sweep 255
plain view doctrine 256
curtilage 256

inevitable discovery rule 261
public safety doctrine 261
booking 262
lineup 262
exclusionary rule 264
good faith exception 266

Doing Research on the Web

For an up-to-date list of Web links, go to http://cj.wadsworth.com/siegel_intro10e.

For much of the past three decades, law enforcement has ruled at the U.S. Supreme Court. The Court has given police more power to stop motorists, search homes, and put defendants in jail. Except for landmark cases such as *Miranda* v. *Arizona* and *Mapp* v. *Ohio,* the justices have allowed the police to crack down on crime and expand their power.

However, the Court has become increasingly suspicious about aggressive techniques that police are using to counter drugs and gun violence. In *Florida* v. *J. L.,* the Court ruled that police may not stop and frisk someone simply because an anonymous tipster said he was carrying a gun. In *Bond* v. *United States,* the Court ruled that police cannot look for drugs by randomly squeezing the luggage of bus passengers.

To research more on how the Supreme Court views the *Miranda* decision, go to the following articles from InfoTrac College Edition: George Thomas, "The

End of the Road for *Miranda* v. *Arizona?" American Criminal Law Review* 37 (2000): 1; Jerry Riggs, "Excluding Automobile Passengers from the Fourth Amendment," *Journal of Criminal Law and Criminology* 88 (1998): 957. Both articles raise important questions regarding the history and future of rules for police interrogation and search and seizure law. To read more about the case, go to the Court TV crime library site: http://www.crimelibrary.com/notorious_murders/not_guilty/miranda/8.html?sect=14.

> Pro/Con discussions and Viewpoint Essays on some of the topics in this chapter may be found at the Opposing Viewpoints Resource Center: http://www.gale.com/OpposingViewpoints.

Discussion Questions

1. Should obviously guilty persons go free because police originally arrested them with less than probable cause?
2. Should illegally seized evidence be excluded from trial, even though it is conclusive proof of a person's criminal acts?
3. Should a person be put in a lineup without the benefit of counsel?
4. Have criminals been given too many rights? Should courts be more concerned with the rights of the victims or the rights of offenders?
5. Can a search and seizure be reasonable if it is not authorized by a warrant?
6. What is the purpose of the *Miranda* warnings?
7. What is a pretext traffic stop? Does it violate a citizen's civil rights?

Notes

1 *United States* v. *Arvizu,* No. 00–1519 (2002).
2 378 U.S. 108, 84 S.Ct. 1509, 12 L.Ed.2d 723 (1964).
3 462 U.S. 213, 103 S.Ct. 2317, 76 L.Ed.2d 527 (1983).
4 *Alabama* v. *White,* 496 U.S. 325 (1990).
5 *Alabama* v. *White,* 496 U.S. 325, 326.
6 *Florida* v. *J. L.,* No. 98–1993 (2000).
7 *Kirk* v. *Louisiana,* No. 01–8419, U.S. Supreme Court, per curiam opinion, decided June 24, 2002.
8 392 U.S. 1, 88 S.Ct. 1868, 20 L.Ed.2d 899 (1968).
9 120 S.Ct. 673 (2000).
10 395 U.S. 752, 89 S.Ct. 2034, 23 L.Ed.2d 685 (1969).
11 267 U.S. 132, 45 S.Ct. 280, 69 L.Ed.2d 543 (1925). See also James Rodgers, "Poisoned Fruit: Quest for Consistent Rule on Traffic Stop Searches," *American Bar Association Journal* 81 (1995): 50–51.
12 456 U.S. 798, 102 S.Ct. 2157, 72 L.Ed.2d 572 (1982). See also Barry Latzer, "Searching Cars and Their Contents: *U.S.* v. *Ross,*" *Criminal Law Bulletin* 6 (1982): 220; Joseph Grano, "Rethinking the Fourth Amendment Warrant Requirements," *Criminal Law Review* 19 (1982): 603.
13 440 U.S. 648, 99 S.Ct. 1391, 59 L.Ed.2d 660 (1979). See also Lance Rogers, "The Drunk-Driving Roadblock: Random Seizure or Minimal Intrusion?" *Criminal Law Bulletin* 21 (1985): 197–217.
14 No. 99–1030, U.S. Supreme Court, 2000–2001.
15 *Michigan* v. *Sitz,* 496 U. S. 444 (1990).
16 434 U.S. 106, 98 S.Ct. 330, 54 L.Ed.2d 331 (1977).
17 *Maryland* v. *Wilson,* 65 U.S.L.W. 4124 (February 19, 1997).
18 *U.S.* v. *Green,* 01–31359 (March 11, 2003).
19 *Ohio* v. *Robinette,* 117 S.Ct. 417 (1996).
20 *Whren* v. *United States,* 116 S.Ct. 1769 (1996); Mark Hansen, "Rousting Miss Daisy?" *American Bar Association Journal* 83 (1997): 22; *Wyoming* v. *Houghton,* 199 S.Ct. (1999).
21 121 S.Ct. 1876, 149 L.Ed.2d 994 (2001).x
22 391 U.S. 543, 88 S.Ct. 1788, 20 L.Ed.2d 797 (1968).
23 412 U.S. 218, 93 S.Ct. 2041, 36 L.Ed.2d 854 (1973).
24 *Florida* v. *Bostick,* 501 U.S. 429, 111 S.Ct. 2382, 115 L.Ed.2d 389 (1991).
25 475 U.S. 106, 106 S.Ct. 960, 89 L.Ed.2d 81 (1986).
26 480 U.S. 321, 107 S.Ct. 1149, 94 L.Ed.2d 347 (1987).
27 466 U.S. 170, 104 S.Ct. 1735, 80 L.Ed.2d 214 (1984).
28 476 U.S. 207, 106 S.Ct. 1809, 90 L.Ed.2d 210 (1986).
29 488 U.S. 445, 109 S.Ct. 693, 102 L.Ed.2d 835 (1989).
30 508 U.S. 366, 113 S.Ct. 2130, 124 L.Ed.2d 334 (1993).
31 *Bond* v. *United States,* 120 S.Ct. 1462 (2000).
32 Gary T. Marx, *Undercover: Police Surveillance in America* (Berkeley: University of California Press, 1988).
33 389 U.S. 347, 88 S.Ct. 507, 19 L.Ed.2d 576 (1967).
34 *Kyllo* v. *United States,* No. 99–8508 (2001).
35 500 U.S. 44, 111 S.Ct. 1661, 114 L.Ed.2d 49 (1991).
36 No. 99–1408, April 24, 2001.
37 384 U.S. 436, 86 S.Ct. 1602, 16 L.Ed.2d 694 (1966).
38 *Colorado* v. *Connelly,* 107 S.Ct. 515 (1986).
39 *Minnick* v. *Miss.,* 498 U.S. 46; 111 S.Ct. 486; 112 L.Ed. 2d. 489 (1990).
40 *Texas* v. *Cobb,* No. 99–1702 (2001).
41 *Harris* v. *New York,* 401 U.S. 222 (1971).
42 *Michigan* v. *Tucker,* 417 U.S. 433 (1974).
43 *Nix* v. *Williams,* 104 S.Ct. 2501 (1984).
44 *Oregon* v. *Elstad,* 105 S.Ct. 1285 (1985).
45 *Colorado* v. *Connelly,* 107 S.Ct. 515 (1986).
46 *Arizona* v. *Fulminante,* 499 U.S. 279, 111 S.Ct. 1246; 113 L.Ed. 2d. 302 (1991).
47 *Moran* v. *Burbine,* 106 S.Ct. 1135 (1986); *Michigan* v. *Mosley,* 423 U.S. 96 (1975); *Fare* v. *Michael C.,* 442 U.S. 23 (1979).

48 *New York* v. *Quarles,* 104 S.Ct. 2626 (1984).

49 *Colorado* v. *Spring,* 107 S.Ct. 851 (1987).

50 *Moran* v. *Burbine,* 106 S.Ct. 1135 (1986).

51 *Davis* v. *United States,* 114 S.Ct. 2350 (1994).

52 *Chavez* v. *Martinez,* No. 01–1444, decided May 27, 2003.

53 Michael Wald and others, "Interrogations in New Haven: The Impact of *Miranda,*" *Yale Law Journal* 76 (1967): 1519. See also Walter Lippman, "*Miranda* v. *Arizona* — Twenty Years Later," *Criminal Justice Journal* 9 (1987): 241; Stephen J. Schulhofer, "Reconsidering *Miranda,*" *University of Chicago Law Review* 54 (1987): 435–461; Paul Cassell, "How Many Criminals Has *Miranda* Set Free?" *Wall Street Journal,* March 1, 1995, p. A12.

54 "Don't Blame *Miranda,*" *Washington Post,* December 2, 1988, p. A26. See also Scott Lewis, "*Miranda* Today: Death of a Talisman," *Prosecutor* 28 (1994): 18–25; Richard Leo, "The Impact of *Miranda* Revisited," *Journal of Criminal Law and Criminology* 86 (1996): 621–48.

55 *Dickerson* v. *United States,* 530 U.S. 428 (2000).

56 Victoria Time and Brian Payne, "Police Chiefs' Perceptions about *Miranda:* An Analysis of Survey Data," *Journal of Criminal Justice* 30 (2002): 77–86.

57 Ibid.

58 388 U.S. 218, 87 S.Ct. 1926, 18 L.Ed.2d 1149 (1967); 406 U.S. 682, 92 S.Ct. 1877, 32 L.Ed.2d 40 (1972).

59 Marvin Zalman and Larry Siegel, *Key Cases and Comments on Criminal Procedure* (St. Paul, Minn.: West Publishing, 1994).

60 390 U.S. 377, 88 S.Ct. 967, 19 L.Ed.2d 1247 (1968).

61 409 U.S. 188, 93 S.Ct. 375, 34 L.Ed.2d 401 (1972).

62 232 U.S. 383, 34 S.Ct. 341, 58 L.Ed. 652 (1914).

63 *Mapp* v. *Ohio,* 367 U.S. 643 (1961).

64 462 U.S. 213, 103 S.Ct. 2317, 76 L.Ed.2d 527 (1983).

65 468 U.S. 897, 104 S.Ct. 3405, 82 L.Ed.2d 677 (1984).

66 *Arizona* v. *Evans,* 514 U.S. 260, 115 S.Ct. 1185, 131 L.Ed.2d 34 (1995).

Part Three Courts and Adjudication

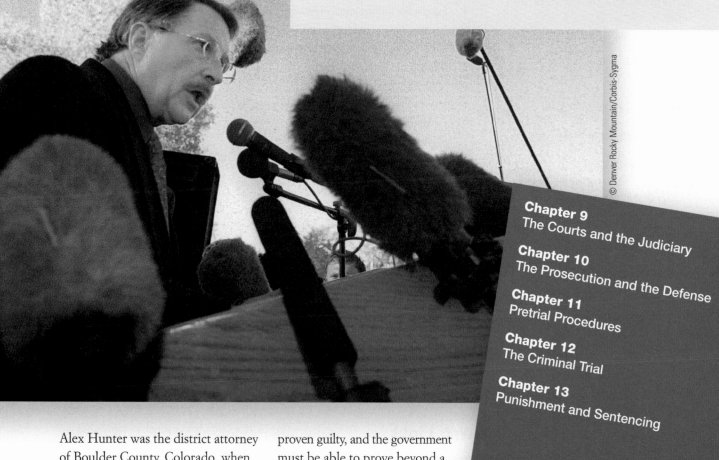

© Denver Rocky Mountain/Corbis-Sygma

Alex Hunter was the district attorney of Boulder County, Colorado, when 6-year-old JonBenet Ramsey was found murdered in her home in 1997. The case drew instant national attention because of the age of the victim, the fact that she was a beauty contest winner, and the many confusing aspects of the crime.

Despite a lack of convincing evidence, a great deal of pressure was placed on Hunter to prosecute Jon-Benet's parents for the murder. The media coverage was widespread, and the prosecutors would have liked to hand down indictments. Doing so probably would have made their job much easier. But in the U.S. system of justice, an individual is innocent until

proven guilty, and the government must be able to prove beyond a reasonable doubt that the defendant committed the crime. The results of DNA and lie detector tests raised serious doubts regarding the sufficiency of the evidence against the parents. Hunter refused to indict them, and the murder remains unsolved.

The JonBenet Ramsey murder was one of a number of notorious cases that the American court system handles each year. In some instances, they receive the full course of rights and processes guaranteed by the U.S. Constitution. In others, the prosecutor curtails his actions for want of evidence or because a plea bargain has been struck.

The chapters in this section cover the court process. Chapter 9 reviews the structure of the courts and the role of the judge. Chapter 10 covers the prosecution and defense. Chapter 11 analyzes the pretrial stage, including bail and plea bargaining. Chapter 12 covers the process of the criminal trial and the legal rules that structure its process. Chapter 13 looks at criminal sentencing, including capital punishment.

Chapter Outline

Chapter Objectives

After reading this chapter, you should be able to:

1. Understand the state and federal court structure.
2. Know the differences between limited and general courts.
3. Recognize the function of the appellate court system.
4. Explain the various levels of federal courts.
5. Describe how a case gets to the U.S. Supreme Court.
6. Know the problems associated with case overload.
7. Discuss the duties of a judge.
8. Know what the Missouri Plan is.
9. Identify the different types of judicial selection.
10. Explain how technology is changing the trial process.

Viewpoints

 Analyzing Criminal Justice Issues: Specialized Courts: Drugs and Mental Health 278

 Law in Review: *Commonwealth* v. *Louise Woodward* 290

 Criminal Justice and Technology: Technology and Court Management 294

Web Links

InfoTrac College Edition Links

Chapter 9 | The Courts and the Judiciary

In 2003 Alabama Chief Justice Roy Moore made national headlines when he was suspended for defying a federal court order to remove a Ten Commandments monument from the rotunda of the Alabama Supreme Court building. Judge Moore had installed the 5,300 pound monument as a symbol of his belief in the Supreme Being. When a suit was filed in federal court charging that it violated the constitutionally mandated separation between Church and state, U.S. District Judge Myron Thompson ordered the monument removed. Judge Moore countered that the ruling violated his right to acknowledge the role of God as the source of our rights and liberties and the law itself. When he refused to obey the federal court ruling, the Alabama Supreme Court ordered that the monument be removed. They held that, regardless of their personal feelings, officers of a lower state court must obey a binding order of a federal court. Judge Moore was suspended and the monument removed. On November 4, 2003, the United States Supreme court refused to hear an appeal by Roy Moore, thereby allowing his suspension to stand. On November 13, 2003, the

Alabama Court of the Judiciary permanently removed Moore from his post as Chief Justice.

While the "Ten Commandments" case is certainly unusual, it does illustrate the role of the court system in regulating human behavior. A legal ruling issued from a superior court must be obeyed even if its target is the Chief Justice of a state court! The case also shows how important it is for the court system to maintain a semblance of impartiality and objec-tivity. Religious and political beliefs cannot shape the contours of justice. Finally, the case illustrates the guiding role of the U.S Constitution in shaping legal policy at every stage of the judicial system: Regardless of personal beliefs, Constitutional mandates must be obeyed.

View the CNN video clip of this story on your Introduction to Criminal Justice 10e CD.

The criminal court is the setting in which many of the most important decisions in the criminal justice system are made. Eyewitness identification, bail, trial, plea negotiations, and sentencing all involve court-made decisions. Within the confines of the court, those accused of crime (defendants) call on the tools of the legal system to provide them with a fair and just hearing, with the burden of proof resting on the state; crime victims ask the government to provide them with justice for the wrongs done them and the injuries they have suffered; and agents of the criminal justice system attempt to find solutions that benefit the victim, the defendant, and society in general. The court process is designed to provide an open and impartial forum for deciding the truth of the matter and reaching a solution that, although punitive, is fairly arrived at and satisfies the rule of law.

It must render fair, impartial justice in deciding the outcome of a conflict between criminal and victim, law enforcement agents and violators of the law, parent and child, federal government and violators of governmental regulations, or other parties. Regardless of the issues involved, the parties' presence in a courtroom should guarantee that they will have a hearing conducted under rules of procedure in an atmosphere of fair play and objectivity and that the outcome of the hearing will be clear. If a party believes that the ground rules have been violated, he or she may take the case to a higher court, where the procedures of the original trial will be reexamined. If it finds that a violation of legal rights has occurred, the appellate court may deem the findings of the original trial improper and either order a new hearing or hold that some other measure must be carried out; for example, the court may dismiss the charge outright.

The court is a complex social agency with many independent but interrelated subsystems — clerk, prosecutor, defense attorney, judge, and probation department — each having a role in the court's operation. Ideally, the judicatory process operates with absolute fairness and equality. The entire process, from filing the initial complaint to final sentencing of the defendant, is governed by precise rules of law designed to ensure fairness. No defendant tried before a U.S. court should suffer or benefit because of his or her personal characteristics, beliefs, or affiliations. However, in today's crowded court system, such abstract goals are often impossible to achieve. The nation's court system is chronically under budgeted and recent economic downturns have not helped matters. In Alabama, funds were so low that in 2002 the state's senior justice called for a five-month moratorium on most jury trials. In Massachusetts, the trial court system, paralyzed by budget cuts, stopped conducting civil trials in 25 superior courtrooms in early May 2002. Kentucky's judicial system was in crisis in 2002 after the legislature failed to pass a budget.[1]

These constraints have a significant impact on the way courts do justice. The U.S. court system often is the scene of accommodation and "working things out," instead of an arena for a vigorous criminal defense. Plea negotiations and other nonjudicial alternatives, such as diversion, are far more common than the formal trial process. Consequently, the U.S. criminal justice can be selective. Discretion accompanies defendants through every step of the process, determining what will happen to them and how their cases will be resolved. Discretion means that two people committing similar crimes will receive highly dissimilar treatment. For example, most people convicted of homicide receive a prison sentence, but about 4 percent receive probation as a sole sentence. More murderers get probation than the death penalty.[2]

Use the term "court crowding" as a subject guide on InfoTrac College Edition to learn more about this social problem.

---

plea negotiations/plea bargaining Discussions between defense counsel and prosecution in which the accused agrees to plead guilty in exchange for certain considerations, such as reduced charges or a lenient sentence.

Perspectives on Justice

Such abstract goals as fairness can be impossible to reach in the crowded U.S. court system. The players in the system often seek accommodation, not a vigorous criminal defense. **Plea negotiations** and other nonjudicial alternatives, such as diversion, are far more common than the formal trial process. In a sense, caseload pressure interferes with due process and in many cases makes the court system an instrument of nonintervention.

The Criminal Court Process

The U.S. court system has evolved over the years into an intricately balanced legal process, which has recently come under siege because of the sheer numbers of cases it must consider and the ways in which it is forced to handle such over-crowding. Overloaded court dockets have given rise to charges of "assembly-line justice," in which a majority of defendants are induced to plead guilty, jury trials are rare, and the speedy trial is highly desired but unattainable.

Overcrowding causes the poor to languish in detention, while the wealthier go free on bail. An innocent person can be frightened into pleading guilty, and conversely, a guilty person released because a trial has been delayed too long.[3] Whether providing more judges or new or enlarged courts will solve the problem of overcrowding remains to be seen. Meanwhile, diversion programs, decriminalization of certain offenses, and bail reform provide other avenues of possible relief. More efficient court management and administration is also seen as a step that might ease the congestion of the courts. The introduction of professional trial court managers — administrators, clerks, and judges with management skills — is one of the more significant waves of change in the nation's courts in recent decades.

To house this complex process, each state maintains its own state court organization and structure. American courts basically have two systems: state and federal. There are 50 state trial and appellate systems and separate courts for the District of Columbia and the Commonwealth of Puerto Rico. Usually three (or more) separate court systems exist within each state jurisdiction.

State Courts

The state court system alone handled about 92 million new cases in 2001 (the last data available).[4] As Table 9.1 shows, that total included about 20 million civil and domestic cases, more than 14 million criminal cases, 2 million juvenile cases, and 56 million traffic and ordinance violations. Significant growth characterized the states' criminal caseloads, which rose about 28 percent from 1987 to 2001 (Figure 9.1). While criminal case filings have risen significantly, traffic cases have declined, probably because the number of driving while intoxicated (DWI) cases dropped about 5 percent. The decline in DWI filings likely reflects stricter law enforcement, media attention to the problem, and alcohol awareness programs. However, the recent uptick between 1997 and 2000 shows that the DWI problem remains a national concern.

Use "criminal court process" as a subject guide on InfoTrac College Edition to learn more about court conditions in the United States and abroad.

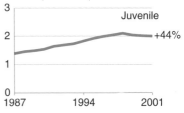
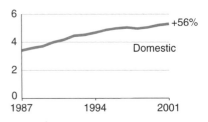
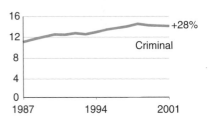
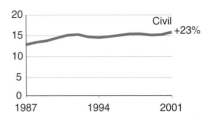

Figure 9.1
State Court Filings by Type of Case, 1987–2001 (in millions)

Source: Brian Ostrom, Neal Kauder, and Robert LaFountain, *Examining the Work of State Courts, 2002* (Williamsburg, Va.: National Center for State Courts, 2003), p. 10.

Table 9.1 Types of Cases Filed in State Courts, 2001 (in millions)

Case Type	Total	Jurisdiction	
		General	Limited
Traffic	55.7	14.1	41.6
Civil	15.8	7.4	8.4
Criminal	14.1	4.8	9.2
Domestic	5.3	3.8	1.5
Juvenile	2.0	1.3	0.7
Total	92.8	31.4	61.4

Source: Brian Ostrom, Neal Kauder, and Robert LaFountain, *Examining the Work of State Courts, 2002* (Williamsburg, Va.: National Center for State Courts, 2003).
Note: Totals may not sum because of rounding.

The National Center for State Courts (NCSC) is an independent, nonprofit organization dedicated to the improvement of justice. NCSC activities include developing policies to enhance state courts, advancing state courts' interests within the federal government, fostering state court adaptation to future changes, securing sufficient resources for state courts, strengthening state court leadership, facilitating state court collaboration, and providing a model for organizational administration. To access its Web site, go to http://www.ncsc.dni.us.

courts of limited jurisdiction
Courts that handle misdemeanors and minor civil complaints.

lower courts
Courts that conduct preliminary hearings and try misdemeanor cases and civil matters of a limited monetary value.

drug courts
Specialty courts with jurisdiction over cases involving illegal substances, often providing treatment alternatives for defendants.

courts of general jurisdiction
Court that try felony cases and more serious civil matters.

felony courts
Courts that try felony cases and civil matters involving significant monetary claims.

Perspectives on Justice

Ironically, evidence shows that an informal justice system, which is often deplored by experts, may provide criminal suspects a greater degree of satisfaction than the more formal criminal trial. This belief is the core of the restorative justice movement whose advocates want the community to play a greater role in the justice process.

Courts of Limited Jurisdiction

There are approximately 14,000 **courts of limited jurisdiction** in the United States. Most are organized along town, municipal, and county lines of government; the rest are controlled by state governments. Limited jurisdiction courts outnumber general jurisdiction courts approximately 5 to 1 (14,000 to 3,000).[5]

Courts of limited jurisdiction (sometimes called municipal courts, or **lower courts**) are restricted in the types of cases they may hear. Usually, they will handle misdemeanor criminal infractions, violations of municipal ordinances, traffic violations, and civil suits in which the damages involve less than a certain amount of money (usually $10,000). These courts also conduct preliminary hearings for felony criminal cases.

The lower criminal courts are restricted in the criminal penalties they can impose. Most can levy a fine of $1,000 or less and incarcerate a person for 12 months or less in the local jail.

Specialty Courts Included within the category of courts of limited jurisdiction are special courts, such as juvenile, family, and probate (divorce, estate issues, and custody) courts. Some states separate limited courts into those that handle civil cases only and those that settle criminal cases. A rise in a particular problem, such as drug use, may cause states to create specialized juvenile and adult **drug courts.** These newest types of specialty courts are discussed in the Analyzing Criminal Justice Issues feature on page 278.

The nation's lower courts are the ones most often accused of providing assembly-line justice. Because the matters they decide involve minor personal confrontations and conflicts — family disputes, divorces, landlord–tenant conflicts, barroom brawls — the rule of the day is "handling the situation" and resolving the dispute.

Courts of General Jurisdiction

Approximately 3,000 **courts of general jurisdiction,** or **felony courts,** exist in the United States. They process about 5 million felony cases each year, doubling since 1984 (see Figure 9.2). Courts of general jurisdiction handle the more serious felony cases (for example, murder, rape, robbery), whereas courts of limited jurisdiction handle misdemeanors (for example, simple assault, shoplifting, bad checks). About 90 percent of the general courts are state-administered, and the remainder are controlled by counties or municipalities. The overwhelming majority of general courts hear both serious civil and criminal matters (felonies). A general jurisdiction trial court is the highest state trial court where felony criminal cases are adjudicated.

Courts of general jurisdiction may also be responsible for reviewing cases on appeal from courts of limited jurisdiction. In some cases, they will base their decision on a review of the transcript of the case. In others, they can grant a new trial in a procedure known as the trial de novo process. Changes in the courts of general jurisdiction, such as increases in felony filing rates, are watched closely because serious crime is of great public concern.

There are currently more than 450 tribal justice forums among the 556 federally recognized tribes in the United States. Sometimes they claim jurisdiction over cases that regularly go to state courts. Kirk Douglas Billie, a Miccosukee Seminole Indian charged with murder in the deaths of his two young sons, sits with his attorneys, Diane Ward, left, and Ed O'Donnell, right, February 6, 2001, in Miami-Dade County Court. The defense maintained that Billie did not know the two boys were asleep in the back seat of the sport utility vehicle he drove into a canal near the reservation; the state argued that he did. Billie's tribe said it had already meted out punishment for the crime and that Billie should be set free. Billie was found guilty of second-degree murder but planned to appeal on the grounds that he had already been tried by the tribal courts.

Appellate Courts

If defendants believe that the procedures used in their case were in violation of their constitutional rights, they may appeal the outcome of their case. For example, defendants can file an appeal if they believe that the law they were tried under violates constitutional standards (for example, it was too vague) or if the procedures used in the case contravened principles of due process and equal protection or were in direct opposition to a constitutional guarantee (for example, denial of the right to have competent legal representation). **Appellate courts** do not try cases; they review the procedures of the case to determine whether an error was made by judicial authorities. Judicial error can include admitting into evidence illegally seized material, improperly charging a jury, allowing a prosecutor to ask witnesses improper questions, and so on. The appellate court can order a new trial, allow the defendant to go free, or uphold the original verdict.

Most criminal appeals are limited to trial convictions, sentences, and guilty plea convictions. The most basic feature of the appellate system is the distinction between mandated appeals by right and discretionary review of certain cases. For example, appeals of trial convictions are ordinarily under the courts' mandatory jurisdiction. The most famous appellate court with discretionary jurisdiction is the U.S. Supreme Court, the nation's highest court.

State criminal appeals are heard in one of the appellate courts in the 50 states and the District of Columbia. Each state has at least one court of last resort, usually

appellate courts

Courts that reconsider cases that have already been tried to determine whether the lower court proceedings complied with accepted rules of criminal procedure and constitutional doctrines.

Figure 9.2 State Filings in Courts of General Jurisdiction

Source: Brian Ostrom, Neal Kauder, and Robert LaFountain, *Examining the Work of State Courts, 2002* (Williamsburg, Va.: National Center for State Courts, 2003), p. 14.

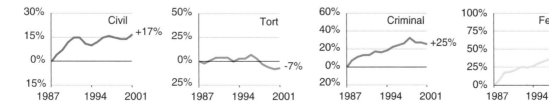

Specialized Courts: Drugs and Mental Health

analyzing criminal justice issues

A growing phenomenon in the United States is the creation of specialty courts that focus on one type of criminal act. All cases within the jurisdiction that involve this particular type of crime are funneled to the specialty court, where presumably they will get prompt resolution.

Drug Courts

Drug courts have jurisdiction over the burgeoning number of cases involving substance abuse and trafficking. The aim is to place nonviolent first offenders into intensive treatment programs instead of putting them in jail or prison. One such court, the Drug Night Court program in Cook County, Illinois, was set up in 1975 as an emergency measure to deal with the rapidly expanding number of narcotics cases being filed. Today there are 327 drug courts across 43 states, the District of Columbia, and Puerto Rico. Drug courts address the overlap between the public health threats of drug abuse and crime: Crimes are often drug-related; drug abusers are frequently involved with the criminal justice system. Drug courts provide an ideal setting to address these problems by linking the justice system with health services and drug treatment providers while easing the burden on the already overtaxed correctional system.

While some recent research finds that drug courts may not be as effective as originally believed, research by Denise Gottfredson and her associates conducted in the Baltimore City Drug Treatment Court in Baltimore, Maryland, found that drug courts did seem to work for reducing crime in a population of offenders who were severely drug-addicted. In one study conducted with Lyn Exum, Gottfredson used a carefully designed experimental model in which cases were randomly sent to either the drug court or a traditional court. The researchers found that drug court judges imposed harsher sentences but suspended these sentences conditional on compliance with the drug court regimen, such as drug testing and treatment. Most important, within a 12-month period, 48 percent of drug treatment court clients compared with 64 percent of the people handled in traditional courts were arrested for new offenses. Among the more serious cases heard, 32 percent of drug court clients versus 57 percent of controls were rearrested. All things considered, cases handled in a traditional court suffered rearrest at a rate nearly three times that of the drug treatment court client. This research finding is not unique. Evaluations of drug courts in Las Vegas, Nevada, and Portland, Oregon, conducted by John Goldkamp reaffirms the utility of the drug court concept.

Mental Heath Courts

Based largely on the organization of drug courts, mental health courts focus their attention on mental health treatment to help people with emotional problems reduce their chances of reoffending. By focusing on the need for treatment, along with providing supervision and support from the community, mental health courts provide a venue for those dealing with mental health issues to avoid the trauma of jail or prison where they will have little, if any, access to treatment.

Though mental health courts tend to vary in their approach, most share a few basic operating procedures.

- Most mental health courts demand active participation by the defendant.
- The participant must be diagnosed with a mental illness, and a direct link must be established between the illness and the crime committed.
- Intervention must occur quickly. Individuals must be screened and referred to the program either immediately after arrest or within three weeks.
- Once in the program, participants are closely monitored by case managers.

called a state supreme court, which reviews issues of law and fact appealed from the trial courts. A few states have two high courts, one for civil appeals and the other for criminal cases. In addition, many states have established intermediate appellate courts (IAC) to review decisions by trial courts and administrative agencies before they reach the supreme court stage. Currently, 39 states have at least one permanent IAC. Mississippi was the last state to create an IAC, which began operations in 1995.

Many people believe that criminal appeals clog the nation's court system because so many convicted criminals try to "beat the rap" on a technicality. Actually, criminal appeals represent a small percentage of the total number of cases processed by the nation's appellate courts. All types of appeals, including criminal ones, continue to inundate the courts, so most courts are having problems processing cases expeditiously.

State courts have witnessed an increase in the number of appellate cases each year. In the meantime, the number of judges and support staff has not kept pace.

Although programs vary, most require that defendants plead guilty in exchange for entering the program. After guilt is established, participants are sent to live in a residential treatment facility where, with help from counselors, they develop a treatment plan, which is rigorous at first and then gradually less restrictive if improvement is shown. Most programs involve the use of medication to help individuals overcome the symptoms of their illness.

While the mental health court concept seems beneficial, it has encountered a few operational difficulties. First, getting community support for programs and institutions treating mentally ill offenders can be challenging. Residents do not want treatment centers to be located close to where they live; that is, the "not in my backyard" syndrome comes into play. Second, most programs accept only the nonviolent mentally ill. The violent-prone are still lost in the correctional system without receiving the proper treatment.

Assessing the benefits of having specialized mental health courts also is difficult. With other specialized courts, measuring offender improvement is relatively easy. For example, people sent to drug court programs must simply prove they can remain drug-free. However,

those involved with mental health court programs suffer from complex mental issues, and case managers must ensure that these individuals have gained control over their illness, which can be hard to determine.

The mental health court movement has prompted development of juvenile mental health courts to treat troubled adolescents who have been accused of committing nonviolent crimes. Juvenile mental health court programs typically involve collaboration between the justice system, mental health professionals, and the parents of the young offenders to devise a treatment plan to treat the child, helping him or her avoid the standard juvenile justice system process.

Critical Thinking

1. Do you believe that specialized courts are needed for other crime types, such as sex offenses or domestic violence?
2. Should a judge preside over a specialized court or should it be administered by treatment personnel?

InfoTrac College Edition Research

 To learn more about the "drug court" movement, use it as a subject guide on InfoTrac College Edition.

Sources: John S. Goldkamp and Cheryl Irons-Guynn, *Emerging Judicial Strategies for the Mentally Ill in the Criminal Caseload: Mental Health Courts in Fort Lauderdale, Seattle, San Bernardino, and Anchorage* (Washington, D.C.: U.S. Department of Justice, Office of Justice Programs, 2000); Melissa Lackman and Susan Solomon, "CABF Endorses Juvenile Mental Health Courts," *Child and Adolescent Bipolar Foundation Bulletin* 4 (2003): 1; John Goldkamp, "The Impact of Drug Courts," *Criminology and Public Policy* 2 (2003): 197–206; Denise Gottfredson, Stacy Najaka, and Brook Kearley, "Effectiveness of Drug Treatment Courts: Evidence from a Randomized Trial," *Criminology and Public Policy* 2 (2003): 171–97; Denise C. Gottfredson and Lyn Exum, "The Baltimore City Drug Treatment Court: One-Year Results from a Randomized Study," *Journal of Research in Crime and Delinquency* 39 (2002): 337–57; Bureau of Justice Assistance, *Drug Night Courts: The Cook County Experience* (Washington, D.C.: National Institute of Justice, 1994); Terance Miethe, Hong Lu, and Eric Reese, "Reintegrative Shaming and Recidivism Risks in Drug Court: Explanations for Some Unexpected Findings," *Crime and Delinquency* 46 (2000): 522–41; Jeffrey A. Butts and Janeen Buck, "Teen Courts: A Focus on Research," *Juvenile Justice Bulletin* (October 2000); Kevin Minor, James Wells, Irinia Soderstrom, Rachel Bingham, and Deborah Williamson, "Sentence Completion and Recidivism among Juveniles Referred to Teen Courts," *Crime and Delinquency* 45 (1999): 467–80; Paige Harrison, James R. Maupin, and G. Larry Mays, "Teen Court: An Examination of Processes and Outcomes," *Crime and Delinquency* 47 (2001): 243–64; Suzanne Wenzel, Douglas Longshore, Susan Turner, and Susan Ridgely, "Drug Courts: A Bridge between Criminal Justice and Health Services," *Journal of Criminal Justice* 29 (2001): 241–53.

The resulting imbalance has led to the increased use of intermediate courts to screen cases.

Use "appellate court" as a subject guide on InfoTrac College Edition to learn more about how these courts operate.

Perspectives on Justice

Crime control advocates believe that criminal appeals clog the nation's court system because so many convicted criminals try to get free on a technicality. They may be overstating the case. For example, less than 20 percent of the appeals in federal courts are criminal matters. The right to appeal an unjust conviction lies at the heart of the due process model.

In sum, most states have at least two trial courts and two appellate courts, but they differ about where jurisdiction over such matters as juvenile cases and

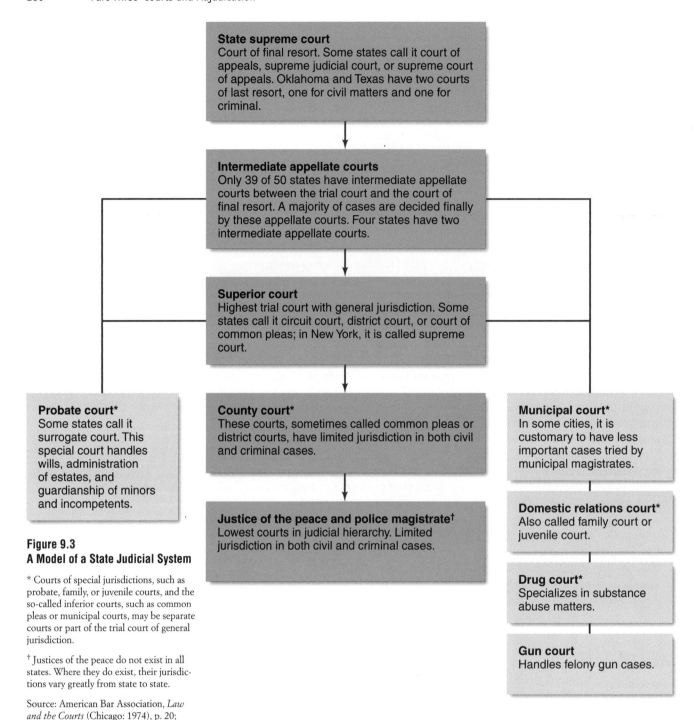

**Figure 9.3
A Model of a State Judicial System**

* Courts of special jurisdictions, such as probate, family, or juvenile courts, and the so-called inferior courts, such as common pleas or municipal courts, may be separate courts or part of the trial court of general jurisdiction.

† Justices of the peace do not exist in all states. Where they do exist, their jurisdictions vary greatly from state to state.

Source: American Bar Association, *Law and the Courts* (Chicago: 1974), p. 20; Bureau of Justice Statistics, *State Court Organization—1998* (Washington, D.C.: Department of Justice, 2000).

felony versus misdemeanor offenses is found. Such matters vary from state to state and between the state courts and the federal system.

Model State Court Structure

Figure 9.3 illustrates the interrelationship of appellate and trial courts in a typical state court structure. Each state's court organization varies from this standard pattern. Each state has a tiered court organization (lower, upper, and appellate courts), but states differ in the way they have delegated responsibility to a particular court system. For example, the court organizations of Texas and New York are complex in comparison with the model court structure (Figures 9.4 and 9.5).

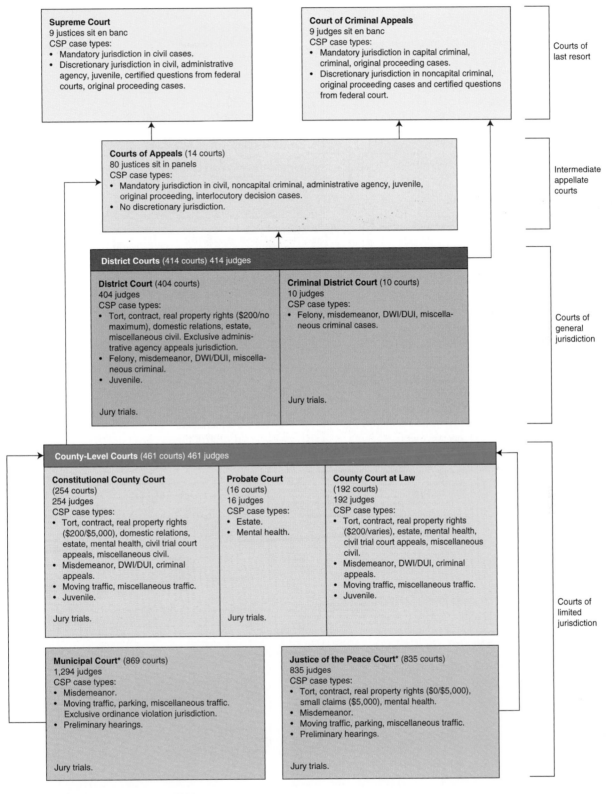

Figure 9.4 Texas Court Structure, 2001

Note: CSP = Court Statistics Project.

* Some municipal and justice of the peace courts may appeal to the district court. DWI/DUI = driving while intoxicated/driving under the influence.

Source: Brian Ostrom, Neal Kauder, and Robert LaFountain, *Examining the Work of State Courts, 2002* (Williamsburg, Va.: National Center for State Courts, 2003), p. 52.

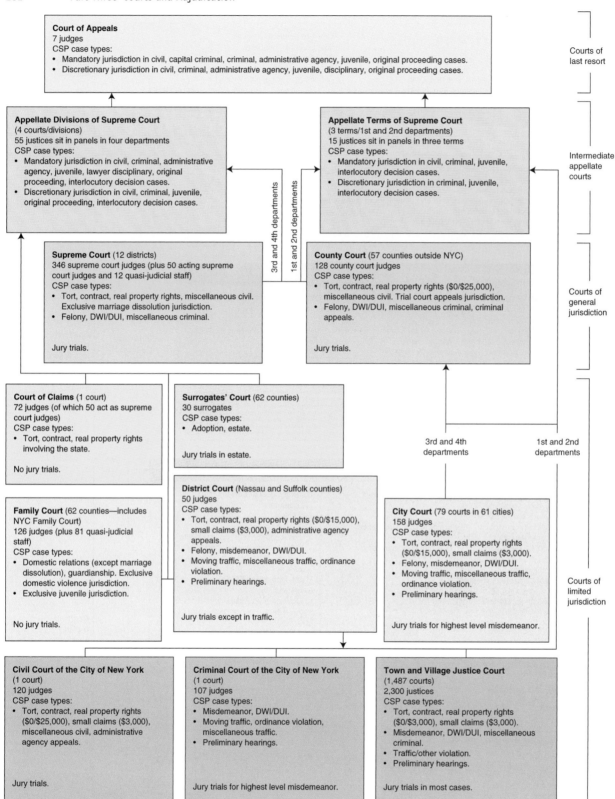

Court of Appeals
7 judges
CSP case types:
- Mandatory jurisdiction in civil, capital criminal, criminal, administrative agency, juvenile, original proceeding cases.
- Discretionary jurisdiction in civil, criminal, administrative agency, juvenile, disciplinary, original proceeding cases.

Courts of last resort

Appellate Divisions of Supreme Court
(4 courts/divisions)
55 justices sit in panels in four departments
CSP case types:
- Mandatory jurisdiction in civil, criminal, administrative agency, juvenile, lawyer disciplinary, original proceeding, interlocutory decision cases.
- Discretionary jurisdiction in civil, criminal, juvenile, original proceeding, interlocutory decision cases.

Appellate Terms of Supreme Court
(3 terms/1st and 2nd departments)
15 justices sit in panels in three terms
CSP case types:
- Mandatory jurisdiction in civil, criminal, juvenile, interlocutory decision cases.
- Discretionary jurisdiction in criminal, juvenile, interlocutory decision cases.

Intermediate appellate courts

3rd and 4th departments

1st and 2nd departments

Supreme Court (12 districts)
346 supreme court judges (plus 50 acting supreme court judges and 12 quasi-judicial staff)
CSP case types:
- Tort, contract, real property rights, miscellaneous civil. Exclusive marriage dissolution jurisdiction.
- Felony, DWI/DUI, miscellaneous criminal.

Jury trials.

County Court (57 counties outside NYC)
128 county court judges
CSP case types:
- Tort, contract, real property rights ($0/$25,000), miscellaneous civil. Trial court appeals jurisdiction.
- Felony, DWI/DUI, miscellaneous criminal, criminal appeals.

Jury trials.

Courts of general jurisdiction

Court of Claims (1 court)
72 judges (of which 50 act as supreme court judges)
CSP case types:
- Tort, contract, real property rights involving the state.

No jury trials.

Surrogates' Court (62 counties)
30 surrogates
CSP case types:
- Adoption, estate.

Jury trials in estate.

3rd and 4th departments

1st and 2nd departments

Family Court (62 counties—includes NYC Family Court)
126 judges (plus 81 quasi-judicial staff)
CSP case types:
- Domestic relations (except marriage dissolution), guardianship. Exclusive domestic violence jurisdiction.
- Exclusive juvenile jurisdiction.

No jury trials.

District Court (Nassau and Suffolk counties)
50 judges
CSP case types:
- Tort, contract, real property rights ($0/$15,000), small claims ($3,000), administrative agency appeals.
- Felony, misdemeanor, DWI/DUI.
- Moving traffic, miscellaneous traffic, ordinance violation.
- Preliminary hearings.

Jury trials except in traffic.

City Court (79 courts in 61 cities)
158 judges
CSP case types:
- Tort, contract, real property rights ($0/$15,000), small claims ($3,000).
- Felony, misdemeanor, DWI/DUI.
- Moving traffic, miscellaneous traffic, ordinance violation.
- Preliminary hearings.

Jury trials for highest level misdemeanor.

Courts of limited jurisdiction

Civil Court of the City of New York (1 court)
120 judges
CSP case types:
- Tort, contract, real property rights ($0/$25,000), small claims ($3,000), miscellaneous civil, administrative agency appeals.

Jury trials.

Criminal Court of the City of New York (1 court)
107 judges
CSP case types:
- Misdemeanor, DWI/DUI.
- Moving traffic, ordinance violation, miscellaneous traffic.
- Preliminary hearings.

Jury trials for highest level misdemeanor.

Town and Village Justice Court (1,487 courts)
2,300 justices
CSP case types:
- Tort, contract, real property rights ($0/$3,000), small claims ($3,000).
- Misdemeanor, DWI/DUI, miscellaneous criminal.
- Traffic/other violation.
- Preliminary hearings.

Jury trials in most cases.

Figure 9.5 New York Court Structure, 2001

Note: Unless otherwise noted, numbers reflect statutory authorization. Many judges sit in more than one court so the number of judgeships indicated in this chart does not reflect the actual number of judges in the system. Fifty County Court judges also serve Surrogates' Court and six County Court judges also serve Family Court. CSP = Court Statistics Project. DWI/DUI = driving while intoxicated/driving under the influence.

Source: Brian Ostrom, Neal Kauder, and Robert LaFountain, *Examining the Work of State Courts, 2002* (Williamsburg, Va.: National Center for State Courts, 2003), p. 40.

Sketch by Jane Collins © AFP/Corbis

Richard Reid, the "Shoe Bomber," shown here in a courtroom drawing was tried in federal court. Reid pleaded guilty to all eight counts against him — including attempted use of a weapon of mass destruction, attempted homicide, and placing an explosive device on an aircraft. He was sentenced to a possible sixty years in prison.

Texas separates its highest appellate divisions into civil and criminal courts. The Texas Supreme Court hears civil, administrative, and juvenile cases, and an independent Court of Criminal Appeals has the final say on criminal matters. New York's unique structure features two separate intermediate appellate courts with different geographic jurisdictions and an independent Family Court, which handles both domestic relations (such as guardianship and custody, neglect, and abuse) and juvenile delinquency. Surrogates' Court handles adoptions and settles disagreements over estate transfers. The Court of Claims handles civil matters in which the state is a party. In contrast to New York, which has 10 independent courts, six states (Idaho, Illinois, Iowa, Massachusetts, Minnesota, and South Dakota) have unified their trial courts into a single system.

To quiz yourself on this material, go to questions 9.1–9.6 on the Introduction to Criminal Justice 10e CD.

Federal Courts

The legal basis for the federal court system is contained in Article 3, Section 1, of the U.S. Constitution, which provides that "the judicial power of the United States shall be vested in one Supreme Court, and in such inferior courts as Congress may from time to time ordain and establish." The important clauses in Article 3 indicate that the federal courts have jurisdiction over the laws of the United States, treaties, and cases involving admiralty and maritime jurisdiction, as well as over controversies between two or more states and citizens of different states.[6] This complex language generally means that state courts have jurisdiction over all legal matters, unless they involve a violation of a federal criminal statute or a civil suit between citizens of different states or between a citizen and an agency of the federal government.

Within this authority, the federal government has established a three-tiered hierarchy of court jurisdiction that, in order of ascendancy, consists of the U.S. district courts, U.S. courts of appeals (circuit courts), and the U.S. Supreme Court (Figure 9.6).

District Courts

U.S. district courts are the trial courts of the federal system. They have jurisdiction over cases involving violations of federal laws, including civil rights abuses, interstate transportation of stolen vehicles, and kidnappings. They may also hear

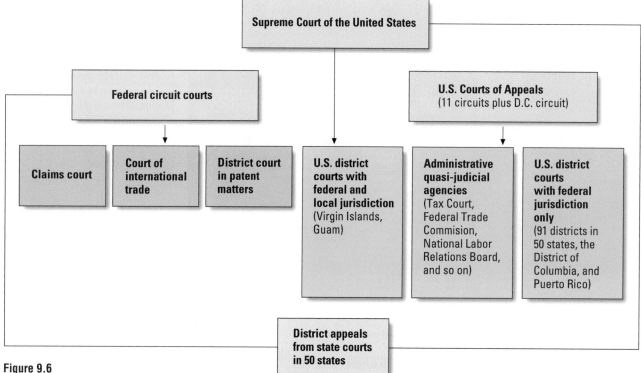

Figure 9.6
The Federal Judicial System

Source: American Bar Association, *Law and the Courts* (Chicago: 1974), p. 21. Updated information provided by the Federal Courts Improvement Act of 1982 and West Publishing Company, St. Paul, Minnesota.

cases on questions involving citizenship and the rights of aliens. The jurisdiction of the U.S. district court will occasionally overlap that of state courts. For example, citizens who reside in separate states and are involved in litigation of an amount in excess of $10,000 may choose to have their cases heard in either of the states or the federal court. Finally, federal district courts hear cases in which one state sues a resident (or firm) in another state, where one state sues another, or where the federal government is a party in a suit. A single judge ordinarily presides over criminal trials; a defendant may also request a jury trial.

Federal district courts were organized by Congress in the Judicial Act of 1789, and today 94 independent courts are in operation. Originally, each state was allowed one court. As the population grew, however, so did the need for courts. Now each state has from one to four district courts, and the District of Columbia has one for itself.

Federal Appeals Courts

Approximately 40,000 appeals from the district courts are heard each year in the 12 federal courts of appeals, sometimes referred to as U.S. circuit courts. This name is derived from the historical practice of having judges ride the circuit and regularly hear cases in the judicial seats of their various jurisdictions. Today, appellate judges are not required to travel (although some may sit in more than one court), and each federal appellate court jurisdiction contains a number of associate justices who share the caseload. Circuit court offices are usually located in major cities, such as San Francisco and New York, and cases to be heard must be brought to these locations by attorneys.

The circuit court is empowered to review federal and state appellate court cases on substantive and procedural issues involving rights guaranteed by the Constitution. Circuit courts neither retry cases nor determine whether the facts brought out during trial support conviction or dismissal. Instead, they analyze judicial interpretations of the law, such as the charge (or instructions) to the jury, and reflect on the constitutional issues involved in each case they hear.

Although federal court criminal cases do make up only a small percentage of appellate cases, they are still of concern to the judiciary. Steps have been taken to make appealing more difficult. For example, the U.S. Supreme Court has tried to limit the number of appeals being filed by prison inmates, which often represent a significant number of cases appealed in the federal criminal justice system.

The U.S. Supreme Court

The U.S. Supreme Court is the nation's highest appellate body and the **court of last resort** for all cases tried in the various federal and state courts.

The Supreme Court is composed of nine members appointed for lifetime terms by the president, with the approval of Congress. (The size of the Court is set by statute.) The Court has discretion over most of the cases it will consider and may choose to hear only those it deems important, appropriate, and worthy of its attention. The Court chooses around 300 of the 5,000 cases that are appealed each year; less than half of these typically receive full opinions.

When the Supreme Court decides to hear a case, it grants a writ of certiorari, requesting a transcript of the proceedings of the case for review. However, the Court is required to hear cases in a few instances, such as decisions from a three-judge federal district court on reapportionment or cases involving the Voting Rights Act.

When the Supreme Court rules on a case, usually by majority decision (at least five votes), the outcome becomes a precedent that must be honored by all lower courts. For example, if the Court grants a particular litigant the right to counsel at a police lineup, all similarly situated clients must be given the same right. This type of ruling is usually referred to as a landmark decision. The use of precedent in the legal system gives the Supreme Court power to influence and mold the everyday operating procedures of the police, trial courts, and corrections agencies. This influence became particularly pronounced during the tenure of Chief Justices Earl Warren (1953–69) and Warren Burger (1969–86), who greatly amplified and extended the power of the Court to influence criminal justice policies. Under William H. Rehnquist, who was elevated to chief justice in 1986, the Court has continued to influence criminal justice matters, ranging from the investigation of crimes to the execution of criminals. The personal legal philosophy of the justices and their orientation toward the civil and personal rights of victims and criminals significantly affect the daily operations of the justice system.

How a Case Gets to the Supreme Court The Supreme Court is unique in several ways. First, it is the only court established by constitutional mandate, instead of federal legislation. Second, it decides basic social and political issues of grave consequence and importance to the nation. Third, the justices shape the future meaning of the U.S. Constitution. Their decisions identify the rights and liberties of citizens throughout the United States.

When the nation was first established, the Supreme Court did not review state court decisions involving issues of federal law. Even though Congress had given the Supreme Court jurisdiction to review state decisions, much resistance and controversy surrounded the relationship between the states and the federal government. However, in a famous decision, *Martin* v. *Hunter's Lessee* (1816), the Court reaffirmed the legitimacy of its jurisdiction over state court decisions when such courts handled issues of federal or constitutional law.[7] This decision allowed the Court to actively review actions by states and their courts and reinforced the Court's power to make the supreme law of the land. Since that time, a defendant who indicates that governmental action — whether state or federal — violates a constitutional law is in a position to have the Court review such action.

court of last resort
A court that handles the final appeal on a matter; in the federal system, the U.S. Supreme Court.

© 2002 AP/Wide World Photos

Supreme Court rulings set precedents that guide the administration of justice. For example, in the 2002 case *Atkins* v. *Virginia,* the Court ruled that executions of mentally retarded criminals are "cruel and unusual punishments" prohibited by the Eighth Amendment. The Court noted that a significant number of states have concluded that death is not a suitable punishment for a mentally retarded criminal. Here, Daryl Renard Atkins, who has an IQ of fifty-nine, sits in a Virginia courtroom during his trial in 1998. His execution was stayed by the Court's decision.

writ of certiorari
An order of a superior court requesting that a record of an inferior court (or administrative body) be brought forward for review or inspection.

To quiz yourself on this material, go to questions 9.7–9.14 on the Introduction to Criminal Justice 10e CD.

To carry out its responsibilities, the Supreme Court had to develop a method for dealing with the large volume of cases coming from the state and federal courts for final review. In the early years of its history, the Court sought to review every case brought before it. Since the middle of the twentieth century, however, the Court has used the **writ of certiorari** to decide what cases it should hear. (Certiorari is a Latin term meaning "to bring the record of a case from a lower court up to a higher court for immediate review.") When applied, it means that an accused in a criminal case is requesting the U.S. Supreme Court to hear the case. More than 90 percent of the cases heard by the Court are brought by petition for a writ of certiorari. Under this procedure, the justices have discretion to select the cases they will review for a decision. Of the thousands of cases filed before the Court every year, only about 100 receive a full opinion. Four of the nine justices sitting on the Court must vote to hear a case brought by a writ of certiorari for review. Generally, these votes are cast in a secret meeting attended only by the justices.

After the Supreme Court decides to hear a case, it reviews written and oral arguments. The written materials are referred to as legal briefs, and oral arguments are normally presented to the justices at the Court in Washington, D.C.

After the material is reviewed and the oral arguments heard, the justices normally meet in what is known as a case conference. At this case conference, they discuss the case and vote to reach a decision. The cases voted on by the Court generally come from the judicial systems of the various states or the U.S. courts of appeals, and they represent the entire spectrum of law.

In reaching a decision, the Supreme Court reevaluates and reinterprets state statutes, the U.S. Constitution, and previous case decisions. Based on a review of the case, the Court either affirms or reverses the decision of the lower court. When the justices reach a decision, the chief justice of the Court assigns someone of the majority group to write the opinion. Another justice normally writes a dissent, or minority, opinion. When the case is finished, it is submitted to the public and becomes the law of the land. The decision represents the legal precedents that add to the existing body of law on a given subject, change it, and guide its future development (Figure 9.7).

In the area of criminal justice, the decisions of the U.S. Supreme Court have had the broadest impact on the reform of the system. The Court's action is the final step in settling constitutional criminal disputes throughout the nation. By discretionary review through a petition for certiorari, the Court requires state courts to accept its interpretation of the Constitution. In doing so, the Court has changed the day-by-day operations of the criminal justice system.

Court Congestion

This vast system has been overloaded by the millions of cases that are brought each year. One reason for the increase in court caseloads is the recent attempt in some communities to lower the crime rate by aggressively prosecuting petty offenses and nuisance crimes such as panhandling or vagrancy. In New York City,

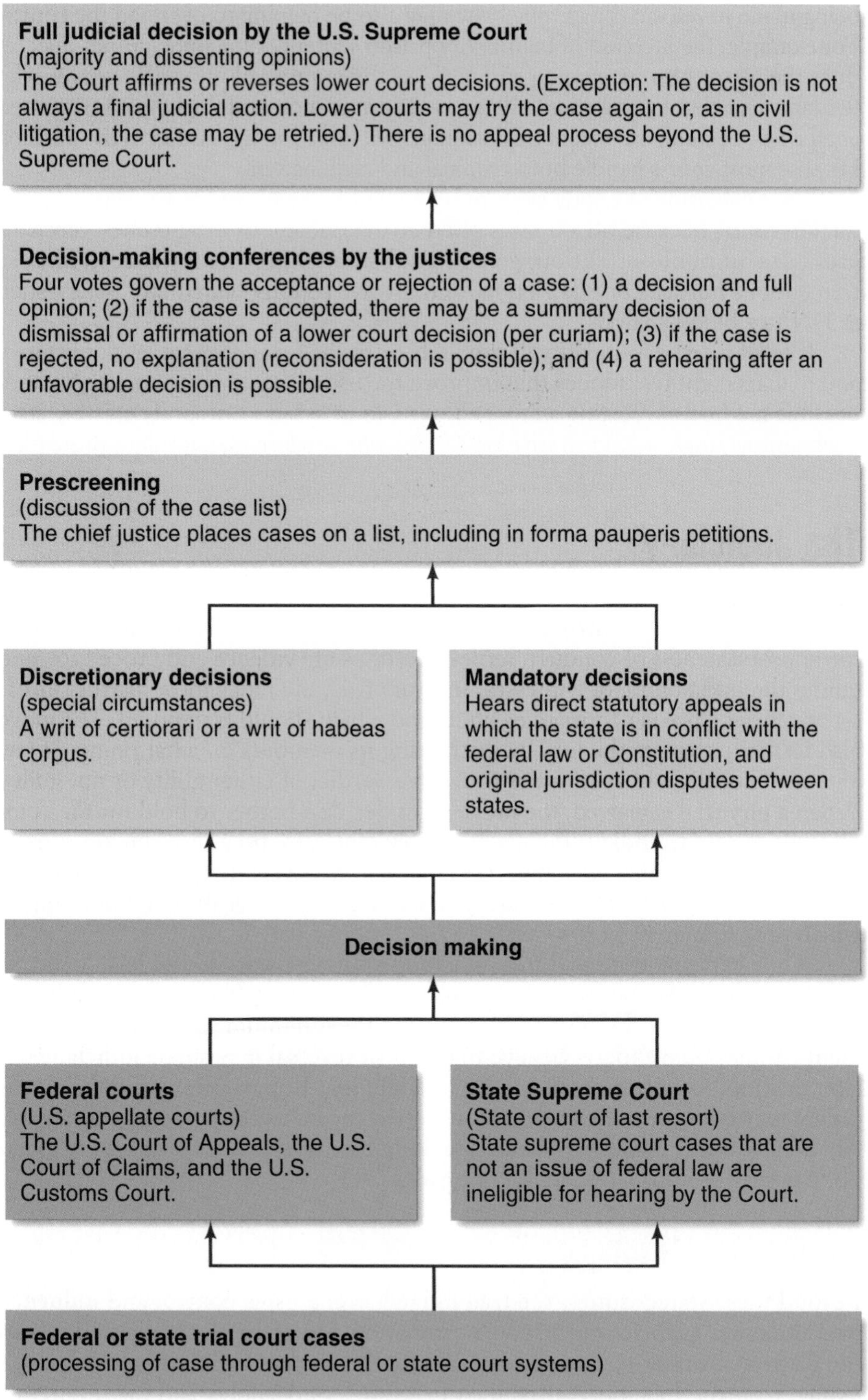

Full judicial decision by the U.S. Supreme Court
(majority and dissenting opinions)
The Court affirms or reverses lower court decisions. (Exception: The decision is not always a final judicial action. Lower courts may try the case again or, as in civil litigation, the case may be retried.) There is no appeal process beyond the U.S. Supreme Court.

↑

Decision-making conferences by the justices
Four votes govern the acceptance or rejection of a case: (1) a decision and full opinion; (2) if the case is accepted, there may be a summary decision of a dismissal or affirmation of a lower court decision (per curiam); (3) if the case is rejected, no explanation (reconsideration is possible); and (4) a rehearing after an unfavorable decision is possible.

↑

Prescreening
(discussion of the case list)
The chief justice places cases on a list, including in forma pauperis petitions.

↑

Discretionary decisions
(special circumstances)
A writ of certiorari or a writ of habeas corpus.

Mandatory decisions
Hears direct statutory appeals in which the state is in conflict with the federal law or Constitution, and original jurisdiction disputes between states.

↑

Decision making

↑

Federal courts
(U.S. appellate courts)
The U.S. Court of Appeals, the U.S. Court of Claims, and the U.S. Customs Court.

State Supreme Court
(State court of last resort)
State supreme court cases that are not an issue of federal law are ineligible for hearing by the Court.

↑

Federal or state trial court cases
(processing of case through federal or state court systems)

Figure 9.7
Tracing the Course of a Case to the U.S. Supreme Court

for example, the number of felonies has stayed roughly the same since the early 1990s, while the number of misdemeanor cases has soared by 85 percent. In 1998, 77 New York City judges heard 275,379 cases — about 3,500 cases each — in the city's lower criminal courts, which handle misdemeanors involving sentences of less than a year in jail. For defendants who want to fight charges, the average waiting time for a misdemeanor trial is 284 days, up from 208 days in 1991.[8]

As the law becomes more complex and involves such issues as computer crimes, the need for a more involved court process has escalated. Ironically, efforts

wWW The Supreme Court maintains a Web site that has a wealth of information on its history, judges, procedures, cases filings, rules, handling guides, opinions, and other relevent Court-related material. To access the site, go to http://www.supremecourtus. gov/.

being made to reform the criminal law may also be helping to overload the courts. For example, the increase of mandatory prison sentences for some crimes may reduce the use of plea bargaining and increase the number of jury trials because defendants fear that a conviction will lead to incarceration and thus must be avoided at all costs. Second, the recent explosion in civil litigation has added to the backlog because most courts handle both criminal and civil matters.

The processing of felony cases poses considerable problems for general jurisdiction courts because the offenses often involve violent or drug crimes, receive a great deal of public attention, generate substantial prosecutorial cost, impose tremendous burdens on the victims, and involve serious evidentiary issues, such as DNA or blood analysis.

If relief is to be found, it will probably be in the form of better administrative and management techniques that improve the use of existing resources. Another possible method of creating a more efficient court system is to unify existing state courts into a single administrative structure using modern management principles.

The Judiciary

The judge is the senior officer in a court of criminal law. His duties are varied and far more extensive than might be expected. During trials, the judge rules on the appropriateness of conduct, settles questions of evidence and procedure, and guides the questioning of witnesses. In a jury trial, the judge must instruct jurors on which evidence is proper to examine and which should be ignored. The judge also formally charges the jury by instructing its members on what points of law and evidence they must consider to reach a verdict of either guilty or not guilty. When a jury trial is waived, the judge must decide whether to hold for the complainant or the defendant. Finally, if a defendant is found guilty, the judge must decide on the sentence (in some cases, this is legislatively determined), which includes choosing the type of sentence and its length as well as the conditions under which probation may be revoked.

The American Judges Association seeks to improve the effective and impartial administration of justice, to enhance the independence and status of the judiciary, to provide for continuing education of its members, and to promote the interchange of ideas of a judicial nature among judges, court organization, and the public. Go to the Web site at http://aja.ncsc.dni.us/.

While carrying out his duties, the judge must be wary of the legal controls placed on the trial process by the appellate court system. If an error is made, the judge's decision may be reversed, causing at the minimum personal embarrassment. While some experts believe that fear of reversal may shape judicial decision making, recent research by David Klein and Robert Hume indicates that judges may be more independent than previously believed, especially if they can use their judicial power as a policy-making tool to influence important social policies such as affirmative action or privacy.[9]

Other Judicial Functions

Beyond these stated duties, the trial judge has extensive control and influence over the other agencies of the court: probation, the court clerk, the police, and the district attorney's office. Probation and the clerk may be under the judge's explicit control. In some courts, the operations, philosophy, and procedures of these agencies are within the magistrate's administrative domain. In others — for example, where a state agency controls the probation department — the attitudes of the county or district court judge greatly influence the way a probation department is run and how its decisions are made. Judges often consult with probation staff on treatment decisions, and many judges are interested in providing the most innovative and up-to-date care possible.

Police and prosecutors are also directly influenced by the judge, whose sentencing discretion affects the arrest and charging processes. For example, if a judge usually chooses minimal sentences — such as a fine for a particular offense — the police may be reluctant to arrest offenders for that crime, knowing that doing so will basically be a waste of time. Similarly, if a judge is known to have an open attitude toward police discretion, the local department may be more inclined to engage in practices that border on entrapment or to pursue cases through easily obtained wiretaps. However, a magistrate oriented toward strict use of due process guarantees would stifle such activities by dismissing all cases involving apparent police abuses of personal freedoms. The district attorney's office may also be sensitive to judicial attitudes. The district attorney might forgo indictments in cases that the presiding magistrate expressly considers trivial or quasi-criminal and in which the judge has been known to take only token action, such as the prosecution of pornographers.

Finally, the judge considers requests by police and prosecutors for leniency (or severity) in sentencing. The judge's reaction to these requests is important if the police and the district attorney are to honor the bargains they may have made with defendants to secure information, cooperation, or guilty pleas. For example, when police tell informers that they will try to convince the judge to go easy on them to secure required information, they will often discuss the terms of the promised leniency with representatives of the court. If a judge ignores police demands, the department's bargaining power is severely diminished, and communication within the criminal justice system is impaired.

There is always concern that judges will discriminate against defendants on the basis of their gender, race, or class. Although this issue is of great social concern, most research efforts have failed to find consistent bias in judicial decision making. Judges tend to dismiss cases that they consider weak and less serious.[10] The role of the judge in guiding the outcome of a high-profile criminal case is nowhere better illustrated than in the trial of Louise Woodward, the British au pair accused in 1997 of killing her eight-month-old charge, Matthew Eappen. This case is discussed in the Law in Review feature on page 290.

www The National Summit on Improving Judicial Selection was convened on January 25, 2001, under the leadership of Texas Supreme Court chief justice Thomas R. Phillips and Texas senator Rodney Ellis. The participants discussed how to best improve judicial selection processes, focusing on those states in which judicial selection is subject to popular election. Read about their findings at http://www.ncsconline.org/WC/Publications/Res_JudSel_CallToActionPub.pdf.

Judicial Qualifications

The qualifications for appointment to one of the existing 30,000 judgeships vary from state to state and court to court. Most typically, the potential judge must be a resident of the state, licensed to practice law, a member of the state bar association, and at least 25 and less than 70 years of age. However, a significant degree of diversity exists in the basic qualification, depending on the level of court jurisdiction. While almost every state requires judges to have a law degree if they are to serve on appellate courts or courts of general jurisdiction, it is not uncommon for municipal or town court judges to lack a legal background, even though they maintain the power to incarcerate criminal defendants.

While judges are held in high esteem, they must sacrifice many financial benefits if they shift careers from lucrative private practices to low-paid government positions. In a recent statement, Alfred Carlton, president of the American Bar Association, noted that judicial salaries are woefully inadequate and that, over the past 30 years, judges' salaries have declined in value almost 25 percent (compared with a 17.5 percent increase for other workers when adjusted for inflation). The salary situation has deteriorated to the point where some federal judges earn less than first-year associates in major law firms, who today make more than $100,000 per year.[11]

A great deal of concern has been raised about the qualifications of judges. In most states, people appointed to the bench have had little or no training in how to be a judge. Others may have held administrative posts and may not have appeared before a court in years. Although judicial salaries may seem impressive, they certainly cannot compare with the high salaries paid to partners in large urban law firms. It may be difficult to attract the most competent attorneys to a relatively low-paying judgeship.

A number of agencies have been created to improve the quality of the judiciary. The National Conference of State Court Judges and the National College

Commonwealth v. Louise Woodward
law in review

On February 4, 1997, British au pair Louise Woodward called the police and said that Matthew Eappen, the eight-month-old baby she had been hired to care for, was having difficulty breathing. The 18-year-old Woodward had been hired by two Newton, Massachusetts, doctors, Sunil and Deborah Eappen, in November 1996 to care for their two young sons. When paramedics arrived at the Eappen household, they found that the baby had a two-and-a-half-inch skull fracture. Matthew's eyes were also bulging, a possible sign of shaken baby syndrome. The baby spent four days on life support before dying on February 9.

Newton police officers on the scene later claimed that Woodward admitted to handling the baby roughly and "dropping" him on the floor. Because they believed that this rough treatment had caused the death of a child, prosecutors were persuaded to charge Woodward with first-degree murder on the grounds that her behavior was heinous and cruel.

At the trial, Woodward's high-powered defense team claimed that her alleged mishandling of the baby did not cause Matthew Eappen's death but that a preexisting medical condition might have killed the baby. Defense experts testified that the skull fracture detected during the autopsy was three weeks old and could have opened spontaneously. On the stand,

Woodward claimed that she might have shaken Matthew, but only to revive a baby already in distress. Moreover, the police officers on the scene did not hear her correctly. Instead of saying she "dropped" the baby on the floor, she had said she had "popped" the baby down, an English expression misunderstood by American police officers.

Despite the scientific evidence and Woodward's testimony, the jury found her guilty of second-degree murder, a charge that carries a minimum of 15 years in prison. Then, in a dramatic turn of events, Judge Hiller Zobel reversed the jury's decision and found Woodward guilty of involuntary manslaughter. Even more surprising to the prosecution, he sentenced her to time served, allowing for her immediate release. Judge Zobel explained his reasoning:

Judges must follow their oaths and do their duty, heedless of editorials, letters, telegrams, picketers, threats, petitions, panelists, and talk shows. In this country, we do not administer justice by plebiscite. A judge, in short, is a public servant who must follow his conscience, whether or not he counters the manifest wishes of those he serves; whether or not his decision seems a surrender to the prevalent demands.

The test here is no longer narrowly legal. The judge, formerly only an um-

pire enforcing the rules, now must determine whether, under the special circumstances of this case, justice requires lowering the level of guilt from murder to manslaughter (or even to battery). The facts, as well as the law, are open to consideration.

In deciding this issue, the judge must, above all, use the power sparingly, and with restraint, taking care not to act arbitrarily or unreasonably. The judge does not sit as a second jury, or even as a thirteenth juror; he should not second-guess the jury. Nonetheless, he is entitled to consider testimony that the jury may have disbelieved, including such of Defendant's own testimony as he finds credible.

After considering the law and the evidence of the whole case "broadly," to determine whether "there was any miscarriage of justice," the judge's duty requires: weighing "the fundamental fairness of the result," deciding whether a reduced verdict would be more consonant with justice, and determining whether justice "will be more nearly achieved" by a reduction, rather than by allowing the jury's verdict to stand. In short, the court may reduce the level of the conviction, for any reason that justice may require. This in turn means that the judge must decide whether failing to reduce the verdict raises a substantial risk that justice has miscarried. The scope of review may be even broader than requiring Defendant to show "grave prejudice" or "substantial

of Juvenile Justice both operate judicial training seminars and publish manuals and guides on state-of-the-art judicial technologies. Their ongoing efforts are designed to improve the quality of the nation's judges.

Judicial Alternatives

Increased judicial caseloads have prompted the use of alternatives to the traditional judge. For example, to expedite matters in civil cases, it has become common for both parties to agree to hire a retired judge and abide by his or her decision. Jurisdictions have set up dispute resolution systems for settling minor complaints informally upon the agreement of both parties. An estimated 700 dispute resolution programs are now handling domestic conflicts, landlord–tenant cases, misdemeanors, consumer–merchant disputes, and so on.[12]

likelihood" that a miscarriage of justice has occurred.

The Court may not, however, take into account the feelings of those the death has affected; the judge must focus entirely on the events of the trial. Thus although as a father and grandfather I particularly recognize and acknowledge the indescribable pain Matthew Eappen's death has caused his parents and grandparents, as a judge I am duty-bound to ignore it. I must look only at the evidence and the defendant.

Viewing the evidence broadly, as I am permitted to do, I believe that the circumstances in which Defendant acted were characterized by confusion, inexperience, frustration, immaturity and some anger, but not malice (in the legal sense) supporting a conviction for second-degree murder. Frustrated by her inability to quiet the crying child, she was "a little rough with him," under circumstances where another, perhaps wiser, person would have sought to restrain the physical impulse. The roughness was sufficient to start (or restart) a bleeding that escalated fatally.

Having considered the matter carefully, I am firmly convinced that the interests of justice mandate my reducing the verdict to manslaughter. I do this in accordance with my discretion and my duty. After intensive, cool, calm reflection, I am morally certain that allowing this defendant on this evidence to re- main convicted of second-degree murder would be a miscarriage of justice.

The *Woodward* case is fascinating for many reasons. It was televised around the globe, making it an international spectacle. The extensive use of expert witnesses who supplied forensic evidence was a key element in the case. Is it possible that only defendants who can afford to hire experts (some of whom charged $900 per hour) may be in a position to acquire evidence sufficient to counteract the prosecution's case (Woodward raised $100,000 in donations to pay for her defense)? But the most important element of the case was the discretion used by the presiding judge. The defense had the option to include manslaughter in the charge to the jury but chose not to, mistakenly believing that no jury could find Woodward guilty of the malicious killing of a child; but it was wrong. If it had allowed the prosecution to include manslaughter, the jury might have convicted on that lesser charge. The judge, then, was left to use his discretion both to reduce the jury's verdict and to hand down a lenient sentence. This aspect of judicial power is not invoked often. Judge Zobel, for example, had overturned only two verdicts in 18 years.

Critical Thinking

The Eappen case illustrates the power that judges have to shape the criminal process. As Judge Zobel states in his decision, the power to change jury verdicts is part of the judicial duty to render fair and impartial justice. He believes that a judge's duty requires "weighing 'the fundamental fairness of the result'" of jury decisions, "deciding whether a reduced verdict would be more consonant with justice, and determining whether justice 'will be more nearly achieved' by a reduction." Do you agree with this approach, or do you feel it undermines the jury process? After all, why spend so much time and effort serving on a jury if a judge can later decide to ignore your decision?

InfoTrac College Edition Research

 To learn more about the Eappen case, read Suzanne Fields, "Why Is Matthew Eappen Sharing Victim Status?" *Insight on the News* 13, no. 45 (December 1997): 48; Wray Herbert, "Why Did Matthew Die?" *U.S. News and World Report,* November 24, 1997, p. 41.

Sources: Sarah Lyall, "An American Jury Shocks Britain," *New York Times,* November 5, 1997; Matt Richtel, "Judge in Au Pair Trial Plans to Use Net to Unveil Decision," *New York Times,* November 2, 1997, p. 1; *Commonwealth* v. *Louise Woodward,* Memorandum and Order, Superior Court No. 97–0433 (November 10, 1997).

Perspectives on Justice

The use of mediation is one of the key components of the restorative justice perspective. By removing cases from the court setting, mediation is designed to be both a money-saving device and a forum in which conflicts can be solved in a nonadversarial manner.

Other jurisdictions have created new quasi-judicial officers, such as referees or magistrates, to relieve the traditional judge of time-consuming responsibilities. The Magistrate Act of 1968 created a new type of judicial officer in the federal district court system who handles pretrial duties.[13] Federal magistrates also handle civil trials if both parties agree to the arrangement.[14]

Other jurisdictions use part-time judges. Many of these are attorneys who carry out their duties pro bono — for no or limited compensation. These judicial adjuncts assist the courts on a temporary basis while maintaining an active law practice.[15] The use of alternative court mechanisms should continue to grow as court congestion increases.

© 2003 AP/Wide World Photos

In many jurisdictions judges are chosen by partisan election and receive campaign contributions from people who may have an interest in how the court conducts its business. Is this a conflict of interest? Here, criminal attorney Andrea Black pauses for a photo on May 29, 2003 in Orlando, Florida. In April 2002, Black contributed $250 to help Circuit Judge A. Thomas Mihok get re-elected, although he faced no opposition. Seven months later, she was in front of the judge defending a client on two first-degree murder charges. Jurors found her client, Kevin Robinson, guilty. Black said she sometimes thinks some judges bend over backward to appear impartial when facing lawyers who have contributed to their campaigns.

Missouri Plan

A method of judicial selection that combines a judicial nominating commission, executive appointment, and nonpartisan confirmation elections.

Selecting Judges

Many methods are used to select judges. In some jurisdictions, the governor appoints judges. In others, the governor's recommendations must be confirmed by the state senate, the governor's council, a special confirmation committee, an executive council elected by the state assembly, or an elected review board. Some states employ a judicial nominating commission that submits names to the governor for approval.

Another form of judicial selection is popular election. In some jurisdictions, judges run as members of the Republican, Democratic, or other parties; in others, they run without party affiliation. In 13 states, partisan elections are used for selecting judges in courts of general jurisdiction; in 17 states, nonpartisan elections are used; and in the remainder, upper–trial court judges are appointed by the governor or the legislature. Of state judges, 87 percent face elections of some type, with 53 percent of appellate judges and 77 percent of trial judges (general jurisdiction) facing contestable elections. However, each judge may face a different election experience because each has a different term of appointment. For example, 39 percent of state supreme court justices have terms of 10–15 years while 45 percent have only 6 years; 19 percent of trial judges have terms of 10–15 years, compared with the 18 percent with only 3–4 years, and 56 percent with 6 years.[16] For a review of judicial selection, see Concept Summary 9.1.

Judicial elections are troubling to some because they involve partisan politics in a process to select people who must be nonpolitical and objective. The process itself has been tainted by charges of scandal; for example, when political parties insist that judicial candidates hire favored people or firms to run their campaigns or have them make contributions to the party to obtain an endorsement.[17]

Many states have adopted some form of what is known as the **Missouri Plan** to select appellate court judges, and six states also use it to select trial court judges. This plan consists of three parts: (1) a judicial nominating commission to nominate candidates for the bench, (2) an elected official (usually from the executive branch) to make appointments from the list submitted by the commission, and (3) subsequent nonpartisan and noncompetitive elections in which incumbent judges run on their records and voters can choose either their retention or dismissal.[18]

The quality of the judiciary is a concern. Although merit plans, screening committees, and popular elections are designed to ensure a competent judiciary, it has often been charged that many judicial appointments are made to pay off political debts or to reward cronies and loyal friends. Also not uncommon are charges that those desiring to be nominated for judgeships are required to make significant political contributions.

Concept Summary 9.1 Judicial Selection

Type	Process
Appointment	Governor selects candidate, confirmed by state senate or other official body
Election	Run as partisan politician during regular election
Missouri Plan	Bar committee searches for qualified candidates, governor chooses among them, judge runs for reappointment in nonpartisan election

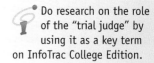

What are the problems with electing judges? Read Michael Scherer, "State Judges for Sale: In the 39 States That Elect Appellate Judges, Politicization of the Bench Is Growing," *Nation*, September 2, 2002, p. 20.

Do research on the role of the "trial judge" by using it as a key term on InfoTrac College Edition.

Judicial Overload

Great concern has arisen about stress placed on judges by case pressure. In most states, people appointed to the bench have had little or no training in the role of judge. Others may have held administrative posts and may not have appeared before a court in a long while. Once they are appointed to the bench, judges are given an overwhelming amount of work that has grown dramatically over the years. The number of civil and criminal filings per state court judge has increased significantly since 1985. Annually there are about 1,500 civil and criminal case filings per state court judge and 450 per federal judge.[19] State court judges deal with far more cases, but federal cases may be more complex and demand more judicial time. In any event, the number of civil and criminal cases, especially in state courts, seems to be outstripping the ability of states to create new judgeships. Judicial caseloads have increased substantially during the past decade.

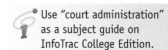

To quiz yourself on this material, go to questions 9.15–9.23 on the Introduction to Criminal Justice 10e CD.

Court Administration

In addition to qualified personnel, a need exists for efficient management of the judicial system. Improved court administration may serve as a way to relieve court congestion. Management goals include improving organization and scheduling of cases, devising methods to allocate court resources efficiently, administering fines and monies due the court, preparing budgets, and overseeing personnel.

The federal courts have led the way in creating and organizing court administration. In 1939 Congress passed the Administrative Office Act, which established the Administrative Office of the United States Courts. Its director was charged with gathering statistics on the work of the federal courts and preparing the judicial budget for approval by the Conference of Senior Circuit Judges. One clause of the act created a judicial council with general supervisory responsibilities for the district and circuit courts.

Unlike the federal government, the states have experienced a slow and uneven growth in the development and application of court management principles. The first state to establish an administrative office was North Dakota in 1927. Today, all states employ some form of central administration.

The federal government has encouraged the development of state court management through funding assistance to court managers. In addition, the federal judiciary has provided the philosophical impetus for better and more effective court management.

Use "court administration" as a subject guide on InfoTrac College Edition.

Despite the multitude of problems in reforming court management, some progress is being made. In most jurisdictions today, centralized court administrative services perform numerous functions with the help of sophisticated computers that free the judiciary to fulfill their roles as arbiters of justice.

The Criminal Justice and Technology feature on page 294 illustrates how the use of technology is reforming court administration.

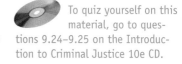

To quiz yourself on this material, go to questions 9.24–9.25 on the Introduction to Criminal Justice 10e CD.

Technology and Court Management
criminal justice and technology

As trial reconvenes, the participants blink into existence on the computer monitors that supply the only commonality applicable to them. Judge, counsel, parties, witnesses, and jury appear in virtual form on each person's monitor. Necessary evidentiary foundations are laid by witnesses with distant counsel's questions; documentary evidence is not seen by the jury until received by the court. A real-time, multi-media record (transcript with digital audio, video, and evidence) is available instantly. Sidebar conferences are accomplished simply by switching the jury out of circuit. During the interim, the jurors can head for their kitchens or for restroom breaks. The public can follow the proceedings on the Internet. Should critical interlocutory motions be argued, the appellate court can directly monitor the proceedings.

This is how court technology expert Fredric I. Lederer foresees the court of the future. His projections may not be too far off. Computers are becoming an important aid in the administration and management of courts. Rapid retrieval and organization of data are now being used for such functions as

- Maintaining case histories and statistical reporting;
- Monitoring and scheduling of cases;
- Preparing documents;
- Indexing cases;
- Issuing summonses;
- Notifying witnesses, attorneys, and others of required appearances;
- Selecting and notifying jurors; and
- Preparing and administering budgets and payrolls.

The federal government has encouraged the states to experiment with computerized information systems. Federal funds were used to begin a 50-state consortium for the purpose of establishing a standardized crime-reporting system called SEARCH (Systems for the Electronic Analysis and Retrieval of Criminal Histories).

Computer technology is also being applied in the courts in such areas as videotaped testimonies, new court-reporting devices, information systems, and data-processing systems to handle such functions as court docketing and jury management. In 1968, only 10 states had state-level automated information systems; today, all states employ such systems for a mix of tasks and duties. A survey of Georgia courts found that 84 percent used computers for three or more court administration applications.

Court jurisdictions are also cooperating with police departments in the installation of communications gear that allows defendants to be arraigned via closed-circuit television while they are in police custody. Closed-circuit television has been used for judicial conferences and scheduling meetings. Courts are using voice-activated cameras as the sole means of keeping trial records.

About 400 courts across the country have videoconferencing capability. It is

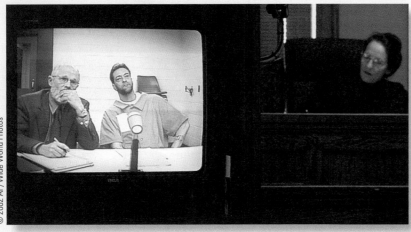

© 2002 AP/Wide World Photos

About 400 courts across the country have videoconferencing capability, and it is now being used for juvenile detention hearings, testimony at trial, oral arguments on appeal, and parole hearings. Here, Sixth Judicial District Associate Judge Sylvia Lewis, right, reads charges of first-degree murder and kidnapping to Richard Dodd, center, and Johnson County pubic defender Dick Klausner, left, in Johnson County District Court on February 1, 2002, in Iowa City, Iowa. Dodd, who is currently serving a life sentence at the Iowa State Penitentiary for a 1984 kidnapping and rape conviction, is charged with the 1981 murder of Vicki Klotzbach. Dodd appeared via closed circuit television from the Johnson County Jail.

now being employed for juvenile detention hearings, expert witness, testimony at trial, oral arguments on appeal, and parole hearings. More than 150 courts are using two-way live, televised remote linkups for first appearance and arraignment. In the usual arrangement, the defendant appears from a special location in the jail where he is able to see and hear and be seen and heard by the presiding magistrate. Such appearances are now being authorized by state statute, for example, Virginia Code § 19.2–3. 1. Televising appearances minimizes delays in prisoner transfer, effects large savings through the elimination of transportation and security costs, and reduces escape and assault risks.

More than 50 high-tech courtrooms are equipped for real-time transcription and translation, audio-video preservation of the court record, remote witness participation, computer graphics displays, television monitors for jurors, and computers for counsel and judge. Attorneys in the case of *Yukiyo* v. *Watanabe,* 114 F.3d 1207 (9th Cir. 1997), filed an appellate brief on a CD-ROM containing hot links to the entire trial transcript, the deposition record, the full opinions of all cases cited by the attorneys, and replications of all exhibits used by expert witnesses during trial. Though the CD-ROM brief was dismissed after opposing counsel objected to its use, it provides a glimpse of how technology can change the court process.

Case management will soon be upgraded. In the 1970s, municipal courts installed tracking systems, which used databases to manage court data. These older systems were limited and could not process the complex interrelationships of information pertaining to persons, cases, time, and financial matters that occur in court cases.

Contemporary relational databases provide the flexibility to handle the complex case management. To help programmers define the multiplicity of relationships that occur in a court setting, the National Center for State Courts in Williamsburg, Virginia, has developed a methodology for structuring a case management system that tracks a person to the case or cases in which he is a defendant, the scheduling of the cases to avoid any conflicts, and, of increasing importance, the fines that have been levied and the accounts to which the money goes.

The Internet has begun finding its way into the court system, too. For example, in the federal system, "J-Net" is the judiciary branch's "intranet" Web site. It allows judges and court personnel to more easily access important information in a timely fashion. The federal courts' Administrative Office has begun sending official correspondence by electronic mail, a method that provides instantaneous communication. In 1999 an automated library management system was developed, which meant that judges could access a Web-based virtual law library. A Web-based electronic network providing the public with access to court records and other information was also implemented. In 2002, 11 federal courts announced that they would allow Internet access to criminal case files as part of a pilot program adopted by the Judicial Conference of the United States (a panel of 27 federal judges responsible for crafting policy in the federal court system). This was the first time the public could gain access to criminal case files.

The computer cannot replace the judge, but it can be used as an ally to help speed the trial process by identifying backlogs and bottlenecks that can be eradicated by applying intelligent managerial techniques. Just as a manager must know the type and quantity of goods on hand in a warehouse, so an administrative judge must have available information concerning those entering the judge's domain, what happened to them once they were in it, and how they have fared since judgment has been rendered.

Critical Thinking

Does the advent of technology in the courtroom spell the eventual demise of the trial system? Can you foresee people sitting in their homes and participating in cases on the Internet? What are the advantages of such a system and what are its drawbacks?

InfoTrac College Edition Research

What are the issues in court administration and technology? To find out, use "court administration" and "court management" as subject guides on InfoTrac College Edition.

Sources: Fredric I. Lederer, "The Road to the Virtual Courtroom? Consideration of Today's — and Tomorrow's — High Technology Courtrooms," *South Carolina Law Review* 50 (1999): 799; "Criminal Court Records Go Online," *Quill* 90 (2002): 39; Donald C. Dilworth, "New Court Technology Will Affect How Attorneys Present Trials," *Trial* 33 (1997): 100–14.

Summary

- The U.S. court system is a complex social institution.
- There is no set pattern of court organization. Courts are organized on federal, state, county, and local levels of government.
- Courts of general jurisdiction hear felony cases and larger civil trials.
- Courts of limited jurisdiction hear misdemeanors and more limited civil cases.
- Specialty courts have developed to focus on particular crime problems such as drug abuse.
- Appellate courts review trials if there is a complaint about the process.
- The U.S. Supreme Court is the highest court in the land and has final jurisdiction over federal and state cases.
- Courts today must deal with almost 100 million cases each year. The heavy caseload leads to congestion and delays.

- The judge's duties including approving plea bargains, trying cases, and determining the sentence given the offender.
- Judges can be selected via executive appointment, election, or the Missouri Plan, which combines both activities.
- Many judges are overworked and underpaid.
- The trial process is undergoing significant change through the introduction of technology and modern court management.
- Caseloads are being more effectively managed, and modern communications allow many aspects of the court process to be conducted in cyberspace.
- Some experts believe that the United States is at the threshold of a new form of trial in which the courthouse of old will be supplanted by the computer, Internet, and wireless communications.

Key Terms

plea negotiations/
    plea bargaining 274
courts of limited jurisdiction 276
lower courts 276

drug courts 276
courts of general jurisdiction 276
felony courts 276
appellate courts 277

court of last resort 285
writ of certiorari 286
Missouri Plan 292

Doing Research on the Web

**For an up-to-date list of Web links, go to
http://cj.wadsworth.com/siegel_intro10e.**

Numerous Web sites can help you with your court-focused research. Foremost among them is the National Center for State Courts Web site at http://www.ncsconline.org/.
    The federal government maintains its own Web site at http://www.uscourts.gov/.

Each state system maintains numerous sites for individual courts or the general court system. Here is a link to Colorado's: http://www.courts.state.co.us/.

Pro/Con discussions and Viewpoint Essays on some of the topics in this chapter may be found at the Opposing Viewpoints Resource Center: http://www.gale.com/OpposingViewpoints.

Discussion Questions

1. What are the benefits and drawbacks of selecting judges through popular elections? Could a judge who considers himself a Republican or a Democrat render fair and impartial justice?
2. Should more specialized courts be created and, if so, what for?
3. Should all judges be trained as attorneys? If not, members of what other professions should be considered for the judiciary?
4. Should a defendant have to be present in the courtroom or would a virtual courtroom suffice? What about witnesses?

5. What is the Missouri Plan? Do you consider it an ideal way to select judges?
6. The Judiciary Act of 1869 increased the U.S. Supreme Court membership to nine. The judicial workload in the aftermath of the Civil War proved more than the seven sitting justices could handle. Considering that the population is now approaching 300 million, do you think the number of justices should be increased once again?

Notes

1 "Courts Hit by Budget Cuts," *State Government News* 45 (June–July 2002): 6

2 Matthew Durose and Patrick A. Langan, *State Court Sentencing of Convicted Felons, 1998* (Washington, D.C.: Bureau of Justice Statistics, February 2001).

3 Thomas Henderson, *The Significance of Judicial Structure: The Effect of Unification on Trial Court Operations* (Washington, D.C.: National Institute of Justice, 1984).

4 The court data used here and in the following sections rely heavily on Brian Ostrom, Neal Kauder, and Robert LaFountain, *Examining the Work of State Courts, 2002* (Williamsburg, Va.: National Center for State Courts, 2002). Herein cited as State Court Statistics, 2002.

5 State Court Statistics, 2002

6 U.S. Constitution, Article 3, Sections 1 and 2.

7 1 Wharton 304, 4 L.Ed. 97 (1816).

8 David Rohde, "Arrests Soar in Giuliani Crackdown," *New York Times,* February 2, 1999.

9 David Klein and Robert Hume, "Fear of Reversal as an Explanation of Lower Court Compliance," *Law and Society Review* 37 (2003): 579–607.

10 Huey-Tsyh Chen, "Dropping In and Dropping Out: Judicial Decisionmaking in the Disposition of Felony Arrests," *Journal of Criminal Justice* 19 (1991): 1–17.

11 "ABA President A. P. Carlton Remarks on the Federal Judicial Pay Report, May 28, 2003," American Bar Association, http://www.manningmedia.net/Clients/ABA/ABA261/ABA261_APRemarks.htm, accessed on August 10, 2003.

12 "State Adoption of Alternative Dispute Resolution," *State Court Journal* 12 (1988): 11–15.

13 Public Law 90-578, Title I, Sec. 101, 82 Stat. 1113 (1968), amended; Public Law

94-577, Sec. 1, Stat. 2729 (1976); Public Law 96-82, Sec. 2, 93 Stat. 643 (1979).

14 See, generally, Carroll Seron, "The Professional Project of Parajudges: The Case of U.S. Magistrates," *Law and Society Review* 22 (1988): 557–75.

15 Alex Aikman, "Volunteer Lawyer–Judges Bolster Court Resources," *NIJ Report* (January 1986): 2–6.

16 Roy Schotland, "2002 Judicial Elections," *Spectrum: The Journal of State Government* 76 (2003): 18–20.

17 Daniel Wise, "Making a Criminal Case over Selection of Judges in Brooklyn," *New York Law Journal* (July 23, 2003): 1.

18 Sari Escovitz with Fred Kurland and Nan Gold, *Judicial Selection and Tenure* (Chicago: American Judicature Society, 1974), pp. 3–16.

19 Ostrom, Kauder, and LaFountain, *Examining the Work of State Courts.*

Chapter Outline

Chapter Objectives

After reading this chapter, you should be able to:

1. Understand the role of the prosecutor.
2. Know the similarities and differences between different types of prosecutors.
3. Recognize the role of prosecutorial discretion in the justice system.
4. Explain the political influences on prosecutorial discretion.
5. Discuss the concept of right to counsel.
6. Recognize the different types of defender services.
7. Know the cases that mandate the right to counsel at trial.
8. Describe the role of the defense attorney in the trial process.
9. Understand the issues involved in legal ethics.
10. Explain what it means to be a legally competent attorney.

Viewpoints

 Law in Review: The Danielle Van
Dam Case: Should Defense Lawyers
Tell the Truth? 315

 Law in Review: *Wiggins* v. *Smith,
Warden et al.* 324

 InfoTrac College
Edition Links

Article: "Sixth Amendment Right to Counsel
   and Its Underlying Values" 316

Web Links

American Bar Association
http://www.abanet.org/abapubs/
crimlaw.html 303

National District Attorneys Association
http://www.ndaa.org/ 303

American Prosecutors Research Institute
http://www.ndaa-apri.org 304

Chicago Police Department
http://www.ci.chi.il.us/communitypolicing 307

National Legal Aid and Defenders Association
http://www.nlada.org/About/About_Home 312

Chapter 10 | The Prosecution and the Defense

Until July 19, 2003, Mark D. Hurlbert was a typical hardworking local prosecutor. He had been appointed district attorney for the Fifth Judicial District in Colorado in December 2002, a position that made him the chief prosecutor for Summit, Eagle, Clear Creek, and Lake Counties.[1] He had lived in Summit County for more than 20 years and was a graduate of Summit High School. He received his bachelor of arts degree from Dartmouth College and his juris doctor from the University of Colorado. Hurlbert had worked since 1993 in the District Attorney's office, where he began his service as an intern. He was appointed deputy district attorney in 1994 and has also held the positions of chief deputy district attorney and assistant district attorney. As district attorney, he tried all first-degree murder cases and many second-degree murder cases in the district. His professional career turned topsy-turvy on that July day, when he filed rape charges against the well-known basketball star Kobe

Bryant (see Exhibit 10.1). Immediately, Hurlbert was thrust in the media limelight, and his every move was second-guessed. Why did it take him so long to file charges (the alleged incident took place on June 30, 2003)? Could his office handle the pressure of a case against a big star? Could Kobe Bryant get a fair trial in a small town? How a

prosecutor such as Hurlbert handles himself amidst unrelenting media attention could help determine the outcome of the case.

CNN *View the CNN video clip of this story on your Introduction to Criminal Justice 10e CD.*

Exhibit 10.1 Text of the Kobe Bryant Charging Document

July 19th, 2003
State of Colorado, County of Eagle against Kobe Bean Bryant

Mark D. Hurlbert, District Attorney in and for the Fifth Judicial District of the State of Colorado, in the name and by the authority of the People of the State of Colorado informs the Court:

COUNT 1: that on or about the 30th day of June, 2003, in the said County of Eagle, State of Colorado, KOBE BEAN BRYANT unlawfully feloniously and knowingly inflicted sexual intrusion or sexual penetration on (name omitted) causing submission of the victim by means of sufficient consequence reasonably calculated to cause submission against victim's will.

Further the defendant caused submission of the victim through the actual application of physical force or physical violence, in violation of section 18–3–402 (1) (a), (4) (a), C.R.S.; against the peace and dignity of the People of the State of Colorado, in violation of C.R.S. 18–3–402 (1)(a), (4)(a), as amended, (F3). SEXUAL ASSAULT — OVERCOME VICTIM'S WILL. Penalty 4 years up to life in the Department of Corrections, 20 years up to life if Probation imposed pursuant to 18–1.3–1004 C.R.S. And possible fine of $3,000 to $750,000.

Respectfully submitted this 18th day of July 2003.

Mark D. Hurlbert, District Attorney

---

prosecutor
The public official who presents the government's case against a person accused of a crime.

Two adversaries face each other in the criminal trial process: the **prosecutor,** who represents the state's interest and is the "people's attorney," and the defense attorney, who represents the accused. While the judge manages the trial process, ensuring that the rules of evidence are obeyed, the prosecution and defense attorneys control the substance of the criminal process. They both share the goal and burden of protecting the civil rights of the criminal defendant while they conduct the trial process in a fair and even-handed manner, a difficult task in the current era of vast media coverage and national fascination with high-profile cases.

The Prosecutor

Depending on the level of government and the jurisdiction in which the prosecutor functions, he or she may be known as a district attorney, a county attorney, a state's attorney, or a U.S. attorney. Whatever the title, the prosecutor is ordinarily a member of the practicing bar who has been appointed or elected to be a public prosecutor responsible for bringing the state's case against the accused. He or she focuses the power of the state on those who disobey the law by charging them with a crime and eventually bringing them to trial or conversely releasing them after deciding that the evidence at hand does not constitute proof of a crime.

Although the prosecutor's primary duty is to enforce the criminal law, his or her fundamental obligation as an attorney is to seek justice as well as convict those who are guilty. For example, if the prosecutor discovers facts suggesting that the accused is innocent, he or she must bring this information to the attention of the court. The American Bar Association's *Model Code of Professional Responsibility* addresses the ethical duties of the attorney as a public prosecutor (Exhibit 10.2).

The senior prosecutor must make policy decisions on the exercise of prosecutorial enforcement powers in a wide range of cases in criminal law, consumer

Exhibit 10.2 Ethical Duties of a Prosecutor

Dr 7-103 Performing the Duty of Public Prosecutor or Other Government Lawyer

A. A public prosecutor or other government lawyer shall not institute or cause to be instituted criminal charges when he knows or it is obvious that the charges are not supported by probable cause.

B. A public prosecutor or other government lawyer in criminal litigation shall make timely disclosure to counsel for the defendant, or to the defendant, if he has no counsel, of the existence of evidence, known to the prosecutor or other government lawyer, that tends to negate the guilt of the accused, mitigate the degree of the offense, or reduce the punishment.

Source: American Bar Association, *Model Code of Professional Responsibility* (Chicago: 1986), p. 87; John Jay Douglas, *Ethical Issues in Prosecution* (Houston, Texas: University of Houston Law Center, National College of District Attorneys, 1988); National District Attorneys Association, *National Prosecution Standards,* 2d ed. (Alexandria, Va.: 1991).

protection, housing, and other areas. In so doing, the prosecutor determines and ultimately shapes the manner in which justice is exercised in society.[2] While these decisions should be rendered in a fair and objective manner, the prosecutor remains a political figure who has a party affiliation, a constituency of voters and supporters, and a need to respond to community pressures and interest groups.

The political nature of the prosecutor's office can heavily influence decision making. When deciding if, when, and how to handle a case, the prosecutor cannot forget that he or she may be up for election soon and may have to answer to an electorate who will scrutinize those decisions. For example, in a murder trial involving a highly charged issue such as child killing, the prosecutor's decision to ask for the death penalty may hinge on his or her perception of the public's will.

Individual prosecutors are often caught between being compelled by their supervisors to do everything possible to obtain a guilty verdict and acting as a concerned public official to ensure that justice is done. Sometimes this conflict can lead to prosecutorial misconduct. According to some legal authorities, unethical prosecutorial behavior is often motivated by the desire to obtain a conviction and by the fact that prosecutorial misbehavior is rarely punished by the courts.[3] Some prosecutors may conceal evidence or misrepresent it or influence juries by impugning the character of opposing witnesses. Even where a court may instruct a jury to ignore certain evidence, a prosecutor may attempt to sway the jury or the judge by simply mentioning the tainted evidence. Appellate courts generally uphold convictions when such misconduct is not considered serious (the *harmless error doctrine*), so prosecutors are not penalized for their behavior. They also are not held personally liable for their conduct. Overzealous, excessive, and even cruel prosecutors, motivated by political gain or notoriety, produce wrongful convictions, thereby abusing their office and the public trust.[4] According to legal expert Stanley Fisher, prosecutorial excesses appear when the government

- Always seeks the highest charges,
- Interprets the criminal law expansively,
- Wins as many convictions as possible, and
- Obtains the most severe penalties.[5]

Today, there are more than 2,300 state court prosecutors' offices employing over 79,000 attorneys, investigators, and support staff, which represents a 39 percent increase from 1992 and a 13 percent increase from 1996 (see Table 10.1). Most of these offices are relatively small. Half employ nine or fewer people and have a budget of about $300,000 or less.

Table 10.1 State Court Prosecutors' Offices, 2001

	All offices	Full-time offices (population served)			Part-time offices
		1,000,000 or more	250,000 to 999,999	Under 250,000	
Number of offices	2,341	34	194	1,581	532
Median population served	36,052	1,478,630	449,737	41,319	9,589
Total staff size	9	456	112	10	3
Salary of chief prosecutor	$85,000	$136,700	$115,000	$90,000	$39,750
Budget for prosecution	$318,000	$32,115,000	$6,100,000	$379,000	$95,000

Source: Bureau of Justice Statistics, http://www.ojp.usdoj.gov/bjs/pros.htm, accessed on August 12, 2003.

© 2002 AP/Wide World Photos

The prosecutor is responsible for bringing the state's case against the accused. Here, prosecutor Jeff Dusek holds a photo of Twin Peaks Cleaners, where David Westerfield dropped off clothes to be cleaned. Store employee Julie Mills points to where Westerfield's motor home was parked when he dropped off the clothes, as she testifies June 17, 2002, at his trial in San Diego. Westerfield was later convicted of killing his neighbor, seven-year-old Danielle van Dam, and sentenced to death.

The Duties of the Prosecutor

The prosecutor is the chief law enforcement officer of a particular jurisdiction. His or her participation spans the entire gamut of the justice system, from the time search and arrest warrants are issued or a grand jury is impaneled to the final sentencing decision and appeal (Concept Summary 10.1). General duties of a prosecutor include enforcing the law, representing the government, maintaining proper standards of conduct as an attorney and court officer, developing programs and legislation for law and criminal justice reform, and being a public spokesperson for the field of law. Of these, representing the government while presenting the state's case to the court is the prosecutor's central activity.

Priority Prosecution

Because they are political figures, prosecutors may respond to the public's demand for action on particular social problems. Sometimes they respond to media campaigns that focus attention on specific crime problems ranging from corporate wrongdoing to drug abuse. In response, many jurisdictions have established special programs aimed at seeking indictments and convictions of those committing major felonies.

White-Collar Crime Well-publicized corporate scandals involving billion-dollar companies such as Enron and Worldcom may be prompting prosecutorial action. In a national survey of prosecutorial practices, Michael Benson and his colleagues found an apparent increase in local prosecution of corporate offenders.[6] According to the research, the federal government historically played a dominant role in controlling white-collar crime, but an increased willingness to prosecute corporate misconduct is evident on a local level if an offense causes substantial harm.

Concept Summary 10.1 Prosecutorial Duties

1. Investigates possible violations of the law.
2. Cooperates with police in investigating a crime.
3. Determines what the charge will be.
4. Interviews witnesses in criminal cases.
5. Reviews applications for arrest and search warrants.
6. Subpoenas witnesses.
7. Represents the government in pretrial hearings and in motion procedures.
8. Enters into plea bargaining negotiations.
9. Tries criminal cases.
10. Recommends sentences to courts upon convictions.
11. Represents the government in appeals.

High-Tech Crimes The federal government is operating a number of organizations that are coordinating efforts to prosecute high-tech crime, including cybercrime. For example, the Interagency Telemarketing and Internet Fraud Working Group brings together representatives of numerous U.S. attorneys' offices, the FBI, the Secret Service, the Postal Inspection Service, the Federal Trade Commission, the Securities and Exchange Commission, and other law enforcement and regulatory agencies to share information about trends and patterns in Internet fraud schemes and open the door for prosecutions. Because cybercrime is so new, existing laws sometimes are inadequate to address the problem. Therefore new legislation is being drafted to protect the public from this new breed of cybercriminals. For example, before October 30, 1998, when the Identity Theft and Assumption Act of 1998 became law, no federal statute made identity theft a crime. Today, federal prosecutors are making substantial use of the statute and have prosecuted more than 90 cases of identity theft.[7]

Environmental Crimes Environmental crime prosecution — a field that mixes elements of law, public health, and science — has also emerged as a new area of specialization. Not only federal prosecutions but also local environmental crime prosecutions have increased dramatically.[8] Approximately half of all U.S. jurisdictions operate special environmental units.

The most common environmental offenses being prosecuted center around waste disposal. Such cases, often involving the illegal disposal of hazardous wastes, are referred to the prosecutor by local law enforcement and environmental regulatory agencies. The two most important factors in deciding to prosecute these crimes are the degree of harm posed by the offense and the criminal intent of the offender. If the prosecutor decides not to prosecute, it is usually because of a lack of evidence or problems with evidentiary standards and the use of expert witnesses.

The National District Attorneys Association has responded to the concerns of prosecutors faced with the need to enforce complex environmental laws by creating the National Environmental Crime Prosecution Center. This center, modeled after the National Center for Prosecution of Child Abuse, lends assistance to district attorneys who are prosecuting environmental crimes.[9]

Career Criminals Another area of priority prosecutions in many jurisdictions is the *career criminal prosecution program.* Such programs involve identifying those dangerous offenders who commit a high proportion of crime so that prosecutors can target them for swift prosecution.[10]

www The American Bar Association (ABA) has published a set of *Standards for Criminal Justice* — a compilation of more than 20 volumes dealing with every aspect of justice. Go to the ABA home page and review the standards for prosecution and defense: http://www.abanet.org/abapubs/crimlaw.html.

www The National District Attorneys Association Web site can be accessed at http://www.ndaa.org/.

Prosecutors and law enforcement officials often cooperate when bringing complex legal cases to trial. Here, Dr. Thomas Hoshour is escorted from Sober Life Alternatives by Indianapolis police Sergeant Michael Thayer, right, and Marion County Prosecutor Carl Brizzi on July 16, 2003, in Noblesville, Indiana. Hoshour was arrested on charges that he diagnosed patients with bogus ailments and charged insurance companies for blood tests and non-existent face-to-face visits.

© 2003 AP/Wide World Photos

Rape and Sexual Assault Local prosecutors' handling of rape crimes continues to undergo changes. In the 1980s, most states imposed a heavy burden on rape victims, such as prompt reporting of the crime to police, corroboration by witnesses, and the need to prove physical resistance. In recent years, many states have removed these restrictions and have also made the victims' sexual history inadmissible as evidence at trial. In addition, the definition of rape has been expanded to include other forms of penetration of the person, and laws now exist making the rape of a woman by her husband a crime. Other areas in which the justice system is expanding its sexual assault prosecution capabilities include more vigorous prosecution of acquaintance rape, testing of defendants for the AIDS virus and for DNA profiling, and improved coordination among police, prosecutors, rape crisis centers, and hospitals.[11]

Public Health Prosecutors have also assumed the role of protector of the public health.[12] They are responsible for such areas as prosecution of physician-assisted suicide, cases in which AIDS transmission is used as a weapon, violence against the elderly, cases in which pregnant women are known drug abusers, and health care fraud cases. Prosecutors are paying special attention to the illegal practices of physicians and other health care professionals who abuse their position of trust. For example, under Medicaid, recipients under 21 are entitled to dental checkups and cleanings twice a year and a limited amount of other treatments. In 2001, prosecutors in Miami filed charges against two former dentists, Joel Berger and Charles Kravitz, for allegedly setting up a Medicaid fraud scheme that cost the state millions in bogus fees. Berger was charged with hiring recruiters to pick up children, some as young as 2, from street corners, school bus stops, and day care centers and taking them to dental facilities for unneeded procedures that included cleanings, X-rays, and extractions. Recruiters received $25 for every child they placed in a dental chair; the kids got $5 for participating. The procedures were frequently administered by untrained dental employees. The scheme involved a dozen dentists and nearly 90 recruiters and dental workers, and it may have cost taxpayers up to $20 million in illegal Medicaid payments. Similar albeit smaller scale frauds have been uncovered in Kansas and Texas, among other states.[13]

The American Prosecutors Research Institute of the National District Attorneys Association conducts research and provides consultation to state and local prosecutors. To learn more about current research on prosecutorial issues, visit http://www.ndaa-apri.org.

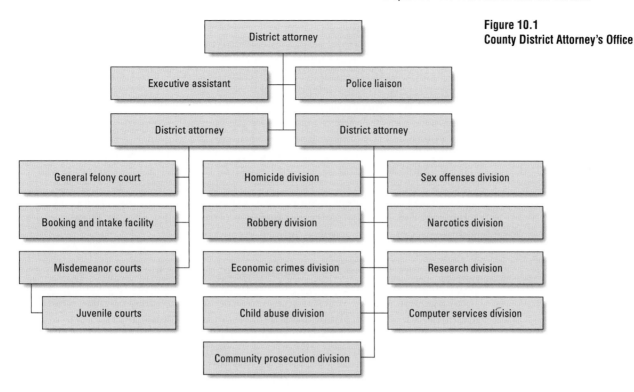

Figure 10.1
County District Attorney's Office

Types of Prosecutors

In the federal system, prosecutors are known as U.S. attorneys and are appointed by the president. They are responsible for representing the government in federal district court. The chief prosecutor is usually an administrator, whereas assistants normally handle the preparation and trial work. Federal prosecutors are professional civil service employees with reasonable salaries and job security.

On the state and county levels, the **attorney general** and the **district attorney,** respectively, are the chief prosecutorial officers. Again, the bulk of the criminal prosecution and staff work is performed by scores of full- and part-time attorneys, police investigators, and clerical personnel. Most attorneys who work for prosecutors on the state and county levels are political appointees who earn low salaries, handle many cases, and in some jurisdictions maintain private law practices. Many young lawyers take these staff positions to gain the trial experience that will qualify them for better opportunities. In most state, county, and municipal jurisdictions, however, the attorneys working within the office of the prosecutor can be described as having the proper standards of professional skill, personal integrity, and adequate working conditions.

In urban jurisdictions, the structure of the district attorney's office is often specialized, with separate divisions for felonies, misdemeanors, and trial and appeal assignments. In rural offices, chief prosecutors handle many of the criminal cases themselves. Where assistant prosecutors are employed in such areas, they often work part time, have limited professional opportunities, and depend on the political patronage of chief prosecutors for their positions. See Figure 10.1 for an organizational chart of a county district attorney's office.

attorney general
The chief legal officer and prosecutor of each state and of the United States.

district attorney
The county prosecutor who is charged with bringing offenders to justice and enforcing the criminal laws of the state.

The Prosecutor within Society

For many years, prosecutors have been criticized for bargaining justice away, for using their positions as a stepping-stone to higher political office, and often for failing to investigate or simply dismissing criminal cases.

In response to this criticism, local, state, and federal prosecutors during the past decade have become extremely aggressive in attacking particular crime problems. For example, federal prosecutors have made extraordinary progress in the war against insider trading and securities fraud on Wall Street, using information, wiretaps, and the federal racketeering law. Some commentators now argue that the government may be going overboard in its efforts to punish white-collar criminals, especially for crimes that are the result of negligent business practices, not intentional criminal conspiracy.[14] Both fines and penalties have been increasing, and in one recent case a food company executive was sentenced to serve more than five years in prison for his in role in a bid-rigging scheme. It was the longest single prison sentence ever obtained for a violation of business law.[15]

In addition, prosecutors are now sharpening their working relationships with both the law enforcement community and the general public. These relationships are key to greater prosecutorial effectiveness.

Prosecutors and Law Enforcement One of the most important of the prosecutor's many functions involves the relationship between the prosecutor and law enforcement agents. When it comes to processing everyday offenses and minor crimes, the prosecutor often relies on law enforcement officers to provide and initiate the formal complaint. With more serious offenses, such as some felonies, the prosecutor's office may become directly involved in the criminal investigation. Some district attorney's offices carry out special investigations of organized crime, corruption of public officials, and corporate and white-collar crime, as well as vice and drug offenses. Much of the investigative work is handled by police personnel directly assigned to the prosecutor.

Police and prosecutorial relationships vary from one jurisdiction to another and often depend on whether the police agency is supplying the charge or the district attorney is investigating the matter. In either case, the prosecutor is required to maintain regular contact with the police department to develop the criminal prosecution properly. Some of the areas in which the police officer and the prosecutor work together include the following.

- *The police investigation report.* This report is one of the most important documents in the prosecutor's file. It is basically a statement by the police of the details of the crime, including all the evidence needed to support each element of the offense. It is a critical first step in developing the government's case against a suspect.
- *Providing legal advice.* Often the prosecutor advises the police officer about the legal issues in a given case. The prosecutor may also assist the officer by limiting unnecessary court appearances, informing the officer of the disposition of the case, and preparing the officer for pretrial appearances. As an officer of the court, the prosecutor enjoys civil immunity when assisting the police in criminal cases. This means that he or she is not liable to a criminal defendant in a civil suit.
- *Training police personnel.* In many jurisdictions, prosecutors help train police officers in securing warrants, making legal arrests, interrogating persons in custody, and conducting legal lineups. Some police departments have police legal advisers who work with the prosecutor in training new and experienced police personnel in legal matters.[16]

The Prosecutor and the Community Today many prosecutors' offices are improving their working relationship with the community. The concept of **community prosecution** recognizes that crime reduction is built on community partnerships.[17] It is not just a program, but also a new strategy for prosecutors to do their job. Just as police officers no longer simply make arrests, prosecutors need to do more than try cases. They become problem solvers looking to improve the overall safety and well-being of the communities over which they have jurisdiction.

community prosecution
A prosecutorial philosophy that emphasizes community support and cooperation with other agencies in preventing crime as well as a less centralized and more proactive role for local prosecutors.

The traditional prosecutorial model is case-oriented and reactive to crime, not problem-oriented and proactive. Prosecutors are centrally located and assigned to teams focusing on specific types of crime (homicide, narcotics, sex offenses, misdemeanors, and so on), with the most senior prosecutors handling the most serious felonies. Most prosecutions are arrest-generated. There is not much direct interaction among prosecutors, police, and members of the community outside of specific cases.

The lack of direct involvement by prosecutors in the community, when combined with an arrest-generated, case-oriented approach, often leads to an inefficient allocation of criminal justice resources. Often, no effort is made to allocate resources on a geographical basis or to assign prosecutors where they are needed. To align resources with community needs, some prosecutors must be in the community daily. In this way, the prosecutor can gauge the seriousness of the crime problem and play a positive role in its solution, along with other law enforcement and community groups. Community prosecution requires that field prosecutors work directly with the police to improve public safety in a particular district.

The main components of such a program include placing prosecutors in selected communities to work at police stations; increasing communication with police and with community groups, schools, and other organizations so prosecutors can be made aware of which cases and problems need the most attention; and using prosecutorial resources to solve community problems, not just to prosecute individual cases.

What is the role of community prosecutors? They meet with the police daily to discuss law enforcement problems, strategize about the methods used to approach criminal behaviors, attend community meetings to learn about criminal incidents ranging from nuisances to felonies, and screen citizen complaints by diverting those cases that should not be in the criminal justice system.

In short, field prosecutors build partnerships with the police, citizen groups, schools, and businesses to ensure public safety for the community.

Community prosecution programs have been started in many jurisictions, with notable accomplishments. For example, prosecutors working with police and business leaders reduced the incidence of robberies near a local theater by implementing measures to make the area less attractive to criminals (better lighting, removal of pay phones, stricter enforcement of trespass laws, and increased police surveillance). In another example, community prosecutors, police, and housing inspectors closed and condemned a drug house where illegal drug activities were consistently taking place.[18]

Establishing partnerships with the community and law enforcement, as well as strong working relationships with other public and private agencies, is the key to a successful community prosecution approach. Community prosecution is not a new program, but rather an important new philosophy. It is the result of efforts similar to community policing to provide better criminal justice service to the community.

Finally, one of the greatest challenges facing community prosecution is the task of evaluating its effectiveness. What is the best measure of success for a prosecutor? Is it the number of prosecutions? What about the percentage of cases won in court? Is it how many offenders are given prison time? Or is it whether crime is reduced in the community? Each of these factors provide a useful measure for determining the success or failure of community prosecution efforts.

 Community prosecution is considered community policing's legal partner. The Chicago Police Department recently launched a Web site granting users public access to a wide range of crime information. Can the same concept be applied to community prosecution? To find out, access Chicago's Web site at http://www. ci.chi.il.us/communitypolicing.

To quiz yourself on this material, go to questions 10.1–10.7 on the Introduction to Criminal Justice 10e CD.

Prosecutorial Discretion

One might expect that after the police arrest and bring a suspect to court, the entire criminal court process would be mobilized. This is often not the case, however. For a variety of reasons, a substantial percentage of defendants are never

Concept Summary 10.2 Common Reasons for Rejection or Dismissal of a Criminal Case

Many criminal cases are rejected or dismissed because of

- **Insufficient evidence** — a failure to find sufficient physical evidence linking the defendant to the offense.
- **Witness problems** — for example, when a witness fails to appear, gives unclear or inconsistent statements, is reluctant to testify, or is unsure of the identity of the offender, or when a prior relationship exists between the victim or witness and the offender.
- **The interests of justice** — deciding not to prosecute certain types of offenses, particularly those that violate the letter but not the spirit of the law (for example, offenses involving insignificant amounts of property damage).
- **Due process problems** — violations of the constitutional requirements for seizing evidence and for questioning the accused.
- **A plea on another case** — for example, when the accused is charged in several cases and the prosecutor agrees to drop one or more of the cases in exchange for a plea of guilty on another case.
- **Pretrial diversion** — agreeing to drop charges when the accused successfully meets the conditions for diversion, such as completion of a treatment program.
- **Referral for other prosecution** — when there are other offenses, perhaps of a more serious nature, in a different jurisdiction, or deferring to a federal prosecution.

brought to trial. The prosecutor decides whether to bring a case to trial or to dismiss it outright. Even if the prosecutor decides to pursue a case, the charges may later be dropped, in a process called nolle prosequi, if conditions are not favorable for a conviction.

Even in felony cases, the prosecutor ordinarily exercises considerable discretion in deciding whether to charge the accused with a crime.[19] After a police investigation, the prosecutor may be asked to review the sufficiency of the evidence to determine if a criminal complaint should be filed. In some jurisdictions, this may involve presenting the evidence at a preliminary hearing. In other cases, the prosecutor may decide to seek a criminal complaint through a **grand jury** or other information procedure. These procedures, representing the formal methods of charging the accused with a felony offense, are discussed in Chapter 11.

Prosecutors exercise a great deal of discretion in even the most serious cases. In one classic study of prosecutorial discretion in three counties, Barbara Boland found that prosecutors used their discretion to dismiss a high percentage of the cases before trial.[20] However, when cases were forwarded for trial, few defendants were acquitted, indicating that prosecutorial discretion was exercised to screen out the weakest cases. The reasons some cases are rejected or dismissed are summarized in Concept Summary 10.2. Evidence problems are the most common reason for rejecting cases; many other cases are dropped because defendants plead guilty to lesser crimes.

The Exercise of Discretion

The power to institute or discontinue formal charges against the defendant is the key to the prosecutorial function, representing the control and power the prosecutor has over an individual's liberty. The prosecutor has broad discretion in the exercise of his or her duties. This discretion is subject to few limitations and often puts the prosecutor in the position of making difficult decisions without appropriate policies and guidelines. Prosecutorial discretion is rarely reviewed by the courts, unless the prosecutor makes a specific violation of a defendant's constitutional rights.[21] As the U.S. Supreme Court stated in *United States* v. *Armstrong:*

grand jury
A group of citizens chosen to hear charges against persons accused of crime and to determine whether there is sufficient evidence to bring the persons to trial.

The Attorney General and the United States Attorneys retain "broad discretion" to enforce the Nation's criminal laws. They have this latitude because they are designated by statute as the President's delegates to help him discharge his constitutional responsibility to "take Care that the Laws be faithfully executed."[22]

As a result, prosecutorial decisions to drop cases are rarely reviewed. More than 70 years ago, legal scholar Newman Baker commented on the problems of prosecutorial decision making.

"To prosecute or not to prosecute?" is a question which comes to mind of this official scores of times each day. A law has been contravened and the statute says he is bound to commence proceedings. His legal duty is clear. But what will be the result? Will it be a waste of time? Will it be expensive to the state? Will it be unfair to the defendant (the prosecutor applying his own ideas of justice)? Will it serve any good purpose to society in general? Will it have good publicity value? Will it cause a political squabble? Will it prevent the prosecutor from carrying the offender's home precinct when he, the prosecutor, runs for Congress after his term as prosecutor? Was the law violated a foolish piece of legislation? If the offender is a friend, is it the square thing to do to reward friendship by initiating criminal proceedings? These and many similar considerations are bound to come to the mind of the man responsible for setting the wheels of criminal justice in motion.[23]

Prosecutors have discretion to either move forward on cases or discontinue their involvement. Here, Martha Stewart waves to supporters on June 19, 2003, as she leaves a federal courthouse. Stewart was indicted on charges stemming from her trading of ImClone Systems stock, which federal prosecutors considered in violation of insider trading laws. Prosecutors have the choice of seeking an indictment in the case or concluding that Stewart was merely a sharp stock trader who had broken no laws. They decided to prosecute.

Once involved in a case, the prosecutor must also determine the formal charge. Deciding whether or not to charge a person with a crime is not easy — nor is determining the appropriate charge. Should a 17-year-old boy be charged with burglary or handled as a juvenile offender in the juvenile court? Would it be more appropriate to reduce a drug charge from the sale of marijuana to mere possession? Should an offense be considered mayhem, battery, or simply assault?

What, then, are the factors that influence prosecutorial decision making?

System Factors In determining what course of action to take, the prosecutor has a significant effect on the criminal justice system. Initiating formal charges against all defendants arrested by the police would clog the courts with numerous petty crimes and cases with little chance of conviction. The prosecutor would waste time on minor cases that could have been better spent on the investigation and prosecution of more serious crimes. Effective screening by prosecutors can eliminate from the judicial system many cases in which convictions cannot reasonably be obtained or that may be inappropriate for criminal action, such as petty thefts, minor crimes by first offenders, and criminal acts involving offenders in need of special services (for example, emotionally disturbed or mentally retarded offenders). The prosecutor can then concentrate on bringing to trial offenders who commit serious personal and property crimes, such as homicide, burglary, rape, and robbery. In meeting this goal, the prosecutor may decide not to press charges in the current case but rely on such mechanisms as revoking the client's probation or, if appropriate, turning the case over to correctional authorities for a parole re-vocation hearing. As a result, many cases that may look as if they were dropped by the prosecutor conclude with the incarceration of the defendant.[24]

Case Factors Because they are ultimately responsible for deciding whether to prosecute, prosecutors must be aware of the wide variety of circumstances that affect their decisions. Frank Miller, in his classic work *Prosecution: The Decision to Charge a Suspect with a Crime,* identified the factors that affect discretion and the charging decision. Among these factors are the attitude of the victim, the cost of prosecution to the criminal justice system, the avoidance of undue harm to the suspect, the availability of alternative procedures, the use of civil sanctions, and the willingness of the suspect to cooperate with law enforcement authorities.[25]

Evidence also indicates that the relationship between the victim and the criminal may greatly influence whether a prosecutor wishes to pursue a case. In a classic study, Barbara Boland found that conviction rates were much lower in cases involving friends (30 percent) or relatives (19 percent) than they were in cases involving strangers (48 percent).[26] Prosecutors who are aware of the lower conviction probability in friend and relative cases may be reluctant to pursue them unless they involve serious offenses.

Convictability is a particular issue in cases involving sexual assault such as the Kobe Bryant case. Prosecutors know that the victim's character and back-ground will be attacked in court and must conclude that their witness and sup-porting evidence can withstand the attack. When Cassia Spohn and David Holleran studied prosecutors' decisions in rape cases, they found that perception of the victim's character was still a critical factor in their decision to file charges. In cases involving an acquaintance (such as the Bryant case), prosecutors were reluctant to file charges when the victim's character was questioned — for exam-ple, when police reports described the victim as sexually active or as being en-gaged in sexually oriented occupations such as stripper. In cases involving strangers, prosecutors were more likely to take action if a gun or knife was used. Spohn and Holleran conclude that prosecutors are still influenced by percep-tions of what constitutes "real rape" and who are "real victims."[27]

Disposition Factors

In determining which cases should be eliminated from the criminal process or brought to trial, the prosecutor has the opportunity to select alternative actions if they are more appropriate. For example, offenders may be alcoholics or narcotic addicts; they may be mentally ill; or they may have been led into crime by their fam-ily situation or their inability to get a job. If they are not helped, they may return to crime. In many cases, only minimal intrusions on defendants' liberty seem necessary. Often it will be enough simply to refer offenders to the appropriate agency in the community and hope that they will take advantage of the help offered. The prosecu-tor might, for example, be willing to drop charges if a man goes to an employment agency and makes a bona fide effort to get a job, seeks help from a social service agency, or resumes his education. The prosecutor retains legal power to file a charge until the period of limitations has expired, but as a practical matter, unless the of-fense is repeated, reviewing the initial charge would be unusual.

Today, particularly in those jurisdictions where alternative programs exist, prosecutors are identifying and diverting offenders to community agencies in cases in which the full criminal process does not appear necessary. This may occur in certain juvenile cases, with alcoholic and drug offenders, and in nonsupport paternity, prostitution, and gambling offenses. The American Bar Association recommends the use of social service programs as an appropriate alternative to prosecution.[28]

Dealing with the accused in a noncriminal fashion has come to be known as pretrial **diversion.** In this process, the prosecutor postpones or eliminates criminal prosecution in exchange for the alleged offender's participation in a rehabilitation program.[29] In recent years, the reduced cost and general utility of such programs have made them an important factor in prosecutorial discretion and a major part of the criminal justice system. A more detailed discussion of pretrial diversion is found in Chapter 11.

diversion
The use of a noncriminal alternative to trial, such as referral to treatment or employment programs.

Political Factors

The prosecutor is a political figure, typically elected to office, whose discretion may be shaped by prevailing political necessities. If the public is outraged by school shootings, the prosecutor may be under media pressure to do something about kids who carry guns to school. Similarly, public interest groups that are interested in curbing particular behaviors, such as domestic violence or possession of handguns, may lobby prosecutors to devote more attention to these social problems. If too successful, lobbying efforts may dilute resources and overextend the prosecutor's office. For example, when prosecutors in Milwaukee, Wisconsin, substantially increased the prosecution of domestic violence cases, the time taken to process the cases doubled, convictions declined, pretrial crimes increased, and victim satisfaction with the justice process decreased.[30]

The Role of Prosecutorial Discretion

The proper exercise of prosecutorial discretion can improve the criminal justice process, preventing unnecessarily rigid implementation of the criminal law. Discretion allows the prosecutor to consider alternative decisions and humanize the operation of the criminal justice system. If prosecutors had little or no discretion, they would be forced to prosecute all cases brought to their attention. According to Judge Charles Breitel, "If every policeman, every prosecutor, every court, and every postsentence agency performed his or its responsibility in strict accordance with the rules of law, precisely and narrowly laid down, the criminal law would be ordered but intolerable."[31]

Meanwhile, too much discretion can lead to abuses that result in the abandonment of law. Prosecutors are political creatures. While they are charged with serving the people, they also must be wary of their reputations. Losing too many high-profile cases may jeopardize their chances of reelection. They therefore may be unwilling to prosecute cases in which the odds of conviction are low. They are worried about *convictability.*[32]

 To quiz yourself on this material, go to questions 10.8–10.10 on the Introduction to Criminal Justice 10e CD.

Perspectives on Justice

Some prosecutor's offices will make liberal use of noncriminal alternatives such as placement in a community program in lieu of being charged with a criminal offense. The availability of these community programs is a function of how advocates of nonintervention have shaped the justice process in an effort to reduce stigma and labeling.

The Defense Attorney

The **defense attorney** is the counterpart of the prosecuting attorney in the criminal process. The accused has a constitutional right to counsel. If the defendant cannot afford an attorney, the state must provide one.

defense attorney
Legal counsel for the defendant in a criminal case, representing the accused person from arrest to final appeal.

www   National Legal Aid and Defenders Association (NLADA) is the nation's leading advocate for frontline attorneys and other equal justice professionals. Representing legal aid and defender programs, as well as individual advocates, NLADA is the oldest and largest national, nonprofit membership association serving the broad equal justice community. Check its Web site at http://www.nlada.org/About/About_Home.

For many years, much of the legal community looked down on the criminal defense attorney and the practice of criminal law. This attitude stemmed from the kinds of legal work a defense attorney was forced to do — working with shady characters, negotiating for the release of known thugs and hoodlums, and often overzealously defending alleged criminals in criminal trials. Lawyers were reluctant to specialize in criminal law because they received comparatively low pay and often provided services without compensation. In addition, law schools in the past seldom offered more than one or two courses in criminal law and trial practice.

In recent years, however, with the implementation of constitutional requirements regarding the right to counsel, interest has grown in criminal law. Almost all law schools today have clinical programs that employ students as voluntary defense attorneys. They also offer courses in trial tactics, brief writing, and appellate procedures. In addition, legal organizations such as the American Bar Association, the National Legal Aid and Defenders Association, and the National Association of Criminal Defense Lawyers have assisted in recruiting able lawyers to do criminal defense work. As the American Bar Association has noted, "An almost indispensable condition to fundamental improvement of American criminal justice is the active and knowledgeable support of the bar as a whole."[33]

The defense attorney's main role is to represent his clients at trial. Here, defense attorney F. R. "Buck" Files Jr. whispers into the ear of Deanna LaJune Laney during a court appearance in Tyler, Texas, on May 12, 2003. Pictured in the background is state District Judge Cynthia Kent. Laney is accused of killing two of her sons, Joshua Keith Laney, 8, and Luke Allen Laney, 6, and critically injuring the third, Aaron James Laney, 14 months.

© 2003 AP/Wide World Photos

The Role of the Criminal Defense Attorney

The defense counsel is an attorney as well as an officer of the court. As an attorney, the defense counsel is obligated to uphold the integrity of the legal profession and to observe the requirements of the *Model Rules of Professional Conduct* in the defense of a client. The duties of the lawyer to the adversary system of justice are as follows.

> Our legal system provides for the adjudication of disputes governed by the rules of substantive, evidentiary, and procedural law. An adversary presentation counters the natural human tendency to judge too swiftly in terms of the familiar that which is not yet fully known; the advocate, by his zealous preparation of facts and law, enables the tribunal to come to the hearing with an open and neutral mind to render impartial judgments. The duty of the lawyer to his client and his duty to the legal system are the same: To represent his client zealously within the boundaries of the law.[34]

The defense counsel performs many functions while representing the accused in the criminal process. Exhibit 10.3 lists some of the major duties of a defense attorney, whether privately employed by the accused, appointed by the court, or serving as a public defender.

Because of the way the U.S. system of justice operates, criminal defense attorneys face many role conflicts. They are viewed as the prime movers in what is essentially an adversary process. The prosecution and the defense engage in conflict over the facts of the case, with the prosecutor arguing the case for the state and the defense counsel using all the means at his or her disposal to aid the client. This system can be compared with a sporting event in which the government and the accused are the players and the judge and the jury are the referees. As members of the legal profession, defense counsel must also be aware of their role as

Exhibit 10.3 Functions of the Defense Attorney

- Investigating the incident.
- Interviewing the client, police, and witnesses.
- Discussing the matter with the prosecutor.
- Representing the defendant at the various pretrial procedures, such as arrest, interrogation, lineup, and arraignment.
- Entering into plea negotiations.
- Preparing the case for trial, including developing tactics and strategy.
- Filing and arguing legal motions with the court.
- Representing the defendant at trial.
- Providing assistance at sentencing.
- Determining the appropriate basis for appeal.

officers of the court. As attorneys, defense counsel are obligated to uphold the integrity of the legal profession and to rely on constitutional ideals of fair play and professional ethics to provide adequate representation for a client.

Ethical Issues

As an officer of the court, along with the judge, prosecutors, and other trial participants, the defense attorney seeks to uncover the basic facts and elements of the criminal act. In this dual capacity as both a defense advocate and an officer of the court, the attorney is often confronted with conflicting obligations to his or her client and profession. In a famous work, Monroe Freedman identified three of the most difficult problems involving the professional responsibility of the criminal defense lawyer.

1. Is it proper to cross-examine for the purpose of discrediting the reliability or credibility of an adverse witness whom you know to be telling the truth?
2. Is it proper to put a witness on the stand when you know he will commit perjury?
3. Is it proper to give your client legal advice when you have reason to believe that the knowledge you give him will tempt him to commit perjury?[35]

Other equally important issues confound a lawyer's ethical responsibilities. Lawyers are required to keep their clients' statements confidential — the attorney–client privilege. Suppose a client confides that he is planning to commit a crime. What are the defense attorney's ethical responsibilities? The lawyer would have to counsel the client to obey the law. If the lawyer assisted the client in engaging in illegal behavior, the lawyer would be subject to charges of unprofessional conduct and criminal liability. If the lawyer felt the danger was imminent, he would have to alert the police. The criminal lawyer needs to be aware of these troublesome situations to properly balance the duties of being an attorney with those of being an officer of the court and a moral person. Often these decisions are difficult to make. What should an attorney do when her client reveals that he committed a murder and that an innocent person has been convicted of the crime and is going to be executed? Should the attorney do the moral thing and reveal the information before a terrible miscarriage of justice occurs? Or should the attorney do the professional thing and maintain her client's confidence? In the aftermath of terrorist attacks and corporate scandals, the government is pressuring lawyers to breach their clients' confidences. In 2003 the Securities and Exchange Commission adopted a rule requiring lawyers to report potential fraud to corporate boards; the Internal Revenue Service is trying to make law firms disclose which clients bought questionable tax shelters; and the Justice Department said that conversations between lawyers and terrorism suspects are subject to eavesdropping.[36]

Because the defense attorney and the prosecutor have different roles, their ethical dilemmas may also differ. The defense attorney must maintain confidentiality and advise his or her client of the constitutional requirements of counsel, the privilege against self-incrimination, and the right to trial. The prosecutor represents the public and is not required to abide by such restrictions in the same way. In some cases, the defense counsel may be justified in withholding evidence by keeping the defendant from testifying at the trial. In addition, whereas prosecutors are prohibited from expressing a personal opinion on the defendant's guilt during summation of the case, defense attorneys are not barred from expressing their belief about a client's innocence.

As a practical matter, therefore, ethical rules may differ because the state is bringing the action against the defendant and must prove the case beyond a reasonable doubt. This is also why a defendant who is found guilty can appeal, whereas a prosecutor must live with an acquittal, and why defense lawyers generally have more latitude in performing their duties on behalf of their clients. However, neither side should encourage unethical practices.[37]

Perspectives on Justice

The defense attorney's obligation to her client is one of the purest illustrations of the due process perspective because it mandates fair and equitable treatment to those accused of a crime even if they are personally obnoxious to those representing them in court. The defense attorney cannot let her personal feelings interfere with her obligation to put on a spirited defense.

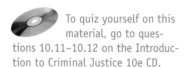

To quiz yourself on this material, go to questions 10.11–10.12 on the Introduction to Criminal Justice 10e CD.

The Law in Review feature on page 315 illustrates an ethical dilemma that emerged in a notorious murder case.

The Right to Counsel

Over the past decade, the rules and procedures of criminal justice administration have become extremely complex. Bringing a case to court involves a detailed investigation of the crime, knowledge of court procedures, the use of rules of evidence, and skills in criminal advocacy. Both the state and the defense must have this specialized expertise, particularly when an individual's freedom or life is at stake. Consequently, the right to the assistance of counsel in the criminal justice system is essential if the defendant is to have a fair chance of presenting a case in the adversary process.

One of the most critical issues in the justice system has been whether an **indigent defendant** has the right to counsel. Can an accused person who is poor and cannot afford an attorney have a fair trial without the assistance of counsel? Is counsel required at preliminary hearings? Should the convicted indigent offender be given counsel at state expense in appeals of the case? Questions such as these have arisen constantly in recent years. The federal court system has long provided counsel to indigent defendants on the basis of the Sixth Amendment to the U.S. Constitution, unless he or she waives this right. This constitutional mandate clearly applies to the federal courts, but its application to state criminal proceedings has been less certain.

In the landmark case of *Gideon* v. *Wainwright* (1963), the U.S. Supreme Court took the first major step on the issue of right to counsel by holding that state courts must provide counsel to indigent defendants in felony prosecutions.[38] Nine years later, in *Argersinger* v. *Hamlin* (1972), the Court extended the obligation to provide counsel to all criminal cases in which the penalty includes imprisonment —

indigent defendant
A poor defendant who lacks the funds to hire a private attorney and is therefore entitled to free counsel.

The Danielle Van Dam Case: Should Defense Lawyers Tell the Truth?

law in review

One of the most highly publicized criminal cases of the past few years was the Danielle Van Dam murder case. The pretty 7-year-old California girl was abducted from her bedroom and later found dead in a wooded area. Suspicion was soon directed at a neighbor, David Westerfield, who subsequently was arrested and charged with the crime.

During the trial, Steven Feldman and Robert Boyce, Westerfield's defense team, put on a vigorous defense. They pointed a finger at the lifestyle of the girl's parents, Brenda and Damon van Dam, who were forced to admit on the stand that they engaged in partner swapping and group sex. The defense lawyers told jurors the couple's sex life brought them in contact with sleazy characters who were much more likely to harm Danielle than Westerfield, a neighbor with no felony record. The defense also told jurors that scientific evidence proved Westerfield could not have dumped Danielle's body by a remote roadside. Forensic entomologists testified that the insects in her decaying body indicated her death occurred during a period for which Westerfield could account for his activities. Despite their efforts, physical evidence found in Westerfield's home proved very damaging in court, and he was convicted of the murder and sentenced to death.

After the trial was over, the *San Diego Union-Tribune* broke the story that Westerfield's lawyers tried to broker a deal before trial in which Westerfield would reveal the location of Danielle's body in exchange for a guarantee that he would not face the death penalty but life without parole. Both sides were about to make the deal when volunteer searchers found Danielle's body. Talk show host Bill O'Reilly

(The O'Reilly Factor) revealed the contents of the *Union Tribune* article on national TV. In reference to Feldman and Boyce, O'Reilly said:

> Would these two men have allowed Westerfield to walk out of the courtroom a free man if he had been acquitted? Remember, these guys knew he killed Danielle and were willing to lead authorities to her body, according to the Trib.
>
> So forget all the smears they made up. Forget about the fact they consciously misled the jury. Would these two men have allowed Westerfield to walk free, knowing he was a child killer?

O'Reilly added, "No American should ever talk to these two people again — that's how sleazy they are." He filed a formal complaint with the State Bar of California.

Members of the legal community in San Diego defended the trial tactics of Feldman and Boyce. Defense lawyers and former prosecutors pointed out that plea discussions are never admissible during trial and that Feldman and Boyce would have been accused of incompetence if they did not try to raise reasonable doubt in the case. A defense attorney's job is not to decide whether the client committed the offense but to provide him with a vigorous defense and ensure that the client is not convicted unless the prosecution can prove its case beyond a reasonable doubt. And it is impossible to make the prosecution meet its burden without aggressively challenging the evidence, even if the defender believes the client committed the crime. San Diego defense lawyer Bill Nimmo defended the lawyers' decision to raise the parents' swinging and the insect evidence. "You [as a defense lawyer] are not personally vouching for

everything. You are arguing what the evidence shows, not what you personally know," said Nimmo. "If the evidence is good enough, if the prosecution has strong enough evidence, what do you care what the defense lawyer knows? He'll get convicted." If Westerfield attempted to take the stand and lie about his involvement in the murder, then Feldman and Boyce would be required to tell the judge, but Westerfield did not testify.

Critical Thinking

Do you agree that defense attorneys should put on a vigorous defense, casting doubt on their client's guilt, even if they know beyond doubt that their client is guilty? If witnesses are not allowed to lie in court, why should attorneys maintain that privilege? An attorney is compelled by professional oath to defend his client to the best of his ability. But does that mean misleading the jury?

InfoTrac College Edition Research

 Use "Danielle Van Dam" and "David Westerfield" as subject guides on InfoTrac College Edition to learn more about this case.

Sources: Harriet Ryan, "Fox Talk Show Host Calls for Disbarment of Westerfield Lawyers," September 19, 2002, http://www.courttv.com/trials/westerfield/091902_ctv.html, accessed on October 15, 2002; Alex Roth, "Experts Make Case for Defense Attorneys," *San Diego Union Tribune,* September 22, 2002, p. 1; Alex Roth, "Story of Plea Attempt Raises Ire of Many," *San Diego Union Tribune,* September 18, 2002, p. 1; "Did Westerfield's Attorneys Mislead the Jury?" Fox News Web page, http://www.foxnews.com/story/0,2933,63596,00.html, accessed on October 15, 2002.

regardless of whether the offense is a felony or a misdemeanor.[39] These two major decisions apply to the Sixth Amendment right to counsel when presenting a defense at the trial stage of the criminal justice system.

In numerous Supreme Court decisions since *Gideon,* the states have been required to provide counsel for indigent defendants at virtually all other stages of the criminal process, beginning with the arrest and concluding with the defendant's release from the system.

The Sixth Amendment right to counsel and the Fifth Amendment guarantee of due process of law have been judicially interpreted together to require state-provided counsel in all types of criminal proceedings. The right to counsel begins at the earliest stages of the justice system, usually when a criminal suspect is interrogated while in police custody. *Miranda* v. *Arizona* (1966) held that any statements made by the accused when in custody are inadmissible at trial unless the accused has been informed of the right to counsel and, if indigent, the right to have an attorney appointed by the state.[40]

The Supreme Court also has extended the right to counsel to postconviction and other collateral proceedings, such as probation and parole revocation and appeal. When, for example, the court intends to revoke a defendant's probation and impose a sentence, the probationer has a right to counsel at the deferred sentence hearing.[41] Where the state provides for an appellate review of the criminal conviction, the defendant is entitled to the assistance of counsel for this initial appeal.[42] The Supreme Court has also required states to provide counsel in other proceedings that involve the loss of personal liberty, such as juvenile delinquency hearings and mental health commitments.[43]

Areas still remain in the criminal justice system where the courts have not required assistance of counsel for the accused. These include preindictment lineups; booking procedures, including the taking of fingerprints and other forms of identification; grand jury investigations; appeals beyond the first review; disciplinary proceedings in correctional institutions; and postrelease revocation hearings. Nevertheless, the general rule is that no person can be deprived of freedom without representation by counsel.

Exhibit 10.4 summarizes the major U.S. Supreme Court decisions granting defendants the right to counsel throughout the criminal justice system.

For further information on the right to counsel, see Martin Gardner, "Sixth Amendment Right to Counsel and Its Underlying Values," *Journal of Criminal Law and Criminology* 90 (2000): 397.

The Private Bar

The lawyer whose practice involves a substantial proportion of criminal cases is often considered a specialist in the field. Most lawyers are not prepared in law school for criminal work, so their skill often results from their experience in the trial courts.

While some criminal lawyers take on big cases and develop national reputations, such as O. J. Simpson's attorney Johnny Cochran, most criminal defendants are represented by lawyers who often accept many cases for small fees. These lawyers may belong to small law firms or work alone, but a sizable portion of their practice involves representing those accused of crime. Other private practitioners occasionally take on criminal matters as part of their general practice. Criminal lawyers often work on the fringe of the legal business, and they receive little respect from colleagues or the community as a whole.

All but the most eminent criminal lawyers are bound to spend much of their working lives in overcrowded, physically unpleasant courts, dealing with people who have committed questionable acts, and attempting to put the best possible construction on those acts. It is not the sort of working environment that most people choose. Sometimes a criminal lawyer is identified unjustifiably in the public eye with the client he or she represents. "How could someone represent a child killer and try to get them off?" is a question many people may ask and few attorneys want to answer.

Another problem associated with the private practice of criminal law is that the fee system can create a conflict of interest. Private attorneys are usually paid in advance and do not expect additional funds whether their client is convicted or acquitted. Many are aware of the guilt of their client before the trial begins, and they earn the greatest profit if they get the case settled as quickly as possible. This usually means bargaining with the prosecutor instead of going to trial. Even

Exhibit 10.4 Major U.S. Supreme Court Cases Granting the Right to Counsel

Case	Stage and ruling
Escobedo v. *Illinois,* 378 U.S. 478 (1964)	The defendant has the right to counsel during the course of any police interrogation.
Miranda v. *Arizona,* 384 U.S. 436 (1966)	Procedural safeguards, including the right to counsel, must be followed at custodial interrogation to secure the privilege against self-incrimination.
Massiah v. *United States,* 377 U.S. 201 (1964)	The defendant has the right to counsel during postindictment interrogation.
Hamilton v. *Alabama,* 368 U.S. 52 (1961)	The arraignment is a critical stage in the criminal process, so that denial of the right to counsel is a violation of due process of law.
Coleman v. *Alabama,* 399 U.S. 1 (1970)	The preliminary hearing is a critical stage in a criminal prosecution requiring the state to provide the indigent defendant with counsel.
United States v. *Wade,* 388 U.S. 218 (1967)	A defendant in a pretrial, postindictment lineup for identification purposes has the right to assistance of counsel.
Moore v. *Michigan,* 355 U.S. 155 (1957)	The defendant has the right to counsel when submitting a guilty plea to the court.
Brady v. *United States,* 397 U.S. 742 (1970)	Counsel is required during the plea bargaining process.
Powell v. *Alabama,* 287 U.S. 45 (1932)	Defendants have the right to counsel at their trial in a state capital case.
Gideon v. *Wainwright,* 372 U.S. 335 (1963)	An indigent defendant charged in a state court with a noncapital felony has the right to the assistance of free counsel at trial under the due process clause of the Fourteenth Amendment.
Argersinger v. *Hamlin,* 407 U.S. 25 (1972)	A defendant has the right to counsel at trial whenever he or she may be imprisoned, even for one day, for any offense, whether classified as a misdemeanor or a felony.
Faretta v. *California,* 422 U.S. 806 (1975)	The defendant has a constitutional right to defend herself or himself if her or his waiver of the right to counsel is knowing and intelligent.
In re Gault, 387 U.S. 1 (1967)	Procedural due process, including the right to counsel, applies to juvenile delinquency adjudication that may lead to a child's commitment to a state institution.
Townsend v. *Burke,* 334 U.S. 736 (1948)	A convicted offender has a right to counsel at the time of sentencing.
Douglas v. *California,* 372 U.S. 353 (1963)	An indigent defendant granted a first appeal from a criminal conviction has the right to be represented by counsel on appeal.
Mempa v. *Rhay,* 389 U.S. 128 (1967)	A convicted offender has the right to assistance of counsel at probation revocation hearings when the sentence has been deferred.
Gagnon v. *Scarpelli,* 411 U.S. 778 (1973)	The defendant has a right to counsel in the court's discretion at probation revocation hearings.
Morrissey v. *Brewer,* 408 U.S. 471 (1972)	The defendant has a right to counsel at parole board revocation hearings.

if attorneys win the case at trial, they may lose personally because the time expended will not be compensated by more than the gratitude of their client. And, many criminal defendants cannot afford even a modest legal fee and therefore cannot avail themselves of the services of a private attorney. For these reasons, an elaborate, publicly funded legal system has developed.

Legal Services for the Indigent

Justice Hugo Black, one of the greatest Supreme Court justices of the twentieth century, acknowledged the need for public defenders when he wrote, in his dissent in *Betts* v. *Brady,* "A fair trial is impossible if an indigent is not provided with a free attorney."[44]

To satisfy the constitutional requirement that indigent defendants be provided with the assistance of counsel at various stages of the criminal process, the federal government and the states have had to evaluate and expand criminal defense services. Prior to the Supreme Court's mandate in *Gideon* v. *Wainwright,* public defense services were provided mainly by local private attorneys appointed

The United States Supreme Court has ruled that all criminal defendants facing jail or prison time are entitled to a lawyer. If they cannot afford one, the state must provide counsel free of charge. Most often, that means a public defender. Here, public defender Kathryn Benson talks with Richard Allen Williams following his arraignment July 22, 2002, in Boone County, Missouri, Circuit Court. Williams, 36, pleaded innocent to ten counts of first-degree murder for allegedly killing patients a decade ago while working as a nurse at the Truman Memorial Veterans Hospital in Columbia, Missouri. On August 6, 2003, Williams was released after prosecutors admitted that the tests that led to the charges against him were flawed. Without his court-appointed counsel, Williams would still be in prison.

© 2002 AP/Wide World Photos

assigned counsel
A private attorney appointed by the court to represent a criminal defendant who cannot afford to pay for a lawyer.

public defender
An attorney employed by the government to represent criminal defendants who cannot afford to pay for a lawyer.

recoupment
Process by which the state later recovers some or all of the cost of providing free legal counsel to an indigent defendant.

and paid for by the court, called **assigned counsel,** or by limited **public defender** programs. In 1961, for example, public defender services existed in only 3 percent of the counties in the United States, serving only about one-quarter of the country's population.[45] The general lack of defense services for indigents traditionally stemmed from the following causes, among others.

- Until fairly recently, laws of most jurisdictions did not require the assistance of counsel for felony offenders and others.
- Only a few attorneys were interested in criminal law practice.
- The organized legal bar was generally indifferent to the need for criminal defense assistance.
- The caseloads of lawyers working in public defender agencies were staggering.
- Financial resources for courts and defense programs were limited.

However, since the *Gideon* case in 1963 and the *Argersinger* decision in 1972, the criminal justice system has been forced to increase public defender services. Today, about 3,000 state and local agencies are providing indigent legal services in the United States.

Providing legal services for indigent offenders is a huge undertaking. More than 4.5 million offenders are given free legal services annually. And although most states have a formal set of rules for determining who is indigent, and many require repayment to the state for at least part of their legal services (known as **recoupment**), indigent legal services still cost more than $1.5 billion annually.

Programs providing assistance of counsel to indigent defendants can be divided into three major categories: public defender systems, assigned counsel systems, and contract systems. Other approaches to the delivery of legal services include mixed systems, such as representation by both public defenders and the private bar; law school clinical programs; and prepaid legal services. Of the three major approaches, assigned counsel systems are the most common; a majority of U.S. courts use this method. However, public defender programs seem to be on the increase, and many jurisdictions use a combination of programs statewide.

Public Defenders The first public defender program in the United States opened in 1913 in Los Angeles, California. Over the years, primarily as a result of efforts by judicial leaders and bar groups, the public defender program became the model for the delivery of legal services to indigent defendants in criminal cases throughout the country.

Most public defender offices can be thought of as law firms whose only clients are criminal offenders. However, they are generally administrated at one of two government levels: state or county. About one-third of the states have a statewide public defender's office headed by a chief public defender who administers the system. In some of these states, the chief defender establishes offices in all counties around the state; in others, the chief defender relies on part-time private attorneys to provide indigent legal services in rural counties. Statewide public defenders may be organized as part of the judicial branch, as part of the executive branch, as an independent state agency, or as a private, nonprofit organization.

Assigned Counsel System In contrast to the public defender system, the assigned counsel system involves the use of private attorneys appointed by the court to represent indigent defendants. The private attorney is selected from a list of attorneys maintained by the court and is reimbursed by the state for any legal services rendered to the client. Assigned counsels are usually used in rural areas, which do not have sufficient caseloads to justify a full-time public defender staff.

There are two main types of assigned counsel systems. In an *ad hoc* assigned counsel system, the presiding judge appoints attorneys on a case-by-case basis. In a *coordinated* assigned counsel system, an administrator oversees the appointment of counsel and sets up guidelines for the administration of indigent legal services. The fees awarded assigned counsels can vary widely, ranging from a low of $10 per hour for handling a misdemeanor out of court to a high of $100 per hour for a serious felony. Some jurisdictions may establish a maximum allowance per case of $750 for a misdemeanor and $1,500 for a felony. Average rates seem to be between $40 and $80 per hour, depending on the nature of the case. Proposals for higher rates are pending. Restructuring the attorney fee system is undoubtedly needed to maintain fair standards for the payment of such legal services.

The assigned counsel system, unless organized properly, suffers from such problems as unequal assignments, inadequate legal fees, and the lack of supportive or supervisory services. Other disadvantages are the frequent use of inexperienced attorneys and the tendency to use the guilty plea too quickly. Some judicial experts believe that the assigned counsel system is still no more than an ad hoc approach that raises serious questions about the quality of representation. However, the assigned counsel system is simple to operate. It also offers the private bar an important role in providing indigent legal services, because most public defender systems cannot represent all needy criminal defendants. Thus, the appointed counsel system gives attorneys the opportunity to do criminal defense work.

Contract System The **contract system** is a relative newcomer in providing legal services to the indigent. It is being used in a small percentage of the counties around the United States. In this system, a block grant is given to a lawyer or law firm to handle indigent defense cases. In some instances, the attorney is given a set amount of money and is required to handle all cases assigned. In other jurisdictions, contract lawyers agree to provide legal representation for a set number of cases at a fixed fee. A third system involves representation at an estimated cost per case until the dollar amount of the contract is reached. At that point, the contract may be renegotiated, but the lawyers are not obligated to take new cases.

The contract system is used often in counties that also have public defenders. Such counties may need independent counsel when a conflict of interest arises or when there is a constant overflow of cases. It is also used in sparsely populated states that cannot justify the structure and costs of full-time public defender programs. Experts have found that contract attorneys are at least as effective as assigned counsel and are most cost-effective.[46]

The per case cost in any jurisdiction for indigent defense services is determined largely by the type of program offered. In most public defender programs, funds are obtained through annual appropriations. Assigned counsel costs relate

contract system (court)
Provision of legal services to indigent defendants by private attorneys under contract to the state or county.

to legal charges for the appointed counsel, and contract programs negotiate a fee for the entire service. No research currently available indicates which is the most effective way to represent the indigent on a cost per case basis. However, Lawrence Spears reports that some jurisdictions have adopted the contract model with much success. Advantages include the provision of comprehensive legal services, controlled costs, and improved coordination in counsel programs.[47]

Mixed Systems A mixed system uses both public defenders and private attorneys in an attempt to draw on the strengths of both. In this approach, the public defender system operates simultaneously with the assigned counsel system or contract system to offer total coverage to the indigent defendant. This need occurs when the caseload increases beyond the capacity of the public defender's office. In addition, many counties supply independent counsel to all codefendants in a single case to prevent a conflict of interest. In most others, separate counsel will be provided if a codefendant requests it or if the judge or the public defender perceives a conflict of interest.

Other methods of providing counsel to the indigent include the use of law school students and prepaid legal service programs (similar to comprehensive medical insurance). Most jurisdictions have a student practice rule of procedure. Third-year law school students in clinical programs provide supervised counsel to defendants in nonserious offenses. In *Argersinger* v. *Hamlin,* Supreme Court justice William Brennan suggested that law students are an important resource in fulfilling constitutional defense requirements.[48]

Costs of Defending the Poor Over the past decade, the justice system has faced extreme pressure to provide counsel for all indigent criminal defendants. However, inadequate funding has made implementation of this Sixth Amendment right an impossible task. The chief reasons for underfunded defender programs are caseload problems, lack of available attorneys, and legislative restraints. Increasing numbers of drug cases, mandatory sentencing, and overcharging have put tremendous stress on defender services.

The system is also overloaded with appeals by indigent defendants convicted at the trial level whose representation involves filing complex briefs and making oral arguments. Such postconviction actions often consume a great deal of time and result in additional backlog problems. Death penalty litigation is another area in which legal resources for the poor are strained.

The indigent defense crisis is a chronic problem. In some jurisdictions, attorneys are just not available to provide defense work. Burnout from heavy caseloads, low salaries, and poor working conditions are generally the major causes for the limited supply of attorneys interested in representing the indigent defendant. Some attorneys refuse to accept appointments in criminal cases because the fees are too low.

Lack of government funding is the most significant problem today. Although the entire justice system is often underfunded, the indigent defense system is usually in the worst shape. Ordinarily, providing funding for indigent criminal defendants is not the most politically popular thing to do. Yet indigent defense services are a critical component of the justice system. If there is growing disparity in the resources allocated to police, courts, and correctional agencies, then few cases will go to trial, and most will have to be settled by informal processing, such as plea bargaining or diversion.[49]

According to Robert Spangenberg and Tessa Schwartz, noted experts on public defense programs, total justice spending in the 1990s was about $75 billion to $100 billion per year. Of this amount, only 3 percent was spent on the indigent defense system. All too often, the limited criminal justice resources available are used to place more police officers on the streets and build more prisons, while ignoring prosecution, courts, and public defense.[50] As the country entered the twenty-first century, the resources spent on public defense were not much higher.

Current funding for defender programs is ordinarily the responsibility of state and local governments. As a result of an amendment to the Crime Control Act of 1990, however, federal funds are also available through the Drug Control Act of 1988.[51] No effort was made to increase available funds in the 1994–95 federal crime legislation, but the Anti-Terrorism Act of 1996 authorized $300 million to improve the federal judiciary's public defender program. According to most experts on public defender spending, jurisdictions whose legislatures have been relatively generous in funding such programs in the past have continued to do so, whereas underfunded programs have become more seriously hampered.

The National Institute of Justice reported that a new Public Defenders in the Neighborhood program has improved the overall quality of justice for indigent clients while reducing the cost of such services. Indigent defendants are often dissatisfied with court-appointed attorneys because of the pressure for quick plea bargains. Known as the Neighborhood Defender Service (NDS), this program has several benefits: Lawyers and clients are more accessible to each other; more contact is made with the client's family during criminal investigation; team representation (lawyers, investigators, and support staff) enables the use of a broad range of social and legal resources; and savings are realized because defendants spend less time in jail or prison. The impact of NDS programs builds on the right of indigent defendants to free counsel.[52] NDS takes cases only from its surrounding vicinity because it believes that staff can acquire a deeper knowledge of clients and their problems this way, as opposed to traditional public defender agency operations.

Public versus Private Attorneys

Do criminal defendants who hire their own private lawyers do better in court than those who depend on legal representatives provided by the state? While having private counsel has some advantages, national surveys indicate that state-appointed attorneys do well in court. According to data compiled by the federal government:

- Conviction rates for indigent defendants and those with their own lawyers were about the same in federal and state courts. About 90 percent of the federal defendants and 75 percent of the defendants in the most populous counties were found guilty regardless of the type of their attorneys.
- Of those found guilty, however, those represented by publicly financed attorneys were incarcerated at a higher rate than those defendants who paid for their own legal representation: 88 percent compared with 77 percent in federal courts and 71 percent compared with 54 percent in the most populous counties.
- On average, sentence lengths for defendants sent to jail or prison were shorter for those with publicly financed attorneys than those who hired counsel. In federal district court, those with publicly financed attorneys were given just under five years on average and those with private attorneys just over five years. In large state courts, those with publicly financed attorneys were sentenced to an average of two and a half years and those with private attorneys to three years.[53]

The data indicate that private counsel may have a slightly better track record in some areas but that court-appointed lawyers acquit themselves quite well.

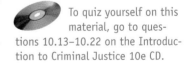 To quiz yourself on this material, go to questions 10.13–10.22 on the Introduction to Criminal Justice 10e CD.

The Defense Lawyer as a Professional Advocate

The problems of the criminal bar are numerous. Private attorneys are often accused of sacrificing their clients' interests for pursuit of profit. Many have a bad reputation in the legal community because of their unsavory clientele and reputation as shysters who hang out in court hoping for referrals. Attorneys who specialize in criminal work base their reputation on their power and influence. A good reputation is based on the ability to get obviously guilty offenders acquitted on legal technicalities, to arrange the best deal for clients who cannot hope to evade punishment, and to protect criminals whose illegal activities are shocking to many citizens. Consequently, the private criminal attorney is not often held in high esteem by his or her colleagues.

Public defenders are often young attorneys who are seeking trial practice before going on to high-paying jobs in established law firms. They are in the unenviable position of being paid by the government, yet acting in the role of the government's adversary. Generally, they find themselves at the bottom of the legal profession's hierarchy because, for limited wages, they represent clients without social prestige. Forced to work under bureaucratic conditions, public defenders can do only routine processing of their cases. Large caseloads prevent them from establishing more than a perfunctory relationship with their clients. To keep their caseload under control, they may push for the quickest and easiest solution to a case — a plea bargain.

Assigned counsel and contract attorneys may also be young lawyers just starting out and hoping to build their practice by taking on indigent cases. Because their livelihood depends on getting referrals from the court, public defender's office, or other government bodies, they risk the problem of conflict of interest. If they pursue too rigorous a defense or handle cases in a way not approved by the presiding judge or other authorities, they may be removed from the assigned counsel lists.

Very often, large firms contribute the services of their newest members for legal aid to indigents, referred to as **pro bono** work. Although such efforts may be made in good spirit, they mean that inexperienced lawyers are handling legal cases in which a person's life may be at stake.

pro bono
The practice by private attorneys of taking the cases of indigent offenders without fee as a service to the profession and the community.

The Informal Justice System

What has emerged is a system in which plea bargaining predominates because little time and insufficient resources are available to give criminal defendants a full-scale defense. Moreover, because prosecutors are under pressure to win their cases, they are often more willing to work out a deal than pursue a case trial. After all, half a loaf is better than none. Defense attorneys, too, often find it easier to encourage their clients to plead guilty and secure a reduced sentence or probation instead of seeking an acquittal and risking a long prison term.

These conflicts have helped erode the formal justice process, which is based on the adversary system. Prosecutors and defense attorneys meet in the arena of the courtroom to do battle over the merits of the case. Through the give-and-take of the trial process, the truth of the matter becomes known. Guilty defendants are punished, and the innocent go free. Yet the U.S. legal system seldom works that way. Because of the pressures faced by defense attorneys and prosecutors, the defense and the prosecution more often work together in a spirit of cooperation to get the case over with, rather than fight it out, wasting each other's time and risking an outright loss. In the process of this working relationship, the personnel in the courtroom — judge, prosecutor, defense attorney — form working groups that leave the defendant on the outside. Criminal defendants may find that everyone they encounter in the courtroom seems to be saying "plead guilty," "take the deal," "let's get it over with."

The informal justice system revolves around the common interest of its members to move the case along and settle matters. In today's criminal justice system, defense attorneys share a common history, goals, values, and beliefs with their colleagues in the prosecution. They are alienated by class and social background from the clients they defend. Considering the reality of who commits crime, who are its victims, and who defends, prosecutes, and tries the case, it should not be surprising that the adversary system has suffered. The key question is whether the adversary system impedes public safety while safeguarding the rights of the accused.

The Competence of Defense Lawyers

The presence of competent and effective counsel has long been a basic principle of the adversary system. With the Sixth Amendment's guarantee of counsel for virtually all defendants, the performance of today's attorneys has come into question.

Inadequacy of counsel may occur in a variety of instances. The attorney may refuse to meet regularly with his or her client, neglect to cross-examine key government witnesses, or fail to investigate the case properly. A defendant's plea of guilty may be based on poor advice, when the attorney may misjudge the admissibility of evidence. When codefendants have separate counsel, conflicts of interest between defense attorneys may arise. On an appellate level, the lawyer may decline to file a brief, instead relying on a brief submitted for one of the co-appellants. Such problems as these are being raised with increasing frequency.

Even a legally competent attorney sometimes makes mistakes that can prejudice a case against his or her client. For example, in *Taylor* v. *Illinois* (1988), a defense lawyer sprung a surprise witness against the prosecution.[54] The judge ruled the witness out of order (invoking the *surprise witness rule*), thereby depriving the defendant of valuable testimony and evidence. The Supreme Court affirmed the conviction despite the defense attorney's error in judgment because the judge had correctly ruled that surprising the prosecution was not legally defensible. The key issue is the level of competence that should be required of defense counsel in criminal cases.

In recent years, the courts have adopted a **reasonable competence standard,** but differences exist in the formulation and application of this standard. For example, is it necessary for defense counsel to answer on appeal every nonfrivolous issue requested by his or her convicted client? What if counsel does not provide the court with all the information at the sentencing stage and the defendant feels counsel's performance is inadequate? Whether counsel should be considered incompetent in such circumstances is a question that requires court review.

reasonable competence standard Minimally required level of functioning by a defense attorney such that defendants are not deprived of their rights to counsel and to a fair trial.

Finally, the concept of attorney competence was defined by the Supreme Court in the case of *Strickland* v. *Washington* in 1984.[55] Strickland had been arrested for committing a string of serious crimes, including murder, torture, and kidnapping. Against his lawyer's advice, Strickland pleaded guilty and threw himself on the mercy of the trial judge at a capital sentencing hearing. He also ignored his attorney's recommendation that he exercise his right to have an advisory jury at his sentencing hearing.

In preparing for the hearing, the lawyer spoke with Strickland's wife and mother but did not otherwise seek character witnesses. A psychiatric examination was not requested because, in the attorney's opinion, Strickland did not have psychological problems. The attorney also did not ask for a presentence investigation because he believed that such a report would contain information damaging to his client.

Although the presiding judge had a reputation for leniency in cases in which the defendant confessed, he sentenced Strickland to death. Strickland appealed on the grounds that his attorney had rendered ineffective counsel, citing his failure to seek psychiatric testimony and present character witnesses.

The case eventually went to the Supreme Court, which upheld Strickland's sentence. The justices found that a defendant's claim of attorney incompetence must have two components. First, the defendant must show that the counsel's performance was deficient and that such serious errors were made as to eliminate the presence of counsel guaranteed by the Sixth Amendment. Second, the defendant must show that the deficient performance prejudiced the case to such an extent that the defendant was deprived of a fair trial (that is, a trial with reliable results). In *Strickland,* the Court found insufficient evidence that the attorney had acted beyond the boundaries of professional competence. Although the strategy he had adopted might not have been the best one possible, it certainly was not unreasonable, considering minimum standards of professional competence.

Wiggins v. *Smith, Warden et al.*

law in review

In 1989, Kevin Wiggins was convicted of murder. In her opening statement at a sentencing hearing, his public defender told members of the jury that they would hear, among other things, about Wiggins's difficult life and troubled family background, but such evidence was never introduced. The jury sentenced Wiggins to death. Later, represented by new counsel, Wiggins sought postconviction relief. He argued that his trial counsel had rendered ineffective assistance by failing to investigate and present mitigating evidence of his dysfunctional background. He presented expert testimony by a forensic social worker about the severe physical and sexual abuse he had suffered at the hands of his mother and while under the care of a series of foster parents. His first public defender testified that a forensic social worker had not been retained to prepare a social history before sentencing, even though state funds were available for that purpose, and explained that the defense team had decided to focus instead on disputing Wiggins's direct responsibility for the murder. On appeal, the state court of appeals denied the claim

and concluded that trial counsel had made a reasoned choice to proceed with what it considered its best defense.

On review, the U.S. Supreme Court found that the performance of Wiggins's attorneys at sentencing violated his Sixth Amendment right to effective assistance of counsel. The justices reasoned that an ineffective assistance claim has two components: A petitioner must show that counsel's performance was deficient and that the deficiency prejudiced the defense. Performance is deficient if it falls below an objective standard of reasonableness, which is defined in terms of prevailing professional norms. The Court ruled that Wiggins's attorneys did not conduct a reasonable investigation and their decision not to expand their investigation fell short of professional standards. Although funds were available to retain a forensic social worker, counsel chose not to commission a report. And though Wiggins's defense team knew about his alcoholic mother and his problems in foster care, the decision to cease investigating when it did was deemed "unreasonable." Any reasonably competent attorney, the Court ruled, would have realized that pursuing such

leads was necessary to making an informed choice among possible defenses.

Wiggins had experienced severe privation and abuse while in the custody of his alcoholic, absentee mother and physical torment, sexual molestation, and repeated rape while in foster care. He spent time homeless and had diminished mental capacities. Given the nature and extent of the abuse, the Court found that a competent attorney, aware of this history, would have introduced it at sentencing and that a jury confronted with such mitigating evidence would have returned with a different sentence. Had it been able to place his excruciating life history on the mitigating side of the scale, a reasonable probability existed that at least one juror would have struck a different balance.

The *Wiggins* case shows that the Court considers attorney competence more than a matter of showing up on time and handing in the correct forms. How the attorney conducts the defense may be called into question if he ignores standard practices and techniques.

Source: *Wiggins* v. *Smith, Warden et al.,* No. 02 — 311, decided June 26, 2003.

The Court recognized the defense attorney's traditional role as an advocate of the defendant's cause, which includes such duties as consulting on important decisions, keeping the client informed of important developments, bringing knowledge and skill to the trial proceeding, and making the trial a reliable adversary proceeding. But the Court found that a mechanical set of rules to define competency would be unworkable. The Law in Review feature (above) shows how the *Strickland* standard was applied in a recent death penalty case.

Relations between Prosecutor and Defense Attorney

In the final analysis, the competence of the prosecutor and the defense attorney depends on their willingness to work together in the interest of the client, the criminal justice system, and the rest of society. However, serious adversarial conflicts have arisen between them in recent years.

The prosecutor, for instance, should exercise discretion in seeking to **subpoena** other lawyers to testify about any relationship with their clients. Although not all communication between a lawyer and his or her client is privileged, confidential information entrusted to a lawyer is ordinarily not available for prosecutorial investigation. Often, however, overzealous prosecutors try to use their subpoena power against lawyers whose clients are involved in drug or organized crime cases to ob-

subpoena
A court order requiring a witness to appear in court at a specified time and place.

© 2003 AP/Wide World Photos

Despite being locked in an adversarial procedure, the prosecution and defense must cooperate during the trial process. Here, Assistant District Attorney Freda Black, holding a piece of evidence, looks over shared witness data with District Attorney Jim Hardin, center, and one of Michael Peterson's attorneys, David Rudolf, Peterson's trial Friday, September 5, 2003, in Durham, North Carolina. The prosecution rested its case against Peterson, who was charged with first-degree murder in the death of his wife, Kathleen. Peterson was found guilty of murder on March 10, 2003, and sentenced to life in prison.

tain as much evidence as possible. Prosecutors interested in confidential information about defendants have subpoenaed lawyers to testify against them. Court approval should be needed before a lawyer is forced to give information about a client. Otherwise, the defendant is not receiving effective legal counsel under the Sixth Amendment. In addition, prosecutors should refrain from using their grand jury subpoena power to obtain information from private investigators employed by the defense attorney. Judicial remedies for violations of these rules often include suppression of subpoenaed evidence and dismissal of a criminal indictment.

By the same token, some criminal defense lawyers ignore situations in which a client informs them of his or her intention to commit perjury. The purpose of the defense attorney's investigation is to learn the truth from the client. The defense attorney also has a professional responsibility to persuade the defendant not to commit perjury, which is a crime.

It is the duty of the prosecutor to seek justice and not merely to obtain a conviction; this goal also applies to the criminal defense attorney. As legal scholar David G. Bress so aptly put it, "A defense attorney does not promote the attainment of justice when he secures his client's freedom through illegal and improper means."[56]

Often, the public image of prosecutors and defense attorneys is shaped by television programs, movies, and newspaper stories. You may hear of a prosecutor who takes a campaign donation and ignores a politician's crime. A defense attorney may use improper influence in representing a client. Unfortunately, corruption is still a fact of life in the justice system. Doing everything possible to deter such behavior is an important feature of a fair justice system.

To quiz yourself on this material, go to questions 10.23–10.25 on the Introduction to Criminal Justice 10e CD.

Summary

- The prosecutor and the defense attorney are the major officers of justice in the judicial system.
- The prosecutor, who is the people's attorney, has discretion to decide the criminal charge and disposition.

- The prosecutor's daily decisions have a significant impact on police and court operations.
- To improve their efficiency, prosecutors' offices have created priority programs such as antirape and white-collar prosecution efforts.

- The prosecutor retains a great deal of discretion in processing cases.
- Political, social, and legal factors all shape the prosecutors' charging decisions.
- Prosecutors are working closely with both police and the community.
- The role of the defense attorney in the criminal justice system has grown dramatically during the past few decades.
- Today, providing defense services to the indigent criminal defendant is an everyday practice. Under landmark decisions of the U.S. Supreme Court, particularly *Gideon* v. *Wainwright* and *Argersinger* v. *Hamlin,* all defendants who could face imprisonment for any offense must be afforded counsel at trial.

- Methods of providing counsel include assigned counsel systems, where an attorney is selected by the court to represent the accused, and public defender programs, where public employees provide legal services.
- Many ethical issues face defense attorneys, such as whether they should keep their clients' statements confidential even though they know they are lying or whether they should defend criminals whom they know are guilty.
- Lawyers doing criminal defense work have discovered an increasing need for their services, not only at trial, but also at the pre- and postjudicial stages of the criminal justice system.
- The issue of defense lawyer competence has become an important one for judicial authorities.

Key Terms

prosecutor 300
attorney general 305
district attorney 305
community prosecution 306
grand jury 308

diversion 311
defense attorney 311
indigent defendant 314
assigned counsel 318
public defender 318

recoupment 319
contract system 319
pro bono 322
reasonable competence standard 323
subpoena 324

Doing Research on the Web

**For an up-to-date list of Web links, go to
http://cj.wadsworth.com/siegel_intro10e.**

In the 1980s, a quiet revolution was shaping American policing — the development of community policing. Organized at the stationhouse level, the initial community policing programs were designed to make citizens aware of police activities, alert them to methods of self-protection, and improve general attitudes toward policing.

In the 1990s, many prosecutors implemented the notion of community prosecution. Both approaches want to make neighborhoods safe.

Go to InfoTrac College Edition and read the following two articles: Catherine M. Coles and George L. Kelling, "Prevention through Community Prosecution:

New Approaches to Fighting Crime," *Public Interest* 36 (1999): 69; Susan P. Weinstein, "Community Prosecution: Community Policing's Legal," *FBI Law Enforcement Bulletin* 67 (1998): 19, http://www.ndaa.org/apri/programs/community_pros/cp_home.htmlPartner.

If you want to do more research about community prosecution on the Web, go to these two sites for starters: http://www.ksg.harvard.edu/criminaljustice/research/community_prosecution.htm and http://www.usdoj.gov/usao/dc/cp/cp.html.

> Pro/Con discussions and Viewpoint Essays on some of the topics in this chapter may be found at the Opposing Viewpoints Resource Center: http://www.gale.com/OpposingViewpoints.

Discussion Questions

1. Should attorneys disclose information given them by their clients concerning participation in earlier unsolved crimes?
2. Should defense attorneys cooperate with prosecutors if it means that their clients will go to jail?
3. Should prosecutors have absolute discretion over which cases to proceed on and which to drop? Do you believe prosecutors should have a great deal of discretion? Why?
4. Should clients be made aware of an attorney's track record in court?

5. Does the assigned counsel system present an inherent conflict of interest because attorneys are hired and paid by the institution they are to oppose?
6. Which kinds of cases do you think are most likely to be handled informally?
7. Explain the following: "It is the duty of the prosecutor to seek justice, not merely a conviction."
8. What are the differences between community prosecution and the traditional approach to prosecution?

Notes

1 Summit County Colorado Web page, http://www.co.summit.co.us/profiles/distattry.htm, accessed on August 11, 2003.

2 *Berger v. United States,* 295 U.S. 78, 88, 55 S.Ct. 629, 633, 79 L.Ed. 1341 (1935).

3 See Bennett Gershman, "Why Prosecutors Misbehave," *Criminal Law Bulletin* 22 (1986): 131–43. See also Joan Jacoby, "The American Prosecutor — from Appointive to Elective Status," *Prosecutor* 31 (1997): 25.

4 American Bar Association, *Model Rules of Professional Conduct* (Chicago: 1983), Rule 3.8. See also Stanley Fisher, "In Search of the Virtuous Prosecutor: A Conceptual Framework," *American Journal of Criminal Law* 15 (1988): 197.

5 Stanley Fisher, "Zealousness and Overzealousness: Making Sense of the Prosecutor's Duty to Seek Justice," *Prosecutor* 22 (1989): 9. See also Bruce Green, "The Ethical Prosecutor and the Adversary System," *Criminal Law Bulletin* 24 (1988): 126–45.

6 Michael Benson, Francis Cullen, and William Maakestad, "Local Prosecutors and Corporate Crime," *Crime and Delinquency* 36 (July 1990): 356–72.

7 Heather Jacobson and Rebecca Green, "Computer Crime," *American Criminal Law Review,* 39 (2002): 273–326; Identity Theft and Assumption Act of 1998 (18 U.S.C. S 1028(a)(7)).

8 American Prosecutors Research Institute, *Environmental Crime Prosecution: Results of a National Survey,* National Institute of Justice Research in Brief (Washington, D.C.: National Institute of Justice, 1994), pp. 1–12, www.ncjrs.org/txtfiles/ENVIR.txt, accessed on October 31, 2003.

9 "NDAA Establishes Environmental Center," *National District Attorneys Association Bulletin* 10 (October 1991): 1.

10 Marcia Chaiken and Jan Chaiken, *Priority Prosecutors of High-Rate Dangerous Offenders* (Washington, D.C.: National Institute of Justice, 1991).

11 Bureau of Justice Statistics, *The Criminal Justice and Community Response to Rape* (Rockville, Md.: National Criminal Justice Reference Service, 1994).

12 Donald Rebovich, "Expanding the Role of Local Prosecution," *National Institute of Justice Journal Research in Action* 28 (1994): 21–24.

13 Dana Canedy, "Children Are Prey in a Medicaid Dental Scheme," *New York Times,* August 17, 2001, p. 1.

14 Mark Cohen, "Environmental Crime and Punishment: Legal/Economic Theory and Empirical Evidence on Enforcement of Federal Environmental Statutes," *Journal of Criminal Law and Criminology* 82 (1992): 1054–1109.

15 Jonathan Lechter, Daniel Posner, and George Morris, "Antitrust Violations," *American Criminal Law Review* 39 (2002): 225–73.

16 American Bar Association, *Standards for Criminal Justice: Prosecution Function and Defense Function,* 3d ed. (Washington, D.C.: 1993). See also American Bar Association, *Standards for Criminal Justice: Providing Defense Sources,* 3d ed. (Washington, D.C.: 1993).

17 Eric Holden, "Community Prosecution," *Prosecutor* 34 (2000): 31.

18 Douglas Gansler, "Implementing Community Prosecution in Montgomery County, Maryland," *Prosecutor* 34 (2000): 30.

19 Kenneth C. Davis, *Discretionary Justice* (Baton Rouge: Louisiana State University Press, 1969), p. 180. See also James B. Stewart, *The Prosecutor* (New York: Simon and Schuster, 1987).

20 Barbara Boland, *The Prosecution of Felony Arrests* (Washington, D.C.: Government Printing Office, 1983).

21 Leslie Griffin, "The Prudent Prosecutor," *Georgetown Journal of Legal Ethics* 14 (2001): 259–308

22 *United States v. Armstrong,* 517 U.S. 456 at 464 (1996).

23 Newman Baker, "The Prosecutor — Initiation of Prosecution," *Journal of Criminal Law, Criminology, and Police Science* 23 (1933): 770–71.

24 Rodney F Kingsnorth, Randall C Macintosh, and Sandra Sutherland, "Criminal Charge or Probation Violation? Prosecutorial Discretion and Implication for Research in Criminal Court Processing," *Criminology* 40 (2002): 553–77

25 Frank W. Miller, *Prosecution: The Decision to Charge a Suspect with a Crime* (Boston: Little Brown, 1970). See also Harvey Wallace, "A Prosecutor's Guide to Stalking," *Prosecutor* 29 (1995): 26–30.

26 Boland, *The Prosecution of Felony Arrests.*

27 Cassia Spohn and David Holleran, "Prosecuting Sexual Assault: A Comparison of Charging Decisions in Sexual Assault Cases Involving Strangers, Acquaintances, and Intimate Partners," *Justice Quarterly* 18 (2001): 651–88.

28 American Bar Association, *Standards for Criminal Justice: Prosecution Function and Defense Function,* Standard 3.8, p. 33.

29 See, generally, Michael Tonry and Richard Frase, *Sentencing and Sanctions in Western Countries* (London, England: Oxford University Press, 2001).

30 Robert Davis, Barbara Smith, and Bruce Taylor, "Increasing the Proportion of Domestic Violence Arrests That Are Prosecuted: A Natural Experiment in Milwaukee," *Criminology and Public Policy* 2 (2003): 263–82.

31 Charles D. Breitel, "Control in Criminal Law Enforcement," *University of Chicago Law Review* 27 (1960): 427.

32 Cassia Spohn, Dawn Beichner, and Erika Davis-Frenzel, "Prosecutorial Justifications for Sexual Assault Case Rejection: Guarding the 'Gateway to Justice,'" *Social Problems* 48 (2001): 206–35.

33 American Bar Association, *Report of Standing Committee on Legal Aid and Indigent Defendants* (Chicago: 1991).

34 See American Bar Association, *Model Rules of Professional Conduct* (Chicago: 1994), Rule 12.

35 Monroe H. Freedman, "Professional Responsibility of the Criminal Defense Lawyer: The Three Hardest Questions," *Michigan Law Review* 64 (1966): 1468.

36 Jonathan Glater, "Lawyers Pressed to Give Up Ground on Client Secrets," *New York Times,* August 10, 2003, p. 1.

37 Bennett Brummer, *Ethics Resource Guide for Public Defenders* (Chicago: American Bar Association, February 1992).

38 372 U.S. 335, 83 S.Ct. 792, 9 L.Ed.2d 799 (1963).

39 407 U.S. 25, 92 S.Ct. 2006, 32 L.Ed.2d 530 (1972).

40 384 U.S. 436, 86 S.Ct. 1602, 16 L.Ed.2d 694 (1966).

41 *Mempa v. Rhay,* 389 U.S. 128, 88 S.Ct. 254, 19 L.Ed.2d 336 (1967).

42 *Douglas v. California,* 372 U.S. 353, 83 S.Ct. 814, 9 L.Ed.2d 811 (1963).

43 *In re Gault,* 387 U.S. 1, 875 S.Ct. 1428, 18 L.Ed.2d 527 (1967); *Specht v. Patterson,* 386 U.S. 605, 87 S.Ct. 1209, 18 L.Ed.2d 326 (1967).

44 See *Betts v. Brady,* 316 U.S. 455, 62 S.Ct. 1252, 86 L.Ed. 1595 (1942). Justice Black subsequently wrote the majority opinion in *Gideon v. Wainwright,* guaranteeing defendants' right to counsel and overruling the *Betts* case.

45 See F. Brownell, *Legal Aid in the United States* (Chicago: National Legal Aid Defender Association, 1961). For an interesting study of Cook County, Illinois, Office of Public Defenders, see Lisa McIntyre, *Public Defenders: Practice of Law in Shadows of Dispute* (Chicago: University of Chicago Press, 1987).

46 Pauline Houlden and Steven Balkin, "Quality and Cost Comparisons of Private Bar Indigent Defense Systems: Contract vs. Ordered Assigned Counsel," *Journal of Criminal Law and Criminology* 76 (1985): 176–200. See also John Arrango, "Defense Services for the Poor," *American Bar Association Journal on Criminal Justice* 12 (1998): 35.

47 Lawrence Spears, "Contract Counsel: A Different Way to Defend the Poor — How It's Working in North Dakota," *American Bar Association Journal on Criminal Justice* 6 (1991): 24–31.

48 407 U.S. 25, 92 S.Ct. 2006, 32 L.Ed.2d 530 (1972).

49 Timothy Murphy, "Indigent Defense and the War on Drugs: The Public Defender's Losing Battle," *American Bar Association Journal on Criminal Justice* 6 (1991): 14–20.

50 Robert Spangenberg and Tessa J. Schwartz, "The Indigent Defense Crisis Is Chronic," *Criminal Justice Journal* 9 (1994): 13–16; *Sourcebook of Criminal Justice Statistics: 1998* (Washington, D.C.: U.S. Department of Justice, 1999).

51 See Drug Control Act of 1988, 42 U.S.C. §375 (G)(10).

52 David Anderson, *Public Defenders in the Neighborhood* (Washington, DC: Office of Justice Programs, March 1997). See also Roger Hanson and others, *Indigent Defenders: Get the Job Done and Done Well* (Williamsburg, Va.: National Center for State Courts, 1992).

53 Data compiled by the Bureau of Justice Statistics, http://www.ojp.usdoj.gov/bjs/id.htm#conviction, accessed on August 8, 2003.

54 *Taylor v. Illinois,* 484 U.S. 400, 108 S.Ct. 646, 98 L.Ed.2d 798 (1988).

55 *Strickland v. Washington,* 466 U.S. 688, 104 S.Ct. 2052, 80 L.Ed.2d 674 (1984).

56 David G. Bress, "Professional Ethics in Criminal Trials," *Michigan Law Review* 64 (1966): 1493; John Mitchell, "The Ethics of the Criminal Defense Attorney," *Stanford Law Review* 32 (1980): 325.

Chapter Outline

Chapter Objectives

After reading this chapter, you should be able to:

1. Understand the concept of grand juries and preliminary hearings.
2. Know the role and actions of pretrial services.
3. Discuss the advantages of bail.
4. Describe the various types of bail systems.
5. Discuss the likelihood of making bail.
6. Recount the history of bail reform.
7. Describe the difference between preventive detention and release on recognizance.
8. Explain what is meant by the term *plea bargain.*
9. Identify the different types of pleas and how they are used.
10. Explain the role of the prosecutor, defense attorney, and judge in the plea negotiation.
11. Comment on the success of plea bargain reform.
12. Discuss pretrial diversion.

Viewpoints

 Analyzing Criminal Justice Issues: Pretrial Services Programs 332

 Law in Review: *United States* v. *Salerno* (1987) 339

Web Links

Pretrial Services Resource Center
http://www.pretrial.org 330

Nolo contendere pleas
http://www.almd.uscourts.gov/
Web%20Orders%20&%20Info/
Guilty%20Plea%20Colloquy.PDF 330

Action Bail Bond
www.actionbail.com 335

Professional Bail Agents of the United States
www.pbus.com/pba2.htm 335

Bail Reform Act of 1984
http://www.law.ukans.edu/research/
bailrfrm.htm 336

Grand juries
http://www.udayton.edu/~grandjur/ 341

Plea bargaining
http://www.lawsguide.com/mylawyer/
guideview.asp?layer=2&article=147 345

**Federal government's pretrial
diversion program**
http://www.usdoj.gov/usao/eousa/foia_reading_
room/usam/title9/22mcrm.htm 353

 **InfoTrac College Edition Links**

Key Term: "bail" 333

Article: "Recommended for Release on Recognizance: Factors Affecting Pretrial Release Recommendations" 336

Key Term: "preventive detention" 338

Key Term: "grand juries" 342

Key Term: "arraignment" 343

Chapter 11 | Pretrial Procedures

Andrew Luster, an heir to the Max Factor cosmetic fortune, had a privileged life of sun and fun. He lived in a beach house in an exclusive community near Santa Barbara, California. However, Luster has a darker side. On July 17, 2000, he was arrested after a young woman accused him of drugging her with GHB, known as the date rape drug, and then having sex with her while she was unconscious. When police searched his home, they found tapes indicating that Luster had a habit of drugging women and raping them while they were comatose. Luster spent five months in jail before a judge lowered his bail from $10 million to $1 million. After that, he was placed on an electronic monitoring device, confined to his house. Two and a half years after Luster was arrested, the case went to trial. But halfway through, Luster jumped bail, disappeared, and was declared a fugitive from justice. In his absence, the jury found him guilty on 86 of the 87 counts, and he was eventually sentenced to more than 100 years in prison. Five months later, he was captured in the resort town of Puerto Vallarta, Mexico, by bounty hunter Duane "Dog" Chapman. On July 3, 2003, an appellate court denied Luster's appeal of his guilty verdicts because he had jumped bail.

Should a dangerous criminal, such as Luster, be let out on bail while he is on trial for raping numerous women? Or, because he is "innocent until proven guilty," should he be allowed his freedom while he prepares his defense? These are some of the questions that surround the pretrial stage of the justice process.

CNN. *View the CNN video clip of this story on your Introduction to Criminal Justice 10e CD.*

pretrial procedures
Legal and administrative actions that take place after arrest and before trial, including grand jury indictments, preliminary hearings, bail, and plea negotiation.

nolle prosequi
Decision by a prosecutor to drop a case after a complaint has been made because of, for example, insufficient evidence, witness reluctance to testify, police error, or office policy.

 The Pretrial Services Resource Center is an independent, nonprofit clearinghouse for information on pretrial issues and a technical assistance provider for pretrial practitioners, criminal justice officials, academicians, and community leaders nationwide. Check out http://www.pretrial.org/.

 To read how nolo contendere pleas are taken, go to http://www.almd.uscourts.gov/Web%20Orders%20&%20Info/Guilty%20Plea%20Colloquy.PDF.

complaint
A sworn written statement addressed to a court or judge by the police, prosecutor, or individual alleging that an individual has committed an offense and requesting indictment and prosecution.

indictment
A written accusation returned by a grand jury, charging an individual with a specified crime after determination of probable cause.

information
A formal charging document, similar to an indictment, based on probable cause as determined at a preliminary hearing.

The plea bargain is just one of a series of events that are critical links in the chain of justice. These include arraignments, grand jury investigations, bail hearings, plea-bargaining negotiations, and predisposition treatment efforts. **Pretrial procedures** are critically important components of the justice process because the great majority of all criminal cases are resolved informally at this stage and never come before the courts. Although the media like to focus on the elaborate jury trial with its dramatic elements and impressive setting, formal criminal trials are relatively infrequent. Consequently, understanding the events that take place during the pretrial period is essential to grasping the reality of criminal justice policy.

Cases are settled during the pretrial stage in a number of ways. Prosecutors can use their discretion to drop cases before formal charges are filed because of insufficient evidence, office policy, witness conflicts, or similar problems. Even if charges are filed, the prosecutor can decide not to proceed against the defendant **(nolle prosequi)** because of a change in the circumstances of the case.

In addition, the prosecution and the defense almost always meet to try to arrange a nonjudicial settlement for the case. Plea bargaining, in which the defendant exchanges a guilty plea for some consideration, such as a reduced sentence, is commonly used to terminate the formal processing of the case. The prosecution or the defense may believe, for example, that a trial is not in the best interests of the victim, the defendant, or society because the defendant is incapable of understanding the charges or controlling her behavior. In this instance, the defendant may have a competency hearing before a judge and be placed in a secure treatment facility until ready to stand trial. Or the prosecutor may waive further action so that the defendant can be placed in a special treatment program, such as a detoxification unit at a local hospital.

Procedures Following Arrest

After arrest, the accused is ordinarily taken to the police station, where the police list the possible criminal charges against him and obtain other information for the booking process. This may include recording a description of the suspect and the circumstances of the offense. The suspect may then be fingerprinted, photographed, and required to participate in a lineup.

An individual arrested on a misdemeanor charge is ordinarily released from the police station on his own recognizance to answer the criminal charge before the court at a later date. He is usually detained by the police until it is decided whether a criminal complaint will be filed. The **complaint** is the formal written document identifying the criminal charge, the date and place where the crime occurred, and the circumstances of the arrest. The complaint is sworn to and signed under oath by the complainant, usually a police officer. The complaint will request that the defendant be present at an initial hearing held soon after the arrest is made. In some jurisdictions, this may be referred to by other names, such as arraignment. The defendant may plead guilty at the initial hearing, and the case may be disposed of immediately. A defendant who pleads not guilty to a minor offense has been informed of the formal charge, provided with counsel if he is unable to afford a private attorney, and asked to plead guilty or not guilty as charged. A date in the near future is set for trial, and the defendant is generally released on bail or on his own recognizance to await trial.

Where a felony or a more serious crime is involved, the U.S. Constitution requires an intermediate step before a person can be tried. This involves proving to an objective body that there is probable cause to believe that a crime has taken place and that the accused should be tried on the matter. This step of the formal charging process is ordinarily an indictment from a grand jury or an information issued by a lower court.

An **indictment** is a written accusation charging a person with a crime. It is drawn up by a prosecutor and submitted to a grand jury, which — after considering the evidence presented by the prosecutor — votes to endorse or deny the indictment. In jurisdictions that do not use the grand jury system, the prosecutor will draw up an **information,** a charging document that is brought before a lower court judge in a **preliminary hearing** (sometimes called a **probable cause hearing**). The purpose of this hearing is to require the prosecutor to present the case so that the judge can determine whether the defendant should be held to answer for the charge in a felony court.

After being indicted, the accused is brought before the trial court for **arraignment,** during which the judge informs the defendant of the charge, ensures that the accused is properly represented by counsel, and determines whether he should be released on bail or some other form of release pending a hearing or trial.

The defendant who is arraigned on an indictment or information can ordinarily plead guilty, not guilty, or **nolo contendere,** which is equivalent to a guilty plea but cannot be used as evidence against the defendant in a civil case on the same matter. In cases in which a guilty plea is entered, the defendant admits to all elements of the crime, and the court begins a review of the person's background for sentencing purposes. A not guilty plea sets the stage for a trial on the merits or for negotiations, known as plea bargaining, between the prosecutor and the defense attorney.

In addition to these steps in the pretrial phase, the defendant is also considered for bail so that he may remain in the community to prepare his criminal defense. Even at this early stage, some may interface with court-based treatment programs.

Pretrial Services

At the pretrial stage, the system is required to balance the often-conflicting goals of ensuring community safety and respecting the civil rights of the arrestee. This delicate balance has been sorely test because of the ongoing "war against drugs." Many jurisdictions today are faced with significant increases in the number of criminal cases involving substance abuse. Of these arrestees, the justice system must determine which can safely be released pending trial and which must be kept in secure detention. Because of this need, courts have begun to rely on pretrial service programs.

Pretrial programs conduct an in-depth analysis on a criminal defendant's suitability for pretrial release. They evaluate community ties and prior criminal justice involvement. The aim is to provide a judge with an objective measure of a defendant's behavior and suitability for pretrial release and later to serve as a tool for controlling possible misconduct during the pretrial release period. For example, some jurisdictions have statutory requirements for defendant drug testing, and the local pretrial release program conducts the tests.[1]

The Analyzing Criminal Justice Issues feature on page 332 examines the pretrial services mechanism in greater detail.

Bail

One of the first and most critical decisions made at the pretrial stage is the defendant's eligibility for bail. A defendant who qualifies for bail posts a money bond or some other security provided to the court to ensure his appearance at every subsequent stage of the criminal justice process. Its purpose is to obtain the release from custody of a person charged with a crime so that he is free in the community to help prepare his defense to the state's criminal charges.

preliminary hearing (probable cause hearing)
Hearing before a magistrate to determine if the government has sufficient evidence to show probable cause that the defendant committed the crime.

arraignment
Initial trial court appearance at which accused is read the charges, advised of his or her rights, and asked to enter a plea.

nolo contendere
A plea of "no contest"; the defendant submits to sentencing without any formal admission of guilt that could be used against him or her in a subsequent civil suit.

To quiz yourself on this material, go to questions 11.1–11.14 on the Introduction to Criminal Justice 10e CD.

Bail hearings are generally held in court, but there are always exceptions. At his bail hearing, carjacking suspect John Powell, 30, hospitalized with a gunshot wound to the head, lies on his bed at Boston Medical Center on September 18, 2002, in Boston, after his arraignment. Judge Edward Redd, left, arraigned Powell in private before opening the room to the media. At center is Court Officer Michael McCusker. At right are defense attorney Beth Eisenberg and intern Jason Benzahn, from the Roxbury Defenders League.

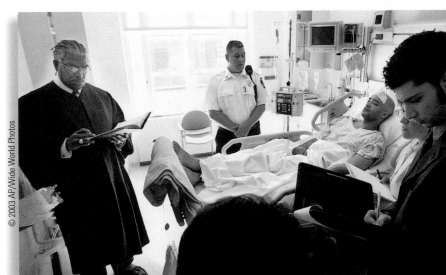

© 2003 AP/Wide World Photos

Pretrial Services Programs

analyzing criminal justice issues

First begun in the 1960s, pretrial services programs now operate in more than 300 counties and in all 94 districts in the federal court system,. They were part of the effort to improve the release or detention decision-making process by improving the breadth and quality of information available to judges at the point of initial decision making. Personnel gathered information on such factors as the defendants' housing arrangements, family ties, and employment. When the federal government passed the Federal Bail Reform Act of 1966, it encouraged judges to consider factors other than the seriousness of the charge in setting conditions of release and to use conditions other than the setting of a money bond amount, further encouraging the development of pretrial service programs. A second generation of pretrial services programs developed during the 1980s and 1990s focused primarily on trying to identify defendants who were unable to make bail but who would be acceptable risks for release either on their own recognizance or under supervision.

Today pretrial services programs perform two critically important functions in the effective administration of criminal justice.

1. They gather and present information about newly arrested defendants and about available release options for use by judicial officers in deciding what (if any) conditions are to be set for defendants' release prior to trial.

2. They supervise the defendants released from custody during the pretrial period by monitoring their compliance with release conditions and by helping to ensure that they appear for scheduled court events.

These tasks are designed to minimize the use of unnecessary pretrial detention, reduce jail crowding, increase public safety, ensure that released defendants appear for scheduled court events, and lessen discrimination between the rich and poor in the pretrial process.

To carry out these stated goals, pretrial service programs have at their core the collection, verification, and analysis of information about newly arrested defendants and available supervisory options. Pretrial programs collect and provide to the court the following defendant information.

- Identity, including date of birth and gender.
- Community ties, including residence, employment, and family status.
- Physical and mental condition, including alcohol or drug abuse.
- Criminal record, including history of adjudication of delinquency.
- Prior record of compliance with conditions of release, including record of appearing for scheduled court dates.

Most pretrial services use the information they collect to develop recommendations or identify options for the judicial officer who makes the release or detention decision. In

addition, pretrial programs monitor offenders, help them avoid missing court dates, and manage their behavior in the community. Defendants who miss a court appearance generally return to court when contacted, but a missed appearance nevertheless disrupts the court schedule, inconveniences victims and other witnesses, delays case disposition, and wastes valuable time. Pretrial services programs use a variety of monitoring and reminder techniques to anticipate and avoid possible nonappearance problems. When a defendant does miss a court appearance, programs seek to contact the defendant immediately to resolve the problem. The following program activities can play an important role, however, in managing the risks that released defendants pose to public safety.

- Monitoring released defendants' compliance with conditions of release designed to minimize pretrial crime, including curfews, orders restricting contact with alleged victims and possible witnesses, home confinement, and drug and alcohol testing.
- Providing direct intensive supervision for some categories of defendants by using program staff and collaborating with the police, other agencies, and community organizations.

Kentucky: A Statewide Pretrial Services Agency

The Kentucky legislature established the Pretrial Services and Court Security

Once the amount of bail is set by the court, the defendant is required to deposit all or a percentage of the entire amount in cash or security (or to pay a professional bonding agent to submit a bond). If the defendant is released on bail but fails to appear in court at the stipulated time, the bail deposit is forfeited. A defendant who fails to make bail is confined in jail until the court appearance.

Bail Today

The most recent national data available indicate that most defendants (64 percent) made bail. An estimated 36 percent of all defendants were detained until the courts disposed of their cases, including 7 percent who were denied bail. Murder defendants (13 percent) were the least likely to be released prior to case disposition, followed by defendants whose most serious arrest charge was robbery (38 percent),

Agency in 1976 to replace the commercial bail bonding system. The new agency immediately assumed responsibility for implementing the pretrial release process, and the enabling act made it a crime to post a bond for profit in Kentucky.

The agency now has 220 staff members located in 60 offices, serving a state population of approximately 4 million. The agency operates within the judicial branch as part of Kentucky's Administrative Office of the Courts. Staff members interview about 180,000 defendants each year, or approximately 84 percent of all arrestees. They conduct interviews around the clock in the state's population centers of Louisville, Lexington, and the Kentucky sector of the Cincinnati metropolitan area. Interviewers are on duty 16 to 20 hours per day in smaller cities and on call at all times in rural regions.

A pretrial officer interviews all arrestees except those who decline to be interviewed or who post bail immediately. The officer's top interview priority is obtaining background information for use by the judge at the defendant's first court appearance. Increasingly, the agency is able to draw on information in its own records system. Interview information is treated as confidential — only the judge is given access to the report, and neither the interview nor the report can be subpoenaed. The information goes into the agency's records system for future reference in subsequent cases involving the defendant and also may be used by the agency's failure to appear (FTA) unit.

Pretrial officers in Kentucky must be prepared to present information to the judge at the court appearance and to provide or renew the search for information the judge may request at that time. Using a point-scoring system that accounts for current charges, prior record, and family and community ties, the agency recommends release on recognizance (ROR) — without money bail — for defendants who score above the cutoff line. Judges are required by law to consider ROR and to identify in writing issues regarding risk of flight or community safety, although this does not always happen in practice. In making the release or detention decision, judges can use a variety of methods in addition to ROR, including placing the defendant in the custody of a person or organization, placing restrictions on the defendant's travel or residence, and requiring the defendant to post a cash bond with the court.

The agency supervises defendants principally through a tracking and notification system, using the system to remind defendants of upcoming court appearances. More intensive supervision is reserved for major felony cases and court requests. Drug testing is done at court request.

The failure to appear rate for defendants under the agency's supervision is a modest 8 percent. Most FTAs occur in cases involving minor offenses, such as public intoxication. In most FTA cases, a warrant is issued and the agency's FTA unit draws on all the information the

agency has collected to locate and return the defendant. The agency has an active in-service training program and is working to broaden officer skills related to domestic violence, cultural diversity, victim advocacy, and driving while intoxicated.

Critical Thinking

Suppose an effective technology is developed that could be installed in a wearable device that monitors an offender's physical and emotional processes. The device would measure heartbeat, skin conductivity, and so on and would alert authorities if the wearer was having an emotional crisis or contemplating some forbidden activity such as committing crime. Would you be inclined to increase the number of offenders given pretrial release if such a device existed?

InfoTrac College Edition Research

 What would happen if the jails were so crowded that all arrestees were given immediate pretrial release? To find out, read Sarah B. Vandenbraak, "Bail, Humbug! Why Criminals Would Rather Be in Philadelphia," *Policy Review* 73 (Summer 1995): 73, on InfoTrac College Edition.

Source: Barry Mahoney, Bruce D. Beaudin, John A. Carver III, Daniel B. Ryan, and Richard B. Hoffman, *Pretrial Services Programs: Responsibilities and Potential* (Washington, D.C.: National Institute of Justice, 2001).

rape (47 percent), burglary (50 percent), or motor vehicle theft (50 percent) (see Figure 11.1).[2] Still, these data indicate that many offenders charged with the most serious violent crimes such as rape are released on bail prior to their trials.

 Use "bail" for a key word search on InfoTrac College Edition.

Receiving Bail

Whether a defendant can be expected to appear at the next stage of the criminal proceedings is a key issue in determining bail.[3] Bail cannot be used to punish an accused, and it cannot be denied or revoked at the indulgence of the court. Critics argue that money bail is one of the most unacceptable aspects of the criminal justice system. They say it is discriminatory because it works against the poor; it is costly because the government must pay to detain those offenders who are unable to make bail but who would otherwise remain in the community; it is unfair because a higher

Most serious arrest charge

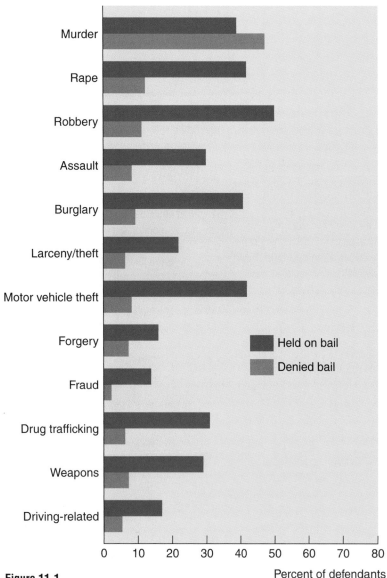

Figure 11.1
Pretrial Detention of Felony Defendants in the 75 Largest Counties, by Most Serious Arrest Charge

Source: Brian A. Reeves, *Felony Defendants in Large Urban Counties, 1998* (Washington, D.C.: Bureau of Justice Statistics, 2001), p. 16.

proportion of detainees receive longer sentences than people released on bail; and it is dehumanizing because innocent people who cannot make bail suffer in the nation's deteriorated jail system.

The Legal Right to Bail

The Eighth Amendment does not guarantee a constitutional right to bail but rather prohibits "excessive bail." Because many state statutes place no precise limit on the amount of bail a judge may impose, many defendants who cannot make bail are placed in detention while awaiting trial. It has become apparent over the years that the bail system is discriminatory because defendants who are financially well off can make bail, whereas indigent defendants languish in pretrial detention in the county jail. In addition, keeping a person in jail imposes serious financial burdens on local and state governments — and, in turn, on taxpayers — who must pay for the cost of confinement. These factors have given rise to bail reform programs that depend on the defendant's personal promise to appear in court for trial (recognizance), instead of on financial ability to meet bail. These reforms have enabled many deserving but indigent offenders to go free, but another trend has been to deny people bail on the grounds that they are a danger to themselves or to others in the community.

The Eighth Amendment restriction on excessive bail may also be interpreted to mean that the sole purpose of bail is to ensure that the defendant returns for trial. Bail may be used neither as a form of punishment nor to coerce or threaten a defendant. In most cases, a defendant has the right to be released on reasonable bail. Many jurisdictions also require a bail review hearing by a higher court in cases in which the initial judge set what might be considered excessive bail.

The U.S. Supreme Court's interpretation of the Eighth Amendment's provisions on bail was set out in the 1951 case of *Stack* v. *Boyle*.[4] In that case, the Supreme Court found bail to be a traditional right to freedom before trial that permits unhampered preparation of a defense and prevents the criminal defendant from being punished prior to conviction. The Court held that bail is excessive when it exceeds an amount reasonably calculated to ensure that the defendant will return for trial. The Court indicated that bail should be in the amount that is generally set for similar offenses. Higher bail can be imposed when evidence supporting the increase is presented at a hearing at which the defendant's constitutional rights can be protected. Although *Stack* did not mandate an absolute right to bail, it did set guidelines for state courts to follow: If a crime is bailable, the amount set should not be frivolous, unusual, or beyond a person's ability to pay.

Exhibit 11.1 Pretrial Release Mechanisms

Stage	Mechanism	Description
Police	Field citation release	An arresting officer releases the arrestee on a written promise to appear in court, at or near the actual time and location of the arrest. This procedure is commonly used for misdemeanor charges and is similar to issuing a traffic ticket.
Police	Station house citation release	The determination of an arrestee's eligibility and suitability for release and the actual release of the arrestee are deferred until after he or she has been removed from the scene of an arrest and brought to the station house or police headquarters.
Police/pretrial	Jail citation release	The determination of an arrestee's eligibility and suitability for citation release and the actual release of the arrestee are deferred until after he or she has been delivered by the arresting department to a jail or other pretrial detention facility for screening, booking, and admission.
Pretrial/court	Direct release authority by pretrial program	To streamline release processes and reduce the length of stay in detention, courts may authorize pretrial programs to release defendants without direct judicial involvement. Where court rules delegate such authority, the practice is generally limited to misdemeanor charges, but felony release authority has been granted in some jurisdictions.
Police/court	Bail schedule	An arrestee can post bail at the station house or jail according to amounts specified in a bail schedule. The schedule is a list of all bailable charges and a corresponding dollar amount for each. Schedules may vary widely from jurisdiction to jurisdiction.
Court	Judicial release	Arrestees who have not been released by either the police or the jailer and who have not posted bail appear at the hearing before a judge, magistrate, or bail commissioner within a set period of time. In jurisdictions with pretrial release programs, program staff often interview arrestees detained at the jail prior to the first hearing, verify the background information, and present recommendations to the court at arraignment.

Source: Andy Hall, *Pretrial Release Program Options* (Washington, D.C.: National Institute of Justice, 1984).

Making Bail

Bail is typically considered at a hearing conducted shortly after a person has been taken into custody. At the hearing, such issues as crime type, flight risk, and dangerousness will be considered before a bail amount is set. Some jurisdictions have developed bail schedules to make amounts uniform based on crime and criminal history. As Exhibit 11.1 shows, bail is considered at numerous points in the criminal justice process.

Because many criminal defendants are indigent, making bail is a financial challenge that, if not met, can result in a long stay in a county jail. In desperation, indigent defendants may turn to bail bondspersons. For a fee, bonding agents lend money to people who cannot make bail on their own. Typically, they charge a percentage of the bail amount. For example, a person who is asked to put up $10,000 will be asked to contribute $2,000 of their own and the bondsman covers the remaining $8,000. After trial, the bondsman keeps the $2,000 as his fee.

Powerful ties often exist between bonding agents and the court, with the result that defendants are steered toward particular bonding agents. Charges of kickbacks and cooperation accompany such arrangements.Consequently, efforts have been made to reform and even eliminate money bail and reduce the importance of bonding agents. Until the early 1960s, the justice system relied primarily on money bonds as the principal form of pretrial release. Many states now allow defendants to be released on their own recognizance without any money bail. **Release on recognizance**

 If you want to understand how a bail bond agency operates, go to Action Bail Bond's home page at www.actionbail.com.

 The Professional Bail Agents of the United States Web site is designed to help bail bondspersons be more competent and effective. You can visit the site at www.pbus.com/pba2.htm.

release on recognizance (ROR) A pretrial release in which a defendant with ties to the community is not required to post bail but promises to appear at all subsequent proceedings.

(ROR) was pioneered by the Vera Institute of Justice in an experiment called the Manhattan Bail Project, which began in 1961 with the cooperation of the New York City criminal courts and local law students.[5] It came about because defendants with financial means were able to post bail to secure pretrial release, while indigent defendants remained in custody. The project found that if the court had sufficient background information about the defendant, it could make a reasonably good judgment about whether the accused would return to court. When release decisions were based on such information as the nature of the offense, family ties, and employment record, most defendants returned to court when released on their own recognizance. The results of the Vera Institute's initial operation showed a default rate of less than 0.7 percent. The bail project's experience suggested that releasing a person on the basis of verified information more effectively guaranteed appearance in court than did money bail. Highly successful ROR projects were set up in major cities around the country, including Philadelphia, Pennsylvania, and San Francisco, California. By 1980 more than 120 formal programs were in operation, and today they exist in almost every major jurisdiction.[6]

The success of ROR programs in the early 1960s resulted in bail reforms that culminated with the enactment of the federal Bail Reform Act of 1966, the first change in federal bail laws since 1789.[7] This legislation sought to ensure that release would be granted in all noncapital cases in which sufficient reason existed to believe that the defendant would return to court. The law clearly established the presumption of ROR that must be overcome before money bail is required, authorized 10 percent deposit bail, introduced the concept of conditional release, and stressed the philosophy that release should be under the least restrictive method necessary to ensure court appearance.

During the 1970s and early 1980s, the pretrial release movement was hampered by public pressure over pretrial increases in crime. As a result, the more recent federal legislation, the Bail Reform Act of 1984, mandated that no defendants shall be kept in pretrial detention simply because they cannot afford money bail, established the presumption for ROR in all cases in which a person is bailable, and formalized restrictive preventive detention provisions. The 1984 act required that community safety, as well as the risk of flight, be considered in the release decision. Consequently, such criminal justice factors as the seriousness of the charged offense, the weight of the evidence, the sentence that may be imposed upon conviction, court appearance history, and prior convictions are likely to influence the release decisions of the federal court.

Bail reform is considered one of the most successful programs in the recent history of the criminal justice system. Yet it is not without critics who suggest that emphasis should be put on controlling the behavior of serious criminals instead of on making sure that nondangerous defendants are released before their trials. Criminal defendants released without bail and those who commit crimes awaiting trial fuel the constant debate over pretrial release versus community protection. While some experts believe that all people — even noncitizens accused of crimes — enjoy the right to bail, others view it as a license to abscond or commit more crimes.[8]

A number of innovative alternative bail programs are described in Exhibit 11.2. The most often used are personal recognizance, unsecured or personal bond, surety or cash bond, and percentage or deposit bail. As Figure 11.2 shows, most bailees receive surety bond followed by ROR.

To see the provisions of the Bail Reform Act of 1984, go to http://www.law.ukans.edu/research/bailrfrm.htm.

To find out which factors influence the release on recognizance decision, read Thomas A. Petee, "Recommended for Release on Recognizance: Factors Affecting Pretrial Release Recommendations," *Journal of Social Psychology* 134, no. 3 (June 1994): 375, on InfoTrac College Edition.

Figure 11.2
Pretrial Release of Felony Defendants in the 75 Largest Counties, by Type of Release

Source: Brian A. Reaves, *Felony Defendants in Large Urban Counties, 1998* (Washington, D.C.: Bureau of Justice Statistics, 2001), p. 17.

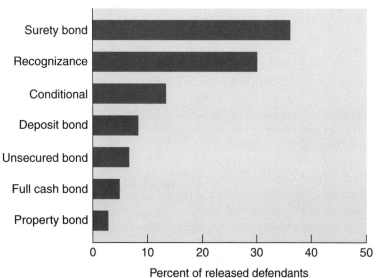

Type of pretrial release

Percent of released defendants

Exhibit 11.2 Innovative Bail Systems

Program	Description
Nonfinancial Release	
Release on recognizance (ROR)	The defendant is released on a promise to appear, without any requirement of money bond. This form of release is unconditional — that is, without imposition of special conditions, supervision, or specially provided services.
Conditional release	The defendant is released on a promise to fulfill some stated requirements that go beyond those associated with ROR. Four types of conditions are placed on defendants: (1) status quo conditions, such as requiring that the defendant retain a residence or employment status; (2) restrictive conditions, such as requiring that the defendant remain in the jurisdiction; (3) contact conditions, such as requiring that the defendant report by telephone or in person to the release program; and (4) problem-oriented conditions, such as requiring that the defendant participate in drug or alcohol treatment programs.
Financial Release	
Unsecured bail	The defendant is released with no immediate requirement of payment. However, if the defendant fails to appear, he or she is liable for the full amount.
Privately secured bail	A private organization or individual posts the bail amount, which is returned when the defendant appears in court.
Property bail	The defendant may post evidence of real property in lieu of money.
Deposit bail	The defendant deposits a percentage of the bail amount, typically 10 percent, with the court. When the defendant appears in court, the deposit is returned, sometimes minus an administrative fee. If the defendant fails to appear, he or she is liable for the full amount of the bail.
Surety bail	The defendant pays a percentage of the bond, usually 10 percent, to a bonding agent who posts the full bail. The fee paid to the bonding agent is not returned to the defendant if he or she appears in court. The bonding agent is liable for the full amount of the bond should the defendant fail to appear. Bonding agents often require posting collateral to cover the full bail amount.
Cash bail	The defendant pays the entire amount of bail set by the judge to secure release. The bail is returned to the defendant when he or she appears in court.

Source: Adapted from Andy Hall, *Pretrial Release Program Options* (Washington, D.C.: National Institute of Justice, 1984), pp. 32–33.

Preventive Detention

More than half of all violent criminals are released on bail, including people on trial for committing murder. The presumption of bail is challenged by those who believe that releasing dangerous criminals before trial poses a threat to public safety. They point to evidence showing that many people released on bail commit new crimes while at large and often fail to appear for trial. Today, about a third of released defendants were either rearrested for a new offense, failed to appear in court as scheduled, or committed some other violation that resulted in the revocation of their pretrial release (Figure 11.3). Those rearrested tend to be on bail longer (nine months or more), have a serious prior record, abuse drugs, have a poor work record, and be disproportionately young, male, and minority group members.

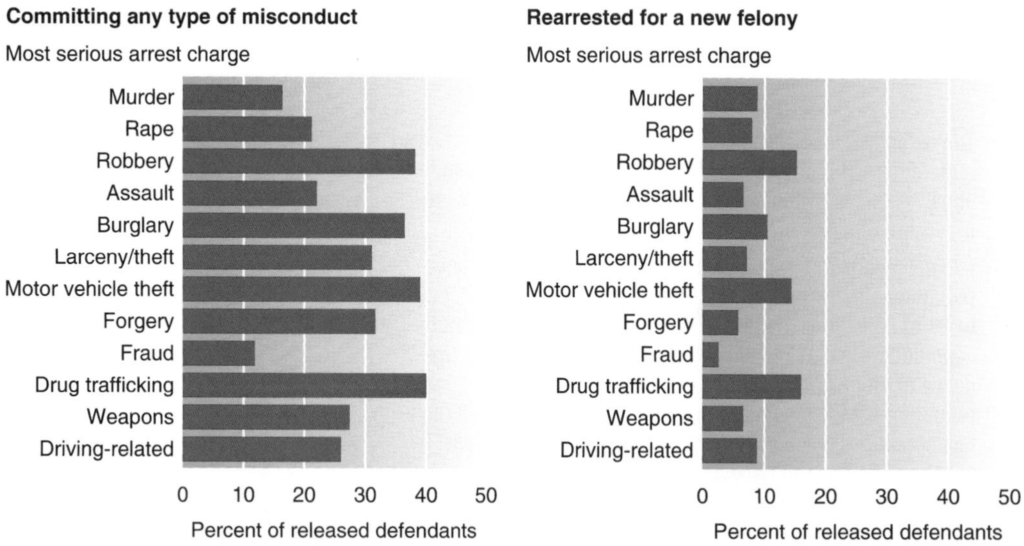

Committing any type of misconduct

Most serious arrest charge

Rearrested for a new felony

Most serious arrest charge

Percent of released defendants

Percent of released defendants

Figure 11.3
Misconduct Prior to Case Disposition by Released Felony Defendants in the 75 Largest Counties, 1998

Source: Brian A. Reaves, *Felony Defendants in Large Urban Counties, 1998* (Washington, D.C.: Bureau of Justice Statistics, 2001), p. 22.

Use "preventive detention" as a key word search item on InfoTrac College Edition to find out about the various forms it can take.

One response to the alleged failure of the bail system to protect citizens is the adoption of preventive detention statutes. These laws require that certain dangerous defendants be confined before trial for their own protection and that of the community. Preventive detention is an important manifestation of the crime control perspective on justice, because it favors the use of incapacitation to control the future behavior of suspected criminals. Often, the key question is whether preventive detention is punishment before trial.

The most striking use of preventive detention can be found in the federal Bail Reform Act of 1984, which contrasted sharply with previous law.[9] Although the act does contain provisions for ROR, it allows judges to order preventive detention if they determine "that no condition or combination of conditions will reasonably assure the appearance of the person as required and the safety of any other person and the community."[10]

A number of state jurisdictions have incorporated elements of preventive detention into their bail systems. Although most of the restrictions do not constitute outright preventive detention, they serve to narrow the scope of bail eligibility. These provisions include exclusion of certain crimes from bail eligibility, definition of bail to include appearance in court and community safety, and the limitations on right to bail for those previously convicted.

Perspectives on Justice

Doesn't preventive detention amount to punishing an individual before he has been brought to trial and found guilty? Even if the defendant is later found not guilty at trial, it is better to err on the side of caution and community safety. Denying defendants the right to bail because they are presumed to be dangerous is at the heart of the crime control perspective.

Preventive detention has also been a source of concern for civil libertarians who believe it violates the due process clause of the U.S. Constitution, because it means that a person will be held in custody before proven guilty. In two important cases, the U.S. Supreme Court disagreed with this analysis. In *Schall* v. *Martin,* the Court upheld the application of preventive detention statutes to juvenile defendants on the grounds that such detention is useful to protect the welfare of the minor and society as a whole.[11] In 1987, the Court upheld the Bail Reform Act's provision on preventive detention as it applied to adults in the case of *United States* v. *Salerno,* which is set out in the Law in Review feature on page 339.[12]

United States v. Salerno (1987)

law in review

On March 21, 1986, Anthony Salerno and codefendant Vincent Cafaro were charged in a 29-count indictment alleging various racketeering violations, including gambling, wire fraud, extortion, and conspiracy to commit murder. At their arraignment, the government moved to have them detained on the grounds that no condition of release could ensure community safety. At a detention hearing, the prosecution presented evidence that Salerno was the "boss" of the Genovese crime family and that Cafaro was a "captain." Wiretap evidence indicated that the two men had participated in criminal conspiracies, including murder. The court heard testimony from two witnesses who had personally participated in the murder conspiracies. In rebuttal, Salerno provided character statements, presented evidence that he had a heart condition, and challenged the veracity of the government's witnesses. Cafaro claimed the wiretaps had merely recorded "tough talk." The trial court allowed the detention on the grounds that the defendants wanted to use their pretrial freedom to continue their "family" business and "when business as usual involves threats, beatings, and murder, the present danger such people pose to the community is self-evident."

On appeal, the U.S. Court of Appeals for the Second Circuit agreed with the defendants' claim that the government could not detain suspects simply because they were thought to represent a danger to the community. The circuit court found that the criminal law system holds people accountable for their past deeds, not their anticipated future actions. The government then reappealed the case to the U.S. Supreme Court.

The Supreme Court held in *United States* v. *Salerno* that the preventive detention act had a legitimate and compelling regulatory purpose and did not violate the due process clause. Preventive detention was not designed to punish dangerous individuals but to find a solution for the social problem of people committing crimes while on bail. Preventing danger to the community is a legitimate societal goal.

The Court also stated that society's need for protection can outweigh an individual's liberty interest. Under some circumstances, individuals can be held without bail. The act provides that only the most serious criminals can be held and mandates careful procedures to ensure that the judgment of future dangerousness is made after careful deliberation. Finally, the Court found that the Eighth Amendment does not limit the setting (or denial) of bail simply to prohibit defendants' flight to avoid trial and held that

considerations of dangerousness are a valid reason to deny pretrial release.

Salerno legitimizes the use of preventive detention as a crime control method. It permits the limitations on bail already in place in many state jurisdictions to continue. *Salerno* further illustrates the concern for community protection that has developed in the past decade. It is a good example of the recent efforts by the Court to give the justice system greater control over criminal defendants. At this time, it is still unclear how often judges will rely on preventive detention statutes that require a hearing on the facts or whether they will simply continue to set extremely high bail for defendants whom they wish to remain in pretrial custody.

Critical Thinking

Do you believe that some dangerous offenders such as rapists and child molesters should never be granted pretrial release? Does preventive detention violate the basic right that a person is innocent until proven guilty?

InfoTrac College Edition Research

 To access articles that discuss the use of preventive detention, use the term "preventive detention" as a subject guide on InfoTrac College Edition.

Pretrial Detention

The criminal defendant who is not eligible for bail or ROR is subject to pretrial detention in the local county jail. The jail has long been a trouble spot for the criminal justice system. Conditions tend to be poor and rehabilitation nonexistent.

In terms of the number of persons affected each year, pretrial custody accounts for more incarceration in the United States than does imprisonment after sentencing. On any given day in the United States, more than 600,000 people were held in more than 3,500 local jails. Over the course of a year, many times that number pass through the jailhouse door. More than 50 percent of those held in local jails have been accused of crimes but not convicted; they are **pretrial detainees.** In the United States, people are detained at a rate twice that of neighboring Canada and three times that of Great Britain. Hundreds of jails are overcrowded, and many are under court orders to reduce their populations and improve conditions. The national jail-crowding crisis has worsened over the years.

pretrial detainees
People who either are denied bail or cannot afford to post bail before trial and are kept in secure confinement.

© 2003 AP/Wide World Photos

Jails are often considered the weakest link in the criminal justice process. They are frequently dangerous, harmful, decrepit, and filled with the poor and friendless. The costs of holding a person in jail range up to more than $100 per day and $36,000 per year. In addition, detainees are often confined with those convicted of crimes and those who have been transferred from other institutions because of overcrowding. Many felons are transferred to jails from state prisons to ease crowding. It is possible to have in close quarters a convicted rapist, a father jailed for nonpayment of child support, and a person awaiting trial for a crime that he did not commit. Thus, jails contain a mix of inmates, which can lead to violence, brutality, and suicide.

Jails can be overcrowded and dangerous. Sometimes it takes a court order to improve conditions. Prisoners in one of the Marion County Lockup cells, sleep on the floor May 22, 2001, in Indianapolis. At least 19 of the state's 92 counties have jail populations that are near or beyond their intended capacities. Many have been using some form of early release to reduce the number of inmates. Despite early releases, crowding at the Marion County Lockup is under new scrutiny as its population continues to soar. On April 16, 2001, it reached 439 inmates — more than twice the limit set in 1999 by a federal judge.

The Effects of Detention   What happens to people who do not get bail or who cannot afford to put up bail money? Traditionally, they find themselves more likely to be convicted and then getting longer prison sentences than those who commit similar crimes but who were released on bail. A federally sponsored study of case processing in the nation's largest counties found that about 63 percent of all defendants granted bail were convicted; in contrast, 78 percent of detainees were convicted.[13] Detainees are also more likely to be convicted of a felony offense than releasees and, therefore, are eligible for a long prison sentence instead of the much shorter term of incarceration given misdemeanants. People being held in jails are in a less attractive bargaining position than those released on bail, and prosecutors, knowing their predicament, may be less generous in their negotiations. It is for these reasons that bail reform advocates have tried so hard to eliminate whenever possible the detention of nondangerous criminal defendants.

Perspectives on Justice

Due process advocates bemoan the fact that bail is one of the few decision points in the justice system where money is the deciding factor. Why should one person be detained for months or years simply because he cannot make bail while a more affluent person can simply write a check? Noninterventionists would argue that a jail experience can be extremely damaging to the future chances of young offenders.

To quiz yourself on this material, go to questions 11.5–11.9 on the Introduction to Criminal Justice 10e CD.

Charging the Defendant

Charging a defendant with a crime is a critical stage in the pretrial process. The charge is selected by the prosecutor depending on the facts of the case, strength of the evidence, availability of witnesses, and so on. The process varies depending on whether it occurs via a grand jury or a preliminary hearing.

The Indictment Process — The Grand Jury

The grand jury was an early development of the English common law. Under the Magna Carta (1215), no "freeman" could be seized and imprisoned unless he had been judged by his peers. To determine fairly who was eligible to be tried, a group of freeman from the district where the crime was committed would be brought together to examine the facts of the case and determine whether the charges had merit. Thus, the grand jury was created as a check against arbitrary prosecution by a judge who might be a puppet of the government.

The concept of the grand jury was brought to the American colonies by early settlers and later incorporated into the Fifth Amendment, which states that "no person shall be held to answer for a capital, or otherwise infamous crime, unless on a presentment or indictment of a grand jury."

Today, the use of the grand jury is diminishing. Relatively few states require a grand jury indictment to begin all felony proceedings; most allow the prosecutor the option of calling a grand jury or proceeding with a preliminary hearing. The federal government employs both the grand jury and the preliminary hearing systems.

The grand jury today has two roles. First, the grand jury has the power to act as an independent investigating body. In this capacity, it examines the possibility of criminal activity within its jurisdiction. These investigative efforts are directed toward general, not individual, criminal conduct. After completing its investigation, the grand jury issues a report called a **presentment,** which contains its findings and also usually a recommendation of indictment.

presentment
The report of a grand jury investigation, which usually includes a recommendation of indictment.

The grand jury's second and better-known role is accusatory in nature. In this capacity, the grand jury acts as the community's conscience in determining whether an accusation by the state (the prosecution) justifies a trial. The grand jury relies on the testimony of witnesses called by the prosecution through its subpoena power. After examining the evidence and the testimony of witnesses, the grand jury decides whether probable cause exists for prosecution. If it does, an indictment, or **true bill,** is affirmed. If the grand jury fails to find probable cause, a **no bill** (meaning that the indictment is ignored) is passed. In some states, a prosecutor can present evidence to a different grand jury if a no bill is returned; in other states, this action is prohibited by statute.

true bill
The action by a grand jury when it votes to indict an accused suspect.

no bill
The action by a grand jury when it votes not to indict an accused suspect.

A grand jury is ordinarily made up of 16 to 23 individuals, depending on the requirements of the jurisdiction. This group theoretically represents a county. Selection of members varies from state to state, but for the most part, they are chosen at random (for example, from voting lists). To qualify to serve on a grand jury, an individual must be at least 18 years of age, a U.S. citizen, and a resident of the jurisdiction for one year or more and possess sufficient English-speaking skills for communication.

The grand jury usually meets at the request of the prosecution. Hearings are closed and secret. The prosecuting attorney presents the charges and calls witnesses who testify under oath to support the indictment. Usually, the accused individuals are not allowed to attend the hearing unless they are asked to testify by the prosecutor or the grand jury.

To get the latest news on grand juries, go to http://www.udayton.edu/~grandjur/.

Reforming the Grand Jury? The grand jury usually meets at the request of the prosecution, and hearings are closed and secret. The defense attorney, defendant, and general public are not allowed to attend. The prosecuting attorney presents the charges and calls witnesses who testify under oath to support the indictment. This process has been criticized as being a rubber stamp for the prosecution because the presentation of the evidence is shaped by the district attorney who is not required by law to reveal information that might exonerate the accused.[14] In the case of *United States* v. *Williams* (1992), the Supreme Court ruled that that no supervisory power in the federal courts requires presentation of **exculpatory evidence**

exculpatory evidence
Includes all information that is material and favorable to the accused defendant because it casts doubt on the defendant's guilt or on the evidence the government intends to use a trial.

The preliminary hearing is used to determine whether there is sufficient evidence to bind felony defendants over for trial. Maryville, Tennessee attorney, David M. Boyd talks with his client, 20-year old Aaron Lee Skeen, June 5, 2003, at the Blount County Justice Center in Maryville after his preliminary hearing. Skeen is charged with murder, rape, kidnapping, and burglary in the killing of Sandy Jeffers. Jeffers body was located at the bottom of a 60-foot cliff off the Foothills Parkway in the Great Smoky Mountains.

© 2003 AP/Wide World Photos

(evidence that can clear a defendant from blame or fault).[15] Some legal scholars find that the *Williams* decision conflicted with the grand jury's historical purpose of shielding criminal defendants from unwarranted and unfair prosecution and overrode the mandate that it be both informed and independent. An alternative might be to change the rule of criminal procedure so that prosecutors would be obliged to present exculpatory evidence to the grand jury even if it might result in the issuance of a no bill or indictment.[16] Another alternative put forth by defense lawyers is to open the grand jury room to the defense and to hold the government to the same types of constitutional safeguards required to protect defendants that are now used at trial.[17] Because the grand jury is often controlled solely by the state prosecutor, some legal experts believe that the system should provide the defendant with more due process protection. The American Bar Association (ABA) publication *Grand Jury Policy and Model Act* suggests the following changes in state grand jury statutes: Witnesses should have their own attorneys when they give testimony; prosecutors should be required to present evidence that might show that a suspect is innocent; witnesses should be granted constitutional privileges against self-incrimination; and grand jurors should be informed of all the elements of the crimes being presented against the suspect.[18]

Use "grand juries" as a key term on InfoTrac College Edition.

The Indictment Process—The Preliminary Hearing

The preliminary hearing is used in about half the states as an alternative to the grand jury. Although the purpose of preliminary and grand jury hearings is the same — to establish whether probable cause is sufficient to merit a trial — the procedures differ significantly.

The preliminary hearing is conducted before a magistrate or lower court judge and, unlike the grand jury hearing, is open to the public unless the defendant requests otherwise. Present at the preliminary hearing are the prosecuting attorney, the defendant, and the defendant's counsel, if already retained. The prosecution presents its evidence and witnesses to the judge. The defendant or the defense counsel then has the right to cross-examine witnesses and to challenge the prosecutor's evidence.

After hearing the evidence, the judge decides whether there is sufficient probable cause to believe that the defendant committed the alleged crime. If so, the defendant is bound over for trial, and the prosecuting attorney's information (same as an indictment) is filed with the superior court, usually within 15 days. When the judge does not find sufficient probable cause, the charges are dismissed, and the defendant is released from custody.

Waiving the Preliminary Hearing A unique aspect of the preliminary hearing is the defendant's right to waive the proceeding. In most states, the prosecutor and the judge must agree to this waiver. A waiver has advantages and disadvantages for both the prosecutor and the defendant. In most situations, a prosecutor will agree to a waiver because it avoids revealing evidence to the defense before trial. However, if the state believes it is necessary to obtain a record of witness testimony because of the possibility that a witness or witnesses may be unavailable for the trial or unable to remember the facts clearly, the prosecutor might override the waiver. In this situation, the record of the preliminary hearing can be used at the trial.

The defendant will most likely waive the preliminary hearing for one of three reasons: (1) He has already decided to plead guilty; (2) he wants to speed the criminal justice process; or (3) he hopes to avoid the negative publicity that might result from the hearing. However, the preliminary hearing is of obvious advantage to the defendant who believes that it will result in a dismissal of the charges. In addition, the preliminary hearing gives the defense the opportunity to learn what evidence the prosecution has. Figure 11.4 outlines the significant differences between the grand jury and the preliminary hearing processes.

Arraignment

After an indictment or information is filed following a grand jury or preliminary hearing, an arraignment takes place before the court that will try the case. At the arraignment, the judge informs the defendant of the charges against her and appoints counsel if one has not yet been retained. According to the Sixth Amendment, the accused has the right to be informed of the nature and cause of the accusation. Thus, the judge at the arraignment must make sure that the defendant clearly understands the charges.

After the charges are read and explained, the defendant is asked to enter a plea. If a plea of not guilty or not guilty by reason of insanity is entered, a trial date is set. When the defendant pleads guilty or nolo contendere, a date for sentencing is arranged. The magistrate then either sets bail or releases the defendant on personal recognizance.

The Plea

Ordinarily, a defendant in a criminal trial will enter one of three pleas: guilty, not guilty, or nolo contendere.

Guilty On July 7, 2001, Lizzie Grubman, a New York publicist with a dazzling roster of clients, was asked her to move her Mercedes sports utility vehicle (SUV) from a fire lane in front of a trendy nightclub in the Hamptons. She angrily slammed her SUV into reverse and drove into a crowd of onlookers, injuring 16 people before she drove away. On August 23, 2002, she plead guilty

Use the term "arraignment" as a key word on InfoTrac College Edition.

On July 7, 2001, Lizzie Grubman, a New York publicist, drove into a crowd in front of a trendy club in the Hamptons, injuring 16 people before she drove away. On August 23, 2002, she plead guilty to third-degree assault and leaving the scene of an accident in exchange for a sentence of two months in jail, 280 hours of community service, and five years' probation. Had she gone to trial, she could have faced up to seven years behind bars if convicted.

**Figure 11.4
Charging the Defendant with
a Crime**

Note the differences betwen the
grand jury and preliminary hearing.

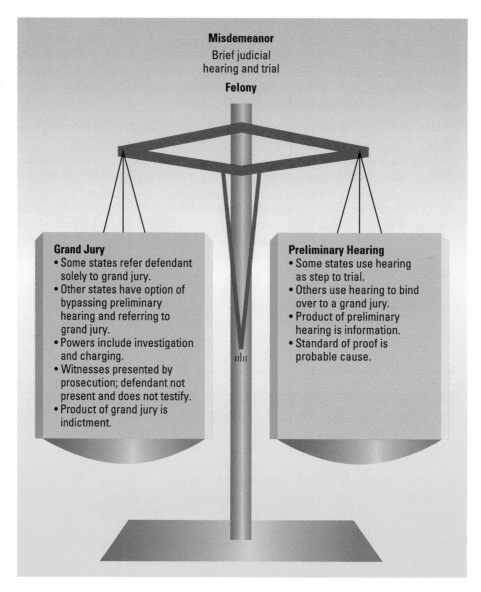

Misdemeanor
Brief judicial
hearing and trial

Felony

Grand Jury
• Some states refer defendant solely to grand jury.
• Other states have option of bypassing preliminary hearing and referring to grand jury.
• Powers include investigation and charging.
• Witnesses presented by prosecution; defendant not present and does not testify.
• Product of grand jury is indictment.

Preliminary Hearing
• Some states use hearing as step to trial.
• Others use hearing to bind over to a grand jury.
• Product of preliminary hearing is information.
• Standard of proof is probable cause.

to third-degree assault and leaving the scene of an accident in exchange for a sentence of two months in jail, 280 hours of community service, and five years' probation. She could have faced up to seven years behind bars if convicted at trial.[19]

The Grubman case is certainly not unique. More than 90 percent of defendants appearing before the courts plead guilty prior to the trial stage (Figure 11.5). A guilty plea has several consequences. It functions not only as an admission of guilt but also as a surrender of the entire array of constitutional rights designed to protect a criminal defendant against unjustified conviction, including the right to remain silent, the right to confront witnesses against her, the right to a trial by jury, and the right to be proven guilty by proof beyond a reasonable doubt. Once a plea is made, it cannot be rescinded or withdrawn even if a change is made in the law that might have made conviction more problematic.[20]

As a result, judges must follow certain procedures when accepting a plea of guilty. First, the judge must clearly state to the defendant the constitutional guarantees automatically waived by this plea. Second, the judge must believe that the facts of the case establish a basis for the plea and that the plea is made voluntarily. Third, the defendant must be informed of the right to counsel during the pleading process. In many felony cases, the judge will insist on the presence of defense counsel. Finally, the judge must inform the defendant of the possible sentencing outcomes, including the maximum sentence that can be imposed.

After a guilty plea has been entered, a sentencing date is arranged. In a majority of states, a guilty plea may be withdrawn and replaced with a not guilty plea at any time prior to sentencing if good cause is shown.

Not Guilty At the arraignment or before the trial, a not guilty plea is entered in two ways: (1) It is verbally stated by the defendant or the defense counsel, or (2) it is entered for the defendant by the court when the defendant stands mute before the bench.

Once a plea of not guilty is recorded, a trial date is set. In misdemeanor cases, trials take place in the lower court system, whereas felony cases are normally transferred to the superior court. At this time, a continuance or issuance of bail is once again considered.

Nolo Contendere The plea nolo contendere ("no contest") is essentially a plea of guilty. This plea has the same consequences as a guilty plea, with one exception: It may not be held against the defendant as proof in a subsequent civil matter because technically no admission of guilt has been made. This plea is accepted at the discretion of the trial court and must be voluntarily and intelligently made by the defendant.

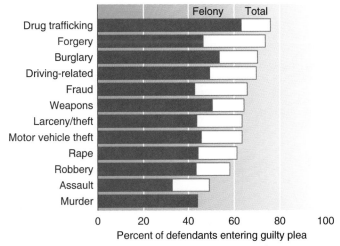

Most serious arrest charge

Figure 11.5
Plea Rate for Felony Defendants in the 75 Largest Counties, by Most Serious Arrest Charge, 1998

Source: Brian A Reaves, *Felony Defendants in Large Urban Counties, 1998* (Washington, D.C.: Bureau of Justice Statistics, 2001), p. 25.

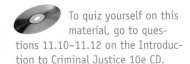

To quiz yourself on this material, go to questions 11.10–11.12 on the Introduction to Criminal Justice 10e CD.

Plea Bargaining

One of the most common practices in the criminal justice system today, and a cornerstone of the informal justice system, is plea bargaining.[21] Plea bargaining is a relatively recent development, taking hold late in the nineteenth century. At first, judges were reluctant to accept pleas, preferring trials to sharing their power with prosecutors (who make the deal). However, plea bargaining became more attractive at the turn of the twentieth century when the mechanization of manufacture and transportation prompted a flood of complex civil cases, which persuaded judges that criminal cases had to be settled quickly lest the court system break down.[22] Today, more than 90 percent of criminal convictions are estimated to result from negotiated pleas of guilty. Even in serious felony cases, some jurisdictions will have several plea-bargaining arrangements for every trial. For example, a recent federal survey of felony sentencing in state courts found that in a single year (2000), of the estimated 924,700 convicted felons, the vast majority (879,200, or 95 percent) pleaded guilty. The rest were found guilty either by a jury or by a judge in a bench trial. Not surprisingly, persons convicted of murder were the least likely to have pleaded guilty (58 percent) and the most likely to have been convicted by a jury (38 percent). However, as Table 11.1 shows, those people who plead guilty to murder were much less likely to get the death penalty or a life sentence than those who were convicted at trial. These data show that plea bargains benefit both the prosecution, which is assured a conviction, and the defendant, who is rewarded with a lenient sentence.[23]

To gain some more insight on plea bargaining, go to http://www.lawsguide.com/mylawyer/guideview.asp?layer=2&article=147.

Table 11.1 The Effect of Trial Type on
Sentencing in Murder Cases

Type of conviction	Type of sentence for murder or nonnegligent manslaughter		
	Life	Death	Other
Trial	41	4	55
Jury	43	4	53
Bench	20	1	79
Guilty plea	15	1	84
Total	23%	2%	75%

Source: Matthew Durose and Patrick Langan, *Felony Sentencing in State Courts, 2000* (Washington, D.C.: Bureau of Justice Statistics, 2003).

The Nature of the Bargain

Plea bargaining is the exchange of prosecutorial and judicial concessions for pleas of guilty. Normally, a bargain can be made between the prosecutor and the defense attorney in four ways: (1) The initial charges may be reduced to those of a lesser offense, thus automatically reducing the sentence imposed; (2) in cases in which many counts are charged, the prosecutor may reduce the number of counts; (3) the prosecutor may promise to recommend a lenient sentence, such as probation; and (4) when the charge imposed has a negative label attached (for example, child molester), the prosecutor may alter the charge to a more socially acceptable one (such as assault) in exchange for a plea of guilty. In a jurisdiction where sentencing disparities exist between judges, the prosecutor may even agree to arrange for a defendant to appear before a lenient judge in exchange for a plea; this practice is known as judge shopping.

Bargains are rarely a one-shot deal and may be negotiated many times as evidence becomes known and the case unfolds.[24] They are negotiated until the defense believes it got the best deal for its client and the prosecutor believes that, considering the totality of the circumstances, it was able to dispense a fair amount of punishment. The defense attorney conducts the bargain as a form of negotiation, putting forth information that will convince the prosecutor that the case is very strong and the chances of an acquittal quite high. If he can magnify the value of the case, the chances of a favorable plea outcome will increase.

Pros and Cons of Plea Bargaining

Plea bargaining is so widespread that it is recognized as one of the major elements of the criminal justice system. Despite its prevalence, its merits are hotly debated. Those opposed to the widespread use of plea bargaining assert that it is coercive in its inducement of guilty pleas, that it encourages the unequal exercise of prosecutorial discretion, and that it complicates sentencing as well as the job of correctional authorities. Others argue that it is unconstitutional and that it results in cynicism and disrespect for the entire system.[25] Some argue that plea bargaining is objectionable because it encourages defendants to waive their constitutional right to trial, while others contend that sentences tend to be less severe when a defendant enters a guilty plea than when the case proceeds to trial. This aspect of plea negotiations convinces the general public that plea bargaining allows the defendant to beat the system and further tarnishes the criminal process. Plea bargaining also raises the danger that an innocent person will be convicted of a crime if he is convinced that the lighter treatment from a guilty

Plea bargains are commonly used in even the most notorious cases that make media headlines. Here, Robert Iler, center, the teenage star of the HBO series *The Sopranos,* returns to court surrounded by friends and family after pleading guilty to misdemeanor petty larceny in return for a sentence of three years' probation, April 23, 2003, outside New York State Supreme Court. Iler, seventeen, agreed to a plea bargain for his role in a robbery in July 2001 on New York City's Upper East Side.

plea is preferable to the risk of conviction with a harsher sentence following a formal trial.

Proponents of plea bargaining contend that the practice ensures the flow of guilty pleas essential to administration efficiency. It allows the system the flexibility to individualize justice and inspires respect for the system because it is associated with certain and prompt punishment. Proponents contend that plea bargaining benefits both the state and the defendant in the following ways.

- The overall costs of the criminal prosecution are reduced.
- The administrative efficiency of the courts is greatly improved.
- The prosecution can devote more time to more serious cases.
- The defendant avoids possible detention and an extended trial and may receive a reduced sentence.
- Resources can be devoted more efficiently to cases that need greater attention.[26]

In recent years, efforts have been made to convert plea bargaining into a more visible, understandable, and fair dispositional process. Some jurisdictions have developed safeguards and guidelines to prevent violations of due process and to ensure that innocent defendants do not plead guilty under coercion. Such safeguards include

- Uniform plea practice,
- Time limits on plea negotiations,
- Presence of defense counsel to advise defendant,
- Open discussions about plea between prosecutor and defense attorney,
- Full information regarding offender and offense,
- Judicial questioning of defendant before accepting plea, and
- Judicial supervision of plea.

Plea negotiations are unlikely to be eliminated or severely curtailed in the near future. Supporters of the total abolition of plea bargaining are in the minority. As a result of abuses, however, efforts are being made to improve plea-bargaining operations. Such reforms include development of uniform plea practices, representation of counsel during plea negotiations, and establishment of time limits on plea negotiations.

Legal Issues in Plea Bargaining

The U.S. Supreme Court has reviewed the propriety of plea bargaining in several decisions. Some of the more important findings are discussed here.

Effective Assistance of Counsel Defendants are entitled to the effective assistance of counsel to protect them from pressure and influence during plea negotiations. In *Hill* v. *Lockhart* (1985), the Supreme Court ruled that, to prove ineffectiveness, the defendant must show a "reasonable probability that, but for counsel's errors, he would not have pleaded guilty and would have insisted on going to trial."[27]

Voluntariness Guilty pleas must be voluntary and the prosecutor cannot threaten or coerce a defendant into pleading guilty. In *Boykin* v. *Alabama* (1969), the Court held that an affirmative action (such as a verbal statement) that the plea was made voluntarily must exist on the record before a trial judge may accept a guilty plea.[28] This is essential because a guilty plea basically constitutes a waiver of the defendant's Fifth Amendment privilege against self-incrimination and Sixth Amendment right to a jury trial. However, a prosecutor can apprise the defendant of the consequences of going to trial. For example, the prosecutor lets the defendant know that the death penalty will be sought in a murder case if a trial is required. The Court ruled in *Brady* v. *United States* (1970) that a guilty plea is not invalid simply because it is entered to avoid the possibility of the death penalty.[29]

How far can prosecutors go to convince a defendant to plead guilty? The Supreme Court ruled in the 1978 case of *Bordenkircher* v. *Hayes* that a defendant's due process rights are not violated when a prosecutor threatens to reindict the accused on more serious charges if the defendant does not plead guilty to the original offense.[30] Though the threat of reindictment seems coercive, the Supreme Court did not see it that way and gave the prosecutor the upper hand in the bargaining process.

Promises Must Be Kept In *Santobello* v. *New York* (1971), the Court held that the promise of the prosecutor must be kept and that a prosecutor's breaking of a plea-bargaining agreement required a reversal for the defendant.[31]

Not only must the prosecutor keep her word in a plea bargain agreement, but the defendant must also. In *Ricketts* v. *Adamson* (1987), the Court ruled that defendants must also keep their side of a bargain to receive the promised offer of leniency.[32] An example of defendant cooperation can be observed in a recent New York appellate case, *People* v. *Hicks* (2002).[33] In *Hicks,* a defendant pleaded guilty to sex-related crimes in exchange for a promised lenient sentence. A condition of the plea included that he truthfully answer all questions asked by probation officers when they investigated the case. After he told the investigators that he was not really guilty and that the children initiated sexual contact with him, the trial judge imposed a more severe sentence. Hicks appealed the longer sentence, but his request was turned down by the appellate court, which ruled that the defendant violated his promise to be truthful, thereby negating the plea bargain agreement.

Need for Guilt When the question arose about whether a guilty plea may be accepted by a defendant maintaining her innocence, the Supreme Court, in *North Carolina* v. *Alford* (1970), said that such action was appropriate when a defen-

Concept Summary 11.1 Control Over Plea Negotiation

Case	Decision
Boykin v. *Alabama* (1969)	The defendant must make an affirmative statement that the plea is voluntary before the judge can accept it.
Brady v. *United States* (1970)	Avoiding the possibility of the death penalty is not grounds to invalidate a guilty plea.
North Carolina v. *Alford* (1970)	Accepting a guilty plea from a defendant who maintains his or her innocence is valid.
Santobello v. *New York* (1971)	The promise of a prosecutor that rests on a guilty plea must be kept in a plea-bargaining agreement.
Bordenkircher v. *Hayes* (1978)	A defendant's constitutional rights are not violated when a prosecutor threatens to reindict the accused on more serious charges if he or she is not willing to plead guilty to the original offense.
Hill v. *Lockhart* (1985)	To prove ineffectiveness of defense counsel, the defendant needs to show a reasonable probability that, except for counsel's errors, the defendant would not have pleaded guilty.
Ricketts v. *Adamson* (1987)	The defendant is required to keep his or her side of the bargain to receive the promised offer of leniency, because plea bargaining rests on an agreement between the parties.
United States v. *Mezzanatto* (1995)	A defendant who wants to plea bargain in federal court can be required to agree that, if he testifies at trial, his statements during the plea bargain negotiations can be used against him.

dant was seeking a lesser sentence. In other words, a defendant could plead guilty without admitting guilt.[34]

Use of Statements In *United States* v. *Mezzanatto* (1995), the Supreme Court declared that statements made by the defendant during plea bargaining can be used at trial for impeachment purposes. This means that a prosecutor can refuse to plea bargain with a defendant unless the defendant agrees that any statements made during the negotiations can be used to impeach him at trial. Therefore, if the plea negotiations break down and the defendant testifies in his own behalf at trial, anything he said during the negotiation process can be used to rebut his testimony. In its decisions, the Court narrowly interpreted Rule 410 of the Federal Rules of Evidence, which says that statements made during plea bargaining are inadmissible at trial. Although the ruling applies only to federal trials, it is likely to be adopted by many state court systems that watch Supreme Court decisions and follow suit.[35]

Repeated actions by the Supreme Court show that plea bargaining is a constitutionally accepted practice in the United States. Concept Summary 11.1 summarizes the major Supreme Court decisions regulating plea-bargaining practices.

The Role of the Prosecutor in Plea Bargaining

The prosecutor in the U.S. system of criminal justice has broad discretion in the exercise of his responsibilities. Such discretion includes deciding whether to initiate a criminal prosecution, determining the nature and number of the criminal charges, and choosing whether to plea bargain a case and under what conditions.

Plea bargaining is one of the major tools the prosecutor uses to control and influence the criminal justice system (the other two are the decision to initiate a charge and the ability to take the case to trial). Few states have placed limits on the discretion of prosecutors in plea-bargaining situations. Instead, in making a plea-bargaining decision, the prosecutor is generally free to weigh competing alternatives and factors, such as the seriousness of the crime, the attitude of the victim, the police report of the incident, and applicable sentencing provisions. Such factors as the offense, the defendant's prior record and age, and the type, strength, and admissibility of evidence are considered important in the plea-bargaining decision.[36] The attitude of the complainant is also an important factor in the decision-making process. For example, in victimless cases, such as heroin possession, the police attitude is most often considered, whereas in victim-related crimes, such as rape, the attitude of the victim is a primary concern. Prosecutors in low-population or rural jurisdictions not only use more information while making their decisions but also seem more likely than their urban counterparts to accept bargains, a finding that suggests case pressure alone is not the incentive for most plea bargains.[37]

Plea bargaining frequently occurs in cases in which the government believes the evidence is weak, as when a key witness seems unreliable or unwilling to testify. Bargaining permits a compromise settlement in a weak case when the criminal trial outcome is in doubt.

Some jurisdictions have established guidelines to provide consistency in plea-bargaining cases. For instance, a given office may be required to define the kinds and types of cases and offenders that may be suitable for plea bargaining. In other jurisdictions, approval to plea bargain may be required. Other controls might include procedures for internally reviewing decisions by the chief prosecutor and the use of written memorandums to document the need and acceptability for a plea bargain in a given case. For example, pleas may be offered on a "take it or leave it" basis. In each case, a special prosecutor, whose job it is to screen cases, sets the bargaining terms. If the defense counsel cannot accept the agreement, there is no negotiation, and the case must go to trial. Only if complications arise in the case, such as witnesses changing their testimony, can negotiations be reopened.[38]

The prosecutor's role in plea bargaining is also important on a statewide or systemwide basis because it involves exercising leadership in setting policy. The most extreme example of a chief prosecutor influencing the plea-negotiation process has occurred when the prosecutor has attempted to eliminate plea bargaining. In Alaska such efforts met with resistance from assistant prosecutors and others in the system, particularly judges and defense attorneys.[39]

The Role of the Defense Counsel in Plea Bargaining

Both the U.S. Supreme Court and such organizations as the American Bar Association have established guidelines for the court receiving a guilty plea and for the defense counsel representing the accused in plea negotiations.[40] No court should accept a guilty plea unless the defendant has been properly advised by counsel and the court has determined that the plea is voluntary and has a factual basis. The court has the discretion to reject a plea if it is inappropriately offered. The defense counsel — a public defender or a private attorney — is required to play an advisory role in plea negotiations. The defendant's counsel is expected to be aware of the facts of the case and of the law and to advise the defendant of the alternatives available. The defense attorney is basically responsible for making certain that the accused understands the nature of the plea-bargaining process and the guilty plea. This means that the defense counsel should explain to the defendant that, by pleading guilty, she is waiving certain rights that would be available if the case went to trial. In addition, the defense attorney has the duty to keep the defendant informed of developments and discussions with the prosecutor regarding plea bargaining. While doing so, the attorney for the accused cannot misrepresent evidence or mislead the client into making a detrimental agreement. The defense counsel is not only ethically but constitutionally required to communicate all plea-bargaining offers to a client even if counsel believes the offers to be unacceptable.[41]

In reality, most plea negotiations occur in the chambers of the judge, in the prosecutor's office, or in the courthouse hallway. Under these conditions, it is often difficult to assess the actual roles played by the prosecutor and the defense attorney. Even so, it is fundamental that a defendant not be required to plead guilty until advised by counsel and that a guilty plea should not be made unless it is done with the consent of the accused.

The Role of the Judge in Plea Bargaining

One of the most confusing problems in the plea-bargaining process has been the proper role of the judge. Should the judge act only in a supervisory capacity or enter into the negotiation process? The leading national legal organization, the ABA, is opposed to judicial participation in plea negotiations.[42] According to ABA standards, judges should not be a party to arrangements for the determination of a sentence, whether as a result of a guilty plea or a finding of guilty based on proof. Furthermore, judicial participation in plea negotiations creates the impression in the mind of the defendant that she could not receive a fair trial, lessens the ability of the judge to make an objective determination of the voluntariness of the plea, is inconsistent with the theory behind the use of presentence investigation reports, and may induce an innocent defendant to plead guilty because he is afraid to reject the disposition desired by the judge.[43] In addition to the ABA, the Federal Rules of Criminal Procedure prohibit federal judges from participating in plea negotiations.[44]

While these learned legal bodies frown on judicial involvement, most states still permit the judge to participate in the negotiation procedure. This approach allows the judge to work closely with prosecutors in securing the conviction of potentially dangerous offenders and shaping sentencing outcomes. When John Kramer and Jeffrey Ulmer examined sentencing practices in Pennsylvania, they found that judges were willing to work with the prosecutor as long as the agreed-upon sentence did not "shock their conscience."[45] For example, one judge commented, when asked about a negotiated plea agreement in which the prosecutor agreed not to seek a mandatory five-year prison sentence:

> When a district attorney comes in and says, "Judge, the defendant is willing to plead to 4–8 years and I think that the public is better off with that than me running the risk of losing this case because I think we have some evidentiary problems. The witness against him is a convicted felon that told two different stories." What are you going to do? Sounds like the best deal to me for everybody [is to accept the plea].

Despite the legal ethics of such a view, especially when evidence is questionable or tainted, there seemed little question that judges were willing to work with prosecutors for the sake of crime control at the expense of due process.

The Victim and Plea Bargaining

What role should victims play in plea bargaining? Crime victims are not empowered at the pretrial stage of the criminal process and should not play a role in the plea negotiations. Statutes do not require that the prosecutor defer to the victim's wishes, and there are no legal consequences for ignoring the victim in a

© 2003 AP/Wide World Photos

Many prosecutors confer with crime victims in their plea bargaining decision and in some cases prosecutors seek approval for the plea from a victim or family member. Here, during his sentencing in Somerset, Kentucky, Jeff Morris turns to the family of slain Pulaski County Sheriff Sam Catron and apologizes for his role in Catron's murder, September 15, 2003. Under a plea bargain, Morris was convicted of murder. Morris, an ex-deputy, was running against Catron in the Republican primary.

plea-bargaining decision. Even the ABA's *Model Uniform Victims of Crime Act* suggests only that the prosecutor "confer" with the victim.[46] Nonetheless, many prosecutors do confer with crime victims, and some critics have suggested that the system today is too victim-driven; that is, in too many cases prosecutors seek approval for the plea from a victim or family member.

Plea-Bargaining Reform

In recent years, efforts have been made to convert plea bargaining into a more visible, understandable, and fair dispositional process. Many jurisdictions have developed safeguards and guidelines to prevent violations of due process and to ensure that innocent defendants do not plead guilty under coercion. Such safeguards include the following: (1) The judge questions the defendant about the facts of the guilty plea before accepting the plea; (2) the defense counsel is present and can advise the defendant of her rights; (3) the prosecutor and the defense attorney openly discuss the plea; and (4) full and frank information about the defendant and the offenses is made available at this stage of the process. In addition, judicial supervision ensures that plea bargaining is conducted in a fair manner.

What would happen if plea bargaining were banned outright, as its critics advocate? Numerous jurisdictions throughout the United States have experimented with bans on plea bargaining. In 1975 Alaska eliminated the practice. Honolulu, Hawaii, has also attempted to abolish plea bargaining. Other jurisdictions, including Arizona, Delaware, the District of Columbia, and Iowa, have sought to limit the use of plea bargaining.[47] In theory, eliminating plea bargains means that prosecutors in these jurisdictions give no consideration or concessions to a defendant in exchange for a guilty plea.

In reality, however, in these and most jurisdictions, sentence-related concessions, charge-reduction concessions, and alternative methods for prosecution continue to be used in one fashion or another.[48] Where plea bargaining is limited or abolished, the number of trials may increase, the sentence severity may change, and more questions regarding the right to a speedy trial may arise. Discretion may also be shifted further up the system. Instead of spending countless hours preparing for and conducting a trial, prosecutors may dismiss more cases outright or decide not to prosecute them after initial action has been taken. Candace McCoy's study of plea reform in California investigated legislative efforts to eliminate the state's plea-bargaining process. Instead of achieving a ban on plea bargaining, the process shifted from the superior to the municipal courts. McCoy found that the majority of defendants plead guilty after some negotiations and that the new law accelerated the guilty plea process. McCoy suggests an alternative model of plea-bargaining reform that includes emphasizing public scrutiny of plea bargaining, adhering to standards of professionalism, and making a greater commitment to due process procedures.[49]

To quiz yourself on this material, go to questions 11.13–11.24 on the Introduction to Criminal Justice 10e CD.

Pretrial Diversion

Another important feature in the early court process is placing offenders into non-criminal diversion programs before their formal trial or conviction. Pretrial diversion programs were first established in the late 1960s and early 1970s, when it became apparent that a viable alternative to the highly stigmatized criminal sentence was needed. In diversion programs, formal criminal proceedings against an accused are suspended while that person participates in a community treatment program under court supervision. Diversion helps the offender avoid the stigma of a criminal conviction and enables the justice system to reduce costs and alleviate prison overcrowding.

Many diversion programs exist throughout the United States. These programs vary in size and emphasis but generally pursue the same goal: to constructively bypass criminal prosecution by providing a reasonable alternative in the form of treatment, counseling, or employment programs.

The prosecutor often plays the central role in the diversion process. Decisions about nondispositional alternatives are based on the nature of the crime, special characteristics of the offender, whether the defendant is a first-time offender, whether the defendant will cooperate with a diversion program, the impact of diversion on the community, and consideration for the opinion of the victim.[50]

Diversion programs can take many forms. Some are separate, independent agencies that were originally set up with federal funds but are now being continued with county or state assistance. Others are organized as part of a police, prosecutor, or probation department's internal structure. Still others are a joint venture between the county government and a private, nonprofit organization that carries out the treatment process.

First viewed as a panacea that could reduce court congestion and help treat minor offenders, diversion programs have come under fire for their alleged failures. Some national evaluations have concluded that diversion programs are no more successful at avoiding stigma and reducing recidivism than traditional justice processing.[51] The most prominent criticism is that they help widen the net of the justice system. By this, critics mean that the people placed in diversion programs are the ones most likely to have otherwise been dismissed after a brief hearing with a warning or small fine.[52]

Those who would have ordinarily received a more serious sentence are not eligible for diversion anyway. Thus, instead of limiting contact with the system, the diversion programs increase it. Not all justice experts agree with this charge, and some have championed diversion as a worthwhile exercise of the criminal justice system's rehabilitation responsibility. Although diversion may not be a cure-all for criminal behavior, it is an important effort that continues to be made in most jurisdictions across the United States. Originally proposed in 1967 by the President's Commission on Law Enforcement and Administration of Justice and supported by federal funds, most existing programs are now underwritten with state funds.[53]

 Read about the federal government's pretrial diversion program at http://www.usdoj.gov/usao/eousa/foia_reading_room/usam/title9/22mcrm.htm.

 To quiz yourself on this material, go to question 11.25 on the Introduction to Criminal Justice 10e CD.

Perspectives on Justice

The diversion movement was one of the cornerstones of the nonintervention movement, which peaked in the 1970s.

Summary

- Many important decisions about what happens to a defendant are made prior to trial.

- Hearings, such as before the grand jury and the preliminary hearing, are held to determine if probable cause exists to charge the accused with a crime. If so, the defendant is arraigned, enters a plea, is informed of his constitutional rights (particularly the right to the assistance of counsel), and is considered for pretrial diversion.

- The use of money bail and other alternatives, such as release on recognizance, allows most defendants to be free pending their trial.
- Bail reform has resulted in the use of release on recognizance to replace money bail for nondangerous offenders.
- Preventive detention has been implemented because many believe that significant numbers of criminals violate their bail and commit further crimes while on pretrial release.
- Research indicates that most cases never go to trial but are bargained out of the system.

- Bargains can be made for a plea of guilty in exchange for a reduced sentence, dropping charges, lowering the charge, or substituting a more socially acceptable charge for one with negative connotations.
- People who plead guilty generally get lighter sentences than those who go to trial.
- The U.S. Supreme Court has shaped the legal contours of the plea system. For example, it has ruled that bargains must be kept on both sides.
- Although plea bargaining has been criticized, efforts to control it have not met with success.
- Diversion programs offering a criminal defendant the ability to enter a treatment program instead of a criminal trial continue to be used throughout the United States.

Key Terms

pretrial procedures 330
nolle prosequi 330
complaint 330
indictment 330
information 331

preliminary hearing (probable cause hearing) 331
arraignment 331
nolo contendere 331
release on recognizance (ROR) 335

pretrial detainees 339
presentment 341
true bill 341
no bill 341
exculpatory evidence 341

Doing Research on the Web

For an up-to-date list of Web links, go to http://cj.wadsworth.com/siegel_intro10e.

Preventive detention is not unique to the United States. It is also used abroad. Some critics accuse governments of illegally detaining political opponents. Use "preventive detention" as a subject guide on InfoTrac College Edition to find out more about where and how it is used around the world. To read about preventive

detention in India, go to http://web.amnesty.org/library/index/engasa200102000.

Pro/Con discussions and Viewpoint Essays on some of the topics in this chapter may be found at the Opposing Viewpoints Resource Center: http://www.gale.com/OpposingViewpoints.

Discussion Questions

1. Should criminal defendants be allowed to bargain for a reduced sentence in exchange for a guilty plea? Should the victim always be included in the plea-bargaining process?
2. Should those accused of violent acts be subjected to preventive detention instead of bail, even though they have not been convicted of a crime? Is it fair to the victim to have his alleged attacker running around loose?

3. What purpose does a grand jury or preliminary hearing serve in adjudicating felony offenses? Should one of these methods be abandoned? If so, which one?
4. Why should pretrial services be provided for defendants?
5. Should a suspect in a terrorist case be allowed bail? Wouldn't that give him license to carry out his plot?

Notes

1 U.S. Department of Justice, *Predicting Pretrial Misconduct with Drug Tests of Arrestees* (Washington, D.C.: National Institute of Justice, 1996), p. 1; William Rhodes, Raymond Hyatt, and Paul Scheiman, "Predicting Pretrial Misconduct with Drug Tests of Arrestees: Evidence from Eight Settings," *Journal of Quantitative Criminology* 12 (1996): 315–47; D. Alan Henry and

John Clark, *Pretrial Drug Testing — An Overview* (Washington, D.C.: Bureau of Justice Assistance, 1999).

2 Brian A. Reaves, *Felony Defendants in Large Urban Counties, 1998* (Washington, D.C.: Bureau of Justice Statistics, 2001).

3 Christopher Stephens, "Bail," *Georgetown Law Journal* 90 (2002): 1395–1416.

4 *Stack* v. *Boyle,* 342 U.S. 1, 72 S.Ct. 1, 96 L.Ed. 3 (1951).

5 *Vera Institute of Justice, 1961–1971: Programs in Criminal Justice* (New York: Vera Institute of Justice, 1972).

6 Chris Eskridge, *Pretrial Release Programming* (New York: Clark Boardman, 1983), p. 27.

7 Public Law 89-465, 18 U.S.C., Sec. 3146 (1966).

8 Ellis M Johnston, "Once a Criminal, Always a Criminal? Unconstitutional Presumptions for Mandatory Detention of Criminal Aliens," *Georgetown Law Journal* 89 (2001): 2593–2636.

9 18 U.S.C., Sec. 3142 (1984).

10 See, generally, Fred Cohen, "The New Federal Crime Control Act," *Criminal Law Bulletin* 21 (1985): 330–37.

11 *Schall* v. *Martin,* 467 U.S. 253, 104 S.Ct. 2403, 81 L.Ed.2d 207 (1984).

12 *United States* v. *Salerno,* 481 U.S. 739, 107 S.Ct. 2095, 95 L.Ed.2d 697 (1987).

13 Reaves, *Felony Defendants in Large Urban Counties.*

14 Ric Simmons, "Reexamining the Grand Jury: Is There Room for Democracy in the Criminal Justice System?" *Boston University Law Review* 82 (2002): 1–76.

15 *United States* v. *Williams,* 504 U.S. 36, 38 (1992).

16 Suzanne Roe Neely, "Preserving Justice and Preventing Prejudice: Requiring Disclosure of Substantial Exculpatory Evidence to the Grand Jury," *American Criminal Law Review* 39 (2002): 171–200.

17 John Gibeaut, "Indictment of a System," *ABA Journal* 87 (2001): 34.

18 American Bar Association, *Grand Jury Policy and Model Act* (Chicago: 1982). See also Deborah Day Emerson, *Grand Jury Reform: A Review of Key Issues* (Washington, D.C.: National Institute of Justice, 1983).

19 Associated Press, "Grubman Pleads Guilty in Hamptons Crash," *New York Times,* August 23, 2002, p. 1.

20 Kirke D. Weaver, "A Change of Heart or a Change of Law? Withdrawing a Guilty Plea under Federal Rule of Criminal Procedure

32(e)," *Journal of Criminal Law and Criminology* 92 (2001): 273–306.

21 See, generally, F. Andrew Hessick and Reshma Saujani, "Plea Bargaining and Convicting the Innocent: The Role of the Prosecutor, the Defense Counsel, and the Judge," *BYU Journal of Public Law* 16 (2002): 189–243.

22 George Fisher, "Plea Bargaining's Triumph," *Yale Law Journal* 109 (2000): 857–1058.

23 Matthew Durose and Patrick Langan, *Felony Sentencing in State Courts, 2000* (Washington, D.C.: Bureau of Justice Statistics, 2003).

24 Debra Emmelman, "Trial by Plea Bargain: Case Settlement as a Product of Recursive Decisionmaking," *Law and Society Review* 30 (1996): 335–61.

25 Fisher, "Plea Bargaining Triumphs," pp. 855–75.

26 Fred Zacharis, "Justice in Plea Bargaining," *William and Mary Law Review* 39 (1998): 1211–40.

27 *Hill* v. *Lockhart,* 474 U.S. 52, 106 S.Ct. 366, 88 L.Ed.2d 203 (1985).

28 *Boykin* v. *Alabama,* 395 U.S. 238, 89 S.Ct. 1709, 23 L.Ed.2d 274 (1969).

29 *Brady* v. *United States,* 397 U.S. 742, 90 S.Ct. 1463, 25 L.Ed.2d 747 (1970).

30 *Bordenkircher* v. *Hayes,* 434 U.S. 357, 98 S.Ct. 663, 54 L.Ed.2d 604 (1978).

31 *Santobello* v. *New York,* 404 U.S. 257, 92 S.Ct. 495, 30 L.Ed.2d 427 (1971).

32 *Ricketts* v. *Adamson,* 483 U.S. 1, 107 S.Ct. 2680, 97 L.Ed.2d 1 (1987).

33 *People* v. *Hicks,* NY2d (July 1, 2002), 2002 NYSlipOp 05513.

34 *North Carolina* v. *Alford,* 400 U.S. 25, 91 S.Ct. 160, 27 L.Ed.2d 162 (1970).

35 *United States* v. *Mezzanatto,* 116 S.Ct. 1480, 134 L.Ed.2d 687 (1995).

36 Stephen P. Lagoy, Joseph J. Senna, and Larry J. Siegel, "An Empirical Study on Information Usage for Prosecutorial Decision Making in Plea Negotiations," *American Criminal Law Review* 13 (1976): 435–71.

37 Ibid., p. 462.

38 Barbara Boland and Brian Forst, *The Prevalence of Guilty Pleas* (Washington, D.C.: Bureau of Justice Statistics, 1984), p. 3. See also Gary Hengstler, "The Troubled Justice System," *American Bar Association Journal* 80 (1994): 44.

39 National Institute of Law Enforcement and Criminal Justice, *Plea Bargaining in the*

United States (Washington, D.C.: Georgetown University, 1978), p. 8.

40 See American Bar Association, *Standards Relating to Pleas of Guilty,* 2d ed. (Chicago: 1988). See also *North Carolina* v. *Alford,* 400 U.S. 25, 91 S.Ct. 160, 27 L.Ed.2d 162 (1970).

41 Keith Bystrom, "Communicating Plea Offers to the Client," in *Ethical Problems Facing the Criminal Defense Lawyer,* ed. Rodney Uphoff (Chicago: American Bar Association, Section on Criminal Justice, 1995), p. 84.

42 American Bar Association, *Standards Relating to Pleas of Guilty,* Standard 3.3; National Advisory Commission on Criminal Justice Standards and Goals, *Task Force Report on Courts* (Washington, D.C.: Government Printing Office, 1973), p. 42.

43 American Bar Association, *Standards Relating to Pleas of Guilty,* p. 73. See also Alan Alschuler, "The Trial Judge's Role in Plea Bargaining," *Columbia Law Review* 76 (1976): 1059.

44 Federal Rules of Criminal Procedure, 11 (C) (1) (Amended December 1, 2002).

45 John Kramer and Jeffrey Ulmer, "Downward Departures for Serious Violent Offenders: Local Court 'Corrections' to Pennsylvania's Sentencing Guidelines," *Criminology* 40 (2002): 897–933.

46 American Bar Association, *Model Uniform Victims of Crime Act* (Chicago: 1992).

47 National Institute of Law Enforcement and Criminal Justice, *Plea Bargaining in the United States,* pp. 37–40.

48 Gary Blankenship, "Debating the Pros and Cons of Plea Bargaining," *Florida Bar News* 30 (July 15, 2003): 6–7.

49 Candace McCoy, *Politics and Plea Bargaining: Victims' Rights in California* (Philadelphia: University of Pennsylvania Press, 1993).

50 National District Attorneys Association, *National Prosecution Standards,* 2d ed. (Alexandria, Va.: 1991), p. 130.

51 Franklyn Dunford, D. Wayne Osgood, and Hart Weichselbaum, *National Evaluation of Diversion Programs* (Washington, D.C.: Government Printing Office, 1982).

52 Sharla Rausch and Charles Logan, "Diversion from Juvenile Court: Panacea or Pandora's Box?" in *Evaluating Juvenile Justice,* ed. James Kleugel (Beverly Hills, Calif.: Sage, 1983), pp. 19–30.

53 See Malcolm Feeley, *Court Reform on Trial* (New York: Basic Books, 1983).

Chapter Outline

Chapter Objectives

After reading this chapter, you should be able to:

1. Understand the concept of the jury trial.
2. Know what it means to confront witnesses.
3. Recognize the term *speedy trial.*
4. Explain the concept of the pro se defense.
5. Discuss what a fair trial means.
6. Argue the right of the press to attend trials.
7. Discuss the issues surrounding the broadcast of criminal trials.
8. Know the difference between a challenge for cause and a peremptory challenge.
9. Identify the different ways evidence is presented in criminal trials.
10. Explain the concept of proof beyond a reasonable doubt.

Viewpoints

 Images of Justice: TV or Not TV? Should Criminal Trials Be Televised? 370

 Law in Review: *Batson* v. *Kentucky* (1986) 373

 Race, Gender, and Ethnicity in Criminal Justice: Jury Selection and Peremptory Challenges 376

Web Links

 # InfoTrac College Edition Links

Chapter 12 | The Criminal Trial

On January 18, 2002, Sara Jane Olson was sentenced to 20 years to life in prison for her role in a failed bomb plot to kill Los Angeles police officers in 1975. Then known as Kathy Soliah, a member of the radical Symbionese Liberation Army (SLA), Olson escaped capture and fled to Minnesota, where she led a quiet life. She married a doctor, raised a family, and became an upstanding member of the community engaging in many charitable works. Then, in a segment of the TV show *America's Most Wanted,* pictures of Soliah and another SLA fugitive, James Kilgore, were broadcast and the FBI offered a $20,000 reward for information leading to Soliah's capture. Identified by someone who watched the show, she peacefully surrendered to the police on June 16, 1999, after being pulled over a few blocks from her home.

During trial, Olson's defense attorneys suffered one setback after another. They argued she could not hope to get a fair hearing in light of the events of September 11, 2001. The judge sided with the prosecutors, who said that international acts of terrorism have no bearing on any case in the court system, even one involving domestic terrorism. The judge also ruled that prosecutors could present evidence of the Symbionese Liberation Army's history of criminal acts during Olson's trial, even though she was not accused of participating in them. The judge said that all the acts were relevant because they showed the deadly intentions of the group.

The Olson case illustrates the difficulty of getting a fair trial in a highly charged political environment. Might she have been found not guilty if the September 11 terrorist acts had never taken place? Can such high-profile cases ever hope to get fair and unbiased juries? The Olson case aptly illustrates the moral and legal dilemmas that are raised when such issues as pretrial publicity and televised trials are considered. It also raises issues about the purpose of prosecuting and punishing criminal defendants. This middle-aged mother hardly presents a danger to society. Given that Sarah Jane Olson had rehabilitated herself, was her prosecution and trial merely a cruel afterthought? Then again, should she be rewarded with lenient treatment because she was able to escape capture and elude the authorities for 25 years? Her sterling record as a wife and mother could have been

accomplished only because she evaded the grasp of the law at the time her crimes were committed. Should a rapist be freed merely because he escaped capture for 20 years?[1]

CNN *View the CNN video clip of this story on your Introduction to Criminal Justice 10e CD.*

WWW On November 6, 2002, Sara Jane Olson, along with three other former members of the Symbionese Liberation Army, agreed to plead guilty to murder in the shotgun slaying of a bank customer during a 1975 holdup. They were charged with first-degree murder but agreed to plead guilty to second-degree murder in a deal with prosecutors to avoid a possible sentence of life in prison. Olson received a six-year sentence for the crime, which she will have to serve after completing her earlier sentence. To read more about the Olson case, go to the Court TV site at http://www.courttv.com/trials/soliah/.

adjudication (adult)
The determination of guilt or innocence; a judgment concerning criminal charges.

The center point of the **adjudication** process is the criminal trial, an open and public hearing designed to examine the facts of the case brought by the state against the accused. Though trials are relatively rare events and most cases are settled by a plea bargain, the trial is an important and enduring fixture in the criminal justice system. By its very nature, it is a symbol of the moral authority of the state. The criminal trial is the symbol of the administration of objective and impartial justice. Regardless of the issues involved, the defendant's presence in a courtroom is designed to guarantee that he will have a hearing conducted under rules of procedure in an atmosphere of fair play and objectivity and that the outcome of the hearing will be clear and definitive. If the defendant believes that his constitutional rights and privileges have been violated, he may appeal the case to a higher court, where the procedures of the original trial will be examined. If, after examining the trial transcript, the appellate court rules that the original trial employed improper and unconstitutional procedures, it may order a new hearing be held or order that the charges against the defendant be dismissed.

bench trial
The trial of a criminal matter by a judge without a jury.

Most formal trials are heard by a jury, though some defendants waive their constitutional right to a jury trial and request a **bench trial** in which the judge alone renders a verdict. In this situation, which occurs daily in the lower criminal courts, the judge may initiate a number of formal or informal dispositions, including dismissing the case, finding the defendant not guilty, finding the defendant guilty and imposing a sentence, or continuing the case indefinitely. Bench trials may also occur in serious felonies. For example, in 2003 James C. Kopp, the accused killer of Dr. Barnett A. Slepian, an abortion provider in Buffalo, New York, waived his right to a jury trial and requested a bench trial. Kopp, who had admitted that he shot and killed Slepian with an assault rifle in 1998, was warned by the trial judge that he was giving up the most logical defense tactic; that is, having his lawyers appeal to the emotions and religious principles of a jury.[2] Kopp proceeded nonetheless, was found guilty, and was given a long prison sentence.

The decision the judge makes often depends on the seriousness of the offense, the background and previous record of the defendant, and the judgment of the court about whether the case can be properly dealt with in the criminal process. Instead of holding a trial, the judge may simply continue the case without a finding, which means the verdict is withheld without a finding of guilt to induce the accused to improve her behavior in the community. If the defendant's behavior does improve, the case is ordinarily closed within a specific amount of time.

Legal Rights during Trial

Underlying every trial are constitutional principles, complex legal procedures, rules of court, and interpretation of statutes, all designed to ensure that the accused will receive a fair trial.

The Right to be Competent at Trial

To stand trial, a criminal defendant must be considered mentally competent to understand the nature and extent of the legal proceedings. If a defendant is considered mentally incompetent, his trial must be postponed until treatment renders him capable of participating in his own defense. Can state authorities force a mentally unfit defendant to be treated so that he can be tried? In *Riggins* v. *Nevada* (1992), the U.S. Supreme Court ruled that forced treatment does not violate a defendant's due process rights if it was medically appropriate and, considering less intrusive alternatives, was essential for the defendant's own safety or the safety of others.[3] In a 2003 case, *Sell* v. *United States,* the Court set out four rules that guide the use of forced medication.[4]

© 2003 AP/Wide World Photos

The right to confront witnesses is guaranteed by the Sixth Amendment.

1.   A court must find that important governmental interests are at stake. Courts must consider each case's facts in evaluating this interest because special circumstances may lessen its importance. For example, a defendant's refusal to take drugs may mean lengthy confinement in an institution, which would diminish the risks of freeing without punishment one who has committed a serious crime.
2.   The court must conclude that forced medication will significantly further state interests. It must find that medication is substantially likely to render the defendant competent to stand trial and substantially unlikely to have side effects that will interfere significantly with the defendant's ability to assist counsel in conducting a defense.
3.   The court must conclude that involuntary medication is necessary to further state interests and find that alternative, less intrusive treatments are unlikely to achieve substantially the same results.
4.   The court must conclude that administering the drugs is medically appropriate.

The Right to Confront Witnesses

The Sixth Amendment states, "In all criminal prosecutions, the accused shall enjoy the right . . . to be confronted with the witnesses against him." The **confrontation clause** is essential to a fair criminal trial because it restricts and controls the admissibility of hearsay evidence. Secondhand evidence, which depends on a witness not available in court, is ordinarily limited; the personal knowledge of a witness or victim of a crime is preferred. The framers of the Constitution sought face-to-face accusations in which the defendant has a right to see and cross-examine all witnesses against him or her. The idea that it is always more difficult to tell lies about people to their face than behind their back underlies the point of the confrontation clause. A witness in a criminal trial may have more difficulty repeating his or her testimony when facing the accused in a trial than in providing information to the police during an investigation. The accused has the right to confront any witnesses and challenge their assertions and perceptions: Did they really see what they believe? Are they biased? Can they be trusted? What about the veracity of their testimony? Generally speaking, the courts have

confrontation clause
The constitutional right of a criminal defendant to see and cross-examine all the witnesses against him or her.

been nearly unanimous in their belief that the right to confrontation and cross-examination is an essential requirement for a fair trial.[5]

This face-to-face presence was reviewed by the Supreme Court in a case involving a child as a witness in criminal proceedings. In *Coy* v. *Iowa* (1988), the Supreme Court limited the protection available to child sex victims at the trial stage.[6] In *Coy,* two girls were allowed to be cross-examined behind a screen that separated them from the defendant. The Court ruled that the screen violated the defendant's right to confront witnesses and overturned his conviction. However, in her supporting opinion, Justice Sandra Day O'Connor made it clear that ruling out the protective screen did not bar the states from using videotapes or closed-circuit television. Although Justice O'Connor recognized that the Sixth Amendment right to confront witnesses was violated, she indicated that an exception to a literal interpretation of the confrontation clause might be appropriate.

In *Maryland* v. *Craig* (1990), the Supreme Court carved out an exception to the Sixth Amendment confrontation clause by deciding that alleged child abuse victims could testify by closed-circuit television if face-to-face confrontation would cause them trauma.[7] In allowing the states to take testimony via closed-circuit television, the Supreme Court found that circumstances exist in child sex abuse cases that override the defendant's right of confrontation.

As a result of these decisions, the confrontation clause does not appear to guarantee criminal defendants the absolute right to a face-to-face meeting with witnesses at their trial. Instead, according to *Maryland* v. *Craig,* it reflects a preference for such a guarantee. *Craig* signals that the Court is willing to compromise a defendant's right to confront his or her accuser to achieve a social objective, the prosecution of a child abuser.

The Right to a Jury Trial

The defendant has the right to choose whether the trial will be before a judge or a jury. Although the Sixth Amendment guarantees the defendant the right to a jury trial, the defendant can and often does waive this right. A substantial proportion of defendants, particularly those charged with misdemeanors, are tried before the court without a jury.

The major legal issue surrounding jury trial has been whether all defendants, those accused of misdemeanors as well as felonies, have an absolute right to a jury trial. Although the U.S. Constitution is silent on this point, the U.S. Supreme Court has ruled that all defendants in felony cases have this right. In *Duncan* v. *Louisiana* (1968), the Court held that the Sixth Amendment right to a jury trial is applicable to all states, as well as to the federal government, and that it can be interpreted to apply to all defendants accused of serious crimes.[8] The Court in *Duncan* based its holding on the premise that in the American states, as in the federal judicial system, a general grant of jury trial for serious offenses is a fundamental right, essential for preventing miscarriages of justice and for assuring that fair trials are provided for all defendants.[9]

The *Duncan* decision did not settle whether all defendants charged with crimes in state courts are constitutionally entitled to jury trials. It seemed to draw the line at only those charged with serious offenses, leaving the decision to grant jury trials to defendants in minor cases to the discretion of the individual states.

In 1970, in *Baldwin* v. *New York,* the Supreme Court departed from the distinction of serious versus minor offenses and decided that a defendant has a constitutional right to a jury trial when facing a possible prison sentence of six months or more, regardless of whether the crime committed was a felony or a misdemeanor.[10] When the possible sentence is six months or less, the accused is not entitled to a jury trial unless it is authorized by state statute. In most jurisdictions, the more serious the charge, the greater likelihood of trial—and of a trial by jury.

The Supreme Court has used six months' potential imprisonment as the dividing line between petty offenses for which the Sixth Amendment gives no right to jury trial and serious offenses that enjoy such a legal right. In *Lewis* v. *United States* (1996), the Court faced the unusual problem of multiple petty offenses that, when added together, could lead to imprisonment in excess of six months.[11] The defendant argued that he was constitutionally entitled to a jury trial. But the Supreme Court said there was no Sixth Amendment right to a jury trial for a string of petty offenses tried together, even when the potential total sentence could exceed six months. The Court's reasoning was that the legislature was responsible for the design of an offense with a maximum possible penalty, and the prosecutor has the right to exercise discretion to join different offenses in one trial without defeating the legislative intent to distinguish between petty and serious offenses.

In sum, the Sixth Amendment guarantees the right to a jury trial. The accused can waive this right and be tried by a judge, who then becomes the fact finder as well as the determiner of the law.

Other important issues related to the defendant's rights in a criminal jury trial include the right to a jury of 12 people and the right to a unanimous verdict.

Jury Size The size of the jury has been a matter of great concern. Can a defendant be tried and convicted of a crime by a jury of fewer than 12 persons? Traditionally, 12 jurors have deliberated as the triers of fact in criminal cases involving misdemeanors or felonies. However, the Constitution does not specifically require a jury of 12 persons. As a result, in *Williams* v. *Florida* (1970), the Supreme Court held that a six-person jury in a criminal trial does not deprive a defendant of the constitutional right to a jury trial.[12] The Court made clear that the 12-person panel is not a necessary ingredient of the trial by jury and upheld a Florida statute permitting the use of a six-person jury in a robbery trial. The majority opinion in the *Williams* case traced the Court's rationale for its decision.

> *We conclude, in short, as we began: the fact that a jury at common law was composed of precisely twelve is a historical accident, unnecessary to effect the purposes of the jury system and wholly without significance "except to mystics."*[13]

Justice Byron R. White, writing further for the majority, said,

> *In short, while sometime in the 14th century the size of the jury came to be fixed generally at 12, that particular feature of the jury system appears to have been a historical accident, unrelated to the great purpose which gave rise to the jury in the first place.*[14]

On the basis of this decision, many states are using six-person juries in misdemeanor cases, and some states, such as Florida, Louisiana, and Utah, use them in felony cases (except in capital offenses). In the *Williams* decision, Justice White emphasized, "We have an occasion to determine what minimum number can still constitute a jury, but do not doubt that six is above the minimum."[15]

The six-person jury can play an important role in the criminal justice system because it promotes court efficiency and also helps implement the defendant's rights to a speedy trial. However, the Supreme Court has ruled that a jury composed of fewer than six people is unconstitutional and that, if a **six-person jury** is used in serious crimes, its verdict must be unanimous.[16] *Williams* v. *Florida,* decided more than 30 years ago, offered a welcome measure of relief to an overburdened crime control system. Today, jury size can be reduced for all but the most serious criminal cases.

In addition to the convention of 12-person juries in criminal trials, tradition had been that the jurors' decision must be unanimous. However, in *Apodaca* v. *Oregon* (1972), the Supreme Court held that the Sixth and Fourteenth Amendments do not prohibit criminal convictions by less than unanimous jury verdicts in noncapital cases.[17] In the *Apodaca* case, the Court upheld an Oregon statute

six-person jury
Because the U.S. Supreme Court has ruled that the Constitution does not require a 12-person jury, states allow juries of lesser size, the minimum being six people.

requiring only 10 of 12 jurors to convict the defendant of assault with a deadly weapon, burglary, and grand larceny.

Nonunanimous verdicts are not unusual in civil matters, but much controversy remains regarding their place in the criminal process. Those in favor of less than unanimous verdicts argue, as the Court stated in *Apodaca,* that unanimity does not materially contribute to the exercise of commonsense judgment. Some also believe that it would be easier for the prosecutor to obtain a guilty plea verdict if the law required only a substantial majority to convict the defendant. Today, the unanimous verdict remains the rule in the federal system and all but two state jurisdictions. Unanimity is required in six-person jury trials.

The Right to Counsel at Trial

Through a series of leading U.S. Supreme Court decisions (*Powell* v. *Alabama* in 1932, *Gideon* v. *Wainwright* in 1963, and *Argersinger* v. *Hamlin* in 1972), the right of a criminal defendant to have counsel in state trials has become fundamental in the U.S. criminal justice system.[18] Today, state courts must provide counsel at trial to indigent defendants who face the possibility of incarceration.

The historical development of the law regarding right to counsel reflects the gradual process of decision making in the Supreme Court. It also reiterates the relationship between the Bill of Rights, which protects citizens against federal encroachment, and the Fourteenth Amendment, which provides that no state shall deprive any person of life, liberty, or property without due process of law. A difficult constitutional question has been whether the Fourteenth Amendment incorporates the Bill of Rights and makes its provisions binding on individual states.

In *Powell* v. *Alabama* (also known as the "Scottsboro boys" case), nine black men were charged in an Alabama court with raping two young white women. They were tried and convicted without the benefit of counsel. The U.S. Supreme Court concluded that the presence of a defense attorney is so vital to a fair trial that the failure of the Alabama trial court to appoint counsel was a denial of due process of law under the Fourteenth Amendment. In this instance, due process meant the right to counsel for defendants accused of a capital offense.

More than 30 years later, in *Gideon* v. *Wainwright,* the Supreme Court in a unanimous and historic decision stated that, although the Sixth Amendment does not explicitly lay down a rule binding on the states, the right to counsel is so fundamental to a fair trial that states are obligated to abide by it under the Fourteenth Amendment's due process clause. Thus, the Sixth Amendment requirement regarding the right to counsel in the federal court system is also binding on the states.

The *Gideon* decision made it clear that a person charged with a felony in a state court has an absolute constitutional right to counsel. But whereas some states applied the *Gideon* ruling to all criminal trials, others did not provide a defendant with an attorney in misdemeanor cases. Then, in 1972, in the momentous decision of *Argersinger* v. *Hamlin,* the Supreme Court held that no person can be imprisoned for any offense—whether classified as a petty offense, a misdemeanor, or a felony—unless he or she is offered representation by counsel at trial. The decision extended this right to virtually all defendants in state criminal prosecutions.

What about a case in which incarceration is not on the table but could be an issue later on? In *Alabama* v. *Shelton* (2002), the Court ruled that a defendant must be represented by counsel if he receives a probation sentence in which a prison or jail term is suspended but can later be imposed if the rules of probation are violated. In other words, if the sentence contains even a threat of future incarceration, the defendant must be afforded the right to counsel at trial.[19] In its decision, the Court stated: "We hold that a suspended sentence that may end up in the actual deprivation of a person's liberty may not be imposed unless the defendant was accorded 'the guiding hand of counsel' in the prosecution for the

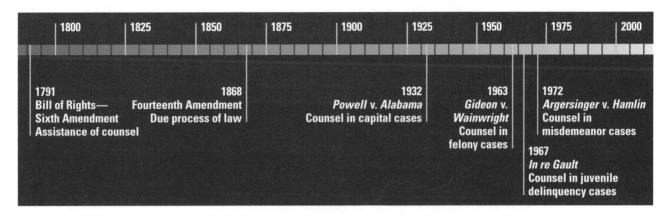

Figure 12.1
Historical Time Line of Right to Counsel

Source: Almost two centuries were needed to establish that adults and juveniles have a right to counsel at trial.

crime charged."[20] *Shelton* may be interpreted as saying any person who is currently in jail on the basis of a probation violation and who did not have legal representation at trial is being held unconstitutionally.

The time line in Figure 12.1 tracks the almost 200 years it has taken to establish what the U.S. Constitution stated in 1791: "In all criminal prosecutions, the accused shall enjoy the right . . . to have the assistance of counsel for his defense."

Perspectives on Justice

Tremendous indigent defense caseload increases have far outpaced increases in funding. Underfunding is the major problem for virtually all of the public defender offices in America. Yet, the emergence and growth of professional criminal defense attorneys for indigent defendants are among the most important contemporary developments in the criminal justice system. Today, criminal defendants are granted the right to an attorney at almost all stages of the legal process. The success of indigent defenders is attributable to the use of the due process model.

The Right to Self-Representation

Are criminal defendants guaranteed the right to represent themselves—that is, to act as their own lawyers? Prior to the 1975 Supreme Court decision in *Faretta* v. *California,* defendants in most state courts and in the federal system claimed the right to proceed **pro se,** or for themselves, by reason of federal and state statutes and on state constitutional grounds.[21] This permitted defendants to choose between hiring counsel or conducting their own defense. Whether a constitutional right to represent oneself in a criminal prosecution existed remained an open question until the *Faretta* decision.

The defendant, Anthony Faretta, was charged with grand theft in Los Angeles County. Before his trial, he requested that he be permitted to represent himself. The judge told Faretta that he believed this would be a mistake but accepted his waiver of counsel. The judge then held a hearing to inquire into Faretta's ability to conduct his own defense and subsequently ruled that Faretta had not made an intelligent and knowing waiver of his right to assistance of counsel. As a result, the judge appointed a public defender to represent Faretta, who was brought to trial, found guilty, and sentenced to prison. He appealed, claiming that he had a constitutional right to self-representation.

Upon review, the U.S. Supreme Court recognized Faretta's pro se right on a constitutional basis, while making it conditional on a showing that the defendant could competently, knowingly, and intelligently waive his right to counsel. The

pro se

To present one's own defense in a criminal trial; self-representation.

Court's decision was based on the belief that the right of self-representation is supported by the Sixth Amendment, as well as by English and colonial jurisprudence from which the amendment emerged. Thus, in forcing Faretta to accept counsel against his will, the California trial court deprived him of his constitutional right to conduct his own defense.

Today, a defendant in a criminal trial is able to waive the right to the assistance of counsel. Generally, however, the courts have encouraged defendants to accept counsel so that criminal trials may proceed in an orderly and fair manner. When defendants ask to be permitted to represent themselves and are found competent to do so, the court normally approves their requests. The defendants in these cases are almost always cautioned by the courts against self-representation. When pro se defendants' actions are disorderly and disruptive, the court can terminate their right to represent themselves.

No ruling, similar to *Faretta,* has been made that a defendant has a federal constitutional right to prosecute his own criminal appeal. In *Martinez* v. *Court of Appeals of California* (2000), the U.S. Supreme Court indicated that historical and practical differences between trials and appeals convinced them that due process does not require a recognition of the right to self-representation in criminal appeals.[22]

The Right to a Speedy Trial

The requirement of the right to counsel at trial in virtually all criminal cases often causes delays in the formal processing of defendants through the court system. Counsel usually seeks to safeguard the interests of the accused and in doing so may employ a variety of legal devices (pretrial motions, plea negotiations, trial procedures, and appeals) that require time and extend the decision-making period in a particular case. The involvement of counsel, along with inefficiencies in the court process—such as the frequent granting of continuances, poor scheduling procedures, and the abuse of time by court personnel—has made the problem of delay in criminal cases a serious constitutional issue. According to the American Bar Association's *Standards Relating to Speedy Trial,* "Congestion in the trial courts of this country, particularly in urban centers, is currently one of the major problems of judicial administration."[23]

The Sixth Amendment guarantees a criminal defendant the right to a speedy trial in federal prosecutions. This right was made applicable to the states by the decision in *Klopfer* v. *North Carolina* (1967).[24] In this case, the defendant Klopfer was charged with criminal trespass. His original trial ended in a mistrial, and he sought to determine if and when the government intended to retry him. The prosecutor asked the court for a *nolle prosequi with leave,* a legal device discharging the defendant but allowing the government to prosecute him in the future. The U.S. Supreme Court held that the government's attempt to postpone Klopfer's trial indefinitely without reason denied him the right to a speedy trial guaranteed by the Sixth and Fourteenth Amendments.

In *Klopfer,* the Supreme Court emphasized the importance of the speedy trial in the criminal process, stating that this right was "as fundamental as any of the rights secured by the Sixth Amendment."[25] Its primary purposes are

- To improve the credibility of the trial by seeking to have witnesses available for testimony as early as possible.
- To reduce the anxiety for the defendant in awaiting trial, as well as to avoid pretrial detention.
- To avoid extensive pretrial publicity and questionable conduct of public officials that would influence the defendant's right to a fair trial.
- To avoid any delay that can affect the defendant's ability to defend himself or herself.

Since the *Klopfer* case in 1967, the Supreme Court has dealt with the speedy trial guarantee on numerous occasions. One example is the 1992 case of *Doggett* v. *United States*, in which the Court found that a delay of eight-and-a-half years between indictment and arrest was prejudicial to the defendant and required a dismissal of the charges.[26]

Because of court backlogs, the government has been forced to deal with the problem of how to meet the constitutional requirement of a speedy trial. The President's Commission on Law Enforcement and the Administration of Justice in 1967 suggested that nine months would be a reasonable period of time in which to litigate the typical criminal felony case through appeal. The process from arrest through trial would take four months, and the decision of an appeals court an additional five months.[27] In 1973, the National Advisory Commission on Criminal Justice Standards and Goals recommended that the period from the arrest of the defendant in a felony prosecution to the beginning of the trial should generally not be longer than 60 days and that the period from arrest to trial in a misdemeanor prosecution should be no more than 30 days.[28]

Today, most states and the federal government have statutes fixing the period of time during which an accused must be brought to trial. These requirements ensure that a person's trial cannot be unduly delayed and that the suspect cannot be held in custody indefinitely. The federal Speedy Trial Act of 1974 established the following time limits.

- An information or indictment charging a person with a crime must be filed within 30 days of the time of arrest.
- The arraignment must be held within 10 days of the time of the information or indictment.
- The trial must be held within 60 days of the arraignment.[29]

This means that the accused must be brought to trial in the federal system within 100 days of arrest. Other special provisions of the Speedy Trial Act include the gradual phasing in of time standards, the use of fines against defense counsels for causing delays, and the allocation of funds with which to plan speedy trial programs in the federal judicial districts. The Speedy Trial Act was amended in 1979 to more precisely define what constitutes the guarantee of a speedy trial and to encourage state jurisdictions to adopt similar procedures. Many state speedy trial statutes provide even shorter time limits when a defendant is detained in jail.

Long delays have been a central feature of the U.S. justice system. Many states have found that dramatic results can be achieved in reducing such extreme delays by establishing special courts to deal with, for example, drug-related crimes or homicide. These courts aim to get cases to trial within 60 days of a defendant's initial appearance. The results often include shortened disposition time, reduced case backlogs, increased convictions, and lowered pretrial jail costs. The success of speedy trial courts also enhances the quality of justice for defendants and the public by getting victims and witnesses to attend court proceedings and to give reliable and accurate testimony.

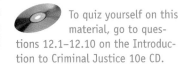

To quiz yourself on this material, go to questions 12.1–12.10 on the Introduction to Criminal Justice 10e CD.

Fair Trial versus Free Press

Every person charged with a crime has a fundamental right to a fair trial. What does it mean to have a fair trial in the criminal justice system? A fair trial is one before an impartial judge and jury in an environment of judicial restraint, orderliness, and fair decision making. Although it is not expressly stated in the U.S. Constitution, the right of the accused to a fair trial is guaranteed by the due process clause of the Fifth Amendment.

This fair trial right can be violated in a number of ways. A hostile courtroom crowd, improper pressure on witnesses, or any behavior that produces prejudice toward the accused can preclude a fair trial. When a defendant was required to go to trial in prison clothing, for example, the U.S. Supreme Court found a violation of the due process clause of the Fourteenth Amendment.[30] Adverse pretrial publicity can also deny a defendant a fair trial. The release of premature evidence by the prosecutor, extensive and critical reporting by the news media, and vivid and uncalled-for details in indictments can all prejudice a defendant's case.

Recently, one of the most controversial issues involving the conduct of a trial has been the apparent conflict between the constitutional guarantees of fair trial and freedom of the press. When there is widespread pretrial publicity, as in the Menendez brothers murder case and the Rodney King police brutality case, can an accused defendant get a fair trial as guaranteed by the Fifth, Sixth, and Fourteenth Amendments? Think about the intense media coverage in the O. J. Simpson double murder trial, the Timothy McVeigh Oklahoma City bombing case, and the Louise Woodward child murder case. The murder conviction of Dr. Sam Sheppard more than 30 years ago was reversed by the U.S. Supreme Court because negative publicity generated by the government denied Sheppard a fair trial.[31] In one of the most highly publicized cases in U.S. history, Claus von Bulow was acquitted of the attempted murder of his wife after two trials.[32] Both the prosecution and the defense used the media to reflect its side. Press conferences, leaked news stories, and daily television and radio coverage all contributed to a media sideshow. Even jury sequestration was not successful because many of the jurors had prior knowledge of the case. In the end, the media played a critical role in both the initial conviction and the subsequent acquittal on retrial of the defendant.

Judges involved in newsworthy criminal trials have attempted to place restraints on media coverage to preserve the defendant's right to a fair trial. At the same time, it is generally believed that the media have a constitutional right to provide news coverage. Judge Lance Ito faced these issues in limiting the media's access in the O. J. Simpson trial. He threatened a television blackout, temporarily banned the *Los Angeles Times* for its early release of the juror questionnaire, and tinkered with television cameras after a broadcast showed jurors from another trial. This represents the classic conflict between the Constitution's First Amendment guarantee of press freedom and the Sixth Amendment guarantee of a fair trial.

Some critics have suggested that the media should be prohibited from reporting about ongoing criminal trials. Such an approach, however, would inhibit the role of the press under the First Amendment. Public information about criminal trials, the judicial system, and other areas of government is an indispensable characteristic of a free society. At the same time, trial by the media violates a defendant's right to a fair trial. Still, publicity is essential to preserving confidence in the trial system, even though this principle may occasionally clash with the defendant's right to a fair trial.

The Law of Fair Trial

The U.S. Supreme Court dealt with the fair trial–free press issue in *Nebraska Press Association* v. *Stuart* (1976).[33] The Court ruled unconstitutional a trial judge's order that prohibited the press from reporting confessions implicating the defendant in the crime. The Court's decision was based primarily on the principle that "prior restraints on speech and publication are the most serious and least tolerable infringement on First Amendment rights."[34]

In *Gannett Co.* v. *DePasquale* (1979), the Court was asked to decide if the public had an independent constitutional right of access to a pretrial hearing, even though all the parties agreed to closure to guarantee a fair trial.[35]Justice Potter Stewart, writing for the Court, said that the trial court was correct in finding that the press had a right of access of constitutional dimensions but that this right was outweighed by the defendant's right to a fair trial.[36] The Court balanced competing social interests and found that denial of access to the public did not violate the First (free press), Sixth (fair trial), or Fourteenth (due process) Amendment rights of the defendant. The interests of justice require that the defendant's case should not be jeopardized, and the desire for a fair trial far outweighed the public's right of access to a pretrial suppression hearing. The *Gannett* decision is not ordinarily cited as a precedent to determine whether a right of access to trials is constitutionally guaranteed, because the Court believes that pretrial hearings are not trials.

The question of the First Amendment right of access to preliminary hearings was raised again in *Press-Enterprise Co.* v. *Superior Court* (1986).[37] The defendant, charged with murder, agreed to have the preliminary hearing closed to the press and the public. But the Supreme Court said that closure is permissible under the First Amendment only if a substantial probability exists that the defendant's right to a fair trial would be prejudiced by publicity that closed proceedings would prevent. According to the Court, preliminary hearings have traditionally been open to the public and should remain so. The *Press-Enterprise* case clearly established the First Amendment right of access to criminal trials.

In an important 1993 case involving pretrial hearings, a reporter for the largest newspaper in Puerto Rico was denied access to a probable cause hearing because of a rule in the Commonwealth of Puerto Rico requiring that the hearings be held privately. The Supreme Court held that this rule violated the First Amendment to the Constitution and, based on the *Press-Enterprise* case, indicated that a pretrial hearing cannot be closed to the press unless prejudice will result to the accused.[38]

The Right to a Public Trial

The U.S. Supreme Court has also interpreted the First Amendment to mean that members of the press (and the public) have a right to attend trials. The most important case on this issue is *Richmond Newspapers Inc.* v. *Commonwealth of Virginia* (1980).[39] Here, the Supreme Court clearly established that criminal trials must remain public.

Although the Court has ruled that criminal trials are open to the press, the right to a public trial is basically for the benefit of the accused.[40] The familiar language of the Sixth Amendment clearly states that "the accused shall enjoy the right to a speedy and public trial." This provision is rooted in the principle that justice cannot survive behind walls of silence. It was enacted because the framers of the Constitution distrusted secret trials and arbitrary proceedings. Settlers brought this concept to colonial America from England, where the wisdom of holding criminal trials in public predates the Norman Conquest.

In the 1948 case of *In re Oliver*, the Supreme Court held that the secrecy of a criminal contempt trial violated the right of the defendant to a public trial under the Fourteenth Amendment.[41] Thus, the Court recognized the constitutional guarantee of a public trial for defendants in state as well as federal courts. Three decades later, the *Richmond Newspapers* decision clearly affirmed the right of the public and the press to attend criminal trials.[42] Thus, criminal trials may not be closed unless findings are sufficient to overcome the presumption of openness.

Concept Summary 12.1 summarizes the decisions guaranteeing the defendant's constitutional rights at trial.

Televising Criminal Trials

Other fair trial–free press issues remain, however. Whether jury trials should be televised, for instance, is one of the most controversial questions in the criminal justice system today. The legal community was divided over the use of television cameras in the courtroom for the highly publicized 10-day rape trial of William Kennedy Smith.[43] Smith's acquittal also raised the question of whether the media

Concept Summary 12.1 Decisions Affirming the Defendant's Constitutional Rights at Trial

Constitutional right	Decision
Confrontation of witnesses	*Coy* v. *Iowa*
Jury trial	*Duncan* v. *Louisiana*
Right to counsel	*Gideon* v. *Wainwright*
Self-representation	*Faretta* v. *California*
Speedy trial	*Klopfer* v. *North Carolina*
Fair trial, free press	*Nebraska Press Association* v. *Stuart*
Public trial	*Richmond Newspapers Inc.* v. *Commonwealth of Virginia*

should protect the privacy rights of the rape victim; that is, whether they should reveal her name and display her picture.

In another case that received a great deal of media coverage, Mike Tyson, the former heavyweight boxing champion, was convicted in 1992 of raping a Miss Black America contestant. She said he lured her to his hotel room and overpowered her. Because of the interest in the trial, closed-circuit television was used to accommodate the more than 100 news organizations that covered the trial.

Judges involved in such high-profile trials are faced with placing restrictions not only on press coverage but also on television coverage. In the Tyson trial, the State of Indiana, which normally does not allow television cameras in its courts, acquiesced in the use of closed-circuit television. Colorado, meanwhile, refused to allow television coverage of the Timothy McVeigh trial. In the so-called trial of the century, *People* v. *O. J. Simpson,* unedited television coverage allowed Americans to see the entire trial. This courtroom drama was seen on two continents and received worldwide attention. Cases of this magnitude have intense emotional appeal, provoke arguments, and generate enormous public interest.

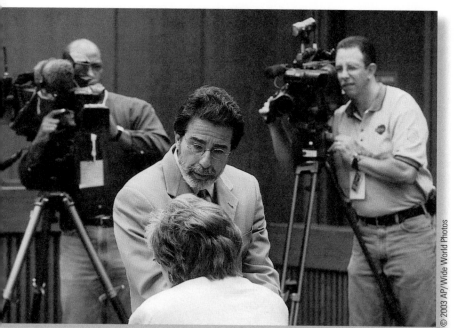

© 2003 AP/Wide World Photos

Today, many state courts permit such coverage, often at the judge's discretion, but the use of television cameras, video recorders, and still photography is banned in the federal court system.[44] In addition, Chief Justice William H. Rehnquist opposes televising Supreme Court proceedings. After a two-year study, the U.S. Judicial Conference decided in 1995 to continue to ban cameras in the federal courts. Camera advocates may try to get federal legislation passed to permit cameras in the federal system.[45]

A defense attorney speaks to one of his assistants during a televised trial. Though broadcasting high-profile cases has become routine, some critics question whether it invades privacy rights and jeopardizes the right to receive a fair trial.

Televising criminal proceedings could have significant advantages. Judges would be better prepared; the public would be informed about important legal issues; and the proceedings would serve an educational function, offsetting the simplistic views offered by television programs and feature films. The extent to which judges, witnesses, and the accused would be influenced by the use of modern technology in the courtroom remains unknown, however, and is the major argument against adopting total media coverage. In extreme cases, the judge might ban the media if televising the case risked igniting violence or if the rights of the accused and the state might be at risk. Also, under the statutes of different jurisdictions, spectators and the press might be excluded from the trial of juvenile cases, certain sordid sex crimes, or national security offenses.

Regardless of the kind of crime committed, a defendant is always permitted to have family, close associates, and legal counsel at his or her trial. Still, the Supreme Court has held, in *Chandler* v. *Florida* (1981), that subject to certain safeguards, a state may allow electronic media coverage by television stations and still photography of public criminal proceedings over the objection of the defendant in a criminal trial.[46] The Supreme Court did not maintain in *Chandler* that the media had a constitutional right to televise trials; it left it up to state courts to decide whether they wanted trials televised in their jurisdictions.

The controversy surrounding the televising of trials has prompted bar and media groups to develop standards in an attempt to find an acceptable middle ground between the First and Sixth Amendment rights concerning public trials. The defendant has a constitutional right to a public trial, and the media must be able to exercise their First Amendment rights. Above all, the court must seek to protect the rights of the accused to a fair trial by an unbiased jury.

The Images of Justice feature on page 370 discusses further the topic of televised trials.

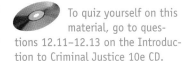

To quiz yourself on this material, go to questions 12.11–12.13 on the Introduction to Criminal Justice 10e CD.

The Trial Process

The trial of a criminal case is a formal process conducted in a specific and orderly fashion in accordance with rules of criminal law, procedure, and evidence. Unlike what transpires in popular television programs involving lawyers—where witnesses are often asked leading and prejudicial questions and where judges go far beyond their supervisory role—the modern criminal trial is a complicated and often time-consuming technical affair. It is a structured adversary proceeding in which both the prosecution and defense follow specific procedures and argue the merits of their cases before the judge and jury.

Each side seeks to present its own case in the most favorable light. When possible, the prosecutor and the defense attorney object to evidence he considers damaging to his side's position. The prosecutor uses direct testimony, physical evidence, and a confession, if available, to convince the jury that the accused is guilty beyond a reasonable doubt. The defense attorney rebuts the government's case with his or her own evidence, makes certain that the rights of the criminal defendant under the federal and state constitutions are considered during all phases of the trial, and determines whether an appeal is appropriate if the client is found guilty. The defense attorney uses his or her skill at cross-examination to discredit government witnesses: Perhaps they have changed their statements from the time they gave them to the police, perhaps their memory is faulty, perhaps their background is unsavory, and so on. From the beginning of the process to its completion, the judge promotes an orderly and fair administration of the criminal trial.

Although each jurisdiction in the United States has its own trial procedures, all jurisdictions conduct criminal trials in a generally similar fashion. The basic steps of the criminal trial, which proceed in an established order, are described in this section and outlined in Figure 12.2 on page 372.

Jury Selection

Jurors are selected randomly in both civil and criminal cases from tax assessment, driver's license, or voter registration lists within each court's jurisdiction. Advocates of more diverse jury pools contend that such lists often do not accurately reflect a

TV or Not TV? Should Criminal Trials Be Televised?

images of justice

On January 18, 2002, a federal judge refused to allow TV cameras into the trial of Zacarias Moussaoui, who was alleged to be one of the September 11, 2001, terrorists. Judge Leonie N. Brinkema, in a 13-page ruling, denied the request of the Court TV cable network to broadcast the trial of Moussaoui, who was charged with six terrorism conspiracy counts. In her ruling, Brinkema wrote that she had no authority to reject a federal court ban on cameras in courtrooms. Even if she did, she would not, she wrote, because, "given the issues raised in this indictment, any societal benefits from photographing and broadcasting these proceedings are heavily outweighed by the significant dangers worldwide broadcasting of this trial would pose to the orderly and secure administration of justice." Her ruling embraced concerns raised by prosecutors that broadcasting the trial would intimidate witnesses, endanger court officers, and provide Moussaoui with a platform to vent his political beliefs. Moussaoui's lawyers favored televising the trial, with restrictions. They argued that the broadcasts would give their client an added layer of protection in getting a fair trial on charges that could result in the death penalty. The decision outraged some commentators who felt the American people were cheated by the decision. Writing in *Newsweek*, Anna Quindlen said that

> the events of September 11 have left a nation of victims, and the number who bear witness should not be determined by the square footage of a courtroom. Let the world see how well the American justice system works. The point of public trials in the first place was to let the people in. In the 21st century, letting the people in means letting the cameras in.

The Supreme Court has upheld the public's right of access to the judicial system but has stopped short of saying the right to a public trial means the right to a televised trial. Justice David H. Souter testified in 1996 before a Senate subcommittee: "The day you see cameras come into our courtroom, it's going to roll over my dead body." Until recently, the justices did not even allow the live audio broadcasting of arguments, though they did permit archival audio taping. In the landmark case of *Bush* v. *Gore*—the case that awarded George W. Bush the presidency after the 2000 election—the justices finally relented and permitted the real-time audio transmission of the final arguments. As Court TV expert Hedieh Nasheri points out, *Bush* v. *Gore* was a good first step, but many Americans wondered why the justices were prepared to be heard but not seen. Today's television cameras require no special lighting, she argues in her book *Crime and Justice in the Age of Court TV,* and can be placed discreetly behind walls so as not to interfere with courtroom proceedings. *Bush* v. *Gore* was a wonderful civics lesson, but it was somewhat incomplete because the television cameras were excluded. One option, she notes, is the Sunshine in the Courtroom Act, which was pending in the 108th Congress (2003–05). This bill would give judges in federal trial and appeals courts discretion to permit cameras in their courtrooms, but it would require them to afford witnesses the option of having their faces and voices obscured.

While federal court rules specifically prohibit the televising of any federal criminal trial, state courts are more flexible. All states now allow some judicial proceedings to be broadcast, and 38 states permit the showing of state criminal trials.

What are the pros and cons for televising criminal trials? Lawyers who represent the news media often point out valid arguments for using cameras in the courtroom.

- Public trials would encourage participants to do a better job;

---

state's ethnic composition. As a result, some jurisdictions are requiring that its poll of prospective jurors include people drawn from welfare and unemployment rolls.

Few states impose qualifications on those called for jury service; many states do mandate a residency requirement.[47] Most jurisdictions also prohibit convicted felons from serving on juries, as well as others exempted by statute, such as public officials, medical doctors, and attorneys. The initial list of persons chosen—called **venire** or *jury array*—provides the state with a group of capable citizens able to serve on a jury. Many states, by rule of law, review the venire to eliminate unqualified persons and to exempt those who by reason of their profession are not allowed to be jurors. The jury selection process begins with those remaining on the list.

The court clerk, who handles the administrative affairs and documents related to the trial, randomly selects enough names (sometimes from a box) to fill the required number of places on the jury. In most cases, the jury in a criminal trial consists of 12 persons, with two alternate jurors standing by to serve should one of the regular jurors be unable to complete the trial. There is little uniformity

venire
The group called for jury duty from which jury panels are selected.

- In a democratic society, the public should have access to all trials, even those of a scandalous nature; and
- TV coverage can contribute to educating the public about the justice system.

Conversely, some defense lawyers and judges believe that televised trials should be restricted because they are only a form of entertainment and suppress the search for truth. Others question whether the public interest outweighs the defendant's ability to obtain a fair trial. Still, resistance to the idea remains firm. The U.S. Judicial Conference, the policy-making body for the federal courts, says cameras in courtrooms raise privacy concerns for witnesses in sensitive cases and put traditionally low-profile, but powerful, federal judges at risk.

One advocate of cameras in the court room is lawyer Ronald Goldfarb, who in his book *TV or Not TV* argues that the proper line between entertainment and education, between exploitation and information, between the negative consequences of televised and nontelevised trials is neither clear nor can it be measured with scientific objectivity. So even though visibility on TV may be a yet unmeasured risk to trial fairness, it is one worth taking. Televising trials keeps the legal system in the "sunlight" and assures that judges, lawyers, and even

witnesses act honestly. Allowing cameras in the courtroom helps the public's perception of the trial as a fair process. The public is more suspicious of the outcome if the trial is held behind closed doors. Goldfarb dismisses critics by stating that "[m]uch of the current criticism of televised trials amounts to killing the messenger while ignoring the message" (p. 164). The media are not at fault for showing that trials are sometimes unfair and boring, or that lawyers may be bullies or incompetent; that is the nature of the trial process and not the media coverage. Instead, he argues, live and inconspicuous television might improve upon some shortcomings of ordinary press coverage of the courts: "One can bribe a reporter, but not a camera" (p. 172).

Goldfarb proposes a regulated system of total media coverage. He foresees cameras in every courtroom, with the broadcast of every trial available for viewing on a publicly run TV station or through the Internet. However, he would also allow for the right to oppose broadcast by a number of people involved in the trial.

Critical Thinking

Three major concerns arise in TV criminal trials: (1) Jurors and potential jurors are exposed to media coverage that may cause

prejudgment; (2) in-court media coverage, especially cameras and TV, can increase community and political pressure on participants and even cause grandstanding by participants; (3) media coverage can erode the dignity and decorum of the courtroom. In a democratic society, shouldn't the public have access to all trials through the TV medium, regardless of these concerns?

InfoTrac College Edition Research

 Televising courtroom dramas in criminal trials has resulted in a boom of lawyer-centered talk shows as well as Court TV. Does the public debate the legal, political, and social issues through these trials? Use InfoTrac College Edition to do research on high-profile criminal trials such as the O. J. Simpson case. Focus on such issues as a defendant's right to a public trial and the rights of the press under the First Amendment.

Source: Hedieh Nasheri, *Crime and Justice in the Age of Court TV* (New York: LFB Scholarly Publishing LLC, 2002); Ronald Goldfarb, *TV or Not TV: Television, Justice, and the Courts* (New York: New York University Press, 1998); Anna Quindlen, "Lights, Camera, Justice for All," *Newsweek,* January 21, 2002, p. 64; "Judge Won't Allow Televising Terror Trial," *Quill* 90 (March 2002): 8.

in the amount of time served by jurors, with the term ranging from one day to months, depending on the nature of the trial.

Once the prospective jurors are chosen, they undergo a process known as **voir dire** (French for "to tell the truth"), in which they are questioned by both the prosecution and the defense to determine their appropriateness to sit on the jury. They are examined under oath by the government, the defense, and sometimes the judge about their background, occupation, residence, and possible knowledge of or interest in the case. Detailed questionnaires are also used for this purpose. A juror who acknowledges any bias for or prejudice against the defendant (if the defendant is a friend or relative, for example, or if the juror has already formed an opinion about the case) is **challenged for cause** and replaced with another. Thus, any prospective juror who declares that he or she cannot be impartial and render a verdict solely on the evidence to be presented at the trial may be removed by either the prosecution or the defense. Because normally no limit is placed on the number of challenges for cause, it often takes

voir dire
The process in which a potential jury panel is questioned by the prosecution and the defense to select jurors who are unbiased and objective.

challenge for cause
Dismissal of a prospective juror by either the prosecution or the defense because he or she is biased, has prior knowledge about a case, or for other reasons that demonstrate the individual's inability to render a fair and impartial judgment.

Figure 12.2
The Steps in a Jury Trial

Source: Marvin Zalman and Larry Siegel, *Criminal Procedure: Constitution and Society* (St. Paul, Minn.: West Publishing, 1991), p. 655.

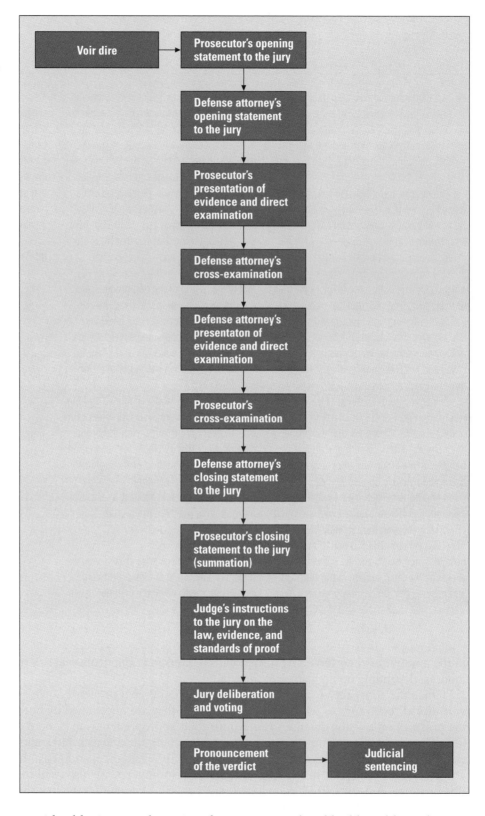

considerable time to select a jury for controversial and highly publicized criminal cases.

Peremptory Challenges In addition to challenges for cause, both the prosecution and the defense are allowed peremptory challenges, which enable the attorneys to excuse jurors for no particular reason or for undisclosed reasons. For example, a

Batson v. Kentucky (1986)

law in review

During the criminal trial of a black defendant in Kentucky, the prosecutor used his peremptory challenges to remove four blacks from the venire. Consequently, an all-white jury was selected. Although defense counsel protested that this deprived Batson, his client, of a fair jury representing a cross section of the community, the trial judge denied the motion. Batson was ultimately convicted. The Kentucky Supreme Court relied on the *Swain* v. *Alabama* (1965) doctrine in upholding the case, arguing that the defense did not demonstrate systematic exclusion of black jurors in other cases.

The U.S. Supreme Court held that defendants have no right to a jury composed of members in whole or in part of their own race. However, the Fourteenth Amendment's equal protection clause guarantees that the state will not exclude jury members on account of race or under the false assumption that members of the defendant's own race cannot render a fair verdict. This would also discriminate against the jury members and undermine public confidence in the jury system. Thus, the state is forbidden to preempt jurors solely on the basis of their race.

In addition, if defendants want to prove racism in the use of the peremptory challenge, they no longer must show a pattern of discrimination as the *Swain* doctrine indicated. Defendants may show purposeful racial discrimination in selection of the venire by relying solely on the facts of their own case. They must show that they are members of a particular race and that the prosecutor has exercised his or her peremptory challenges to remove members of that racial group from the jury. They may rely on the fact that such practices permit "those to discriminate who have a mind to discriminate." The burden is then on the prosecutor to come forward with a neutral explanation for challenging the jurors.

Finally, the Court argued that the peremptory challenge can still play an important role in the adversarial process. It can be used in most criminal cases as long as it is not employed in a racially biased manner.

Batson v. *Kentucky* struck down a legal procedure that was out of sync with modern ideas of justice and fairness. It prevented an element of racial discrimination from entering into the trial stage of justice, which is one of the cornerstones of American freedom. Yet it preserved, under controlled circumstances, the use of the peremptory challenge, which is an integral part of the jury selection process.

Critical Thinking

The U.S. Supreme Court has limited the ways the prosecution and defense can exercise peremptory challenges based on race or gender. In what other areas can the *Batson* rule be expanded?

InfoTrac College Edition Research

Jury selection is often the most important part of a case. Preparation, evidence, and eyewitnesses do not mean anything without a good jury. For a discusson of this issue, go to InfoTrac College Edition and read Kathryn Barnett, "Letting Focus Groups Work for You," *Trial* 35 (1999): 74.

Source: *Batson* v. *Kentucky,* 476 U.S. 79 (1986).

prosecutor might not want a bartender as a juror in a drunk-driving case, believing that a person with that occupation would be sympathetic to the accused. Or the defense might excuse a prospective male juror because the attorney prefers to have a predominantly female jury. The number of peremptory challenges permitted is limited by state statute and often varies by case and jurisdiction.

The **peremptory challenge** has been criticized by legal experts who question the fairness and propriety with which it has been used.[48] The most significant criticism is that it has been used to exclude blacks from hearing cases in which the defendant is also black. In *Swain* v. *Alabama* (1965), the U.S. Supreme Court upheld the use of peremptory challenges in isolated cases to exclude jurors by reason of racial or other group affiliation.[49] This policy was extremely troublesome because it allowed what seemed to be legally condoned discrimination against minority group members. In 1986, the Court struck down the *Swain* doctrine in *Batson* v. *Kentucky,* holding that the use of peremptory challenges by prosecutors in criminal cases, if based on race, violated the Constitution.[50] Because of the importance of this landmark case, it is discussed in the Law in Review feature, above.

In an analysis of the peremptory challenge after the *Batson* decision, James Archer suggested that this legal procedure can still be used fairly, with improved systematic jury selection, appropriate judicial discretion, and the identification of

peremptory challenge
Dismissal of a prospective juror by either the prosecution or the defense for unexplained, discretionary reasons.

Exhibit 12.1 U.S. Supreme Court Decisions Regarding the Peremptory Challenge

Court case	Decision
Batson v. *Kentucky* (1986)	Under the Fourteenth Amendment, the Supreme Court ruled that prosecutors were barred from using peremptory challenges to remove black jurors because of their race.
Powers v. *Ohio* (1991)	The Supreme Court concluded that a defendant has the standing to object to race-based exclusion of jurors by the use of peremptory challenges on the grounds of equal protection, even if the defendant is not of the same race as the challenged jurors.
Edmonson v. *Leesville Concrete Co.* (1991)	The Court held that the *Batson* ruling applies to attorneys in civil lawsuits. A private party in a civil action may not raise peremptory challenges to exclude jurors on the basis of race.
Georgia v. *McCollum* (1992)	On the basis of *Batson,* the Court prohibited the exercise of race-based peremptory challenges by defense attorneys in criminal cases.
J. E. B. v. *Alabama* (1994)	The Supreme Court held that the equal protection clause of the Fourteenth Amendment bars discrimination in jury selection on the basis of sex. Discrimination in jury selection, whether based on race or gender, causes harm to the litigants, the community, and the individual jurors who are wrongfully excluded from participation in the judicial process.

prima facie (evident "on its face") constitutional violations in the jury process.[51] Other authors believe that the success of the *Batson* standard depends primarily on the discretion of the trial judge.[52] Marvin Steinberg makes a case for eliminating peremptory challenges altogether to end racial discrimination in the jury system.[53]

Since the *Batson* decision, the issue of racial discrimination in the use of peremptory challenges has been raised by defendants in numerous cases. In *Powers* v. *Ohio* (1991), for instance, the Supreme Court was faced with deciding the legality of peremptory challenges involving jurors not of the same race as the defendant. The Court held that a defendant may object to the race-based removal of a juror even when the defendant is a member of a different racial group. The equal protection clause prohibits a prosecutor from using the peremptory challenge to exclude qualified and unbiased persons from a jury solely by reason of race. In so ruling, the Court rejected the government's contention that the rule applied only to jurors of the same race as the defendant. Similarly, in the 1992 case of *Georgia* v. *McCollum,* the Supreme Court found that criminal defendants may not seek to exclude potential jurors strictly on the basis of race. Race-based peremptory challenges to potential jurors in civil lawsuits have also been declared unconstitutional.[54]

In 1994, the Supreme Court, in *J. E. B.* v. *Alabama,* ruled that prosecutors and defense attorneys may not use peremptory challenges to strike men or women from juries solely on the basis of gender. Such discrimination also violates the equal protection clause of the Fourteenth Amendment, the Court said.[55] Supreme Court decisions regarding peremptory challenges are summarized in Exhibit 12.1 Some state courts have ruled that peremptory challenges cannot be based on religion. Some day, states may rule that they cannot be based on age or disability.[56]

Impartial Juries The Sixth Amendment provides for the right to a speedy trial by an impartial jury, but the concept of an impartial jury has always been controversial. Research indicates that jury members often have little in common with their criminal peers. Moreover, remaining impartial may be a struggle. Studies of jury deliberations indicate that the dynamics of decision making often involve pressure to get the case over with and convince recalcitrant jurors to join the majority. Nevertheless, jurors also appear to take cases seriously and to reach decisions not too different from those made by legal professionals.[57] Judges, for instance, often agree with jury decisions. However, jurors often have problems understanding judicial instructions and legal rule making in criminal trials, and this may cause confusion in determining the appropriate verdict.

The Supreme Court has sought to ensure compliance with the constitutional mandate of impartiality by eliminating racial discrimination in jury selection. For instance, in *Ham* v. *South Carolina* (1973), the Court held that the defense counsel of a black civil rights leader was entitled to question each juror on the issue of racial prejudice.[58] In *Taylor* v. *Louisiana* (1975), the Court overturned the conviction of a man by an all-male jury because a Louisiana statute allowed women but not men to exempt themselves from jury duty.[59]

The issue of racial composition of the jury is particularly acute in cases involving the death penalty. In *Turner* v. *Murray* (1986), the Court ruled that a defendant accused of an interracial crime in which the death penalty is an option can insist that prospective jurors be informed of the victim's race and be questioned on the issue of their bias. A trial judge who refuses this line of questioning during voir dire risks having the death penalty vacated, but not having the conviction reversed.[60] These and other, similar decisions have had the effect of providing safeguards against jury bias.

Jury selection can be even more difficult in capital punishment cases, when jurors are asked about their views on the death penalty. In *Lockhart* v. *McCree* (1986), the Supreme Court decided that jurors who strongly oppose capital punishment may be disqualified from determining a defendant's guilt or innocence in capital cases.[61] The *Lockhart* decision raises certain questions, however. Juries are not supposed to represent only one position or another. An impartial jury of one's peers is rooted in the idea that the defendant should be judged by a cross section of members of the local community. Their views should not be disproportionate on any one issue. Consequently, a ruling such as *Lockhart* could theoretically result in higher conviction rates in murder cases.

The Supreme Court has not yet fully answered all of the important questions regarding impartiality in the role and qualifications of jurors in criminal cases. The Race, Gender, and Ethnicity in Criminal Justice feature on page 376 provides additional information on discrimination in jury selection.

Another safeguard against bias, used in highly publicized and celebrated cases, is to sequester jury members, once selected, for the duration of the trial, isolating them from contact with the outside world. Sequestration is discretionary with the trial judge, and most courts believe "locking a jury up" is needed only in sensational cases, such as the O. J. Simpson trial.

Opening Statements

Once the jury has been selected and has heard the criminal complaint read by the court clerk, the prosecutor and the defense attorney may each make an opening statement to the jury. The purpose of the prosecutor's statement is to introduce the judge and jury to the particular criminal charges, to outline the facts, and to describe how the government will prove the defendant guilty beyond a reasonable doubt. The defense attorney reviews the case and indicates how the defense intends to show that the accused is not guilty of the charge. The defense attorney's opening statement ordinarily follows that of the prosecution.

The opening statement gives the jury a concise overview of the evidence that is to follow. In the opening statement, neither attorney is allowed to make prejudicial remarks or inflammatory statements or to mention irrelevant facts. Both are free, however, to identify what they will eventually prove by way of evidence—witnesses, physical evidence, and expert testimony. The actual content of the statement is left to the discretion of the trial judge. As a general rule, the opening statements used in jury trials are important because they provide the finders of fact (the jury) with an initial summary of the case. They are less effective and are infrequently used in bench trials, however, where juries are not employed. Most lower court judges have handled hundreds of similar cases and do not need the benefit of an opening statement.

Jury Selection and Peremptory Challenges

race, gender, and ethnicity in criminal justice

Jury selection often accounts for a large share of criminal trial time, particularly in high-profile cases involving serious crimes. Jury selection procedures include the voir dire examination, in which prospective jurors are questioned for the purpose of ascertaining their fitness to serve on the jury; the challenge for cause, in which jurors are eliminated because of prejudice; and the peremptory challenge, in which an objection is made to a juror for no apparent reason.

Of all these procedures, the peremptory challenge poses the greatest actual and potential risk of jury discrimination. The U.S. Supreme Court, in *Batson* v. *Kentucky,* recognized the widespread abuses of peremptory challenges by deciding that purposeful discrimination in their use is a violation of the defendant's right to an impartial jury. The Court later extended the *Batson* rule beyond racial discrimination to the category of gender.

Despite the expansion of the *Batson* rule, peremptory challenges may still involve discrimination along other dimensions. Race-neutral explanations may be used to justify what may be discriminatory peremptory challenges of minorities. For instance, it may be possible to strike Spanish-speaking minorities if a prosecutor claims that they would have difficulty understanding the testimony. Also, the social class of jurors could be as impor-

tant as race and gender in explaining disproportionate jury representation.

Based on the cases addressing peremptory challenges decided by the U.S. Supreme Court, excluding potential jurors from criminal trials because of race or gender clearly violates the defendant's rights under the Fourteenth Amendment. Justice Thurgood Marshall recognized the seriousness of this issue when he suggested in the *Batson* case that peremptory challenges should be eliminated entirely from the criminal justice system.

Professor Charles Ogletree points out that the seemingly neutral explanations of prosecutors for peremptory challenges undermine the protection against jury discrimination established by the *Batson* case. Ogletree suggests that, if a prosecutor violates *Batson,* the criminal case should be dismissed and that prosecution peremptory challenges should be eliminated. However, a state court or legislature is unlikely to establish such rules.

Critical Thinking

1. Would criminal trials be fairer without peremptory challenges?
2. Differences exist in the number of peremptory challenges available in each state and in the federal court system. The American Bar Association has recommended allowing 10 peremptory challenges per side

in capital cases, five per side if a sentence of imprisonment of more than six months may be imposed, and three per side if the maximum sentence is incarceration of six months or less. Are these standards reasonable?
3. Should social class indicators (income, occupation, and authority position of prospective jurors) be considered in determining jury participation?

InfoTrac College Edition Research

The peremptory challenge has been weakened in recent decades by U.S. Supreme Court decisions holding that challenges based on either race or gender violate the equal protection clause of the Fourteenth Amendment. But the Court has not yet considered the constitutionality of religion-based challenges. See Jean Hellwege, "Religion-Based Peremptory Challenges Are Unconstitutional," *Trial Magazine* 35 (1999): 15.

Sources: Charles Ogletree, "Just Say No! A Proposal to Eliminate Racially Discriminatory Uses of Peremptory Challenges," *American Criminal Law Review* 31 (1994): 1099–1151; Marvin Zalman and Larry Siegel, *Criminal Procedure: Constitution and Society,* 2d ed. (Belmont, Calif.: West/Wadsworth, 1997); Hiroshi Fukurai, "Race, Social Class, and Jury Participation: New Dimensions for Evaluating Discrimination in Jury Service," *Journal of Criminal Justice* 24 (1996): 71–88.

Presentation of the Prosecutor's Evidence

direct examination
The initial questioning of one's own (prosecution or defense) witness during a trial.

Following the opening statements, the government begins its case by presenting evidence to the court through its witnesses. Those called as witnesses, such as police officers, victims, or experts, provide testimony via direct examination. During **direct examination,** the prosecutor questions the witness to reveal the facts believed pertinent to the government's case. Testimony involves what the witness saw, heard, or touched and does not include opinions. However, a witness's opinion can be given in certain situations, such as when describing the motion of a vehicle or indicating whether a defendant appeared to act intoxicated or insane. Witnesses may also qualify to give opinions because they are experts on a particular subject relevant to the case; for example, a psychiatrist may testify about a defendant's mental capacity at the time of the crime.

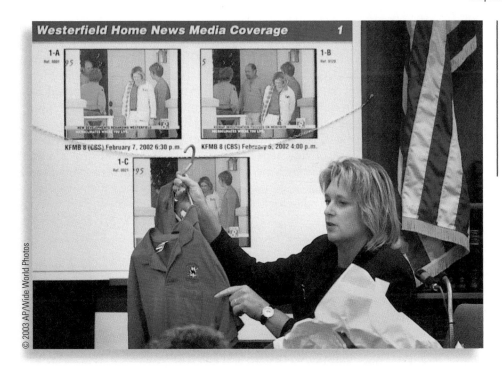

The prosecutor calls witnesses in order to present a sufficient level of evidence to gain a conviction. Here, a San Diego police detective testifies during the trial of David Westerfield, who was accused of killing Danielle van Dam. The physical evidence presented at trial was sufficient to gain a conviction on murder charges.

After the prosecutor finishes questioning a witness, the defense may cross-examine the same witness by asking questions that seek to clarify the defendant's role in the crime. The right to cross-examine witnesses is an essential part of a trial, and except in extremely unusual circumstances (such as a person's being hospitalized), witness statements will not be considered unless they are made in court and open for question. For example, in *Lee* v. *Illinois* (1986), the U.S. Supreme Court ruled that a confession made to police by a codefendant in a criminal trial cannot be used in court unless the person making the confession is available for cross-examination.[62] If desired, the prosecutor may seek a second direct examination after the defense attorney has completed **cross-examination.** This allows the prosecutor to ask additional questions about information brought out during cross-examination. Finally, the defense attorney may question or cross-examine the witness once again. All witnesses for the trial are sworn in and questioned in the same basic manner.

Types of Evidence at a Criminal Trial

In addition to testimonial evidence given by police officers, citizens, and experts, the court acts on real (nonverbal) evidence.[63] **Real evidence** may include exhibits such as a revolver that may have been in the defendant's control at the time of a murder, tools found in the possession of a suspect charged with a burglary, a bottle allegedly holding narcotics, or blood samples from a murder victim. The criminal court judge will also review documentary evidence, such as writings, government reports, public records, and business or hospital records.

In general, the primary test for the admissibility of evidence in either a criminal or civil proceeding is its relevance. The court must ask itself whether the gun, shirt, or photograph, for instance, has relevant evidentiary value in determining the issues of the case. Ordinarily, evidence that establishes an element of the crime is acceptable to the court. For example, in a prosecution for possession of drugs, evidence that shows the defendant to be a known drug user might be relevant.

Circumstantial (indirect) evidence is also often used in trial proceedings. Such evidence is often inferred or used indirectly to prove a fact in question. On

Can a psychiatrist be liable for civil actions because of his appearance as an expert witness? To find out, read Barbara Boughton, "Immunity for Expert Witnesses Dwindling Due to Case Law (Psychiatrists Can Sometimes Be Held Liable)," *Clinical Psychiatry News* 30, no. 18 (August 2002): 37, on InfoTrac College Edition.

cross-examination
The questioning of a prosecution witness by the defense, or of a defense witness by the prosecution.

real evidence
Any object, such as a weapon or a photograph, produced for inspection at a trial; physical evidence.

circumstantial (indirect) evidence
Indirect evidence from which a fact may be inferred.

How can lawyers use technology to present evidence at trial? Go to InfoTrac College Edition and read Brian Panish and Christine Spagnoli, "Take Technology to Trial: Jurors Remember Best What They See and Hear, So Use Visual Technology to Make Your Message Stick," *Trial* 38, no. 7 (July 2002): 39.

the issue of malice in a criminal murder trial, for instance, circumstantial evidence could be used to prove the defendant's state of mind. Circumstantial evidence bearing on or establishing the facts in a crime is ordinarily admissible, but evidence that is prejudicial, remote, or unrelated to the crime should be excluded by the court. In general, the admissibility of such evidence remains governed by constitutional law, such as the right to be free from unreasonable search and seizure, the privilege against self-incrimination, and the right to counsel.

In recent years, a considerable amount of real evidence has come from video recordings. Courtroom use of videotape originated with undercover surveillance operations. Today, citizens are being filmed regularly. Security cameras are mounted everywhere. The plethora of cameras makes evidentiary videotape widely available and an important part of the technology of criminal evidence collection.[64]

Motion for a Directed Verdict

Once the prosecution has provided all the government's evidence against a defendant, it will inform the court that it rests the people's case. The defense attorney at this point may enter a motion for a **directed verdict.** This is a procedural device by which the defense attorney asks the judge to order the jury to return a verdict of not guilty. In essence, the defense attorney argues that the prosecutor's case against the defendant is insufficient to prove the defendant guilty beyond a reasonable doubt. The judge must rule on the motion and will either sustain it or overrule it, depending on whether he or she believes that the prosecution has proved all the elements of the alleged crime. If the motion is sustained, the trial is terminated. If it is rejected, the case continues with the defense portion of the trial.

directed verdict
A judge's order directing a jury to acquit a defendant because the state has not proven the elements of the crime or otherwise has not established guilt according to law.

The defense usually makes a motion for a directed verdict so that a finding of guilt can later be appealed to a higher court. If the judge refuses to grant the motion, this decision can be the focus of an appeal charging that the judge did not use proper procedural care in making his or her decision. In some cases, the judge may reserve decision on the motion, submit the case to the jury, and consider a decision on the motion before the jury verdict.

Presentation of Evidence by the Defense Counsel

The defense attorney has the option of presenting many, some, or no witnesses on behalf of the defendant. In addition, the defense attorney must decide if the client should take the stand and testify in his or her own behalf. In a criminal trial, the defendant is protected by the Fifth Amendment right against self-incrimination, which means that a person cannot be forced by the state to testify against himself or herself in a criminal trial. However, defendants who choose voluntarily to tell their side of the story can be subject to cross-examination by the prosecutor.

rebuttal evidence
Evidence presented by the prosecution at the conclusion of the defense case, with the permission of the court, to rebut or disprove defense evidence.

After the defense concludes its case, the government may then present **rebuttal evidence.** This normally involves bringing evidence forward that was not used when the prosecution initially presented its case. The defense may examine the rebuttal witnesses and introduce new witnesses in a process called a **surrebuttal.** After all the evidence has been presented to the court, the defense attorney may again submit a motion for a directed verdict. If the motion is denied, both the prosecution and the defense prepare to make closing arguments, and the case on the evidence is ready for consideration by the jury.

surrebuttal evidence
At the end of rebuttal, the defense may be allowed to refute the evidence presented by the prosecution with its own surrebuttal evidence. Surrebuttal is not an opportunity for the defense to present new evidence but simply to refute the prosecution's rebuttal evidence.

Closing Arguments

The attorneys use closing arguments to review the facts and evidence of the case in a manner favorable to each of their positions. At this stage of the trial, both the prosecution and the defense are permitted to draw reasonable inferences and to

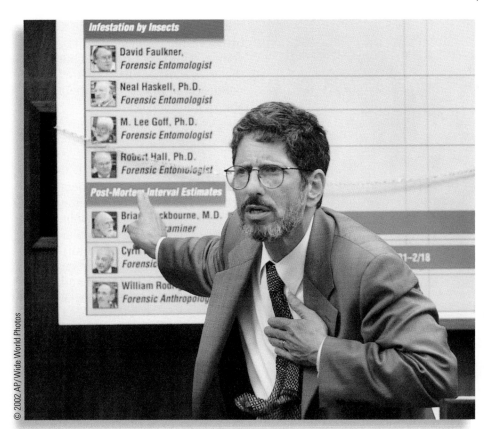

The defense may also present experts to convince the jury of the innocence of their client. Here, entomologist Steven Feldman presents evidence during the Van Dam murder trial that allegedly proved that David Westerfield could not have committed the murder. Feldman's testimony failed to sway the jury, who returned a guilty verdict.

show how the facts prove or refute the defendant's guilt. Both attorneys have a relatively free hand in arguing about the facts, issues, and evidence, including the applicable law. They cannot comment on matters not in evidence, however, or on the defendant's failure to testify in a criminal case. Normally, the defense attorney makes a closing statement first, followed by the prosecutor. Either party can elect to forgo the right to make a final summation to the jury. Because the prosecution gives the opening statement first and makes the closing argument last, some experts believe that the government has a decided advantage over the defense.

Instructions to the Jury

In a criminal trial, the judge will instruct, or charge, the jury members on the principles of law that ought to guide and control their decision on the defendant's innocence or guilt. Included in the charge is information about the elements of the alleged offense, the type of evidence needed to prove each element, and the burden of proof required for a guilty verdict. Although the judge commonly provides the instruction, he or she may ask the prosecutor and the defense attorney to submit instructions for consideration; the judge then uses discretion in determining whether to use any of their instructions. The instructions that cover the law applicable to the case are particularly important because they may serve as the basis for a subsequent appeal.

A good example of an improper jury instruction that voided a conviction occurred in *Sullivan* v. *Louisiana* (1993).[65] In this murder case, the defendant's lawyer argued that there was reasonable doubt concerning the identity of the killer. The trial judge in his instructions said that reasonable doubt must have a "substantial" basis that would give rise to a "grave uncertainty" that the defendant was the killer. The Supreme Court declared that this instruction violated the Fifth Amendment due process clause because using the word "substantial"

© 2000 AP/Wide World Photos

At the completion of a trial, the jury verdict is publicly announced. Here, a packed courtroom in Las Vegas listens as guilty verdicts on all charges for the murder of casino heir Ted Binion, are read, May 19, 2000. From left, defense attorney John Momot, defendants Sandy Murphy and Rick Tabish, Tabish's attorney Louis Palazzo, attorney Rob Murdock, and Linda Norvell show little emotion. Prosecutors said Binion was forced to ingest a lethal dose of heroin and the prescription anti-anxiety drug Xanax, then was suffocated by Murphy, Binion's live-in girlfriend, and Tabish, her lover. In 2003, their murder convictions were overturned and a new trial was ordered.

wWW A great deal of research is being conducted regarding criminal sanctions. One of the best sources of information is the Sentencing Project. Check the Web site at http://www.sentencingproject.org.

downplayed the duty of the state to prove all the elements of a crime beyond a reasonable doubt. Thus, even the use of one word can create further confusion in interpreting the reasonable doubt standard.

The Verdict

Once the charge is given to the jury members, they retire to deliberate on a verdict. The verdict in a criminal case is usually required to be unanimous. A review of the case by the jury may take hours or even days. The jurors are always sequestered during their deliberations, and in certain lengthy and highly publicized cases, they are kept overnight in a hotel until the verdict is reached. In less sensational cases, the jurors may be allowed to go home, but they are cautioned not to discuss the case with anyone.

The rules of procedure for most jurisdictions permit only two possible verdicts in a criminal trial: *guilty* and *not guilty.* In a criminal trial, the government has the responsibility to convince the judge or jury that the defendant is guilty. If the government fails, the defendant is then found not guilty. Contrary to what is often observed on television or in the movies, where a person accused of a crime is found "innocent," criminal courts do not make such a determination. If a verdict cannot be reached, the trial may result in a hung jury. If the prosecution still wants a conviction, it must bring the defendant to trial again.

If found not guilty, the defendant is released from the criminal process. If the defendant is found guilty, the judge normally orders a presentence investigation by the probation department before imposing a sentence. Prior to sentencing, the defense attorney will probably submit a motion for a new trial, alleging that legal errors occurred in the trial proceedings. The judge may deny the motion and impose a sentence immediately, a practice common in misdemeanor offenses. In felony cases, however, the judge sets a date for sentencing and the defendant is either released on bail or held in custody until that time.

The Sentence

Imposing the criminal sentence is normally the responsibility of the trial judge. In some jurisdictions, the jury may determine the sentence or make recommendations for leniency for certain offenses. Often, the sentencing decision is based on information and recommendations given to the court by the probation department after a presentence investigation of the defendant. The sentence itself is determined by the statutory requirements for the particular crime, as established by the legislature. In addition, the judge ordinarily has a great deal of discretion in sentencing. The different criminal sanctions available include fines, probation, imprisonment, and commitment to a state hospital, as well as combinations of these.

The Appeal

Defendants have three possible avenues of appeal: the direct appeal, federal court review, and postconviction remedy.[66] Both the direct appeal and federal court review provide the convicted person with the opportunity to appeal to a higher state or federal court on the basis of an error that affected the conviction in the trial court. Extraordinary trial court errors, such as the denial of the right to counsel or the inability to provide a fair trial, are subject to the "plain error" rule of the federal courts.[67] "Harmless errors," such as the use of innocuous identification procedures or the denial of counsel at a noncritical stage of the proceeding, would not necessarily result in overturning a criminal conviction.

A postconviction remedy—often referred to as a "collateral attack"—is the primary means by which state prisoners can have their conviction or sentence reviewed in federal court. It takes the form of a legal petition, such as for a writ of habeas corpus. A writ of habeas corpus (meaning "you should have the body") seeks to determine the validity of detention by asking the court to release the person or give legal reasons for the incarceration.

Take a look at the appeal petition in the famous Louise Woodward child abuse case: http://www.courttv.com/trials/woodward/appeal.html.

In most jurisdictions, direct criminal appeal to an appellate court is a matter of right. This means that the defendant has an automatic right to appeal a conviction based on errors that may have occurred during the trial proceedings. A substantial number of criminal appeals are the result of disputes over points of law, such as the introduction at the trial of illegal evidence detrimental to the defendant or statements made during the trial that were prejudicial to the defendant. Through objections made at the pretrial and trial stages of the criminal process, the defense counsel preserves specific legal issues on the record as the basis for appeal. A copy of the transcript of these proceedings serves as the basis on which the appellate court will review any errors that may have occurred during the lower court proceedings. Although the defendant has an automatic right to an appeal in the first instance, all further appeals are discretionary, including an appeal "all the way to the U.S. Supreme Court."

Because an appeal is an expensive, time-consuming, and technical process, involving a review of the lower court record, the research and drafting of briefs, and the presentation of oral arguments to the appellate court, the defendant has been granted the right to counsel at this stage of the criminal process. In *Douglas* v. *California* (1963), the Supreme Court held that an indigent defendant has a constitutional right to the assistance of counsel on a direct first appeal.[68] If the defendant appeals to a higher court, the defendant must have private counsel or apply for permission to proceed in forma pauperis, meaning that the defendant may be granted counsel at public expense if the court believes the appeal has merit.

The right of appeal normally does not extend to the prosecution in a criminal case. At one extreme are states that grant no right of appeal to the prosecution in criminal cases. At the other, some jurisdictions permit the prosecution to appeal in those instances that involve the unconstitutionality of a statute or a motion granting a new trial to the defendant. However, the prosecutor cannot bring the defendant to trial again on the same charge after an acquittal or a conviction, as this would violate the defendant's right to be free from double jeopardy under the Fifth Amendment. The purpose of the double jeopardy guarantee is to protect the defendant from a second prosecution for the same offense.

After an appeal has been fully heard, the appeals court renders an opinion on the procedures used in the case. If an error of law is found, such as an improper introduction of evidence or an improper statement by the prosecutor that was prejudicial to the defendant, the appeals court may reverse the decision of the trial court and order a new trial. If the lower court's decision is upheld, the case is finished, unless the defendant seeks a discretionary appeal to a higher state or federal court.

Over the past decade, criminal appeals have increased significantly in almost every state and the federal courts. Criminal case appeals make up a majority of

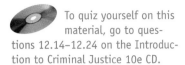

To quiz yourself on this material, go to questions 12.14–12.24 on the Introduction to Criminal Justice 10e CD.

the state appellate and federal caseload, which includes prisoner petitions and ordinary criminal appeals. Today, a substantial number of these appeals involve drug-related cases.

Evidentiary Standards

The standard required to convict a defendant at the trial stage of the criminal process is proof beyond a reasonable doubt. This requirement dates back to early American history and, over the years, has become the accepted measure of persuasion needed by the prosecutor to convince the judge or jury of the defendant's guilt. Many twentieth-century U.S. Supreme Court decisions reinforced this standard by making "beyond a reasonable doubt" a constitutional due process requirement.[69]

The reasonable doubt standard is an essential ingredient of the criminal justice process. It is the prime instrument for reducing the risk of convictions based on factual errors. The underlying premise of this standard is that it is better to release a guilty person than to convict someone who is innocent. In applying the reasonable doubt standard to juvenile trials, in *In re Winship* (1970), the Supreme Court noted:

> *If the standard proof for a criminal trial were preponderance of evidence rather than proof beyond a reasonable doubt, there would be a smaller risk of factual errors that result in freeing guilty persons, but a far greater risk of factual errors that result in convicting the innocent.*[70]

Because the defendant is presumed innocent until proven guilty, this standard forces the prosecution to overcome the presumption of innocence with the highest standard of proof. Unlike the civil law, where a mere preponderance of the evidence is the standard, the criminal process requires proof beyond a reasonable doubt for each element of the offense. These and other evidentiary standards of proof are defined and compared in Concept Summary 12.2.

Concept Summary 12.2 Evidentiary Standards of Proof: Degrees of Certainty

Standard	Definition	Where used
Absolute certainty	No possibility of error; 100 percent certainty	Not used in civil or criminal law
Beyond a reasonable doubt; moral certainty	Conclusive and complete proof, without leaving any reasonable doubt as to the guilt of the defendant; allowing the defendant the benefit of any possibility of innocence	Criminal trial
Clear and convincing evidence	Prevailing and persuasive to the trier of fact	Civil commitments, insanity defense
Preponderance of evidence	Greater weight of evidence in terms of credibility; more convincing than an opposite point of view	Civil trial
Probable cause	U.S. constitutional standard for arrest and search warrants, requiring existence of facts sufficient to warrant that a crime has been committed	Arrest, preliminary hearing, motions
Sufficient evidence	Adequate evidence to reverse a trial court	Appellate review
Reasonable suspicion	Rational, reasonable belief that facts warrant investigation of a crime on less than probable cause	Police investigations
Less than probable cause	Mere suspicion; less than reasonable to conclude that criminal activity exists	Prudent police investigation when safety of an officer or others is endangered

Trials are currently undergoing significant changes as technology begins to have an impact on the adjudication process. The use of DNA evidence has now become routine. Here, Marvin Anderson smiles as he holds the unconditional pardon issued August 21, 2002, by Virginia Governor Warner. Anderson's sister, Garnetta Bishop, left, and other family members surround him in front of the Capitol in Richmond, Virginia. Anderson, who served 15 years in prison for a rape he did not commit, was cleared of the crime by DNA evidence hours after he was paroled.

Over the years, the courts have struggled to define many of the standards of evidence, particularly reasonable doubt. The Federal Judicial Center's model standard states it best:

> *Proof beyond a reasonable doubt is proof that leaves you firmly convinced of the defendant's guilt. There are very few things in this world that we know with absolute certainty, and in criminal cases the law does not require proof that overcomes every possible doubt. If, based on your consideration of the evidence, you are firmly convinced that the defendant is guilty of the crime charged, you must find him guilty. If, on the other hand, you think there is a real possibility that he is not guilty, you must give him the benefit of the doubt and find him not guilty.*[71]

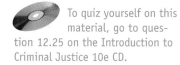

To quiz yourself on this material, go to question 12.25 on the Introduction to Criminal Justice 10e CD.

Trial Reform in the Twenty-First Century

Criminal trial practices will likely undergo considerable change during coming decades. What innovations can be expected in the twenty-first century? What are the trends in the trial process and in the role of the jury? Where is the criminal trial heading?

Trials will likely continue to be adversarial in nature. Prosecutors, defense attorneys, and judges will reshape their roles, stressing community organization, sentencing reform, and mediation of criminal cases. The number of minority and female members of the judiciary should continue to grow.

Another change that will continue to have an impact on the trial is the use of DNA evidence. DNA profiling involves scientifically matching the genetic material from hair, blood, and other bodily tissues and fluids found at a crime scene with samples taken from known suspects.

The use of DNA profiling in criminal trials received a boost in 1997 when the FBI announced that DNA testing has become so precise that experts no longer have to supply statistical estimates of accuracy while testifying at trial. They can now state in court that there exists "a reasonable degree of scientific certainty" that evidence came from a single suspect.

The FBI has implemented the Combined DNA Index System (CODIS). This computerized database allows DNA taken at a crime scene to be searched electronically to find matches against samples taken from convicted offenders and from other crime scenes. One database allows suspects to be identified; the second allows investigators to establish links between crimes. So far there have been more than 100 instances in which offenders have been linked to unsolved cases. In addition, 67 convicts (some on death row) have been exonerated by DNA evidence.[72] The use of DNA evidence should become commonplace in the twenty-first century.

Trial courts also are tapping into new communiation technologies to improve the effectiveness of the criminal trial. Cellular phones, fax machines, computers, and teleconferencing systems that provide both audio and video linkages are routinely used by judges, prosecutors, and defense attorneys. Legal experts are still uncertain about the viability of televising all criminal trials. Some support the idea, because it exposes the judicial process to public scrutiny. Others believe the tabloid approach of a commercial enterprise such as Court TV will continue to scare off the federal courts from ever allowing cameras into the courtroom.

According to some legal experts, the present U.S. criminal trial process is inadequate because it is too complicated and requires an inordinate amount of time. The accuracy of jury verdicts is often questioned by the public, and serious issues remain regarding the use of unanimous verdicts and peremptory challenges. The past decade has seen criticism of the jury system by the legal profession, the press, and the public.[73] Two areas of the jury system that require attention are (1) jury selection procedures and (2) jury service during conduct of the trial.[74]

The peremptory challenge has led to scientific jury selection and has even given birth to a new profession, jury consulting. Selecting a jury has become a complicated process, as attorneys seek to stack the jury with people who fit their ideal demographic profile. Even the unlimited "for cause" challenges delay the trial process and often lead the courts to search for the least informed citizens to serve as jurors. The present system has put an increased time burden on the judicial system and decreased public confidence in the accuracy of jury verdicts.

The treatment of jurors during the trial is also a problem. Most jurors consider jury service a hassle. It means taking time off from work or finding someone to care for children at home. It may even mean a loss of income. Jurors need to be treated with respect and consideration in keeping with their critical role in the legal system. Consequently, shortening the in-court voir dire examination of prospective jurors would make practical sense. Allowing the jury to ask questions during the trial and to discuss evidence among themselves would also be helpful, particularly in complex cases with scientific testimony.

Another question is whether judges need to summarize the law and the facts for the jury. Presently, judges read to the jury a statement of the law along with a definition of reasonable doubt. Research has found that jurors often have a poor understanding of the judge's instructions. Jurors often need assistance in applying the law to the facts in a given case. These reforms would give the jury more information when it seeks the truth and also create a more efficient jury system.[75]

Yet another issue is whether jury verdicts should always be unanimous. The U.S. Supreme Court has ruled that the Sixth Amendment's guarantee of a jury trial does not require a unanimous verdict. Proponents of less than unanimous jury verdicts argue that such an approach would largely eliminate hung juries and even reduce the possibility of one juror's corrupting the jury process. Opponents counter that nonunanimous verdicts tend to reduce juror deliberation and devalue dissenting opinions.

WWW For information on violations of civil liberties in criminal trial practice, as well as on racial profiling in the justice system, visit the Web site of the American Civil Liberties Union at http://www.aclu.org.

Summary

- The jury trial is the centerpiece of the criminal justice system because it provides every defendant with the right to be judged by his peers and not the government.
- A defendant may choose between a trial before a judge alone or a trial by jury. In either case, the purpose of the trial is to adjudicate the facts, ascertain the truth, and determine the guilt or innocence of the accused.
- Criminal trials represent the adversary system at work. The state uses its authority to seek a conviction, and the defendant is protected by constitutional rights, particularly those under the Fifth and Sixth Amendments.
- When they involve serious crimes, criminal trials are complex legal affairs. Each jurisdiction relies on rules and procedures that have developed over many years to resolve legal issues.

- During trials criminal defendants are afforded particular rights guaranteed by the Constitution and applied by the U.S. Supreme Court.
- These include the right to confront witnesses, to have a fair and public trial, to have a speedy trial, and to be represented by counsel.
- The right to have or not have trials televised is still open to debate, though many notorious cases have been broadcast.
- An established order of steps is followed throughout a criminal trial, beginning with the selection of a jury, proceeding through opening statements and the introduction of evidence, and concluding with closing arguments and a verdict.
- For a defendant to be found guilty at trial, the allegations must be proven beyond a reasonable doubt.
- The trial is the central test of the facts and law involved in a criminal case.

Key Terms

adjudication 358
bench trial 358
confrontation clause 359
six-person jury 361
pro se 363
venire 370

voir dire 371
challenge for cause 371
peremptory challenge 373
direct examination 376
cross-examination 377
real evidence 377

circumstantial (indirect) evidence 377
directed verdict 378
rebuttal evidence 378
surrebuttal evidence 378

Doing Research on the Web

For an up-to-date list of Web links, go to http://cj.wadsworth.com/siegel_intro10e.

You are a superior court judge. A local television station has asked you to allow cameras to be placed in the jury room while the jurors consider whether to recommend the death penalty in a high-profile murder trial. The station argues that the recording would serve an important purpose and shed light on the death penalty process. The prosecutor is opposed to this tactic and believes it would disrupt jury deliberations, invade the jurors' privacy, and inhibit some jurors from giving their opinions. It is one thing, she argues, to have cameras in the courtroom, it is another to have them in the

jury room. Should jury deliberations be turned into a kind of TV reality show? What would you decide to do? To help in your decision, go to InfoTrac College Edition and use "cameras in the court room" as a subject guide. You also might want to read this editorial: "Camera in the Jury Room? Not Yet," *News Photographer* 58 (January 2003): 8.

Pro/Con discussions and Viewpoint Essays on some of the topics in this chapter may be found at the Opposing Viewpoints Resource Center: http://www.gale.com/OpposingViewpoints.

Discussion Questions

1. What are the steps involved in the criminal trial?
2. What are the pros and cons of a jury trial versus a bench trial?

3. What are the legal rights of the defendant in a trial process?
4. Should people be denied the right to serve as jurors without explanation or cause? In other

words, should the peremptory challenge be maintained?

5. "In the adversary system of criminal justice, the burden of proof in a criminal trial to show that the defendant is guilty beyond a reasonable doubt is on the government." Explain the meaning of this statement.

6. What is testamentary evidence?

Notes

1 James Sterngold, "A Radical's Tale: Compassion Then Led to Prison Now," *New York Times,* December 14, 2001, p. A24; James Sterngold, "70s Radical Is Sentenced, Then Arraigned in New Case," *New York Times,* January 19, 2002, p. A10.

2 Thomas J. Lueck, "Man Who Killed Abortion Provider Asks for Trial by Judge," *New York Times,* March 12, 2003, p. A12.

3 *Riggins* v. *Nevada,* 504 U.S. 127 (1992).

4 *Sell* v. *United States,* No. 02—5664, June 16, 2003.

5 *Pointer* v. *State of Texas,* 380 U.S. 400, 85 S.Ct. 1065, 13 L.Ed.2d 923 (1965).

6 487 U.S. 1012, 108 S.Ct. 2798, 101 L.Ed.2d 867 (1988).

7 497 U.S. 836, 110 S.Ct. 3157, 111 L.Ed.2d 666 (1990).

8 391 U.S. 145, 88 S.Ct. 1444, 20 L.Ed.2d 491 (1968).

9 Ibid., at 157–58, 88 S.Ct., at 1451–52.

10 399 U.S. 66, 90 S.Ct. 1886, 26 L.Ed.2d 437 (1970).

11 See *Blanton* v. *City of Las Vegas,* 489 U.S. 538, 109 S.Ct. 1289, 103 L.Ed.2d 550 (1989). See also *Lewis* v. *United States,* 116 S.Ct. 2163 (1996).

12 399 U.S. 78, 90 S.Ct. 1893, 26 L.Ed.2d 446 (1970).

13 Ibid., at 102–3, 90 S.Ct., at 1907.

14 Ibid., at 101, 90 S.Ct., at 1906.

15 Ibid., at 102, 90 S.Ct., at 1907.

16 *Ballew* v. *Georgia,* 435 U.S. 223, 98 S.Ct. 1029, 55 L.Ed.2d 234 (1978); *Burch* v. *Louisiana,* 441 U.S. 130, 99 S.Ct. 1623, 60 L.Ed.2d 96 (1979).

17 406 U.S. 404, 92 S.Ct. 1628, 32 L.Ed.2d 184 (1972).

18 287 U.S. 45, 53 S.Ct. 55, 77 L.Ed. 158 (1932); 372 U.S. 335, 83 S.Ct. 792, 9 L.Ed.2d 799 (1963); Yale Kamisar, "*Gideon* v. *Wainwright:* A Quarter Century Later," *Pace Law Review* 10 (1990): 343; 407 U.S. 25, 92 S.Ct. 2006, 32 L.Ed.2d 530 (1972).

19 *Shelton* v. *Alabama,* 122 U.S. 1764 (2002).

20 *Shelton,* quoting *Argersinger* v. *Hamlin,* 407 U.S. 25, 40 (1972).

21 422 U.S. 806, 95 S.Ct. 2525, 45 L.Ed.2d 562 (1975).

22 120 S.Ct. 684, 2000.

23 See American Bar Association, *Standards Relating to Speedy Trial* (New York: Institute of Judicial Administration, 1986), p. 1.

24 386 U.S. 213, 87 S.Ct. 988, 18 L.Ed.2d 1 (1967).

25 Ibid., at 223, 87 S.Ct., at 993.

26 *Doggett* v. *United States,* 505 U.S. 647, 112 S.Ct. 2686, 120 L.Ed.2d 520 (1992).

27 President's Commission on Law Enforcement and the Administration of Justice, *Task Force Report: The Courts* (Washington, D.C.: Government Printing Office, 1967), pp. 86–87. See also B. Mahoney and others, *Implementing Delay Reduction and Delay Prevention: Programs in Urban Trial Courts* (Williamsburg, Va.: National Center for State Courts, 1985); *The State of Criminal Justice: An Annual Report, 1994* (Chicago: American Bar Association, 1994).

28 National Advisory Commission on Criminal Justice Standards and Goals, *Courts,* pp. xx–xxi. See also Gregory S. Kennedy, "Speedy Trial," *Georgetown Law Journal* 75 (1987): 953–64.

29 18 U.S.C.A. § 3161 (Supp. 1975). For a good review of this legislation, see Marc I. Steinberg, "Right to Speedy Trial: The Constitutional Right and Its Applicability to the Speedy Trial Act of 1974," *Journal of Criminal Law and Criminology* 66 (1975): 229. See also Thomas Schneider and Robert Davis, "Speedy Trial and Homicide Courts," *American Bar Association Journal of Criminal Justice* 9 (1995): 24.

30 *Estelle* v. *Williams,* 425 U.S. 501, 96 S.Ct. 1691, 48 L.Ed.2d 126 (1976).

31 *Sheppard* v. *Maxwell,* 384 U.S. 333, 86 S.Ct.1507, 16 L.Ed.2d 600 (1966).

32 See *State* v. *von Bulow,* 475 A.2d 995 (R.I. 1984). See also Alan Dershowitz, *Reversal of Fortune: The von Bulow Affair* (New York: Random House, 1986).

33 427 U.S. 539, 96 S.Ct. 2791, 49 L.Ed.2d 683 (1976).

34 Ibid., at 547, 96 S.Ct., at 2797.

35 443 U.S. 368, 99 S.Ct. 2898, 61 L.Ed.2d 608 (1979).

36 Ibid., at 370, 99 S.Ct., at 2900.

37 478 U.S. 1, 106 S.Ct. 2735, 92 L.Ed.2d 1 (1986).

38 *Caribbean International News Corp.* v. *Puerto Rico,* 508 U.S. 147, 113 S.Ct. 2004, 124 L.Ed.2d 60 (1993).

39 448 U.S. 555, 100 S.Ct. 2814, 65 L.Ed.2d 1 (1980).

40 Nicholas A. Pellegrini, "Extension of Criminal Defendant's Right to Public Trial," *St. John's University Law Review* 611 (1987): 277–89.

41 *In re Oliver,* 333 U.S. 257, 68 S.Ct. 499, 92 L.Ed. 682 (1948).

42 448 U.S. 555, 100 S.Ct. 2814, 65 L.Ed.2d 1 (1980)

43 See *Chandler* v. *Florida,* 449 U.S. 560, 101 S.Ct. 802, 66 L.Ed.2d 740 (1981).

44 T. Dyk and B. Donald, "Cameras in the Supreme Court," *American Bar Association Journal* 75 (1989): 34.

45 "Rally for Court Cameras Falls Short," *American Bar Association Journal* 81 (1995): 30.

46 449 U.S. 560, 101 S.Ct. 802, 66 L.Ed.2d 740 (1981).

47 Conference of State Court Administrators, *State Court Organization, 1987* (Williamsburg, Va.: National Center for State Courts, 1988).

48 George Hayden, Joseph Senna, and Larry Siegel, "Prosecutorial Discretion in Peremptory Challenges: An Empirical Investigation of Information Use in the Massachusetts Jury Selection Process," *New England Law Review* 13 (1978): 768.

49 380 U.S. 202, 85 S.Ct. 824, 13 L.Ed.2d 759 (1965).

50 476 U.S. 79, 106 S.Ct. 1712, 90 L.Ed.2d 69 (1986).

51 James Archer, "Exercising Peremptory Challenges after *Batson,*" *Criminal Law Bulletin* 24 (1988): 187–211.

52 Brian Sern and Mark Maney, "Racism, Peremptory Challenges, and Democratic Jury: The Jurisprudence of Delicate Balance," *Journal of Criminal Law and Criminology* 79 (1988): 65.

53 Marvin Steinberg, "The Case for Eliminating Peremptory Challenges," *Criminal Law Bulletin* 27 (1991): 216–29.

54 *Powers* v. *Ohio,* 499 U.S. 400, 111 S.Ct. 1364, 113 L.Ed.2d 411 (1991); *Georgia* v. *McCollum* 505 U.S. 42, 112 S.Ct. 2348, 120 L.Ed.2d 33 (1992).

55 *J. E. B.* v. *Alabama,* ex rel. T. B., 511 U.S. 142, 114 S.Ct. 1419, 128 L.Ed.2d 89 (1994).

56 "Peremptory Challenges Can't Be Based on Religion," *Lawyers Weekly USA,* February 13, 1995, p. 1.

57 For a review of jury decision making, see John Baldwin and Michael McConville, "Criminal Juries," in *Crime and Justice,* vol. 2, ed. Norval Morris and Michael Tonry (Chicago: University of Chicago Press, 1980), pp. 269–320. See also Reid Hastie, ed., *Inside the Juror* (New York: Cambridge University Press, 1993).

58 409 U.S. 524, 93 S.Ct. 848, 35 L.Ed.2d 46 (1973).

59 419 U.S. 522, 95 S.Ct. 692, 42 L.Ed.2d 690 (1975).

60 476 U.S. 28, 106 S.Ct. 1683, 90 L.Ed.2d 27 (1986). See James Gobert, "In Search of an Impartial Jury," *Journal of Criminal Law and Criminology* 79 (1988): 269.

61 476 U.S. 162, 106 S.Ct. 1758, 90 L.Ed.2d 137 (1986).

62 476 U.S. 530, 106 S.Ct. 2056, 90 L.Ed.2d 514 (1986).

63 See Charles McCormick, *Handbook on Evidence* (St. Paul, Minn.: West Publishing, 1987), Chapter 1.

64 Deborah Mahan, "Forensic Image Processing," *American Bar Association Journal of Criminal Justice* 10 (1995): 2.

65 *Sullivan* v. *Louisiana,* 508 U.S. 275, 113 S.Ct. 2078, 124 L.Ed.2d 182 (1993).

66 Bureau of Justice Statistics, *Report to the Nation on Crime and Justice,* 2d ed. (Washington, D.C.: Government Printing Office, 1988), p. 88.

67 *Chapman* v. *California,* 386 U.S. 18, 87 S.Ct. 824, 17 L.Ed.2d 705 (1967).

68 372 U.S. 353, 83 S.Ct. 814, 9 L.Ed.2d 811 (1963).

69 Barry Scheck, Peter Newfeld, and Jim Dugen, *Actual Innocence* (New York: Doubleday, 2000).

70 Benjamin Austin, "Right to Jury Trial," *Georgetown University Law Review* 85 (1997): 1240.

71 *Model Jury Standards for Criminal Trial* (Washington, D.C.: Federal Judicial Center, 1987). See also Michael Higgins, "Not So Plain English," *American Bar Association Journal* 84 (1998): 40

72 Scheck, Newfeld, and Jim Dugen, *Actual Innocence.*

73 Benjamin Austin, "Right to Jury Trial," *Georgetown University Law Review* 85 (1997): 1240.

74 Sandra Day O'Connor, "Juries: They May Be Broken—But We Can Fix Them," *Federal Lawyer* 44 (1997): 20.

75 Eugene Sullivan and Akhil Amar, "Jury Reform: A Return to the Old Country," *American Criminal Law Review* 33 (1996): 1141.

Chapter Outline

Chapter Objectives

After reading this chapter, you should be able to:

1. Understand the concept of criminal punishment.
2. Know the different stages of punishment used throughout history.
3. Recognize the differences between concurrent and consecutive sentences.
4. Explain the various reasons for criminal sanctions.
5. Discuss the concept of indeterminate sentencing.
6. Recognize why determinate sentencing was instituted.
7. Describe the role of sentencing guidelines.
8. Know what is meant by "three strikes and you're out."
9. Understand the concept of mandatory sentencing.
10. Know the arguments for and against capital punishment.
11. Describe the legal issues in capital sentencing.
12. Discuss the issue of whether the death penalty deters murder.

Viewpoints

 Analyzing Criminal Justice Issues: Getting Tough: Three Strikes Laws 406

 Race, Gender, and Ethnicity in Criminal Justice: Race and Sentencing 412

 International Justice: The Death Penalty Abroad 414

 Analyzing Criminal Justice Issues: The Capital Jury Project 418

InfoTrac College Edition Links

Key Term: "torture" 390

Article: "Putting Severity of Punishment Back in the Deterrence Package" 394

Article: "Why Do Increased Arrest Rates Appear to Reduce Crime? Deterrence, Incapacitation, or Measurement Error? 394

Article: "Sentencing Guidelines: The Problem of Conditional Sentences" 404

Key Term: "capital punishment" 410

Web Links

Trial and execution of William Wallace
http://www.lawbuzz.com/justice/braveheart/
betrayed.htm 392

Minnesota Sentencing Guidelines Commission
http://www.msgc.state.mn.us/ 401

Federal Sentencing
http://www.ussc.gov/ 401

Mandatory sentencing and the Sentencing Project
www.sentencingproject.org/ 404

Capital punishment and the American Civil Liberties Union
http://www.aclu.org/death-penalty/ 416

Capital Jury Project
http://www.lawschool.cornell.edu/
lawlibrary/death/cjp_publ.htm 417

Chapter 13 | Punishment and Sentencing

On July 15, 2002, Samantha Runnion, 5, was kidnapped while playing in front of her California home. The police received an anonymous tip and found her body soon afterward. She had been raped and murdered. A playmate of Samantha gave the police a good description of her attacker. Alejandro Avila was arrested and charged with four felonies — one count of kidnapping, two of forcible lewd acts on a child, and one of murder. Avila had been charged in a previous child molestation case but had not been convicted. After Avila's arrest, prosecutors cited "special circumstances" in the killing, kidnapping, and sexual assault on a minor, a standard that would allow them to seek the death penalty. Tony Ruckauckas, the Orange County district attorney, told reporters that he would consult with the victim's family and members of his staff before coming to a decision on whether Avila, if convicted, should be put to death. But, he said, "Anyone who commits this kind of crime in Orange County will either die in prison of natural causes or will be executed." The District Attorney's Office also let it be known that DNA evidence found at the crime scene linked Avila to the crime. Ruckauckas told reporters that the evidence was "very, very compelling, and we are satisfied that we have the right person."[1]

CNN. *View the CNN video clip of this story on your Introduction to Criminal Justice 10e CD.*

While such terrible incidents are relatively rare, the Runnion case raises important issues for the criminal justice system. First, the suspect's name and picture were broadcast almost instantly after his arrest, along with statements testifying to the incriminating evidence that had been gathered at the crime scene. Does such pretrial publicity make it virtually impossible for a suspect in a high-profile murder case to get a fair trial? In this age of pervasive media exposure, should limits be placed on press coverage? Or does this violate the Constitution's guarantee of free speech and press?

The Runnion case also illustrates the system's growing dependence on technology to solve crimes. How did the district attorney conclude that Avila was the real culprit? Because of DNA matches found at the crime scene. Is it fair to convict someone of a crime based on relatively new technologies that have not been proven over years of use? Avila may face the death penalty in the case. Should a person be executed based solely on a DNA match?

Finally, the Runnion case shows the complex issues surrounding the application of capital punishment in the United States. The district attorney told the press that he would consult with the family before making the decision to seek the death penalty. Should family members, justifiably emotional after their loss, be part of the decision to take the defendant's life? Why should a murder suspect's fate rest in the hands of the victim's family? Would the outcome be altered if the victim did not have any living family members? What role does public opinion play in the distribution of the death penalty? Samantha Runnion was a beautiful girl. Her death caused understandable public outrage. But should her killer be treated more harshly than another person who killed someone less vulnerable and less attractive? Should not all crime victims be considered equal? And finally, should the death penalty be employed if Samantha's killer suffered from some mental defect that caused him to have uncontrollable violent sexual urges? The U.S. Supreme Court has ruled that the death penalty cannot be used with people who are insane at the time they committed their offense. But what about people who are not legally insane but still suffer from severe psychological problems? Skeptics might suggest that all killers must suffer from psychological deficits. Should they be immune from punishments?

Historically, a full range of punishments has been inflicted on criminal defendants, including physical torture, branding, whipping, and, for most felony offenses, death. During the Middle Ages, the philosophy of punishment was to "torment the body for the sins of the soul."[2] People who violated the law were considered morally corrupt and in need of strong discipline. If punishment were harsh enough, it was assumed, they would never repeat their mistakes. Punishment was also viewed as a spectacle that taught a moral lesson. The more gruesome and public the sentence, the greater the impact it would have on the local populace.[3] Harsh physical punishments would control any thoughts of rebellion and dissent against the central government and those who held political and economic control. Such barbaric use of state power is no longer tolerated in the United States.

Today the major issue regarding criminal punishment involves both its nature and extent: Are too many people being sent to prison?[4] Do people get widely different sentences for similar crimes?[5] Is there discrimination in sentencing based on race, gender, or social class?[6] These are but a few of the most significant issues in the sentencing process.

Is torture still being used today? Use "Torture" as a subject guide on InfoTrac College Edition to find out.

The History of Punishment

The punishment and correction of criminals has changed considerably through the ages, reflecting custom, economic conditions, and religious and political ideals.[7]

The Granger Collection, New York

In earlier times, punishment was quite severe. Even kings, such as Charles I of England, were not immune from death by beheading.

From Exile to Fines, Torture to Forfeiture

In early Greece and Rome, the most common state-administered punishment was banishment, or exile. Only slaves were commonly subjected to harsh physical punishment for their misdeeds. Interpersonal violence, even attacks that resulted in death, was viewed as a private matter. These ancient peoples typically used economic punishments, such as fines, for such crimes as assault on a slave, arson, or housebreaking.

During the Middle Ages (fifth to fifteenth centuries), there was little law or governmental control. Offenses were settled by blood feuds carried out by the families of the injured parties. When possible, the Roman custom of settling disputes by fine or an exchange of property was adopted as a means of resolving interpersonal conflicts with a minimum of bloodshed. After the eleventh century, during the feudal period, forfeiture of land and property was common punishment for persons who violated law and custom or who failed to fulfill their feudal obligations to their lord. The word felony comes from the twelfth century, when the term *felonia* referred to a breach of faith with one's feudal lord.

During this period the main emphasis of criminal law and punishment was on maintaining public order. If in the heat of passion or while intoxicated a person severely injured or killed her neighbor, freemen in the area would gather to pronounce a judgment and make the culprit do penance or pay compensation called wergild. The purpose of the fine was to pacify the injured party and ensure that the conflict would not develop into a blood feud and anarchy. The inability of the peasantry to pay a fine led to the use of corporal punishment, such as whipping or branding, as a substitute penalty.

The development of the common law in the eleventh century brought some standardization to penal practices. However, corrections remained an amalgam of fines and brutal physical punishments. The criminal wealthy could buy their way out of punishment and into exile, but capital and corporal punishment were used to control the criminal poor, who were executed and mutilated at ever-increasing rates. Execution, banishment, mutilation, branding, and flogging were used on a whole range of offenders, from murderers and robbers to vagrants and Gypsies. Punishments became unmatched in their cruelty, featuring a gruesome variety of physical tortures often part of a public spectacle, presumably so that the sadistic **sanctions** would act as deterrents. But the variety and imagination of the tortures inflicted on even minor criminals before their death suggest that retribution, sadism, and spectacle were more important than any presumed deterrent effect.

sanctions
Social control mechanisms designed to enforce society's laws and standards.

 The trial and execution of William Wallace was depicted by Mel Gibson in the film *Braveheart*. The execution was a textbook case of medieval punishment. Read about it at http://www.lawbuzz.com/justice/braveheart/betrayed.htm.

Public Work and Transportation to the Colonies

By the end of the sixteenth century, the rise of the city and overseas colonization provided tremendous markets for manufactured goods and spurred the need for labor. **Punishment** of criminals changed to meet the demands created by these social conditions. Instead of being tortured or executed, many offenders were made to do hard labor for their crimes. **Poor laws,** developed at the end of the sixteenth century, required that the poor, vagrants, and vagabonds be put to work in public or private enterprises. Houses of correction were developed to make it convenient to assign petty law violators to work details. In London a workhouse was developed at Brideswell in 1557. Its use became so popular that by 1576 Parliament ordered a Brideswell-type workhouse to be built in every county in England. Many convicted offenders were pressed into sea duty as galley slaves. Galley slavery was considered a fate so loathsome that many convicts mutilated themselves to avoid servitude on the high seas.

punishment
Pain, suffering, loss, or sanction inflicted on a person because they committed a crime or offense.

poor laws
Seventeenth-century English laws under which vagrants and abandoned and neglected children were bound to masters as indentured servants.

The constant shortage of labor in the European colonies also prompted authorities to transport convicts overseas. In England, an Order in Council of 1617 granted a reprieve and stay of execution to people convicted of robbery and other felonies who were strong enough to be employed overseas. Similar measures were used in France and Italy to recruit galley slaves and workers.

Transporting convicts to the colonies became popular. It supplied labor, cost little, and was profitable for the government, because manufacturers and plantation owners paid for convicts' services. The Old Bailey Court in London supplied at least 10,000 convicts between 1717 and 1775. Convicts would serve a period as workers and then become free again.

The American Revolution ended the transportation of felons to North America, although it continued in Australia and New Zealand. Between 1787 and 1875, when the practice was finally abandoned, more than 135,000 felons were transported to Australia.

Although transportation in lieu of a death sentence may at first glance seem advantageous, transported prisoners endured enormous hardships. Those who were sent to Australia suffered incredible physical abuse, including severe whippings and mutilation. Many of the British prison officials placed in charge of the Australian penal colonies could best be described as sociopaths or sadists.

The Rise of the Prison

Between 1776, when the American colonies declared their independence from the British Crown, and the first decades of the nineteenth century, the population of Europe and the United States increased rapidly. Transportation of convicts to North America was no longer an option. The increased use of machinery made industry capital-intensive, not labor-intensive. As a result, there was less need for unskilled laborers in England, and many workers could not find suitable employment.

The gulf between poor workers and wealthy landowners and merchants widened. The crime rate rose significantly, prompting a return to physical punishment and increased use of the death penalty. During the latter part of the eighteenth century, 350 types of crime in England were punishable by death. Although many people sentenced to death for trivial offenses were spared the gallows, the use of capital punishment was common in England during the mid-eighteenth century. Prompted by the excessive use of physical and capital punishment, legal philosophers argued that physical punishment should be replaced by periods of confinement and incapacitation. Jails and workhouses were commonly used to hold petty offenders, vagabonds, the homeless, and debtors. However, these institutions were not meant for hard-core criminals. One solution to imprisoning a growing criminal population was to keep prisoners in abandoned ships anchored in rivers and harbors throughout England. The degradation under which prisoners lived in these ships inspired John Howard, the sheriff of Bedfordshire, in 1777 to write *The State of the Prisons,* which inspired Parliament to pass legislation mandating the construction of secure and sanitary structures to house prisoners.

By 1820 long periods of incarceration in walled institutions called reformatories or **penitentiaries** began to replace physical punishment in England and the United States. These institutions were considered liberal reforms during a time when harsh physical punishment and incarceration in filthy holding facilities were the norm. Incarceration has remained the primary mode of punishment for serious offenses in the United States since it was introduced in the early nineteenth century. Ironically, in America's high-tech society, some of the institutions constructed soon after the Revolutionary War are still in use today. In recent times, prison as a method of punishment has been supplemented by a sentence to community supervision for less serious offenders, and the death penalty is reserved for those considered to be the most serious and dangerous.

penitentiary
A state or federal correctional institution for the incarceration of felony offenders for terms of one year or more; prison.

 To quiz yourself on this material, go to questions 13.1–13.4 on the Introduction to Criminal Justice 10e CD.

The Goals of Modern Sentencing

When a notorious criminal, such as serial killers Jeffrey Dahmer or Ted Bundy, receives a long prison sentence or the death penalty for a particularly heinous crime, each person has a distinct reaction. Some are gratified that a truly evil person "got just what he deserved"; many people feel safer because a dangerous person is now "where she can't harm any other innocent victims"; others hope the punishment serves as a warning to potential criminals that "everyone gets caught in the end"; some may feel sorry for the defendant — "He got a raw deal, he needs help, not punishment"; and still others hope that "when she gets out, she'll have learned her lesson." And when an offender is forced to pay a large fine, someone says, "What goes around comes around."

Each of these sentiments may be at work when criminal sentences are formulated. After all, sentences are devised and implemented by judges, many of whom are elected officials and share the general public's sentiments and fears. The objectives of criminal sentencing today can usually be grouped into six distinct areas: general deterrence, incapacitation, specific deterrence, retribution/just desert, rehabilitation, and equity/restitution.

General Deterrence

One of the goals of sentencing is **general deterrence.** By severely punishing those people convicted of crime, it is believed that others who are contemplating future criminal activity will be deterred or dissuaded from their planned actions.

What is the impact on the community when a criminal offender is punished? By punishing an offender severely, the state can demonstrate its determination to control crime. Too lenient a sentence might encourage criminal conduct; too severe a sentence might reduce the system's ability to dispense fair and impartial justice and may encourage criminality. For example, if the crime of rape were punished with death, rapists might be encouraged to kill their victims to dispose of the one person who could identify them. Because they would already be facing

general deterrence
A crime control policy that depends on the fear of criminal penalties.

the death penalty for rape, they would have nothing more to lose. Maintaining a balance between fear and justice is an ongoing quest in the justice system.

Sentencing for the purposes of general deterrence, then, is designed to give a signal to the community at large: Crime does not pay.

Expected Punishment   The general deterrence concept relies on the fact that people will forgo criminal activity if they expect to be punished for their crimes. As the likelihood of getting punished increases, crime rates should go down. Similarly, if punishments become more severe, they should have a greater deterrent power.

Some justice experts attribute the recent decline in the crime rates to the fact that criminal penalties have been toughened for many crimes. Once arrested, people have a greater chance of being convicted today than in the past. This is referred to as "expected punishment" or the number of days in prison a typical criminal can expect to serve per each crime they commit.[8] According to the National Center for Policy Analysis (NCPA), crime rates dropped dramatically during the past two decades because expected punishment rose:

- For murder, nearly tripled from 14 months to 41 months.
- For rape, tripled to 128 days.
- For robbery, increased by 70 percent to 59 days.
- For serious assault, more than doubled to 18 days.
- For burglary, more than doubled from 4 days to 9 days.

Despite these increases, expected punishment is still low because most criminals are never apprehended and many that are have their cases dropped. Still others are given probation instead of prison sentences. For example, the NCPA figures that for every 100 burglaries, only about 7 are cleared by arrest and less than 2 convicted burglars are sentenced to prison.[9] Such inefficiency limits the deterrent effect of punishment. Other people may be too desperate or psychologically impaired by drugs and alcohol to be deterred by the threat of distant criminal punishment, or their economic circumstances may be too desperate for the threat of punishment to have an effect. Nonetheless, some experts believe that severe and draconian sentences can eventually bring down crime rates. They call for a get-tough policy featuring long, mandatory prison terms with little chance for early release.

Incapacitation

Incapacitation of criminals is a justifiable goal of sentencing because inmates will not be able to repeat their criminal acts while they are under state control. For some offenders, this means a period in a high-security state prison where behavior is closely monitored. According to this strategy, choosing the type of sentence and fixing its length involves determining how long a particular offender needs to be incarcerated to ensure that society is protected.

To some critics, incapacitation strategies seem of questionable utility because little association seems to exist between the number of criminals behind bars and the crime rate. Although the prison population jumped between 1980 and 1990, the crime rate also increased. This indicates that crime rates have little to do with incarceration trends and that reductions in crime are related to other factors such as population makeup, police effectiveness, declining drug use, and a strong economy.

In contrast, those who favor an incapacitation policy claim that the crime-reducing effect of putting people in prison has just taken a little longer than expected. The number of people and percentage of the general population behind bars escalated rapidly between 1990 and 2002, and the crime rate fell. This correlation is not a mere coincidence but a true incapacitation effect.

Would increasing the severity of punishment deter more crimes? To find out, read Silvia M. Mendes and Michael D. McDonald, "Putting Severity of Punishment Back in the Deterrence Package," *Policy Studies Journal* 29, no. 4 (Winter 2001): 588, on InfoTrac College Edition.

incapacitation
The policy of keeping dangerous criminals in confinement to eliminate the risk of their repeating their offense in society.

Which has a greater crime reducing effect, deterrence or incapacitation? To find out, read Steven D. Levitt, "Why Do Increased Arrest Rates Appear to Reduce Crime? Deterrence, Incapacitation, or Measurement Error?" *Economic Inquiry* 36, no. 3 (July 1998): 353, on InfoTrac College Edition.

Specific Deterrence

Experiencing harsh criminal punishments should convince convicted offenders that crime does not pay and **recidivism** is not in their best interests. The suffering caused by punishment should inhibit future law violations. A few research efforts have found that punishment can have significant specific deterrence on future criminality, but they are balanced by research that has failed to find specific deterrence effects. For example, a number of research studies have found little association between severity of punishment for past spousal abuse and rearrest on subsequent charges. Abusers seem just as likely to recidivate if their case is dismissed, if they are given probation, or if they are sent to jail.[10] The effect of **specific deterrence** is further undermined by data showing that most inmates (more than 80 percent) who are released from prison have had prior convictions and the great majority (68 percent) will reoffend soon after their release. The specific deterrent goal of sentencing is weakened by the fact that a prison stay seems to have little effect on reoffending.[11]

recidivism
Repetition of criminal behavior; habitual criminality.

specific deterrence
Punishment severe enough to convince convicted offenders never to repeat their criminal activity.

Retribution/Just Desert

According to the retributive goal of sentencing, the essential purpose of the criminal process is to punish deserving offenders — fairly and justly — in a manner that is proportionate to the gravity of their crimes.[12]

Offenders are punished simply and solely because they deserve to be disciplined for what they have done; "the punishment should fit the crime."[13] It would be wrong to punish people to set an example for others or to deter would-be criminals, as the general deterrence goal demands. Punishment should be no more or less than the offender's actions deserve. It must be based on how **blameworthy** the person is; this is referred to as the concept of **just desert**.[14]

According to this view, punishments must be equally and fairly distributed to all people who commit similar illegal acts. Determining just punishments can be difficult because there is generally little consensus about the treatment of criminals, the seriousness of crimes, and the proper response to criminal acts. Nonetheless, an ongoing effort has been made to calculate fair and just sentences by creating guidelines to control judicial decision making.

blameworthy
A person who is deserving of blame or punishment because of evil or injurious behavior.

just desert
The view that those who violate the rights of others deserve punishment commensurate with the seriousness of the crime.

Perspectives on Justice

The just desert basis of criminal sentencing is at the heart of the justice perspective, which maintains that people should be punished fairly, equally, and in proportion to the severity of their crimes.

Rehabilitation

Can criminal offenders be effectively treated so that they can eventually readjust to society? It may be fair to offer offenders an opportunity for rehabilitation instead of harsh criminal punishments. In a sense, society has failed criminal offenders, many of whom have grown up in disorganized neighborhoods and dysfunctional families. They may have been the target of biased police officers and, once arrested and labeled, placed at a disadvantage at home, at school, and in the job market.[15] Society is therefore obligated to help these unfortunate people who, through no fault of their own, experience social and emotional problems that are often the root of their criminal behavior.

The rehabilitation aspect of sentencing is based on a prediction of the future needs of the offender, not on the gravity of the current offense. For example, if a

felony
A more serious crime that carries a penalty of incarceration in a state or federal prison, usually for one year or more.

judge sentences a person convicted of a **felony** to a period of community supervision, the judge's actions reflect her belief that the offender can be successfully treated and presents no future threat to society.

The rehabilitation goal of sentencing has also been criticized by those who find little conclusive evidence exists that correctional treatment programs can prevent future criminality.[16] While the rehabilitative ideal has been undermined by such attacks, surveys indicate that the general public still supports the treatment goal of sentencing.[17] Many people express preferences for programs that are treatment-oriented, such as early childhood intervention and services for at-risk children, rather than those that espouse strict punishment and incarceration policies.[18] And evidence is growing that offender rehabilitation can be effective if the proper methods are used.[19]

Equity/Restitution

Because criminals gain from their misdeeds, it seems both fair and just to demand that they reimburse society for its loss caused by their crimes. In the early common law, **wergild** and fines represented the concept of creating an equitable solution to crime by requiring the convicted offender to make restitution to both the victim and the state. Today, judges continue to require that offenders pay victims for their losses.

wergild
During the Middle Ages, the compensation paid to the victim by a defendant found guilty of a crime.

equity
Sanction designed to compensate victims and society for the losses caused by crime; restitution.

The **equity** goal of punishment means that convicted criminals must pay back their victims for their loss, the justice system for the costs of processing their case, and society for any disruption they may have caused. In a so-called victimless crime, such as drug trafficking, the social costs might include the expense of drug enforcement efforts, drug treatment centers, and care for infants born to drug-addicted mothers. In predatory crimes, the costs might include the services of emergency room doctors, lost workdays and productivity, and treatment for long-term psychological problems. To help defray these costs, convicted offenders might be required to pay a fine, forfeit the property they acquired through illegal gain, do community service work, make financial restitution to their victim, and reimburse the state for the costs of the criminal process. Because the criminals' actions helped expand their personal gains, rights, and privileges at society's expense, justice demands that they lose rights and privileges to restore the social balance.

Each factor that influences sentencing decisions is illustrated in Figure 13.1.

One of the goals of punishment is equity: If the criminal benefited from his or her crime, it is only fair that he/she make restitution to the victim and society. Here, defense attorney Greg Jackson, left of center, leads convicted felons Darryl Willis, second from right, and Dale Erickson, right, from the courtroom after their sentencing hearing May 12, 2003, in Powell District Court in Deer Lodge, Montana. Willis and Erickson were sentenced according to a plea agreement giving each 25 years imprisonment with 10 years suspended for allegedly defrauding Una Anderson of millions of dollars including her family ranch. They were also ordered to pay $6.5 million in restitution.

© 2003 AP/Wide World Photos

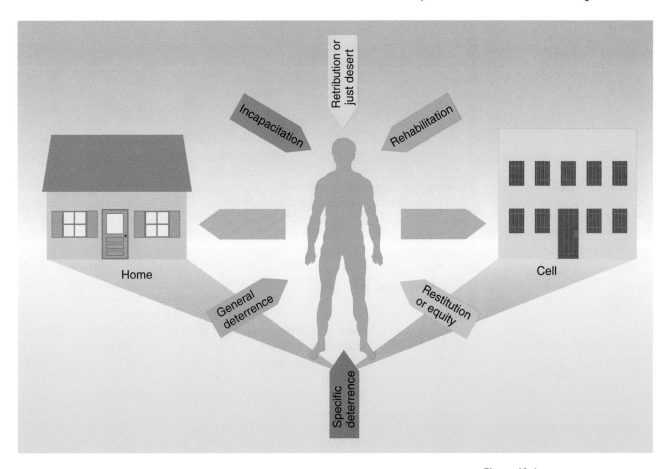

Figure 13.1
The Goals behind Sentencing Decisions

Imposing the Sentence

Regardless of the factors that influence the sentence, it is generally imposed by the judge, and sentencing is one of the most crucial functions of judgeship. Sentencing authority may also be exercised by the jury, or it may be mandated by statute (for example, a mandatory prison sentence for a certain crime).

In most felony cases, except when the law provides for mandatory prison terms, sentencing is usually based on a variety of information available to the judge. Some jurisdictions allow victims to make impact statements that are considered at sentencing hearings. Most judges also consider a presentence investigation report by the probation department in making a sentencing decision. This report is a social and personal history, as well as an evaluation of the defendant's chances for rehabilitation within the community. Some judges give the presentence investigation report great weight; others may dismiss it completely or rely on only certain portions.

When an accused person is convicted of two or more charges, he must be sentenced on each charge. If the sentences are *concurrent,* they begin the same day and are completed when the longest term has been served. For example, a defendant is convicted of burglarizing an apartment and assaulting its occupant. He is sentenced to 3 years on a charge of assault and 10 years for burglary, with the sentences to be served concurrently. After 10 years in prison, the sentences would be completed.

In contrast, receiving a **consecutive sentence** means that on completion of the sentence for one crime the offender begins serving time for the second of multiple crimes. If the defendant in the above example had been sentenced consecutively, he would serve 3 years on the assault charge and then 10 years for the burglary. Therefore, the total term on the two charges would be 13 years.

consecutive sentence
Incarceration for more than one offense such that each sentence begins only after the previous one has been completed.

**Figure 13.2
Consecutive versus
Concurrent Sentences**

Example: In state X	**Consecutive sentence**	**Concurrent sentence**
1. Rape is punishable by 10 years in prison 2. Possession of a handgun by 3 years 3. Possession of heroin by 4 years	Rape + possession of a handgun + possession of heroin 10 + 3 + 4 = 17 years (each sentence must be served)	Rape + possession of a handgun + possession of heroin 10 years (all sentences served simultaneously)

concurrent sentence
Incarceration for more than one offense such that all sentences begin on the same day and are completed after the longest term has been served.

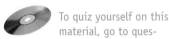
To quiz yourself on this material, go to questions 13.5–13.10 on the Introduction to Criminal Justice 10e CD.

indeterminate sentence
A term of incarceration with a stated minimum and maximum length; the prisoner is eligible for parole after serving the minimum.

Concurrent sentences are the norm. Consecutive sentences are requested for the most serious criminals and for those who are unwilling to cooperate with authorities. Figure 13.2 shows the difference between a consecutive and concurrent sentence.

Sentencing Models

When a convicted offender is sentenced to prison, the statutes of the jurisdiction in which the crime was committed determine the penalties that may be imposed by the court. Over the years, a variety of sentencing structures have been used in the United States. They include indeterminate sentences, determinate sentences, and mandatory sentences.

Indeterminate Sentences

In the 1870s, prison reformers, such as Enoch Wines and Zebulon Brockway, called for creation of **indeterminate sentences,** tailored to fit individual needs. Offenders, the argument went, should be placed in confinement only until they were rehabilitated and then they should be released on parole. Criminals were believed to be sick, not bad. They could be successfully treated in prison. Instead of holding that "the punishment should fit the crime," reformers believed "the treatment should fit the offender."

The indeterminate sentence is still the most widely used type of sentence in the United States. Convicted offenders are typically given a light minimum sentence that must be served and a lengthy maximum sentence that is the outer boundary of the time that can be served. For example, the legislature might set a sentence of a minimum of 3 years and a maximum of 20 years for burglary. The convicted offender thus must be sentenced to no less than 3 years but no more than 20 years in prison. Under this scheme, the actual length of time served by the offender is controlled both by the judge and the correctional agency. A judge could sentence a burglar between 3 and 20 years. The inmate could then be paroled from confinement soon after serving the minimum sentence if the correctional authorities believe that she is ready to live in the community. If the inmate accumulates good time, she could be released in 18 months; a troublesome inmate would be forced to do all 20 years.

The basic purpose of the indeterminate sentence is to individualize each sentence in the interests of rehabilitating the offender. This type of sentencing allows for flexibility not only in the type of sentence to be imposed but also in the length of time to be served.

Most jurisdictions that use indeterminate sentences employ statutes that specify minimum and maximum terms but allow judicial discretion to fix the actual sentence within those limits. The typical minimum sentence is at least one year; a few state jurisdictions require at least a two-year minimum sentence for felons.[20]

Determinate Sentences

The indeterminate sentence has come under attack in recent years for a variety of reasons. It is alleged to produce great disparity in the way people are treated in the correctional system. For example, one offender may serve 1 year, and another may serve 20 years, for the same crime. Further, the indeterminate sentence is believed to take control of sentencing out of the hands of the judiciary and place it within the framework of corrections, especially when the minimum sentence is short. Every time an inmate who is granted early release via discretionary parole and commits a violent crime, the call goes up to get tough on prison inmates. In contrast, many inmates feel cheated by the system when they are denied parole, despite having a good prison record. The protections of due process maintained in the courtroom are absent in the correctional setting. Dissatisfaction with the disparity and uncertainty of indeterminate sentencing has prompted some states and the federal government to abandon it in favor of determinate sentencing models or structured sentencing models.

Determinate sentences, the first kind used in the United States, are still being used today. As originally conceived, a determinate sentence was a fixed term of years, the maximum set in law by the legislature, to be served by the offender sentenced to prison for a particular crime. For example, if the law provided for a sentence of up to 20 years for robbery, the judge might sentence a repeat offender to a 15-year term. Another, less experienced felon might receive a more lenient sentence of 5 years.

determinate sentence
A fixed term of incarceration.

Good Time Although determinate sentences provide a single term of years to be served without benefit of parole, the time spent in prison is reduced by the implementation of "time off for good behavior." This concept was first used in 1817 in New York, and it was quickly adopted in most other jurisdictions. **Good time** is still in use today. Inmates can accrue standard good time at a rate ranging from 10 to 15 days per month. In addition, some correctional authorities grant earned sentence reductions to inmates who participate in treatment programs, such as educational and vocational training, or who volunteer for experimental medical testing programs. More than half of a determinate sentence can be erased by accumulating both standard and earned good time.

good time
Reduction of a prison sentence by a specified amount in exchange for good behavior within the institution.

Good-time laws allow inmates to calculate their release date at the time they enter prison by subtracting the expected good time from their sentence. However, good time can be lost if inmates break prison rules, get into fights, or disobey correctional officers. In some jurisdictions, former inmates can be returned to prison to serve the balance of their unexpired sentence when their good time is revoked for failing to conform to conditions set down for their release (for example, not reporting to a postrelease supervisor or for abusing drugs).

Structured Sentences

Coinciding with the development of determinate sentencing has been the development of sentencing guidelines to control and structure the process and make it more rational. Guidelines are usually based on the seriousness of a crime and the background of an offender: The more serious the crime and the more extensive the offender's criminal background, the longer is the prison term recommended by the guidelines. For example, guidelines might require that all people convicted of robbery who had no prior offense record and who did not use excessive force or violence be given an average of a five-year sentence; those who used force and had a prior record will have three years added to their sentence. By eliminating judicial discretion, structured sentences are designed to reduce racial and gender disparity.[21] Exhibit 13.1 lists some of the goals of sentencing guidelines.

Exhibit 13.1 The Goals of Sentencing Guidelines

- Reduce judicial disparity in sentencing.
- Promote more uniform and consistent sentencing.
- Project the amount of correctional resources needed.
- Prioritize and allocate correctional resources.
- Increase punishments for certain categories of offenders and offenses.
- Decrease punishment for certain categories of offenders and offenses.
- Establish truth-in-sentencing.
- Make the sentencing process more open and understandable.
- Encourage the use of particular sanctions for particular categories of offenders.
- Encourage increased use of nonincarceration sanctions (intermediate and community-based).
- Reduce prison crowding.
- Provide a rational basis for sentencing.
- Increase judicial accountability.

Source: Robin Lubitz and Thomas Ross, *Sentencing Guidelines: Reflections on the Future* (Washington, D.C.: National Institute of Justice, June 2001).

How Are Guidelines Used? Today, about 18 states use some form of structured sentencing. About 7 states employ voluntary/advisory sentencing guidelines (sometimes called descriptive guidelines), which are used merely to suggest rather than mandate sentencing. In the other states, presumptive sentencing guidelines (sometimes called prescriptive guidelines) are used. These require judges to use the guidelines to shape their sentencing decisions, and their sentencing decisions may be open to appellate review if they stray from the mandated sentences. Michigan, Minnesota, North Carolina, Oregon, Pennsylvania, Washington, and the federal government mandate that judges follow a set of comprehensive presumptive guidelines.[22]

Prescriptive guidelines are created by appointed sentencing commissions. The commission members determine what an ideal sentence would be for a particular crime and offender. However, a great deal of variation exists within prescriptive sentencing.[23]

Sentencing guidelines such as the ones used in Minnesota are designed to create fair punishments while reducing sentencing disparity. With the help of physical therapist Mary Mentone, left, and student Jennifer Roun, Rick Hennek walks January 10, 2002, at Bethesda Rehabilitation Hospital in St. Paul, Minnesota, as his mother, sister, and father follow. In October 2001, Hennek was beaten and left for dead at an apartment building outside St. Cloud. Waite Park detective Ben Theisen tracked down Jakub Drewiczak, who was convicted in the beating and sentenced to nine years in prison. Considering the seriousness of Hennek's injuries is a sentence of nine years in prison sufficient punishment? What would you recommend? Does your sentence match the one suggested by the guidelines?

© 2003 AP/Wide World Photos

Within this basic framework are many different approaches to using guidelines. Some coexist with discretionary parole release, while others replace parole with mandatory release from prison once the statutory guideline sentence has been fulfilled. Some deal with all crimes and others only with felonies. Some set narrow sentencing ranges, and some set broad ones.[24] Some states provide for a wide range of sentences, while others prescribe a narrow range. Some states link use of guidelines to the availability of correctional resources, while others do not take resources into account. There are states that address only confinement and those that incorporate a range of intermediate sentencing options. Finally, there are states whose guidelines incorporate an appellate review process for all sentences and those with no appellate review.[25]

The Minnesota Guidelines Guidelines can be formulated in a number of ways. One method is to create a grid with prior record and current offense as the two coordinates and setting out specific punishment. Figure 13.3 shows Minnesota's guidelines. As prior record and offense severity increase, so does recommended sentence length. After a certain point, probation is no longer an option, and the defendant must do prison time. A burglar with no prior convictions can expect to receive probation or an 18-month sentence for a house break-in; an experienced burglar with six or more prior convictions can get four years for the same crime, and probation is not an option.

Minnesota judges do retain some discretion and are allowed to depart from the guidelines when substantial and compelling aggravating (or mitigating) circumstances exist. If they depart from the guidelines, the judge must provide written reasons that articulate the substantial and compelling circumstances and that demonstrate why the sentence given is more appropriate or fair than the presumptive sentence.[26] The prosecution or defense may appeal the sentence if the judge departs from the guidelines. If an offender is sent to prison, the sentence consists of two parts: a *term of imprisonment* equal to two-thirds of the total executed sentence and a *supervised release* term equal to the remaining one-third. The amount of time the offender serves in prison may be extended by the commissioner of corrections, if the offender violates disciplinary rules while in prison or violates conditions of supervised release. This extension period could result in the offender serving the entire sentence in prison.[27]

Federal Guidelines The federal guidelines use a somewhat different cookbook approach to determine sentences. A magistrate must first determine the base penalty that a particular charge is given in the guidelines. For example, the federal guidelines give a base score (20) and mitigation factors for robbery. The base level can be adjusted upward if the crime was particularly serious or violent. Seven points could be added to the robbery base if a firearm was discharged during the crime, or 5 points if the weapon was simply in the offender's possession. Similarly, points can be added to a robbery if a large amount of money was taken, a victim was injured, a person was abducted or restrained to facilitate an escape, or the object of the robbery was to steal weapons or drugs. Upward adjustments can also be made if the defendant was a ringleader in the crime, obstructed justice, or used a professional skill or position of trust (such as doctor, lawyer, or politician) to commit the crime. Offenders designated as career criminals by a court can likewise receive longer sentences.

Once the base score is computed, judges determine the sentence by consulting a sentencing table that converts scores into months to be served. Offense levels are set out in the vertical column, and the criminal history (ranging from one to six prior offenses) is displayed in a horizontal column, forming a grid that contains the various sentencing ranges (similar to the Minnesota guideline grid). By matching the applicable offense level and the criminal history, the judge can determine the sentence that applies to the particular offender.

To access the Minnesota Sentencing Guidelines Commission home page, go to http://www.msgc.state.mn.us/.

The Federal Sentencing Web site is located at http://www.ussc.gov/.

Criminal history score

Severity level of conviction offense		0	1	2	3	4	5	6 or More
Murder, second degree (intentional murder; drive-by shootings)	XI	306 *299–313*	326 *319–333*	346 *339–353*	366 *359–373*	386 *379–393*	406 *399–413*	426 *419–433*
Murder, third degree Murder, second degree (unintentional murder)	X	150 *144–156*	165 *159–171*	180 *174–186*	195 *189–201*	210 *204–216*	225 *219–231*	240 *234–246*
Criminal sexual conduct, first degree* Assault, first degree	IX	86 *81–91*	98 *93–103*	110 *105–115*	122 *117–127*	134 *129–139*	146 *141–151*	158 *153–163*
Aggravated robbery, first degree	VIII	48 *44–52*	58 *54–62*	68 *64–72*	78 *74–82*	88 *84–92*	98 *94–102*	108 *104–112*
Felony driving while intoxicated (DWI)	VII	36	42	48	54 *51–57*	60 *57–63*	66 *63–69*	72 *69–75*
Criminal sexual conduct, second degree (a) and (b)	VI	21	27	33	39 *37–41*	45 *43–47*	51 *49–53*	57 *55–59*
Residential burglary Simple robbery	V	18	23	28	33 *31–35*	38 *36–40*	43 *41–45*	48 *46–50*
Nonresidential burglary	IV	12†	15	18	21	24 *23–25*	27 *26–28*	30 *29–31*
Theft crimes (over $2,500)	III	12†	13	15	17	19 *18–20*	21 *20–22*	23 *22–24*
Theft crimes ($2,500 or less) Check forgery ($200–$2,500)	II	12†	12†	13	15	17	19	21 *20–22*
Sale of simulated controlled substance	I	12†	12†	12†	13	15	17	19 *18–20*

☐ Presumptive commitment to state imprisonment. First-degree murder is excluded from the guidelines by law and continues to have a mandatory life sentence. See section II.E. Mandatory Sentences for policy regarding those sentences controlled by law, including minimum periods of supervision for sex offenders released from prison.

▨ Presumptive stayed sentence; at the discretion of the judge, up to a year in jail or other non-jail sanctions or both can be imposed as conditions of probation. However, certain offenses in this section of the grid always carry a presumptive commitment to state prison. These offenses include third-degree controlled substance crimes when the offender has a prior felony drug conviction, burglary of an occupied dwelling when the offender has a prior felony burglary conviction, second and subsequent criminal sexual conduct offenses and offenses carrying a mandatory minimum prison term due to the use of a dangerous weapon (second-degree assault). See sections II.C. Presumptive Sentence and II.E. Mandatory Sentences.

* Pursuant to M.S. § 609.342, subd. 2, the presumptive sentence for criminal sexual conduct in the first degree is a minimum of 144 months (see II.C. Presumptive Sentence and II.G. Convictions for Attempts, Conspiracies, and Other Sentence Modifiers).

† One year and one day.

Note: Italicized numbers within the grid denote the range within which a judge may sentence without the sentence being deemed a departure. Offenders with nonimprisonment felony sentences are subject to jail time according to law.
Source: Minnesota Sentencing Guidelines Commission, August 1, 2002.

Figure 13.3
Sentencing Guidelines Grid
(Presumptive Sentence Lengths in Months)

How Effective Are Guidelines? Despite the widespread acceptance of guidelines, some nagging problems remain. A number of critics, including Michael Tonry, argue that they are rigid, harsh, and overly complex; disliked by the judiciary; and should be substantially revised or totally eliminated.[28]

One important criticism is that guidelines are biased against African Americans and Hispanics despite their stated goal of removing discrimination from the

sentencing process. One recent research effort found that, in some federal jurisdictions, Hispanic defendants are often perceived as "villains" instead of "victims" in drug-trafficking cases and receive sentences that are longer than those
given to other minority group members.[29] The most notorious element of the
federal guidelines is the one mandating that the possession of crack cocaine be
punished far more severely than possession of powdered cocaine. Critics charge
that this amounts to racial bias because African Americans are much more likely
to be charged with possessing crack cocaine than Caucasians, who are more commonly charged with possessing powdered cocaine.[30] The disparity in sentencing
seems ludicrous to critics because there is no pharmacological difference between crack cocaine and powder cocaine. However, the former can be broken
into bits and sold relatively cheaply on the street, while the latter is usually bought
and sold more discreetly indoors.[31]

Some jurisdictions give enhanced sentences if defendants have a prior juvenile conviction or if they were on juvenile probation or parole at the time of an
arrest. African American offenders are more likely than white offenders to have a
prior record as a juvenile and therefore receive harsher sentences for their current crime.[32] These fears are confirmed by some recent research conducted by
Barbara Koons-Witt, who found that the Minnesota guidelines influenced sentencing outcomes in a number of unexpected ways. During the pre-guidelines
and early guidelines periods, white males had the highest probability of receiving
a prison sentence, followed by white females, nonwhite males, and then nonwhite females. After guidelines were implemented, white male offenders no
longer had the highest probability of imprisonment; nonwhite male offenders
did. Nonwhite female offenders eventually had a higher probability of being sent
to prison than white female offenders.[33] The Koons-Witt research indicates that
guidelines may cause racial injustice to increase, not decrease.

Some defense attorneys oppose the use of guidelines because they result in
longer prison terms, prevent judges from considering mitigating circumstances,
and reduce the use of probation. Even the widely heralded federal guidelines
have had and will continue to have some dubious effects. The use of probation
has diminished and the size of the federal prison population is increasing because guideline sentences are tougher and defendants have little incentive to plea
bargain. They require incarceration sentences for petty offenders who in pre-
guideline days would have been given community release. Many of these petty
offenders might be better served with cheaper alternative sanctions.[34] Evidence
also exists that judges in different courts interpret elements of the guidelines differently, for example, assigning different crime seriousness scores, so that the effect is to create jurisdictional differences in the way guidelines are applied.[35]
Nationally, in approximately 36 percent of all cases, judges depart from the guidelines. In some jurisdictions, such as the Northern District of New York and the
Southern District of California, the majority of defendants were not sentenced
within the guidelines' range. In contrast, approximately 90 percent of all defendants in both the Northern District of West Virginia and the Eastern District of
Virginia were sentenced within the guidelines' range. It is hard to argue that the
guidelines create sentence uniformity when less than half of the defendants in
some jurisdictions are sentenced in accordance with the guidelines' calculation
while in others 90 percent of all defendants meet the guideline standards.[36]

Because of these problems, sentencing expert Michael Tonry calls the federal
guidelines "the most controversial and disliked sentencing reform initiative in
United States history."[37] In his important book *Sentencing Matters,* Tonry offers
a prescription to improve structured sentencing guidelines that calls in part for
the creation of ongoing sentencing commissions, establishment of realistic guidelines, reliance on alternative sanctions, and a sentencing philosophy that stresses
the "least punitive and intrusive appropriate sentence."[38] Tonry's claims have not
gone unnoticed. In August 2003, Supreme Court justice Anthony M. Kennedy in

To read about the use of sentencing guidelines abroad, read Martin Wasik, "Sentencing Guidelines: The Problem of Conditional Sentences," *Criminal Justice Ethics* 13, no. 1 (Winter–Spring 1994): 50–57, on InfoTrac College Edition.

a speech to the American Bar Association said that too many people are imprisoned in the United States and called for the end of mandatory minimum prison terms. He also said that U.S. sentencing guidelines should be more lenient: "Our resources are misspent; our punishments too severe, our sentences too long." Kennedy urged the lawyers to ask Congress to repeal federal mandatory minimum sentences and "let the judges be judges." In response, the association took on the challenge of examining whether the nation's sentencing policies are too tough.[39]

Mandatory Sentences

Another effort to limit judicial discretion and at the same time get tough on crime has been the development of the mandatory sentence. Some states, for example, prohibit people convicted of certain offenses, such as violent crimes, and chronic offenders (recidivists) from being placed on probation. They must serve at least some time in prison. Other statutes bar certain offenders from being considered for parole. Mandatory sentencing legislation may impose minimum and maximum terms, but typically it requires a fixed prison sentence.

mandatory sentence
A statutory requirement that a certain penalty be set and carried out in all cases on conviction for a specified offense or series of offenses.

Mandatory sentencing generally limits the judge's discretionary power to impose any disposition but that authorized by the legislature. As a result, it limits individualized sentencing and restricts sentencing disparity. Mandatory sentencing provides equal treatment for all offenders who commit the same crime, regardless of age, sex, or other individual characteristics.

More than 35 states have replaced discretionary sentencing with fixed-term mandatory sentences for such crimes as the sale of hard drugs, kidnapping, gun possession, and arson. The results have been mixed. Mandatory sentences have helped increase the size of the correctional population to record levels. They have also failed to eliminate racial disparity from the sentencing process.[40] Some state courts have ruled such practices unconstitutional. As a result, many offenders who in the past might have received probation are now being incarcerated. The use of mandatory sentencing is discussed in the Analyzing Criminal Justice Issues feature on page 406, which describes a recent development in mandatory sentencing, the three strikes law.

 For more on mandatory sentencing, the Sentencing Project has news publications and a search engine on its Web site: www.sentencingproject.org/.

Truth-in-Sentencing

truth-in-sentencing
Sentencing reform sponsored by the federal government mandating that any defendant who has plead guilty to or has been found guilty of a felony shall be required to serve a minimum prison term of 85 percent of the sentence imposed by the court.

Truth-in-sentencing laws, another get-tough measure designed to fight a rising crime rate, require offenders to serve a substantial portion of their prison sentence behind bars.[41] Parole eligibility and good-time credits are restricted or eliminated. The movement was encouraged by the Violent Offender Incarceration and Truth-in-Sentencing Incentive Grants Program, part of the federal government's 1994 Crime Act, which offered funds to support the state costs associated with creating longer sentences. To qualify for federal funds, states must require persons convicted of a violent felony crime to serve not less than 85 percent of the prison sentence. Today more than half the states and the District of Columbia met the federal Truth-in-Sentencing Incentive Grant Program eligibility criteria. Eleven states adopted truth-in-sentencing laws in 1995, one year after the 1994 Crime Act.

How People Are Sentenced Some of the most important information about how people are sentenced comes from national studies sponsored by the Bureau of Justice Statistics.[42]

According to the latest data available (Table 13.1), covering 2000, nearly a million adults were convicted in state and federal courts. About 68 percent of all felons were sentenced to a period of confinement — 40 percent to state prisons

Table 13.1 Lengths of Felony Sentences Imposed by State Courts, 2000

	Average maximum sentence length (in months) for felons sentenced to incarceration			
Most serious conviction offense	*Total*	*Prison*	*Jail*	*Probation*
All offenses	36	55	6	38
Violent offenses	66	91	7	44
Property offenses	27	42	6	38
Drug offenses	30	47	6	36
Weapons offenses	25	38	7	36
Other offenses	22	38	6	40

Note: Means exclude sentences to death or to life in prison. Sentence length data were available for 852,616 incarceration and probation sentences.

Source: Bureau of Justice Statistics, 2003.

and 28 percent to local jails. About 32 percent of convicted felons were given straight probation with no jail or prison time to serve. Besides being sentenced to incarceration or probation, about 40 percent of convicted felons were ordered to pay a fine, provide victim restitution, receive treatment, perform community service, or comply with some other penalty. About 25 percent of convicted felons had to pay a fine in addition to their incarceration or community sentence.

How long was the average sentence? Felons sentenced to a state prison in 2000 had an average sentence of four-and-a-half years. As Table 13.1 shows, those sentenced to prison for violent crimes received the longest sentences — almost eight years. However, most did not serve their term but were released via parole or other sentencing reduction programs after serving a little more than half their sentence.

Doing More Time Though the crime rate has dropped significantly during the past decade, the correctional population has not followed suit. One reason may be that the percentage of the criminal sentence spent behind bars before release has been increasing. As Table 13.2 and Figure 13.4 show, the percentage of convicted offenders now receiving a prison sentence is less than it was in 1992. Meanwhile, community sentences are being used more frequently. In addition, as the data in Table 13.3 indicate, the lengths of sentences are less than they were a decade ago. Then why hasn't the prison population plummeted? The answer is that for many crime categories inmates are serving a greater percentage of their sentence than they did in the past. In 1992 the typical felon received six-and-a-half years and served about two-and-a-half years, or a third of that sentence, before being released. By contrast, in 2000 the typical felon received only five years but served about half before being released, or two-and-a-half years (Table 13.4). The increased percentage of sentence time spent behind bars is the result of passage of tough sentencing laws

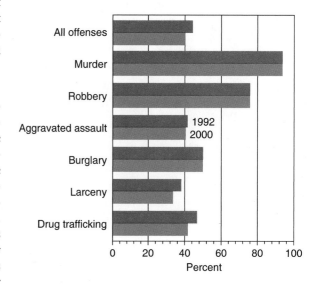

Figure 13.4 Percent of Convicted Felons Who Received a Prison Sentence, 1992–2000

Source: Matthew Durose and Brian Reaves, *Felony Sentences in State Courts, 2000* (Washington, D.C.: Bureau of Justice Statistics, 2003); p. 11.

Getting Tough: Three Strikes Laws

analyzing criminal justice issues

During his lifetime, Michael Riggs had been convicted eight times in California for such offenses as car theft and robbery. In 1996 he was once again in trouble, this time for shoplifting a $20 bottle of vitamins. Riggs was sentenced to a term of 25 years to life under California's three strikes law, which mandates a life sentence for anyone convicted of a third offense. The law enables a trial judge to treat a defendant's third offense, even a petty crime such as shoplifting, as if it were a felony for purposes of applying the law's mandatory sentencing provisions. Riggs must serve a minimum of 20.8 years before parole eligibility. Without the three strikes law, he would ordinarily have earned a maximum sentence of six months. If he had been convicted of murder, he would have had to serve only 17 years. Riggs appealed his conviction to the U.S. Supreme Court in 1999, but the justices refused to rule on the case, letting his sentence stand.

While the punishment given Riggs seems excessive, public concern over crime has convinced lawmakers to toughen sentences for repeat offenders and those who commit serious crimes.

Three Strikes Laws

Three strikes and you're out laws provide these lengthy terms for any person convicted of three felony offenses, even if the third crime is relatively trivial. California's statutory three strikes law is

Leandro Andrade was sentenced to 50 years in prison for stealing four videotapes from a Wal-Mart in 1995.

© 2003 AP/Wide World Photos

aimed at getting habitual criminals off the street. The federal Crime Act of 1994 also adopted a three strikes provision, requiring a mandatory life sentence for any offender convicted of three felony offenses. Twenty-six states have so far followed suit and passed some form of the three strikes law.

Although welcomed by conservatives looking for a remedy for violent crime, the three strikes policy is controversial because a person convicted of a minor felony can receive a life sentence. Some judges reportedly are defying three strikes provisions because they consider them

unduly harsh. Much to the chagrin of three strikes advocates, two California court decisions, *People* v. *Romero* (1996) and *People* v. *Garcia* (1999), allow judges to disregard an earlier conviction if the judge believes a life term is unjustified.

The Costs Are High

Three strikes laws have undeniable political appeal to legislators being pressured by their constituents to "do something about crime." Yet even if possibly effective against crime, any effort to deter criminal behavior through tough laws is not without costs. In California alone the

requiring that offenders spend a considerable portion of their sentence behind bars.

What Factors Affect Sentencing?

What factors influence judges when they decide on criminal sentences? Crime seriousness and the offender's prior record are certainly considered. State sentencing codes usually include various factors that can legitimately influence the length of prison sentences, including the following:

- The severity of the offense.
- The offender's prior criminal record.

three strikes law is estimated to increase correctional spending $4.5 billion to $6.5 billion per year.

Three strikes laws may in fact help put some chronic offenders behind bars, but can they realistically be expected to lower the crime rate? Criminologist Marc Mauer, a leading opponent of the three strike law, finds that the approach may satisfy the public's hunger for retribution but makes little practical sense. First, three-time losers are at the brink of aging out of crime. Locking them up for life should have little effect on the crime rate. In addition, current sentences for chronic violent offenders are already severe, yet their punishment seems to have had little influence on reducing national violence rates. A three strikes policy also suffers because criminals typically underestimate their risk of apprehension while overestimating the rewards of crime. Given their inflated view of the benefits of crime, coupled with a seeming disregard of the risks of apprehension and punishment, a three strikes policy is unlikely to have a measurable deterrent effect on the crime rate. Even if such a policy could reduce the number of career offenders on the street, the drain in economic resources that might have gone for education and social welfare ensures that a new generation of young criminals will fill the offending shoes of their incarcerated brethren. Mauer also suggests that a three strikes policy will enlarge an already overburdened prison system, driving up costs, and, presumably,

reducing resources available to house other inmates. Mauer warns that African Americans face an increased risk of being sentenced under three strikes statutes, expanding the racial disparity in sentencing. More ominous is the fact that police officers may be put at risk because two-time offenders would violently resist arrest, knowing that they face a life sentence.

Two recent cases have upheld the legality of the three strikes concept. In *Lockyer* v. *Andrade* (2003), the U.S. Supreme Court ruled that it was permissible to send a criminal to prison for 50 years for stealing $153 worth of videotapes. In *Ewing* v. *California* (2002), the Court also upheld the three strikes concept for a petty theft. These cases indicate that those states wishing to bear the financial burden of incarcerating petty offenders for long periods of time will be permitted to do so by the nation's highest court.

Critical Thinking

1. Is a policy that calls for spending billions on incarceration throwing money into the wind? Why or why not? After all, the number of people in prison already exceeds 1 million, and little conclusive evidence shows that incarceration alone can reduce crime rates. Might the funds earmarked for prison construction be used elsewhere with greater effect? Explain.
2. A large portion of the prison population consists of drug offenders. Al-

though the number of people incarcerated for violent and property crimes has decreased in recent years, the number of incarcerated drug offenders has skyrocketed. Are the nation's interests best served by giving a life sentence to someone convicted of his third drug-trafficking charge, even if the crime involves selling a small amount of cocaine? Explain.

InfoTrac College Edition Research

 To learn more about three strikes laws, read Kelly McMurry, "Three-Strikes Laws Proving More Show Than Go," *Trial* 33 (1997): 12; Chi Chi Sileo, "Are Three-Strikes Laws Handcuffing the Courts?" *Insight on the News* 11 (1995): 14.

Sources: *Lockyer* v. *Andrade,* 01–1127 (2003); *Ewing* v. *California,* 01–6978 (2003); Riggs v. *California,* No. 98–5021 (1999); Public Law No. 103-322; "California Supreme Court Undercuts Three-Strikes Law," *Criminal Justice Newsletter,* July 1, 1996, p. 2; "Three-Strikes Laws Rarely Used, Except California's, Study Finds," *Criminal Justice Newsletter,* September 17, 1996, p. 4; "California Passes a Tough Three-Strikes-You're-Out Law," *Criminal Justice Newsletter,* April 4, 1993, p. 6; *California's New Three-Strikes Law: Benefits, Costs, and Alternatives,* RAND Research Brief (Santa Monica, Calif.: RAND Corp., 1994); *Marc Mauer Testimony before the U.S. Congress House Judiciary Committee on "Three Strikes and You're Out,"* March 1, 1994 (Washington, D.C.: Sentencing Project, 1994); Lois Forer, *A Rage to Punish: The Unintended Consequences of Mandatory Sentencing* (New York: Norton, 1994).

*   Whether the offender used violence.
*   Whether the offender used weapons.
*   Whether the crime was committed for money.

Research shows a strong correlation between these legal variables and the type and length of sentence received. For example, judges seem less willing to use discretion in cases involving the most serious criminal charges such as terrorism, while employing greater control in low-severity cases.[43]

Besides these legally appropriate factors, sentencing experts suspect that judges may be influenced by the defendant's age, race, gender, and income. Considerations of such variables would be a direct violation of constitutional due process and equal protection, as well as of federal statutes, such as the Civil Rights

Table 13.2 Percentage of Convicted Offenders Receiving a Prison Sentence

	Convicted felons who received a prison sentence (percent)		
	1992	*1996*	*2000*
All Offenses	44	38	40
Murder	93	92	93
Robbery	74	73	74
Aggravated assault	44	42	40
Burglary	52	45	52
Larceny	38	31	33
Drug trafficking	48	39	41

Source: Matthew Durose and Brian Reaves, *Felony Sentences in State Courts, 2000* (Washington, D.C.: Bureau of Justice Statistics, 2003), p. 11.

Table 13.3 Average Prison Sentences, 1992–2000

	Average imposed prison sentence length (in months)		
	1992	*1996*	*2000*
All Offenses	79	62	55
Murder	251	257	248
Robbery	117	101	94
Aggravated assault	87	69	59
Burglary	76	60	52
Larceny	53	40	34
Drug trafficking	72	55	52

Source: Matthew Durose and Brian Reaves, *Felony Sentences in State Courts, 2000* (Washington, D.C.: Bureau of Justice Statistics, 2003), p. 11.

Table 13.4 Percentage of Sentence Served behind Bars

	Imposed prison sentence actually served (percent)		
	1992	*1996*	*2000*
All Offenses	38	45	55
Murder	44	50	64
Robbery	46	47	58
Aggravated assault	48	54	64
Burglary	35	42	55
Larceny	38	44	59
Drug trafficking	34	42	49

Source: Matthew Durose and Brian Reaves, *Felony Sentences in State Courts, 2000* (Washington, D.C.: Bureau of Justice Statistics, 2003), p. 11.

Act. Limiting judicial bias is one of the reasons that states have adopted determinate and mandatory sentencing statutes. Do extralegal factors influence judges when they make sentencing decisions?

Social Class Evidence supports an association between social class and sentencing outcomes. Members of the lower class may expect to get longer prison sentences than more affluent defendants. One reason is that poor defendants may be unable to obtain quality legal representation or to make bail, factors that influence sentencing.[44]

Not all research efforts have found a consistent class–crime relationship, however, and the relationship may be more robust for some crime patterns than others.[45]

Gender Does a defendant's gender influence how he or she is sentenced? Some theorists believe that women benefit from sentence disparity because the criminal justice system is dominated by men who have a paternalistic or protective attitude toward women; this is referred to as the **chivalry hypothesis.** Others argue that female criminals can be the victim of bias because their behavior violates what men believe is proper female behavior.[46]

© 2002 AP/Wide World Photos

Most research indicates that women receive more favorable outcomes the further they go in the criminal justice system. They are more likely to receive preferential treatment from a judge at sentencing than they are from the police officer making the arrest or the prosecutor seeking the indictment.[47] Favoritism crosses both racial and ethnic lines, benefiting African American, white, and Hispanic women.[48] Gender bias may be present because judges perceive women as better risks than men. Women have been granted more lenient pretrial release conditions and lower bail amounts than men. Women are also more likely to spend less time in pretrial detention.[49] Recent research indicates that women with dependent children are the ones most likely to receive leniency, probably because judges are reluctant to incarcerate a child's most essential care-giver.[50]

Age Another extralegal factor that may play a role in sentencing is age. Judges may be more lenient with elderly defendants and more punitive toward younger ones.[51] Although sentencing leniency may be a result of judges' perception that the elderly pose little risk to society, such practices are a violation of the civil rights of younger defendants.[52] However, judges may wish to protect the youngest defendants, sparing them the pains of a prison experience.[53]

Victim Characteristics Victim characteristics may also influence sentencing. Victims may be asked to make a **victim impact statement** before the sentencing judge. This gives victims an opportunity to tell of their experiences and describe their ordeal. In the case of a murder trial, the surviving family members can recount the effect the crime has had on their lives and well-being.[54] The effect of victim and witness statements on sentencing has been the topic of some debate. Some research finds that victim statements result in a higher rate

Although most research shows that there is a gender gap in sentencing, there are some crimes that are considered inappropriate for women and for which they may receive relatively harsh punishments. Here, defense attorney David Allen speaks to his client Susan G. Lemery at her sentencing hearing in Snohomish County Superior Court in Everett, Washington, July 26, 2002. Lemery, a second-grade teacher convicted of sexually abusing two fourteen-year-old-boys, was sentenced to five years in prison, the maximum sentence for three counts of third-degree child rape and two counts of third-degree child molestation.

chivalry hypothesis
The idea that female defendants are treated more leniently in sentencing (and are less likely to be arrested and prosecuted in the first place) because the criminal justice system is dominated by men who have a paternalistic or protective attitude toward women.

victim impact statement
A victim impact statement is a written statement that describes the harm or loss suffered by the victim of an offense. The court considers the statement when the offender is sentenced.

of incarceration, but other efforts find that victim and witness statements are insignificant.[55]

A victim's personal characteristics may influence sentencing. Sentences may be reduced when a victim has negative personal characteristics or qualities. For example, rapists whose victims are described as prostitutes or substance abusers or who have engaged in risky behaviors, such as hitchhiking or going to bars alone, receive much shorter sentences than those who assault women without such characteristics.[56]

Race No issue concerning personal factors in sentencing is more important than the suspicion that race influences sentencing outcomes. Racial disparity in sentencing has been suspected because a disproportionate number of African American inmates are in state prisons and on death row. The war on drugs has been centered in African American communities, and politically motivated punitive sentencing policies aimed at crack cocaine have had a devastating effect on young African American men. If, charges Michael Tonry, such punitive measures are allowed to continue or are even expanded, an entire cohort of young African Americans may be placed in jeopardy.[57] Because this issue is so important, it is the focus of the Race, Gender, and Ethnicity in Criminal Justice feature on page 412.

To quiz yourself on this material, go to questions 13.11–13.21 on the Introduction to Criminal Justice 10e CD.

Capital Punishment

The most severe sentence used in the United States is capital punishment, or execution. More than 14,500 confirmed executions have been carried out in America under civil authority, starting with the execution of Captain George Kendall in 1608. Most of these executions were for murder and rape. However, federal, state, and military laws have conferred the death penalty for other crimes, including robbery, kidnapping, treason (offenses against the federal government), espionage, and desertion from military service.

InfoTrac College Edition has more than 1,000 articles on capital punishment. Use "capital punishment" as a subject guide.

In recent years, the U.S. Supreme Court has limited the death penalty to first-degree murder and only then when aggravating circumstances, such as murder for profit or murder using extreme cruelty, are present.[58] The federal government still has provisions for granting the death penalty for espionage by a member of the armed forces, treason, and killing during a criminal conspiracy, such as drug trafficking. Some states still have laws assessing capital punishment for such crimes as aircraft piracy, ransom kidnapping, and the aggravated rape of a child, but it remains to be seen whether the courts will allow criminals to be executed today for any crime less than aggravated first-degree murder.

The death penalty for murder is used in 38 states and by the federal government. After many years of abolition, New York reinstated the use of the death penalty in 1995 and expanded its use to cover numerous acts, including serial murder, contract killing, and the use of torture.[59]

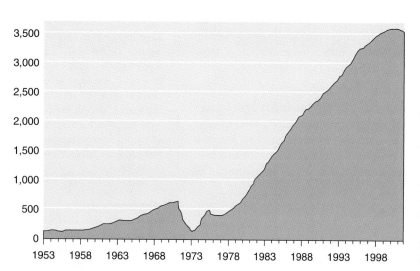

Figure 13.5 Prisoners on Death Row, 1953–2002

Source: Thomas Bonczan and Tracy Snell, *Capital Punishment 2002* (Washington, D.C.: Bureau of Justice Statistics, 2003).

More than 3,500 people currently are on death row.[60] However, as Figure 13.5 shows, the number of people on death row declined in both 2001 and 2002, the first such reductions since 1976. Between 70 and 100 people are executed each year, most having served 10 years on death row before their execution. In 2002, 71 people were executed, which was 5 more than in 2001. California has the most people on death row, while Texas executes the most (around 40 per year, or almost half the total executions in the United States). Almost all executions are carried out in Southern and Western states (Figure 13.6).

The decline in executions and death row admissions may be a product of several factors, including a lower murder rate. However, uneasiness seems to be growing with the administration of the death penalty, and the recent use of scientific evidence based on DNA has resulted in numerous exonerations of death row inmates. Even though the general public remains in support of capital sentences, those in political power have become concerned about charges of racial bias and sloppy investigations. The number of people on death row could continue to decline, if other political leaders emulate the January 11, 2003, decision of Illinois governor George Ryan to commute all death sentences in the state. His action spared the lives of 163 men and 4 women who served a collective 2,000 years for the murders of more than 250 people. While it is difficult to determine how many of these people were innocent, in the previous 25 years, of the 298 men and women sentenced to death in Illinois, 17 were later exonerated and released — a rate of 5.7. If the same held true for this group, at least 9 innocent people may have been on death row at the time of Ryan's action.

Lethal injection is the predominant method of death, though a number of states maintain the gas chamber and electric chair. In 1999 the U.S. Supreme Court refused to hear a case concerning Florida's use of the electric chair as the sole means of execution. Even though the chair has malfunctioned several times, sending up smoke and flames, the Court refused to consider whether this amounted to cruel and unusual punishment. Of the 38 death penalty states, only Alabama, Florida, Georgia, and Nebraska still use the electric chair as the sole means of execution.[61] Although the death penalty is generally approved of in the United States, it fairs less well abroad. See the International Justice feature on page 414.

No issue in the criminal justice system is more controversial or emotional than the implementation of the death penalty. Opponents and proponents have formulated a number of powerful arguments in support of their positions.

Arguments for the Death Penalty

Supporters have a number of arguments for retaining the death penalty in the United States.

Incapacitation Supporters argue that death is the "ultimate incapacitation" and the only one that can ensure that convicted killers can never be pardoned, be paroled, or escape. Most states that do not have capital punishment provide the sentence of "life in prison without the chance of parole." However, 48 states grant their chief executive the right to grant clemency and

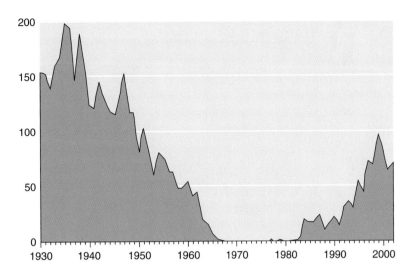

Figure 13.6 Number of Executions, 1930–2002

Source: Thomas Bonczan and Tracy Snell, *Capital Punishment 2002* (Washington, D.C.: Bureau of Justice Statistics, 2003).

Paul Hill was convicted for the killing of an abortion provider and his bodyguard. Before his death, Hill claimed to be a martyr for his cause. The state considered him a cold-blooded killer and Hill was executed on September 3, 2003. Hill was willing to kill people who opposed his political views. Is society justified in taking the life of someone who opposes its political views?

Race and Sentencing

race, gender, and ethnicity in criminal justice

While critics of American race relations may think otherwise, research on sentencing has failed to show a definitive pattern of racial discrimination. While some works do indicate that a defendant's race has a direct impact on sentencing outcomes, other efforts show that the influence of race on sentencing is less clear-cut than anticipated. The disproportionate number of minority group members in prison could be a result of crime and arrest patterns and not racial bias by judges when they hand out criminal sentences. Racial and ethnic minorities commit more crime, the argument goes, and therefore they are more likely to wind up in prison.

Some studies, however, find that minorities receive significantly longer sentences than Caucasians merely because of their race. For example, Shawn Bushway and Anne Morrison Piehl studied sentencing outcomes in Maryland and found that on average African Americans have 20 percent longer sentences than whites, even when holding constant age, gender, and recommended sentence length. Tracy Nobiling, Cassia Spohn, and Miriam De-Lone found that racial status influences sentencing partially because minority group members have a lower income than Caucasians and are more likely to be unemployed. Judges may view their status as social dynamite, considering them more dangerous and likely to recidivate than white offenders.

Patterns of Racial Disparity

Why is the critical issue of racial disparity so murky? One reason may be that if disparity is a factor in sentencing its cause may lay outside of judicial sentencing practices. For example, research efforts show that minority defendants suffer discrimination in a variety of court actions:

They are more likely to be detained before trial than whites and, upon conviction, are more likely to receive jail sentences instead of fines. Prosecutors are less likely to divert minorities from the legal system than whites who commit the same crimes; minorities are less likely to win appeals than white appellants.

The relationship between race and sentencing may be difficult to establish because their association may not be linear. While minority defendants may be punished more severely for some crimes, they are treated more leniently for others, under some circumstances. The most recent sentencing data indicate that minorities receive longer and harsher sentences for some crimes (robberies) while Caucasians receive longer sentences for other criminal offenses (drug trafficking). Sociologist Darnell Hawkins explains this phenomenon as a matter of "appropriateness."

> *Certain crime types are considered less "appropriate" for blacks than for whites. Blacks who are charged with committing these offenses will be treated more severely than blacks who commit crimes that are considered more "appropriate." Included in the former category are various white collar offenses and crimes against political and social structures of authority. The latter groups of offenses would include various forms of victimless crimes associated with lower social status (e.g., prostitution, minor drug use, or drunkenness). This may also include various crimes against the person, especially those involving black victims.*

Race may impact on sentencing because some race-specific crimes are punished more harshly than others. African Americans receive longer sentences for drug crimes than Anglos because they are more likely to be arrested for crack pos-

session and sales and because crack dealing is more severely punished by state and federal laws than other drug crimes. Given that Caucasians are more likely to use marijuana and methamphetamines, prosecutors are more willing to plea bargain and offer shorter jail terms.

Racial bias has also been linked to the victim–offender status. Minority defendants are sanctioned more severely if their victim is white than if their target is a fellow minority group member. Minorities who kill whites are more likely to get the death penalty than those who kill other minorities. Judges may base sentencing decisions on the race of the victim and not the race of the defendant. For example, Charles Crawford, Ted Chiricos, and Gary Kleck found that African American defendants are more likely to be prosecuted under habitual offender statutes if they commit crimes in which a greater likelihood exists that the victim is white — for example, larceny and burglary — than if they commit violent crimes that are largely intraracial. Where there is a perceived racial threat, punishments are enhanced.

System Effects

Sentencing disparity may also reflect race-based differences in criminal justice practices and policies associated with sentencing outcome. Probation presentence reports may favor white over minority defendants, causing judges to award whites probation more often than minorities. Caucasians are more likely to receive probation in jurisdictions where African Americans and Caucasians receive prison sentences of similar duration; this is referred to as the "in-out" decision.

Defendants who can afford bail receive more lenient sentences than those who remain in pretrial detention. Minority defendants are less likely to make bail because they suffer a higher degree of income inequality. That is, minorities earn less on average and therefore are less likely to be able to make bail. Sentencing outcome is also affected by the defendant's ability to afford a private attorney and put on a vigorous legal defense that makes use of high-paid expert witnesses. These factors place the poor and minority group members at a disadvantage in the sentencing process and result in sentencing disparity. And while considerations of prior record may be legitimate in forming sentencing decisions, evidence shows that minorities are more likely to have prior records because of organizational and individual bias on the part of police.

Are Sentencing Practices Changing?

If racial discrepancies exist, new sentencing laws featuring determinate and mandatory sentences may be helping to reduce disparity. For example, Jon'a Meyer and Tara Gray found that jurisdictions in California using mandatory sentences for crimes such as drunk driving show little racial disparity in sentences between Caucasians and minority group members. Similarly, a national survey of sentencing practices conducted by the Bureau of Justice Statistics found that while white defendants are somewhat more likely to receive probation and other nonincarceration sentences than black defendants, little racial disparity showed up in the length of prison sentences. Black males averaged four months longer than white males (41 versus 37), and the average sentence of white females was one month less than of black females (23 versus 24).

While these results are encouraging, some studies could miss a racial effect because they combine Anglo and Hispanic cases into a single category of "white" defendants and then compare them with the sentencing of black defendants. Darrell Steffensmeier and Stephen Demuth's analysis of sentencing in Pennsylvania found that Hispanics are punished considerably more severely than non-Hispanic Caucasians and that combining the two groups masks the ethnic differences in sentencing. Steffensmeier and Demuth also found that federal court judges in Pennsylvania were less likely to consider race and ethnic origin in their sentencing decisions than state court judges. This outcome suggests that federal judges, insulated from community pressures and values and holding lifetime appointments, are better able to render objective decisions. By implication, justice may become more objective if judges held life tenure and were selected from a pool of qualified applicants who reside outside the county in which they serve.

Critical Thinking

Critics have called for change in the way federal sentencing guidelines are designed, asking that the provisions that punish crack possession more heavily than powdered cocaine possession be repealed because African Americans are more likely to use crack and Caucasians powdered cocaine. Do you approve of such a change? Should sentences be altered because a particular racial or ethnic group is more likely to engage in that behavior?

InfoTrac College Edition Research

Use "race" and "sentencing" as key terms on InfoTrac College Edition to find out more about the relationship between these two factors.

Sources: Shawn Bushway and Anne Morrison Piehl, "Judging Judicial Discretion: Legal Factors and Racial Discrimination in Sentencing," *Law and Society Review* 35 (2001): 733–65; Barbara Koons-Witt, "The Effect of Gender on the Decision to Incarcerate before and after the Introduction of Sentencing Guidelines," *Criminology* 40 (2002): 97–129; Marian R. Williams and Jefferson E. Holcomb, "Racial Disparity and Death Sentences in Ohio," *Journal of Criminal Justice* 29 (2001): 207–18; Rodney Engen and Randy Gainey, "Modeling the Effects of Legally Relevant and Extra-Legal Factors under Sentencing Guidelines: The Rules Have Changed," *Criminology* 38 (2000) 1207–30; Darrell Steffensmeier and Stephen Demuth, "Ethnicity and Judges' Sentencing Decisions: Hispanic–Black–White Comparisons," *Criminology* 39 (2001): 145–78; Tracy Nobiling, Cassia Spohn, and Miriam DeLone, "A Tale of Two Counties: Unemployment and Sentence Severity," *Justice Quarterly* 15 (1998): 459–86; Travis Pratt, "Race and Sentencing: A Meta-Analysis of Conflicting Empirical Research Results," *Journal of Criminal Justice* 26 (1998): 513–25; Charles Crawford, Ted Chiricos, and Gary Kleck, "Race, Racial Threat, and Sentencing of Habitual Offenders," *Criminology* 36 (1998): 481–511; Jon'a Meyer and Tara Gray, "Drunk Drivers in the Courts: Legal and Extra-Legal Factors Affecting Pleas and Sentences," *Journal of Criminal Justice* 25 (1997): 155–63; Alexander Alvarez and Ronet Bachman, "American Indians and Sentencing Disparity: An Arizona Test," *Journal of Criminal Justice* 24 (1996): 549–61; Carole Wolff Barnes and Rodney Kingsnorth, "Race, Drug, and Criminal Sentencing: Hidden Effects of the Criminal Law," *Journal of Criminal Justice* 24 (1996): 39–55; Samuel Walker, Cassia Spohn, and Miriam DeLone, *The Color of Justice, Race, Ethnicity and Crime in America* (Belmont, Calif.: Wadsworth, 1996), pp. 145–46; Jo Dixon, "The Organizational Context of Sentencing," *American Journal of Sociology* 100 (1995): 1157–98; Celesta Albonetti and John Hepburn, "Prosecutorial Discretion to Defer Criminalization: The Effects of Defendant's Ascribed and Achieved Status Characteristics," *Journal of Quantitative Criminology* 12 (1996): 63–81; Darnell Hawkins, "Race, Crime Type and Imprisonment," *Justice Quarterly* 3 (1986): 251–69.

The Death Penalty Abroad

international justice

In March 2002, a Nigerian woman, Amina Lawal, 30, was convicted and sentenced to death by stoning by an Islamic Shariah court after giving birth to a baby girl more than nine months after divorcing her husband. Bowing to international pressure, the Nigerian court upheld her appeal of the sentence, and she was freed on September 26, 2003. However, not everyone is as lucky as Lawal. Two Saudi brothers, Saud and Musaid bin Abdul-Rahman al-Aulian, were beheaded for kidnapping, raping, and robbing a woman who they had lured to a secluded area. The Saudis behead about 125 people each year for such crimes as murder, rape, drug trafficking, and armed robbery. But not all Saudi executions concern violent crime. On February 28, 2001, Hassan bin Awad al-Zubair, a Sudanese national, was beheaded after he was convicted on charges of "sorcery." He claimed the power to heal the sick and to "separate married couples."

The United States is not alone in using the death penalty. According to the latest data from watchdog group Amnesty International, about 76 nations have abolished the death penalty for ordinary crimes and another 36 retain it but have abolished it in practice. Another 83 nations retain the death penalty.

Most executions international executions take place in China, the Democratic Republic of Congo, Iran, and Saudi Arabia. Amnesty International estimates that, during 2002, at least 1,526 prisoners were executed in 31 countries and 3,248 people were sentenced to death in 67 countries. These figures include only cases known to Amnesty International; the true figures are certainly higher. The execution figures were lower in 2002 than in 2001, when more than 3,000 people were executed, many during the "Strike Hard" campaign that China instituted against crime. That country alone executed about 2,500 people in 2001. In ad-

dition to violent crimes, executions were carried out for crimes such as stealing gasoline, bribery, pimping, embezzlement, tax fraud, drug offenses, and selling harmful foodstuffs.

While opposition to executions is growing in many areas, the public in some nations still demands the use of the death penalty. In addition to China, nations operating under Islamic law routinely employ the death penalty. At least 79 executions were carried out in Saudi Arabia during 2002 and 113 in Iran, but the real numbers may be higher. The governments of Barbados, Guyana, and Jamaica have expressed interest in speeding the use of the death penalty, and more than 250 prisoners are currently on death row across the English-speaking Caribbean.

Japan, a nation that prides itself on nonviolence, routinely uses the death penalty. Prisoners are informed less than two hours before execution, and their families and lawyers are never told of the decision to carry out the death penalty.

Executions of Juveniles

International human rights treaties prohibit anyone under 18 years of age at the time of the crime from being sentenced to death. The International Covenant on Civil and Political Rights, the American Convention on Human Rights, and the United Nations Convention on the Rights of the Child all have provisions to this effect. More than 100 countries have laws specifically excluding the execution of juvenile offenders or may be presumed to exclude such executions by being parties to one or another of the above treaties. A small number of countries, however, continue to execute juvenile offenders. Seven countries since 1990 are known to have executed prisoners who were under 18 years old at the time of the crime — the Democratic Republic of Congo, Iran, Nigeria, Pakistan, Saudi Arabia, the United

States, and Yemen. Since 1994, 20 juvenile offenders have been executed, including 13 in the United States.

Critical Thinking

1. The movement toward abolition of capital punishment in the United States is encouraged by the fact that so many nations have abandoned the death penalty. Should Americans model their system of punishments after other nations or does the U.S. crime problem require the use of capital punishment?

2. Do you believe that someone who joins a terrorist group and trains to kill Americans deserves the death penalty even if they have never killed anyone?

InfoTrac College Edition Research

Are innocent people on death row? To find out, read Peter Vilbig, "Innocent on Death Row," *New York Times Upfront,* September 18, 2000, p. 10. The death penalty remains a controversial issue around the world. To learn more, read Stefanie Grant, "A Dialogue of the Deaf? New International Attitudes and the Death Penalty in America," *Criminal Justice Ethics* 17 (1998): 19.

Sources: Amnesty International's most recent data on the death penalty can be accessed at http://web.amnesty.org/rmp/dplibrary.nsf/index?openview; "Nigeria: Stoning Sentence Stands," *New York Times,* September 10, 2002, p. A6; "Saudi Arabia Executes Man for Sorcery," *Death Penalty News,* March 2000; "USA Set to Break a Global Consensus — Execution of Child Offender Due," news release, Amnesty International, October 22, 2001; "China 'Striking Harder' Than Ever Before," news release, Amnesty International, June 7, 2001; Associated Press, "Saudi Brothers Beheaded for Raping," *New York Times,* July 20, 2001, p. 3; Larry Rohter, "In Caribbean, Support Growing for Death Penalty," *New York Times,* October 4, 1998, p. A1; Associated Press, "Chechen Pair Executed in Public," *Boston Globe,* September 19, 1997, p. 9; Reuters, "Saudi Beheadings Over 100 for 1997," *Boston Globe,* September 28, 1997, p. A29.

commute a life sentence and may give lifers eligibility for various furlough and re-lease programs.

Death penalty advocates believe that the potential for recidivism is a serious enough threat to require that murderers be denied further access to the public. Stephen Markman and Paul Cassell analyzed the records of 52,000 state prison inmates serving time for murder and found that 810 had previously been con-victed of homicide and that these recidivists had killed 821 people following their first convictions.[62] More than 250 inmates on death row today had prior homi-cide convictions. If they had been executed for their first offense, 250 innocent people would still be alive.[63]

Deterrent Proponents of capital punishment argue that executions serve as a strong deterrent for serious crimes. Although capital punishment would proba-bly not deter the few mentally unstable criminals, it could have an effect on the cold, calculating murderer, such as the hired killer or someone who kills for profit. The fear of death may also convince felons not to risk using handguns during armed robberies.

Proponents argue that the deterrent effect of an execution can produce a substantial decline in the murder rate.[64] Some supporters use a commonsense approach, not relying on scientific analysis. They argue, for example, that homi-cide rates increased dramatically in the 1960s and 1970s, when executions were halted by the courts and death penalty laws were subsequently abolished. Propo-nents also maintain that even if homicide rates increase after the death penalty is adopted in a state, murder rates may have been much higher if capital punish-ment had never been legislated.[65]

Other proponents rely on more scientific analysis of data. In one assessment of 16 well-publicized executions, Steven Stack found that they may have saved 480 lives by immediately deterring potential murderers.[66] In a more recent sur-vey, he concluded that well-publicized executions of criminals in California re-duced the homicide rate 12 percent during the month of the execution.[67]

Morally Correct Advocates of capital punishment justify its use on the grounds that it is morally correct because it is mentioned in the Bible and other religious works. Although the U.S. Constitution forbids "cruel and unusual punishments," this prohibition would not include the death penalty because capital punishment was widely used at the time the Constitution was drafted. The original intent of the founders was to allow the states to use the death penalty. Capital punishment may be cruel, but it is not unusual.

The death penalty is morally correct because it provides the greatest justice for the victim and helps alleviate the psychic pain of the victim's family and friends. It has even been accepted by criminal justice experts who consider themselves hu-manists, people who are concerned with the value and dignity of human beings. As the noted humanist David Friedrichs argues, a civilized society has no choice but to hold responsible those who commit horrendous crimes. The death penalty makes a moral statement: Some behavior is so unacceptable to a community of human beings that one who engages in such behavior forfeits his right to live.[68]

Proportional Putting dangerous criminals to death also conforms to the require-ment that the punishment must be proportional to the seriousness of the crime. Because the United States uses a system of escalating punishments, it follows that the most serious punishment should be used to sanction the most serious crime. Before the brutality of the death penalty is considered, the cruelty with which the victim was treated should not be forgotten.

Reflects Public Opinion Those who favor capital punishment charge that a majority of the public believes that criminals who kill innocent victims should forfeit their own lives. Public opinion polls show that up to 67 percent of the public favors the death penalty, almost double the percentage of 20 years ago (though the numbers have declined somewhat in the last five years from a high of 75 percent).[69] Public approval is based on the rational belief that the death penalty is an important instrument of social control, can deter crime, and is less costly than maintaining a murderer in prison for life.[70] The 67 percent approval rating could underestimate public opinion. Research by Alexis Durham and his associates found that almost everyone (95 percent) would give criminals the death penalty under some circumstances, and the most heinous crimes are those for which the public is most likely to approve capital punishment.[71]

Unlikely Chance of Error The many legal controls and appeals currently in use make it almost impossible for an innocent person to be executed or for the death penalty to be used in a racist or capricious manner. Although some unfortunate mistakes may have been made in the past, the current system makes it virtually impossible to execute an innocent person. Federal courts closely scrutinize all death penalty cases and rule for the defendant in an estimated 60 percent to 70 percent of the appeals. Such judicial care should ensure that only those who are both truly guilty and deserving of death are executed.

In sum, those who favor the death penalty find it to be traditional punishment for serious crimes, one that can help prevent criminality; is in keeping with the traditional moral values of fairness and equity; and is highly favored by the public.

Arguments against the Death Penalty

Arguments for the death penalty are matched by those that support its abolition.

Possibility of Error Critics of the death penalty believe capital punishment has no place in a mature democratic society.[72] They point to the finality of the act and the real possibility that innocent persons can be executed. Examples of people wrongfully convicted of murder abound. Critics point to miscarriages of justice such as the case of Rolando Cruz and Alejandro Hernandez who, wrongfully convicted of murder, were released in 1995 after spending more than a decade on death row in the Illinois prison system. Three former prosecutors and four deputy sheriffs who worked on the case were charged with fabricating evidence against the pair.[73] Cruz and Hernandez are certainly not alone. Jeffrey Blake went to prison for a double murder in 1991 and spent seven years behind bars before his conviction was overturned in 1998. The prosecution's star witness conceded that he lied on the stand, forcing Blake to spend a quarter of his life in prison for a crime he did not commit.[74] These wrongful convictions would have been even more tragic if the defendants had been executed for their alleged crimes. A congressional report cited 48 cases in the past two decades in which people who served time on death row were released because of new evidence proving their innocence. One Maryland man served nine years on death row before DNA testing proved that he could not have committed the crime.[75] These findings show that, even with the best intentions, grave risk exists that an innocent person can be executed.[76] In Illinois, 17 men on death row were freed within the past two decades, causing the governor to impose a moratorium on executions there because of the high number of mistaken convictions.[77]

According to classic research by Michael Radelet and Hugo Bedeau, about 350 wrongful murder convictions were handed down in the twentieth century, of

www Does capital punishment present ethical problems that make its use morally dubious? Read what the American Civil Liberties Union has to say at http://www.aclu.org/death-penalty/.

which 23 led to executions. They estimate that about three death sentences are returned every two years in cases in which the defendant has been falsely accused. More than half the errors stem from perjured testimony, false identifications, coerced confessions, and suppression of evidence. In addition to the 23 who were executed, 128 of the falsely convicted served more than six years in prison, 39 served more than 16 years in confinement, and 8 died while serving their sentence.[78] Radelet and Bedeau's view is that, even though the system attempts to be especially cautious in capital cases, unacceptable mistakes can occur. Although death penalty sentences are carefully reviewed, relatively few stays of execution are granted (about 2 out of 50). Obviously, there is room for judicial error.[79] Some states have placed a moratorium on executions until the possibility of error can be investigated.

Unfair Use of Discretion Critics also frown on the tremendous discretion used in seeking the death penalty and the arbitrary manner in which it is imposed. Of the approximately 10,000 persons convicted each year on homicide charges, only 250 to 300 are sentenced to death, while an equal number receive a sentence of probation or community supervision only. Many convicted murderers do not commit first-degree murder and therefore are ineligible for execution, but many serious criminals who could have received the death penalty likely are not sentenced to death because of prosecutorial discretion. Some escape death by cooperating or giving testimony against their partners in the crime. A person who commits a particularly heinous crime and knows full well that she will receive the death penalty if convicted may be the one most likely to plea bargain to avoid capital punishment. Is it fair to spare the life of a dangerous killer who cooperates with the prosecutor while executing another who does not?

Abolitionists also argue that juries use inappropriate discretion when making capital punishment recommendations. The ongoing Capital Jury Project has been interviewing members of juries involved in making death penalty decisions and finds that many are motivated by ignorance and error. Read more about the project in the Analyzing Criminal Justice Issues feature on page 418.

WWW To get a bibliography of articles published in conjunction with the Capital Jury Project, go to http://www.lawschool.cornell.edu/lawlibrary/death/cjp_publ.htm.

Vicious Criminals Often Go Free Some vicious criminals who grievously injure victims during murder attempts are spared the death penalty because a physician's skill saved the victim. Some notable cases come to mind. Lawrence Singleton used an axe to cut off the arms of a woman he raped, yet he served only eight years in prison because the victim's life was saved by prompt medical care. (After being released from prison, Singleton killed a female companion in 1997.) "David," a boy severely burned in a murder attempt, lives in fear because his assailant, his father, Charles Rothenberg, was paroled from prison after serving a short sentence.[80] Although these horrific crimes received national attention and the intent to kill the victim was present, the death penalty could not be applied because of the availability of effective medical treatment. Areas that have superior medical resources have lower murder rates than less well-equipped areas. For example, ambulance response time can reduce the death rate by expeditiously transporting victims to an appropriate treatment center.[81] It makes little sense to punish someone for an impulsive murder while sparing the life of those who intentionally maim and torture victims who happen by chance to live because of prompt medical care.

Misplaced Vengeance Although critics acknowledge that the general public approves of the death penalty, they maintain that prevailing attitudes reflect a primitive desire for revenge and not just desert. Public acceptance of capital punishment has been compared with the approval of human sacrifices practiced

The Capital Jury Project

analyzing criminal justice issues

The Capital Jury Project (CJP), begun by sociologist William Bowers in 1990, has sent research teams to 15 states to interview jurors in death penalty cases. The interviews, which run for more than three hours, are taped and coded for analysis.

CJP findings show that the decision making in capital cases often strays from legal and moral guidelines. Some jurors express overwhelming racial prejudice in making their decisions. Others say that they have decided on the punishment before the trial is completed and the defendant found guilty.

Others are confused about the law and are influenced by factual misconceptions. For example, many believe that prison terms are far shorter than they are, and many underestimate the time served for murder by 10 years or more. Many jurors mistakenly believe that the death penalty is mandatory in cases in which it was not, while others reject capital punishment in situations in which the law clearly mandates its use. The greater the factual errors, the most likely the juror will vote for death.

Many capital jurors are unwilling to accept primary responsibility for their punishment decisions. They vote for the death penalty in the mistaken belief that most defendants will never be executed, absolving them of responsibility. They often place responsibility for the defen-

dant's punishment elsewhere, such as with the judge or other jurors. For example, one female juror who had recommended death told CJP interviewers that she had voted only to go along with the other jurors and that she had never believed the man should be executed. "I really had no thought about it," she said. "It wasn't my choice to make. It was a judgment call. It really doesn't mean a whole lot what I say because it's ultimately up to the judge." These feelings were most often expressed in states where the law allows judges to override a jury's decisions and either impose or reject a capital sentence.

Recent research by Wanda Foglia on CJP data from Pennsylvania found that many jurors make up their minds before the sentencing stage and were confused by or misunderstood judicial instructions. Most admitted discussing the death penalty during jury deliberations before the defendant was even found guilty. Some based their decisions on legally irrelevant concepts, such as whether the defendant would be dangerous in the future. Disturbingly, many jurors seem to make more than one error in their decision making. They misunderstand the judge, ignore relevant facts, underestimate life sentences, and make up their minds without considering all the evidence.

Critical Thinking

The Capital Jury Project clearly shows that, instead of being a precise and objective decision-making process, the imposition of the death penalty is often a legal crapshoot. Considering this finding, would you advocate that the death penalty be abolished? Or, considering the right to appeal and to have the case reviewed by an appellate court, would you advocate that capital punishment be retained?

InfoTrac College Edition Research

To read more about how capital jurists make their decisions, go to Margaret Gonzalez-Perez, "A Model of Decisionmaking in Capital Juries," *International Social Science Review* (Fall-Winter 2001): 79.

Sources: Wanda Foglia, "They Know Not What They Do: Unguided and Misguided Discretion in Pennsylvania Capital Cases," *Justice Quarterly* 20 (2003): 187–212; William J. Bowers, "The Capital Jury Project: Rationale, Design, and Preview of Early Findings," *Indiana Law Journal* 70 (1995): 1043–1102; William J. Bowers, Marla Sandys, and Benjamin Steiner, "Foreclosed Impartiality in Capital Sentencing: Jurors' Predispositions, Guilt Trial Experience, and Premature Decision Making," *Cornell Law Review* 83 (1998): 1476–1556; Margaret Vandiver, "Race in the Jury Room: A Preliminary Analysis of Cases from the Capital Jury Project," paper presented to the American Academy of Criminal Justice Sciences, March 1997.

by the Aztecs in Mexico 500 years ago.[82] It is ironic that many death penalty advocates also oppose abortion on the grounds that it is the taking of human life.[83] The desire to be vengeful and punitive outweighs their concern about taking life.

Even if the majority of the general public favors the death penalty, support has been associated with prejudice against racial minorities and the approval of revenge as a rationale for punishment.[84] Public support is not as strong as death penalty advocates believe. When surveys ask about a choice of punishments, such as life without parole, support for the death penalty declines from 80 percent to 50 percent.[85] Public opinion is influenced by such factors as the personal characteristics of the offender and the circumstances of the offense. Therefore, the public does not support death in many cases of first-degree murder.[86] Politicians could favor the death penalty in the mistaken belief that the public supports such harsh punishment for criminal offenders.[87]

No Deterrent Effect Those opposed to the death penalty also find little merit in the argument that capital punishment deters crime. They charge that insufficient evidence exists that the threat of a death sentence can convince potential murderers to forgo their criminal activity. Most murders involve people who knew each other, very often friends and family members. Given that murderers frequently are under the influence of alcohol or drugs at the time of the crime or are suffering severe psychological turmoil, no penalty will likely be a deterrent. Most research concludes that the death penalty is not an effective deterrent.[88] For example, Keith Harries and Derral Cheatwood studied differences in homicide rates in 293 contiguous counties within the United States and found higher violent crime rates in counties that routinely employed the death penalty than in those in which the use of the death penalty was rare.[89]

Hope of Rehabilitation The death sentence also rules out any hope of offender rehabilitation. Evidence indicates that convicted killers make good parole risks. Convicted murderers are model inmates and, once released, commit fewer crimes than other parolees. The general public, including people who sit on juries, could be overestimating the dangerousness of people who commit murder. One recent study found that capital jurors predicted an 85 percent likelihood that the defendant would commit a future violent crime and a 50 percent likelihood that the defendant would commit a new homicide if he had been given a sentence of life imprisonment. In reality, those people given a life sentence for capital murder have a less than 1 percent (0.2 percent) chance of committing another homicide over a 40-year term. The risk of their committing an assault is about 16 percent.[90]

Racial, Gender, and Other Bias Capital punishment may be tarnished by gender, racial, and ethnic and other biases. Evidence suggests that homicides with male offenders and female victims are more likely to result in a death sentence than homicides involving female offenders and male victims.[91] Homicides involving strangers are more likely to result in a death sentence than homicides involving nonstrangers and acquaintances.

Prosecutors are more likely to recommend the death sentence for people who kill white victims than they are in any other racial combination of victim and criminal, for example, whites who kill blacks.[92] Not surprisingly, since the death penalty was first instituted in the United States, a disproportionate number of minorities have been executed. Charges of racial bias are supported by the disproportionate numbers of African Americans who have received the death sentence, are currently on death row, and who have been executed (53.5 percent of all executions). While white victims account for approximately one-half of all murder victims, 81 percent of all capital cases involve white victims. Furthermore, as of October 2002, 12 people have been executed in cases in which the defendant was white and the murder victim black, compared with 178 black defendants executed for murders with white victims.[93]

Racism was particularly blatant when the death penalty was invoked in rape cases. Of those receiving the death penalty for rape, 90 percent in the South and 63 percent in the North and West were black.[94] Today, about 40 percent of the inmates on death row are African Americans, a number disproportionate to the minority representation in the population (see Figure 13.7).

Causes More Crime than It Deters Some critics fear that the introduction of capital punishment will encourage criminals to escalate their violent behavior, consequently putting police officers at risk. For example, a suspect who kills someone during a botched robbery may be inclined to fire away upon encountering police rather than surrender peacefully. The killer faces the death penalty

Figure 13.7 Prisoners on Death Row by Race, 1968–2002

Source: Thomas Bonczan and Tracy Snell, *Capital Punishment 2002* (Washington, D.C.: Bureau of Justice Statistics, 2003).

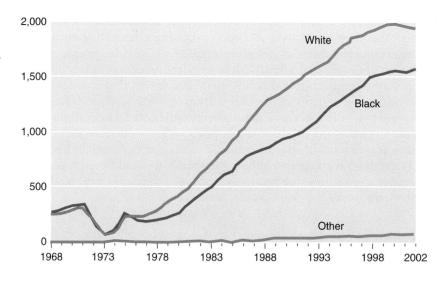

already, what does he have to lose? Geoffrey Rapp studied the effect of capital punishment on the killings of police and found that, all other things being equal, the greater number of new inmates on death row, the greater the number police officers killed by citizens.[95] Rapp concludes that the death penalty seems to create an extremely dangerous environment for law enforcement officers because it does not deter criminals and it may lull officers into a false sense of security. They come to believe that the death penalty will deter violence directed against them, which causes them to let down their guard.

Brutality Abolitionists believe that executions are unnecessarily cruel and inhuman and come at a high moral and social cost. American society does not punish criminals by subjecting them to the same acts they themselves committed. Rapists are not sexually assaulted, and arsonists do not have their house burned down. Why, then, should murderers be killed?

Robert Johnson has described the execution process as a form of torture in which the condemned are first tormented psychologically by being made to feel powerless and alone while on death row. Suicide is a constant problem among those on death row.[96] The execution itself is a barbaric affair marked by the smell of burning flesh and stiffened bodies. The executioners suffer from delayed stress reactions, including anxiety and a dehumanized personal identity.

brutalization effect

The belief that capital punishment creates an atmosphere of brutality, reinforces the view that violence is an appropriate response to provocation, and thus encourages rather than deters the criminal use of violence.

The brutality of the death penalty may produce more violence than it prevents — the so-called **brutalization effect.**[97] Executions may increase murder rates because they raise the general violence level in society and because violence-prone people identify with the executioner, not with the target of the death penalty. When someone gets in a conflict with such individuals or challenges their authority, they execute them in the same manner the state executes people who violate its rules.[98] The brutalization effect was encountered by John Cochran and his associates when they studied the influence of a well-publicized execution in Oklahoma. After the execution, murders of strangers increased by one per month.[99] Follow-up research by William Bailey finds that the brutalization effect extends to other types of murder (for example, nonstranger murder) and a vicarious brutalization effect may occur in which people in a state that does not practice capital punishment are influenced by news reports of executions in death penalty states.[100]

Because of its brutality, many enlightened nations have abandoned the death penalty with few ill effects. Abolitionists point out that such nations as Denmark and Sweden have long abandoned the death penalty and that 40 percent of the countries with a death penalty have active abolitionist movements.[101] Ironically, citizens of countries that have eliminated the death penalty sometimes find themselves on death row in the United States. For example, a Paraguayan citizen, Angel Francisco Breard, age 32, was executed on April 14, 1998, in Virginia, for murder and attempted rape, despite a plea from the International Court of Justice that he be spared and intense efforts by the Paraguayan government to stay the execution.[102]

Expense Some people complain that they do not want to support "some killer in prison for 30 years." Abolitionists counter that legal appeals drive the cost of executions far higher than the cost of years of incarceration. If the money spent on the judicial process were invested, the interest would more than pay for the lifetime upkeep of death row inmates. For example, in 1998 there were 508 men and 9 women on death row in California. Because of numerous appeals, the median time between conviction by a jury, sentencing by a judge, and execution averaged 14 years. The cost of processing appeals is extremely costly, and the annual budget for the state's public defender staff of 45 lawyers who represent inmates in death cases is $5 million.[103]

At least 30 states now have a sentence of life in prison without parole, and this can more than make up for an execution. Being locked up in a hellish prison without any chance of release (barring a rare executive reprieve) may be a worse punishment than a painless death by lethal injection. If vengeance is the goal, life without parole may eliminate the need for capital punishment.

Legal Issues in the Death Penalty

The constitutionality of the death penalty has been a major concern to both the nation's courts and its concerned social scientists. In 1972 the U.S. Supreme Court in *Furman* v. *Georgia* decided that the discretionary imposition of the death penalty was cruel and unusual punishment under the Eighth and Fourteenth Amendments.[104] This case not only questioned whether capital punishment is a more effective deterrent than life imprisonment but also challenged the very existence of the death penalty on the grounds of its brutality and finality. The Supreme Court did not completely rule out the use of capital punishment as a penalty. Rather, it objected to the arbitrary and capricious manner in which it was imposed. After *Furman,* many states changed statutes that had allowed jury discretion in imposing the death penalty. In some states this was accomplished by enacting statutory guidelines for jury decisions; in others, the death penalty was made mandatory for certain crimes only. Despite these changes in statutory law, no further executions were carried out while the Court pondered additional cases concerning the death penalty.

In July 1976 the Supreme Court ruled on the constitutionality of five state death penalty statutes. In the first case, *Gregg* v. *Georgia,* the Court found valid the Georgia statute holding that a finding by the jury of at least one "aggravating circumstance" out of 10 is required in pronouncing the death penalty in murder cases.[105] In the *Gregg* case, for example, the jury imposed the death penalty after finding beyond a reasonable doubt two aggravating circumstances: (1) The offender was engaged in the commission of two other capital felonies, and (2) the offender committed the offense of murder for the purpose of receiving money and other financial gains (for example, an automobile).[106]

In probably one of the most important death penalty cases, *McKlesky* v. *Kemp,* the Court upheld the conviction of a black defendant in Georgia, despite social science evidence that black criminals who kill white victims have a significantly greater chance of receiving the death penalty than white offenders who kill black victims. The Court ruled that the evidence of racial patterns in capital sentencing was not persuasive without a finding of racial bias in the immediate case.[107] Many observers believe that *McKlesky* presented the last significant legal

The Supreme Court has banned the death penalty for the mentally challenged. But sometimes the line defining normal intelligence is hard to draw. Death row inmate Travis Walters, 23, is shown July 25, 2003, at Central Prison in Raleigh, North Carolina. Walters received federal disability payments for mental retardation from age 13 until police say he walked into a Lumberton, North Carolina fast-food restaurant in 1998 and shot a supervisor in the head. A judge has ruled Walters is not retarded, which means he remains sentenced to die by lethal injection instead of spending life in prison without parole.

© 2003 AP/Wide World Photos

obstacle that death penalty advocates had to overcome and that, as a result, capital punishment will be a sentence in the United States for years to come. (Warren McKlesky was executed in 1991.)

Although the Court has generally supported the death penalty, it has placed some limitations on its use. Rulings have promoted procedural fairness in the capital sentencing process. For example, the Court has limited the death penalty sentence to capital murder cases, ruling that it is not permissible to punish rapists with death.[108] It has prohibited prosecutors from presenting damaging evidence about the defendant's background unless it is directly relevant to the case.[109]

Age and Mental Capacity   The Court has also reinforced the idea that it would be cruel to execute someone who, because of his age or mental capacity, could not fully appreciate the wrongfulness of his acts. It has ruled that the defendant's age, though not excusing criminal behavior, can be considered as a mitigating factor in capital sentencing decisions. In *Wilkins* v. *Missouri* and *Stanford* v. *Kentucky,* the Court set a limit of 16 years as the age of defendants who could be sentenced to death.[110] These rulings effectively barred the use of capital punishment from minors under the age of 16 who have been waived or transferred from the juvenile to the adult court system.

In a 2002 case, *Atkins* v. *Virginia,* the Court ruled that executions of mentally retarded criminals are "cruel and unusual punishments" prohibited by the Eighth Amendment. The Court noted that a significant number of states have concluded that death is not a suitable punishment for a mentally retarded criminal and the direction states have taken is to prohibit executing retarded offenders.[111] While death penalty opponents welcomed the *Atkins* decision, some commentators cautioned that it opened the door to both confusion and arbitrariness because the definition of mental retardation (and mental illness) relies on the often-conflicting diagnosis and testimony of mental health professionals. In this case, experts defined Daryl Atkins as mentally retarded. However, as legal expert Douglas Mossman points out, the mentally retarded are not a group that is clearly distinct from the nonretarded. Mental retardation is an artificial category, and the line that separates persons with mental retardation from those who are only well below average is both changing and arbitrary.[112]

Jury Issues

The role of the jury has become an important legal issue in the debate over capital punishment.

Death-Qualified Juries One area of interest is the **death-qualified jury,** in which any person opposed in concept to capital punishment has been removed during voir dire. Defense attorneys are opposed to death qualification because it bars from serving on juries those citizens who oppose the death penalty and who may be more liberal and less likely to convict defendants. Death qualification creates juries that are nonrepresentative of the 20 percent of the public that opposes capital punishment.

In *Witherspoon* v. *Illinois* (1968), the Supreme Court upheld the practice of excusing jurors who are opposed to the death penalty.[113] The Court has made it easier to convict people in death penalty cases by ruling that jurors can be excused if their views on capital punishment are deemed by a trial judge to "prevent or substantially impair the performance of their duties."[114] The Court has also ruled that jurors can be removed because of their opposition to the death penalty at the guilt phase of a trial, even though they would not have to consider the issue of capital punishment until a separate sentencing hearing. In *Lockhart* v. *McCree* (1986), the Court also ruled that removing anti–capital punishment jurors does not violate the Sixth Amendment provision that juries represent a fair cross section of the community and does not unfairly tip the scale toward juries that are prone to convict people in capital cases.[115] So, it appears that for, the present, prosecutors will be able to excuse jurors who feel that the death penalty is wrong or immoral.

Jury Decisions A second jury issue is whether it is the judge or jury that makes the decision to use the death penalty. Some states had left this critical decision to the judge alone. However, in a 2002 ruling, *Ring* v. *Arizona,* the U.S. Supreme Court ruled that juries, not judges, must make the critical findings that send convicted killers to death row. The 7–2 ruling should force states that allow judge-only decisions such as Arizona, Colorado, Idaho, Montana, and Nebraska to redo their death penalty statutes. It also will affect states such as Alabama, Delaware, Florida, and Indiana that allow a judge to impose a death sentence despite a jury's recommendation of life in prison. Many people now on death row may have to have their sentence reconsidered or reduced. The Court reasoned that the Sixth Amendment's right to a jury trial would be "senselessly diminished" if it did not allow jurors to decide whether a person deserves the death penalty.[116]

Racial Bias The Court has also ruled that jury selection cannot be tainted by racial bias. In 2003, the Court ruled against selecting biased juries in the case of *Miller-El* v. *Cockrell.* Thomas Miller-El, who is an African American, was convicted of capital murder and sentenced to death in 1986. He appealed, arguing that prosecutors excluded African Americans from the jury in Dallas County, Texas. The lower courts refused to consider his claim. The Supreme Court disagreed, noting that the prosecution had used its peremptory challenge to eliminate 91 percent of the eligible African Americans. Also, the stated reasons given by the prosecutor for eliminating the African American jurors — ambivalence about the death penalty, hesitancy to vote to execute defendants capable of being rehabilitated, and the jurors' own family history of criminality — applied to some white jurors who were not challenged and who did serve on the jury. The Court noted that the prosecutor used underhanded techniques to limit or eliminate African American (the so-called Texas shuffle) and used disparate questioning of

death-qualified jury
A jury formed to hear a capital case, with any person opposed in principle to capital punishment automatically excluded.

potential jurors based on race. Furthermore, a memo instructed prosecutors to eliminate jurors based on race, religion, and ethnic background.[117]

Does the Death Penalty Deter Murder?

The key issue in the capital punishment debate is whether it can lower the murder rate and save lives. Despite its inherent cruelty, capital punishment might be justified if it proved to be an effective crime deterrent that could save many innocent lives. Abolitionists claim it has no real deterrent value; advocates claim it does. Who is correct?

Considerable empirical research has been carried out on the effectiveness of capital punishment as a deterrent. In particular, studies have tried to discover whether the death sentence serves as a more effective deterrent than life imprisonment for capital crimes such as homicide. Three methods have been used.

1. Immediate-impact studies, which calculate the effect a well-publicized execution has on the short-term murder rate.
2. Time-series analysis, which compares long-term trends in murder and capital punishment rates.
3. Contiguous-state analysis, which compares murder rates in states that have the death penalty with a similar state that has abolished capital punishment.

Using these three methods over a 60-year period, most researchers have failed to show any deterrent effect of capital punishment.[118] These studies show that murder rates do not seem to rise when a state abolishes capital punishment any more so than they decrease when the death penalty is adopted. The murder rate is also similar both in states that use the death penalty and neighboring states that have abolished capital punishment. Finally, little evidence shows that executions can lower the murder rate. For example, a test of the deterrent effect of the death penalty in Texas found no association between the frequency of execution during the years 1984–97 and murder rates.[119]

Only a few studies have found that the long-term application of capital punishment may reduce the murder rate.[120] However, these have been disputed by researchers who have questioned the methodology used and indicate that the deterrent effects that the studies uncover are an artifact of the statistical techniques used in the research.[121]

The general consensus among death penalty researchers today is that the threat of capital punishment has little effect on murder rates. It is still unknown why capital punishment fails as a deterrent, but the cause may lie in the nature of homicide. Murder is often a crime of passion involving people who know each other, and many murders are committed by people under the influence of drugs and alcohol — more than 50 percent of all people arrested for murder test positive for drug use. People involved in interpersonal conflict with friends, acquaintances, and family members and who may be under the influence of drugs and alcohol are not likely to be capable of considering the threat of the death penalty.

Murder rates have also been linked to the burdens of poverty and income inequality. Desperate adolescents who get caught up in the cycle of urban violence and become members of criminal groups and gangs may find that their life situation gives them little choice except to engage in violent and deadly behavior. They have few chances to ponder the deterrent impact of the death penalty.

The failure of the "ultimate deterrent" to deter the "ultimate crime" has been used by critics to question the value of capital punishment.

Despite the less than conclusive empirical evidence, many people still hold to the efficacy of the death penalty as a crime deterrent, and recent U.S. Supreme Court decisions seem to justify its use. Even if the death penalty were no greater a deterrent than a life sentence, some people would still advocate its use on the grounds that it is the only way to permanently rid society of dangerous criminals who deserve to die.

To quiz yourself on this material, go to questions 13.22–13.25 on the Introduction to Criminal Justice 10e CD.

Summary

- Punishment and sentencing have gone through various phases throughout the history of Western civilization.
- Initially, punishment was characterized by retribution and the need to fix sentences for convicted offenders. The prison developed as a place of reform.
- At the tail end of the nineteenth century, individualized sentencing was created and became widely accepted. The concept of rehabilitation was used to guide sentencing.
- During the 1970s, experts began to become disenchanted with rehabilitation and concepts related to treating the individual offender. There was less emphasis on treatment and more on the legal rights of offenders. A number of states returned to the concept of punishment in terms of mandatory and fixed sentences.
- The philosophy of sentencing has thus changed from a concentration on rehabilitation to a focus on incapacitation and deterrence, where the goal is to achieve equality of punishment and justice in the law and to lock up dangerous criminals for as long as possible.
- Sentencing in today's criminal justice system is primarily based on deterrence, incapacitation, retribution, and rehabilitation. Traditional dispositions include fines, probation, and incarceration, with probation being the most common choice.
- Though sentences are getting shorter and fewer people are sent to prison per crime, people are serving a greater proportion of their sentence than they did a decade ago. Consequently, prison populations are not dropping despite a drop in the crime rate.
- Most states use indeterminate sentences, which give convicted offenders a short minimum sentence after which they can be released on parole if they are considered rehabilitated.
- A number of states have developed determinate sentences that eliminate parole and attempt to restrict judicial discretion so that convicted criminals are given a single sentence that they must serve without parole.
- Efforts have been made to control judicial discretion and reduce sentencing disparity. Methods for making dispositions more uniform include sentencing guidelines that create uniform sentences based on offender background and crime characteristics.
- Jurisdictions that use either determinate or indeterminate sentences also allow inmates to be released early on good behavior.
- Social and personal factors continue to influence sentencing. Some evidence suggests that young males, especially if they are members of a minority group, are more likely to receive longer sentences than older, Caucasian females.
- The death penalty continues to be the most controversial sentence, with over half the states reinstituting capital punishment laws since the 1972 *Furman* v. *Georgia* decision.
- Although little evidence exists that the death penalty deters murder, supporters still view it as necessary in terms of incapacitation and retribution and cite the public's support for the death penalty and the low chance of error in its application.
- Opponents point out that mistakes can be made, that capital sentences are apportioned in a racially biased manner, and that the practice is cruel and barbaric.
- Nonetheless, the courts have generally supported the legality of capital punishment, and it has been used more frequently in recent years.
- The death penalty is used abroad, though it has been abolished in many nations. The United States leads the world in the execution of juveniles.

Key Terms

sanctions 392
punishment 392
poor laws 392
penitentiary 393
general deterrence 393
incapacitation 394
recidivism 395
specific deterrence 395

blameworthy 395
just desert 395
felony 396
wergild 396
equity 396
consecutive sentence 397
concurrent sentence 398
indeterminate sentence 398

determinate sentence 399
good time 399
mandatory sentence 404
truth-in-sentencing 404
chivalry hypothesis 409
victim impact statement 410
brutalization effect 420
death-qualified jury 423

Doing Research on The Web

For an up-to-date list of Web links, go to http://cj.wadsworth.com/siegel_intro10e.

Capital punishment provokes more debate than almost any other criminal justice issue. Some opponents oppose the death penalty on moral and religious grounds. They argue, for example, that many innocent people are on death row. Read about this issue at Ramesh Ponnuru, "Bad List: A Suspect Roll of Death Row 'Innocents,'" *National Review,* September 16, 2002.

Another criticism is that the United States is one of the few nations that executes people who committed crimes while they were juveniles. Read more about this provocative topic at Allyssa D. Wheaton-Rodriguez, "The United States' Choice to Violate International Law by Allowing the Juvenile Death Penalty," *Houston Journal of International Law* 24, no. 1 (Fall 2001): 209.

While most academics are opposed to the death penalty for these and other reasons, some still believe it is a valuable criminal justice policy. Use the "death penalty" as a subject guide on Info-Trac College Edition to research the utility and benefits of the death penalty. Do you agree with those who advocate its use?

To read what Amnesty International has to say about the death penalty, go to http://web.amnesty.org/pages/deathpenalty-index-eng.

> Pro/Con discussions and Viewpoint Essays on some of the topics in this chapter may be found at the Opposing Viewpoints Resource Center: http://www.gale.com/OpposingViewpoints.

Discussion Questions

1. Discuss the sentencing dispositions in your jurisdiction. What are the pros and cons of each?
2. Compare the various types of incarceration sentences. What are the similarities and differences? Why are many jurisdictions considering the passage of mandatory sentencing laws?
3. Discuss the issue of capital punishment. In your opinion, does it serve as a deterrent? What new rulings has the U.S. Supreme Court made on the legality of the death penalty?
4. Why does the problem of sentencing disparity exist? Do programs exist that can reduce disparate sentences? If so, what are they? Should all people who commit the same crime receive the same sentence? Explain.
5. Should convicted criminals be released from prison when correctional authorities are convinced they are rehabilitated? Why or why not?

Notes

1 Nick Madigan, "Man Accused of Killing Girl in California Postpones Plea," *New York Times,* July 22, 2002, p. 1.
2 Michel Foucault, *Discipline and Punishment* (New York: Vintage Books, 1978).
3 Graeme Newman, *The Punishment Response* (Philadelphia: Lippincott, 1978), 13.
4 Peter Greenwood with Allan Abrahamse, *Selective Incapacitation* (Santa Monica, Calif.: RAND Corp., 1982).
5 Kathleen Auerhahn, "Selective Incapacitation and the Problem of Prediction," *Criminology* 37 (1999): 703–34.
6 Kathleen Daly, "Neither Conflict nor Labeling nor Paternalism Will Suffice: Intersections of Race, Ethnicity, Gender, and Family in Criminal Court Decisions," *Crime and Delinquency* 35 (1989): 136–68.
7 Among the most helpful sources for this section are Benedict Alper, *Prisons Inside-Out* (Cambridge, Mass.: Ballinger, 1974); Gustave de Beaumont and Alexis de Tocqueville, *On the Penitentiary System in the United States and Its Applications in France* (Carbondale: Southern Illinois University Press, 1964); Orlando Lewis, *The Development of American Prisons and Prison Customs, 1776–1845* (Montclair, N.J.: Patterson-Smith, 1967); Leonard Orland, ed., *Justice, Punishment, and Treatment*

(New York: Free Press, 1973); J. Goebel, *Felony and Misdemeanor* (Philadelphia: University of Pennsylvania Press, 1976); George Rusche and Otto Kircheimer, *Punishment and Social Structure* (New York: Russell and Russell, 1939); Samuel Walker, *Popular Justice* (New York: Oxford University Press, 1980); Newman, *The Punishment Response;* David Rothman, *Conscience and Convenience* (Boston: Little, Brown, 1980); George Ives, *A History of Penal Methods* (Montclair, N.J.: Patterson-Smith, 1970); Robert Hughes, *The Fatal Shore* (New York: Knopf, 1986); Leon Radzinowicz, *A History of English Criminal Law,* vol. 1 (London: Stevens, 1943), p. 5.
8 *Crime and Punishment in America, 1999,* Report 229 (Washington, D.C.: National Center for Policy Analysis, 1999).
9 Ibid.
10 Christopher D. Maxwell, Joel H. Garner, and Jeffrey A. Fagan, *The Effects of Arrest in Intimate Partner Violence: New Evidence from the Spouse Assault Replication Program* (Washington, D.C: National Institute of Justice, 2001); Robert Davis, Barbara Smith, and Laura Nickles, "The Deterrent Effect of Prosecuting Domestic Violence Misdemeanors," *Crime and Delinquency* 44 (1998): 434–42.

11 Patrick Langan and David Levin, *Recidivism of Prisoners Released in 1994* (Washington, D.C.: Bureau of Justice Statistics, 2002).
12 Charles Logan, *Criminal Justice Performance Measures for Prisons* (Washington, D.C.: Bureau of Justice Statistics, 1993), p. 3.
13 Alexis Durham, "The Justice Model in Historical Context: Early Law, the Emergence of Science, and the Rise of Incarceration," *Journal of Criminal Justice* 16 (1988): 331–46.
14 Andrew von Hirsh, *Doing Justice: The Choice of Punishments* (New York: Hill and Wang, 1976).
15 Shawn Bushway, "The Impact of an Arrest on the Job Stability of Young White American Men," *Journal of Research in Crime and Delinquency* 35 (1998): 454–79.
16 Charles Logan and Gerald Gaes, "Meta-Analysis and the Rehabilitation of Punishment," *Justice Quarterly* 10 (1993): 245–64.
17 Richard McCorkle, "Research Note: Punish and Rehabilitate? Public Attitudes toward Six Common Crimes," *Crime and Delinquency* 39 (1993): 240–52; D. A. Andrews, Ivan Zinger, Robert Hoge, James Bonta, Paul Gendreau, and Francis Cullen, "Does Correctional Treatment Work? A Clinically Relevant and Psycho-

logically Informed Meta-Analysis," *Criminology* 28 (1990): 369–404.

18 Francis Cullen, John Paul Wright, Shayna Brown, Melissa Moon, and Brandon Applegate, "Public Support for Early Intervention Programs: Implications for a Progressive Policy Agenda," *Crime and Delinquency* 44 (1998): 187–204.

19 Lawrence W. Sherman, David P. Farrington, Doris Layton MacKenzie, Brandon Walsh, Denise Gottfredson, John Eck, Shawn Bushway, and Peter Reuter, *Evidence-Based Crime Prevention* (London: Routledge and Kegan Paul, 2002). See also Arnulf Kolstad, "Imprisonment as Rehabilitation: Offenders' Assessment of Why It Does Not Work," *Journal of Criminal Justice* 24 (1996): 323–35.

20 Paula Ditton and Doris James Wilson, *Truth in Sentencing in State Prisons* (Washington, D.C.: Bureau of Justice Statistics, 1999).

21 Jo Dixon, "The Organizational Context of Criminal Sentencing," *American Journal of Sociology* 100 (1995): 1157–98.

22 Michael Tonry, *Reconsidering Indeterminate and Structured Sentencing Series: Sentencing and Corrections: Issues for the 21st Century* (Washington, D.C.: National Institute of Justice, 1999).

23 Michael Tonry, *The Fragmentation of Sentencing and Corrections in America* (Washington, D.C.: National Institute of Justice, 1999).

24 Ibid., p. 11.

25 Robin Lubitz and Thomas Ross, *Sentencing Guidelines: Reflections on the Future* (Washington, D.C.: National Institute of Justice, June 2001).

26 Minnesota Sentencing Guideline Commission, 2002, http://www.msgc.state.mn.us/msgcwork.htm, accessed on November 10, 2003.

27 Ibid.

28 Michael Tonry, "The Failure of the U.S. Sentencing Commission's Guidelines," *Crime and Delinquency* 39 (1993): 131–49.

29 Lisa Pasko, "Villain or Victim: Regional Variation and Ethnic Disparity in Federal Drug Offense Sentencing," *Criminal Justice Policy Review* 13 (2002): 307–28.

30 Michael Tonry, "Racial Politics, Racial Disparities, and the War on Crime," *Crime and Delinquency* 40 (1994): 475–94.

31 Louis F. Oberdorfer, "Mandatory Sentencing: One Judge's Perspective, 2002," *American Criminal Law Review* 40 (2003): 11–19.

32 Joan Petersilia and Susan Turner, *Guideline-Based Justice: The Implications for Racial Minorities* (Santa Monica, Calif.: RAND Corp., 1985).

33 Barbara Koons-Witt "The Effect of Gender on the Decision to Incarcerate before and after the Introduction of Sentencing Guidelines," *Criminology* 40 (2002): 97–129.

34 Elaine Wolf and Marsha Weissman, "Revising Federal Sentencing Policy: Some Consequences of Expanding Eligibility for Alternative Sanctions," *Crime and Delinquency* 42 (1996): 192–205.

35 Paula Kautt, "Location, Location, Location: Interdistrict and Intercircuit Variation in Sentencing Outcomes for Federal Drug-Trafficking Offenses," *Justice Quarterly* 19 (2002): 633–72.

36 Kirby Behre and A. Jeff Ifrah, "Foreword: You Be the Judge: The Success of Fifteen Years of Sentencing under the United States Sentencing Guidelines," *American Criminal Law Review* 40 (2003): 5–11.

37 Tonry, "The Failure of the U.S. Sentencing Commission's Guidelines," p. 131.

38 Michael Tonry, *Sentencing Matters* (New York: Oxford University Press, 1996), p. 5.

39 Gail Appleson, "ABA Set to Review Sentencing Policies," *Boston Globe,* August 12, 2003, p. 12.

40 Henry Scott Wallace, "Mandatory Minimums and the Betrayal of Sentencing Reform: A Legislative Dr. Jekyll and Mr. Hyde," *Federal Probation* 57 (1993): 9–16.

41 Paula M. Ditton and Doris James Wilson, *Truth in Sentencing in State Prisons* (Washington, D.C.: Bureau of Justice Statistics, 1999).

42 Matthew Durose and Patrick A. Langan, *State Court Sentencing of Convicted Felons, 1998* (Washington, D.C.: Bureau of Justice Statistics, February 2001).

43 Brent Smith and Kelly Damphouse, "Terrorism, Politics, and Punishment: A Test of Structural–Contextual Theory and the Liberation Hypothesis," *Criminology* 36 (1998): 67–92.

44 For a general look at the factors that affect sentencing, see Susan Welch, Cassia Spohn, and John Gruhl, "Convicting and Sentencing Differences among Black, Hispanic, and White Males in Six Localities," *Justice Quarterly* 2 (1985): 67–80.

45 Stewart D'Alessio and Lisa Stolzenberg, "Socioeconomic Status and the Sentencing of the Traditional Offender," *Journal of Criminal Justice* 21 (1993): 61–77.

46 Cecilia Saulters-Tubbs, "Prosecutorial and Judicial Treatment of Female Offenders," *Federal Probation* 57 (1993): 37–41.

47 See, generally, Janet Johnston, Thomas Kennedy, and I. Gayle Shuman, "Gender Differences in the Sentencing of Felony Offenders," *Federal Probation* 87 (1987): 49–56; Cassia Spohn and Susan Welch, "The Effect of Prior Record in Sentencing Research: An Examination of the Assumption That Any Measure Is Adequate," *Justice Quarterly* 4 (1987): 286–302; David Willison, "The Effects of Counsel on the Severity of Criminal Sentences: A Statistical Assessment," *Justice System Journal* 9 (1984): 87–101.

48 Cassia Spohn, Miriam DeLone, and Jeffrey Spears, "Race/Ethnicity, Gender and Sentence Severity in Dade County, Florida: An Examination of the Decision to Withhold Adjudication," *Journal of Crime and Justice* 21 (1998): 111–32.

49 Ellen Hochstedler Steury and Nancy Frank, "Gender Bias and Pretrial Release: More Pieces of the Puzzle," *Journal of Criminal Justice* 18 (1990): 417–32.

50 Koons-Witt, "The Effect of Gender on the Decision to Incarcerate before and after the Introduction of Sentencing Guidelines."

51 Dean Champion, "Elderly Felons and Sentencing Severity: Interregional Variations in Leniency and Sentencing Trends," *Criminal Justice Review* 12 (1987): 7–15.

52 Darrell Steffensmeier, John Kramer, and Jeffery Ulmer, "Age Differences in Sentencing," *Justice Quarterly* 12 (1995): 583–601.

53 Darrell Steffensmeier, Jeffery Ulmer, and John Kramer, "The Interaction of Race, Gender, and Age in Criminal Sentencing: The Punishment Cost of Being Young, Black, and Male," *Criminology* 36 (1998): 763–98.

54 *Payne* v. *Tennessee,* 111 S.Ct. 2597, 115 L.Ed.2d 720 (1991).

55 Robert Davis and Barbara Smith, "The Effects of Victim Impact Statements on Sentencing Decisions: A Test in an Urban Setting," *Justice Quarterly* 11 (1994): 453–69; Edna Erez and Pamela Tontodonato, "The Effect of Victim Participation in Sentencing on Sentence Outcome," *Criminology* 28 (1990): 451–74.

56 Rodney Kingsworth, Randall MacIntosh, and Jennifer Wentworth, "Sexual Assault: The Role of Prior Relationship and Victim Characteristics in Case Processing," *Justice Quarterly* 16 (1999): 276–302.

57 Michael Tonry, *Malign Neglect: Race, Crime, and Punishment in America* (New York: Oxford University Press, 1995), 105–09.

58 *Coker* v. *Georgia,* 433 U.S. 584, 97 S.Ct. 2861, 53 L.Ed.2d 982 (1977).

59 "Many State Legislatures Focused on Crime in 1995, Study Finds," *Criminal Justice Newsletter,* January 2, 1996, p. 2.

60 The most recent data on capital punishment used here is from Thomas Bonczar and Tracy Snell, *Capital Punishment 2002* (Washington, D.C.: Bureau of Justice Statistics, 2003).

61 *Lopez* v. *Singletary,* No. 98–6065.

62 Stephen Markman and Paul Cassell, "Protecting the Innocent: A Response to the Bedeau–Radelet Study," *Stanford Law Review* 41 (1988): 121–70.

63 Bonczar and Snell, *Capital Punishment 2002,* p. 2.

64 Stephen Layson, "United States Time-Series Homicide Regressions with Adaptive Expectations," *Bulletin of the New York Academy of Medicine* 62 (1986): 589–619.

65 James Galliher and John Galliher, "A 'Commonsense' Theory of Deterrence and the 'Ideology' of Science: The New York State Death Penalty Debate," *Journal Criminal Law and Criminology* 92 (2002): 307.

66 Steven Stack, "Publicized Executions and Homicide, 1950–1980," *American Sociological Review* 52 (1987): 532–40. For a study challenging Stack's methods, see William Bailey and Ruth Peterson, "Murder and Capital Punishment: A Monthly Time-Series Analysis of Execution Publicity," *American Sociological Review* 54 (1989): 722–43.

67 Steven Stack, "The Effect of Well-Publicized Executions on Homicide in California," *Journal of Crime and Justice* 21 (1998): 1–12.

68 David Friedrichs, "Comment — Humanism and the Death Penalty: An Alternative Perspective," *Justice Quarterly* 6 (1989): 197–209.

69 Kathleen Maguire and Ann L. Pastore, eds., *Sourcebook of Criminal Justice Statistics,* http://www.albany.edu/sourcebook/ [2002], accessed on November 13, 2003.

70 For an analysis of the formation of public opinion on the death penalty, see Kimberly Cook, "Public Support for the

Death Penalty: A Cultural Analysis," paper presented at the annual meeting of the American Society of Criminology, San Francisco, California, November 1991.

71 Alexis Durham, H. Preston Elrod, and Patrick Kinkade, "Public Support to the Death Penalty: Beyond Gallup," *Justice Quarterly* 13 (1996): 705–36.

72 See, generally, Hugo Bedeau, *Death Is Different: Studies in the Morality, Law, and Politics of Capital Punishment* (Boston: Northeastern University Press, 1987); Keith Otterbein, *The Ultimate Coercive Sanction* (New Haven, Conn.: HRAF Press, 1986).

73 "Illinois Ex-Prosecutors Charged with Framing Murder Defendants," *Criminal Justice Newsletter* 28 (1997): 3.

74 Jim Yardley, "Convicted in Murder Case, Man Cleared 7 Years Later," *New York Times,* October 29, 1998, p. A3.

75 House Subcommittee on Civil and Constitutional Rights, *Innocence and the Death Penalty: Assessing the Danger of Mistaken Executions* (Washington, D.C.: Government Printing Office, 1993).

76 David Stewart, "Dealing with Death," *American Bar Association Journal* 80 (1994): 53.

77 Editorial, "The Innocence Protection Act," *America* 187 (September 23, 2002): 2–3.

78 Michael Radelet and Hugo Bedeau, "Miscarriages of Justice in Potentially Capital Cases," *Stanford Law Review* 40 (1987): 121–81.

79 Stewart, "Dealing with Death."

80 "A Victim's Progress," *Newsweek,* June 12, 1989, p. 5.

81 William Doerner, "The Impact of Medical Resources on Criminally Induced Lethality: A Further Examination," *Criminology* 26 (1988): 171–77.

82 Elizabeth Purdom and J. Anthony Paredes, "Capital Punishment and Human Sacrifice," in *Facing the Death Penalty: Essays on Cruel and Unusual Punishment,* ed. Michael Radelet (Philadelphia: Temple University Press, 1989), 152–53.

83 Kimberly Cook, "A Passion to Punish: Abortion Opponents Who Favor the Death Penalty," *Justice Quarterly* 15 (1998): 329–46.

84 Steven Barkan and Steven Cohn, "Racial Prejudice and Support for the Death Penalty by Whites," *Journal of Research in Crime and Delinquency* 31 (1994): 202–09; Robert Bohm and Ronald Vogel, "A Comparison of Factors Associated with Uninformed and Informed Death Penalty Opinions," *Journal of Criminal Justice* 22 (1994): 125–43.

85 Kathleen Maguire and Ann Pastore, *Sourcebook of Criminal Justice Statistics, 1995* (Washington, D.C.: Government Printing Office, 1996), p. 183.

86 Gennaro Vito and Thomas Keil, "Elements of Support for Capital Punishment: An Examination of Changing Attitudes," *Journal of Crime and Justice* 21 (1998): 17–25.

87 John Whitehead, Michael Blankenship, and John Paul Wright, "Elite versus Citizen Attitudes on Capital Punishment: Incongruity between the Public and Policy Makers," *Journal of Criminal Justice* 27 (1999): 249–58.

88 William Bowers and Glenn Pierce, "Deterrence or Brutalization: What Is the Effect of Executions?" *Crime and Delinquency* 26 (1980): 453–84.

89 Keith Harries and Derral Cheatwood, *The Geography of Executions: The Capital Punishment Quagmire in America* (Lanham, Md.: Rowman and Littlefield Publishers, 1997).

90 Jonathan R. Sorensen and Rocky L. Pilgrim, "An Actuarial Risk of Assessment of Violence Posed by Murder Defendants," *Journal of Criminal Law and Criminology* 90 (2000): 1251–71.

91 Marian Williams and Jefferson Holcomb, "Racial Disparity and Death Sentences in Ohio," *Journal of Criminal Justice* 29 (2001): 207–18.

92 Jon Sorenson and Danold Wallace, "Prosecutorial Discretion in Seeking Death: An Analysis of Racial Disparity in the Pretrial Stages of Case Processing in a Midwestern County," *Justice Quarterly* 16 (1999): 559–78.

93 Data from the American Civil Liberties Web site, http://www.aclu.org/Death-Penalty/DeathPenalty.cfm?ID=9312&c=6 2, accessed on August 14, 2003.

94 Lawrence Greenfield and David Hinners, *Capital Punishment, 1984* (Washington, D.C.: Bureau of Justice Statistics, 1985).

95 Geoffrey Rapp, "The Economics of Shootouts: Does the Passage of Capital Punishment Laws Protect or Endanger Police Officers?" *Albany Law Review* 65 (2002): 1051–84.

96 Robert Johnson, *Death Work: A Study of the Modern Execution Process* (Pacific Grove, Calif.: Brooks/Cole, 1990).

97 William Bailey, "Disaggregation in Deterrence and Death Penalty Research: The Case of Murder in Chicago," *Journal of Criminal Law and Criminology* 74 (1986): 827–59.

98 Gennaro Vito, Pat Koester, and Deborah Wilson, "Return of the Dead: An Update on the Status of *Furman*-Commuted Death Row Inmates," in *The Death Penalty in America: Current Research,* ed. Robert Bohm (Cincinnati, Ohio: Anderson, 1991), pp. 89–100; Gennaro Vito, Deborah Wilson, and Edward Latessa, "Comparison of the Dead: Attributes and Outcomes of *Furman*-Commuted Death Row Inmates in Kentucky and Ohio," in *The Death Penalty in America: Current Research,* ed. Robert Bohm (Cincinnati, Ohio: Anderson, 1991), pp. 101–12.

99 John Cochran, Mitchell Chamlin, and Mark Seth, "Deterrence or Brutalization? An Impact Assessment of Oklahoma's Return to Capital Punishment," *Criminology* 32 (1994): 107–34.

100 William Bailey, "Deterrence, Brutalization, and the Death Penalty: Another Examination of Oklahoma's Return to Capital Punishment," *Justice Quarterly* 36 (1998): 711–34.

101 Joseph Schumacher, "An International Look at the Death Penalty," *International Journal of Comparative and Applied Criminal Justice* 14 (1990): 307–15.

102 David Stout, "Clemency Denied, Paraguayan Is Executed," *New York Times,* April 15, 1998, p. A2.

103 Don Terry, "California Prepares for Faster Execution Pace," *New York Times,* October 17, 1998, p. A7.

104 *Furman* v. *Georgia,* 408 U.S. 238, 92 S.Ct. 2726, 33 L.Ed.2d 346 (1972).

105 *Gregg* v. *Georgia,* 428 U.S. 153, 96 S.Ct. 2909, 49 L.Ed.2d 859 (1976).

106 Ibid., at 205–207, 96 S.Ct. at 2940–41.

107 *McKlesky* v. *Kemp,* 428 U.S. 262, 96 S.Ct. 2950, 49 L.Ed.2d 929 (1976).

108 *Coker* v. *Georgia,* 430 U.S. 349, 97 S.Ct. 1197, 51 L.Ed.2d 393 (1977).

109 *Dawson* v. *Delaware,* 503 U.S. 159, 112 S.Ct. 1093, 117 L.Ed.2d 309 (1992).

110 *Wilkins* v. *Missouri* and *Stanford* v. *Kentucky,* 492 U.S. 361, 109 S.Ct. 2969, 106 L.Ed.2d 306 (1989).

111 *Atkins* v. *Virginia,* No. 00–8452, 2002.

112 Douglas Mossman, "Psychiatry in the Courtroom," *Public Interest* 150 (200): 22–37.

113 *Witherspoon* v. *Illinois,* 391 U.S. 510, 88 S.Ct. 1770, 20 L.Ed.2d 776 (1968).

114 *Wainwright* v. *Witt,* 469 U.S. 412, 105 S.Ct. 844, 83 L.Ed.2d 841 (1985).

115 *Lockhart* v. *McCree,* 476 U.S. 162, 106 S.Ct. 1758, 90 L.Ed.2d 137 (1986).

116 *Ring* v. *Arizona,* No. 01–488 (2002).

117 *Miller-El* v. *Cockrell, Director, Texas Department of Criminal Justice, Institutional Division,* No. 01–7662, decided February 25, 2003.

118 Walter C. Reckless, "Use of the Death Penalty," *Crime and Delinquency* 15 (1969): 43; Thorsten Sellin, "Effect of Repeal and Reintroduction of the Death Penalty on Homicide Rates," in *The Death Penalty,* ed. Thorsten Sellin (Philadelphia: American Law Institute, 1959); Robert H. Dann, "The Deterrent Effect of Capital Punishment," *Friends Social Service Series* 29 (1935): 1; William Bailey and Ruth Peterson, "Murder and Capital Punishment: A Monthly Time-Series Analysis of Execution Publicity," *American Sociological Review* 54 (1989): 722–43; David Phillips, "The Deterrent Effect of Capital Punishment," *American Journal of Sociology* 86 (1980): 139–48; Sam McFarland, "Is Capital Punishment a Short-Term Deterrent to Homicide? A Study of the Effects of Four Recent American Executions," *Journal of Criminal Law and Criminology* 74 (1984): 1014–32; Richard Lempert, "The Effect of Executions on Homicides: A New Look in an Old Light," *Crime and Delinquency* 29 (1983): 88–115.

119 Jon Sorenson, Robert Wrinkle, Victoria Brewer, and James Marquart, "Capital Punishment and Deterrence: Examining the Effect of Executions on Murder in Texas," *Crime and Delinquency* 45 (1999): 481–93.

120 Isaac Ehrlich, "The Deterrent Effect of Capital Punishment: A Question of Life or Death," *American Economic Review* 65 (1975): 397.

121 For a review, see William Bailey, "The General Prevention Effect of Capital Punishment for Non-Capital Felonies," in *The Death Penalty in America: Current Research,* ed. Robert Bohm (Cincinnati, Ohio: Anderson, 1991), 21–38.

Part Four Corrections

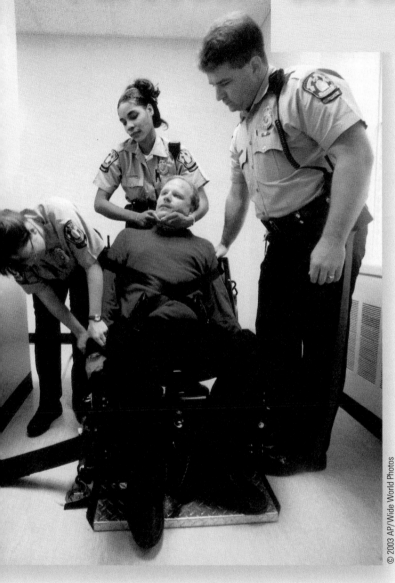

© 2003 AP/Wide World Photos

Could an enlightened nation such as the United States be subduing correctional inmates with painful jolts of electricity? Hard to believe, but the use of stun belts, which deliver up to 50,000 volts of electricity, has become a somewhat routine practice in American correctional institutions. Critics of the practice, such as Amnesty International, have called for the abolition of the device, which they view as a form of torture. While the use of stun belts may be troubling to some, the correctional system has also developed restorative programs that seek to reintegrate the offender back into society with a minimum of coercion and harm.

The contemporary correctional system, which controls and treats more than 4 million people, is immense and intricate. The chapters in this section attempt to describe its operations, philosophies, and programs. Chapter 14 looks at community sentences such as probation, alternative sanctions, and restorative justice. Chapters 15 and 16 cover secure correctional institutions, including prisons and jails. A number of important issues are covered, ranging from the development of new generation jails to the reentry of prisoners into society.

Chapter Outline

Chapter Objectives

After reading this chapter, you should be able to:

1. Understand the concept of community sentencing.
2. Know how probation developed.
3. Recognize the different types of probation sentences.
4. Identify the rules of probation.
5. Discuss the issue of probation revocation.
6. Describe the effectiveness of probation.
7. Understand the concept of alternative sanctions.
8. Know the various alternative sanctions, from fines to community incarceration.
9. Describe the concept of the punishment ladder.
10. Explain the principles of restorative justice.
11. Understand the concept of reintegrative shaming.
12. List the various types of restorative justice programs in use.

Viewpoints

 International Justice: Alternatives to Incarceration Abroad 445

 Analyzing Criminal Justice Issues: DTAP: Drug Treatment Alternative-to-Prison 455

 Analyzing Criminal Justice Issues: Reintegrative Shaming 459

 Analyzing Criminal Justice Issues: Restorative Justice in the Community 462

Web Links

Probation in England
http://www.syps.org.uk/syindex.htm 433

Extent of probation
http://www.ojp.usdoj.gov/bjs/pandp.htm 435

New York probation professional organization
http://www.nyspoa.com/ 438

RAND Corporation
http://www.rand.org/ 441

Center for Restorative Justice and Peacemaking
http://ssw.che.umn.edu/rjp/default.html 460

Sentencing circles
http://www.ojp.usdoj.gov/nij/rest-just/CH5/3_sntcir.htm 461

 # InfoTrac College Edition Links

Article: "Professionalizing Probation Work in Chicago, 1900–1935" 433

Article: "Spotlight on Probation in the Netherlands" 433

Article: "Probation: Strength through Association" 438

Key Term: "probation treatment supervision" 439

Article: "The Keys to the Castle: A New Standard for Warrantless Home Searches in *United States* v. *Knights*" 442

Article: "License to Loot? A Critique of Follow-the-Money Methods in Crime Control Policy" 448

Chapter 14 | Community Sentences: Probation, Intermediate Sanctions, and Restorative Justice

On December 12, 2001, actress Winona Ryder was apprehended by Saks Fifth Avenue store detectives as she attempted to leave the premises with clothes, socks, hats, hair accessories, and handbags worth some $5,500. Store detectives found her in possession of designer tops and handbags bearing holes where security tags had been removed. They later found security tags in the pocket of a coat in a section of the store that Ryder had been seen to visit. Three of them contained material that matched holes in two handbags and a hair bow allegedly stolen by Ryder. She was also found in possession of eight forms of painkillers, ranging from Valium to Vicodin to a generic form of Oxycodone (drug possession charges were later dropped).

On November 6, 2002, Ryder was found guilty of grand theft and vandalism and sentenced to probation. Under the terms of her three-year probation sentence, Ryder was required to perform 480 hours of community service and undergo both drug and personal counseling. She also had to pay $6,555.40 in restitution to the Beverly Hills, California, Saks Fifth Avenue where she was caught shoplifting, plus $2,700 in

fines. To fulfill her community service requirement, Ryder had to spend 240 hours at City of Hope, a cancer treatment center outside of Los Angeles; 120 hours at the Foundation for the Junior Blind; and 120 hours at Caring for Babies with AIDS.

After the trial was over, Ann Rundle, the prosecutor who tried the case, was quoted as saying, "We never thought about jail time. . . . We won't be asking for it. We simply want Ms. Ryder to take responsibility for her conduct."[1] Because shoplifting is not

a violent crime, Rundle said, an appropriate sentence would be some combination of probation, community service, and restitution. "And that's what we're going to ask for," she said.

On December 15, 2003 Judge Elden Foy publicly praised Ryder's efforts to complete her community treatment.

CNN. *View the CNN video clip of this story on your Introduction to Criminal Justice 10e CD.*

431

The Winona Ryder case illustrates the difficulty of reaching appropriate sentences in the criminal justice system. While some people may believe she was given special treatment because she is a celebrity, it is a rare occurrence for first-time offenders to be incarcerated for shoplifting. If they were, the correctional system would be even more crowded than it is today. Her treatment reflects the evolution of punishment that has continued for thousands of years and has produced the widespread use of community sentencing, which includes probation, alternative sanction, and restorative justice.

The core value of community sentencing is that many convicted in criminal courts are deserving of a second chance; most present little threat to society. If they can be reintegrated into the community and given the proper treatment they are unlikely to recidivate. Considering these circumstances, it seems foolish to incarcerate them in an overcrowded and dangerous prison system, which inmates describe as "criminal universities" where deviant identities are reinforced.[2] It may be both more effective and less costly to have them remain in the community under the supervision of a trained court officer where they can receive treatment that will help them turn around their lives. Rehabilitation would be aided immensely if those who commit crime could be made to understand the problems their actions caused their family, friends, and community.

Considering the potential benefits and cost-effectiveness of a community sentence, it is not surprising that the number of community sentences is at an all-time high. There are now a great variety of community sentences, including traditional probation and probation plus (also called **alternative sanctions** or **intermediate sanctions**), which typically involves probation and a fine, forfeiture, restitution, shock probation, split sentencing, intensive probation supervision (IPS), house arrest, electronic monitoring (EM), or residential community corrections (RCC). These programs are designed to provide greater control over an offender and to increase the level of sanction without resorting to a prison sentence. In addition, restorative justice programs are being implemented that involve the offender in new forms of treatment typically designed to reintegrate them back into society.

Both traditional probation and the newer forms of community sentences have the potential to become reasonable alternatives to many of the economic and social problems faced by correctional administrators. They are less costly than jail or prison sentences, they help the offender maintain family and community ties, they can be structured to maximize security and maintain public safety, they can be scaled in severity to correspond to the seriousness of the crime, and they can feature restoration and reintegration instead of punishment and ostracism. No area of the criminal justice system is undergoing more change and greater expansion than community sentencing.

History of Probation

The roots of probation can be traced back to the traditions of the English common law. During the Middle Ages, judges wishing to spare deserving offenders from the pains of the then commonly used punishments of torture, mutilation, and death used their power to grant clemency and stays of execution. The common law practice of **judicial reprieve** allowed judges to suspend punishment so that convicted offenders could seek a pardon, gather new evidence, or demonstrate that they had reformed their behavior. Similarly, the practice of **recognizance** enabled convicted offenders to remain free if they agreed to enter into a debt obligation with the state. The debt would have to be paid only if the offender was caught engaging in further criminal behavior. Sometimes **sureties** were required — these were people who made themselves responsible for the behavior of an offender after he was released.

alternative sanctions
Community sentences featuring probation plus additional requirements such as restitution, fines, home confinement, or electronic monitoring, designed to provide more control and sanctions than traditional probation but less than secure incarceration in jail or prison.

intermediate sanctions
A group of punishments falling between probation and prison; community-based sanctions including house arrest and intensive supervision.

judicial reprieve
In medieval England, a judge's suspension of punishment, enabling a convicted offender to seek a pardon, gather new evidence, or demonstrate reformed behavior.

recognizance
Medieval practice of letting convicted offenders remain free if they agreed to enter a debt relation with the state to pay for their crimes.

sureties
During the Middle Ages, people who made themselves responsible for people given release or a reprieve.

Early U.S. courts continued the practice of indefinitely suspending sentences of criminals who seemed deserving of a second chance, but it was John Augustus of Boston who is usually credited with originating the modern probation concept.[3] As a private citizen, Augustus began in 1841 to supervise offenders released to his custody by a Boston judge. Over an 18-year period, Augustus supervised close to 2,000 probationers and helped them get jobs and establish themselves in the community. Augustus had an amazingly high success rate, and few of his charges became involved in crime again.

In 1878 Augustus's work inspired the Massachusetts legislature to pass a law authorizing the appointment of a paid probation officer for the city of Boston. In 1880 probation was extended to other jurisdictions in Massachusetts, and by 1898 the probation movement had spread to the superior (felony) courts.[4] The Massachusetts experience was copied by Missouri (1887), by Vermont (1898), and soon after by most other states. In 1925 the federal government established a probation system for the U.S. district courts. The probation concept soon became the most widely used correctional mechanism in the United States.[5]

To learn more about the early history of probation and the movement toward professionalism, read Anne Meis Knupfer, "Professionalizing Probation Work in Chicago, 1900–1935," *Social Service Review* 73, no. 4 (December 1999): 478, on InfoTrac College Edition.

Probation Today

Probation is a criminal sentence mandating that a convicted offender be placed and maintained in the community under the supervision of a duly authorized agent of the court. Once on probation, the offender is subject to certain rules and conditions that must be followed to remain in the community. The probation sentence is managed by a probation department that supervises the offender's behavior and treatment and carries out other tasks for the court. Although the term has many meanings, probation usually indicates a nonpunitive form of sentencing for convicted criminal offenders and delinquent youth, emphasizing maintenance in the community and treatment without institutionalization or other forms of punishment.

probation
A sentence entailing the conditional release of a convicted offender into the community under the supervision of the court (in the form of a probation officer), subject to certain conditions for a specified time.

Not only is probation used extensively in the United States, but it also is popular abroad. Read about probation in Holland at Donald G. Evans, "Spotlight on Probation in the Netherlands," *Corrections Today* 64, no. 4 (July 2002): 104.

Perspectives on Justice

Probation is at the heart of both the rehabilitation and noninterventionist perspective. It rests on the assumption that the average offender is not a dangerous criminal or a menace to society and can be rehabilitated without further risk to the community. When offenders are institutionalized, the prison community becomes their new reference point. They are forced to interact with hardened criminals, and the "ex-con" label prohibits them from making successful adjustments to society. Probation provides offenders with the opportunity to prove themselves, gives them a second chance, and allows them to be closely supervised by trained personnel who can help them reestablish proper forms of behavior in the community.

Why Probation?

The philosophy of probation is that the average offender is not a dangerous criminal or a menace to society. Advocates of probation suggest that when offenders are institutionalized instead of being granted community release, the prison community becomes their new reference point, they are forced to interact with hardened criminals, and the "ex-con" label prohibits them from making successful adjustments to society. Probation is not limited to minor or petty criminals. A significant proportion of people convicted of felony offenses receives probation, including about 4 percent of murderers and 16 percent of rapists.[6]

Probation is not unique to the United States. Read about probation in England at http://www.syps.org.uk/syindex.htm.

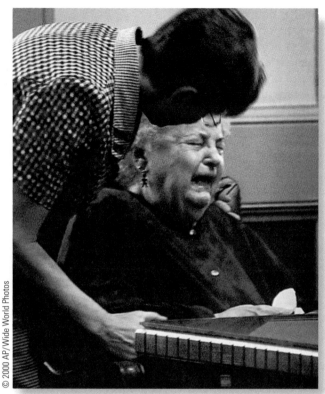

Probation provides an opportunity for nondangerous offenders to receive treatment in the community. A probation sentence is often combined with a variety of other sentencing alternatives. Here, former county clerk Juanita Wright is comforted by her daughter Paula Hughes prior to her sentencing on embezzlement charges, May 17, 2000, in Ashland County Common Pleas Court in Ashland, Ohio. The seventy-eight-year-old grandmother pleaded guilty to embezzling $178,000 in county funds over a ten-year period. She received thirty days in jail, eleven months house arrest, four hundred hours of community service, five years probation, and a $5,000 fine and repayment of the embezzled funds out of her retirement account. In addition, she would have to undergo treatment for a gambling addiction, take financial management classes, and get a job.

Probation usually involves suspension of the offender's sentence in return for the promise of good behavior in the community under the supervision of the probation department. As practiced in all 50 states and by the federal government, probation implies a contract between the court and the offender in which the former promises to hold a prison term in abeyance while the latter promises to adhere to a set of rules or conditions mandated by the court. If the rules are violated, and especially if the probationer commits another criminal offense, probation may be revoked. **Revocation** means that the contract is terminated and the original sentence is enforced. If an offender on probation commits a second offense that is more serious than the first, she may also be indicted, tried, and sentenced on the second offense. However, probation may be revoked simply because the rules and conditions of probation have not been met; it is not necessary for an offender to commit another crime.

Each probationary sentence is for a fixed period of time, depending on the seriousness of the offense and the statutory law of the jurisdiction. Probation is considered served when offenders fulfill the conditions set by the court for that period of time. They can then live without state supervision.

Awarding Probation

Probationary sentences may be granted by state and federal district courts and state superior (felony) courts. In some states, juries may recommend probation if the case meets certain legally regulated criteria (for example, if it falls within a certain class of offenses as determined by statute). Even in those jurisdictions that allow juries to recommend probation, judges have the final say in the matter and may grant probation at their discretion. In non-jury trials, probation is granted solely by judicial mandate.

In most jurisdictions, all juvenile offenders are eligible for probation, as are most adults. Some state statutes prohibit probation for certain types of adult offenders, usually those who have engaged in repeated and serious violent crimes, such as murder or rape, or those who have committed crimes for which mandatory prison sentences have been legislated.

In about half of all cases a probationary sentence is imposed without an incarceration sentence being formulated or threatened; this is referred to as straight probation or a probation only sentence. It is also common for the judge to formulate a prison sentence and then suspend it if the offender agrees to obey the rules of probation while living in the community (a **suspended sentence**).[7] The term of a probationary sentence may extend to the limit of the suspended prison term, or the court may set a time limit that reflects the sentencing period. For misdemeanors, probation usually extends for the entire period of the jail sentence, and felonies are more likely to warrant probationary periods that are shorter than the suspended prison sentences. Some offenders (about 10 percent) receive some form of split sentence in which they must first serve a jail term before being released on probation. In about 10 percent of all cases, the imposition of the sentence to probation is suspended.[8] This step is usually taken to encourage the defendant to pursue a specific rehabilitation program, such as treatment for alcohol abuse. If the program is successfully completed, further legal action is not usually taken.

Exhibit 14. 1 Profile of the Probationer

- Nationwide, women represented a slightly larger percentage of the probation population in 2002 than in 1995. Women were 23 percent of the adults on probation in 2002 (906,600), up from 21 percent in 1995.

- At year-end 2002 more than half of all probationers were white (2,212,700); a third were black (1,228,300); and an eighth were of Hispanic origin (485,600). Persons of other races comprised about 2 percent of probationers (68,700).

- Half of all probationers were convicted of a felony; a quarter were convicted of a drug law violation.

- Sixty percent of probationers had a direct sentence to probation; 22 percent had received a sentence of incarceration that had been suspended; and 9 percent had received a split sentence that included incarceration followed by probation. An additional 10 percent had entered probation before completion of all court proceedings (including those who entered probation before final verdict).

- Approximately 3 of every 4 probationers were under active supervision and were required to regularly report to a probation authority in person, by mail, or by telephone. The percent of probationers required to report regularly has dropped steadily, from 79 percent in 1995 to 76 percent in 2000 and to 75 percent in 2002.

- In 2002, 24 percent of probationers had a drug law violation; 17 percent were sentenced for driving while intoxicated or under the influence of alcohol; 13 percent for larceny/theft; and 10 percent for other assault, excluding sexual assault and domestic violence. Less than 10 percent were sentenced to probation for burglary (8 percent), domestic violence (7 percent), minor traffic offenses (6 percent), fraud (5 percent), and sexual assault (2 percent).

Source: Lauren E. Glaze, *Probation and Parole in the United States, 2002* (Washington, D.C.: Bureau of Justice Statistics, 2003), p. 3.

revocation
Removing a person from probation (or parole) in response to a violation of law or of the conditions of probation (or parole).

suspended sentence
A sentence of incarceration that is not carried out if the offender agrees to obey the rules of probation while living in the community.

The Extent of Probation

There are approximately 2,000 adult probation agencies in the United States. Slightly more than half are associated with a state-level agency, while the remainder are organized at the county or municipal level of government. About 30 states combine probation and parole supervision into a single agency.

Today, almost 4 million adults are under federal, state, or local probation.[9] Among offenders on probation, half had been convicted for committing a felony, 49 percent for a misdemeanor, and 1 percent for other infractions. In 1980, 1.1 million people were on probation, so the number of probationers has quadrupled in two decades (Exhibit 14.1). And while the growth rate has slowed down, the probation caseload increased about 1.6 percent between 2001 and 2002. Some states, such as California and Texas, are maintaining hundreds of thousands of probationers in their caseloads. Without probation, the correctional system would rapidly become overcrowded, overly expensive, and unmanageable. Exhibit 14. 1 provides a profile of the average probationer.

The most recent data on the extent of probation is provided by the Bureau of Justice Statistics: http://www.ojp.usdoj.gov/bjs/pandp.htm.

Eligibility for Probation

Several criteria are used in granting probation. The statutes of many states determine the factors that a judge should take into account when deciding whether to grant probation. For example, California's probation statute directs judges to consider probation under certain circumstances.

(2) A fact or circumstance not amounting to a defense, but reducing the defendant's culpability for the offense, including:

(i) The defendant participated in the crime under circumstances of great provocation, coercion, or duress not amounting to a defense, and the defendant has no recent record of committing crimes of violence.

(ii) The crime was committed because of a mental condition not amounting to a defense, and there is a high likelihood that the defendant would respond favorably to mental health care and treatment that would be required as a condition of probation.

(iii) The defendant is youthful or aged, and has no significant record of prior criminal offenses.[10]

Some states limit the use of probation in serious felony cases and for specific crimes with penalties that are controlled by mandatory sentencing laws. However, the granting of probation to serious felons is common. More than half of all probationers were convicted on felony offenses.

Some states have attempted to control judicial discretion by creating guidelines for granting probation. Judges often follow these guidelines, but probation decision making is varied: An individual offender granted probation in one jurisdiction might not be if tried in another. Probation is most often granted by a discretionary decision based on the beliefs and attitudes of the presiding judge and the probation staff.

Conditions of Probation

When probation is fixed as a sentence, the court sets down certain conditions for qualifying for community treatment. Some conditions are standard and are applied in every probation case (for example, "Do not leave the jurisdiction"), but the sentencing judge usually has broad discretion to set specific conditions on a case-by-case basis. A presiding judge may not impose capricious or cruel conditions, such as requiring an offender to make restitution out of proportion to the seriousness of the criminal act.[11]

Judges may, however, legally impose restrictions tailored to fit the probationer's individual needs or to protect society from additional harm or both. For example, in 2003 Albert Lee, who had plead guilty to transporting child pornography via computer and enticing a minor by computer to engage in sex, was given a probation sentence with conditions that required him to register as a sex offender, avoid contact with his victims, have no contact with persons under the age of 18, not own or operate a personal computer or other devices that allow Internet access, not be housed in an area where minors congregate, not hire any minors to perform household chores or yard work, and allow his residence to be subject to random searches

A judge may impose special conditions of probation depending on the circumstances of the case. Here, Kevin Kelly looks back towards his family as he waits for his sentencing hearing to begin February 21, 2003, at the Prince William County Courthouse in Manassas, Virginia. Kelly, a father of 13 who allowed his youngest daughter to die in a sweltering van, was given probation, but will spend one night in jail every February 21st for the next seven years. Kelly was convicted of involuntary manslaughter and reckless endangerment in the May 29th death. Passers-by found Frances Kelly, 21 months, strapped into her car seat inside the family's van, which was parked at their Manassas home.

© 2003 AP/Wide World Photos

for the presence of sexual risk factors. He was also required to submit to periodic polygraph questioning about his activities to see if he had violated any of these conditions. He appealed, saying this final condition was a violation of his Fifth Amendment right against self-incrimination. However, the Third U.S. Circuit Court of Appeals ruled that the conditions of Lee's probation were appropriate for his crime and that the use of a polygraph did not violate his constitutional rights as long as his probation would be not revoked simply because he refused to answer a question.[12]

While Lee's Internet use was restricted, in another related case, *U.S.* v. *Freeman,* a different three-judge panel ruled that it was an error to forbid a probationer to possess any computer in his home or use any online computer service without the written approval of the probation officer. It found this condition too restrictive.[13] In sum, a great deal of discretion is evident in the formulation of specific probation rules.

While some probationers may be forced to obey exotic conditions, most are asked to enter some sort of treatment program as part of their probationary sentence. Alcohol- or drug-abuse treatment and testing and mental health counseling are the most commonly required conditions.

Administration of Probation Services

Probation services are organized in a variety of ways, depending on the state and the jurisdiction in which they are located. Some states have a statewide probation service, but each court jurisdiction controls its local department. Other states maintain a strong statewide authority with centralized control and administration. Thirty states combine probation and parole services in a single unit. Some combine juvenile and adult probation departments, whereas others maintain these departments separately.

The typical probation department is situated in a single court district, such as juvenile, superior, district, or municipal court. The relationship between the department and court personnel (especially the judge) is extremely close.

The chief probation officer (CPO) sets policy, supervises hiring, determines training needs, and may personally discuss with or recommend sentencing to the judge. In state-controlled departments, some of the CPO's duties are mandated by the central office. Training guidelines, for example, may be determined at the state level. If, however, the department is locally controlled, the CPO is invested with great discretion in the management of the department.

The probation officers (POs), or the line staff, may be in direct and personal contact with the entire supervisory staff, or they may be independent of the CPO and answer mainly to the assistant chiefs. Line staff members perform the following major functions.

1. Supervise or monitor cases assigned to them to ensure that the rules of probation are followed.
2. Attempt to rehabilitate their cases through specialized treatment techniques.
3. Investigate the lives of convicted offenders to enable the court to make intelligent sentencing decisions.
4. Occasionally collect fines due the court or oversee the collection of delinquent payments, such as child support.
5. Interview complainants and defendants to determine whether further criminal action is warranted, whether cases can be decided informally, whether diversion should be advocated, and so on. This last procedure, called **intake,** is common in juvenile probation.

Probation Style Like police officers, probation officers also maintain a working style. An officer's style is influenced by both personal values and the department's general policies and orientation toward the goals of probation.[14] Some POs view themselves as social workers and maintain a treatment orientation. Their goal is

intake
The process by which a probation officer settles cases at the initial court appearance, before the onset of formal criminal proceedings; the screening process in which a juvenile is referred to the juvenile court, referred elsewhere, or released.

To find out about professional associations connected with probation, go to InfoTrac College Edition and read Donald G. Evans, "Probation: Strength through Association," *Corrections Today* 57, no. 5 (August 1995): 100.

Many states have their own probation professional organization. Here is the Web site for the one in New York: http://www.nyspoa.com/.

to help offenders adjust in the community. Others are law enforcers who are more concerned with supervision, control, and public safety. For example, in 2003 New York City probation officers were for the first time authorized to carry handguns under a new departmental policy intended to enhance the supervision of their clients, the majority of whom are felons. Arming the officers became necessary when the department began to reduce its probation caseload — from 200 down to 65 — and required officers to spend more time visiting their clients in their neighborhoods and homes. Other departments have armed their officers as the number of probationers increased and duties became more dangerous.[15]

Duties of Probation Officers

Staff officers in probation departments are usually charged with four primary tasks: intake, diagnosis, presentence investigation, and treatment supervision.

Intake Probation officers are asked to interview defendants who have been summoned to the court for initial appearances. Intake is most commonly used with juvenile offenders but may also be used with adult misdemeanant cases. During juvenile court intake, the petitioner (the juvenile) and the complainant (the private citizen or the police officer) may work with the PO to determine an equitable resolution of the case. The PO may settle the case without further court action, recommend restitution or other compensation, initiate actions that result in a court hearing, or recommend unofficial or informal probation.

presentence investigation
A postconviction investigation, performed by a probation officer attached to the trial court, of the defendant's background, education, employment, family, acquaintances, physical and mental health, prior criminal record, and other factors that may affect sentencing.

Presentence Investigations In the investigative stage, the PO conducts an inquiry within the community to discover the factors related to the criminality of the offender. The **presentence investigation** is conducted primarily to gain information for judicial sentences, but in the event that the offender is placed on probation, the investigation elicits useful testimony on which to base treatment and supervision. An important task of POs is the investigation and evaluation of defendants coming before the court for sentencing. The court uses presentence investigation reports in deciding whether to grant probation, incarcerate, or use other forms of treatment.

At the conclusion of most presentence investigations, a recommendation is made to the presiding judge that reflects the department's sentencing posture on the case at hand. This is a crucial aspect of the report because the probation department's recommendation is followed in many but not all cases.

With the use of sentencing guidelines, some probation departments are now being asked to evaluate the facts of the case to help judges formulate sentences. For example, in *United States* v. *Anthony Capanelli,* the defendant was convicted of conspiring to commit armed robbery. The probation department's presentence report suggested that Anthony Capanelli's sentence be increased because he had "intended" to take in excess of $1.5 million. Capanelli appealed his sentence on the grounds that the probation department could not know what he "intended" to steal because he was caught before the robbery took place. The appellate court agreed and ordered him resentenced.[16] The *Capanelli* case illustrates how probation departments are being called upon by judges to evaluate a case in light of sentencing guidelines to render sentencing decisions.

Diagnosis Probation officers are asked to review the new probationer's personality profile and develop a personality profile that may be helpful in treating the offender. Diagnosis involves evaluating the probationer, based on information from an initial interview (intake) or the presentence investigation, for the purpose of planning a proper treatment program.

risk classification
Assigning probationers to a level and type of supervision based on their particular needs and the risks they pose for the community.

Part of diagnosis may be a **risk classification,** which involves assigning cases to a level and type of supervision on the basis of the clients' particular needs and the risks they present to the community. For example, some clients may need frequent (intensive) supervision, whereas others are assigned to minimum monitoring by a PO.

A number of risk assessment approaches are used, but most employ such objective measures as the offender's age, employment status, drug abuse history, prior felony convictions, and number of address changes in the year prior to sentencing. Efforts are under way to create more effective instruments using subjective information obtained through face-to-face interviews and encounters.[17]

Does classification make a dramatic difference in the success of probation? Though little clear-cut evidence exists that classification has a substantial impact on reducing recidivism, its use has become commonplace and administrators believe that it may be a useful tool in case management and treatment delivery. The scales may validate the PO's self-perception of being a rational and scientific decision maker.[18] The classification of offenders aids the most important goal of supervision: reducing the risk the probationer presents to the community. In addition, classification schemes are in sync with desert-based sentencing models: The most serious cases get the most intensive supervision.[19]

Treatment Supervision

Based on a knowledge of psychology, social work, or counseling and the diagnosis of the offender, the PO plans a treatment program that will, it is hoped, allow the probationer to fulfill the probation contract and make a reasonable adjustment to the community.

In years past, the probation staff had primary responsibility for supervision and treatment. Probation officers today rarely have hands-on treatment responsibility and instead employ the resources of the community to carry out this function.

The treatment function is a product of both the investigative and diagnostic aspects of probation. It is based on the PO's perceptions of the probationer, including family problems, peer relationships, and employment background. Treatment may also involve the use of community resources. For example, a PO who discovers that a client has a drinking problem may find a detoxification center willing to accept the client, a chronically underemployed offender may be given job counseling or training, and a person undergoing severe psychological stress may be placed in a therapeutic treatment program. In the case of juvenile delinquency, a PO may work with teachers and other school officials to help a young offender stay in school. The need for treatment is critical and the vast size of probation caseloads, especially the large numbers of narcotics abusers, often overwhelms the availability of community-based substance abuse programs.[20]

Failure to adequately supervise probationers and determine whether they are obeying the rules of probation can result in the officer and the department being held legally liable for civil damages. For example, if a probationer with a history of child molestation attacks a child while working as a school custodian, the probationer's case supervisor could be held legally responsible for failing to check on the probationer's employment activities.[21]

Use "probation treatment supervision" as a subject guide on InfoTrac College Edition.

How Successful Is Probation?

Probation is the most commonly used alternative sentence for a number of reasons. It is humane, it helps offenders maintain community and family ties, and it is cost-effective. Incarcerating an inmate costs more than $20,000 per year, while probation costs about $2,000 per year.[22]

Although unquestionably inexpensive, is probation successful? If most probation orders fail, the costs of repeated criminality would certainly outweigh the cost savings of a probation sentence. Overall, most probation orders do seem successful. National data indicate that about 60 percent of probationers successfully complete their probationary sentence while about 40 percent either are re-arrested, violate probation rules, or abscond.[23] Most revocations occur for technical violations that occur during the first three months of the probation sentence.[24] While a 40 percent failure rate seems high, even the most serious criminals who receive probation are less likely to recidivate than those who are sent to prison for committing similar crimes.[25]

Perspectives on Justice

The revocation of probation represents the inherent conflict between its rehabilitation and crime control aspects. On the one hand, probation is viewed as a second chance that enables deserving offenders to rehabilitate themselves in the community. On the other hand, probationers are convicted offenders who must obey stringent rules unless they want to be sent to prison. Rehabilitation advocates may not want to pull the revocation trigger unless it is absolutely necessary, whereas those who espouse a crime control approach may be less charitable to breaches of probation rules

---

Felony Probation A significant issue involving eligibility for probation is community supervision of convicted felons. Many people believe that probation is given to minors or first offenders who are deserving of a break. This is not the case. Many serious criminal offenders are given probation sentences (32 percent of felons), including people convicted on homicide (about 5 percent), sexual assault and rape (about 16 percent), and robbery (11 percent) charges (see Table 14.1).[26]

Although originally conceived as a way to provide a second chance for young offenders, probation today is also a means of reducing the population pressures on an overcrowded and underfunded correctional system. So there are two distinct sides to the probation, one involving the treatment and rehabilitation of nondangerous offenders deserving of a second chance and the other the supervision and control of criminals who might otherwise be incarcerated.

Though probationers are less likely to recidivate than former prison inmates, the fact that many felons who commit violent offenses are granted probation is an issue of some concern. Tracking the outcome of felony probation was the goal of Joan Petersilia and her colleagues at the RAND Corporation, a private think tank, when they traced 1,672 men convicted of felonies who had been granted probation in Los Angeles and Alameda Counties in California.[27] In this now classic study, Petersilia found that 1,087 (65 percent) were rearrested; of those rearrested, 853 (51 percent) were convicted; and of those convicted, 568 (34 percent) were sentenced to jail or prison. Of the probationers who had new charges filed against them, 75 percent were charged with burglary, theft, robbery, and other predatory crimes; 18 percent were convicted of serious, violent crimes.

The RAND researchers found that probation is by far the most common sentencing alternative to prison, used in about 60 to 80 percent of all criminal convictions. What is disturbing, however, is that the crimes and criminal records of about 25 percent of all probationers are indistinguishable from those of offenders who go to prison.

Who is most likely to fail on probation? Young males who are unemployed or who have a very low income, a prior criminal record, and a history of instability are most likely to be rearrested. In contrast, probationers who are married with children, have lived in the area for two or more years, and are adequately employed are the most likely to be successful on probation.[28] Among female probationers, those who have stable marriages, who are better educated, and who are employed full or part time are more likely to successfully complete probation orders than male pro-

Table 14.1 Distribution of Types of Felony Sentences Imposed
by State Courts, by Offense, 2000

Most serious conviction offense	Total	Percent of felons sentenced to incarceration			
		Total	Prison	Jail	Probation
All offenses	100	68	40	28	32
Violent offenses	100	78	54	24	22
Murder[a]	100	95	93	2	5
Sexual assault[b]	100	84	64	20	16
Rape	100	90	70	20	10
Other sexual assault	100	80	60	20	20
Robbery	100	89	74	15	11
Aggravated assault	100	71	40	31	29
Other violent[c]	100	71	42	29	29
Property offenses	100	64	37	27	36
Burglary	100	76	52	24	24
Larceny[d]	100	63	33	30	37
Motor vehicle theft	100	73	41	32	27
Fraud[e]	100	54	29	25	46
Drug offenses	100	67	38	29	33
Possession	100	64	33	31	36
Trafficking	100	69	41	28	31
Weapons offenses	100	70	41	29	30
Other offenses[f]	100	66	32	34	34

Note: For persons receiving a combination of sentences, the sentence designation came from the most severe penalty imposed—prison being the most severe, followed by jail, then probation. Prison includes death sentences. Felons receiving a sentence other than incarceration or probation are classified under "probation." This table is based on an estimated 919,387 cases.

[a]Includes nonnegligent manslaughter.
[b]Includes rape.
[c]Includes offenses such as negligent manslaughter and kidnapping.
[d]Includes motor vehicle theft.
[e]Includes forgery and embezzlement.
[f]Composed of nonviolent offenses such as receiving stolen property and vandalism.

Source: Matthew Durose and Patrick A. Langan, *Felony Sentences in State Courts, 2000* (Washington, D.C.: Bureau of Justice Statistics, 2002), p. 2.

bationers or those who are single, less educated, and unemployed. Prior record is also related to probation success. Clients who have a history of criminal behavior, prior probation, and previous incarceration are the most likely to fail.[29]

To read more about the RAND Corporation, go to http://www.rand.org/.

Why Do People Fail on Probation? Probationers bring with them a considerable amount of emotional baggage that may reduce their chances of successful rehabilitation. Many are felons who have long histories of offending. More than 75 percent of all probationers have had prior convictions. Others suffer from a variety of social and psychological disabilities. Surveys indicate that a significant number (16 percent) suffer from mental illness.[30] Whether mentally ill or mentally sound, probationers are likely to have grown up in households in which family members were incarcerated and so have lived part of their lives in foster homes or state institutions. Many had parents or guardians who abused drugs. They also suffered high rates of physical and sexual abuse. They are now unemployed or underemployed, and almost half are substance abusers. Considering their harsh and abusive backgrounds and their current economic distress and mental illness, many, not surprisingly, find it difficult to comply with the rules of probation and forgo criminal activity. In contrast, those probationers who have a stake in conformity, such as a good job and economic resources, are the ones most likely to succeed on probation. For many probationers, a strong stake in society may be a more powerful determinant of probation success than participation in a treatment program.[31]

Although the recidivism rate of probationers seems high, it is still lower than the recidivism rate of prison inmates.[32] To improve probation effectiveness, it could be supplemented with more stringent rules, such as curfews, and closer supervision. Even though such measures can dramatically increase the cost of probation, they would still be far less expensive than the cost of incarceration.

Legal Rights of Probationers

A number of important legal issues surround probation, one set involving the civil rights of probationers and another involving the rights of probationers during the revocation process.

Civil Rights   The U.S. Supreme Court has ruled that probationers have a unique status and therefore are entitled to fewer constitutional protections than other citizens. One area of law involves the Fifth Amendment right of freedom from self-incrimination. The Supreme Court dealt with this issue in the case of *Minnesota* v. *Murphy* (1984).[33] In *Murphy,* the Supreme Court ruled that the probation officer–client relationship is not confidential, like physician–patient or attorney–client relationships. If a probationer admits to committing a crime to his probation supervisor, the information can be passed on to the police or district attorney. Furthermore, the *Murphy* decision held that a probation officer could use trickery or psychological pressure to get information and turn it over to the police.

A second area of law involving probationers is search and seizure. In *Griffin* v. *Wisconsin* (1987), the Supreme Court held that a probationer's home may be searched without a warrant on the grounds that probation departments "have in mind the welfare of the probationer" and must "respond quickly to evidence of misconduct."[34] But what if a probationer is believed to have committed another crime and the search is for evidence and not to protect his or her "welfare"? In *United States* v. *Knights* (2001), the Supreme Court upheld the legality of a warrantless search of a probationer's home for the purposes of gathering criminal evidence. In *Knights,* the Court ruled that the home of a probationer who is suspected of a crime can be searched without a warrant if the search was based on a reasonable suspicion that he had committed another crime while on probation and a condition of his previous probation was that he would submit to searches. The Court reasoned that the government's interest in preventing crime, combined with the defendant's diminished expectation of privacy, required only a reasonable suspicion to make the search fit within the protections of the Fourth Amendment. Although the Court recognized that society has a legitimate interest in the rehabilitation of probationers, it embraced the state's argument that a probationer is more likely to commit a crime than a nonprobationer.[35]

Read more about *United States* v. *Knights* at Jonathan T. Skrmetti, "The Keys to the Castle: A New Standard for Warrantless Home Searches in *United States* v. *Knights,*" *Harvard Journal of Law and Public Policy* 25, no. 3 (Summer 2002): 1201.

Revocation Rights   During the course of a probationary term, a violation of the rules or terms of probation or the commitment of a new crime can result in probation being revoked, at which time the offender may be placed in an institution. Revocation is not often an easy decision, given that it conflicts with the treatment philosophy of many probation departments.

When revocation is chosen, the offender is notified, and a formal hearing is scheduled. If the charges against the probationer are upheld, the offender can then be placed in an institution to serve the remainder of the sentence. Most departments will not revoke probation unless the offender commits another crime or seriously violates the rules of probation.

Because placing a person on probation implies that probation will continue unless the probationer commits some major violation, the defendant has been given certain procedural due process rights at this stage of the criminal process. In three significant decisions, the U.S. Supreme Court provided procedural safeguards to apply at proceedings to revoke probation (and parole). In *Mempa* v. *Rhay* (1967), the Court unanimously held that a probationer was constitutionally entitled to counsel in a revocation-of-probation proceeding when the imposition of sentence had been suspended.[36] Then, in 1972, the Supreme Court in the case of *Morrissey* v. *Brewer* handed down an important decision detailing the procedures required for parole revocation.[37] Because the revocations of probation and parole are similar, the standards in the *Morrissey* case affected the probation process as well. In *Morrissey,* the Court required an informal inquiry to determine whether there was probable cause to believe the arrested parolee had violated the conditions of parole, as well as a formal revocation hearing with minimum due process requirements. However, in *Morrissey* the Court did not deal with the issue of right to counsel. Chief Justice Warren Burger stated, "We do not reach or decide the question whether the parolee is entitled to the assistance of retained counsel or to appointed counsel if he is indigent."

The question of the right to counsel in revocation proceedings came up again in the 1973 case of *Gagnon* v. *Scarpelli.*[38] In that decision, which involved a probationer, the Supreme Court held that both probationers and parolees have a constitutionally limited right to counsel in revocation proceedings. The *Gagnon* case can be viewed as a step forward in the application of constitutional safeguards to the correctional process. The provision of counsel helped give control over the unlimited discretion exercised in the past by probation and parole personnel in revocation proceedings.

With the development of innovative probation programs, courts have had to review the legality of changing probation rules and their effect on revocation. For example, courts have in general upheld the demand that restitution be made to the victim of crime.[39] Because restitution is designed to punish and reform the offender, instead of simply repaying the victim, the probationer can be made legally responsible for paying restitution.

In *United States* v. *Granderson* (1994), the Supreme Court helped clarify what can happen to a probationer whose community sentence is revoked. Ralph Granderson was eligible for a six-month prison sentence but instead was given 60 months of probation. When he tested positively for drugs, his probation was revoked. The statute he was sentenced under required that he serve one-third his original sentence in prison. When the trial court sentenced him to 20 months, he appealed. Was his original sentence six months or 60 months? The Supreme Court found that it would be unfair to force a probationer to serve more time in prison than he would have if originally incarcerated and ruled that the proper term should have been one-third of the six months, or two months.[40]

If during a hearing a judge rules that the conditions of probation have been violated, probation may be revoked. Here, actor Nick Nolte turns to address the prosecutor during a progress hearing on Nolte's probation on an earlier driving under the influence case, in a Malibu, California courtroom July 18, 2003. Judge Lawrence Mira determined that an anonymous tip that Nolte was drinking and driving was unfounded and refused to find the actor in violation of probation.

© 2003 AP/Wide World Photos

The Future of Probation

Probation remains the sentence of choice for about one-third of all felony cases.[41] Because it costs far less to maintain an offender in the community than in prison, and because prison overcrowding persists, there is constant economic pressure to grant probation to serious felony offenders. Even if probation is no more successful than prison, it costs less and is therefore extremely attractive to policy makers. However, some believe that the risk of probation failure is too high and that judges should think carefully before sentencing felons to probation.

Probation will continue to be a sentence of choice in both felony and misdemeanor cases because it holds the promise of great cost savings at a time when many state budgets are being reduced. Defraying the cost of probation may be possible by asking clients to pay fees for probation services, a concept that would be impossible with prison inmates. At least 25 states now impose some form of fee on probationers to defray the cost of community corrections. Massachusetts initiated **day fees,** which are based on the probationer's wages (the usual fee is between one and three days' wages each month).[42] Texas requires judges to impose supervision fees unless the offender is truly unable to pay. Fees make up more than half the probation department's annual budget.[43]

Another probation initiative, borrowing from the hot spot approach to policing, is Maryland's **HotSpot probation** initiative. Here, police officers, probation agents, neighbors, and social service professionals have collaborated to form community probation supervision teams. Using a team approach, they provide increased monitoring of offenders through home visits, drug testing, and regular meetings. They also work with the offenders to ease reentry through offender creation of work crews, which aid in community cleanups, work on vacant houses, and participate in other projects. Recent evaluations find that the recidivism rates of HotSpot probationers was not significantly different from that of traditional probation, but the initiative seems to have a great deal of utility and warrants further study.[44]

Probation is unquestionably undergoing dramatic changes. During the past decade, it has been supplemented and used as a restrictive correctional alternative. Expanding the scope of probation has created a new term, *intermediate sanctions,* to signify penalties that fall between traditional community supervision and confinement in jail or prison.

Intermediate Sanctions

Community sentencing has traditionally emphasized offender rehabilitation. The probation officer has been viewed as a caseworker or counselor whose primary job is to help the offender adjust to society. Offender surveillance and control has seemed more appropriate for law enforcement, jails, and prisons than for community corrections.[45]

But since 1980 a more conservative justice system has reoriented toward social control. Although the rehabilitative ideals of probation have not been abandoned, new programs have been developed that add a control dimension to community corrections. These programs can be viewed as probation plus, because they add restrictive penalties and conditions to community service orders. Being more punitive than probation, intermediate sanctions can be sold to conservatives, while they remain attractive to liberals as alternatives to incarceration.[46]

Intermediate sanctions include programs typically administered by probation departments: intensive probation supervision, house arrest, electronic monitoring, restitution orders, shock probation or split sentences, and residential community corrections.[47] Some experts also include high-impact shock incarceration, or boot camp experiences, within the definition of intermediate sanctions, but these programs are typically operated by correctional departments (and are discussed separately in Chapter 15). Intermediate sanctions also involve sentences administered independently of probation staffs: fines and forfeiture, pretrial programs, and pretrial and posttrial residential programs. Intermediate sanctions therefore range from the barely intrusive, such as restitution orders, to the highly restrictive, such as house arrest accompanied by electronic monitoring and a stay in a community correctional center.

day fees
Fees imposed on probationers to offset the costs of probation.

HotSpot probation
A program using community supervision teams to monitor offenders.

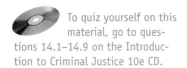
To quiz yourself on this material, go to questions 14.1–14.9 on the Introduction to Criminal Justice 10e CD.

Alternatives to Incarceration Abroad

international justice

While the crime rate has been declining in the United States for nearly a decade, get-tough measures such as "three strikes and you're out" have resulted in a steadily increasing prison population. Western European countries have crime rates similar to the United States, but their incarceration rates are much lower. Criminal penalties there are not nearly as harsh as those in the United States. This disparity in punishment has not been lost on researchers such as legal scholar Michael Tonry, who has explored the differences between the United States and other Western democracies.

Tonry points out that crime trends seem to have an important impact on U.S. incarceration policies. As the crime rate goes up, so, too, does the media coverage of crime stories. Political figures, especially those running for office, feed off the media coverage and make crime an election focus. Because these events fuel public anxiety, there is an outcry for punitive measures to be taken against criminals. Politicians are happy to oblige their constituents and pass tough sanctions against criminals to show their sensitivity to the voters.

Tonry finds that crime has taken on increasing political importance since the 1964 presidential election. In the 1990s the overused phrase "get tough on crime" crossed party lines as lawmakers promised to implement harsh measures against criminals, regardless of whether the measures would reduce crime or

were needed. As crime rates fall, both the politicians and the public credit the get-tough stance for success, though little evidence shows that draconian measures reduce crime. For example, crime rates were already trending downward before harsh reform laws such as mandatory minimum sentencing and truth-in-sentencing laws were created. Yet conservatives believe that these get-tough measures helped reduce crime rates.

Western European nations have taken a different approach to crime control. When rates of crime rose in European democracies, lawmakers focused on making punishment fair as opposed to harsh. Instead of mandatory sentencing, individual circumstances and the reasons for committing a crime are considered. Western European lawmakers also focus on punishments that are utilitarian and effective in reducing crime, not punitive and retributive. They often rely on community sentences such as day fines, which are based on the offender's earnings and economic circumstances. The money collected from day fines not only punish the offender but also serve to benefit society. Western European judges have also been more likely to sentence offenders to community service. Community service, which was created in the United States, has quickly become the sentence of choice for minor crimes in European nations. Where community service hours can number in the thousands for an American criminal, Euro-

pean sentences often limit the number of hours to 240.

Critical Thinking

Incarceration sentences in Europe are substantially shorter than those in the United States. No European country has implemented mandatory sentences or truth-in-sentencing laws. Almost all efforts to control or reduce judicial discretion has been met with disapproval. Michael Tonry points out this may be because Western European judges and prosecutors are career civil servants, free from political concerns. Not having to worry about an upcoming election allows them to focus on what they believe is just, not what is politically expedient. Would you encourage such practices in the United States? Why or why not?

InfoTrac College Edition Research

To learn more about community sentences abroad, read Donald G. Evans, "Ontario's New Probation Supervision Model," *Corrections Today* 60 (1998): 126; Donald G. Evans, "'What Works' in the United Kingdom," *Corrections Today* 60 (1998): 124.

Sources: Michael Tonry, "Why Are U.S. Incarceration Rates So High?" *Crime and Delinquency* 45 (1999): 419–38; Michael Tonry, "Parochialism in U.S. Sentencing Policy," *Crime and Delinquency* 45 (1999): 48–66.

What are the advantages of creating a system of intermediate sanctions? Primary is the need to develop alternatives to prisons and jails, which have proved to be costly, ineffective, and injurious. Little evidence exists that incapacitation is either a general deterrent to crime or a specific deterrent against future criminality. Some correctional systems have become inundated with new inmates. Even states that have extensively used alternative sanctions have experienced rapid increases in their prison population. The pressure on the correctional system if alternative sanctions had not been an option is almost inconceivable. Other nations have embraced alternative sanctions and despite rising crime rates have not experienced the explosion in the prison population that has occurred in the United States. This issue is explored further in the International Justice feature, above.

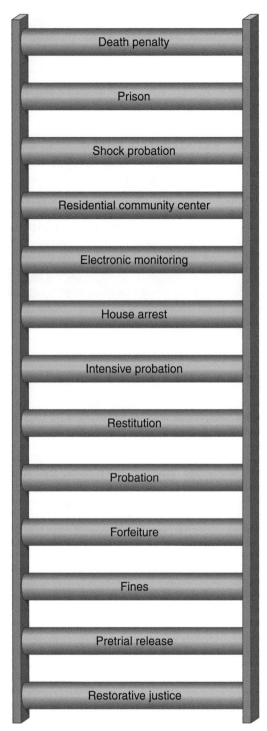

Figure 14.1
The Punishment Ladder

The ladder (top to bottom) shows:

- Death penalty
- Prison
- Shock probation
- Residential community center
- Electronic monitoring
- House arrest
- Intensive probation
- Restitution
- Probation
- Forfeiture
- Fines
- Pretrial release
- Restorative justice

Advantages of Intermediate Sanctions

Intermediate sanctions also have the potential to save money. Although they are more expensive than traditional probation, they are far less costly than incarceration. If those offenders given alternative sanctions would have otherwise been incarcerated, the extra cost would be significant. In addition, offenders given intermediate sanctions generate income, pay taxes, reimburse victims, perform community service, and provide other cost savings that would be nonexistent had they been incarcerated. Intermediate sanctions are not likely to pay an immediate corrections dividend because many correctional costs are fixed, but they may reduce the need for future prison and jail construction.

Intermediate sanctions also help meet the need for developing community sentences that are fair, equitable, and proportional.[48] It seems unfair to treat both a rapist and a shoplifter with the same type of probationary sentence, considering the differences in their crimes. As Figure 14.1 illustrates, intermediate sanctions can form the successive steps of a meaningful ladder of scaled punishments outside of prison, thereby restoring fairness and equity to nonincarceration sentences.[49] For example, forgers may be ordered to make restitution to their victims, and rapists can be placed in a community correctional facility while they receive counseling at a local psychiatric center. This feature of intermediate sanctions allows judges to fit the punishment to the crime without resorting to a prison sentence. Intermediate sentences can be designed to increase punishment for people whose serious or repeat crimes make a straight probation sentence inappropriate yet for whom a prison sentence would be unduly harsh and counterproductive.[50]

In the broadest sense, intermediate sanctions can serve the needs of a number of offender groups. The most likely candidates are convicted criminals who would normally be sent to prison but who either pose a low risk of recidivism or are of little threat to society (such as nonviolent property offenders). Used in this sense, intermediate sanctions are a viable solution to the critical problem of prison overcrowding.

Intermediate sanctions can also reduce overcrowding in jails by providing alternatives to incarceration for misdemeanants and cut the number of pretrial detainees who currently make up about half the inmate population.[51] Some forms of bail already require conditions, such as supervision by court officers and periods of home confinement (conditional bail), that are a form of intermediate sanctions.

Intermediate sanctions can also potentially be used as halfway-back strategies for probation and parole violators. Probationers who violate the conditions of their community release could be placed under increasingly more intensive supervision before incarceration is required. Parolees who pose the greatest risk of recidivism might receive conditions that require close monitoring or home confinement. Parole violators could be returned to a community correctional center instead of a walled institution.

The forms of intermediate sanctions currently in use are fines, forfeiture, restitution, shock probation and split sentencing, intensive probation supervision, house arrest, electronic monitoring, and residential community corrections.

Fines

Fines are monetary payments imposed on offenders as an intermediate punishment for their criminal acts. They are a direct offshoot of the early common law practice of requiring compensation be paid to the victim and the state (wergild) for criminal acts. Fines are still commonly used in Europe, where they are often the sole penalty, even in cases involving chronic offenders who commit fairly serious crimes.[52]

In the United States, fines are most commonly used in cases involving misdemeanors and lesser offenses. Fines are also frequently used in felony cases when the offender benefited financially. Fines may be used as a sole sanction or combined with other punishments, such as probation or confinement. Judges commonly levy other monetary sanctions along with fines, such as court costs, public defender fees, probation and treatment fees, and victim restitution, to increase the force of the financial punishment. However, evidence suggests that many offenders fail to pay fines and that courts are negligent in their efforts to collect unpaid fees.

In most jurisdictions, little guidance is given to the sentencing judge directing the imposition of the fine. Judges often have inadequate information on the offender's ability to pay, resulting in defaults and contempt charges. Because the standard sanction for nonpayment is incarceration, many offenders held in local jails are confined for nonpayment of criminal fines. Although the U.S. Supreme Court in *Tate* v. *Short* (1971) recognized that incarcerating a person who is financially unable to pay a fine discriminates against the poor, many judges continue to incarcerate offenders for noncompliance with financial orders.[53]

Research indicates that, given the facts of a case, judges do seem to use fines in a rational manner: Low-risk offenders are the ones most likely to receive fines instead of a jail sentence; the more serious the crime, the higher the amount of the fine. Offenders who are fined seem less likely to commit new crimes than those who receive a jail sentence.[54]

Day Fines Because judges rely so heavily on offense seriousness to fix the level of fines, financial penalties may have a negative impact on success rates. The more serious the offense and the higher the fine, the greater are the chances that the offender will fail to pay the fine and risk probation revocation. To overcome this sort of problem, some jurisdictions, such as New York City, began experimenting with **day fines**.[55]

A concept originated in Europe, day fines are geared to an offender's net daily income. In an effort to make them equitable and fairly distributed, fines are based on the severity of the crime, weighted by a daily-income value taken from a chart similar to an income tax table. The number of the offender's dependents is also taken into account. The day fine concept means that the severity of punishment is based on the offender's ability to pay. Day fines hold the promise of becoming an equitable solution to the problem of setting the amount of a fine according to the offender's ability to pay. However, there is little conclusive evidence whether the day fine program works as intended.[56]

Forfeiture

Another intermediate sanction with a financial basis is criminal (in personam) and civil (in rem) **forfeiture.** Both involve the seizure of goods and instrumentalities related to the commission or outcome of a criminal act. The difference is that

© 2003 AP/Wide World Photos

Fines may be a condition of probation. Here, Madelyne Toogood leaves the St. Joseph County Courthouse February 14, 2003 in South Bend, Indiana. Toogood accepted a plea offer to resolve the criminal charges filed against her after she was caught by a security camera hitting her 4-year-old daughter in a parking lot. The judge sentenced Toogood, 26, under misdemeanor guidelines, giving her a one-year suspended sentence, with a year on probation and a $500 fine.

fine
A sum imposed as punishment for an offense.

day fine
A fine geared to an offender's net daily income, as well as number of dependents and the seriousness of the crime, in an effort to make sentences more equitable.

forfeiture
The seizure of personal property by the state as a civil or criminal penalty.

criminal forfeiture proceedings target criminal defendants and can only follow a criminal conviction. In contrast, civil forfeiture proceedings target property used in a crime and do not require that formal criminal proceedings be initiated against a person or that he is proven guilty of a crime.[57] For example, federal law provides that, after arresting drug traffickers, the government may seize the boats they used to import the narcotics, the cars they used to carry the drugs overland, the warehouses in which the drugs were stored, and the homes paid for with the drug profits. On conviction, the drug dealers lose permanent ownership of these instrumentalities of crime.

Forfeiture is not a new sanction. During the Middle Ages, "forfeiture of estate" was a mandatory result of most felony convictions. The Crown could seize all of a felon's real and personal property. Forfeiture derived from the common law concept of "corruption of blood" or "attaint," which prohibited a felon's family from inheriting or receiving his property or estate. The common law mandated that descendants could not inherit property from a relative who may have attained the property illegally: "[T]he Corruption of Blood stops the Course of Regular Descent, as to Estates, over which the Criminal could have no Power, because he never enjoyed them."[58]

Forfeiture was reintroduced to U.S. law with the passage of the Racketeer Influenced and Corrupt Organization (RICO) Act and the Continuing Criminal Enterprises Act, both of which allow the seizure of any property derived from illegal enterprises or conspiracies. Although these acts were designed to apply to ongoing criminal conspiracies, such as drug or pornography rings, they are now being applied to a far-ranging series of criminal acts, including white-collar crimes. More than 100 federal statutes use forfeiture of property as a punishment.

Although law enforcement officials at first applauded the use of forfeiture as a hard-hitting way of seizing the illegal profits of drug law violators, the practice has been criticized because the government has often been overzealous in its application. For example, million-dollar yachts have been seized because someone aboard possessed a small amount of marijuana; this confiscatory practice is referred to as **zero tolerance.** This strict interpretation of the forfeiture statutes has come under fire because it is often used capriciously, the penalty is sometimes disproportionate to the crime involved, and it makes the government a "partner in crime."[59] It is also alleged that forfeiture unfairly targets a narrow range of offenders. For example, government employees involved in corruption commonly forfeit their pensions; employees of public companies are exempt from such punishment.[60] There is also the issue of conflict of interest. Because law enforcement agencies can use forfeited assets to supplement their budgets, they may direct their efforts to cases that promise the greatest payoff instead of ones that have the highest law enforcement priority.[61]

Restitution

Another popular intermediate sanction is **restitution,** which can take the form of requiring offenders to either pay back the victims of crime (monetary restitution) or serve the community to compensate for their criminal acts (**community service restitution**).[62] Restitution programs offer offenders a chance to avoid a jail or prison sentence or a lengthier probation period. It may help them develop a sense of allegiance to society, better work habits, and some degree of gratitude for being given a second chance. Restitution serves many other purposes, including giving the community something of value without asking it to foot the bill for an incarceration stay and helping victims regain lost property and income.

If **monetary restitution** is called for, the probation department typically makes a determination of victim loss and develops a plan for paying fair compensation. To avoid the situation in which a wealthy offender can fill a restitution order by merely writing a check, judges will sometimes order that compensation be paid out of income derived from a low-paid social service or public works job.

---

zero tolerance
A practice in which criminal defendants forfeit homes, cars, and so on for the slightest law violation.

To read more about the conflict of interest inherent in a forfeiture policy, read R. T. Naylor, "License to Loot? A Critique of Follow-the-Money Methods in Crime Control Policy," *Social Justice* 28, no. 3 (Fall 2001): 121.

restitution
Criminal sanction that requires the offender to repay the victim or society or both for damage caused by the criminal act.

community service restitution
Criminal sanction that requires the offender to work in the community at such tasks as cleaning public parks or helping handicapped children as an alternative to incarceration.

monetary restitution
Criminal sanction that requires the offender to compensate the victim for property damage, lost wages, medical costs, or other losses.

Community service orders usually require duty in a public nursing home, shelter, hospital, drug treatment unit, or works program. Some young vandals may find that they must clean up the damage they caused to the school or the park. Judges sometimes have difficulty gauging the length of community service orders. One suggestion is that the maximum order should be no more than 240 hours and that this should be considered the equivalent of a 6- to 12-month jail term.[63] Whether these terms are truly equivalent remains a matter of personal opinion.

Judges and probation officers have embraced the concept of restitution because it appears to benefit the victim, the offender, the criminal justice system, and society.[64] Financial restitution is inexpensive to administer, helps avoid stigma, and provides compensation for victims of crime. Offenders ordered to do community service work have been placed in schools, hospitals, and nursing homes. Helping them avoid a jail sentence can mean saving the public thousands of dollars that would have gone to maintaining them in a secure institution, frees up needed resources, and gives the community the feeling that equity has been returned to the justice system.

Does restitution work? Most reviews rate it as a qualified success. The majority of restitution clients successfully complete their restitution orders and most have no subsequent contact with the justice system.[65]

Community restitution has become a common addition to probation. William Ligue Jr., left, leaves the Cook County Courts building August 6, 2003, in Chicago, with Kelly Chomer, right. Ligue, who ran onto a baseball field in Chicago with his son during a major league baseball game and attacked the visiting team's first-base coach, was sentenced to two years probation and 80 hours of community service.

Shock Probation and Split Sentencing

Shock probation and **split sentences** are alternative sanctions designed to allow judges to grant offenders community release only after they have sampled prison life. These sanctions are based on the premise that if offenders are given a taste of incarceration sufficient to shock them into law-abiding behavior, they will be reluctant to violate the rules of probation or commit another crime.

In a number of states and in the federal court system, a jail term can be a condition of probation, known as split sentencing. About 10 percent of probationers are now given split sentences. The shock probation approach involves resentencing an offender to probation after a short prison stay. The shock comes because the offender originally received a long maximum sentence but is then eligible for release to community supervision at the discretion of the judge (usually within 90 days of incarceration).

Shock probation and split sentencing have been praised as ways to limit prison time, reintegrate the client quickly into the community, maintain family ties, and reduce prison populations and the costs of corrections. An initial jail sentence probably makes offenders more receptive to the conditions of probation, because it amply illustrates the problems they will face if probation is violated. Shock probation and split sentencing have been criticized by those who believe that even a brief period of incarceration can interfere with the purpose of probation, which is to provide the offender with nonstigmatizing, community-based treatment. Even a short-term commitment subjects probationers to the destructive effects of institutionalization, disrupts their life in the community, and stigmatizes them for having been in jail.

shock probation
A sentence in which offenders serve a short term in prison to impress them with the pains of incarceration before they begin probation.

split sentence
Giving a brief term of incarceration as a condition of probation.

Intensive Probation Supervision

Intensive probation supervision programs are another important form of intermediate sanctions (these programs are also referred to as intensive supervision programs). IPS programs, which have been implemented in some form in about

intensive probation supervision (IPS)
A type of intermediate sanction involving small probation caseloads and strict daily or weekly monitoring.

40 states and today include about 100,000 clients, involve small caseloads of 15 to 40 clients who are kept under close watch by probation officers.[66]

The primary goal of IPS is decarceration: Without intensive supervision, clients would normally be sent to already overcrowded prisons or jails. The second goal is control: High-risk offenders can be maintained in the community under much closer security than traditional probation efforts can provide. A third goal is reintegration: Offenders can maintain community ties and be reoriented toward a more productive life while avoiding the pains of imprisonment.

In general, IPS programs rely on a great degree of client contact to achieve the goals of decarceration, control, and reintegration. Most programs have admissions criteria based on the nature of the offense and the offender's criminal background. Some programs exclude violent offenders; others will not take substance abusers. In contrast, some jurisdictions do not exclude offenders based on their prior criminal history.

IPS programs are used in several ways. In some states, IPS is a direct sentence imposed by a judge; in others, it is a post-sentencing alternative used to divert offenders from the correctional system. A third practice is to use IPS as a case management tool to give the local probation staff flexibility in dealing with clients. Other jurisdictions use IPS in all three ways, in addition to applying it to probation violators to bring them halfway back into the community without resorting to a prison term.

The Effectiveness of IPS Evaluations indicate that IPS programs are generally successful, deliver more services than would normally be received by probationers, are cost-effective, and produce recidivism rates equal to or better than those of offenders who have been confined. However, evaluations have so far not been definitive, often ignoring such issues as whether the program met its stated goals, whether IPS is more attractive than other alternative sanctions, and which types of offenders are particularly suited for IPS. For example, IPS seems to work better for offenders with good employment records than it does for the underemployed or unemployed. Younger offenders who commit petty crimes are the most likely to fail on IPS. Ironically, people with these characteristics are the ones most likely to be included in IPS programs.[67]

Indications also exist that the failure rate in IPS caseloads is high, in some cases approaching 50 percent. IPS clients may even have a higher rearrest rate than other probationers.[68] It should come as no surprise that IPS clients fail more often because, after all, they are more serious criminals who might otherwise have been incarcerated and are now being watched and supervised more closely than probationers. Probation officers may also be more willing to revoke the probation of IPS clients because they believe the clients are a risk to the community and, under normal circumstances, would have been incarcerated. Why risk the program to save a few bad apples?

Although evidence that it can significantly reduce offending rates is still insufficient, IPS might be an attractive alternative to traditional correctional methods if it can be restricted to offenders who would most likely have been incarcerated without the availability of the IPS program. IPS may also be more effective if it is combined with particular treatment modalities such as cognitive-behavioral treatment that stresses such life skills as problem solving, social skills, negotiation skills, management of emotion, and values enhancement.[69]

After thoroughly reviewing the impact of IPS, Betsy Fulton and her associates concluded that IPS programs are among the most popular alternatives to imprisonment in the United States and that, although IPS has not provided a solution to prison crowding, it is useful for those not meriting imprisonment but at high risk for probation.[70]

The house arrest concept requires convicted offenders to spend extended periods of time in their own homes as an alternative to an incarceration sentence. Dontee Stokes, center, leaves jail May 17, 2002, with family members after being released on $150,000 bail in Baltimore. Stokes, 26, accused of shooting a priest he had accused of molesting him, was released after a psychiatrist testified that he posed no danger to himself or others. Stokes was to remain under house arrest and fitted with an electronic monitoring device.

House Arrest

The **house arrest** concept requires convicted offenders to spend extended periods of time in their own home as an alternative to an incarceration sentence. For example, persons convicted on a drunk-driving charge might be sentenced to spend between 6 p.m. Friday and 8 a.m. Monday and every weekday after 5:30 p.m. in their home for six months. Current estimates indicate that more than 10,000 people are under house arrest.

house arrest
A sentence that requires convicted offenders to spend extended periods of time in their own home as an alternative to incarceration.

As with IPS programs, a great deal of variation exists in house arrest initiatives. Some are administered by probation departments, while others are simply judicial sentences monitored by surveillance officers. Some check clients 20 or more times a month (such as the Florida Community Control Program), while others do only a few curfew checks. Some use 24-hour confinement, while others allow offenders to attend work or school.

No definitive data exist indicating that house arrest is an effective crime deterrent, and sufficient evidence is not available to conclude that it has utility as a device to lower the recidivism rate. One evaluation of the Florida program found that nearly 10 percent of the house arrest sample had their probation revoked for technical violations within 18 months of their sentencing.[71] Another evaluation of the same program found that recidivism rates were almost identical to a matched sample of inmates released from secure correctional facilities; 4 out of 5 offenders in both forms of correction recidivated within five years.[72]

Although these findings are troublesome, the advantages of house arrest in reducing costs and overcrowding in the correctional system probably make further experimentation inevitable. There may also be some unanticipated benefits. For example, to older offenders, house arrest with electronic monitoring may be appealing because it allows them to stay clear of the perceived dangerous prison environment and keep their family relations intact. Those with health problems can maintain better access to health care while in the community, especially if they have their own insurance. Furthermore, the state is relieved of the economic burden of paying for the inmate's health care needs when they are on a community-based sanction such as house arrest as opposed to incarceration in a prison.[73]

Exhibit 14.2 Available Electronic Monitoring Systems

- Identity verification devices can range from personal identification numbers to biometric verification that recognizes different parts of the human body to ensure the reporting person is the intended offender.

- **Remote alcohol detection devices** require users to blow into the device, which is usually in the offender's home, to measure blood alcohol content. The results are recorded by a computer to determine compliance with conditions of alcohol consumption.

- **Ignition interlock devices** are linked to the electrical systems of automobiles. The driver must expel deep lung air into the device to operate the vehicle. If the driver's blood alcohol content is registered above a predetermined level deemed unsafe to drive, the vehicle will not start.

- **Programmed contact systems** are used to contact and verify the location of offenders in their homes or elsewhere. They utilize a central computer that either receives telephone calls from or makes calls to offenders in one or more locations.

- **Continuous signaling devices** are battery-powered and transmit a radio signal two or more times per minute. These are placed on the offender's wrist or ankle with a tamper-resistant strap and must be worn at all times. A receiver detects the transmitter's signals and conveys a message via telephone report to a central computer when either it stops receiving the radio frequency or the signal resumes. Receivers can detect transmitter signals from a range of up to, and in some cases exceeding, 150 feet when installed in a typical home environment.

- **Victim notification systems** alert the victim when the offender is approaching his or her residence. A transmitter is worn by both the offender and the victim, and a receiver is placed at both residences.

- **Field monitoring devices,** or drive-by units, are another type of continuous signaling technology. Probation or parole officers or other authorities use a portable device that can be handheld or used in a vehicle with a roof-mounted antenna. When within 200 to 800 feet of an offender's ankle or wrist transmitter, the portable device can detect the radio signals of the offender's transmitter.

- **Group monitoring units** allow supervisors to monitor several offenders in the same location, such as for verifying attendance of multiple offenders in a day-reporting program or monitoring offenders confined in a residential group setting.

- **Location tracking systems,** also known as global positioning systems, have receivers that detect satellite signals relating the exact time the signal is sent and the identity of the satellite sending the signal. This information is processed to determine the person's location. This more expensive technology typically is used for high-risk offenders. It can determine when an offender leaves an area where he or she is supposed to be (inclusion zone) or enters an area where he or she is not allowed to be (exclusion zone).

Source: Ann Crowe, "Electronic Supervision: From Decision-Making to Implementation," *Corrections Today* 64 (2002): 131–32.

Electronic Monitoring

electronic monitoring (EM) Electronic equipment that enables probation officers to monitor the location of those under house arrest or other forms of supervision.

For house arrest to work, sentencing authorities must be assured that arrestees are actually at home during their assigned times. Random calls and visits are one way to check on compliance with house arrest orders. However, one of the more interesting developments in the criminal justice system has been the introduction of **electronic monitoring** devices to manage offender obedience to home confinement orders.[74]

Electronically monitored offenders wear devices, which send signals to a control office, around their ankles, wrists, or necks. Two basic types of systems are used: active and passive. Active systems constantly monitor offenders by continuously sending a signal to the central office. If offenders leave their home at an unauthorized time, the signal is broken, and the failure is recorded. In some cases, the control officer is automatically notified electronically through a beeper. Passive systems usually involve random phone calls generated by computers to which the offenders have to respond within a particular time (such as 30 seconds). In addition to probationers, EM can be used at the front end of the system with bailees and at the back end with parolees.

The various kinds of EM devices are described in Exhibit 14.2.

More than 150,000 offenders are being monitored at home.[75] Electronic monitoring supporters claim the EM has the benefits of relatively low cost and high security, while helping offenders avoid the pains of imprisonment in overcrowded, dangerous state facilities. Electronic monitoring is capital-intensive, not labor-intensive. Because offenders are monitored by computers, an initial investment in hardware rules out the need for hiring many more supervisory officers to handle large numbers of clients. EM can also benefit from rapidly expanding technological advances. For example, more than 1,000 probationers are now being tracked by Global Positioning Satellite (GPS) systems. Veridian Information Solutions has developed a software system called VeriTracks, which records the GPS data of its wearer (typically every 10 or 15 minutes) and then at night creates a log of the position of the EM client. The position coordinates are then stored in a database application and compared the next morning with crime incident data reported by law enforcement agencies. Crime-mapping software can then be used to pinpoint whether monitored offenders were in the vicinity of a reported crime close to the time it was committed.[76]

The public, not surprisingly, supports EM as a cost-effective alternative to prison sentences that have proven ineffective.[77] EM can be a welcomed addition to the galaxy of intermediate sanctions, providing the judiciary with an enhanced supervision tool.[78] For example, when Kevin Courtright and his associates examined the cost-saving potential of using house arrest with EM as an alternative to incarceration for a drunk-driving population in a Pennsylvania county, they found that the program saved money and avoided new construction costs, without widening the net of social control.[79] However, not all evaluations have been successful and some find that parolees monitored on EM are no less likely to recidivate than those released without such supervision.[80]

Some civil libertarians are troubled by the fact that EM can erode privacy and liberty. Should U.S. citizens be watched over by a computer? What are the limits of EM? Can it be used with mental patients? HIV carriers? Suicidal teenagers? Those considered high-risk future offenders?

While promising to reduce the correctional population, EM has the potential to substantially increase it by turning homes into prisons. Nonetheless, both its effectiveness and its acceptance by state agencies have not been fully determined. For example, one survey of supervision agencies in Texas found that about two-thirds still did not use EM most often because of its presumed cost and perceptions that is ineffective.[81] Consequently, the future of EM is still uncertain.

Residential Community Corrections

The most secure intermediate sanction is a sentence to a **residential community corrections** facility. Such a facility has been defined as "a freestanding nonsecure building that is not part of a prison or jail and houses pretrial and adjudicated adults. The residents regularly depart to work, to attend school, and/or participate in treatment activities and programs."[82]

Traditionally, the role of community corrections was supplied by the nonsecure halfway house, designed to reintegrate soon-to-be-paroled prison inmates back into the community. Inmates spend the last few months in the halfway house, acquiring suitable employment, building up cash reserves, obtaining an apartment, and developing a job-related wardrobe.

The traditional concept of community corrections has expanded. Today, the community correctional facility is a vehicle to provide intermediate sanctions as well as a prerelease center for those about to be paroled from the prison system. For example, RCC has been used as a direct sentencing option for judges who believe particular offenders need a correctional alternative halfway between traditional probation and a stay in prison. Placement in an RCC center can be used as a condition of probation for offenders who need a nonsecure community facility that provides a more structured treatment environment than traditional probation. It is commonly used in the juvenile justice system for youths who need a more secure environment than can be provided by traditional probation yet who are not deemed a threat to the community and do not require a secure placement.

Probation departments and other correctional authorities have been charged with running RCC centers that serve as a pre-prison sentencing alternative. In

residential community corrections (RCC)
An intermediate sanction, as well as a parole or pretrial option, in which convicted offenders are housed in a non-secure facility from which they go to work, attend school, or participate in treatment activities and programs.

addition, some RCC centers are operated by private, nonprofit groups that receive referrals from the county or district courts and from probation or parole departments. For example, Portland House, a private residential center in Minneapolis, operates as an alternative to incarceration for young adult offenders. The 25 residents regularly receive group therapy and financial, vocational, educational, family, and personal counseling. Residents may work to earn a high school equivalency degree. With funds withheld from their earnings at work-release employment, residents pay room and board, family and self-support, and income taxes. Portland House appears to be successful. It is significantly cheaper to run than a state institution, and the recidivism rate of clients is much lower than that of those who have gone through traditional correctional programs.[83]

Besides being sole sentence and halfway houses, RCC facilities have also been residential pretrial release centers for offenders who are in immediate need of social services before their trial and as halfway-back alternatives for both parole and probation violators who might otherwise have to be imprisoned. In this capacity, RCC programs serve as a base from which offenders can be placed in outpatient psychiatric facilities, drug and alcohol treatment programs, job training, and so on. Some programs make use of both inpatient and outpatient programs to provide clients with specialized treatment, such as substance abuse management.[84]

day reporting center (DRC)
Nonresidential, community-based treatment program.

One recent development has been the use of RCC facilities as **day reporting centers (DRCs)**.[85] Day reporting centers provide a single location to which a variety of clients can report for supervision and treatment. Used in Delaware, Georgia, Utah, and other jurisdictions, DRCs utilize existing RCC facilities to service nonresidential clients. They can be used as a step up for probationers who have failed in the community and a step down in security for jail or prison inmates.[86] For example, the Atlanta Day Reporting Center, opened in June 2001, was developed as a joint project by the Georgia Parole Board and the Georgia Department of Corrections. It provides 125 probationers and parolees with structured daily programs in general equivalency diploma (GED) preparation, substance abuse recovery, and cognitive skills training. Although offenders return to their homes at night, the center intensifies training and support and therefore affords many of the well-documented benefits of traditional halfway houses.[87]

More than 2,000 state-run community-based facilities are in use today. In addition, up to 2,500 private, nonprofit RCC programs operate in the United States. About half also have inmates who have been released from prison (halfway houses) and use the RCC placement to ease back into returning to society. The remainder are true intermediate sanctions, including about 400 federally sponsored programs. The Analyzing Criminal Justice Issues feature on page 455 describes one program being used with substance abusers.

Despite the thousands of traditional and innovative RCC programs in operation around the United States, relatively few efforts have been made to evaluate their effectiveness. Those evaluations that do exist suggest that many residents do not complete their treatment regimen in RCC facilities, violating the rules or committing new offenses. Those that do complete the program have lower recidivism rates than the unsuccessful discharges.[88]

One reason that it is so difficult to assess RCC facilities is that programs differ considerably with respect to target population, treatment alternatives, and goals. While some are rehabilitation-oriented and operate under loose security, others are control-oriented and use such security measures as random drug and alcohol testing. Although critics question their overall effectiveness, RCC facilities appear to work for some types of offenders, and some treatment orientations seem to work better than others. Instead of being used as a last-resort community alternative before sentence to a jail or prison, RCC placement might work better with first-time offenders who have relatively little experience with the criminal or juvenile justice systems.[89]

DTAP: Drug Treatment Alternative-to-Prison

analyzing criminal justice issues

The Drug Treatment Alternative-to-Prison Program (DTAP) was established in Brooklyn, New York. The program incorporates drug treatment in place of incarceration and has been used with repeat felony offenders who are nonviolent and are facing New York's second felony law, which mandates a prison term for anyone convicted of a second felony. The program is directed at those individuals who were drug users or drug dealers of heroin, crack, and powder cocaine, among other dangerous drugs.

All candidates must apply for the program and the District Attorney's Office chooses who will be permitted into the program after close scrutiny of all applicants. Most of the participants chosen have been arrested for drug charges on approximately five occasions and have spent about four years in incarceration. The DTAP program provides 15 to 24 months of residential drug treatment, educational classes, vocational training, employment strategies, and social, mental health, and family services. The average stay is about 18 months. Participants plead guilty to a felony, thereby ensuring a mandatory prison sentence if they abscond from the program. Sentencing is deferred upon program participation. If participants complete the program, their guilty plea is withdrawn and the charges dismissed. If at any time an individual does not comply with the rigid rules established by the program, by either using drugs or partaking in violent behavior, he faces being kicked out of the program and will begin the incarceration sentence he would have been sentenced to.

Although the program was established in 1990, it has recently been evaluated by the Center on Addiction and Substance Abuse. The study consisted of 280 DTAP participants who were compared with 130 individuals who went through the regular process of incarceration. Preliminary findings suggest the program is very beneficial. In fact, studies that were completed on DTAP participants who had graduated from the program two years before found that, when compared with the other sample, DTAP graduates experienced a 26 percent lower rearrest rate and a 36 percent lower reconviction rate. And they were 67 percent less likely to return to prison than their counterparts.

Such findings suggest that the program is useful in helping to deter future crime by these individuals. Some of the reasons this program has been so useful is that it offers not only drug treatment to these individuals but also additional help in other aspects of their lives. For example, the program has an employer counselor who works with the participants to develop skills in gaining employment. After release from the program, it is important that the individual has legitimate activities to partake in so he will not be as likely to resort back to his drug-related ways. In addition, many of the program's participants have relied on drug dealing to make a living. By working with an employer counselor and also receiving vocational training, which the program also offers, an individual is more likely to gain tactics that will help him succeed when he returns back to the streets. Furthermore, research shows that those who participated in the program are three times more likely to be employed after release from the program compared with their employee rates of when they initially entered the program.

Not only does the program appear to be successful in lowering recidivism rates but the program is also cost-effective when compared with the expense of incarceration. The program costs on average about $32,975, while the average cost of prison is $64,338. Thus, the program allows for a savings of roughly 50 percent.

With approximately 80 percent of incarcerated individuals having some sort of connection to drugs, either through dealing, using, or committing crime to support their habits, the DTAP program appears to be needed. Society cannot expect individuals with drug-use problems to be incarcerated and then be released back to the streets without returning to their old ways if they have not received any help. By allowing individuals who want to change their ways an opportunity to enter the DTAP program, not only do the individuals themselves benefit, but so does society when recidivism rates are lowered. For now the Center on Addiction and Substance Abuse praises the program and only suggests that the DTAP program be replicated in other sites. If results from other sites show consistently positive results, then it would be wise for other states to also incorporate the program.

Critical Thinking

Should felony offenders and drug abusers be given the privilege of remaining in the community while they receive treatment? Should they not be punished for their criminal activity? Why should a white-collar offender go to prison for embezzlement while a drug-addicted burglar be given community treatment in a program such as DTAP?

InfoTrac College Edition Research

Use "community drug treatment" as a subject guide on InfoTrac college edition to learn more about this important topic.

Source: Columbia University, National Center on Addiction and Substance Abuse, *Crossing the Bridge: An Evaluation of the Drug Treatment Alternative-to-Prison (DTAP) Program* (New York: 2003).

Concept Summary 14.1 Intermediate Sanctions

	Goal	Problems
Fines	Monetary sanction	Overburdens the poor
Forfeiture	Monetary sanction, equity	Can be overreaching
Restitution	Pay back victim	Does not reduce recidivism
Shock incarceration and split sentence	"Taste of bars" as a deterrent	Can cause labeling and stigma
Intensive probation	Small caseloads, more supervision	High failure rate
House arrest	Avoids jail	Lacks treatment possibility
Electronic monitoring	Supervision by computer	Technology-dependent, no treatment
Residential community corrections	Less secure than prison	Expensive, high failure rate

Can Intermediate Sanctions Work?

Intermediate community-based sanctions hold the promise of providing cost-effective crime control strategies without widening the net of the criminal justice system (see Concept Summary 14.1). They reduce overreliance on incarceration and exploding correctional construction costs.[90] And as Table 14.2 shows, they are routinely being used in conjunction with probation. Nonetheless, indications are that, as currently situated, intermediate sanctions are no more effective in reducing recidivism than traditional forms of probation. Because of the more intense monitoring involved, intermediate sanctions may result in more offenders being discovered to have committed technical violations.[91] Revocation for technical reasons helps increase instead of decrease the correctional population, an outcome in opposition to the stated goals of alternative sentencing.[92]

Some criminal justice professionals welcome the use of intermediate sanctions as a practical alternative to prison, whereas others are skeptical about the ability of community sentences to significantly reduce the correctional population. Skeptics John DiIulio and Charles Logan argue that it is a myth that prison crowding can be reduced, that new construction can be avoided, and that annual operating costs can be cut if greater advantage is taken of intermediate sanctions. The great majority of those under correctional supervision, they argue, have already been on probation and will eventually be supervised in the community. In other words, most convicted criminals are already experiencing an intermediate sanction for at least some part of their sentence. Of inmates currently in state prisons, 67 percent were given probation as an intermediate sanction one or more times on prior convictions, and over 80 percent have had prior convictions resulting in either probation or incarceration. On any day of the week, argue DiIulio and Logan, you will find three times as many convicts under alternative supervision as you will find under the watchful eye of a warden. And most of those in the warden's custody are probably there at least partly because they did not do well under some prior alternative.[93]

In contrast to this view, Michael Tonry and Mary Lynch suggest that intermediate sanctions can be a useful correctional tool. Not everyone who commits a crime is the same, and all should not receive identical punishments. Clients for intermediate sanction programs might be chosen from those already incarcerated, eliminating the threat of net widening. It might be possible, they suggest, to establish exchange rates that create equivalent sentences for prison and community alternatives, such as three days in home confinement instead of one day in jail. Although intermediate sanctions are not a panacea for all offenders (as Tonry

Table 14.2 Felons Sentenced to an Additional Penalty by State Courts, by Offense, 2000

	Percent of felons with an additional penalty of				
Most serious conviction offense	Fine	Restitution	Treatment	Community service	Other
All offenses	25	14	7	5	7
Violent offenses	20	13	7	4	7
Murder	9	11	3	1	3
Sexual assault	19	11	9	3	8
Rape	14	10	8	2	8
Other sexual assault	22	11	9	4	8
Robbery	13	13	3	3	4
Aggravated assault	22	13	8	6	10
Other violent	36	15	6	5	4
Property offenses	24	26	7	6	7
Burglary	21	24	6	5	6
Larceny	24	25	6	7	9
Motor vehicle theft	19	27	5	5	19
Fraud	27	31	8	6	7
Drug offenses	27	6	7	6	7
Possession	20	4	12	7	12
Trafficking	31	6	5	5	4
Weapons offenses	19	6	4	5	8
Other offenses	27	10	7	6	9

Source: Matthew Durose and Patrick A. Langan, *Felony Sentences in State Courts, 2000* (Washington, D.C.: Bureau of Justice Statistics, 2003), p. 10.

and Lynch put it, "There is no free lunch"), they conclude that for offenders who do not present unacceptable risks of violence, well-managed intermediate sanctions offer a cost-effective way to keep them in the community.[94]

Perspectives on Justice

The premise of alternative sanctions is attractive, but there is still little evidence that they reduce recidivism. Increased monitoring and surveillance almost guarantees a higher probation failure rate. The more intensive monitoring involved results in more offenders committing technical violations. Revocation for technical reasons helps increase, not decrease, the correctional population, an outcome in opposition to the stated goals of alternative sentencing. In this sense, alternative sentencing programs may work counter to the noninterventionist philosophy that underpins traditional probation. Instead of resocializing offenders, they may help to widen the net.

To quiz yourself on this material, go to questions 14.10–14.19 on the Introduction to Criminal Justice 10e CD.

Restorative Justice

Some crime experts believe that, ironically, instead of reducing crime and recidivism, policies based on getting tough on crime can cause crime rates to fluctuate higher and offenders to commit more crime. Punishment does not work because

Exhibit 14.3 Definitions of Restorative Justice

- Restorative justice is a philosophical framework that has been proposed as an alternative to the current way of thinking about crime and criminal justice. Restorative justice empha- sizes the ways in which crime harms relationships in the context of community. (Minnesota Department of Corrections)

- Restorative justice gives priority to repairing the harm done to victims and communities, and offender accountability is defined in terms of assuming responsibility and taking action to repair harm. (Pennsylvania Juvenile Court Judges Commission)

- Restorative justice emphasizes the importance of elevating the role of crime victims and community members through more active involvement in the justice process, holding of- fenders directly accountable to the people and communities they have violated, restoring the emotional and material losses of victims, and providing a range of opportunities for dialogue, negotiation, and problem solving, whenever possible, which can lead to a greater sense of community safety, social harmony, and peace for all involved. (Mark Umbreit, University of Minnesota)

- Authentic restorative justice is a continuum that includes underlying principles, basic tenets, general public policies, and specific practices, programs, and procedures. It is a sound, com- prehensive understanding of the relationships affected by crime that recognizes that the crimi- nal justice system must focus on the full circle of injuries, needs, and responsibilities of crime victims, offenders, the community, and the government. (Restorative Justice Institute)

- "The concept of restorative justice is . . . a new paradigm for doing justice that starts at the grassroots with ordinary members of the community as well as victims and offenders . . . inclusive of all whose lives are affected by wrongdoing." (Ottawa, Ontario Church Council on Justice and Corrections)

- Restorative justice: apology and forgiveness, including participation in culture-based cleansing ceremonies, traditional counseling and advisement, and so on. (Ada Melton, au- thor and development consultant in Navajo country)

- A way of dealing with victims and offenders by focusing on the settlement of conflicts arising from crime and resolving the underlying problems that cause it. It is also, more widely, a way of dealing with crime generally in rational problem solving way. Central to restorative justice is the recognition of the community, not criminal justice agencies, as the prime site of crime control. (Tony Marshall, author and researcher from Great Britain)

Source: National Institute of Justice, "Working Definition of Restorative Justice," http://www.ojp.usdoj.gov/nij/rest-just/ch1/cjdef3.htm, accessed on August 14, 2003.

it destroys the offender's dignity and piece of mind. Traditional community-based correctional models such as probation have proven ineffective. And when they are supplemented by the new alternative or intermediate sanctions, the effect is to add a punitive aspect that can further hinder rehabilitation efforts. Instead, **restorative justice** advocates suggest a policy based on restoring the damage caused by crime and creating a system of justice that includes all the parties harmed by the criminal act — the victim, offender, community, and society.[95] Exhibit 14.3 helps define restorative justice.

While the restoration movement has many sources, one of the key pillars is Australian criminologist John Braithwaite's influential book *Crime, Shame, and Reintegration.*[96] Braithwaite's ideas are discussed in the Analyzing Criminal Jus- tice Issues feature on page 459.

The Concept of Restoration

According to the restorative view, crimes can seem quite different, ranging from a violent assault to a white-collar fraud scheme. Nonetheless, they all share one common trait: They bring harm to the community in which they occur. The tra- ditional justice system did little to involve the community in the justice process.

restorative justice

A perspective on justice that views the main goal of the criminal justice system to be a systematic response to wrongdoing that emphasizes healing the wounds of victims, of- fenders, and communities caused or revealed by crime. It stresses non- coercive and healing approaches whenever possible.

Reintegrative Shaming

analyzing criminal justice issues

John Braithwaite, a prominent Australian criminologist, notes that shame is a powerful tool of informal social control. Countries such as Japan, in which conviction for crimes brings an inordinate amount of personal shame, have extremely low crime rates. In contrast, citizens in cultures in which crime is not shameful, such as the United States, cast themselves as victims of the justice system. Because their punishment comes at the hands of strangers, such as police and judges who are being paid to act, they fail to understand the harm their actions caused. The adversary system turns their case over to lawyers and prosecutors who argue legal rules while ignoring the plight of the victim and the community. In nations that rely on shame and personal responsibility, criminal prosecution proceeds only when the normal process of public apology, compensation, and the victim's forgiveness breaks down.

Braithwaite divides the concept of shame into two distinct types. The most common form of shaming typically involves stigmatization, which occurs during a process of degradation in which the offender is branded as an evil person and cast out of society. Shaming can occur at a school disciplinary hearing or a criminal court trial. Bestowing stigma and degradation is doomed to failure: People who suffer humiliation at the hands of the justice system are turned into outcasts with little choice but to reject society. They may join with fellow rejects and collectively resist social control. An example

is the student who is expelled from high school and joins a teenage gang. Despite these dangers, an ongoing effort has been made to brand offenders and make their shame both public and permanent. For example, most states have passed sex offender registry and notification laws that make public the names of those convicted of sex offenses and warn neighbors of their presence in the community. Such efforts leave little hope of successful reintegration into conventional society.

Braithwaite argues that crime control can be better achieved through a policy of reintegrative shaming. Here disapproval is limited to the offenders' evil deeds, and not to the offender himself. The law violator must be made to realize that while his actions have caused harm he is still a valuable person who can be reaccepted by society. A critical element of reintegrative shaming occurs when the offender begins to understand and recognize his wrongdoing and shames himself. To be reintegrative, shaming must be brief and controlled and then followed by ceremonies of forgiveness, apology, and repentance.

To prevent crime, society must encourage reintegrative shaming and eschew vengeance, stigma, and labeling. For example, the incidence of domestic violence might be reduced by mounting a crusade to shame spouse abusers and help them understand the harm they have caused. Similarly, parents who use reintegrative shaming techniques in their child-rearing practices may improve parent–child rela-

tionships and ultimately reduce the delinquent involvement of their children. Efforts such as these can humanize a system of justice that today relies on repression instead of forgiveness.

Critical Thinking

Considering the reasons that people commit crime in the first place, is it reasonable to believe that a reintegrative shaming policy can restore them to conventional society? Can there be a simple solution to the crime problem such as reintegrative shaming if offenders suffer from multiple social and personal problems, including impulsivity, long-term substance abuse, and economic deprivation?

InfoTrac College Edition Research

On InfoTrac College Edition, read John Braithwaite, "Shame and Criminal Justice," *Canadian Journal of Criminology* 42, no. 3 (July 2000): 281; John Braithwaite, *Crime, Shame, and Reintegration* (Melbourne, Australia: Cambridge University Press, 1989); Anthony Petrosino and Carolyn Petrosino, "The Public Safety Potential of Megan's Law in Massachusetts: An Assessment from a Sample of Criminal Sexual Psychopaths," *Crime and Delinquency* 45 (1999): 140–58; Carter Hay, "An Exploratory Test of Braithwaite's Reintegrative Shaming Theory," *Journal of Research in Crime and Delinquency* 38 (2001): 132–53.

What has developed was a system of coercive punishments, administered by bureaucrats, that is inherently harmful to offenders and reduces the likelihood they will ever become productive members of society. This system relies on punishment, stigma, and disgrace. What is needed instead is a justice policy that repairs the harm caused by crime and includes all parties having suffered from that harm, including the victim, the community, and the offender. The principles of this approach are set out in Exhibit 14.4.

An important aspect of achieving these goals is for the offender to accept accountability for her actions and responsibility for the harm her actions caused. Only then can she be restored as a productive member of her community.

Exhibit 14.4 The Basic Principles of Restorative Justice

- Crime is an offense against human relationships.
- Victims and the community are central to justice processes.
- The first priority of justice processes is to assist victims.
- The second priority is to restore the community, to the degree possible.
- The offender has personal responsibility to victims and to the community for crimes committed.
- The offender will develop improved competency and understanding as a result of the restorative justice experience.
- Stakeholders share responsibilities for restorative justice through partnerships for action.

Source: Anne Seymour, "Restorative Justice/Community Justice," in *National Victim Assistance Academy Textbook,* ed. Grace Colman, Mario Gaboury, Morna Murray, and Anne Seymour (Washington, D.C.: National Victim Assistance Academy, 2001; updated July 2002), Chapter 4.

restoration
A vision of justice that attempts to heal the rift between criminal and victim to provide healing instead of punishment.

The Web site for the Center for Restorative Justice and Peacemaking provides links and information on the ideals of restoration and programs based on its principles. Check http://ssw.che.umn.edu/rjp/default.html.

Restoration involves turning the justice system into a healing process rather than being a distributor of retribution and revenge.

Most people involved in offender–victim relationships know one another or were related in some way before the criminal incident took place. Instead of treating one of the involved parties as a victim deserving of sympathy and the other as a criminal deserving of punishment, it is more productive to address the issues that produced conflict between these people. Instead of taking sides and choosing whom to isolate and punish, society should try to reconcile the parties involved in conflict.[97] The effectiveness of justice ultimately depends on the stake a person has in the community (or a particular social group). If a person does not value his membership in the group, he will be unlikely to accept responsibility, show remorse, or repair the injuries caused by his actions.

The Process of Restoration

The restoration process begins by redefining crime in terms of a conflict among the offender, the victim, and affected constituencies (families, schools, workplaces, and so on). Therefore, it is vitally important that the resolution take place within the context in which the conflict originally occurred and not be transferred to a specialized institution that has no social connection to the community or group from which the conflict originated. In other words, most conflicts are better settled in the community than in a court.

By maintaining ownership or jurisdiction over the conflict, the community is able to express its shared outrage about the offense. Shared community outrage is directly communicated to the offender. The victim is also given a chance to voice his or her story and the offender can directly communicate his or her need for social reintegration and treatment.

All restoration programs involve an understanding between all the parties involved in a criminal act: the victim, offender, and community. Although processes differ in structure and style, they generally include the following.

- An element in which the offender is asked to recognize that he caused injury to personal and social relations, a determination and acceptance of responsibility (ideally accompanied by a statement of remorse).
- A commitment to both material (for example, monetary restitution) and symbolic reparation (for example, an apology).
- A determination of community support and assistance for both victim and offender.

The intended result of the process is to repair injuries suffered by the victim and the community while assuring reintegration of the offender.

Restoration Programs

Negotiation, mediation, consensus building, and peacemaking have been part of the dispute resolution process in European and Asian communities for centuries.[98] Native American and Native Canadian people have long used the type of community participation in the adjudication process (for example, sentencing circles, sentencing panels, elders panels) that restorative justice advocates are now embracing.[99]

 To read more about sentencing circles, go to http://www.ojp.usdoj.gov/nij/rest-just/CH5/3_sntcir.htm.

In some Native American communities, people accused of breaking the law will meet with community members; victims, if any; village elders; and agents of the justice system in a **sentencing circle.** Each member of the circle expresses his or her feelings about the act that was committed and raises questions or concerns. The accused can express regret about his or her actions and a desire to change the harmful behavior. People may suggest ways the offender can make things up to the community and those he or she harmed. A treatment program, such as Alcoholics Anonymous, can be suggested, if appropriate.

sentencing circle
In native communities, a group of citizens, leaders, victims, and so on who meet to deal with conflicts between people in an equitable way.

Restorative justice is being embraced on many levels within the justice system.

Schools Some schools have adopted restorative justice practices to deal with students who are involved in drug and alcohol abuse, without having to resort to more punitive measures such as expulsion. School in Colorado, Minnesota, and elsewhere are trying to involve students in relational rehabilitation programs, which strive to improve the person's relationships with key figures in the community who may have been harmed by their actions.[100]

Police Restorative justice has also been implemented when crime is first encountered by police. The new community policing models are an attempt to bring restorative concepts into law enforcement. Restorative justice relies on the fact that criminal justice policy makers need to listen and respond to the needs of those who are to be affected by their actions, and community policing relies on policies established with input and exchanges between officers and citizens.[101]

In addition, police may be included in Family Group Conference (FGC) programs. Developed in New Zealand, FGCs are conferences in which victims are invited to meet offenders and their families, with the police and a justice coordinator present, to discuss the crime and its outcome.[102] Victims are thereby given a voice to tell of the impact of the crime and ask the offender: Why were they victimized? Will they be victimized again? How will the offender put things right? In New Zealand, victims have the right to attend the mandated FGC and to tell offenders face to face about the personal impact of the crime.

Courts In the court system, restorative programs typically involve diverting the formal court process. These programs, instead, encourage meeting and reconciling the conflicts between offenders and victims via victim advocacy, mediation programs, and sentencing circles, in which crime victims and their families are brought together with offenders and their families in an effort to formulate a sanction that addresses the needs of each party. Victims are given a chance to voice their stories and offenders can help compensate them financially or provide some service (for example, fixing damaged property).[103] The goal is to enable offenders to appreciate the damage they have caused, to make amends, and to be reintegrated back into society.

The Analyzing Criminal Justice Issues feature on page 462 describes four restorative justice programs.

Restorative Justice in the Community

analyzing criminal justice issues

A number of new and innovative community programs based on restorative justice principles, four of which are discussed here, are being tested around the nation.

Minnesota

Minnesota has been a groundbreaker in restorative justice. Its Department of Corrections created the Restorative Justice Initiative in 1992, hiring Kay Pranis as a full-time restorative justice planner in 1994 — the first such position in the country. The initiative offers training in restorative justice principles and practices, provides technical assistance to communities in designing and implementing practices, and creates networks of professionals and activists to share knowledge and provide support.

Besides promoting victim–offender mediation, family group conferencing, and neighborhood conferencing, the department has introduced sentencing circles. Citizen volunteers and criminal justice officials from Minnesota have participated in training in the Yukon Territory, Canada, where peacemaking circles have been held since the late 1980s. In Minnesota the circle process is used by the Mille Lacs Indian Reservation and in other communities in several counties. The circle process usually has several phases. First, the Community Justice Committee conducts an intake interview with offenders who want to participate. Then, separate healing circles are held for the victim (and others who feel harmed) and the offender. The committee tries to cultivate a close personal relationship with victims and offenders and to create support networks for them. In the end, a sentencing circle, open to the community, meets to work out a sentencing plan.

Vermont

A pilot reparative probation program began in Vermont in 1994, and the first cases were heard by a reparative citizen board the following year. Three features distinguish this restorative justice initiative from most others in the United States. The Department of Corrections designed the program, it is implemented statewide, and it involves a sizable number of volunteer citizens. The process is straightforward. Following an adjudication of guilt, the judge sentences the offender to probation, with the sentence suspended and only two conditions imposed. The offender will commit no more crimes and will complete the reparative program. The volunteer board members meet with the offender and the victim and together discuss the offense, its effects on victim and community, and the life situations of victim and offender. All participants must agree on a contract, to be fulfilled by the offender. It is based on five goals. The victim is restored and healed, the community is restored, the offender understands the effects of the crime, the offender learns ways to avoid reoffending, and the community offers reintegration to the offender. Because reparative probation targets minor crimes, it is not meant as a prison diversion program. In 1998 the 44 boards handled 1,200 cases, accounting for more than one-third of the probation caseload. More than 300 trained volunteers serve as board members. Ten coordinators handle case management and organization for the boards. The goal is to have the boards handle about 70 percent of the targeted probation cases. That only about 17 percent of offenders fail to complete their agreements or attend follow-up board meetings is a measure of the program's success. These offenders are referred back to the courts.

Travis County, Texas

Texas law authorizes that each county develop a community justice council and community justice task force. The task force includes representatives of criminal justice agencies, social and health services, and community organizations. With task force assistance, the council, consisting of elected officials, handles planning and policy making and prepares a community justice plan.

Many efforts are directed at juvenile offenses. In Austin, the Juvenile Probation Office offers victim–offender mediation for young people in trouble. For misdemeanors, juveniles may be diverted from court to neighborhood conference committees. These consist of panels of trained adult citizens who meet with juvenile offenders and their parents, and together they develop contracts tailored to the case.

Critical Thinking

Restorative justice may be the model that best serves alternative sanctions. How can this essentially humanistic approach be sold to a general public that supports more punitive sanctions? For example, would it be feasible that using restorative justice with nonviolent offenders frees up resources for the relatively few dangerous people in the criminal population? Explain.

InfoTrac College Edition Research

To learn more about the restorative justice approach, see Gordon Bazemore, "Restorative Justice and Earned Redemption: Communities, Victims, and Offender Reintegration," *American Behavioral Scientist* 41 (1998): 768; Tag Evers, "A Healing Approach to Crime," *Progressive* 62 (1998): 30; Carol La Prairie, "The Impact of Aboriginal Justice Research on Policy: A Marginal Past and an Even More Uncertain Future," *Canadian Journal of Criminology* 41 (1999): 249.

Source: Leena Kurki, *Incorporating Restorative and Community Justice into American Sentencing and Corrections* (Washington, D.C.: National Institute of Justice, 1999).

Exhibit 14.5 Victim Concerns about Restorative Justice

- Restorative justice processes can cast victims as little more than props in a psychodrama focused on the offender, to restore him and thereby render him less likely to offend again.

- A victim, supported by family and intimates while engaged in restorative conferencing and feeling genuinely free to speak directly to the offender, may press a blaming instead of restorative shaming agenda.

- The victims' movement has focused for years on a perceived imbalance of rights. Criminal defendants enjoy the presumption of innocence, the right to proof beyond a reasonable doubt, the right not to have to testify, and lenient treatment when found guilty of crime. Victims were extended no rights at all in the legal process. Is restorative justice another legal giveaway to criminals?

- A victim's rights are threatened by some features of the restorative justice process, such as respectful listening to the offender's story and consensual dispositions. These features seem affronts to a victim's claim of the right to be seen as a victim, to insist on the offender being branded a criminal, to blame the offender, and not to be "victimized all over again by the process."

- Many victims do want apology, if it is heartfelt and easy to get. But some want, even more, to put the traumatic incident behind them, to retrieve stolen property being held for use at trial, and to be assured that the offender will receive treatment he is thought to need if he is not to victimize someone else. For victims such as these, restorative justice processes can seem unnecessary at best.

- Restorative processes depend, case by case, on a victim's active participation, in a role more emotionally demanding than that of a complaining witness in a conventional criminal prosecution — which is itself a role avoided by many, and perhaps most, victims.

Source: Michael E. Smith, *What Future for "Public Safety" and "Restorative Justice" in Community Corrections?* (Washington, D.C.: National Institute of Justice, 2001).

The Challenge of Restorative Justice

Restorative justice programs must be wary of cultural and social differences, which can be found throughout America's heterogeneous society.[104] What may be considered restorative in one subculture may be considered insulting and damaging in another.[105] Similarly, so many diverse programs call themselves restorative that evaluating them is difficult. Each one may be pursuing a unique objective. In other words, no single definition has been derived of what constitutes restorative justice.[106]

Possibly the greatest challenge to restorative justice is the difficult task of balancing the needs of offenders with those of their victims. If programs focus solely on the reconciliation of the victim's needs, they may risk ignoring the offender's needs and increasing the likelihood of reoffending. Sharon Levrant and her colleagues suggest that restorative justice programs featuring short-term interactions with victims fail to help offenders learn prosocial ways of behaving. Restorative justice advocates may falsely assume that relatively brief interludes of public shaming will change deeply rooted criminal predispositions.[107]

In contrast, programs focusing on the offender may turn off victims and their advocates. Some victim advocacy groups have voiced concerns about the focus of restorative justice programs (see Exhibit 14.5).

These are a few of the obstacles that restorative justice programs must overcome for them to be successful and productive. Yet, because the method holds so much promise, criminologists are conducting numerous demonstration projects to find the most effective means of returning the ownership of justice to the people and the community.

To quiz yourself on this material, go to questions 14.20–14.25 on the Introduction to Criminal Justice 10e CD.

Summary

- Probation can be traced to the common law practice of granting clemency to deserving offenders.
- The modern probation concept was developed by John Augustus of Boston, who personally sponsored 2,000 convicted inmates over an 18-year period.
- Today, probation is the community supervision of convicted offenders by order of the court. It is a sentence reserved for defendants whom the magistrate views as having potential for rehabilitation without needing to serve prison or jail terms.
- Probation is practiced in every state and by the federal government and includes both adult and juvenile offenders.
- In the decision to grant probation, most judges are influenced by their personal views and the presentence reports of the probation staff.
- Once on probation, the offender must follow a set of rules or conditions, the violation of which may lead to revocation of probation and reinstatement of a prison sentence. These rules vary from state to state but usually involve such demands as refraining from using alcohol or drugs, obeying curfews, and terminating past criminal associations.
- Probation officers are usually organized into countywide departments, although some agencies are statewide and others are combined parole–probation departments.
- Probation departments have instituted a number of innovative programs designed to bring better services to their clients. These include restitution and diversionary programs, intensive probation, and residential probation.
- In recent years, the U.S Supreme Court has granted probationers greater due process rights. Today, when the state wishes to revoke probation, it must conduct a full hearing on the matter and provide the probationer with an attorney when that assistance is warranted.
- To supplement probation, a whole new family of intermediate sanctions has been developed. These range from pretrial diversion to residential community corrections. Other widely used intermediate sanctions include fines and forfeiture, house arrest, and intensive probation supervision.
- Electronic monitoring involves a device worn by an offender under home confinement. While some critics complain that EM smacks of a "Big Brother Is Watching You" mentality, it would seem an attractive alternative to a stay in a dangerous, deteriorated, secure correctional facility.
- A stay in a community correctional center is one of the most intrusive alternative sentencing options. Residents may be eligible for work and educational release during the day while attending group sessions in the evening. Residential community correction is less costly than more secure institutions, while being equally effective.
- It is too soon to determine whether alternative sanction programs are successful, but they provide a hope of being lost-cost, high-security alternatives to traditional corrections. Alternatives to incarceration can help reduce overcrowding in the prison system and spare nonviolent offenders the pains of a prison experience. Although alternatives may not be much more effective than a prison sentence in reducing recidivism rates, they are far less costly and can free up needed space for more violent offenders.
- A promising approach to community sentencing is the use of restorative justice programs.
- Restorative justice programs stress healing and redemption, not punishment and deterrence. Restoration means that the offender accepts accountability for her actions and responsibility for the harm her actions caused. Restoration involves turning the justice system into a healing process, instead of being a distributor of retribution and revenge.
- Restoration programs are being used around the nation and involve mediation, sentencing circles.

Key Terms

alternative sanctions 432
intermediate sanctions 432
judicial reprieve 432
recognizance 432
sureties 432
probation 433
revocation 435
suspended sentence 435
intake 437
presentence investigation 438
risk classification 438

day fees 444
HotSpot probation 444
fine 447
day fine 447
forfeiture 447
zero tolerance 448
restitution 448
community service restitution 448
monetary restitution 448
shock probation 449
split sentence 449

intensive probation
    supervision (IPS) 449
house arrest 451
electronic monitoring (EM) 452
residential community
    corrections (RCC) 453
day reporting center (DRC) 454
restorative justice 458
restoration 460
sentencing circles 461

Doing Research on the Web

For an up-to-date list of Web links, go to http://cj.wadsworth.com/siegel_intro10e.

Some people believe that offenders have taken from society and they should be forced to give back. Is this truly part of restorative justice? To find out the answer, read Gregg W. Etter and Judy Hammond, "Community: Service Work as Part of Offender Rehabilitation," *Corrections Today* 63, no. 7 (December 2001): 114.

Can restorative justice truly work? Does it impact equally on men and women? Read Stephanie Coward-Yaskiw, "Restorative Justice: What Is It? Can It Work? What Do Women Think?" *Herizons* 15, no. 5 (Spring 2002): 22.

To learn more about restorative justice and to do research on recent developments in the field, go to Restorative Justice Online, a comprehensive, nonpartisan Web site devoted to restorative justice principles, practice, programs, and theory: http://www.restorativejustice.org/.

The National Institute of Justice maintains a restorative justice Web site at http://www.ojp.usdoj.gov/nij/rest-just/.

> Pro/Con discussions and Viewpoint Essays on some of the topics in this chapter may be found at the Opposing Viewpoints Resource Center: http://www.gale.com/OpposingViewpoints.

Discussion Questions

1. What is the purpose of probation? Identify some conditions of probation and discuss the responsibilities of the probation officer.
2. Discuss the procedures involved in probation revocation. What are the rights of the probationer?
3. Is probation a privilege or a right? Explain.
4. Should a convicted criminal make restitution to the victim? Why or why not? When is restitution inappropriate?
5. Should offenders be fined based on the severity of what they did or according to their ability to pay? Is it fair to gear day fines to wages? Why or why not? Should offenders be punished more severely because they are financially successful? Explain.
6. Does house arrest involve a violation of personal freedom? Does wearing an ankle bracelet smack of "Big Brother"? Would you want the government monitoring your daily activities? Could this be expanded, for example, to monitor the whereabouts of AIDS patients? Explain.
7. Do you agree that criminals can be restored through community interaction? Considering the fact that recidivism rates are so high, are traditional sanctions a waste of time and restorative ones the wave of the future?

Notes

1 Rick Lyman, "Winona Ryder Found Guilty of 2 Counts in Shoplifting Case," *New York Times,* November 6, 2002, p. A1; Matt Bean, "Wynona Ryder Gets Probation for Shoplifting," Court TV.com, April 4, 2003, http://www.courttv.com/archive/trials/ryder/sentence.html, accessed on November 21, 2003.

2 Arnulf Kolstad, "Imprisonment as Rehabilitation: Offenders' Assessment of Why It Does Not Work," *Journal of Criminal Justice* 24 (1996): 323–35.

3 For a history of probation, see Edward Sieh, "From Augustus to the Progressives: A Study of Probation's Formative Years," *Federal Probation* 57 (1993): 67–72.

4 Ibid.

5 David Rothman, *Conscience and Convenience* (Boston: Little, Brown, 1980), pp. 82–117.

6 Matthew Durose and Patrick A. Langan, *State Court Sentencing of Convicted Felons, 1998* (Washington, D.C.: Bureau of Justice Statistics, February 2001).

7 Lawrence Bonczar and Lauren Glaze, *Probation and Parole, 1998* (Washington, D.C.: Bureau of Justice Statistics, 1999).

8 Ibid.

9 Data in this section come from Lauren E. Glaze, *Probation and Parole in the United States, 2002* (Washington, D.C.: Bureau of Justice Statistics, 2003).

10 California Rules of Court, Rule 4.413, amended effective July 1, 2003; adopted as Rule 413, effective January 1, 1991; previously renumbered, effective January 1, 2001.

11 *Higdon* v. *United States,* 627 F.2d 893 (9th Cir., 1980).

12 *United States* v. *Lee,* No. 01–4485, January 7, 2003; *United States* v. *Lee,* PICS N. 03–0023.

13 *U.S.* v. *Freeman,* No. 01–34750, January 8, 2003.

14 Todd Clear and Edward Latessa, "Probation Officers' Roles in Intensive Supervision: Surveillance versus Treatment," *Justice Quarterly* 10 (1993): 441–62.

15 Paul von Zielbauer, "Probation Dept. Is Now Arming Officers Supervising Criminals," *New York Times,* August 7, 2003, p. 5.

16 "*United States* v. *Anthony Capanelli,*" *New York Law Journal,* July 21, 2003, p. 1.

17 Patricia Harris, "Client Management Classification and Prediction of Probation Outcome," *Crime and Delinquency* 40 (1994): 154–74.

18 Anne Schneider, Laurie Ervin, and Zoann Snyder-Joy, "Further Exploration of the Flight from Discretion: The Role of Risk/Need Instruments in Probation Supervision Decisions," *Journal of Criminal Justice* 24 (1996): 109–21.

19 Todd Clear and Vincent O'Leary, *Controlling the Offender in the Community* (Lexington, Mass.: Lexington Books, 1983), pp. 11–29, 77–100.

20 David Duffee and Bonnie Carlson, "Competing Value Premises for the Provision of Drug Treatment to Probationers," *Crime and Delinquency* 42 (1996): 574–92.

21 Richard Sluder and Rolando Del Carmen, "Are Probation and Parole Officers Liable for Injuries Caused by Probationers and Parolees?" *Federal Probation* 54 (1990): 3–12.

22 Joan Petersilia, "An Evaluation of Intensive Probation in California," *Journal of Criminal Law and Criminology* 82 (1992): 610–58.

23 Glaze, *Probation and Parole in the United States.*

24 M. Kevin Gray, Monique Fields, and Sheila Royo Maxwell, "Examining Probation Violations: Who, What, and When," *Crime and Delinquency* 47 (2001): 537–57.

25 Cassia Spohn and David Holleran, "The Effect of Imprisonment on Recidivism Rates of Felony Offenders: A Focus on Drug Offenders," *Criminology* 40 (2002): 329–59.

26 Matthew Durose and Patrick Langan, *Felony Sentences in the United States, 2000* (Washington, D.C.: Bureau of Justice Statistics, 2003).

27 Joan Petersilia, Susan Turner, James Kahan, and Joyce Peterson, *Granting Felons Probation: Public Risks and Alternatives* (Santa Monica, Calif.: RAND Corp., 1985).

28 Kathryn Morgan, "Factors Influencing Probation Outcome: A Review of the Literature," *Federal Probation* 57 (1993): 23–29.

29 Kathryn Morgan, "Factors Associated with Probation Outcome," *Journal of Criminal Justice* 22 (1994): 341–53.

30 Paula M. Ditton, *Mental Health and Treatment of Inmates and Probationers* (Washington, D.C.: Bureau of Justice Statistics, 1999).

31 Lynette Feder and Laura Dugan, "A Test of the Efficacy of Court-Mandated Counseling for Domestic Violence Offenders: The Broward Experiment," *Justice Quarterly* 19 (2002): 343–76.

32 Spohn and Holleran, "The Effect of Imprisonment on Recidivism Rates of Felony Offenders."

33 *Minnesota v. Murphy,* 465 U.S. 420, 104 S.Ct. 1136, 79 L.Ed.2d 409 (1984).

34 *Griffin v. Wisconsin,* 483 U.S. 868, 107 S.Ct. 3164, 97 L.Ed.2d 709 (1987).

35 *United States v. Knights,* 122 S.Ct. 587 (2001).

36 *Mempa v. Rhay,* 389 U.S. 128, 88 S.Ct. 254, 19 L.Ed.2d 336 (1967).

37 *Morrissey v. Brewer,* 408 U.S. 471, 92 S.Ct. 2593, 33 L.Ed.2d 484 (1972).

38 *Gagnon v. Scarpelli,* 411 U.S. 778, 93 S.Ct. 1756, 36 L.Ed.2d 656 (1973).

39 *United States v. Carson,* 669 F.2d 216 (5th Cir., 1982).

40 *United States v. Granderson,* 114 Ct. 1259, 127 L.Ed.2d 611 (1994).

41 Durose and Langan, *State Court Sentencing of Convicted Felons.*

42 "Law in Massachusetts Requires Probationers to Pay 'Day Fees,'" *Criminal Justice Newsletter,* September 15, 1988, p. 1.

43 Peter Finn and Dale Parent, *Making the Offender Foot the Bill: A Texas Program* (Washington, D.C.: National Institute of Justice, 1992).

44 Nicole Leeper Piquero, "A Recidivism Analysis of Maryland's Community Probation Program," *Journal of Criminal Justice* 31 (2003): 295–308.

45 Richard Lawrence, "Reexamining Community Corrections Models," *Crime and Delinquency* 37 (1991): 449–64.

46 Todd Clear and Patricia Hardyman, "The New Intensive Supervision Movement," *Crime and Delinquency* 36 (1990): 42–60.

47 For a thorough review of these programs, see James Byrne, Arthur Lurigio, and Joan Petersilia, eds., *Smart Sentencing: The Emergence of Intermediate Sanctions* (Newbury Park, Calif.: Sage, 1993).

48 Norval Morris and Michael Tonry, *Between Prison and Probation: Intermediate Punishments in a Rational Sentencing System* (New York: Oxford University Press, 1990).

49 Michael Tonry and Richard Will, *Intermediate Sanctions* (Washington, D.C.: National Institute of Justice, 1990).

50 Ibid., p. 8.

51 Michael Maxfield and Terry Baumer, "Home Detention with Electronic Monitoring: Comparing Pretrial and Postconviction Programs," *Crime and Delinquency* 36 (1990): 521–56.

52 Sally Hillsman and Judith Greene, "Tailoring Fines to the Financial Means of Offenders," *Judicature* 72 (1988): 38–45.

53 *Tate v. Short,* 401 U.S. 395, 91 S.Ct. 668, 28 L.Ed.2d 130 (1971).

54 Margaret Gordon and Daniel Glaser, "The Use and Effects of Financial Penalties in Municipal Courts," *Criminology* 29 (1991): 651–76.

55 "'Day Fines' Being Tested in New York City Court," *Criminal Justice Newsletter,* September 1, 1988, pp. 4–5.

56 Doris Layton MacKenzie, "Evidence-Based Corrections: Identifying What Works," *Crime and Delinquency* 46 (2000): 457–72.

57 John L. Worrall, "Addicted to the Drug War: The Role of Civil Asset Forfeiture as a Budgetary Necessity in Contemporary Law Enforcement," *Journal of Criminal Justice* 29 (2001): 171–87.

58 C. Yorke, *Some Consideration on the Law of Forfeiture for High Treason,* 2d ed. (London, England: Printed by Mr. Thomas Cadell, 1746), p. 26, cited in David Freid, "Rationalizing Criminal Forfeiture," *Journal of Criminal Law and Criminology* 79 (1988): 329.

59 Fried, "Rationalizing Criminal Forfeiture," p. 436.

60 James B. Jacobs, Coleen Friel, and Edward O'Callaghan, "Pension Forfeiture: A Problematic Sanction for Public Corruption," *American Criminal Law Review* 35 (1997): 57–92.

61 Worrall, "Addicted to the Drug War."

62 For a general review, see Burt Galaway and Joe Hudson, *Criminal Justice, Restitution, and Reconciliation* (New York: Criminal Justice Press, 1990); Robert Carter, Jay Cocks, and Daniel Glazer, "Community Service: A Review of the Basic Issues," *Federal Probation* 51 (1987): 4–11.

63 Morris and Tonry, *Between Prison and Probation,* pp. 171–75.

64 Frederick Allen and Harvey Treger, "Community Service Orders in Federal Probation: Perceptions of Probationers and Host Agencies," *Federal Probation* 54 (1990): 8–14.

65 Sudipto Roy, "Two Types of Juvenile Restitution Programs in Two Midwestern Counties: A Comparative Study," *Federal Probation* 57 (1993): 48–53.

66 Jodi Brown, *Correctional Populations in the United States, 1996* (Washington, D.C.: Bureau of Justice Statistics, 1999), p. 39.

67 James Ryan, "Who Gets Revoked? A Comparison of Intensive Supervision Successes and Failures in Vermont," *Crime and Delinquency* 43 (1997): 104–18.

68 Peter Jones, "Expanding the Use of Noncustodial Sentencing Options: An Evaluation of the Kansas Community Corrections Act," *Howard Journal* 29 (1990): 114–29; Michael Agopian, "The Impact of Intensive Supervision Probation on Gang-Drug Offenders," *Criminal Justice Policy Review* 4 (1990): 214–22.

69 Angela Robertson, Paul Grimes, and Kevin Rogers, "A Short-Run Cost-Benefit Analysis of Community-Based Interventions for Juvenile Offenders," *Crime and Delinquency* 47 (2001): 265–84.

70 Betsy Fulton, Edward Latessa, Amy Stichman, and Lawrence Travis, "The State of ISP: Research and Policy Implications," *Federal Probation* 61 (1997): 65–75.

71 S. Christopher Baird and Dennis Wagner, "Measuring Diversion: The Florida Community Control Program," *Crime and Delinquency* 36 (1990): 112–25.

72 Linda Smith and Ronald Akers, "A Comparison of Recidivism of Florida's Community Control and Prison: A Five-Year Survival Analysis," *Journal of Research in Crime and Delinquency* 30 (1993): 267–92.

73 Brian Payne and Randy Gainey, "The Influence of Demographic Factors on the Experience of House Arrest," *Federal Probation* 66 (2002): 64–70.

74 Robert N. Altman, Robert E. Murray, and Evey B. Wooten, "Home Confinement: A '90s Approach to Community Supervision," *Federal Probation* 61 (1997): 30–32.

75 Jennifer Lee, "Some States Track Parolees by Satellite," *New York Times,* January 31, 2002, p. A3.

76 Cecil Greek, "The Cutting Edge," *Federal Probation* 66 (2002): 51–53; Veridian's Web site at http://www.veridian.com/, accessed on November 18, 2003.

77 Preston Elrod and Michael Brown, "Predicting Public Support for Electronic House Arrest: Results from a New York County Survey," *American Behavioral Scientist* 39 (1996): 461–74.

78 Joseph Papy and Richard Nimer, "Electronic Monitoring in Florida," *Federal Probation* 55 (1991): 31–33.

79 Kevin E. Courtright, Bruce L. Berg, and Robert J. Mutchnick, "The Cost Effectiveness of Using House Arrest with Electronic Monitoring for Drunk Drivers," *Federal Probation* 61 (1997): 19–22.

80 Mary Finn and Suzanne Muirhead-Steves, "The Effectiveness of Electronic Monitoring with Violent Male Parolees," *Justice Quarterly* 19 (2002): 293–313.

81 Brian McKay, "The State of Sex Offender Probation Supervision in Texas,"*Federal Probation* 66 (2002): 16–21.

82 See, generally, Edward Latessa and Lawrence Travis III, "Residential Community Correctional Programs," in James Byrne, Arthur Lurigio, and Joan Petersilia, eds., Smart Sentencing: *The Emergence of Intermediate Sanctions* (Newbury Park, Calif.: Sage, 1993).

83 Updated with personal correspondence, Portland House personnel, September 22, 2002.

84 Harvey Siegal, James Fisher, Richard Rapp, Casey Kelliher, Joseph Wagner, William O'Brien, and Phyllis Cole, "Enhancing Substance Abuse Treatment with Case Management," *Journal of Substance Abuse Treatment* 13 (1996): 93–98.

85 Dale Parent, *Day Reporting Centers for Criminal Offenders — A Descriptive Analysis of Existing Programs* (Washington, D.C.: National Institute of Justice, 1990).

86 David Diggs and Stephen Pieper, "Using Day Reporting Centers as an Alternative to Jail," *Federal Probation* 58 (1994): 9–12.

87 Information on the Atlanta program can be reached at http://www.pap.state.ga.us/2001%20Annual%20Report%20Web/day_reporting_centers.htm, accessed on November 18, 2003.

88 David Hartmann, Paul Friday, and Kevin Minor, "Residential Probation: A Seven-Year Follow-Up of Halfway House Discharges," *Journal of Criminal Justice* 22 (1994): 503–15.

89 Banhram Haghighi and Alma Lopez, "Success/Failure of Group Home Treatment Programs for Juveniles," *Federal Probation* 57 (1993): 53–57.

90 Richard Rosenfeld and Kimberly Kempf, "The Scope and Purposes of Corrections: Exploring Alternative Responses to Crowding," *Crime and Delinquency* 37 (1991): 481–505.

91 For a thorough review, see Michael Tonry and Mary Lynch, "Intermediate Sanctions," in *Crime and Justice: A Review of Research*, vol. 20, ed. Michael Tonry (Chicago: University of Chicago Press, 1996), pp. 99–144.

92 Francis Cullen, "Control in the Community: The Limits of Reform?" paper presented at the International Association of Residential and Community Alternatives, Philadelphia, Pennsylvania, November 1993.

93 John DiIulio and Charles Logan, "The Ten Deadly Myths about Crime and Punishment in the U.S.," *Wisconsin Interest* 1 (1992): 21–35.

94 Tonry and Lynch, "Intermediate Sanctions."

95 Kathleen Daly and Russ Immarigeon, "The Past, Present and Future of Restorative Justice: Some Critical Reflections," *Contemporary Justice Review* 1 (1998): 21–45.

96 John Braithwaite, *Crime, Shame, and Reintegration* (Melbourne, Australia: Cambridge University Press, 1989).

97 Gene Stephens, "The Future of Policing: From a War Model to a Peace Model," in *The Past, Present, and Future of American Criminal Justice*, ed. Brendan Maguire and Polly Radosh (Dix Hills, N.Y.: General Hall Pub., 1996), pp. 77–93.

98 Kay Pranis, "Peacemaking Circles: Restorative Justice in Practice Allows Victims and Offenders to Begin Repairing the Harm," *Corrections Today* 59 (1997): 74–78.

99 Carol LaPrairie, "The 'New' Justice: Some Implications for Aboriginal Communities," *Canadian Journal of Criminology* 40 (1998): 61–79.

100 David R. Karp and Beau Breslin, "Restorative Justice in School Communities," *Youth and Society* 33 (2001): 249–72.

101 Paul Jesilow and Deborah Parsons, "Community Policing as Peacemaking," *Policing and Society* 10 (2000): 163–83.

102 Donald J. Schmid, *Restorative Justice in New Zealand* (Wellington, New Zealand: Fullbright New Zealand, 2001).

103 Gordon Bazemore and Curt Taylor Griffiths, "Conferences, Circles, Boards, and Mediations: The 'New Wave' of Community Justice Decision Making," *Federal Probation* 61 (1997): 25–37.

104 John Braithwaite, "Setting Standards for Restorative Justice," *British Journal of Criminology* 42 (2002): 563–77.

105 David Altschuler, "Community Justice Initiatives: Issues and Challenges in the U.S. Context," *Federal Probation* 65 (2001): 28–33.

106 Lois Presser and Patricia Van Voorhis, "Values and Evaluation: Assessing Processes and Outcomes of Restorative Justice Programs," *Crime and Delinquency* 48 (2002): 162–89.

107 Sharon Levrant, Francis Cullen, Betsy Fulton, and John Wozniak, "Reconsidering Restorative Justice: The Corruption of Benevolence Revisited? *Crime and Delinquency* 45 (1999): 3–28.

Chapter Outline

Chapter Objectives:

After reading this chapter, you should be able to:

1. Describe the history of penal institutions.
2. Know the differences between the Auburn (congregate) and Pennsylvania (isolate) systems.
3. Understand the history of penal reform.
4. Explain the concept of the jail.
5. Discuss the issue of the new generation jails.
6. Describe different levels of prison security.
7. Discuss the super-maximum-security prison.
8. Know what is meant by the term *penal harm.*
9. Discuss the benefits and drawbacks of boot camps.
10. Explain the current trends in the prison population.

Viewpoints

 International Justice: The Development of Parole 477

 Analyzing Criminal Justice Issues: Penal Harm: The No-Frills Movement 480

 Criminal Justice and Technology: You've Got Mail? 486

 Criminal Justice and Technology: Ultramaximum-Security Prisons 488

InfoTrac College Edition Links

Web Links

Chapter 15 | Corrections: History, Institutions, and Populations

The fact that prison can be a dangerous place was graphically demonstrated on August 23, 2003, when ex-priest John Geoghan, a convicted pedophile, was strangled by Joseph L. Druce, 38, another inmate inside a maximum-security Massachusetts prison. Geoghan, who faced accusations of molesting more than 150 boys in his parishes over three decades, had been serving a nine-year sentence for fondling a boy in a public swimming pool in 1991. Druce, who was serving a life sentence without parole for strangling a trucker who he believed was gay, later told investigators that he had plotted to murder Geoghan for at least a month. He had come up with a plan to jam the priest's cell door shut with part of a book, tie him up with a T-shirt, and use stretched out socks to strangle him.

Druce is an all-too-familiar figure in the American prison system. Named Darrin Smiledge at birth, Druce was an unplanned child, who by age 9 was obsessed with sex and violent fantasies, often venting his rage on smaller children. In 1999, he changed

his name to Joseph L. Druce, allegedly because he hated his mother.[1] Mental health professionals who evaluated Druce found that he suffered from a personality disorder as a child and from severe attention deficit disorder. Bullying people half his strength was a pattern that apparently started when Druce attended the Lakeside School in Peabody, Massachusetts, an alter- native facility for children. "If there is a child in a group who is weaker than Darrin," one psychologist wrote, "he will focus his provocative behavior and teasing toward that child."

View the CNN video clip of this story on your Introduction to Criminal Justice 10e CD.

Although the Geoghan case is unusual, it is not atypical. Despite ongoing efforts to improve security, violence is an ever-present occurrence in the prison system. Many prisoners come from troubled backgrounds. Many have serious emotional problems and grew up in abusive households. A majority are alcohol and drug dependent at the time of their arrest. Is it realistic to expect that a significant portion of these troubled individuals will successfully adjust to society after a lengthy stay in an overcrowded and dangerous penal institution?

Today, the correctional system has branches in the federal, state, and county levels of government. Felons may be placed in state or federal penitentiaries (prisons), which are usually isolated, high-security structures. Misdemeanants are housed in county jails, sometimes called reformatories or houses of correction. Juvenile offenders have their own institutions, sometimes euphemistically called schools, camps, ranches, or homes. Typically, the latter are non-secure facilities, often located in rural areas, that provide both confinement and rehabilitative services for young offenders.

Other types of correctional institutions include ranches and farms for adult offenders and community correctional settings, such as halfway houses, for inmates who are about to return to society. Today's correctional facilities encompass a wide range, from maxi-maxi security institutions, such as the federal prison in Florence, Colorado, where the nation's most dangerous felons are confined, to low-security camps that house white-collar criminals convicted of such crimes as insider trading and mail fraud.

One of the great tragedies of the current era is that correctional institutions, whatever form they take, do not seem to correct. They are, in most instances, overcrowded, understaffed, outdated warehouses for social outcasts. The overcrowding crisis is the most significant problem faced by the prison today. Prisons, which contain more than 1.3 million inmates (Figure 15.1), seem more suited for control, punishment, and security than rehabilitation and treatment.

A sad but unfortunately accurate observation is that today's correctional institution has become a revolving door and that too many of its residents return time and again. More than half of all inmates will be back in prison within six years of their release.

Despite the apparent lack of success of penal institutions, great debate continues over the direction of their future operations. Some penal experts maintain that prisons and jails are not places for rehabilitation and treatment but should be used to keep dangerous offenders apart from society and give them the "just deserts" for their crimes.[2] In this sense, prison success would be measured by such factors as physical security, length of incapacitation, relationship between the crime rate and the number of incarcerated felons, and inmates' perceptions that their treatment was fair and proportionate. The dominance of this correctional philosophy is illustrated by the three strikes presumptive and mandatory sentencing structures, which are used in such traditionally progressive states as California, Illinois, and Massachusetts; the number of people under lock and key, which has risen rapidly in the past few years even though the crime rate has declined; and commentators taking note that the crime rate has declined as the prison population increases.

Although the conservative tide in corrections is self-evident, many penal experts still maintain that prisons can be useful places for offender rehabilitation, and numerous examples of the treatment philosophy still flourish in prisons. For example, educational programs allow inmates to get college credits, vocational training has become more sophisticated, counseling and substance abuse pro-

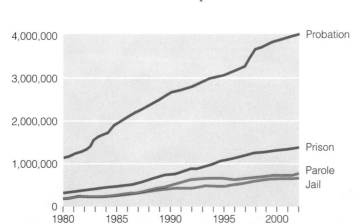

Figure 15.1
Adult Correctional Populations, 1980–2002

Sources: Bureau of Justice Statistics correctional surveys (Annual Probation Survey, National Prisoner Statistics, Survey of Jails, and Annual Parole Survey) as presented in Bureau of Justice Statistics, *Correctional Populations in the United States* (Washington, D.C.: 2003); Paige M. Harrison and Allen J. Beck, *Prisoners in 2002* (Washington, D.C.: Bureau of Justice Statistics, 2003); Lauren Glaze, *Probation and Parole in the United States, 2002* (Washington, D.C.: Bureau of Justice Statistics, 2003).

Despite a spotty track record, the cost of corrections keeps escalating. To find out more about this issue, go to Elizabeth B. Guerard, "Analysis: Prison Spending Outpaces Higher Education," *Education Daily* 35, no. 165 (August 30, 2002): 3.

The American Correctional Association is a multidisciplinary organization of professionals representing all facets of corrections and criminal justice, including federal, state, and military correctional facilities and prisons, county jails and detention centers, probation and parole agencies, and community corrections and halfway houses. It has more than 20,000 members. To learn about what the association does, check http://www.corrections.com/aca/.

van Gogh, Vincent: Prisoner's Round (detail), 1890. Pushkin Museum of Fine Arts, Moscow. Scala/ArtResource, New York.

"Prisoners Exercising" by Vincent van Gogh. Painted in 1890, this work captures the despair of the nineteenth-century penal institution. The face of the prisoner near the center of the picture looking at the viewer is van Gogh's.

grams are almost universal, and every state maintains some type of early-release and community correctional programs.

While this debate is ongoing, there is little question that the correctional system is vast and, despite a drop in the crime rate, still growing. The total number of state and federal inmates has increased from 400,000 in 1982 to more than 1,300,000 in 2003. To accommodate these inmates, more than 650 new federal and state institutions were opened during this period. The number of local jail inmates also tripled, from approximately 200,000 in 1982 to more than 600,000 in 2003. The number of adults serving community sentences increased from more than 1.3 million to about 4 million persons. And the number of corrections employees more than doubled from nearly 300,000 to more than 716,000 during this period.[3]

History of Correctional Institutions

The original legal punishments were typically banishment or slavery, restitution, corporal punishment, and execution. The concept of incarcerating convicted offenders for long periods of time as a punishment for their misdeeds did not become the norm of corrections until the nineteenth century.[4]

Although the use of incarceration as a routine punishment began much later, some early European institutions were created specifically to detain and punish criminal offenders. Penal institutions were constructed in England during the tenth century to hold pretrial detainees and those waiting for their sentence to be carried out.[5] During the twelfth century, King Henry II of England constructed a series of county jails to hold thieves and vagrants prior to the disposition of their sentence. In 1557, the workhouse in Brideswell, England, was built to hold people convicted of relatively minor offenses who would work to pay off their debt to society. Those committing more serious offenses were held there pending execution.

Le Stinche, a prison in Florence, Italy, was used to punish offenders as early as 1301.[6] Prisoners were enclosed in separate cells, classified on the basis of gender, age, mental state, and crime seriousness. Furloughs and conditional release were permitted, and perhaps for the first time, a period of incarceration replaced corporal punishment for some offenses. Although Le Stinche existed for 500 years, relatively little is known about its administration or whether this early example of incarceration was unique to Florence.

The first penal institutions were foul places devoid of proper care, food, or medical treatment. The jailer, usually a **shire reeve** (sheriff) — an official appointed by king or noble landholder as chief law enforcement official of a county — ran the jail under a fee system, whereby inmates were required to pay for their own food and services. Those who could not pay were fed scraps until they starved to death.

> In 1748 the admission to Southwark prison was eleven shillings and four pence. Having got in, the prisoner had to pay for having himself put in irons, for his bed, of whatever sort, for his room if he was able to afford a separate room. He had to pay for his food, and when he had paid his debts and was ready to go out, he had to pay for having his irons struck off, and a discharge fee. . . . The gaolers [jailers] were usually "low bred, mercenary and oppressive, barbarous fellows, who think of nothing but enriching themselves by the most cruel extortion, and have less regard for the life of a poor prisoner than for the life of a brute."[7]

Jail conditions were deplorable because jailers ran them for personal gain. The fewer the services provided, the greater their profit. Early jails were catchall institutions that held not only criminal offenders awaiting trial but also vagabonds, debtors, the mentally ill, and assorted others.

From 1776 to 1785, a growing inmate population that could no longer be transported to North America forced the English to house prisoners on **hulks,** abandoned ships anchored in harbors. The hulks became infamous for their degrading conditions and brutal punishments but were not abandoned until 1858. The writings of John Howard, the reform-oriented sheriff of Bedfordshire, drew attention to the squalid conditions in British penal institutions. His famous book, *The State of the Prisons* (1777), condemned the lack of basic care given English inmates awaiting trial or serving sentences.[8] Howard's efforts to create humane standards in the British penal system resulted in the Penitentiary Act, by which Parliament established a more orderly penal system, with periodic inspections, elimination of the fee system, and greater consideration for inmates.

The Origin of Corrections in the United States

Although Europe had jails and a variety of other penal facilities, correctional reform was first instituted in the United States. The first American jail was built in James City in the Virginia colony in the early seventeenth century. However, the modern American correctional system had its origin in Pennsylvania under the leadership of William Penn.

At the end of the seventeenth century, Penn revised Pennsylvania's criminal code to forbid torture and the capricious use of mutilation and physical punishment. These penalties were replaced with imprisonment at hard labor, moderate flogging, fines, and forfeiture of property. All lands and goods belonging to felons were to be used to make restitution to the victims of their crimes, with restitution being limited to twice the value of the damages. Felons who owned no property were assigned by law to the prison workhouse until the victim was compensated.

shire reeve
In early England, the chief law enforcement official in a county, forerunner of today's sheriff.

hulk
Mothballed ship used to house prisoners in eighteenth-century England.

Penn ordered that a new type of institution be built to replace the widely used public forms of punishment — stocks, pillories, gallows, and branding irons. Each county was instructed to build a house of corrections similar to today's jails. County trustees or commissioners were responsible for raising money to build the jails and providing for their maintenance, although they were operated by the local sheriff. Penn's reforms remained in effect until his death in 1718, when the criminal penal code was changed back to open public punishment and harsh brutality.

Identifying the first American prison is difficult. Alexis Durham has described the opening of the Newgate Prison of Connecticut in 1773 on the site of an abandoned copper mine. However, Newgate, which closed in the 1820s, is often ignored by correctional historians.[9] In 1785, Castle Island prison was opened in Massachusetts and operated for about 15 years.

The Pennsylvania System

The origin of the modern correctional system is usually traced to eighteenth-century developments in Pennsylvania. In 1776, postrevolutionary Pennsylvania again adopted William Penn's code, and in 1787, a group of Quakers led by Benjamin Rush formed the Philadelphia Society for Alleviating the Miseries of Public Prisons. The aim of the society was to bring some degree of humane and orderly treatment to the growing penal system. The Quakers' influence on the legislature resulted in limiting the use of the death penalty to cases involving treason, murder, rape, and arson. Their next step was to reform the institutional system so that the prison could serve as a suitable alternative to physical punishment.

The only models of custodial institutions at that time were the local county jails that Penn had established. These facilities were designed to detain offenders, to securely incarcerate convicts awaiting other punishment, or to hold offenders who were working off their crimes. The Pennsylvania jails placed men, women, and children of all ages indiscriminately in one room. Liquor was often freely sold.

Under pressure from the Quakers to improve these conditions, the Pennsylvania legislature in 1790 called for the renovation of the prison system. The ultimate result was the creation of a separate wing of Philadelphia's **Walnut Street Jail** to house convicted felons (except those sentenced to death). Prisoners were placed in solitary cells, where they remained in isolation and did not have the right to work.[10] Quarters that contained the solitary or separate cells were called the **penitentiary house,** as was already the custom in England.

The new Pennsylvania prison system took credit for a rapid decrease in the crime rate — from 131 convictions in 1789 to 45 in 1793.[11] The prison became known as a school for reform and a place for public labor. The Walnut Street Jail's equitable conditions were credited with reducing escapes to none in the first four years of its existence (except for 14 on opening day).

The Walnut Street Jail was not a total success. Overcrowding undermined the goal of solitary confinement of serious offenders, and soon more than one inmate was placed in each cell. Isolation had a terrible psychological effect on inmates, and eventually inmates were given in-cell piecework on which they worked up to eight hours a day. Despite these difficulties, similar institutions were erected in New York (Newgate in 1791) and New Jersey (Trenton in 1798).

The Auburn System

As the nineteenth century got under way, both the Pennsylvania and the New York prison systems were experiencing difficulties maintaining the ever-increasing numbers of convicted criminals. Initially, administrators dealt with the problem by increasing the use of pardons, relaxing prison discipline, and limiting supervision.

Walnut Street Jail
The birthplace of the modern prison system and of the Pennsylvania system of solitary confinement.

penitentiary house
A correctional institution for those convicted of major crimes.

tier system
A type of prison in which cells are located along corridors in multiple layers or levels.

congregate system
The prison system, originated in New York, in which inmates worked and ate together during the day and then slept in solitary cells at night.

Auburn system
Prison system, developed in New York during the nineteenth century, based on congregate (group) work during the day and separation at night.

In 1816, New York built a new prison at Auburn, hoping to alleviate some of the overcrowding at Newgate. The Auburn Prison design became known as the **tier system,** because cells were built vertically on five floors of the structure. It was also referred to as the **congregate system,** because most prisoners ate and worked in groups. In 1819, construction began on a wing of solitary cells to house unruly prisoners. Three classes of prisoners were then created. One group remained continually in solitary confinement as a result of breaches of prison discipline; the second group was allowed labor as an occasional form of recreation; and the third and largest class worked and ate together during the day and were separated only at night.

The philosophy of the **Auburn system** was crime prevention through fear of punishment and silent confinement. The worst felons were to be cut off from all contact with other prisoners, and although they were treated and fed relatively well, they had no hope of pardon to relieve their solitude or isolation. For a time, some of the worst convicts were forced to remain alone and silent during the entire day. This practice, which led to mental breakdowns, suicides, and self-mutilations, was abolished in 1823.

The combination of silence and solitude as a method of punishment was not abandoned easily. Prison officials sought to overcome the side effects of total isolation while maintaining the penitentiary system. The solution adopted at Auburn was to keep convicts in separate cells at night but allow them to work together during the day under enforced silence. Hard work and silence became the foundation of the Auburn system wherever it was adopted. Silence was the key to prison discipline. It prohibited the formulation of escape plans, it prevented plots and riots, and it allowed prisoners to contemplate their infractions.

Developing Prisons

Why did prisons develop at this time? One reason was that, during this period of enlightenment, a concerted effort was made to alleviate the harsh punishments and torture that had been the norm. The interest of religious groups, such as the Quakers, in prison reform was prompted in part by humanitarian ideals. Another factor was the economic potential of prison industry, viewed as a valuable economic asset in times of short labor supply.[12]

The concept of using harsh discipline and control to retrain the heart and soul of offenders was the subject of an important book on penal philosophy, *Discipline and Punish* (1978) by French sociologist Michel Foucault.[13] Foucault's thesis was that as societies evolve and become more complex, they create increasingly more elaborate mechanisms to discipline their recalcitrant members and make them docile enough to obey social rules. In the seventeenth and eighteenth centuries, discipline was directed toward the human body itself, through torture. However, physical punishment and torture turned some condemned men into heroes and martyrs. Prisons presented the opportunity to rearrange, not diminish, punishment — to make it more effective and regulated. In the development of the nineteenth-century prison, the object was to discipline the offender psychologically; "the expiation that once rained down on the body must be replaced by a punishment that acts in the depths of the heart."[14]

Regimentation became the standard mode of prison life. Convicts did not simply walk from place to place; instead, they went in close order and single file, each looking over the shoulder of the preceding person, faces inclined to the right, feet moving in unison. The lockstep prison shuffle was developed at Auburn and is still used in some institutions today.[15]

When discipline was breached in the Auburn system, punishment was applied in the form of a rawhide whip on the inmate's back. Immediate and effective, Auburn discipline was so successful that when 100 inmates were used to

The Eastern State Penitentiary, in Philadelphia, Pennsylvania, became the most expensive and most copied building of its time. It is estimated that more than 300 prisons worldwide are based on its wagon-wheel or radial floor plan. Some of America's most notorious criminals were held in this penitentiary's vaulted, sky-lit cells, including Al Capone. After 142 years of consecutive use, Eastern State Penitentiary was abandoned in 1971. For more information, check http://www.EasternState.com/.

build the famous Sing Sing Prison in 1825, not one dared try to escape, although they were housed in an open field with only minimal supervision.[16]

In 1818, Pennsylvania took the radical step of establishing a prison that placed each inmate in a single cell for the duration of his sentence. Classifications were abolished, because each cell was intended as a miniature prison that would prevent the inmates from contaminating one another.

The new Pennsylvania state prison, called the Western Penitentiary, had an unusual architectural design. It was built in a semicircle, with the cells positioned along its circumference. Built back to back, some cells faced the boundary wall while others faced the internal area of the circle. Its inmates were kept in solitary confinement almost constantly, being allowed out for about an hour a day for exercise. In 1829, a second, similar penitentiary using the isolate system was built in Philadelphia and was called the Eastern Penitentiary.

Supporters of the **Pennsylvania system** believed that the penitentiary was truly a place to do penance. By removing the sinner from society and allowing the prisoner a period of isolation in which to consider the evils of crime, the Pennsylvania system reflected the influence of religion and religious philosophy on corrections. Its supporters believed that solitary confinement with in-cell labor would make work so attractive that upon release the inmate would be well suited to resume a productive existence in society.

The Pennsylvania system eliminated the need for large numbers of guards or disciplinary measures. Isolated from one another, inmates could not plan escapes or collectively break rules. When discipline was a problem, however, the whip and the iron gag were used.

Many fiery debates occurred between advocates of the Pennsylvania system and adherents of the Auburn system. Those supporting the latter claimed that it was the cheapest and most productive way to reform prisoners. They criticized the Pennsylvania system as cruel and inhumane, suggesting that solitary confinement was both physically and mentally damaging. The Pennsylvania system's devotees argued that their system was quiet, efficient, humane, and well ordered and provided the ultimate correctional facility.[17] They chided the Auburn system for tempting inmates to talk by putting them together for meals and work and then punishing them when they did talk. Finally, the Auburn system was accused of becoming a breeding place for criminal associations by allowing inmates to get to know one another.

The Auburn system eventually prevailed and spread throughout the United States. Many of its features are still used today. Its innovations included congregate working conditions, the use of solitary confinement to punish unruly inmates, military regimentation, and discipline. In Auburn-like institutions, prisoners were marched from place to place. Their time was regulated by bells telling them to wake up, sleep, and work. The system was so like the military that many of its early administrators were recruited from the armed services.

Although the prison was viewed as an improvement over capital and corporal punishment, it quickly became the scene of depressed conditions. Inmates were treated harshly and routinely whipped and tortured. Prison brutality flourished in these institutions, which had originally been devised as a more humane correctional alternative. In these early penal institutions, brutal corporal punishment took place indoors where, hidden from public view, it could become even more savage (Concept Summary 15.1).[18]

Pennsylvania system
Prison system, developed in Pennsylvania during the nineteenth century, based on total isolation and individual penitence.

The Late Nineteenth Century

The prison of the late nineteenth century was remarkably similar to that of today. The congregate system was adopted in all states except Pennsylvania. Prisons were overcrowded, and the single-cell principle was often ignored. The prison, like the

Concept Summary 15.1 Early Correctional Systems

Prison	Structure	Living conditions	Activities	Discipline
Auburn system	Tiered cells	Congregate	Group work	Silence, harsh punishment
Pennsylvania system	Single cells set in semicircle	Isolated	In-cell work, Bible study	Silence, harsh punishment

police department, became the scene of political intrigue and efforts by political administrators to control the hiring of personnel and dispensing of patronage.

Prison industry developed and became the predominant theme around which institutions were organized. Some prisons used the **contract system,** in which officials sold the labor of inmates to private businesses. Sometimes the contractor supervised the inmates inside the prison itself. Under the **convict-lease system,** the state leased its prisoners to a business for a fixed annual fee and gave up supervision and control. Finally, some institutions had prisoners produce goods for the prison's own use.[19]

The development of prison industry quickly led to the abuse of inmates, who were forced to work for almost no wages, and to profiteering by dishonest administrators and business owners. During the Civil War era, prisons were major manufacturers of clothes, shoes, boots, furniture, and the like. Beginning in the 1870s, opposition by trade unions sparked restrictions on interstate commerce in prison goods.

The National Congress of Penitentiary and Reformatory Discipline, held in Cincinnati, Ohio, in 1870, heralded a new era of prison reform. Organized by penologists Enoch Wines and Theodore Dwight, the congress provided a forum for corrections experts from around the nation to call for the treatment, education, and training of inmates. Overseas another penal reform was being developed in which inmates could earn early release and serve out their sentence in the community. Called parole, it is the subject of the International Justice feature on page 477.

One of the most famous people to attend the congress, Zebulon Brockway, warden at the Elmira Reformatory in New York, advocated individualized treatment, the indeterminate sentence, and **parole.**

The reformatory program initiated by Brockway included elementary education for illiterates, designated library hours, lectures by faculty members of the local Elmira College, and a group of vocational training shops. From 1888 to 1920, Elmira administrators used military-like training to discipline the inmates and organize the institution. The military organization could be seen in every aspect of the institution: schooling, manual training, sports, supervision of inmates, and even parole decisions.[20] The cost to the state of the institution's operations was to be held to a minimum.

Although Brockway proclaimed Elmira to be an ideal reformatory, his achievements were limited. The greatest significance of his contribution was the injection of a degree of humanitarianism into the industrial prisons of that day (although accusations were made that excessive corporal punishment was used and that Brockway personally administered whippings).[21] Although many institutions were constructed across the nation and labeled reformatories based on the Elmira model, most of them continued to be industrially oriented.[22]

Prisons in the Twentieth Century

The early twentieth century was a time of contrasts in the U.S. prison system.[23] At one extreme were those who advocated reform, such as the Mutual Welfare League led by Thomas Mott Osborne. Prison reform groups proposed better treatment for inmates, an end to harsh corporal punishment, the creation of meaningful prison industries, and educational programs. Reformers argued that prisoners should not be

---

contract system (prison)
System whereby officials sold the labor of prison inmates to private businesses, for use either inside or outside the prison.

convict-lease system
Contract system in which a private business leased prisoners from the state for a fixed annual fee and assumed full responsibility for their supervision and control.

 The Oregon State Penitentiary is the oldest prison and the only maximum-security institution currently operated in Oregon. To read about its history, go to http://www.doc.state.or.us/institutions/osp/histidx.htm.

parole
The early release of a prisoner from incarceration subject to conditions set by a parole board.

 The penitentiary movement spread around the world. In Australia, between 1850 and 1860, convicts built Fremantle Prison. Convicts were brought to western Australia to help in the building of roads, bridges, port facilities, and public buildings. To read about the history of the prison and get a virtual tour, go to http://www.fremantleprison.com.au/home.htm.

The Development of Parole

international justice

Parole was a concept that developed overseas and was later brought to the United States. The term *parole* itself comes from the French word for "promise," referring to the practice of releasing captured enemy soldiers if they promised not to fight again with the threat that they would be executed if recaptured.

In the early seventeenth century, English judges began to spare the lives of offenders by banishing them to the newly formed overseas colonies. In 1617, the Privy Counsel of the British Parliament standardized this practice by passing an order granting reprieves and stays of execution to convicts willing to be transported to the colonies. Transportation was viewed as an answer to labor shortages caused by war, disease, and the opening of new commercial markets.

By 1665, transportation orders were modified to include specific conditions of employment and to provide for reconsideration of punishment if the conditions were not met — for example, if the person returned to England before the expiration of the sentence. In 1717, the British Parliament passed legislation creating the concept of *property in service*, which transferred control of prisoners to a contractor or shipmaster until the expiration of their sentences. When the prisoners arrived in the colonies, their services could be resold to the highest bidder. After sale, an offender's status changed from convict to indentured servant.

Transportation quickly became the most common sentence for theft offenders. In the American colonies, property in service had to be abandoned after the revolution. Thereafter, Australia, claimed as a British colony in 1770, became the destination for most transported felons. From 1815 to 1850, large numbers of inmates were shipped to Australia to serve as indentured servants working for plantation owners, in mines, or on sheep stations.

In England, opposition to penal servitude and the deprivations associated with transportation produced such organizations as the Society for the Improvement of Prison Discipline. This group asked the famous reformer Alexander Maconochie to investigate conditions in Australia. Maconochie condemned transportation and eventually helped end the practice. Later, when appointed director of the infamous Australian prison on Norfolk Island, Maconochie instituted reforms, such as classification and rehabilitation programs, that became models for the treatment of convicted offenders. Recalled from Australia, Maconochie returned to England, where his efforts led to the English Penal Servitude Act of 1853, which all but ended transportation and substituted imprisonment as a punishment.

Part of this act made it possible to grant a *ticket-of-leave* to those who had served a sufficient portion of their prison sentence. This form of conditional release permitted former prisoners to be at large in specified areas. The conditions of their release were written on a license that the former inmates were required to carry with them at all times. Conditions usually included sobriety, lawful behavior, and hard work. Many releasees violated these provisions, prompting criticism of the system. Eventually, prisoner aid society members helped supervise and care for releasees.

In Ireland, Sir Walter Crofton, a disciple of Maconochie's reforms, liberalized Irish prisons. He instituted a mark system in which inmates could earn their ticket-of-leave by accumulating credits for good conduct and hard work in prison. Crofton also instituted a system in which private volunteers or police agents could monitor ticket-of leave offenders in the community. Crofton's work is considered an early form of parole.

The concept of parole spread to the United States. As early as 1822, volunteers from the Philadelphia-based Society for Alleviating the Miseries of Public Prisons began to help offenders once they were released from prison. In 1851, the society appointed two agents to work with inmates discharged from Pennsylvania penal institutions. Massachusetts appointed an agent in 1845 to help released inmates obtain jobs, clothing, and transportation.

In the 1870s, using a carefully weighted screening procedure, Zebulon Brockway selected rehabilitated offenders from Elmira Reformatory for early release under the supervision of citizen volunteers known as *guardians.* The guardians met with the parolees at least once a month and submitted written reports on their progress. The parole concept spread rapidly. Ohio created the first parole agency in 1884. By 1901, as many as 20 states had created some type of parole agency. By 1927, only three states, Florida, Mississippi, and Virginia, had not established some sort of parole release. Parole had become institutionalized as the primary method of release for prison inmates, and half of all inmates released in the United States were paroled.

Critical Thinking

The new sentencing models attempt to restrict parole and early release. Does this do a disservice to offenders by restricting the rewards given to rehabilitation efforts?

InfoTrac College Edition Research

The National Parole Board of Canada is preparing to celebrate 100 years of conditional release. Read about the history of parole in Canada in Donald Evans, "One Hundred Years of Conditional Release in Canada," *Corrections Today* 61, no. 5 (August 1999): 132.

Source: William Parker, *Parole: Origins, Development, Current Practices, and Statutes* (College Park, Md.: American Correctional Association, 1972); Samuel Walker, *Popular Justice* (New York: Oxford University Press, 1980).

American Correctional Association

Elmira Reformatory, training course in drafting, 1909. Inmates stand at drafting tables as guards watch and a supervisor sits at fenced-off desk at the front of the hall. Elmira was one of the first institutions to employ education and training programs.

isolated from society and that the best elements of society — education, religion, meaningful work, self-governance — should be brought to the prison. Osborne went so far as to spend a week in New York's notorious Sing Sing Prison to learn firsthand about its conditions.

In time, some of the more rigid prison rules gave way to liberal reform. By the mid-1930s, few prisons required inmates to wear the red-and-white-striped convict suit; nondescript gray uniforms were substituted. The code of silence ended, as did the lockstep shuffle. Prisoners were allowed "the freedom of the yard" to mingle and exercise an hour or two each day.[24] Movies and radio appeared in the 1930s. Visiting policies and mail privileges were liberalized.

A more important trend was the development of specialized prisons designed to treat particular types of offenders. In New York, for example, the prisons at Clinton and Auburn were viewed as industrial facilities for hard-core inmates, Great Meadow was an agricultural center for non-dangerous offenders, and Dannemora was a facility for the criminally insane. In California, San Quentin housed inmates considered salvageable by correctional authorities, while Folsom was reserved for hard-core offenders.[25]

Perspectives on Justice

Prison reform challenged the crime control orientation of prisons. Opposed to the reformers were conservative prison administrators and state officials who believed that stern disciplinary measures were needed to control dangerous prison inmates. They continued the time-honored system of regimentation and discipline. Although the whip and the lash were eventually abolished, solitary confinement in dark, bare cells became a common penal practice.

Prison industry also evolved. Opposition by organized labor helped put an end to the convict-lease system and forced inmate labor. By 1900, a number of states had restricted the sale of prisoner-made goods on the open market. The worldwide Great Depression that began in 1929 prompted industry and union leaders to further pressure state legislators to reduce competition from prison industries. A series of ever more restrictive federal legislative initiatives led to the Sumners–Ashurst Act (1940), which made it a federal offense to transport in interstate commerce goods made in prison for private use, regardless of the laws of the state receiving the goods.[26] The restrictions imposed by the federal government helped to severely curtail prison industry for 40 years. Private entrepreneurs shunned prison investments because they were no longer profitable. The result was inmate idleness and make-work jobs.[27]

Despite some changes and reforms, the prison in the mid-twentieth century remained a destructive total institution. Although some aspects of inmate life improved, severe discipline, harsh rules, and solitary confinement were the way of life in prison.

The Modern Era

The modern era has been a period of change and turmoil in the nation's correctional system. Three trends stand out. First, between 1960 and 1980, came the prisoners' rights movement. After many years of indifference (the so-called

hands-off doctrine), state and federal courts ruled in case after case that institutionalized inmates had rights to freedom of religion and speech, medical care, procedural due process, and proper living conditions. Inmates won rights unheard of in the nineteenth and early twentieth centuries. Since 1980, however, an increasingly conservative judiciary has curtailed the growth of inmate rights.

Second, violence within the correctional system became a national concern. Well-publicized riots at New York's Attica Prison and the New Mexico State Penitentiary drew attention to the potential for death and destruction that lurks in every prison. Prison rapes and killings have become commonplace. The locus of control in many prisons shifted from the correctional staff to violent inmate gangs. In reaction, some administrators have tried to improve conditions and provide innovative programs that give inmates a voice in running the institution. Another reaction has been to tighten discipline and build new super-maximum-security prisons to control the most dangerous offenders. The problem of prison overcrowding has made attempts to improve conditions extremely difficult.

Third, the view that traditional correctional rehabilitation efforts have failed has prompted many penologists to reconsider the purpose of incarcerating criminals. Between 1960 and 1980, it was common for correctional administrators to cling to the **medical model,** which viewed inmates as sick people who were suffering from some social malady that prevented them from adjusting to society. Correctional treatment could help cure them and enable them to live productive lives once they returned to the community. In the 1970s, efforts were also made to help offenders become reintegrated into society by providing them with new career opportunities that relied on work release programs. Inmates were allowed to work outside the institution during the day and return in the evening. Some were given extended furloughs in the community. Work release became a political issue when Willie Horton, a furloughed inmate from Massachusetts, raped a young woman. Criticism of the state's "liberal" furlough program helped Vice President George Bush defeat Massachusetts governor Michael S. Dukakis for the U.S. presidency in 1988. In the aftermath of the Horton case, a number of states, including Massachusetts, restricted their furlough policies.

Prisons have come to be viewed as places for control, incapacitation, and punishment, instead of sites for rehabilitation and reform. Advocates of the no-frills or penal harm movement believe that, if prison is a punishing experience, would-be criminals will be deterred from crime and current inmates will be encouraged to go straight. Nonetheless, efforts to use correctional institutions as treatment facilities have not ended, and such innovations as the development of private industries on prison grounds have kept the rehabilitative ideal alive.

While historians sometimes find the conditions in these early prisons severe, some modern administrators have sought to copy the harsh regime in an effort to convince inmates that their institution is no country club and they better not return. This no-frills movement is the subject of the Analyzing Criminal Justice Issues feature on page 480.

hands-off doctrine
The judicial policy of not interfering in the administrative affairs of prisons.

medical model
The view that convicted offenders are victims of their environment who need care and treatment to be transformed into valuable members of society.

The Corrections Connection's mission is to provide a comprehensive and unbiased online community for professionals and businesses working in the corrections industry and to "inform, educate and assist" corrections practitioners by providing best practices, online resources, weekly news, products and services, career opportunities, access to post and review bids, partnership opportunities, innovative technologies, and educational tools. Find out more about the organization at http://www.corrections.com.

Perspectives on Justice

The alleged failure of correctional treatment coupled with constantly increasing correctional costs has prompted advocates of the nonintervention perspective to develop alternatives to incarceration, such as intensive probation supervision, house arrest, and electronic monitoring. The idea is to move as many nonviolent offenders as possible out of the correctional system by means of community-based programs. These efforts have been compromised by a growing get-tough stance in judicial and legislative sentencing policy, including mandatory minimum sentences for gun crimes and drug trafficking.

 To quiz yourself on this material, go to questions 15.1–15.11 on the Introduction to Criminal Justice 10e CD.

Penal Harm: The No-Frills Movement

analyzing criminal justice issues

According to the penal harm movement, punishment is a planned governmental act in which a law violator is harmed. While some may consider punishment for the sake of harming someone immoral, those who advocate this position find it justifiable because it is an offender who has harmed others who is suffering. Penal harm has dominated correctional thinking for the past 30 years. The incarceration rate per 100,000 citizens has doubled during this period, and sentencing reform has meant more people behind bars than ever before. Parole has been limited.

One aspect of the penal harm movement is the no-frills approach to prison whose advocates want to return to the early days of corrections when prisons were places of harsh punishment and strict confinement. Some correctional administrators believe that system may not have been as bad as reformers suggest and that prisons should still be places of punishment only. If inmate privileges and treatment programs were curtailed, they argue, then the return rate would not be so high. Who would recidivate and chance a return to a harsh penal environment without TV or sports facilities?

Inmates in some states have suffered reduced visiting hours, removal of televisions and exercise gear, and substitution of cold sandwiches for hot meals. In some jails, inmates are forced to wear stun belts while on work details. After detonation, the belts give fleeing inmates an eight-second,

50,000-volt jolt of electricity, which renders them helpless for up to 10 minutes. Developed by Stun Tech Inc., more than 1,000 belts have been sold to law enforcement and correctional agencies. Amnesty International has asked Congress to ban the belts, in part because they can be used for torture. Amnesty charges that the belts are "cruel, inhuman, and degrading."

Advocates of the no-frills movement claim to be responding to the public's desire to get tough on crime. They are tired of hearing that some prison inmates get free education, watch cable TV, or get special educational programs. Some of the efforts to restrict inmates' rights include the following.

- The Alabama Department of Corrections (DOC) introduced no-frills chain gangs in each of the state's three prisons in 1994. Inmates in the gangs do not have telephones or visitation privileges, and recreation is limited to basketball on the weekends. Chain gang members include primarily parole violators and repeat offenders, especially offenders who are former gang members. After six months of good behavior, chain gang members return to the general population and are given standard inmate privileges.
- Throughout the 1990s, the Arizona DOC, supplementing the legislature's ban on weightlifting equipment, reduced the amount of property and clothing inmates may keep in their cells, the number of

items for sale in the store, the number and types of movies and television programs inmates may watch, and the frequency of telephone calls.
- Effective January 1, 1996, the Kansas DOC introduced a formal incentive program in which incoming inmates have to earn a range of privileges, including television, handicrafts, use of outside funds, canteen expenditures, personal property, and visitation. Under a three-level system, new inmates who spend their first 120 days (Incentive Level I) without disciplinary reports and participate in educational programs or work assignments earn increased privileges (Incentive Level II). After another 120 days of similar behavior, additional privileges are made available (Incentive Level III). Inmates are reduced one level for misbehavior. Furloughs were the only privilege the DOC banned permanently for all inmates.
- Complementing the action of the state's governor, the commissioner of corrections in Wisconsin reduced the amount of personal property inmates may own, established limits on the amount of personal clothing and electronic equipment they may keep, and introduced monitoring of telephone calls.
- A number of sheriffs have eliminated privileges in their jails. Seven sheriffs in Florida have eliminated television and weightlifting; seven jails in Los Angeles County have eliminated weightlifting equipment; the Niagara County, New

Jails

The nation's jails are institutional facilities with five primary purposes: (1) they detain accused offenders who cannot make or are not eligible for bail prior to trial; (2) they hold convicted offenders awaiting sentence; (3) they serve as the principal institution of secure confinement for offenders convicted of misdemeanors; (4) they hold probationers and parolees picked up for violations and waiting for a hearing; and (5) they house felons when state prisons are overcrowded. Today, the **jail** is a multipurpose correctional institution whose other main functions are set out in Exhibit 15.1.

A number of formats are used to jail offenders. About 15,000 local jurisdictions maintain short-term police or municipal lockups that house offenders for

jail
A county correctional institution used to hold people awaiting trial or sentencing, as well as misdemeanor offenders sentenced to a term of less than one year.

York, sheriff has eliminated free coffee. The sheriff of Maricopa County (Phoenix) has eliminated "girlie" magazines, hot lunches, most hot breakfasts, and coffee and has reduced recreation time, television programming, visitation, and the number of items in the commissary.

- In 1995, the Federal Bureau of Prisons ordered — and federal legislation now requires — wardens to stop purchasing or repairing new televisions in individual cells.

Some correctional administrators are charging fees for jail services, just like in the original eighteenth-century institutions. In Massachusetts, Sheriff Thomas Hodgson, who runs Bristol county's correctional facilities, has taken out the televisions from inmates' cells. He charges for haircuts and even for medical care co-payments. "The fact that you commit a crime and had to be incarcerated doesn't alleviate your responsibility for your life after that," Hodgson said. "If you have money to buy things extra in canteen, you have money to help the tax payer help pay your way. That's how it is in the real world."

Will the no-frills movement continue? In 2003 a new bill was introduced into Congress that was aimed at restricting federal funds that might be used for inmate amenities such as TVs or musical instruments.

Federal No Frills Prisons Act of 2003.

SEC. 2. PROHIBITION ON USE OF FEDERAL FUNDS FOR CERTAIN AMENITIES AND PERSONAL COMFORTS IN THE FEDERAL PRISON SYSTEM.

No Federal funds may be used to provide any of the following amenities or personal comforts in the federal prison system:

(1) In-cell television viewing, except for prisoners who are segregated from the general prison population for their own safety.

(2) Viewing of any motion picture rated R, X, or NC-17, without regard to the medium through which the motion picture is presented.

(3) Instruction (whether live or through broadcasts), or training equipment, for boxing, wrestling, judo, karate, or any other martial art, or any bodybuilding or weightlifting equipment of any sort.

(4) Possession of any in-cell coffee pot, hot plate, or heating element.

(5) Use or possession of any electric or electronic musical instrument.

Although this bill has not yet been enacted into law, many politicians embrace the no-frills prison idea to appeal to their vengeful, conservative constituents. Wardens and prison administrators are more wary of a policy that restricts inmate activities, increases boredom, and threatens their control over inmates. One approach is to limit privileges at first but return them as rewards for good behavior. Whether the no-frills approach is a political fad or a long-term correctional policy trend remains to be seen.

Critical Thinking

Do you believe that inmates should be harmed by their prison experience to shock them into conformity? The penal harm movement is the antithesis of the rehabilitation ideal. By harming inmates and taking away privileges, are correctional administrators giving up on the prison as a place of reform?

InfoTrac College Edition Research

 The no-frills movement is not unique to the United States. To read about the Canadian counterpart, go to InfoTrac College Edition and read Brian Stewart, "Not a Country Club: Most Inmates Do Hard Time behind Twenty Rows of Razor Wire," *MacLean's,* April 9, 2001, p. 34.

Sources: *H. R. 2296: A Bill to Prohibit the Use of Federal Funds for Certain Amenities and Personal Comforts in the Federal Prison System,* 108th Cong., 1st sess., 2003; Thomas Hodgson interview transcript, http://www.greaterboston.tv/features/gb_071002_prisons.html; Peter Finn, "No-Frills Prisons and Jails: A Movement in Flux," *Federal Probation* 60 (1996): 35–49; W. Wesley Johnson, Katherine Bennett, and Timothy Flanagan, "Getting Tough on Prisoners: Results from the National Corrections Executive Survey, 1995," *Crime and Delinquency* 43 (1997): 24–41; Peter Kilborn, "Revival of Chain Gangs Takes a Twist," *New York Times,* March 11, 1997, p. A18.

no more than 48 hours before a bail hearing can be held. Thereafter, detainees are kept in the county jail. In some jurisdictions, such as Massachusetts and New Hampshire, a house of corrections holds convicted misdemeanants, and a county jail holds pretrial detainees.

Jails are typically a low-priority item in the criminal justice system. Because they are usually administered on a county level, jail services have not been sufficiently regulated and a unified national policy has not been developed to mandate what constitutes adequate jail conditions. Many jails have consequently developed into squalid, crumbling holding pens.

Jails are considered to be holding facilities for the county's undesirables, not correctional institutions that provide meaningful treatment. They may house indigents who, looking for a respite from the winter's cold, commit a minor offense; the

© 2002 AP/Wide World Photos

mentally ill who will eventually be hospitalized after a civil commitment hearing; and substance abusers who are suffering the first shocks of confinement. The jail rarely holds "professional" criminals, most of whom are able to make bail.[28] Instead, the jail holds the people considered detached from and disreputable in local society and who are frequently arrested because they are considered offensive by the local police. A recent survey in New York City found that on any given day more than 2,800 people with serious mental illness were being confined in jail, about 20 percent of the total inmate population.[29] The purpose of the jail is to manage these persons and keep them separate from the rest of society. By intruding in their lives, jailing them increased their involvement with the law.

Because of a lack of resources and budget cuts, some jails have developed into squalid, crumbling holding pens and others are extremely overcrowded. Here, an inmate in the Garfield County Jail fills out paperwork needed to get a lawyer for an upcoming court date in Enid, Oklahoma, May 7, 2002. Many Oklahoma jails, including Garfield County's, must balance shrinking jail space with an increase in inmate population.

Jail Populations

According to the most recent statistics, 665,000 offenders were confined in jail facilities, up about 20,000 from the year before.[30] Of these, about 10 percent or 70,000 are in alternative programs outside the jail facilities while another 630,000 persons were housed in local jails. About half of the jailed inmates are awaiting formal charges (arraignment), bail, or trial. The remaining half are convicted offenders who are serving time, are awaiting parole or probation revocation hearings, or have been transferred from a state prison because of overcrowding.

A national effort has been made to remove as many people from local jails as possible through the adoption of both bail reform measures and pretrial diversion. Nonetheless, jail populations have been steadily increasing between 4 and 5 percent per year, due in part to the increased use of mandatory jail sentences

Exhibit 15.1 Jail Functions and Services

- Receive individuals pending arraignment and hold them awaiting trial, conviction, or sentencing.
- Readmit probation, parole, and jail-bond violators and absconders.
- Temporarily detain juveniles pending transfer to juvenile authorities.
- Hold mentally ill persons pending their movement to appropriate health facilities.
- Hold individuals for the military, for protective custody, for contempt, and for the courts as witnesses.
- Release convicted inmates to the community on completion of sentence.
- Transfer inmates to federal, state, or other authorities.
- House inmates for federal, state, or other authorities because of crowding of their facilities.
- Relinquish custody of temporary detainees to juvenile and medical authorities.
- Sometimes operate community-based programs as alternatives to incarceration.
- Hold inmates sentenced to short terms (generally under one year).

Source: Paige Harrison and Jennifer Karberg, *Prison and Jail Inmates at Midyear 2002* (Washington, D.C.: Bureau of Justice Statistics, 2003), p. 7.

for such common crimes as drunk driving. Jail populations also respond to prison overcrowding. Correctional departments sometimes use local jails to house inmates for whom there is no room in state prisons.

Who Are Jail Inmates?

Although removing juveniles from adult jails has long been a national priority, over 50,000 youths probably are admitted to adult jails each year. As of 2002, about 7,000 persons under age 18 were housed in adult jails on a given day. Almost 90 percent of these young inmates have been convicted or are being held for trial as adults in criminal court.

Males still predominate and, as Figure 15.2 shows, still make up about 90 percent of the jail population.

On average the adult female jail population has grown 6 percent annually since 1990, while the adult male inmate population has grown about 4 percent. The female-to-male jail inmate ratio reflects developments in the crime rate; that is, female crime rates are increasing at a faster pace than male crime rates.

The majority of local jail inmates are either black or Hispanic. White non-Hispanics made up about 40 percent of the jail population; black non-Hispanics, 40 percent; Hispanics, 15 percent; other races, about 1.6 percent. Relative to their number in the U.S. population, black non-Hispanics were over five-and-a-half times more likely than white non-Hispanics, over two-and-a-half times more likely than Hispanics, and over nine times more likely than persons of other races to have been held in a local jail.

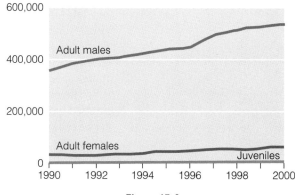

Number of jail inmates (one-day count)

Figure 15.2
Jail Population by Age and Gender, 1990–2000

Source: Bureau of Justice Statistics.

Perspectives on Justice

The racial disparity in the jail population is a red flag for those who advocate the due process perspective. If justice were fair, they maintain, this disproportionality would diminish or end.

A strong association also exists between prior physical and sexual abuse and jail inmate status. About 13 percent of males and 47 percent of female inmates report either physical or sexual abuse.[31] Not surprisingly, about 16 percent of those in local jails report having either a mental condition or an overnight stay in a mental hospital at least once in their lives.[32]

Jail Conditions

Jails are the oldest and most deteriorated institutions in the criminal justice system. Because they are usually run by the county government (and controlled by a sheriff), persuading taxpayers to support increased funding for improved facilities is difficult. In fact, jails are usually administered under the concept of custodial convenience, which involves giving inmates minimum standards of treatment and benefits while controlling the cost of jail operations. Jail employees are often underpaid, ill-trained, and lacking in professional experience.

A number of factors lead to overcrowded and ineffective jails. One is the concerted effort being made to reduce or control particular crime problems, including substance abuse, spousal abuse, and driving while intoxicated (DWI). For example, some jurisdictions have passed legislation requiring that people arrested on suspicion of domestic violence be held in confinement for a number of hours to cool off before becoming eligible for bail. Other jurisdictions have attempted to deter drunk driving by passing mandatory jail sentences for people convicted of DWI. Such legislation can quickly result in overcrowded jails.[33]

New Generation Jails

To relieve overcrowding and improve effectiveness, a jail building boom has been under way. Many of the new jails are using modern designs to improve effectiveness; these are referred to as new generation jails.[34] Traditional jails are constructed and use what is referred to as the linear or intermittent surveillance model. Jails using this design are rectangular, with corridors leading to either single- or multiple-occupancy cells arranged at right angles to the corridor. Correctional officers must patrol to see into cells or housing areas, and when they are in a position to observe one cell, they cannot observe others. Unobserved inmates are essentially unsupervised.

The new generation jails allow for continuous observation of residents. There are two types: direct and indirect supervision. Direct supervision jails contain a cluster of cells surrounding a living area or pod, which contains tables, chairs, TVs, and other material. A correctional officer is stationed within the pod. The officer has visual observation of inmates and maintains the ability to relate to them on a personal level. By being in the pod, the officer has an increased awareness of the behaviors and needs of the inmates. This results in creating a safer environment for both staff and inmates. Because interaction between inmates is constantly and closely monitored, dissension can be quickly detected before it escalates. During the day, inmates stay in the open area (dayroom) and typically are not permitted to go into their rooms except with permission of the officer in charge. The officer controls door locks to cells from the control panel. In case of trouble or if the officer leaves the station for an extended period of time, command of this panel can be switched to a panel at a remote location, known as central control. The officer usually wears a device that permits immediate communication with central control in case of trouble, and the area is also covered by a video camera monitored by an officer in the central control room. Indirect supervision jails use similar construction, but the correctional officer's station is located inside a secure room. Microphones and speakers inside the living unit permit the officer to hear and communicate with inmates. While these institutions have not yet undergone extensive evaluation, research shows that they may help reduce post-release offending in some situations.[35]

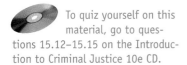

To quiz yourself on this material, go to questions 15.12–15.15 on the Introduction to Criminal Justice 10e CD.

Prisons

The Federal Bureau of Prisons and every state government maintain closed correctional facilities, also called **prisons,** penitentiaries, or reformatories.[36] It is a vast and costly system. According to the Bureau of Justice Statistics, local, state, and the federal government spend about $49 billion per year on corrections, an amount that has risen a whopping 946 percent since 1977.[37]

Types of Prisons

As of 2003, more than 1,600 public and private adult correctional facilities housed state prisoners. In addition, 84 federal facilities and 26 private facilities housed federal inmates. The number of institutions increased 14 percent since 1995.

Usually, prisons are organized or classified on three levels — maximum, medium, and minimum security — and each has distinct characteristics.

Maximum-Security Prisons Housing the most famous criminals and subject to films and stories, **maximum-security prisons** are probably the institutions most familiar to the public. Famous "max prisons" have included Sing Sing, Joliet, Attica, Walpole, and the most fearsome prison of all, the now-closed federal facility on Alcatraz Island known as The Rock.

prison
A state or federal correctional institution for the incarceration of felony offenders for terms of one year or more; penitentiary.

maximum-security prison
A correctional institution that houses dangerous felons and maintains strict security measures, including high walls, guard towers, and limited contact with the outside world.

A typical maximum-security facility is fortress-like, surrounded by stone walls with guard towers at strategic places. These walls may be 25 feet high, and sometimes inner and outer walls divide the prison into courtyards. Barbed wire or electrified fences are used to discourage escapes. High security, armed guards, and stone walls give the inmate the sense that the facility is impregnable and reassure the citizens outside that convicts will be completely incapacitated.

Inmates live in interior, metal-barred cells that contain their own plumbing and sanitary facilities and are locked securely by either key or electronic device. Cells are organized in sections called blocks, and in large prisons, a number of cell blocks make up a wing. Thus, an inmate may be officially located in, for example, Block 3 of E Wing. During the evening, each cell block is sealed off from the others, as is each wing.

© 2001 AP/Wide World Photos

In maximum-security prisons correctional staff are made aware that each inmate may be a dangerous violent criminal, and that as a result, the utmost in security must be maintained. In keeping with this philosophy, prisons are designed to eliminate hidden corners where people can congregate, and passages are constructed so they can be easily blocked off to quell disturbances.

Every inmate is assigned a number and a uniform on entering the prison system. Unlike the striped, easily identifiable uniforms of old, the maximum-security inmate today wears khaki attire not unlike military fatigues. Dress codes may be strictly enforced in some institutions, but closely cropped hair and other strict features are vestiges of the past.

During the day, the inmates engage in closely controlled activities: meals, workshops, education, and so on. Rule violators may be confined to their cells, and working and other shared recreational activities are viewed as privileges. As the Criminal Justice and Technology feature on page 486 shows, prison administrators are making use of technology to maintain security.

The byword of the maximum-security prison is security. Guards and other correctional workers are made aware that each inmate may be a dangerous criminal or violent and that, as a result, the utmost in security must be maintained. In keeping with this philosophy, prisons are designed to eliminate hidden corners where people can congregate, and passages are constructed so that they can be easily blocked off to quell disturbances. Some states have constructed **super-maximum-security prisons** (supermax prisons) to house the most predatory criminals. These high-security institutions can be independent correctional centers or locked wings of existing prisons.[38] Some supermax prisons lock inmates in their cells 22 to 24 hours a day, never allowing them out unless they are shackled.[39] The Criminal Justice and Technology feature on page 488 discusses supermax prisons.

super-maximum-security prison
A high-security prison in which inmates are kept in solitary confinement up to 23 hours per day.

Perspectives on Justice

Critics of super-maximum prisons believe that they are a direct threat to inmate due process rights because they deprive inmates of basic human rights such as human contact. They also eliminate the chance for rehabilitation.

medium-security prison
A correctional institution that houses nonviolent offenders, characterized by a less tense and vigilant atmosphere and more opportunities for contact with the outside world.

Medium-Security Prisons While **medium-security prisons** are similar in appearance to maximum-security prisons, the security and atmosphere within them are neither so tense nor so vigilant. Medium-security prisons are also surrounded by

You've Got Mail?

criminal justice and technology

Prisoners enjoy receiving mail. It gives them something to look forward to and provides a link to the outside world. However, because of security reasons, inmate mail must be processed repeatedly to check for contraband to ensure that illegal substances such as mood altering drugs are not entering the correctional facility through letters, stamps, or envelopes. The problem is serious because about 3 percent of the 2 billion drug tests conducted on inmates each year come back positive. If inmates test positive for drugs they lose privileges, including use of the telephone, television, yard, day room, commissary, weight room, library, and alternative dress, as well as receipt of packages, higher-level jobs and furloughs, and attendance at events or club meetings. Restrictions are placed on visitation, and affected inmates may be housed in segregation units or in otherwise restricted circumstances. Other sanctions for positive drug tests include accelerated sentencing in extension of parole, loss of job status, denial of a parole review for one year, extra duty and 30-day lock-up, monthly urine testing, and mandatory payment of fines.

Even mail sent by the inmates' legal representatives is suspect, become some lawyers have been willing to send drugs to their clients. Stamps, address labels, letters, and every crevice of a magazine must be inspected. With several hundred pieces of mail entering a correctional facility per day, closer to a thousand near holidays, the search process becomes very time-consuming.

Different search techniques have been implemented in prison mail centers and post offices. Some correctional facilities require that prepaid postage envelopes or metered mail be used so that drugs that are potent in small amounts, such as LSD (lysergic acid diethylamide), cannot be put on or under stamps. In other institutions, inmates are required to open all mail in front of a correctional officer.

Some institutions rely on technology to locate forbidden substances. Early efforts focused on the use of ultraviolet lights, which have the ability to locate and identify a variety of banned substances. While their use continues, ultraviolet lights have proven ineffective if an entire envelope and its contents are soaked in a drug-laden solution.

One answer to the contraband dilemma has been the development of a variety of *trace detectors* at the Sandia National Laboratories. Trace detectors can distinguish vapors emanating from chemical and biological compounds, which can include narcotics. They come in two varieties, *vapor detectors,* which are able to identify substance from trace amounts of molecules they give off into the air, and *swipe detectors,* which use a cloth-like object to swab the suspected item. The cloth is then inserted into a detector and an alarm is sounded if particles taken from the sample contain traces of the target substance. While a valuable asset, vapor detectors work best when a large amount of the target substance is available. Swipe detectors, which come in a handheld model, can be used throughout the prison.

So far trace detectors have been very effective. The systems have been credited with finding drugs in seemingly innocuous items as a child's drawings, in which drugs have been impregnated within the crayon sketches, and also under stamps and within envelopes.

Critical Thinking

While security is important, should inmates be allowed to get unopened letters from their family members and friends? Should inmates lose their right to privacy once they are incarcerated?

InfoTrac College Edition Research

Use "inmate mail" as a subject guide on InfoTrac College Edition to learn more about this topic.

Sources: "Drug Testing," *Corrections Compendium* 28 (2003): 10–23; National Law Enforcement and Corrections Technology Center, "The Check Is in the Mail," *TECH Beat* (2002): 13; National Law Enforcement and Corrections Technology Center, "You Don't Have Mail," *TECH Beat* (2003): 1–2.

walls, but there may be fewer guard towers or other security precautions. For example, visitor privileges may be more extensive, and personal contact may be allowed, whereas in a maximum-security prison visitors may be separated from inmates by Plexiglas or other barriers (to prohibit the passing of contraband). While most prisoners are housed in cells, individual honor rooms in medium-security prisons are used to reward those who make exemplary rehabilitation efforts. Finally, medium-security prisons promote greater treatment efforts, and the relaxed atmosphere allows freedom of movement for rehabilitation workers and other therapeutic personnel.

minimum-security prison
A correctional institution that houses white-collar and other non-violent offenders, characterized by few security measures and liberal furlough and visitation policies.

Minimum-Security Prisons Operating without armed guards or walls, **minimum-security prisons** usually house the most trustworthy and least violent offenders. White-collar criminals may be their most common occupants. Inmates are allowed a great deal of personal freedom. Instead of being marched to activities by guards, they are summoned by bells or loudspeaker announcements and assemble on their own. Work furloughs and educational releases are encouraged, and vocational training is of the highest level. Dress codes are lax, and inmates are allowed to grow beards or mustaches or demonstrate other individual characteristics.

Minimum-security facilities may have dormitories or small private rooms for inmates. Prisoners are allowed to own personal possessions that might be deemed dangerous in a maximum-security prison, such as radios.

Minimum-security prisons have been criticized for being like country clubs. Some federal facilities for white-collar criminals even have tennis courts and pools (they are called derisively "Club Fed"). Yet they remain prisons, and the isolation and loneliness of prison life deeply affects the inmates.

Prison Inmate Characteristics

Surveys of prison inmates indicate that, as might be expected, the personal characteristics of prison inmates reflect common traits of arrestees. Inmates tend to be young, single, poorly educated, disproportionately male, and minority group members. Many are either underemployed or unemployed prior to their arrest. Many have incomes of less than $10,000 and suffer drug abuse and other personal problems.

Gender Gender differences in the prison population are considerable. Women are underrepresented in prison, and not solely because they commit less serious crimes. The Uniform Crime Reports arrest statistics indicate that the overall male–female arrest ratio is about 3.5 male offenders to 1 female offender; for violent crimes, the ratio is closer to 6 males to 1 female. Yet, men were about 15 times more likely than women to be in a state or federal prison. As 2003 began, there were 60 sentenced female inmates per 100,000 women, compared with 906 sentenced male inmates per 100,000 men.

Race and Ethnicity Today black males (586,700) outnumber white males (436,800) and Hispanic males (235,000) among inmates with sentences of more than one year. African American inmates represented an estimated 45 percent of all inmates with sentences of more than one year, while white inmates accounted for 34 percent and Hispanic inmates, 18 percent. This ratio has remained stable since 1995.

Because of this imbalance, there were 3,437 sentenced black male prisoners per 100,000 black males in the United States, compared with 1,176 sentenced Hispanic male inmates per 100,000 Hispanic males and 450 white male inmates per 100,000 white males. An estimated 10 percent of black males, age 25–29, are in prison.

Type of Offense What did the inmates do to earn their sentence? About half of all inmates are serving time for violent crimes, and the growth in the prison population during the past decade was fueled by the increasing number of violent offenders whose numbers grew by more than 273,000. During the past decade the number of drug offenders grew by 101,400 (see Figure 15.3).

Figure 15.3
State Prison Population by Offense Type, 1980–2001

Sources: Allen Beck, *Correctional Populations in the United States, 1997* (Washington, D.C.: Bureau of Justice Statistics, 2000); Paige Harrison and Allen Beck, *Prisoners in 2002* (Washington, D.C.: Bureau of Justice Statistics, 2003).

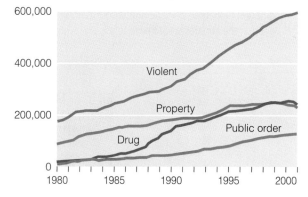

Substance Abuse A strong association exists between substance abuse and inmate status. For example, one study of 400 Texas inmates found that almost 75 percent suffered from lifetime substance abuse or dependence.[40] About 80 percent of inmates report using drugs sometime during their life, and more than 60 percent are regular users. About half of the inmates report being either drunk,

Ultramaximum-Security Prisons

criminal justice and technology

At least 42 American states operate super-maximum- or ultramaximum-security prisons or units, providing nearly 20,000 beds and accounting for 1.8 percent of the state prison population. These high-security institutions can be independent correctional centers or locked wings of existing prisons operating under such names as the secure housing unit or the maximum control unit.

The first federal maxi-prison, in Marion, Illinois, was infamous for its tight security and isolated conditions. Marion has been supplanted by a new 484-bed facility in Florence, Colorado. This new prison has the most sophisticated security measures in the United States, including 168 video cameras and 1,400 electronically controlled gates. Inside the cells, all furniture is unmovable; the desk, bed, and TV stand are made of cement. All potential weapons, including soap dishes, toilet seats, and toilet handles, have been removed. The cement walls are 5,000-pound quality, and steel bars are placed so they crisscross every eight inches inside the walls. Cells are angled so that inmates can see neither each other nor the outside scenery (see Figure 15.A). This cuts down on communications and denies inmates a sense of location, to prevent escapes.

Getting out of the prison seems impossible. Six guard towers are situated at different heights to prevent air attacks. To get out, the inmates would have to pass through seven three-inch-thick steel doors, each of which can be opened only after the previous one has closed. If a guard tower is ever seized, all controls are switched to the next station. If the whole prison is seized, it can be controlled from the outside. The only way out appears to be via good works and behavior, through which an inmate can earn transfer to another prison within three years.

Threat of transfer to a maxi-maxi institution is used to deter inmate misbehavior in less restrictive institutions. Civil rights watchdog groups charge that these maxi-maxi prisons violate the United Nations standards for the treatment of inmates. They are typically located in rural areas, which makes staffing difficult in the professional areas of dentistry, medicine, and counseling. Senior officers prefer not working in these institutions, leaving the most difficult inmates in the hands of the most inexperienced correctional officers.

A recent survey by Leena Kurki and Norval Morris found that, although conditions vary from state to state, many supermax prisons subject inmates to nearly complete isolation and deprivation of sensory stimuli. While the long-term effects of such conditions on inmates is still uncertain, they believe it likely to have an extremely harmful effect, especially on those who suffer from preexisting mental illness or those with subnormal intelligence.

The development of the ultramax prison represents a shift from previous correc-tional policy, which favored dispersing the most troublesome inmates to different prisons to prevent them from joining forces or planning escapes. The supermax model finds that housing the most dangerous inmates in an ultrasecure facility eases their control while reducing violence levels in the general prison population. Kurki and Morris, however, argue that, while the supermax prison is considered the ultimate control mechanism for disruptive inmates, individuals are less to blame for prison violence and disruption than the dysfunctional prison regimes and misguided prison administrators, which make prisons the violent institutions they are.

Critical Thinking

Ultramaximum-security prisons are reminiscent of the old Pennsylvania system, which made use of solitary confinement and high security. Is this inhumane in this more enlightened age? Why or why not?

InfoTrac College Edition Research

To read about the conditions in the new super-maximum-security prisons, go to InfoTrac College Edition and read "Cruel and Unusual Punishment," *Harper's Magazine,* July 2001, p. 92.

Source: Leena Kurki and Norval Morris, "The Purpose, Practives, and Problems of Supermax Prisons," in *Crime and Justice:*

high, or both when they committed the crime that landed them in prison. Considering this background, it should come as no surprise that more inmates die from HIV-related disease than from prison violence.[41]

Physical Abuse Like jail inmates, prison inmates also report a long history of physical abuse and mental health problems. About 19 percent report some form of physical abuse, including 57 percent of female offenders.[42] In addition, about 16 percent of state prison inmates report having some form of mental problems.[43] Mentally ill inmates are more likely to be arrested for violent offenses and to have suffered a variety of personal and emotional problems than the general inmate population. The picture that emerges is that

An Annual Edition, ed. Michael Tonry (Chicago: University of Chicago Press, 2001), pp. 385–422; Richard H. Franklin, "Assessing Supermax Operations," *Corrections Today* 60 (1998): 126–28; Chase Riveland, *Supermax Prison: Overview and General Considerations* (Longmont, Colo.: National Institute of Corrections, 1998); Federal Bureau of Prisons, *State of the Bureau, 1995* (Washington, D.C.: Government Printing Office, 1996); Dennis Cauchon, "The Alcatraz of the Rockies," *USA Today,* November 16, 1994, p. 6A.

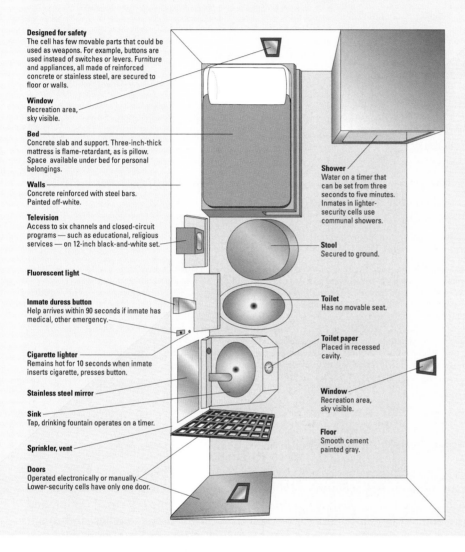

Designed for safety
The cell has few movable parts that could be used as weapons. For example, buttons are used instead of switches or levers. Furniture and appliances, all made of reinforced concrete or stainless steel, are secured to floor or walls.

Window
Recreation area, sky visible.

Bed
Concrete slab and support. Three-inch-thick mattress is flame-retardant, as is pillow. Space available under bed for personal belongings.

Walls
Concrete reinforced with steel bars. Painted off-white.

Television
Access to six channels and closed-circuit programs — such as educational, religious services — on 12-inch black-and-white set.

Fluorescent light

Inmate duress button
Help arrives within 90 seconds if inmate has medical, other emergency.

Cigarette lighter
Remains hot for 10 seconds when inmate inserts cigarette, presses button.

Stainless steel mirror

Sink
Tap, drinking fountain operates on a timer.

Sprinkler, vent

Doors
Operated electronically or manually. Lower-security cells have only one door.

Shower
Water on a timer that can be set from three seconds to five minutes. Inmates in lighter-security cells use communal showers.

Stool
Secured to ground.

Toilet
Has no movable seat.

Toilet paper
Placed in recessed cavity.

Window
Recreation area, sky visible.

Floor
Smooth cement painted gray.

Figure A
Typical Cell in a Super-Maximum Security Prison

Some of the toughest felons in the federal prison system are held in a new penitentiary in Florence, Colorado. It is designed to be the most secure ever built by the government. Many inmates live in isolation, except for an hour a day of recreation. A high-security cell in the 575-bed facility has these features.

Source: Louis Winn, United States Penitentiary, Administrative Maximum, Florence, Colorado.

prisons hold those people who face the toughest social obstacles in society. Only a few members of the educated middle-class wind up behind bars, and these people are usually held in low-security, country club institutions (see Table 15.1).

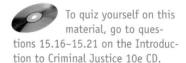

To quiz yourself on this material, go to questions 15.16–15.21 on the Introduction to Criminal Justice 10e CD.

Alternative Correctional Institutions

In addition to prison and jails, a number of other correctional institutions are operating around the United States. Some have been in use for some time, whereas others have been developed as part of an innovative or experimental program.

Table 15.1   Prior Abuse of Correctional Populations, by Sex

| | | Percent experiencing abuse before sentence | | | |
| | | Ever | | Before 18 | |
Correctional population	Total	Male	Female	Male	Female
Ever abused before admission					
State prison inmates	18.7	16.1	57.2	14.4	36.7
Federal prison inmates	9.5	7.2	39.9	5.0	23.0
Jail inmates	16.4	12.9	47.6	11.9	36.6
Probationers	15.7	9.3	40.4	8.8	28.2
Physically abused					
State prison inmates	15.4	13.4	46.5	11.9	25.4
Federal prison inmate	7.9	6.0	32.3	5.0	14.7
Jail inmates	13.3	10.7	37.3	—	—
Probationers	12.8	7.4	33.5	—	—
Sexually abuse					
State prison inmates	7.9	5.8	39.0	5.0	25.5
Federal prison inmate	3.7	2.2	22.8	1.9	14.5
Jail inmates	8.8	5.6	37.2	—	—
Probationers	8.4	4.1	25.2	—	—

Note: — = Not available. A third of women in state prison, a sixth in federal prison, and a quarter in jail said they had been raped before their sentence. Another 3 percent to 6 percent reported that someone had tried unsuccessfully to rape them. More than half of the abused women said they were hurt by spouses or boyfriends, and less than a third, by parents or guardians. More than half of the abused men in correctional populations identified parents or guardians as abusers. Among state prison inmates, 1 in 20 men and 1 in 4 women said they had been sexually abused before age 18; 1 in 10 men and 1 in 4 women, physically abused. Among state prisoners reporting prior abuse, 89 percent had used illegal drugs; 76 percent of the men and 89 percent of the women had used them regularly. Of those not reporting prior abuse, 82 percent had used illegal drugs; 68 percent of the men and 65 percent of the women had used them regularly.

Source: Caroline Wolf Harlow, *Prior Abuse Reported by Inmates and Probationers* (Washington, D.C.: Bureau of Justice Statistics, 1999), p. 2.

Prison Farms and Camps

Prison farms and camps are used to detain offenders. These types of facilities are found primarily in the South and the West and have been in operation since the nineteenth century. Today, about 40 farms, 40 forest camps, 80 road camps, and more than 60 similar facilities (vocational training centers, ranches, and so on) exist in the nation. Prisoners on farms produce dairy products, grain, and vegetable crops that are used in the state correctional system and other governmental facilities, such as hospitals and schools. Forestry camp inmates maintain state parks, fight forest fires, and do reforestation work. Ranches, primarily a western phenomenon, employ inmates in cattle raising and horse breeding, among other activities. Road gangs repair roads and state highways.

Shock Incarceration in Boot Camps

shock incarceration
A short prison sentence served under military discipline at a boot camp facility.

boot camp
A short-term militaristic correctional facility in which inmates, usually young first-time offenders, undergo intensive physical conditioning and discipline.

A recent approach to correctional care that is gaining popularity around the United States is **shock incarceration** in **boot camps.** Such programs typically include youthful, first-time offenders and feature military discipline and physical training (Figure 15.4). The concept is that short periods (90 to 180 days) of high-intensity exercise and work will shock the inmate into going straight. Tough physical training is designed to promote responsibility and improve decision-making

Boot camps use strict discipline regimes, which some critics find demeaning to inmates. Here at the Prison Boot Camp in Illinois, one correctional officer bangs the metal waste basket against the cement floor. Two officers yell at the new inmate, demanding that he hurry and gather his newly-cut hair into the basket. They hurl a barrage of non-profane insults at him. Profanity by correctional officers as well as inmates is forbidden at the boot camp.

skills, build self-confidence, and teach socialization skills. Inmates are treated with rough intensity by drillmasters who may call them names and punish the entire group for the failure of one of its members. Discipline is so severe that some critics warn that it can amount to "cruel and unusual punishment" and generate costly inmate lawsuits.[44]

Wide variation is found in the more than 75 programs operating around the United States.[45] Some programs include educational and training components, counseling sessions, and treatment for special-needs populations, whereas others devote little or no time to therapeutic activities. Some receive program participants directly from court sentencing, whereas others choose potential candidates from the general inmate population. Some allow voluntary participation and others voluntary termination.[46]

Shock incarceration programs can provide some important correctional benefits. New York houses inmates in these programs in separate institutions and provides most, but not all, graduates with extensive follow-up supervision. Although recidivism rates for these programs in New York are similar to those of traditional prisons, indications are that both inmates and staff view shock incarceration as a positive experience.[47] It is estimated that the New York program has saved taxpayers hundreds of millions of dollars because boot camps are cheaper to build and maintain than traditional prisons. Other evaluations have found that a boot camp experience can improve inmates' attitudes and have the potential for enhancing their postcorrection lifestyle.[48]

Shock incarceration has the advantage of being a lower-cost alternative to overcrowded prisons because inmates are held in non-secure facilities and sentences are short. Both staff and inmates seem excited by the programs, and even those who fail on parole report that they felt the shock incarceration was a valuable experience.[49] If shock incarceration is viewed as an exciting or helpful experience by its graduates, however, they could be encouraged to recidivate, given that the threat of the prison experience has been weakened.

Evaluating Shock Incarceration Is shock incarceration a correctional panacea or another fad doomed to failure? The results so far are mixed. The costs of boot camps are no lower than those of traditional prisons, but because sentences are

Figure 15.4
Shock Incarceration

Typical daily routines and schedule in a boot camp program.

Source: Cherie Clark, David Aziz, and Doris Mackenzie, *Shock Incarceration in New York: Focus on Treatment* (Washington, D.C.: National Institute of Justice, 1994), p. 5.

Rita finishes 50 sit-ups and springs to her feet. At 6 a.m. her platoon begins a five-mile run, the last portion of this morning's physical training. After five months in New York's Lakeview Shock Incarceration Correctional Facility, the morning workout is easy. Rita even enjoys it, taking pride in her physical conditioning.

When Rita graduates and returns to New York City, she will face six months of intensive supervision before moving to regular parole. More than two-fifths of Rita's platoon did not make it this far. Some withdrew voluntarily, and the rest were removed for misconduct or failure to participate satisfactorily. By completing shock incarceration, she will enter parole 11 months before her minimum release date.

The requirements for completing shock incarceration are the same for male and female inmates. The women live in a separate housing area of Lakeview. Otherwise, men and women participate in the same education, physical training, drill and ceremony, drug education, and counseling programs. Men and women are assigned to separate work details and attend network group meetings held in inmates' living units.

Daily schedule

A.M.

5:30	Wake up and standing count
5:45-6:30	Calisthenics and drill
6:30-7:00	Run
7:00-8:00	Mandatory breakfast and cleanup
8:15	Standing count and company formation
8:30-11:55	Work/school schedules

P.M.

12:00-12:30	Mandatory lunch and standing count
12:30-3:30	Afternoon work and school schedule
3:30-4:00	Shower
4:00-4:45	Network community meeting
4:45-5:45	Mandatory dinner, prepare for evening
6:00-9:00	School, group counseling, drug counseling, prerelease counseling, decision-making classes
9:00	Count while in programs
9:15-9:30	Squad bay, prepare for bed
9:30	Standing count, lights out

shorter they do provide long-term savings. Some programs suffer high failure-to-complete rates, which makes program evaluations difficult (even if graduates are successful, success could be achieved because troublesome cases drop out and are placed back in the general inmate population). What evaluations exist indicate that the recidivism rates of inmates who attend shock programs are in some cases no lower than for those released from traditional correctional experiences.[50]

Many of these evaluations have been conducted by Doris Layton Mackenzie and her associates. One study with James Shaw found that, although boot camp inmates may have lower recidivism rates than probationers and parolees, they have higher rates of technical violations and revocations.[51] Even though these results are disappointing, Mackenzie reports that both staff and inmates seem excited by the programs, and even those who fail on parole report that they felt boot camp was a valuable experience.[52] She also found, with Alex Piquero, that carefully managed boot camp programs can make a major dent in prison overcrowding.[53]

Extensive evaluations of the boot camp experience generate little evidence that they can significantly lower recidivism rates. Programs that seem to work best, such as those in New York, stress treatment and therapeutic activities, are voluntary, and are longer in duration.[54]

Community Correctional Facilities

One of the goals of correctional treatment is to help reintegrate the offender into society. Placing offenders in a prison makes them more likely to adopt an inmate lifestyle than to reassimilate conventional social norms. As a result, the **community treatment** concept began to take off in the 1960s. State and federal correctional systems created community-based correctional models as an alternative to closed institutions. Many are **halfway houses** to which inmates are transferred just before their release into the community. These facilities are designed to bridge the gap between institutional living and the community. Specialized treatment may be offered, and the residents use the experience to cushion the shock of reentering society.

Commitment to a community correctional center may also be used as an intermediate sanction and sole mode of treatment. An offender may be assigned to a community treatment center operated by the state department of corrections or to probation. Or the corrections department can contract with a private community center. This practice is common in the treatment of drug addicts and other nonviolent offenders whose special needs can be met in a self-contained community setting that specializes in specific types of treatment.

Halfway houses and community correctional centers can look like residential homes and, in many instances, were originally residences. In urban centers, older apartment buildings can be adapted for the purpose. Usually, these facilities have a central treatment theme — such as group therapy or reality therapy — that is used to rehabilitate and reintegrate clients.

Another popular approach in community-based corrections is the use of ex-offenders as staff members. These individuals have made the transition from the closed institution to living in society and can be invaluable in helping residents overcome the many hurdles they face in proper readjustment.

Despite the encouraging philosophical concept presented by the halfway house, evaluation of specific programs has not led to a definite endorsement of this type of treatment.[55] One significant problem has been a lack of support from community residents, who fear the establishment of an institution housing what they perceive as dangerous offenders in their neighborhood. Court actions and zoning restrictions have been brought in some areas to foil efforts to create halfway houses.[56] As a result, many halfway houses are located in decrepit neighborhoods in the worst areas of town — certainly a condition that must influence the attitudes and behavior of the inmates. Furthermore, the climate of control exercised in most halfway houses, where rule violation can be met with a quick return to the institution, may not be one that the average inmate can distinguish from his former high-security penal institution.

Despite these problems, the promise held by community correctional centers, coupled with their low cost of operations, has led to their continued use into the new millennium.

Private Prisons

On January 6, 1986, the U.S. Corrections Corporation opened the first private state prison in Marion, Kentucky — a 300-bed minimum-security facility for inmates who are within three years of parole.[57] Today, more than 264 privately operated facilities were under contract with state or federal authorities to house prisoners, an increase of 140 percent since 1995. The number of inmates held in these facilities rose 459 percent, from 16,663 inmates in June 1995 to 93,077 in June 2000.[58]

There are a number of different models of private correctional facilities. In some instances, a private corporation will finance and build an institution and

community treatment
Correctional treatment services located within the community such as the halfway house.

halfway house
A community-based correctional facility that houses inmates before their outright release so that they can become gradually acclimated to conventional society.

Private prisons are being used abroad. Read about a private women's prison in Australia by going to Amanda George, "Tales of a Private Women's Prison: Writ in Women's Lives," *Hecate* 28, no. 1 (May 2002): 145, on InfoTrac College Edition.

recidivism
Repetition of criminal behavior; habitual criminality.

then contract with correctional authorities to provide services for convicted criminals. Sometimes the private concern will finance and build the institution and then lease it outright to the government. This model has the advantage of allowing the government to circumvent the usually difficult process of getting voters to approve a bond issue and raising funds for prison construction. Another common method of private involvement is with specific service contracts; for example, a private concern might be hired to manage the prison health care system, food services, or staff training.

A recent review of private prisons by Richard Harding finds that they now play an important correctional role in United States, Australia, and the United Kingdom. Harding finds clear evidence not only that the development of private prisons has stimulated improvement in the correctional system but also that private prisons can experience the same failures and problems as public institutions.[59]

Can Private Prisons Work? Some evaluations of **recidivism** among inmates released from private and public facilities find that recidivism rates are lower among the private prison group than the state prison inmates.[60] Inmates released from private prisons who reoffend commit less serious crimes than those released from public institutions. These findings help support the concept of the private correctional institution. Nonetheless, some experts question reliance on private prisons, believing that their use raises a number of vexing problems. For example, will private providers be able to effectively evaluate programs, knowing that a negative evaluation might cause them to lose their contract? Will they skimp on services and programs to reduce costs? Might they not skim off the easy cases and leave the hard-core inmate to the state's care? And will the need to keep business booming require widening the net to fill empty cells? Must they maintain state-mandated liability insurance to cover inmate claims?[61] So far, private and state institutions cost about the same to operate.[62]

Private corrections firms also run into opposition from existing state correctional staff and management who fear the loss of jobs and autonomy. Moreover, the public may be skeptical about an untested private concern's ability to provide security and protection. Private corrections also face administrative problems. How will program quality be controlled? To compete on price, a private facility may have to cut corners to beat out the competition. Determining accountability for problems and mishaps will be difficult when dealing with a corporation that is a legal fiction and protects its officers from personal responsibility for their actions.

Legal Issues Unresolved legal problems also can emerge quickly: Can privately employed guards patrol the perimeter and use deadly force to stop escape attempts? Do private correctional officers have less immunity from lawsuits than state employees? The case of *Correctional Services Corp.* v. *Malesko* (2001) helps define the rights and protections of inmates in private correctional facilities. John Malesko had a heart condition but was forced to walk the stairs instead of being allowed to take an elevator. When he suffered a heart attack, he sued the Correctional Services Corp., which was operating the prison. He alleged that, under the Federal Civil Rights Act, the denial of proper medial care violated his civil rights. Citizens are generally allowed to seek damages against federal agents who violate their civil rights. However, the U.S. Supreme Court ruled that, although Malesko could sue an individual employee of the private correctional corporation for allegedly violating his or her constitutional rights, he may not sue the correctional corporation itself. This decision shields the private prison corporation from suits brought under federal civil rights statutes. The *Malesko* decision upholds the concerns of some critics who view the private prison as an insidious expansion of state control over citizens: a state-supported entity that has more freedom to exert control than the state itself.[63]

In the abstract, a private correctional enterprise may be an attractive alternative to a costly correctional system, but these legal, administrative, and cost

Use "prison management companies" as a subject guide on InfoTrac College Edition.

issues need to be resolved before private prisons can become widespread.[64] A balance must be reached between the need for a private business to make a profit and the integrity of a prison administration that must be concerned with such complex issues as security, rehabilitation, and dealing with highly dangerous people in a closed environment.[65]

 To quiz yourself on this material, go to questions 15.22–15.25 on the Introduction to Criminal Justice 10e CD.

Correctional Populations

The nation's vast system of penal institutions holds about 2,033,331 prisoners in federal or state prisons or in local jails, an increase of 3.7 percent from 2001. There are now an estimated 476 prison inmates per 100,000 U.S. residents, up from 411 at year-end 1995.

The U.S. prison population has had a number of cycles of growth and decline.[66] Between 1925 and 1939, it increased about 5 percent a year, reflecting the nation's concern for the lawlessness of that time. The incarceration rate reached a high of 137 per 100,000 U.S. population in 1939. During World War II, the prison population declined by 50,000, as potential offenders were drafted into the armed services. By 1956, the incarceration rate had dropped to 99 per 100,000 U.S. population.

The late 1950s saw a steady increase in the prison population until 1961, when 220,000 people were in custody, a rate of 119 per 100,000. From 1961 to 1968, with the escalation of the Vietnam War, the prison population declined by about 30,000. The incarceration rate remained fairly stable until 1974, when the current dramatic rise began. Between 1995 and 2003, the number of state and federal prisoners grew 24 percent, reaching more than 1,300,000 in 2003.

The most recent data indicate, however, that the prison population finally began to stabilize and then to decline in the latter half 2002 (Figure 15.5).

Whether this is a short-term correction or long-term trend remains to be seen.[67]

Number of offenders per 100,000 population

Figure 15.5
Incarceration Rate, 1980–2002

Source: Allen Beck, *Correctional Populations in the United States, 1997* (Washington, D.C.: Bureau of Justice Statistics, 2000); Paige Harnison and Allen Beck, *Prisoners in 2002* (Washington, D.C.: Bureau of Justice Statistics, 2003).

Going to Prison during Your Lifetime

The prison boom means that a significant portion of American citizens will one day be behind bars. Today, more than 5.6 million adult U.S. residents were serving time or had previously served time in a state or federal prison.[68] This means that 1 in 37 adults living in the United States on December 31, 2001, had been confined in prison at some time during his or her life. Between growth in the population and increases in life expectancy, the number of current or former inmates increased by 3.8 million men and women between 1974 and 2002.

Significant racial differences exist in the likelihood of going to prison. About 16.6 percent of adult black males were current or former inmates, compared with 7.7 percent of Hispanic males and 2.6 percent of white males. Among black males 35 to 44 years of age, 22 percent were current or former prisoners, compared with 10 percent of Hispanic males and 3.5 percent of white males in the same age group. The lifetime chances of going to prison were six times higher for men (11.3 percent) than women (1.8 percent). If the current rates of incarceration were to continue indefinitely, a black male in the United States would have about a 1 in 3 chance of going to prison during his lifetime; a Hispanic male, a 1 in 6 chance; and a white male, a 1 in 17 chance. Making the same assumptions, black females (5.6 percent) would be almost as likely to go to prison as white males (5.9 percent). Hispanic females (2.2 percent) and white females (0.9 percent) would have much lower lifetime chances of imprisonment.

Prison populations are also rising abroad. Read about recent developments in Holland, at Kees Boeij, "Developments in the Netherlands Penitentiary System," *Corrections Today* 64, no. 1 (February 2002): 50.

Many prisons have experienced overcrowded conditions. Administrators at the Deuel Vocational Institute in California were forced to turn a gym into inmate housing in order to accommodate the influx of new inmates. It is likely that a declining crime rate will one day reduce overcrowding.

© 2003 AP/Wide World Photos

Explaining Prison Population Trends

Why did the prison population grow so rapidly over the past decade despite the fact that the crime rate fell? One reason may be politicians responding to the general public's more punitive response to criminal offenders, creating the penal harm movement. Public concern about drugs and violent crime has not been lost on state lawmakers. Mandatory sentencing laws, which have been implemented by a majority of states and the federal government, increase eligibility for incarceration and limit the availability for early release via parole.

Although probation and community sentences still predominate, structural changes in criminal codes and crime rates also have helped produce an expanding correctional population. The amount of time served in prison has increased because of such developments as truth-in-sentencing laws that require inmates to serve at least 85 percent of their sentence behind bars.[69] The conviction rate is increasing for crimes that are traditionally punished with a prison sentence, such as robbery and burglary. In addition, get-tough policies have helped curtail the use of parole and have reduced judicial discretion to impose non-incarceration sentences.[70] Some states have implemented laws mandating that violent juveniles be waived or transferred to the adult court for treatment.[71] Thousands of juveniles are being tried as adults each year and may end up in adult prisons.

Also swelling the prison population is an increasing number of ex-inmates who have failed on community release. Today about one-third of new admissions to prison were parole or other conditional release violators, up from 29 percent in 1990.

The slowing of the prison population increase, which began in 2002, may signal that the declining crime rate has overcome harsh sentencing policies. As costs skyrocket, some states are spending more on prisons than on higher education. The public may begin to question the wisdom of a strict incarceration policy. There may also be fewer criminals to incarcerate. The waning of the crack cocaine epidemic in large cities may hasten this decline because street crimes will decline and fewer offenders will be eligible for the long penalties associated with the possession of crack.[72] In the final analysis, change in the correctional population may depend on the faith judges and legislators place in incarceration as a crime control policy. As long as policy makers believe that incarcerating predatory criminals can bring down crime rates, the likelihood of a significant decrease in the institutional population seems remote. If little evidence exists that this costly system lowers crime rates, less costly and equally effective alternatives may be sought.

Summary

- Today's correctional institutions can trace their development from European origins.
- Punishment methods developed in Europe were modified and improved by American colonists, most notably William Penn. He replaced the whip and other methods of physical punishment with confinement in county institutions or penitentiaries.
- Later, as needs grew, the newly formed states created their own large facilities. Discipline was harsh within them, and most enforced a code of silence.
- New York developed the system of congregate working conditions during the day and isolation at night at Auburn Prison.
- Pennsylvania adopted an isolate system that required inmates be locked into their cells for the duration of their sentence. While secure, it drove many inmates mad.
- The congregate system, developed in New York, has been adopted by the present U.S. penal system.
- Correctional rehabilitation programs began to develop in the late nineteenth century.
- Parole developed abroad but was imported to the United States and became the predominant type of prison release.
- A number of correctional reforms have been instituted over the centuries, including the development of specialized prisons.
- A number of institutions currently house convicted offenders. Jails are used for misdemeanants and minor felons. Because conditions are so poor in jails, they have become a major trouble spot for the criminal justice system. New generation jails have improved security and reduced violence.
- Federal and state prisons — classified as minimum, medium, and maximum security — house most of the nation's incarcerated felons.
- The poor track record of prisons has spurred the development of new correctional models, specifically the boot camp, the halfway house, and the community correctional center.
- The success of these institutions has been challenged by research efforts indicating that their recidivism rates are equal to those of state prisons. One newer development has been the correctional institution operated by private companies, which receive a fee for their services. There are more than 240 of these institutions around the nation.
- The prison population has skyrocketed in the past few years, but recent data indicate that the boom may be leveling off.
- A significant percentage of the American public will serve a prison sentence during their lifetime. Significant racial discrepancies exist in the likelihood of going to prison.

Key Terms

shire reeve 472
hulk 472
Walnut Street Jail 473
penitentiary house 473
tier system 474
congregate system 474
Auburn system 474
Pennsylvania system 475

contract system 476
convict-lease system 476
parole 476
hands-off doctrine 479
medical model 479
jail 480
prison 484
maximum-security prison 484

super-maximum-security prison 485
medium-security prison 485
minimum-security prison 486
shock incarceration 490
boot camp 490
community treatment 493
halfway house 493
recidivism 494

Doing Research on the Web

For an up-to-date list of Web links, go to http://cj.wadsworth.com/siegel_intro10e.

Is it possible for prison authorities to introduce policies that have an impact on crime rates? While some experts may remain skeptical, authorities in Oklahoma believe they have found the answer. To discover their blueprint for success, read, on InfoTrac College Edition, Frank Keating, "The Oklahoma Turnaround: How One State Rethought Prison Policies — and Reduced Crime," *Corrections Today* 64, no. 5 (August 2002): 96.

For another view, go to this Sentencing Project site: http://www.sentencingproject.org/pdfs/9039smy.pdf. And this one from the National Institute of Justice: http://www.ncjrs.org/rr/vol2_3/11.html.

Pro/Con discussions and Viewpoint Essays on some of the topics in this chapter may be found at the Opposing Viewpoints Resource Center: http://www.gale.com/OpposingViewpoints.

Discussion Questions

1. Would you allow a community correctional center to be built in your neighborhood? Why or why not?
2. Should pretrial detainees and convicted offenders be kept in the same institution? Explain.
3. What can be done to reduce correctional overcrowding?
4. Should private companies be allowed to run correctional institutions? Why or why not?
5. What are the drawbacks to shock incarceration?

Notes

1 Michael S. Rosenwald, "Court Records Show Druce's Troubled, Deviant Life," *Boston Globe,* August 28, 2003 p. A1.
2 See David Fogel, *We Are the Living Proof,* 2d ed. (Cincinnati, Ohio: Anderson, 1978); Andrew von Hirsch, *Doing Justice: The Choice of Punishments* (New York: Hill and Wang, 1976); R. G. Singer, *Just Deserts — Sentencing Based on Equality and Desert* (Cambridge, Mass.: Ballinger, 1979).
3 Sidra Lee Gifford, *Justice Expenditure and Employment in the United States, 1999* (Washington, D.C.: Bureau of Justice Statistics, 2002).
4 Among the most helpful sources in developing this section were Mark Colvin, *Penitentiaries, Reformatories, and Chain Gangs* (New York: St. Martin's Press, 1997); David Duffee, *Corrections: Practice and Policy* (New York: Random House, 1989); Harry Allen and Clifford Simonsen, *Correction in America,* 5th ed. (New York: Macmillan, 1989); Benedict Alper, *Prisons Inside-Out* (Cambridge, Mass.: Ballinger, 1974); Harry Elmer Barnes, *The Story of Punishment,* 2nd ed. (Montclair, N.J.: Patterson-Smith, 1972); Gustave de Beaumont and Alexis de Tocqueville, *On the Penitentiary System in the United States and Its Applications in France* (Carbondale: Southern Illinois University Press, 1964); Orlando Lewis, *The Development of American Prisons and Prison Customs, 1776–1845* (Montclair, N.J.: Patterson-Smith, 1967); Leonard Orland, ed., *Justice, Punishment, and Treatment* (New York: Free Press, 1973); J. Goebel, *Felony and Misdemeanor* (Philadelphia: University of Pennsylvania Press, 1976); Georg Rusche and Otto Kircheimer, *Punishment and Social Structure* (New York: Russell and Russell, 1939); Samuel Walker, *Popular Justice* (New York: Oxford University Press, 1980); Graeme Newman, *The Punishment Response* (Philadelphia: J. B. Lippincott, 1978); David Rothman, *Conscience and Convenience* (Boston: Little, Brown, 1980).
5 F. Pollock and F. Maitland, *History of English Law* (London, England: Cambridge University Press, 1952).
6 Marvin Wolfgang, "Crime and Punishment in Renaissance Florence," *Journal of Criminal Law and Criminology* 81 (1990): 567–84.
7 Margaret Wilson, *The Crime of Punishment,* Life and Letters Series, no. 64 (London, England: Johnathon Cape, 1934), p. 186.

8 John Howard, *The State of Prisons,* 4th ed. (1792; reprint, Montclair, N.J.: Patterson-Smith, 1973).
9 Alexis Durham III, "Newgate of Connecticut: Origins and Early Days of an Early American Prison," *Justice Quarterly* 6 (1989): 89–116.
10 Lewis, *Development of American Prisons and Prison Customs,* p. 17.
11 Ibid., p. 29.
12 Dario Melossi and Massimo Pavarini, *The Prison and the Factory: Origins of the Penitentiary System* (Totowa, N.J.: Barnes and Noble, 1981).
13 Michel Foucault, *Discipline and Punish* (New York: Vintage Books, 1978).
14 Ibid., p. 16.
15 David Rothman, *The Discovery of the Asylum* (Boston: Little, Brown, 1970).
16 Orland, *Justice, Punishment, and Treatment,* p. 143.
17 Ibid., p. 144.
18 Walker, *Popular Justice,* p. 70.
19 Ibid., p. 71.
20 Beverly Smith, "Military Training at New York's Elmira Reformatory, 1880–1920," *Federal Probation* 52 (1988): 33–41.
21 Ibid.
22 See Z. R. Brockway, "The Ideal of a True Prison System for a State," in *Transactions of the National Congress on Penitentiary and Reformatory Discipline* (reprint, Washington, D.C.: American Correctional Association, 1970), pp. 38–65.
23 This section leans heavily on Rothman, *Conscience and Convenience.*
24 Ibid., p. 23.
25 Ibid., p. 133.
26 18 U.S.C. 1761.
27 Barbara Auerbach, George Sexton, Franlin Farrow, and Robert Lawson, *Work in American Prisons: The Private Sector Gets Involved* (Washington, D.C.: National Institute of Justice, 1988), p. 72.
28 John Irwin, *The Jail: Managing the Underclass in American Society* (Berkeley: University of California Press, 1985).
29 Correctional Association of New York, *Prison and Jails: Hospitals of Last Resort* (New York: 1998).
30 Paige M. Harrison and Jennifer Karberg, *Prison and Jail Inmates at Midyear 2002* (Washington, D.C.: Bureau of Justice Statistics, 2003).
31 Caroline Wolf Harlow, *Prior Abuse Reported by Inmates and Probationers* (Washington, D.C.: Bureau of Justice Statistics, 1999).

32 Paula M. Ditton, *Mental Health and Treatment of Inmates and Probationers* (Washington, D.C.: Bureau of Justice Statistics, 1999).
33 Fred Heinzlemann, W. Robert Burkhart, Bernard Gropper, Cheryl Martorana, Lois Felson Mock, Maureen O'Connor, and Walter Philip Travers, *Jailing Drunk Drivers: Impact on the Criminal Justice System* (Washington, D.C.: National Institute of Justice, 1984).
34 Brandon Applegate, Ray Surette, and Bernard McCarthy, "Detention and Desistance from Crime: Evaluating the Influence of a New Generation of Jail on Recidivism," *Journal of Criminal Justice* 27 (1999): 539–48.
35 Ibid.
36 Data in this section come from Allen J. Beck and Paige M. Harrison, *Prisoners in 2000* (Washington, D.C.: Bureau of Justice Statistics, 2001).
37 Gifford, *Justice Expenditure and Employment in the United States.*
38 Human Rights Watch, *Cold Storage: Super-Maximum Security Confinement in Indiana* (New York: 1997); Jamie Fellner, *Red Onion State Prison: Super-Maximum Security Confinement in Virginia* (New York: Human Rights Watch, 1999).
39 "Suit Alleges Violations in California's 'Super-Max' Prison," *Criminal Justice Newsletter,* September 1, 1993, p. 2.
40 Roger Peters, Paul Greenbaum, John Edens, Chris Carter, and Madeline Ortiz, "Prevalence of DSM-IV Substance Abuse and Dependence Disorders among Prison Inmates," *American Journal of Drug and Alcohol Abuse* 24 (1998): 573–80.
41 Craig Hemmens and James Marquart, "Fear and Loathing in the Joint: The Impact of Race and Age on Inmate Support for Prison AIDS Policies," *Prison Journal* 78 (1998): 133–52.
42 Harlow, *Prior Abuse Reported by Inmates and Probationers,* p. 1.
43 Ditton, *Mental Health and Treatment of Inmates and Probationers,* p. 1.
44 James Anderson, Laronistine Dyson, and Jerald Burns, *Boot Camps: An Intermediate Sanction* (Lanham, Md.: University Press of America, 1999), pp. 1–17.
45 Doris Layton Mackenzie, Robert Brame, David McDowall, and Claire Souryal, "Boot Camp Prison and Recidivism in Eight States," *Criminology* 33 (1995): 327–57.
46 Ibid., pp. 328–29.

47 "New York Correctional Groups Praise Boot Camp Programs," *Criminal Justice Newsletter,* April 1, 1991, pp. 4–5.

48 Velmer Burton, James Marquart, Steven Cuvelier, Leanne Fiftal Alarid, and Robert Hunter, "A Study of Attitudinal Change among Boot Camp Participants," *Federal Probation* 57 (1993): 46–52.

49 Doris Layton Mackenzie, "Book Camp Prisons: Components, Evaluations, and Empirical Issues," *Federal Probation* 54 (1990): 44–52.

50 See, for example, Jeanne Stinchcomb and W. Clinton Terry III, "Predicting the Likelihood of Rearrest among Shock Incarceration Graduates: Moving beyond Another Nail in the Boot Camp Coffin," *Crime and Delinquency* 47 (2001): 221–42.

51 Doris Layton Mackenzie and James Shaw, "The Impact of Shock Incarceration on Technical Violations and New Criminal Activities," *Justice Quarterly* 10 (1993): 463–87.

52 Mackenzie, "Boot Camp Prisons."

53 Doris Layton Mackenzie and Alex Piquero, "The Impact of Shock Incarceration Programs on Prison Crowding," *Crime and Delinquency* 40 (1994): 222–49.

54 Mackenzie, Brame, McDowell, and Souryal, "Boot Camp Prison and Recidivism in Eight States," pp. 352–53.

55 Correctional Research Associates, *Treating Youthful Offenders in the Community: An Evaluation Conducted by A. J. Reiss* (Washington, D.C.: Correctional Research Associates, 1966).

56 Kevin Krajick, "Not on My Block: Local Opposition Impedes the Search for Alternatives," *Corrections Magazine* 6 (1980): 15–27.

57 "Many State Legislatures Focused on Crime in 1995, Study Finds," *Criminal Justice Newsletter,* January 2, 1996, p. 2.

58 *Census of State and Federal Correctional Facilities, 2000* (Washington, D.C.: Bureau of Justice Statistics, 2003)

59 Richard Harding, "Private Prisons," in *Crime and Justice: An Annual Edition,* ed. Michael Tonry (Chicago: University of Chicago Press, 2001), 265–347.

60 Lanza-Kaduce, Parker, and Thomas, "A Comparative Recidivism Analysis of Releases from Private and Public Prisons," *Crime and Delinquency* 45 (1999): 28–47.

61 Ira Robbins, *The Legal Dimensions of Private Incarceration* (Chicago: American Bar Association, 1988).

62 Travis Pratt and Jeff Maahs, "Are Private Prisons More Cost-Effective Than Public Prisons? A Meta-Analysis of Evaluation Research Studies," *Crime and Delinquency* 45 (1999): 358–71.

63 Ahmed A. White, "Rule of Law and the Limits of Sovereignty: The Private Prison in Jurisprudential Perspective," *American Criminal Law Review* 38 (2001): 111–47.

64 Lawrence Travis, Edward Latessa, and Gennaro Vito, "Private Enterprise and Institutional Corrections: A Call for Caution," *Federal Probation* 49 (1985): 11–17.

65 Patrick Anderson, Charles Davoli, and Laura Moriarty, "Private Corrections: Feast or Fiasco," *Prison Journal* 65 (1985): 32–41.

66 Data in this section come from Bureau of Justice Statistics, *Prisoners, 1925–1981* (Washington, D.C.: Government Printing Office, 1982).

67 Allen J. Beck and Paige M. Harrison, *Prisoners in 2001* (Washington, D.C.: Bureau of Justice Statistics, 2002).

68 Thomas Bonzcar, *Prevalence of Imprisonment in the U.S. Population, 1974–2001* (Washington, D.C.: Bureau of Justice Statistics, 2003).

69 Todd Clear, *Harm in American Penology: Offenders, Victims and Their Communities* (Albany: State University of New York Press, 1994).

70 Daniel Nagin, "Criminal Deterrence Research: A Review of the Evidence and a Research Agenda for the Outset of the 21st Century," in *Crime and Justice: An Annual Review,* vol. 23, ed. Michael Tonry (Chicago: University of Chicago Press, 1997), pp. 1–42.

71 For more on this issue, see Marcy Rasmussen Podkopacz and Barry Feld, "The End of the Line: An Empirical Study of Judicial Waiver," *Journal of Criminal Law and Criminology* 86 (1996): 449–92.

72 Andrew Lang Golub, Farrukh Hakeem, and Bruce Johnson, *Monitoring the Decline in the Crack Epidemic with Data from the Drug Use Forecasting Program: Final Report* (Washington, D.C.: National Institute of Justice, 1996).

Chapter Outline

Chapter Objectives

After reading this chapter, you should be able to:

1. Understand the experience of living in prison.
2. Describe the various elements of the inmate social code.
3. Recognize the differences between the prison culture today and at mid-twentieth century.
4. Know what is meant by the make-believe family.
5. Discuss the problems of women in prison.
6. Recognize the recent changes in correctional law.
7. Describe the role of the prison rehabilitation efforts.
8. Know about the problems faced by correctional officers.
9. Understand the different forms of parole.
10. Show how the problem of reentry has influenced the correctional system.

Viewpoints

 Analyzing Criminal Justice Issues: Girl Scouts Beyond Bars 514

 Images of Justice: *Newjack* 522

 Criminal Justice and Technology: Technocorrections: Contemporary Correctional Technology 526

 Law in Review: *Hope* v. *Pelzer et al.* 531

 Analyzing Criminal Justice Issues: The Problems of Reentry 536

 Analyzing Criminal Justice Issues: Residential Substance Abuse Treatment 539

InfoTrac College Edition Links

Web Links

Chapter 16 | Prison Life: Living in and Leaving Prison

Kathy Boudin served 20 years in prison at the Bedford Hills Correctional Facility for her role in the October 20, 1981, robbery of a Brinks truck at the Nanuet Mall in Rockland County, New York. During the robbery, Peter Paige, a Brinks employee, was killed. Boudin, a member of the 1960s radical group the Weathermen, drove the getaway truck in what was considered a revolutionary act by members of the Black Revolutionary Army. After the police closed in, Boudin surrendered, but two officers were killed in the resulting shootout with the other robbers. Though at trial it was determined she was unarmed and unaware that the conspirators would use violence, under New York's felony murder law Boudin was liable for any death that occurred during the course of the robbery. However, Boudin could not be held legally responsible for the killings of the officers because she had already surrendered and was in custody.

While in prison Boudin was considered an exemplary prisoner who worked with AIDS patients, supported incarcerated parents and their children, and taught educational programs for inmates. In prison, she earned a master's degree and started on a doctorate. After being denied parole twice she was granted release

on August 20, 2003. Her victim's surviving relatives treated the decision with bitterness, questioning whether she was at all remorseful. Her supporters endorsed her release, proclaiming that she was ashamed and contrite about her earlier life. Barbara Hanson Treen, a former member of the New York State Division of Parole who got to know Boudin, told the media:

"Kathy is really an example of the best that prison could provide for people. . . . People are so much more complex than that one crime that defines them. The best thing for people

coming home is to treat them with dignity, as individual human beings, and to get them ready."[1]

Three other surviving participants in the robbery, including Boudin's estranged husband, David Gilbert, cannot be considered for parole before 2056. A fourth defendant, Abdul Majid, is up for parole in 2015. A fifth defendant, Kuwasi Balagoon, died in prison in 1986.

CNN *View the CNN video clip of this story on your Introduction to Criminal Justice 10e CD.*

Boudin's release, which made national headlines in 2003, illustrates the fact that most inmates, even those involved in notorious crimes, do not serve their entire sentence in prison but are released on parole or other early release mechanisms. It also illustrates how many inmates try to turn their lives around while inside prison walls, entering treatment programs and even earning graduate degrees. Unfortunately, most inmates are not rehabilitated, and a majority return to prison soon after their release. The spotty record of correctional rehabilitation is not surprising considering the overcrowded correctional system. A significant percentage of facilities are old, decrepit, archaic structures. Twenty-five prisons were built before 1875, 79 between 1875 and 1924, and 141 between 1925 and 1949. Some of the first prisons ever constructed, such as the Concord Reformatory in Massachusetts, are still in operation.

Although a majority of prisons are classified as medium security, more than half of all inmates are being held in large, maximum-security institutions. Despite the continuous outcry by penologists against the use of fortress-like prisons, institutions holding 1,000 or more inmates still predominate. Prison overcrowding is a significant problem. The prison system now holds more than 1.3 million people. Many institutions are operating above stated capacity. Recreation and workshop facilities have been turned into dormitories housing 30 or more inmates in a single room. Most prison experts agree that a minimum of 60 square feet is needed for each inmate, but many prisons fail to reach this standard.

This giant, overcrowded system designed to reform and rehabilitate offenders is instead undergoing a crisis of massive proportions. Institutions are so overcrowded that meaningful treatment efforts are often a matter of wishful thinking; recidivism rates are shockingly high. Inmates are resentful of the deteriorated conditions, and correctional officers fear that the institution is ready to explode. Some may resort to violence themselves.

Men Imprisoned

total institution
A regimented, dehumanizing institution, such as a prison, in which like-situated people are kept in social isolation, cut off from the world at large.

According to prevailing wisdom, prisons in the United States are **total institutions.** This means that inmates locked within their walls are segregated from the outside world, kept under constant scrutiny and surveillance, and forced to obey strict official rules to avoid facing formal sanctions. Their personal possessions are taken from them, and they must conform to institutional dress and personal appearance norms. Many human functions are strictly curtailed — heterosexual relationships and sex, friendships, family relationships, education, and participation in groups, and even smoking become privileges of the past, Vermont and other states, for example, are about to ban a cigarettes in 2004.[2]

Living in Prison

Inmates quickly learn what the term *total institution* means. When they arrive at the prison, they are stripped, searched, shorn, and assigned living quarters. Before they get there, though, their first experience occurs in a classification or reception center, where they are given a series of psychological and other tests and are evaluated on the basis of their personality, background, offense history, and treatment needs. Based on the classification they are given, they will be assigned to a permanent facility. Hard-core, repeat, and violent offenders will go to the maximum-security unit; offenders with learning disabilities may be assigned to an institution that specializes in educational services; mentally disordered offenders will be held in a facility that can provide psychiatric care; and so on. Some states such as California have instituted rigorous classification instruments designed to maximize the effectiveness of placements, thereby cutting down on the cost of incarceration. If classification can be conducted in an efficient and effective manner, non-dangerous offenders would not needlessly be kept in expensive high-security facilities.[3]

Once they arrive at the long-term facility, inmates may be granted a short orientation period and then given a permanent cell assignment in the general population. Because of overcrowding, they may be sharing a cell designed for a single inmate with one or more others. All previous concepts of personal privacy and dignity are soon forgotten. Personal losses include the deprivation of liberty, goods, services, heterosexual relationships, autonomy, and security.[4] Inmates may be subject to verbal and physical attack and threats, with little chance of legal redress. Although the criminal law applies to inmates as to any other citizen, it is rarely enforced within prison walls.[5] Therefore, part of living in prison involves learning to protect oneself and developing survival instincts.

Inmates in large, inaccessible prisons may find themselves physically cut off from families, friends, and associates. Visitors may find it difficult to travel great distances to see them. Mail is censored and sometimes destroyed.

Adjusting to Prison

Inmates may go through a variety of attitude and behavior changes, or cycles, as their sentence unfolds. During the early part of their prison stay, inmates may become easily depressed while considering the long duration of the sentence and the loneliness and dangers of prison life. They must learn the ins and outs of survival in the institution: Which persons can be befriended, and which are best avoided? Who will grant favors and for what repayment? Some inmates will request that regular payments be made to them in exchange for protection from rape and beatings. To avoid victimization, inmates must learn to adopt a lifestyle that shields them from victimization.[6] They must discover areas of safety and danger. Some learn how to fight back to prove they are not people who can be taken advantage of. While some kill their attackers and get even longer sentences, others join cliques that provide protection and the ability to acquire power within the institution.

Inmates may find that some prisoners have formed cliques, or groups, based on ethnic backgrounds or personal interests. They are likely to encounter Mafia-like or racial terror groups that must be dealt with. Inmates may be the victim of homosexual attacks. They may find that power in the prison is shared by terrified guards and inmate gangs. The only way to avoid being beaten and raped may be to learn how to beat and rape.[7] If they are weak and unable to defend themselves, new inmates may find that they are considered a "punk." If they ask a guard for help, they are labeled a "snitch." After that, they may spend the rest of their sentence in protective custody, sacrificing the "freedom of the yard" and rehabilitation services for personal protection.[8]

Because so many inmates are now returnees, the adjustment to prison for many inmates is relatively painless. They may have only just left.

Coping Behavior Despite all these hardships, many inmates learn to adapt to the prison routine. Each prisoner has his own method of coping: He may stay alone, become friends with another inmate, join a group, or seek the advice of treatment personnel. Inmates may soon learn that their lifestyle and activities can contribute to their being victimized by more aggressive inmates. The more time they spend in closely guarded activities, the less likely they are to become the victims of violence; the more they isolate themselves from others who might protect them, the greater is their vulnerability to attack; the more visitors they receive, the more likely they are to be attacked by fellow inmates jealous of their relationship with the outside world.[9]

New inmates must learn to deal with the guards and other correctional personnel. These relationships will determine whether the inmates do "hard time"

Sexual abuse is a constant danger in prison. Read about the threat at Christopher Man and John Cronan, "Forecasting Sexual Abuse in Prison: The Prison Subculture of Masculinity as a Backdrop for 'Deliberate Indifference,'" *Journal of Criminal Law and Criminology* (Fall 2001): 127, on InfoTrac College Edition.

or "easy time." For example, when inmates housed in open institutions are sent out to work on roads or to do farm work, they may be forced to wear stun belts for security. Once confined in a stun belt, the inmate can receive a shock of 50,000 volts and three to four milliamps for a period of eight seconds. Although not fatal, the shock is very painful, and victims are immediately incapacitated. Burns, which may take months to heal, may develop where the electrodes touch the skin above the left kidney. Critics charge that stun guns are brutal and can be used by correctional workers to terrorize or torture inmates whom they dislike or find offensive.[10]

Regardless of adaptation style, the first stage of the inmates' prison cycle is marked by a growing awareness that they can no longer depend on their traditional associates for help and support and that, for better or worse, the institution is a new home to which they must adjust. Unfortunately for the goal of rehabilitation, the predominant emotion that inmates must confront is boredom. The absence of anything constructive to do, the forced idleness, is what is often so frustrating and so damaging.[11]

Conflict and Hustling   Part of new inmates' early adjustment involves becoming familiar with and perhaps participating in the black market, the hidden economy of the prison — the hustle. Hustling provides inmates with a source of steady income and the satisfaction that they are beating the system.[12] Hustling involves sales of such illegal commodities as drugs (uppers, downers, pot), alcohol, weapons, or illegally obtained food and supplies. When prison officials crack down on hustled goods, it merely serves to drive up the price — giving hustlers greater incentive to promote their activities. Drugs and other contraband are smuggled into prison by visitors, carried in by inmates who are out on furlough or work release programs, or bought from corrupt prison officials. Control of the prison drug trade is often the spark that creates violence and conflict.

Inmates must also learn to deal with the racial conflict that is a daily fact of life. Prisoners tend to segregate themselves, and if peace is to reign in the institution, they learn to stay out of each other's way. Often, racial groupings are exact; for example, Hispanics will separate themselves according to their national origin (Mexican, Puerto Rican, Colombian, and so on). Because racial disparity in sentencing is common in many U.S. courts, prisons are one place where minorities often hold power.

Inmates may find that the social support of inmate peers can make incarceration somewhat less painful. They may begin to take stock of their situation and enter into educational or vocational training programs, if they are available. Many turn to religion and take Bible classes. They heed the inmate grapevine to determine what the parole board considers important in deciding to grant community release. They may become more politically aware in response to the influence of other inmates, and the personal guilt they may have felt may be shifted to society at large. Why should they be in prison when those equally guilty go free? They learn the importance of money and politics. Eventually, they may be called on by new arrivals to aid them in adapting to the system.

Even in the harsh prison environment, inmates may learn to find a niche for themselves. They may be able to find a place, activity, or group in which they can feel comfortable and secure.[13] An inmate's niche is a kind of insulation from the pains of imprisonment, enabling him to cope and providing him with a sense of autonomy and freedom. Finding a niche may insulate inmates from attack, and research indicates that prison victimization may be less prevalent than commonly believed. Not surprisingly, the relatively few victims of prison violence seem less psychologically healthy, more fearful than nonvictims, and less able to avoid the pains of imprisonment.[14]

Not all inmates learn to cope. Some inmates repeatedly violate institutional rules. One reason is that in the United States and abroad many inmates suffer from serious psychological and emotional problems. A review of inmate mental health in

Inmates must learn how to adapt to the prison culture. Some are able to participate in activities, such as the baseball players shown here, while others fearful of victimization may spend most of their time alone in protective custody.

12 countries including the United States found that almost 4 percent of the male inmates suffered from psychotic illnesses, 10 percent were diagnosed with major depression, and 65 percent had a personality disorder, including 47 percent with antisocial personality disorder. Prisoners were several times more likely to have psychosis and major depression, and about 10 times more likely to have antisocial personality disorder, than the general population.[15] The prevalence of psychological problems in the inmate population makes coping problematic.

Predicting who will become an institutional troublemaker is difficult, but rule-breaking behavior has been associated with being a younger inmate with a low intelligence quotient (IQ), possessing numerous juvenile convictions, being a repeat offender, and having victimized a stranger. Inmates who have limited intelligence and maintain low self-control may not be able to form adaptive coping mechanisms and manage the stress of being in prison.[16]

Prison Culture

For many years, criminal justice experts maintained that inmates formed their own world with a unique set of norms and rules, known as the **inmate subculture.**[17] A significant aspect of the inmate subculture was a unique **inmate social code,** unwritten guidelines that expressed the values, attitudes, and type of behavior that older inmates demanded of young ones. Passed on from one generation of inmates to another, the inmate social code represented the values of interpersonal relations within the prison.

National attention was first drawn to the inmate social code and subculture by Donald Clemmer's classic book *The Prison Community,* in which he presented a detailed sociological study of life in a maximum-security prison.[18] Referring to thousands of conversations and interviews, as well as to inmate essays and biographies, Clemmer was able to identify a unique language, or argot, that prisoners use. In addition, Clemmer found that prisoners tend to group themselves into cliques on the basis of such personal criteria as sexual preference, political beliefs, and offense history. He found complex sexual relationships in prison and

inmate subculture
The loosely defined culture that pervades prisons and has its own norms, rules, and language.

inmate social code
The informal set of rules that govern inmates and shape the inmate subculture.

Exhibit 16.1 Elements of the Inmate Social Code

1. Don't interfere with inmates' interests. Within this area of the code are maxims concerning serving the least amount of time in the greatest possible comfort. For example, inmates are warned never to betray another inmate to authorities; in other words, grievances must be handled personally. Other aspects of the noninterference doctrine include "Don't be nosy," "Don't have a loose lip," "Keep off the other inmates' backs," and "Don't put another inmate on the spot."

2. Don't lose your head. Inmates are also cautioned to refrain from arguing, quarreling, or engaging in other emotional displays with fellow inmates. The novice may hear such warnings as "Play it cool" and "Do your own time."

3. Don't exploit inmates. Prisoners are warned not to take advantage of one another — "Don't steal from cons," "Don't welsh on a debt," and "Be right."

4. Be tough and don't lose your dignity. Although Rule 2 forbids conflict, once it starts, an inmate must be prepared to deal with it effectively and thoroughly. Maxims include "Don't cop out," "Don't weaken," and "Be tough; be a man."

5. Don't be a sucker. Inmates are cautioned not to make fools of themselves and support the guards or prison administration over the interest of the inmates — "Be sharp."

Source: Gresham Sykes, *The Society of Captives* (Princeton, N.J.: Princeton University Press, 1958).

concluded that many heterosexual men will turn to homosexual relationships when faced with long sentences and the loneliness of prison life.

prisonization
Assimilation into the separate culture in the prison that has its own rewards and behaviors.

Clemmer's most important contribution may have been his identification of the **prisonization** process. This he defined as the inmate's assimilation into the existing prison culture through acceptance of its language, sexual code, and norms of behavior. Those who become the most "prisonized" will be the least likely to reform on the outside.

Using Clemmer's work as a jumping-off point, a number of prominent sociologists have set out to more fully explore the various roles in the prison community. The most important principles of the dominant inmate subculture are listed in Exhibit 16.1.

While some inmates violate the code and exploit their peers, the "right guy" is someone who uses the inmate social code as his personal behavior guide. He is always loyal to his fellow prisoners, keeps his promises, is dependable and trustworthy, and never interferes with inmates who are conniving against the officials.[19] The right guy does not go around looking for a fight, but he never runs away from one. He acts like a man.

Developing a Prison Culture How do prison cultures develop? What are the forces that shape inmate roles? There are three views on the matter. First, some prison experts believe that the prison experience transforms people and forces them to accept the inmate culture. According to this deprivation model, inmate behavior is a product of the prison environment. Developed by experts such as Clemmer and Gresham Sykes, the "pains of imprisonment," which include loss of liberty, possessions, and freedom, alter people and cause them to change their values and behaviors.[20]

A second view, referred to as the importation perspective, suggests that an inmate's early socialization, which occurs before he enters prison, is what shapes his behavior and values. In other words, the prison culture is imported from the outside world.[21] Inmate culture is affected as much by the values of newcomers and events on the outside as it is by traditional inmate values. People who view violence as an acceptable alternative before entering prison are the ones most likely to adopt the inmate social code.[22]

A third view, referred to as the administrative control model, suggests that inmate culture is deeply influenced by the management style of the prison administration. Prisons managed with a formal organizational structure that features a strict division of labor, detailed rules, routines, and a strong leader at the top of the organization will have significantly less prison disorder.[23] When there is an administrative breakdown, for example, when the organizational structure of the prison is unsound, security cannot protect weaker inmates and overall prison conditions and services deteriorate. Under these conditions, inmates band together for self-protection as prison misconduct increases as a result of organizational breakdown.[24] Research shows that administrative behaviors can influence inmate behaviors and that positive enforcements may have a more significant impact on inmate behavior and attitudes than punitive measures.[25]

The effects of prisonization may be long term and destructive. Many become hostile to the legal system, learning to use violence as a means of solving problems and to value criminal peers.[26] For some this change may be permanent. For others it is temporary, and they may revert to their normal life after release.

The New Inmate Culture The importation of outside values into the inmate culture has had a dramatic effect on prison life. Although the old inmate subculture may have been harmful because its norms and values insulated the inmate from rehabilitation efforts, it did help create order within the institution and prevent violence among the inmates. People who violated the code and victimized others were sanctioned by their peers. An understanding developed between guards and inmate leaders: The guards would let the inmates have things their own way; the inmates would not let things get out of hand and draw the attention of the administration.

The old system may be dying or already dead in most institutions. The change seems to have been precipitated by the Black Power movement in the 1960s and 1970s. Black inmates were no longer content to fill a subservient role and challenged the power of established white inmates. As the Black Power movement gained prominence, racial tension in prisons created divisions that severely altered the inmate subculture. Older, respected inmates could no longer cross racial lines to mediate disputes. Predatory inmates could victimize others without fear of retaliation. Consequently, more inmates than ever are now assigned to protective custody for their own safety.

In the new culture, African American and Latino inmates are much more cohesively organized than whites.[27] Their groups sometimes form out of religious or political affiliations, such as the Black Muslims; out of efforts to combat discrimination in prison, such as the Latino group La Familia; or from street gangs, such as the Vice Lords or Gangster Disciples in the Illinois prison system and the Crips in California. Where white inmates have successfully organized, it is in the form of a neo-Nazi group called the Aryan Brotherhood. Racially homogenous gangs are so cohesive and powerful that they are able to supplant the original inmate code with one of their own.

 To read about the California prison system, go to http://www.cdc.state.ca.us/index.htm.

To quiz yourself on this material, go to questions 16.1–16.7 on the Introduction to Criminal Justice 10e CD.

Women Imprisoned

Before 1960 few women were in prison. Women's prisons were relatively rare and were usually an outgrowth of male institutions. Only four institutions for women were built between 1930 and 1950. In comparison, 34 women's prisons were constructed during the 1980s as crime rates soared.

At the turn of the twentieth century, female inmates were viewed as morally depraved people who flaunted conventional rules of female behavior. The treatment of white and African American women differed significantly. In some states, white women were placed in female-only reformatories designed to improve their deportment. Black women were placed in male prisons, where they were subject to the chain gang and beatings.[28]

While the number of women in prison is still far smaller than the number of men, their population has been increasing at a much faster pace. The female offender population has increased so rapidly for a number of reasons. Women have accelerated their crime rate at a higher rate than men. The get-tough policies that produced mandatory and determinate sentencing statutes also helped reduce the judicial discretion that has traditionally benefited women. As Meda Chesney-Lind points out, women are swept up in the get-tough movement and no longer receive the benefits of male chivalry. The use of sentencing guidelines means that such factors as family ties and employment record, two elements that usually benefit women during sentencing, can no longer be considered by judges.[29] Chesney-Lind notes that judges seem willing once again to view female offenders as "depraved" and outside the ranks of "true womanhood."[30]

Female Institutions

State jurisdictions have been responding to the influx of female offenders into the correctional system by expanding the facilities for housing and treating them.[31] Women's prisons tend to be smaller than those housing male inmates.[32] Although some female institutions are strictly penal, with steel bars, concrete floors, and other security measures, the majority are non-secure institutions similar to college dormitories and group homes in the community. Women's facilities, especially those in the community, commonly offer a great deal of autonomy to inmates and allow them to make decisions affecting their daily life.

Like men's prisons, women's prisons suffer from a lack of adequate training, health, treatment, and educational facilities. Psychological counseling often takes the form of group sessions conducted by laypeople, such as correctional officers. Most trained psychologists and psychiatrists restrict themselves to such activities as conducting intake classifications and court-ordered examinations and prescribing mood-controlling medication. Although many female inmates are parents and had custody of their children before their incarceration, little effort is made to help them develop better parenting skills. And while most female (and male) inmates have at least one child, less than a quarter get an annual visit. Who takes care of the children while their mothers are incarcerated? Most children of incarcerated women are placed with their father, grandparent, other relative, or a family friend. About 10 percent wind up in foster homes or state facilities.

Job-training opportunities are also a problem. Where vocational training exists, it is in areas with limited financial reward, hindering adjustment on release. Female inmates, many of whom were on the economic margin before their incarceration began, find little opportunity for improvement during their prison experience.[33] Surveys also indicate that the prison experience does little to prepare women to reenter the workforce after their sentence has been completed. Gender stereotypes still shape vocational opportunities.[34] Female inmates are still being trained for "women's roles," such as child rearing, and not given the programming to make successful adjustments in the community.[35]

Female Inmates

Like their male counterparts, female inmates are young (most are under age 30), minority group members, unmarried, undereducated (more than half are high school dropouts), and either unemployed or underemployed.

Incarcerated women also have had a troubled family life. Significant numbers were at-risk children, products of broken homes and the welfare system. Over half had received welfare at some time during their adult lives. They experienced a pattern of harsh discipline and physical abuse. Many claim to have been physically or sexually abused. Many female inmates were victims of domestic violence.

Female offenders are more likely than males to be convicted of a nonviolent crime and be incarcerated for a low-level involvement in drug offenses, such as driving a boyfriend to make a drug deal. The female offender may end up serving a longer sentence than the boyfriend simply because she is less likely to work out a plea arrangement.[36]

Not surprisingly, many female offenders display psychological problems, including serious psychopathology.[37] One recent survey found that 4.0 percent of incarcerated women in 12 nations including the United States had psychotic illnesses; 12 percent, depression; and 42 percent, a personality disorder, including 21 percent with antisocial personality disorder.[38]

A significant number of female inmates report having substance abuse problems. About three-fourths have used drugs at some time in their lives, and almost half were involved with addictive drugs, such as cocaine, heroin, or PCP. Little difference exists in major drug use between male and female offenders when measured over their life span or at the time of their current arrest. The incarceration of so many women who are low-criminal risks yet face a high risk of exposure to HIV (human immunodeficiency virus, which causes AIDS) and other health issues because of their prior history of drug abuse presents a significant problem. For example, one recent study of incarcerated women found that one-third of the sample reported that before their arrest they had traded sex for money or drugs. Twenty-four percent of the women reported trading sex for money or drugs "weekly or more often."[39] Such risky behavior significantly increases the likelihood of their carrying the AIDS virus or other sexually transmitted diseases.

The picture that emerges of the female inmate is troubling. After a lifetime of emotional turmoil, physical and sexual abuse, and drug use, it seems improbable that overcrowded, underfunded correctional institutions can forge a dramatic turnaround in the behavior of at-risk female inmates.

Sexual Exploitation   Numerous reports have surfaced of female prisoners being sexually abused and exploited by male correctional workers who either use brute force or psychological coercion to gain sexual control over inmates.[40] Staff-on-inmate sexual misconduct covers a wide range of behaviors, from lewd remarks to voyeurism to assault and rape. A recent survey by the federal government's General Accounting Office (GAO) found that the federal government, 41 states, and the District of Columbia have been forced to pass laws criminalizing some types of staff sexual misconduct in prisons. The GAO's in-depth analysis of the three correctional systems with the largest number of female inmates — the federal Bureau of Prisons, the California Department of Corrections, and the Texas Department of Criminal Justice — found that sexual misconduct persists despite efforts to correct problems and train staff.[41]

Criminologist Meda Chesney-Lind finds that the movement to eliminate gender inequality has triggered an increase in sexual abuse in male-dominated institutions. She sites the example of New York State, which created a policy of videotaping male inmates while they were being strip searched. For the sake of gender equality, the state instituted a policy of also taping women's strip searches. The videotaping was done while male officers were in the vicinity, and the female inmates sued and won damages when they suspected that the videos were being watched by prison officials. Such sexually charged situations are particularly damaging to women who have a history of sexual and physical abuse. Because male correctional officers now are commonly assigned to women's prisons, major scandals have erupted involving the sexual exploitation and rape of female inmates. Few, if any, of these incidents are reported, and perpetrators rarely go to trial. Institutional workers cover for each other, and women who file complaints are offered little protection from vengeful guards.[42]

On InfoTrac College Edition, read Susie Day, "Cruel But Not Unusual: The Punishment of Women in U.S. Prisons," *Monthly Review* 53, no. 3 (July 2001): 42, to learn more about the problems faced by women in prison.

© Max Whittaker/Getty Images

Female inmates, such as the ones shown here at the Leo Chesney Correctional Center in Live Oak, California, tend to be young (most are under age 30), unmarried, undereducated (more than half are high school dropouts), and either unemployed or underemployed.

Adapting to the Female Prison

Daily life in women's prisons differs somewhat from that in male institutions. For one thing, unlike male inmates, women usually do not present an immediate physical danger to staff and fellow inmates. Relatively few engage in violent behavior, and incidents of inmate-initiated sexual aggression, so common in male institutions, are rare in women's prisons.[43] Recent research conducted in the California prison system finds that few female inmates either experience the violent atmosphere common in male institutions or suffer the racial and ethnic conflict and divisiveness.[44] However, the female inmate experience is not a bed of roses. When Mark Pogrebin and Mary Dodge interviewed former female inmates who had done time in a Western state, they discovered that an important element of prison life for many women was dealing with fear and violence. Some reported that violence in women's prisons is common and that many female inmates undergo a process of socialization fraught with danger and volatile situations.[45]

The rigid, antiauthority inmate social code found in many male institutions does not exist in female institutions.[46] Confinement for women, however, may produce severe anxiety and anger because of separation from families and loved ones and the inability to function in normal female roles. Unlike men, who direct their anger outward, female prisoners may turn to more self-destructive acts to cope with their problems. Female inmates are more likely than males to maim themselves and attempt suicide. For example, one common practice among female inmates is self-mutilation, or carving. This ranges from simple scratches to carving the name of their boyfriend on their body or even complex statements or sentences ("To mother, with hate").[47]

Another form of adaptation to prison used by women is the make-believe family. This group contains masculine and feminine figures acting as fathers and mothers; some even act as children and take on the role of brother or sister. Formalized marriages and divorces may be conducted. Sometimes one inmate holds multiple roles, so that a "sister" in one family may "marry" and become the "wife" of another inmate. About half of all female inmates are members of make-believe families.[48]

Why do make-believe families exist? Experts suggest that they provide the warm, stable relationships otherwise unobtainable in the prison environment. People both in and out of prison have needs for security, companionship, affection, attention, status, prestige, and acceptance that can be filled only by having primary group relationships. Friends fill many of these needs, but the family better represents the ideal or desire for these things in a stable relationship.

To quiz yourself on this material, go to questions 16.8–16.10 on the Introduction to Criminal Justice 10e CD.

Correctional Treatment Methods

Almost every prison facility uses some mode of treatment for inmates. This may come in the form of individual or group therapy programs or educational or vocational training.

Despite good intentions, rehabilitative treatment within prison walls is extremely difficult to achieve. Trained professional treatment personnel usually command high salaries, and most institutions do not have sufficient budgets to adequately staff therapeutic programs. Usually, a large facility may have a single staff psychiatrist or a few social workers. Another problem revolves around the philosophy of less eligibility, which has been interpreted to mean that prisoners should always be treated less well than the most underprivileged law-abiding citizen. Translated into today's terms, less eligibility usually involves the question, Why should inmates be treated to expensive programs denied to the average honest citizen? Enterprising state legislators use this argument to block expenditures for prison budgets, and some prison administrators may agree with them.

Finally, correctional treatment is hampered by the ignorance surrounding the practical effectiveness of one type of treatment program over another. What constitutes proper treatment has not yet been determined, and studies evaluating treatment effectiveness have suggested that few, if any, of the programs currently used in prisons produce significant numbers of rehabilitated offenders.

The following is a description of a selected number of therapeutic methods that have been used nationally in correctional settings.

Counseling and Treatment

Prison inmates typically suffer from a variety of cognitive and psychosocial deficits, such as poor emotional control, social skills, and interpersonal problem solving. These deficits are often linked to long-term substance abuse. Modern counseling programs help them to control emotions (for example, understanding why they feel the way they do; how not to get too nervous or anxious; solving their problems creatively), to communicate with others (for example, understanding what people tell them; communicating clearly when they write), to deal with legal concerns (for example, keeping out of legal trouble; avoiding breaking laws), to manage general life issues (for example, finding a job; dealing with difficult coworkers; being a good parent), and to develop and maintain social relationships (for example, getting along with others; making others happy; making others proud).[49] To achieve these goals, correctional systems use a variety of intensive individual and group techniques, including behavior modification, aversive therapy, milieu therapy, reality therapy, transactional analysis, and responsibility therapy.

Therapeutic Communities Because drug abuse is so prevalent among inmates, some institutions have been organized into therapeutic communities (TC) to best serve their clientele. The TC approach to substance abuse treatment uses a psychosocial, experiential learning process that relies on positive peer pressure within a highly structured social environment.[50] The community itself, including staff and program participants, becomes the primary method of change. They work together as members of a family to create a culture where community members confront each other's negative behavior and attitudes and establish an open, trusting, and safe environment. TC relies then on mutual self-help. The TC approach encourages personal disclosure, not the isolation of the general prison culture. Participants view staff as role models and rational authorities instead of custodians or treatment providers.

Therapeutic communities have several distinctive characteristics.

- They present an alternative concept of inmates that is usually much more positive than prevailing beliefs.
- Their activities embody positive values, help to promote positive social relationships, and start a process of socialization that encourages a more responsible and productive way of life.
- Their staff, some of whom are recovering addicts and former inmates, provide positive role models.
- They provide transition from institutional to community existence, with treatment occurring just prior to release and with continuity of care in the community.[51]

Treating the Special-Needs Inmate

One of the challenges of correctional treatment is to care for special-needs inmates. These individuals can have a variety of social problems. Some are mentally ill but have been assigned to prison because the state has toughened its insanity laws. Others suffer mental problems developed during their imprisonment. An additional 1 to 6 percent of the inmate population is mentally retarded. Treating the mentally ill inmate has required the development and use of new therapies in the prison environment. Although some critics warn of the overuse of "chemical straitjackets" — psychotropic medications — to keep disturbed inmates docile, prison administrators have been found to have a genuine concern for these special-needs inmates.[52]

Elderly Inmates Restrictive crime control policies have also produced another special-needs group — elderly inmates who require health care, diets, and work and recreational opportunities that are different from those of the general population. Some correctional systems have responded to the growing number of elderly inmates by creating facilities tailored to their needs.[53] There are about 40,000 inmates age 55 and over in the correctional system. In 1990 there were 49 people over 55 for every 100,000 residents; by 1996 the number had jumped to 69, and today it is more than 141.[54]

Research indicates that older prisoners tend to be loners who may experience symptoms of depression or anxiety. They suffer from an assortment of physical and health problems associated with aging including arthritis, ulcers, prostate problems, hypertension, and emphysema. Because many have had a long-term history with smoking and of alcohol consumption, they may suffer incontinence as well as heart, respiratory, and degenerative diseases. After reviewing available evidence, one study came to the following conclusions.

- The proportion of state and federal inmates 55 years of age and older is steadily increasing. The number of inmates older than 75 will continue to increase in the future if current sentencing practices remain in place.
- The older inmate was most likely an unmarried white man with children, who did not graduate from high school.
- Older offenders are most likely to be incarcerated for violent crimes, often perpetrated against family members in the home.
- Older inmates are likely to report one or more chronic health problems. Cigarette and alcohol use is common.
- Most states and the Federal Bureau of Prisons have implemented limited provisions to accommodate older inmates with special needs.[55]

The Drug-Dependent Inmate Another special-needs group in prison are drug-dependent inmates. Although most institutions attempt to provide drug and alcohol treatment, these efforts are often inadequate.

Although the ideal drug treatment has yet to be identified, experimental efforts around the country use counseling sessions, instruction in coping strategies, employment counseling, and strict security measures featuring random urinalysis.

The AIDS-Infected Inmate The AIDS-infected prisoner is another acute special-needs inmate. Two groups of people at high risk of contracting HIV are intravenous drug users who share needles and males who engage in homosexual sex. Both are common in prison. Although the numbers are constantly changing, the rate of HIV infection among state and federal prisoners has stabilized at around 2 percent. There are about 25,000 HIV-infected inmates.

Correctional administrators have found it difficult to arrive at effective policies to confront AIDS. Although all state and federal jurisdictions do some AIDS

To read how corrections departments are trying to treat drug-dependent inmates in the prison setting, go to http://www.ojp.usdoj.gov/docs/psrsa.txt.

© 2003 AP/Wide World Photos

Most institutions have programs designed to help the substance abusing inmate. Here, inmates enrolled in the Substance Abuse Program (SAP) at the Special Unit of the Limestone Correctional Facility in Capshaw, Alabama, sit in a circle during their meeting. The Special Unit is home to every man confined in the state's prison system known to have the AIDS virus. Those in the SAP, limited to 25 inmates at a time, engage in candid, sometimes confrontational group-therapy sessions.

testing, only 18 states and the Federal Bureau of Prisons conduct mass screenings of all inmates. Most states test inmates only if there are significant indications that they are HIV-positive. About 40 percent of all state prison inmates have never been tested for AIDS.

Most correctional systems are now training staff about AIDS. Educational programs for inmates are often inadequate because administrators are reluctant to give them information on the proper cleaning of drug paraphernalia and safe sex (because both drug use and homosexual sex are forbidden in prison).

Inmates with Families Many inmates are married, and a stay in prison strains relationships with both spouses and children. To help inmates deal with the disruption caused by a prison sentence, some institutions allow **conjugal visits,** which are private family visits designed to maintain and strengthen family bonds.[56]

Private family visits are typically 48 hours or more in length and provide inmates and their families the opportunity to interact in a private setting. Programs make use of quarters that are separate from the rest of the inmate population to ensure privacy. Private family visits are currently allowed in California, Mississippi, New York, and Washington. In addition, 4,500 such visits were made in Canada last year. While proponents believe that conjugal visits are an ideal method of maintaining family bonds, critics point out that they may cause resentment among the unmarried inmate population and result in pregnancies and children whom inmates are ill equipped to support or raise.

Some programs have been developed specifically to help institutionalized women maintain relationships with their children. The Analyzing Criminal Justice Issues feature describes one such program.

conjugal visit
A prison program that allows inmates to receive visits from spouses for the purpose of maintaining normal interpersonal relationships.

Educational and Vocational Programs

Besides treatment programs stressing personal growth through individual analysis or group process, inmate rehabilitation is pursued through vocational and educational training. Although these two kinds of training sometimes differ in style and content, they can overlap when, for example, education involves practical, job-related study. Educational programs are critical in prison because about 41 percent

Girl Scouts Beyond Bars

analyzing criminal justice issues

Hundreds of thousands of children have mothers in correctional facilities. Research has shown that children of incarcerated parents are likely to experience many negative impacts, such as anxiety, aggression, stress, decrease in schoolwork, and a lack of motivation. Studies have shown that many girls, whose mothers are incarcerated, display social and emotional problems, such as self-esteem issues, partaking in high-risk behavior, and attachment problems. Some refuse to get close to other individuals or, conversely, latch on to every adult that enters her life regardless of the risk. These children are also much more likely to one day be incarcerated themselves than children of non-incarcerated parents.

Knowing the risk of parental incarceration and given that approximately 80 percent of incarcerated females are mothers, the Girl Scouts of America has teamed with correctional departments to help ensure that mother–daughter relationships are maintained during the time a mother spends in prison. The program, known as Girl Scouts Beyond Bars, began in 1992 and is available to girls ages 5–17 whose mothers have been incarcerated. It provides a number of important services including transportation to visit mothers in prison. Young girls and their mothers are placed in a program whose curriculum strives to decrease the chance of family dissolution and also teaches good decision-making strategies. The program is designed to prevent the daughters of prisoners

from making the same poor decisions that led their mother's into trouble with the law. Girls visit their mothers in prison two Saturdays out of the month, and they spend the remaining Saturdays in Girl Scout meetings without their mothers. Some activities focus strictly on having fun, such as arts and crafts and recreational activities, while other activities incorporate serious educational lessons, such as practicing the "Girl Scout law," which stresses the importance of respecting authority, being honest, and taking responsibility for your own actions. In addition, through role-playing activities, mothers and daughters learn to deal with issues that might arise in a girl's daily life, such as drug abuse, birth control, unexpected pregnancies, and so on. Because these women will be released and will continue taking care of their daughters on the outside, they may also attend meetings without their daughters to develop better parenting skills.

In most facilities, women of all security levels are allowed to partake in the Girl Scouts Beyond Bars program, as long as they meet criteria set forth by the facility. These requirements usually include that the prisoner has no history of child abuse and that she has not violated any prison rules within the past six months. Once participation in the program begins, prisoners can be removed from the program if they violate any prison rules.

The program has been so successful that it has won numerous recognition

awards and is currently being implemented in 20 correctional facilities throughout the country. The program's cost is approximately $30 per hour for each girl. Costs include paying for transportation to and from the facility, paying social workers and others to instruct classes, and paying for supplies for different activities. For $6,000 per year, girls are helped to avoid future incarcerations that would cost the state 10 times more.

Critical Thinking

Do you agree that programs designed to bring children into prisons to be with their mothers can have long-term benefits? Does this discriminate between inmates with children and those without? Should society pay $30 per hour to facilitate such meetings?

InfoTrac College Edition Research

 To read more about "women in prison," use it as a subject guide on InfoTrac College Edition.

Sources: Rose Arce, "Girl Scouts Go behind Bars to Teach, Learn Values," February 26, 2001, www.cnn.com/2001/US/02/26/girl.scouts, accessed on July 18, 2003, pp. 1–3; Girl Scout Totem Council, *Girl Scouts Beyond Bars* (Seattle, Wash.: Girl Scouts Inc., 2000), pp. 1–2, www.girlscout-stotem.org, July 18, 2003; Marilyn Moses, "Keeping Incarcerated Mothers and Their Daughters Together: Girl Scouts Beyond Bars," *National Institute of Justice Program Focus* (Washington, D.C.: National Institute of Justice, 1995): 1–12.

of inmates in the nation's state and federal prisons had not completed high school or its equivalent. In comparison, 18 percent of the general population age 18 or older had not finished the 12th grade.[57]

The first prison treatment programs were educational. A prison school was opened at the Walnut Street Jail in Philadelphia in 1784. Elementary courses were offered in New York's prison system in 1801 and in Pennsylvania's in 1844. A school system was established in Detroit's House of Corrections in 1870, and Elmira Reformatory opened a vocational trade school in 1876. Today, most institutions provide some type of educational program. At some prisons, inmates can obtain a high school diploma or a general educational development (GED) certificate through equivalency exams. Other institutions provide a classroom education, usually staffed by certified teachers employed full time at the prison or by part-time teachers who also teach full time at nearby public schools.

The number of hours devoted to educational programs and the quality and intensity of these efforts vary greatly. Some are full-time programs employing highly qualified and concerned educators, whereas others are part-time programs without any real goals or objectives. Although worthwhile attempts are being made, prison educational programs often suffer from inadequate funding and administration. The picture is not totally bleak, however. In some institutions, programs have been designed to circumvent the difficulties inherent in the prison structure. They encourage volunteers from the community and local schools to tutor willing and motivated inmates. Some prison administrators have arranged flexible schedules for inmate students and actively encourage their participation in these programs. In several states, statewide school districts serving prisons have been created. Forming such districts can make better-qualified staff available and provide the materials and resources necessary for meaningful educational programs.

Recent surveys indicate how prevalent and successful prison-based educational programs have become. About 26 percent of state prison inmates said they had completed the GED while serving time in a correctional facility. And although the percentage of state prison inmates who reported taking education courses while confined fell from 57 percent in 1991 to 52 percent at last count (1997), the number who participated in an educational program since admission increased from 402,500 inmates in 1991 to 550,000 in 2002.[58]

© Sam Dean/The Roanoke Times

Even inmates facing long sentences can become involved in prison vocational training programs. Here, inmate John Bumgarner plays with Buddy, a puppy brought to him by the Saint Francis of Assisi service dog foundation. Bumgarner, serving a 30-plus-year sentence in Bland, Virginia, is part of the first-ever inmate dog training program in Virginia. He will walk, feed, and train the dog in basic commands under the supervision of Assisi counselors for 12 to 16 months.

Vocational Services

Every state correctional system also has some job-related services for inmates. Some have elaborate training programs within the institution, whereas others have instituted prerelease and post-release employment services. Inmates who hope to obtain parole need to participate in prison industry. Documenting a history of stable employment in prison is essential if parole agents are to convince prospective employers that the ex-offender is a good risk. Post-release employment is usually required for parole eligibility.[59]

WWW Prison education is also important in Europe. Read about some efforts there at http://users.tibus.com/epea/.

Basic Prison Industries Prisoners are normally expected to work within the institution as part of their treatment program. Aside from saving money for the institution, prison work programs are supposed to help inmates develop good habits and skills. Most prominent among traditional prison industries are those designed to help maintain and run the institution and provide services for other public or state facilities, such as mental hospitals. These include the following.

Food Services. Inmates are expected to prepare and supply food for prisoners and staff. These duties include baking bread, preparing meat and vegetables, and cleaning and maintaining kitchen facilities.

Maintenance. The buildings and grounds of most prisons are cared for by inmates. Electrical work, masonry, plumbing, and painting are all inmate activities. Requiring less skills are such duties as garbage collection, gardening, and cleaning.

Laundry. Most prisons have their own inmate-run laundries. Prison laundries often will also furnish services to other state institutions.

Agriculture. In western and southern states, many prisons farm their own land. Dairy herds, crops, and poultry are all managed by inmates. The products are used in the prison and in other state institutions.

Vocational Training Most institutions also provide vocational training programs. In New York, Corcraft is the manufacturing division of the department of correctional services, which employees 2,500 inmates. Corcraft products include inmate and officers' clothing and uniforms, cleaning supplies, furniture, and prescription eyeglasses, which must be used by the corrections department or sold to other state agencies and local governments. By law, Corcraft products and services cannot be sold on the open market to private organizations or individuals. The products of most of these programs save the taxpayers money, and the programs provide the inmates with practical experience. Many other states offer this type of vocational programming.

Despite the promising aspects of such programs, they have also been seriously criticized. Inmates often have trouble finding skill-related, high-paying jobs on their release; equipment in prisons is often secondhand, obsolete, and hard to come by; some programs are thinly disguised excuses for prison upkeep and maintenance; and unions and other groups resent the intrusion of prison labor into their markets.

Work Release To supplement programs stressing rehabilitation via in-house job training or education, more than 44 states have attempted to implement **work release** or **furlough** programs. These allow deserving inmates to leave the institution and hold regular jobs in the community.

Inmates enrolled in work release may live at the institutions at night while working in the community during the day. However, security problems (for example, contraband may be brought in) and the usual remoteness of prisons often make this arrangement difficult. More typical is the extended work release, where prisoners are allowed to remain in the community for significant periods of time. To help inmates adjust, some states operate community-based prerelease centers where inmates live while working. Some inmates may work at their previous jobs, while others seek new employment.

Like other programs, work release has its good and bad points. Inmates are sometimes reluctantly received in the community and find that certain areas of employment are closed to them. Citizens are often concerned about prisoners "stealing" jobs or working for lower than normal wages. Consequently, such practices are prohibited by federal statute (Public Law 89-176), which controls the federal work release program.

However, inmates gain many benefits from work release, including the ability to maintain work-related skills, to foster community ties, and to make an easier transition from prison to the outside world. For those who have learned a skill in the institution, work release offers an excellent opportunity to test out a new occupation. For others, the job may be a training situation in which new skills are acquired. A number of states have reported that few work release inmates abscond while in the community.

Vocational Training for Female Offenders Critics have charged that educational and vocational programs are especially deficient in female institutions, which typically have offered only remedial-level education or occasional junior college classes. Female inmates were not being provided with the tools needed to succeed on the outside because the limited vocational training stressed what was considered traditional women's work: cosmetology, secretarial work, and food services.

Today, 47 states have instituted some sort of vocational training programs for women; the other states provide supplemental services for their few female in-

To read more about Corcraft, go to its Web site at http://www.corcraft.org/03_corn.html.

work release (furlough)
A prison treatment program in which inmates leave the institution to work in the community, sometimes returning to prison or another supervised facility at night.

While some critics want to end work release, the program is supported by the American Civil Liberties Union. Check http://www.aclu.org/news/2002/n042402b.html.

mates. Although the traditional vocation of sewing is the most common industrial program, correctional authorities are beginning to teach data processing, and female inmates are involved in such other industries as farming, printing, telemarketing, and furniture repair. Clearly, greater efforts are needed to improve the quality of work experiences for female inmates.

Private Prison Enterprise Opposition from organized labor ended the profitability of commercial prison industries, but a number of efforts have been made to vary the type and productivity of prison labor.[60] The federal government helped put private industry into prisons when it approved the Free Venture Program in 1976. Seven states, including Connecticut, Minnesota, and South Carolina, were given grants to implement private industries within prison walls. This successful program led to the Percy Amendment (1979), federal legislation that allowed prison-made goods to be sold across state lines if the projects complied with strict rules, such as making sure unions were consulted and preventing manufacturers from undercutting the existing wage structure.[61] The new law authorized a number of Prison Industry Enhancement pilot projects. These were certified as meeting the Percy Amendment operating rules and were therefore free to ship goods out of state. By 1987, 15 projects had been certified.

Today, private prison industries have used a number of models. One approach, the state-use model, makes the correctional system a supplier of goods and services to state-run institutions. For example, the California Prison Industry Authority (PIA) is an inmate work program that provides work assignments for approximately 7,000 inmates and operates 70 service, manufacturing, and agricultural industries in 23 prisons. These industries produce a variety of goods and services including flags, printing services, signs, binders, eyewear, gloves, office furniture, clothing, and cell equipment. PIA products and services are available to government entities, including federal, state, and local government agencies. Court-ordered restitutions or fines are deducted from the wages earned by PIA inmates and are transferred to the Crime Victims' Restitution Fund. PIA inmates receive wages between 30 and 95 cents per hour, before deductions.[62]

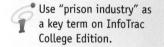 You can access the Prison Industry Authority at http://www.pia.ca.gov/piawebdev/pia_facts.html.

In another approach, the free enterprise model, private companies set up manufacturing units on prison grounds or purchase goods made by inmates in shops owned and operated by the corrections department. In the corporate model, a semi-independent business is created on prison grounds, and the profits go to the state government and inmate laborers.[63] Despite widespread publicity, the partnership between private enterprise and the prison community has been limited to a few experimental programs. However, it is likely to grow in the future.

Use "prison industry" as a key term on InfoTrac College Edition.

Post-release Programs A final element of job-related programming involves helping inmates obtain jobs before they are released and keep them once they are on the outside. A number of correctional departments have set up employment services designed to ease the transition between institution and community. Employment program staff assess inmates' backgrounds to determine their abilities, interests, goals, and capabilities. They also help them create job plans essential to receiving early release (parole) and successfully reintegrating into the community. Some programs maintain community correctional placements in sheltered environments that help inmates bridge the gap between institutions and the outside world. Services include job placement, skill development, family counseling, and legal and medical assistance.

Inmate Self-Help

Recognizing that the probability of failure on the outside is acute, inmates have attempted to organize self-help groups to provide the psychological tools needed to prevent recidivism.[64] Membership in these programs is designed to improve inmates' self-esteem and help them cope with common problems, such as alcoholism, narcotics abuse, or depression.

Some groups are chapters of common national organizations, such as Alcoholics Anonymous. Other groups are organized along racial and ethnic lines. For example, in prisons stretching from California to Massachusetts are chapters of the Chicanos Organizados Pintos Aztlan, the Afro-American Coalition, and the Native American Brotherhood. These groups try to establish a sense of brotherhood so that members will work together for individual betterment. They hold literacy, language, and religion classes and offer counseling, legal advice, and pre-release support. Ethnic groups seek ties with outside minority organizations, such as the National Association for the Advancement of Colored People (NAACP), the Black Muslims, the Urban League, La Raza, and the American Indian Movement, as well as the religious and university communities.

Another type of self-help group assists inmates in finding the strength to make it on the outside. The best known is the Fortune Society, which claims more than 7,000 members. Staffed by ex-offenders, the Fortune Society provides counseling, education, and vocational training to parolees. The group also helps supervise offenders in the community in alternatives to incarceration programs. The staffers run a substance abuse treatment unit that provides individual and group counseling to clients sent by the New York City Department of Probation, provide HIV-prevention information, and work as an advocate group to improve prison conditions.[65]

WWW Staffed primarily by ex-prisoners, the Fortune Society is a nonprofit community-based organization dedicated to educating the public about prisons, criminal justice issues, and the root causes of crime. It also helps ex-prisoners and at-risk youth break the cycle of crime and incarceration through a broad range of services. Check the Web site at http://www.fortunesociety.org/.

Can Rehabilitation Work?

Despite the variety and number of treatment programs in operation, questions remain about their effectiveness. In their oft-cited research, Robert Martinson and his associates found that a majority of treatment programs were failures.[66] Through a national study they discovered that, with few exceptions, rehabilitative efforts seemed to have no appreciable effect on recidivism. The research produced a "nothing works" view of correctional treatment.

The research by Martinson and his colleagues was followed by efforts showing that some high-risk offenders were more likely to commit crimes after they had been placed in treatment programs than before the onset of rehabilitation efforts.[67] A slew of reviews has claimed that correctional treatment efforts aimed at youthful offenders provide little evidence that rehabilitation can take place within correctional settings. Evidence is scant that treatment efforts — even those that include vocational, educational, and mental health services — can consistently lower recidivism rates.[68]

The so-called failure of correctional treatment has helped promote a conservative view of corrections in which prisons are considered places of incapacitation and punishment, not treatment centers. Current policies stress eliminating the non-serious offender from the correctional system while increasing the probability that serious, violent offenders will be incarcerated and serve longer sentences. This view supports the utility of mandatory and determinate sentences for serious offenders and the simultaneous use of intermediate sanctions, such as house arrest, restitution, and diversion, to limit the non-serious offender's involvement in the system.

Although the concept of correctional rehabilitation is facing considerable challenges, many experts still believe strongly in the rehabilitative ideal.[69] Recent analysis of education, vocation, and work programs indicate that they may be able to lower recidivism rates and increase post-release employment.[70] Inmates who have completed higher levels of education find it easier to gain employment upon release and consequently are less likely to recidivate over long periods.[71] Programs that teach interpersonal skills, utilize individual counseling, make use

Exhibit 16.2 What Works in Correctional Rehabilitation?

Rehabilitation is effective in reducing the criminal behavior of at least some offenders. The evidence suggests that effective correctional treatment programs appear to follow some basic principles. To effectively reduce recidivism, treatment programs appear to need to

- Be carefully designed to target the specific characteristics and problems of offenders that can be changed in treatment (dynamic characteristics) and those that are predictive of the individual's future criminal activities (criminogenic) such as antisocial attitudes and behavior, drug use, anger responses;

- Be implemented in a way that is appropriate for the participating offenders and utilizes therapeutic techniques that are known to work (for example, designed by knowledgeable individuals, programming provided by appropriately educated and experienced staff, use of adequately evaluated programs) and require offenders to spend a reasonable length of time in the program considering the changes desired (deliver sufficient dosage);

- Give the most intensive programs to offenders who are at the highest risk of recidivism; and

- Use cognitive and behavioral treatment methods based on theoretical models such as behaviorism, social learning, or cognitive behavioral theories of change that emphasize positive reinforcement contingencies for prosocial behavioral and is individualized as much as possible. Intensive, behavior-based programs that target offenders.

Rehabilitation programs that are successful tend to

- Be structured and focused;

- Use multiple treatment components, focus on developing skills, and use behavioral (including cognitive-behavioral) methods (with reinforcements for clearly identified, overt behaviors as opposed to non-directive counseling focusing on insight, self-esteem, or disclosure);

- Provide for substantial, meaningful contact between the treatment personnel and the participant;

- Be designed to address the characteristics of the offenders that are associated with criminal activities and can be changed; and

- Be of sufficient integrity to ensure that what is delivered is consistent with the planned design.

Among those that work best are the following.

- Prison-based therapeutic community treatment of drug-involved offenders and in-prison therapeutic communities (TC) with follow-up community treatment.

- Intensive, behavior-based programs that target offenders' drug use, a behavior that is clearly associated with criminal activities.

- Programs that combine the TCs with follow-up community treatment.

- Cognitive behavioral therapy. Reasoning and rehabilitation and moral development theory focus on changing participants' thoughts and attitudes, either through problem solving (reasoning and rehabilitation) or moral development (moral reconation).

- Non-prison-based sex offender treatment programs. Sex offender treatment provided outside of prison in a hospital or other residential setting using cognitive-behavioral methods is effective in reducing the sexual offense recidivism of sex offenders.

- Vocational education programs provided in prison or residential settings. Research on vocational education programs demonstrates that these programs are effective in reducing the recidivism of offenders.

- Multicomponent correctional industry programs.

- Community employment programs.

Source: Lawrence W. Sherman, Denise Gottfredson, Doris MacKenzie, John Eck, Peter Reuter, and Shawn Bushway, *Preventing Crime: What Works, What Doesn't, What's Promising: A Report to the United States Congress* (Washington, D.C.: National Institute of Justice, 1998); Doris Layton MacKenzie, "Evidence-Based Corrections: Identifying What Works," *Crime and Delinquency* 46 (2000): 457–71.

of behavioral modification techniques, and improve cognitive reasoning and the development of social skills have produced positive results both in the community and within correctional institutions.[72]

Other researchers have shown through careful analysis that, although not all programs are successful for all inmates, many treatment programs are effective and that participants, especially younger clients, have a better chance of success on the outside than those who forgo treatment. If administered properly, correctional treatment programs have success rates in the magnitude of 20 to 35 percent.[73] The characteristics associated with the most successful programs are described in Exhibit 16.2.

Treatment Problems While this research indicates promising results, correctional treatment is often hampered by a lack of funds and facilities. Even where programs exist, there has been low-level participation of inmates (both men and

Table 16.1 Treatment of Mentally Ill Inmates

	Mentally ill inmates	
	State prison	Jail
Mental health treatment		
Any treatment	60.5%	40.9%
Medication	50.1	34.1
Counseling	44.1	16.2

Source: Paula M. Ditton, *Mental Health and Treatment of Inmates and Probationers* (Washington, D.C.: Bureau of Justice Statistics, 1999).

To quiz yourself on this material, go to questions 16.11–16.17 on the Introduction to Criminal Justice 10e CD.

women) in work, vocational, mental health, substance abuse, and parent counseling programs.[74] For example, one federal survey found that although more than 80 percent of inmates report using drugs and almost 60 percent reported using drugs in the month before their arrest, only one-third of state inmates and one-fourth of federal prisoners said they had participated in drug or alcohol treatment or other substance abuse programs since admission. Reported levels of drug treatment since admission were lower for both state (10 percent) and federal (9 percent) prisoners than those reported in 1991 (25 percent and 16 percent, respectively).[75] Similarly, as the data in Table 16.1 show, about 40 percent of inmates diagnosed as being mentally ill receive no treatment in prison; 60 percent of mentally ill jail inmates receive no treatment.

Guarding the Institution

Control of a prison is a complex task. On one hand, a tough, high-security environment may meet the goals of punishment and control but fail to reinforce positive behavior changes. On the other hand, too liberal an administrative stance can lower staff morale and place inmates in charge of the institution.

For many years, prison guards were viewed as ruthless people who enjoyed their positions of power over inmates, fought rehabilitation efforts, were racist, and had a "lock psychosis" developed from years of counting, numbering, and checking on inmates. This view has changed in recent years. Correctional officers are now viewed as public servants who are seeking the security and financial rewards of a civil service position.[76] Most are in favor of rehabilitation efforts and do not hold any particular animosity toward the inmates. The correctional officer has been characterized as a "people worker" who must be prepared to deal with the problems of inmates on a personal level and also as a member of a complex bureaucracy who must be able to cope with its demands. Consequently, most state jurisdictions now require at least a high school diploma or GED as a hiring prerequisite for correctional officer positions. Some states such as Minnesota require an associate's or bachelor's degree. Another 12 states give monetary incentives to correctional officers as encouragement to continue their education after they are hired. For example, Florida will pay up to $1,560 per year, while Massachusetts provides an incentive of $1,500 per year for an associate's degree, $2,500 for a bachelor's degree, and $3,000 for a master's degree.[77]

Corrections officers play a number of roles within the institution. They supervise cell houses, dining areas, shops, and other facilities as well as perch up on the walls, armed with rifles to oversee the yard and prevent escapes. Corrections officers also sit on disciplinary boards and escort inmates to hospitals and court appearances.

The greatest problem faced by correctional officers is the duality of their role: maintainers of order and security and advocates of treatment and rehabilitation. Added to this basic dilemma is the changing inmate role. In earlier times, corrections officers could count on inmate leaders to help them maintain order, but now they are faced with a racially charged atmosphere in which violence is a way of life. Today, correctional work is filled with danger, tension, boredom, and little evidence that efforts to help inmates lead to success. Research indicates that next to police officers the correctional worker is the most high-risk job in the United States and abroad.[78] And, unlike police officers, correctional officers apparently do not form a close-knit subculture with unique values and a sense of intergroup loyalty. Correctional officers experience alienation and isolation from inmates, the administration, and each other. This sense of alienation seems great-

© 2002 AP/Wide World Photos

Violence is a constant threat in the prison environment and administrators must be vigilant in order to maintain order. Here, prison guard Tatum Lodish opens a gate in the Berks County Prison near Reading, Pennsylvania. Lodish graduated with a bachelor's degree in criminal justice and the intention of working with troubled teenagers. But for the past eight months, the 23-year-old has been a correctional officer at the prison.

est in younger officers. Evidence exists that later in their careers officers enjoy a revival of interest in their work and take great pride in providing human services to inmates.[79] Not surprisingly, correctional officers perceive significant levels of stress related to such job factors as lack of safety, inadequate career opportunities, and work overload.[80]

Many state prison authorities have developed training programs to prepare guards for the difficulties of prison work. Guard unions have also commonly been formed to negotiate wages and working conditions with corrections departments.

Female Correctional Officers

The issue of female correctional officers in male institutions comes up repeatedly. Today, an estimated 5,000 women are assigned to all-male institutions.[81] The employment of women as guards in close contact with male inmates has spurred many questions of privacy and safety and a number of legal cases. In one important case, *Dothard* v. *Rawlinson* (1977), the U.S. Supreme Court upheld Alabama's refusal to hire female correctional officers on the grounds that it would put them in significant danger from the male inmates.[82] Despite such setbacks, women now work side by side with male guards in almost every state, performing the same duties. Research indicates that discipline has not suffered because of the inclusion of women in the guard force. Sexual assaults have been rare, and more negative attitudes have been expressed by the female guards' male peers than by inmates. Most commentators believe that the presence of female guards can have an important beneficial effect on the self-image of inmates and improve the guard–inmate working relationship.

Little research has been conducted on male correctional officers in female prisons, although almost every institution housing female offenders employs male officers. What research there is indicates that male officers are generally well received, and although there is evidence of sexual exploitation and privacy violations, female inmates generally believe that the presence of male correctional officers helps create a more natural environment and reduces tension. Both male and female inmates are concerned about opposite-sex correctional workers intruding on their

Newjack
images of justice

The daily operations of criminal justice are not only portrayed on TV and in the movies but they are also the focus of the print media. While the number of novels focusing on police work are too numerous to count, there is also an extensive true-crime literature. One unique addition to this literature (*Newjack: Guarding Sing Sing*) was recently produced by Ted Conover, a well-known author (*Whiteout, Coyotes*) who wanted to write about what it meant to be a correctional officer in a maximum-security prison.

He soon found out that a civilian (especially a writer) would not be allowed to enter a prison and be given needed access to inmates and correctional personnel. So, to get the data he needed, he applied to become a correctional officer, was given a position, and underwent seven weeks of preparation at the Correctional Officer Training Academy in Albany, New York. After graduation he was ready, so he thought, to become a newjack, a rookie correctional officer. He was assigned as a gallery officer who oversaw a prison pod in Sing Sing. This infamous 170-year-old institution, one of the first built in the

United States, is the kind of maximum security institution where men instantly size each other up to see who can be dominated and who will dominate.

On his first day on the job, Conover was asked to stand before a camera, holding a piece of paper showing his name and Social Security number. When he asked why, Conover was told that the pictures were "hostage shots" and were kept on file in case a correctional officer is injured or taken hostage, at which time the photographs are released to the press. He at first laughed but then realized that "hostage shots" are not all that funny and that correctional officers can be injured or killed at any moment. It comes as no surprise that, while some of his colleagues were hardworking and sincere, others were brutal and vicious.

Conover soon learned that correctional officers cannot show a trace of fear because it attracts abuse from inmates and the loss of respect of fellow officers. Inmates will grant respect if the correctional officer is firm but willing to make an exception to the rules once in a while. Too many exceptions, and the respect vanishes as the

residents start taking advantage. Inmates are described as the "lowest of the low" and officers describe themselves as "warehousers" and "baby-sitters." Some recollect what they call the "good old days" when they could beat up inmates at will; some suggest that a correctional officer can still beat up an inmate with immunity in some isolated institutions.

Conover felt the aggression, frustration at the procedures, and perpetually tense interaction between inmates and correctional personnel, which permeated the institution. Officers bragged about how at some institutions unruly inmates are savagely beaten and how they would not mind doing the same at Sing Sing. Horrified at first, Conover realized that he himself has a violent side, which he never knew existed, and learned the tricks that can be used to protect himself when his aggression emerged. He learned to yell "stop resisting" as he roughed up an inmate to avoid brutality charges; he was shown how logbooks can be fudged to conceal undeserved discipline. He considered some of his duties demeaning and ugly, especially body cavity searches. He

To quiz yourself on this material, go to questions 16.18–16.19 on the Introduction to Criminal Justice 10e CD.

privacy, such as being given assignments in which they may observe inmates dressing or bathing or in which they may come into physical contact, such as during searches or pat-downs.

The difficulties faced by correctional officers, both male and female, have been captured in a new book called *Newjack* (slang for a rookie officer), which is the subject of the Images of Justice feature above.

Prison Violence

On August 9, 1973, Stephen Donaldson, a Quaker peace activist, was arrested for trespassing after participating in a pray-in at the White House. Sent to a Washington, D.C., jail for two nights, Donaldson was gang-raped approximately 60 times by numerous inmates. Donaldson later became president of Stop Prisoner Rape, a nonprofit organization that advocates for the protection of inmates from sexual assault and offers support to victims. On July 18, 1996, at the age of 49, Donaldson passed away from infections complicated by AIDS after he contracted HIV through his prisoner rape.[83]

The Stop Prisoner Rape Web site can be reached at http://www.spr.org/.

Conflict, violence, and brutality are sad but ever-present facts of institutional life. Violence can involve individual conflict: inmate versus inmate, inmate versus

was attacked and punched in the head by an inmate and forced to wrestle with powerful muscle-bound men. For all this he earned about $23,000 per year.

Conover experienced what he considered to be the essence of correctional life: unending tedium interrupted by a sudden adrenaline rush when an incident occurs. He began to understand why correctional officers develop a feeling that they are in confinement themselves. It is a consequence of dealing all day and night with men who can do almost nothing for themselves on their own and who depend on their gallery officer to take care of their most personal needs. Instead of feeling tough and in control, at the end of the day the correctional officer feels like a waiter who has served 100 tables or a mother with too many dependent children. Because of their dependence, the inmates are often made to feel like infants, and those who do not take it well may revert to violence to ease their frustrations. The potential for violence in the prison setting is so great that it makes even routine assignments seem dangerous. Yet, Conover was astonished that there were not even more violent incidents considering that 1,800 rapists, murderers, and assaulters were trapped together in a hellish environment.

Conover did find that some inmates were intelligent and sensitive. One prisoner pointed out that the United States is now planning prisons that will be built in 12 years. By planning that far into the future, he told Conover, the government is planning on imprisoning people who are now children. Instead of spending millions on future prisons, why not spend thousands on education and social services to ensure that child will not be just another statistic? Conover could not think of an adequate answer.

Probably most disturbing was the effect the institution had on Conover's personal life. Though he got to go home to his wife and children, he could not leave his prison experiences at the gate. Prison gets into your skin, he said. If you stayed long enough, "some of it seeped into your soul." His wife was troubled by the changes she saw in him and begged him to quit. He in turn implored her to let him finish out the year. If a man such as Conover experienced such personal stress knowing that he was a writer incognito on temporary assignment, what must the stress be like for professional officers who do not share the luxury of having another career waiting over the horizon?

Critical Thinking

Can a writer truly experience what it must be like to be a prison guard when he is only playing a role, one that he can step out of any time he chooses? If a writer wanted to experience college life and enrolled at your school, would he truly begin to understand what it means to be a student?

InfoTrac College Edition Research

 How do correctional officers perceive their job? Are they different from law enforcement personnel? To find out go to InfoTrac College Edition and read Charles Mesloh, Ross Wolf, and Mark Henych, "Perceptions of Misconduct: An Examination of Ethics at One Correctional Institution," *Corrections Compendium* 25 (2003): 1–9.

Source: Ted Conover, *Newjack: Guarding Sing Sing* (New York: Random House, 2000).

---

staff, staff versus inmate. One common threat is sexual assault. Research has shown that prison rapes usually involve a victim who is viewed as weak and submissive and a group of aggressive rapists who can dominate the victim through their collective strength. Sexual harassment leads to fights, social isolation, fear, anxiety, and crisis. Nonsexual assaults may stem from an aggressor's desire to shake down the victim for money and personal favors, may be motivated by racial conflict, or may simply be used to establish power within the institution. Surveys indicate that at least 20 percent of all inmates are raped during their prison stay.[84] The problem is so severe that Congress is considering funding for the Prison Rape Reduction Act of 2003 that would assist correctional institutions in dealing with sexual violence.[85]

Violence can also involve large groups of inmates, such as the famous Attica riot in 1971, which claimed 39 lives, or the New Mexico State Penitentiary riot of February 1980, in which the death toll was 33. More than 300 prison riots have occurred since the first one in 1774, 90 percent of them since 1952.[86]

A number of factors can spark such damaging incidents. They include poor staff–inmate communications, destructive environmental conditions, faulty classification, and promised but undelivered reforms. The 1980 New Mexico State Penitentiary riot drew national attention to the problem of prison riots. The prison was designed for 800 but held 1,135 prisoners. Conditions of overcrowding, squalor, poor food, and lack of medical treatment abounded. The state government had

To read about the history of correctional violence, go to InfoTrac College Edition and access Curtis R. Blakely, "A History of Correctional Violence: An Examination of Reported Causes of Riots and Disturbances," *Corrections Today* 61, no. 1 (February 1999): 80.

been called on to improve guard training, physical plant quality, and relief from overcrowding but was reluctant to spend the necessary money.

Although revulsion over the violent riots in New Mexico and the earlier riot in New York's Attica prison led to calls for prison reform, prison violence has continued unabated. About 75–100 inmates are killed by their peers each year in U.S. prisons, 6 or 7 staff members are murdered, and some 120 suicides are recorded.

Individual Violence

A number of explanations are offered for individual violence by prisoners.[87] One position holds that inmates are often violence-prone individuals who have always used force to get their own way. What are the causes of prison violence? There is no single explanation for either collective or individual violence, but theories abound. One position holds that many inmates suffer from personality disorders. Recent research shows that, among institutionalized offenders, psychopathy is the strongest predictor of violent recidivism and indifferent response to treatment.[88] In the crowded, dehumanizing world of the prison, it is not surprising that people with extreme psychological distress may resort to violence to dominate others.[89]

Another view is that prisons convert people to violence by their inhuman conditions, including overcrowding, depersonalization, and the threat of sexual assault. Even in the most humane prisons, life is a constant put-down, and prison conditions are a threat to the inmates' sense of self-worth. Violence is an expected consequence of these conditions.

Violence may also result because prisons lack effective mechanisms to enable inmate grievances against either prison officials or other inmates to be handled fairly and equitably. Prisoners who complain about other inmates are viewed as "rats" or "snitches" and are marked for death by their enemies. Similarly, complaints or lawsuits filed against the prison administration may result in the inmate being placed in solitary confinement — "the hole." The frustration caused by living in a prison with a climate that promotes violence — that is, one that lacks physical security and adequate mechanisms for resolving complaints and where the "code of silence" protects violators — is believed to promote individual violence by inmates who might otherwise be controlled.

Here, members of a prison tactical team made up of officers from 10 different prisons stand watch over inmates at Big Muddy Correctional Center in Ina, Illinois. The team surprised inmates with a drug and weapons sweep that resulted in more than 30 positive drug tests and the recovery of one weapon.

© 2003 AP/Wide World Photos

Collective Violence

Two distinct theories have been put forth to explain the cause of collective violence. The first, called the inmate-balance theory, suggests that riots and other forms of collective action occur when prison officials make an abrupt effort to take control of the prison and limit freedoms. Crackdowns occur when officials perceive that inmate leaders have too much power and take measures to control their illicit privileges such as gambling or stealing food.[90]

According to the administrative control theory, collective violence may be caused by prison mismanagement, lack of strong security, and inadequate control by prison officials. Poor management may inhibit conflict management and set the stage for violence. Repressive administrations give inmates the feeling that nothing will ever change, that they have nothing to lose, and that violence is the only means for change.

Overcrowding caused by the rapid increases in the prison population has also been linked to prison violence. As the prison population continues to climb, unmatched by expanded capacity, prison violence may increase.

Future prison officials could lean on technology to control the prison environment. This issue is discussed in the Criminal Justice and Technology feature on page 526.

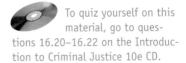

To quiz yourself on this material, go to questions 16.20–16.22 on the Introduction to Criminal Justice 10e CD.

Prisoners' Rights

Before the early 1960s it was accepted that on conviction an individual forfeited all rights not expressly granted by statutory law or correctional policy; inmates were civilly dead. The U.S. Supreme Court held that convicted offenders should expect to be penalized for their misdeeds and that part of their punishment was the loss of rights that free citizens take for granted.

One reason that inmates lacked rights was that state and federal courts were reluctant to intervene in the administration of prisons unless the circumstances of a case clearly indicated a serious breach of the Eighth Amendment protection against cruel and unusual punishment. This judicial policy is referred to as the **hands-off doctrine.** The courts used three basic justifications for their neglect of prison conditions.

hands-off doctrine
The judicial policy of not interfering in the administrative affairs of prisons.

1. Correctional administration was a technical matter best left to experts instead of to courts ill equipped to make appropriate evaluations.
2. Society as a whole was apathetic to what went on in prisons, and most individuals preferred not to associate with or know about the offender.
3. Prisoners' complaints involved privileges, not rights. Prisoners were considered to have fewer constitutional rights than other members of society.[91]

As the 1960s drew to a close, the hands-off doctrine was eroded. Federal district courts began seriously considering prisoners' claims concerning conditions in the various state and federal institutions and used their power to intervene on behalf of the inmates. In some ways, this concern reflected the spirit of the times, which saw the onset of the civil rights movement, and subsequently was paralleled in such areas as student rights, public welfare, mental institutions, juvenile court systems, and military justice.

Beginning in the late 1960s, such activist groups as the NAACP Legal Defense Fund and the American Civil Liberties Union's National Prison Project began to search for appropriate legal vehicles to bring prisoners' complaints before state and federal courts. The most widely used device was the federal Civil Rights Act, 42 U.S.C. 1983.

Every person who, under color of any statute, ordinance, regulation, custom, or usage of any State or Territory subjects, or causes to be subjected, any citizen of the United States or other person within the jurisdiction thereof to the deprivation of any rights, privileges, or immunities secured by the Constitution and laws shall be liable to the party injured in an action at law, suit in equity, or other proper proceeding for redress.

The legal argument went that, as U.S. citizens, prison inmates could sue state officials if their civil rights were violated — for example, if they were the victims of racial or religious discrimination.

The U.S. Supreme Court first recognized the right of prisoners to sue for civil rights violations in cases involving religious freedom brought by the Black Muslims. This well-organized group had been frustrated by prison administrators who feared its growing power and desired to place limits on its recruitment

Technocorrections: Contemporary Correctional Technology
criminal justice and technology

Contemporary technological forces are converging with the forces of law and order to create technocorrections. The correctional establishment — the managers of the jail, prison, probation, and parole systems — and their sponsors in elected office are seeking more cost-effective ways to increase public safety as the number of people under correctional supervision continues to grow. A correctional establishment that takes advantage of all the potential offered by the new technologies to reduce the costs of supervising criminal offenders and minimize the risk they pose to society will define the field of technocorrections.

A few recent advances, some of which have been deployed and others of which are in the development stage, are discussed below.

Ground Penetrating Radar. The Special Technologies Laboratories (STL) has developed a new technology called ground-penetrating radar (GPR), which is able to locate tunnels that inmates use to escape. GPR works almost like an old-fashioned Geiger counter, held in the hand and swept across the ground by an operator. Only instead of detecting metal, the GPR system detects changes in ground composition, including voids, such as those created by a tunnel.

Heartbeat Monitoring. The weakest security link in any prison has always been the sally port, where trucks unload their supplies and where trash and laundry are taken out of the facility. Over the years, inmates have hidden in loads of trash, old produce, laundry — any possible container that might be exiting the facility. Now escapes can be prevented by monitoring inmates' heartbeats. The Advanced Vehicle Interrogation and Notification System (AVIAN), being marketed by

Geo Vox Security, works by identifying the shock wave generated by the beating heart, which couples to any surface the body touches. The system takes all the frequencies of movement, such as the expansion and contraction of an engine or rain hitting the roof, and determines if a pattern is present similar to a human heartbeat.

Satellite Monitoring. Pro Tech Monitoring Inc. of Palm Harbor, Florida, has developed a system to monitor offenders by satellite using cellular technology combined with the federal government's global positioning system of satellites. While in the community, each offender wears an ankle bracelet and carries a three-pound portable tracking device (smart box), programmed with information on his or her geographical restrictions. For instance, a sex offender may be forbidden to come within five miles of his victim's home or workplace, or a pedophile may be barred from getting close to a school. A satellite monitors the geographic movements of the offender, either in real time or by transmitting the information to the smart box for later retrieval. The smart box and the ankle bracelet sound an alarm when boundaries are breached, alerting potential victims.

Pulsed Radar. Special Technologies Laboratories has developed the GPR-X, ground-penetrating radar that transmits energy into the ground and, by measuring the time it takes for that energy to be reflected, detects changes in ground material. GPR can detect contraband buried in the recreation yard, for instance, or a tunnel being built under the prison.

Sticky Shocker. This less-than-lethal projectile uses stun gun technology to temporarily incapacitate a person at standoff range. The Sticky Shocker is a

low-impact, wireless projectile fired from compressed gas or powder launchers and is accurate to within 10 meters.

Back-Scatter Imaging System for Concealed Weapons. This system utilizes a back-scatter imager to detect weapons and contraband. The major advantage of this device over current walk-through portals is that it can detect nonmetallic as well as metallic weapons. It uses low-power X-rays equal to about five minutes of exposure to the sun at sea level. While these X-rays penetrate clothing, they do not penetrate the body.

Body Scanning Screening System. This is a stationary screening system to detect nonmetallic weapons and contraband in the lower body cavities. It uses simplified magnetic resonance imaging (MRI) as a noninvasive alternative to X-ray and physical body cavity searches. The stationary screening system makes use of first-generation medical MRI.

Transmitter Wristbands. Developed by Technology Systems International, these broadcast a unique serial number via radio frequency every two seconds so that antennas throughout the prison can pick up the signals and pass the data via a local area network to a central monitoring station computer. The bands can sound an alert when a prisoner gets dangerously close to the perimeter fence or when an inmate does not return from a furlough on time. They can even tag gang members and notify guards when rivals get into contact with one another.

Personal Health Status Monitor. Correctional authorities are now developing a personal health status monitor that, in its initial form, will use acoustics to track the heartbeat and respiration of a person in a cell. The monitor does not need to be located on the person of the inmate but,

activities. In the 1964 case of *Cooper* v. *Pate,* however, the Supreme Court ruled that inmates who were being denied the right to practice their religion were entitled to legal redress under 42 U.S.C. 1983.[92] Although *Cooper* applied to the narrow issue of religious freedom, it opened the door to providing other rights for inmates.

because it is the size of two packs of cigarettes, it can be placed on the ceiling or just outside a cell. The device is similar to ones that are installed inside the cribs of infants in hospitals.

More advanced health status monitors are now being developed that can monitor more than five or more vital signs at once and, based on the combination of findings, produce an assessment of an inmate's state of health. While this more advanced version of the personal health status monitor may take another decade to develop, the current version will be able to help save lives that would otherwise be lost to suicide and will be positional in the near future.

All-in-One Drug Detection Spray. For the past several years, Mistral Security of Bethesda, Maryland, has marketed drug detection sprays for marijuana, methamphetamines, heroin, and cocaine. A specially made piece of paper is wiped on a surface. When sprayed with one of the aerosol sprays, it changes color within 15 seconds if as little as 4 to 20 micrograms of drugs are present. A new detection device is being developed that uses a single spray that will test for all drugs at once. The test paper will turn different colors depending on which drugs the spray contacts, and several positive results will be possible with a single use of the spray.

Radar Vital Signs Monitor, Radar Flashlight. Researchers at Georgia Tech have developed a handheld radar flashlight that can detect the respiration of a human in a cell from behind a 20-centimeter hollow-core concrete wall or an eight-inch cinder block wall. It instantly gives the user a bar-graph readout that is viewed on the apparatus itself. Other miniature radar detectors give users heartbeat and respiration readings. The

equipment is expected to be a useful tool in searches for people who are hiding, because the only thing that successfully blocks its functioning is a wall made of metal or conductive material in the direction it is pointed. The radars can also be used in telemedicine and for individuals to whom electrodes would be difficult to apply. Future applications for this technology include advanced lie detectors and using the human heartbeat as a biometric for personnel identification.

Personal Alarm Location System. Prison employees can carry a tiny transmitter linking them with a computer in a central control room. In an emergency, they can hit an alarm button and transmit to a computer that automatically records whose distress button had been pushed. An architectural map of the facility instantly appears on-screen showing the exact location of the staff member.

Although sensors are placed only inside the prison, the Personal Alarm Location System (PALS) works up to 300 feet outside prison walls. It locates within a range of four meters inside the room that the duress button is pushed and also locates signals in between floors. The PALS system also has an option that tracks the movement of employees who have pressed their duress buttons. If an officer moves after hitting the duress button, the red dot that represents him or her on the computer screen will move as well. The PALS system is being used in six correctional institutions in the United States and Canada and is scheduled to be adopted in more.

Future Technology. Not yet employed but in the planning stage are the following technological breakthroughs.

Angel Chip. This microchip would be implanted underneath the skin of the user and would contain vital and identifying

information. To avoid future legal entanglements, it is being developed by Sun Microsystems with the assistance of the American Civil Liberties Union.

Noninvasive Body Cavity Scanner. Eliminating the necessity of a physical search, this machine uses magnetic resonance imaging technology to scan body cavities.

Noninvasive Drug Detection. A swab or patch that, when placed on the skin, absorbs perspiration and detects the presence of illegal drugs.

Critical Thinking

Should the use of technology for prison security be unrestricted or must it follow the same legal guidelines, guaranteeing privacy, when used in the outside world? That is, do inmates lose their First Amendment rights when they enter prison?

InfoTrac College Edition Research

 To read more about the issues surrounding the use of prison technology, go to Ann H. Crowe, "Electronic Supervision: From Decision-Making to Implementation," *Corrections Today* 64, no. 5 (August 2002): 130.

Sources: Mark Robert, "Big Brother Goes behind Bars," *Fortune,* September 30, 2002, p. 44; Tony Fabelo, " 'Technocorrections': The Promises, the Uncertain Threats," *Sentencing and Corrections: Issues for the 21st Century* (Washington, D.C.: National Institute of Justice, 2000); Irwin Soonachan, "The Future of Corrections: Technological Developments Are Turning Science Fiction into Science Fact," *Corrections Today* 62 (2000): 64–66; Steve Morrison, "How Technology Can Make Your Job Safer," *Corrections Today* 62 (2000): 58-60; Gabrielle deGroot, "Hot New Technologies," *Corrections Today* 59 (1997): 60–63.

The subsequent prisoners' rights crusade, stretching from 1960 to 1980, paralleled the civil rights and women's movements. Battle lines were drawn between prison officials hoping to maintain their power and resenting interference by the courts and inmate groups and their sympathizers, who used state and federal courts as a forum for demanding better living conditions and personal rights.

Each decision handed down by the courts was viewed as a victory for one side or the other. This battle continues today.

Substantive Rights

substantive right
A specific right, such as the right to medical care or freedom of religion.

Through a slow process of legal review, the courts have granted inmates a number of **substantive rights** that have significantly influenced the entire correctional system. The most important of these rights are discussed in the following sections.

Access to Courts, Legal Services, and Materials Without the ability to seek judicial review of conditions causing discomfort or violating constitutional rights, the inmate must depend solely on the slow and often insensitive administrative mechanism of relief within the prison system. Therefore, the right of easy access to the courts gives inmates hope that their rights will be protected during incarceration. Courts have held that inmates are entitled to have legal materials available and be provided with assistance in drawing up and filing complaints. Inmates who help others, so-called **jailhouse lawyers,** cannot be interfered with or harassed by prison administrators.

jailhouse lawyer
An inmate trained in law or otherwise educated who helps other inmates prepare legal briefs and appeals.

- *DeMallory* v. *Cullen* (1988) — An untrained inmate paralegal is not a constitutionally acceptable alternative to law library access.[93]
- *Lindquist* v. *Idaho State Board of Corrections* (1985) — Seven inmate law clerks for a prison population of 950 were sufficient legal representation because they had a great deal of experience.[94]
- *Smith* v. *Wade* (1983) — An inmate who has been raped can have access to the state court to sue a correctional officer for failing to protect the inmate from aggressive inmates.[95]
- *Bounds* v. *Smith* (1977) — State correctional systems are obligated to provide inmates with either adequate law libraries or the help of people trained in the law.[96]

Freedom of the Press and of Expression Correctional administrators traditionally placed severe limitations on prisoners' speech and expression. For example, they have read and censored inmate mail and restricted their reading material. With the lifting of the hands-off doctrine, courts have consistently ruled that only when a compelling state interest exists can prisoners' First Amendment rights be modified. Correctional authorities must justify the limiting of free speech by showing that granting it would threaten institutional security. In a 2001 case, *Shaw* v. *Murphy,* the Court ruled that inmates do not have a right to correspond with other inmates even if they are requesting legal advice. If prison administrators believe such correspondence undermines prison security, the First Amendment rights of inmates can be curtailed.[97]

- *Turner* v. *Safley* (1987) — Prisoners do not have a right to receive mail from one another. Inmate-to-inmate mail can be banned if the reason is "related to legitimate penological interests."[98]
- *Ramos* v. *Lamm* (1980) — The institutional policy of refusing to deliver mail in a language other than English is unconstitutional.[99]
- *Procunier* v. *Martinez* (1974) — Censorship of a prisoner's mail is justified only when there exists substantial government interest in maintaining the censorship to further prison security, order, and rehabilitation, and the restrictions are not greater or more stringent than is demanded by security precautions.[100]
- *Nolan* v. *Fitzpatrick* (1971) — Prisoners may correspond with newspapers unless their letters discuss escape plans or contain contraband or otherwise objectionable material.[101]

Freedom of Religion Freedom of religion is a fundamental right guaranteed by the First Amendment. In general, the courts have ruled that inmates have the right to assemble and pray in the religion of their choice but that religious symbols and practices that interfere with institutional security can be restricted. Administrators can draw the line if religious needs become cumbersome or impossible to carry out for reason of cost or security. Granting special privileges can also be denied on the grounds that they will cause other groups to make similar demands.

- *Mumin* v. *Phelps* (1988) — If there is a legitimate penological interest, inmates can be denied special privileges to attend religious services.[102]
- *O'Lone* v. *Estate of Shabazz* (1987) — Prison officials can assign inmates work schedules that make it impossible for them to attend religious services as long as no reasonable alternative exists.[103]
- *Rahman* v. *Stephenson* (1986) — A prisoner's rights are not violated if the administration refuses to use the prisoner's religious name on official records.[104]

Medical Rights In early prisons, inmates' right to medical treatment was restricted through the "exceptional circumstances doctrine." Using this policy, the courts would hear only those cases in which the circumstances disregarded human dignity, while denying hearings to less serious cases. The cases that were allowed access to the courts usually represented a situation of total denial of medical care.

To gain their medical rights, prisoners have resorted to class action suits (for example, suits brought on behalf of all individuals affected by similar circumstances, in this case, poor medical attention). In the most significant case, *Newman* v. *Alabama* (1972), the entire Alabama prison system's medical facilities were declared inadequate.[105] The Supreme Court cited the following factors as contributing to inadequate care: insufficient physician and nurse resources, reliance on untrained inmates for paramedical work, intentional failure in treating the sick and injured, and failure to conform to proper medical standards. The *Newman* case forced corrections departments to upgrade prison medical facilities.

It was not until 1976, in *Estelle* v. *Gamble,* that the Supreme Court clearly mandated an inmate's right to have medical care.[106] J. W. Gamble had hurt his back in a Texas prison and filed suit because he contested the type of treatment he had received and questioned the lack of interest that prison guards had shown in his case. The Supreme Court said, "Deliberate indifference to serious medical needs of prisoners constitutes the 'unnecessary and wanton infliction of pain,' proscribed by the Eighth Amendment."[107] Gamble was allowed to collect monetary damages for his injuries.

The *Gamble* decision means that lower courts can decide, on a case-by-case basis, whether "deliberate indifference" to an inmate's medical needs occurred and to what damages the inmate is entitled. Yet, when budgets are tight, correctional systems may be forced to cut back on medical care. For example, in 1993 Pennsylvania announced a plan to treat far fewer inmates found to be infected with hepatitis C, but those who were treated would get better care. The cutback meant that instead of the 5–7 percent of infected inmates being treated, only 1-2 percent of infected inmates would be treated. The right to medical care goes only so far.[108]

Cruel and Unusual Punishment The concept of **cruel and unusual punishment** is founded in the Eighth Amendment. The term itself has not been specifically defined by the Supreme Court, but the Court has held that treatment constitutes cruel and unusual punishment when it

- Degrades the dignity of human beings.[109]
- Is more severe (disproportional) than the offense for which it has been given.[110]
- Shocks the general conscience and is fundamentally unfair.[111]
- Is deliberately indifferent to a person's safety and well-being.[112]
- Punishes people because of their status, such as race, religion, and mental state.[113]
- Is in flagrant disregard of due process of law, such as punishment that is capriciously applied.[114]

cruel and unusual punishment
Treatment that degrades human dignity, is disproportionately severe, or shocks the general conscience; prohibited by the Eighth Amendment to the U.S. Constitution.

State and federal courts have placed strict limits on disciplinary methods that may be considered inhumane. Corporal punishment all but ended after the practice was condemned in *Jackson* v. *Bishop* (1968).[115] Although the solitary confinement of disruptive inmates continues, its prolonged use under barbaric conditions has been held in violation of the Eighth Amendment. Courts have found that inmates placed in solitary have the right to adequate personal hygiene, exercise, mattresses, ventilation, and rules specifying how they earn their release.

In *Hope* v. *Pelzer et al.,* the Supreme Court in 2002 ruled that correctional officials who knowingly violate the Eighth Amendment rights of inmates can be held liable for damages.[116] The *Hope* case is set out in the Law in Review feature on page 531.

© 2003 AP/Wide World Photos

Prisoners have the right to the minimal conditions necessary for human survival, such as the necessary food, clothing, shelter, and medical attention. However, increasing inmate populations and declining budgets may curtail adequate treatments.

Overall Prison Conditions Prisoners have long had the right to the minimal conditions necessary for human survival, such as the food, clothing, shelter, and medical care to sustain human life. A number of attempts have been made to articulate reasonable standards of prison care and to make sure they are carried out. Courts have held that, although people are sent to prison for punishment, it does not mean that prison should be a punishing experience.[117] In the 1994 case of *Farmer* v. *Brennan,* the Court ruled that prison officials are legally liable if, knowing that an inmate faces a serious risk of harm, they disregard that risk by failing to take measures to avoid or reduce it. Furthermore, prison officials should be able to infer the risk from the evidence at hand; they need not be warned or told.[118]

Although inmates retain the right to reasonable care, if a legitimate purpose exists for the use of governmental restrictions, they may be considered constitutional. For example, it might be possible to restrict reading material, allow strip searches, and prohibit inmates from receiving packages from the outside if the restrictions are legitimate security measures. If overcrowded conditions require it, inmates may be double-bunked in cells designed for a single inmate.[119]

Courts have also reviewed entire correctional systems to determine whether practices are unfair to inmates. In a critical case, *Estelle* v. *Ruiz,* the Texas Department of Corrections was ordered to provide new facilities to alleviate overcrowding; to abolish the practice of using inmate trustees; to lower the inmate-to-staff ratio; to improve treatment services, such as medical, mental health, and occupational rehabilitation programs; and to adhere to the principles of procedural due process in dealing with inmates.[120] A court-ordered master was appointed to oversee the changes and served from 1981 to 1990, when the state was deemed in compliance with the most critical of the court-ordered reforms.[121] A period of tension and violence followed this decision, in part perhaps because the staff and administration felt that the court had undermined their authority. It took more than 18 years for the case to be settled.

Because of the large numbers of lawsuits filed by inmates, the federal government has moved to limit inmate access to the courts. The Prison Litigation Reform Act (PLRA) of 1996 limited the number of prison cases in federal court by providing that "no action shall be brought with respect to prison conditions" by an inmate in either state or federal prison "until such administrative remedies as are available are exhausted."[122] The PLRA includes a new form of "three strikes and you're out": If a prisoner has filed three suits that are dismissed because they fail to state a claim for relief (or are frivolous), he or she is barred from filing future actions unless in imminent danger of serious physical harm. Although such measures are designed to limit litigation, the overcrowding crisis likely will prompt additional litigation requesting overall prison relief.

To quiz yourself on this material, go to questions 16.23–16.24 on the Introduction to Criminal Justice 10e CD.

Hope v. *Pelzer et al.*

law in review

Larry Hope, an Alabama prison inmate, was twice handcuffed to a hitching post for disruptive conduct. During a two-hour period in May 1995, he was offered drinking water and a bathroom break every 15 minutes, and his responses were recorded on an activity log. He was handcuffed above shoulder height, and when he tried moving his arms to improve circulation, the handcuffs cut into his wrists, causing pain and discomfort. After an altercation with a guard at his chain gang's work site in June, Hope was subdued, handcuffed, placed in leg irons, and transported back to the prison. Once there, he was ordered to take off his shirt and thus was exposed to the sun. He spent seven hours on the hitching post, during which he was given one or two water breaks but no bathroom breaks, and a guard taunted him about his thirst. Hope filed a suit against three guards charging them with violating his civil rights. Without deciding whether placing Hope on the hitching post as punishment violated the Eighth Amendment, the lower courts found that the guards were entitled to qualified immunity from lawsuits on the grounds that Hope could not show that the guards' behavior violated "clearly established statutory or constitutional rights of which a reasonable person would have known."

On appeal, the U.S. Supreme Court ruled that Hope's allegations established an Eighth Amendment violation. It ruled that among the "'unnecessary and wanton' inflictions of pain [constituting cruel and unusual punishment forbidden by the Amendment] are those that are 'totally without penological justification.'" This determination is made in the context of prison conditions by ascertaining whether an official acted with "deliberate indifference" to the inmates' health or safety, a

state of mind that can be inferred from the fact that the risk of harm is obvious. The Court reasoned that any safety concerns had long since ended by the time Hope was handcuffed to the hitching post, because he had already been subdued, handcuffed, placed in leg irons, and transported back to prison. He was separated from his work squad and not given the opportunity to return. Despite the clear lack of emergency, the guards knowingly subjected him to a substantial risk of physical harm, unnecessary pain, unnecessary exposure to the sun, prolonged thirst and taunting, and a deprivation of bathroom breaks that created a risk of particular discomfort and humiliation.

Qualified immunity operates to ensure that, before they are subjected to suit, officers are on notice that their conduct is unlawful. A reasonable officer would have known that using a hitching post as Hope alleged was unlawful. The obvious cruelty inherent in the practice should have provided respondents with some notice that their conduct was unconstitutional. In addition, binding legal precedent from earlier cases should have given them notice that several forms of corporal punishment are impermissible, including handcuffing inmates to fences or cells for long periods, and that "physical abuse directed at [a] prisoner after he terminate[s] his resistance to authority would constitute an actionable eighth amendment violation."

The *Hope* case shows that correctional officials can be sued if their behavior violates an inmate's constitutional rights and that they or any reasonable person should have surmised that the behavior was in violation of accepted practices. Courts have recognized the need to protect government employees from meritless litiga-

tion that may interfere with the exercise of lawful job-related discretion; that is, qualified immunity. Nonetheless, government officials are not immune from damages if their behavior violates basic human rights. If it does, then the court must determine whether a reasonable officer would have thought that the alleged act was lawful in light of clearly established law and the factual information in possession at the time. If the court finds their behavior was unreasonable, then they are liable for damages. The fact that officers can be sued is critical because most state and local governments indemnify their employees against such judgments and also assume the costs of their defense. Judgments such as this can cost states millions of dollars.

Critical Thinking

To prove cruel and unusual treatment in prison, the courts have ruled that there must be a showing of "unnecessary and wanton" inflictions of pain, especially those that are "totally without penological justification." This determination is typically made in the context of prison conditions by determining whether a prison official acted with "deliberate indifference" to the inmates' health or safety. Do you believe the facts of the *Hope* case met this condition?

InfoTrac College Edition Research

 Use "cruel and unusual punishment" as a subject guide on InfoTrac College Edition to learn more about this topic.

Source: *Hope* v. *Pelzer et al.*, Docket 01–309, decided June 27, 2002.

Leaving Prison

At the expiration of their prison term, most inmates return to society and try to resume their life there. For some inmates, their reintegration into society comes by way of parole, the planned community release and supervision of incarcerated offenders before the expiration of their full prison sentences. In states where determinate sentencing statutes have eliminated discretionary parole, offenders are released after having served their determinate sentence, less time off for good behavior and other credits designed to reduce the term of incarceration. Their release may involve supervision in the community, and rule violations can result in return to prison for the balance of their unexpired sentence.

In a few instances, inmates are released after their sentence has been commuted by a board of pardons or directly by a governor or even the president of the United States. About 15 percent of prison inmates are released after serving their entire maximum sentence without any time excused or forgiven. And despite the efforts of correctional authorities, about 7,000 inmates escape every year from state and federal prisons (the number of escapes is declining, due in part to better officer training and more sophisticated security measures).[123]

Regardless of the method of their release, former inmates face the formidable task of having to readjust to society. This means regaining legal rights they may have lost on their conviction, reestablishing community and family ties, and finding employment. After being in prison, these goals are often difficult to achieve.

Parole

The decision to **parole** is determined by statutory requirement. In some states parole is granted by a parole board, a duly constituted body of men and women who review inmate cases and determine whether offenders have reached a rehabilitative level sufficient to deal with the outside world. The board also dictates what specific parole rules parolees must obey. In other jurisdictions, the amount of time a person must remain in prison is a predetermined percentage of the inmate's sentence, assuming that there are no infractions or escape attempts. Referred to as **mandatory parole release,** the inmate is released when the unserved portion of the maximum prison term equals the inmate's earned good time (less time served in jail awaiting trial). In some states, sentences can be reduced by more than half with a combination of statutory and earned good time. If the conditions of their release are violated, mandatory releasees can have their good time revoked and be returned to the institution to serve the remainder of their unexpired term. The remaining inmates are released for a variety of reasons, including expiration of their term, commutation of their sentence, and court orders to relieve overcrowded prisons.

People on Parole Today there were more than 650,000 people on parole, up 30 percent since 1990. About 312 adults per 100,000 adult U.S. residents were on state-supervised parole, compared with 271 in 1990.[124] The popularity of determinate sentencing has radically changed the way people are being released from prison. The number of state inmates released from prison as a result of a parole board decision making has dropped from 39 percent of all releases in 1990 to about 24 percent today. During the same period, mandatory releases increased from 29 percent to 41 percent of all parole releases.[125]

The Parole Board

In those states that have maintained discretionary parole, the authority to release inmates is usually vested in the parole board. State parole boards have four primary functions.

To learn more about today prison release methods, use the term "parole" as a subject guide on InfoTrac College Edition.

parole
The early release of a prisoner from incarceration subject to conditions set by a parole board.

mandatory parole release
A release date determined at the beginning of the confinement period based on a percentage of the inmate's sentence to be served. Inmate can have their expected time served increased if they violate prison rules or conditions.

How has parole changed in the era of three strikes laws and determinate sentencing? Read the following article to find the answer: George M. Anderson, "Parole Revisited," *America,* March 4, 2002, p. 10.

The Federal Parole board maintains a Web site at http://www.usdoj.gov/uspc/.

1. To select and place prisoners on parole.
2. To aid, supervise, and provide continuing control of parolees in the community.
3. To determine when the parole function is completed and to discharge from parole.
4. To determine whether parole should be revoked, if violations of conditions occur.

Most parole authorities are independent agencies with their own staff and administration, and a few parole boards are part of the state department of corrections. Arguments for keeping the board within a corrections department usually include the improved communication and availability of more intimate knowledge about offenders.

Most boards are relatively small, usually numbering fewer than 10 members. Their size, coupled with their large caseloads and the varied activities they are expected to perform, can prevent board members from becoming as well acquainted with the individual inmates as might be desired.

Parole Hearings

The actual (discretionary) parole decision is made at a parole-granting hearing. At this hearing the full board or a selected subcommittee reviews information, may meet with the offender, and then decides whether the parole applicant has a reasonable probability of succeeding outside of prison. Each parole board has its own way of reviewing cases. In some, the full board meets with the applicant; in others, only a few members do that. In a number of jurisdictions, a single board member can conduct a personal investigation and submit the findings to the full board for a decision.

At the hearing, parole board members consider such information as police reports of the crime, the presentence investigation, psychological testing and scores developed by prison mental health professionals, and institutional reports of disciplinary actions, treatment, and adjustment.[126] Letters may be solicited from the inmate's friends and family members. In some jurisdictions, victims may appear and make statements of the losses they suffered.

By speaking directly to the applicant, the board can also promote and emphasize the specific types of behavior and behavior changes it expects to see if the inmate is to eventually qualify for or effectively serve parole.

The inmate's specific rights at a parole-granting hearing also vary from jurisdiction to jurisdiction. In about half of the parole-granting jurisdictions, inmates are permitted counsel or are allowed to present witnesses on their behalf; other jurisdictions do not permit these privileges. Because the federal courts have declared that the parole applicant is not entitled to any form of legal representation, the inmate may have to pay for legal services when this privilege is allowed. In almost all discretionary parole-granting jurisdictions, the reasons for the parole decision must be given in writing, and in about half of the jurisdictions, a verbatim record of the hearing is made.

In the case of *Pennsylvania Board of Probation and Parole* v. *Scott,* the U.S. Supreme Court held that the exclusionary rule for illegally obtained evidence did not apply to parole revocation proceedings. The Court reasoned that the social costs of excluding incriminating evidence outweigh any benefits of protecting parolees from invasion of their privacy. *Scott* then allows evidence to be used in a parole revocation hearing that would be excluded from a criminal prosecution.[127]

The Parolee in the Community

Once released into the community, a parolee is given a standard set of rules and conditions that must be obeyed. As with probation, the offender who violates these rules may have parole revoked and be sent back to the institution to serve the remainder of the sentence. Once in the community, the parolee is supervised by a trained staff of parole officers who help the offender search for employment and monitor the parolee's behavior and activities to ensure that the conditions of parole are met.

Parole is generally viewed as a privilege granted to deserving inmates on the basis of their good behavior while in prison. Parole has two conflicting sides, however. On one hand, the paroled offender is allowed to serve part of the sentence in the community, an obvious benefit for the deserving offender. On the other hand, because parole is a privilege and not a right, the parolee is viewed as a dangerous criminal who must be carefully watched and supervised. The conflict between the treatment and enforcement aspects of parole has not been reconciled by the criminal justice system, and the parole process still contains elements of both.

To overcome these roadblocks to success, the parole officer may have to play a much greater role in directing and supervising clients' lives than the probation officer. In some instances, parole programs have become active in creating new post-release treatment-oriented programs designed to increase the chances of parole success. For example, the Kansas parole department has adopted a restorative justice approach and is now having parolees work in community service settings upon their release. Jobs may include work at soup kitchens, homeless shelters, and halfway houses. Reports indicate the program is quite successful.[128] In other instances, parole agencies have implemented law enforcement–oriented services that work with local police agencies to identify and apprehend parolees who may have been involved in criminal activity. The California Department of Corrections established the Special Service Unit, which among its others tasks acts as a liaison with local police agencies in helping them solve major crimes when inmates or state parolees are the known or suspected offenders.[129]

Intensive Supervision Parole To aid supervision, some jurisdictions are implementing systems that classify offenders on the basis of their supervision needs. Typically, a point or guideline system (sometimes called a salient factor score) based on prior record and prison adjustment divides parolees into three groups: (1) those who require intensive surveillance, (2) those who require social service instead of surveillance, and (3) those who require limited supervision.

intensive supervision parole (ISP)
A form of parole characterized by smaller caseloads and closer surveillance; may include frequent drug testing or, in some cases, electronic monitoring.

In some jurisdictions, parolees in need of closer surveillance are placed on **intensive supervision parole (ISP).** These programs use limited caseload sizes, treatment facilities, the matching of parolee and supervisor by personality, and shock parole (which involves immediate short-term incarceration for parole violators to impress them with the seriousness of a violation). ISP clients are required to attend more office and home visits than routine parolees. ISP may also require frequent drug testing, a term in a community correctional center, and electronic monitoring in the home. More than 17,000 parolees are under intensive supervision, 1,400 of whom are monitored electronically by computer.

Although ISP seems like an ideal way of limiting already overcrowded prison populations, little evidence shows that ISP programs are effective. In fact, they may produce a higher violation rate than traditional parole supervision. Limiting caseload size allows parole officers to supervise their clients more closely and spot infractions more easily.[130]

The Effectiveness of Parole

According to Joan Petersilia,

> [p]ersons released from prison face a multitude of difficulties. They remain largely uneducated, unskilled, and usually without solid family support systems — to which are added the burdens of a prison record. Not surprisingly, most parolees fail, and rather quickly — rearrests are most common in the first six months after release.[131]

Despite all efforts to treat, correct, and rehabilitate incarcerated offenders, the fact remains that a majority return to prison shortly after their release. A 2002 federal study of nearly 300,000 prisoners released in 15 states in 1994 provides data that underscores the problem. Of the total number of releasees, 67.5 percent were rearrested within three years of leaving prison for a felony or serious misdemeanor.[132] About 47 percent were reconvicted for a new crime and 25 percent resentenced to prison for a new crime. Within three years, about 52 percent were back in prison, serving time for a new prison sentence or for a technical violation of their release, such as failing a drug test, missing an appointment with their parole officer, or being arrested for a new crime.

Who was most likely to fail on parole or other release mechanisms? Released prisoners with the highest rearrest rates were robbers (70.2 percent), burglars (74.0 percent), larcenists (74.6 percent), motor vehicle thieves (78.8 percent), those in prison for possessing or selling stolen property (77.4 percent), and those in prison for possessing, using, or selling illegal weapons (70.2 percent). Ironically, those committing murder, sexual assault, or rape had the lowest recidivism rates.

The cost of recidivism is acute. The 272,111 offenders discharged in 1994 had accumulated 744,000 charges within three years of release. Put another way, about a quarter of a million U.S. citizens are victimized each year by people released on parole in just 15 states. Another federal survey of 156,000 parole violators serving time in the nation's prison system estimated that these offenders committed at least 6,800 murders, 5,500 rapes, 8,800 assaults, and 22,500 robberies while under supervision in the community an average of 13 months.[133]

Crime experts believe that the large numbers of former inmates returning to their neighborhoods can destabilize the area and increase existing crime rates. This issue is further explored in the Analyzing Criminal Justice Issues feature on page 536.

© 2003 AP/Wide World Photos

Parole is controversial because it allows convicted criminals back on the street before they have served their full sentence. Sometimes the outcome can be disastrous. Here, David Zink is being escorted into a Missouri courtroom after being charged with the murder of a young woman. Zink, a parolee, abducted the woman after they had a minor traffic accident.

The Problems of Parole

Parole failure is still a significant problem, and a growing portion of the correctional population consists of parolees who failed on the outside. Why has the phenomenon of parole failure remained so stubborn and hard to control? One reason may be the nature of the prison experience itself. The psychological and economic problems that lead inmates to recidivism are rarely addressed by a stay in prison. Despite rehabilitation efforts, the typical ex-convict is still the same undereducated, unemployed, substance-abusing lower-class male he was when arrested. Being separated from friends and family, not sharing in conventional society, associating with dangerous people, and adapting to a volatile lifestyle probably has done little to improve offenders' personality or behavior. And when they return to society, it may be to the same destructive neighborhood and social groups that prompted their original law-violating behavior. It seems naïve to think that incarceration alone can help someone overcome these lifelong disabilities. As correctional expert Stephen Daguid maintains, by their very nature prisons seek to impose and maintain order and conformity instead of helping inmates develop skills such as independence and critical thinking, factors that may be essential once the inmate is forced to cope outside the prison's walls.[134]

Parole failure also could be tied to the releasee's own personal deficits. Most research efforts indicate that a long history of criminal behavior, an antisocial personality, and childhood experiences with family dysfunction are all correlated with post-release recidivism.[135] Many releasees have suffered from a lifetime of

The Problems of Reentry

analyzing criminal justice issues

Because of America's two-decade-long imprisonment boom, more than 500,000 inmates are being released back into the community each year. In New York City alone, the New York State Department of Correctional Services releases approximately 25,000 people a year to the city, and the New York City jails release almost 100,000. In the state of California, more than 125,000 prisoners are released annually, almost 10 times the number of releases only 20 years earlier.

Criminologist Joan Petersilia warns that a number of unfortunate collateral consequences result from releasing people back into the community, many of whom have not received adequate treatment and are unprepared for life in conventional society. The risks they present to the community include increases in child abuse, family violence, the spread of infectious diseases, homelessness, and community disorganization.

Reentry risks can be tied to legal change in the way people are released from prison. In the past, offenders were granted early release only if a parole board believed they were rehabilitated and had ties to the community, such as a family or a job. Inmates were encouraged to enter treatment programs to earn parole. Changes in sentencing law have resulted

in the growth of mandatory release and the limits on discretionary parole. People now serve a fixed sentence and the discretion of parole boards has been blunted. Inmates may be discouraged from seeking involvement in rehabilitation programs (they do not influence the chance of parole), and the lack of incentive means that fewer inmates leaving prison have participated in programs to address work, education, and substance use deficiencies. For example, only 13 percent of inmates who suffer addiction receive any kind of drug abuse treatment in prison. And the situation does not improve upon release. Many inmates are not assigned to supervision caseloads once released into the community; about 100,000 released inmates go unsupervised each year.

Petersilia argues that, once back in the community, offenders may increase their criminal activity because they want to make up for lost time and resume their criminal careers. The majority leave prison with no savings, no immediate entitlement to unemployment benefits, and few employment prospects. One year after release, as many as 60 percent of former inmates are not employed in the regular labor market, and employers are increasingly reluctant to hire ex-offenders. Unemployment is closely related to drug

and alcohol abuse. Losing a job can lead to substance abuse, which in turn is related to child and family violence. Mothers released from prison have difficulty finding services such as housing, employment, and child care, and this causes stress for them and their children. Children of incarcerated and released parents often suffer confusion, sadness, and social stigma, and these feelings often result in school-related difficulties, low self-esteem, aggressive behavior, and general emotional dysfunction. If the parents are negative role models, children fail to develop positive attitudes about work and responsibility. Children of incarcerated parents are five times more likely to serve time in prison than are children whose parents have not been incarcerated.

Prisoners have significantly more medical and mental health problems than the general population, because of lifestyles that often include crowded or itinerant living conditions, intravenous drug use, poverty, and high rates of substance abuse. Inmates with mental illness (about 16 percent of all inmates) also are increasingly being imprisoned — and being released. Even when public mental health services are available, many mentally ill individuals fail to use them because they fear institutionalization,

substance abuse or dependence disorder.[136] A history of physical and sexual abuse has also been linked to recidivism.[137] Other parolees have substance abuse and mental health problems, and more than 10 percent exhibit both mental illness and substance abuse (see Table 16.2).

For example, one study of 400 Texas inmates found that almost 75 percent suffered from lifetime substance abuse or dependence disorder.[138] It seems naïve to think that incarceration alone can help someone overcome these disabilities.

Social and Economic Consequences The prison experience — being separated from friends and family, not sharing in conventional society, associating with dangerous people, and adapting to a volatile lifestyle — probably does little to improve offenders' personality or behavior. And when they return to society, it may deny they are mentally ill, or distrust the mental health system. The situation will become more serious as more and more parolees are released back into the disorganized communities whose deteriorated conditions may have motivated their original crimes.

Fear of a prison stay has less of an impact on behavior than ever before. As the prison population grows, the negative impact of incarceration may be lessening. In neighborhoods where doing time is more a rule than the exception, it becomes less of a stigma and more of a badge of acceptance. It also becomes a way of life from which some ex-convicts do rebound. Teens may encounter older men who have gone to prison and have returned to begin their lives again. With the proper skills and survival techniques, prison is considered manageable. While a prison stay is still unpleasant, it has lost its aura of shame and fear. By becoming commonplace and mundane, the prison experience has been exposed and its deterrent power reduced.

The Effect on Communities

Parole expert Richard Seiter has written on the effect returnees have on communities. When there were only a few hundred thousand prisoners, and a few thousand releasees per year, the issues surrounding the release of offenders did not overly challenge communities. Families could house ex-inmates, job-search organizations could find them jobs, and community social service agencies could respond to their individual needs for mental health or substance abuse treatment. Today, the sheer number of reentering inmates has taxed communities. The results of this system overload were recently encountered in Tallahassee, Florida, by Todd Clear and his associates. Data collected indicated that crime rates increase markedly one year after large numbers of inmates are released into the community. Disturbingly, the Clear research found that high rates of prison admissions produce high crime rates. The national policy of relying on prison as a deterrent to crime may produce results that policy makers had not expected nor wanted.

Critical Thinking

1. All too often, government leaders jump on the incarceration bandwagon as a panacea for the nation's crime problem. Is it a quick fix whose long-term consequences may be devastating for the nation's cities or are these problems counterbalanced by the crime-reducing effect of putting large numbers of high-rate offenders behind bars?

2. If you agree that incarceration undermines neighborhoods, can you think of some other indirect ways that high incarceration rates help increase crime rates?

InfoTrac College Edition Research

Alternatives to prison are now being sought because high incarceration rates may undermine a community's viability. What do you think? For some interesting developments, check out Joe Loconte, "Making Criminals Pay: A New York County's Bold Experiment in Biblical Justice," *Policy Review* 87 (January-February 1998): 26; Katarina Ivanko, "Shifting Gears to Rehabilitation," *Corrections Today* 59, no. 2 (April 1997): 20.

Sources: Joan Petersilia, "When Prisoners Return to Communities: Political, Economic, and Social Consequences," *Federal Probation* 65 (2001): 3-9; Todd Clear, Dina Rose, Elin Waring, and Kristen Scully, "Coercive Mobility and Crime: A Preliminary Examination of Concentrated Incarceration and Social Disorganization," *Justice Quarterly* 20 (2003): 33–65; Richard Seiter, "Prisoner Reentry and the Role of Parole Officers," *Federal Probation* 66 (2002): 50–54.

---

be to the same destructive neighborhood and social groups that prompted their original law-violating behavior. Some ex-inmates may have to prove that the prison experience has not changed them: Taking drugs or being sexually aggressive may show friends that they have not lost their "heart."[139]

Ex-inmates may find their home life torn and disrupted. Wives of inmates report that they must face the shame and stigma of having an incarcerated spouse while withstanding a barrage of calls from jealous husbands on the inside who try to monitor their behavior and control their lives. Family visits to the inmate become traumatic and strain interpersonal relationships because they often involve strip searches and other invasions of privacy.[140] One study of youthful ex-offenders trying to make it on the outside found that many experience delayed emotional and cognitive development because of early drug use. Most have never learned to use problem-solving or coping skills outside of the

Table 16.2 Levels of Substance Abuse and Mental Illness among State Prisoners Reentering Society

	Percent of reentering inmates
Drug or alcohol involved	*73.6*
Drug use	
In month before offense	59.2
At time of offense	33.7
Intravenous use in past	22.2
Alcohol abuse	
Binge drinkers	41.8
Alcohol dependent	25.2
At time of offense	35.7
Identified as mentally ill	14.4
Co-occurring disorders (substance abuse and mentally ill)	11.4

Source: Allen Beck, "State and Federal Prisoners Returning to the Community: Findings from the Bureau of Justice Statistics," paper presented at the First Reentry Courts Initiative Cluster Meeting, Washington, D.C., April 2000.

correctional setting, and most remain drug dependent.[141] Sensitive to these problems, some states have instituted support groups designed to help inmates' families adjust to their loneliness and despair.[142]

Even if familial and spousal support are present, former inmates soon find that imprisonment reduces their income and employment opportunities.[143] Ex-convicts by law are denied the right to work in certain occupations. And even if a criminal record does not automatically prohibit employment, many employers are reluctant to hire people who have served time. Why would someone hire an ex-con when other applicants are available? Many find that it is difficult to get jobs because potential employers are unconvinced that reform is possible or doubt that former inmates have the people skills that will enable them to succeed in the workplace. Some business owners are concerned about customers' reactions if they knew an employee was an ex-inmate.[144] If ex-offenders lie about their prison experience and are later found out, they could be dismissed for misrepresentation. The stress of economic deprivation, in turn, can lead to family breakup and to less involvement with children.[145] Research shows that former inmates who gain and keep meaningful employment are more likely to succeed on parole than those who are unemployed or underemployed.[146]

The specter of recidivism is especially frustrating to the American public. It is so difficult to apprehend and successfully prosecute criminal offenders that it seems foolish to grant them early release so they can prey on more victims. This problem is exacerbated when the parolee is a chronic, frequent offender. Research indicates that many of these returning prisoners are less prepared for reintegration and less connected to community-based social structures than in the past.[147] There seems to be a strong association between prior and future offending: The parolees most likely to fail on release are the ones who have failed in the past; chronic offenders are the ones most likely to reoffend. Because of these issues, some state jurisdictions are creating programs that ease the reentry process. The Analyzing Criminal Justice Issues feature on page 539 describes one such innovative program.

Residential Substance Abuse Treatment

analyzing criminal justice issues

The Residential Substance Abuse Treatment (RSAT) program has been implemented in Idaho. The state had found that too many people were being released from prison only to find themselves back in the correctional facility usually because of their substance-using behavior. Thus, the correctional facility located in southern Idaho incorporated the RSAT program to target parole violating individuals who have substance abuse problems.

The program consists of 9–12 months of rigorous drug treatment, which is provided by a private contractor who specializes in drug and alcohol use and also criminality. To partake in the program, an individual must be recommended by both parole officers and commission hearing officers. Specifications of the individual to enter the program include being a low risk, having a habitual substance abuse problem, and being sentenced to approximately 18 months in lockup. Individuals who have a desire to change, have a positive attitude, and have legitimate resources on the outside that will assist them when released are a few other aspects that increase the chances of a person to be selected to enter the program. Those who are chosen to participate are generally awarded an earlier release date from their sentence compared with those individuals who do not partake in the program.

The program is delivered in a therapeutic community environment within the correctional facility. The participants are grouped together and are urged to overcome their enemies together: substance abuse and criminality. During their treatment, participants are to better themselves by learning to think before they act. By thinking of the consequences of their behavior before they act, it is hoped that they will change their ways of decision making. In addition, they are to write down their thoughts and feelings, expressing what motivates their destructive behavior and how they can change their ways with more constructive choices. Furthermore, participants work on their social, behavioral, and vocational skills.

Another important aspect of the program is its incorporation of a 12-step model, similar to that used by Alcoholics Anonymous and Narcotics Anonymous. The 12-steps model promotes group counseling along with individual counseling. Plus, it incorporates meetings and physical activity. In addition to the current curriculum, an aftercare component has been considered for the program. Aftercare would provide assistance to those who have completed the program but who need a little more support to make it.

So far the program seems to be successful. Evaluations have suggested that the program is similar to other successful substance abuse treatment programs used in correctional facilities. Unfortunately, evaluations have been done to analyze only the changes of participants that have occurred as a result of the program. So far results show that, overall, participants have developed more positive attitudes regarding their substance abuse after completing the program. However, no evaluations have been completed on recidivism. With hope, recidivism rates will be the focus of future research to see if this program is successful in reaching its ultimate goal, which is to reduce recidivism rates.

Critical Thinking

1. How does the use of a program such as Residential Substance Abuse Treatment jibe with the no-frills movement? Would it be "cruel and unusual punishment" not to offer inmates the opportunity to control their substance abuse or are programs such as RSAT a privilege and not a right?

InfoTrac College Edition Research

 Use "Residential Substance Abuse Treatment" as a key term on InfoTrac College Edition.

Source: Mary K. Stohr, Craig Hemmens, Diane Baune, Jed Dayley, Mark Gornik, Kirstin Kjaer, and Cindy Noon, *Residential Substance Abuse Treatment for State Prisoners: Breaking the Drug-Crime Cycle among Parole Violators* (Washington, D.C.: National Institute for Justice, May 2003).

Losing Rights   One reason that ex-inmates find it so difficult to make it on the outside is the legal restrictions they are forced to endure.[148] These may include bars on certain kinds of employment, limits on obtaining licenses, and restrictions on their freedom of movement. Surveys have found that a significant number of states still restrict the activities of former felons.[149] Some of the more important findings are listed in Exhibit 16.3.

In general, states have placed greater restrictions on former felons, part of the get-tough movement. However, courts have considered individual requests by convicted felons to have their rights restored. It is common for courts to look at such issues as how recently the criminal offense took place and its relationship to the particular right before deciding whether to restore it.

Exhibit 16.3 Rights Lost by Convicted Felons

- Forty-seven jurisdictions restrict the right to vote; 38 of these allow for restoration.
- Forty-eight jurisdictions allow for termination of parental rights.
- Twenty-nine states consider a felony conviction to be legal grounds for divorce.
- Forty-seven states deny convicted felons the right to serve on juries; 37 allow restoration of the right.
- Forty jurisdictions prevent convicted felons from holding public office; 31 allow for restoration of the right.
- Federal law prevents ex-convicts from owning guns. Forty-four employ additional legal measures to prevent felons from possessing firearms. Twelve states allow for restoration of the right.
- Forty-six states require that felons register with law enforcement agencies. This requirement is up sharply in recent years; in 1986, only eight states required felons to register. All states require criminal registration of sex offenders.
- Civil death, or the denial of all civil rights, is still practiced in two states.

Source: Kevin Buckler and Lawrence Travis, "Reanalyzing the Prevalence and Social Context of Collateral Consequences Statutes," *Journal of Criminal Justice* 31 (2003): 435–53; Kathleen Olivares, Velmer Burton, and Francis Cullen, "The Collateral Consequences of a Felony Conviction: A National Study of State Legal Codes 10 Years Later," *Federal Probation* 60 (1996): 10–17.

A number of experts and national commissions have condemned the loss of rights of convicted offenders as a significant cause of recidivism. Consequently, courts have generally moved to eliminate the most restrictive elements of postconviction restrictions.[150]

Making Good Though most inmates recidivate soon after they are released, some do not and somehow are able to turn their lives around. What helps them go straight, while so many others fail? One reason may be tied to the social and economic support inmates receive on the outside. Maintaining family ties and gaining steady employment may help. Parolees who had a good employment record before their incarceration and who are able to find jobs after their release are the ones most likely to avoid recidivating.[151]

Some inmates undergo a cognitive change while inside. When justice expert Shadd Maruna interviewed a group of serious criminals to understand how they were able to reform their lives, he found that going straight was a long process, not an instantaneous event.[152] Those who do well after prison have undergone a long-term cognitive change in which they begin to see themselves as a new person or have a new outlook on life. They begin to try to understand their past and develop insights into why they behaved the way they did and why and how things went wrong. Those who leave a life of crime begin to feel a sense of fulfillment in engaging in productive behaviors and in so doing become agents of their own change. They start feeling in control of their future and have a newfound purpose in life. Instead of running from the past, they view their prior history as a learning experience, finding a silver lining in an otherwise awful situation.

Maruna finds that ex-offenders who desist from crime almost always attribute their deviant pasts to environmental factors outside of their control.[153] Similarly, they believe that their radical change in lifestyle — from convict to conventional success story — stems from outside forces over which they have little control. Often success is linked to some person or persons who, being forgiving and generous, can see past the ex-offender's mistakes. They give the ex-offender an opportunity to finally become his or her true self (a good productive person). This kindness does not go unappreciated. As a way of trying to give something back to the society from which they have taken so much, they make every effort to go straight, to become the man or woman their benefactor believed they could be.

To quiz yourself on this material, go to questions 16.25 on the Introduction to Criminal Justice 10e CD.

Summary

- On entering a prison, offenders must make tremendous adjustments to survive. Usual behavior patterns or lifestyles are radically changed. Opportunities for personal satisfaction are reduced. Passing through a number of adjustment stages or cycles, inmates learn to cope with the new environment.
- Inmates also learn to obey the inmate social code, which dictates proper behavior and attitudes. If inmates break the code, they may be unfavorably labeled.
- Inmates must learn how to cope and deal with sexual and physical predators.
- Inmates are eligible for a large number of treatment devices designed to help them readjust to the community once they are released.
- A number of treatment programs have offered inmates individualized and group psychological counseling. Some make use of the therapeutic community idea.
- There are many educational programs at the high school and even college levels.
- There are vocational training programs. Work furloughs have also been employed.
- Violence is common in prisons. Women often turn their hatred inward and hurt themselves, and male inmates engage in collective and individual violence against others. The Attica and New Mexico riots are examples of the most serious collective prison violence.
- In years past, society paid little attention to the incarcerated offender. The majority of inmates confined in jails and prisons were basically deprived of the rights guaranteed them under the Constitution.
- Today, however, the judicial system is actively involved in the administration of correctional institutions. Inmates can now take their grievances to courts and seek due process and equal protection under the law.
- The courts have recognized that persons confined in correctional institutions have rights — which include access to the courts and legal counsel, the exercise of religion, the rights to correspondence and visitation, and the right to adequate medical treatment.
- Most inmates return to society before the completion of their prison sentence. The majority earn early release through time off for good behavior or other sentence-reducing mechanisms.
- In addition, inmates are paroled before the completion of their maximum term.
- Most state jurisdictions maintain an independent parole board whose members decide whether to grant parole. Their decision making is discretionary and is based on many factors, such as the perception of the needs of society, the correctional system, and the client.
- Once paroled, the client is subject to control by parole officers who ensure that the conditions set by the board (the parole rules) are maintained. Parole can be revoked if the offender violates the rules of parole or commits a new crime.
- At one time most inmates were released on discretionary parole, but today changes in sentencing provisions have resulted in a significant increase in mandatory parole releases.
- Ex-inmates have a tough time adjusting on the outside, and the recidivism rate is disturbingly high. One reason is that many states restrict their rights and take away privileges granted to other citizens.

Key Terms

total institution 502
inmate subculture 505
inmate social code 505
prisonization 506
conjugal visit 513
work release (furlough) 516
hands-off doctrine 525
substantive right 528
jailhouse lawyer 528
cruel and unusual punishment 529
parole 532
mandatory parole release 532
intensive supervision
   parole (ISP) 534

Doing Research on the Web

For an up-to-date list of Web links, go to http://cj.wadsworth.com/siegel_intro10e.

Prison administrators are beginning to pay more attention to the communications and other technologies that have been developed for correctional facilities. In some cases, technology has been used for security purposes; in others, to keep down costs. There is abundant information on correctional technology at the National Law Enforcement and Corrections Technology Center, http://www.nlectc.org/.

To read more about how technology is influencing prison security, go to http://www.ojp.usdoj.gov/nij/sciencetech/aca/04_01.pdf.

Pro/Con discussions and Viewpoint Essays on some of the topics in this chapter may be found at the Opposing Viewpoints Resource Center: http://www.gale.com/OpposingViewpoints.

Discussion Questions

1. What are the benefits and drawbacks of conjugal visits?
2. Should women be allowed to work as guards in male prisons? What about male guards in female prisons? Why or why not?
3. Should prison inmates be allowed a free college education while noncriminals are forced to pay tuition? Why or why not? Do you believe in less eligibility for prisoners? Explain.
4. Define parole, including its purposes and objectives. How does it differ from probation?
5. What is the role of the parole board?
6. Should a former prisoner have all the civil rights afforded the average citizen? Explain. Should people be further penalized after they have paid their debt to society? Why or why not?

Notes

1 Darryl McGrath, "Brinks Case Decision: Ex-Militant's Parole Buoys Son, Angers Bereaved," *Boston Globe,* September 1, 2003, p.1.

2 Vanessa O'Connell, "Bans on Smoking in Prison Shrink a Coveted Market," *Wall Street Journal,* August 27, 2003, pp. A1–3.

3 Richard Berk, Heather Ladd, Heidi Graziano, and Jong-Ho Baek, "A Randomized Experiment Testing Inmate Classification Systems,"*Criminology and Public Policy* 2 (2003): 215–42.

4 Gresham Sykes, *The Society of Captives* (Princeton, N.J.: Princeton University Press, 1958).

5 David Eichenthal and James Jacobs, "Enforcing the Criminal Law in State Prisons," *Justice Quarterly* 8 (1991): 283–303.

6 John Wooldredge, "Inmate Lifestyles and Opportunities for Victimization," *Journal of Research in Crime and Delinquency* 35 (1998): 480–502.

7 David Anderson, *Crimes of Justice: Improving the Police, Courts, and Prison* (New York: Times Books, 1988).

8 Robert Johnson, *Hard Time: Understanding and Reforming the Prison* (Monterey, Calif.: Brooks/Cole, 1987), p. 115.

9 Wooldredge, "Inmate Lifestyles and Opportunities for Victimization."

10 Lawrence Hinman, "Stunning Morality: The Moral Dimensions of Stun Belts," *Criminal Justice Ethics* 17 (1998): 3–6.

11 Kevin Wright, *The Great American Crime Myth* (Westport, Conn.: Greenwood Press, 1985), p. 167.

12 Sandra Gleason, "Hustling: The Inside Economy of a Prison," *Federal Probation* 42 (1978): 32–39.

13 Hans Toch, *Living in Prison* (New York: Free Press, 1977), pp. 179–205.

14 Angela Maitland and Richard Sluder, "Victimization and Youthful Prison Inmates: An Empirical Analysis," *Prison Journal* 77 (1998): 55–74.

15 Seena Fazel and John Danesh, "Serious Mental Disorder in 23,000 Prisoners: A Systematic Review of 62 Surveys," *Lancet* 359 (2002): 545–61.

16 Leonore Simon, "Prison Behavior and Victim–Offender Relationships among Violent Offenders," paper presented at the annual meeting of the American Society of Criminology, San Francisco, California, November 1991.

17 John Irwin, "Adaptation to Being Corrected: Corrections from the Convict's Perspective," in *Handbook of Criminology,* ed. Daniel Glazer (Chicago: Rand McNally, 1974), pp. 971–93.

18 Donald Clemmer, *The Prison Community* (New York: Holt, Rinehart, and Winston, 1958).

19 Gresham Sykes and Sheldon Messinger, "The Inmate Social Code," in *The Sociology of Punishment and Corrections,* ed. Norman Johnston and others (New York: Wiley, 1970), pp. 401–08.

20 Gresham Sykes , *The Society of Captives: A Study of a Maximum Security Prison* (Princeton, N.J.: Princeton University Press, 1958).

21 John Irwin and Donald Cressey, "Thieves, Convicts, and the Inmate Culture," *Social Problems* 10 (1962): 142–55.

22 Brent Paterline and David Petersen, "Structural and Social Psychological Determinants of Prisonization," *Journal of Criminal Justice* 27 (1999): 427–41.

23 John Dilulio, *Governing Prisons: A Comparative Study of Correctional Management* (New York, Free Press, 1987).

24 B. Useem and M. Reisig, "Collective Action in Prisons: Protests, Disturbances, and Riots," *Criminology* 37 (1999): 735–59.

25 Beth Huebner, "Administrative Determinants of Inmate Violence: A Multilevel Analysis," *Journal of Criminal Justice* 31 (2003): 107–17.

26 Paterline and Petersen, "Structural and Social Psychological Determinants of Prisonization," p. 439.

27 James B. Jacobs, ed., *New Perspectives on Prisons and Imprisonment* (Ithaca, N.Y.: Cornell University Press, 1983).

28 Nicole Hahn Rafter, *Partial Justice* (New Brunswick, N.J.: Transaction Books, 1990), pp. 181–82.

29 Meda Chesney-Lind, "Patriarchy, Prisons, and Jails: A Critical Look at Trends in Women's Incarceration," paper presented at the International Feminist Conference on Women, Law, and Social Control, Mont Gabriel, Quebec, Canada, July 1991.

30 Meda Chesney-Lind, "Vengeful Equity: Sentencing Women to Prison," in *The Female Offender: Girls, Women, and Crime,* ed. Meda Chesney-Lind (Thousand Oaks, Calif.: Sage, 1997).

31 Elaine DeCostanzo and Helen Scholes, "Women behind Bars, Their Numbers Increase," *Corrections Today* 50 (1988): 104–06.

32 This section synthesizes the findings of a number of surveys of female inmates, including DeCostanzo and Scholes, "Women behind Bars"; Ruth Glick and Virginia Neto, *National Study of Women's Correctional Programs* (Washington, D.C.: Government Printing Office, 1977); Ann Goetting and Roy Michael Howsen, "Women in Prison: A Profile," *Prison Journal* 63 (1983): 27–46; Meda Chesney-Lind and Noelie Rodrigues, "Women under Lock and Key: A View from Inside," *Prison Journal* 63 (1983): 47–65; Contact Inc., "Women Offenders," *Corrections Compendium* 7 (1982): 6–11.

33 Merry Morash, Robin Harr, and Lila Rucker, "A Comparison of Programming for Women and Men in U.S. Prisons in the 1980s," *Crime and Delinquency* 40 (1994): 197–221.

34 Pamela Schram, "Stereotypes about Vocational Programming for Female Inmates," *Prison Journal* 78 (1998): 244–71.

35 Morash, Harr, and Rucker, "A Comparison of Programming for Women and Men in U.S. Prisons in the 1980s."

36 Polly Radosh, "Reflections on Women's Crime and Mothers in Prison: A Peacemaking Approach," *Crime and Delinquency* 48 (2002): 300–16.

37 Rebecca Jackson, Richard Rogers, Craig Neuman, and Paul Lambert, "Psychopathy in Female Offenders: An Investigation of Its Underlying Dimensions," *Criminal Justice and Behavior* 29 (2002): 692–705.

38 Fazel and Danesh, "Serious Mental Disorder in 23,000 Prisoners."

39 Gary Michael McClelland, Linda Teplin, Karen Abram, and Naomi Jacobs, "HIV and AIDS Risk Behaviors among Female Jail Detainees: Implications for Public Health Policy," *American Journal of Public Health* 92 (2002): 818–26.

40 "Sex Abuse of Female Inmates Is Common, Rights Group Says," *Criminal Justice Newsletter,* December 16, 1996, p. 2.

41 General Accounting Office, *Women in Prison: Sexual Misconduct by Correctional Staff* (Washington, D.C.: Government Printing Office, 1999).

42 Chesney-Lind, "Vengeful Equity."

43 Candace Kruttschnitt and Sharon Krmpotich, "Aggressive Behavior among Female Inmates: An Exploratory Study," *Justice Quarterly* 7 (1990): 370–89.

44 Candace Kruttschnitt, Rosemary Gartner, and Amy Miller, "Doing Her Own Time? Women's Responses to Prison in the Context of the Old and New Penology," *Criminology* 38 (2000): 681–718.

45 Mark Pogrebin and Mary Dodge, "Women's Accounts of Their Prison Experiences: A Retrospective View of Their Subjective Realities," *Journal of Criminal Justice* 29 (2001): 531–41.

46 Edna Erez, "The Myth of the New Female Offender: Some Evidence from Attitudes toward Law and Justice," *Journal of Criminal Justice* 16 (1988): 499–509.

47 Robert Ross and Hugh McKay, *Self-Mutilation* (Lexington, Mass.: Lexington Books, 1979).

48 Alice Propper, *Prison Homosexuality* (Lexington, Mass.: Lexington Books, 1981).

49 Dianna Newbern, Donald Dansereau, and Urvashi Pitre, "Positive Effects on Life Skills Motivation and Self-Efficacy: Node-Link Maps in a Modified Therapeutic Community," *American Journal of Drug and Alcohol Abuse* 25 (1999): 407–10.

50 Therapeutic Communities of America, Therapeutic Communities in Correctional Settings, *Appendix B: Revised TCA Standards for TCs in Correctional Settings* (Washington, D.C.: White House Office of National Drug Control Policy, 1998).

51 William Burdon, David Farabee, Michael Prendergast, Nena Messina, and Jerome Cartier, "Prison-Based Therapeutic Community Substance Abuse Programs: Implementation and Operational Issues," *Federal Probation* 66 (2002): 3–9.

52 Ira Sommers and Deborah Baskin, "The Prescription of Psychiatric Medication in Prison: Psychiatric versus Labeling Perspectives," *Justice Quarterly* 7 (1990): 739–55.

53 Judy Anderson and R. Daniel McGehee, "South Carolina Strives to Treat Elderly and Disabled Offenders," *Corrections Today* 53 (1991): 124–27.

54 Paige M. Harrison and Allen Beck, *Prisoners in 2002* (Washington, D.C.: Bureau of Justice Statistics, 2003); Darrell Gilliard and Allen Beck, *Prisoners in 1997* (Washington, D.C.: Bureau of Justice Statistics, 1998).

55 Catherine Lemieux, Timothy Dyeson, and Brandi Castiglione, "Revisiting the Literature on Prisoners Who Are Older: Are We Wiser?" *Prison Journal* 82 (2002): 432–56.

56 Charles Sullivan, "Private Family Visits Are a Matter of Logic," *Corrections Today* 65 (2003): 18–19.

57 Caroline Wolf Harlow, *Education and Correctional Populations* (Washington, D.C.: Bureau of Justice Statistics, 2003).

58 Harlow, *Education and Correctional Populations.*

59 Howard Skolnik and John Slansky, "A First Step in Helping Inmates Get Good Jobs after Release," *Corrections Today* 53 (1991): 92.

60 This section leans heavily on Barbara Auerbach, George Sexton, Franklin Farrow, and Robert Lawson, *Work in American Prisons: The Private Sector Gets Involved* (Washington, D.C.: National Institute of Justice, 1988).

61 Public Law 96-157, Sec. 827, codified as 18 U.S.C., Sec. 1761(c).

62 Courtesy of the Prison Industry Authority, 560 East Natoma Street, Folsom, CA 95630-2200.

63 Diane Dwyer and Roger McNally, "Public Policy, Prison Industries, and Business: An Equitable Balance for the 1990s," *Federal Probation* 57 (1993): 30–35.

64 This section leans heavily on Mark Hamm, "Current Perspectives on the Prisoner Self-Help Movement," *Federal Probation* 52 (1988): 49–56.

65 For more information, contact the Fortune Society, 39 West 19th Street, New York, NY 10011, (212) 206-7070. The e-mail address is info@fortunesociety.org.

66 Douglas Lipton, Robert Martinson, and Judith Wilks, *The Effectiveness of Correctional Treatment: A Survey of Treatment Evaluation Studies* (New York: Praeger, 1975).

67 Charles Murray and Louis Cox, *Beyond Probation: Juvenile Corrections and the Chronic Delinquent* (Beverly Hills, Calif.: Sage, 1979).

68 Steven Lab and John Whitehead, "An Analysis of Juvenile Correctional Treatment," *Crime and Delinquency* 34 (1988): 60–83.

69 Francis Cullen and Karen Gilbert, *Reaffirming Rehabilitation* (Cincinnati, Ohio: Anderson Publications, 1982).

70 David Wilson, Catherine Gallagher, and Doris MacKenzie, "A Meta-Analysis of Corrections-Based Education, Vocation, and Work Programs for Adult Offenders," *Journal of Research in Crime and Delinquency* 37 (2000): 347–68.

71 Mary Ellen Batiuk, Paul Moke, and Pamela Wilcox Rountree, "Crime and Rehabilitation: Correctional Education as an Agent of Change — A Research Note," *Justice Quarterly* 14 (1997): 167–80.

72 Frank Pearson, Douglas Lipton, Charles Cleland, and Dorline Yee, "The Effects of Behavioral/Cognitive-Behavioral Programs on Recidivism," *Crime and Delinquency* 48 (2002): 476–97; Mark Lipsey and David Wilson, "Effective Intervention for Serious Juvenile Offenders: A Synthesis of Research," in *Serious and Violent Juvenile Offenders: Risk Factors and Successful Interventions,* ed. Rolf Loeber and David Farrington (Thousand Oaks, Calif.: Sage, 1998).

73 Paul Gendreau and Claire Goffin, "Principles of Effective Correctional Programming," *Forum on Correctional Research* 2 (1996): 38–41.

74 Morash, Harr, and Rucker, "A Comparison of Programming for Women and Men in U.S. Prisons in the 1980s."

75 Christopher J. Mumola, *Substance Abuse and Treatment, State and Federal Prisoners, 1997* (Washington, D.C.: Bureau of Justice Statistics, 1999)

76 Lucien X. Lombardo, *Guards Imprisoned* (New York: Elsevier, 1981); James Jacobs and Norma Crotty, "The Guard's World," in *New Perspectives on Prisons and Imprisonment,* ed. James Jacobs (Ithaca, N.Y.: Cornell University Press, 1983), 133–41.

77 Correctional Officer Education and Training," *Corrections Compendium* 28 (2003): 11–13.

78 Claire Mayhew and Duncan Chappell, "An Overview of Occupational Violence," *Australian Nursing Journal* 9 (2002): 34–35.

79 John Klofas and Hans Toch, "The Guard Subculture Myth," *Journal of Research in Crime and Delinquency* 19 (1982): 238–54.

80 Ruth Triplett and Janet Mullings, "Work-Related Stress and Coping among Correctional Officers: Implications from the Organizational Literature," *Journal of Criminal Justice* 24 (1996): 291–308.

81 Peter Horne, "Female Correction Officers," *Federal Probation* 49 (1985): 46–55.

82 *Dothard* v. *Rawlinson,* 433 U.S. 321 (1977).

83 Christopher D. Man and John P. Cronan, "Forecasting Sexual Abuse in Prison: The Prison Subculture of Masculinity as a Backdrop for 'Deliberate Indifference,'" *Journal of Criminal Law and Criminology* (2001): 127–66.

84 Jesse Walker, "Rape behind Bars," *Reason* 35 (2003): 10–12.

85 Daphne Retter, "Prison Rape Measure Advances through House Judiciary Panel," *CQ Weekly* 61 (2003): 10–12.

86 David Duffee, *Corrections, Practice, and Policy* (New York: Random House, 1989), p. 305.

87 Randy Martin and Sherwood Zimmerman, "A Typology of the Causes of Prison Riots and an Analytical Extension to the 1986 West Virginia Riot," *Justice Quarterly* 7 (1990): 711–37.

88 Grant Harris, Tracey Skilling, and Marnie Rice, "The Construct of Psychopathy, in *Crime and Justice: An Annual Edition,* ed. Michael Tonry (Chicago: University of Chicago Press, 2001), 197–265.

89 For a series of papers on the position, see A. Cohen, G. Cole, and R. Baily, eds., *Prison Violence* (Lexington, Mass.: Lexington Books, 1976).

90 Bert Useem and Michael Resig, "Collective Action in Prisons: Protests, Disturbances,

and Riots," *Criminology* 37 (1999): 735–60.

91 National Advisory Commission on Criminal Justice Standards and Goals, *Corrections* (Washington, D.C.: Government Printing Office, 1973), p. 18.

92 *Cooper* v. *Pate,* 378 U.S. 546 (1964).

93 *DeMallory* v. *Cullen,* 855 F.2d 422 (7th Cir. 1988).

94 *Lindquist* v. *Idaho State Board of Corrections,* 776 F.2d 851 (9th Cir. 1985).

95 *Smith* v. *Wade,* 461 U.S. 30, 103 S.Ct. 1625 (1983).

96 *Bounds* v. *Smith,* 430 U.S. 817 (1977).

97 *Shaw* v. *Murphy* (99–1613), 2001.

98 *Turner* v. *Safley,* 482 U.S. 78, 107 S.Ct. 2254 (1987) at 2261.

99 *Ramos* v. *Lamm,* 639 F.2d 559 (10th Cir. 1980).

100 *Procunier* v. *Martinez,* 411 U.S. 396 (1974).

101 *Nolan* v. *Fitzpatrick,* 451 F.2d 545 (1st Cir. 1971). See also *Washington Post Co.* v. *Kleindienst,* 494 F.2d 997 (D.C. Cir. 1974).

102 *Mumin* v. *Phelps,* 857 F.2d 1055 (5th Cir. 1988).

103 *O'Lone* v. *Estate of Shabazz,* 482 U.S. 342, 107 S.Ct. 2400 (1987).

104 *Rahman* v. *Stephenson,* 626 F.Supp. 886 (W.D. Tenn. 1986).

105 *Newman* v. *Alabama,* 92 S.Ct. 1079, 405 U.S. 319 (1972).

106 *Estelle* v. *Gamble,* 429 U.S. 97 (1976).

107 Ibid.

108 "Pennsylvania's State Prisons Changing Way They Treat Inmates," *Health and Medicine Week* (August 11, 2003): 259–61.

109 *Trop* v. *Dulles,* 356 U.S. 86, 78 S.Ct. 590 (1958). See also *Furman* v. *Georgia,* 408 U.S. 238, 92 S.Ct. 2726, 33 L.Ed.2d 346 (1972).

110 *Weems* v. *United States,* 217 U.S. 349, 30 S.Ct. 544, 54 L.Ed. 793 (1910).

111 *Lee* v. *Tahash,* 352 F.2d 970 (8th Cir., 1965).

112 *Estelle* v. *Gamble,* 429 U.S. 97 (1976).

113 *Robinson* v. *California,* 370 U.S. 660 (1962).

114 *Gregg* v. *Georgia,* 428 U.S. 153 (1976).

115 *Jackson* v. *Bishop,* 404 F.2d 571 (8th Cir. 1968).

116 *Hope* v. *Pelzer et al.,* No. 01–309. June 27, 2002.

117 *Bell* v. *Wolfish,* 99 S.Ct. 1873–1974 (1979). See also "*Bell* v. *Wolfish:* The Rights of Pretrial Detainees," *New England Journal of Prison Law* 6 (1979): 134.

118 *Farmer* v. *Brennan,* 144 S.Ct. 1970 (1994).

119 *Rhodes* v. *Chapman,* 452 U.S. 337 (1981). For further analysis of *Rhodes,* see Randall Pooler, "Prison Overcrowding and the Eighth Amendment: The Rhodes Not Taken," *New England Journal on Criminal and Civil Confinement* 8 (1983): 1–28.

120 *Estelle* v. *Ruiz,* No. 74-329 (E.D. Texas 1980).

121 "Ruiz Case in Texas Winds Down: Special Master to Close Office," *Criminal Justice Newsletter,* January 15, 1990, p. 1.

122 Prison Litigation Reform Act of 1995, Pub. L. No. 104-134 (codified as amended in scattered titles and sections of the U.S.C.). See also H.R. 3019, 104th Cong., 2d sess. (1996).

123 *Prison Escape Survey* (Lincoln, Neb.: Corrections Compendium, 1991).

124 Bureau of Justice Statistics, "Forty-two Percent of State Parole Discharges Were Successful," news release, October 3, 2001.

125 Timothy A. Hughes, Doris James Wilson, and Allen J. Beck, *Trends in State Parole, 1990–2000* (Washington, D.C.: Bureau of Justice Statistics, 2001).

126 Ronald Burns, Patrick Kinkade, Matthew Leone, and Scott Phillips, "Perspectives on Parole: The Board Members' Viewpoint," *Federal Probation* 63 (1999): 16–22.

127 Duncan N. Stevens, "Off the *Mapp:* Parole Revocation Hearings and the Fourth Amendment," *Journal of Criminal Law and Criminology* 89 (1999): 1047–60.

128 Gregg Etter and Judy Hammond, "Community: Service Work as Part of Offender Rehabilitation," *Corrections Today* 63 (2001): 114–17.

129 Brian Parry, "Special Service Unit: Dedicated to Investigating and Apprehending Violent Offenders," *Corrections Today* 63 (2001): 120.

130 Thomas Hanlon, David N. Nurco, Richard W. Bateman, and Kevin E. O'-Grady, "The Response of Drug Abuser Parolees to a Combination of Treatment and Intensive Supervision," *Prison Journal* 78 (1998): 31–44; Susan Turner and Joan Petersilia, "Focusing on High-Risk Parolees: An Experiment to Reduce Commitments to the Texas Department of Corrections," *Journal of Research in Crime and Delinquency* 29 (1992): 34–61.

131 Joan Petersilia, "When Prisoners Return to Communities: Political, Economic, and Social Consequences," *Federal Probation* 65 (2001): 3-9.

132 Patrick A. Langan and David J. Levin, *Recidivism of Prisoners Released in 1994* (Washington, D.C.: Bureau of Justice Statistics, 2002).

133 Robyn L. Cohen, *Probation and Parole Violators in State Prison, 1991: Survey of State Prison Inmates, 1991* (Washington, D.C.: Bureau of Justice Statistics, 1995).

134 Stephen Duguid, *Can Prisons Work? The Prisoner as Object and Subject in Modern Corrections* (Toronto, Canada: University of Toronto Press, 2000).

135 James Bonta, Moira Law, and Karl Hanson, "The Prediction of Criminal and Violent Recidivism among Mentally Disordered Offenders: A Meta-Analysis," *Psychological Bulletin* 123 (1998): 123–42.

136 Roger Peters, Paul Greenbaum, John Edens, Chris Carter, and Madeline Ortiz, "Prevalence of DSM-IV Substance Abuse and Dependence Disorders among Prison Inmates," *American Journal of Drug and Alcohol Abuse* 24 (1998): 573–80.

137 Catherine Hamilton, Louise Falshaw, and Kevin D. Browne, "The Link between Recurrent Maltreatment and Offending Behavior," *International Journal of Offender Therapy and Comparative Criminology* 46 (2002): 75–95.

138 Peters, Greenbaum, Edens, Carter, and Ortiz, "Prevalence of DSM-IV Substance Abuse and Dependence Disorders among Prison Inmates."

139 J. E. Ryan, "Who Gets Revoked? A Comparison of Intensive Supervision Successes and Failures in Vermont," *Crime and Delinquency* 43 (1997): 104–118.

140 Laura Fishman, *Women at the Wall: A Study of Prisoners' Wives Doing Time on the Outside* (New York: State University of New York Press, 1990).

141 Bonnie Todis, Michael Bullis, Miriam Waintrup, Robert Schultz, and Ryan D'ambrosio, "Overcoming the Odds: Qualitative Examination of Resilience among Formerly Incarcerated Adolescents," *Exceptional Children* 68 (2001): 119–40.

142 Leslee Goodman Hornick, "Volunteer Program Helps Make Inmates' Families Feel Welcome," *Corrections Today* 53 (1991): 184–86.

143 Jeffrey Fagan and Richard Freeman, "Crime and Work," in *Crime and Justice: A Review of Research,* vol. 25, ed. Michael Tonry (Chicago: University of Chicago Press, 1999), pp. 211–29.

144 Rachelle Giguere and Lauren Dundes, "Help Wanted: A Survey of Employer Concerns about Hiring Ex-Convicts," *Criminal Justice Policy Review* 13 (2002): 396–408.

145 John Hagan and Ronit Dinovitzer, "Collateral Consequences of Imprisonment for Children, Communities, and Prisoners," in *Crime and Justice: A Review of Research,* vol. 26, ed. Michael Tonry and Joan Petersilia (Chicago: University of Chicago Press, 1999), pp. 89–107.

146 Hanlon, Nurco, Bateman, and O'Grady, "The Response of Drug Abuser Parolees to a Combination of Treatment and Intensive Supervision."

147 Jeremy Travis and Joan Petersilia, "Reentry Reconsidered: A New Look at an Old Question," *Crime and Delinquency* 47 (2001): 291–313.

148 Hanlon, Nurco, Bateman, and O'Grady, "The Response of Drug Abuser Parolees to a Combination of Treatment and Intensive Supervision."

149 Kevin Buckler and Lawrence Travis, "Reanalyzing the Prevalence and Social Context of Collateral Consequences Statutes," *Journal of Criminal Justice* 31 (2003): 435–53; Kathleen Olivares, Velmer Burton, and Francis Cullen, "The Collateral Consequences of a Felony Conviction: A National Study of State Legal Codes 10 Years Later," *Federal Probation* 60 (1996): 10–17.

150 See, for example, *Bush* v. *Reid,* 516 P.2d 1215 (Alaska, 1973); *Thompson* v. *Bond,* 421 F.Supp. 878 (W.D. Mo., 1976); *Delorne* v. *Pierce Freightlines Co.,* 353 F.Supp. 258 (D. Or., 1973); *Beyer* v. *Werner,* 299 F.Supp. 967 (E.D. N.Y., 1969).

151 Hanlon, Nurco, Bateman, and O'Grady, "The Response of Drug Abuser Parolees to a Combination of Treatment and Intensive Supervision."

152 Shadd Maruna, *Making Good : How Ex-Convicts Reform and Rebuild Their Lives* (Washington, D.C.: American Psychological Association, 2000).

153 Shadd Maruna, "Going Straight: Desistance from Crime and Self-Narratives of Reform," *Narrative Study of Lives* 5 (1997): 59-93.

Part Five The History and Nature of the Juvenile Justice System

© 2003 AP/Wide World Photos

Chapter 17
The Juvenile Justice System

Nathaniel Abraham was 11 years old when he fired a shot from a .22-caliber rifle, fatally wounding Ronnie Lee Greene Jr. As his trial began, Abraham's defense attorney told jurors that the shooting was a "very tragic, tragic accident" and that Abraham had the developmental abilities of a boy 6 to 8 years old at the time of the killing. He argued that Abraham was not capable of forming the intent to kill, as is required for a first-degree murder conviction. The prosecutor retorted that Abraham bragged to friends about the killing. Prosecutors also noted that Abraham had had 22 scrapes with police and that

his mother had tried to have him ruled incorrigible in juvenile court.

After Abraham's conviction for murder, prosecutors sought a blended sentence of incarceration in a juvenile facility until age 21, followed by imprisonment in an adult facility. However, the sentencing judge ordered him to be held in juvenile detention until age 21, when he would be released. "While there is no guarantee Nathaniel will be rehabilitated at 21, it is clear 10 years is enough to accomplish this goal," said Judge Eugene Moore at the sentencing hearing.

The Abraham case, while extreme, is representative of the difficult choices that agents of the juvenile justice system are continually asked to make: How should troubled children be treated? What can be done to save dangerous young offenders? Should youthful law violators be given unique treatment because of their age, or should they be treated in a similar fashion to an adult committing the same crime? In this section, the juvenile justice system is examined in some detail.

Chapter Outline

Chapter Objectives

After reading this chapter, you should be able to:

1. Understand why the juvenile justice system developed.
2. Discuss the differences between delinquents and status offenders.
3. Recognize the problems associated with the child-saving movement.
4. Describe the efforts to create the first juvenile court.
5. Know the similarities and differences between adult and juvenile justice.
6. Understand the rights of children.
7. Describe the various stages in the juvenile justice process.
8. Discuss the concept of deinstitutionalizaton.
9. Describe the various juvenile institutions.
10. Understand the argument for abolishing the juvenile court.

Viewpoints

 Law in Review: *In re Gault* 564

 Analyzing Criminal Justice Issues: Teen Courts 565

 Analyzing Criminal Justice Issues: The Juvenile Mentoring Program (JUMP) 573

 Analyzing Criminal Justice Issues: Should the Juvenile Court Be Abolished? 574

InfoTrac College Edition Links

Article: " 'The Cop Will Get You': The Police and Discretionary Juvenile Justice, 1890–1940" 552

Article: "Exploring 'Youth' in Court: An Analysis of Decision-Making in Youth Court Bail Hearings" 560

Article: "Juvenile Justice? In the 1990s, Many States Passed Laws That Made It Easier to Try Teens as Adults: Does Youth Crime Deserve 'Adult Time'?" 563

Article: "Failure of Mental Health Policy — Incarcerated Children and Adolescents" 569

Article: "Prevention as Public Policy" 571

Web Links

**Office of Juvenile Justice and
Delinquency Prevention**
http://ojjdp.ncjrs.org/ 553

**Pasadena, California,
police juvenile division**
http://www.ci.pasadena.tx.us/police/
investigations/juveniles/juveniles.htm 557

National Center for Youth Law
http://www.youthlaw.org 557

Prosecution of juvenile offenders
http://www.ncjrs.org/html/ojjdp/
jjbul2000_03_5/pag4.html 558

National Juvenile Detention Association
http://www.njda.com/default.html 560

In re Gault
http://caselaw.lp.findlaw.com/scripts/getcase.
pl?court=us&vol=387&invol=1 563

**National Council of Juvenile and
Family Court Judges**
http://www.ncjfcj.org/ 563

McKeiver* v. *Pennsylvania
http://caselaw.lp.findlaw.com/scripts/getcase.
pl?navby=search&court=US&case=/us/403/528.
html 563

**Council of Juvenile Correctional
Administrators**
http://www.corrections.com/cjca/ 568

Parenting Resources for the 21st Century
http://www.parentingresources.ncjrs.org/ 572

Chapter 17 | The Juvenile Justice System

Lee Boyd Malvo, the 17-year-old identified as one of the two snipers who went on a shooting spree in the Washington, D.C., area in October 2002, was an enigma to those who knew him. Some described him as "unremarkable" and others as "caring and very respectful." To his classmates at a Bellingham, Washington, high school, Malvo, a Jamaican native, seemed quiet and studious.[1] The prosecutor in the sniper case announced after Malvo's arrest that he would be tried as an adult and eligible for the death penalty.

On December 23, 2003, Malvo was spared capital punishment and sentenced instead to life in prison without the possibility of parole.

While unique, the Malvo case is representative of the difficult choices that agents of the juvenile justice system are continually asked to make: How should troubled children be treated? What can be done to save

dangerous young offenders? Should youthful law violators be given unique treatment because of their age, or should they be treated in a similar fashion to an adult committing the same crime?

CNN. *View the CNN video clip of this story on your Introduction to Criminal Justice 10e CD.*

parens patriae
The power of the state to act on behalf of a child and provide care and protection equivalent to that of a parent.

Independent yet interrelated with the adult criminal justice system, the juvenile justice system is primarily responsible for dealing with juvenile and youth crime, as well as with incorrigible and truant children and runaways. First conceived at the turn of the twentieth century, the juvenile justice system was viewed as a quasi-social welfare agency that was to act as a surrogate parent in the interests of the child; this is referred to as the **parens patriae** philosophy. Today, some authorities still hold to the original social welfare principles of the juvenile justice system and argue that it is primarily a treatment agency that acts as a wise parent, dispensing personalized, individual justice to needy children who seek guidance and understanding. They recognize that many children who are arrested and petitioned to juvenile court come from the lowest economic classes. These at-risk children have grown up in troubled families, attend inadequate schools, and live in deteriorated neighborhoods. They are deserving of care and concern, not punishment and control.

In contrast to this view, those with a crime control orientation suggest that the juvenile justice system's parens patriae philosophy is outdated. They point to nationally publicized incidents of juvenile violence, such as the D.C. sniper case and shootings at Columbine High School in Colorado, as indicators that serious juvenile offenders should be punished and disciplined, instead of treated and rehabilitated. They note that juveniles 17 years and under commit about 10 percent of all murders in the United States.[2] Not surprisingly, they applaud when court rulings enhance the state's ability to identify and apprehend youthful law violators. For example, in 1995 the U.S. Supreme Court held in *Vernonia School District* v. *Acton* that a public school athlete in middle and high schools can be required to submit to random drug testing even though the student did not engage in suspicious behavior.[3] On June 27, 2002, the Court in *Board of Education of Independent School District No. 92 of Pottawatomie County et al.* v. *Earls et al.* ruled permissible a school drug testing policy that established random, suspicionless urinalysis testing of any students participating in extracurricular competitive activities.[4] These and similar rulings encourage those who want the state to be given a free hand to deal with juveniles who are disruptive at school and in the community.

It remains to be seen whether the juvenile justice system will continue on its path toward identification and control or return to its former role of a treatment-dispensing agency. Some call for a new approach to the juvenile justice system, using the balanced and restorative justice model, which relies on offender–victim reconciliation, personal accountability, and community-based program developments.[5]

The History of Juvenile Justice

The modern practice of legally separating adult and juvenile offenders can be traced to two developments in English custom and law: poor laws and chancery court. Both were designed to allow the state to take control of the lives of needy but not necessarily criminal children.[6] They set the precedent for later American developments.

poor laws
Seventeenth-century English laws under which vagrants and abandoned and neglected children were bound to masters as indentured servants.

As early as 1535 the English passed statutes known as **poor laws,** which in part mandated the appointment of overseers who placed destitute or neglected children with families who then trained them in agricultural, trade, or domestic services; this practice was referred to as indenture. The Elizabethan poor laws of 1601 created a system of church wardens and overseers who, with the consent of the justices of the peace, identified vagrant, delinquent, and neglected children and took measures to put them to work. Often this meant placing them in poorhouses or workhouses or, more commonly, apprenticing them until their adulthood. The indenture, or involuntary apprentice, system set the precedent, which continues today, of allowing the government to take control of youths who had committed no illegal acts but who were deemed unable to care for themselves.

In contrast, **chancery courts** were concerned primarily with protecting the property rights and welfare of more affluent minor children who could not care for themselves — children whose position and property were of direct concern to the monarch. They dealt with issues of guardianship and the use and control of property. Chancery courts operated under the parens patriae philosophy, which held that children were under the protective control of the state and its rulers were justified in intervening in their lives.[7] In the famous English case *Wellesley* v. *Wellesley,* a duke's children were taken from him in the name of parens patriae because of his scandalous behavior.[8]

The concept of parens patriae came to represent the primacy of the state and its power to act in "the best interests of the child." The idea that the state was legally obligated to protect the immature, the incompetent, the neglected, and the delinquent subsequently became a major influence on the development of the U.S. juvenile justice system in the twentieth century.

chancery courts
English courts assigned with the protection of the property rights of minor children.

child savers
Civic leaders who focused their attention on the misdeeds of poor children to control their behavior.

Care of Children in Early America

The forced apprenticeship system and the poor laws were brought from England to colonial America. Poor laws were passed in Virginia in 1646 and in Connecticut and Massachusetts in 1678 and continued in force until the early nineteenth century. They mandated care for wayward and destitute children. However, those youths who committed serious criminal offenses were tried in the same courts as adults.

To accommodate dependent youths, local jurisdictions developed almshouses, poorhouses, and workhouses. Crowded and unhealthy, these accepted the poor, the insane, the diseased, and vagrant and destitute children. Middle-class civic leaders, who referred to themselves as **child savers,** began to develop organizations and groups to help alleviate the burdens of the poor and immigrants by sponsoring shelter care for youths, educational and social activities, and the development of settlement houses. In retrospect, their main focus seems to have been on extending governmental control over a whole range of youthful activities that previously had been left to private or family control, including idleness, drinking, vagrancy, and delinquency.[9]

The Granger Collection/New York

The Child-Saving Movement

The child savers were responsible for creating a number of programs for indigent youths, including the New York House of Refuge, which began operations in 1825.[10] Its creation was effected by prominent Quakers and influential political leaders, such as Cadwallader Colden and Stephen Allen. In 1816 they formed the Society for the Prevention of Pauperism, which was devoted to the concept of protecting indigent youths who were at risk of leading a life of crime by taking them off the streets and reforming them in a family-like environment.[11]

The first House of Refuge constructed in New York City was the product of their reform efforts. Though the program was privately managed, the state legislature began providing funds partly through a head tax on arriving transatlantic passengers and seamen, plus the proceeds from license fees for New York City's taverns, theatres, and circuses. These revenue sources were deemed appropriate,

Boys on the steps of an abandoned tenement building in New York City, about 1889. The child savers were concerned that, if left alone, children such as these would enter a life of crime. Critics accused them of class and race discrimination and thought they sought to maintain control over the political system.

given that supporters blamed immigration, intemperance, and commercial entertainment for juvenile crime.

The reformatory opened January 1, 1825, with only six boys and three girls. However, within the first decade of its operation, 1,678 youths were admitted. Most kids were sent because of vagrancy and petty crimes and were sentenced or committed indefinitely until they reached adulthood. Originally, the institution accepted inmates from across the state, but when a Western House of Refuge was opened in Rochester, New York, in 1849, residents came from the eastern quarters.

Once a resident, a large part of the adolescent's daily schedule was devoted to supervised labor, which was regarded as beneficial to education and discipline. Inmate labor also supported operating expenses for the reformatory. Male inmates worked in shops that produced brushes, cane chairs, brass nails, and shoes. The female inmates sewed uniforms, did laundry, and carried out other domestic work. A badge system was used to segregate inmates according to their behavior. Although students received rudimentary educational skills, greater emphasis was placed on evangelical religious instruction; non-Protestant clergy were excluded. The reformatory had the authority to commit inmates to indenture agreements with private employers. Most males became farm workers; females, domestic laborers.

The Reform Movement Spreads

When the House of Refuge opened, the majority of children admitted were status offenders placed there because of vagrancy or neglect. Children were put in the institution by court order, sometimes over parents' objections. Their length of stay depended on need, age, and skill. Critics complained that the institution was run like a prison, with strict discipline and absolute separation of the sexes. Such a harsh program drove many children to run away, and the House of Refuge was forced to take a more lenient approach. Despite criticism, the concept enjoyed expanding popularity. In 1826, the Boston City Council founded the House of Reformation for juvenile offenders.[12] The courts committed children found guilty of criminal violations, or found to be beyond the control of their parents, to these schools. Because the child savers considered parents of delinquent children to be as guilty as convicted offenders, they sought to have the reform schools establish control over the children. Refuge managers believed they were preventing poverty and crime by separating destitute and delinquent children from their parents and placing them in an institution.[13]

The child savers also influenced state and local governments to create independent correctional institutions to house minors. The first of these reform schools opened in Westboro, Massachusetts, in 1848 and in Rochester, New York, in 1849. Other states soon followed suit — Ohio in 1850 and Maine, Michigan, and Rhode Island in 1860. Children lived in congregate conditions and spent their days working at institutional jobs, learning a trade when possible, and receiving some basic education. They were racially and sexually segregated, discipline was harsh and often involved whipping and isolation, and the physical care was of poor quality.

Children's Aid Society
Group created by Charles Loring Brace to place indigent city kids with farm families.

In 1853 New York philanthropist Charles Loring Brace helped develop the **Children's Aid Society** as an alternative for dealing with neglected and delinquent youths. Brace proposed rescuing wayward youths from the harsh environment of the city and providing them with temporary shelter and care. He then sought to place them in private homes in rural communities where they could engage in farming and agricultural work outside the harsh influence of the city. Although some placements proved successful, others resulted in the exploitation of children in a strange environment with few avenues of escape.

Establishment of the Juvenile Court

As the nation expanded, it became evident that private charities and public organizations were not caring adequately for the growing number of troubled youths. The child savers lobbied for an independent, state-supported juvenile court, and their efforts prompted the development of the first comprehensive juvenile court in Illinois in 1899. The Illinois Juvenile Court Act set up an independent court to handle criminal law violations by children under 16 years of age, as well as to care for neglected, dependent, and wayward youths. The act also created a probation department to monitor youths in the community and to direct juvenile court judges to place serious offenders in secure schools for boys and industrial schools for girls. The ostensible purpose of the act was to separate juveniles from adult offenders and provide a legal framework in which juveniles could get adequate care and custody. By 1925 most states had developed juvenile courts. The enactment of the Juvenile Court Act of 1899 was a major event in the history of the juvenile justice movement in the United States.

Although the efforts of the child savers to set up independent juvenile courts were originally seen as liberal reforms, modern scholars commonly view them as attempts to control and punish. Justice historians have suggested that the reform movement expressed the vested interests of the "ruling class."[14] Thus, according to this revisionist approach, the reformers applied the concept of parens patriae for their own purposes, including the continuance of middle- and upper-class values, the control of the political system, and the furtherance of a child labor system consisting of lower-class workers with marginal skills.

The Development of Juvenile Justice

The juvenile court movement quickly spread across the United States. In its early form it provided youths with quasi-legal, quasi-therapeutic, personalized justice. The main concern was the "best interests of the child," not strict adherence to legal doctrine, constitutional rights, or due process of law. The court was paternalistic, not adversarial. For example, attorneys were not required. Hearsay evidence, inadmissible in criminal trials, was commonly employed in the adjudication of juvenile offenders. Children were encouraged to admit their guilt in open court in violation of their Fifth Amendment rights. Verdicts were based on a "preponderance of the evidence," instead of "beyond a reasonable doubt." Juvenile courts then functioned as quasi-social service agencies.

Reform Schools Youngsters found delinquent in juvenile court could spend years in a state training school. Though priding themselves as nonpunitive, these early reform schools were generally aimed at punishment and based on the concept of reform through hard work and discipline. In the second half of the nineteenth century, the emphasis shifted from massive industrial schools to the cottage system. Juvenile offenders were housed in a series of small cabins, each one holding 20 to 40 children, run by cottage parents, who attempted to create a homelike atmosphere. The first cottage system was established in Massachusetts, the second in Ohio. The system was generally applauded for being a great improvement over the industrial training schools. The general movement was away from punishment and toward rehabilitation through attending to the needs of the individual and by implementing complex programs of diagnosis and treatment.[15] By the 1950s the influence of such therapists as Karen Horney and Carl Rogers promoted the introduction of psychological treatment in juvenile corrections. Group counseling techniques became standard procedure in most juvenile institutions.

Legal Change In the 1960s and 1970s the U.S. Supreme Court radically altered the juvenile justice system when it issued a series of decisions that established the right of juveniles to receive due process of law:[16] The Court ruled that juveniles had the same rights as adults in important areas of trial process, including the right to confront witnesses, notice of charges, and the right to counsel. Figure 17.1

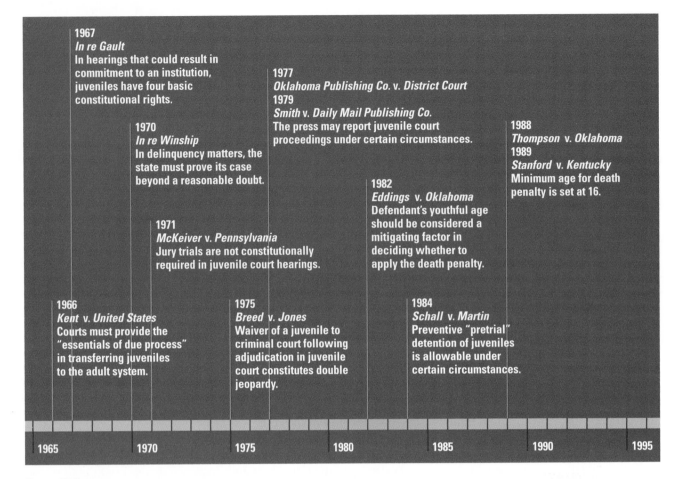

Figure 17.1
Leading Supreme Court Cases on Juvenile Justice

Source: Howard Snyder and Melissa Sickmund, *Juvenile Offenders and Victims: 1999 National Report* (Washington, D.C.: Office of Juvenile Justice and Delinquency Prevention, 1999), p. 91.

To read about decision making in the early juvenile justice system, go to David Wolcott, "'The Cop Will Get You': The Police and Discretionary Juvenile Justice, 1890–1940," *Journal of Social History* 35, no. 2 (Winter 2001): 349, on InfoTrac College Edition.

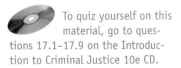

To quiz yourself on this material, go to questions 17.1–17.9 on the Introduction to Criminal Justice 10e CD.

illustrates some of the most important legal cases bringing procedural due process to the juvenile justice process.

Besides the legal revolution brought about by the Supreme Court, Congress passed the Juvenile Justice and Delinquency Prevention Act of 1974 (JJDP Act), which established the federal Office of Juvenile Justice and Delinquency Prevention (OJJDP).[17] This legislation was enacted to identify the needs of youths and to fund programs in the juvenile justice system. Its main goal was to separate wayward, nondangerous youths from institutions housing delinquents and to remove adolescents from institutions housing adult offenders. In 1996, in a move reflecting the growing national frustration with serious delinquent offenders, the act was amended to make it easier to hold delinquents in adult penal institutions. The various stages in juvenile justice history are set out in Concept Summary 17.1.

Juvenile Justice Today

Today, the juvenile justice system has jurisdiction over two distinct categories of offenders — delinquents and status offenders.[18] Juvenile delinquency refers to children who fall under a jurisdictional age limit, which varies from state to state, and who commit an act in violation of the penal code. Status offenders include truants and habitually disobedient and ungovernable children. They are commonly characterized in state statutes as persons or children in need of supervision (PINS or CHINS). Most states distinguish such behavior from delinquent

Concept Summary 17.1 Shifting Philosophies of Juvenile Justice

Pre-1899	Juveniles treated similarly to adult offenders. No distinction by age or capacity to commit criminal acts.
1899 to 1950s	Children treated differently, beginning with the Illinois Juvenile Court Act of 1899. By 1925, juvenile court acts established in virtually every state. Parens patriae philosophy dominates.
1950s to 1970	Recognition by experts that the rehabilitation model and the protective nature of parens patriae had failed to prevent delinquency.
1970 to 1980	Introduction of constitutional due process into the juvenile justice system. Experimentation with diversion and concern about stigma and labeling. Juvenile Justice and Delinquency Prevention Act of 1974 enacted.
1980 to 1990	Failure of rehabilitation and due process protections to control delinquency leads to a shift to a crime control and punishment philosophy similar to that of the adult criminal justice system.
1990-today	Reliance on punishment and deterrence. Focus on expanding options for handling juvenile offenders. Emphasis on "what works" and implementing the best intervention and control programs. Calls for use of the restorative justice model.

conduct to lessen the effect of any stigma on children as a result of their involvement with the juvenile court. In addition, juvenile courts generally have jurisdiction over situations involving conduct directed at (rather than committed by) juveniles, such as parental neglect, deprivation, abandonment, and abuse.

The states have also set different maximum ages below which children fall under the jurisdiction of the juvenile court. Many states include all children under 18 years of age, others set the limit at 17, and still others at 16. States may retain jurisdiction over children's sentence to juvenile institutions while they complete their sentence.

Some states exclude certain classes of offenders or offenses from the juvenile justice system. For example, youths who commit serious violent offenses such as

The Office of Juvenile Justice and Delinquency Prevention is an excellent resource for information on the juvenile justice system. Check http://ojjdp.ncjrs.org/.

© Sean Clayton/ The Image Works

Does scaring youth help keep them out of trouble? Shape-Up participants tour cell house 5, dubbed "The Zoo," at the Colorado Territorial Prison. The two-day program is designed to show delinquent teens what life is like inside prison and how to avoid it. Reviews of such programs have been mixed, and there is some evidence that participants actually commit more crime than non-participants!

Concept Summary 17.2 Similarities and Differences between Juvenile and Adult Justice Systems

Similarities	Differences
• Discretion used by police officers, judges, and correctional personnel.	• The primary purpose of juvenile procedures is protection and treatment; with adults, the aim is to punish the guilty.
• Right to receive *Miranda* warning.	• Jurisdiction is determined by age in the juvenile system; by the nature of the offense in the adult system.
• Protection from prejudicial lineups or other identification procedures.	• Juveniles can be apprehended for acts that would not be criminal if committed by an adult (status offenses).
• Procedural safeguards when making an admission of guilt.	• Juvenile proceedings are not considered criminal; adult proceedings are.
• Advocacy roles of prosecutors and defense attorneys.	• Juvenile court proceedings are generally informal and private; adult court proceedings are more formal and are open to the public.
• Right to counsel at most key stages of the court process.	• Courts cannot release to the press identifying information about a juvenile, but they must release such information about an adult.
• Availability of pretrial motions.	• Parents are highly involved in the juvenile process but not in the adult process.
• Plea negotiation or plea bargaining.	• The standard of arrest is more stringent for adults than for juveniles.
• Right to a hearing and an appeal.	• Juveniles are released into parental custody; adults are generally given bail.
• Standard of proof beyond a reasonable doubt.	• Juveniles have no constitutional right to a jury trial; adults do. Some states extend this right to juveniles by statute.
• Pretrial detention possible.	• Juveniles can be searched in school without probable cause or a warrant.
• Detention without bail if defendant considered dangerous.	• A juvenile's record is generally sealed when the age of majority is reached; an adult's record is permanent.
• Determinate sentencing in some states.	• A juvenile court cannot sentence juveniles to county jails or state prisons, which are reserved for adults.
• Probation as a sentencing option.	• The U.S. Supreme Court has declared that the Eighth Amendment prohibits the death penalty for juveniles ages 15 and under, but not for juveniles ages 16 and 17.
• Community treatment as a sentencing option.	

rape or murder may be automatically excluded from the juvenile justice system and treated as adults on the premise that they stand little chance of rehabilitation within the confines of the juvenile system. Juvenile court judges may also transfer, or waive, repeat offenders whom they deem untreatable by the juvenile authorities.

The juvenile justice system has evolved into a parallel yet independent system of justice with its own terminology and rules of procedure. Concept Summary 17.2 describes the basic similarities and differences between the juvenile and adult justice systems, and Concept Summary 17.3 points out how the language used in the juvenile court differs from that used in the adult system.

The juvenile justice system is responsible for processing and treating almost 2 million cases of youthful misbehavior annually. Each state's system is unique, so it is difficult to give a precise accounting of the justice process. Moreover, depending on local practice and tradition, case processing often varies from community to community within a single state. Keeping this in mind, the following

Concept Summary 17.3 Comparison of Terms Used in Adult and Juvenile Justice Systems

	Juvenile term	Adult term
The person and the act	Delinquent child	Criminal
	Delinquent act	Crime
Preadjudicatory stage	Take into custody	Arrest
	Petition	Indictment
	Agree to a finding	Plead guilty
	Deny the petition	Plead not guilty
	Adjustment	Plea bargain
	Detention facility	Jail
	Child care shelter	Jail
Adjudicatory stage	Substitution	Reduction of charges
	Fact-finding hearing	Trial
	Adjudication	Trial
Postadjudicatory stage	Dispositional hearing	Sentencing hearing
	Disposition	Sentence
	Commitment	Incarceration
	Training school	Prison
	Community resdential facility	Halfway house
	Aftercare	Parole

sections provide a general description of some of the key processes and decision points within juvenile justice. Figure 17.2 illustrates a model of the juvenile justice process.

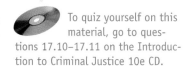 To quiz yourself on this material, go to questions 17.10–17.11 on the Introduction to Criminal Justice 10e CD.

Police Processing of the Juvenile Offender

According to the Uniform Crime Reports, police officers arrest more than 1.6 million juveniles under age 18 each year, including almost 500,000 under age 15. The number of juvenile arrests has been in decline (for example, more than 2 million youths were arrested in 1995, including 677,000 index crime arrests), an indication that — like the adult crime problem — juvenile delinquency has diminished during the past decade.[19]

Most larger police departments have separate juvenile detectives who handle delinquency cases and focus their attention on the problems of youth. In addition to conducting their own investigations, they typically take control of cases after an arrest is made by a uniformed officer.

Most states do not have specific statutory provisions distinguishing the arrest process for children from that for adults. Some jurisdictions, however, give broad arrest powers to the police in juvenile cases by authorizing the officer to make an arrest whenever it is believed that the child's behavior falls within the jurisdiction of the juvenile court. Consequently, police may arrest youths for behavior considered legal for adults, including running away, curfew violations, and being in possession of alcohol.

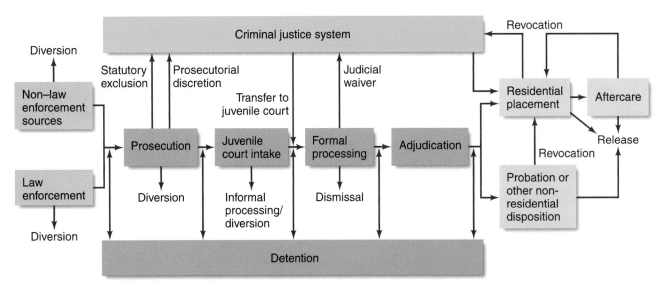

Figure 17.2
Case Flow through the Juvenile Justice Process

Source: Office of Juvenile Justice and Delinquency Prevention, www.ojjdp.ncjrs.org/facts/casejpg.html.

Use of Discretion

When a juvenile is found to have engaged in delinquent or incorrigible behavior, police agencies are charged with the decision to release or to detain the child and refer her to juvenile court. Because of the state's interest in the child, the police generally have more discretion in the investigatory and arrest stages of the juvenile process than they do when dealing with adult offenders.

This discretionary decision — to release or to detain — is based not only on the nature of the offense but also on police attitudes and the child's social and personal conditions at the time of the arrest. The following is a partial list of factors believed to be significant in police decision making regarding juvenile offenders.

- The type and seriousness of the child's offense.
- The ability of the parents to be of assistance in disciplining the child.
- The child's past contacts with police.
- The degree of cooperation obtained from the child and parents and their demeanor, attitude, and personal characteristics.
- Whether the child denies the allegations in the petition and insists on a court hearing.

Research indicates that most police decisions involve discretion.[20] The Project on Policing Neighborhoods — a comprehensive study of police patrols in Indianapolis, Indiana, and St. Petersburg, Florida — found that only 13 percent of police encounters with juveniles resulted in arrest.[21] As shown in Table 17.1, the most likely disposition of police encounters with juveniles is a command or threat to arrest (38 percent), followed by searching or interrogation of the suspects (24 percent). Furthermore, these studies show that many juvenile offenders are never referred to the juvenile court.

Legal Rights

Once a juvenile has been taken into custody, the child has the same Fourth Amendment right to be free from unreasonable searches and seizures as an adult does. Children in police custody can be detained prior to trial, interrogated, and placed in lineups. However, because of their youth and inexperience, children are generally afforded more protections than adults. Police must be careful that the juve-

Table 17.1 Disposition of Police Encounters with Juveniles

Disposition	Juveniles
Release	14%
Advise	11
Search or interrogate	24
Command or threaten	38
Arrest	13

Source: Robert E. Worden and Stephanie M. Myers, *Police Encounters with Juvenile Suspects* (Albany, N.Y.: State University of New York, University at Albany, Hindelang Criminal Justice Research Center and School of Criminal Justice, 2001), Table 3.

nile suspect understands his constitutional rights and, if there is some question, must provide access to a parent or guardian to protect the child's legal interests. For example, police often questioned juveniles in the absence of their parents or an attorney. Any incriminatory statements or confessions made by juveniles could be placed in evidence at their trials. That is no longer permissible, and children have the same (or more) *Miranda* rights as adults, a right that was confirmed in the case of *Fare* v. *Michael C.* (1979).[22] Today, police will interrogate a juvenile without an adult present only if they believe that the youth is unquestionably mature and experienced enough to understand her legal rights.

Policing in Schools

Because a great deal of juvenile crime occurs on school grounds, police departments have been stationing officers within schools. These police officers are generally referred to as school resource officers or SROs. The increased presence of law enforcement officers within schools raises the question of the legal rights of students within the educational environment. The issue of student privacy relates not only to police but also to school officials who often assume quasi-police powers over children. Both police officers and school officials may wish to search students to determine whether they are in possession of contraband, such as drugs or weapons; search their lockers and desks; and question them about illegal activities.

In *New Jersey* v. *T.L.O.* (1985), the U.S. Supreme Court held that a school official had the authority to search a student's purse, even though no warrant was issued and no probable cause existed that a crime had been committed, only a suspicion that T.L.O. had violated school rules.[23] This case involved an assistant principal's search of the purse of a 14-year-old female student who had been observed smoking a cigarette in a school lavatory. The assistant principal found cigarette-rolling papers when a pack of cigarettes was removed from the purse. A further search revealed marijuana and several items indicating marijuana selling. As a result, T.L.O. was adjudicated as a delinquent. The Supreme Court held that the Fourth Amendment protections against unreasonable searches and seizures apply to students but that the need to maintain an orderly educational environment modified the usual Fourth Amendment requirements of warrants and probable cause. The Court relaxed the usual probable cause standard and found the search to be reasonable. It declared that the school's right to maintain discipline on school grounds allowed it to search students and their possessions as a safety precaution. The Court, which had guarded the warrant requirement and its exceptions in the past, now permits warrantless searches in school, based on the lesser standard of "reasonable suspicion." This landmark decision did not deal with other thorny issues, however, such as the search and seizure of contraband from a student's locker or desk.

Searching for Drugs Faced with crime by students in public schools, particularly illicit drug use, school administrators have gone to extreme measures to enforce drug control statutes and administrative rules. Some urban schools are using breathalyzers, drug-sniffing dogs, hidden video cameras, and routine searches of students' pockets, purses, lockers, and cars. In general, courts consider such searches permissible when they are not overly offensive and when reasonable grounds are found to suspect that the student may have violated the law. School administrators are walking a tightrope between a student's constitutional right to privacy and school safety.

In 1995, the U.S. Supreme Court held that public school athletes in middle and high school may be required to submit to random drug testing without violating their Fourth Amendment rights. James Acton, a seventh-grader, was kept off a football team because his parents refused to sign a urinalysis consent form. On appeal, the Supreme Court held that such testing is constitutional even though the student does not engage in suspicious behavior.[24]

 To read more about a police juvenile division, go to the Web page of the Pasadena, California, Police Department at http://www.ci.pasadena.tx.us/police/investigations/juveniles/juveniles.htm.

 One of the best sources of information on juveniles and the law is the National Center for Youth Law: Visit the Web site at http://www.youthlaw.org.

 To quiz yourself on this material, go to questions 17.12–17.15 on the Introduction to Criminal Justice 10e CD.

To read about the prosecution of juvenile gun offenders, go to http://www.ncjrs.org/html/ojjdp/jjbul2000_03_5/pag4.html.

The Juvenile Court Process

After the police have determined that a case warrants further attention, they will bind it over to the prosecutor's office, which then has the responsibility for channeling the case through the juvenile court. The juvenile court plays a major role in controlling juvenile behavior and delivering social services to children in need.

The most recent data available indicates that U.S. juvenile courts process an estimated 1.7 million delinquency cases (cases involving juveniles charged with criminal law violations) each year. The number of delinquency cases handled by juvenile courts increased 44 percent during the 10-year period between 1989 and 1998. During this time, cases involving crimes against people (such as assaults and robberies) increased 88 percent, public order offenses (prostitution, traffic offenses) increased 73 percent, and property offense cases increased 11 percent.[25] Drug offenses more than doubled between 1993 and 1998. Drug offense cases accounted for 11 percent of all delinquency cases in 1998, compared with 8 percent in 1994. The number of drug offense cases processed during 1998 was 108 percent greater than in 1993 and 148 percent greater than 1989.[26] Like the crime rate, the number of youth petitioned to juvenile court has stabilized during the past few years. The most recent data available indicates a decline of about 3 percent between 1997 and 1998.[27]

Distinct gender- and race-based differences are found in the juvenile court population. About three-fourths of all 1998 juvenile cases involved a male. However, the percentage of females processed by juvenile courts has increased about 25 percent during the past decade. African American youth made up about 30 percent of the juvenile court population, but only about 15 percent of the general population.

The Intake Process

intake
The process by which a probation officer settles cases at the initial court appearance, before the onset of formal criminal proceedings; the screening.

After police processing, the juvenile offender is typically remanded to the local juvenile court's **intake** division. Court intake officers or probation personnel or both review and screen the child and the family to determine if the child needs to be handled formally or whether the case can be settled without the necessity of costly and intrusive official intervention. Their report helps the prosecutor decide whether to handle the case informally or bind it over for trial. The intake stage represents an opportunity to place a child in informal programs both within the court and in the community. The intake process also is critically important because more than half of the referrals to the juvenile courts never go beyond this stage.

The Detention Process

detention
Temporary care of a child alleged to be a delinquent or status offender who requires secure custody pending court disposition.

After a juvenile is formally taken into custody, either as a delinquent or as a status offender, the prosecutor usually makes a decision to release the child to the parent or guardian or to detain the child in a secure shelter pending trial.

Detention has always been a controversial area of juvenile justice. Far too many children have been routinely placed in detention while awaiting court appearances. Status offenders and delinquents have been held in the same facility, and in many parts of the country, adult county jails were used to detain juvenile offenders. The JJDP Act of 1974 emphasized reducing the number of children placed in inappropriate detention facilities, and although successful, the practice continues.

Despite efforts to reduce detention, caseloads increased 25 percent between 1989 and 1998, reflecting the increase in juvenile court cases from 1.2 million in 1989 to 1.8 million in 1998 (see Figure 17.3). While the likelihood of being detained decreased, the population increase in juvenile offenders meant that the number of kids in detention increased.

© 2003 AP/Wide World Photos

Among the duties of the juvenile court judge is to decide whether a youngster should remain in pre-trial detention or be released to his parents or guardian. Here, Assistant District Attorney Ken Fladager reads the charges to defendant Steven Sedillo, 13, right, and his attorney, Dennis Martinez, during Sedillo's detention hearing in Children's Court in front of Children's Judge John Romero on July 1, 2003. Ricky Navarette, 16, Fernando Anaya, 13, and Sedillo pleaded innocent on charges in connection with a fire along the Rio Grande.

Another reason for the increase in the number of detained youth has been a surge in the detention of female offenders, whose numbers in detention increased 56 percent compared with 20 percent for males. The large increase was tied to the growth in the number of delinquency cases involving females charged with violent offenses (157 percent).[28]

Between 1989 and 1998, the number of cases involving detention increased more for white juveniles (33 percent, from 149,000 to 198,000) than for black juveniles (15 percent, from 100,900 to 115,800). This most likely happened because of the use of detention in cases involving violence and drug offenses increased more for whites than blacks. The increase in detention for juveniles charged with violent person offenses was 3 times greater for whites than blacks (95 percent versus 30 percent), and the increase for drug offenses was 12 times greater.

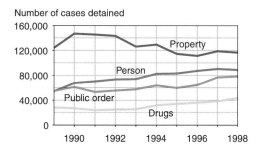

Figure 17.3
Detention Trends

Note: Although the percentage of cases involving detention dropped from 1989 to 1998, the number of cases involving detention increased. Overall, youth were detained in 19 percent of delinquency cases handled in 1998. The number of delinquency cases involving detention rose 25 percent from 1989 to 1998. Person offense cases had the largest relative increase in detained cases (63 percent). Although there was a 6 percent decline in detained property cases between 1989 and 1998, they accounted for the largest volume of cases involving detention in every year. In 1998, the percentage of cases that involved detention was lower for property offense cases (15 percent) than for the other general offense categories (22–23 percent). For all four general offense categories, the probability of detention was lower in 1998 than in 1989. This was especially true for drug cases.

Source: Melissa Sickmund, *Juveniles in Court,* National Report Series Bulletin (Washington, D.C.: Office of Juvenile Justice and Delinquency Prevention, 2003), p. 1.

Legal Issues Most state statutes ordinarily require a hearing on the appropriateness of detention if the initial decision is to keep the child in custody. At this hearing, the child has a right to counsel and may be given other procedural due process safeguards, notably the privilege against self-incrimination and the right to confront and cross-examine witnesses. Most state juvenile court acts provide criteria to support a decision to detain the child. These include the need to protect the child, whether the child presents a serious danger to the public, and the likelihood that the juvenile will return to court for adjudication. Whereas in adult cases the sole criterion for pretrial release may be the offender's availability for trial, juveniles may be detained for other reasons, including their own protection. Normally, the finding of the judge that the child should be detained must be supported by factual evidence. In the 1984 case of *Schall* v. *Martin,* the U.S. Supreme Court upheld the right of the states to detain a child before trial to protect his welfare and the public safety.[29]

Reforming Detention An ongoing effort has been made to reform detention. The most important reform has been to remove status offenders from lockups containing delinquents. After decades of effort, almost all states have passed laws requiring that status offenders be placed in non-secure shelters, not secure detention facilities, thereby reducing their contact with more dangerous delinquent youth.

Another serious problem is the detention of youths in adult jails. The practice is common in rural areas where relatively few separate facilities are available for young offenders.[30] The OJJDP has given millions of dollars in aid to encourage the removal of juveniles from adult lockups. These grants have helped jurisdictions develop intake screening procedures, specific release or detention criteria, and alternative residential and nonresidential programs for juveniles awaiting trial. By 1980 amendments to the act mandating the absolute removal of juveniles from jails had been adopted. Despite such efforts, many states are not complying with the removal provisions, and thousands of youths are annually detained in adult jails. Whatever the actual number jailed today, placing young offenders in adult jails continues to be a significant problem in the juvenile justice system. Juveniles detained in adult jails often live in squalid conditions and are subject to physical and sexual abuse. The practice is widely condemned, but eliminating the confinement of juveniles in adult institutions remains a difficult task.[31] Many youths who commit non-serious acts are still being held in adult jails — for example, runaways who are apprehended in rural areas. Minority juveniles may be spending greater amounts of time in jail than white offenders for the same offense.[32] While this is troubling, the fact that a smaller percentage of juvenile cases now involve detention indicates reforms may be working.

With offices based at Eastern Kentucky University and at Michigan State University, the National Juvenile Detention Association exists exclusively to advance the science, processes, and art of juvenile detention services through the overall improvement of the juvenile justice profession. Go to the Web site at http://www.njda.com/default.html.

Bail

If a child is not detained, the question of bail arises. Federal courts have not found it necessary to rule on the issue of a juvenile's constitutional right to bail because liberal statutory release provisions act as appropriate alternatives. Although only a few state statutes allow release on money bail, many others have juvenile code provisions that emphasize the release of the child to the parents as an acceptable substitute. A constitutional right to bail that on its face seems to benefit a child may have unforeseen results. For example, money bail might impose a serious economic strain on the child's family while conflicting with the protective and social concerns of the juvenile court. Considerations of economic liabilities and other procedural inequities have influenced the majority of courts confronting this question to hold that juveniles do not have a right to bail.

To read about the bail process in Canada, go to Kimberly N. Varma, "Exploring 'Youth' in Court: An Analysis of Decision-Making in Youth Court Bail Hearings," *Canadian Journal of Criminology* 44, no. 2 (April 2002): 143.

Plea Bargaining

Before trial, juvenile prosecutors may attempt to negotiate a settlement to the case. For example, if the offender admits to the facts of the petition, she may be offered a placement in a special community-based treatment program in lieu of a term in a secure state facility. Or a status offense petition may be substituted for one of delinquency so that the adolescent can avoid being housed in a state training school and instead be placed in a more treatment-oriented facility.

If a bargain can be reached, the child will be asked to admit in open court that he did in fact commit the act of which he stands accused. State juvenile courts tend to minimize the stigma associated with the use of adult criminal standards by using other terminology, such as "agree to a finding" or "accept the petition" instead of "admit guilt." When the child makes an admission, juvenile courts require the following procedural safeguards: The child knows of the right to a trial, the plea or admission is made voluntarily, and the child understands the charges and consequences of the plea.

Waiver of Jurisdiction

Prior to the development of the first modern juvenile court in Illinois in 1899, juveniles were tried for violations of the law in adult criminal courts. The consequences were devastating. Many children were treated as criminal offenders and often sentenced to adult prisons. Although the subsequent passage of state legislation creating juvenile courts eliminated this problem, the juvenile justice system did recognize that certain forms of conduct require that children be tried as adults. Today, most jurisdictions provide by statute for **waiver,** or transfer, of juvenile offenders to the criminal courts. The decision of whether to waive a juvenile to the adult, or criminal, court is made in a transfer hearing.

The **transfer** of a juvenile to the criminal court is often based on statutory criteria established by the state's juvenile court act, so waiver provisions vary considerably among jurisdictions. Most commonly considered are the child's age and nature of the offense alleged in the petition. For example, some jurisdictions require that the child be over a certain age (typically, 14) before he or she can be waived. Some mandate that the youth be charged with a felony before being tried as an adult, whereas others permit waiver of jurisdiction to the criminal court regardless of the seriousness of the offense (for example, when a child is a petty albeit chronic offender).

Legal Controls Because of the nature of the waiver decision and its effect on the child in terms of status and disposition, the U.S. Supreme Court has imposed procedural protections for juveniles in the waiver process. In *Kent* v. *United States* (1966), the Court held that the waiver proceeding is a critically important stage in the juvenile justice process and that juveniles must be afforded minimum requirements of due process of law at such proceedings, including the right to legal counsel.[33] Then, in *Breed* v. *Jones* (1975), the Court held that the prosecution of juveniles as adults in the California Superior Court violated the double jeopardy clause of the Fifth Amendment if they previously had been tried on the same charge in juvenile court.[34] The Court concluded that jeopardy attaches when the juvenile court begins to hear evidence at the adjudicatory hearing; this requires that the waiver hearing take place prior to any adjudication.

Youths in Adult Courts All states allow juveniles to be tried as adults in criminal courts in one of four ways.

1. *Concurrent jurisdiction.* The prosecutor has the discretion of filing charges for certain offenses in either juvenile or criminal court.
2. *Excluded offenses.* State laws exclude from juvenile court jurisdiction certain offenses that are either very minor, such as traffic or fishing violations, or very serious, such as murder or rape.
3. *Judicial waiver.* After a formal hearing at which both prosecutor and defense attorney present evidence, a juvenile court judge may decide to waive jurisdiction and transfer the case to criminal court. This procedure is also known as binding over or certifying juvenile cases to criminal court.
4. *Reverse waiver.* State laws mandate that certain offenses be tried in adult court. However, judges may decide that the case be tried in juvenile court.

Nearly every state has provisions for handling juveniles in adult criminal courts, and the trend is to make the waiver broader.[35] In 31 states, once a juvenile is tried in adult court, she is no longer eligible for juvenile justice on any subsequent offense. To get tough on juvenile crime, these efforts have limited the judge's ability to consider the individual circumstances that apply in each case.

Extent of Waiver For every 1,000 formally handled delinquency cases, about 8 are waived to criminal court. The number of delinquency cases judicially waived to criminal court peaked in 1994 with 12,100 cases, an increase of more than 50 percent

waiver
The voluntary and deliberate relinquishing of a known right, such as those guaranteed under the Fifth and Sixth Amendments; the transfer of a juvenile offender to criminal court for prosecution as an adult.

transfer
The process of sending a case from the juvenile to adult courts.

over the number of cases waived in 1998 (8,000), or less than 1 percent of the formally processed delinquency caseload. One reason may be that the number of youth waived for drug cases is in decline, falling from 4.1 percent (1,800 cases) in 1991 and declining since then (1.1 percent, or 1,300 cases in 1998).[36] The proportion of youths waived for personal offenses involving violence is now equal to the waived cases involving property crimes.

Should the Waiver Process Be Maintained? Though the percentage of waived cases may be in decline, the problem of youths processed in adult courts is still a serious one. What is accomplished by treating juveniles like adults? There are experts who support waiver and those who are opposed to its usage.

Against Waiver. Some experts criticize waiver because in the final tally juveniles whose cases are waived to criminal court are sentenced more leniently than they would have been in juvenile court. This outcome contradicts the purpose of waiver. In many states, even when juveniles are tried in criminal court and convicted on the charges, they may still be sentenced to a juvenile or youthful offender institution, instead of an adult prison. Some studies show that only a small percentage of juveniles tried as adults are incarcerated for periods longer than the terms served by offenders convicted on the same crime in the juvenile court. Others have found that waived juveniles serve more time behind bars.[37] For example, they spend more time in juvenile detention awaiting trial. In the end, what began as a get-tough measure has had the opposite effect, while costing taxpayers more money.[38]

Transfer decisions are not always carried out fairly or equitably, and evidence suggests that minorities are waived at a rate that is greater than their representation in the population.[39] About 40 percent of all waived youth are African Americans, even though they represent less than a third (31 percent) of the juvenile court population.[40]

Some critics view waiver as inefficient, ineffective, and philosophically out of step with the original concept of the juvenile court. They believe that youths transferred to the criminal system are more likely to commit new offenses, especially if they have spent time in jail or prison. They also reoffend more quickly and more frequently. Furthermore, no evidence exists that youths who are transferred are more mature or responsible than others their age or less amenable to treatment.[41] Exacerbating this problem is that a significant portion of younger teens are mentally incompetent to stand trial, if the same criteria are employed with adults who are mentally ill.[42]

Little in the way of national policy has been offered on how to treat juveniles once they are waived or provide them with treatment different from the adult offender. Their position is summed up in this statement by Shay Bilchick, director of the Child Welfare League of America.

> [T]oo many communities are failing to determine which offenders are beyond the reach of the juvenile justice system and failing to provide programs to hold those youths accountable in a timely manner, for the duration and intensity needed. As we increasingly transfer juveniles blindly, we are failing both our youths and our communities. We deserve better.[43]

For Waiver. Supporters view the waiver process as a sound method of getting the most serious juvenile offenders off the streets while ensuring that rehabilitation plays a less critical role in the juvenile justice system. They point to data showing that minors are involved in serious violent crimes and that society must be protected from predatory youth. When the juvenile justice system was first formulated early in the twentieth century, it was aimed at treating petty offenders and not the gun-toting super-predators of the twenty-first century.

Kids are most likely to be transferred to criminal court if they have injured someone with a weapon or if they have a long juvenile court record.[44] Also, even if transferred, juveniles are typically not placed in an adult facility until they are at least 18. Until then they are detained in juvenile facilities or special institutions for younger offenders. Their position is aptly summed up by this statement made by U.S. representative Lamar Smith of Texas.

> *It is common sense public policy when states pass laws that allow or require violent juveniles to be transferred to adult courts. I strongly believe that we can no longer tolerate young people who commit violent crimes simply because of their age. Young people have the ability to decide between right and wrong, as the vast majority do every day. But those youths who choose to prey on other juveniles, senior citizens, merchants or homeowners will be held responsible. If that choice results in confinement in an adult prison system, perhaps youths who have a propensity to commit violent crimes will think twice before acting.*[45]

For another take on the waiver decision, go to Patricia Smith, "Juvenile Justice? In the 1990s, Many States Passed Laws That Made It Easier to Try Teens as Adults: Does Youth Crime Deserve 'Adult Time'?" *Junior Scholastic* 104, no. 13 (February 25, 2002): 10, on InfoTrac College Edition.

The Trial

There are typically two judicial hearings in the juvenile court process. The first, usually called an **initial appearance,** is similar to the arraignment in the adult system. The child is informed of the charges against him, attorneys are appointed, bail is reviewed, and in many instances cases are settled with an admission of the facts, followed by a community sentence. If the case cannot be settled at this initial stage, it is bound over for trial.

During the **adjudication** or trial process, often called the **fact-finding hearing** in juvenile proceedings, the court hears evidence on the allegations stated in the delinquency petition. In its early development, the juvenile court did not emphasize judicial rule making similar to that of the criminal trial process. Absent were such basic requirements as the standard of proof, rules of evidence, and similar adjudicatory formalities. Proceedings were to be nonadversarial, informal, and noncriminal. However, the juvenile trial process was the target of criticism because judges were handing out punishments to children without affording them legal rights. This changed in 1967 when the U.S. Supreme Court's landmark *In re Gault* decision radically altered the juvenile justice system.[46] Because of its importance, the facts of the *Gault* case are set out in the Law in Review feature on page 564.

The *Gault* decision completely altered the juvenile trial process. Instead of dealing with children in a benign and paternalistic fashion, the courts were forced to process juvenile offenders within the framework of appropriate constitutional procedures. And though *Gault* was technically limited to the adjudicatory stage, it has spurred further legal reform throughout the juvenile system. Today, the right to counsel, the privilege against self-incrimination, the right to treatment in detention and correctional facilities, and other constitutional protections are applied at all stages of the juvenile process, from investigation through adjudication to parole. *Gault* ushered in an era of legal rights for juveniles.

After *Gault,* the Supreme Court continued its trend toward legalizing and formalizing the juvenile trial process with the decision in *In re Winship* (1970), which held that a finding of delinquency in a juvenile case must be made with the same level of evidence used in an adult case: beyond a reasonable doubt.[47]

Although the informality of the traditional juvenile trial court was severely altered by *Gault* and *Winship,* the trend of increased rights for juveniles was somewhat curtailed when the Supreme Court held in *McKeiver* v. *Pennsylvania* (1971) that children do not have the same right to a jury trial as an adult.[48] The Court reasoned that juries were not an essential element of justice and, if used in juvenile cases, would end confidentiality.

Once an adjudicatory hearing has been completed, the court is normally required to enter a judgment against the child. This may take the form of declaring the child delinquent or a ward of the court or possibly even suspending judgment to avoid the stigma of a juvenile record. Following the entering of a judgment, the court can begin its determination of possible dispositions for the child.

initial appearance
The first hearing in juvenile court.

adjudication (juvenile)
The juvenile court hearing at which the juvenile is declared a delinquent or status offender, or no finding of fact is made.

fact-finding hearing
The trial in the juvenile justice system.

To read the *In re Gault* case, go to http://caselaw.lp.findlaw.com/scripts/getcase.pl?court=us&vol=387&invol=1.

One group that has struggled to upgrade the juvenile court system is the National Council of Juvenile and Family Court Judges. Learn about this important organization at http://www.ncjfcj.org/.

To read *McKeiver* v. *Pennsylvania,* go to http://caselaw.lp.findlaw.com/scripts/getcase.pl?navby=search&court=US&case=/us/403/528.html.

In re Gault

law in review

Gerald Gault, age 15, was taken into custody by the sheriff of Gila County, Arizona, because a woman complained that he and another boy had made an obscene telephone call to her. At the time, Gerald was under a six-month probation as a result of being found delinquent for stealing a wallet. As a result of the woman's complaint, Gerald was taken to a children's home. His parents were not informed that he was being taken into custody. His mother subsequently was told by the superintendent of detention when a hearing would be held in juvenile court. On the day in question, the police officer who had taken Gerald into custody filed a petition alleging his delinquency. Gerald, his mother, and the police officer appeared before the judge in his chambers. The complainant was not at the hearing. Gerald was questioned about the telephone calls and sent back to the detention home, then released a few days later.

On the day of Gerald's release, his mother received a letter indicating that a hearing would be held on Gerald's delinquency a few days later. A hearing was held, and again the complainant was not present. No transcript or recording was made of the proceedings. The juvenile officer stated that Gerald had admitted making the lewd telephone calls. Neither the boy nor his parents were advised of any right to remain silent, the right to be represented by counsel, or any other constitutional rights. At the conclusion of the hearing, the juvenile court committed Gerald as a juvenile delinquent to the state industrial school in Arizona for the period of his minority.

This meant that, at the age of 15, Gerald was sent to the state school until he reached the age of 21, unless discharged

sooner. The maximum punishment for an adult charged with the same crime was a $50 fine or two months in prison.

Gerald's attorneys filed a writ of habeas corpus, which was denied by the Arizona Superior Court. That decision was subsequently affirmed by the Arizona Supreme Court. On appeal to the U.S. Supreme Court, Gerald's counsel argued that the juvenile code of Arizona under which Gerald was found delinquent was invalid because it was contrary to the due process clause of the Fourteenth Amendment. In addition, Gerald was denied the following basic due process rights: notice of the charges with regard to their timeliness and specificity, right to counsel, right to confrontation and cross-examination, privilege against self-incrimination, right to a transcript of the trial record, and right to appellate review.

In deciding the case, the Supreme Court had to determine whether procedural due process of law within the context of fundamental fairness under the Fourteenth Amendment applies to juvenile delinquency proceedings in which a child is committed to a state industrial school. The Court, in a far-reaching opinion written by Justice Abe Fortas, agreed that Gerald's constitutional rights had been violated. Notice of charges was an essential ingredient of due process of law, as were the right to counsel, the right to confront and cross-examine witnesses, and the privilege against self-incrimination. The Court did not answer the questions of appellate review and right to a transcript in this case.

The *Gault* case established that a child has procedural due process constitutional rights in delinquency adjudication proceedings when the child could be commit-

ted to a state institution. While recognizing the history and development of the juvenile court, the Court sought to reconcile the motives of rehabilitation and treatment with children's rights. It recognized the principle of fundamental fairness of the law for children as well as for adults.

Although the *Gault* decision was confined to proceedings at the adjudication stage of the juvenile process, it has had a far-reaching impact throughout the entire juvenile justice system. *Gault* initiated the development of due process standards at the pretrial, trial, and posttrial stages of the juvenile process. Judged in the context of today's juvenile justice system, *Gault* redefined the relationships between juveniles, their parents, and the state. It remains the single most significant constitutional case in the area of juvenile justice.

Critical Thinking

Comment on the following statement: The introduction of lawyers into the criminal justice system criminalizes what had heretofore been a noncriminal procedure. Adding lawyers justifies such measures as determinate sentencing for juveniles and nullifies the informal treatment style preferred by the creators of the juvenile justice system. By creating a quasi-criminal system, *Gault* negates the need for a juvenile justice system.

InfoTrac College Edition Research

To read more about "juvenile law" in the United States and abroad, use the term as a subject guide on InfoTrac College Edition.

Source: *In re Gault,* 387 U.S. 1; 87 S.Ct. 1248 (1967).

Alternatives to the Juvenile Trial

There has also been a movement to create alternatives to the traditional juvenile court adjudication process. One approach has been the development of teen courts to supplement the traditional juvenile court process. Teen courts are the subject of the Analyzing Criminal Justice Issues feature on page 565.

Teen Courts

analyzing criminal justice issues

To relieve overcrowding and provide an alternative to traditional forms of juvenile courts, more than 300 jurisdictions are experimenting with teen courts. These differ from other juvenile justice programs because young people, not adults, determine the disposition in a case. Cases handled in these courts typically involve young juveniles (ages 10 to 15), with no prior arrest records, who are being charged with minor law violations (shoplifting, vandalism, and disorderly conduct). Typically, young offenders are asked to volunteer to have their case heard in a teen court instead of the more formal court of the traditional juvenile justice system.

As in a regular juvenile court, teen court defendants may go through an intake process, a preliminary review of charges, a court hearing, and sentencing. In a teen court, however, other young people are responsible for much of the process. Charges may be presented to the court by a 15-year-old "prosecutor." Defendants may be represented by a 16-year-old "defense attorney." Other youth may serve as jurors, court clerks, and bailiffs. In some teen courts, a youth "judge" (or panel of youth judges) may choose the best disposition or sanction for each case. In a few teen courts, youth even determine whether the facts in a case have been proven by the prosecutor (similar to a finding of guilt). Offenders are often ordered to pay restitution or perform community service. Some teen courts require offenders to write formal apologies to their victims; others require offenders to serve on a subsequent teen court jury. Many courts use other innovative dispositions, such as requiring offenders to attend classes designed to improve their decision-making skills, enhance their awareness of victims, and deter them from future theft.

Though decisions are made by juveniles, adults are also involved in teen courts. They often administer the programs, and they are usually responsible for essential functions such as budgeting, planning, and personnel. In many programs, adults supervise the courtroom activities, and they often coordinate the community service placements,

where youth work to fulfill the terms of their dispositions. In some programs, adults act as the judges while teens serve as attorneys and jurors.

Proponents of teen court argue that the process takes advantage of one of the most powerful forces in the life of an adolescent — the desire for peer approval and the reaction to peer pressure. According to this argument, youth respond better to prosocial peers than to adult authority figures. Thus, teen courts are seen as a potentially effective alternative to traditional juvenile courts that are staffed with paid professionals such as lawyers, judges, and probation officers. Teen court advocates also point out that the advantages extend beyond defendants. Teen courts may benefit the volunteer youth attorneys and judges, who probably learn more about the legal system than they ever could in a classroom. The presence of a teen court may also encourage the entire community to take a more active role in responding to juvenile crime. In sum, teen courts offer at least four potential benefits.

1. *Accountability.* Teen courts may help to ensure that young offenders are held accountable for their illegal behavior, even when their offenses are relatively minor and would not likely result in sanctions from the traditional juvenile justice system.
2. *Timeliness.* An effective teen court can move young offenders from arrest to sanctions within a matter of days instead of the months that may pass with traditional juvenile courts. This rapid response may increase the positive impact of court sanctions, regardless of their severity.
3. *Cost savings.* Teen courts usually depend heavily on youth and adult volunteers. If managed properly, they may handle a substantial number of offenders at relatively little cost to the community.
4. *Community cohesion.* A well-structured and expansive teen court program may affect the entire community by increasing public appreciation of the legal system, enhancing community–court relationships, encouraging greater re-

spect for the law among youth, and promoting volunteerism among both adults and youth.

The teen court movement is just beginning and its effectiveness is still a matter of debate. But currently there are over 300 of these courts in operation around the United States. Recent evaluations of teen courts have found that they did not widen the net of justice by handling cases that in the absence of the peer court would have been subject to a lesser level of processing. However, research by Kevin Minor and his associates of teen courts in Kentucky and by Paige Harrison and her colleagues in New Mexico indicate that recidivism levels range from 25 to 30 percent. Considering that these cases typically involve offenses of only moderate seriousness, the findings do not suggest that the program can play a significant role in reducing teenage crime rates.

Critical Thinking

1. Could teen courts be used to try serious criminal acts such as burglary and robbery?
2. Is a conflict of interest created when teens judge the behavior of other teens? Does the fact that they themselves may one day become defendants in a teen court influence decision making?

InfoTrac College Edition Research

To read more about teen courts, go to Kathiann M. Kowalski, "Courtroom Justice for Teens-by Teens," *Current Health* 2 (April 1999): 29.

Sources: Jeffrey A. Butts and Janeen Buck, "Teen Courts: A Focus on Research," *Juvenile Justice Bulletin October 2000* (Washington, D.C.: Office of Juvenile Justice and Delinquency Prevention, 2000); Kevin Minor, James Wells, Irinia Soderstrom, Rachel Bingham, and Deborah Williamson, "Sentence Completion and Recidivism among Juveniles Referred to Teen Courts," *Crime and Delinquency* 45 (1999): 467–80; Paige Harrison, James Maupin, and G. Larry Mays, "Are Teen Courts an Answer to Our Delinquency Problems?" *Juvenile and Family Court Journal* 51 (2000): 27–33; Paige Harrison, James R. Maupin, and G. Larry Mays, "Teen Court: An Examination of Processes and Outcomes, *Crime and Delinquency* 47 (2001): 243–64.

Disposition and Treatment

dispositional hearing
A court hearing to determine the appropriate treatment for a youth found to be a delinquent.

At the **dispositional hearing,** the juvenile court judge imposes a sentence on the juvenile offender based on her offense, prior record, and family background. Normally, the judge has broad discretionary power to issue a range of dispositions from dismissal to institutional commitment. In theory, the dispositional decision is an effort by the court to serve the best interests of the child, the family, and the community. In many respects, this post-adjudicative process is the most important stage in the juvenile court system because it represents the last opportunity for the court to influence the child and control his behavior.

To ensure that only relevant and appropriate evidence is considered by the court during trial, most jurisdictions require a separate hearing to consider the disposition. The bifurcated hearing process ensures that the adjudicatory hearing is used solely to determine the merits of the allegations, whereas the dispositional hearing determines whether the child is in need of rehabilitation.

In theory, the juvenile court seeks to provide a disposition that represents an individualized treatment plan for the child. This decision is normally based on the presentence investigation of the probation department, reports from social agencies, and possibly a psychiatric evaluation. The judge generally has broad discretion in dispositional matters but is limited by the provisions of the state's juvenile court act. Typical juvenile court dispositions are suspended judgment; probation; placement in a community treatment program; and commitment to the state agency responsible for juvenile institutional care.

In addition, the court may place the child with parents or relatives, make dispositional arrangements with private youth-serving agencies, or order the child committed to a mental institution.

Disposition Outcomes In 1998 (the most recent data available) juveniles were adjudicated delinquent in 63 percent of the 1,000,300 cases brought before a judge. Once adjudicated, juveniles in 58 percent (365,100) of the cases were placed on formal probation; in 26 percent (163,800) of the cases, juveniles were placed in a residential facility.[49] Eleven percent of adjudicated cases resulted in other dispositions, such as referral to an outside agency, community service, or

Peer courts are becoming a popular alternative to traditional juvenile courts. Here, youth peer court prosecutor Dante Ballensky, a freshman at Mazama High School, confers with David Schutt, the court's judge, and a Klamath County deputy district attorney, during a session of court in Klamath Falls, Oregon.

© 2000 AP/Wide World Photos

restitution. Between 1989 and 1998, the number of cases in which the court ordered an adjudicated delinquent to be placed in a residential facility increased 37 percent, while the number of formal probation cases increased 73 percent.[50] While the juvenile court has been under pressure to get tough on youth crime, probation is still the disposition of choice in even the most serious cases. Fewer youths are being waived to the adult court today than a decade ago; conversely, more on being placed on probation.[51]

There were racial differences in out-of-home placements. About 24 percent of adjudicated cases involving white youth resulted in out-of-home placement, compared with 30 percent of cases involving black youth and 25 percent involving other minority youth.[52]

Juvenile Sentencing

Over the past decade, juvenile justice experts and the general public have become aroused about the serious juvenile crime rate in general and about violent acts committed by children in particular. As a result, some law enforcement officials and conservative legislators have demanded that the juvenile justice system take a more serious stand with dangerous juvenile offenders. In the past two decades, many state legislatures have responded by toughening their juvenile codes. Some jurisdictions have passed mandatory or determinate incarceration sentences for juveniles convicted of serious felonies. The get-tough approach even allows the use of the death penalty for minors transferred to the adult system.[53] Numerous commentators have called for the abolition of the death penalty for minors, arguing that it is a sad misuse of the principles that govern the legal system.[54]

Many jurisdictions, however, have not abandoned rehabilitation as a primary dispositional goal and still hold to the philosophy that placements should be based on the least detrimental alternative. This view requires that judges employ the least intrusive measures possible to safeguard a child's growth and development.[55]

A second reform has been the concerted effort to remove status offenders from the juvenile justice system and restrict their entry into institutional programs. Because of the development of numerous diversion programs, many children who are involved in truancy and incorrigible behavior who ordinarily would have been sent to a closed institution are now being placed in community programs. There are far fewer status offenders in detention or institutions than ever before.

A third reform effort has been to standardize dispositions in juvenile court. As early as 1977, Washington passed one of the first determinate sentencing laws for juvenile offenders, resulting in other states adopting similar statutes.[56] All children found to be delinquent are evaluated on a point system based on their age, prior juvenile record, and type of crime committed. Minor offenders are handled in the community. Those committing more serious offenses are placed on probation. Children who commit the most serious offenses are subject to standardized institutional penalties. As a result, juvenile offenders who commit such crimes as rape or armed robbery are being sentenced to institutionalization for two, three, and four years. This approach is different from the indeterminate sentencing under which children who had committed a serious crime might be released from institutions in less than a year if correctional authorities believe that they have been rehabilitated.

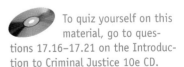 To quiz yourself on this material, go to questions 17.16–17.21 on the Introduction to Criminal Justice 10e CD.

The Juvenile Correctional Process

After disposition in juvenile court, delinquent offenders may be placed in some form of correctional treatment. Although many are placed in the community, more than 100,000 are now in secure facilities.

Juvenile probation officers provide supervision and treatment in the community. The treatment plan is a product of the intake, diagnostic, and investigative aspects of probation. Treatment plans vary in approach and structure. Some juveniles simply report to the probation officer and follow the conditions of probation. In other cases, juvenile probation officers supervise young people more intensely, monitor their daily activities, and work with them in directed treatment programs. Here, a juvenile probation officer and police officer talk with Crips gang members in California.

© A. Ramey/Photo Edit

Probation

Probation is the most commonly used formal sentence for juvenile offenders, and many states require that a youth fail on probation before being sent to an institution (unless the criminal act is serious). Probation involves placing the child under the supervision of the juvenile probation department for the purpose of community treatment. Conditions of probation are normally imposed on the child by either statute or court order. There are general conditions, such as those that require the child to stay away from other delinquents or to obey the law. More specific conditions of probation include requiring the child to participate in a vocational training program, to attend school regularly, to obtain treatment at a child guidance clinic, or to make restitution. Restitution can be in the form of community service — for example, a youth found in possession of marijuana might be required to work 50 hours in a home for the elderly. Monetary restitution requires delinquents to pay back the victims of their crimes. Restitution programs have proven successful and have been adopted around the country.[57]

Juvenile probation is a major component of the juvenile justice system. Juvenile courts place more than 80 percent of adjudicated delinquents on some form of probation. It is the most widely used method of community treatment. The cost savings of community treatment, coupled with its nonpunitive intentions, are likely to keep probation programs growing.

Institutionalization

The most severe of the statutory dispositions available to the juvenile court involves commitment of the child to an institution. The committed child may be sent to a state training school or private residential treatment facility. These are usually minimum-security facilities with small populations and an emphasis on treatment and education. Some states, however, maintain facilities with populations over 1,000.

Most state statutes vary when determining the length of the child's commitment. Most jurisdictions have the ability to commit the child up to their majority age, which can range from 15 to 17. Once a juvenile has been committed by a

www The Council of Juvenile Correctional Administrators is dedicated to the improvement of juvenile correctional services and practices. Its Web site is at http://www.corrections.com/cjca/.

court, there is a great deal of difference in the way the states determine the juvenile's placement, length of stay, and eventual release. In some states, the agency that runs the state's juvenile correctional facilities determines the place of confinement, the level of security, treatment methods, length of stay, and conditions of release. In other states, the juvenile court judge may make some or all of these decisions. Some states allow judges to pass down definite periods of confinement similar to a determinate sentence in adult court, while others use purely indeterminate sentences in which the juvenile is released when the correctional agency believes he is rehabilitated. In some states, the juvenile court judge makes or at least reviews the release decision, and in other states a juvenile parole board operates independently of the court and secure correctional system.[58]

Ninety-five percent of incarcerated juveniles are held for delinquent offenses — offenses that would be crimes if committed by adults. Thirty-five percent were held for person-oriented offenses; about 20 percent for alcohol, drug, and public order offenses; and more than 40 percent for property crimes.[59] Just over 5 percent were confined for a juvenile status offense, such as truancy, running away, or incorrigibility. The efforts made in recent years to keep status offenders out of institutions seem to have paid off.

Population Trends At last count, there were almost 110,000 juveniles being held in public (70 percent) and private (30 percent) facilities in the United States.[60] The juvenile custody rate varies widely among states. The District of Columbia makes the greatest use of custodial treatment, incarcerating just over 700 delinquents in public and private facilities per 100,000 juveniles in the general population. In contrast, about half of the states had rates of about 300 juveniles per 100,000. Some states rely heavily on privately run facilities, while others place many youths in out-of-state facilities. Whereas most delinquents are held in public facilities, most status offenders are held in private facilities.

The typical resident of a juvenile facility is a 15- to 16-year-old white male incarcerated for an average stay of five months in a public facility or six months in a private facility. Private facilities tend to house younger youths, while public institutions provide custodial care for older youths, including a small percentage of youths between 18 and 21 years of age. Most incarcerated youths are person, property, or drug offenders.

Minorities in Juvenile Institutions Minority youths are incarcerated at a rate two to five times that of white youths. The difference is greatest for black youths, with a custody rate of 1,004 per 100,000 juveniles; for white youths the rate is 212.[61] Research has found that this overrepresentation is not a result of differentials in arrest rates but often stems from disparity at early stages of case processing.[62] Of equal importance, minorities are more likely to be confined in secure public facilities instead of open private facilities that might provide more costly and effective treatment.[63]

Minority youths accused of delinquent acts are less likely than white youths to be diverted from the court system into informal sanctions and are more likely to receive sentences involving incarceration.

Deinstitutionalization

Some experts in delinquency and juvenile law question the policy of institutionalizing juvenile offenders. Many believe that large institutions are too costly to operate and only produce more sophisticated criminals. This dilemma has produced a number of efforts to remove youths from juvenile facilities and replace large institutions with smaller community-based facilities. For example, Massachusetts closed all its state training schools more than 20 years ago (subsequently,

*Many incarcerated youth have serious social and psychological problems. To learn more, read Deborah Shelton, "Failure of Mental Health Policy — Incarcerated Children and Adolescents," *Pediatric Nursing* 28, no. 3 (May-June 2002): 278, on InfoTrac College Edition.

however, public pressure caused a few secure facilities to be reopened). Many other states have established small residential facilities operated by juvenile care agencies to replace larger units.

Despite the daily rhetoric on crime control, public support for community-based programs for juveniles still exists. Although such programs are not panaceas, many experts still recommend more treatment and less incarceration for juvenile offenders. Maryland, Pennsylvania, Utah, and Vermont, for example, have dramatically reduced their reform school populations while setting up a wide range of intensive treatment programs for juveniles. Many large, impersonal, and expensive state institutions with unqualified staff and ineffective treatment programs have been eliminated.

Status Offenders An ongoing effort has been made for almost 30 years to deinstitutionalize status offenders (DSO).[64] This means removing noncriminal youths from institutions housing delinquents to prevent them from interacting with violent or chronic offenders.

Since its inception, the DSO approach has been hotly debated. Some have argued that early intervention is society's best hope of forestalling future delinquent behavior and reducing victimization. Other experts maintain that legal control over status offenders is a violation of youths' rights. Still others have viewed status-offending behavior as a symptom of some larger trauma or problem that requires attention. These diverse opinions still exist today.

Since Congress passed the JJDP Act in 1974, all 50 states have complied with some aspect of the deinstitutionalization mandate. Millions of federal, state, and local dollars have been spent on the DSO movement. Vast numbers of programs have been created around the country to reduce the number of juveniles in secure confinement. What remains to be done, however, is to study the effect DSO has had on juveniles and the justice system.

Aftercare

Aftercare marks the final stage of the formal juvenile justice process. Its purpose is to help youths make the transition from residential or institutional settings back into the community. Effective aftercare programs provide adequate supervision and support services to help juvenile offenders avoid criminal activity. Examples of programs include electronic monitoring, counseling, treatment and community service referrals, education, work training, and intensive parole supervision.

Most juvenile aftercare involves parole. A juvenile parole officer provides the child with counseling, school referral, vocational training, and other services. Children who violate the conditions of parole may have their parole revoked and be returned to the institution. Unlike the adult postconviction process, where the U.S. Supreme Court has imposed procedural protections in probation and parole revocations, juveniles do not have such due process rights. State courts have also been reluctant to grant juveniles rights in this area, and those that have generally refuse to require that the whole array of rights be made available as they are to adult offenders. Since the *Gault* decision, however, many states have adopted administrative regulations requiring juvenile agencies to incorporate due process, such as proper notice of the hearing and the right to counsel in postconviction proceedings.

To quiz yourself on this material, go to questions 17.22–17.25 on the Introduction to Criminal Justice 10e CD.

Preventing Delinquency

delinquency prevention
Intervening in a young person's life to help them avoid involvement in delinquent activities.

While the juvenile justice system has been concerned with controlling delinquent behavior, important efforts are being made to prevent delinquency before it occurs. **Delinquency prevention** refers to intervening in a young person's life prior to him or her engaging in delinquency in the first place; that is, preventing involvement in delinquency in the first instance. In the past, delinquency prevention was the responsibility of treatment oriented agencies such as the YMCA (Young Men's Christian Association), Boys and Girls Clubs of America, and other private and public agencies. Today, many community-based treatment programs involve a combination of juvenile justice and treatment agencies.

Community Strategies

Comprehensive community-based delinquency prevention programs are made up of a range of different types of interventions and typically involve an equally diverse group of community and government agencies that are concerned with the problem of juvenile delinquency. Today these are being supplemented with a systematic approach or comprehensive planning model to develop preventive interventions. This includes an analysis of the delinquency problem, an identification of available resources in the community, development of priority delinquency problems, and the identification of successful programs in other communities and tailoring them to local conditions and needs.[65] Not all comprehensive community-based prevention programs follow this model, but evidence suggests that this approach will produce the greatest reductions in juvenile delinquency.[66]

© 2003 AP/Wide World Photos

Many jurisdictions are developing new intervention programs for at-risk teenage youths. Some are treatment-oriented programs that rely on rehabilitation ideals. For example, the federal Children at Risk program was set up to help improve the lives of young people at high-risk for delinquency, gang involvement, substance abuse, and other problem behaviors. It was delivered to a large number of young people in poor and high-crime neighborhoods in five cities across the country. It involved a wide range of preventive measures, including case management and family counseling, family skills training, tutoring, mentoring, after-school activities, and community policing. The program was different in each neighborhood. A study of all five cities showed that one year after the program ended the young people who received the program, compared with a control group, were less likely to have committed violent delinquent acts and used or sold drugs. Some of the other beneficial results for those in the program included less association with delinquent peers, less peer pressure to engage in delinquency, and more positive peer support.[67]

Other large-scale comprehensive community-based delinquency prevention programs include Communities That Care (CTC) and the SafeFutures Initiative.[68] Both programs are funded by OJJDP. The CTC strategy emphasizes the reduction of risk factors for delinquency and the enhancement of protective factors against delinquency for different developmental stages from birth through adolescence.[69] CTC follows a rigorous, multilevel planning process that includes

Former Clinton administration attorney general Janet Reno is a firm advocate of prevention in the juvenile justice system. See Janet Reno, "Prevention as Public Policy," *Reclaiming Children and Youth* 10, no. 4 (Winter 2002): 207, on InfoTrac College Edition.

Jacqueline Castillo, 13, left, Jasmin Amaya, 13, top, and Jacquelyn Rodriguez, 20, right, posed for a portrait after a news conference about Aspira, a national organization devoted to developing leadership and community among Latino youth, in the Southwest Regional Library in Pembroke Pines, Florida, on July 24, 2002. Florida's Department of Juvenile Justice awarded $7.5 million to fund new delinquency prevention programs around the state, targeting Zip codes where high concentrations of child offenders live. Aspira is one of the programs that received a grant.

Exhibit 17.1 SafeFutures Initiative to Reduce Juvenile Delinquency and Youth Violence

Nine program areas constitute the SafeFutures Initiative.

1. After-school programs.
2. Juvenile mentoring programs (JUMP).
3. Family strengthening and support services.
4. Mental health services for at-risk and adjudicated youth.
5. Delinquency prevention programs in general.
6. Comprehensive community-wide approaches to gang-free schools and communities.
7. Community-based day treatment programs.
8. Continuum-of-care services for at-risk and delinquent girls.
9. Serious, violent, and chronic juvenile offender programs (with an emphasis on enhancing graduated sanctions).

Source: Elaine Morley, Shelli B. Rossman, Mary Kopczynski, Janeen Buck, and Caterina Gouvis, *Comprehensive Responses to Youth at Risk: Interim Findings from the SafeFutures Initiative* (Washington, D.C.: Office of Juvenile Justice and Delinquency Prevention, 2000), p. x.

WWW Parenting Resources for the 21st Century links parents and other adults responsible for the care of a child with information on issues covering the full spectrum of parenting. It provides information on delinquency prevention in the community. Check out http://www.parentingresources.ncjrs.org/.

drawing upon interventions that have previously demonstrated success and tailoring them to the needs of the community.[70]

The SafeFutures Initiative operates much like CTC; for example, by emphasizing the reduction of risk factors for delinquency and protective factors against delinquency, using what works, and following a rigorous planning model to implement different interventions. It also aims to build or strengthen existing collaborations among the many community groups and government departments working to prevent delinquency. However, unlike CTC, the SafeFutures Initiative is only targeted at youths, those who are both at high risk for delinquency and adjudicated offenders (see Exhibit 17.1). An important part of the SafeFutures Initiative is the Juvenile Mentoring Program (JUMP), which is set out in the Analyzing Criminal Justice Issues feature on page 573.

Enforcement Strategies

While these programs are primarily treatment-oriented, many new programs combine treatment with enforcement. Some important ones are now targeting teenage gun use. Easy availability of guns is a significant contributor to teen violence. Research indicates a close tie among gun use, control of drug markets, and teen violence. Gang-related homicides almost always involve firearms. Unless significant efforts are made to control the spread of handguns, teenage murder rates should continue to rise.

At least 35 states have adopted legislation dealing with guns and children. In 1995 alone, 19 states passed laws requiring schools to expel or suspend students for possessing weapons on school grounds.[71] At the federal level, laws have also been passed to restrict the possession, sale, and transfer of guns to juveniles. The Gun-Free Schools Act of 1994 requires local educational agencies receiving financial assistance to expel for one year any student who brings a firearm to school. The Youth Handgun Safety Act (part of the Omnibus Violent Crime Control and Law Enforcement Act of 1994) prohibits the possession or private transfer of a handgun to a juvenile. Although this legislation was enacted by the federal government, it is the state and local officials who can deal most effectively with juvenile gun violations.

The Juvenile Mentoring Program (JUMP)

analyzing criminal justice issues

The Juvenile Mentoring Program, referred to as JUMP, is a program that aides children who are at risk of failing out of school or demonstrate delinquent behavior such as gang involvement or substance abuse. The program is directed by the Office of Juvenile Justice and Delinquency Prevention, which resides within the Department of Justice. JUMP provides funds to community-based organizations, such as schools, to provide the proper elements needed to incorporate one-to-one mentoring for these children, which in turn helps them rise from their current delinquent level. Currently, the program has been incorporated in 47 states. Mentors generally come from religious establishments, community organizations, schools, local law enforcement agencies, medical organizations, and businesses within the community. Mentors must be 18 years of age or older to work for the program. Once recruited, these mentors assist kids, both male and female, who have different problems. Some are victims of abuse or neglect or both, some have parents who are incarcerated, some are involved with the court system, while others are battling disabilities.

The program was established with the three goals in mind. First, JUMP was developed to deter children from partaking in delinquent behavior as well as reducing their involvement with gang activities. Second, the program strives to demonstrate the importance of staying in school. Third, JUMP hopes that kids will realize the importance of school and, thus, improve their class work. Through mentoring, children are to gain assistance in partaking in non-delinquent activities. Through these activities it is hoped that children will be discouraged from using drugs and from being involved in violent activities. In addition, the program encourages children to take responsibility for their own actions. Furthermore, mentors stress participation in community service.

A community must meet certain criteria to obtain funding for the JUMP program. The program is used for high-risk children, those who are at risk in their homes, schools, or communities. These risks are likely to cause a child to drop out of school, join a gang, begin drug use, or get involved in other delinquent

behavior. More specifically, schools that wish to participate in this program must show that the juvenile arrest rate of the targeted community is as great as or greater than the overall juvenile arrest rate for the county or municipality in which the school is located. In addition, the drop out rate at the school must be as great as or greater than the entire school districts drop out rate.

Evaluations of the program are being conducted on the multiple sites that have implemented the JUMP curriculum. The Information Technology International Incorporation has begun to collect data from these sites to make a cumulative report on the success of the program in its different locations.

Sources: *Juvenile Mentoring Program* (Washington, D.C.: Department of Justice, Office of Juvenile Justice and Delinquency Prevention, June 2003), www.ojjpd.ncjrs.org/jump/oview.html, accessed on November 25, 2003; Laurence Novotney, Elizabeth Mertinko, James Lange, and Tara Kelley, "Juvenile Mentoring Program: A Progress Review," *Juvenile Justice Bulletin* (September 2000): 1–5.

Keep the Juvenile Court?

Over the past century, the juvenile court has struggled to provide treatment for juvenile offenders while guaranteeing them constitutional due process. The juvenile court system has been transformed from a rehabilitative to a quasi-criminal court. Many states are toughening juvenile codes. With limited resources and procedural deficiencies, much change is unlikely in the near future.

The system has been so overwhelmed by violent juvenile crime and family breakdown that some judges and politicians have suggested abolishing the juvenile system. Even those experts who want to retain an independent juvenile court have called for its restructuring. Crime control advocates want to reduce the court's jurisdiction over juveniles charged with serious crimes and liberalize the prosecutor's ability to try them in adult courts. In contrast, child advocates suggest that the court scale back its judicial role and transfer its functions to community groups and social service agencies.[72] Despite these differing opinions, the juvenile court will likely remain a critical societal institution; there are few viable alternatives. This issue is addressed in the Analyzing Criminal Justice Issues feature on page 574.

Should the Juvenile Court Be Abolished?

analyzing criminal justice issues

In an important work, *Bad Kids: Race and the Transformation of the Juvenile Court*, legal expert Barry C. Feld makes the controversial suggestion that the juvenile court system should be discontinued or replaced by an alternative method of justice. He says that the current structure of current court makes it almost impossible to fulfill or achieve the purpose for which it was originally intended.

Feld maintains that the juvenile court was intended to create a process that was more lenient than that used against adult criminals. While a worthwhile goal, the juvenile court system was doomed to failure even from the beginning, because it was thrown into the role of providing child welfare while at the same time being an instrument law enforcement, two missions that are often at cross-purposes. During its history, various legal developments have further undermined its purpose. Most notable was the *In re Gault* ruling, which led to juveniles receiving similar legal protections as adults and to children being treated like adults. The juvenile courts vision of leniency was further undercut by fear and racism created by postwar migration and economic trends, which led to the development of large enclaves of poor and underemployed African Americans living in Northern cities. Then, in the 1980s, the sudden rise in gang membership, gun violence, and homicide committed by juveniles further undermined the juvenile court mission and resulted in legislation that created mandatory sentences for juvenile offenders and mandatory waiver to the adult court. As a result, the focus of the court has been on dealing with the offense instead of treating the offender. In Feld's words, the juvenile court has become a "deficient second-rate criminal court."

The welfare and rehabilitative purposes of the juvenile court have been subordinated to its role of law enforcement agent.

Can juvenile court be reformed? Feld maintains that it is impossible because of the court's conflicting purposes and shifting priorities. The money spent on serving the court and its large staff would be better spent on child welfare, which would target a larger audience and prevent antisocial acts before they occur. In lieu of juvenile court, youths who violate the law should receive full procedural protections in the criminal court system. The special protections given youth in the juvenile court could be provided by altering the criminal law and recognizing age as a factor in the creation of criminal liability. Because youth have had a limited opportunity to develop self-control, their criminal liability should also be curtailed or restricted.

Is Feld's dour assessment of the juvenile court valid? Not so, according to John Johnson Kerbs, who suggests that Feld's assumptions may not be wedded to the reality of the American legal system. First, Kerbs finds that it is naïve to assume the criminal courts can provide the same or greater substantive and procedural protections as the juvenile court. Many juvenile court defendants are indigent, especially those coming from the minority community, and they may not be able to obtain adequate legal defense in the adult system. Second, Feld's assumption that criminal courts will take a defendant's age into close consideration may be illusory. In this get-tough era, criminal courts likely will provide harsher sentences and the brunt of these draconian sentences will fall squarely on the shoulders of minority youth. Research efforts routinely show that African American

adults are unduly punished in adult courts. Sending juvenile offenders to these venues will most likely further enmesh them in an already unfair system. Finally, Kerb finds that the treatment benefits of the juvenile courts should not be overlooked or abandoned. Ample research, he maintains, shows that juvenile courts can create lower recidivism rates than criminal courts. Though the juvenile court is far from perfect and should be improved, it would be foolish to abandon a system that is aimed at helping kids find alternatives to crime for one that produces higher recidivism rates, lowers future prospects, and has a less than stellar record of providing due process and equal protection for the nation's most needy citizens.

Critical Thinking

Should the juvenile court be abolished? Given that the trend has been to transfer the most serious criminal cases to the adult court, is there still a purpose for an independent juvenile court? Should the juvenile court be reserved for non-serious first offenders?

InfoTrac College Edition Research

Before you make up your mind about the future of juvenile court, read Joseph V. Penn, "Justice for Youth? A History of the Juvenile and Family Court," *Brown University Child and Adolescent Behavior Letter* 17, no. 9 (September 2001): 1.

Sources: Barry C. Feld, *Bad Kids: Race and the Transformation of the Juvenile Court* (New York: Oxford University Press, 1999); John Johnson Kerbs, "(Un)equal Justice: Juvenile Court Abolition and African Americans," *Annals of the American Academy of Political and Social Science,* 564 (1999): 109–25.

Summary

- The juvenile justice system is concerned with delinquent children, as well as with those who are beyond the care and protection of their parents.
- The juvenile justice system was established at the turn of the twentieth century after decades of effort by child-saving groups. These reformers sought to create an independent category of delinquent offender and keep their treatment separate from adults.
- Juveniles involved in antisocial behavior come under the jurisdiction of juvenile or family court systems.
- These courts belong to a system of juvenile justice agencies, including law enforcement, child care, and institutional services. Representatives from different disciplines, such as lawyers, social workers, and psychiatrists, all play major roles in the judicial process.
- In recent years the juvenile court system has become more legalistic by virtue of U.S. Supreme Court decisions that have granted children procedural safeguards. The child has a right to counsel and is generally given other procedural due process safeguards, notably the privilege against self-incrimination and the right to confront and cross-examine witnesses.
- The juvenile justice process consists of a series of steps: the police investigation, the intake procedure in the juvenile court, the pretrial procedures used for juvenile offenders, and the adjudication, disposition, and post-dispositional procedures.
- Kids who are considered dangerous are detained in secure facilities. A major effort has been made to remove juveniles from detention in adult jails

- and to make sure status offenders are not placed in secure detention facilities.
- Those who are held for trial are generally released to their parents, on bail or through other means. An issue related to bail is preventive detention, which refers to the right of a judge to deny persons release before trial on the grounds that they may be dangerous to themselves or others.
- Each year, thousands of youths are transferred to adult courts because of the serious nature of their crimes. This process, known as waiver, is an effort to remove serious offenders from the juvenile process and into the more punitive adult system. Today, virtually all jurisdictions provide for waiver of juvenile offenders to the criminal courts.
- Juveniles alleged to be delinquent have virtually all the rights given a criminal defendant at trial — except possibly the right to a trial by jury. In addition, juvenile proceedings are generally closed to the public.
- Types of dispositional orders in juvenile court include dismissal, fine, probation, and institutionalization. Legislatures have begun to take a tougher position with regard to the sentencing of some juvenile offenders
- In recent years a number of states have made drastic changes in juvenile sentencing law, moving away from the indeterminate sentence and embracing more determinate forms of disposition.
- The future of the juvenile justice system is in doubt. A number of state jurisdictions are revising their juvenile codes to restrict eligibility in the juvenile justice system and eliminate the most serious offenders.

Key Terms

parens patriae 548
poor laws 548
chancery courts 549
child savers 549
Children's Aid Society 550

intake 558
detention 558
waiver 561
transfer 561
initial appearance 563

adjudication 563
fact-finding hearing 563
dispositional hearing 566
delinquency prevention 570

Doing Research on the Web

For an up-to-date list of Web links, go to http://cj.wadsworth.com/siegel_intro10e.

InfoTrac College Edition provides numerous articles on juvenile justice. You can use it to review many

of the topics discussed in this chapter. For example, if you want to research the issues related to the abolition of the juvenile court, read Barry C. Feld, "Abolish the Juvenile Court: Youthfulness, Criminal Responsibility, and Sentencing Policy," *Journal of Criminal Law and Criminology* 88 (1997): 68–136; Stephen J. Morse, "Immaturity and Irresponsibility," *Journal of Criminal Law and Criminology* 88 (1997): 15–67.

For information on detention and incarceration issues, check out Steven H. Rosenbaum, "Civil Rights Issues in Juvenile Detention and Correctional Systems," *Corrections Today* 61 (1999): 148.

An important site for research on the Web is the Office of Juvenile Justice and Delinquency Prevention: http://ojjdp.ncjrs.org/.

> Pro/Con discussions and Viewpoint Essays on some of the topics in this chapter may be found at the Opposing Viewpoints Resource Center: http://www.gale.com/OpposingViewpoints.

Discussion Questions

1. Should status offenders be treated by the juvenile court? Explain. Should they be placed in confinement for running away or cutting school? Why or why not?
2. Should a juvenile ever be waived to adult court at the risk that the child will be incarcerated with adult felons? Why or why not?
3. Do you support the death penalty for children? Explain.
4. Should juveniles be given mandatory incarceration sentences for serious crimes, as adults are? Explain.
5. Is it fair to deny juveniles a jury trial? Why or why not?
6. Do you think the trend toward treating juveniles like adult offenders is desirable? Explain.

Notes

1 Jeordan Legon, "Teen Sniper Suspect Remains a Mystery," CNN News, April 28, 2003, http://www.cnn.com/2002/US/10/28/sproject.sniper.malvo.profile/index.html, accessed on November 27, 2003.

2 Federal Bureau of Investigation, *Crime in the United States, 2002* (Washington, D.C.: Government Printing Office, 2003); Howard Snyder and Melissa Sickmund, *Juvenile Offenders and Victims: 1999 National Report* (Washington, D.C.: Office of Juvenile Justice and Delinquency Prevention, 1999).

3 *Vernonia School District* v. *Acton,* 515 U.S. 646, 115 S.Ct. 2386, 132 L.Ed.2d (1995).

4 *Board of Education of Independent School District No. 92 of Pottawatomie County* v. *Earls et al.* (No. 01–332), 2002.

5 Gordon Bazemore, "What's 'New' about the Balanced Approach?" *Juvenile and Family Court Journal* 48 (1997): 1–21. See also Office of Justice Programs, *Balanced and Restorative Justice for Juveniles — A Framework for Juvenile Justice in the 21st Century* (Washington, D.C.: Office of Juvenile Justice and Delinquency Prevention, 1997).

6 Material in this section depends heavily on Sanford J. Fox, "Juvenile Justice Reform: A Historical Perspective," *Stanford Law Review* 22 (1970): 1187–1205; Lawrence Stone, *The Family, Sex, and Marriage in England: 1500–1800* (New York: Harper and Row, 1977); Philippe Aries, *Century of Childhood: A Social History of Family Life* (New York: Vintage Press, 1962); Douglas

R. Rendleman, "Parens Patriae: From Chancery to the Juvenile Court," *South Carolina Law Review* 23 (1971): 205–29; Anthony Platt, "The Rise of the Child-Saving Movement: A Study in Social Policy and Correctional Reform," *Annals of the American Academy of Political and Social Science* 381 (1979): 21–38; Anthony M. Platt, *The Child Savers: The Intervention of Delinquency* (Chicago: University of Chicago Press, 1969); Robert S. Pickett, *House of Refuge: Origins of Juvenile Reform in New York State, 1815–1857* (Syracuse, N.Y.: Syracuse University Press, 1969).

7 Douglas Besharov, *Juvenile Justice Advocacy: Practice in a Unique Court* (New York: Practicing Law Institute, 1974), p. 2. See also Jay Albanese, *Dealing with Delinquency — The Future of Juvenile Justice* (Chicago: Nelson-Hall, 1993).

8 4 Eng.Rep. 1078 (1827).

9 Platt, *The Child Savers,* pp. 11–38.

10 See, generally, Anne Meis Knupfer, *Reform and Resistance: Gender, Delinquency, and America's First Juvenile Court* (London, England: Routledge, 2001).

11 This section is based on material from the New York State Archives, *The Greatest Reform School in the World: A Guide to the Records of the New York House of Refuge: A Brief History 1824–1857* (Albany, N.Y.: 2001); Sanford J. Fox, "Juvenile Justice Reform: A Historical Perspective," *Stanford Law Review* 22 (1970):1187.

12 Pickett, *House of Refuge.*

13 Robert Mennel, "Origins of the Juvenile Court: Changing Perspectives on the Legal Rights of Juvenile Delinquents," in *Juvenile Justice Philosophy,* ed. Frederick Faust and Paul Brantingham (St. Paul, Minn. West Publishing, 1974)," pp. 69–70.

14 Platt, *The Child Savers,* p. 116.

15 LaMar T. Empey, *American Delinquency: Its Meaning and Construction* (Homewood, Ill.: Dorsey Press, 1978), p. 515.

16 *Kent* v. *United States,* 383 U.S. 541, 86 S.Ct. 1045, 16 L.Ed.2d 84 (1966); *In re Gault,* 387 U.S. 1, 87 S.Ct. 1428, 18 L.Ed.2d 527 (1967); *In re Winship,* 397 U.S. 358, 90 S.Ct. 1068, 25 L.Ed.2d 368 (1970); *Breed* v. *Jones,* 421 U.S. 519, 95 S.Ct. 1779, 44 L.Ed.2d 346 (1975).

17 Public Law 93-415 (1974).

18 For a comprehensive view of juvenile law, see, generally, Joseph J. Senna and Larry J. Siegel, *Juvenile Law: Cases and Comments,* 2d ed. (St. Paul, Minn.: West, 1992).

19 Federal Bureau of Investigation, *Crime in the United States,* p. 220.

20 Joan McCord, Cathy Spatz-Widom, and Nancy A. Crowell, eds., *Juvenile Crime, Juvenile Justice,* Panel on Juvenile Crime: Prevention, Treatment, and Control (Washington, D.C.: National Academy Press, 2001), p. 163.

21 Robert E. Worden and Stephanie M. Myers, *Police Encounters with Juvenile Suspects* (Albany, N.Y.: State University of New York, University at Albany, Hindelang Criminal Justice Research Center and School of Criminal Justice, 2001), Table 3.

22 *Fare* v. *Michael C.,* 442 U.S. 707 (1979).

23 *New Jersey v. T.L.O.*, 469 U.S. 325 (1985).

24 *Vernonia School District v. Acton* (1995).

25 Anne L. Stahl, *Delinquency Cases in Juvenile Courts, 1998* (Washington, D.C.: Office of Juvenile Justice and Delinquency Prevention, 2001).

26 Anne L. Stahl, *Drug Offense Cases in Juvenile Courts, 1989–1998* (Washington, D.C.: Office of Juvenile Justice and Delinquency Prevention, 2001).

27 Stahl, *Delinquency Cases Juvenile Courts, 1998.*

28 Paul Harms, *Detention in Delinquency Cases, 1989–1998* (Washington, D.C.: Officer of Juvenile Justice and Delinquency Prevention, 2002).

29 *Schall v. Martin,* 467 U.S. 253, 104 S.Ct. 2403, 81 L.Ed.2d 207 (1984).

30 See Juvenile Justice and Delinquency Prevention Act of 1974, 42 U.S.C., Sec. 5633.

31 Ira Schwartz, Linda Harris, and Laurie Levi, "The Jailing of Juveniles in Minnesota," *Crime and Delinquency* 34 (1988): 131. See also Barry Krisberg and Robert DeComo, *Juveniles Taken into Custody — 1991* (San Francisco: National Council on Crime and Delinquency, 1993), p. 25.

32 Schwartz, Harris, and Levi, "The Jailing of Juveniles in Minnesota," p. 134.

33 383 U.S. 541, 86 S.Ct. 1045, 16 L.Ed.2d 84 (1966).

34 421 U.S. 519, 528, 95 S.Ct. 1779, 1785, 44 L.Ed.2d 346 (1975).

35 Alan Karpelowitz, *State Legislative Priorities — 1995* (Denver, Colo.: National Conference of State Legislatures, 1995), p. 10.

36 Charles M. Puzzanchera, *Delinquency Cases Waived to Criminal Court, 1989–1998* (Washington, D.C.: Office of Juvenile Justice and Delinquency Prevention, 2001).

37 Dale Parent and others, *Key Issues in Criminal Justice: Transferring Serious Juvenile Offenders to Adult Courts* (Washington, D.C.: National Institute of Justice, 1997).

38 Barry Feld, "The Juvenile Court Meets the Principle of the Offense: Legislative Changes in Juvenile Waiver Statutes," *Journal of Criminal Law and Criminology* 78 (1987): 471–533. See also John Kramer, Henry Sontheimer, and John Lemmon, "Pennsylvania Waiver to Adult Court," paper presented at the annual meeting of the American Society of Criminology, San Francisco, California, November 1991. The authors confirm that juveniles tried in adult courts are generally male, age 17 or older, and disproportionately minorities.

39 Puzzanchera, *Delinquency Cases Waived to Criminal Court;* James Howell, "Juvenile Transfers to Criminal Court," *Juvenile and Family Justice Journal* 6 (1997): 12–14.

40 Anne L. Stahl, *Delinquency Cases in Juvenile Courts, 1997* (Washington, D.C.: Office of Juvenile Justice and Delinquency Prevention, 2000); Puzzanchera, *Delinquency Cases Waived to Criminal Court.*

41 Jeffrey Fagan and Franklin Zimring, eds., *The Changing Borders of Juvenile Justice: Transfer of Adolescents to the Criminal Court* (Chicago: University of Chicago Press, 2000).

42 Thomas Grisso and Robert Schwartz, *Juveniles' Competence to Stand Trial: A Comparison of Adolescents' and Adults' Capacities as Trial Defendants* (Philadelphia, Pa.: MacArthur Foundation Research Network on Adolescent Development and Juvenile Justice, 2003).

43 Shay Bilchik, "Sentencing Juveniles to Adult Facilities Fails Youths and Society," *Corrections Today* 65 (2003): 21.

44 Howard N. Snyder, Melissa Sickmund, and Eileen Poe-Yamagata, *Juvenile Transfers to Criminal Court in the 1990s: Lessons Learned from Four Studies* (Washington, D.C.: Office of Juvenile Justice and Delinquency Prevention, 2000).

45 Lamar Smith, "Sentencing Youths to Adult Correctional Facilities Increases Public Safety," *Corrections Today* 65 (2003): 20.

46 387 U.S. 1, 87 S.Ct. 1428, 18 L.Ed.2d 527 (1967).

47 397 U.S. 358, 90 S.Ct. 1068, 25 L.Ed.2d 368 (1970).

48 403 U.S. 528, 91 S.Ct. 1976, 29 L.Ed.2d 647 (1971).

49 Paul Harms, *Robbery Cases in Juvenile Court, 1989–1998* (Washington, D.C.: Office of Juvenile Justice and Delinquency Prevention, 2002).

50 Stahl, *Delinquency Cases in Juvenile Courts, 1998.*

51 Harms, *Robbery Cases in Juvenile Court.*

52 Charles Puzzanchera, *Juvenile Court Placement of Adjudicated Youth, 1989–1998* (Washington, D.C.: Office of Juvenile Justice and Delinquency Prevention, 2002).

53 Victor Streib, *Death Penalty for Juveniles* (Bloomington: Indiana University Press, 1987).

54 Biko Agozino, "The Crisis of Authoritarianism in the Legal Institutions," *Journal of Contemporary Criminal Justice* 19 (2003): 315–50.

55 See Joseph Goldstein, Anna Freud, and Albert Solnit, *Beyond the Best Interest of the Child* (New York: Free Press, 1973).

56 See Michael Serrill, "Police Write a New Law on Juvenile Crime," *Police Magazine* (September 1979): 47. See also A. Schneider and D. Schram, *Assessment of Juvenile Justice Reform in Washington State,* vols. 1–4 (Washington, D.C.: Institute of Policy Analysis, 1983); T. Castellano, "Justice Model in the Juvenile Justice System — Washington State's Experience," *Law and Policy* 8 (1986): 479.

57 Anne Schneider, *Guide to Juvenile Restitution* (Washington, D.C.: Department of Justice, 1985).

58 *Following Commitment, How Are Placement, Length of Stay, and Release Decisions Made?* (Pittsburgh, Pa.: National Center for Juvenile Justice, April 18, 2003).

59 Melissa Sickmund, Howard Snyder, and Eileen Poe-Yamagata, *Juvenile Offenders and Victims: 1997 Update on Violence* (Washington, D.C.: Office of Juvenile Justice and Delinquency Prevention, 1997), p. 18.

60 Melissa Sickmund and Yi-chun Wan, "Census of Juveniles in Residential Placement Databook," 2001, http://www.ojjdp.ncjrs.org/ojstatbb/cjrp, accessed on November 25, 2003.

61 Sickmund and Wan, "Census of Juveniles in Residential Placement Databook."

62 Howard N. Snyder and Melissa Sickmund, *Juvenile Offenders and Victims: 1999 National Report* (Pittsburgh, Pa.: National Center for Juvenile Justice, 1999), p. 192.

63 Ibid, p. 195.

64 National Conference of State Legislatures, *A Legislator's Guide to Comprehensive Juvenile Justice, Juvenile Detention, and Corrections* (Denver, Colo.: 1996).

65 J. David Hawkins, Richard F. Catalano, and Associates, *Communities That Care: Action for Drug Abuse Prevention* (San Francisco, Calif.: Jossey-Bass, 1992).

66 Richard F. Catalano, Michael W. Arthur, J. David Hawkins, Lisa Berglund, and Jeffrey J. Olson, "Comprehensive Community- and School-Based Interventions to Prevent Antisocial Behavior," in *Serious and Violent Juvenile Offenders: Risk Factors and Successful Interventions,* ed. Rolf Loeber and David P. Farrington (Thousand Oaks, Calif.: Sage, 1998).

67 Adele V. Harrell, Shannon E. Cavanagh, and Sanjeev Sridharan, *Evaluation of the Children at Risk Program: Results 1 Year after the End of the Program* (Washington, D.C.: NIJ Research in Brief, 1999).

68 Hawkins, Catalano, and Associates, *Communities That Care;* Elaine Morley, Shelli B. Rossman, Mary Kopczynski, Janeen Buck, and Caterina Gouvis, *Comprehensive Responses to Youth at Risk: Interim Findings from the SafeFutures Initiative* (Washington, D.C.: Office of Juvenile Justice and Delinquency Prevention, 2000).

69 Catalano, Arthur, Hawkins, Berglund, and Olson, "Comprehensive Community- and School-Based Interventions to Prevent Antisocial Behavior," p. 281.

70 James C. Howell and J. David Hawkins, "Prevention of Youth Violence," in *Youth Violence: Crime and Justice: A Review of Research,* vol. 24, ed. Michael Tonry and Mark H. Moore (Chicago: University of Chicago Press, 1998), pp. 303–04.

71 Office of Justice Programs, *Reducing Youth Gun Violence* (Washington, D.C.: Office of Juvenile Justice and Delinquency Prevention, 1996).

72 Fox Butterfield, "Justice Besieged," *New York Times,* July 21, 1997, p. A16.

Appendix A | Careers in Criminal Justice

Employment in criminal justice fields can be found in government, the private sector, educational institutions, and nonprofit organizations. Criminal justice fields are evolving to include specialization in areas of technology and computer security as well as new approaches to treatment and rehabilitation of offenders. Over the past decades, the employment possibilities within the traditional police, courts, and corrections areas are being expanded.

Criminal justice careers cover a variety of jobs and professions. Typically, they do not require that the applicant major in criminal justice but may welcome people with backgrounds in criminology, sociology, political science, psychology, social work, and other social science and human services disciplines. So, while a criminal justice degree may be preferred, the door will not be closed to those majoring in another subject.

The search for the right career within the criminal justice system begins by deciding where your personal interests lay or at least by forming a general idea of your career goals: law enforcement, human services, research, teaching, and so on. Once you have decided which general areas of criminal justice best suits you, you could contact the campus career services program, which typically assists students with résumé writing and in developing interviewing skills.

Many Web sites are available that help students find out about the many different types of criminal justice employment. While it is difficult to keep current with job openings around the country, a number of sites have fairly up-to-date listings.

• The Web site http://www.govtjobs.com concentrates on public sector jobs (cities, counties, and states) and can be searched by job type. You can sign up to receive an e-mail when job listings change.
• GOVJOBS.com seeks to provide cost-efficient, user-friendly ways of sharing employment information to worldwide job seekers and all government and commercial employers.
• The Web site for the University of South Carolina, College of Criminal Justice (http://www.cla.sc.edu/crju/resources.html) provides a listing of key sites in general but is especially helpful in identifying career-related sites. Govtjob.net has a section on public safety and criminal justice employment that lists current openings around the country.

In addition to these generalized sites, many others provide more specific information.

• The Web site for the Wackenhut Corporation (http://www.wackenhut.com) has detailed information about employment opportunities with this worldwide private security enterprise.
• The Corrections Corporation of America (http://www.correctionscorp.com) provides an employment page with information about careers with this leading private sector provider of detention and corrections services to all government levels.
• Cornell Corrections, a leading provider of privatized institutional, prerelease, and juvenile services in the United States, offers information about career opportunities via a link from the company's home page (http://www.cornellcompanies.com/crn/crn.nsf/index2.htm).

You can also contact the various agencies in your local area to find out about hiring programs, needs, and requirements. For example, state police agencies offer regularly scheduled hiring tests, which typically include psychological, physical, and intellectual components. Those scoring high will be invited to the police academy for further training.

Law Enforcement

More than half a million people are employed in policing and law enforcement in the United States at the municipal, county, state, and federal levels.

The majority of people in law enforcement work for city police departments. The work of the patrol officer, traffic cop, and detective is familiar to anyone who watches television or goes to movies (although the accuracy of the portrayal by those entertainment vehicles is highly suspect). Beyond these familiar roles, however, police work also includes a great many administrative and service jobs, such as officer training, communications, records management, purchasing, and so on. Salaries in municipal police agencies are competitive, and larger cities may offer higher starting salaries and provide a full range of benefits. For example, the Dallas Police Department has the following pay scales and benefits.[1]

Pay Scales

	Police officer Base	Bachelor's degree
Trainee	$35,053	$36,253
Apprentice	35,403	36,603
Probationary	35,752	36,952
Police officer	37,805	39,005
2 years of service	39,683	40,883
3 years of service	41,671	42,871
5 years of service	43,763	44,967
7 years of service	45,951	47,151
9 years of service	48,245	49,445
11 years of service	50,669	51,862
13 years of service	53,180	54,380
15 years of service	55,845	57,045
Senior corporal		
Start	38,875	40,075
Maximum	61,567	62,767

Note: Trainee police officers receive $1,000 lump sum upon graduation.

Health Insurance On the date you are hired, you become eligible for one of the City of Dallas' major medical insurance programs. The city offers several separate insurance packages, each providing coverage for hospital room and medical expenses, outpatient care and maternity care. The packages offer different supplemental dental and vision plans and varying coverage for dependents. Non-city health coverage plans also are available.

Life Insurance Once you are hired, you are enrolled in the City of Dallas group life insurance program. You can choose from among three plans — Option 1 is paid by the City of Dallas, and Options 2 and 3 are available at a reduced rate premium.

Option 1 is a $40,000 basic insurance policy.

Option 2 pays the equivalent of your annual salary plus $40,000.

Option 3 pays the amount of double your annual salary plus $40,000.

Retirement Once you are hired, you will be enrolled in the Dallas Police and Fire Pension Fund. You will contribute 8.5% of your paycheck to the pension fund, while the City of Dallas contributes 27.5%. You become eligible for full retirement at age 50, with a minimum 5 years of service. The retirement plan pays up to 96% of the average of your highest paid 36 months of salary. Upon reaching retirement age, officers may choose to participate in the Deferred Retirement Option Plan (DROP). This option places your calculated monthly pension into an investment account with the Pension Fund as you continue to draw your salary and work as a Dallas Police Officer. The account will earn an 8–10% return. Upon entering DROP at age 50, a Senior Corporal with 20 years of service and 5 years in DROP can have in excess of $100,000 in the account upon retiring, depending on the individual pension contribution. This is in addition to receiving the calculated monthly pension. Upon leaving the Department, you will be paid for all accrued vacation time and up to 720 hours of sick leave at your present hourly rate of pay.

Equipment All officers are provided with uniforms and other necessary equipment including a regulation service weapon.

In addition, officers can get salary increases for completing college courses and becoming language specialists. In Massachusetts, salaries start at about $30,000 a year. However, under the Quinn bill, if police officers earn an undergraduate degree, they get an extra 20 percent on their base pay; a master's or law degree increases their starting pay by 25 percent. Overtime and special detail pay can add to this sum. It is not uncommon for uniformed police officers to top $100,000 in a single year.

Civil service rules usually apply to the hiring of police officers. Candidates must be American citizens, at least 20 years old, and in good physical condition. They compete for positions based on their scores on a written exam, as well as their education and experience. Physical exams test vision, strength, and agility. Candidates must also be of good character. They undergo a background investigation, drug testing, and a lie detector test.

In large, urban police departments, where most of the jobs are, applicants usually must have at least a high school education. Increasingly, departments prefer some college education as well. Some departments will pay tuition if officers pursue degrees in law enforcement, police science, administration of justice, or public administration.

Civilian Employees

In addition to sworn personnel, many police agencies hire civilian employees who bring special skills to the department. For example, departments employ information resource managers who are charged with improving data processing, integrating the department's computer information database with others in the state, operating computer-based fingerprint identification systems and other high-tech investigation devices, and linking with national computer systems such as the FBI's national crime information system, which holds the records of millions of criminal offenders.

State and County Law Enforcement

In addition to city police agencies, state and county governments provide career opportunities in law enforcement. The state police and county sheriff's department do much the same work as city police agencies — traffic, patrol, and investigation — depending on their area of jurisdiction. These agencies commonly take on a greater law enforcement role in more rural areas and provide ancillary services, such as running the local jail or controlling traffic, in urban centers. State agencies also hire investigators as part of their enforcement mandate. For example, the California Department of Insurance employs fraud investigators to conduct felony investigations of insurance fraud and related statutes. It also employs property controllers to handle property seized in investigations of insurance fraud. Similarly, the California Division of Consumer Affairs employs investigators to enforce rules and regulations relating to consumer protection. State investigators carry out many of the tasks of other law enforcement officers, including serving warrants, making arrests, and conducting undercover investigations.

Federal Law Enforcement

The federal government employs thousands of law enforcement personnel in such agencies as the Federal Bureau of Investigation, the Drug Enforcement Agency, the Secret Service, and so on. These agencies are often considered the elite of the law enforcement profession, and standards for entry are high. The duties of these federal agencies include upholding federal laws controlling counterfeiting, terrorism, espionage, bank robbery, and importation and distribution of controlled substances, among others.

Private Security

The field of private security offers many career opportunities. Some positions are in large security companies, such as Pinkerton or Wackenhut. Others are in company security forces, such as those maintained by large retail chains, manufacturing companies, and railroads. Public institutions such as hospitals, airports, and port facilities also have security teams. For example, large retail chains typically employ loss prevention agents who are responsible for the protection of company assets. Other private companies maintain their own enforcement branches. Insurance firms hire field investigators to determine the origin and cause of accidents, fires, and other events for which the company is liable. Insurance investigators also handle claims in which client fraud is suspected.

These are but a few of the many careers in law enforcement. Box A provides a more complete list of law enforcement job titles.

Starting a Career in Law Enforcement

What are the best ways to begin a career in law enforcement? Plan your career as best you can by keeping current on employment trends and job descriptions. Both are available from the Bureau of Labor Statistics at its Employment Projections site (http://www.bls.gov/emp/home/htm) and its *Occupational Outlook Handbook* site (http://www.bls.gov/oco/home.htm), where you can find listed the fastest growing jobs in the nation (frequently requested information). Look at state-by-state analyses, and avoid states that have had cutbacks in law enforcement (or courts and correctional agencies). Make use of the career services center at your local college or library. Utilize the people you know: faculty, alumni, fellow students, and professionals. Trade magazines can be informative. Attend a meeting of a professional association, such as the Academy of Criminal Justice Sciences. Consider joining one of these or other professional associations (as a student member with reduced fees) as their newsletters will prove invaluable. Subscribe to Internet discussion groups and post questions. Furthermore, the following monthly newsletters list jobs (although they require a fee).

Public Safety Recruitment
802 Maple St.
East Jordan, MI 49727
1-800-880-9018

Police Career Digest
P.O. Box 7772, Dept. GA
Winter Haven, FL 33883
1-800-359-6260

Try to be as certain as you can about what is important to you on the job; for example, geographic location, pay, security, praise, promotion, chances to learn, opportunities to do something worthwhile.

Choosing a Particular Career Option

Each level of government (federal, state, county, local) offers its own benefits and costs, and all the different positions have different pay grades. Federal and state jobs have the most pay and prestige, but you will almost certainly have to relocate. Some entry-level salaries are listed below; make sure you do not sell yourself short.

- Federal jobs should start at minimum at $33,000.
- State jobs should start at minimum at $27,000.
- County jobs should start at minimum at $22,000.
- City jobs should start at minimum at $24,000.

Try to maximize your salary potential by choosing large agencies with lots of job titles, especially civilian

Box A Law Enforcement Job Titles

Arson investigator	Director of standards and training	Pilot
Attaché or police liaison officer	Dispatcher	Polygraph examiner
Ballistics expert	Drug enforcement agent	Psychologist, psychiatrist, psychometrician
Booking officer	Emergency medical service (EMS) coordinator	Public relations officer
Border patrol agent	Evidence technician	Public safety director
Chaplain	FBI special agent	Radio communications
Chief of police	Fingerprint expert	Records management
Chief of staff	Firearms instructor	School liaison
Commander	Forensic scientist	Scientist
Commissioner	Gaming enforcement officer	Secret service
Communications specialist	Gang crimes investigator	Security specialist
Community policing officer	Inspector	Serologist
Community safety officer	Instructor	Sheriff
Community service officer	Intelligence analyst	Street crimes investigator
Conservation officer	Investigator	Superintendent
Crime prevention specialist	Jailer	Special Weapons and Tactics (SWAT) officer
Crime lab technician	Juvenile specialist	Technologist
Crime scene technician	K–9 handler	Traffic analyst
Customs agent	Lawyer	Trainer
Data processing specialist	Law enforcement planner	Treasury agent
Deputy chief	Law enforcement representative	Trooper
Deputy sheriff	Manpower allocation specialist	Undercover operative
Detective	Narcotics officer	Undersheriff
Detention officer	Patrol officer	U.S. marshal
Document examiner	Personnel specialist	Water patrol officer
Director of research and development	Photographer	Witness protection
Director of scientific services		

ones. Big cities are your best bet, but bigger is not necessarily better in some cases. Expect to start out no less than $24,000 in a metropolitan department, and as high as $38,000 in others.

Getting Prepared for a Career in Law Enforcement

The 10 steps to getting an appointment are (1) application, (2) entrance exam, (3) physical testing, (4) medical examination, (5) interview, (6) psychological testing, (7) background check, (8) academy training, (9) field training, and (10) civil service exam (for promotional purposes).

Steps 3 and 4 are the most critical in terms of general preparation. Find a sport or exercise regimen that you are comfortable with and develop your physical fitness. Fitness is one of the most important criteria for ob-

taining a job in criminal justice, and you cannot achieve it overnight. Plan to impress employers with your stamina and strength. Some of the tougher physical standards are as follows.

- Pull-ups (palms out) — average 10, maximum 25 in one minute.
- Sit-ups or an alternative — average 70, maximum 100 in one minute.
- Push-ups — average 40, maximum 85 in one minute.
- 300-yard run — average 60 seconds.
- 2-mile run — average 12 minutes.

If you have any kind of functional or organic disorder such as high blood pressure, high cholesterol level, smoking status, drug use, diabetes, or epilepsy, it becomes the duty of your medical examiner to qualify or disqualify you. If you smoke, stop, because recently quitting tobacco is not held against you. If you used drugs (including alcohol abuse, casual use of marijuana, or psychotropic medication), you will be excluded by about 75 percent of the agencies. Some will accept the fact that you experimented with marijuana as long as it was not prolonged or recent usage, but they are generally not forgiving of the slightest experimentation with hallucinogens, cocaine, and so on. Most agencies will accept corrected vision (no worse than 20/40 uncorrected, but in some cases as bad as 20/100 if at least one eye is correctable to 20/20) but not color blindness or deafness. The Americans with Disabilities Act allows anyone to apply and prohibits any disability-related inquiry prior to a conditional job offer. The job offer will be conditioned on the results of a confidential medical exam, which is used to determine if the department can make reasonable accommodations.

Your criminal history should be clear of felonies and serious misdemeanors (anything punishable by one year or more). Many people have had run-ins with the law sometime in their lives, so most examiners are sympathetic, but expect sympathies and interpretations of what constitutes a "serious misdemeanor" to vary. Above all, do not try to hide anything. In general, agencies are more forgiving the younger you were when the incident occurred. Some agencies still use a "moral turpitude" clause, which includes any sexual offense; indecent liberties; use, sale, or manufacture of any controlled substance; or any offense addressing public morality. The criminal records division of the state police will allow you to look at your record beforehand and assist you with correcting errors, but to wipe something out will more than likely require a petition for removal with the district attorney from the jurisdiction where it was recorded. It is a definite plus to have a clean driving record as the time of appointment rolls around. You should also have a clean credit history, or at least no signs of continual poor financial responsibility, such as records of late payments, wage garnishments, or bankruptcy.

Although some jurisdictions have outlawed polygraph evidence in courts of law, most police agencies still rely on it for employment purposes. Try to breathe steadily and act normally; your best bet is to be honest about your past. Some agencies have substituted other types of assessment exercises to get at your honesty and integrity. You may find that someone "accidentally" left his or her wallet in the restroom (to see if you turn it in); you may be asked how serious a colleague's misconduct has to be before you would report him or her; or you may have to address hypothetical scenarios such as if your senior patrol partner disappears into a tavern for over an hour. In general, examiners like it when you show a willingness to be tough and hard, but they also do not like whistle-blowers and snitches.

Anticipate that finding the ideal job will take at least three months of hard work. For this effort, you may have to wait approximately six months to two years before an agency offers you a position. Given that some places make you wait as long as two years, you should begin a serious job search sometime in your sophomore or junior year of college. Anything you can do to get your foot in the door or build up some experience (which often substitutes for education) during this waiting period is useful. Does the agency need volunteers? Does it have a police auxiliary or a reserve program? Can you voluntarily attend classes and workshops held at a training center?

Ads and Applications

Often, a job advertisement will appear one day only in a newspaper, usually the Sunday edition. Such ads will usually say respond with a cover letter and résumé, and you should respond in such manner by the required date, but remember that some agencies do not treat you as having technically filed unless you fill out their application form. If a job exists, a document called the "Job Announcement" will list detailed instructions for applicants. Remember that the purpose of filling out an application is to be notified by mail when and where to appear for the entrance examination.

In responding to an ad, your cover letter should be specific to the job advertised and addressed to an individual, if possible. Keep the cover letter to one page, match your qualifications to any requirements listed in the ad, and strive for a combination of modesty and self-confidence. One- to two-page résumés are sufficient for entry-level positions; three to four pages for management jobs. Education and training (dates, course titles, and degrees) should be listed first in an easy-to-read format. Then provide your job experience, but be cautious with job titles. If you once attended a neighborhood watch meeting, do not put down that you were a crime prevention specialist. Copies of diplomas and photographs are usually unnecessary. It is better to provide names and means of contacting your references on the résumé instead of simply saying "available on request." Consider sending your material by a priority mail service as this indicates you are concerned enough to make sure it arrived, and do not rule out the option of hand-delivering your material. Remember, including too much data is the main fault of résumés. Keep it brief, but well documented, with no gaps in employment dates. And do not forget a follow-up letter about a week or two later.

Correctional Service Work

A significant number of people who work in the field of criminal justice become involved in its social service side. Many opportunities are available to provide di-

Box B Correctional Job Titles

Administrator	Employee development specialist	Psychiatrist, psychologist
Affirmative action officer	Facility manager	Public relations officer
Budget analyst	Food service supervisor	Records office manager
Business office manager	Health systems administrator	Teacher
Chaplain	Juvenile detention officer	Trainer
Chief of programs	Juvenile worker	Transport officer
Chief of security	Leisure time activities specialist	Unit manager
Computer specialist	Medical records supervisor	Vocational specialist
Correctional clerk	Ombudsman	Warden
Correctional counselor	Personnel officer	
Correctional officer	Placement officer	

rect service to people both before they get involved with the law and after they have come to the attention of criminal justice agencies.

Salaries in the correctional field vary widely based on skill level, experience, responsibilities, and the size of the institution. Correctional pay varies tremendously from state to state. States with big prison systems such as New Jersey and New York may start their entry-level correctional officers as high as $32,000. Jobs in probation and parole also have salaries that vary widely. Federal probation has some of the highest salaries in corrections, usually around $40,000 or more to start, and some states such as Massachusetts offer similar wages. The various correctional positions are listed in Box B.

Probation Officers

Probation officers — who, in some states, may be referred to as community supervision officers — monitor offenders' behavior through personal contact with the offenders and their families.[2] Officers also may arrange for offenders to get substance abuse rehabilitation or job training. Probation officers usually work with either adults or juveniles exclusively. Only in small, usually rural, jurisdictions do probation officers counsel both adults and juveniles.

Another part of the probation officer's job involves working in the courts. Officers investigate the background of offenders brought before the court, write presentence reports, and make sentencing recommendations for each offender; review sentencing recommendations with offenders and their families before submitting the recommendations to the court; and testify in court regarding their findings and recommendations. Probation officers also attend hearings to update the court on an offender's probation compliance status and on the of-

fender's efforts at rehabilitation. Occasionally, probation officers in the federal courts system work as pretrial services officers, conducting pretrial investigations and making bond recommendations for defendants.

The number of cases a probation officer has depends on both the counseling needs of offenders and the risks they pose to society. High-risk offenders and those who need more counseling usually command more of an officer's or specialist's time and resources. Those who work with these offenders handle fewer cases. Caseloads also vary by agency jurisdiction. Consequently, officers may handle 20 to more than 300 active cases at a time.

Probation officers specialists usually work a standard 40-hour week, but they may be required to work longer or to be on call 24 hours a day to supervise and assist offenders. In addition, meeting with offenders who are on probation or parole may require extensive travel or fieldwork. However, this burden may be eased somewhat for workers whose agencies allow them to telecommute from home via computers and other equipment and to make use of other technology, such as electronic monitoring devices worn by offenders that allow probation officers to keep track of their activities.

Probation officers may find their jobs stressful for a variety of reasons. They work with convicted criminals, some of whom may be dangerous. In the course of supervising offenders, officers and specialists' usually interact with many other individuals, including family members and friends of their clients, who may be angry, upset, or uncooperative. Officers and specialists also may be required to collect and transport urine samples of offenders for drug testing.

Although stress makes these jobs difficult at times, the work also can be rewarding. Many probation officers gain personal satisfaction from counseling members of their community and helping them become productive citizens.

Jobs for probation officers are more plentiful in urban areas. More opportunities for employment also are found in states that have numerous men and women on probation, such as California and Texas, which currently have the largest such populations. Median annual earnings of probation officers is a bout $36,130. The middle 50 percent earned between $29,260 and $44,890. The lowest 10 percent earned less than $24,310, and the highest 10 percent earned more than $54,810. Officers and specialists who worked in urban areas usually had higher earnings than those working in rural areas.

Employment of probation officers is projected to grow through 2008. Vigorous law enforcement is expected to result in a continuing increase in the prison population. Overcrowding in prisons also has swelled the probation population as judges and prosecutors search for alternative forms of punishment, such as electronic monitoring and day reporting centers. In addition to openings because of growth, vacancies will result from the need to replace workers who leave the occupation permanently, including the large number expected to retire over the next several years.

Prospective probation officers must be in good physical condition and be emotionally stable. Most agencies require applicants to be at least 21 years old and, for federal employment, not older than 37. Those convicted of felonies may not be eligible for employment in these occupations.

Probation officers need strong writing skills because of the large number of reports they must prepare. Familiarity with computers often is required. Job candidates also should be knowledgeable about laws and regulations pertaining to corrections.

Educational requirements for probation officers vary by state, but a bachelor's degree in social work or criminal justice usually is required. In addition, some states require probation officers to have one year of work experience in a related field or one year of graduate study in criminal justice, social work, or psychology. Most probation officers must complete a training program sponsored by their state government or the federal government. Most work as trainees for about six months. Candidates who successfully complete the training period obtain a permanent position. Some states require applicants to take a certification test during or after training. Applicants usually must also pass written, oral, psychological, and physical examinations.

Agencies that employ probation officers have several levels of officers and specialists, as well as supervisors. A graduate degree — such as a master's degree in criminal justice, social work, or psychology — may be helpful for advancement.

Secure Correctional Work

Numerous opportunities exist for working in secure correctional settings. Although some may view correctional work as a matter of guarding incarcerated inmates, that narrow perspective is far from accurate. Correctional workers are charged with overseeing a great variety of activities that may involve them in budgeting, management, training, counseling, classification, planning, and human services. Correctional treatment staff engage in such tasks as vocational and educational training, counseling, recreational work, and so on. Almost every correctional institution has a social service staff that helps inmates adjust to the institution and prepare for successful reentry into the outside world. In addition, correctional settings require security staff, maintenance workers, medical staff, clergy, and other types of personnel.

Parole and Aftercare

Parole and aftercare workers supervise offenders upon their release from correctional treatment. This work involves helping individuals find jobs, achieve their educational objectives, sort out their family problems, and so on. Parole officers employ various counseling techniques to help clients clarify their goals and find ways of surmounting obstacles so that they can make a successful readjustment to the community.

Law and the Courts

The criminal justice system provides many opportunities for people interested in working in the legal system and the courts (see Box C). In most instances, these careers require postgraduate education, such as law school or a course in court management. Prosecutors represent the state in criminal matters. They bring charges against offenders, engage in plea bargaining, conduct trials, and help determine sentences. Prosecutors work at the local, county, state, and federal levels of government. For example, an assistant U.S. attorney general would prosecute violations of federal law in one of the U.S. district courts.

Defense Counsel

All criminal defendants are entitled to legal counsel. Therefore, agencies such as the public defender's office have been created to provide free legal services to indigent offenders. In addition, private attorneys often take

Box C Court-Related Job Titles

Arbitrator	Defense attorney	Manager
Assistant administrator	Deputy assistant	Mediation specialist
Assistant prosecutor	Diversion specialist	Paralegal
Background investigator	Expert witness	Parole officer
Bailiff	Grants administrator	Probation officer
Bondsman	Investigator	Process server
Criminal justice systems planner	Judicial assistant	Sentencing analyst
Court clerk	Law clerk	Victim restitution
Court reporter	Lawyer	
Courthouse security	Legal research	

on criminal cases without compensation as a gesture of community service or are assigned cases by the court for modest compensation (referred to as pro bono cases). Defense attorneys help clients gather evidence to support their innocence; represent them at pretrial, trial, and sentencing hearings; and serve as their advocate if an appeal is filed upon conviction. A legal career is quite desirable and lucrative, with starting salaries in major big-city firms in excess of $100,000. Law school admissions are highly competitive, and students interested in attending are cautioned to maintain the highest levels of academic achievement.

Judge

Judges carry out many functions during the trial stage of justice. They help in jury selection, oversee the admission of evidence, and control the flow of the trial. Most important, they are entrusted with the duty of ensuring that the trial is conducted within the boundaries of legal fairness. Although many criminal defense attorneys and prosecutors aspire to become judges, few are chosen for this honor. Senior judges are paid well, and six-figure salaries for senior court judges are not uncommon.

Staff Counsel

A number of public agencies will hire a staff counsel to give legal advice, prepare legal memoranda and reports, respond to inquiries, draft proposed legislation, and advise administrators on the legal ramifications of policy changes. Staff counsel typically are paid in the $50,000 range to start, depending on their experience and specialized knowledge; more senior staff counsel might be hired at $60,000 plus.

Court Administrator

Most court jurisdictions maintain an office of court administration. These individuals help in case management and ensure that the court's resources are used in the most efficient manner. Court administrators are usually required to receive advanced education in programs that specialize in court management and are involved in financial management, human resources, case flow management, and statistical analysis, among other duties. Pay is high, typically between $75,000 and $100,000.

Research, Administration, and Teaching

In addition to work within the agencies of justice themselves, a career in criminal justice can involve teaching, research, or administration.

Private Sector Research

A number of private sector institutes and research firms — such as the RAND Corporation in Santa Monica, California — employ research scientists who conduct criminal justice–related research. Some private nonprofit organizations are devoted to the study of criminal justice issues, including the Police Executive Research Forum, the Police Foundation, and the International Association of Chiefs of Police, all located in the Washington, D.C., area, and the National Council on Crime and Delinquency in San Francisco, California. Many universities maintain research centers that for many years have conducted ongoing efforts in criminal justice, often with funding from the government and private foundations. For example, the Institute for

Social Research at the University of Michigan has conducted an annual survey of teenage substance abuse; the Hindelang Research Center at the University at Albany produces the *Sourcebook of Criminal Justice Statistics,* an invaluable research tool.

Most people who work for these research centers hold advanced degrees in criminal justice or other applied social sciences. Some of the projects carried out by these centers, such as the study of career criminals conducted by RAND Corporation scientists and the Police Foundation's study of the deterrent effect of police patrol, have had a profound effect on policy making within the criminal justice system.

Public Sector Research

Most large local, state, and federal government agencies contain research arms that oversee the evaluation of ongoing criminal justice programs and plan for the development of innovative efforts designed to create positive change in the system. For example, most state corrections departments have planning and research units that monitor the flow of inmates in and out of the prison system and help evaluate the effectiveness of prison programs, such as work furloughs. On a local level, larger police departments commonly employ civilian research coordinators who analyze police data to improve the effectiveness and efficiency of police services.

The most significant contribution to criminal justice research made by the public sector is probably that of the federal government's Bureau of Justice Statistics and National Institute of Justice (NIJ), which are the research arms of the U.S. Justice Department. In recent years, these agencies have supported some of the most impressive and important of all research studies on criminal justice issues, such as sentencing, plea bargaining, and victimization. Research salaries are generally high, typically $65,000 and up.

System Administration

Federal and state governments usually maintain central criminal justice planning offices that are responsible for setting and implementing criminal justice policy or for distributing funds for policy implementation. For example, the NIJ sets priorities for criminal justice research and policy on an annual basis, then distributes funds to local and state applicants willing to set up and evaluate demonstration projects. The NIJ has targeted the following areas: apprehension, prosecution, and adjudication of criminal offenders; public safety and security; punishment and control of offenders; victims of crime; white-collar and organized crime; criminal careers; drugs and alcohol and crime; forensic science; offender classification; and violent criminal behavior.

A number of states also have criminal justice administrative agencies that set policy agendas and coordinate state efforts to improve the quality of the system. Planners and analysts working for these agencies are expected to hold a master's degree and are typically hired in the $40,000 to $50,000 range.

College Teaching

The United States has more than 600 criminal justice education programs. These include specialized criminal justice programs, programs in which criminal justice is combined with another department (such as sociology or political science), and programs that offer a concentration in criminal justice as part of another major.

Criminal justice educators have a career track similar to that of most other teaching specialties. Regardless of the level at which they teach — associate, baccalaureate, or graduate — their courses will reflect the core subject matter of criminal justice, including courses on policing, the courts, and the correctional system. Starting salaries for assistant professors typically range from $40,000 to $60,000, and senior full professors at prestigious universities average in the $100,000 range.

Notes

1 See http://recruiting.dallaspolice.net/index.cfm?page_ID=2683& subnav=0.

2 Andrew D. Alpert, "Probation Officers and Correctional Treatment Specialists," *Occupational Outlook Quarterly* 45, no. 3 (Fall 2001): 28; Matthew Mariani, "Peacemakers," *Occupational Outlook Quarterly* 40, no. 2 (Summer 1996): 38.

Appendix B | The Constitution of the United States

Preamble

We the People of the United States, in Order to form a more perfect Union, establish Justice, insure domestic Tranquility, provide for the common defence, promote the general Welfare, and secure the Blessings of Liberty to ourselves and our Posterity, do ordain and establish this Constitution for the United States of America.

Article I

Section 1 All legislative Powers herein granted shall be vested in a Congress of the United States, which shall consist of a Senate and House of Representatives.

Section 2 The House of Representatives shall be composed of Members chosen every second Year by the People of the several States, and the Electors in each State shall have the Qualifications requisite for Electors of the most numerous Branch of the State Legislature.

No Person shall be a Representative who shall not have attained to the Age of twenty five Years, and been seven Years a Citizen of the United States, and who shall not, when elected, be an Inhabitant of that State in which he shall be chosen.

Representatives and direct Taxes shall be apportioned among the several States which may be included within this Union, according to their respective Numbers, which shall be determined by adding to the whole Number of free Persons, including those bound to Service for a Term of Years, and excluding Indians not taxed, three fifths of all other Persons. The actual Enumeration shall be made within three Years after the first Meeting of the Congress of the United States, and within every subsequent Term of ten Years, in such Manner as they shall by Law direct. The Number of Representatives shall not exceed one for every thirty Thousand, but each State shall have at Least one Representative; and until such enumeration shall be made, the State of New Hampshire shall be entitled to choose three, Massachusetts eight, Rhode Island and Providence Plantations one, Connecticut five, New York six, New Jersey four, Pennsylvania eight, Delaware one, Maryland six, Virginia ten, North Carolina five, South Carolina five, and Georgia three.

When vacancies happen in the Representation from any State, the Executive Authority thereof shall issue Writs of Election to fill such Vacancies.

The House of Representatives shall choose their Speaker and other Officers; and shall have the sole Power of Impeachment.

Section 3 The Senate of the United States shall be composed of two Senators from each State, chosen by the Legislature thereof, for six Years; and each Senator shall have one Vote.

Immediately after they shall be assembled in Consequence of the first Election, they shall be divided as equally as may be into three Classes. The Seats of the Senators of the first Class shall be vacated at the Expiration of the second Year, of the second Class at the Expiration of the fourth Year, and of the third Class at the Expiration of the sixth Year, so that one third may be chosen every second Year; and if Vacancies happen by Resignation, or otherwise, during the Recess of the Legislature of any State, the Executive thereof may make temporary Appointments until the next Meeting of the Legislature, which shall then fill such Vacancies.

No Person shall be a Senator who shall not have attained to the Age of thirty Years, and been nine Years a Citizen of the United States, and who shall not, when elected, be an Inhabitant of that State for which he shall be chosen.

The Vice-President of the United States shall be President of the Senate, but shall have no Vote, unless they be equally divided.

The Senate shall choose their other Officers, and also a President pro tempore, in the Absence of the Vice-President, or when he shall exercise the Office of President of the United States.

The Senate shall have the sole Power to try all Impeachments. When sitting for that Purpose, they shall be on Oath or Affirmation. When the President of the United States is tried the Chief Justice shall preside: And no Person shall be convicted without the Concurrence of two thirds of the Members present.

Judgment in Cases of Impeachment shall not extend further than to removal from Office, and disqualification to hold and enjoy any Office of honor, Trust or Profit under the United States: but the Party convicted shall nevertheless be liable and subject to Indictment, Trial, Judgment, and Punishment, according to Law.

Section 4 The Times, Places and Manner of holding Elections for Senators and Representatives, shall be prescribed in each State by the Legislature thereof; but the Congress may at any time by Law make or alter such Regulations, except as to the Places of choosing Senators.

The Congress shall assemble at least once in every Year, and such Meeting shall be on the first Monday in December, unless they shall by Law appoint a different Day.

Section 5 Each House shall be the Judge of the Elections, Returns and Qualifications of its own Members, and a Majority of each shall constitute a Quorum to do Business; but a smaller Number may adjourn from day to day, and may be authorized to compel the Attendance of absent Members, in such Manner, and under such Penalties as each House may provide.

Each House may determine the Rules of its Proceedings, punish its Members for disorderly Behaviour, and, with the Concurrence of two thirds, expel a Member.

Each House shall keep a Journal of its Proceedings, and from time to time publish the same, excepting such Parts as may in their Judgment require Secrecy; and the Yeas and Nays of the Members of either House on any question shall, at the Desire of one fifth of those Present, be entered on the Journal.

Neither House, during the Session of Congress, shall, without the Consent of the other, adjourn for more than three days, nor to any other Place than that in which the two Houses shall be sitting.

Section 6 The Senators and Representatives shall receive a Compensation for their Services, to be ascertained by Law, and paid out of the Treasury of the United States. They shall in all Cases, except Treason, Felony and Breach of the Peace, be privileged from Arrest during their Attendance at the Session of their respective Houses, and in going to and returning from the same; and for any Speech or Debate in either House, they shall not be questioned in any other Place.

No Senator or Representative shall, during the Time for which he was elected, be appointed to any civil Office under the Authority of the United States, which shall have been created, or the Emoluments whereof shall have been increased during such time; and no Person holding any Office under the United States, shall be a Member of either House during his Continuance in Office.

Section 7 All Bills for raising Revenue shall originate in the House of Representatives; but the Senate may propose or concur with Amendments as on other Bills.

Every Bill which shall have passed the House of Representatives and the Senate, shall, before it become a Law, be presented to the President of the United States; If he approve he shall sign it, but if not he shall return it, with his Objections to that House in which it shall have originated, who shall enter the Objections at large on their Journal, and proceed to reconsider it. If after such Reconsideration two thirds of that House shall agree to pass the Bill, it shall be sent, together with the Objections, to the other House, by which it shall likewise be reconsidered, and if approved by two thirds of that House, it shall become a Law. But in all such Cases the Votes of both Houses shall be determined by Yeas and Nays, and the Names of the Persons voting for and against the Bill shall be entered on the Journal of each House respectively. If any Bill shall not be returned by the President within ten Days (Sundays excepted) after it shall have been presented to him, the Same shall be a Law, in like Manner as if he had signed it, unless the Congress by their Adjournment prevent its Return, in which Case it shall not be a Law.

Every Order, Resolution, or Vote to which the Concurrence of the Senate and House of Representatives may be necessary (except on a question of Adjournment) shall be presented to the President of the United States; and before the Same shall take Effect, shall be approved by him, or being disapproved by him, shall be repassed by two thirds of the Senate and House of Representatives, according to the Rules and Limitations prescribed in the Case of a Bill.

Section 8 The Congress shall have Power To lay and collect Taxes, Duties, Imposts and Excises, to pay the Debts and provide for the common Defence and general Welfare of the United States; but all Duties, Imposts and Excises shall be uniform throughout the United States;

To borrow Money on the credit of the United States;

To regulate Commerce with foreign Nations, and among the several States, and with the Indian Tribes;

To establish an uniform Rule of Naturalization, and uniform Laws on the subject of Bankruptcies throughout the United States;

To coin Money, regulate the Value thereof, and of foreign Coin, and fix the Standard of Weights and Measures;

To provide for the Punishment of counterfeiting the Securities and current Coin of the United States;

To establish Post Offices and post Roads;

To promote the Progress of Science and useful Arts, by securing for limited Times to Authors and Inventors the exclusive Right to their respective Writings and Discoveries;

To constitute Tribunals inferior to the supreme Court;

To define and punish Piracies and Felonies committed on the high Seas, and Offences against the Law of Nations;

To declare War, grant Letters of Marque and Reprisal, and make Rules concerning Captures on Land and Water;

To raise and support Armies, but no Appropriation of Money to that Use shall be for a longer Term than two Years;

To provide and maintain a Navy;

To make Rules for the Government and Regulation of the land and naval Forces;

To provide for calling forth the Militia to execute the Laws of the Union, suppress Insurrections and repel Invasions;

To provide for organizing, arming, and disciplining, the Militia, and for governing such Part of them as may be employed in the Service of the United States, reserving to the States respectively, the Appointment of the Officers, and the Authority of training the Militia according to the discipline prescribed by Congress;

To exercise exclusive Legislation in all Cases whatsoever, over such District (not exceeding ten Miles square) as may, by Cession of particular States, and the Acceptance of Congress, become the Seat of the Government of the United States, and to exercise like Authority over all Places purchased by the Consent of the Legislature of the State in which the Same shall be, for the Erection of Forts, Magazines, Arsenals, dock-Yards, and other needful Buildings;—And

To make all Laws which shall be necessary and proper for carrying into Execution the foregoing Powers, and all other Powers vested by this Constitution in the Government of the United States, or in any Department or Officer thereof.

Section 9 The Migration or Importation of such Persons as any of the States now existing shall think proper to admit, shall not be prohibited by the Congress prior to the Year one thousand eight hundred and eight, but a Tax or duty may be imposed on such Importation, not exceeding ten dollars for each Person.

The privilege of the Writ of Habeas Corpus shall not be suspended, unless when in Cases of Rebellion or Invasion the public Safety may require it.

No Bill of Attainder or ex post facto Law shall be passed.

No Capitation, or other direct, Tax shall be laid, unless in Proportion to the Census or Enumeration herein before directed to be taken.

No Tax or Duty shall be laid on Articles exported from any State.

No Preference shall be given by any Regulation of Commerce or Revenue to the Ports of one State over those of another: nor shall Vessels bound to, or from, one State be obliged to enter, clear, or pay Duties in another.

No Money shall be drawn from the Treasury, but in Consequence of Appropriations made by Law; and a regular Statement and Account of the Receipts and Expenditures of all public Money shall be published from time to time.

No Title of Nobility shall be granted by the United States: And no Person holding any Office of Profit or Trust under them, shall, without the Consent of the Congress, accept of any present, Emolument, Office, or Title, of any kind whatever, from any King, Prince, or foreign State.

Section 10 No State shall enter into any Treaty, Alliance, or Confederation; grant Letters of Marque and Reprisal; coin Money; emit Bills of Credit; make any Thing but gold and silver Coin a Tender in Payment of Debts; pass any Bill of Attainder, ex post facto Law, or Law impairing the Obligation of Contracts, or grant any Title of Nobility.

No State shall, without the Consent of the Congress, lay any Imposts or Duties on Imports or Exports, except what may be absolutely necessary for executing its inspection Laws: and the net Produce of all Duties and Imposts, laid by any State on Imports or Exports, shall be for the Use of the Treasury of the United States; and all such Laws shall be subject to the Revision and Control of the Congress.

No State shall, without the Consent of Congress, lay any Duty of Tonnage, keep Troops, or Ships of War in time of Peace, enter into any Agreement or Compact with another State, or with a foreign Power, or engage in War, unless actually invaded, or in such imminent Danger as will not admit of delay.

Article II

Section 1 The executive Power shall be vested in a President of the United States of America. He shall hold his Office during the Term of four Years, and, together with the Vice-President, chosen for the same Term, be elected, as follows:

Each State shall appoint, in such Manner as the Legislature thereof may direct, a Number of Electors, equal to the whole Number of Senators and Representatives to which the State may be entitled in the Congress; but no Senator or Representative, or Person holding an Office of Trust or Profit under the United States, shall be appointed an Elector.

The Electors shall meet in their respective States, and vote by Ballot for two Persons, of whom one at least shall not be an Inhabitant of the same State with themselves. And they shall make a List of all the Persons voted for, and of the Number of Votes for each; which List they shall sign and certify, and transmit sealed to the Seat of Government of the United States, directed to the President of the Senate. The President of the Senate shall, in the Presence of the Senate and House of Representatives, open all the Certificates, and the Votes shall then be counted. The Person having the greatest Number of Votes shall be the President, if such Number be a Majority of the whole Number of Electors appointed; and if there be more than one who have such Majority, and have an equal Number of Votes, then the House of Representatives shall immediately choose by Ballot one of them for President; and if no Person have a Majority, then from the five highest on the List the said House shall in like Manner choose the President. But in choosing the President, the Votes shall be taken by States, the Representation from each State having one Vote; A quorum for this Purpose shall consist of a Member or Members from two thirds of the States, and a Majority of all the States shall be necessary to a Choice. In every Case, after the Choice of the President, the Person having the greatest Number of Votes of the Electors shall be the Vice-President. But if there should remain two or more who have equal Votes, the Senate shall choose from them by Ballot the Vice-President.

The Congress may determine the Time of choosing the Electors, and the Day on which they shall give their Votes; which Day shall be the same throughout the United States.

No Person except a natural born Citizen, or a Citizen of the United States, at the time of the Adoption of this Constitution, shall be eligible to the Office of President; neither shall any Person be eligible to that Office who shall not have attained to the Age of thirty five Years, and been fourteen Years a Resident within the United States.

In Case of the Removal of the President from Office, or of his Death, Resignation, or Inability to discharge the Powers and Duties of the said Office, the same shall devolve on the Vice-President, and the Congress may by Law provide for the Case of Removal, Death, Resignation or Inability, both of the President and Vice-President declaring what Officer shall then act as President, and such Officer shall act accordingly, until the Disability be removed, or a President shall be elected.

The President shall, at stated Times, receive for his Services, a Compensation, which shall neither be increased nor diminished during the Period for which he shall have been elected, and he shall not receive within that Period any other Emolument from the United States, or any of them.

Before he enter on the Execution of his Office, he shall take the following Oath or Affirmation: "I do solemnly swear (or affirm) that I will faithfully execute the Office of President of the United States, and will to the best of my Ability, preserve, protect and defend the Constitution of the United States."

Section 2 The President shall be Commander in Chief of the Army and Navy of the United States, and of the Militia of the several States, when called into the actual Service of the United States; he may require the Opinion, in writing, of the principal Officer in each of the executive Departments, upon any Subject relating to the Duties of their respective Offices, and he shall have Power to grant Reprieves and Pardons for Offenses against the United States, except in Cases of Impeachment.

He shall have Power, by and with the Advice and Consent of the Senate, to make Treaties, provided two thirds of the Senators present concur; and he shall nominate, and by and with the Advice and Consent of the Senate, shall appoint Ambassadors, other public Ministers and Consuls, Judges of the supreme Court, and all other Officers of the United States, whose Appointments are not herein otherwise provided for, and which shall be established by Law; but the Congress may by Law vest the Appointment of such inferior Officers, as they think proper, in the President alone, in the Courts of Law, or in the Heads of Departments.

The President shall have Power to fill up all Vacancies that may happen during the Recess of the Senate, by granting Commissions which shall expire at the End of their next Session.

Section 3 He shall from time to time give to the Congress Information of the State of the Union, and recommend to their Consideration such Measures as he shall judge necessary and expedient; he may, on extraordinary Occasions, convene both Houses, or either of them, and in Case of Disagreement between them, with Respect to the Time of Adjournment, he may adjourn them to such Time as he shall think proper; he shall receive Ambassadors and other public Ministers; he shall take Care that the Laws be faithfully executed, and shall Commission all the Officers of the United States.

Section 4 The President, Vice-President and all civil Officers of the United States, shall be removed from Office on Impeachment for, and Conviction of, Treason, Bribery, or other high Crimes and Misdemeanors.

Article III

Section 1 The judicial Power of the United States, shall be vested in one supreme Court, and in such inferior Courts as the Congress may from time to time ordain and establish. The Judges, both of the supreme and inferior Courts, shall hold their Offices during good Behaviour, and shall, at stated Times, receive for their Services a Compensation which shall not be diminished during their Continuance in Office.

Section 2 The judicial Power shall extend to all Cases, in Law and Equity, arising under this Constitution, the Laws of the United States, and Treaties made, or which shall be made, under their Authority;—to all Cases affecting Ambassadors, other public Ministers and Consuls;—to all Cases of admiralty and maritime Jurisdiction;—to Controversies to which the United States shall be a Party;—to Controversies between two or more States;—between a State and Citizens of another State;—between Citizens of different States;—between Citizens of the same State claiming Lands under Grants of different States, and between a State, or the Citizens thereof, and foreign States, Citizens or Subjects.

In all Cases affecting Ambassadors, other public Ministers and Consuls, and those in which a State shall be Party, the supreme Court shall have original Jurisdiction. In all the other Cases before mentioned, the supreme Court shall have appellate Jurisdiction, both as to Law and Fact, with such Exceptions, and under such Regulations as the Congress shall make.

The Trial of all Crimes, except in Cases of Impeachment, shall be by Jury; and such Trial shall be held in the State where the said Crimes shall have been committed; but when not committed within any State, the Trial shall be at such Place or Places as the Congress may by Law have directed.

Section 3 Treason against the United States shall consist only in levying War against them, or in adhering to their Enemies, giving them Aid and Comfort. No Person shall be convicted of Treason unless on the Testimony of two Witnesses to the same overt Act, or on Confession in open Court.

The Congress shall have Power to declare the Punishment of Treason, but no Attainder of Treason shall work Corruption of Blood, or Forfeiture except during the Life of the Person attainted.

Article IV

Section 1 Full Faith and Credit shall be given in each State to the public Acts, Records, and judicial Proceedings of every other State. And the Congress may by general Laws prescribe the Manner in which such Acts, Records and Proceedings shall be proved, and the Effect thereof.

Section 2 The Citizens of each State shall be entitled to all Privileges and Immunities of Citizens in the several States.

A Person charged in any State with Treason, Felony, or other Crime, who shall flee from Justice, and be found in another State, shall on Demand of the executive Authority of the State from which he fled, be delivered up, to be removed to the State having Jurisdiction of the Crime.

No Person held to Service or Labour in one State, under the Laws thereof, escaping into another, shall, in Consequence of any Law or Regulation therein, be discharged from such Service or Labour, but shall be delivered up on Claim of the Party to whom such Service or Labour may be due.

Section 3 New States may be admitted by the Congress into this Union; but no new State shall be formed or erected within the Jurisdiction of any other State; nor any State be formed by the Junction of two or more States, or Parts of States, without the Consent of the Legislatures of the States concerned as well as of the Congress.

The Congress shall have Power to dispose of and make all needful Rules and Regulations respecting the Territory or other Property belonging to the United States; and nothing in this Constitution shall be so construed as to Prejudice any Claims of the United States, or of any particular State.

Section 4 The United States shall guarantee to every State in this Union a Republican Form of Government, and shall protect each of them against Invasion; and on Application of the Legislature, or of the Executive (when the Legislature cannot be convened) against domestic Violence.

Article V

The Congress, whenever two thirds of both Houses shall deem it necessary, shall propose Amendments to this Constitution, or, on the Application of the Legislatures of two thirds of the several States, shall call a Convention for proposing Amendments, which, in either Case, shall be valid to all Intents and Purposes, as Part of this Constitution, when ratified by the Legislatures of three fourths of the several States, or by Conventions in three fourths thereof, as the one or the other Mode of Ratification may be proposed by the Congress; Provided that no Amendment which may be made prior to the Year One thousand eight hundred and eight shall in any Manner affect the first and fourth Clauses in the Ninth Section of the first Article; and that no State, without its Consent, shall be deprived of its equal Suffrage in the Senate.

Article VI

All Debts contracted and Engagements entered into, before the Adoption of this Constitution, shall be as valid against the United States under this Constitution, as under the Confederation.

This Constitution, and the Laws of the United States which shall be made in Pursuance thereof; and all Treaties made, or which shall be made, under the Authority of the United States, shall be the supreme Law of the Land; and the Judges in every State shall be bound thereby, any Thing in the Constitution or Laws of any State to the Contrary notwithstanding.

The Senators and Representatives before mentioned, and the Members of the several State Legislatures, and all executive and judicial Officers, both of the United States and of the several States, shall be bound by Oath or Affirmation, to support this Constitution; but no religious Test shall ever be required as a Qualification to any Office or public Trust under the United States.

Article VII

The Ratification of the Conventions of nine States shall be sufficient for the Establishment of this Constitution between the States so ratifying the Same.

Done in Convention by the Unanimous Consent of the States present the Seventeenth Day of September in the Year of our Lord one thousand seven hundred and Eighty seven and of the Independence of the United States of America the Twelfth IN WITNESS whereof We have hereunto subscribed our Names,

Amendment 1 [1791]

Congress shall make no law respecting an establishment of religion, or prohibiting the free exercise thereof; or abridging the freedom of speech, or of the press; or the right of the people peaceably to assemble, and to petition the Government for a redress of grievances.

Amendment 2 [1791]

A well regulated Militia, being necessary to the security of a free State, the right of the people to keep and bear Arms, shall not be infringed.

Amendment 3 [1791]

No Soldier shall, in time of peace be quartered in any house, without the consent of the Owner, nor in time of war, but in a manner to be prescribed by law.

Amendment 4 [1791]

The right of the people to be secure in their persons, houses, papers, and effects, against unreasonable searches and seizures, shall not be violated, and no Warrants shall issue, but upon probable cause, supported by Oath or affirmation, and particularly describing the place to be searched, and the persons or things to be seized.

Amendment 5 [1791]

No person shall be held to answer for a capital, or otherwise infamous crime, unless on a presentment or indictment of a Grand Jury, except in cases arising in the land or naval forces, or in the Militia, when in actual service in time of War or public danger; nor shall any person be subject for the same offence to be twice put in jeopardy of life or limb; nor shall be compelled in any criminal case to be a witness against himself, nor be deprived of life, liberty, or property, without due process of law; nor shall private property be taken for public use, without just compensation.

Amendment 6 [1791]

In all criminal prosecutions, the accused shall enjoy the right to a speedy and public trial, by an impartial jury of the State and district wherein the crime shall have been committed, which district shall have been previously ascertained by law, and to be informed of the nature and cause of the accusation; to be confronted with the witnesses against him; to have compulsory process for obtaining witnesses in his favor, and to have the Assistance of Counsel for his defence.

Amendment 7 [1791]

In Suits at common law, where the value in controversy shall exceed twenty dollars, the right of trial by jury shall be preserved, and no fact tried by a jury, shall be otherwise re-examined in any Court of the United States, than according to the rules of the common law.

Amendment 8 [1791]

Excessive bail shall not be required, nor excessive fines imposed, nor cruel and unusual punishments inflicted.

Amendment 9 [1791]

The enumeration in the Constitution, of certain rights, shall not be construed to deny or disparage others retained by the people.

Amendment 10 [1791]

The powers not delegated to the United States by the Constitution, nor prohibited by it to the States, are reserved to the States respectively, or to the people.

Amendment 11 [Jan. 8, 1798]

The Judicial power of the United States shall not be construed to extend to any suit in law or equity, commenced or prosecuted against one of the United States by Citizens of another State, or by Citizens or Subjects of any Foreign State.

Amendment 12 [Sept. 25, 1804]

The Electors shall meet in their respective states, and vote by ballot for President and Vice-President, one of whom, at least, shall not be an inhabitant of the same state with themselves; they shall name in their ballots the person voted for as President, and in distinct ballots the person voted for as Vice-President, and they shall make distinct lists of all persons voted for as President, and of all persons voted for as Vice-President, and of the number of votes for each, which list they shall sign and certify, and transmit sealed to the seat of the government of the United States, directed to the President of the Senate;—The President of the Senate shall, in the presence of the Senate and House of Representatives, open all the certificates and the votes shall then be counted;—The person having the greatest number of votes for President, shall be the President, if such number be a majority of the whole number of Electors appointed; and if no person have such majority, then from the persons having the highest numbers not exceeding three on the list of those voted for as President, the House of Representatives shall choose immediately, by ballot, the President. But in choosing the President, the votes shall be taken by states, the representation from each state having one vote; a quorum for this purpose shall consist of a member or members from two-thirds of the states, and a majority of all the states shall be necessary to a choice. And if the House of Representatives shall not choose a President whenever the right of choice shall devolve upon them, before the fourth day of March next following, then the Vice-President shall act as President, as in the case of the death or other constitutional disability of the President.—The person having the greatest number of votes as Vice-President, shall be the Vice-President, if such number be a majority of the whole number of Electors appointed, and if no person have a majority, then from the two highest numbers on the list, the Senate shall choose the Vice-President; a quorum for the purpose shall consist of two-thirds of the whole number of Senators, and a majority of the whole number shall be necessary to a choice. But no person constitutionally ineligible to the office of President shall be eligible to that of Vice-President of the United States.

Amendment 13 [Dec. 18, 1865]

Section 1 Neither slavery nor involuntary servitude, except as a punishment for crime whereof the party shall have been duly convicted, shall exist within the United States, or any place subject to their jurisdiction.

Section 2 Congress shall have power to enforce this article by appropriate legislation.

Amendment 14 [July 28, 1868]

Section 1 All persons born or naturalized in the United States, and subject to the jurisdiction thereof, are citizens of the United States and of the State wherein they reside. No State shall make or enforce any law which shall abridge the privileges or immunities of citizens of the United States; nor shall any State deprive any person of life, liberty, or property, without due process of law; nor deny to any person within its jurisdiction the equal protection of the laws.

Section 2 Representatives shall be apportioned among the several States according to their respective numbers, counting the whole number of persons in each State, excluding Indians not taxed. But when the right to vote at any election for the choice of electors for President and Vice-President of the United States, Representatives in Congress, the Executive and Judicial officers of a State, or the members of the Legislature thereof, is denied to any of the male inhabitants of such State, being twenty-one years of age, and citizens of the United States, or in any way abridged, except for participation in rebellion, or other crime, the basis of representation therein shall be reduced in the proportion which the number of such male citizens shall bear to the whole number of male citizens twenty-one years of age in such State.

Section 3 No person shall be a Senator or Representative in Congress, or elector of President and Vice-President, or hold any office, civil or military, under the United States, or under any State, who, having previously taken an oath, as a member of Congress, or as an officer of the United States, or as a member of any State legislature, or as an executive or judicial officer of any State, to support the Constitution of the United States, shall have engaged in insurrection or rebellion against the same, or given aid or comfort to the enemies thereof. But Congress may by a vote of two-thirds of each House, remove such disability.

Section 4 The validity of the public debt of the United States, authorized by law, including debts incurred for payment of pensions and bounties for services in suppressing insurrection or rebellion, shall not be questioned. But neither the United States nor any State shall assume or pay any debt or obligation incurred in aid of insurrection or rebellion against the United States, or any claim for the loss or emancipation of any slave; but all such debts, obligations and claims shall be held illegal and void.

Section 5 The Congress shall have power to enforce, by appropriate legislation, the provisions of this article.

Amendment 15 [March 30, 1870]

Section 1 The right of citizens of the United States to vote shall not be denied or abridged by the United States or by any State on account of race, color, or previous condition of servitude.

Section 2 The Congress shall have power to enforce this article by appropriate legislation.

Amendment 16 [Feb. 25, 1913]

The Congress shall have power to lay and collect taxes on incomes, from whatever source derived, without apportionment among the several States, and without regard to any census or enumeration.

Amendment 17 [May 31, 1913]

Section 1 The Senate of the United States shall be composed of two Senators from each State, elected by the people thereof, for six years; and each Senator shall have one vote. The electors in each State shall have the qualifications requisite for electors of the most numerous branch of the State legislatures.

Section 2 When vacancies happen in the representation of any State in the Senate, the executive authority of such State shall issue writs of election to fill such vacancies: Provided, That the legislature of any State may empower the executive thereof to make temporary appointments until the people fill the vacancies by election as the legislature may direct.

Section 3 This amendment shall not be so construed as to affect the election or term of any Senator chosen before it becomes valid as part of the Constitution.

Amendment 18 [Jan. 29, 1919; repealed Dec. 5, 1933]

Section 1 After one year from the ratification of this article the manufacture, sale, or transportation of intoxicating liquors within, the importation thereof into, or the exportation thereof from the United States and all territory subject to the jurisdiction thereof for beverage purposes is hereby prohibited.

Section 2 Congress and the several States shall have concurrent power to enforce this article by appropriate legislation.

Section 3 This article shall be inoperative unless it shall have been ratified as an amendment to the Constitution by the legislatures of the several States, as provided in the Constitution, within seven years from the date of the submission hereof to the States by the Congress.

Amendment 19 [Aug. 26, 1920]

Section 1 The right of citizens of the United States to vote shall not be denied or abridged by the United States or by any State on account of sex.

Section 2 Congress shall have power to enforce this article by appropriate legislation.

Amendment 20 [Feb. 6, 1933]

Section 1 The terms of the President and Vice-President shall end at noon on the 20th day of January, and the terms of Senators and Representatives at noon on the third day of January, of the years in which such terms would have ended if this article had not been ratified; and the terms of their successors shall then begin.

Section 2 The Congress shall assemble at least once in every year, and such meeting shall begin at noon on the third day of January, unless they shall by law appoint a different day.

Section 3 If, at the time fixed for the beginning of the term of the President, the President elect shall have died, the Vice-President elect shall become President. If a President shall not have been chosen before the time fixed for the beginning of his term, or if the President elect shall have failed to qualify, then the Vice-President elect shall act as President until a President shall have qualified; and the Congress may by law provide for the case wherein neither a President elect nor a Vice-President elect shall have qualified, declaring who shall then act as President, or the manner in which one who is to act shall be selected, and such person shall act accordingly until a President or Vice-President shall have qualified.

Section 4 The Congress may by law provide for the case of the death of any of the persons from whom the House of Representatives may choose a President whenever the right of choice shall have devolved upon them, and for the case of the death of any of the persons from whom the Senate may choose a Vice-President whenever the right of choice shall have devolved upon them.

Section 5 Sections 1 and 2 shall take effect on the 15th day of October following the ratification of this article.

Section 6 This article shall be inoperative unless it shall have been ratified as an amendment to the Constitution by the legislatures of three-fourths of the several States within seven years from the date of its submission.

Amendment 21 [Dec. 5, 1933]

Section 1 The eighteenth article of amendment to the Constitution of the United States is hereby repealed.

Section 2 The transportation or importation into any State, Territory, or possession of the United States for delivery or use therein of intoxicating liquors, in violation of the laws thereof, is hereby prohibited.

Section 3 This article shall be inoperative unless it shall have been ratified as an amendment to the Constitution by conventions in the several States, as provided in the Constitution, within seven years from the date of the submission hereof to the States by the Congress.

Amendment 22 [March 1, 1951]

Section 1 No person shall be elected to the office of the President more than twice, and no person who has held the office of President, or acted as President, for more than two years of a term to which some other person was elected President shall be elected to the office of the President more than once. But this Article shall not apply to any person holding the office of President when this Article was proposed by the Congress, and shall not prevent any person who may be holding the office of President, or acting as President, during the term within which this Article becomes operative from holding the office of President or acting as President during the remainder of such term.

Section 2 This article shall be inoperative unless it shall have been ratified as an amendment to the Constitution by the legislatures of three-fourths of the several States within seven years from the date of its submission to the States by the Congress.

Amendment 23 [April 3, 1961]

Section 1 The District constituting the seat of Government of the United States shall appoint in such manner as the Congress may direct:

A number of electors of President and Vice-President equal to the whole number of Senators and Representatives in Congress to which the District would be entitled if it were a State, but in no event more than the least populous State; they shall be in addition to those appointed by the States, but they shall be considered, for the purposes of the election of President and Vice-President, to be electors appointed by a State; and they shall meet in the District and perform such duties as provided by the twelfth article of amendment.

Section 2 The Congress shall have power to enforce this article by appropriate legislation.

Amendment 24 [Feb. 4, 1964]

Section 1 The right of citizens of the United States to vote in any primary or other election for President or Vice-President, for electors for President or Vice-President, or for Senator or Representative in Congress, shall not be denied or abridged by the United States or any State by reason of failure to pay any poll tax or other tax.

Section 2 The Congress shall have power to enforce this article by appropriate legislation.

Amendment 25 [Feb. 10, 1967]

Section 1 In case of the removal of the President from office or his death or resignation, the Vice-President shall become President.

Section 2 Whenever there is a vacancy in the office of the Vice-President, the President shall nominate a Vice-President who shall take the office upon confirmation by a majority vote of both houses of Congress.

Section 3 Whenever the President transmits to the President pro tempore of the Senate and the Speaker of the House of Representatives his written declaration that he is unable to discharge the powers and duties of his office, and until he transmits to them a written declaration to the contrary, such powers and duties shall be discharged by the Vice-President as Acting President.

Section 4 Whenever the Vice-President and a majority of either the principal officers of the executive departments, or of such other body as Congress may by law provide, transmit to the President pro tempore of the Senate and the Speaker of the House of Representatives their written declaration that the President is unable to discharge the powers and duties of his office, the Vice-President shall immediately assume the powers and duties of the office as Acting President.

Thereafter, when the President transmits to the President pro tempore of the Senate and the Speaker of the House of Representatives his written declaration that no inability exists, he shall resume the powers and duties of his office unless the Vice-President and a majority of either the principal officers of the executive department, or of such other body as Congress may by law provide, transmit within four days to the President pro tempore of the Senate and the Speaker of the House of Representatives their written declaration that the President is unable to discharge the powers and duties of his office. Thereupon Congress shall decide the issue, assembling within forty-eight hours for that purpose if not in session. If the Congress, within twenty-one days after receipt of the latter written declaration, or, if Congress is not in session, within twenty-one days after Congress is required to assemble, determines by two-thirds vote of both Houses that the President is unable to discharge the powers and duties of his office,

the Vice-President shall continue to discharge the same as Acting President; otherwise, the President shall resume the powers and duties of his office.

Amendment 26 [June 30, 1971]

Section 1 The right of citizens of the United States, who are eighteen years of age or older, to vote shall not be denied or abridged by the United States or any state on account of age.

Section 2 The Congress shall have power to enforce this article by appropriate legislation.

Amendment 27 [May 7, 1992]

No law, varying the compensation for the services of Senators and Representatives, shall take effect until an election of Representatives shall have intervened.

Glossary

actus reus An illegal act, or failure to act when legally required.

adjudication (adult) The determination of guilt or innocence; a judgment concerning criminal charges.

adjudication (juvenile) The juvenile court hearing at which the juvenile is declared a delinquent or status offender, or no finding of fact is made.

alternative sanctions Community sentences featuring probation plus additional requirements such as restitution, fines, home confinement, or electronic monitoring, designed to provide more control and sanctions than traditional probation but less than secure incarceration in jail or prison.

anomie The absence or weakness of rules, norms, or guidelines as to what is socially or morally acceptable.

appellate courts Courts that reconsider cases that have already been tried to determine whether the lower court proceedings complied with accepted rules of criminal procedure and constitutional doctrines.

arraignment Initial trial court appearance at which accused is read the charges, advised of his or her rights, and asked to enter a plea.

arrest Taking a person into legal custody for the purpose of restraining the accused until he or she can be held accountable for the offense at court proceedings.

arrest warrant Written court order authorizing and directing that an individual be taken into custody to answer criminal charges.

assigned counsel A private attorney appointed by the court to represent a criminal defendant who cannot afford to pay for a lawyer.

attorney general The chief legal officer and prosecutor of each state and of the United States.

Auburn system Prison system, developed in New York during the nineteenth century, based on congregate (group) work during the day and separation at night.

beats Designated police patrol areas.

bench trial The trial of a criminal matter by a judge without a jury.

blameworthy A person who is deserving of blame or punishment because of evil or injurious behavior.

blue curtain The secretive, insulated police culture that isolates officers from the rest of society.

booking The administrative record of an arrest listing the offender's name, address, physical description, date of birth, employer, time of arrest, offense, and name of arresting officer; also includes photographing and fingerprinting of the offender.

boot camp A short-term militaristic correctional facility in which inmates, usually young first-time offenders, undergo intensive physical conditioning and discipline.

broken windows model Role of the police as maintainers of community order and safety.

brutalization effect The belief that capital punishment creates an atmosphere of brutality, reinforces the view that violence is an appropriate response to provocation, and thus encourages rather than deters the criminal use of violence.

bus sweep Police investigation technique in which officers board a bus or train without suspicion of illegal activity and question passengers, asking for identification and seeking permission to search their baggage.

career criminals Persistent repeat offenders who organize their lifestyle around criminality.

challenge for cause Dismissal of a prospective juror by either the prosecution or the defense because he or she is biased, has prior knowledge about a case, or for other reasons that demonstrate the individual's inability to render a fair and impartial judgment.

chancery courts English courts assigned with the protection of the property rights of minor children.

child savers Civic leaders who focused their attention on the misdeeds of poor children to control their behavior.

Children's Aid Society Group created by Charles Loring Brace to place indigent city kids with farm families.

chivalry hypothesis The idea that female defendants are treated more leniently in sentencing (and are less likely to be arrested and prosecuted in the first place) because the criminal justice system is dominated by men who have a paternalistic or protective attitude toward women.

chronic offenders As defined by Marvin Wolfgang, Robert Figlio, and Thorsten Sellin, delinquents arrested five or more times before the age of 18 who commit a disproportionate amount of all criminal offenses.

circumstantial (indirect) evidence Indirect evidence from which a fact may be inferred.

civil law All law that is not criminal, including tort, contract, personal property, maritime, and commercial law.

cleared An offense is cleared by arrest or solved when at least one person is arrested or charged with the commission of the offense and is turned over to the court for prosecution. If the following questions can all be answered "yes," the offense can then be cleared "exceptionally": (1) Has the investigation definitely established the identity of the offender? (2) Is there enough information to support an arrest, charge, and turning over to the court for prosecution? (3) Is the exact location of the offender known so that the subject could be taken into custody now? (4) Is there some reason outside law enforcement control that precludes arresting, charging, and prosecuting the offender?

community-oriented policing (COP) Programs designed to bring police and the public closer together and create a more cooperative working environment between them.

community policing A law enforcement program that seeks to integrate officers into the local community to reduce crime and gain good community relations. It typically involves personalized service and decentralized policing, citizen empowerment, and an effort to reduce community fear of crime, disorder, and decay.

community prosecution A prosecutorial philosophy that emphasizes community support and cooperation with other agencies in preventing crime as well as a less centralized and more proactive role for local prosecutors.

community service restitution Criminal sanction that requires the offender to work in the community at such tasks as cleaning public parks or helping handicapped children as an alternative to incarceration.

community treatment Correctional treatment services located within the community such as the halfway house.

complaint A sworn written statement addressed to a court or judge by the police, prosecutor, or individual alleging that an individual has committed an offense and requesting indictment and prosecution.

concurrent sentence Incarceration for more than one offense such that all sentences begin on the same day and are completed after the longest term has been served.

conflict theory The view that crime results from the imposition by the rich and powerful of their own moral standards and economic interests on the rest of society.

confrontation clause The constitutional right of a criminal defendant to see and cross-examine all the witnesses against him or her.

congregate system The prison system, originated in New York, in which inmates worked and ate together during the day and then slept in solitary cells at night.

conjugal visit A prison program that allows inmates to receive visits from spouses for the purpose of maintaining normal interpersonal relationships.

consecutive sentence Incarceration for more than one offense such that each sentence begins only after the previous one has been completed.

constable In early English towns, an appointed peacekeeper who organized citizens for protection and supervised the night watch.

contract system (court) Provision of legal services to indigent defendants by private attorneys under contract to the state or county.

contract system (prison) System whereby officials sold the labor of prison inmates to private businesses, for use either inside or outside the prison.

convict-lease system Contract system in which a private business leased prisoners from the state for a fixed annual fee and assumed full responsibility for their supervision and control.

court of last resort A court that handles the final appeal on a matter; in the federal system, the U.S. Supreme Court.

courtroom work group All parties in the adversary process working together in a cooperative effort to settle cases with the least amount of effort and conflict.

courts of general jurisdiction Courts that try felony cases and more serious civil matters.

courts of limited jurisdiction Courts that handle misdemeanors and minor civil complaints.

crime control perspective A model of criminal justice that emphasizes the control of dangerous offenders and the protection of society through harsh punishment as a deterrent to crime.

criminal justice system The various sequential stages through which offenders pass, from initial contact with the law to final disposition, and the agencies charged with enforcing the law at each of these stages.

criminal law The body of rules that define crimes, set out their punishments, and mandate the procedures for carrying out the criminal justice process.

criminology The scientific study of the nature, extent, cause, and control of criminal behavior.

cross-examination The questioning of a prosecution witness by the defense, or of a defense witness by the prosecution.

cruel and unusual punishment Treatment that degrades human dignity, is dispro-

portionately severe, or shocks the general conscience; prohibited by the Eighth Amendment to the U.S. Constitution.

culture of poverty The view that people in the lower class of society form a separate culture with its own values and norms that are in conflict with those of conventional society.

curtilage Grounds or fields attached to a house.

cynicism The belief that most people's actions are motivated solely by personal needs and selfishness.

DARE Drug Abuse Resistance Education, a school-based program designed to give students the skills to resist peer pressure to experiment with tobacco, alcohol, and illegal drugs.

day fees Fees imposed on probationers to offset the costs of probation.

day fine A fine geared to an offender's net daily income, as well as number of dependents and the seriousness of the crime, in an effort to make sentences more equitable.

day reporting center (DRC) Nonresidential, community-based treatment program.

deadly force Police killing of a suspect who resists arrest or presents a danger to an officer or the community.

death-qualified jury A jury formed to hear a capital case, with any person opposed in principle to capital punishment automatically excluded.

decriminalization Reducing the penalty for a criminal act without legalizing it.

defense attorney Legal counsel for the defendant in a criminal case, representing the accused person from arrest to final appeal.

deinstitutionalization The movement to remove as many offenders as possible from secure confinement and treat them in the community.

delinquency prevention Intervening in a young person's life to help them avoid involvement in delinquent activities.

demeanor The way in which a person outwardly manifests his or her personality.

Department of Homeland Security (DHS) A federal agency created to coordinate national efforts to prevent terrorist attacks from occurring within the United

States, to respond if an attack takes place, and to reduce or minimize the damage from attacks that do happen.

detention Temporary care of a child alleged to be a delinquent or status offender who requires secure custody pending court disposition.

determinate sentence A fixed term of incarceration.

deterrent Preventing crime before it occurs by means of the threat of criminal sanctions.

developmental theories A view of crime holding that as people travel through the life course their experiences along the way influence behavior patterns. Behavior changes at each stage of the human experience.

differential association theory The view that criminal acts are related to a person's exposure to antisocial attitudes and values.

direct examination The initial questioning of one's own (prosecution or defense) witness during a trial.

directed verdict A judge's order directing a jury to acquit a defendant because the state has not proven the elements of the crime or otherwise has not established guilt according to law.

discretion The use of personal decision making and choice in carrying out operations in the criminal justice system.

disinhibition Unrestricted behavior resulting from a loss of inhibition produced by an external influence, such as drugs or alcohol, or from a brain injury.

displacement An effect that occurs when criminals move from an area targeted for increased police presence to another that is less well protected.

dispositional hearing A court hearing to determine the appropriate treatment for a youth found to be a delinquent.

district attorney The county prosecutor who is charged with bringing offenders to justice and enforcing the criminal laws of the state.

diversion The use of a noncriminal alternative to trial, such as referral to treatment or employment programs.

DNA profiling The identification (or elimination) of criminal suspects by comparing DNA samples (genetic material) taken from them with specimens found at crime scenes.

double marginality According to Nicholas Alex, the social burden African American police officers carry by being both minority group members and law enforcement officers.

drug courts Specialty courts with jurisdiction over cases involving illegal substances, often providing treatment alternatives for defendants.

due process perspective A model of criminal justice that emphasizes individual rights and constitutional safeguards against arbitrary or unfair judicial or administrative proceedings.

electronic monitoring (EM) Electronic equipment that enables probation officers to monitor the location of those under house arrest or other forms of supervision.

equity Sanction designed to compensate victims and society for the losses caused by crime; restitution.

exclusionary rule The principle that prohibits using illegally obtained evidence in a trial.

exculpatory evidence Includes all information that is material and favorable to the accused defendant because it casts doubt on the defendant's guilt or on the evidence the government intends to use a trial.

exigent Emergency or immediate circumstance.

ex post facto law A law that makes an act criminal after it was committed or retroactively increases the penalty for a crime.

expressive crimes Criminal acts that serve to vent rage, anger, or frustration.

fact-finding hearing The trial in the juvenile justice system.

Federal Bureau of Investigation (FBI) The arm of the Justice Department that investigates violations of federal law, gathers crime statistics, runs a comprehensive crime laboratory, and helps train local law enforcement officers.

felony A more serious crime that carries a penalty of incarceration in a state or federal prison, usually for one year or more.

felony courts Courts that try felony cases and civil matters involving significant monetary claims.

fine A sum imposed as punishment for an offense.

focal concerns Central values and goals that, according to Walter Miller, differ by social class.

foot patrol Police patrol that takes officers out of cars and puts them on a walking beat to strengthen ties with the community.

forfeiture The seizure of personal property by the state as a civil or criminal penalty.

Gang Tactical Detail A police unit created to combat neighborhood gang problems by targeting known offenders who have shown a propensity toward gang violence or criminal activity.

general deterrence A crime control policy that depends on the fear of criminal penalties.

good faith exception The principle that evidence may be used in a criminal trial even though the search warrant used to obtain it was technically faulty, so long as the police acted in good faith when they sought the warrant from a judge.

good time Reduction of a prison sentence by a specified amount in exchange for good behavior within the institution.

grand jury A group of citizens chosen to hear charges against persons accused of crime and to determine whether there is sufficient evidence to bring the persons to trial.

grass eater A term used for a police officer who accepts payoffs when everyday duties place him or her in a position to be solicited by the public.

halfway house A community-based correctional facility that houses inmates before their outright release so that they can become gradually acclimated to conventional society.

hands-off doctrine The judicial policy of not interfering in the administrative affairs of prisons.

hearsay evidence Testimony that is not firsthand but relates information told by a second party.

hot spots of crime The view that a significant portion of all police calls in metropolitan areas typically radiate from a relatively few locations: bars, malls, the bus depot, hotels, and certain apartment buildings.

HotSpot probation A program using community supervision teams to monitor offenders.

house arrest A sentence that requires convicted offenders to spend extended periods of time in their own home as an alternative to incarceration.

hue and cry In medieval England, a call for mutual aid against trouble or danger.

hulk Mothballed ship used to house prisoners in eighteenth-century England.

hundred In medieval England, a group of 100 families responsible for maintaining order and trying minor offenses.

incapacitation The policy of keeping dangerous criminals in confinement to eliminate the risk of their repeating their offense in society.

indeterminate sentence A term of incarceration with a stated minimum and maximum length; the prisoner is eligible for parole after serving the minimum.

index crimes The eight serious crimes — murder, rape, assault, robbery, burglary, arson, larceny, and motor vehicle theft — whose incidence is reported in the annual Uniform Crime Report (UCR).

indictment A written accusation returned by a grand jury, charging an individual with a specified crime after determination of probable cause.

indigent defendant A poor defendant who lacks the funds to hire a private attorney and is therefore entitled to free counsel.

inevitable discovery rule Evidence can be used in court even though the information that led to its discovery was obtained in violation of the *Miranda* rule if a judge finds it would have been discovered anyway by other means or sources.

information A formal charging document, similar to an indictment, based on probable cause as determined at a preliminary hearing.

initial appearance The first hearing in juvenile court.

inmate social code The informal set of rules that govern inmates and shape the inmate subculture.

inmate subculture The loosely defined culture that pervades prisons and has its own norms, rules, and language.

in presence requirement A police officer cannot arrest someone for a misdemeanor unless the officer sees the crime occur. To make an arrest for a crime he did not witness, the officer must obtain a warrant.

instrumental crimes Criminal acts intended to improve the financial or social position of the criminal.

intake The process by which a probation officer settles cases at the initial court appearance, before the onset of formal criminal proceedings; the screening process in which a juvenile is referred to the juvenile court, referred elsewhere, or released.

intensive probation supervision (IPS) A type of intermediate sanction involving small probation caseloads and strict daily or weekly monitoring.

intensive supervision parole (ISP) A form of parole characterized by smaller caseloads and closer surveillance; may include frequent drug testing or, in some cases, electronic monitoring.

intermediate sanctions A group of punishments falling between probation and prison; community-based sanctions including house arrest and intensive supervision.

internal affairs Unit that investigates allegations of police misconduct.

jail A county correctional institution used to hold people awaiting trial or sentencing, as well as misdemeanor offenders sentenced to a term of less than one year.

jailhouse lawyer An inmate trained in law or otherwise educated who helps other inmates prepare legal briefs and appeals.

judicial reprieve In medieval England, a judge's suspension of punishment, enabling a convicted offender to seek a pardon, gather new evidence, or demonstrate reformed behavior.

just desert The view that those who violate the rights of others deserve punishment commensurate with the seriousness of the crime.

justice of the peace Official appointed to act as the judicial officer in a county.

justification A defense for a criminal act claiming that the criminal act was reasonable or necessary under the circumstances.

Knapp Commission A public body that conducted an investigation into police corruption in New York City in the early

1970s and uncovered a widespread network of payoffs and bribes.

labeling theory The view that society produces criminals by stigmatizing certain individuals as deviants, a label that they come to accept as a personal identity.

latent trait theories A view that human behavior is controlled by a master trait, present at birth or soon after, which influences and directs their behavior.

Law Enforcement Assistance Administration (LEAA) Agency funded by the federal Safe Streets and Crime Control Act of 1968 that provided technical assistance and hundreds of millions of dollars in aid to local and state justice agencies between 1969 and 1982.

left realism A branch of conflict theory that accepts the reality of crime as a social problem and stresses its impact on the poor.

legalization The removal of all criminal penalties from a previously outlawed act.

legislature The branch of government in a state invested with power to make and repeal laws.

liberal feminist theory An ideology holding that women suffer oppression, discrimination, and disadvantage as a result of their sex. Calls for gender equality in pay, opportunity, child care, and education.

life course The course of social and developmental changes through which an individual passes as he or she travels from birth through childhood, adolescence, adulthood, and finally old age.

lineup Placing a suspect in a group for the purpose of being viewed and identified by a witness.

low-visibility decision making Decision making by police officers that is not subject to administrative review; for example, when a decision is made not to arrest someone or not to stop a speeding vehicle.

lower courts Courts that conduct preliminary hearings and try misdemeanor cases and civil matters of a limited monetary value.

mala in se In common law, offenses that are from their own nature evil, immoral, and wrong. Mala in se offenses include murder, theft, and arson.

mandatory parole release A release date determined at the beginning of the confinement period based on a percentage of the inmate's sentence to be served. Inmates can have their expected time served increased if they violate prison rules or conditions.

mandatory sentence A statutory requirement that a certain penalty be set and carried out in all cases on conviction for a specified offense or series of offenses.

masculinity hypothesis The view that women who commit crimes have biological and psychological traits similar to those of men.

maximum-security prison A correctional institution that houses dangerous felons and maintains strict security measures, including high walls, guard towers, and limited contact with the outside world.

meat eater A term used to describe a police officer who actively solicits bribes and vigorously engages in corrupt practices.

medical model The view that convicted offenders are victims of their environment who need care and treatment to be transformed into valuable members of society.

medium-security prison A correctional institution that houses nonviolent offenders, characterized by a less tense and vigilant atmosphere and more opportunities for contact with the outside world.

mens rea A guilty mind; the intent to commit a criminal act.

methadone A synthetic narcotic used as a substitute for heroin in drug-control efforts.

Metropolitan Police Act In 1829, when Sir Robert Peel was home secretary, the first Metropolitan Police Act was passed and the Metropolitan Police Force was established to replace the local watch and constable system in the London area.

minimum-security prison A correctional institution that houses white-collar and other nonviolent offenders, characterized by few security measures and liberal furlough and visitation policies.

Missouri Plan A method of judicial selection that combines a judicial nominating commission, executive appointment, and nonpartisan confirmation elections.

Mollen Commission An investigative unit set up to inquire into police corruption in New York City in the 1990s.

monetary restitution Criminal sanction that requires the offender to compensate the victim for property damage, lost wages, medical costs, or other losses.

National Crime Victimization Survey (NCVS) The NCVS is the nation's primary source of information on criminal victimization. Each year, data are obtained from a national sample that measure the frequency, characteristics, and consequences of criminal victimization by such crimes as rape, sexual assault, robbery, assault, theft, household burglary, and motor vehicle theft.

National Incident-Based Reporting System (NIBRS) A new form of crime data collection created by the FBI requiring local police agencies to provide at least a brief account of each incident and arrest within 22 crime patterns, including the incident, victim, and offender information.

neighborhood-oriented policing (NOP) A philosophy of police suggesting that problem solving is best done at the neighborhood level, where issues originate, not at a far-off central headquarters.

neurotransmitters Chemical substances that carry impulses from one nerve cell to another. Neurotransmitters are found in the space (synapse) that separates the transmitting neuron's terminal (axon) from the receiving neuron's terminal (dendrite).

no bill The action by a grand jury when it votes not to indict an accused suspect.

nolle prosequi Decision by a prosecutor to drop a case after a complaint has been made because of, for example, insufficient evidence, witness reluctance to testify, police error, or office policy.

nolo contendere A plea of "no contest"; the defendant submits to sentencing without any formal admission of guilt that could be used against him or her in a subsequent civil suit.

nonintervention perspective A model of criminal justice that favors the least intrusive treatment possible: decarceration, diversion, and decriminalization.

obitiatry Helping people take their own lives; assisted suicide.

order maintenance (peacekeeping) Maintaining order and authority without the need for formal arrest; "handling the situation"; keeping things under control by means of threats, persuasion, and understanding.

parens patriae The power of the state to act on behalf of a child and provide care and protection equivalent to that of a parent.

parole The early release of a prisoner from incarceration subject to conditions set by a parole board.

Part I crimes Those crimes in the FBI's Crime Index, which is composed of offenses used to gauge fluctuations in the overall volume and rate of crime. The offenses included are the violent crimes of murder and non-negligent manslaughter, forcible rape, robbery, and aggravated assault and the property crimes of burglary, larceny-theft, motor vehicle theft, and arson.

Part II crimes All other crimes reported to the FBI not included in the Crime Index. These are less serious crimes and misdemeanors, excluding traffic violations.

particularity The requirement that a search warrant state precisely where the search is to take place and what items are to be seized.

peacemaking criminology A branch of conflict theory that stresses humanism, mediation, and conflict resolution as means to end crime.

penitentiary A state or federal correctional institution for the incarceration of felony offenders for terms of one year or more; prison.

penitentiary house A correctional institution for those convicted of major crimes.

Pennsylvania system Prison system, developed in Pennsylvania during the nineteenth century, based on total isolation and individual penitence.

penumbral crimes Criminals act defined by a high level of noncompliance with the stated legal standard, an absence of stigma associated with violation of the stated standard, and a low level of law enforcement or public sanction.

peremptory challenge Dismissal of a prospective juror by either the prosecution or the defense for unexplained, discretionary reasons.

plain view doctrine Evidence that is in plain view of police officers may be seized without a search warrant.

plea negotiations/plea bargaining Discussions between defense counsel and prosecution in which the accused agrees to plead guilty in exchange for certain considerations, such as reduced charges or a lenient sentence.

police brutality Actions such as using abusive language, making threats, using force or coercion unnecessarily, prodding with nightsticks, and stopping and searching people to harass them.

police styles The working personalities adopted by police officers that can range from being a social worker in blue to a hard-charging crime fighter.

poor laws Seventeenth-century English laws under which vagrants and abandoned and neglected children were bound to masters as indentured servants.

preliminary hearing (probable cause hearing) Hearing before a magistrate to determine if the government has sufficient evidence to show probable cause that the defendant committed the crime.

presentence investigation A postconviction investigation, performed by a probation officer attached to the trial court, of the defendant's background, education, employment, family, acquaintances, physical and mental health, prior criminal record, and other factors that may affect sentencing.

presentment The report of a grand jury investigation, which usually includes a recommendation of indictment.

pretrial detainees People who either are denied bail or cannot afford to post bail before trial and are kept in secure confinement.

pretrial diversion Informal, community-based treatment programs that are used in lieu of the formal criminal process.

pretrial procedures Legal and administrative actions that take place after arrest and before trial, including grand jury indictments, preliminary hearings, bail, and plea negotiation.

prison A state or federal correctional institution for the incarceration of felony offenders for terms of one year or more; penitentiary.

prisonization Assimilation into the separate culture in the prison that has its own rewards and behaviors.

pro bono The practice by private attorneys of taking the cases of indigent offenders without fee as a service to the profession and the community.

pro se To present one's own defense in a criminal trial; self-representation.

proactive policing An aggressive law enforcement style in which patrol offices take the initiative against crime instead of waiting for criminal acts to occur. For example, they stop motor vehicles to issue citations and aggressively arrest and detain suspicious persons.

probable cause The evidentiary criterion necessary to sustain an arrest or the issuance of an arrest or search warrant; a set of facts, information, circumstances, or conditions that would lead a reasonable person to believe that an offense was committed and that the accused committed that offense.

probable cause hearing If a person is taken into custody for a misdemeanor, a hearing is held to determine if probable cause exists that he committed the crime.

probation A sentence entailing the conditional release of a convicted offender into the community under the supervision of the court (in the form of a probation officer), subject to certain conditions for a specified time.

problem-oriented policing A style of police management that stresses proactive problem solving instead of reactive crime fighting.

profile (profiling) The practice of police targeting members of particular racial or ethnic groups for traffic and other stops because they believe that members of that group are more likely to be engaged in criminal activity even though the individual being stopped has not engaged in any improper behavior.

prosecutor The public official who presents the government's case against a person accused of a crime.

psychopath A person whose personality is characterized by a lack of warmth and feeling, inappropriate behavioral responses, and an inability to learn from experience; also called sociopath or antisocial personality.

public defender An attorney employed by the government to represent criminal defendants who cannot afford to pay for a lawyer.

public safety doctrine A suspect can be questioned in the field without a *Miranda* warning if the information the police seek is needed to protect public safety.

public safety or strict liability crime A criminal violation — usually one that endangers the public welfare — that is defined by the act itself, irrespective of intent.

punishment Pain, suffering, loss, or sanction inflicted on a person because they committed a crime or offense.

radical feminism A branch of conflict theory that focuses on the role of capitalist male dominance in female criminality and victimization.

real evidence Any object, such as a weapon or a photograph, produced for inspection at a trial; physical evidence.

reasonable competence standard Minimally required level of functioning by a defense attorney such that defendants are not deprived of their rights to counsel and to a fair trial.

rebuttal evidence Evidence presented by the prosecution at the conclusion of the defense case, with the permission of the court, to rebut or disprove defense evidence.

recidivism Repetition of criminal behavior; habitual criminality.

recognizance Medieval practice of letting convicted offenders remain free if they agreed to enter a debt relation with the state to pay for their crimes.

recoupment Process by which the state later recovers some or all of the cost of providing free legal counsel to an indigent defendant.

rehabilitation perspective A model of criminal justice that sees crime as an expression of frustration and anger created by social inequality that can be controlled by giving people the means to improve their lifestyle through conventional endeavors.

release on recognizance (ROR) A pretrial release in which a defendant with ties to the community is not required to post bail but promises to appear at all subsequent proceedings.

residential community corrections (RCC) An intermediate sanction, as well as a parole or pretrial option, in which convicted offenders are housed in a nonsecure facility from which they go to work, attend school, or participate in treatment activities and programs.

restitution Criminal sanction that requires the offender to repay the victim or society or both for damage caused by the criminal act.

restoration A vision of justice that attempts to heal the rift between criminal and victim to provide healing instead of punishment.

restorative justice A perspective on justice that views the main goal of the criminal justice system to be a systematic response to wrongdoing that emphasizes healing the wounds of victims, offenders, and communities caused or revealed by crime. It stresses noncoercive and healing approaches whenever possible.

revocation Removing a person from probation (or parole) in response to a violation of law or of the conditions of probation (or parole).

risk classification Assigning probationers to a level and type of supervision based on their particular needs and the risks they pose for the community.

routine activities theory The view that crime is a product of three everyday factors: motivated offenders, suitable targets, and a lack of capable guardians.

sanctions Social control mechanisms designed to enforce society's laws and standards.

search incident to a lawful arrest An exception to the search warrant rule; limited to the immediate surrounding area.

search warrant An order, issued by a judge, directing officers to conduct a search of specified premises for specified objects or persons and to bring them before the court.

self-report survey A research approach that questions large groups of subjects, typically high school students, about their own participation in delinquent or criminal acts.

sentencing circle In native communities, a group of citizens, leaders, victims, and so on who meet to deal with conflicts between people in an equitable way.

sheriff The chief law enforcement officer in a county.

shire reeve In early England, the chief law enforcement official in a county, forerunner of today's sheriff.

shock incarceration A short prison sentence served under military discipline at a boot camp facility.

shock probation A sentence in which offenders serve a short term in prison to impress them with the pains of incarceration before they begin probation.

six-person jury Because the U.S. Supreme Court has ruled that the Constitution does not require a 12-person jury, states allow juries of lesser size, the minimum being six people.

social capital Positive relations with individuals and institutions that foster self-worth and inhibit crime.

social control The ability of society and its institutions to control, manage, restrain, or direct human behavior.

social control theory The view that most people do not violate the law because of their social bonds to family, peer group, school, and other institutions. If these bonds are weakened or absent, they become free to commit crime.

social learning theory The view that human behavior is learned through observation of human social interactions, either directly from those in close proximity or indirectly from the media.

social structure The stratifications, classes, institutions, and groups that characterize a society.

source control Attempting to cut off the supply of illegal drugs by destroying crops and arresting members of drug cartels in drug-producing countries.

specific deterrence Punishment severe enough to convince convicted offenders never to repeat their criminal activity.

split sentence Giving a brief term of incarceration as a condition of probation.

spree killer A killer of multiple victims whose murders take place over a relatively short period of time.

stalking The willful, malicious, and repeated following, harassing, or contacting of another person. It becomes a criminal act when it causes the victim to feel fear for his or safety or the safety of others.

stare decisis To stand by decided cases; the legal principle by which the decision or holding in an earlier case becomes the standard by which subsequent similar cases are judged.

sting operation Organized groups of detectives who deceive criminals into openly committing illegal acts or conspiring to engage in criminal activity.

stop and frisk The situation in which police officers who are suspicious of an individual run their hands lightly over the suspect's outer garments to determine if the person is carrying a concealed weapon; also called a threshold inquiry or pat-down.

strain The emotional turmoil and conflict caused when people believe they cannot achieve their desires and goals through legitimate means.

subpoena A court order requiring a witness to appear in court at a specified time and place.

substantive right A specific right, such as the right to medical care or freedom of religion.

super-maximum-security prison A high-security prison in which inmates are kept in solitary confinement up to 23 hours per day.

sureties During the Middle Ages, people who made themselves responsible for people given release or a reprieve.

surrebuttal evidence At the end of rebuttal, the defense may be allowed to refute the evidence presented by the prosecution with its own surrebuttal evidence. Surrebuttal is not an opportunity for the defense to present new evidence but simply to refute the prosecution's rebuttal evidence.

suspended sentence A sentence of incarceration that is not carried out if the offender agrees to obey the rules of probation while living in the community.

three strikes laws Sentencing codes that require that an offender receive a life sentence after conviction for a third felony. Some states allow parole after a lengthy prison stay, for example, 25 years.

threshold inquiry A term used to describe a stop and frisk.

tier system A type of prison in which cells are located along corridors in multiple layers or levels.

time-in-rank system The promotion system in which a police officer can advance in rank only after spending a prescribed amount of time in the preceding rank.

tithings During the Middle Ages, groups of about 10 families responsible for maintaining order among themselves and dealing with disturbances, fire, wild animals, or other threats.

total institution A regimented, dehumanizing institution, such as a prison, in which like-situated people are kept in social isolation, cut off from the world at large.

transfer The process of sending a case from the juvenile to adult courts.

true bill The action by a grand jury when it votes to indict an accused suspect.

truth-in-sentencing Sentencing reform sponsored by the federal government mandating that any defendant who has plead guilty to or has been found guilty of a felony shall be required to serve a minimum prison term of 85 percent of the sentence imposed by the court.

Uniform Crime Reports (UCRs) The official crime data collected by the FBI from local police departments.

venire The group called for jury duty from which jury panels are selected.

vice squads Police officers assigned to enforce morality-based laws, such as those on prostitution, gambling, and pornography.

victim impact statement A victim impact statement is a written statement that describes the harm or loss suffered by the victim of an offense. The court considers the statement when the offender is sentenced.

victim precipitation The role of the victim in provoking or encouraging criminal behavior.

victimless crime A crime typically involving behavior considered immoral or in violation of public decency that has no specific victim, such as public drunkenness, vagrancy, or public nudity.

vigilantes In the old west, members of a vigilance committee or posse called upon to capture cattle thieves or other felons.

voir dire The process in which a potential jury panel is questioned by the prosecution and the defense to select jurors who are unbiased and objective.

waiver The voluntary and deliberate relinquishing of a known right, such as those guaranteed under the Fifth and Sixth Amendments; the transfer of a juvenile offender to criminal court for prosecution as an adult.

Walnut Street Jail The birthplace of the modern prison system and of the Pennsylvania system of solitary confinement.

watch system In medieval England, men organized in church parishes to guard at night against disturbances and breaches of the peace under the direction of the local constable.

wergild During the Middle Ages, the compensation paid to the victim by a defendant found guilty of crime.

white-collar crime White-collar crimes involve the violation of rules that control business enterprise. They can range from employee pilferage, bribery, commodities law violations, mail fraud, computer fraud, environmental law violations, embezzlement, Internet scams, extortion, forgery, insurance fraud, price fixing, and environmental pollution.

widening the net To enmesh more offenders for longer periods in the criminal justice system — a criticism of pretrial diversion programs.

work release (furlough) A prison treatment program in which inmates leave the institution to work in the community, sometimes returning to prison or another supervised facility at night.

writ of certiorari An order of a superior court requesting that a record of an inferior court (or administrative body) be brought forward for review or inspection.

zero tolerance A practice in which criminal defendants forfeit homes, cars, and so on for the slightest law violation.

Table of Cases

Name Index

Subject Index

Credits